Tools & Techniques of LIFE INSURANCE PLANNING

3rd EDITION

LEIMBERG
DOYLE

The National Underwriter Company

A Unit of Highline Media LLC

5081 Olympic Boulevard • Erlanger, KY 41018 • www.NUCO.com

Library of Congress Control Number: 2004109661

ISBN 0-87218-654-7

THE NATIONAL UNDERWRITER COMPANY

Copyright © 1993, 1999, 2004

The National Underwriter Company
P.O. Box 14367
Cincinnati, Ohio 45250-0367

Third Edition

Printed in the United States of America

DEDICATION

<u>To:</u>

ROBERT J. DOYLE, JR.

STEPHEN N. KANDELL

JERRY A. KASNER

ROBERT T. LeCLAIR

CHARLES K. PLOTNICK

JOHN J. McFADDEN

RALPH G. MILLER

MOREY S. ROSENBLOOM

JOSEPH M. YOHLIN

HOWARD M. ZARITSKY

*"Working with you has enriched me in many ways
but most importantly through your friendship."*

ACKNOWLEDGMENTS

We thank Morey S. Rosenbloom, Esq. of Blank, Rome, Comisky, and McCauley, for his outstanding guidance on both the life insurance product and its uses as well as for his firm's careful review of this text. We would also like to express appreciation to attorney Howard Zaritsky for his constant suggestions and tax planning advice. We highly recommend his book, *Tax Planning with Life Insurance*, for its many excellent specimen documents and indepth legal treatment of tax matters related to life insurance. Edward Graves served the authors as special consultant with regard to the life insurance product.

Barton Francis, CPA, authored a special appendix chapter on "Accounting for Life Insurance" which we are sure our readers will find highly informative. Martin J. Satinsky, J.D., CPA and Charles S. DiLullo, CPA, were invaluable technical advisors to this most important chapter. Ron Bachrach, J.D., CLU, of MONY, provided valuable assistance and information in the appendix chapter on Section 1035 exchanges.

The Tools and Techniques of Life Insurance Planning could not have been created in its present form without the massive effort of the technical staff of The National Underwriter Company. We applaud Deborah A. Miner, J.D., CLU, ChFC, and the following members of her staff for their extraordinary effort and meticulous attention to detail in bringing this third edition to press: William J. Wagner, J.D., LL.M., CLU, April K. Caudill, J.D., CLU, ChFC, Joseph F. Stenken, J.D., Sonya E. King, J.D., LL.M., and John H. Fenton, J.D.

As our loyal followers know, more than most books, *The Tools and Techniques of Life Insurance Planning* was "a long time commin." It was a massive effort interrupted by numerous changes and upheavals not only in the economy and tax law but also in the lives of the authors. It's birth was not unlike the gestation of a not so small whale. But it is a work of which we are proud. We wish to thank all of you who have "hung in there" and have on your shelves other copies of the *Leimberg Tools and Techniques* library.

We want you to know you are important to us and we will continue to acknowledge that importance by keeping *Tools and Techniques* loaded with creative ideas and practical information that is easy to find, understand, and use. We've worked hard to make sure that this second edition significantly expands, as well as updates, the coverage of life insurance and its taxation.

Stephan R. Leimberg

Robert J. Doyle, Jr.

ABOUT THE AUTHORS

Stephan R. Leimberg

Stephan R. Leimberg is CEO of LISI, Leimberg Information Services, Inc., a provider of e-mail/internet news and commentary for professionals on recent cases, rulings, and legislation; CEO of Leimberg and LeClair, Inc., an estate and financial planning software company; and President of Leimberg Associates, Inc., a publishing and software company in Bryn Mawr, Pennsylvania.

Leimberg is the author of numerous books on estate, financial, and employee benefit and retirement planning and a nationally known speaker. Leimberg is the creator and principal author of the entire eight book *Tools and Techniques* series including *The Tools and Techniques of Estate Planning, The Tools and Techniques of Financial Planning, The Tools and Techniques of Employee Benefit and Retirement Planning, The Tools and Techniques of Life Insurance Planning, The Tools and Techniques of Charitable Planning, The Tools and Techniques of Income Tax Planning, The Tools and Techniques of Investment Planning, and The Tools and Techniques of Risk Management*. Leimberg is co-author, with noted attorney Howard Zaritsky, *Tax Planning with Life Insurance, The New, New Book of Trusts* with attorneys Charles K. Plotnick and Daniel Evans, and *How to Settle an Estate* with Charles K. Plotnick.

Leimberg is creator or co-creator of many software packages for the financial services professional including *NumberCruncher* (estate planning), *IRS Factors Calculator* (actuarial computations), *Financial Analyzer II, Estate Planning Quickview* (Estate Planning Flow Charts), *Toward a Zero Estate Tax* (PowerPoint Estate Planning Client Seminar), *Gifts That Give, Gifts That Give Back* (Powerpoint Client Charitable Planning Seminar), and Long-Term Care (Powerpoint Client Seminar).

A nationally known speaker, Professor Leimberg has addressed the Miami (Heckerling) Estate Planning Institute, the NYU Tax Institute, the Notre Dame Law School and Duke University Law School's Estate Planning Conference, The American Bar Association Planning Techniques for Large Estate and Sophisticated Planning Techniques courses of study, the National Association of Estate Planners and Councils, and the AICPA's National Estate Planning Forum. Leimberg has also spoken to the Federal Bureau of Investigation, and the National Aeronautics and Space Administration.

Leimberg was named 1998 Edward N. Polisher Lecturer of the Dickinson School of Law, and was awarded the Excellence in Writing Award of the American Bar Association's Probate and Property Section. He has been honored as Estate Planner of the Year by the Montgomery County Estate Planning Council and as Distinguished Estate Planner by the Philadelphia Estate Planning Council. He is also recipient of the President's Cup of the Philadelphia Life Underwriters, a two time Boris Todorovitch Lecturer, and the first Ben Feldman Lecturer.

Robert J. Doyle, Jr.

Robert J. Doyle, Jr. is an independent financial consultant, writer and speaker, and software developer specializing in executive compensation, retirement planning, investment and insurance tax planning, business valuation, and business continuation planning. He is currently affiliated with Surgent & Associates in Devon, Pennsylvania, as a writer and speaker. Surgent & Associates is a CPA firm and publisher of continuing professional education courses for CPAs. It is the largest vendor in the United States of continuing professional CPA education courses in the topic areas of taxation and advisory services.

Prior to his affiliation with Surgent & Associates, Mr. Doyle was Senior Vice President of Mandeville Financial Services, Inc., a diversified insurance, real estate, employee benefits, and executive compensation consulting firm and life insurance agency. Before joining Mandeville Financial Services, Mr. Doyle spent 15 years as Associate Professor of Finance and Insurance at The American College where he was responsible for courses in retirement and wealth accumulation planning in the College's CLU and ChFC professional designation programs. Mr. Doyle also has served as Adjunct Professor of Taxation in the graduate tax program of Widener University Graduate School of Management where he has taught courses in taxation of investments and taxation for financial planning.

He is an author or co-author of over a dozen books and monographs including *The Tools & Techniques of Financial Planning, The Tools & Techniques of Life Insurance*

Planning, Can You Afford to Retire? and *Solutions Handbook For Personal Financial Planning, Business Planning, Employee Benefits, Estate Planning*. He has written and presented numerous professional education courses for CPAs for Surgent & Associates on tax, retirement, investment, business, and other financial planning topics. Beyond his book and education courses, Mr. Doyle has published nearly fifty articles in the academic, professional, and trade press and he has appeared as a financial planning expert on radio and television talk shows around the country.

In addition to speaking at dozens of conferences sponsored by The American College and at several hundred CPA continuing education seminars, Mr. Doyle has addressed audiences in regional and national conferences sponsored by The Widener Tax Institute,

The International Association of Financial Planners, The Institute of Certified Financial Planners, Commerce Clearing House, The American Society of CLU & ChFC, TIAA-CREF, and a number of state CPA Institutes. He has spoken before dozens of chapters of The American Society of CLU & ChFC and numerous regional Estate Planning Councils as well as various community groups and charitable organizations.

Mr. Doyle did his graduate study as a Huebner Fellow at the Wharton School of the University of Pennsylvania. He holds the MA and MBA degrees from Wharton, a BA from Macalester College, is a CLU and a Chartered Financial Consultant (ChFC).

Mr. Doyle resides in Wayne, Pennsylvania with his wife, Kathryn, and their three children.

PREFACE TO THE THIRD EDITION

The Tools and Techniques of Life Insurance Planning is one of many books and online resources in the *Tools and Techniques* series.

In each of our books we had one major goal in mind:

"To create the single best source of up-to-date, pragmatic, and transferable information on the topics you need to help others."

With the growing labyrinth of highly technical and interrelated tax and other laws that have an impact upon clients and their plans, our task – and yours – has become exceedingly difficult.

But we believe that *The Tools and Techniques of Life Insurance Planning* will be of significant help. In the following pages, you'll find six introductory chapters, twelve chapters on planning tools, twelve chapters on tax techniques, and a set of extensive tax appendices. You'll find unique charts, checklists, graphs, examples, and references to assist you in absorbing and in turn conveying highly complex concepts to clients in a clear and simple manner.

You'll find our opinions as to what should be done about problems your estate and business planning clients will face with respect to life insurance decisions. These should help you quickly identify problems, determine appropriate solutions, decide upon the most efficient and effective course to take, and convey to your clients the urgency and significance of action.

Although it is not designed as an exhaustive treatise on the laws regarding life insurance, it will be highly useful to students, CPAs, attorneys, trust officers, and others whose professional task is to advise others. Because it carefully defines each new term, it will also be of immense use to the layperson searching for a reliable objective source of information and to the professional searching for perspective.

The Tools and Techniques of Life Insurance Planning will be a timely, invaluable learning tool, reference manual, and practical guide for helping others make major life insurance decisions and for those who must make those decisions for themselves.

Please let us know how well we've met our objectives.

Stephan R. Leimberg

Robert J. Doyle, Jr.

GUIDELINES FOR THE PROFESSIONAL

Life insurance is the only certain way to create "instant" capital. That capital, in turn, can be used by clients to solve a multiplicity of personal and business problems.

To understand how life insurance can, and should, be used (the planners' imagination and creativity are the only major boundaries limiting the scope of life insurance's uses), you must first focus on the problems. Then, the planning team must

MATCH THE PRODUCTS WITH THE PROBLEMS TO BE SOLVED

in the priority order the client assigns to those problems.

Here are the major problems the client's family will face:

1. *Lack of liquidity* - Not enough cash to pay death taxes, administrative costs, attorneys' fees, appraisal fees, and other death-generated expenses as they fall due. (This is one of the major and most obvious reasons for life insurance.)

2. *Improper disposition of assets* - The wrong thing goes to the wrong person at the wrong time in the wrong manner. Many times the awesome responsibility of safeguarding, investing, and distributing the income from complex property or the task of running a business interest is thrust upon persons who are unable or unwilling to handle it. (Life insurance is often used as a substitute for such property, i.e., life insurance can be paid to or owned by a trust for the benefit of a beneficiary who cannot or should not manage a complex portfolio or run a business while the more competent, capable, and willing beneficiaries can be left securities or a business interest.)

3. *Inadequate amounts of income or capital at the client's death, disability, retirement, or for special needs* - College costs continue to climb. This in turn exhausts funds that might otherwise have been used for retirement and leaves many facing retirement with debt rather than assets. Clients are living longer, and having greater medical expenses during retirement and surprisingly higher (rather than as expected lower) standards of living and consequent mainte-

nance costs. In many cases they have more leisure time to travel, try new hobbies, and spend money than they did before they retired and less of their expenses are paid for after retirement by their companies. (Cash value life and disability insurance are obvious answers to part of these problems if the protection is coordinated with other investment planning.)

4. The value of the client's assets (particularly real estate portfolios or business interests) has not been stabilized or maximized: When all or the bulk of an estate consists of real estate, the cash required to pay taxes often far outstrips the cash available to pay those taxes. The result is often a forced sale of the real estate at the worst possible time. Likewise, a business which loses a key employee through death (or disability) often loses value needlessly. Without a "buy-sell" agreement, the client's family will seldom obtain a full and fair price for a business interest. The result of the absence of a buy-sell agreement between business owners is a total lack of a market for the business interest or at best a forced sale at pennies on the dollar (a "fire sale"). (Life and disability income insurance have been the traditional means of "shock absorbers" to stabilize a business at a key employee's death or to buy-out and bail out the heirs of a shareholder-employee.)

5. Excessive transfer costs: The cost of transferring wealth from one generation to another continues to increase because of increasing federal and state taxes, probate costs, attorneys' fees, and other "slippage." When property is owned in more than one state, "ancillary administration" (multiple probates) results in unexpected aggravation, delay, and expense. In many cases the ownership of property is set up in a manner that aggravates rather than minimizes the tax burden and other costs. (Life insurance can be set up in a manner that avoids all of these problems.)

6. Special needs: Successful clients often express a strong desire to "give back" to their schools, churches, synagogues, communities, or other charitable organizations. Many clients have spouses or children with certain gifts or handicaps which require larger than usual amounts of both capital and income — or who have asset management needs that would not be served by

an outright disposition of property to them. (Life insurance is often the most effective means — and sometimes the only way — of raising large amounts of cash to create financial security for an organization or an individual.)

Only when the planner has identified the need(s) and the client has expressed preference as to the order of needs should the planner attempt to formulate a strategy. Few clients can solve all their financially-oriented problems simultaneously. Resources must therefore be allocated to the tools or techniques which are most cost effective in solving these problems.

EXAMINE THE PROS AND CONS OF THE VIABLE ALTERNATIVES

Life insurance is a unique product in that a small premium payment can generate a vastly disproportionate amount of capital and guarantee the availability of that capital almost instantly. Death, the event which creates the need for large amounts of capital, creates the capital to satisfy that need through life insurance.

Clearly, life insurance is one of the most important of all the wealth creation and wealth transfer tools. Yet, the planner should never choose ANY tool or use ANY technique without asking:

"What are the no-cost or less costly alternatives to this product or device that could also solve the client's problem — and what are their pros and cons?"

Once the advantages and disadvantages of the viable alternatives are examined, the planner can objectively ask and ascertain

"Which course(s) of action will result in the highest present value of capital and income for the family unit as a whole and which course(s) of action will result in the lowest present value in terms of financial and other costs?"

In many cases life insurance will be the indicated tool. How that life insurance is arranged makes a considerable difference in the tax implications and ultimate cost effectiveness. One last question that the planner and every member of the client's advisory team — and the client — must ask is:

"What if I (we) do nothing?" "What happens — or doesn't happen?"

Decisions in financial, estate, business and employee benefit planning with respect to life insurance (or any

other tool or technique) must not be made in a vacuum. *A planner will be held accountable — not only for what is said and done — but also for the advice which is not given that should have been.*

LIFE INSURANCE AS A PROBLEM SOLVING TOOL

Only when the thought process described above has been employed should the planner arrive at a particular tool or technique — and the process should continue even after that selection.

Assuming life insurance has been chosen as the best vehicle for the job of solving one or more of these client problems and it has been ascertained that it can be used in a cost-efficient manner, the question then becomes, "what specific life insurance ownership and beneficiary strategy would best meet the client's objectives?"

Planners must continue to ask and answer many additional questions such as:

"What is the right type of life insurance for this client and how much is needed?"

"What specific life insurance ownership and beneficiary strategy would best meet the client's objectives?"

"What company (or combination of companies) could answer the identified product needs best?"

Use *The Tools and Techniques of Life Insurance Planning* as a complementary text to the other *Tools and Techniques* books to round out your ability to ask and answer questions such as these.

The Tools and Techniques of Life Insurance Planning will focus on life insurance as a problem solver and

(a) define each tool or technique,

(b) explain when the tool or technique is indicated and should be considered,

(c) illustrate through an example how the tool or technique is implemented,

(d) cover the tax ramifications of the strategy, and

(e) cover various questions regarding the practical application of the strategy.

TABLE OF CONTENTS

PART I TOOLS

PART II TECHNIQUES

APPENDICES

Chapter 1

INTRODUCTION TO LIFE INSURANCE

Life insurance is a complex amalgamation of legal, tax, and economic elements. But basically it is a unique wealth creation tool that assures the accumulation of a desired amount of liquid capital at death. Depending on the plan of insurance, it may also create more or less capital for lifetime needs.

Through its unique capital creation feature and tax advantages, it can be used to solve a host of personal and business problems. However, there is a wide variety of life insurance policies. Once the client's problems are identified, the insurance advisor must match the appropriate life insurance product to the problem. To do so, the planner must first fully understand the legal, tax, and economic elements of life insurance and the particular features of each type of policy.

This chapter will provide an overview of, as well as an introduction to, the multi-faceted aspects of life insurance. Use this chapter to gain and maintain perspective and balance. Because life insurance is not really one product but a multiplicity of products, above all learn to "MATCH THE PRODUCT WITH THE PROBLEM!"

PRINCIPAL USES OF LIFE INSURANCE

Broadly stated, life insurance is indicated only when there is a NEED.

The following is a checklist of common *estate building* and *estate conservation* needs that life insurance can satisfy:

- Provide for income needs of surviving dependent family members;

- Pay federal and state death taxes and other estate settlement costs;

- Pay debts;

- Provide for children's education;

- Shift wealth from one generation to another in the most cost effective manner possible;

- Meet "special" financial demands of physically or mentally handicapped or learning-disabled children or parents or other dependents with physical or mental limitations;

- Benefit a charity;

- Relieve survivors of financial management burdens by providing an inexhaustible lifetime annuity; and

- Create an "instant estate."

The following is a checklist of *business insurance* needs that life insurance can satisfy:

- Fund a buy-sell agreement;

- Finance nonqualified deferred compensation arrangements;

- Finance death benefit only (DBO) plans;

- Provide a basic level of financial security for families of all employees; and

- Recruit, retain, retire, and reward key employees.

The operative word is NEED. Life insurance should be recommended only if, and to the extent, any need exists. Thus, the financial services professional must first find a need and match the type and amount of the product to that need.

ADVANTAGES

The advantages offered by life insurance vary with the type of policy and the problem to which the policy is applied. These advantages are highlighted in subsequent chapters that describe the particular types of policies and the applications to which they are most suited. However, all types of life insurance policies provide certain favorable features, which are listed below.

1. Life insurance provides a guarantee of large amounts of cash payable immediately at the death of the insured. The amount of the death benefit payable is usually significantly greater than the premiums paid for the policy.

2. Life insurance proceeds are not part of the probate estate. The only way life insurance benefits become part of probate is when they are paid to or for the benefit of the estate of the insured. Therefore, the proceeds can be paid to the beneficiary without delay caused by administration of the estate.

3. There will be no public record of the death benefit amount or to whom it is payable.

4. Life insurance policies generally have some protection against creditors of both the policyowner and of the beneficiary. The amount of protection varies from state to state.

5. Life insurance cash values provide instant availability to cash through policy loans. The interest rate for policy loans is known in advance and is usually lower than the rate applicable to loans from other sources.

6. The death benefit proceeds from a life insurance policy are generally not subject to federal income taxes.

7. The increases in the cash value of a life insurance policy enjoy federal income tax deferral. Interest earned on policy cash values is generally not taxable unless or until the policy is surrendered for cash.

8. Life insurance proceeds are often exempt from state inheritance taxes.

9. Despite some highly publicized life insurance company insolvencies, the life insurance industry remains unparalleled in safety among the financial intermediaries such as the savings and loan, banking, and mutual fund industries. It is commonly noted that not a single dollar of death claim has been lost or denied because of a life insurance company insolvency or failure.

DISADVANTAGES

1. Life insurance is not available to persons in extremely poor health (although almost all individuals in poor health can obtain insurance).

2. Life insurance is an extremely complex product that is hard to evaluate and compare. The time required to gather policy information, decipher it, and compare it with other policies discourages purchasers from engaging in comparison shopping.

3. The cost of coverage reduces the amount of funds available for current consumption or investment.

LEGAL ASPECTS OF LIFE INSURANCE

Legally, life insurance is a contract, governed principally by state law, that promises to pay a specified amount of money to a designated beneficiary when the insured person dies. The contract is between the insurance company and the policyowner, who pays premiums in exchange for the promised death (and other) benefits. Frequently the policyowner is the person insured, but the policy can be owned by someone other than the insured.

In return for its promise to pay death and other benefits under the contract, the insurance company charges a premium to provide adequate funds to pay death benefits when they come due and to cover insurance company expenses and profits. (Ultimately, though, the death benefit may be significantly larger than the premium(s) paid for the individual policy.)

Although there are variations among the state laws, life insurance contracts are issued with a number of standard provisions. In the typical policy, these provisions:

1. Spell out who the parties to the contract are;

2. Explain the need for an insurable interest by the policyowner in the life of the insured;

3. Describe the legal form and contents of the contract;

4. Describe the insured's rights to name and change the beneficiary;

5. Limit the insurer's right to contest or challenge the validity of the contract after (usually) two years, even if the policyowner made a material or fraudulent misrepresentation in acquiring the policy;

6. Provide a one-month grace period for the payment of premiums;

7. Limit the insurer's obligation to pay death benefits if the insured commits suicide within (usually) two years of policy issue;

8. Provide for an adjustment in the death benefit in the event the insured's age is misstated;

9. Describe how the policyowner may apply or use dividends, if the policy is participating;

10. Assure minimum cash values in the event of lapse or termination of the policy and provide certain standard options as to how these "nonforfeiture" values may be received;

11. Explain the policyowner's right to reinstate and the procedures for reinstating the policy in the event of lapse;

12. Provide a number of alternative settlement options that beneficiaries may elect when receiving proceeds from the insurer;

13. Explain the policyowner's right to borrow cash values, and spell out the conditions and terms of such loans, including the method of determining the interest rate;

14. Give the policyowner the right to automatically have policy loans pay premiums if premiums are not paid by the end of the grace period; and

15. Explain the policyowner's right to assign the policy to another person or entity.

Each of these legal provisions is discussed in detail in Chapter 5, "Legal Aspects of Life Insurance."

In addition, in order for a contract to qualify as life insurance for income and other tax purposes it must exhibit risk shifting and risk sharing and it must meet the Internal Revenue Code's definition of life insurance, as provided in Code section 7702. Code section 7702 limits the amount of cash value relative to the face amount of coverage.

If the cash value were allowed to be too high relative to the face amount of coverage, there would be, first, insufficient risk shifting, and, second, an incentive to shelter otherwise taxable investment income in life insurance products. Increases in the cash values inside

a contract that fails to meet the standards of Code section 7702 are taxable to the policyowner as earned, rather than being tax deferred, as in qualifying life insurance contracts.

TAX ASPECTS OF LIFE INSURANCE

1. In general, no deduction is permitted for premium payments on life insurance policies. The notable exceptions are for premium payments for group life insurance provided by an employer for employees and for "bonus" payments to employees for payment of premiums under Code section 162 plans.

2. Dividends received by the policyowner generally are not subject to federal income taxation. Dividends are not usually taxable income until the aggregate of dividends paid exceeds the aggregate of premiums paid by the policyowner.

3. The cash value increases in a life insurance policy attributable to investment income are not usually taxable income as long as the policy remains in force. The cash value buildup in a life insurance policy generally enjoys an indefinite deferral from taxation while it remains in force and an exemption from taxation if the policy terminates in a death claim. However, if the policy is surrendered for cash, the gain on the policy is subject to federal income taxation. The gain on a surrendered policy is the amount by which the net cash value payable plus any policy loan forgiven exceed the owner's basis in the policy. Basis in the policy equals the premiums actually paid in cash less policyowner dividends and withdrawals recovered tax free, if any.

4. Withdrawals of cash values, when permitted, are usually taxed on a first-in, first-out basis, or under what is called the cost-recovery rule. Specifically, a withdrawal is considered to be a nontaxable recovery of cost basis or premiums until the policyowner's entire cost basis has been withdrawn. Only then are additional withdrawals treated as taxable distributions of interest or gain in the policy.

5. A withdrawal of cash values within the first 15 policy years may be taxed on a last-in, first-out basis, or under what is called the interest-first rule, if a reduction in the face amount of coverage accompanies the withdrawal. Specifically, in these cases a withdrawal will be taxable to the extent of gain in the policy. The excess is then treated as a nontaxable recovery of basis in the policy.

6. Distributions or withdrawals under the contract at any time before death from policies that are classified as modified endowment contracts (MECs) are taxed under the interest-first rule, even if they are not accompanied by a reduction in the face amount of coverage. In addition, if such distributions are received before age 59½, the taxable portion may be subject to an additional 10% penalty tax. (For the definition of a modified endowment contract, see Appendix D.)

7. Policy loans, except from modified endowment contracts, are generally not treated as taxable distributions, even if the loan exceeds the policyowner's cost basis in the policy.

8. Any interest paid or accrued on debt with respect to corporate-owned life insurance or annuity or endowment contracts is generally not deductible. This rule bars the deduction for interest even if the deduction would not be disallowed under any other rule (e.g., the four-out-of-seven rule). (See Appendix F for a further discussion of deductibility of policy loan interest.)

    For contracts issued before June 9, 1997, in tax years ending before that date, the interest disallowance rule applies only to corporate-owned life insurance policies and certain corporate-owned annuity or endowment contracts covering any individual who is or was an officer or employee of, or is or was financially interested in, any trade or business currently or formerly carried on by the business/taxpayer.

    There is an exception to the general corporate-owned life insurance interest disallowance rule for interest paid after October 13, 1995. Under this rule, a corporation may deduct a limited amount of interest subject to certain rate limitations. The exception applies only to interest paid or accrued on debt with respect to corporate-owned insurance policies or endowment or annuity contracts covering a "key person" (an officer or 20% owner). Furthermore, the interest is deductible only to the extent that the aggregate amount of the debt with respect to the policies and contracts covering that person does not exceed $50,000. This exception applies only to a limited number of key persons (not more than the greater of: (1) five individuals, or (2) the lesser of 5% of total officers and employees, or 20 individuals).

    For policies purchased before June 21, 1986, the limit on the deduction does not apply. However,

IRS has privately held that interest on contracts governed by prior law had to be valid interest to be deductible, that is, paid for the use or forbearance of money for a valid underlying debt obligation. According to IRS, policies with a high premium structure together with loading dividend and partial withdrawal mechanisms served no economic purpose and did not produce debt for tax purposes.

Generally, even if a policy qualifies under the exceptions described above, the interest paid on loans secured by a key employee life insurance policy is not deductible unless one or more of the following exceptions are met:

a) *"Four out of seven" exception* – At least four of the first seven annual premiums are paid without recourse to policy loans.

b) *"$100 a year" exception* – If the interest does not exceed $100 for any taxable year, the interest deductions will not be disallowed even if there is a systematic plan of borrowing.

c) *"Unforeseen event" exception* – If the debt was incurred because of an unforeseen substantial loss of income or substantial increase in obligations, the deduction will not be disallowed even though the policy loan was used to pay premiums.

d) *"Trade or business" exception* – If the debt is incurred in connection with the client's trade or business, the interest deduction will not be disallowed. Generally, the amounts to finance key employee coverage will not be considered to fall within this exception.

9. Personal interest, including interest on policy loans used for personal purposes, is no longer deductible. In general, if policy loans are used to pay premiums on the policy or for any other personal purpose other than to finance an investment or for business use, the interest is subject to the personal interest limitations.

10. Interest paid on policy loans used for investment purposes is subject to different deductibility limits. In general, the interest on all the taxpayer's loans, including life insurance policy loans, used to finance investments is deductible each year but only to the extent it does not exceed the taxable investment income from all investments. If interest expense

exceeds investment income in one year, the excess carries forward and may be deducted in future years when there is adequate investment income.

11. In general, life insurance death proceeds are not subject to federal income taxation. However, life insurance policies that have been sold from one policyowner to another may be subject to the transfer for value rule. Under this rule, the portion of the death proceeds in excess of the sum of the purchase price and any premiums paid after the transfer is subject to taxation as income. In other words, if an existing life insurance policy or an interest in an existing policy is transferred for any type of valuable consideration in money or money's worth, all or a significant portion of the proceeds may lose their income-tax-free status when the insured dies. However, certain transfers are exempt from the transfer for value rule. Policies can be transferred safely to (1) the insured, (2) a partner of the insured, (3) a partnership in which the insured is a partner, or (4) a corporation in which the insured is a shareholder or officer, without subjecting the policy proceeds to income tax.

12. Proceeds from corporate-owned life insurance policies paid to the corporation may generate an alternative minimum tax (AMT). Under a worst case scenario, this tax could amount to roughly 15% of the total policy proceeds paid to a corporate beneficiary. The AMT is basically an alternative tax calculation that assures at least a minimum amount of tax is paid if certain "preferred" types of income that are excludable for regular tax purposes or special deductions reduce the regular income tax "too much."

13. The proceeds of a life insurance policy will be included in the estate of the insured for federal estate tax purposes if the insured held "incidents of ownership" at any time during the three years prior to death or if the proceeds from the policy were payable to or for the benefit of the estate of the insured. Incidents of ownership include such things as the right to (a) change the beneficiary, (b) take out a policy loan, or (c) surrender the policy for cash.

14. Death benefits paid to someone other than the owner-insured or the owner-insured's estate are not treated as gifts for gift tax purposes.

15. Premium payments by an owner-insured on a policy where someone other than the insured or the insured's estate is named as beneficiary are generally not considered gifts for gift tax purposes.

However, premium payments by anyone on a policy owned by someone other than the person paying the premiums are generally considered gifts and may be subject to gift tax if the annual premiums exceed the annual exclusion ($11,000 in 2004 as indexed for inflation). Such premiums generally qualify for the annual exclusion.

Later chapters and appendices discuss the income, estate, gift, and generation-skipping transfer taxation of life insurance in detail. Also, any special tax considerations with respect to particular types of policies and their use in various particular applications are discussed where appropriate in the chapters describing the policies or in the "techniques" section of the book.

ECONOMIC ASPECTS OF LIFE INSURANCE

Life Insurance as an Investment

The principal economic purpose of life insurance is to accumulate capital. Although most commentators stress that life insurance should not be viewed principally as an investment, the authors of this text disagree. That is what life insurance really is: a superb "investment" vehicle. All conventional investment vehicles serve the same purpose, but the unique feature of life insurance is that it assures a desired accumulation at a specific, but uncertain, time, namely at the time of the insured's death. No other investment makes such a guarantee.

If the time of death were not uncertain, life insurance would be unnecessary. A person could accumulate any desired target amount by investing in a traditional investment vehicle and employing a systematic plan of saving, or what is called a sinking fund. For example, if a person's objective is to accumulate $1,000 in five years and he or she could be assured of surviving that long, this person could simply invest a specific lump-sum amount today in a traditional investment vehicle that with interest would grow to $1,000 in 5 years. For instance, if $620.92 is invested today at 10% interest, the fund will grow to $1,000 in 5 years. Alternatively, if this person does not have $620.92 to invest today, he or she could finance the accumulation over time, for instance, by investing $148.91 at the beginning of each year for the next five years. However, if this person died anytime before the end of the 5-year period, the amount accumulated at the time of death would be less than the desired $1,000. Life insurance is essentially an investment mechanism that assures the desired accumulation by the time of death regardless of when death occurs.

Figure 1.1

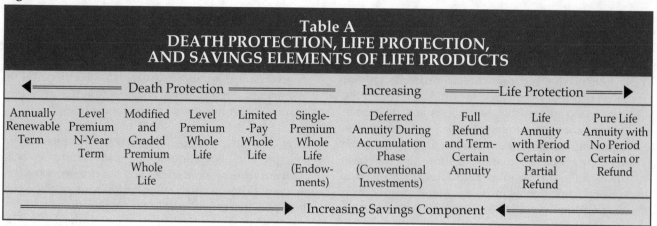

Table A
DEATH PROTECTION, LIFE PROTECTION,
AND SAVINGS ELEMENTS OF LIFE PRODUCTS

Most discussions of life insurance describe it as a combination of "pure death protection" that decreases and "savings" or "investment" that increases over a person's lifetime. This distinction can be confusing and misleading since life insurance should be viewed in its entirety as a special type of investment or accumulation vehicle that matures at death. However, this bifurcation between "death protection" and "savings" elements can be useful, if it is understood for what it really is. The savings component is the non-contingent part of the overall investment accumulation that is available not just at death, but also during life, similar to any conventional investment or savings instrument.

What is described as the pure death protection component is properly viewed as a contingent investment – the part of the overall investment accumulation that matures or becomes available only at death. The relative size of these two components depends on the life product and how the life insurance is financed. At one extreme is annually renewable term insurance, which is essentially 100% pure death protection and 0% savings. At the other extreme are deferred annuities during the accumulation phase (and other conventional investments), which are essentially 0% pure death protection and 100% savings.[1] The other life insurance products fall somewhere between these extremes.

Making the distinction between the "pure death protection" and "savings" components actually ignores half the spectrum of "life" products. Annuities may be described in a manner analogous to life insurance, as a combination of "pure *life* protection" and "savings" elements after the annuity starting date. The savings component of annuities is the non-contingent part of the overall investment that is available regardless of whether one lives or dies, similar to any conventional investment or savings instrument. In other words, the savings component is the guaranteed or refund amount provided by

some annuities that is payable even if the annuitant dies. The pure life protection component is a contingent investment that matures or is available only if the annuitant lives. At one end of this spectrum is full-refund or term-certain annuities (or conventional investments) that are essentially 100% savings and 0% pure life protection. At the other end of the spectrum are no-refund life annuities that are 0% savings (theoretically) and 100% pure life protection.[2]

Figure 1.1 shows how various "life" products from term insurance to annuities fall within the pure death/life protection and savings element spectra. But keep in mind that both components make up the total investment. Any assessment that evaluates the "investment" potential of a life product by looking only at the savings element (the amounts that are available regardless of whether a person lives or dies) ignores the fact that the pure death/life protection component is properly viewed as a type of contingent investment that matures or is available only when the death or life contingency occurs.

Simplified Life Insurance Financial Mathematics

The basic operation of life insurance as a capital accumulation vehicle with both death-protection and savings components can be illustrated with the following simplified example. Suppose 5 people form a capital accumulation lottery pool or syndicate with the objective that each of them will receive $1,000 from the pool over a 5 year period. Each person will contribute the same amount to the pool in each year that he or she still participates. However, at the end of each year, one of them, selected by lot, will be paid his or her $1,000 payout and will drop out of the pool. Only those persons remaining continue to make whatever contributions are necessary to fund for the $1,000 distributions in subsequent years. The expected or average number of years until any given participant in this pool will receive his or her payout is 3 years.[3] Assuming a 10% rate of return, the amount any one of them would have to save at the beginning of each year for 3 years to accumulate $1,000 is $274.65.

Figure 1.2 shows how much each participant would have to contribute each year to assure the necessary funds to pay $1,000 out of the pool each year to the person selected by lot using various funding or financing arrangements that are similar to typical insurance premium payment plans.

For example, in the "level-annual payment" section of Figure 1.2 each participant is assumed to contribute a level $284.99 at the beginning of each year that he or she is still a participant in the pool. With these contributions the pool will be adequately funded throughout the 5 year period. Specifically, each of the 5 participants pays $284.99 the first year for a total of $1,424.96. With interest credited at 10%, the end of year balance before distribution of the first $1,000 lottery payout is $1,567.46. The lucky winner is selected and paid $1,000, leaving $567.46 in the pool to help fund later distributions. This works out to $141.87 for each person who remains in the pool. In the second year, each of the remaining 4 participants again contributes $284.99, totaling $1,139.97. This amount, together with the carryover balance from the prior year, $567.46, will grow at 10% to $1,878.17 by the end of the second year when the second payout occurs. After paying $1,000 to the lucky winner, $878.17, or $292.72 per remaining participant, is left in the pool. The aggregate amount in the pool first increases and then declines as participants receive their $1,000 payouts and drop out. However, the balance or "reserve" per participant continues to increase each year until the last year when the remaining balance plus the last year contribution and interest earnings thereon equal the final required payout of $1,000.

This lottery pool arrangement is a simplified description of how a level-premium life insurance plan works. If this were a level-premium life insurance plan, the probabilities used would represent the chance of any given person dying each year rather than the chance of winning the lottery.[4] The "premium" each participant would pay ($284.99) is very close to the amount he or she would save each year ($274.65) to accumulate $1,000 by the end of his or her "life expectancy," which, in this simplified case is 3 years. However, just like in real life, although each participant can expect to live a certain period of additional years, in this case 3 years, some will die sooner and some will die later. The pool-

ing arrangement is a risk sharing mechanism that assures each participant that he or she will receive $1,000 regardless of when he or she dies, just as if he or she were certain to live to life expectancy and saved virtually the same amount as the premium each year.

Those participants who die sooner may be losers in the "game of life," but they are compensated by winning the lottery. They obviously receive more from the pool than they could have accumulated outside the pool arrangement by the time they die. For comparison, column (L) in Figure 1.2 shows how much any given participant would have accumulated by the end of each year if contributions had been invested outside the pool at the same 10% rate of return. For example, in the level-payment plan, the person who dies the first year and receives $1,000 would have accumulated only $313.49, or $686.51 less if the "premium" had been invested outside the plan.

The participants who die late are winners in the "game of life," but losers in the lottery. They actually receive less than they would have accumulated outside the pool by the time they die. For example, once again looking at the level-payment plan, the person who dies in year 5, receiving $1,000, would have accumulated almost twice as much, $1,913.88, if premiums had been invested outside the plan.[5] However, since nobody knows who will die sooner and who will die later, all participants are "winners" if their mutual objective is to assure that they will receive no less than $1,000 regardless of when they die. For essentially the same annual payment as it would take to accumulate the desired sum if they each lived to life expectancy, they eliminate the risk of under-accumulating if they should die early. And, if they happen to be one of the longer lived participants, they are still assured they will accumulate at least the minimum desired amount of $1,000.

As is characteristic of level-premium and other cash-value life insurance, the pool builds up reserves or cash values that are necessary to cover shortfalls that arise when there are fewer participants remaining who pay into the pool in later years. These values are shown in column (K). Although the aggregate reserves or cash value balances in the pool decline in the later years (columns (E) and (G)), they continue to increase throughout the 5-year payout period on a per-participant basis, which is analogous to how level-premium life plans work. This per-person reserve or cash balance is the "savings" element of the arrangement and is the source for policy loans, cash surrender values, and other "living" benefits in cash-value insurance plans. If a person dropped out of the pool before dying, he or she could take his or her individual cash balance without jeopardizing the cash accumulation necessary to ultimately pay $1,000 to the remaining participants.

The second section of Figure 1.2 shows a "pay-as-you-go" lottery pool that is analogous to an annually renewable term insurance plan. Similar to the level-annual payment lottery pool described above, the pool pays $1,000 at the end of each year to one participant determined by lot. Each remaining participant's contribution each year is equal to the amount that when aggregated and invested at 10% interest is just sufficient to pay $1,000 out of the pool at the end of the year with nothing left over. In contrast with the level-annual payment lottery pool and level-premium life insurance plans, there is no accumulated reserve or cash balance, which is analogous to an annually renewable term insurance plan. As this example clearly demonstrates, the pay-as-you-go annually renewable term plan starts with lower required premium payments than the level-premium plan, but they quickly increase and exceed the level-premium payments by the third year. The annually renewable term plan creates bigger economic "winners" and bigger economic "losers" than the level-premium plan. Those who die sooner, get a much greater effective return on their "investment" since their total payments into the pool are much less. Those who die later, get a much lower (negative) return on their investment, since they must make much greater total payments to the pool. However, once again, all participants may be viewed as "winners" under this arrangement relative to a savings plan outside the pool if their principal objective is sharing the risk to assure they each accumulate at least $1,000 regardless of when they die.

The last two sections of Figure 1.2 use the lottery analogy to show how single-premium life and limited-pay life compare to level-premium life and annually renewable term plans in this simplified example. When the paying period is shortened relative to the payout period, the total contributions necessary to fund later payouts are accelerated and the annual amounts paid in must necessarily increase. However, the per-person reserves or cash balances also increase. In other words the savings component of each participant's total investment increases while the pure death protection component decreases. Furthermore, the total amount any given participant must pay, even the longest surviving participant, declines. In other words, from an economic standpoint there is a smaller difference in the total cost of the program between the "winners" who die early and the "losers" who die late since the contingent or pure death protection component of the total investment has decreased.

Elements of Life Insurance Premium Pricing and Cash Value Calculations

Risk Shifting and Risk Sharing

A common misconception about life insurance is that the risk of premature death is transferred to the insurance company. Although insurance companies must have a certain amount of surplus or paid-in capital to cover potential excess losses, they price their products to maintain or even increase the surplus and paid-in capital over time. Therefore, risk is shifted to or shared among all insureds in the insurance pool. Those policyowners who live a long time carry the economic burden for those who do not. However, there is less risk sharing with premium-payment plans that generate a greater "savings" component, such as single-premium life insurance, than with those that have a greater "pure death protection" component, such as annually renewable term. The savings component, similar to other investments, can be viewed as a form of self-insurance, since it is available regardless of whether the insured lives or dies. If the self-insurance component is greater, the amount of risk that must be shared among all participants in the pool is obviously less.

Premiums and Costs

Another common misconception is that higher premiums mean higher cost. The various payment plans in Figure 1.2 demonstrate the fallacy of that conception. By design, each of the premium payment plans in Figure 1.2 is actuarially equivalent. In each case, the expected value of each participant's payments is exactly equal to his or her expected return, $1,000. In principle, life insurance companies determine premiums in the same way. From an actuarial standpoint, there are no differences between one premium-payment plan and another for a given level and term of coverage since they are all priced to be equivalent on a present value or prospective basis.

The actual after-the-fact cost to the insured may vary substantially from one premium-payment plan to another, as is also clearly demonstrated by the illustrated values in Figure 1.2. If a person dies soon, the pay-as-you-go term insurance plan is relatively the best economic deal. But it is also the worst deal for a person who lives a long time. Conversely, the single-premium plan is relatively the best deal if a person lives a long time, but the worst deal if death comes early. Clearly, all else being equal (which it is not because of the unique income and estate tax features as well as other characteristics of life insurance), if a person could be sure that he

Figure 1.2

	(A)	(B)	(C)	(D)	(E)	(F)	(G)	(H)	(I)	(J)	(K)	(L)
							Table B					
				LOTTERY ANALOGY TO THE OPERATION OF LIFE INSURANCE								
Year	BOP Balance	# In BOP	Pmt Per Person	Total Pmts (BxC)	Balance Before Interest (A+D)	Interest (at 10%) (Ex10%)	Balance After Interest (E+F)	EOP Payout	Balance After Payout (G-H)	# In EOP (B-1)	Balance Per Person (I÷J)	Amt Outside Each Person
Level-Annual Payment (Level Premium Whole Life)												
1	$ 0.00	5	$284.99	$1,424.96	$1,424.96	$142.50	$1,567.46	($1,000)	$567.46	4	$141.87	$ 313.49
2	567.46	4	284.99	1,139.97	1,707.43	170.74	1,878.17	(1,000)	878.17	3	292.72	658.33
3	878.17	3	284.99	854.98	1,733.15	173.32	1,906.47	(1,000)	906.47	2	453.23	1,037.65
4	906.47	2	284.99	569.99	1,476.45	147.65	1,624.10	(1,000)	624.10	1	624.10	1,454.90
5	624.10	1	284.99	284.99	909.09	90.91	1,000.00	(1,000)	0.00	0	0.00	1,913.88
Pay-As-You-Go (Annually Renewable Term)												
1	$0.00	5	$181.82	$909.09	$909.09	$90.91	$1,000.00	($1,000)	$0.00	4	$0.00	$ 200.00
2	0.00	4	227.27	909.09	909.09	90.91	1,000.00	(1,000)	0.00	3	0.00	470.00
3	0.00	3	303.03	909.09	909.09	90.91	1,000.00	(1,000)	0.00	2	0.00	850.33
4	0.00	2	454.55	909.09	909.09	90.91	1,000.00	(1,000)	0.00	1	0.00	1,435.37
5	0.00	1	909.09	909.09	909.09	90.91	1,000.00	(1,000)	0.00	0	0.00	2,578.91
One-Time Payment (Single-Premium Life)												
1	$ 0.00	5	$758.16	$3,790.79	$3,790.79	$379.08	$4,169.87	($1,000)	$3,169.87	4	$792.47	$ 833.98
2	3,169.87	4	0.00	0.00	3,169.87	316.99	3,486.85	(1,000)	2,486.85	3	828.95	917.37
3	2,486.85	3	0.00	0.00	2,486.85	248.69	2,735.54	(1,000)	1,735.54	2	867.77	1,009.11
4	1,735.54	2	0.00	0.00	1,735.54	173.55	1,909.09	(1,000)	909.09	1	909.09	1,110.02
5	909.09	1	0.00	0.00	909.09	90.91	1,000.00	(1,000)	0.00	0	0.00	1,221.02
3-Period Payment (Limited-Pay Life)												
1	$ 0.00	5	$341.03	$1,705.15	$1,705.15	$170.51	$1,875.66	($1,000)	$ 875.66	4	$218.92	$ 375.13
2	875.66	4	341.03	1,364.12	2,239.78	223.98	2,463.76	(1,000)	1,463.76	3	487.92	787.78
3	1,463.76	3	341.03	1,023.09	2,486.85	248.69	2,735.54	(1,000)	1,735.54	2	867.77	1,241.69
4	1,735.54	2	0.00	0.00	1,735.54	173.55	1,909.09	(1,000)	909.09	1	909.09	1,365.86
5	909.09	1	0.00	0.00	909.09	90.91	1,000.00	(1,000)	0.00	0	0.00	1,502.45

or she would live longer than average for his or her age, the best deal would be to invest outside of life insurance in conventional investments. But nobody can ever have that assurance.

Interest Rates

The required contribution levels (premiums) under the various payment plans in the Figure 1.2 illustrations were computed using an interest assumption of 10% and highly simplified mortality factors. Similarly, insurance companies must make assumptions about the interest they will earn on assets and the mortality experience of their pool of insureds to compute the required premiums. If it is assumed that reserves (the "savings" component) can be invested to earn high interest rates, the required premiums will be lower. If the assumed interest rate is lower, premiums will be higher. Life insurance companies guarantee that the interest rate that will be credited to the policyowner's "savings" component will equal or exceed a certain minimum rate, ranging from 4% to 6% (except on variable life products). The maximum interest rate that an insurer may assume when computing required premiums and reserves is limited by statute.

Mortality and Morbidity and the Law of Large Numbers

Mortality refers to the number of deaths in a given time or a given community. Generally, it is expressed as a rate reflecting the proportion of deaths to population, or to a specific number of the population such as per 1,000, 10,000, or 100,000 lives. Actuaries compute mortality for various large groups of people based upon demographic factors such as sex, age, race, and country or area or residence, and other factors such as occupation, educational level, income level, and habits or hobbies (e.g., smoker versus non-smoker). They create tables of mortality exhibiting the average relative number of persons who survive, or who have died, at the end of each year of life, out of a given number supposed to have been born at the same time.

The term morbidity is sometimes used in the same sense as mortality, but it is actually a more general term relating to the incidence of disease within a community, including both fatal and non-fatal cases.

Insurance companies base their mortality assumptions on the experience of large groups of people. By the law of large numbers, the proportion of a large group of people with similar characteristics of a given age who will die within a given year can be estimated with remarkable accuracy. Technically, the law of large numbers says that in repeated, independent trials with the same probability p of success in each trial, the chance that the percentage of successes differs from the probability p by more than a fixed positive amount, e > 0, converges to zero as the number of trials n goes to infinity, for every positive e. In other words, as the number of people of the same age and with similar characteristics increases, the rate of actual deaths experienced by the group will get closer and closer to the expected rate of deaths for the group at any given age.[6]

Adverse Selection and Moral Hazard

Adverse selection is one of two main sorts of market failure often associated with insurance. The other is moral hazard. Adverse selection can be a problem when there is asymmetric information between the seller of insurance and the buyer. What this means is that insurance may not be profitable when buyers have better information about their risk of claiming than does the insurer. Ideally, insurance premiums should be set according to the risk of a randomly selected person in the insured slice of the population (55-year-old male smokers, say). In practice, this means pricing based upon the average risk of that group. However, people who know they have a higher risk of claiming than the average of the group will tend to find the price attractive and buy the insurance, whereas those who have a below-average risk may tend to feel it is too expensive to be worth buying. In this case, premiums set according to the average risk will not be sufficient to cover the claims that eventually arise because, among the people who have bought the policy, more will have above-average risk than below-average risk. In general, raising the premium will not solve this problem, for as the premium rises the insurance policy will become unattractive to more of the people who know they have a lower risk of claiming.

The concept of moral hazard is related to the fact that people with insurance may take greater risks than they would tend to take without the insurance because they know they are protected. Consequently, the insurer may get more or earlier claims, on average, than expected. Insurers try to avoid these problems by requiring prospective insureds to take physical exams and by employing comprehensive underwriting procedures. They also negotiate with employers, associations, and other groups, to provide group coverage where essentially every member of the group is covered, so there is relatively little opportunity for adverse selection.

Underwriting Process

Through their underwriting process, insurance companies classify or rate insureds by their risk characteristics. Health, occupation, avocations, sex, and habits, such as whether or not the insured smokes or drinks are the types of factors considered when rating insureds. Depending on the rating, premiums may be based on "standard" or "preferred" mortality charges or multiples of up to 5 or even more times the standard mortality charges. Many insurers specialize in substandard risks. They will insure people with certain high-risk health characteristics, such as heart conditions, diabetes, or other diseases or debilitating conditions, or who are employed in high-risk occupations or practice high-risk avocations. Except for people in extremely poor health, almost anyone can acquire insurance, but perhaps only at very high rates. Insurers guarantee that mortality charges will not exceed certain maximums. But similar to interest rates, mortality rates insurers may use when computing required premiums and reserves must exceed certain statutory minimums by age and classification of insured.

Expenses and Risk Loadings

Although interest and mortality are the two principle factors in premium calculations, in reality other factors must also be included. Various expenses as well as risk loadings must be included when the insurer sets premiums. One major expense is agent sales commissions, which for a level-premium whole life insurance policy typically run about 55% or more of the annual premium in the first year and about equal to one annual premium in total over the life of the contract. Although this may seem high, it is not out of line with commissions and sales fees on other types of investments such as stocks, bonds, and mutual funds over the same period as a whole life insurance policy would typically be in force. For instance, in the case where the total commission is equal to one annual premium, the total commission expense would be equal to 4% of the total premiums a 40-year-old would pay to age 65. The sales fees or commissions on stocks and bonds and other types of investments are lower as a percent of the amount invested, but they are typically incurred both when buying and selling. If instead of paying premiums, this same person bought and held stocks and paid only a 2% commission on each purchase, he or she would have paid total commissions equal to only 2% of total investments by age 65. But this person would still have to pay 2% of the accumulated balance when selling the stocks. Since the accumulated balance would presumably be much greater than the total amount invested as a result of the growth in the value of the stock, the selling commissions would be considerably greater than another 2% of the total amount invested over the years.

The total "round trip" commissions on the stocks would almost certainly be greater than the total commissions paid for the insurance. Furthermore, it would be a rare individual indeed who never had any turnover (sales and repurchases) of his or her investments in the intervening years. Sell/buy transactions in the intervening years would further increase the commissions paid on the stock investment relative to the life insurance purchase. Compared with other types of investments, the sales commissions paid on life insurance look more and more favorable the longer the policy is expected to remain in force.

In addition, the insurance company must recover other typical business expenses for home office salaries and administrative costs, advertising and promotion, research and product development costs, underwriting, investment management fees, rent, and other operating and overhead expenses. These expenses together with agent sales commissions are typically recovered through some combination of front- and/or back-end charges and annual policy fees that must be recovered from premiums or from the "savings" component of the policy.

Finally, the insurance company must charge loading for various risks in addition to mortality risk. Since the bulk of the expenses associated with a policy is incurred when the policy is first issued, but the majority of these expenses are not recovered through expense charges for several years, policies that are lapsed or terminated within the first few years are a drain on the company's surplus. Therefore, the company must estimate lapse rates when setting premiums. It also adds a risk charge or load to cover the risk that the actual lapse rate will exceed projected rates. Also, since there is a risk that the company will not actually earn the guaranteed minimum rate on their investments, it must include a risk loading to the premium to cover this contingency. Similarly, although the number of people who will die each year out of a large group of people with similar characteristics and of the same age can be predicted with remarkable accuracy, there is always a residual risk that the company's actual mortality experience will be worse than was anticipated. Since a life insurance company guarantees that mortality charges will not exceed certain maximums, it adds a risk loading when setting premiums to help cover the risk that its actual mortality experience is worse than projected.

Similar to the lottery illustrated in Figure 1.2, insurance companies combine their interest, mortality, lapse and expense assumptions, and loading factors to determine the premium that is necessary for any given premium-payment plan to equate the present value of the expected future benefit payouts and expenses with the present value of the expected premium pay-ins from the group of similar policies. If the premium-payment plan is other than a pay-as-you-go annually-renewable term plan, per-policy reserves (the savings component) will build up and serve as the basis for cash values that are available for policy loans or as surrender values if a policy is terminated. Based on statutorily mandated conservative assumptions, the insurance company can guarantee a minimum schedule of cash values. In the initial years, the cash value available to the policyowner is usually less than the reserve, since either front- or back-end charges are imposed to recover the high initial policy issue costs. However, as the years pass and issue costs are fully recovered, the cash value that is available to policyowners grows ever closer to the entire reserve.

Participating and Nonparticipating Policies

Since insurance companies must guarantee death benefits and a minimum schedule of cash values in most policies (except variable life policies), they must be conservative when estimating the values of the various premium pricing factors (interest, mortality, expenses, lapse rates, and risk loading factors) used to compute the required premiums under any particular premium-payment plan of insurance.

In the case of nonparticipating policies, all elements – premiums, death benefits, and the schedule of cash values – are guaranteed and fixed. If a company's experience is more favorable than assumed with respect to any or all of the pricing factors, the premiums in excess of the amount needed to pay the company's obligations add to the company's profit or surplus. However, competitive pressures within the industry as well as from alternative investments have made such entirely guaranteed but nonparticipating policies unattractive in the marketplace. Now most policies issued are participating in one way or another, meaning that they share the benefits of the company's favorable mortality, investment, expense, or lapse experience with the policyowners.

In what are called traditional participating life insurance products (typically, but not exclusively issued by mutual rather than stock insurance companies[7]), policyowners participate in the favorable experience of the company through dividends. Life insurance dividends are not like stock dividends, which represent a return *on* investment. Instead, they are more like a return *of* investment and are generally treated for tax and other purposes as a nontaxable return of prior overpayment of premiums. Policyowners are typically given a number of options as to how such dividends may be used, such as to reduce current premiums, to buy paid-up additional insurance, to buy additional one-year term insurance, to repay policy loans, to increase policy cash values and shorten the premium paying period, or to accumulate at interest. In any case, dividends reduce the overall cost of insurance and make participating life insurance policies more attractive and competitive with alternative investments.

Purchasers of participating policies are presented with a schedule of projected dividends when they buy the policy. Basically, the projected dividends generally reflect the company's best estimate of the values of the various pricing factors as compared with the conservative assumptions built into their premium calculations. But in contrast with quoted premiums, death benefits, and cash value schedules, dividends are *not* guaranteed. They cannot be guaranteed since they depend on the company's actual experience relative to its conservative pricing assumptions, which cannot be known until the experience actually unfolds.

In relatively recent years, a new type of participating life insurance, generically called current-assumption life insurance, has become popular.[8] In contrast with traditional participating policies, these types of policies do not pay dividends. Rather, if the company's experience is more favorable than assumed in its premium-pricing computations, the favorable experience is reflected directly in the amounts credited to the policy's cash values. In other words, if the company's experience is favorable, cash values grow larger and more quickly than shown on the schedule of guaranteed minimum cash values.

Depending on the type of policy, the policyowner may have several options as to how these additional cash value increases may be used. In some cases, policyowners may withdraw the additional cash value without otherwise affecting their death benefits, premium payments, and minimum guaranteed cash values; they may be permitted to reduce the level of future premium payments while maintaining the same face amount of coverage; they may be allowed to increase the face amount of coverage while maintaining the same premium level; they may keep the face amount and the premium payment level the same but shorten the required premium-payment period; or they may choose some combination or variation of these options.

Purchasers of current-assumption policies are presented with an illustration of projected premiums, cash values, and death benefits that uses the company's current assumptions regarding the various premium pricing factors as well as an illustration showing the minimum guaranteed values based on the current premium and the statutorily mandated conservative pricing assumptions. Similar to projected dividends with traditional participating policies, the projected cash values and any projected death benefit increases above those shown using the required conservative pricing assumptions are *not* guaranteed. In many cases, even the premiums and the term of the policy are not guaranteed. If the company's experience turns out less favorably than currently assumed, the policyowner may

Figure 1.3

		Table C			
	LIFE INSURANCE POLICY COMPARISON CHART				
PRODUCT	**CHARACTERISTICS**	**MARKET**	**DEATH BENEFIT**	**PREMIUM**	**CASH VALUE (CV)**	**CV AND/OR DIVIDENDS USE CURRENT INTEREST?**
Annual Renewable Term	"Pure" life insurance with no cash value element; initially, the highest death benefit for the lowest premium.	Short to intermediate term need; need max. death benefit for min. initial premium.	Fixed, level.	Fixed, increasing.	No cash value.	N/A
Participating Ordinary Life	Most common and easily understood form of lifetime coverage; known max. cost and min. death benefit levels; dividends may reduce premiums, pay-up policy, buy paid-up additions, accum. at interest, be paid in cash.	Anybody who needs lifetime coverage.	Fixed, level.	Fixed, level.	Fixed with min. guaranteed interest rate; excess through dividends.	Yes.
Current Assumption Whole Life	Mixes characteristics of universal life and traditional ordinary life; future premiums, face amount, and/or cash value based on interest, expense, mortality experience.	Upper and middle income prospects.	Fixed, level.	May change based on insurer's experience; Max. guaranteed but insurer may charge less.	May change based on insurer's experience; guaranteed min.; Min. guaranteed interest; excess lowers premium or increases CV.	Yes.
Variable Life	Whole life contract with assets supporting policy held in separate account; choice of investment assets; death benefits depend on investment results.	Upper and middle income prospects with investment acumen.	Guaranteed min.; can increase based on investment performance.	Fixed, level.	Based on investment performance; not guaranteed.	N/A.
Adjustable Life	May select death benefit and, within limits, choose premiums; face amount and premiums are fixed between adjustment periods; usual features of whole life.	Young families starting insurance program; need for flexibility with guarantees.	Adjustable.	Adjustable at option of policyowner.	Varies depending on premium/death benefit mix; fixed with min. guaranteed interest; excess through dividends.	Yes.
Universal Life	Flexible premium current-assumption adjustable death benefit policy; policy elements unbundled; two death benefit options.	Middle and upper income looking for ultimate in flexibility.	Adjustable; Option A like Ord. Life; Option B like Ord. Life plus term rider equal to cash value.	Flexible at option of policyowner.	Varies depending on face amount and premium; min. guaranteed interest excess interest increases cash value.	Yes.
Universal Life III — Universal Variable Life	Combines features of universal and variable life.	Middle and upper income with investment acumen looking for ultimate in flexibility.	Adjustable.	Flexible at option of policyowner.	Varies depending on face amount, premium, and investment performance; not guaranteed.	N/A
Annuities	Combine tax advantages, investment choice, flexibility and guarantees with various lifetime payout options that cannot be outlived.	Middle and upper income; qualified (IRA) and non-qualified retirement arrangements.	Accumulation period: max. of premiums or cash value; payout period: depends on option.	Fixed or flexible.	Varies depending on investment performance; min. guaranteed interest rate unless variable annuity.	Yes.

Figure 1.3 (cont'd)

		Table C			
LIFE INSURANCE POLICY COMPARISON CHART					
PARTIAL SURRENDERS PERMITTED?	**POLICY ELEMENTS**	**DIRECT BORROWING RECOGNITION**	**ADVANTAGES TO BUYER**	**DISADVANTAGES TO BUYER**	**RISKS TO BUYER**
N/A	Bundled.	N/A	Low outlay for large face amounts; develop outside investment program.	Increasing outlay; buyer may not invest difference or may realize lower return.	Increasing premium. Failure to earn more aftertax on investments than insurer.
Yes, but through paid up additions only.	Bundled.	Yes, with many policies.	Familiar product; predictable; helps buyer discipline; share in favorable interest, mortality and expense experience.	Costly if lapsed early.	Failure to meet premium commitment.
Yes.	Unbundled.	Yes.	Take advantage of high current interest rates and improved mortality.	Premiums can be higher or cash value lower than projected; policy can lose paid-up status.	If assumptions change adversely, premiums can be higher or cash value can be lower than with traditional products.
No.	Bundled, but to some degree shown in prospectus.	No.	Take advantage of growth in economy.	Must decide on underlying investments and monitor them for change; few guarantees.	Investment risk is great. Typically higher expenses than traditional products.
Yes.	Bundled.	Yes.	Flexibility to adjust to changing needs; only one policy needed.	If needs are known and not likely to change, other products may be less costly per unit of protection.	Changes made by buyer to satisfy short-term needs may have an impact on the satisfaction of long-term goals.
Yes.	Unbundled.	Yes.	Greater transparency and more flexibility than Adj. Life.	Flexibility places greater responsibility on buyer; buyer assumes greater investment and mortality risks.	Adverse change in assumptions can affect satisfaction of long-term goals and drop cash value below that of ordinary life.
Yes.	Unbundled.	No.	Epitome of flexibility in all respects.	Equity performance unpredictable; relatively high expenses; few guarantees.	Combined risks of universal and variable life products.
Yes.	Partially unbundled.	Yes, if permitted.	Cannot outlive benefits if life option elected.	Expenses can be higher than alternative investments.	Under life options, payouts cease at death: if death occurs early, total benefits less than with alternative investments.

have to pay premiums for a longer period than anticipated or pay increased premiums in order to maintain
the face amount of coverage. Alternatively, the
policyowner may have to accept a reduction in the face
amount of coverage or a shortened term of coverage.

Variable life policies are the ultimate in participating
policies, at least with respect to investment performance. The policyowner bears all the investment risk
and reaps all the investment rewards from the underlying investments; the insurer provides no minimum
interest guarantee with respect to cash values. In most
cases the policyowner may choose to invest premium
dollars among a number of mutual fund type investments. As in other types of policies, the insurer guarantees that mortality charges will not exceed certain maximums and that the death benefit will not fall below a
certain minimum, regardless of the investment performance of the underlying assets. However, the insurer
makes no assurances regarding cash values. Depending
on the type of variable life policy, favorable investment
performance may increase the face amount of coverage
or the policyowner may be given a number of flexible
options similar to those described above for certain
current-assumption policies.

SUMMARY COMPARISON OF POLICIES

Figure 1.3 summarizes and compares the characteristics, markets, advantages and disadvantages, and other
features of various types of life contracts. More complete information is provided in separate chapters on
the various products.

WHERE CAN I FIND OUT MORE ABOUT IT?

1. B. Anderson, *Anderson on Life Insurance* (Waltham,
    MA: Little, Brown and Company, 1991).

2. B. Baldwin, *The Complete Book of Insurance: Protecting
    Your Life, Health, Property and Income* (Chicago, IL:
    Probus Publishing Company, 1991).

3. B. Baldwin, *New Life Insurance Investment Advisor:
    Achieving Financial Security for You and Your Family
    Through Today's Insurance Products*, 2nd ed.
    (Hightstown, NJ: McGraw-Hill Trade, 2001).

4. J. Belth, *Life Insurance: A Consumer's Handbook*, 2nd
    ed. (Bloomington, IN: Indiana University Press,
    1985).

5. K. Black, Jr. and H. Skipper, Jr., *Life Insurance*, 13th ed.
    (Old Tappan, NJ: Prentice Hall Inc., 1999).

6. W. Brownlie and J. Seglin, *The Life Insurance Buyer's
    Guide* (Hightstown, NJ: McGraw-Hill Publishing
    Company, 1989).

7. G. Daily, *The Individual Investor's Guide to Low-Load
    Insurance Products* (Chicago, IL: American Associa-
    tion of Individual Investors, 1989).

8. *Journal of the American Society of CLU and ChFC*
    (Bimonthly), (Bryn Mawr, PA: The American Soci-
    ety of CLU and ChFC).

9. *Best's Review — Life/Health Edition* (Monthly),
    (Oldwick, NJ: A. M. Best Company).

10. H. Zaritsky and S. Leimberg, *Tax Planning with Life
    Insurance*, 2nd ed. (Boston, MA: Warren, Gorham &
    Lamont, updated yearly).

11. E. Graves, Editor, *McGill's Life Insurance*, 5th ed.
    (Bryn Mawr, PA: The American College, 2004).

CHAPTER ENDNOTES

1. The life insurance product "closest" to a 0% pure death protec-
    tion and 100% savings combination is a single-premium endow-
    ment policy. An endowment policy is essentially a whole life
    policy that will mature or "endow," that is, pay the face amount
    of coverage, if the insured is still alive at a specified age, such as
    age 65. Similar to other life insurance products, it also pays the
    face amount if the insured dies before the policy endows. By
    analogy, traditional whole life policies are really endowment
    policies that endow at age 95 or 100. Since policies that endow
    before age 95 or 100 build substantial cash values relative to the
    face amount of coverage, they usually will be classified as
    modified endowment contracts (MECs) for tax purposes or will
    fail the Code section 7702 definition of life insurance altogether.
    In either case, the adverse tax consequences of such classification
    has made endowment policies unpopular. (MECs and the Code
    section 7702 definition of life insurance are covered in Appendi-
    ces D and F, respectively.)

    Although some endowment policies that meet the Code
    section 7702 definition of life insurance (but are generally classi-
    fied as MECs) are offered by some insurance companies, in
    general consumers have turned to deferred annuities to accom-
    plish the same basic tax-advantaged accumulation objective.
    Deferred annuities enjoy the same tax-deferred accumulation as
    endowments and other cash-value life insurance products with-
    out the risk and adverse tax consequences of failing the Code
    section 7702 definition of life insurance.

    In reality, most deferred annuities provide a slight measure
    of pure death protection during the accumulation period before
    payout. In general, if the insured-annuitant dies before the time
    when payouts are scheduled to begin, the insurance company
    guarantees that the gross amount payable will not be less than
    the total premiums paid, even if the investment performance is
    such that the accumulated value would otherwise be less than
    the total premiums paid.

2. Even "pure" no-refund life annuities may be considered to have some "savings" component or provide some element of recovery even in the event of death since (1) they may sometimes be exchanged for annuities with refund or guaranteed features, (2) companies may permit the annuitant to "surrender" all or a part of the annuity for its commuted value, or (3) in very limited circumstances and in limited amounts, the annuitant may be permitted to take loans.

3. The expected or average number of years until payout may be determined by summing the number of years all participants must wait in total until each receives a payout and dividing that total by the number of participants. In this simple example, one participant must wait 1 year, another 2 years, another 3 years, another 4 years, and the last participant, 5 years. The sum is 15 years. Therefore, the expected or average number of years each participant must wait is 3 years.

    The expected or average number of years until payout is analogous to the concept of life expectancy when dealing with probabilities of death and should not be confused with the number of years until there is a 50% chance that a given participant will receive a payout or the number of years until half the participants will have received a payout. The initial probability that any particular participant will *receive* the payout in any given year, given that he or she is still a participant at the beginning of the year is 20% for each year. This probability is determined by multiplying the probability of "winning" the lottery in any particular year, given the number of participants remaining in the pool, by the probability of being one of the remaining participants going into that year. Specifically, in the first year, the probability of winning the lottery is 1/5, since all 5 participants are in the pool in the first year. The probability of winning the lottery in the second year, given that a person is still in the pool, is 1/4, since there will then be only 4 participants remaining. The probability of being one of the 4 participants remaining in the pool is 4/5. Therefore, the initial probability of winning the lottery in the second year is also 20% (1/4 x 4/5). Similarly, the initial probability of winning the lottery in the third, fourth, or fifth years is 20% [(1/3 x 3/5), (1/2 x 2/5), (1 x 1/5), respectively].

    The probability of winning the lottery on or before a given year is determined by summing the probabilities up to and including that year. Specifically, for any given participant, there is a 20% chance of winning the lottery in the first year, a 40% chance of winning the lottery within the first two years, a 60% chance of winning within 3 years, and 80% chance of winning within 4 years, and a certainty (probability of 1) of receiving the payout within 5 years. Since there is a 40% chance of receiving the payout within two years and a 60% chance of receiving the payout within 3 years, the expected or average number of years until half the participants receive a payout (that is, there is a 50% chance of receiving the payout) is 2.5 years (although this number is purely theoretical in this case since payments are never made in the middle of the year and, furthermore, half the number of participants is 2.5). (If the pool had been set up for 6 years, rather than 5, and with 6 participants, rather than 5, the number of years until half the participants (3) received payouts – the number of years until any given participant had a 50% chance of winning the lottery – would be exactly 3 years. However, the expected or average number of years until any given participant could expect a payout in this case would still be greater, 3.5 years.)

    It is a common misconception with respect to the use of life expectancy tables that the life expectancy for a given age represents the additional number of years until half the people that age can be expected to die, or alternatively, beyond which half the people can be expected to live. Depending on the "force of mortality" over the relevant range of years, the life expectancy may be longer or shorter than the number of years until half the people of a given age can be expected to die. For virtually any age for most of the commonly used life expectancy tables, life expect-

ancy is *less* than the number of years until half the people that age can be expected to die.

4. The probabilities used in Figure 1.2 are unlike real mortality probabilities since the number of people assumed to die each period (1) is known with certainty, the only uncertainty is which of the participants is the unlucky one. By the law of large numbers, the proportion of a population of people of the same age and characteristics that will die each year can be predicted with greater and greater accuracy as the number of people in the population increases. However, there is always some residual risk that more or less than the predicted number will die in any given year. The only certainty with a group of real lives is that, ultimately, they will all die.

5. The comparison of the amount that could be accumulated "outside" with the amount accumulated inside the plan assumes all else is equal, which is unrealistic. Life insurance has tax and other favorable features, other than the payment of death benefits, that would be difficult if not impossible to reproduce outside the life insurance vehicle. However, regardless of the specifics of how one should best compare investments outside the life insurance plan with the total investment aspects of a life insurance plan, the general principle remains true. Life insurance is a risk-sharing pool where, by necessity, some people (those who die early) will receive more than they could ever have accumulated without life insurance and others (those who die later) may receive less than they could have accumulated without life insurance. The various tax advantages and other advantageous features of life insurance help to increase the number of economic "winners" relative to "losers." But for every pool of insureds there will always be some, those who live the longest (if they could have only known beforehand), who might have done better by investing their premium dollars in something other than insurance.

6. Note two things: The difference between the number of successes and the number of trials times the chance of success in each trial (the expected number of successes) tends to grow as the number of trials increases. (In fact, this difference tends to grow like the square-root of the number of trials.) Although the chance of a large difference between the percentage of successes and the chance of success gets smaller and smaller as n grows, nothing prevents the difference from being large in some sequences of trials. The assumption that this difference always tends to zero, as opposed to this difference having a large probability of being arbitrarily close to zero, is the difference between the Law of Large Numbers, which is a mathematical theorem, and the Empirical Law of Averages, which is an assumption about how the world works that lies at the base of the Frequency Theory of probability.

7. Stock insurance companies are, like regular corporations, owned by stockholders who put up the required capital with the objective of earning profits on the difference between the premiums paid for policies and the various death and living benefits paid out. Mutual insurance companies are in principle owned by the policyowners rather than stockholders. "Profits," as such, do not exist. Premiums paid in excess of the amount necessary for the company to pay benefits increase the company's surplus (similar to a stock company's capital account or owner's equity account). A certain amount of surplus is required as a reserve to assure payment of all of the company's obligations under their life insurance contracts and to finance the company's growth, but any excess, called divisible surplus, may be shared with and distributed to policyowners.

8. Originally, current-assumption policies were developed and sold by stock insurance companies to compete with the participating policies offered by mutual insurers. Today, current-assumption types of policies are the bread-and-butter of stock companies but they are also offered in various forms by many mutual insurers.

Chapter 2

HOW TO ESTIMATE THE INSURANCE NEED

INTRODUCTION

Financial planning professionals apply diversified techniques to determine the life insurance needs of a family. There are essentially three principal, but often overlapping, life insurance planning areas:

- income replacement and family needs analysis;

- business insurance needs analyses; and

- estate preservation and liquidity needs analysis.

Life insurance planning is best conducted with a comprehensive study of the client's financial needs and concerns. The process of life insurance planning must begin and end with the objectives and goals of the client being paramount, even if such objectives and goals do not conform to what the advisor considers proper or appropriate values or concerns. This is not to suggest that the advisor does not have a responsibility to "educate" the client about the potential uses and abuses of insurance, issues normally considered when assessing life insurance needs, ownership issues, tax effects, and the like. However, ethics and prudence require that the insurance plan satisfy the client's objectives; a plan, however well conceived and however "appropriate," will simply not be implemented if the client is not satisfied that it meets his or her objectives.

INCOME REPLACEMENT AND FAMILY NEEDS ANALYSIS

Any method of determining a family's insurance needs will be an estimate. Future circumstances will change in unexpected ways and basic assumptions about earnings, interest rates, inflation, and similar factors will never replicate actual experience. Consequently, every insurance program must be monitored and periodically updated to assure that the client's needs are still being met.

Personal computers have made it possible to perform increasingly comprehensive and sophisticated analyses of insurance needs. The problem with this trend is that, as the analyses become more comprehensive and sophisticated, what is already an inherently confusing subject becomes even more so, often further reducing the client's ability to understand and accept the insurance plan. There is frequently an unfortunate, but necessary, tradeoff between comprehensiveness and comprehension.

Insurance advisors use basically three approaches to estimate family life insurance needs:

- rules of thumb;

- income replacement approach; and

- needs approach.

Rules of Thumb

The simplest methods to understand, and the least reliable, are various rules of thumb that are frequently used to estimate either the amount of insurance that is needed or the amount of premium one should be spending on insurance.

One rough guide used to estimate the amount of insurance required is six to eight times annual gross income. For example, a parent earning $50,000 per year should have between $300,000 and $400,000 of life insurance under this rule.

A similar rule that takes immediate cash needs at death into account is five times gross income plus mortgage, debts, final expenses, and any other special funding need (e.g., college fund). For example, assume once again that a parent earns $50,000 per year but also that the mortgage is $60,000, other personal debts are $10,000, final expenses are expected to be $15,000, and that $35,000 is needed for the children's college expenses. Using this rule, the parent should be insured for $250,000 (5 x $50,000) plus $120,000 ($60,000 + $10,000 + $15,000 + $35,000), or $370,000 total.

Another rule is that 6% of the breadwinner's gross income plus another 1% for each dependent should be spent on premiums for life insurance. Under this rule, a person with a nonworking spouse and three children should be spending about 10% of gross income on premiums for life insurance. In some cases, the amount of premium may be expressed as a percent, ranging from 5 to 15%, of after-tax take-home pay.

Such rules of thumb can be useful as a very rough starting point. They can give clients a broad sense of the scope of the problem in terms they can quickly understand, but they are, at best, very limited. Individual needs vary widely and the rules of thumb do not take such variations into account. They do not take account of the insured's age, the dependents' ages, or whether the family is a one- or two-income household. Stating the objective in terms of required premium outlays is even more limited, since premiums will vary greatly for the same amount of coverage depending on the insured's age and plan of insurance.

Multiples–of–Salary Method

A somewhat more precise rule-of-thumb method is the use of multiples-of-salary charts such as presented below. This approach is actually a hybrid method combining the simpler rule-of-thumb methods with elements of the income replacement and needs analysis approaches discussed below. The chart is based on the assumption that the average family can live adequately and maintain its standard of living on 75% of the wage earner's after-tax income and that the insured is the only breadwinner in the family. If income were to drop below 60%, the family's living standard would suffer. The chart also assumes social security coverage and that insurance proceeds are invested at a net annual rate of 5%.[1]

To use this chart:

1. Find the column showing the spouse's current age.

2. Locate the point in the column at which the client's earnings intersect the spouse's age (the 75% column is recommended).

3. Multiply the client's salary by the appropriate factor.

MULTIPLES-OF-SALARY CHART

Your Client's Present Gross Earnings	Present Age of Your Client's Spouse							
	25 Years		35 Years		45 Years		55 Years	
	75%	60%	75%	60%	75%	60%	75%	60%
$ 7,500	4.0	3.0	5.5	4.0	7.5	5.5	6.5	4.5
9,000	4.0	3.0	5.5	4.0	7.5	5.5	6.5	4.5
15,000	4.5	3.0	6.5	4.5	8.0	6.0	7.0	5.5
23,500	6.5	4.5	8.0	5.5	8.5	6.5	7.5	5.5
30,000	7.5	5.0	8.0	6.0	8.5	6.5	7.0	5.5
40,000	7.5	5.0	8.0	6.0	8.0	6.0	7.0	5.5
65,000	7.5	5.5	7.5	6.0	7.5	6.0	6.5	5.0

Source: Cady, *Field Guide to Estate Planning, Business Planning & Employee Benefits*, (National Underwriter Company, 2004).

If the age or earnings differ from those shown in the chart, interpolate using the nearest salaries and ages. For example, assume your client's salary is $35,000 and the spouse is age 40. Since $35,000 is halfway between the $30,000 and $40,000 earnings rows and also halfway between the age 35 and age 45 columns shown in the chart, the multiplier would be found by averaging the four factors shown in these row/column combinations ($30,000 row and age 35 column: 8.0; $30,000 row and age 45 column: 8.5; $40,000 row and age 35 column: 8.0; $40,000 row and age 45 column: 8.0). Therefore, the multiplier is 8.1 [(8.0 + 8.0 + 8.0 + 8.5) ÷ 4]. The estimated amount needed to meet the family's income requirements is $283,500 ($35,000 x 8.1).

In general, this amount would be increased to account for immediate capital or cash needs at death. Such capital needs would commonly include funds to pay funeral and other final expenses, to pay off debts, such as mortgages or personal loans, to fund special projects, such as children's educations, and to set up an emergency reserve. For example, assuming your client had a $50,000 mortgage and estimated final expenses of $20,000, wanted $40,000 to fund the children's educations, and felt that the equivalent of one year's salary ($35,000) should be set aside for emergencies; the total capital needs would be $145,000. Adding the $145,000 required to fund capital needs to the $283,500 required to fund income needs would result in a total need of $428,500.

Finally, the amount of additional insurance needed is determined by subtracting any insurance already in force and the value of other assets available from the total calculated need. For example, assume your client already has $150,000 of group insurance provided through his or her employer and has otherwise saved $30,000. The amount of additional insurance needed would be computed by subtracting $180,000 from the estimated total need of $428,500 to derive the final result, $248,500.

The multiples-of-salary chart method still suffers from many of the limitations associated with the simple rules of thumb. It does not take account of the age of the insured, premium costs, or the number of dependents who must be protected. Although it does adjust for the spouse's age (and implicitly, the number of years in which income must be provided), it does not adjust for the ages of children. In addition, it is not a suitable method in the increasingly common case where both spouses work. Similar to the simpler rules of thumb, it does not take into account differences in tax rates or investment rates of return that may apply in different family situations.

However, if these limitations are kept in mind, this method can provide reasonable first approximations of the insurance need in simple situations.

The Income Replacement Approach

A second approach used to estimate life insurance needs is based on the human life value concept. The human life value concept has often been applied in wrongful death litigation and basically holds that the measure of the economic value of a life to those who depend on that person is the present value of the future earnings potential of that person. The income replacement approach to life insurance needs analysis is based on the premise that the basic objective of life insurance is to replace some or all of the earnings lost if an income-producing family member should die. In other words, the insurance should be equal to the value of that person's future earnings potential to the surviving family members.

Although the basic premise may be questionable because it ignores other equally valid reasons why life insurance may be purchased, the method does allow one to estimate a theoretical maximum based on the idea that a person should never be worth more economically to beneficiaries dead than alive. This method may provide a more accurate starting point than simple rules of thumb while still being relatively easy conceptually – if not computationally – to understand.

Human Life Value

A person's human life value depends on numerous factors including future income levels, taxes, education,

training, promotions, and various normal decremental factors such as the possibility of illness, disability, periods of unemployment, and the like. However, reasonable estimates of the present value of future earnings can usually be determined using basically four inputs or assumptions:

1. current annual after-tax earnings (C);

2. the projected rate of growth of earnings (g);

3. the future working lifetime (n); and

4. an after-tax discount rate (r).

Given these four factors, the present value of future earnings may be computed using the present value of an annuity formula, equation 2.1, as follows:[2]

Equation 2-1:

$$\text{PV Future Earnings} = C \times \left[\frac{1 - \left(\frac{1}{1+i^n} \right)}{i} \right] \times \left(\frac{1+i}{1+\frac{r}{2}} \right)$$

where $i = \left[\frac{r-g}{1+g} \right]$, the growth-adjusted discount rate, and $r \neq g$.

If $r = g$, the present value is simply equal to n x C.

The formula assumes earnings are paid annually in the middle of the year, which is a reasonable approximation to monthly or other periodic payments throughout the year.

For example, assume (1) your client's after-tax income is currently $50,000 per year, (2) he estimates it will grow at an average annual rate of 5%, (3) he is age 35 and expects to work for 30 more years until age 65, and (4) an appropriate after-tax discount rate is 6%. The present value of his future earnings is about $1,275,000, computed as follows:

PV Future Earnings

$$= \$50,000 \times \left[\frac{1 - \left(\frac{1}{1.009524} \right)^{30}}{0.009524} \right] \times \left(\frac{1.009524}{1 + \frac{0.06}{2}} \right)$$

$$= \$50,000 \times \left[\frac{1 - 0.75249}{0.009524} \right] \times \left(\frac{1.009524}{1.03} \right)$$

$$= \$50,000 \times 25.988062 \times 0.98012$$

$$= \$1,273,575 \approx \$1.275 \text{ million}$$

The value of $1,275,000 is the amount that, if invested today at a 6% after-tax rate of return, could provide an after-tax income stream payable in the middle of each year for the next 30 years, with the initial after-tax amount starting at $50,000 and each subsequent payment growing by 5%. After 30 years, the entire $1,275,000 would be used up.

Basic Assumptions

The present value of future earnings is very sensitive to changes in the underlying earnings growth and discount rate assumptions. For example, if earnings are assumed to grow at 2% rather than 5% and the discount rate remains at 6%, the present value is $881,000, or almost 1/3 less. If instead, earnings are assumed as before to grow at 5%, but the discount rate is only 3%, the present value is just over $1,980,000, or more than half again greater.

What are reasonable assumptions for the earnings growth and discount rates?

Earnings growth rate – The earnings growth rate will usually depend on inflation rates and tax rates, as well as career opportunities. As a guideline, keep in mind that the average annual compound U.S. growth rate of inflation-adjusted disposable (after-tax) income has been just over 2% over the long run. In other words, on average, after-tax incomes have increased by about 2% more than inflation each year. Year to year, the rate has varied widely, but for estimation purposes, long-term trends are most appropriate.

Inflation itself has averaged slightly more than 3% per year over the long run, but it too varies widely from year to year or from subperiod to subperiod. For the 11 year period ending in 1990, inflation averaged 5.2% per year. This is considerably lower than the 7.2% average in the decade of the seventies but still high by long-term historical standards. The recent trend of inflation rates has been down, however. Since the end of 1985, the average annual inflation rate has been slightly less than 3%.[3] As we learned in the 1970's, we can at times experience long periods where inflation rates remain quite high. However, if we assume a reversion to the long-run averages, a reasonable starting point for estimating long-term earnings growth rates might be the combined long-run trend for inflation, 3%, plus the average 2% real growth above inflation, or 5%.

The 2% U.S. average growth in inflation-adjusted disposable earnings is an average across all industries and occupations and all age groups. But it is not necessarily a good estimate of real average annual earnings growth for any particular individual. First, every individual is unique and may advance faster or slower than others within his or her occupation. Second, earnings growth rates vary among industries and occupations.

Some occupations or occupations within certain industries experience greater than average earnings increases as computed across all occupations while other occupations are experiencing less than average increases.[4] So estimates of earnings growth rates must take close account of the particular talents and potential of the client and the character of the lifetime earnings profile of his or her chosen occupation.

As a practical matter, estimates of future real inflation-adjusted earnings growth rates are unnecessary in many cases. Many family breadwinners desire to provide a standard of living comparable to that the family currently enjoys if they should die. However, they do not feel quite the same responsibility to insure the increasing standard of living the family might enjoy while they live. If the objective is to maintain the family's current standard of living, it is only necessary to estimate future inflation rates, not also earnings growth rates in excess of inflation. In these cases, an estimate of the average future inflation rate would be substituted for the earnings growth rate in equation 2.1. The value so calculated is the amount that if invested today at the assumed after-tax rate of return could replace the wage earner's current level of real inflation-adjusted after-tax income each year for the rest of what would be the wage earner's remaining working lifetime.

After-tax discount rates – Estimating reasonable after-tax discount rates can be just as problematic. The basic question is: at what after-tax rate of return could the life insurance proceeds be invested over the long run? That depends on the risk one is willing to assume, tax rates, and inflation rates. As a guideline, Figure 2.1 presents average nominal and real (inflation-adjusted) compound returns for principal categories of marketable assets and inflation for the period 1974 to 2003.

Using the period 1974 to 2003 as a basis for estimating returns, an investment in long-term high-quality corporate bonds could be expected to return about 9.92% before tax compounded annually. A 50/50 mix of high quality corporate bonds and common stocks, which is perhaps about as aggressively as one would want to assume the assets would be invested, could be expected to return about 11.06%. As Figure 2.1 shows, the real annual inflation-adjusted compound return for corporate bonds over this period was just 4.97% after adjusting for inflation (which averaged 4.72%); for a 50/50 bond/stock mix, about 6.06%. Chances are that returns for all asset classes will tend toward the long run average over time, but there is no assurance of when or even if that will actually happen.

Figure 2.1

AVERAGE ANNUAL NOMINAL AND REAL COMPOUND RETURNS (1974-2003)		
	Nominal	**Real**
Large Stocks (S&P 500)	12.20%	7.15%
Corporate Bonds (Moody's AAA)	9.92%	4.97%
Government Bonds (10 Year)	9.03%	4.12%
Treasury Bills (3 Month)	6.48%	1.68%
Inflation (Consumer Price Index)	4.72%	4.72%

Source: Based on data obtained from Global Financial Data, Los Angeles, CA, www.globalfindata.com.

Since the values computed will vary substantially depending on the assumed rate of return, it is best to discuss alternative assumptions with your client and let him or her be your guide, within informed reason, on selecting the appropriate discount rate. Since present values vary inversely with the assumed discount rate, the conservative and prudent practice is to err on the side of lower, rather than higher, assumed rates.

To determine the appropriate discount rate, whatever estimate of return is used must be adjusted for taxes. The tendency is to overstate tax rates since appropriate adjustments for standard deductions and personal exemptions, as well as the tax-free recovery of investment, are neglected. The effect of the standard deduction and personal exemptions is to reduce the appropriate tax rate for use in equation 2.1 to about 20% to 80% of the marginal tax bracket rate for a comparable level of adjusted gross income. The effect of the exclusion of amounts treated as a recovery of the initial investment further reduces the effective average tax rate by 1/3 or more. In general, it is suitable to apply tax rates ranging from about 4% to about 10% when determining after-tax discount rates to use in equation 2.1.[5]

Family Support Ratio

Under the income replacement approach, insurance value is always less than human life value. The portion of after-tax income spent for self-maintenance is not available for the family so only the remaining portion may be devoted to or spent in support of the family. It is often assumed that about 25% of after-tax income is spent for self-maintenance and the remaining 75% for family support. However, this ratio may vary widely from family to family. In general, the proportion spent in support of the family is somewhat less at higher incomes than at lower incomes and is higher the greater the number of children. In addition, under the basic premise of this method, one of the important elements of family support is the cost of the insurance itself. Since the amount spent for insurance is not otherwise available to support the family's standard of living, this cost should further reduce the proportion of income that is insured to support the surviving family members' standard of living.

Therefore, once an estimate of the breadwinner's human life value is determined, that amount should be multiplied by the family support ratio. For example, if the present value of future earnings is determined to be $1 million and if it is also assumed that 70% of the breadwinner's after-tax income is needed to support the surviving family members' standard of living, then the amount needed to maintain the family in the event of the breadwinner's death is $700,000.

Other Adjustments

The amount so determined is not necessarily the amount of additional insurance required. This amount should be further reduced by the amount of any assets that are currently available to fund the survivor's income needs and by any life insurance currently in force. Among the assets that should be counted are marketable securities, savings account balances, and the like, as well as current vested account or benefit balances in employer-sponsored pension and profit-sharing plans, IRC Section 403(a) or (b) tax-deferred annuity plans, individual retirement arrangements (IRAs), simplified employee pensions (SEPs), and Keogh plans.

Many advisers feel that the family support ratio should also be increased to account for contributions or credits that would be made to employer-sponsored retirement plans (qualified and nonqualified) while the breadwinner lives. For example, assume the employer sponsors a 401(k) plan that will match 50% of employee contributions up to 6% of pay. If the employee has 6% of pay deducted for the 401(k), the reported after-tax salary is reduced by about 6%. However, the 401(k) plan is increased by 9% of pay. Assuming, for simplicity that the employee is in the 33% tax bracket, this is effectively equivalent to an offsetting 6% increase in the employee's after-tax income. Therefore, the family support ratio should be computed based on the reported after-tax income increased by the effective after-tax value of the 401(k) contributions. If the family support ratio is otherwise assumed to be 70%, it should be increased to 74.2% to account for the equivalent after-tax value of the employer-sponsored plan (70% x 6% = 4.2%).

In addition, many advisers strongly suggest that the amount should be increased by any outstanding debts, such as personal loans and the home mortgage, and by anticipated final death expenses. Although it violates the general premise of the income replacement method (which is to provide a fund sufficient, but no larger than that necessary, to replace what the breadwinner would provide to the family if and while he or she lives), in some cases advisers further recommend that additional insurance be acquired to fund special objectives, such as college education funds for the children. In general, such funding objectives would be considered part of the normal support obligation and would be implicitly included when selecting the family support ratio.

Adjustment for Social Security Survivor Benefits

Most workers are covered by Social Security or some other government program that provides survivor benefits to surviving spouses with dependent children and surviving spouses alone after age 60. This is a form of income-replacement insurance and should reduce the present value of the family support obligation accordingly. The amount paid to a surviving spouse with one eligible child is 150% of the deceased spouse's primary insurance amount (PIA) at the date of death. For each additional eligible child an additional 75% of the PIA is payable. Children are eligible until age 16, or until age 18 if in high school, or as long as they are disabled if disability occurs before age 22. A spouse alone is eligible for reduced benefits equal to 71.5% of the PIA starting at age 60, or if receipt of benefits is delayed, up to 100% of the PIA starting at normal retirement age.[6] A disabled spouse is eligible for 71.5% of the PIA starting at age 50. The total amount payable to the family is subject to a limit, called the maximum family benefit, which can range from 150% to about 187.5% of the PIA.

The PIA depends on both the level of pay and the number of years in covered employment. Information regarding a person's current insurance status in the Social Security program, earnings history, current PIA, and estimates of benefits may be acquired by filing Form SSA-7004-PC (SPEC) (9-89) with the Social Security Administration. It is generally advisable to file this form at least once every three years to check the accuracy of the Social Security Administration's records, since corrections generally have to be made within three years of the time of the error. Currently, the Social Security Administration automatically sends out statements containing such information, so it may not be necessary to request the information.[7]

Figure 2.2 can be used to estimate survivor benefits. The figures are for 2004 and are based on the assumption that the worker has been employed steadily and received 5% pay raises throughout his or her working career. In the case of the $87,900 wages, wages are assumed to be equal to or greater than the maximum OASDI wage base for all years. Normal retirement age depends on when a person was born. Like other Social Security benefits, survivor benefits are increased each year to reflect changes in the cost of living. Therefore the table may be used to estimate benefits in 2004 and later years by scaling the appropriate figures up by the rate of increase in the CPI since 2004.

For example, assume your client, Mike Fox, is married and is currently earning $60,000 in FICA wages, is age 45 (wife, Mary, age 40), and has two children, ages nine and five. According to Figure 2.2, Mary and each of Mike's two children are eligible for $1,215 a month, or $3,645 total in 2004 dollars. However, the maximum monthly family benefit is $2,836 in 2004 dollars. The annual benefit of $34,032 (12 x $2,836) would be payable for nine years until Mike's nine-year-old turns age 18 (assuming the child is in high school). (All benefits would be increased each year for inflation.) After that, $29,160 (12 x $1,215 x 2: the maximum family benefit limit is higher at this point and no longer applies) would be payable for two years until Mike's second child reaches age 16. At this point, Mary would lose her benefit until age 60. Mike's second child would continue to receive a child's benefit of $14,580 (12 x $1,215 x 1) for two more years until age 18 if a full time high school student.

When Mary reaches age 60, she will be eligible for $1,158 per month (in 2004 dollars) for life, or if she waits until age 67 (her normal retirement age) to begin receiving payments, $1,620 (in 2004 dollars). Of course, Mary's benefits must also be adjusted for anticipated increases due to inflation until benefits begin. The mechanics of this adjustment are explained in the following section.

Figure 2.2

		Earnings in 2004				
Age	**Family**	**$30,000**[1]	**$45,000**[1]	**$60,000**[1]	**$75,000**[1]	**$87.900 or More**[2]
35	Your spouse and one child[3]	$1,605	$2,142	$2,479	$2,730	$3,041
	Your spouse and two children[4]	1,957	2,517	2,893	3,186	3,549
	One child only	802	1,071	1,239	1,365	1,520
	Your spouse at NRA[5]	1,070	1,428	1,652	1,820	2,027
	Your spouse at age 60[6]	765	1,021	1,181	1,301	1,449
45	Your spouse and one child[3]	1,554	2,065	2,430	2,670	3,000
	Your spouse and two children[4]	1,864	2,448	2,836	3,116	3,501
	One child only	777	1,032	1,215	1,335	1,500
	Your spouse at NRA[5]	1,036	1,376	1,620	1,780	2,000
	Your spouse at age 60[6]	740	984	1,158	1,272	1,430
55	Your spouse and one child[3]	1,585	2,099	2,433	2,636	2,914
	Your spouse and two children[4]	1,920	2,479	2,839	3,076	3,400
	One child only	792	1,049	1,216	1,318	1,457
	Your spouse at NRA[5]	1,056	1,399	1,622	1,757	1,942
	Your spouse at age 60[6]	755	1,000	1,159	1,256	1,389

APPROXIMATE MONTHLY SURVIVORS' BENEFITS FOR YOUR FAMILY ASSUMING STEADY EARNINGS AND DEATH IN 2004

1. Assumes earnings increased at 5% annual growth rate from age 22 through 2004.
2. Assumes earnings equal to or greater than the OASDI wage base from age 22 through 2004.
3. Amounts shown also equal to the benefits paid to two children, if no parent survives or surviving parent has substantial earnings.
4. Equals the maximum family benefit.
5. Normal retirement age (66 to 67) depends on year of birth. Amounts payable in 2004. Spouses reaching NRA in the future would receive higher benefits.
6. Amounts payable in 2004. Spouses turning 60 in the future would receive higher benefits.

Note: The accuracy of these estimates depends on actual earnings, which may vary significantly from those shown here.

Converting Social Security Survivor Benefits to Present Values

To account for these Social Security benefits when determining the amount of insurance required, Social Security benefits must be converted into a present value. This can be easily accomplished using equation 2.1. Using the prior example to demonstrate the procedure, the benefits payable during the children's eligibility period are best viewed in three components:[8]

1. a stream of $14,580 (12 x $1,215 in 2004 dollars) annual payments for 13 years (the youngest child's benefit until reaching age 18); and

2. a stream of $14,580 (12 x $1,215 in 2004 dollars) payable for 11 years (Mary's benefit until the youngest child reaches age 16); and

3. a stream of $4,872 ($34,032 Maximum Family Benefit - [$14,580 x 2: Mary's and youngest child's benefits] in 2004 dollars) payable for 9 years (the incremental benefit payable to the oldest child as limited by the maximum family benefit).

Assuming benefits continue to inflate at a 3% rate each year and that 6% is a reasonable interest rate assumption, equation 2.1 would be used to determine the present values as follows:

$$i = \frac{0.06 - 0.03}{1.03} = 0.02913$$

$$\text{PV Benefit Stream (1)} = \$14,580 \times \left[\frac{1 - \left(\frac{1}{1.02913^{13}} \right)}{0.02913} \right]$$

$$\times \left(\frac{1.02913}{1 + \frac{0.06}{2}} \right)$$

$$= \$14,580 \times 10.69437 \times 0.999155 = \underline{\$155,792}$$

PV Benefit Stream (2) = $14,580 x $\left[\dfrac{1 - \left(\frac{1}{1.02913^{1}}\right)}{0.02913}\right]$

$\qquad$ x $\left(\dfrac{1.02913}{1 + \frac{0.06}{2}}\right)$

= $14,580 x 9.29737 x 0.999155 = $135,441

PV Benefit Stream (3) = $4,872 x $\left[\dfrac{1 - \left(\frac{1}{1.02913^{9}}\right)}{0.02913}\right]$

$\qquad$ x $\left(\dfrac{1.02913}{1 + \frac{0.06}{2}}\right)$

= $4,872 x 7.81779 x 0.999155 = $38,056

PV Streams (1) + (2) + (3) = $155,792 + $135,441 + $38,056 = $329,289

The present value of Social Security benefits payable to the spouse, Mary in this case, is determined in a similar manner, except that the present value must be adjusted for the fact benefits will not be paid until Mary reaches at least age 60.[9] This can be accomplished in several ways, but the easiest method is to use a two-step procedure where you first calculate the present value as if the payments were to begin today and then discount this value at the assumed inflation-adjusted rate of return for the number of years until payments would actually begin. The formula for finding the present value of a future lump-sum value of the spouse's benefits is:

Equation 2-2:

Present Value of Future Lump Sum (FLS) =

FLS x $\left(\dfrac{1}{1+i}\right)^{n}$

where i is computed using the assumed before-tax discount rate. The before-tax discount rate is used since Social Security benefits are generally paid free of income tax.[10]

Equation 2.1 can be used in the first-step calculation to determine the lump-sum value of the benefit stream payable to Mary, assuming that Mary were currently age 60 (or at normal retirement age, depending on which age benefits are assumed to start). The term of the payment period should be Mary's life expectancy at the age payments are assumed to begin. Based on IRS Table V (see Figure 2.3),[11] life expectancy for a 60-year-old is 24.2 years. Of course, adjustments should probably be made for any known health problems, the family history of longevity, and the fact that females still tend to live longer than males, although the gap is narrowing slightly.[12] Assuming payments will begin at Mary's age 60, her monthly payments will be $1,158, or $13,896 annually. If the appropriate life expectancy is 24.2 years,

the discount rate is 6%, and the inflation rate is 3% (that is, i = 0.02913), the future lump-sum value of Mary's benefit stream when she is age 60 using 2004 dollars is

Future Lump-Sum Value
Spouse's Benefit Age 60 = $13,896 x $\left[\dfrac{1 - \left(\frac{1}{1.02913^{24.2}}\right)}{0.02913}\right]$

$\qquad$ x $\left(\dfrac{1.02913}{1 + \frac{0.06}{2}}\right)$

Future Lump-Sum Value Spouse's Benefit Age 60 = $13,896 x 17.19404 x 0.99915 = $238,725

Equation 2.2 is now applied to complete the second step of the calculation. In this case, Mary is currently age 40, so the future Social Security benefits will begin in 20 years at age 60. The present value of the future lump-sum value of Mary's benefits is computed as follows:

Present Value of Future Lump Sum (FLS)

= $238,725 x $\left(\dfrac{1}{1.02913}\right)^{20}$

= $238,725 x 0.56311 = $134,428

The present values of all Social Security benefits to the family are summed to determine the current insurance value of the Social Security benefits. In this case, the present value of the Social Security benefits payable to Mary and the children while the children are young is approximately $329,000, and payable to Mary upon reaching age 60 is approximately $134,000, for a total of about $463,000. The present value of the family support obligation otherwise determined should then be reduced by this amount in deriving the required amount of insurance.

Income Replacement Approach – Step by Step

Figure 2.4 presents a work sheet that summarizes the nine basic steps in using the income replacement approach to determine insurance need.

For example, in the case of the Mike Fox family, the analysis would proceed as follows. Assume Mike's after-income-and-FICA tax take-home pay is $50,000. Assume also that Mike expects his income to grow at 4% [about 1% more than the rate of inflation, which is assumed to be 3% (to be consistent with assumptions regarding Social Security benefits)]. Also assume, that a 2% after-tax return in excess of inflation is reasonable, or about 5%. In this case, then, the earnings-adjusted discount rate for computing the present value of Mike's future earnings is about 1% (5% less 4%). Further

Figure 2.3

	TABLE V.				
	ORDINARY LIFE ANNUITIES – ONE LIFE – EXPECTED RETURN MULTIPLES				
Age	Multiple (Life Expectancy)	Age	Multiple (Life Expectancy)	Age	Multiple (Life Expectancy)
5	76.6	42	40.6	79	10.0
6	75.6	43	39.6	80	9.5
7	74.7	44	38.7	81	8.9
8	73.7	45	37.7	82	8.4
9	72.7	46	36.8	63	7.9
10	71.7	47	35.9	84	7.4
11	70.7	48	34.9	85	6.9
12	69.7	49	34.0	86	6.5
13	68.8	50	33.1	87	6.1
14	67.8	51	32.2	88	5.7
15	66.8	52	31.3	89	5.3
16	65.8	53	30.4	90	5.0
17	64.8	54	29.5	91	4.7
18	63.9	55	28.6	92	4.4
19	62.9	56	27.7	93	4.1
20	61.9	57	26.8	94	3.9
21	60.9	58	25.9	95	3.7
22	59.9	59	25.0	96	3.4
23	59.0	60	24.2	97	3.2
24	58.0	61	23.3	98	3.0
25	57.0	62	22.5	99	2.8
26	56.0	63	21.6	100	2.7
27	55.1	64	20.8	101	2.5
28	54.1	65	20.0	102	2.3
29	53.1	66	19.2	103	2.1
30	52.2	67	18.4	104	1.9
31	51.2	68	17.6	105	1.8
32	50.2	69	16.8	106	1.6
33	49.3	70	16.0	107	1.4
34	48.3	71	15.3	108	1.3
35	47.3	72	14.6	109	1.1
36	46.4	73	13.9	110	1.0
37	45.4	74	13.2	111	.9
38	44.4	75	12.5	112	.8
39	43.5	76	11.9	113	.7
40	42.5	77	11.2	114	.6
41	41.5	78	10.6	115	.5

assume Mike's employer provides an insurance benefit equal to one and one-half times Mike's gross pay, or $90,000 and that he has $30,000 in marketable assets and cash available to help fund the family's income need. Assume further that Mike's current mortgage balance is $110,000, which he would like paid off in the event of his death, and that final death expenses are expected to be about $15,000. Finally, assume about 75% of Mike's after-tax income would be necessary to support the family's current standard of living should he die.

Based on these assumptions and using equation 2.1, the present value of Mike's 20 years of future after-tax earnings is about $892,186, which is entered in Step 1 of the work sheet (see Figure 2.5). Multiplying this present value by the 75% family support ratio determines the present value of the family support obligation, which is $669,140. As described above, the present value of the survivorship benefits under Social Security is $463,000. This amount, together with the $90,000 of employer-provided life insurance and $30,000 of available assets,

Figure 2.4

INCOME REPLACEMENT APPROACH WORK SHEET		
Step	**Description**	**Values**
1	PV of future after-tax earnings stream [Equation (1)]	_____
2	Family support ratio	_____
3	PV of family support obligation (1 x 2)	_____
4	PV of Social Security benefits	_____
5	Other decremental adjustments[1]	_____
6	Total decrements (4 + 5)	_____
7	Net family support obligation (3 - 6)	_____
8	Special adjustments[2]	_____
9	Insurance Required (7 - 8)	_____

1. Includes insurance already in place on insured plus marketable assets, cash, and other assets such as vested retirement benefits.
2. Such as final expenses, debt repayment, college education funds.

reduces the present value of the family support obligation by $583,000 to just $86,140. When the special funding needs totaling $125,000 are added, the amount of insurance required is determined to be about $211,140. This amount represents just over 3.5 times Mike's current gross income of $60,000.

Income Replacement as a Multiple of Gross Pay

Figures 2.6, 2.7, and 2.8 show multiples-of-salary tables, similar to the multiples of salary chart above, but using the income replacement approach with actual income and Social Security tax rates and Social Security benefit levels. Since the number of alternative situations is virtually endless, the authors have restricted their analyses to three different cases based on family size that they consider "representative" of many family insurance situations. The tables are indicative of how the amount necessary to replace 75% of a "representative" family's after-tax income may vary by age of insured, gross pay level, and number of children. The following assumptions are common to each table:

1. The insured's earnings are assumed to grow at the rate of inflation (that is, it is assumed that the objective is to maintain the family's current standard of living, but not to insure any real increases in family income that might occur if the insured survives).

2. The insured's current after-tax income is computed based on the current tax rate schedule for married persons filing jointly.

3. Social Security taxes are computed assuming gross pay is employment (as opposed to self-employment) income subject to a 7.65% tax rate up to the Social Security OASDI wage base and to a 1.45% tax rate on all earned income.

4. The Social Security OASDI and HI wages bases are indexed for inflation.

5. Itemized deductions are assumed equal to 15% of current gross pay.

6. Personal exemptions, standard deductions, and tax brackets are indexed for inflation.

7. The single taxpayer tax schedule is used to compute taxes on replacement income for a

Figure 2.5

	INCOME REPLACEMENT APPROACH WORK SHEET: THE MIKE FOX CASE		
Step	**Description**	**Values**	
1	PV of future after-tax earnings stream [Equation (1)]		$892,186
2	Family support ratio		0.75
3	PV of family support obligation (1 x 2)		$699,140
4	PV of Social Security benefits	$463,000	
5	Other decremental adjustments[1]	120,000	
6	Total decrements (4 + 5)		(583,000)
7	Net family support obligation (3 - 6)		$86,140
8	Special adjustments[2]		125,000
9	Insurance Required (7 - 8)		$211,140

1. Includes insurance already in place on insured plus marketable assets, cash, and other assets such as vested retirement benefits.
2. Such as final expenses, debt repayment, college education funds.

surviving spouse with no children. The head-of-household tax schedule is used for a surviving spouse with children.

8. Social Security survivor benefits and family maximums are assumed to maintain the same level relative to the insured's pay in future years as shown in Figure 2.2.

9. Social Security benefit levels and family maximums are indexed for inflation.

10. The after-tax inflation-adjusted discount rate is assumed to be 3% (that is, the actual rate of return is assumed to exceed the inflation rate by about 3%, regardless of the actual level of inflation).

11. The surviving spouse will elect to receive Social Security survivor benefits at age 60 and the value of the benefits is computed assuming a life expectancy of 24.2 years (IRS Table V).

12. The family income replacement ratio is 75% of after-tax income.

13. The insured and spouse are the same age.

14. The amount required to replace family income is computed using the IRC Section 72 annuity taxation rules. That is, it is the investment that would be necessary to provide a cost-of-living-adjusted fixed-term annuity paying an amount before tax sufficient to reproduce the after-tax family replacement income over the term until the insured would have reached age 65. The tax-favorable annuity taxation rules of IRC Section 72 defer the tax on investment earnings until they are actually paid. In addition, a fixed proportion of each payment is excluded from tax as recovery of the initial investment.

Figure 2.6 shows the amount of insurance required to replace 75% of *after-tax* pay as a multiple of gross pay over various assumed ages for the insured ranging from 25 to 55. The multiples are computed assuming there are no children eligible for Social Security survivor benefits and that the surviving spouse's benefits will begin at age 60. Because of the shorter income-replacement period,

Figure 2.6

INSURANCE REQUIREMENTS IN ADDITION TO SOCIAL SECURITY* TO REPLACE 75% OF EARNINGS AFTER TAXES** TO INSURED'S AGE 65 – NO CHILDREN (EXPRESSED AS A MULTIPLE OF GROSS ANNUAL PAY.)							
Gross Annual Pay	**Age of Insured at Death**						
	25	**30**	**35**	**40**	**45**	**50**	**55**
$15,000	14.7	13.4	11.9	10.2	8.2	5.9	3.2
30,000	14.5	13.2	11.6	9.9	7.9	5.7	3.2
45,000	14.3	12.9	11.4	9.7	7.8	5.6	3.2
60,000	14.3	12.9	11.4	9.7	7.8	5.6	3.2
75,000	14.4	13.1	11.6	9.9	8.0	5.8	3.4
87,900	14.4	13.1	11.7	10.1	8.2	6.1	3.8
100,000	14.6	13.3	11.9	10.3	8.5	6.4	4.1
125,000	14.8	13.5	12.1	10.4	8.6	6.6	4.3
150,000	15.0	13.7	12.2	10.6	8.7	6.7	4.4
200,000	15.0	13.7	12.2	10.6	8.8	6.8	4.6
250,000	14.9	13.6	12.1	10.5	8.7	6.8	4.6
500,000	14.7	13.3	11.9	10.3	8.6	6.7	4.6

* Assumes spouse is the same age as insured and elects to receive Social Security survivor benefits based on insured's PIA beginning at age 60.

** Taxes considered include federal income and Social Security taxes only.

the multiples decline with the age of insured. At each age, the multiples tend to increase with gross income (in some cases, multiples may actually decrease inversely to increases in income at certain low or high levels of income), but the difference between the lowest and highest multiples is not generally large. Some of the differences are attributable to the lower tax rates and the higher Social Security spouse's survivor benefit levels relative to income at the lower income levels. Since the value of the surviving spouse's benefits becomes larger at later ages (because the discount period is shorter), the difference in the multiples between lower and higher income levels increases slightly at later ages.

Figures 2.7 and 2.8 present the same type of information as Figure 2.6, except that they assume there are two and four children, respectively, who qualify for Social Security survivor benefits. The children's Social Security survivor benefits greatly reduce the multiples at the ages where the children are assumed to receive benefits, especially at the lower income levels where the benefits are higher relative to the insured's gross pay. The children's Social Security benefits also have a much greater effect on the multiples at lower income levels than at higher income levels; once again, because of the relatively higher benefit levels at lower income levels.

The tables can be used to estimate the required insurance amount for a sufficiently "representative" family as follows:

1. Find the multiple in the column corresponding to the breadwinner's current age and the row corresponding to the breadwinner's current gross pay and multiply it by the breadwinner's gross pay. (If necessary, interpolate.)

2. Reduce the amount determined in step 1 by the value of any assets or insurance currently available to fund the income need in the event of death.

3. Add the current value of any special additional funding objectives, such as final expenses, mortgage debts, etc.

4. The result is the amount of additional insurance required.

For example, assume the breadwinner and spouse are age 35, the breadwinner earns $50,000, and they have two children, ages six and nine. The multiple, estimated by interpolation from Figure 2.7 is about 3.1 times gross pay. The lump-sum amount necessary to replace 75% of the inflation-adjusted after-tax income for 30 years (until the insured would be age 65) after

Figure 2.7

Gross Annual Pay	Age of Insured at Death						
	25	30	35	40	45	50	55
$15,000	14.7	1.9	3.7	5.3	7.1	5.6	3.0
30,000	14.5	0.3	2.6	4.8	6.8	5.4	3.0
45,000	14.3	1.0	2.9	4.8	6.7	5.4	3.0
60,000	14.3	2.0	3.5	5.0	6.5	5.2	2.9
75,000	14.4	3.4	4.5	5.6	6.7	5.3	3.1
87,900	14.4	5.5	6.0	6.6	7.1	5.6	3.5
100,000	14.6	7.4	7.5	7.5	7.5	5.9	3.8
125,000	14.8	8.4	8.2	8.0	7.6	6.0	3.9
150,000	15.0	9.0	8.7	8.3	7.7	6.1	4.0
200,000	15.0	9.9	9.3	8.6	7.8	6.1	4.1
250,000	14.9	10.4	9.6	8.8	7.8	6.2	4.2
500,000	14.7	11.6	10.5	9.4	8.1	6.3	4.3

INSURANCE REQUIREMENTS IN ADDITION TO SOCIAL SECURITY* TO REPLACE 75% OF EARNINGS AFTER TAXES** TO INSURED'S AGE 65 – CHILDREN BORN AT INSURED'S AGE 26 AND 29 (EXPRESSED AS A MULTIPLE OF GROSS ANNUAL PAY.)

* Assumes spouse is the same age as insured and elects to receive Social Security survivor benefits based on insured's PIA beginning at age 60.
** Taxes considered include federal income and Social Security taxes only.

adjusting for Social Security benefits would be $155,000 ($50,000 x 3.1) if the death proceeds are invested at a 3% real (inflation-adjusted) after-tax rate of return.

Similar to the general replacement income analysis described above, the amount determined using the table multiples should be reduced by the amount of resources currently available to fund this need in the event of death, such as investment assets and insurance currently in force.

Needs Analysis

In contrast with the income replacement approach, which is founded on the premise that the insurance need should be based on the income that would be lost if the insured dies, the needs approach estimates the insured's family income needs directly. The typical needs of a family can be divided into two categories.

The first category of needs consists of lump-sum cash needs at death, typically including:

- administrative/final expenses;
- estate settlement costs;
- debt liquidation;

- tax liabilities;
- an education fund;
- an emergency fund; and
- any other special funding needs.

The second category of needs consists of multi-period income needs and is comprised of:

- an adjustment period income;
- the surviving spouse's income needs;
- the children's income needs; and
- the spouse's retirement needs.

Four common special needs and the types of policies used to fund those needs are as follows:

- *Mortgage-repayment policy* – Here, all we need to know is the current amount at risk and how long that risk or need will need to be covered;
- *Other major-debt-repayment policies* – These could be for cars or any other type of nonmortgage long-term debt;

Figure 2.8

Gross Annual Pay	INSURANCE REQUIREMENTS IN ADDITION TO SOCIAL SECURITY* TO REPLACE 75% OF EARNINGS AFTER TAXES** TO INSURED'S AGE 65 – CHILDREN BORN AT INSURED'S AGE 23, 26, 29, 32. (EXPRESSED AS A MULTIPLE OF GROSS ANNUAL PAY.)						
	Age of Insured at Death						
	25	**30**	**35**	**40**	**45**	**50**	**55**
$15,000	3.9	1.6	1.8	5.3	4.9	5.5	2.9
30,000	4.1	0.2	0.7	4.8	4.6	5.4	3.0
45,000	4.4	0.9	1.1	4.8	4.6	5.4	3.0
60,000	5.4	1.9	1.7	4.9	4.6	5.2	2.9
75,000	6.5	3.3	3.0	5.5	5.0	5.3	3.1
87,900	8.2	5.4	4.8	6.5	5.7	5.6	3.5
100,000	9.8	7.3	6.5	7.4	6.4	5.9	3.8
125,000	10.8	8.4	7.5	7.9	6.8	6.0	4.0
150,000	11.6	9.0	8.1	8.2	7.0	6.1	4.0
200,000	12.4	9.8	8.8	8.5	7.3	6.1	4.1
250,000	12.6	10.4	9.2	8.7	7.4	6.2	4.2
500,000	13.5	11.6	10.3	9.3	7.8	6.3	4.3

* Assumes spouse is the same age as insured and elects to receive Social Security survivor benefits based on insured's PIA beginning at age 60.

** Taxes considered include federal income and Social Security taxes only.

- *Education-fund-accumulation policy* – This would be a policy to pay projected education costs for family members, if death occurred prematurely; and

- *Estate-tax-liability policy* – On estates below $1,500,000 (in 2004, with living spouse: $3,000,000) there would be little or no estate tax liability. Above these amounts, an estate tax may be due. The purchase of life insurance could obviate the necessity of the surviving spouse selling off assets to pay estate taxes.

The income needs are met from various sources including Social Security (survivor's income), spouse's earnings, annuity payments, employer-provided pension survivor benefits, and investment income. The excess of income needs over the expected income from these sources must be covered by income from reinvesting a lump-sum life insurance death benefit or by taking an annuity settlement from the insurance company.

The lump sum required to generate a predetermined monthly income depends on whether or not the capital will be depleted or preserved. Essentially, the decision to preserve some or all of the capital can be viewed as a third category of need or objective – the desire to leave something to heirs, or perhaps to a favorite charity, after the surviving spouse dies.

As a practical matter, the capital necessary to fund the spouse's income needs is often calculated in two ways that provide an upper and lower boundary on the required capital. First, the more conservative approach is to plan to preserve capital. The required capital is then the amount that is sufficient to pay the required cash income from interest on the capital alone. This approach assures income to the surviving spouse regardless of how long he or she may live and provides an extra margin of security. However, the cost of insurance may exceed the amount that the insured feels is affordable. The second approach is to assume that both income and capital will provide the required cash income and capital will be entirely consumed over a specified period. In general, the payout period is set equal to or slightly greater than the spouse's remaining life expectancy. If the spouse's remaining life expectancy is long and the assumed interest rate sufficiently high, the difference between the amount necessary if capital is preserved and the amount necessary if capital is depleted is relatively small.

Insurance Needs Analysis Work Sheet

The "Insurance Needs Analysis Work Sheet" shown in Figure 2.9 summarizes the steps in applying this approach. First, current cash needs are estimated and totaled. Then the capital necessary to fund the lifetime income needs of the spouse and children is estimated. Finally, the total value of assets currently available is subtracted from the sum of the current cash needs and the capital necessary to fund the income needs to determine the current surplus or deficit. Additional insurance is required if there is a deficit.

The work sheet calculates the capital necessary to fund the spouse's income needs, both if capital is preserved and if it is consumed over a period equal to or greater than the spouse's remaining life expectancy. Given the prevalence of two-income families, the capital necessary to fund the spouse's income needs should be reduced by the present value of his or her estimated lifetime earnings, if any.

The interest rate assumption is critical. As discussed earlier in regard to the income replacement approach, the assumed interest rate should be an after-tax interest rate. Also, if the objective is to maintain the family's real inflation-adjusted standard of living, the assumed interest rate should be an inflation-adjusted after-tax interest rate. For example, if inflation is expected to average 4% per year and the after-tax rate of return is expected to average 7% per year, about a 3% interest rate should be used in the work sheet to estimate the required capital.

Since the income needs of the children usually terminate when they leave the home, typically after they complete school, begin their own careers, and start their own families, the capital necessary to fund their income needs is computed assuming that it is depleted, rather than preserved. The children's Social Security benefits may be accounted for either by reducing their required monthly income on the work sheet by their estimated monthly Social Security survivor benefits or by including the present value of their benefits in the section of the work sheet listing the capital assets that are currently available. If there is an objective to provide children with a nest egg or hope chest to start their independent careers, the present value of the desired amount may be included in the current cash needs. Alternatively, the number of years of income funding may be extended beyond the time when the children would normally be expected to leave the home. The work sheet aggregates the income needs of all children into one calculation, but it can be modified to calculate the capital required for each child separately.

Most insurance advisors also recommend funding for an adjustment period income for one to two years. The adjustment period income helps to defray costs that continue until the family is able to adjust to its new situation. For example, the family may be locked into certain obligations of the insured, such as car leases, rents, or health club memberships, which may not terminate until sometime after the insured's death. Also, the confusion and disorientation that often follows the death of a loved one frequently may affect the family's ability to manage its financial affairs. The adjustment income provides an extra income cushion until they can adapt.

Insurance Needs Analysis Case Study

Figure 2.10 shows the work sheet filled out for the Sam Sample family. If Sam were to die today, it is estimated that final expenses would be $20,000, $100,000 would be required to pay off the mortgage, and $24,000 would be required to pay off other debts and taxes ($10,000 + $4,000 + $10,000). It is also assumed, based on the current cost for a private college, that $75,000 would be required today to fund Sam's 12-year-old son's college education starting in six years. Finally, Sam would also like to set up an emergency fund of $25,000 in the event he dies. Therefore, a total cash need in the event of Sam's death is $244,000.

Based on his family's current lifestyle, Sam estimates that his wife would need $3,500 per month after tax in current dollars to maintain her standard of living if Sam died. Assuming available assets could be invested at an average annual after-tax return (6%) that is 3% greater than inflation (3%), the capital required to provide this level of real inflation-adjusted income indefinitely (that is, by preserving the real purchasing power of the capital) is about $1,403,500. Sam's wife, who is age 40, has a life expectancy of 42.5 years, according to Table V. The capital required to provide Sam's wife with an inflation-adjusted after-tax monthly income equivalent to $3,500 in current dollars for 45 years is less, at about $1,029,000.

Sam's wife works and earns about $1,200 per month after-tax. Assuming that she would continue to work until age 65 (for 25 years) and her earnings would increase at the rate of inflation, the present value of her income stream is about $250,650. This amount reduces the amount of capital required to fund Sam's wife's income needs. The amount of income currently required to maintain Sam's son's standard of living is about $1,000 per month. Sam wants to provide for his son until he graduates from college, which should occur in 12 years. The capital required to fund this need, once again adjusted for inflation, is about $119,400.

Finally, Sam would like to provide an additional income of about $1,000 per month (adjusted for inflation) for two years to help the family through the adjustment period in the event he dies. He needs about $23,000 to provide this income.

The total capital required to fund the family's income needs is about $1,295,000 if the capital required to fund Sam's wife's income is to be preserved, or $921,000, if it is to be depleted over 45 years. The difference, $374,000, is significant. The difference in the two approaches is especially striking if it is couched in future value terms. If the capital is liquidated, in 45 years no capital will remain. If the capital is preserved, and inflation averages 3% per year, in 45 years the capital value will exceed $5.3 million.[13]

The assets available to fund the current cash and income needs total $600,000. Therefore, the insurance need is somewhere between $565,000 and $940,000 depending on whether or not the capital required to fund Sam's wife's income needs is preserved or liquidated. By selecting an intermediate amount, Sam can assure adequate income at least until his wife reaches age 85 with a reserve in case she lives longer or an inheritance for Sam's son if she does not survive beyond age 85. The choice will usually depend on the insured's overall objectives and ability to pay insurance premiums.

Static Versus Dynamic Analysis

Each of the approaches discussed above is a static analysis that bases the estimate of the required insurance on the needs that must be funded if the insured were to die immediately. But in most cases the insured will not die immediately. A dynamic analysis looks at how the insurance need is expected to change over time based on current expectations if the insured lives. How the insurance need is expected to change over time may have a strong effect on the most appropriate insurance plan and the selection of the most suitable policies.

The first impression is usually that the insurance need should decline as the insured ages, since the period of the family's income need should be shorter. However, first impressions can be mistaken. For example, Figure 2.11 shows an analysis of Sam's insurance need in 6 years. All of the cash needs are assumed to grow at about the rate of inflation, 3%, except the mortgage fund, notes payable, the education expenses, and the taxes payable. The mortgage is assumed to be paid down from $100,000 to $80,000. The notes payable are assumed to remain the same. The taxes payable are assumed to have been entirely repaid. The education fund that is necessary to fund college expenses imme-

diately is estimated to be $120,000, not $75,000, since it must be increased both for inflation plus the interest that was implicitly assumed would be earned on the education fund had Sam died six years earlier. Therefore, current cash needs increase by $31,670, from $244,000 to $275,670.

The income needs for Sam's wife and son and the adjustment period income are each increased by the assumed 3% rate of inflation from $3,500, $1,000, and $1,000, to $4,179, $1,194, and $1,194, respectively. Similarly, Sam's wife's wages are also expected to increase with the rate of inflation from $1,200 to $1,433. In six years, at age 46, Sam's wife's life expectancy will be 36.8 years (from Table V). Adding the 2.5 year margin that was included in the original analysis, the liquidation period is down from 45 years to 38.3 years. Also, Sam's wife's remaining working career is reduced by six years from 25 years to 19 years. Similarly, the income payout period for Sam's son is reduced by six years from 12 years to six years.

Finally, all of the capital assets available to fund the family's needs are assumed to grow by about 10% except the insurance amount and the Social Security benefits. The life insurance is the same on the assumption that Sam had not purchased additional insurance six years earlier. The Social Security benefits are $60,000, or $40,000 less, since the period when Sam's son would receive survivor benefits has been eliminated. The only amount remaining is the present value of Sam's wife's survivor benefit which will not be payable for another 19 years. Therefore, the total assets available to fund the family's needs increases by $191,600, from $600,000 to $791,600.

Based on these quite reasonable assumptions, the required insurance has increased by about $80,000, from approximately $939,000 to $1,019,000, if the objective is to fund Sam's wife's income needs without liquidating capital. However, if the capital liquidation approach is used, the insurance need declines slightly, from approximately $565,000 to about $475,000, or by about $90,000.

As this example demonstrates, it is important to look beyond an immediate "snapshot" of the insurance need to future needs based upon reasonable assumptions. Beyond this, it is critical to periodically update and review insurance plans, since the future virtually never unfolds exactly as projected. The greater the uncertainty of future events, the more important it is to build flexibility into the insurance plan to handle all eventualities.

Figure 2.9

INSURANCE NEEDS ANALYSIS WORK SHEET

Current cash needs:

Final expenses .... $_____
Emergency fund .... $_____
Mortgage fund .... $_____
Notes & loans payable .... $_____
Taxes payable .... $_____
Education expenses (NPV) .... $_____
Other .... $_____

Total cash need .... _____

Plus capital needs:

	Preserving Capital	Liquidating Capital

For spouse's income:
_____ per month forever at
_____ % annual interest (r) with
_____ % annual growth rate (g) .... $_____ †
_____ years only (n) .... $_____ ‡

Less spouse's wages:
_____ per month with
_____ % annual growth rate for
_____ years till retire .... ($_____)‡

For children's income:
_____ per month for
_____ % annual growth rate for
_____ years .... $_____ ‡

For adjustment period income:
_____ per month for
_____ % annual growth rate for
_____ year(s) .... $_____

Total capital needs .... $_____ $_____

Total needs .... $_____ $_____

Less capital assets:

Life insurance .... $_____
Cash, savings, etc. .... $_____
Investment assets .... $_____
Social Security (NPV) .... $_____
Pension benefits .... $_____
Other .... $_____

Total capital assets .... $_____

Surplus or (deficit) .... $_____ $_____

† This value is determined by adding one month's income to the quotient of the monthly income divided by 1/12th of the annual growth-adjusted interest rate or, equivalently: Monthly Income x [1 + (12 ÷ i)]. If I <= 0, there is no solution.

‡ Apply equation 2.1 using 12 times the monthly income as the annual income replacement amount

Figure 2.10

INSURANCE NEEDS ANALYSIS WORK SHEET

Current cash needs:

Final expenses .... $ 20,000
Emergency fund .... $ 25,000
Mortgage fund $100,000
Notes & loans payable .... $ 10,000
Taxes payable .... $ 4,000
Education expenses (NPV) .... $ 75,000
Other .... $ 10,000

Total cash need $244,000

Plus capital needs:	Preserving Capital	Liquidating Capital

For spouse's income:
$3,500.00   per month at
6.09%   annual interest (r) with
3.00%   annual growth rate (g) .... $1,403,500†
45   years only (n) .... $1,029,336‡

Less spouse's wages:
$1,200.00   per month for
3.00%   annual growth rate for
25   years till retire .... ($250,640)‡

For children's income:
$1,000.00   per month for
3.00%   annual growth rate for
12   years .... $119,396 ‡

For adjustment period income:
$1,000.00   per month for
3.00%   annual growth rate for
2   year(s) $22,952

Total capital needs $1,295,208 $921,044

Total needs $1,539,208 $1,165,044

Less capital assets:

Life insurance $200,000
Cash, savings, etc. $25,000
Investment assets $200,000
Social Security (NPV) $100,000
Pension benefits $50,000
Other $25,000

Total capital assets $600,000

Surplus or (deficit) .... ($939,208)   ($565,044)

†   This value is determined by adding one month's income to the quotient of the monthly income divided by 1/12th of the annual growth-adjusted interest rate or, equivalently: Monthly Income x [1 + (12 ÷ i)]. If I <= 0, there is no solution.
‡   Apply equation 2.1 using 12 times the monthly income as the annual income replacement amount.

Figure 2.11

INSURANCE NEEDS ANALYSIS WORK SHEET

Current cash needs:

Final Expenses	$ 23,880
Emergency Fund	$ 29,850
Mortgage Fund	$ 80,000
Notes & Loans Payable	$ 10,000
Taxes Payable	$ 0
Education Expenses (NPV)	$120,000
Other	$ 11,940
Total Cash Needs:	$275,670

Plus capital needs:

		Preserving Capital	Liquidating Capital
For spouse's income:			
$4,179	per month at		
6.09%	annuall interest (r) with		
3.00%	annual growth rate (g)	$1,675,779†	
38.3	years only (n)		$1,132,257‡
Less Spouse's Wages:			
$1,433	per month for		
19	years till retire	($264,204)‡	
For Children's Income:			
$1,194	per month for		
6	years	$77,584‡	
For Adjustment Period Income:			
$1,194	per month for		
2	year(s)	$27,404	
Total Capital Needs		$1,534,563	$991,041
Total Needs		$1,810,233	$1,266,311

Less capital assets:

Life Insurance	$200,000
Cash, Savings, Etc.	$ 44,300
Investment Assets	$354,400
Social Security (NPV)	$ 60,000
Pension Benefits	$ 88,600
Other	$ 44,300
Total Capital Assets	$791,500
Surplus or (Deficit)	($1,018,633) ($475,111)

† This value is determined by adding one month's income to the quotient of the monthly income divided by 1/12th of the annual growth-adjusted interest rate or, equivalently: Monthly Income x [1 + (12 ÷ i)]. If I <= 0, there is no solution.

‡ Apply equation 2.1 using 12 times the monthly income as the annual income replacement amount.

BUSINESS INSURANCE NEEDS ANALYSIS

Life insurance is used in business applications to insure key employees, fund buy-sell agreements, and in various compensation arrangements, such as in death-benefit only plans, Section 162 plans, split dollar arrangements, and in qualified pension and nonqualified deferred compensation plans. The insurance need in most of these cases depends on circumstances peculiar to each case, and is beyond the scope of the current discussion. However, the insurance need in most key employee situations is amenable to a systematic and generic type of analysis, which is presented in the following paragraphs.

Key Employee Insurance

In most businesses, especially in smaller firms, one or a few key employees are responsible for a significant portion of the firm's earning capacity. The premature death or disability, or an untimely resignation, of these employees can have a severe impact on the firm's profitability, and may even cause the firm to fail. Noncompete clauses in employment/severance agreements, cross-training among key employees, and a management philosophy and practice of mentoring subordinates, along with attractive and properly-designed compensation packages, can help to prevent or minimize the risk of early resignation. Life and disability insurance on key employees is the logical choice to help the firm weather the financial loss of a premature death or serious disability. But the critical question remains – how do you determine the insurable value of the key employee to the firm?

A commonly held maxim of management is that no one is irreplaceable. That is generally true, but it does not mean that replacement is costless and that full value can always be recouped. In any event, the loss of a key employee will generally cause business and management disruptions and will entail a period of adjustment before a new replacement is up to speed and the company can adapt to the new arrangements. A properly designed insurance plan can provide the funds necessary to finance the transition period. Since most companies, and especially smaller firms, do not have unlimited cash resources for insurance premiums, it is critical to have enough, but not too much insurance.

Critique of Ad Hoc Rules of Thumb and Common Key Employee Valuation Approaches

Various ad hoc rules of thumb and approaches have been used to estimate the value of a key employee. These rules, although simple to apply, are conceptually limited. For example, estimating an employee's value as some multiple of salary is entirely arbitrary. What multiple is appropriate? In addition, it takes no account of the timing of cash losses. The effect, in many cases, may not actually appear in revenues until future periods.

Alternatively, a key employee's value is sometimes estimated by capitalizing the corporate earnings attributable to the employee's efforts, skills, knowledge, talents, contacts, sales results, or other attributes. A similar approach is to estimate the percentage reduction in the firm's going concern value that would result from loss of the key employee and to multiply that percentage by the firm's going concern value. One problem with these approaches is that they implicitly or explicitly require a valuation of the firm in order to value key employees. Although key employees are an important component contributing to a firm's value, the relationship is not often clear or direct. And although up-to-date and continuous knowledge of a firm's going-concern value would always be welcome for a host of reasons, it is usually neither easy nor inexpensive to perform such valuations, especially in small closely held businesses.

A second and more basic problem with these approaches is that they implicitly assume the key employee is irreplaceable, and his or her loss is a dead weight and irrecoverable loss to the firm. These approaches tend to overestimate the loss to the firm. In virtually all cases, if there is adequate liquidity to cover the transition period, a replacement can ultimately be found who can fulfill many, if not all, of the functions of the lost key employee and the company's management practices can be adapted over time to compensate for the loss.

Basic Principles of Key Employee Valuation

A conceptually sound approach to key employee valuation should:

- measure the financial loss based on what the employee would have contributed to the future success of the firm;

- adjust the financial consequences for the timing of those lost contributions;

- account for trends in the employee's contributions;

- realize that, in every case, a key employee's contribution to the firm will terminate at some

point, either through death, disability, resignation, or retirement; and

- recognize that most, if not all, of the value of the
key employee's contribution to the firm can and
will be recovered over time, either by hiring and
training a replacement, adapting or changing
the management practices and functions of other
key employees, or some combination.

Although an employee's past contributions are often
a major component in determining his or her present
compensation, the cost to the firm of his or her loss
depends on the *future* – on what he or she could be
expected to contribute in subsequent years. In this
regard, both the timing and trend of these future contributions are critical. The loss of an employee who is
essential to the successful close of a major deal is much
more costly if the deal is expected to close within the
next few months than if it is not expected to close for a
year or two. Similarly, the trend is important. It is much
more costly to lose a relatively new "rainmaker," who is
still in the process of bringing new accounts within the
firm, than to lose the same employee later, after many of
those accounts have been acquired and become accus-
tomed to and comfortable with the firm.

One mistake frequently encountered in key employee
valuations is the failure to account for the fact that every
key employee, sooner or later, for one reason or another,
will *terminate* employment with the firm. It is not a
question of if the key employee is lost, but when. This is
a simple fact of life that every firm must face. And while
it is true that without proper planning the loss of a key
employee could, in some circumstances, sound the death
knell for a firm, it is usually entirely avoidable. If a firm
can anticipate and survive a key employee's retirement,
it should also be able to plan for and survive the loss as
a result of death, disability, or resignation.

Any valuation based on the presumption of a permanent and irrecoverable loss will usually be invalid and
overstated. The impact of the loss of a key employee's
contributions to the firm will virtually always diminish
over time as the firm adjusts its practices and reallocates
or replaces lost resources. And although a replacement
may not be able to exactly replicate the contributions of
the lost employee, over time much of the lost contributions can be recovered through training and experience.
In addition, the replacement will frequently bring his or
her own unique talents to the job, adding dimensions
that the key employee may have lacked. Therefore,
ultimately no permanent or ongoing loss to the firm
should result.[14]

Key Employee Valuation Method

Figure 2.12 presents a key employee valuation work
sheet that incorporates the principal elements of a complete and systematic method of valuation.[15] The method
estimates the difference between the key employee's
and a replacement employee's contributions to the firm
each year over a transition training period. The present
value of the differences is an estimate of the amount of
insurance required to carry the firm through the transition period.

The following factors are required inputs:

1. The number of years that would be necessary to
   locate, hire, train, and develop a replacement
   for the key employee until he or she could be
   expected to match the contributions expected
   from the key employee. In general, this would
   be expected to take five years or less, but the
   worksheet could be expanded beyond five years,
   if necessary.

2. The firm's estimated gross revenues for each
   year of the transition period assuming the key
   employee were still with the firm. (Line 1)

3. An estimate of the percentage of gross revenues
   attributable to activities of the key employee.
   (Line 2)

   This percentage may be assumed to be equal
   each year, or it may be varied, depending on the
   firm's development plans and the key
   employee's role in those developments.

4. The expected total compensation to the key
   employee each year over the transition period.
   (Line 4)

   This may be determined as a percentage of
   revenues or sales, as might often be the case
   with a key salesperson, or as some anticipated
   combination of salary and bonus, as might often
   be the case with key executives. This amount
   should include all compensation, including
   various employee benefits, such as medical
   benefits and pension contributions, as well as
   Social Security payments.

5. The total direct (and indirect) costs of locating,
   recruiting, hiring, installing, compensating, and
   training a replacement for each year of the
   transition period. (Line 8)

Figure 2.12

		Year 1	Year 2	Year 3	Year 4	Year 5
	KEY EMPLOYEE VALUATION WORK SHEET					
1	Estimated Total Revenues (I)					
2	% of (1) Attributed to KE (I)					
3	Total of (1) Due to KE (1x2)					
4	KE's Total Compensation (I)					
5	KE's Net Contribution (3-4)					
6	Relative Value of RE (I)					
7	Revenue from RE (3x6)					
8	Total Cost of RE (I)					
9	RE's Net Contribution (7-8)					
10	Loss in Net Contribution (5-9)					
11	Present Value Factor (I)†					
12	PV of Loss (10x11)					
13	Cumulative PV of Loss (Year1 + Year2 +...+ Year5)					

Key:
KE — Key Employee
RE — Replacement Employee
(I) — Input cell
(x#y) — Indicates calculation:
x,y — Row of values
\# — Mathematical operator

†Discount Rate: _____ = r

$$1/(1+r)^n$$

$n = 1,2,3,4,5$
for each year.

Direct costs, especially in the first year, would include payments for the services of a professional recruiter; advertising; reimbursement of travel, meals, lodging, and local transportation expenses for replacement candidates; moving expenses and the like for the new hire; office outfitting and other possible expenses, such as the cost for a salesperson's automobile; and the similar costs of recruitment for necessary new support positions, such as an administrative assistant to the replacement key employee; as well as the legal fees often associated with negotiating employment contracts with high-level executives and top salespersons. Indirect costs that should not be overlooked are the opportunity cost of management time spent in the recruitment effort as well as the additional burdens placed on remaining key employees and management, both to cover the lost key employee's duties until the replacement employee can fully shoulder the burden and to help train or acclimate the new employee.

6. An estimate of the contribution the replacement employee could be expected to make each year to the revenues of the firm relative to the contributions projected for the key employee (as a percent). (Line 6)

Virtually nobody can be expected to step in and immediately match the performance of a true key employee. (If it were easy, the employee would not be considered a key or vital contributor to the firm's success.) The transition period generally depends on the qualifications and experience of the specific person hired, which is difficult to estimate before the fact. However, there is usually a tradeoff between the time it takes for the replacement employee to develop his or her full contributory potential and the initial compensation level of the replacement employee. Trying to attract a person who is extremely well qualified and a better immediate match for the key employee will usually require a premium compensation package and may take more search time, sometimes a year or longer for specialized positions. Thus, it may be more an issue of management preference, than total cost, which route is taken to replace the key employee. If management plans to go the "premium" replacement route, higher compensation levels (generally even higher than that paid to the key employee) and recruitment expenses should be entered in line 8. Also, correspondingly higher relative performance percentages should be entered in line 6, but perhaps deferred for a year or so to reflect the

Figure 2.13

		Year 1	**Year 2**	**Year 3**	**Year 4**	**Year 5**
	KEY EMPLOYEE VALUATION WORK SHEET **(VALUE EXPRESSED IN $1,000S)**					
1	Estimated Total Revenues (I)	2,200	2,420	2,700	3,100	3,500
2	% of (1) Attributed to KE (I)	0.20	0.19	0.18	0.16	0.15
3	Total of (1) Due to KE (1x2)	440.00	459.80	486.00	496.00	525.00
4	KE's Total Compensation (I)	120.0	130.0	140.0	145.0	150.0
5	KE's Net Contribution (3-4)	320.00	329.80	346.00	351.00	375.00
6	Relative Value of RE (I)	0.50	0.60	0.70	0.85	1.00
7	Revenue from RE (3x6)	220.00	275.88	340.20	421.60	525.00
8	Total Cost of RE (I)	150.0	100.0	110.0	130.0	150.0
9	RE's Net Contribution (7-8)	70.00	175.88	230.20	291.60	375.00
10	Loss in Net Contribution (5-9)	250.00	153.92	115.80	59.40	0.00
11	Present Value Factor (I)†	0.909091	0.826446	0.751315	0.683013	0.620921
12	PV of Loss (10x11)	227.27	127.21	87.00	40.57	0.00
13	Cumulative PV of Loss (Year1 + Year2 +...+ Year5)	227.27	354.48	441.48	482.05	**482.05**

Key:	KE	Key Employee
	RE	Replacement Employee
	(I)	Input cell
	(x#y)	Indicates calculation:
	x,y	Row of values
	#	Mathematical operator

†Discount Rate: 0.10 = r

$$1/(1+r)^n$$

n = 1,2,3,4,5
for each year.

longer expected time to find the "premium" replacement. The work sheet can be used to help evaluate the relative benefit or cost of each replacement strategy.

7. The discount rate for calculating present values. (Bottom of Work Sheet)

The discount rate should reflect the firm's cost of capital or borrowing rate. The rate should be adjusted for the firm's tax rate. Although death benefits will (usually[16]) be tax free, the returns on investment will be subject to tax.

The rest of the work sheet operates as follows. Line 3 computes the total projected revenues attributable to the key employee. Line 5 shows the key employee's net projected contribution to the firm based on the difference between the key employee's compensation and his or her contribution. The replacement employee's contribution to the firm relative to the contribution of the current key employee is calculated in line 7. The replacement employee's net contribution (plus or minus) is computed in line 9. Line 10 computes the difference between the net contribution of the current key employee and the replacement employee. The discount factors for computing present values should be entered

in line 11. The formula for computing each year's discount factor is shown at the bottom of the work sheet. Line 12 computes the present value of each year's loss in net contribution. Finally, line 13 shows the cumulative present value of the loss in net contributions to the firm each year. The value in the last year of the transition period is the present value of the total loss and represents the amount that should be insured.

Figure 2.13 illustrates the use of the key employee valuation method described here. In this case, the firm's plans are such that the key employee's relative contribution is expected to decline somewhat (as indicated by the percentages in line 2) as the firm moves into some new operations. However, as indicated in line 3, the key employee's contribution is still expected to be substantial and growing. It is assumed the relative contribution of a replacement employee will start at only 50% of the key employee's contribution but grow to 100% in five years. Although the replacement employee's compensation is expected to be less than the key employee's, the first year expenses of recruitment and placement, together with compensation, are expected to exceed the key employee's compensation. In subsequent years, the replacement employee's compensation is expected to be less than the key employee's, but his or her net contribution will still remain lower than what the key employee

Figure 2.14

AGI	Taxable Income	Marginal Tax Rate	Federal Income Tax	Avg. Tax Rate On TI	Average Tax Rate On AGI	After Tax Income	Ratio of Avg. to Marg. Rate
$10,000	2,050	10.00%	205	10.00%	2.05%	9,795	20.50%
20,000	12,050	15.00%	1,450	12.03%	7.25%	18,550	48.33%
30,000	22,050	15.00%	2,950	13.38%	9.83%	27,050	65.56%
40,000	30,900	25.00%	4,463	14.44%	11.16%	35,538	44.63%
50,000	39,400	25.00%	6,588	16.72%	13.18%	43,413	52.70%
60,000	47,900	25.00%	8,713	18.19%	14.52%	51,288	58.08%
70,000	56,400	25.00%	10,838	19.22%	15.48%	59,163	61.93%
80,000	64,900	25.00%	12,963	19.97%	16.20%	67,038	64.81%
90,000	73,400	28.00%	15,179	20.68%	16.87%	74,821	60.23%
100,000	81,900	28.00%	17,559	21.44%	17.56%	82,441	62.71%
125,000	103,150	28.00%	23,509	22.79%	18.81%	101,491	67.17%
150,000	124,805	29.53%	29,572	23.69%	19.71%	120,428	66.75%
175,000	147,425	34.81%	35,940	24.38%	20.54%	139,060	59.00%
200,000	170,045	34.81%	43,404	25.53%	21.70%	156,596	62.35%
250,000	215,285	34.81%	58,334	27.10%	23.33%	191,666	67.03%
300,000	259,719	33.99%	72,997	28.11%	24.33%	227,003	71.59%
500,000	435,719	36.05%	133,409	30.62%	26.68%	366,591	74.01%
1,000,000	875,719	36.05%	287,409	32.82%	28.74%	712,591	79.73%

SINGLE TAXPAYER — MARGINAL AND AVERAGE TAX RATES (2004 TAX SCHEDULES)

Assumptions: Total itemized deductions equal 15% of AGI; medical, theft and casualty, and investment interest expense deductions equal 3% of AGI.

would have contributed. Based on the projected figures, the insurable value of the key employee is about $482,000.

The work sheet may be a useful tool in justifying the desired amount of key employee coverage and convincing the insurer that there is sufficient insurable interest to issue the policy. In addition, it may be helpful in supporting the accumulation of contingency funds in excess of what may otherwise be allowed under the excess accumulated earnings provisions if challenged by the IRS.[17]

ESTATE PRESERVATION AND LIQUIDITY NEEDS ANALYSIS

For large estates, planning to minimize estate taxes and to assure adequate liquidity to pay estate taxes that cannot be avoided is of paramount importance. Planning should consider a host of techniques, including lifetime gifts, optimal use of the marital deduction, various marital and family trust arrangements, and charitable gifts, as well as life insurance. Estate and gift tax planning is beyond the scope of this chapter, but see Appendices A, B, and C for discussions of federal estate, gift, and generation-skipping tax issues and planning.

CHAPTER ENDNOTES

1. The table was developed by the staff of First National Bank (Citibank).

2. The first part of equation 2.1 is the standard formula for the present value of an annuity with payments at the end of each period (year). The second part of the equation is an adjustment factor to move the payments to the middle of each period (year) rather than the end. The value can be computed easily using a financial calculator.

3. The long-term inflation rate statistic was derived from the data series presented in *Stocks, Bond, Bills, and Inflation, 2004 Yearbook*, (Ibbotson Associates, 8 South Michigan Avenue, Suite 700, Chicago, Illinois 60603; 312-263-3435).

4. National or industry occupational averages may be misleading when trying to estimate earnings growth for a particular occupation for another reason. In many occupations, especially in the professions and in executive or managerial positions, the normal lifetime profile of any average individual's earnings growth may show greater real growth than the average increase for that occupation as a whole.

5. The standard deduction and personal exemptions will shelter the first dollars received from tax. In 2004, the personal exemption is $3,100 per person. The standard deduction for a head of household is $7,150 and for a single person is $4,850. Therefore, if the spouse is the only other family member, at least the first $7,950 ($3,100 + $4,850) of income on the investment of death

Figure 2.15

HEAD OF HOUSEHOLD WITH TWO CHILDREN: MARGINAL AND AVERAGE TAX RATES (2004 TAX SCHEDULES)

AGI	Taxable Income	Marginal Tax Rate	Federal Income Tax	Avg. Tax Rate On TI	Average Tax Rate On AGI	After Tax Income	Ratio of Avg. to Marg. Rate
$10,000	0	0.00%	0	N/A	0.00%	10,000	N/A
20,000	3,550	10.00%	355	10.00%	1.78%	19,645	17.75%
30,000	13,550	15.00%	1,523	11.24%	5.08%	28,478	33.83%
40,000	23,550	15.00%	3,023	12.83%	7.56%	36,978	50.38%
50,000	33,200	15.00%	4,470	13.46%	8.94%	45,530	59.60%
60,000	41,700	25.00%	6,025	14.45%	10.04%	53,975	40.17%
70,000	50,200	25.00%	8,150	16.24%	11.64%	61,850	46.57%
80,000	58,700	25.00%	10,275	17.50%	12.84%	69,725	51.38%
90,000	67,200	25.00%	12,400	18.45%	13.78%	77,600	55.11%
100,000	75,700	25.00%	14,525	19.19%	14.53%	85,475	58.10%
125,000	96,950	25.00%	19,838	20.46%	15.87%	105,163	63.48%
150,000	118,419	28.84%	25,742	21.74%	17.16%	124,258	59.51%
175,000	140,419	28.84%	31,902	22.72%	18.23%	143,098	63.21%
200,000	164,093	36.45%	38,601	23.52%	19.30%	161,399	52.96%
250,000	211,813	36.45%	54,348	25.66%	21.74%	195,652	59.65%
300,000	259,533	36.45%	70,096	27.01%	23.37%	229,904	64.11%
500,000	435,719	36.05%	130,570	29.97%	26.11%	369,430	72.44%
1,000,000	875,719	36.05%	284,570	32.50%	28.46%	715,430	78.94%

Assumptions: Total itemized deductions equal 15% of AGI; medical, theft and casualty, and investment interest expense deductions equal 3% of AGI.

proceeds will likely be received tax free (assuming no other taxable income). Of course, if itemized deductions exceed the standard deduction, an even a greater amount will be sheltered.

In families with dependent children, at least the first $10,250 ($3,100 standard deduction plus $7,150 spouse's personal exemption) plus $3,100 for each dependent child will be received tax free. For example, with two children, the amount of investment income that may be received essentially tax free is $16,450 (assuming no other sources of taxable income). The following table presents these "tax-free" amounts, based on 2004 values (the standard deduction and personal exemption are indexed for inflation each year).

"TAX-FREE" INCOME AMOUNTS BY FILING STATUS AND NUMBER OF DEPENDENTS
(2004 Tax Schedules)

Filing Status	Number of Dependents	"Tax-Free" Income Amount
Single	0	$ 7,950
Head of Household	1	13,350
Head of Household	2	16,450
Head of Household	3	19,550
Head of Household	4	22,650
Head of Household	5	25,750

Figures 2.14, 2.15, and 2.16 show the impact of these exemptions on the effective tax rate. Figure 2.14 presents marginal and average tax rates for a typical single taxpayer for various levels of income. Figures 2.15 and 2.16 present marginal and average tax rates for typical head-of-household taxpayers with two and four dependents, respectively. The tables also show taxable income, federal taxes, after-tax income, and the ratio of the average to the marginal tax rate for each level of adjusted gross income. Since equation 2.1 assumes virtually all of the breadwinner's income is being replaced, the tax rate implicit in the after-tax discount rate should not be a marginal tax rate but an effective average tax rate, as it would apply to the total replacement income as received by the surviving spouse.

These figures show that the effective average tax rate ranges from about 20% (at low levels of AGI) to 80% (at high levels of AGI) of the marginal tax rate applicable to the last and highest dollar of income. For example, in order for a surviving spouse filing as head of household with two dependents to have $53,975 after paying federal income tax, the total before-tax payment would have to be about $60,000. This amount of income would place the surviving spouse in the 25% marginal tax bracket. However, the effective average tax rate on the entire payment would be only slightly higher than 10%.

In addition, the present value equation 2.1 is similar to a sinking fund or loan amortization formula that assumes that the initial death benefits are recovered tax free over the term of the payout. In other words, only a portion of each payment is taxable. The tax-free portion of each payment can be estimated by dividing the initial investment by the number of years in the

Figure 2.16

AGI	**Taxable Income**	**Marginal Tax Rate**	**Federal Income Tax**	**Avg. Tax Rate On TI**	**Average Tax Rate On AGI**	**After Tax Income**	**Ratio of Avg. to Marg. Rate**
$10,000	0	0.00%	0	N/A	0.00%	10,000	N/A
20,000	0	0.00%	0	N/A	0.00%	20,000	N/A
30,000	7,350	10.00%	735	10.00%	2.45%	29,265	24.50%
40,000	17,350	15.00%	2,093	12.06%	5.23%	37,908	34.88%
50,000	27,000	15.00%	3,540	13.11%	7.08%	46,460	47.20%
60,000	35,500	15.00%	4,815	13.56%	8.03%	55,185	53.50%
70,000	44,000	25.00%	6,600	15.00%	9.43%	63,400	37.71%
80,000	52,500	25.00%	8,725	16.62%	10.91%	71,275	43.63%
90,000	61,000	25.00%	10,850	17.79%	12.06%	79,150	48.22%
100,000	69,500	25.00%	12,975	18.67%	12.98%	87,025	51.90%
125,000	90,750	25.00%	18,288	20.15%	14.63%	106,713	58.52%
150,000	112,219	28.84%	24,006	21.39%	16.00%	125,994	55.49%
175,000	134,219	28.84%	30,166	22.48%	17.24%	144,834	59.77%
200,000	159,009	32.31%	37,108	23.34%	18.55%	162,892	57.42%
250,000	209,209	38.08%	53,489	25.57%	21.40%	196,511	56.18%
300,000	259,409	38.08%	70,055	27.01%	23.35%	229,945	61.32%
500,000	435,719	36.05%	130,570	29.97%	26.11%	369,430	72.44%
1,000,000	875,719	36.05%	284,570	32.50%	28.46%	715,430	78.94%

HEAD OF HOUSEHOLD WITH FOUR CHILDREN: MARGINAL AND AVERAGE TAX RATES (2004 TAX SCHEDULES)

Assumptions: Total itemized deductions equal 15% of AGI; medical, theft and casualty, and investment interest expense deductions equal 3% of AGI.

term of the payout. For example, if the insurance amount is $800,000 and the term of payout is 30 years, on average about $26,667 ($800,000 ÷ 30) of each year's payment will be tax-free recovery of the initial investment. Assuming that payments computed on a level annual basis before tax would be $60,000 (6.3% before-tax return), approximately 45% of the average payment ($26,667 ÷ $60,000) would be treated as tax-free recovery of the initial investment. Only $33,333 of each payment, on average, would be subject to tax. Assume, as in the previous paragraph, that the objective is to provide a surviving spouse and two children with $53,362 of after-tax income. If approximately $36,667 of a $60,000 payment is received tax free, the taxable income before consideration of the standard deduction and personal exemptions is only $33,333. The effective average tax rate on this level of AGI is about 5.91% (determined by interpolation in Figure 2.15) not 10.04% as would be the case if no part of the $60,000 payment were excludable.

Therefore, although $60,000 of AGI would normally put a head of household with two dependents in the 25% marginal tax bracket, the effective average tax rate on the investment earnings of the fund necessary to produce an equivalent after-tax income in this case is less than 1/4 of 25%, or just about 5.91%.

The method described in the reading uses a sinking fund equation 2.1 to determine the insurance need. In many cases, it would be more appropriate to assume insurance proceeds are paid under an annuity settlement option which has tax-favored features. The alternative approach is presented in the reading

since working with actual annuity formulas is difficult, virtually requiring the use of a computer. However, the following discussion may shed some light on how the insurance need is estimated if commercial annuities are employed as the vehicle to replace the family income.

Under the rules of IRC Section 72, a fixed portion of each fixed-term annuity payment is treated as tax-free recovery of the initial capital amount. In general, only a portion of each payment will be treated as taxable income. In addition, interest earnings are taxable only when payments are received. Undistributed income accumulates tax-deferred. Assuming payment in the form of an annuity, the exclusion amount will vary with both the interest rate and the payout period. The table below presents exclusion ratios for various interest rates and payout periods. For example, assuming a 6% rate of return and a 20-year payout period, the exclusion ratio is 57.3%. (The exclusion ratios are computed using the rules of Section 72 for fixed period annuities.) In other words, $57.30 of each $100 paid under the annuity is treated as tax-free recovery of the initial investment.

FIXED-PERIOD ANNUITY EXCLUSION RATIOS

Interest	Years in Payout Period			
	10	**20**	**30**	**40**
1%	94.7%	90.2%	86.0%	82.1%
2	89.8	81.8	74.7	68.4
3	85.3	74.4	65.3	57.8
4	81.1	68.0	57.6	49.5

Interest	Years in Payout Period			
	10	20	30	40
5	77.2	62.3	51.2	42.9
6	73.6	57.3	45.9	37.6
7	70.2	53.0	41.4	33.3
8	67.1	49.1	37.5	29.8
9	64.2	45.6	34.2	26.9
10	61.4	42.6	31.4	24.4

The standard deduction and personal exemptions together with the exclusion ratio combine to allow quite large annual annuity payments without any tax, assuming the annuity is the only source of taxable income. Figure 2.17 shows the maximum amounts that may be paid in annuity form to a single taxpayer before any part of the payment is subject to tax. For example, assuming the annuity earns a net 7% interest rate, the first $16,596 of a 20-year annuity will escape tax altogether. Based on the exclusion ratio shown in the table of exclusion ratios, 53% of any additional payment will also be received as a tax-free recovery of investment.

Figure 2.18 is similar to Figure 2.17, except that the "tax-free" amount is determined for a taxpayer filing as a head of household with one dependent. A surviving spouse with dependent children uses the head of household tax schedule. The values in this table are considerably higher than those in Figure 2.17 because of the higher standard deduction ($7,150 vs. $4,850 in 2004) and the presence of two, rather than one, personal exemptions worth $3,100 each (in 2004). Figure 2.19 shows the additional amount of "tax-free" income an annuity may provide to a taxpayer filing as head of household for each additional dependent.

For example, a surviving spouse with four dependent children could receive annual payments of $48,192 ($28,404 from Figure 2.18 plus 3 x $6,596 from Figure 2.19) tax free from a 20-year annuity earning 7% net interest. Once again, based on values in the exclusion ratio table, 53% of any payment in excess of $48,192 would be treated as a tax-free recovery of investment.

The 2004 15% tax bracket for a taxpayer filing as head of household ends at $38,900 of taxable income. Since only 47 cents [$1 x (1 – 53%)] of each annuity payment in excess of $48,192 in this case is subject to tax, an additional $82,766 of annuity payments ($38,900 ÷ 0.47), or $130,958 in total, may be paid in the form of an annuity before any income is taxed at the 25% rate. The total tax payable in this case on a $130,958 annual annuity would be only $5,325. The after-tax annuity payment would be $125,633, or 95.9% of the before tax payment. Although the taxpayer is "in" the 15% tax bracket, the effective or average tax rate (on the entire $130,958 annual amount) is only 4.07%.

6. The amount a spouse will get is a percentage of the deceased's basic Social Security benefit. The percentage depends on your age and the type of benefit you are eligible for. Normal retirement age (NRA), the age at which full Social Security retirement benefits are generally available, had been 65 for many years. However, beginning with people born in 1938 or later, NRA gradually increases until it reaches 67 for people born after 1962. The following chart shows the steps in which the NRA will increase. For more information on widow(er)s benefits, see http://www.ssa.gov/pubs/10084.html.

Year of Birth*	Normal Retirement Age	Age 60 Reduction Months	Monthly % Reduction**
1939 or earlier	65	60	.475
1940	65 and 2 months	62	.460
1941	65 and 4 months	64	.445
1942	65 and 6 months	66	.432
1943	65 and 8 months	68	.419

Year of Birth*	Normal Retirement Age	Age 60 Reduction Months	Monthly % Reduction**
1944	65 and 10 months	70	.407
1945—1956	66	72	.396
1957	66 and 2 months	74	.385
1958	66 and 4 months	76	.375
1959	66 and 6 months	78	.365
1960	66 and 8 months	80	.356
1961	66 and 10 months	82	.348
1962 and later	67	84	.339

* Persons born on January 1 of any year should refer to the previous year.

** Monthly reduction percentages are approximate due to rounding. The total % reduction for anyone who receives benefits at age 60 is always 28.50.

7. An excellent and concise source of information on Social Security benefits is *The Social Security Manual*, The National Underwriter Company, published annually.

8. Where the maximum family benefit applies, individual social security benefits are generally reduced proportionately. The three categories here are not shown proportionately in order to facilitate calculation of the present value of the total benefits.

9. The question of whether a surviving spouse should begin taking Social Security benefits at age 60 or later depends on a number of factors. There is a trade-off. Although if payments are started at age 60, they will be paid longer, the amount is reduced. In general, it is optimal for a normal healthy surviving spouse to begin taking benefits at age 60, rather than delaying the start to normal retirement age, even though payments are lower, if the appropriate inflation-adjusted discount rate for those future payments is above 3%. If the discount rate is below 3%, the spouse will be better off waiting to take payments. For a comprehensive discussion of the factors involved in this decision, see "When to Take Early Social Security Benefits," Robert J. Doyle, Jr., *The Journal of the American Society of CLU & ChFC*, Vol. XLIV, No. 1 (January, 1990), pp. 30-37.

10. Up to 85% of Social Security benefits are taxable under current law if modified taxable income – defined basically as normal taxable income plus tax-exempt bond interest income plus 50% of Social Security income – exceeds $34,000 for single taxpayers or $44,000 for married taxpayers.

11. Table V is the unisex annuity life expectancy table described in Treas. Reg. §1.72-9.

12. Based on Table 90CM, the IRS table used for valuing annuities, life estates, and remainders for income, gift, and estate tax purposes, the unisex life expectancy at age 60 is 20.9 years. These values represent a more conservative estimate of life expectancy and, as a result, produce a smaller present value for surviving spouse Social Security benefits. The effect is to increase the amount of insurance needed, all else being equal.

13. In order to provide a level real inflation-adjusted income from interest only, that is, a nominal income that increases at the rate of inflation, the capital value must increase each year by the rate of inflation. By using a 3% inflation-adjusted interest rate to compute the required capital, the work sheet implicitly assumes the capital value grows at the rate of inflation. If inflation averages 3% per year, the capital value will grow by 3% per year. At a 3% annual growth rate, a dollar invested today will increase 3.7816 times in 45 years (1.03^{45} = 3.7816). Therefore, after subtracting the first month's interest, which is assumed to

Figure 2.17

	TAX-FREE "ANNUITY PAYMENT" SINGLE TAXPAYER (2004 TAX SCHEDULE)			
Interest Rate	**Years in Payout Period**			
	10	**20**	**30**	**40**
1%	150,000	81,122	56,786	44,413
2%	77,941	43,681	31,423	25,158
3%	54,082	31,055	22,911	18,839
4%	42,063	24,844	18,750	15,743
5%	34,868	21,088	16,291	13,923
6%	30,114	18,618	14,695	12,740
7%	26,678	16,915	13,567	11,919
8%	24,164	15,619	12,720	11,325
9%	22,207	14,614	12,082	10,876
10%	20,596	13,850	11,589	10,516

* The payments are "tax-free" because of the combination of the exclusion amount with the standard deduction ($4,850) and personal exemption ($3,100) for single taxpayers. That is, after applying the exclusion ratio, only $7,950 of each payment is taxable, which is completely sheltered by the standard deduction and personal exemption.

Figure 2.18

	TAX-FREE "ANNUITY PAYMENT" HEAD OF HOUSEHOLD AND 1 DEPENDENT (2004 TAX SCHEDULE)			
Interest Rate	**Years in Payout Period**			
	10	**20**	**30**	**40**
1%	251,887	136,224	95,357	74,581
2%	130,882	73,352	52,767	42,247
3%	90,816	52,148	38,473	31,635
4%	70,635	41,719	31,486	26,436
5%	58,553	35,411	27,357	23,380
6%	50,568	31,265	24,677	21,394
7%	44,799	28,404	22,782	20,015
8%	40,578	26,228	21,360	19,017
9%	37,291	24,540	20,289	18,263
10%	34,585	23,258	19,461	17,659

* The payments are "tax-free" because of the combination of the exclusion amount with the standard deduction ($7,150) and two personal exemptions ($3,100) for a head of household with one dependent. That is, after applying the exclusion ratio, only $13,350 of each payment is taxable, and this amount will be completely sheltered by the standard deduction and personal exemption.

Figure 2.19

Interest Rate	TAX-FREE "ANNUITY PAYMENT" FOR EACH ADDITIONAL PERSONAL EXEMPTION (2004 TAX SCHEDULE)			
	Years in Payout Period			
	10	20	30	40
1%	58,491	31,633	22,143	17,318
2%	30,392	17,033	12,253	9,810
3%	21,088	12,109	8,934	7,346
4%	16,402	9,688	7,311	6,139
5%	13,596	8,223	6,352	5,429
6%	11,742	7,260	5,730	4,968
7%	10,403	6,596	5,290	4,648
8%	9,422	6,090	4,960	4,416
9%	8,659	5,699	4,711	4,241
10%	8,031	5,401	4,519	4,101

* The payments are "tax-free" because of the combination of the exclusion amount with the personal exemption ($3,100). That is, after applying the exclusion ratio, only $3,100 of each amount shown is taxable and that amount is completely sheltered by the standard deduction and personal exemption.

be paid in advance, the remaining $1,400,000 should grow to $5.3 million in 45 years. Of course, the required monthly income will also grow correspondingly to $13,236 ($3,500 x 3.7816), or to $158,827 per year.

If the after tax inflation-adjusted interest is assumed to be 3% and inflation is 3%, the after tax rate of return must be 6.09% [which is determined by solving for x in the equation for the inflation-adjusted interest rate: $0.03 = (x - 0.03) \div (1.03)$]. For example, if $100 is invested to earn an after tax rate of return of 6.09%, the total income and principal at the end of the year would be $106.09. If inflation is 3%, the real inflation-adjusted end-of-period value is $103 ($106.09 ÷ 1.03). Therefore, the real inflation-adjusted return is 3%. If the objective is to provide $3 of real income and inflation is 3%, $3.09 must be distributed at the end of the year ($3 x 1.03). After paying the $3.09, the remaining balance is $103. Since inflation is assumed to be 3%, the real inflation-adjusted value of the capital remains intact. In other words, since the capital value increases by the rate of inflation each year, the fund is able to distribute 3% in real terms each year indefinitely.

14. In those relatively rare cases where the key employee is the firm, for all practical purposes, his or her death would constitute a permanent and irreplaceable loss. In these cases, insurable value could be determined using a human life value income replacement approach as described earlier in this chapter.

15. This work sheet is adapted from one developed by Robert Crowe as presented in *The Financial Services Professional's Guide to the State of the Art*, Chapter 8, (The American College, 1989).

16. Insurance proceeds may be subject to regular income tax if the policy was acquired in a transaction subject to the transfer for value rule, which should generally be avoided, if possible. (See Appendix G.) Otherwise, life insurance proceeds will generally be received by the corporation tax free if it has a legitimate insurable interest in the insured. However, corporate-owned life insurance proceeds are an item of tax preference and may be subject to an effective maximum alternative minimum tax rate of 15%. See Appendix F and Chapter 24 for further discussion of the tax issues with respect to corporate-owned life insurance in general and key employee insurance in particular.

17. Suggested references for further information on the subject of key employee valuation include:

Black, Jr. and Black III, "Insurable Interest and Key Man Life Insurance Benefits," *The CPA Journal*, August 1987, p. 46.

Robert M. Crowe, Time and Money: Using the Time Value Analysis in Financial Planning (Dow Jones-Irwin, 1987).

Chapter 3

HOW TO DETERMINE THE RIGHT COMPANY

The financial strength of most life insurance companies used to rarely be seriously questioned and was usually only a cursory consideration when selecting life, annuity, and health insurance policies. However, the collapses of the junk-bond and real-estate markets have had an unprecedented impact on the financial stability of many insurance companies. Thirty-four life and health insurers with total assets of $1 billion went bust over an 18-month period in 1990-91, compared with a mere five with total assets of $41 million in 1981. Others started facing serious financial or solvency problems.

Selecting the best insurance company involves more than evaluating its financial stability and operations, although that should be the paramount consideration. Additional factors include product availability and reputation for service and fairness to policyholders.

Since policy illustrations are only as good as the underlying mortality, expense, and investment assumptions, the first and most important step in selecting a life insurance policy is to assess the financial strength of the insurance company. Once a group of strong companies has been selected, then pricing, illustrations, contracts, and service can be compared.

LIFE INSURANCE COMPANY DUE CARE[1]

To serve the best interests of their clients, as well as to protect themselves from potential malpractice claims, planners should research insurance companies using an analytical methodology similar to the due diligence process required for limited partnership and similar investments. This process should include essentially three steps:

1. An assessment of the company's rating by the major rating services.

2. An evaluation of the general characteristics and financial information of the company.

3. A review of recent trends for various "indicative" tests of profitability, leverage, and liquidity.

In the past, a rating of A+ or A from A.M. Best or a similar rating from one of the other rating agencies was usually considered satisfactory evidence of a company's financial strength. However, since many companies are not rated by these agencies and recent history has shown that even A rated ("Excellent") companies have faced financial difficulties, relying on the company's rating alone is insufficient.[2]

Company Rating Services

For some years, the A.M. Best Company was the only player in the life insurance company rating business. Four other major financial rating companies now provide a similar service – Moody's, Standard & Poor's, Fitch, and Weiss Research. Each of these companies provides extensive reports on company operations and related statistics as well as letter rating classifications. In addition, the National Association of Insurance Commissioners (NAIC) has developed the Insurance Regulatory Information System (IRIS) to assist state insurance departments in overseeing the financial condition of insurance companies.

A.M. Best

The A.M. Best Company has been rating life insurance companies for over 85 years and provides full ratings for the largest number of insurance companies among the rating agencies. It charges a relatively low fee for a company to be included in its rating service. Perhaps the most important of Best's publications for assessing the financial soundness of an insurance company is *Best's Insurance Reports – Life/Health*, which provides detailed statistical reports on the financial position, history, and operating results of life insurance companies.

Best's Insurance Reports provides one-year assessments of each company's financial situation and Best's letter ratings. The objective of Best's rating system is to provide an opinion concerning a company's relative financial strength as well as the company's ability to meet its contractual obligations by reviewing the factors that can impact the company's performance. The letter ratings are intended to categorize each company with respect to its claims-paying ability. The letter ratings range from A++ to F. Some companies are not rated because of their relative newness in the market. A listing of the rating categories is presented in Figure 3.1.

In addition, A.M. Best uses several rating modifiers, including:

(g) – group rating

(p) – pooled rating

(r) – reinsured rating

(u) – under review

Companies that are not assigned ratings by Best are given one of five "Not Rated" (NR) designations:

- NR-1 – insufficient data

- NR-2 – insufficient size or operating experience

- NR-3 – rating procedure is inapplicable

- NR-4 – company request

- NR-5 – not formally followed

As a first level of review, planners should favor companies that have received at least an A+ rating for a number of years (e.g., 10 years). Traditionally, many commentators have recommended avoiding companies with a ranking lower than A.

Best also ranks companies according to financial size using categories from FSC I through FSC XV. This designation is based on the company's size as determined by capital, surplus, and conditional reserve funds. Although the larger companies do not necessarily have the best products, they may be more capable of weathering adverse mortality experience, market changes, and other financial or economic fluctuations than smaller companies.

Moody's

Moody's Investors Service assigns "financial strength ratings" to life insurance companies that range from Aaa (the highest) to C (the lowest). A listing of Moody's rating categories is included in Figure 3.1.

The fee Moody's charges a company to be included in its rating service can be substantial. As a result of the relatively high rating fees, Moody's rates a limited self-selected universe of companies that would probably not choose to be rated if they did not expect high ratings. Differences in the numerical ranking order of Best's and Moody's (e.g., the highest ranking from one company versus the third highest ranking from another) should be a red flag indicating that the company's financials should be given especially close scrutiny.

Fitch Ratings

Fitch Ratings rates the "claims-paying ability" of life insurance companies. Fitch categorizes companies from AAA (the highest rating) to D (the lowest rating). Figure 3.1 lists their rating categories. Similar to Moody's, Fitch charges insurance companies substantial fees to be included in their rating service. But if a relative ranking differs from the ranking provided by Best's or Moody's, it is an indication that the planner should look more closely at other indicators of the company's financial condition.

Standard & Poor's

Standard and Poor's Corporation now provides two types of rating services for life insurance companies. First, is a rating of a life insurance company's "claims-paying ability." Similar to Moody's and Fitch, S&P charges companies substantial fees to be included in their claims-paying ability rating service. S&P rates companies from AAA (highest) to R (lowest). Figure 3.1 lists S&P's rating categories.

As with both Moody's and Fitch's ratings, it appears that basically only the better companies are willing to pay the substantial fee to be included in S&P's rating listings. The relatively high ratings may also reflect the fact that companies are permitted to withdraw from the S&P listing if they find S&P's rating unacceptable.

In addition, S&P provides a system of "qualified solvency ratings" for insurance companies. In contrast with the claims-paying ability rating service that requires the cooperation of the insurance company's management and access to proprietary company information, the qualified solvency rating is a mechanical rating system based solely on public information from financial statements filed with state regulators. Qualified solvency ratings are issued for each company that is in the NAIC data base of public filings for insurance companies and that does not have an S&P claims-paying ability rating.

The qualified solvency rating system was developed in order to provide some financial stability rankings to the public for companies that do not choose to pay to be listed in the claims-paying ability rating service. Companies are assigned to one of three broad categories:

- BBBq – Above average

- BBq – Average

- Bq – Below average

Although S&P admits that their assessments are limited by the lack of the "inside" information they use to make their claims-paying ability ratings, they consider insurers rated BBBq to be candidates for claims-paying ability ratings in the secure range. Some insurers rated BBq may qualify for secure claims-paying ability ratings while insurers rated Bq are unlikely to be viewed as secure.

Figure 3.1

RATING CATEGORIES USED BY BEST, S&P, MOODY'S, FITCH, AND WEISS

RATINGS

Best	S&P	Moody's	Fitch	Weiss
A++	AAA	Aaa	AAA	A+
A+	AA+	Aa1	AA+	A
A	AA	Aa2	AA	A-
A-	AA-	Aa3	AA-	B+
B++	A+	A1	A+	B
B+	A	A2	A	B-
B	A-	A3	A-	C+
B-	BBB+	Baa1	BBB+	C
C++	BBB	Baa2	BBB	C-
C+	BBB-	Baa3	BBB-	D+
C	BB+	Ba1	BB+	D
C-	BB	Ba2	BB	D-
D	BB-	Ba3	BB-	E+
E	B+	B1	B+	E
F	B	B2	B	E-
	B-	B3	B-	F
	CCC	Caa1	CCC+	
	CC	Caa2	CCC	
	R	Caa3	CCC-	
		Ca	CC	
		C	C	
			DD	
			D	

Weiss Research

Weiss Research is a relative newcomer to insurance company ratings. They have their own proprietary rating system that, in contrast with the other services, is almost exclusively dependent on publicly available information.

Included in Weiss's statistical analysis is a measure of how well each insurer would fare, given their financial position today, in "average" and "severe" recessions. Companies with considerable liquidity and low-risk investments are rated higher than companies with less liquidity or less-secure investments that might have to drop a weak product line or upgrade the quality of financial assets to weather a financial crisis. Figure 3.1 lists Weiss' rating categories.

In general, the Weiss ratings have been much more severe than those of the other rating services. They have tended to rate insurers lower, sometimes much more so, than their competitors. The Weiss ratings tend to look like a typical academic bell curve. Only a small portion earns an A or B rating, reflecting "excellent" or "good" financial health. The largest portion of the companies rated fall into the C (average/fair) range. Unlike the same grade from the other rating services, a C from Weiss may not be that bad a grade. The last portion of companies rated get D (weak), E (very weak), or F (failed) grades. The companies that get a B+ or better grade earn a spot on Weiss' list of companies that are recommended for safety.

The Weiss ratings appear to be much more conservative than the ratings given by the other rating services; as a result, it would seem that companies with high ratings from Weiss are the most secure companies. However, Weiss uses less information in making its rankings than the other services. In addition, it does not consider the quality and history of management to avoid financial crisis when overall economic conditions turn sour.

Life Insurance Company Due Care Checklist

Figure 3.2 presents a checklist that planners may use to perform the life insurance company due diligence process.[3] The form begins with basic information regarding the name, address, and phone number of the company, its ratings by the various rating services, its size, and age. Clearly, if a company does not have sufficiently high ratings, the process is complete. What follows is a discussion of some key items on the checklist.

Company Size and Age

The size and age of the company may be important if a history of growth and survival are indications of a company's likelihood of surviving the future decades over which policies purchased today must be secured. While there is no direct relationship between size and stability, large, well-established companies are likely to weather adverse trends more successfully than smaller and newer, less well-established companies.

Company Financial Information

Beyond the ratings, company size, and age, the financial issues raised on the checklist should help planners to focus on other important financial variables.

Percent of premium that is individual life premium – The percentage of the company's total premium that is individual life premium may be important for several reasons. First, if life insurance is not the largest segment of the company's business, the company may become distracted and place more emphasis on its other lines, such as health insurance, to the detriment of life insurance policyholders.

Average policy size – Another factor is the average policy size issued by the company. Statistics show that larger policies, which are purchased by more affluent people as part of estate or business continuation planning, lapse less frequently than smaller policies. Since the first year commission and the cost of putting a policy on the books are a large portion of the total expenses associated with a policy, companies with longer persistency tend to have lower average expenses than companies with shorter persistency. Keep in mind that average policy size and company size are not related. For example, the two largest insurers, Prudential and Metropolitan, have the lowest average policy sizes among the ten largest insurers.

Quality of investment assets – The quality and composition of the underlying assets is the key to the potential long-run performance and financial stability of the company. The most critical categories of assets are bonds, mortgages, real estate, and policy loans. Many insurers that have faced financial difficulties have had a large portion of their portfolio invested in junk (below investment grade) bonds and/or have had large portions invested in nonperforming real estate or mortgages that are in arrears. Each of the rating services lists company assets by category and investment grade. Avoid companies whose portfolio is heavily invested in junk bonds.

Also, companies with a shorter weighted average bond maturity are more liquid than those with longer bond maturities. All else being equal, shorter average maturities are considered less risky than longer maturities.

Assessing the quality of a company's real estate and mortgage investments is difficult; planners should be wary of insurers whose real estate and mortgage holdings exceed industry averages.

Policy loans are typically relatively low-yielding investments, especially if a large portion of the loans are attributable to older policies with fixed loan rates of 5% to 8%. Therefore, if policy loans represent a relatively large proportion of the company's portfolio, the overall performance of the portfolio may suffer. Also, since policy loan interest is generally no longer tax deductible, this may tend to increase the lapse ratio and overall expenses.

The following table showing the asset distribution of U.S. life insurers in 2002 may serve as a helpful guideline when evaluating an individual company's investment asset mix.

Asset Distribution
All U.S. Insurers –2002

	Percentage of Portfolio		
Asset	General Account	Separate Accounts	Combined
Corporate Bonds	56.1	12.0	43.6
Government Bonds	16.8	7.8	14.2
Mortgages	10.1	0.7	7.4
Stocks	3.5	73.7	23.4
Real Estate	0.9	1.2	1.0
Policy Loans	4.3	0.1	3.1
Misc. Other (incl. cash)	8.3	4.5	7.3

Source: The American Council of Life Insurance, *Life Insurance Fact Book* (2003), p. 17.

Investment yield – The return on an insurer's general portfolio is the principle source of funds supporting its dividends on participating policies and the basis for interest credited to interest-sensitive and universal life (UL) policies. Planners should compare the portfolio yield to the interest rate assumed in the dividend projections on participating policies or the quoted current interest rate for UL policies. If the rate assumed for dividend scales for par policies or the current interest rate for UL policies exceeds the portfolio rate, the probability that the company can support the projected dividends for par policies or actually credit

Figure 3.2

LIFE INSURANCE COMPANY DUE CARE CHECKLIST

COMPANY: ADDRESS: TELEPHONE	RATING: Best S&P Fitch Moody COMPANY SIZE: COMPANY AGE:

PART 1: FINANCIAL INFORMATION

1. Percent of total premium which is individual life premium:
2. Investments (percent of total assets with comments)
   a) Bonds:
   b) Stocks:
   c) Mortgages:
   d) Real estate:
   e) Short term (cash):
   f) Policy loans:
   g) Other:
3. Investment yield comments:
4. Separate account comments (if applicable):
5. Company history (stability, growth, unusual comments):
6. Management and operations
   a) Mutual/Stock:
   b) Management experience:
   c) Participating/Nonparticipating/Both:
7. Operating ratios
   a) Lapse ratio and trend
   b) Average policy size issued:
   c) Average ordinary premium/thousand:
   d) Renewal expense ratios   Trends:
8. Operating comments
   a) Net yield:
   b) Reserves:
   c) Expenses: Comments:
   d) Mortality:
   e) Lapses:
   f) Policy loans:
   g) Dividends:

9. Business trends	Increasing	Level	Decreasing

a) New business issued:
  b) Insurance in force:
  c) Company development:			

PART 2: TRENDS

FROM: TO: TESTS	TREND ADJUSTMENTS	MIN.	NORM.	MAX.

1. Profitability
  a) Return on equity:
  b) Change in capital and surplus:
2. Leverage
  a) Change in net premiums written:
  b) Net premiums written to capital and surplus:
  c) Surplus relief:
  d) Insurance exposure to capital and surplus:
3. Liquidity
  a) Current liquidity:
  b) Affiliated investments to capital and surplus:				

interest on UL policies at the current rate in future years is questionable.

As a standard for comparison, the following table shows the net rate of investment income for U.S. life insurance companies (before federal income taxes) for recent years.

Net Rate of Return for
U.S. Life Insurance Companies
(Before Federal Income Tax)

Percentage Return

Year	Total Assets	General Account Only
1980	8.02	8.06
1981	8.57	8.53
1982	8.91	8.87
1983	8.96	9.08
1984	9.45	9.65
1985	9.63	9.87
1986	9.35	9.64
1987	9.10	9.39
1988	9.03	9.41
1989	9.10	9.47
1990	8.89	9.31
1991	8.63	9.09
1992	8.08	8.58
1993	7.52	8.04
1994	7.14	7.63
1995	7.41	7.90
1996	7.25	7.75
1997	7.35	7.86
1998	6.95	7.58
1999	6.71	7.49
2000	7.05	7.40
2001	6.31	7.13
2002	5.38	6.64

Source: The American Council of Life Insurance, *Life Insurance Fact Book* (2003), p. 67.

Separate accounts – The separate account item only applies if a variable life, variable annuity, or variable universal life product is being evaluated. By law, variable products must be kept in separate accounts. Planners should inspect several key items. The percentage of the company's total assets that is in separate accounts indicates how important this type of product is within the company's overall product offerings. The breakdown between stocks, bonds, real estate, and other assets will indicate the overall risk level of the separate account portfolio and whether or not it meets the potential policyowner's investment objectives. Planners should assess the quality of the investment assets of the separate account in the same way they would when evaluating a company's general portfolio when considering non-variable policies. The liabilities and payments to surplus accounts indicate the level of charges applied against the funds. The account's net investment income for the current and recent years should be compared with net investment income on separate accounts from competing companies. Also, disbursements for management fees, changes in reserves, and credited income to contract holders should be compared with similar types of disbursements from other companies' separate accounts.

Company history, management and operations – These sections of the checklist can be used to document and compare various items related to company history and management. When was the company founded? Is it a stock or mutual company, has it changed its status, and if so why? Is it a subsidiary of another company? Have there been recent changes in management and, if so, why? Has it shown better-than-average growth and stability of growth? How does its size compare industry-wide? How are its products distributed and what is the size of its agent/broker field force? In which states is the company licensed to do business? If it is not admitted to do business in New York, is it to avoid the generally stricter regulatory requirements of that state? What are the company's most important product lines and the proportion of its business in each line?

Operating ratios – The lapse ratio tells how many ordinary policies are lapsing annually. As a general rule of thumb, planners should look for companies with lapse ratios less than 11% and renewal persistencies greater than 87%.

Greater than average lapse ratios will usually mean higher than average expenses and may mean less than average service to policyowners. In extreme cases, it may suggest that policyowners are being "churned," that is, being systematically encouraged by agents to surrender policies in force for new policies (on which, the agent receives new, high first-year commissions). The trend in lapses should be decreasing if interest rates are declining since it should be difficult for the company's policyowners to find higher rates with new policies. The trend in lapses relative to the industry in general may offer a clue to policyowners' satisfaction and the overall quality of the company's book of business.

As discussed above, the expense of issuing policies generally decreases as the policy size increases and larger policies have tended to experience lower lapse rates than smaller policies. Therefore, all else being equal, it is generally considered better to buy policies with companies with larger average policies.

The average ordinary premium per thousand dollars of coverage should generally have declined in recent years. If premiums have risen, it probably means the company has issued more substandard or rated policies or has had adverse mortality experience.

Industry-wide, renewal expenses have been declining as a percentage of premiums. If a company's renewal expense ratio is not declining in a similar manner it may indicate poor management of expenses or other cost-control problems.

Operating comments – Planners should compare the company's net yield with the industry-wide average and look for suitable reasons why the company's net yield may be higher or lower than the norm. Higher-than-average net yield may be attributable to better-than-average investment management and control of investment expenses. It could also mean higher-than-average risk in the company's portfolio. Analogously, lower-than-average net yields may indicate poor investment management and control of investment expenses. It could also mean the company has invested its portfolio more conservatively, and safely, than the industry average.

Reserves represent the security, or set-aside, required to pay the benefits promised from the company's policies. Surrender values are related to reserves in that the reserves represent the claim against the assets by policyowners who discontinue their policies. Most simply, but somewhat incompletely stated, the statutory reserve is the amount that, together with future net premiums and interest, will be sufficient, according to certain valuation assumptions, to pay future claims.

Companies may use one of several valuation methods to compute reserves. The net level premium method is generally considered the strongest valuation method, but companies have significant latitude in the interest rates and mortality tables they use for valuation. In addition, companies that are growing swiftly (which may be an indication of strength), may have a "capacity" problem (since new policies require increases in reserves in excess of the premiums received). Consequently, these companies may use alternative reserve valuation methods that are less restrictive than the net level premium method. A full assessment of a company's reserve method requires technical knowledge that is beyond the scope of this discussion.[4]

Overall, expenses vary greatly from company to company. Clearly, companies with lower expenses are presumably better managed than those with higher expenses and should be preferred. Commonly used measures of expenses include:

- the ratio of total expenses to the total amount of insurance in force;

- the ratio of total expenses to premiums received; and

- the ratio of total expenses to total income.

These ratios should be used carefully when comparing companies, since they can be misleading, unless applied to similar companies. The first ratio is more appropriate for comparing insurers who are almost exclusively life insurers with little or no annuity, health, disability, or accidental-death business. It gives no weight to annuities, supplementary contracts, health insurance, disability and accidental death benefits, and miscellaneous company operations and, therefore, would tend to be biased against companies that offer these other products by skewing the ratio upward. In addition, it makes no allowance for the difference between first-year and renewal-year expenses and would, therefore, tend to be biased against faster-growing companies. The first ratio also makes no distinction between expenses on ordinary, group, credit, and industrial business and is, therefore, difficult to use when comparing companies with different mixes between these product lines. It also makes no allowance for differences in the companies' books of business by age, sex, and plan or type of insurance which would tend to bias the measure against those companies that may place more of their book of business in the higher expense areas.

The second ratio gives some weight to annuities, health insurance, and disability and accidental-death benefits (but not necessarily the proper weight), but it gives no weight to supplementary contracts. Therefore, the second ratio would be more appropriate than the first ratio for comparing companies with this broader book of business. It otherwise still has the same limitations described for the first ratio.

The third ratio is the broadest overall measure, including weighting for supplementary contracts. However, it still suffers from most of the criticisms of the other two ratios related to variations in companies' books of business, age distribution of policies, differences in ages, sex, and types of plans, etc. Consequently, each of these ratios may provide some relative indication of a company's ability to manage its expenses, but each ratio should be used with the cited limitations clearly in mind.

Mortality experience also varies widely among companies. Companies with better mortality experience typically have higher underwriting standards and better "risks" among their policyowners. All else being equal, it is preferable to acquire a policy from a company with tough standards, if one can qualify. Future mortality experience, and therefore the amounts potentially available to pay dividends or to credit to cash values, is more likely to be favorable. In addition, lapse rates and expenses tend to be lower in policies from companies with tougher underwriting standards.

Dividends – How a company has performed in relation to its promises is indicated by the actual history of dividend payments and interest rates in comparison with the dividend scales and interest rates shown on whole life, universal life, and interest-sensitive policy illustrations. Planners should also compare dividends paid with the net operating gain before dividend payments. Surplus will be depleted if dividends exceed net operating gain.

Business trends – This area of the checklist is used to report on trends in new business issued, management plans for new lines of business, changes in the amount of insurance in force, and other company developments. Clearly, the best companies are those with the best trends. For companies that are introducing, or have introduced, new lines of business or new types of policies, expenses can be expected to be higher than average. Look for trends of declining expenses and evidence of success in any new offerings.

Trends

This section of the checklist is used to summarize trends in profitability and liquidity.

Profitability – Return on equity: Look for companies with a history of increasing earnings and better-than-average returns on equity.

Change in capital and surplus: The change in net capital and surplus is essentially a measure of net worth. Capital and surplus represent the excess of assets over liabilities. The greater a company's surplus, the less risk of insolvency, all else being equal. Experts often compare companies using the ratio of surplus plus mandatory securities valuation reserve (MSVR) to

total assets. The MSVR is a reserve for losses on securities held in the company's general portfolio. Higher values should be preferred and planners should look for growth in surplus.

Leverage – Change in net premiums written: The leverage tests measure whether a company's obligations are growing at a rate that may exceed its ability to handle them. The change in net premiums written should be positive, but not excessive. As discussed above in regard to reserves, putting new policies on the books is a drain on surplus since reserves initially must increase faster than the premium income.

Net premiums written to capital and surplus: The ratio of net premiums written to capital and surplus is often considered a more useful measure for comparing companies with respect to excess growth. Companies with lower ratios should generally be preferred.

Surplus relief: The surplus relief ratio is the ratio of net commissions and expense allowances on reinsurance to capital and surplus. Virtually all insurance companies reinsure a portion of their business. That is, they cede or pass on to another insurer some of the risk of their policies and pay the other company a premium to assume the risk. Similarly, many companies of the companies who reinsure a portion of their own business also serve as reinsurers for other companies. In this way, large risks are shared among many insurance companies. For insurers whose commissions on reinsurance assumed exceed the commissions on reinsurance ceded, this ratio will be negative. Large positive values for this ratio may indicate that the company's management believes the surplus is inadequate. Extreme negative values may indicate that the additional reserves required for the reinsurance assumed is beginning to strain capital and surplus or that excessive commissions and expenses are being incurred by the company acquiring that business.

Insurance exposure to capital and surplus: This ratio, sometimes expressed inversely as the ratio of capital and surplus per $1,000 of insurance in force, is a measure of mortality exposure or mortality leverage. It is a relative measure of how much adverse mortality the company can handle. A lower ratio of insurance exposure to capital and surplus or a higher ratio of capital and surplus per $1,000 of insurance is preferred.

Liquidity – Current liquidity: Liquidity tests measure whether a company can meet its current and future obligations. The current liquidity test is the most important since it measures whether the company could pay all net obligations if they came due in 30 days. The value should be as high as possible.

Affiliated investments to capital and surplus: This test applies when a company is part of an affiliated group of companies. It consolidates the investments of all affiliated companies and compares it to the consolidated capital and surplus. Once again, a higher ratio is preferred.

MUTUAL COMPANIES VERSUS STOCK COMPANIES

Most life insurance companies are either stock or mutual companies. Fraternal benefit societies provide a small fraction of life insurance coverage, and the Department of Veterans Affairs also provides coverage for veterans under six different insurance programs and it oversees three other life insurance programs for members of the uniformed services. Among mutual and stock companies, the vast majority are stock companies – 1,076, or 92% of the industry, in 2002.[5]

A mutual company is a corporation that has no shareholders.[6] The policyholders are the members of the corporation, and they have membership rights. These rights derive from the insurance contract, the corporation's bylaws and charter or articles of incorporation, state laws, and case law. These membership rights are similar to stock owners' rights in a regular corporation and include: (1) the right to contractual benefits, including dividends declared by the board of directors; (2) the right to participate in corporate governance, usually by electing directors to oversee the operation of the company ; (3) the right to receive any remaining value if the corporation is liquidated or demutualized (converted to a stock company); (4) the right to expect that the corporation will be run primarily for the benefit of the members; and (5) the right to bring legal action against the directors and officers for violating their fiduciary duties. Individual members cannot sell their rights to someone else and these membership rights terminate when a member cancels the policy or dies.

Stock life insurance companies are corporations that have shareholders, who may or may not be policyholders. In contrast with mutual policyholders, shareholders may generally sell their ownership interest in a stock company. The corporation is run primarily for the benefit of the shareholders, although its relationship with its customers must respect commercial laws and the need to compete in the marketplace.

What are the advantages and disadvantages of the mutual and stock forms of organization?

Because a mutual company has no shareholders, there is no conflict of interest between shareholders and policyholders. This makes it possible to fulfill the company's primary mission: to provide insurance at its cost. However, mutual companies still must make profits to remain afloat. Mutual companies need profits to maintain financial strength and to support future growth. In contrast with stock companies that can issue new shares of common stock to raise capital to expand their growth, mutual companies generally raise capital by retaining a portion of the premiums they receive in excess of the amount they expect to pay out to cover expenses and benefit payments. In general, however, mutual companies have a lower profit goal than stock companies, because they do not have to satisfy the demands of outside investors. Management can also tend to take a long-term view in running the business, because they do not have to pay attention to daily fluctuations of a stock price. As a result, it is probably true that the net return on cash values has been somewhat higher and the net cost of insurance somewhat lower to mutual policyholders than to stock company policyholders, although this is not unquestionably so in all cases.

These advantages are offset by several disadvantages.

- Mutual companies have limited flexibility to raise capital and to merge with or acquire other companies, because they cannot issue stock.

- Financial reporting is less flexible, because all transactions are reflected on the parent's books.

- Non-insurance subsidiaries may receive a valuation penalty for being associated with a heavily-regulated parent.

- A mutual company's identification as a life insurance company may hinder efforts to provide other comprehensive financial services (as compared to a stock company with subsidiaries in various financial services).

- Management performance is not subject to the same level of scrutiny as it is at stock companies, because there are no outside investors. In most cases, unhappy policyholders find it almost impossible to replace directors who are not fulfilling their duties. Policyholders have to rely on rating agencies to place constraints on management actions.

- Mutual companies may also have a higher tax burden than stock companies, although this has been a subject of debate.

From the insurance buyer's point of view, the major distinction between mutual and stock companies originally was in the types of policies they issued. Stock companies originally issued "non-participating" policies where premiums, cash values, benefit levels, and dividends, if any, were guaranteed, but fixed. Any investment performance above that assumed in setting the guaranteed cash values and dividends (if any) and any savings in expenses, mortality rates, and any of the other assumptions involved in pricing the policy (such as lapse rates and the like), went to the companies' shareholders, not the policyholders. In contrast, mutual companies issued "participating" policies where premiums, cash values, and benefit levels were also guaranteed at some level. However, if the company had favorable investment results or better than anticipated expense or mortality experience, or better experience with respect to the other factors involved in policy pricing, the benefits would be passed on to the policyholders through higher than projected dividends. Of course, if results were unfavorable, the dividends could fall below the projected dividend level, since dividends are not guaranteed.

So in general, policyholders in stock companies had a fixed and guaranteed and, therefore, known cost for the insurance. In contrast, mutual companies tended to charge somewhat higher premiums, all else being equal, but gave the policyholders the opportunity to participate in the favorable experience of the company through higher than projected future dividend payments. As a result, the real cost over time to policyholders in mutual companies tended to be less than that for policyholders in stock companies.

Competition and innovation over time tended to blur the distinction between policies offered by mutual and stock companies. To compete, stock companies first started to offer interest-sensitive policies that paid higher dividends or, more frequently, credited higher cash value accumulations (rather than pay dividends) over time if the investment performance of the insurer's general fund earned rates of return in excess of those rates assumed when setting the premiums. These types of policies evolved over time into the current-assumption policies where favorable experience with respect to virtually all variables used in the premium pricing decision (expenses, mortality rates, lapse rates, etc.) would be passed through to policyholders, generally in the form of higher credits to the accumulating cash value.

Similarly, mutual companies expanded their product offerings and began to offer current-assumption type policies similar to those offered by stock companies. Consequently, today, potential insurance buyers have a whole assortment of policies ranging from the traditional "non-par" (infrequently offered) to traditional dividend-paying "par" policies to "interest-sensitive" to "current-assumption" to "flexible-premium current-assumption" (universal life) policies offered by both stock and mutual companies.

REINSURANCE

Reinsurance refers to the situations where insurance companies insure against losses they may incur. Insurance companies have a limited amount of capital and to protect this capital they will often cap the losses they may incur by purchasing reinsurance. Typically, the smaller the insurer the more reinsurance they will buy. Reinsurance also can reduce the risk facing a company when policies are issued with a high probability of lapse or surrender, as in policies whose premiums rise sharply from one year to the next. Similarly, reinsurance may limit the investment risk inherent in high concentrations from single products – especially annuities.

A second reason for reinsurance is to obtain the reinsurer's underwriting assistance and expertise. The risk pool from which reinsurers develop and provide underwriting knowledge is generally much larger and wider than that of a single primary insurer.

A third reason companies reinsure is to help them either enter or exit given lines of business or product lines. A company associated with a given product line that wants to discontinue that line can reinsure most or all of the risk on that product. Alternatively, a company desiring to offer a new product line can obtain the help of reinsurers to develop and underwrite the product until the company develops its own expertise in the underwriting of that particular line of business. In some cases, the reinsurance agreement (or treaty, as the reinsurance agreement is typically called) has provisions that permit the ceding company to take back some of the risk the reinsurer had assumed as the ceding company's ability to assume the risk grows over time.

Another reason for the use of reinsurance is to help a company manage its financial position. A reinsurer can provide allowances based upon its anticipation of future profits. This may increase the ceding company's statutory earnings and surplus during the year paid. By ceding business, the reinsurer sets up reserves on its books and lessens the amount the ceding company has to set up in reserves. If a company is growing quickly, this is especially advantageous since initial costs (expenses plus reserves) are higher than premiums received.

Sixty-nine percent of life insurers ceded life premiums from some of their policies as reinsurance in 2002.

In traditional reinsurance, or indemnity reinsurance, the company transferring the risk (the ceding company) retains its financial relationship with, and legal obligation to, the policyholders. In most cases, the policyholders are not even aware that part of the risk on their policies is covered by a reinsurer (the assuming company).

A number of different types of reinsurance are available. The two main types are proportional reinsurance and non-proportional reinsurance.

Proportional reinsurance is an arrangement where the reinsurer takes a share of each loss the insurer incurs. This is also sometimes referred to as *quota share* reinsurance – the risk is allocated by a specified percentage that the ceding company and reinsurer will assume. The capital held by the insurer might only allow it to accept a risk with a value of $1 million but purchasing proportional reinsurance might allow it to, for example, double or triple its acceptance limit.

Four main categories of reinsurance arrangements are considered proportionate reinsurance:

1. *Yearly renewable term (YRT) reinsurance* – YRT reinsurance permits the ceding company to transfer mortality risk, but leaves the ceding company entirely responsible for establishing reserves. The premium the ceding company pays to transfer the risk to the reinsurer varies each year with the net amount at risk and the ages of the insureds.

2. *Coinsurance* V The ceding company transfers a proportionate share of all the policy risks and cash flows except the policy fee. Therefore, the reinsurer receives its proportionate share of premiums, pays its share of benefits, sets up its share of reserves, and pays an allowance to the ceding company. In contrast with YRT reinsurance, coinsurance helps to relieve the strain on the ceding company's surplus because it is not entirely responsible for setting up the reserve.

3. *Coinsurance with funds withheld* – The ceding company keeps the premiums normally paid to the reinsurer and the reinsurer keeps the allowances normally paid to the ceding company, thereby limiting the cash flow between the companies.

4. *Modified coinsurance* – The reinsurer transfers its share of reserves back to the ceding company while the risk remains with the reinsurer. In return, the ceding company must pay interest to the reinsurer to compensate for what the reinsurer would have earned had it retained the reserves.

Both coinsurance with funds withheld and modified coinsurance permit a ceding company to take statutory credit for reserves in certain circumstances, reduce its credit risk, secure credit, and retain control over investments.

Non-proportional reinsurance only pays if the loss suffered by the insurer exceeds a certain amount. This type of arrangement, sometimes, called *excess of retention* reinsurance, allocates risk by amount. The ceding company sets a dollar amount on the level of risk it is willing to retain and cedes the excess to the reinsurer, up to what is called the reinsurer's retention limit. The retention limit is the maximum amount the reinsurer is willing to assume. In many cases, the reinsurer will itself reinsure risks above its retention limit, thereby permitting the original ceding company to transfer all risks over the level it is willing to assume to the reinsurer who then handles the problem of reinsuring risks even beyond its retention level.

Non-proportionate plans include several different arrangements:

1. *Stop loss* – The reinsurer covers some or all of a ceding company's aggregate claims above a predetermined dollar amount or above a percentage of premium during a specified period.

2. *Catastrophe* – The reinsurer covers losses exceeding a specified amount or number of insureds due to a single event resulting in more than one loss, such as from an airplane crash, train wreck, or natural disaster.

3. *Excess of loss* – In this form of reinsurance, the insurer is prepared to accept a loss of, say, $1 million for any loss that may occur and purchases a layer of reinsurance of, say, $5 million in excess of $1 million. If a loss of $3 million occurs the insurer pays $1 million themselves and recovers $2 million from the reinsurer. In this example, the insurer will incur for their

own account any loss exceeding $6 million unless they have purchased a further layer of reinsurance

Companies often reinsure with reinsurance syndicates or groups, rather than with single-company reinsurers. The reinsurer who sets the terms (premium and policy conditions) for the reinsurance program is called the *lead* reinsurer; the other companies subscribing to the program are called *follow* reinsurers.

The life, health, property reinsurance market is dominated by a small number of very large companies such as Munich Re, Swiss Re, and Berkshire Hathaway, who own several reinsurers including General Re and Faraday in London. However, there is a wide range of smaller reinsurers who may lead reinsurance programs less frequently but who may often participate as a follow market. Most of the above reinsurance programs or treaties cover every risk accepted by the insurer of the type described in the reinsurance policy. However, companies may purchase reinsurance on a per risk basis, in which case it is known as *facultative* reinsurance. The range of companies accepting facultative reinsurance is far wider than those underwriting treaty programs.

Reinsurance companies themselves also purchase reinsurance and this is typically known as retrocessional coverage.

FEDERAL AND STATE LAWS AND REGULATION

Insurance companies are entrusted with huge amounts of money – in the $50 billion to $200 billion range in the case of the largest life insurance companies, such as the Prudential, Metropolitan Life, and New York Life. The insurance business thus is regulated in an effort to ensure that the public and its funds are dealt with honestly, and to prevent the insurers from taking unwarranted risks with the money they are holding.

The primary purposes of insurance regulation historically have been as follows: (1) to maintain the insurers' financial solvency and soundness so they can carry out their long-term obligations to policyholders and pay claims; and (2) to guarantee the fair treatment of current and prospective policyholders and beneficiaries by both insurers and the people who sell their policies.

Insurance companies in the United States are primarily regulated by the individual states. There is no one Federal regulatory agency that specifically oversees insurance companies (such as the Securities and Exchange Commission that has a central role in regulating the securities industry, or the Comptroller of the Currency who oversees national banks). The name of the state insurance regulatory agency typically is the "Insurance Department," "Division of Insurance," "Insurance Bureau," or something similar. A state government official, usually called the "Commissioner of Insurance," "Superintendent of Insurance," or "Director of Insurance", or something similar heads these state agencies. The Governor of the state appoints the head of the insurance regulatory agency in most states. However, in some states the insurance commissioner is an elected office.

Each state assumes primary responsibility for overseeing the financial operations and management of insurance companies that are incorporated in that state. For example, Prudential is incorporated in New Jersey, so that state has a primary role in its regulation, while Metropolitan is incorporated in New York, which has the primary regulatory role. (Companies have their statutory home office in the state where they are incorporated.) Each state also regulates the local operations of insurance companies it has licensed to do business within the state, particularly as they relate to policy forms, rates, sales agents, and their practices.

The National Association of Insurance Commissioners, made up of the states' insurance regulators, is a group that coordinates the regulatory processes for each of the 50 states and the District of Columbia, Puerto Rico, and the US Virgin Islands. This organization discusses current issues and works to cooperate (more or less) in developing a common form for financial statements. In addition, it suggests model laws that the states' legislatures then sometimes enact and it promulgates model regulations that the state regulators sometimes adopt.

Most states have laws regulating the conduct of insurance business to ensure fairness in the way companies deal with applicants for insurance and policyholders. One of the functions of a Department of Insurance is to enforce these so-called "unfair trade practices" and "unfair claims practices" laws by investigating complaints by consumers and taking action, when appropriate, to get companies to stop conduct that violates the laws and impose penalties for violations. Other duties of a Department of Insurance include reviewing and approving the policy forms used by insurance companies and approving rates charged for various types of insurance to assure compliance with state laws that regulate insurance rates.

UNDERWRITING

Life insurance companies each have their own extensive policy and procedure manuals they are supposed to follow in determining whether or not to issue an individual life insurance policy, and in pricing that policy. The insurer's underwriters typically use a combination of factors that experience shows equates with the risk of death (and premature death).

They include the applicant's answers to a series of questions such as:

1. age;

2. sex (except in several states that require "unisex" rates, even though actuarial data shows women live longer than men);

3. height and weight;

4. health history (and often family health history – parents and siblings);

5. the purpose of the insurance (such as for estate planning or business or family protection);

6. marital status and number of children;

7. the amount of insurance the applicant already has, and any additional insurance the applicant proposes to buy (as people with far more life insurance than they need tend to be poor insurance risks);

8. occupation (some are hazardous and increase the risk of death);

9. income (to help determine suitability);

10. credit history (relates to character and responsibility);

11. smoking or tobacco use (this is an important factor, as smokers have shorter lives);

12. alcohol (excessive drinking seriously hurts life expectancy);

13. certain hobbies (such as race car driving, hanggliding, or piloting non-commercial aircraft); and

14. prevalence or frequency of foreign travel (certain foreign travel is risky).

Most life insurers require the applicant to undergo a physical examination by a doctor, nurse, or a paramedical technician on large policies. At that time, the examiner typically takes samples of the applicant's blood and urine. The insurer will also typically request the applicant's medical records from his or her physicians, and have the underwriters review them. The underwriters usually will also check the applicant's health history with the Medical Information Bureau, the driving record, credit records, and do other investigations that seem warranted. Usually, the greater the amount of insurance sought by the applicant, the greater the extent of the investigation into the applicant's medical, financial, and personal history.

After the application and medical information is completely gathered, the underwriters make their underwriting decisions. First – if the policy has underwriting requirements – they decide whether the applicant qualifies for insurance at all. For example if someone had cancer within the past year, or has AIDS, the applicant might not be unable to buy underwritten life insurance at any price or only at a very high cost from a company that specializes in issuing policies to those who have the applicant's high-risk profile.

Second, underwriters classify the risk – which affects the price of the coverage. Most applicants receive either a "preferred" classification (intended for those who are above average risks) or a "standard" classification. If a person has a history or characteristics that suggest the applicant is riskier than average (perhaps because the applicant is 50 pounds heavier than average for his or her age and height, has high cholesterol, or had heart bypass surgery 5 years ago) the policy would be "rated," and offered at a higher price based on that rating, given the applicant's age.

Each insurer may evaluate an applicant differently, so that a person one company would regard as "preferred" would be "standard" at another company, and perhaps even "rated" at yet another company. Also, some companies rate up to 70% of all applicants as "preferred" (to make applicants and agent feel good about themselves and the company) but charge more than other companies would charge for a "standard" rating.

COMPANY SERVICE AND FAIRNESS TO POLICYHOLDERS

The quality of a company's service is difficult to quantify, but nonetheless an important criterion in company selection. Look for evidence regarding the company's turnaround time for requests for information, policy loans, initial underwriting and application processing, and processing of death claims as well as other administrative matters. The company may provide statistics on such matters, if requested. Also, it is wise to inquire among life insurance professionals who are familiar with the service provided by various companies.

Also, the level of services provided by agents varies greatly from company to company. Some companies spend considerably more than others on training and efforts to keep their agents informed about legal, tax, and planning issues that affect their ability to provide on-going service to policyowners. In general, if a large proportion of the company's agent force has professional designations – such as the CLU (Chartered Life Underwriter), ChFC (Chartered Financial Consultant), or CFP (Certified Financial Planner) – or other credentials certifying their competence in a specialty area, it is evidence of strong support for and encouragement of education and training of their agency force. In addition, since these professional designations generally take some years to earn, it suggests the company appeals to long-term and committed life insurance professionals. Presumably, these professionals prefer to work for companies that provide the highest standards of service to the field force and their clients.

Whether a company has a history of fairness to its policyowners is also difficult to quantify but of considerable importance when selecting a company. A key fairness issue is whether policyowners share equitably in the company's favorable performance. Are distributions to owners of participating or interest-sensitive types of policies equitable relative to the total distributable surplus? Similarly, are existing policyowners (or blocks of policies) treated equitably with respect to new policyowners (or new blocks of policies)? Do policyowners of one type or class of policies receive their equitable share of distributable surplus relative to other types or classes of policies? Each of these questions is difficult to answer but some evidence may be gained by inspecting company financial statements regarding distribution of surplus. Further clues may be unearthed by comparing a company's past dividend illustrations with the amounts of dividends actually paid.[7] Many companies have a history of paying higher dividends than they originally illustrated, quite often by design, so a careful analysis may require comparisons among a number of different classes or types of policies and with differing issue dates to uncover any systematic "unfairness" by class or age of policy. If actual dividend payments are frozen or below the amounts shown in illus-

trations, it should arouse suspicions. However, under the current competitive and financially uncertain environment, we are likely to see far more policies than in the past that are not paying dividends or crediting interest at the rate originally illustrated.

SELECTED REFERENCES and SOURCES

1. A. M. Best Company, Ambest Road, Oldwick, NJ 08858.

    *   *Best's Insurance Reports, Life/Health*

    *   *Best's Insurance Management Reports, Life/Health*

    *   *Best's Key Rating Guide, Life/Health*

    *   *Best's Review, Life/Health*

    *   *Best's Agent's Guide*

    *   *Best's Advanced Rating Reporting Service*

2. Standard and Poor's Insurance Rating Services, 25 Broadway, New York, NY 10004.

    *   *S&P's Insurer Solvency Review, Life/Health*

3. Moody's Investor Services, 99 Church Street, New York, NY 10007.

    *   *Moody's Insurance Credit Report Service*

    *   *Moody's Investor Service Life Insurance Handbook*

4. Joseph M. Belth, P.O. Box 245, Ellettsville, IN 47429.

    *   *The Insurance Forum*

5. American Bar Association, Section of Real Property, Probate and Trust Law, 750 N. Lake Shore Drive, Chicago, IL 60611.

    *   *The Life Insurance Counselor, Vol. I, Life Insurance Products, Illustrations and Due Diligence*

6. The Townsend and Schupp Company, 100 Wells Street, Suite 802, Hartford, CT 06103.

    *   *Life Insurance Business Risk Analysis*

7. Fitch Ratings., One State Street Plaza, New York, NY 10004.

    *   *Fitch Ratings Delivery Service*

8.   Prentice Hall, Englewood Cliffs, New Jersey 07632.

   •   K. Black, Jr. and H. Skipper, Jr., *Life Insurance* (12th ed. 1994)

9.   Weiss Research, Inc., 15430 Endeavour Dr., Jupiter, FL 33478.

   •   *Weiss Ratings' Guide to Life, Health and Annuity Insurers*

QUESTIONS AND ANSWERS

Question – What protection is there for persons who own policies in shaky or financially insolvent companies?

Answer – So far, no one has lost any death benefit from life insurance.

In general, policyowners are protected in two ways. In many cases, smaller insolvent companies are taken over by larger, more secure companies that assume the obligations of the smaller company to its policyowners. In addition, in the event an insurer fails (and its obligations are not assumed by another company), policyowners have one primary source of protection, the state "guaranty fund." To help protect policyowners in the event of insolvency, most states maintain guaranty funds for life and health insurers. When necessary, the guaranty fund intervenes to pay insurance claims, settle policy surrenders, etc. Most state guaranty funds set an upper limit of $100,000 for life insurance cash values or annuities and $300,000 for death benefits. (The state insurance department of an individual state can provide information about the terms of the state's guaranty fund.) These limits are quite generous when compared to the banking and savings and loan industries' deposit insurance programs.

However, the state guaranty system is not without its problems. Some states' guaranty funds are unfunded, relying essentially on current contributions from other insurers in the state to pay claims as they arise. If several large companies experience difficulties at the same time, it could, at worst, overtax the remaining insurers and force the guaranty fund to leave some claims unpaid or, at best, force the guaranty fund to defer the payment of claims, perhaps for years.

Question – Should policyowners in financially troubled companies switch insurers?

Answer – The answer depends on many factors, including the type of policy and the method of switching. In most cases, surrendering an ordinary cash-value life insurance policy with the intention of investing cash values more safely elsewhere and acquiring a new policy from a more financial stable company is inadvisable. A policyowner who hangs on to the policy may earn a lower rate of dividend interest and may be inconvenienced if the company fails. But, the death benefit is generally safe up to the limit of the state's guaranty fund.

Switching might even be expensive. For example, a whole life policyowner switching policies (i.e., surrendering the old policy and purchasing a new one) will enter the new policy at a higher age and higher premium. In addition, the policyowner will pay a new commission, probably have to take a new medical exam, and, if the old policy has been in force for a number of years, may have to pay tax on the excess of the cash surrender value over the amount of premiums paid. However, if the company becomes insolvent, the policyowner may not be able to borrow against cash values. Therefore, it may be advisable to borrow cash values and invest them somewhere else. The cost of assuring this liquidity is essentially the difference between the borrowing rate in the policy and the rate earned on the invested proceeds (also, some companies will reduce the amount earned on cash values by about 2%).

For similar reasons, it is probably inadvisable to surrender universal life or interest-sensitive policies in financially troubled companies. The principal risks of keeping a policy are that the interest credited to cash values may be reduced to the guaranteed rate (typically 4%) if the insurer becomes insolvent and, in the case of universal life policies, mortality and expense charges may be increased to their maximums. In general, it may be wise to put universal life policies into term mode and use accumulated cash values to continue premiums or to pay only the minimum amount necessary to maintain the face amount of coverage. The amount that would otherwise be paid in premiums may be invested elsewhere.

As with whole life and universal life policies, death benefits on variable life policies are generally secure to the level set by the state guaranty fund. Since the cash values are secured by the specific assets of the separate account, rather than the company's general portfolio, variable life policyowners may always cash their policies in at market value. A possible risk of keeping the policy with a financially troubled company is that borrowing against the policy may be restricted during a period of reorganization if the company becomes insolvent.

Although surrenders of cash value policies held by financially troubled companies with the intent of purchasing policies in more financially secure companies do not seem advisable, IRC Section 1035 exchanges should be seriously considered. Such an exchange may avoid taxation of gain, if any, and avoid some, but generally not all, of the expenses associated with the purchase of a new policy. See Appendix E.

In addition, it may be advisable to consider the reduced paid-up insurance option or the extended term option for existing policies together with the purchase of new policies with more financially secure companies to cover the difference.

In the case of term policies held by financially troubled insurers, death benefits are generally secure to the level set by the state's guaranty fund. The principal risk is that the company will raise renewal premiums to the maximum permitted under the policy, which may be considerably higher than premiums charged by more financially secure competitors. Also, if the policyowner is in poor health and the company becomes insolvent, another company can refuse to pick up the coverage. Therefore, if the policyowner is healthy and can qualify for coverage from a more financially secure company, it is advisable to switch companies.

Annuity contracts present some more difficult problems. If a financially troubled company becomes insolvent during the accumulation phase, the new guarantor may pay interest at a lower rate than the original insurer. Annuity owners who surrender an annuity contract within the first seven years will usually pay a surrender charge ranging from about 7% in the first year to 1% in year seven. In addition, annuity owners must pay income tax on gains and a 10% tax penalty on the taxable portion of the distribution if it is received before age 59_ (and none of the other exceptions to the premature distribution penalty applies). These tax disadvantages can be avoided if the contract is properly exchanged for another one under IRC Section 1035.

Question – How reliable are insurance company ratings in predicting long-term solvency and financial strength?

Answer – Critics have questioned the reliability and predictive power of insurance company ratings. Since company obligations are long-term, the question naturally arises, do insurance company ratings predict solvency or indicate relative financial strength over the long term horizons that most policyowners and annuitants are concerned with? Since policy surrenders within the first few years of ownership may be costly, especially for annuity contracts, and surrenders and access to cash values and loans may be severely restricted if a company becomes insolvent or is placed under state supervision, insurance consumers are not likely to view ratings that downgrade a company one or two years before failure as adequate warning.

Dr. Lee Slavutin did a study assessing the likelihood of an insurer's failure in 5, 10, or 15 years, given its Best rating.[8] The study is based on an historical analysis of company failures and Best ratings since 1978. Since Moody's, S&P, and Fitch have been rating insurers for only a few years, it is still too early to assess the long-term predictive power of their ratings. However, according to Moody's, their corporate bond ratings and insurance financial strength ratings are intended to be comparable. Consequently, as a basis for comparison, Dr. Slavutin's study does contrast the predictive power of Best's insurance ratings with the predictive power of comparable bond ratings issued by Moody's and S&P. The highlights of Slavutin's study follow.

Company Failure Rates in Relation to A.M. Best's Ratings Classifications:

Figure 3.3 presents the proportions of all companies rated by Best's in categories A+ through C in the years 1978 through 1981 that have failed within five to 13 years of receiving the indicated rating.

The figure shows virtually no correlation between insurers' failure rates and Best's ratings for failures that occur within five years of Best's rating. In other words, Best's ratings have had little value in predicting which companies may fail within five years of receiving the rating. However, the overall insurer failure rate within five years of rating for all rated insurers was quite low, less than 2% for every rating category and less than 1% for all rating categories combined. In addition, the five-year failure rate for A+ rated companies was only about three per thousand.

Figure 3.3

A.M. BEST RATINGS AND COMPANY FAILURE RATES[1] FOR COMPANIES RATED IN 1978-1981						
Best's Rating by class[3]	5-yr.failure rate (%)		10-yr. failure rate (%)		13-yr. failure rate[2] (%)	
	by class[3]	cumulative[4]	by class[3]	cumulative[4]	by class[3]	cumulative[4]
A+	0.3	0.3	1.3	1.3	3.3	3.3
A	1.4	0.9	3.0	2.2	3.7	3.5
B+	0.4	0.8	3.4	2.5	6.0	4.2
B	1.1	0.8	6.4	3.0	10.5	4.9
C+	1.9	0.9	8.9	3.5	11.3	5.5
C	1.0	0.9	19.6	3.9	23.1	6.0

1. The average percentages of rated companies that failed.
2. The 13-yr. failure rate columns include only companies rated in 1978.
3. The "by class" columns show failure rates for each rating category. For example, 3.0 percent of the companies rated A in 1978 through 1981 failed within 10 years.
4. The "cumulative" columns show that aggregate or cumulative failure rates for all companies in the indicated rating category and all higher-rated categories. For example, 2.5 percent of all companies rated B+ or better in 1978 through 1981 failed within 10 years.

Source: Based on tables found in Slavutin, "Life Insurance Company Ratings — How Reliable is A.M. Best?", *Financial and Estate Planning*, CCH, Inc., August, 1991, at p. 24,997.

The correlation is significant between Best's ratings and insurer failures within ten years and even more so for failures within 13 years. Failure rates progressively increased for each lower rating category. In other words, Best's ratings have had predictive power in identifying the companies with a higher risk of failure over longer periods. However, insurance consumers may consider failure rates of 1.3% within ten years and 3.3% within 13 years as unacceptably high for insurers who received Best's highest rating at that time, A+. The substantial increase in the 13-year failure rates over the ten-year failures is largely attributable to the recent upswing in the number of failing companies. Although the difference in failure rates within ten years between A+ (1.3%) and A (3.0%) rated companies was significant, the difference diminished considerably for failure rates within 13 years (3.3% and 3.5%, for A+ and A, respectively).

A.M. Best's Insurance Ratings Compared with Moody's and S&P's Bond Ratings:

In the absence of sufficient data to evaluate Moody's and S&P's insurance ratings, Slavutin compared insurer failure rates for each of Best's rating categories with bond default rates for comparable bond rating categories for Moody's and S&P. The rationale for this procedure was that "both Moody's and S&P's ratings have been shown to discriminate between 'investment-grade' and 'speculative' bonds and therefore serve as a model of a 'successful' rating system."[9] In addition, according to Moody's, they intend that their corporate bond and insurer ratings should be comparable. Figure 3.4 shows the results of this comparison of insurer failures and bond defaults within ten years of receiving their respective ratings.

This figure shows that the ten year insurer failure rate for insurers with Best's highest A+ rating (1.3% at 10 years) is comparable to the default rate of bonds with Moody's highest bond rating of Aaa (1.1% at 10 years), but higher than the S&P's AAA default rate of 0%. The A ("Excellent") and B+ ("Very Good") Best's ratings show significantly higher failure rates for insurers than the default rates on bonds rated comparably by Moody's and S&P. For example, 3% of the companies Best rated as A failed within 10 years but only 1% of the bonds rated comparably by Moody's defaulted. This sug-

Figure 3.4

	Best's	Moody's		S&P
Class[1]	**By Class[2]**	**Average[3]**	**Aggregate[4]**	**Aggregate (1971-1986)[5]**
1	1.3	1.1	1.0	0.0
2	3.0	1.0	1.4	0.2
3	3.4	2.0	1.8	0.3
4	6.4	4.7	4.4	2.5
5	8.9	17.2	16.1	6.3
6	19.6	27.8	31.6	32.2

10-YEAR INSURER FAILURE RATES AND 10-YEAR CORPORATE BOND DEFAULTS

1. Classes 1-6 correspond, each respectively to Best's ratings A+, A, B+, B, C+, C; Moody's ratings Aaa, Aa, A, Baa, Ba, B; S&P's ratings AAA, AA, A, BBB, BB, B.
2. From Figure 3.3.
3. Average cumulative 10-year default rates [for bonds rated by Moody's] in 1978, 1979, 1980, and 1981.
4. Average cumulative default rates [for bonds rated by Moody's] in the years 1971 through 1990.
5. Adjusted cumulative mortality rates by original S&P bond rating covering issues from 1971-1986.

Source: Based on tables found in Slavutin, "Life Insurance Company Ratings — How Reliable is A.M. Best?", *Financial and Estate Planning*, CCH, Inc., August, 1991, at p. 24,997.

gests that the A rating is actually weaker than Best claims it to be.

Lack of Discrimination in Ratings for Large Insurer:

Slavutin also showed that Best's may award the A+ rating to insurers more easily than S&P, Moody's, and Duff & Phelps (now Fitch). He used a weighting scheme to rank the ratings for the major GIC issuers. The weighting scheme gives a progressively higher numerical score for each lower rating. The weighted-averaged ratings were as follows:

Rater	Weighted Score	Average Rating
Best's	1.07	A+
S&P	2.27	AA+
D&P	2.67	AA
Moody's	3.38	Aa2

In other words, for this group of insurance companies, the average rating given by Best's was its top rating whereas the average rating given by Moody's was its third highest rating. This suggests that Moody's ratings are more conservative. Slavutin similarly compared the rating services based on ratings of 59 life insurance companies published in the April

1991 issue of *The Insurance Forum*.[10] The scores were as follows:

Rater	Weighted Score
Best's	1.41
S&P	2.66
Moody's	3.32

Once again, both S&P and Moody's appear to rate companies more conservatively than Best's, with Moody's the most conservative of all.

Recommendations:

Based on his analysis, Slavutin makes the following recommendations for selecting a strong insurance company:[11]

1. The Best rating system should be used in conjunction with the other major rating agencies.

2. Look only at insurers whose A M. Best rating is A+ for at least 10 consecutive years and, to be even safer, for every year since the letter ratings began in 1976, together with the strongest policyholder recommendation ("most favorable" operating results

and "most substantial" margins for contingencies) in 1975.

3. Avoid insurers rated A+(contingent), A, or lower by A.M. Best.

4. The insurer should be rated by Best and at least two out of three of the other major rating agencies.

5. Look for a rating of AAA or AA with S&P and/or Fitch.

6. Look for a rating of Aaa or Aa with Moody's.

7. Avoid companies on the NAIC watchlist with 4 or more IRIS ratios outside the "usual" ranges.

8. Use multiple insurers when buying large amounts of insurance to diversify and spread risk.

Question – What is the best way to locate the home office of a life insurance company?

Answer – There are many situations where it is necessary to locate the home office of an insurer. One place to start is a local phone book and the number of the company's local office. This office, in turn, can often refer callers to the address of their home office. Here is a list of some alternatives:

1. Many company websites have the company's contact information, including the location of the home office. These websites can usually be found by using common internet search engines such as Google.

2. Call the office of the State Insurance Commissioner. Detailed records of insurance companies licensed to do business in the state will be available here. State Insurance Commissioner offices will also track the mergers, acquisitions, and liquidations of insurance companies.

3. Visit the web site of the National Association of Insurance Commissioners (NAIC)

at "www.naic.org". The NAIC is an organization of insurance regulators from the 50 states, the District of Columbia and four United States territories. From this web site there is a direct link to most state insurance departments.

4. Visit the web site of The A.M. Best Company at "www.ambest.com/resource/insdir.html". This is the location of A.M. Best's searchable database of nearly 6,000 insurance companies.

5. Visit the web site of "www.insurance.about.com/blbiglist.htm". This is About.com's "Big List" of insurance company home pages.

CHAPTER ENDNOTES

1. The following discussion draws heavily upon Slavutin and Kaplan, "Life Insurance Companies and Products: Evaluation and Due Diligence – Part One," *Financial and Estate Planning*, Commerce Clearing House, Inc., June 1990, p. 24,777.

2. The principal point is not that A M. Best's rating was incorrect or that A M. Best should have detected the problem sooner, but rather that relying on ratings alone may be inadequate.

3. This checklist is based on the one discussed in Bevington, "Covered Assets," 18 *Financial Planning* 31, 34 (January 1989).

4. See K. Black, Jr. and H. Skipper, Jr., *Life Insurance* (Prentice Hall Inc., 12th ed. 1994), pp. 559-571.

5. The American Council of Life Insurance, *Life Insurance Fact Book* (2003), p. 1.

6. Portions of the following discussion are adapted from "Mutual Life Insurance Company Reorganizations: An Overview," by Glenn S. Daily, at www.glenndaily.com.

7. For example, see *Best's Review*, Life/Health edition, (published monthly).

8. See Slavutin, "Life Insurance Company Ratings – How Reliable is A.M. Best?" *Financial and Estate Planning*, Commerce Clearing House, Inc., August, 1991, p. 24,991.

9. See Slavutin, "Life Insurance Company Ratings – How Reliable is A.M. Best?" *Financial and Estate Planning*, Commerce Clearing House, Inc., August, 1991, p. 24,993.

10. See "Ratings of Life-Health Insurance Companies by A M. Best, Standard & Poor's, Moody's, and Duff & Phelps," 18 *The Insurance Forum* 199 (April 1991).

11. See Slavutin, "Life Insurance Company Ratings – How Reliable is A.M. Best?" *Financial and Estate Planning*, Commerce Clearing House, Inc., August, 1991, p. 24,995.

Chapter 4

HOW TO DETERMINE THE RIGHT POLICY

Attorneys, accountants, life insurance agents, and other financial services professionals are constantly required to provide an opinion as to the efficacy of a policy for the particular client and to assist in selecting between competing policies. This discussion will focus on the factors that must be considered by professionals in determining the right policy. Rule of thumb guidelines will be stated that should speed up the decision-making process and help the professional determine if the factors he or she is considering follow generally accepted life insurance planning principles. Once the proper amount of coverage or insurance need has been determined (see Chapter 2), professionals have a responsibility to perform analyses in the following four areas:

- Selecting the type of insurance product (or product mix) that is appropriate for the client;

- Deciphering life insurance policy illustrations;

- Reviewing policy comparison measurements; and

- Studying company comparison measurements.

Although the life insurance industry as a whole has an incredibly good record for safety, performance, and service, the past insolvencies of a few major life insurance companies make it more important than ever to select the insurance company carefully. Given such importance and timeliness, company comparison measurements are discussed in a separate chapter, Chapter 3.

HOW TO SELECT THE TYPE OF INSURANCE PRODUCT OR PRODUCT MIX APPROPRIATE FOR THE CLIENT

Above all, the planner must always "MATCH THE PRODUCT TO THE PROBLEM." The particular type of life insurance coverage appropriate for a given client is a function of four factors:

- The client's personal preferences, prejudices, and priorities;

- The amount of insurance needed;

- The client's ability and willingness to pay a given level of premiums (cash flow considerations); and

- Holding period probabilities (duration of need considerations).

Preferences, Prejudices, and Priorities

The selection of a particular type of life insurance policy or policy mix is to a great extent a very personal decision. Just as some individuals prefer, by psychological nature, to lease an automobile or rent an apartment, others prefer to make their purchases with a minimum down payment and stretch out the length of payments as long as possible, while others prefer to make a relatively large down payment and to pay off the loan or mortgage as quickly as possible. To many clients, there is emotional comfort in "owning," while others feel that owning ties them down and restricts their freedom of choice and flexibility. Similar comparisons can be made to life insurance policies. Some clients do not want to "pay, pay, pay … and have nothing to show for it at the end of the term," while others have been told all their lives to "buy term and invest the difference." In the real world, both positions are correct, and not correct. Even the advice of knowledgeable planners has been tainted by their own prejudices. For most clients, the right course of action usually lies where they are most comfortable – since peace of mind is really the impetus for the purchase of life insurance in the first place.

Another useful analogy is the purchase of technology tools by professionals. Some tend to purchase the highest quality, most expensive tools that they can afford to so that the tools will serve them well over a lifetime (or at least the reasonably expected lifetime of the tools). They do not tend to purchase lower priced, lower quality tools that will have to be replaced by other tools because they wear out, were inadequate to begin with, or break. But others cannot afford to (or will choose not to) purchase top quality tools. They may have other priorities. They may prefer to have the money to invest or to spend on current consumption. They may end up spending more over the length of their careers on tools and may be inconvenienced in the process of continually replacing the original tools.

Although this "preference/priority"-based decision making is not necessarily the most logical, it is a strong and important process that requires the planner to take into consideration the client's psychological makeup. The rules of thumb here are as follows:

1. Buy term if the client has a high risk-taking propensity.

2. Buy term if the client has a "lease rather than own" preference.

3. Buy some type of whole life insurance if the client has an "own rather than loan" type personality.

4. Buy some type of whole life insurance if the client wants something to show for his money at any given point. The more important it is for the client to have cash values and dividends at any given point, the more whole life type coverage is indicated.

5. Buy a mix of term and whole life if the client is –like most clients – not solidly on one end of the spectrum or the other.

Amount of Insurance Needed

When the amount of insurance needed is so great (as it often is for families with young children or for couples with high living standards relative to their incomes) that only term insurance or a term/whole life combination is feasible, the need for death protection should be given first priority. This results in simple rules of thumb:

1. Buy term insurance when there is no way to satisfy the death need without it. The term insurance can be converted to another form of protection at a later date, if and when appropriate.

2. Buy a combination of term and permanent insurance when the client can cover the entire death need and is able and willing to allocate additional dollars to appropriate permanent coverage.

Keep in mind, however, that buying term insurance means paying ever increasing premiums for a constant amount of coverage. People with little prospect of increasing their income sufficiently to pay ever-increasing term premiums face a difficult trade-off. They can buy term insurance for the amount of coverage they think they currently need, and face the prospect of being unable to afford that coverage in the future. Or they can purchase as much permanent insurance (e.g., level-premium whole life) as they can afford and be relatively assured that they can maintain the coverage for the long term, but have less coverage than they think they need.

Cash Flow Considerations

There are a large number of premium payment configurations that provide considerable flexibility for policyowners. Some clients will prefer to fully prepay for their coverage and take advantage of the tax-deferred internal buildup of investment return. This limits the total amount of premium that will be paid, even if the insured lives well beyond life expectancy. Other clients will be more comfortable with the payment of premiums at regular intervals for a fixed period or for the life of the insured (or for the working life of the insured). This "installment" purchase of life insurance benefits the policyowner who dies shortly after the policy is purchased, since a much lower total premium would be paid before death.

Conceptually, the insurance company itself is indifferent to the premium payment method selected; all of these patterns of payment, if applied to the same level of death benefit and continued for the same duration of time, will have the same actuarial value. So client abilities to pay and preferences are the major factors in the decision. The rules of thumb are as follows:

1. Prepay coverage (buy vanishing premium or limited payment whole life permanent insurance) if the client expects to live longer than average.

2. Pay on the installment basis (purchase term or low outlay whole life coverage) if the client thinks he or she faces a greater than average mortality risk.

3. Purchase YRT (yearly renewable term) if the client wants or needs to pay absolutely minimal initial premiums, but is willing to pay increasingly larger premiums each consecutive year to keep the same level of coverage in force.

Duration Of Need Considerations

In many cases, the planner's decision must be dictated at least in part by how long the need is expected to last. Some rules of thumb here are:

1. Buy term insurance if the need will probably last for 10 years or less.

2. Buy term and/or whole life if the need will probably last for ten to 15 years.

3. Buy some type of whole life coverage if the need will probably last for 15 years or longer.

4. Buy some type of whole life coverage if the policy will probably be continued up to or beyond the insured's age 55.

5. Buy some type of whole life coverage if the policy is purchased to solve a buy-sell need.

6. Buy some type of whole life coverage if the policy is designed to pay death taxes, or to transfer capital efficiently from one generation to another, or to replace capital given to charity or otherwise diverted from the client's intended beneficiaries.

HOW TO DECIPHER POLICY ILLUSTRATIONS OR LEDGER STATEMENTS

The policy illustration or ledger statement is the principal source of financial information regarding a new-issue policy. The separate chapters on the various types of policies provide ledger statement illustrations and describe in considerable detail what to look for in these statements. Here, we present a general overview. Understanding these ledger statements is important, because the information they provide serves as the basis for the various policy comparison measures that are discussed below.

The first step in understanding a policy illustration is to identify the columns that state the following:

- yearly premium payments;

- year-end policy cash values;

- projected policy dividends;

- cumulative cash value at given policy durations;

- the death benefit from the basic policy; and

- the death benefit provided by any dividends.

The critical questions are:

1. What does the client pay, year by year – compared to what he gets if he lives and what his family receives if he dies?

2. What portion of those amounts is guaranteed – and what portion of those amounts is projected?

3. What interest or other assumptions are built into these figures?

Financial services professionals should examine a policy illustration with particular emphasis on the following:

- surrender charges;

- cash value projections;

- policy loans; and

- dividends.

Surrender Charges

Determine what the company charges if the client surrenders the policy in a given year by looking at the cash value columns. Where there are two columns for cash values – one that reflects the net surrender value of the contract and the other the year-end cash value for the policy – the difference between these two amounts is the surrender charge for the given year.

Cash Value Projections

Ascertain the "premium level safety" by looking at the cash value projections on universal life and interest-sensitive life products. It is common under these two types of policies to show future cash values based on: (1) the guaranteed interest rate; and, also, (2) one or more higher interest rates related to either: (a) current portfolio earnings, or (b) whatever earnings level the agent has selected for the illustration.

Question the long term reasonableness of the assumptions. Are they unrealistic? Does the cash value associated with the guaranteed interest rate drop to zero after some years of duration? This indicates that the premium being charged for the contract will at that point become inadequate to support the coverage in force if the insurer is only able to credit cash values with the guaranteed interest rate. The client will be forced to pay higher premiums unless the contract earns interest higher than the guaranteed rate. If the illustration shows positive cash values at all policy durations, the premium will be adequate to carry the policy indefinitely.

Policy Loans

The notes to the ledger statement should explain what interest rate is being charged on the policy loans and if the rate is fixed or variable. If the rate is variable, is the rate being used for illustration reasonable over the period shown?

Check the illustration to see if loans are part of a systematic plan of borrowing to pay premiums. This is called a "minimum deposit" plan. Although no longer a popular approach to financing insurance premium payments, this is evidenced by a regular pattern of increasing outstanding loan balances where the increases are tied closely to the interest rate applicable to the previous outstanding balance and the premium payment due under the contract.

Dividends

Remember that dividends are not guaranteed. Many insurance companies have recently, and significantly, reduced dividends below their original projections. If the ledger statement shows policy loans, the notes to the ledger statement should explain whether dividends are reduced when loans are outstanding. Check to see whether the projected dividends reflect reductions attributable to any projected policy loans. Also, determine what interest rate the company assumes it must earn to pay the projected dividends. If the assumed interest rate seems too high or too optimistic over the long run, run another ledger with projected dividends based on a more supportable long-run interest assumption. Also, check the interest rate that the insurer will pay on any dividend left with it to earn interest. (The interest is currently taxable, even though the dividend itself will not be taxable to the policyowner.)

The ledger statement should reflect how the dividends will be used. For example, if the client desires additional insurance to build up at net (no commission or overhead) cost, dividends could be used to purchase "paid-up additional insurance" ("paid-up ads") or to purchase one-year term insurance (also a very cost-effective purchase). Alternatively, the dividends could be used to reduce premiums or as additional premiums ("vanishing premium" option) or to repay any projected policy loans. Obtain a ledger statement with dividends used in whatever manner is planned.

Here are some questions to ask:

1. Is the illustration from the home office or is it printed on the agent's (or some other source's) computer? Demand a ledger printout from the insurance company's home office to compare one policy with another.

2. Is the interest rate used reasonable over a long period of time?

3. Are dividends "puffed"? (Does a comparison of the company's past projected dividends with its past actual dividends – or with the records of other companies' products you are examining – suggest that the company has been overly optimistic?) This can have a significant impact upon when, or if, premiums will "vanish" or when they will unexpectedly reappear.

4. Are cash flow amounts in one illustration comparable with those in another? Cash flow amounts will be similar only if death benefit amounts and premium payments, as well as any projected policy loans or withdrawals, are for similar amounts for each policy duration. The more the values of these variables differ from one illustration to another, the less meaningful are differences in cash values, death benefits, or dividends levels.

5. In comparing universal life products, demand to know what variables are incorporated in the illustration and then insist that all competitive illustrations us the same (reasonable) assumptions.

HOW TO COMPARE POLICIES

At best, life insurance is a very complicated product that is extremely difficult to evaluate and compare. Life insurance policies are complex amalgams of varying legal, financial, and probabilistic elements that cannot really be reduced to an all encompassing unitary measure for comparison purposes. However, there are a number of commonly used measures or methods for policy comparison that can be of aid in evaluating purchase alternatives. Keep in mind that none of these methods does, or could, take into account all of the factors that should be considered when making the purchase decision. But, if several methods are used and the planner keeps in mind the strengths and weaknesses of each during the comparison process, they will be quite helpful in at least eliminating policies that should not be considered. The following are commonly used policy comparison techniques:

- the "traditional net cost" method;

- the "interest-adjusted net surrender cost" method;

- the "interest-adjusted net payment cost" method;

- the "equal outlay" method;

- the "cash accumulation" method;

- the "Linton yield" method;

- the "Belth yearly yield" method;

- the "Belth yearly price of protection" method; and

- the "Baldwin" method.

Traditional Net Cost Method

The traditional net cost method works like this:

1. Add up the premiums on the ledger sheet over a stated period of time such as 10, 15, or 20 years.

2. Add up the dividends projected on the ledger sheet over the same period of time.

3. Subtract the total dividends from the total premiums to find the total net premiums paid over the period being measured.

4. Add the cash value and any "terminal dividends" shown on the ledger statement as of the end of such period (and minus any surrender charge) to find the net cash value.

5. Subtract the net cash value from the total net premiums to arrive at the total net cost of the policy over the selected period.

6. Divide the total net cost by the face amount of the policy (in thousands) and again by the num-

ber of years in the selected period to arrive at the net cost of insurance per thousand dollars of coverage per year. [In Figure 4.1, numbers were calculated per $1,000 of coverage from the start.]

This is the easiest method to understand and use. But its simplicity is its weakness. This measure ignores the time value of money. This makes it possible to manipulate policy illustrations by shifting cash flows. Even without intentional manipulation, the traditional net cost method grossly understates the cost of insurance coverage and, in many cases, implies that the average annual cost of coverage is zero or negative. The result could be misleadingly low measures of policy costs. Few states sanction this method for comparing policy costs, although it can be used by the planner, together with the other methods described below, to make a quick and rough first-level relative comparison of policies.

Interest–Adjusted Cost Methods

The interest-adjusted methods of comparing the cost of life insurance policies consider the fact that money spent on premium dollars could have been invested elsewhere and earned a minimum after-tax return. (5% is usually assumed.) Since a policy may terminate, either when the policyowner surrenders the policy or when the insured dies, there are two different interest-adjusted indexes to measure the cost: (1) the net surrender cost index, and (2) the net payment cost index. The indexes do not necessarily define the true cost of policies, but they are useful in comparing the relative costs of similar policies. All other things being equal, a low index represents a better value than a high index. Note, however, that the interest-adjusted indexes are only indexes and nothing more. The true cost of a life insurance policy, if it can actually be measured prospectively, depends on when and how a policy is terminated.

Interest–Adjusted Net Surrender Cost Index

This index is a relative measure of the cost of a policy assuming the policy is surrendered. It works like this:

1. Accumulate each year's premium at some specified rate of interest. (Most policy illustrations use a 5% rate.) Do the calculation over a selected period of time such as 10, 15, or 20 years.

2. Accumulate each year's dividends projected on the ledger sheet at the same assumed rate of interest over the same period of time.

Figure 4.1

			Cash	Terminal	Surrender
Year	Premium	Dividends	Value	Dividends	Charges
1	$22.24	$0.00	$ 0.00	$0.00	$0.00
2	22.24	3.40	16.00	0.00	1.75
3	22.24	4.00	33.00	0.00	1.50
4	22.24	4.70	51.00	0.00	1.00
5	22.24	5.50	69.00	0.00	0.50
6	22.24	6.00	84.00	1.05	0.00
7	22.24	6.75	104.00	2.35	0.00
8	22.24	7.50	122.00	3.25	0.00
9	22.24	8.25	141.00	4.25	0.00
10	22.24	9.00	160.00	5.25	0.00
TOTALS	$222.40	$55.10	$160.00	$5.25	$0.00

TRADITIONAL NET COST METHOD
$25,000 POLICY FOR A MALE AGE 35
(per $1,000 of coverage)

(1)	Total premiums	$222.40
(2)	Minus total dividends	- 55.10
(3)	Equals total net premiums	$167.30
(4)	Cash value in year 10	$160.00
	Plus terminal dividend	+ 5.25
	Minus surrender charge	- 0.00
	Equals net cash value	$165.25
	Total net premiums	$167.30
	Minus net cash value	-165.25
(5)	Equals total net cost	$ 2.05
	Total net cost	$ 2.05
(6)	Divided by number of years	÷ 10
	Equals traditional net cost per $1,000 per year	**$0.205**

3. Subtract the total dividends (plus interest) from total premiums (plus interest) to find the future value of the total net premiums paid over the period being measured.

4. Add the cash value and any "terminal dividends" shown on the ledger statement as of the end of such period (and minus any surrender charge) to find the net cash value.

5. Subtract the net cash value from the future value of the net premiums to arrive at the future value of the total net cost of the policy over the selected period.

6. Divide the result by the future value of the annuity due factor for the rate assumed and the period selected. Assuming 5% interest, the factors for 5, 10, 15, 20, 25, and 30 years are 5.8019, 13.2068, 22.6575, 34.7193, 50.1135, and 69.7608, respectively. The result is the level annual cost for the policy.

7. Divide the level annual cost for the policy by the number of thousands in the face amount of coverage. The result is the interest-adjusted net annual cost per thousand dollars of coverage using the surrender cost index. [In Figure 4.2, numbers were calculated per $1,000 of coverage from the start.]

Figure 4.2

INTEREST-ADJUSTED COST METHOD $25,000 POLICY FOR A MALE AGE 35 (per $1,000 of coverage)						
Premiums			Dividends			
Year	Per Year	Accum. at 5.00%	Per Year	Accum. at 5.00%	Cash Value	Terminal Dividends
1	$22.24	$23.35	$0.00	$0.00	$0.00	$0.00
2	22.24	47.87	3.40	3.57	16.00	0.00
3	22.24	73.62	4.00	7.95	33.00	0.00
4	22.24	100.65	4.70	13.28	51.00	0.00
5	22.24	129.03	5.50	19.72	69.00	0.00
6	22.24	158.84	6.00	27.01	184.00	1.05
7	22.24	190.13	6.75	35.44	104.00	2.35
8	22.24	222.99	7.50	45.09	122.00	3.25
9	22.24	257.49	8.25	56.01	141.00	4.25
10	22.24	293.72	9.00	68.26	160.00	5.25
TOTALS	$222.40	$293.72	$55.10	$68.26	$160.00	$5.25

Surrender Cost Index

(1)	Premiums compounded at 5.00%	$293.72
(2)	Minus dividends compounded at 5.00%	- 68.26
(3)	Equals future value of net premiums	$225.46
(4)	Cash value	$160.00
	Plus terminal dividends	+ 5.25
	Minus surrender charge	- 0.00
	Equals net cash value	$165.25
	Future value of net premiums	$225.46
	Minus net cash value	165.25
(5)	Equals future value of net cost	$ 60.21
	Future value of net cost	$ 60.21
(6)	Divided by annuity due factor	÷13.2068
	Equals surrender cost index **(per $1,000 of coverage)**	**$ 4.56**

Payment Cost Index

(1)	Premiums compounded at 5.00%	$293.72
(2)	Minus dividend's compounded at 5.00%	- 68.26
(3)	Future Value of net premiums	$225.46
	Future Value of net premiums	$225.46
	Divided by annuity due factor	÷13.2068
	Equals payment cost index **(per $1,000 of coverage)**	**$ 17.07**

Interest–Adjusted Net Payment Cost Index

This index is a relative measure of the cost of a policy assuming the insured dies. It works like this:

1. Accumulate each year's premium at some specified rate of interest. (Most policy illustrations use a 5% rate.) Do the calculation over a selected period of time such as 10, 15, or 20 years.

2. Accumulate each year's dividends projected on the ledger sheet at the same assumed rate of interest over the same period of time.

3. Subtract the total dividends (plus interest) from the total premiums (plus interest) to find the future value of the total net premiums paid over the period you are measuring.

4. Divide the result by the future value of the annuity due factor for the rate assumed and the period selected. Assuming 5% interest, the factors for 5, 10, 15, 20, 25, and 30 years are 5.8019, 13.2068, 22.6575, 34.7193, 50.1135, and 69.7608, respectively. The result is the level annual cost for the policy.

5. Divide the level annual cost for the policy by the number of thousands in the face amount of coverage. The result is the interest-adjusted net annual cost per thousand dollars of coverage using the payment cost index. [In Figure 4.2, numbers were calculated per $1,000 of coverage from the start.]

Planners usually will not have to do these computations since most ledger sheets will contain these indexes at the bottom of the front page of the ledger statement. However, the ledger statement usually shows the indexes only for 10 and 20 years, and sometimes for the insured's age 65.

Most states require that prospective policyowners be provided with a policy's interest-adjusted indexes. Planners should therefore understand how this measure works, understand its limitations, and be able to explain it to sophisticated clients. Among the weaknesses of the interest-adjusted methods are these:

1. If the policies being compared are not quite similar, the index results may be misleading. For instance, if the outlays differ significantly, a hypothetical side fund should be established to accumulate the differences in the annual outlays at the assumed rate of interest to properly adjust for the differences. This will be the case where an existing policy is compared with a potential replacement. There will almost always be a material difference in the projected cash flows. This makes the interest-adjusted methods unsuitable (unless adjusted) for "replacement" comparisons.

2. The interest-adjusted methods are subject to manipulation (although to a lesser extent than the traditional net cost method) and in the commonly used measuring periods, such as 10 or 20 years, can be made to provide more favorable estimates of cost than for other selected periods.

3. The interest-adjusted methods are valid only to the extent that the projections of cash flows materialize as assumed. Therefore, the calculations cannot consider the impact of an overly optimistic dividend scale.

4. It is possible in the comparison between two policies for each policy to be superior when ranked on one of the two indexes and inferior when ranked on the other index. However, relative rankings on each index tend to be highly

correlated. That is, a policy that is ranked higher than others using one index tends to also rank similarly using the other index.

The Equal Outlay Method

The equal outlay method works like this: The client is assumed to outlay (pay out) the same premium for each of the policies to be compared. Likewise, the client is assumed to purchase, in each policy under comparison, essentially equal amounts of death benefits year by year.

The equal outlay method is easiest to employ when comparing flexible premium type policies such as universal life since it is easy for the illustration to be generated with equal annual contributions.

Planners should demand that:

*   Cash values are projected using the guaranteed rates for the policy;

*   Separate illustrations are run showing a selected intermediate interest rate assumption; and

*   Separate illustrations are run showing the current interest rate the company credits to policies.

An inspection of the projected cash values in future years should make it possible to identify the policy with the highest cash values and, therefore, to determine which is the best purchase. The procedure will be more complicated where the equal outlay method is used to compare a fixed premium contract with one or more flexible premium polices. Here, the net premium level (adjusted for any dividends) and the death benefit of the flexible premium policies must be made to match the corresponding values for the fixed premium contract for all years over the period of comparison. This makes it possible to compare future cash values in the same manner as when comparing two flexible premium policies.

As shown in Figure 4.3, the equal outlay method can also be used to compare two or more fixed-premium policies, or to compare a term policy to a whole life policy, in the following manner: Hypothetically, "invest" the differences in net annual outlay in a side fund at some reasonable after-tax rate of return that essentially keeps the two alternatives equal in annual outlay. Compare: (1) cash values including side fund amounts, and (2) total death benefits including side fund amounts.

Figure 4.3

				Diff.	OL	YRT	OL with
	OL	YRT	Diff. in	Accum.	Surrend.	Plus Side	Paid-up
Year	Prem.	Prem.	Prem.	at 6%	Values	Fund	Ads
1	$1,445	$145	$1,300	$1,378	$0	$101,378	$100,010
2	1,445	148	1,297	2,836	175	102,836	100,111
3	1,445	154	1,291	4,375	1,670	104,375	100,309
4	1,445	162	1,283	5,997	3,324	105,997	100,848
5	1,445	172	1,273	7,706	5,167	107,706	101,817
6	1,445	185	1,260	9,504	7,189	109,504	103,231
7	1,445	200	1,245	11,394	9,435	111,394	105,105
8	1,445	219	1,226	13,377	11,986	113,377	107,458
9	1,445	242	1,203	15,455	14,768	115,455	110,316
10	1,445	268	1,177	17,630	17,898	117,630	113,678
11	1,445	299	1,146	19,903	21,243	119,903	117,611
12	1,445	333	1,112	22,276	25,007	122,276	122,056
13	1,445	373	1,072	24,749	29,147	124,749	127,057
14	1,445	417	1,028	27,324	33,634	127,324	132,669
15	1,445	466	979	30,001	38,579	130,001	138,903
16	1,445	521	924	32,780	44,126	132,780	145,821
17	1,445	581	864	35,663	50,167	135,663	153,454
18	1,445	646	799	38,650	56,913	138,650	161,813
19	1,445	716	729	41,741	64,238	141,741	171,062
20	1,445	791	654	44,939	72,295	144,939	181,159

EQUAL OUTLAY METHOD
Ordinary Life (OL) versus Yearly Renewable Term (YRT)
$100,000 face value for age 35 male nonsmoker

* This table assumes that dividends are used to purchase paid-up additions.

In this case, the yearly renewable term option is superior if the policy is surrendered before about year 10, or if the policy is maintained and death occurs before about year 13. By the end of the tenth year, the surrender cash value of the whole life policy exceeds the side fund accumulated with the yearly renewable term option. However, the whole life policy's death benefit, assuming dividends are used to buy paid-up additions, does not exceed the total death benefit (term insurance plus side fund) of the YRT option until after year 12. This example demonstrates that term policies will often be a better choice when insurance needs are short term. But term policies are generally increasingly less attractive the longer the duration of the insurance need.

Note, quite often the result of this computation will show that term insurance (or a lower-outlay whole life policy) with a side fund will outperform a permanent type whole life plan during a period of perhaps the first seven to ten years but then lose that edge when the projection is carried to a longer duration.

There are a number of disadvantages to the equal outlay method:

1. When comparing a fixed to a flexible premium contract, the underlying assumptions of the contracts are not the same and, therefore, the analysis cannot fairly compare them. For instance,

many universal life cash value projections are based on "new money assumptions," while ordinary life policy dividends are usually based on the "current portfolio rate" of the insurer (a rate that often varies significantly from the new money rate). Since the portfolio of the insurance company includes investments made in prior years that will not mature for several years, the portfolio rate tends to lag behind new money rates. If new money rates are relatively high, the portfolio rate will generally be less than new money rates. However if new money rates are trending down, portfolio rates will generally be higher than new money rates.

This difference in the rate used to make illustrations can be misleading. For example, if new money rates are greater than the portfolio rate and the trend of high new money rates continues for some time, cash values in universal life contracts are more likely to materialize as projected. But if these economic conditions hold true, then it is likely that the portfolio rate will also rise. This means dividends paid would increase relative to those projected based on the current portfolio rate. The equal outlay method does not take into consideration either the fluctuations in rates or the differences in how they are computed.

2. The required adjustments in most comparisons can quickly become burdensome. In many cases, it is quite difficult to equate death benefits under the comparison policies while maintaining equal outlays.

3. When comparing an existing policy with a potential replacement policy, the analysis must consider any cash value in the existing policy at the time of the comparison. Generally, it is easiest to assume that the cash value will be paid into the new policy. Otherwise, the analysis should probably account for the time value of that cash value and should, as closely as possible, equate total death benefits including any side fund.

4. The results, even after many adjustments have been made, may be ambiguous. Quite often the results can be interpreted as favoring one policy for certain durations, favoring another policy for certain durations, and favoring even another policy for other durations.

Cash Accumulation Method

The cash accumulation method works like this:

1. Equate outlays (much in the same manner as the equal outlay method) for the policies being compared.

2. Change the face amount of the lower premium policy so that the sum of the side fund plus the face amount equals the face amount of the higher premium policy. Note that this would yield the same result as where it is possible to set both death benefits and premium payments exactly equal – in flexible premium policies.

3. Accumulate any differences in premiums at an assumed rate of interest.

4. Compare the cash value/side fund differences over given periods of time to see which policy is preferable to the other.

The cash accumulation method is ideal for comparing term with permanent insurance. But the analysis must be done with caution; the use of the appropriate interest rate is critical since, as is the case with any time-value measurement, a higher assumed interest rate will generally favor a lower premium policy/side fund combination relative to a higher premium policy.

We suggest a two part approach: If the comparison is performed without regard to a specific client and merely to determine the relative ranking of the polices, the planner should assume a relatively conservative risk-free after-tax rate comparable to the rate that one would expect to earn on the cash values of the higher premium policy. This will more closely equate the combination of the lower premium/side fund with the risk-return characteristics of the higher premium policy. Alternatively, if the comparison is being conducted for a specific client, the planner should use that individual's long-run after-tax opportunity cost rate of return, which may be considerable higher than the rate of return anticipated on the cash value of the higher premium policy.

A full and fair comparison is made more difficult because of the impact of death taxes, probate costs, and creditor laws. This is because the cash accumulation method uses a hypothetical side fund to make the comparison. But money in a side fund–if it in fact were accumulated–would not be eligible for the exemptions or special rate reductions afforded to the death proceeds of life insurance. Therefore, each dollar from that side fund would be subjected to a level of transfer tax that life insurance dollars would not. Likewise, the side fund would be subjected to the normal probate fees and attorney's costs to which cash or other property is subject. Furthermore, this method does not consider the value of state law creditor protection afforded to the death benefits in a life insurance policy, but not to amounts held in most other types of investments.

The bottom line is that the side fund money may appear to have more value than it actually would have in the hands of those for whom it was intended. It is therefore apparent that, while the cash accumulation method has strengths that overcome many of the weaknesses of other comparison methods, it also has weaknesses that prevent it from being the single best answer to the financial planner's policy comparison problem.

Figure 4.4

			CASH ACCUMULATION METHOD Ordinary Life (OL) versus Yearly Renewable Term (YRT) $100,000 face value for age 35 male nonsmoker					

Year	OL Prem.	YRT Prem.	Diff. in Prem.	Side Fund at 6.00%	OL Surrend. Value	YRT Face Amount	YRT Plus Side Fund	OL with Paid-up Ads
1	$1,445	$143	$1,302	$1,380	$0	$98,630	$100,010	$100,010
2	1,445	144	1,301	2,842	175	97,269	100,111	100,111
3	1,445	148	1,297	4,388	1,670	95,921	100,309	100,309
4	1,445	154	1,291	6,020	3,324	94,828	100,848	100,848
5	1,445	162	1,283	7,741	5,167	94,076	101,817	101,817
6	1,445	173	1,272	9,554	7,189	93,677	103,231	103,231
7	1,445	187	1,258	11,460	9,435	93,645	105,105	105,105
8	1,445	206	1,239	13,461	11,986	93,997	107,458	107,458
9	1,445	229	1,216	15,557	14,768	94,759	110,316	110,316
10	1,445	257	1,188	17,750	17,898	95,928	113,678	113,678
11	1,445	292	1,153	20,037	21,243	97,574	117,611	117,611
12	1,445	332	1,113	22,420	25,007	99,636	122,056	122,056
13	1,445	381	1,064	24,893	29,147	102,164	127,057	127,057
14	1,445	439	1,006	27,453	33,634	105,216	132,669	132,669
15	1,445	507	938	30,094	38,579	108,809	138,903	138,903
16	1,445	589	856	32,807	44,126	113,014	145,821	145,821
17	1,445	685	760	35,582	50,167	117,872	153,454	153,454
18	1,445	797	648	38,403	56,913	123,410	161,813	161,813
19	1,445	929	516	41,254	64,238	129,808	171,062	171,062
20	1,445	1,084	361	44,112	72,295	137,047	181,159	181,159

* This table assumes that dividends are used to purchase paid-up additions.

The whole life policy and the term rates used in this example are the same as those used in the equal outlay example (see Figure 4.3). The cash accumulation example differs from the equal outlay example chiefly in that it keeps the total death benefits equal each year under each option by adjusting the face amount of the term coverage. This method unambiguously identifies the whole life policy as the superior strategy for years 10 and beyond.

Linton Yield Method

The Linton yield method works like this: The planner computes the rate of return that the policyowner must earn on a hypothetical (or real) side fund assuming death benefits and outlays are held equal for every year over the period being studied. The policy that should be selected according to this method is the one that has the highest Linton yield, that is, the policy that–given an assumed schedule of costs (term rates)–has the highest rate of return.

In essence, this method is just the reverse of the interest-adjusted surrender cost method, which holds the assumed interest rate level and solves for cost; the Linton method holds cost level and solves for interest. It should therefore be an excellent way to check the inter-

est-adjusted method results since the two methods should rank policies virtually identically.

As demonstrated in Figure 4.5, planners can compare dissimilar policies through the Linton yield method. Note, however, that the same term rates must be used for each policy that is being evaluated or the results will be misleading. The higher the term rate that is used, the higher the Linton yield that will be produced–and, of course, the reverse is also true. This emphasizes the importance of using this method only for a relative comparison of policies and not to measure the "true rate of return" actually credited to the cash value of a give policy.

Computationally, the Linton yield method is a variation on the cash accumulation method. Using the cash

Figure 4.5

20-YEAR LINTON YIELD								
Ordinary Life (OL) versus Yearly Renewable Term (YRT)								
$100,000 face value for age 35 male nonsmoker								
Year	**OL Prem.**	**YRT Prem.**	**Diff. in Prem.**	**Side Fund at 9.696%**	**OL Surrend. Value**	**YRT Face Amount**	**YRT Plus Side Fund**	**OL with Paid-up Ads**
1	$1,445	$143	$1,302	$1,428	$3	$98,582	$100,010	$100,010
2	1,445	144	1,301	2,994	175	97,117	100,111	100,111
3	1,445	147	1,298	4,708	1,670	95,601	100,309	100,309
4	1,445	153	1,292	6,582	3,324	94,266	100,848	100,848
5	1,445	160	1,285	8,630	5,167	93,187	101,817	101,817
6	1,445	171	1,274	10,864	7,189	92,367	103,231	103,231
7	1,445	184	1,261	13,301	9,435	91,804	105,105	105,105
8	1,445	200	1,245	15,956	11,986	91,502	107,458	107,458
9	1,445	221	1,224	18,846	14,768	91,470	110,316	110,316
10	1,445	246	1,199	21,988	17,898	91,690	113,678	113,678
11	1,445	276	1,169	25,403	21,243	92,208	117,611	117,611
12	1,445	310	1,135	29,112	25,007	92,944	122,056	122,056
13	1,445	350	1,095	33,135	29,147	93,922	127,057	127,057
14	1,445	397	1,048	37,498	33,634	95,171	132,669	132,669
15	1,445	451	994	42,225	38,579	96,678	138,903	138,903
16	1,445	513	932	47,341	44,126	98,480	145,821	145,821
17	1,445	584	861	52,875	50,167	100,579	153,454	153,454
18	1,445	665	780	58,857	56,913	102,956	161,813	161,813
19	1,445	757	688	65,319	64,238	105,743	171,062	171,062
20	1,445	861	584	72,293	72,295	108,866	181,159	181,159

* This table asumes that dividends are used to purchase paid-up additions.

The difference between the OL premiums and the YRT premiums is invested at 9.696% in the side fund. The side fund virtually equals the cash value in year 20.

accumulation methodology described above, the Linton yield is the rate of return that equates the side fund with the cash surrender value for a specified period of years. For example, in the cash accumulation method example above, see Figure 4.4, the side fund was just about equal to the cash surrender value in year 10 when the side fund was invested at 6%. Therefore, the Linton yield for the whole life policy (assuming the YRT rates are competitive) is about 6% for 10 years. The example in Figure 4.5 shows that the 20-year Linton yield for this policy is 9.696%.

Belth Method

Joseph M. Belth, Ph.D., professor of insurance at Indiana University, has been a leading researcher, constructive critic, and writer on life insurance policy comparison methods and other life insurance issues. He has devised two comparison methods that give comparable ranking results: (1) the yearly rate of return method, and (2) the yearly price of protection method. The reason he developed two methods follows from what has already been said (implicitly, if not explicitly) about comparison methods: If you prefer to compare policies based on a measure of the price of protection, you must specify or assume the cost of protection. In contrast with the methods discussed earlier, which essentially reduce comparisons to relative measure of one rate of one cost index for each policy being compared for a specified term, the Belth methods compute the rates of return or the prices of protection for all years, or any subset of years, the policies may be in force. One of the more attractive features of Belth's methods is that they are easier to use (with caveats) than the other methods when trying to decide whether to replace an existing policy with a new policy.

Belth Yearly Rate of Return Method

The Belth yearly rate of return method works like this:

1. Compute "benefits" from the policy for the year. The benefits are the sum of:

   a) the cash value at the end of the year;

   b) the dividends paid during the year; and

   c) the net death benefit for the policy year.

2. Compute the "investment" in the policy for the year. The investment is defined as the sum of:

   a) the premium paid for the year; plus

   b) the cash value at the beginning of the year.

3. Divide the benefits for the year by the investment for the year and subtract one from the result. Stated as a formula, the computation is:

$$\text{Yearly Rate of Return} = \frac{\text{Benefits}}{\text{Investment}} - 1$$

4. Repeat the calculations for each year over the desired duration or planning period.

This yearly rate of return method is especially useful in comparing policies over many different durations. The policy with the highest yearly rates in the greatest number of years is generally the best choice.

As is the case with the comparison methods described above, this system has its weaknesses and potential flaws:

1. The calculated yearly rates of return may be misleading where cash values are small.

2. The results can be manipulated or unintentionally affected by the term rate assumed. The planner must specify an assumed yearly cost for insurance in order to calculate the benefits for the policy year. In other words, one year term rates must be used. But if the term rates used are neither competitive nor realistic, the results would not accurately portray how well a "buy term and invest the difference" plan performs in comparison to a "buy whole life and build the cash values" plan.

3. Typically, no one policy will be better than another year after year. This means the "best policy" may not be easy to select. One policy may provide the higher yearly rates of return in early years, but not in later years.

Belth Yearly Price of Protection Method

The Belth yearly price of protection method works like this:

1. Accumulate the "investment" in the policy for one year at an assumed rate of interest. The investment is the sum of:

   a) the cash surrender value at the end of the previous year; plus

   b) the current premium.

2. Compute the year end policy surrender value. The year end policy surrender value is the sum of:

   a) the year end cash surrender value; plus

   b) any dividend.

3. Subtract the year end policy surrender value from the year's accumulated investment.

4. Divide the result of (3) by the year's net amount at risk (face amount minus current year's cash surrender value) in thousands to derive the cost of protection (per thousand dollars of coverage) for the year. Stated as a formula, the computation is:

$$\text{Cost per } \$1000 = \frac{(P + CVP) \times (1 + i) - (CSV + D)}{(F - CSV) \times (0.001)}$$

where
P = **P**remium
CVP = **C**ash surrender **V**alue **P**revious year
i = net aftertax **i**nterest rate
CSV = **C**ash **S**urrender **V**alue current year
D = **D**ividend current year
F = **F**ace amount of coverage

The result is an estimate of the cost in any given year of the net death benefit (death benefit minus cash value). The policy with the lowest yearly price of protection in the most years is generally the contract that should be selected under this method.

Figure 4.6

	BELTH YEARLY RATE OF RETURN (YROR) AND YEARLY PRICE OF PROTECTION METHODS (YPOP) Ordinary Life (OL) policy of $100,000 face value for age 35 male nonsmoker, assuming certain Yearly Renewable Term (YRT) rates per $1,000 of coverage							
Year	OL Prem.	Dividends	OL Cash Value	YRT Rate Per $1000	Yearly Benefits	Yearly Invest.	YROR	YPOP at 9.00%
1	$1,445	$3	$0	$1.45	$148	$1,445	-89.779%	$15.72
2	1,445	26	122	1.48	296	1,445	-79.494%	14.28
3	1,445	53	1,352	1.54	1,557	1,567	-0.640%	3.07
4	1,445	149	2,618	1.62	2,925	2,797	4.569%	2.89
5	1,445	278	3,919	1.72	4,363	4,063	7.377%	2.41
6	1,445	418	5,252	1.85	5,845	5,364	8.961%	1.87
7	1,445	572	6,619	2.00	7,378	6,697	10.168%	1.16
8	1,445	742	8,020	2.19	8,963	8,064	11.146%	0.31
9	1,445	928	9,455	2.42	10,602	9,465	12.011%	(0.73)
10	1,445	1,133	10,923	2.68	12,294	10,900	12.797%	(1.97)
11	1,445	1,355	12,423	2.99	14,039	12,368	13.516%	(3.39)
12	1,445	1,584	13,960	3.33	15,830	13,868	14.150%	(4.97)
13	1,445	1,837	15,527	3.73	17,679	15,405	14.764%	(6.78)
14	1,445	2,116	17,127	4.17	19,588	16,972	15.415%	(8.97)
15	1,445	2,424	18,757	4.66	21,559	18,572	16.087%	(11.54)
16	1,445	2,766	20,418	5.21	23,598	20,202	16.811%	(14.62)
17	1,445	3,140	22,105	5.81	25,698	21,863	17.541%	(18.16)
18	1,445	3,552	23,823	6.46	27,867	23,550	18.332%	(22.39)
19	1,445	4,011	25,570	7.16	30,114	25,268	19.178%	(27.39)
20	1,445	4,514	27,345	7.91	32,434	27,015	20.059%	(33.21)

* Dividends are not used to buy paid-up additions.

Yearly benefit = cash value + dividend + net death protection benefit
Net death protection benefit = YRT rate x ($100,000 - cash value) x .001
Yearly investment = premium + prior year's cash value
YROR = (yearly benefit ÷ yearly investment) - 1
YPOP = [(premium + cash value prior year) x (1 + interest rate) - (cash value + dividend)]
        ÷ ($100,000 - cash value) x .001

As a complement to the yearly price of protection method, Belth has developed: (1) benchmark costs per thousand dollars of term insurance for various age ranges, see table below; and (2) rules of thumb for using this method in replacement situations. He describes the benchmark rates (see below) as follows:

The benchmarks were derived from certain United States population death rates. The benchmark figure for each 5-year age bracket is slightly above the death rate per $1,000 at the highest age in the bracket. What we are saying is that, if the price of your life insurance protection per $1,000 is in the vicinity of the 'raw material cost'

(that is the amount needed just to pay death claims based on population death rates), your life insurance protection is reasonably priced.[1]

Belth suggests the following rules of thumb for applying the benchmarks in replacement situations:

1. If the policy price per thousand is less than the benchmark for the insured's age, replacement would probably be inadvisable.

2. If the price per thousand is between one and two times the benchmark, probably no change is indicated.

3. If the price is greater than two times the bench-mark, consider replacing the policy.

JOSEPH BELTH'S BENCHMARK PRICE OF INSURANCE

Age	Price
Under Age 30	$ 1.50
30-34	2.00
35-39	3.00
40-44	4.00
45-49	6.50
50-54	10.00
55-59	15.00
60-64	25.00
65-69	35.00
70-74	50.00
75-79	80.00
80-84	125.00

The flaws and potential weaknesses of this method are:

1. The yearly prices of protection may have no relation to the actual mortality costs charged against the policy in any given year. To compare the calculated yearly "prices" (which have been critically affected by the rate of return assumed by the planner) with term insurance rates may be misleading. But, if the same assumed rate of interest is used when computing the yearly prices for all policies under consideration, the yearly rates for each policy should provide a good indication of where various polices stand in relation to others. Planners should use an assumed rate as close as possible to the rate actually used by the insurance company in its cash value and dividend illustrations. This will enable a fair comparison of the yearly prices of protection from the policy to yearly renewable term insurance.

2. Where the net amount at risk for the year is relatively small, the yearly prices of protection will tend to fluctuate widely and have little meaning.

3. As is the case with previous methods, in some years one policy may look better, while in other years another policy will appear more favorable. This method may not always lead to an unambiguous choice.

4. Like other methods, this method does not take policy loans into consideration. Since policy loans do affect the amount of investment in the

contract, the rate of return and the price of protection may be miscalculated if loans are ignored. Also, policy loans will generally affect (usually reduce) dividend payments.

Baldwin Method[2]

The Baldwin method is a somewhat more complete variation of the Belth yearly rate of return method that seeks to cure some of the inadequacies of the previously discussed comparison methods. Perhaps its most notable feature is that it combines both rate of return with the value of the insurance actually received into one measure. It also adjusts for policy loans and for the opportunity cost of funds and incorporates tax considerations. Despite this relative comprehensiveness, it is basically a simple to use system. It works like this:

1. Determine how much life insurance is provided by the policy in any given year. This is computed by subtracting the total current asset value (what you would get if you cashed the policy in today) from the total death benefit to determine the "net amount at risk."

2. Determine what has been paid to maintain the life insurance in force for the year. This is computed by adding the premium, the net after-tax loan interest cost (if any), and the net after-tax (opportunity) cost of cash left in the policy. The opportunity cost of the cash left in the policy is the cost of not borrowing from the policy if you could have invested policy loans at a greater after-tax return than the after-tax cost of borrowing from the policy.

3. Determine the cash benefits received as a result of maintaining the policy in force for the year. This is computed by adding the current year's divided, if any, to the current year's increase in cash value, account value, or asset value.

4. Determine the investment in the contract. This is computed by subtracting any loans outstanding (plus any unpaid interest) from the total asset or cash value.

5. Determine the dollar amount of return (net gain or loss) earned in the current policy year. To derive this amount, subtract the costs derived in (2) from the benefits derived in (3).

6. Determine the cash-on-cash return for the year. This is computed by dividing the net gain or loss (from (5) by the amount invested (from (4)).

7. Determine the equivalent taxable return. To derive the before-tax rate of return that is necessary to provide an after-tax return that is equal to the currently tax-free return in the policy, divide the rate of return in (6) by (one minus the combined tax rate). For example, if the combined local, state, and federal tax rate is 40% and the rate of return in the policy is 5.4, you would need to earn 9% in taxable investments to have 5.4% left after tax [5.4% ÷ (1 – 40%) = 9%].

8. Determine the value of the life insurance protection received for the year. This is the truly new element added by Baldwin's method. It recognizes that the value of life insurance protection can vary from person to person and is at least partly subjective. Some people have no need for insurance protection and place no value on the life insurance protection provided by the policy. For these people, the equivalent taxable rate of return in the policy (see (7)) is the total measure of the value of the policy. However, most people will place at least some value on the insurance protection. In general, if protection is desired, its value should be equal to at least the absolute minimum term insurance cost for an equivalent amount of protection available to the insured. That is, the most accurate cost per thousand dollars of coverage would be the figure you could obtain as a result of applying to an insurance company for an equivalent amount of term insurance, submitting to medical examination, and receiving an offer for term insurance at a contractually guaranteed rate. Once the equivalent retail value of term insurance is determined, it is multiplied by the amount of life insurance (in thousands) provided by the contract (from (1)) to determine the value of the insurance in the contract.

9. Determine the total value received (total benefits) as a result of continuing the life insurance contract. The total value is equal to the year's net gain or loss (from (5)) plus the life insurance value (from (8)).

10. Determine the percentage return on the total benefits. This is computed by dividing the total benefits (from (9)) by the amount invested (from (4)).

11. Determine the equivalent after-tax return that matches the tax-deferred/tax-free return from the life insurance contract. Divide the percentage rate of return (from (10)) by (one minus the combined tax rate).

The Baldwin method overcomes some of the problems associated with the other comparison methods, but still depends on the values shown on the ledger statement, which must be closely scrutinized for accuracy and the reasonableness of the underlying assumptions. Also, like the Belth methods, it provides a series of annual rate of return figures for as many policy years as you wish to measure. It is quite possible for each of two policies to show superior performance for some years and inferior performance for others relative to each other. Therefore, rankings of policies may be ambiguous.

Policy Comparison Measures Summary

The Summary of Policy Comparison Measures in Figure 4.7 should prove helpful in reviewing these methods and in deciding which should be used or how to properly overcome their flaws. Other considerations in using these techniques are listed below.

1. Remember that a policy comparison based on policy illustrations created by a source other than an insurance company's home office may not be officially sanctioned, accurate, or complete. Demand computer printouts from the insurer's home office for comparative purchasing purposes.

2. Policy dividends are not guarantees – a point the consumer often does not hear or understand (or sometimes does not want to hear or understand). The financial advisor should not only emphasize this in comparing policies but also in making presentations to clients.

3. The longer the period into the future that values are projected or illustrated, the less likely they are to be accurate.

4. The method used to decide rates credited to cash values and to allocate the amount of dividends to policyowners and then apportion them among policyowners will significantly affect policy comparisons. Check to see if the company is using the "portfolio" method or the "investment year" method (sometimes called the "new money" method). Most companies now use the investment year method. Under the investment year method, the assets acquired with the premiums paid during a particular

year are treated as a separate cell of the insurance company's general asset account. The investment returns earned by the assets in each calendar-year cell are credited to the cell. Each year as the composition of the cell changes due to maturities, repayments, sales, and other transactions, the changing investment performance of the cell is allocated to the policies that paid the premiums to acquire the assets in the cell. This method promotes equity, since policyholders receive the investment results that are directly attributable to their premium contributions. If the portfolio method is used, all policies are credited with the rate earned on the company's overall portfolio, despite the fact that earnings on premium dollars received in some years may actually be earning higher or lower returns than the portfolio rate. For instance, in periods of declining interest rates, the premium dollars received on new policies will probably be invested by the company at rates that are lower than the company earns on its existing portfolio. If the portfolio method is used, these new policyholders will benefit at the expense of the prior policyholders, because they will be credited with higher returns than their premium dollars are actually earning. Conversely, if interest rates are increasing, use of the portfolio method will be disadvantageous for new policyholders, but beneficial to existing policyholders. Make sure all the illustrations are based on the same method, if possible.

5. Supplementary benefits and riders impact upon policy comparisons. For example, the total premium for a policy with waiver of premium should be adjusted to take into account the extra charge.

6. In deciding whether to purchase whole life insurance or to "buy term and invest the difference," be sure to consider the value of: (a) protection from creditors, (b) probate savings, (c) federal gift/estate tax savings implications, (d) state gift/death tax savings implications, (e) dividend options (such as one year term), (f) loan/collateral uses, and (g) settlement (annuity) options.

POLICY REPLACEMENT

The previous discussions of the various policy comparison methods and the summary table of the common policy comparison methods suggest which of these methods is potentially suitable for evaluating replacement policies. As those discussions indicate, some of the comparison methods are not suitable for comparisons between existing and new policies, and planners may need to adjust or modify a method when applying it in certain circumstances. Even those methods planners can use to compare existing to new policies may give ambiguous results. In addition, there are other broader implications and considerations that insureds and planners should address when evaluating whether to replace an existing policy with a new policy.

When evaluating whether to replace an existing policy, insureds and planners should return to the original admonition: "MATCH THE PRODUCT TO THE PROBLEM." Often when an insured's objectives change and an existing policy is not entirely suitable for the revised objectives, it may be best to keep the existing policy in place and to purchase additional coverage with the flexibility and features one needs. Sometimes it may be wise to keep an existing policy in place and to use borrowing from the cash value to pay premiums on new supplemental coverage, rather than to exchange the old policy for a new policy.

In almost all replacement cases where the old policy is just not suitable and must be replaced (or where replacement is being considered because of the financial weakness of the company that issued the old policy), the insured should consider using the provisions of IRC Section 1035 to assure that the exchange is treated as a nontaxable event. If the insured surrenders the old policy and uses the cash surrender value to help finance the new policy, two adverse tax consequences could ensue. First, to the extent of gain in the policy (that the cash value exceeds the net premiums paid), the surrender value will be subject to income tax at the policy owner's ordinary tax rate. Second, if a large after-tax surrender value is placed in the new policy, the new policy could be treated as a modified endowment contract (MEC) with very adverse tax consequences with respect to any lifetime withdrawals or loans.[3] Even if the policy is not treated as a MEC, the insured may be subject to the 15-year rule with respect to withdrawals, where amounts withdrawn within the first 15 years may be taxed on the interest-first rule rather than the cost-first rule.[4]

Finally, whenever an old policy is exchanged for a new policy, the insured surrenders certain rights. For example, the new policy generally is issued with a new suicide period and a new incontestable period, even if

Figure 4.7

SUMMARY OF KEY POINTS OF COMMON POLICY COMPARISON METHODS

	Traditional Net Cost	Interest Adjusted Net Cost	Interest Adjusted Payments Index	Equal Outlay	Cash Accumulation	Linton Yield	Belth Yield	Belth Price	Baldwin Method
Technique	Net premiums less cash value and dividends; ignores interest	Net premiums at interest less dividends at interest and cash value, divided by annuity due factor	Average time value adjusted difference between net premiums at interest and dividends at interest	Accumulate premium differences at interest	Accumulate premium differences at interest while holding death benefits constant	Accumulate premium differences at interest rate that causes equal future values and equal death benefits	Ratio of "benefits" to "investment"	Policy "investment" less "benefits"	Rate of cash and life insurance "benefits" to "investment"
Solves for	"Net cost"	Average net cost	Average net cost	Surrender value and death benefit differences	Surrender value differences	Average rate of return that causes equality	Yearly rate of return	Yearly price of protection	Yearly rate of return
Assumptions needed	Money has no time value	Rate of return	Rate of return	1 Rate of return 2 Equal outlay	1 Rate of return 2 Equal outlay 3 Equal death benefits	1 YRT rates 2 Equal outlay 3 Equal death benefits	YRT rates	Rate of return	YRT rates
Compares similar policies?	No	Yes	Yes	Yes, but results often ambiguous	Yes	Yes, if common YRT rates used	Yes, if common YRT rates used	Yes	Yes, if common YRT rates used
Compares dissimilar policies?	No	No	No	Yes, but results often ambiguous	Yes	Yes	Yes	Yes	Yes
Requires computer?	No	No, but time consuming	No, but time consuming	No, but time consuming	Yes	Yes	No	No	No, but recommended
Good for replacement evaluation?	No	No	No	Yes, with modification	Yes, with modification	Yes, with modification	Yes, but results often ambiguous	Yes, but results often ambiguous	Yes, but results may be ambiguous

the old policy had long surpassed the reach of those provisions. In addition, the insured may forfeit more favorable guarantees as to minimum rates credited to the cash values, and more favorable provisions and rates for policy loans. The insured and the planner should compare the relative merit of all the provisions of the existing policy as compared to the provisions and promises of the new policy.

WHERE TO FIND POLICY RATING INFORMATION

The most authoritative independent sources of information on premiums, cash values, dividends, interest adjusted indexes, dividend histories, settlement option values, and other essential data for policy comparison are:

1. *Best's Flitcraft Compend,* available from the A.M. Best Company in Oldwick, New Jersey, is an excellent source of information on the current and historical performance of various policies offered by many insurance companies. For currently offered ordinary whole life policies, it shows 10 and 20 year interest-adjusted cost indices. It also includes a historical policy performance section showing projected and actual dividend and interest histories and projected and actual interest-adjusted net payments and surrender cost indices for various issue ages for

many of the policies that have been offered in the market over the past 20 years.

2. *Life Rates & Data,* published by the National Underwriter Company in Cincinnati, Ohio. While last published in 1989 and no longer available from the publisher, it remains an excellent source for historical comparisons.

3. *Best's Review,* a monthly magazine, runs policy comparisons and each year compares dividend histories of different companies. This magazine is also a valuable source of information about new products.

4. *Consumer Reports* does some evaluations for nonprofessionals but is unfortunately limited in the number of companies and policies reviewed.

CHAPTER ENDNOTES

1. *The Insurance Forum* 168 (June 1982).

2. This discussion of the Baldwin method is adapted from B. Baldwin and W. Droms, *Life Insurance Investment Advisor: A Guide to Understanding and Selecting Today's Insurance Products* (Probus Publishing Company, 1988), pp. 145-155.

3. See Appendix E for a complete discussion of the operation of the Section 1035 provisions.

4. See Appendix F, under "Policy Withdrawals" for a discussion of the potential tax implications.

Chapter 5

LEGAL ASPECTS OF LIFE INSURANCE

INTRODUCTION

This chapter will provide an overview of some of the general principles that govern life insurance as a legally enforceable contract and examine the terms and conditions under which life insurance is sold.[1] Keep in mind that this chapter is not meant to be a legal treatise and can only provide a basic survey. Each state's law may (and often does) differ from another's, or its courts' interpretations of a general principle may vary (from slightly to radically) when compared with the conclusions of courts in another state. Nor will this chapter cover the formation of the life insurance contract because the legal aspects will depend on the insurer's policies and contract terminology in addition to state law.

While reading this chapter, planners should consider the documentation necessary to create a "paper trail" to evidence "what happened," "who said and who did what," and "when and how" each step of the contractual process occurred. Careful record keeping can prove invaluable for tax purposes as well as in the event of a dispute among the parties.

A more thorough understanding of the legal safeguards and peculiarities of the life insurance contract with respect to the few duties it imposes on the policyowner or his or her beneficiaries as well as the multitude of privileges, powers, and rights it bestows will enhance the planner's appreciation for this incredibly unique and socially useful product.

Topics included in this chapter include:

1. parties to the contract;

2. requirement of insurable interest;

3. legal form and contents of the contract;

4. one-month grace period for premium payments;

5. incontestable clause;

6. suicide clause;

7. misstatement-of-age adjustment clause;

8. dividend clause;

9. nonforfeiture provisions (cash surrender, extended term and paid up insurance);

10. policy lapse and reinstatement clause;

11. naming and changing the beneficiary;

12. modes of settlement;

13. policy loans;

14. automatic premium loan provision;

15. assignments of a life insurance policy; and

16. waiver and estoppel.

PARTIES TO THE CONTRACT

A life insurance policy is a legally enforceable contract issued by the insurer in consideration of the application and the payment of premiums. The essence of that contract is that:

> If the insured dies while this policy is in force, we will pay the Sum Insured to the Beneficiary, when we receive at our Home Office due proof of the Insured's death, subject to the provisions of this policy.

There are four "parties" to the life insurance contract: the insurer, the insured, the applicant-policyowner, and the beneficiary.[2]

The first party to a life insurance contract is the "insurer." The insurer almost always operates in corporate form and must be licensed in each state in which it does business.

The "insured" is the second party to the contract.[3] Almost any natural person can be an insured.[4]

A third party, often but not always the same as the insured, is the applicant-policyowner who applies for and "owns" the contract that has been made with the insurer. Again, generally, almost any natural person and most entities such as trusts, corporations, partnerships, limited liability companies, or sole proprietorships can apply for and own life insurance on one or more person's lives.[5] Some state laws give those with "limited contractual capacity" (e.g., a minor) a statutory right to enter into a contract of life insurance and then to void that contract and regain the premiums paid.[6]

Recent cases have created a "fourth" party to the contract (the "third person," assuming the insured and the policyowner are the same) – the beneficiary. Although the beneficiary does not sign the application for insurance and may not even be aware of the existence of the insurance, since the contract is for that party's direct benefit, that party can sue the insurer after the insured's death to collect the policy proceeds. So in a very real sense, at the instant the policy matures through the insured's death, a life insurance policy is a contract for the benefit of the third party beneficiary.

REQUIREMENT OF INSURABLE INTEREST

"Insurable interest" is a key principle in life insurance law. It is the requirement imposed by law (and by insurers) to prevent a "gaming" or "wagering" by one party on the life of another through insurance. Simply put, to insure the life of an individual, the applicant must have an insurable interest, i.e., a greater concern in the insured's living than dying. Courts (and insurers) look for "a reasonable ground . . . to expect some benefit or advantage from the continuance of the [insured]."[7] Stated in another manner, the public has an interest in preventing the contract of insurance where the applicant has no interest in the continuation of the insured's life other than the prospect of profiting from the insured's early demise.

It is almost universally accepted that a person has an unquestionable insurable interest in his or her own life. "The mere fact that a man of his own motion insures his life for the benefit of either himself or of another is sufficient evidence of good faith to validate the contract."[8] So most applicant-insureds will face no insurable interest issue in obtaining life insurance. Nor will their naming of someone other than their estates as beneficiary usually pose a problem since it is generally assumed that the insured will not name as beneficiary someone who wished him harm or who would wager on his life.[9] (Of course, if the policy was obtained expressly for the purpose of wagering or if the policy was really purchased by and soon after issue assigned to the third party beneficiary, the courts will declare such a contract void.[10] Public policy will not allow one to accomplish by fraudulent indirection what one clearly is prohibited from doing directly.)

Every state has either statutory law or case law on insurable interest and all require that either the beneficiary or applicant hold such interest at the inception of the contract. Most states do not require that either the beneficiary or assignee of a policy have an insurable interest. The majority of states hold that there is nothing conclusively illegal about an assignment to one who holds no insurable interest – even where the insured is paid value for the assignment.[11] But some states do require that the assignee have an insurable interest – even though some of the same states allow the insured to name a beneficiary who does not have an insurable interest.

Because each state is free to create its own laws on insurable interest and because different state courts have come to different conclusions on the issue, it is impossible to develop rules that apply without question in every state. Most state laws do not question the insured's insurable interest in his own life nor the interest of close relatives related by blood or law and bonded through natural love and affection with the insured. With respect to others, statutes favor persons who stand to profit by the insured's continued life, suffer economic loss at the insured's death, and who have more to gain by the insured's continued life than death.

Generally, the following rules regarding insurable interest apply:

Blood relatives –

- A parent usually is deemed to have an insurable interest in his or her child's life.

- A child usually is deemed to have an insurable interest in his or her parent's life. (But once the child becomes a financially independent adult, it is not certain that all courts would hold that the blood relationship alone would be sufficient to meet insurable interest tests).

- A grandchild usually is deemed to have an insurable interest in the life of a grandparent.

- A grandparent usually is deemed to have an insurable interest in the life of a grandchild.

- Siblings usually are deemed to have an insurable interest in the life or lives of brothers and sisters.

- Other relatives, such as an aunt, uncle, niece, nephew, or cousin, generally are not deemed to have an insurable interest merely by virtue of their blood relationship (but may have an insurable interest arising out of a business or financial transaction or out of financial dependency on the insured).

Marriage –

- Spouses have an insurable interest on each other's lives.[12]

- A few courts have held that a person engaged to another has an insurable interest in the other's life.[13]

- Other individuals related to the insured by marriage are usually deemed not to have an insurable interest based solely on a marriage relationship (but may have an insurable interest based on financial dependency). In-laws, for example, or step-sons or daughters, or foster children have no per se insurable interest based on family relationships but can obtain insurable interest because of dependency.

Business –

- A person (or business or financial enterprise) that would suffer a financial loss at the insured's death will usually be deemed to have an insurable interest (assuming that the amount of coverage bears a reasonable relationship to the loss that would be suffered at the death of the insured).[14] This means an employer can insure an employee, an employee can insure an employer, a partner can insure a partner, and a partnership can insure its partners, a surety can insure the life of his principal, and a member of a commercial enterprise can insure an individual if that person's death would adversely affect the financial stability or profits of the enterprise. (Although a business generally has an insurable interest in the lives of officers, directors, and managers, or others on whose continued life or lives the business' success may depend upon, a corporation may not have insurable interest in the life of a shareholder who has no working or other financial relationship with the business. The point is that it is not the mere legal relationship that creates the insurable interest, but rather the "existence of circumstances which arise out of or by reason of" the entity.)

- Where business associates have insured each other to fund a purchase of the business interest at the insured's death or the business itself has insured an owner to fund a purchase of that person's interest at death, usually there will be an insurable interest.

- Creditors have been allowed to purchase policies on debtors as long as the relationship between the amount of insurance and the debt were proportionate. But at the point where the transaction was more of a wager than an effort to secure a debt (decided on a case by case basis), the policy is void as lacking insurable interest.[15] So the closer the insurance amount is to the debt owed, the more likely insurable interest will not be an issue.[16] (However, once the policy has been issued to a creditor, the creditor typically is allowed to keep the entire amount of the proceeds even if the amount exceeds the debt.)

Most states require that insurable interest be present only at the time when the life insurance contract is entered into, i.e., at the inception of the policy and need not be present at the insured's death.[17] Therefore, a wife who is married at the time the insurance is purchased on her husband's life but divorced from him at his death is not barred from collecting. Likewise, if a corporation purchases insurance on the life of a key employee, by definition there is an insurable interest at that time. If the employee later leaves the firm, the corporation can still collect the proceeds of the policy on his life.[18]

Even if the insurable interest tests are met by a third party applicant, state law will void the contract if the insured is not informed and the insured's consent is not obtained.[19] Even a spouse cannot lawfully purchase a policy on the other spouse's life in most states without that person's knowledge and consent.[20] However, there is a practical exception to this general rule: a parent can, without the child's consent, purchase relatively small amounts of life insurance on the life of a minor child since the child does not have the legal capacity to consent and so such consent would be meaningless.

Passing of the contestable period will not bar an insurer from asserting a lack of insurable interest since the strength and validity of the incontestable clause is predicated on the existence of a valid contract. Absent insurable interest, there never was a valid contract.

An insurer has a legal duty to use reasonable care in ascertaining the existence of insurable interest and in assuring that the insured did in fact consent to the coverage. If the insurer does not use reasonable care in both duties, it may be liable for the harm that occurs to the insured and/or beneficiaries.[21] For this (and sound underwriting economic) reason(s), insurance companies are often more stringent than state law requires.

LEGAL FORM AND CONTENTS OF THE CONTRACT

The life insurance policy is highly consumer-protection oriented and unique in the law of contracts. In legal parlance, it is an "aleatory, unilateral contract of adhesion."

Aleatory means that the insurer's promise to pay the policy proceeds is conditioned upon an uncertain event, i.e., the insured's death within the term of the contract.

Unilateral describes the fact that the insurance company is the only party to the contract which makes a legally enforceable promise. (The policyowner's payment of premiums is technically a "condition precedent" to the insurer's liability.) The insurer promises to pay a specific dollar amount if the insured dies while the policy is in force. Note that the policyowner makes no promise to continue paying premiums and there is no way the insurer can require that premiums be paid.

Adhesion is a legal recognition that the policyowner was not in a position to negotiate with the insurer on the terms of the contract and the resulting document is not evidence of the normal "give and take" negotiation and bargaining found in a standard contract. The insured may "adhere" to the terms of the policy but cannot change them. Furthermore, the legal terms of the life insurance contract and underlying mathematical assumptions make it difficult for the policyowner to understand. For these reasons, courts will not insist that the policyowner meet the same degree of strict compliance to the terms of the life insurance contract as it might in the case of the typical agreement. Because the insurance contract is a "take it or leave it" agreement in which the insurer selects all wording and there is no negotiation of the terms, ambiguities are typically interpreted in the policyowner's (and beneficiary's) favor and against the insurer.[22]

For these reasons, many courts have adopted one or more theories that have made it possible to construe insurance policy language strictly against the insurer.[23] But since the life insurance contract is one requiring a great deal of reliance on the statements of the insured and/or applicant-owner, honesty – rather than reliance on the leniency of the courts – should be the watchword in the contractual process.

Almost all life insurance contracts have a similar format; there will be a "face page" and both required and optional provisions on succeeding pages. Most contracts also have a page that contains the definitions of terms used in the contract.

The face page contains the basic promise of the insurer to pay a stated amount upon the insured's death, a statement as to the type of policy that is issued (for example, term or whole life), the length of time premiums are payable (most provide premiums are payable for a stated period or until the insured's death) and whether or not dividends are payable, a table of contents guide to the other provisions of the policy, and a statement regarding any additional benefits. It must contain the signatures (facsimile is sufficient) of the president and secretary of the insurer.

Certain provisions are required by state law to safeguard the interests of the policyowner and the beneficiary. These almost universally required provisions[24] include:

1. one-month grace period for premium payments;

2. incontestable clause;

3. suicide clause;

4. misstatement-of-age adjustment clause;

5. dividend clause;

6. extended term and paid up insurance clause; and

7. policy lapse and reinstatement clause;

Some states prohibit the insurer from inserting certain types of provisions for the same reasons. There are prohibitions in various states against such provisions which:

1. limit (to less than the period fixed by that state's general statute of limitations) the time in which a suit may be brought against the insurer;

2. permit "backdating" the policy more than a specified period of time (usually 6 months);

3. allow a forfeiture of the policy for failure to repay a policy loan;

4. make the insurer's agent the client's agent; and

5. cut back the insurance ostensibly provided on the face page.

Almost all states forbid the use of the term "warranty" (a statement guaranteed true in every respect) and now hold that a statement by an applicant or by the insured is a "representation" (a statement that must be true only as to facts material to the risk). The distinction is crucial to the protection of the policyowner and his or her beneficiaries. A warranty is part of the contract but a representation is not. Therefore, the breach of a warranty makes the contract rescindable by the insurer but in the event the insurer proves misrepresentation by the applicant and/or insured, the insurer cannot rescind the contract – unless the fact misrepresented is material to acceptance of the risk. Almost every state requires that the policy itself must provide that – *in the absence of fraud* – all statements by or for the insured are deemed to be representations and not warranties.

Each policy contains an "entire contract" provision stating that the policy – together with the copy of the application that is attached and is legally a part of the policy – is the entire contract. The insurer agrees in this provision not to fight a lawsuit on the basis of any statement unless that statement is made in the application and a copy of the application was attached to the policy when it was issued.[25] The insured and/or policyowner is then put on notice that no one (including the agent, the insured, or the policyowner) has the authority to waive or change a provision in the policy.

Many states allow (and some require) an insurer to insert a provision on the face page of the policy that provides a "free look" – a "trial examination" period to examine and decline the policy within a given period of time (usually 10 days but in some cases as much as 20 days). If declined, the contract would be deemed void from inception and the insurer would be obligated to return the policyowner's money (typically without interest).

ONE–MONTH GRACE PERIOD FOR PREMIUM PAYMENTS

The policyowner's payment of the premium is a "condition precedent" to the insurer's duty to pay a death claim. So nonpayment of premiums will cause a life insurance policy to "lapse."[26] Even an insured in a coma or a person legally adjudicated mentally incompetent must pay premiums in a timely manner or the coverage will end. The insured's rights under the contract end if the specified premium is not paid at the dates specified in the contract.[27]

Most states' laws require that the contract of life insurance contain a "grace period" provision. A grace period gives the policyowner an additional period of time after the due date of the premium during which the policy remains in full force. So if the insured dies during that period of grace, (typically 31 days from the due date[28]) the insurer will pay the full death benefit (less the premium that should have been paid but was not[29]). If the premium is not paid by the last day of the grace period and the insured is still alive, the policy owner does not owe the insurer for the unpaid premium, but of course, the policy lapses.

INCONTESTABLE CLAUSE

The incontestable clause typically is stated as follows:

We will not contest the validity of this Policy, except for nonpayment of premiums, after it has been in force during the Insured's lifetime for two years from the policy date. This Provision does not apply to any rider providing disability or accidental death benefits.

So after the specified period of time (usually two years[30]) starting on the "policy date"[31] and running for such period of time during the insured's lifetime,[32] the insurance company is barred from challenging the validity[33] of the contract. Stated in a more legalistic manner, the insurer is "estopped from contesting even a material or fraudulent misrepresentation in the policy."

The incontestable clause provides a balance between the legitimate interests of the parties:

Insurer – The incontestable clause allows a reasonable time for the insurer to discover and resist fraud by the insured and/or applicant-policyowner and deny liability, repudiate the policy, and return the policyowner's premiums.

Policyowner and beneficiaries – The incontestable clause avoids the necessity of a long, expensive, and uncertain litigation to prove the truth of statements made in the application for the policy while the insured was alive and to obtain the policy proceeds after the insured's death.[34]

In other words, the incontestable clause can be considered a "statute of limitations" on the insurer to investigate statements made in the application for insurance and deny coverage on the basis of that inquiry. Once the contestable period expires, even fraud will not vitiate the contract.

Planners should note that the typical incontestable clause will carve out certain exceptions. For instance, the insurer is not barred from resisting a claim if premiums are not paid. Many clauses also except from the protection of the incontestable clause any accidental death or disability payable under a policy rider or exclude from the incontestable clause's scope "war hazards" (where the insured is killed as the result of military service).[35] Some policies will provide within the incontestable clause a statement that if the insured's age is misstated, the amount payable will be appropriately adjusted.

There are also other reasons why payment under a life insurance contract may be legally refused in spite of the incontestable clause. If these are proved by the insurer, the policy will be void (i.e., there never was a valid contract with the proposed insured).

Fraudulent impersonation[36] (i.e., someone, claiming to be the insured, signs the application and/or takes the physical examination using the insured's name) – Either there never was a valid contract or if the contract was valid, it was with someone other than the insured. So the incontestable clause does not bar the insurer from contesting the policy even after the expiration of the contestable period.

Lack of insurable interest[37] – If there is no reasonable expectation of benefit or advantage from the continued life of the proposed insured, the life insurance contract becomes a form of wagering or gaming. To prevent profiting on the lives of others, all states void a contract in which there was no insurable interest at the inception of the contract regardless of the contestable period expiring.

Procurement of the policy with intent to murder – Public policy will not allow a contract to come into existence where it was entered into with the express purpose of murdering the insured. "Where the contract falls, it brings with it all of its constituent parts" and so the incontestable clause, being "no more a part of the contract than any of its provisions" must fall with the contract.[38]

SUICIDE CLAUSE

Suicide is the intentional killing of oneself. A typical policy will provide that:

If the insured commits suicide, while sane or insane, within two years from the Policy Date, our liability will be limited to the amount of the premiums paid, less any debt and partial surrenders, and less the costs of any riders.

If the insured commits suicide, while sane or insane, within two years from the effective date(s) of any increase in insurance or any reinstatement, our total liability shall be the cost of the increase or reinstatement.

The insurer is stating that the promised death benefit will not be paid if the insured dies as the result of a suicide within the specified period of (usually) two years.[39]

Like the incontestable provision, the suicide clause provides a legitimate balance between the interests of the parties:

Insurer – The insurer is responsible to other policyowners (in a mutual company) or to shareholders (in a stock company) for matching premium charges with risk. If individuals contemplating suicide were allowed to purchase life insurance without restriction, the insurer's increased and accelerated liability would be reflected in higher costs that eventually would be passed on to policyowners (or shareholders). The mere knowledge that suicide within two years would not accomplish the intended goal of enriching beneficiaries at the insurer's expense is thought to discourage those who would take a policy out with the specific intent of committing suicide. The imposition of what amounts to a relatively short "waiting period" for full coverage substantially reduces the threat of unfair additional costs levied upon other policyowners.

Policyowner and beneficiaries – The policyowner and his or her beneficiaries need the insurance regardless of the cause of the insured's death and should not have to bare the expense, aggravation, and uncertainty of litigation if suicide, no matter how long after the contract was purchased, would cause a loss of the proceeds the contract was designed to furnish. Regardless of whether the insured was sane or insane, once the suicide period expires, the insurer is liable at the death of the insured.[40]

Most cases dealing with the suicide clause are concerned with one (or both) of two issues:

- Was the cause of death suicide or some outside force? (Was the insured murdered?)

- Assuming the insured killed himself, did he or did he not intend to do so? (Was the death accidental rather than intentional?)

The presumption is that the insured did not commit suicide and the insurer must prove that the facts reasonably demonstrate death did not occur by accident. This burden of proof shifts, however, in the case of accidental death riders. There, the beneficiary must prove that the insured died accidentally and not by self-destruction.

Absent a suicide provision, if the insured dies as a result of suicide, in most cases the insurer will be required to pay no matter how soon death occurs after the policy is issued – unless the insurer can prove that the insured purchased the policy with the deliberate intent of killing himself and enriching his beneficiaries at the expense of the insurer by that fraud (the implicit agreement that when a policy is purchased the insured is not intending to do himself in).[41]

Because a suicide is by definition a deliberate act, it will mean the insurer is not liable to pay any accidental death benefits. "A suicide is not an accidental death."[42]

When the clock starts to tick on the (typically two year) suicide exclusion time period varies depending upon the following:

Policy backdated to "save age" – Most courts will start the time at the "issue date" if it is clearly stated in the policy.[43] But, if the terms of the contract are ambiguous, the time may start at the backdate rather than the issue date.

Conversion of term to permanent – Assuming the new policy is obtained through an individual term or group option to convert, many courts will treat the transaction as a continuance of the original contract. This means if the original individual term or group term life was covered by a suicide clause, it continues (and the clock ticks) from the original date. If there was no suicide clause in the original, the new policy would not carry one.

After the suicide period has expired, the insurer is liable for paying the death proceeds regardless of the cause of death.

MISSTATEMENT–OF–AGE ADJUSTMENT CLAUSE

Yet another protection for the policyowner of an individual contract and policy beneficiaries is the "mis-statement-of-age" clause[44] that is required by law in most states and will typically read similarly to this:

> This policy is issued at the age shown on page ___, which should be the age attained by the insured on the last birthday before the Policy Date. If the Policy Date falls on the Insured's birthday, the age should be the Insured's attained age on the Policy Date.
>
> If the insured's age is incorrectly shown on page ___, the proceeds payable under this policy will be adjusted to the proceeds that would have been purchased at the correct age based upon our rates in effect when this policy was issued.

Mortality can vary considerably with age. So obviously, age is a crucial factor in the calculation of the proper life insurance premium for a given class of risk. If the wrong age is stated on the application (regardless of whether by deliberate misstatement or because the insured just did not know his date of birth), the insurer cannot charge the appropriate premium and the policyowner may pay much more or much less than what should have been paid. The insurance company trusts the applicant to be truthful and as a matter of convenience to both parties (and as a good marketing practice) does not require a birth certificate or other proof of age at the time of purchase. In fact, it is not until the insured dies and the death certificate accompanies the claim for payment that the insurer has documentation as to when the insured was born. So it is not until then that the insurer can compare the ages, meet its burden of proving that the age in the application was incorrect,[45] and make the appropriate adjustment.

The misstatement-of-age provision provides a legitimate balance between the interests of the parties:

Insurer – The insurer pays neither more nor less than is appropriate for the proper age of the insured at issue and avoids expensive litigation and loss of public goodwill inherent in defenses of claims on the grounds of improper age. This serves as a cost-effective "escape valve" for handling innocent mistakes.[46]

Policyowner and beneficiaries – Even if a misstatement-of-age (a material misrepresentation) is found after the death of the insured,[47] there is assurance that the proper amount of proceeds will be paid, uncertainty will be avoided, and litigation to obtain the rightful amount from the insurer will not be necessary.

An insurer that finds it charged premiums based on an incorrect age can make the adjustment of benefits even if the discovery is made after the policy became incontestable on the grounds that the insurer is not denying the liability to make payments but is merely adjusting an error in how much should be paid.

DIVIDEND CLAUSE

Owners of "participating" life insurance contracts are entitled to "dividends" if the insurer has sufficient earned surplus. The term "participating" means that the policyowner can participate in that surplus – if there is one. Confusion may result for the following reasons:

1. Both mutual insurance companies (owned solely by policyowners) and stock companies (owned solely by outside shareholders) can legally issue participating ("par") policies (although stock companies traditionally have issued "nonparticipating" ("nonpar") contracts).

2. Both types of companies can write checks called dividends.

Profits enjoyed by a stock company are not typically shared with the policyowners; they usually go only to investors (shareholders) in the company's stock and are taxed in the same manner dividends from General Motors or IBM would be.

But the distributed surplus paid to owners of participating policies is very different than the profits paid out to owners of a stock company even though both distributions may be called "dividends." A dividend paid to an owner of a participating contract is a return of "excess premium" due to the generous margins built into the premium calculation assumptions.[48] In other words, the premium in a participating contract is set high enough to provide not only the amount the insurer expects to need to pay its bills and meet its obligations but also an extra amount to provide a margin of safety. Planners should note that policyholders of participating insurance cannot be surcharged by the insurer. Although dividends may not be as favorable as projected, the policyowner will not have to pay more than the set premium regardless of how poorly the insurer does financially.

Three factors – actually, the insurer's experience in three areas – influence *if* (dividends are projections only and NOT guaranteed) and how much dividends will be paid:

1. mortality;

2. interest; and

3. loading.[49]

"Mortality" represents the insurer's ability to match risk with premiums, i.e., how carefully the insurer underwrites policies and how closely the experience (rate of deaths) that actually occurs parallels what was projected by the insurer in setting its rates. If more deaths occur in a given period than expected, dividends will be adversely affected. If fewer deaths occur than projected, dividends will be positively affected.

"Interest" really represents the insurer's investment success with net after-cost premium dollars. If assets earn less than projected, dividends will be adversely affected. If earnings and growth are greater than projected, dividends will be positively affected.

"Loading" is a term that encompasses all the insurer's business expenses in marketing, issuing, administering, and paying claims on policies. If the insurer's cost of doing business is greater than projected, dividends will be adversely affected. If the insurer is able to contain costs and keep them below the projected amounts, dividends will be positively affected.

The interplay between all three of these factors and the level of additional financial safety the insurer's officers deem necessary determines, as stated above, whether the company will be able to refund the excess amounts of premium the policyowner paid in and the extent of that refund. Once this refund is decided upon, it must be "fair." This does not mean that every class of policyowners must be treated equally. For instance, policies purchased twenty years ago may be entitled to higher dividends than those issued five years ago (perhaps because the premiums charged to policyowners twenty years ago were higher than those charged to policyowners five years ago). Likewise, "preferred risk" policies (i.e., those requiring the purchase of larger amounts and/or more stringent underwriting) may be awarded higher dividends than standard policies. But fairness does imply that distributions among the policyowners in any class must be equal.

Dividends are payable to and legally the property of the policyowner and can therefore be assigned with or separately from the policy itself.[50] At the policyowner's death, dividends that were held by the insurer to earn interest technically should pass to the policyowner's estate unless previously assigned or disposed of in another manner in the policy.

Most participating policies provide five ways a policyowner can choose to accept dividends:

1. take dividends in cash;

2. have the insurer automatically use the dividend to reduce the next premium;

3. have the insurer automatically use the amount of the dividend to purchase "paid-up" additional insurance ("paid up" adds) in the same type as the basic policy;[51]

4. have the insurer automatically hold the dividends in an account for the policyowner and pay interest on that account; or

5. have the insurer automatically purchase units of one-year term insurance equal in amount to the cash value of the policy at the date the term insurance is purchased (this is the "fifth dividend option" that is often used in split dollar arrangements but can also be used to considerably increase insurance coverage on a very cost effective net rate basis for other reasons such as the repayment of a policy loan).

Policy dividends are also commonly used to help pay up the policy more quickly than otherwise expected. High levels of dividends have been used to help create the appearance that premiums would "vanish." Of course, premiums do not really vanish. This marketing presentation of dividends depends on dividends being paid at the (sometimes optimistic) level projected by the insurer and, in difficult economic times, the "vanish" may not occur when scheduled.

Dividend options can be prospectively changed. Policyowners can also "mix and match" these options. For example, a policyowner might choose to use dividends to purchase one-year term insurance to the extent allowable and have the balance of the dividend – if any – to reduce premiums, purchase paid up additions, or take the remainder in cash.

If no dividend option is elected by the policyowner and the contract is silent, state law directs the disposition of that money. But insurers are allowed to specify in the policy what will happen if the policyowner does not select a dividend option. For instance, the contract might state that if the policyowner has not selected an option (or if there is excess money from a dividend after another option is elected), the dividend (or any excess) will be used to purchase paid up additional insurance. This is called the "automatic dividend option."

If dividends are used to pay premiums, a policy can not lapse if the insurer holds a sufficient amount of the policyowner's dividends to pay a full premium. If any of the other four options have been selected, the insurer will not apply dividends to pay premiums even if the policy will lapse.

NONFORFEITURE PROVISIONS

State laws and policy provisions combine to provide a number of protective options for the policyowner who stops paying premiums (for whatever reason) after the policy has been in force for a number of years.[52] The equity in the policy (assuming a type of policy in which the premiums exceed the current cost of carrying term insurance) is not lost but can be used advantageously in several ways. In other words, in level premium contracts where a policy requires that a "reserve" be established in early years to meet higher insurance costs as the insured grows older and the probability of death grows greater, that reserve is "released" to the policyowner when the insurer is no longer obligated under the contract. The policyowner will receive an equitable portion of the total values his or her premiums have helped to accumulate.

How much the policyowner will receive is a function of (1) a statutory formula and (2) the insurer's internal policies (the insurer can promise to pay more than the statutory minimum). The values the insurer will pay are printed in the policy. Generally, at least 20 years' (or the term of the policy if less) values are shown.

The policyowner usually has three nonforfeiture options:

Cash surrender – Cashing in (technically called a "cash surrender" of) a policy is the simplest nonforfeiture option.[53] The contract is physically surrendered to the insurer and the insurer issues a check to the policyowner for the policy's "cash value." The cash value (also called "cash surrender value") is the amount shown in the policy itself (sometimes "per thousand dollars" of face amount) as the cash available at the end of specified policy years (reduced by any loans against the policy).[54] The contract will contain a table showing year by year the amount that is available if the policy is cashed in and will make certain other statements in compliance with state law nonforfeiture rules. Although the insurer is allowed in most states to defer the payment of this cash surrender value for up to six months after the contract is tendered to the insurer (to insulate insurers from a "run" on its cash reserves and the consequent self-generating economic crisis such a drain could precipitate), payments are almost always made within days or weeks of the policyowner's surrender of the policy.

Extended term option – If the policyowner elects to use the cash in the policy to create "extended term," the face amount of the coverage is undiminished. The same death benefit payable under the original contract remains payable after the option becomes operative (less any outstanding loan). In essence, the insurer takes the cash in the policy and purchases term insurance (without the payment of commissions or charging of other expenses against the policy). Since the death benefit is the same, only the term of time for which coverage will last changes. If the insured dies during the term, the insurer must pay. If the insured dies after the term, the insurer has no liability. Once the term expires, the policyowner cannot continue the coverage – except by formal reinstatement according to the provisions of the contract (see below). The extended term option would be a good choice where the insured had a shortened life expectancy because of an accident or illness. No policy loan can be taken since extended term coverage makes no provision for policy loan values.

Reduced paid up insurance option – As its name implies, an insurer takes the cash values of the policyowner's contract and uses that money to pay up the contract for the life of the insured. Unlike extended term where the face amount is unchanged but the term is shortened, when the reduced paid up option is elected, the face amount is reduced to what a net single premium in the amount of the policy's cash value will purchase at the attained age of the insured. The same type of insurance continues at that reduced amount for the insured's life no matter how long he lives (up until the maturity date of the policy). The amount of paid up coverage is listed in the contract itself. The amount of coverage purchased is a function of the insured's age at the date the option is elected as well as the type of coverage being purchased and the level of cash values available. But the death benefit is reduced by loans against the policy (and increased by dividend accumulations). Reduced paid up insurance, unlike extended term, has both cash and loan values and is therefore more flexible than extended term. The reduced paid up option would be a good choice where the insured was in average or superior health but for whatever reason the policyowner stopped paying premiums.

State law requires that the policy state an "automatic nonforfeiture benefit" if no option has been selected upon (or within 60 days of) the lapse of a policy. In the case of a "rated" (premiums adjusted to reflect a higher than standard mortality risk) policy, the automatic nonforfeiture benefit is reduced paid up insurance. With respect to all other policies, the automatic nonforfeiture benefit is extended term insurance.

Where an insured dies after selecting a nonforfeiture option but before receiving any benefits from it, the general rule is that, even if the insured dies before the insurer has completed its obligation under the nonforfeiture option, the option and not the death benefit is payable.[55]

POLICY LAPSE AND REINSTATEMENT CLAUSE

A policy "lapses" when premiums are not paid by the end of the grace period.[56] (A policy "expires" when it has run past its grace period with premiums unpaid and has exhausted any benefits available under the nonforfeiture option or the policyowner has allowed the policy to lapse by not paying the next premium due and then decides to cash in the policy.)

However, a lapsed policy can be resuscitated if the insured meets certain tests and the policyholder puts the insurer back to the position it would have been in had the policy never been allowed to lapse. Almost all states require that life insurance contracts contain a clause allowing "reinstatement" – a restoration and, according to most courts, a continuation of the original contract.[57]

Such a clause might read as follows:

This policy may be reinstated at any time by a request, in writing and submitted to the Company's Home Office within five years from the date of default in premium payments, unless the policyowner has surrendered the policy for its cash value, if the policyowner:

1. applies for reinstatement;

2. provides evidence of insurability satisfactory to the insurer;

3. pays all overdue premiums with interest at a rate not exceeding 6% per year compounded annually; and

4. pays or reinstates any policy indebtedness with interest at a rate not in excess of the applicable policy loan rate or rates determined in accordance with the policy's provisions.

There are many reasons why this reinstatement provision can be quite valuable:[58]

1. Annuity purchase rates in the original contract may be more favorable than those currently offered.

2. More favorable policy loan rates may be available in the original contract than those currently offered.

3. Mortality or interest assumptions may be more favorable in the original contract than in contracts issued currently.

4. Premium payments will almost inevitably be lower in the older original contract than in one which may be purchased at a later date.

5. A new policy would take a considerable amount of time to start to build up cash values and dividends.

6. The process of reinstatement is often quicker and simpler than applying for a new contract.

7. Typically, the suicide clause does not run anew from the date of reinstatement but instead starts to run from the original date of the contract.[59] (This assumes the reinstatement was not procured with the intention of committing suicide and also assumes the reinstatement clause itself did not start another suicide period to run.)

8. On a new contract, the incontestable and suicide clauses start anew.

Of course, there are also reasons why reinstatement may not be the appropriate course of action for a particular client to take. Reasons for applying for a new policy rather than reinstating an older one include:[60]

1. A type of policy not available when the policyowner applied for the original coverage may be available now and the new coverage may be more appropriate than the old.

2. Reinstatement often requires a large outlay since the policyowner must not only pay all unpaid premiums but also interest.

3. Rates for new insurance may be lower than the rates charged per thousand of death benefit on the original coverage.

Insurers are usually more liberal than state law requires them to be with respect to policy reinstatement.[61] But to prevent those who are ill or at greater risk from "selecting against the insurer" (this is called "adverse selection"), state statutes and policy provisions uniformly require that the insured must be "insurable" – to the insurer's satisfaction[62] – at the date of reinstatement. Were it not for such a provision, former insureds who have become uninsurable would uniformly seek to become insureds again and by doing so adversely affect the mortality experience of the insurer.

Merely completing the application for reinstatement is not sufficient to restore the policy's benefits. The insured and policyowner must meet all the conditions of reinstatement before the insurer becomes liable to pay anything other than any nonforfeiture benefits that already existed before the application for reinstatement. So if the proposed re-insured dies after signing the reinstatement form but before satisfying all the requisite tests, the insurer is not liable to pay the policy death benefit.

But once all of these "conditions precedent" to the insurer's liability are met (such as full compliance with all the contractual terms including insurability and payment of back premiums and interest), if the insured then dies from a cause such as an accident unrelated to insurability before the reinstatement is approved, most courts will hold that the reinstatement holds and dates back to the time the application and back premiums were tendered to the insurer.[63] An unreasonable delay on the insurer's part may be held to bar the insurer from declining coverage.[64]

Can a reinstated policy be contested? Most courts have held that for other purposes the reinstated contract should be considered the exercise of a contractual right under the original policy, i.e., a continuation of the original. This follows the ordinary meaning of the term "reinstatement," "to restore to the former state or position." But for purposes of contestability, a new period applies – but solely to statements made in the reinstatement application.[65] In other words, the incontestable clause runs anew as to fraud or misrepresentations in the application for reinstatement. Generally, the same contestable period that applied to the original contract applies to the reinstatement.[66]

NAMING AND CHANGING THE BENEFICIARY

A "beneficiary" is a person (or entity) named (or designated such as by a check off) by the policyowner to receive the death benefits under a life insurance policy at the death of the insured.[67] A revocable beneficiary is one whose potential receipt of the proceeds can be cut off at any time. An irrevocable beneficiary is one whose interest in the contract cannot be changed or reduced without his consent. Such a beneficiary has a vested right to the death benefit as soon as he or she is named irrevocably.

Within reasonable limits, the policyowner can change the beneficiary as often during lifetime as he wants – and name anyone he or she wants – subject to the procedures specified in the policy[68] and the following limitations:

1. Some states require that the beneficiary have an insurable interest in the insured's life where the policyowner is someone other than the insured.

2. A community property resident is, during marriage, unable to freely dispose of community assets without the written consent of the other spouse. This is because (aside from gifts and inheritances received before or during the marriage) each spouse is deemed to own a one-half, undivided interest in property acquired during the marriage while living in a community property state. If community funds are used to pay premiums, each spouse has an interest in the policy. So neither spouse can name someone else as beneficiary of the entire proceeds – even a child – without the other spouse's consent (but can name anyone he or she wants with respect to the policyowner's one-half interest).

3. State laws frequently limit the class of beneficiaries that can be named where a minor is the insured. Typically, such statutes allow the naming of the insured's parent, spouse, sibling, or grandparent. A minor, upon reaching the age of legal competency, can change the beneficiary designation at that time.

4. Many states bar an insured under group-term life coverage from naming the employer as beneficiary.

5. If an "irrevocable" beneficiary has been named, the policyowner cannot change the beneficiary without that party's written consent. An irrevocable beneficiary has a vested right to receive the proceeds of the policy – but contingent on surviving the insured. If the irrevocable beneficiary predeceases the insured, his or her rights are terminated at death.

6. Divorce does not, per se, affect the policyowner's right to change the beneficiary nor does it effect a change of beneficiary in most states. However, in some states, there is automatic termination of a spouse's interest after divorce while in others the policyowner can change the beneficiary even if it was "irrevocable" before the divorce. Furthermore, the right to change the beneficiary may be restricted by the divorce decree or property settlement agreement. On the other hand, sometimes at the remarriage of a spouse or upon the legal majority of the children, the policyowner regains the right to change the beneficiary.

7. A legally adjudicated incompetent cannot make or change a policy beneficiary nor can one who is mentally incompetent though not legally declared so. However, the test in the latter case is essentially the same as the test for competency to make a will: Does the policyowner have sufficient capacity to understand the extent of the property (i.e., the amount of the proceeds), the nature of the disposition, and the people who were the natural objects of his bounty? Usually, there is a presumption of competency. The burden of proof of incompetency is placed on the party that alleges it (typically the person who would have been the beneficiary had it not been changed).

8. A beneficiary can collect the proceeds of a life insurance policy if he or she kills the insured in an accident (even through gross carelessness or manslaughter) or in self defense. But every state bars an "intentional and wrongful killer" from enrichment because of that act.[69] Typically, once such a person is disqualified, a secondary beneficiary or the insured's estate will receive the proceeds. (In most situations the issue is not whether the insurer is liable to pay but rather who is the payee. However, if the beneficiary was also the applicant-policyowner and purchased the policy with the express intent of killing the insured, it is likely that the contract is void and the insurer will not be liable to anyone.[70]) The insurer may have no legal liability to make payment to anyone where the insured is legally executed[71] but in a number of states unless the insurer has specifically

excluded death by legal execution, the insurer is liable to pay (particularly if the contestable period has passed).

9. Where the beneficiary and the insured die in a common disaster, the disposition of the proceeds is generally governed by the Uniform Simultaneous Death Act (USDA) that has now been enacted in some form in almost every state. The general rule is as follows:

> Where the insured and the beneficiary die and there is no sufficient evidence that they have died in a manner other than simultaneously, the proceeds of the policy shall be distributed as if the insured survived the beneficiary.

The USDA does, however, specifically allow the policyowner to override that result in the policy's beneficiary form by making a presumption of a "reverse simultaneous death" (as if the insured was survived by his or her beneficiary). Planners should note that such a clause may be used to reduce federal estate taxes by fully utilizing the surviving spouse's unified credit.[72]

The USDA will not apply if: (a) there is evidence that the insured and beneficiary died other than simultaneously, or (b) one of the parties did in fact survive the other for any length of time no matter how short.[73] The problem here is that if the named beneficiary survives for even one minute the proceeds are paid to her estate and pass under her will (if she has a valid will, otherwise by intestate law) and not necessarily to the person the policyowner-insured wanted to benefit.

A solution is the "time clause" or "delay clause." This requires the beneficiary to survive the insured by a given period of time, such as 30 or 60 days, before he or she will be entitled to the proceeds. Beware, however, of a time delay clause lasting for more than 180 days as this will cause the loss of the federal estate tax marital deduction.[74] A simple and practical solution is for the policyowner to elect a settlement option and name contingent payees to receive any proceeds not payable to the primary payee at his or her death. The insurance contract itself will provide the mechanism for payments to continue with almost no delay or cost at the death of the primary payee.

10. A policyowner can, of course, name children as beneficiaries of life insurance but, except for very small amounts, insurers generally will not make settlements directly to minors. This means a guardian would have to be appointed (and suggests to the planner the use of a trust).

A policyowner can – and should – name more than one beneficiary. A planner is derelict in duty if the policyowner is not told of the privilege and advantages of naming both a "primary beneficiary" (which can be more than one person or entity) and one or more "contingent" or "secondary" beneficiaries. Throughout this book are numerous examples of tax savings and creditor protection available through properly arranged life insurance. The authors have found few instances where allowing the policyowner's estate to dispose of insurance proceeds (by default in not naming a contingent beneficiary) is advantageous in comparison to shifting wealth directly through the insurance contract.

The primary beneficiary is the first person (or class of persons) in line to receive the proceeds when the insured dies. But to be entitled to the proceeds, the primary beneficiary must be living on the date the insured dies. Otherwise, the proceeds are paid to the class of beneficiary whose interest is contingent upon surviving both the insured and the primary beneficiary. This class is appropriately called the "contingent" beneficiary.

There can be more than one individual, entity, or combination of individuals and entities in each class. For example, a policyholder may name his spouse if living and otherwise his two children. Where more than one beneficiary is in a given class, they typically share the proceeds equally unless the policyowner specifies otherwise in the beneficiary designation.

Policyowners can (and in the opinion of the authors should) even name a third level of beneficiaries or "final" beneficiaries in case all beneficiaries in a higher class have predeceased the insured. Often, parents, nieces, nephews, cousins, or a charity such as a church, synagogue, or university are named at this level. Alternatively, "the estate of the insured" can be designated and the proceeds will then be added to the other probate assets and be disposed of according to the insured's will or under state intestate laws.

Usually, a lower class' rights are extinguished if payment is made to members of a higher class. For instance, a contingent beneficiary will receive nothing if the primary beneficiary is alive when the insured dies. Likewise, the final beneficiary has no expectancy of a share of the proceeds if the contingent beneficiary survives the insured and the primary beneficiary predeceased the insured. Even if proceeds are taken in installments, once payable to a higher class of beneficiaries, any remainder payable at the death of a member of that higher class will be payable to the decedent's estate (or contingent payee) rather than to the next class of beneficiary.

Even where it seems inherently unfair, the insurer is almost always held by the courts to be bound to pay the proceeds to the named beneficiary. There are numerous cases where the proceeds were payable to a spouse long divorced by the insured because the policyowner had forgotten to designate a new beneficiary.

Specificity is essential. The beneficiary designation should describe the person with sufficient clarity and certainty so that the insurer can easily identify the proper person, make payment, and obtain a valid release.

Planners should therefore take special care in the following beneficiary situations:

The policyowner's spouse is specifically named – Courts look to the person's name rather than description as "husband" or "wife" or "fiancée." So even if that person is no longer a husband, wife, or fiancée when the insured dies, absent specific state law to the contrary, the proceeds will still be payable to the named person.[75] Courts do not pass on the morality of its citizens and recognize the right of the policyowner to make any beneficiary designation he or she pleases.

The policyowner merely says, "To my husband" or "To my wife" but does not name the person – Here, proceeds are payable to the person who, at the time of the insured's death, meets that description.[76]

The policyowner names each child individually and describes the relationship – This is the clearest and safest approach. But a child born after the beneficiary form is signed may be excluded.

The policyowner names his children as a class rather than naming them individually – The insurer may have difficulty in verifying who is included in the class – especially if name changes have occurred. The term "my children" may also cause legal problems and in many cases will include illegitimate, legally adopted, and children from a prior marriage as well as children born after the beneficiary form is signed and even those born after the insured's death.[77] The term "lawful children" will disqualify illegitimate children.

The policyowner names "My Issue and Heirs" – "Issue" is a term far broader than "children" and includes any lineal descendant no matter how far down the line. So grandchildren and even great grandchildren would be included. "Heirs" means those who would inherit under state intestacy laws (i.e., in the absence of a valid will). This designation is not generally recommended.

The policyowner names a class of beneficiaries "per capita" or "per stirpes" – A per capita (by the heads) distribution means that the proceeds will be split according to the number of beneficiaries in the class. If there are three children, each takes one-third. If there are only two out of the three that survive the insured, each takes one-half. A per stirpes (by the branches) distribution means that the distribution is first divided among the class – including a share for any predeceased member that is then split among that member's children. If two out of three children survive, the proceeds are split three ways with the deceased child's children equally splitting the share the deceased child would have had.[78] The choice between per capita and per stirpes is personal but often causes confusion. The authors recommend the policyowner's intent be specified with an example.

The policyowner names a minor as beneficiary – Few states would allow payment of policy proceeds to a minor and few companies would agree to do so even if not forbidden by law since minors cannot give a valid release to the insurer. For this reason, a trustee should be named as beneficiary in most cases involving minors.[79]

The policyowner names a trust as beneficiary – This designation provides the ultimate in flexibility, by assuring that the trustee will survive the insured and spouse, and increasing the chances of proper investment management and higher returns.[80]

The policyowner names a corporation, partnership, limited liability company, or charity – It is essential that the full legal name of the entity be specified.

The policyholder names himself – This is common and proper practice where one party owns life insurance on the life of another. In fact, there are almost always income or gift tax problems where one party owns insurance on the life of another but makes a third party the beneficiary. We call this the "Unholy Trinity."

The policyowner has failed to name a beneficiary – Some smaller policies and group-term life contracts provide a "facility-of-payment" clause that enables the insurer to pay a limited amount directly to the providers of the insured's last illness and burial expenses. Most larger amounts will be paid according to the policy provisions that specify the recipient when no beneficiary has been designated (or where all primary and contingent beneficiaries predecease the insured). Selecting a beneficiary by default is obviously not the preferable manner for disposing of policy proceeds.

Planners have an obligation to suggest to clients that they review the beneficiary designations made under life insurance policies (as well as employee benefit and retirement contracts) at least every two to three years or upon the occurrence of circumstances marking changes in marital status (the client's or the beneficiaries'), the beneficiaries' needs or abilities to handle money, or tax law. It is also important that life insurance beneficiary designations be coordinated with the entire estate plan.

Planners should note that a designation in a will typically does not result in a change of life insurance beneficiary (especially if the method of beneficiary change in the policy is exclusive which it almost always is) nor, as stated previously, does divorce make a change effective in most states.[81]

MODES OF SETTLEMENT

Beneficiaries can chose to "settle" with the insurer in a number of ways aside from the obvious and common method of a lump sum payment.[82] These "optional modes of settlement" include the following:

1. leave the proceeds with the insurer and receive annual interest payments;

2. accept the proceeds in installments for a specified period of time ("fixed-years installments");

3. accept the proceeds in installments of a specified amount ("fixed-amount option"); and

4. accept the proceeds as a life annuity (systematic liquidation of principal and interest) for the life of one or more persons.

Interest option – Here, the interest rate payable by the insurer is guaranteed and may be increased by payments of "excess" interest (also called a "dividend," "extra interest" or "surplus interest") to keep the insurer competitive with alternative investments.

Payment intervals such as annually, semiannually, quarterly, or monthly, are agreed upon by the insurer and beneficiary (unless pre-selected by the policyowner). The payee can be given the right to change to another settlement option and can have either a limited or unlimited right to take all or any portion of the principal. In some cases, the income beneficiary may be given no right to make a withdrawal of capital in which case it will pass to the payee's estate or to a third party depending on the terms of the agreement. The principal may be paid, at the option of the beneficiary, to someone other than the interest recipient. A successor-payee should always be named to receive any amount remaining payable at the primary payee's death.

Planners utilize this option as a temporary investment repository to give the beneficiary time to make a rational and studied decision as to how the proceeds should be invested. It is also convenient if the beneficiary does not currently need income under one of the other options but is planning to utilize one of them at a later date.

Fixed-period of years installments – Payments under this option are paid in equal amounts over a specified period selected by the beneficiary. If the primary payee does not survive to the end of the payment period, the balance of payments will be made to the contingent payee. The contract contains a table that shows the amount of the individual payments (usually per $1,000 of death benefits) that can be made over various periods of time ranging from one to 30 years. Extra interest will increase the amount of income paid (rather than extending the period). This option is indicated where the beneficiary needs the largest possible guaranteed income over a relatively short and fixed period of time.

Fixed-amount option – Payments under this fixed-amount option are paid to the beneficiary (and to the beneficiary's successor-payee after the original beneficiary's death) for as long as the proceeds (compounded at guaranteed interest) last. If the insurer pays excess interest, the period over which payments will be made increase accordingly (but the amount of each payment remains the same). Planners use this easy-to-explain option to augment Social Security benefits and other income.

Unpaid installments under either the fixed-years or fixed-amount option can generally be commuted (i.e., the present value of the future stream of income can be taken in an immediately payable lump sum) or applied under another option.

Life income option – Payments under this option are made over the lifetime of the beneficiary. The insurer uses the proceeds to "purchase" (no commissions or other acquisition costs are charged) a single premium life annuity for the designated payee. That annuity then pays out to the named payee an income of a guaranteed amount for the payee's lifetime. A "period certain" guarantee – a guarantee that payments will continue for a selected period of years, regardless of whether the payee is alive or dead – can be chosen. Ten-, fifteen-, and twenty-year period certains are common.

There are four basic forms that the life income option can take:

1. *Straight life (annuity) income* – Payments will last for as long as the payee lives and stop at the payee's death. This provides the highest annual income of the four forms of life income because it stops when the payee dies.

2. *Life income with period certain* – The insurer makes payments for a period selected by the beneficiary. Payments will be continued to a contingent payee for the balance of the period if the primary payee dies before the period ends.[83]

3. *Life refund annuity* – Payments are made to the payee (and or contingent payee) until an amount at least equal to the proceeds paid at the insured's death has been paid out.

4. *Joint and survivor annuity* – Payments are made to two individuals as long as both are alive and then continue for the life of the survivor. Payments of a smaller amount can be selected to continue at the same level for both lives or payments of a larger amount can be paid until the first of the two payees dies and then the amount of each payment will be reduced.

Planners should consider settlement options where the amount of insurance is relatively small and the cost of establishing a trust is relatively high. Some consider a settlement option the "poor man's trust." These optional modes of settlement do have a number of advantages including:

1. no separate charge is made by the insurer;

2. no other commercial institution can pay a life income; and

3. both principal and a minimum rate of interest are guaranteed.

But planners should also consider the following downside costs and disadvantages:

1. higher earnings may be possible from alternative investments;

2. a trust may prove more flexible; and

3. a trust may be more responsive to the beneficiaries' needs and circumstances.

Figure 5.1 compares settlement options to trusts.

POLICY LOANS

The ability to use the contract as a source of emergency or opportunity cash is one of the most valuable attributes of permanent life insurance. A policy loan provision can be found in almost every cash value policy.[84] As property, the policy can also serve as collateral for a loan from a bank or other lender but more often the insurer will provide the cash under the more favorable terms of the policy's loan provisions.[85]

When a policyowner borrows money directly from the insurer what is actually occurring is something other than a "loan" in common parlance. The difference is this: In a true loan the borrower must agree to repay the money. A policy loan does not require repayment. It is more like an advance of the money the insurer will eventually pay out under the contract.[86] The policyholder is receiving an advance – of his own money.

Even though federal tax law treats a policy loan as a classic loan, it is not. There is never a "debt" or a debtor-creditor relationship. During the insured's lifetime, the insurer is always 100% secured against loss because the amount that can be borrowed can never exceed the amount the insurer would have to pay the policyholder if he chose to surrender the policy. In fact, during lifetime, the "loan" can never exceed that amount (less the interest payable on it). Furthermore, the loan value, plus interest, can be deducted by the insurer from the proceeds otherwise payable if the "loan" has not been repaid before the death of the insured.

Once the insurer advances money to the policyowner, that person or entity can use the money for any purpose. Nor is the permission of a revocable beneficiary required since that party has a mere expectancy in the net (face amount less indebtedness) proceeds. Even an irrevocable beneficiary has no right to demand consent to a

Figure 5.1

	SETTLEMENT OPTIONS	TRUSTS
A COMPARISON OF SETTLEMENT OPTIONS TO TRUSTS		
Discretion	Must be administered strictly in accordance with policy provisions and terms of the settlement agreement.	Trustee can exercise considerable discretion if the grantor directs the trustee to do so.
Flexibility	Although some flexibility can be provided, variations must be specified in advance.	Generally, trusts are more flexible than settlement agreements; amounts payable to the beneficiary can be changed frequently.
Guarantees	Safety of proceeds is guaranteed; minimum rate of interest is guaranteed; a share of any excess interest earned by the insurer is guaranteed.	No guarantees whatsoever are offered, either as to principal or income.
Return on Investments	Investment possibilities open to an insurer are, by law, limited and conservative.	The prospects for gain (and loss) may be enhanced if a grantor chooses to free the trustee from investment restrictions typically imposed on trusts.
Life Income	Proceeds under a life income option can be guaranteed when left with the insurer.	Income for life can be specified but neither the amount nor the duration can be guaranteed.
Expense	Available from insurers at no additional cost.	A corporate trustee charges a fee to administer a trust.
Counseling	Insurers will not function as personal counselors.	A trustee can act as personal counselor to the trust beneficiary.
Title	The insurer and the payee have a debtor-creditor relationship.	A trustee has legal title to the proceeds, and a trust beneficiary has equitable title.
Segregation of Funds	Insurance proceeds retained by a life insurer are commingled for investment purposes with the insurer's other funds.	The property of an individual trust is generally kept separate from the property of other trusts.

policy loan – if the policy states clearly that such consent is not required.[87] Once the policyowner makes an "absolute assignment" (i.e., a total and irrevocable transfer of all interests in the policy) to a third party beneficiary, even if the former policyowner is the insured, he may take no further loans from the policy.[88]

The amount of the loan is limited essentially to the policy's cash value (less a "holdback" for interest). Technically, the policy might state something to the effect of:

The loan value is the amount which, with interest at a daily loan interest rate of ___ %,[89] will equal the policy's cash value.[90] Interest on the loan will be payable on each policy anniversary but if not paid when due it will be added to the loan.

Every year the amount that can be advanced to the policyowner increases as the cash value grows. But if the point is reached where the total of principal and accumulated unpaid interest equals or exceeds the policy's cash surrender value, the policy will (after a one month's notice) terminate and all benefits are canceled.[91]

Why does the insurer charge interest on an "advance" of money that will someday be paid to the policyowner? Because the insurer's statement of what policy values will be year after year is based on the assumption that the insurer will have a "reserve" (i.e., an amount in excess of that needed to pay for the current year's costs) to invest so that future contractual promises can be kept. If premiums unused for costs in early years are not on hand, the insurer cannot invest that money and pay the amounts promised in the future. The charge made to policyowners who accept these advances puts the insurer back where it would have been had it been able to invest the money. (In fact the interest rate may be somewhat higher than the amount assumed by the insurer in calculating policy loan values because the insurer needs to pay for administrative costs in making, keeping track of, and repaying these "loans" and, to some extent, to create a disincentive to "borrowing".)

Repayment of a policy loan is allowed at any time while the insured is alive (subject to a minimum payment for administrative aggravation and cost purposes). Once the insured has died (or the policy has been placed on extended term status), typically the insurer will not accept repayment of a loan.[92] If the advance is not repaid, either the cash value of the policy available to the policyowner or the death proceeds paid to beneficiaries will be reduced.

AUTOMATIC PREMIUM LOAN (APL) PROVISION

"Premium loans are advances of policy cash values that the insurer makes to the policyowner for the purpose of paying the premium. Automatic premium loans are advances the insurer makes under a policy clause providing that, if the policyowner fails to pay a premium by the end of the grace period, the insurer will automatically advance the amount of the premium if the policy has a sufficient net cash value."[93] Usually, the policyowner is notified of this action by the insurer.

If the loan value of the policy is insufficient to pay an annual premium, the insurer will typically pay a semiannual, quarterly, or monthly premium[94] although it is not required to do so.[95] When the loan value is so small that even a monthly premium cannot be paid, nonforfeiture benefit options will apply.

In most states, the payment of premiums by APL has the same result as paying premiums with cash, so the death benefit continues (decreased by the policy loan) and cash values continue to increase. Most states do not require an insurer to notify a policyowner that there is insufficient cash value to make a policy loan through APL or to tell a policyowner how long the loan will keep the policy in force.

A device that pays premiums at the end of a grace period by automatic loan from policy values is an incredibly valuable safety device to keep insurance protection in full force.[96] But the automatic premium loan is effective to prevent a policy lapse only if it is requested by the policy-applicant (or at some later date by the policyowner at a time when no premium is unpaid beyond the policy's grace period). The authors suggest that this provision is extremely valuable and should be considered in every case – especially since it may be canceled at any time.

There is a downside to the automatic premium loan when abused; "the automatic premium loan provision makes it too easy for the insured to avoid the payment of premium in cash."[97] Furthermore, to the extent interest is still deductible, it is not deductible in the case of an automatic premium loan since the interest is borrowed from the insurer rather than paid by the policyowner in cash.[98] A third potential disadvantage is that the contract may last longer if placed on extended term rather than allowing the policy to exhaust itself through automatic premium payments. But planners should keep in mind what this provision is really intended to do: prevent an accidental lapse.

ASSIGNMENTS OF A LIFE INSURANCE POLICY

As property,[99] the life insurance contract can be transferred to another person or entity. The policyowner can transfer either all or only some of the "bundle of rights" that comprises a life insurance policy to almost any person or entity.[100]

The two basic ways of making a lifetime transfer[101] of a policy are (1) the "absolute" assignment, and (2) the collateral assignment. An absolute assignment, as its name implies, transfers all the policyowner's rights irrevocably. A collateral assignment, again as its name implies, assigns so much of the death benefit as necessary for as long as necessary to secure a lender's rights. But no more of the proceeds will go to the lender than the amount of debt owed.

The assignment does not have to be of any particular form (absent specific provision in state law or the contract to the contrary). Since life insurance is treated as "personal" property, ownership rights may be transferred not only by many different types of documents[102] but also by many different actions. For example, if a business is sold and the business owns a life insurance policy, the sale of all the assets of the business carries with it the personal property the business owned – including the life insurance. Likewise, a property settlement in connection with a divorce may have the effect of transferring the ownership of life insurance on the life of one or the other (or both) spouse(s) even though the word "assignment" has not been used. But this type of transfer (where a clause in the divorce decree disposes of life insurance) is both very dangerous and very awkward. If a policyowner names his new spouse as beneficiary of the insurance proceeds and the insurer has no notice or knowledge of the divorce decree's change, both spouses are likely to claim the proceeds.[103] Furthermore, if the decree requires the policyowner spouse to maintain the policy for the benefit of his or her ex-spouse, the policyowner cannot obtain a policy loan – even to keep the policy in force through a premium loan.

But before either the absolute or collateral type of assignment or any other instance of a policy ownership transfer is valid, the insurer must be notified by the policyowner (and where required by the terms of the contract must consent to the assignment). Once notified in writing at the insurer's home office, the insurer must honor the policyowner's transfer – unless the terms of the contract itself forbid assignments. So if the insurer then disregards (by intention or neglect) the assignee's rights and makes payment to someone else, the courts may force the insurer to make a second payment to the assignee. If no notice is given to the insurer, it will be protected in a transaction initiated by a former owner. For instance, if the former owner applies for a policy loan and the insurer has not been given notice that the policy has been assigned, the insurer is protected in making that loan.[104]

The insurer does not, however, have to verify the bona fides of the transaction between the policyowner and the transferee nor the validity of the transaction. In other words, the insurer is not accountable for the mental or legal capacity of the policyowner to make the assignment (unless it had knowledge that the policyowner was not legally competent to make it or there were irregularities in the assignment form).

Reasons for an absolute assignment – An absolute assignment is used in life insurance planning when the policyowner wants to sell or give away all of his or her rights under the contract. The goal might be to obtain valuable consideration, to save estate taxes, avoid creditors, or may be made purely for love and affection and to assure the transferee of financial security. There are many common examples of sales and gifts:

- A client might sell a policy on his life to his business.

- A business might sell a policy on an employee's life to the employee or to the employee's spouse or child or trust (or to a pension plan).

- A shareholder might sell a policy on his life to a new business associate.

- A client might give a policy on her life to her spouse.

- A client might give a policy on his life to his children or to a family trust.

Both sales and gift transactions have important and sometimes unexpectedly expensive tax implications.[105]

Non-tax implications of an absolute assignment – Planners must be aware of the non-tax implications of an absolute assignment in order to avoid them and/or alert the client to their potential effect. Some of these are:

- Although an absolute assignment itself may not per se change the interest of a revocable beneficiary, as a practical matter the new owner can immediately change the beneficiary and often makes that change almost simultaneously with the assignment. Some absolute assignment forms state that the new owner is automatically the primary policy beneficiary until a further change is made.[106]

- If the beneficiary before an absolute assignment was named irrevocably, in most states the assignment will not defeat that designation (without the written consent of the beneficiary) and the transferee should be apprised of this fact.

- Absolute assignments may put the policy and its proceeds beyond the claims of the policyowner's creditors – but the policyowner should be informed that – like diamonds – an absolute assignment is forever. There is a loss of both control and flexibility from the transferor's viewpoint.

Reasons for a collateral assignment – A collateral assignment ("as the creditor's interest may appear") form of transfer is used almost exclusively as a secondary source of payment when a policy is pledged on a temporary basis as collateral for a loan.[107] The term "collateral" implies that the policyowner-debtor is primarily liable for the loan and only if he or she defaults will the policy be called upon to back up that obligation. The cash values in the policy serve as protection to the lender as long as the insured lives and the death benefit protects the lender if the insured dies. Once the loan is repaid, all rights in the policy automatically revert to the policyowner.

What is – and what is not – transferred – Policy rights transferred when the collateral assignment form of transfer is used generally include the right to:

1. receive the death benefit (but the excess over the debt unpaid at the insured's death must be transferred to the beneficiary specified by the policyowner);[108]

2. cash in the policy in the event the policyowner defaults on a loan or fails to pay premiums[109] (but the lender must give reasonable notice and the excess over the debt unpaid at that time must be transferred to the policyowner);

3. exercise nonforfeiture options; and

4. receive policy dividends.

The major right retained by the policyowner is the right to change the beneficiary.

After the debt is repaid, the transferee must reassign all policy rights back to the policyowner. Again, the insurer must be informed in writing at its home office before it will allow the policyowner to exercise all policy rights.

WAIVER

"Waiver," the intentional and voluntary surrender of a "known right,"[110] is an act which the insurer may (or may not) have committed in many situations.[111] A waiver occurs if the insurer knew it had the right to do or demand some action but acted with the deliberate intention of giving up that right.[112] For example, an insurer who gives a policyowner extra time after the grace period has expired to pay premiums and agrees to keep the policy in force during that time may have waived its right to deny a claim in that time period for nonpayment of premiums.

Planners should be conscious of potential waiver (and estoppel) situations in the following situations:

- the taking and submission of the application (e.g., the agent or medical examiner writes false answers on the application or the insurer fails to follow up on an incomplete answer);

- the premium payment process (e.g., the insurer routinely lets the policyowner "slide" with respect to the prompt payment of premiums or customarily accepts an overdue premium or accepts a late payment after it has knowledge that the insured has died or fails to send premium notices as required by state law),

- the submission of claims under a life insurance contract (e.g., the insurer does not promptly send proof of loss forms upon request by the beneficiary or fails to notify a beneficiary that it intends to dispute a claim or the insurer receives what it feels is a defective proof of loss but does not request additional documentation or the insurer promises to pay a claim it has grounds to resist).

Three types of rights cannot be waived or otherwise abrogated or contracted away by the insurer.[113] These include:

1. Rights designed to protect not only a party to the contract but also the public. An example would be the right of an insurer to demand that

an applicant have an insurable interest in the life of the insured. Other examples would include the right of the policyowner to be notified of premiums due or the right to take policy values under nonforfeiture options. "The public policy involved overrides the freedom of contract of the parties."[114]

2. Rights that would create coverage where none previously existed. Waivers cannot create "risk" (legal exposure) if that risk was not already encompassed in the contract nor can coverage be established by waiver where the contract specifically excluded it. In short, the doctrine of waiver cannot be invoked to create liability for benefits that were never contracted for.[115] For instance, if the contract provided benefits for ten years from the date of issue, the insurer's acceptance of a premium beyond the tenth year would not create a right in the policyowner to continue coverage into the 11th year. The insurer would have the right to refund any premium for coverage beyond the 10th year even if the insured died while the insurer held the excess premium and could not waive the expiration of insurance.

3. Rights to receive a sum of money cannot be waived. An agent, for example, cannot waive the insurer's right to receive premiums. A person can, of course, sign a "release" to an insurer stating that the claim of legal liability is satisfied. But a release can only be given in return for consideration. For instance, when a beneficiary signs the check for the policy death proceeds, he or she is acknowledging that the insurer is released from its obligation in return for that money.

Waivers are made by people. In the case of an insurer those people are its authorized "agents" (used here in a broader sense than sales force). So the term "authorized agent" may encompass sales personnel, officers, medical examiners, underwriters, and "others whose actions affect the insurer's contractual relationships."[116] In many cases, the central issue is whether the party making the waiver was in fact "authorized" by the insurer to do so. If the agent has no power to make a waiver, it will be ineffective assuming the applicant-policyowner knows (or has reasonable notice that) the agent lacks such authority. Notice to the applicant-policyowner of limitations of an agent's authority is usually spelled out in both the application and the life insurance contract itself in a "nonwaiver clause" similar to the one that follows:

No agent is authorized to make or modify contracts, to waive any of the Company's rights or requirements, or to bind the Company by making or receiving any promise, representation, or information, unless it is (1) in writing, (2) submitted to the Company, and (3) made part of the contract.[117]

Quite often, the contract will contain a further statement to the effect that:

Only the President of the Company, our Executive Vice President, or our Secretary has the authority to waive or modify any policy provision. Such waiver must be made in writing. No agent or any other person has the authority to change or waive any provision of this policy.

Since the statement appears in the contract and many states hold the applicant-policyowner responsible for reading the contract, he or she will be bound by a limitation-of-right-to-make-a-waiver clause appearing in both the application and policy. This, of course, does not typically bind a beneficiary (who has no reasonable notice of the existence or contents of the nonwaiver clause) to conditions that must be met after a loss occurs. Therefore, an agent of the insurer could waive such policy provisions as those regarding notice to the insurer or the documents required for proof of the insured's death regardless of the nonwaiver clause.

There are three types of waivers that occur in life insurance situations: (1) express waivers, (2) implied waivers, and (3) waivers by silence.

Express waivers – The surrender of a legal right expressly declared by written or oral words of an agent empowered to act for the insurance company are called express waivers. An insurer might deliberately waive a right, despite a breach of condition by the policyowner or beneficiary, in order to "keep the business on the books" or to maintain or obtain good public relations.

Implied waivers – Here, the conduct of the waiving party clearly infers the intention to forego a legal right – even though that surrender is not stated in writing or even orally. For instance, if an insurer time after time accepted premiums tendered by the policyowner well after the grace period expires, a court is likely to conclude that by its repeated inaction (not lapsing the policy) and pattern of actions (acceptance of the premiums beyond the grace period), the insurer, with full knowledge of its rights to lapse the policy, knowingly and voluntarily failed to assert that right. So if the insured died after the grace period but within the time the insurer had customarily accepted late premiums, the insurer would be liable to pay the death benefit.[118] It had waived its right to deny the claim.

Waivers by silence – Where an insurer has the legal duty to speak but fails to do so, the rights of the policyowner or beneficiary that would be lost by the inaction are instead protected.[119] Waiver by silence could occur, for instance, where the insurer gains knowledge of some material misrepresentation but deliberately (or negligently) withholds its knowledge more than a reasonable period of time and the insured dies within the contestable period. Most courts would hold the insurer waived its rights by lulling the policyowner or beneficiary into a false sense of security when it should have taken action in sufficient time for the policyowner to redress the situation with the insurer or obtain alternative coverage elsewhere.

Once a waiver has been made, it cannot then be retroactively revoked. For instance, assume a policyowner breached a condition of the contract (such as payment of premiums) but the insurer notified the policyowner that it would allow the contract to continue for a specified period of time (say one month) after the grace period in spite of the breach. If the insured died during the extra allotted time, the insurer would be liable. It could not revoke its waiver. But if the insurer notified the policyowner within a reasonable time that with respect to future nonpayments, the grace period limitation on coverage would be strictly enforced, the former waiver would not protect the policyowner in the future.

ESTOPPEL

"Estoppel" is a legal way of arriving at a fair and just result when one party (typically the insurer) has through words or conduct either directly or through its agent mislead the policyowner or beneficiary into an action or inaction that results in that party's loss. The key elements of estoppel are therefore that the policyholder or beneficiary suffers a detriment by acting to his prejudice in reliance upon a belief engendered by the insurer through its agent's words or actions.[120] Words and actions of the insurer must have lead the policyowner to act (or not act) so that the policyowner was harmed, the policyowner must not know the true facts, and because of a good faith belief in the insurer's (or insurer's agent's) words or actions acted (or failed to act).

For instance, if an insurance agent (the insurer's agent) tells an applicant that:

"You can ignore that one time you fainted. The insurance company is only concerned with a long history of fainting or blackouts."

If the insurer denies the death claim on the grounds that the fainting was not admitted by the applicant, the policy beneficiary can ask the court to estop the insurer from using misrepresentations as grounds for denial. Even though there was in fact misrepresentation, the insurer, through its agent's statement that one blackout does not count induced the applicant into taking action based on that misstatement and is therefore estopped (forbidden) from using the misstatement to deny liability (even if it can be proven that there was in fact a material misrepresentation).

There has been (and continues to be) confusion between the concepts of waiver and estoppel with some courts separating and distinguishing between the two while others treat them as essentially synonymous (and others seem to blend the two). What is important to the planner is (in the opinion of the authors) this: The law will generally try by whatever means necessary and available to balance the interests of the parties and the public. It will insist on a meeting of the responsibilities of the relationships between them by using one or the other doctrine to prevent the insurer from taking an unfair advantage of the policyowner and his or her beneficiaries (and vice versa).[121]

CHAPTER ENDNOTES

1. The following two texts will prove invaluable in reviewing the essential elements of contract law and researching the non-tax oriented legal aspects of life insurance: M. Crawford, *Law and the Life Insurance Contract*, 7th ed. (Burr Ridge, IL: Irwin Professional Publishing, 1994); B. Anderson, *Anderson on Life Insurance* (Boston, MA: Little, Brown and Company, 1991).

2. Although technically, a beneficiary is not a "party" to the contract, if a contract is for the direct benefit of a third person who is not a party to the contract, that person can sue for damages incurred as the result of a breach of contract. For this reason, the authors have included the beneficiary among the parties to the contract.

3. It is the insurability of the insured that is the linchpin of the agreement between the insurer and the policyowner. It is the termination of the insured's life that marks the liability of the insurer to pay the "face amount" of the policy at death, and it is the insured's life that determines the date of the policy's lifetime maturity. Although the insured may not be viewed by some authorities as a party to the contract, it is the authors' opinion that this position is less than complete. Without the insured's consent to the issuance of the policy, there is no legally binding contract.

4. State law may bar a legally adjudicated insane or mentally infirm person from being an insured. Generally, other legal incompetents such as minors are not prohibited from being an insured.

5. Life insurance contracts between "enemy aliens" or citizens of a country at war with the United States will be void. A corporation's capacity to purchase a life insurance contract depends on the provisions in its charter, by-laws, and the laws of the state where it is domiciled. A corporation can purchase a life insurance policy even if that power is not expressly granted in its charter or the state laws under which it was created if that action is necessary to exercise its express powers. Most corporations and other business entities can therefore purchase life insurance. However, the corporation's board of directors should formally endorse such an action and document its approval in the corporation's minutes.

6. Many states allow a minor 15 years old or over to purchase a life insurance contract on his or her own life but upon reaching the age of majority, he or she can void the contract. The insurer is bound by a life insurance contract made with a minor unless and until it is disaffirmed by the minor. That disaffirmation (voiding of the contract) can generally be made at any time while the child is a minor under state law or within a reasonable amount of time after reaching legal majority. If the policy is voided, the former minor is entitled to a return of whatever premiums he or she has paid but must return any dividends or other money received from the policy.

   Note that many of these statutes allow the minor to make benefits payable only to close family members such as parents or siblings or the minor's estate. Some, but not all states, limit the insured to the minor himself. Others allow the minor to insure the life of a child or spouse.

7. *Black's Law Dictionary*, 5th ed. (West Publishing Company 1979), p. 720.

8. See Anderson, note 1 above, p. 360.

9. See, e.g., *Continental Cas. Co. v. Brightman*, 437 F.2d 67 (10 Cir. 1971). A few states do require that a party cannot be named as beneficiary unless that party has an insurable interest in the life of the insured.

10. If, as part of a scheme to avoid the insurable interest rule and pursuant to a plan with a third party, the insured-applicant purchases a policy on his own life and then transfers the policy to that third party (who never had an insurable interest), the court will probably declare the policy void. See *Lakin v. Postal Life & Cas. Ins. Co.*, 316 S.W.2d 542 (Mo. 1958). See also, 17 *Couch on Insurance* 63A:23 (Lawyers Co-Operative Publishing Co. 1983).

11. Beware, however, the transfer for value rule discussed in Appendix G.

12. See, e.g., *Mutual Life Ins. Co. v. Allen*, 138 Mass. 24 (1884).

13. In an era where many couples live together without the benefit of marriage, it would seem that an applicant-beneficiary co-habiting with the insured could claim to be a dependent and as such show an insurable interest. But see the (in the authors' opinion relatively ancient) case of *Mikesell v. Mikesell*, 40 Pa. Super. 392 (1909).

14. The opposite is also true; if the applicant has no valid relationship with the insured other than merely as a business associate, this relationship will not per se be sufficient to generate an insurable interest. The courts (and the insurer) are likely to ask:

    (a) Did the insured contribute capital or make some other financial contribution to the business that would be lost or jeopardized at his or her death?

    (b) Does the insured have any particular skill, technical knowledge, or ability as a worker or manager that would be lost by the enterprise at his or her death?

    (c) Is there anything special (such as experience or business contacts) that the insured brings to the firm that would die when he or she dies?

15. See, e.g., *Nuuanu Mem. Park v. Briggs*, 434 P.2d 750 (Haw. 1967).

16. See, e.g., *Equitable Life Ins. Co. v. Hazlewood*, 12 S.W. 621 (Tex. 1889), where no more would be collected by the creditor than would be necessary to discharge the debt.

17. Almost all states adhere to this principle including Texas which up until 1981 required the beneficiary to have an insurable interest when the proceeds were payable. See Tex. Rev. Civ. Stat. Ann. art.3.49-1 (Vernon 1981). See also, "Insurable Interest in Life," 18 *Col. L. Rev.* 381, 394 (1921).

18. See, e.g., *Secor v. Pioneer Foundry Co.*, 173 N.W.2d 780 (Mich. 1969).

19. See, e.g., *Metropolitan Life Ins. Co. v. Manahon*, 42 S.W. 924 (Ky. 1897).

20. See, e.g., *Ramey v. Carolina Life Ins. Co.*, 135 S.E.2d 362 (S.C. 1964).

21. For instance, say a relative other than a parent insured the life of a niece or nephew and then murdered the child. If it can be shown that the applicant-policyowner-beneficiary never obtained the consent of the child's parent, a court is likely to hold that the insurer failed to exercise due care. In this instance, such negligence could easily result in contributing to the insured's murder. See *Liberty National Life Ins. Co. v. Weldon*, 100 So.2d 696 (Ala. 1957).

22. This is why constraints are imposed on the form and content of a contract. More and more states are insisting that – to the degree possible – a life insurance contract be written in language that is simple and understandable by the typical client. There is a "Life and Health Insurance Policy Language Simplification Model Act" adopted by the National Association of Insurance Commissioners (NAIC) in 1977. This act forbids fine print, encourages short sentences, requires an index or table of contents for most contracts, and suggests a physical format that lends itself to a balanced emphasis throughout the policy.

    If a provision required by law is omitted from the contract, it will be construed as though the clause were included. The "adhesion" concept is also why statutes require certain provisions while forbidding others.

23. Two such theories are the "doctrine of reasonable expectation" and the "doctrine of constructive ambiguity." The first of these suggests an open disregard of policy language, i.e., that the courts should honor the objectively reasonable expectations of applicants and beneficiaries regarding policy terms even though a careful study of the policy terms or language might negate those expectations. See R. Keeton, *Insurance Law – Basic Text* (West Publishing Company 1971), p. 351. See also *Keene Corp. v. Ins. Co. of North America*, 667 F.2d 1034 (D.C. Cir. 1981), *cert. denied*, 455 U.S. 1007 (1982). The latter doctrine holds that ambiguities in contract language should be resolved against the party who drafted the contract. See Keeton, above. Others describe constructive ambiguity as courts disregarding clear policy language and finding ambiguity where none reasonably exists in order to come to the "right" result. See Anderson, note 1 above, at p. 187.

    As Anderson in the text cited above properly points out, "The function of the insurer is to distribute the risk and in fairness to individual policy holders to fix a premium rate commensurate with its estimate of the risk. This is difficult enough when a court indulges in what other courts refer to as 'constructive ambiguity,' meaning ambiguity is found where none reasonably exists, but when a court in the absence of legislative authority completely disregards clear policy language, the insurer's task is almost impossible."

24. Many states pattern their statutes on these required provisions on the New York standard policy provision law. Most provide that the actual wording in the policy does not have to be exactly the same as long as it conveys the same substance. In most cases, these laws allow the insurer to insert more favorable terms (from the consumer's viewpoint). There is usually an exemption allowing omission of the "required provisions" if they would be inappropriate for the type of policy in question. For instance, no dividend statement would be necessary in a nonparticipating contract.

25. Thus, the policyowner must be provided with a copy of the application that both eliminates uncertainties as to what is contained on it and also assures the policyowner that the policy in his or her hands contains every relevant document. The insured and/or policyowner is given a chance to be sure that his or her responses to the agent's (and/or medical examiner's) questions were properly recorded and request changes if they were not.

However, the entire contract provision works both ways. The policyowner cannot claim ignorance of the statements made in the application. This serves as notification of all the terms and conditions and imposes a responsibility on the insured (and/or policyowner) to read and, if appropriate, to apprise the insurer of errors.

As a practical matter, then, the insurance agent should review the copy of the application attached to the policy with the client and the terms of the policy when it is delivered. Of course, the problems discussed above generally will not be of concern if the insured has survived the period after which the policy becomes incontestable by the insurer.

26. Under common usage, a lapse is what occurs after the policy has "run out of steam." Legalistically, however, a lapse is defined as "a default in premiums before a policy has a nonforfeiture value." L. Davids, *Dictionary of Insurance*, p. 173. According to this definition, a policy could lapse "except as to its nonforfeiture benefits" or lapse and then be cashed in for its surrender value. Then it would be said to "expire."

In certain situations during war when timely payment was impossible, or where some action or inaction by the insurer prevented timely payment, some courts have held that the insurer could not lapse the policy for lack of premium payments.

27. Many states require that the insurance company must notify the policyowner not more than 45 days or less than 15 days before the due date of the premium. That notice must specify the amount payable, when it is due (the "due date"), and where it is payable. Some of these statutes penalize the insurer who does not give timely notice by extending the life of the contract for some period of time (e.g., 6 months to a year) after the due date. But these laws (to prevent fraud on the part of the policyowner) allow the insurance company's mail department to testify that notice was mailed. Once that occurs, the burden often shifts to the policyowner to prove that it was not mailed. Even if this presumption is successfully rebutted, the policyowner must also have brought suit within the statutory limit after the due date.

28. Some insurers make what is known as a "late remittance offer." This gives the policyowner an additional period of time after the grace period expires during which a lapsed policy can be reinstated without the requirement that the insured prove insurability. The insured must, however, be alive on the date payment is tendered to the insurer. This late remittance offer does not extend the grace period.

29. Some statutes also allow the insurer to add interest on the unpaid and overdue premium but, for public relations purposes, many insurers will waive the interest charge even if they have the legal right to collect it.

30. Some companies substitute a one year period of time rather than the customary two year limit on contests. This is done for marketing and public relations reasons and obviously is a consideration that should be added to the checklist of a planner deciding upon which policy is best for a client.

31. Usually the contestable period runs from the "date of issue" which is typically the same as the policy date. But the policy date is not necessarily the date of issue. For instance, if an applicant wants to "backdate" the policy to "save age" (i.e., obtain a lower premium by paying a premium for which no insurance was in force in return for a continuing lower premium), the policy date could be as much as six months earlier than the actual issue date. The contestable period starts at the earlier policy date rather than the issue date in this case. (Most states limit dating back a policy to a six-month period starting at the date of the application.) Backdating is one way to provide incontestability to the policyowner and beneficiary at the earliest possible time.

32. The phrase "during the insured's lifetime" makes it clear that if the insured dies before the end of the contestable period, the policy never becomes incontestable since it was not in force for two years during the lifetime of the insured.

33. "Void" means no contract exists. "Void ab initio" means no contract ever existed. From the beginning, there was never any legally enforceable contract. A "voidable" contract is one which is legally enforceable and valid – unless and until a party who has the right to do so disaffirms (avoids) the obligations and benefits of the contract. A minor, for example, can upon reaching legal majority, void a contract. Lack of capacity, mutual mistake, and material misrepresentation can all make a contract voidable.

34. See the statement of Justice Holmes in *Northwestern Mutual Life Ins. Co. v. Johnson*, 254 U.S. 96, 101 (1920), that says, "The object of the clause is plain and laudable – to create an absolute assurance of the benefit, as free as may be from any dispute of fact except the fact of death . . ."

35. There are conflicts in various state courts as to the effect of adding to the incontestable clause an exclusion for certain items but not others. Some say that if the insurer specifies one or more items to be excluded, although those are exempted from the incontestable clause protection, any exclusion clause not mentioned is automatically meant to be ineffective after the incontestable period. (i.e., "the insurer could not contest its obligation to pay except for a reason plainly reserved in the wording of the incontestable clause itself." *Bernier v. Pacific Mutual Life Ins. Co.*, 139 So. 629 (La. 1932). But most courts now hold that an insurer is free to specify risks it is unwilling to assume throughout the life of the contract (even though – after two years – the validity of the contract itself has become incontestable). See, e.g., *Metropolitan Life Ins. Co. v. Conway*, 169 N.E. 642 (N.Y. 1930). So the incontestable clause in most jurisdictions is not "a mandate as to coverage." It implies only – within the limits of the coverage the contract intended – that after the contestable period has expired, the company cannot protest that the policy was invalid in its inception or became invalid because a condition of coverage was broken.

36. See, e.g., *Obartuch v. Security Mutual Life Ins. Co.*, 114 F.2d 873 (7th Cir. 1940), *cert. denied*, 312 U.S. 696 (1941).

37. See, e.g., *Aetna Life Ins. Co. v. Hooker*, 62 F.2d 805 (6th Cir. 1933), *cert. denied*, 289 U.S. 748 (1933).

38. *Henderson v. Life Ins. Co. of Va.*, 179 S.E. 680 (S.C. 1935).

39. A few states impose a one year limit. Some insurers for competitive and public relations purposes use only a one year period even though state law permits a two year period. Planners should consider this factor when deciding upon the appropriate policy for a client.

40. See, e.g., *John Hancock Mutual Life Ins. Co. v. Moore*, 34 Mich. 46 (1876); *Connecticut Mutual Life Ins. Co. v. Akens*, 150 U.S. 468 (1893).

41. Self destruction of the insured, even though deliberately done while sane, is one of the risks assumed by the insurer unless it is by express terms excepted. *Grand Lodge Independent Order of Mut. Aid v. Wieting*, 48 N.E. 59 (Ill. 1897).

42. See Crawford, note 1 above, at p. 430.

43. See, e.g., *New York Life Ins. Co. v. Noonan*, 215 F.2d 905 (9th Cir. 1954).

44. Many insurers are now calling this clause an "Incorrect Age or Sex" clause and adjusting the proceeds if sex is incorrectly shown in the same manner as if age had been incorrectly stated.

45. The presumption is that the age stated by the applicant-insured is correct. See, e.g., *Southern Ins. Co. v. Wilson*, 108 So. 5 (Ala. 1926).

46. This provision is not intended to shield fraud or collusion. The insurer can deny payment of the proceeds if it can prove the parties intended to cheat the insurer. See, e.g., *Lucas v. American Bankers' Ins. Co.*, 141 So. 394 (La. Ct. App. 1932).

47. If the error as to age is discovered by the insurer prior to the insured's death, either premiums or coverage can be adjusted. Usually, if the insured's age was higher than stated in the application, the insurer will allow the policyowner to pay the difference in premiums (with interest) and keep the original policy or it may issue a new policy with a lower death benefit with the original premium level. If the insured was younger than stated in the application, the insurer will almost always refund the excess premiums (often with interest).

48. When a stock company issues a contract which is "nonpar," the company usually fixes the premium at a lower amount than a mutual company issuing a similar "par" policy. This nonpar policy's lower premium, of course, is initially appealing from a consumer's viewpoint. However, the buyer has no hope of sharing in the financial success of the company (unless he or she also buys stock in the insurer). From the insurer's perspective, the marketing advantage gained by a lower premium is offset to some extent by lower-per-thousand of insurance investable revenue, the fact that premiums once set cannot be changed even if the company experiences financial difficulties, and the lack of any "cushion" in the premium to take up the slack in that event.

49. State law is also a factor in how much is paid and under what conditions. Most states specify what the term "participate" means in terms of legal rights. Almost always, state laws will specify how soon the policy will share in the insurer's surplus (typically not later than the end of the second or third policy year), how the dividend may be applied, and what the insurer must state in the contract about those rights.

50. This ownership exposes dividends and the interest they earn to the claims of the policyowner's creditors to the extent state law does not exempt or otherwise protect them.

51. This is the most frequently selected dividend choice for the automatic option. One reason is that an insured who is insurable only at a higher-than-standard rate or even one who has become uninsurable can purchase additional coverage at net (no commissions or other acquisition charges are added to the cost of this coverage) rates. Paid up additions may be cashed in separately from the underlying policy which adds to the policyowner's flexibility.

52. During the first year or two of a contract, the insurer's costs to put the contract in force and provide current coverage far exceed the amount paid in by the policyowner. So no benefit is required to be provided under state law until the policy has been in force for two (or, in some states, three) years.

53. If the beneficiary of the policy is revocable, no consent is needed for the policyowner to exercise any of the nonforfeiture provisions. If the beneficiary is irrevocable, consent of the irrevocable beneficiary is required to cash in the policy (unless the policy specifies consent is not required) but no consent is usually required to select extended term or reduced paid up insurance.

54. Actually, the amounts shown in the policy assume premiums are paid to the end of the year. Since surrenders rarely occur exactly on that date, the insurer will interpolate and calculate for the policyowner the exact amount due on any given date.

55. The rationale is that the right to exercise a nonforfeiture option is a continuing irrevocable offer made by the insurer to the policyowner. That offer becomes binding on both parties as soon as it is accepted by the policyowner.

56. Technically, once a policy develops a nonforfeiture value, if the policy lapses, it lapses "except as to the nonforfeiture benefits."

57. See *Trapp v. Metropolitan Life Ins. Co.*, 70 F.2d 976 (8th Cir. 1934). Although a few courts have held that reinstatement is actually the start of a new contract, most follow the rule in *Trapp*. The distinction is important for many reasons. For instance, the continuation theory bars an insurer from imposing new contractual restrictions or burdens on the policyowner at the time of reinstatement. This means the insurer cannot add an exclusion (e.g., for death while in military service) that was not in the original policy. See *Schiel v. New York Life Ins. Co.*, 178 F.2d 729 (9th Cir. 1949), *cert. denied*, 339 U.S. 931 (1950). So no new conditions or restrictions can be imposed at the time of or as a condition of reinstatement. See Smith, "What Conditions May an Insurer Impose Upon Reinstatement of a Life Policy?" *Legal Proceedings* (American Life Convention 1948), p. 130.

58. Crawford, note 1 above, at p. 358.

59. See, e.g., *Tatum v. Guardian Life Ins. Co.*, 75 F.2d 476 (2nd Cir. 1935).

60. Crawford, note 1 above, at p. 359.

61. For instance, some insurers provide for reinstatement in term insurance contracts even when there is no state law requirement that they do so. Likewise, although state law does not generally require insurers to allow reinstatement when extended term insurance runs out, quite often the insurer will not deny a policyowner's application.

62. In most states, the insurer may consider the same factors as if underwriting the contract for the first time when considering "insurability." These factors include not only the insured's physical, mental, and emotional health, but also his or her habits, finances, occupation, and avocations. See, e.g., *Volis v. Puritan Life Ins. Co.*, 548 F.2d 895 (10th Cir. 1977).

Of course, most courts will not allow an insurer to act arbitrarily and capriciously in determining if the proposed "re-insured" should be insured again according to its standards and will hold the insurer to a reasonable position based on industry practices. See, e.g., *Sunset Life Ins. Co. v. Crosby*, 380 P.2d 9 (Idaho 1963).

63. See, e.g., *Bowie v. Bankers Life*, 105 F.2d 806 (10th Cir. 1936).

64. See, e.g., *Gressler v. New York Life Ins. Co.*, 163 P.2d 324 (Utah 1945).

65. See, e.g., *Sellwood v. Equitable Life Ins. Co. of Iowa*, 42 N.W.2d 346 (Minn. 1950).

66. See, e.g., *Johnson v. Great Northern Life Ins. Co.*, 17 N.W.2d 337 (N.D. 1945).

67. Crawford, note 1 above, at p. 241. Crawford points out that there are two types of beneficiaries: "intended" and "incidental."

Intended beneficiaries are the only type with standing (i.e., a legal position that bestows the right) to sue the insurer to enforce their rights under the contract. As its name implies, an intended beneficiary is one who the parties to the contract expected would benefit from its performance. Such parties include those who were named without consideration (so called "donee beneficiaries") and those named in satisfaction of a debt (so called "creditor beneficiaries").

An incidental beneficiary is one who only incidentally benefits because of the existence of the insurance. For instance, if a policy were payable to the policyowner's estate, a creditor of the policyowner could satisfy that debt by informing the estate's executor. All or a portion of the proceeds might incidentally be used for payment. But an incidental beneficiary never acquires rights under the life insurance policy and so cannot sue the insurer. The policy was not taken out for that party's benefit. Crawford, note 1 above, at p. 245-46.

68. To name a new beneficiary, the policyowner must meet the terms of the policy. Commonly, it will require the policyowner to file a written request (usually on the insurer's form) with the insurer. The policy itself is not filed. A copy of the change is sent to the policyowner. Usually, that change becomes retroactively effective to the date the policyowner signed the insurer's change of beneficiary request form (but must first be recorded at the insurer's home office).

Under the doctrine of "substantial compliance," once the policyowner has done everything reasonably possible to comply with the insurer's procedure, the change will not fail if circumstances beyond the policyowner's control make it impossible to meet every condition. See, e.g., *Dooley v. James Dooley Assocs.*, 442 N.E.2d 222 (Ill. 1982).

On the other hand, anything less than substantial compliance will be inadequate to make an effective change in benefit. Mere intent without positive action is insufficient. The policyowner must have taken every reasonable step in his power to effect a change of beneficiary. This rule is to protect the interests of the prior beneficiary. See, e.g., *O'Connell v. Brady*, 72 A.2d 493 (Conn. 1950).

69. Neither the killer nor anyone claiming under or through the killer (such as an assignee) can benefit from the life insurance. See McGovern, "Homicide and Succession to Property," 64 *Mich. L. Rev.* 65, 78 (1969) and Statler, "The Wrongful Killing of the Insured by the Beneficiary," *XXII Proceedings* (Association of Life Insurance Counsel 1971), p. 521. Note that intent to kill must be present before the beneficiary will be denied the policy proceeds.

70. See, e.g., *New York Life Ins. Co. v. Henriksen*, 415 N.E.2d 146 (Ind. Ct. App. 1981).

71. See, e.g., *Northwestern Mutual Life Ins. Co. v. McCue*, 223 U.S. 234 (1912). National Service Life Insurance will not pay if death is inflicted as lawful punishment for crime or for military or naval offense (unless inflicted by an enemy of the U.S.). Only the cash value must be paid to the designated beneficiary. 38 U.S.C. 1911. This provision also applies to Servicemen's Group Life Insurance. 38 U.S.C. 1973.

72. To utilize the marital deduction at the first spouse's death, he or she must be survived by a U.S. citizen spouse.

What is the value of a life insurance policy where the owner and beneficiary was the spouse of the insured and both died in a common accident? Since the insured is deemed to have survived, the value the instant before the deaths (rather than the face amount) was held to be the proper figure. See *Estate of Wien v. Comm.*, 441 F.2d 32 (5th Cir. 1971); *Chown v. Comm.*, 428 F.2d 1395 (9th Cir. 1970); *Old Kent Bank and Trust Co. v. U.S.*, 430 F.2d 392 (6th Cir. 1970).

73. The burden of proof is on the party trying to prove the deaths were not simultaneous where the deaths occur in a common disaster.

74. See Appendix A.

75. The name is controlling even if the relationship no longer applies. See, e.g., *Outling v. Young*, 398 So. 2d 256 (Ala. 1981). Even if the description is not correct, where the insured's intention is clear, courts will carry out that desire. See, e.g., *Burkett v. Mott*, 733 P.2d 673 (Ariz. Ct. App. 1986).

76. There are both advantages and disadvantages to this designation. Obviously, if the policyowner changes marital status, a new wife would be benefited under a "to my wife" designation. This is probably the result desired. On the other hand, the ambiguity and therefore litigation potential is significantly enhanced. The best course of action is to properly name and describe each beneficiary, back up each beneficiary with a contingent beneficiary, and quickly change beneficiary designations when marital status changes.

77. Stepchildren are not generally included. Planners should suggest that clients specify which children are not to be included – especially if children from a prior marriage are to be excluded. See, e.g., *Pape v. Pape*, 119 N.E. 11 (Ind. Ct. App. 1918).

78. If the deceased child had left no children, the surviving two children would split the entire amount of the proceeds. It is best when making a per stirpes distribution to specify what is meant since different jurisdictions have varying interpretations of the per stirpes rule. For example, the insured might say something to the effect of:

"I leave the proceeds of this policy in equal shares to my children who survive me but if any predecease me and leave issue who survive me, that deceased child's share is to pass to his or her issue in equal shares, per stirpes."

79. Naming a guardian can cause problems because:

(a) it is not certain that the guardian will survive the insured and the insured's spouse,

(b) the court may not appoint the same individual as the policyowner selected, and

(c) the children may be legally competent by the time the insured dies. Crawford, note 1 above, p. 251

Some states, such as Pennsylvania, provide for what is sometimes called a "naked" or "informal" guardian. This is a perhaps misnamed but highly useful creature of statutory law that allows a policyowner to invoke that statute in the beneficiary designation without the trouble and expense of setting up a formal trust during lifetime by appointing a guardian in a life insurance policy. Pennsylvania's statute provides that a person may appoint a guardian of a minor or otherwise incompetent on the insurer's beneficiary form. Payment by an insurance company to the guardian discharges the insurer to the same extent as if it made payment to an otherwise duly appointed and qualified guardian. This type of procedure is a good compromise when the total proceeds do not warrant the creation of a formal trust.

80. When naming a trustee as policy beneficiary, it is good practice to name a backup beneficiary in case the trust is terminated (or for some reason never comes into existence or is for any reason found to be defective). Consider providing that if the trustee cannot accept the proceeds within a specified number of days (such as 90) after the insured's death, the insurer may make settlement to the insured's estate. This prevents an indefinite delay and benefits both insurer and beneficiaries. Usually, if a bank is trustee or co-trustee a provision should be inserted in the beneficiary designation exonerating the insurer from liability once it pays the proceeds to the trustee.

81. See, e.g., *United Benefit Life Ins. Co. v. Cody*, 286 F.Supp. 552 (W.D. Wash. 1968); *Cook v. Cook*, 111 P.2d 322 (Cal. 1941).

82. Settlement options are sometimes forbidden to assignees, trustees, and corporations who are restricted to lump sum cash payments (or are allowed to choose options only with the consent of the insurer). This is because some insurers do not wish to provide settlement options (which are expensive) for no charge to entities who are in the business of providing similar services at a charge to the consumer.

83. Planners should carefully compare this option with the interest option. Payees may actually be better off taking interest only. Female payees will not receive as much each year under this option as males because their life expectancies are so much longer. At older ages, the "straight life annuity" might have a significant payout advantage over an annuity with period certain.

84. Extended term does not have loan values so no loans are available from it but loans can be made from a policy placed on "reduced paid up" status. When there is a loan outstanding at the time a policy is placed on reduced paid up status (or extended term or cash surrendered), the amount available is reduced by the amount of that loan.

85. Mechanically, a policy loan is typically made through loan forms and insurers can but do not require the policyowner to send in a contract for a stamped endorsement (notice) stating that there is a loan against the contract. The policy loan agreement usually requires the policyowner to certify that the policy has not already been pledged as collateral for a loan.

86. See, e.g., *Board of Assessors v. New York Life Ins. Co.*, 216 U.S. 517 (1910). Typically, the beneficiary of a life insurance policy subject to a loan is entitled only to the net proceeds, i.e., the proceeds remaining after the loan is deducted from the amount otherwise payable. Compare this with the beneficiary of a policy pledged as collateral for a loan; such a beneficiary is generally entitled to have the loan paid from the assets of the estate and may be entitled to the full face amount of the policy. See, e.g., *Chaplin v. Merchants National Bank of Aurora*, 186 F.Supp. 273 (N.D. Ill. 1959).

87. See, e.g., *Mallon v. Prudential Ins. Co.*, 5 F.Supp. 290 (W.D. Mo. 1934).

88. See, e.g., *State Mutual Life Assur. Co. v. Webster*, 148 F.2d 315 (9th Cir. 1945).

89. Most companies now use a variable policy loan interest rate (such as Moody's Monthly Corporate Bond Yield Average) to prevent "disintermediation" (i.e., a strong flow of cash out of the insurer's hands when interest rates that can be earned outside the life insurance contract are far higher than the fixed interest rates charged by the insurer a policy loan). Variable loan rates presently

incorporated in newly-issued policies are not retroactive to older contracts. The older contracts may provide fixed rates as low as 5 percent. Planners should keep this potential advantage in mind in analyzing the value of older as compared to newer policies (but some insurers have lowered dividends payable on policies with 5 and 6 percent loan rates).

90. Interest is typically computed to the following premium date (or if the policy is paid up or single premium to the next policy anniversary). For this reason, the later in the year the loan is made, the more money can be advanced to the policyowner – because less interest need be charged.

91. See, e.g., *Keeley v. Mutual Life Ins. Co.*, 113 F.2d 633 (7th Cir. 1940); *Protective Life Ins. Co. v. Thomas*, 134 So. 488 (Ala. 1931); *Cory v. Mass. Mutual Life Ins. Co.*, 170 A. 494 (R.I. 1934).

92. Some insurers will waive this so that total proceeds can be distributed under a settlement option.

93. Crawford, note 1 above, at p. 325.

94. The terms of the automatic premium loan provision usually give the insurer the right to change the frequency of premium payments.

95. See, e.g., *First Nat'l Bank v. Lincoln Nat'l Life Ins. Co.*, 824 F.2d 277 (3rd Cir. 1987).

96. It is deemed so valuable that the insurer is allowed to continue using policy cash values to pay premiums even if the policyowner is declared legally bankrupt. 11 U.S.C. 542(d).

97. Anderson, note 1 above, at p. 296.

98. See Appendix F.

99. Personal property has been defined as any property which is not land or attached to land. The Supreme Court in *Grigsby v. Russell*, 222 U.S. 149, 156 (1911), held that life insurance is personal property. Writing for the Court, Justice Holmes said,

> [L]ife insurance has become in our days one of the best recognized forms of investment and selfcompelled saving. So far as reasonable safety permits, it is desirable to give to life policies the ordinary characteristics of property.... To deny the right to sell... is to diminish appreciably the value of the contract in the owner's hands.

100. Among the "sticks" in the bundle of rights are the right to obtain a policy loan, the right to withdraw or direct the application of dividends, and the right to surrender the policy for its cash value.

> The policyowner should be free to give away or sell his rights under a life insurance policy for his own advantage according to *Mutual Life Ins. Co. v. Allen*, 138 Mass. 24 (1884). (But that well-seasoned case assumed the insured and the policyholder would be the same and therefore ignored the potential for the "gaming element" in a sale). Even if the assignee has no insurable interest (defined above), the assignment will be valid in almost every state – unless it is shown that there was a lack of good faith and an intent to sidestep the insurable interest rule. See, e.g., *Butterworth v. Mississippi Valley Trust Co.*, 240 S.W.2d 676 (Mo. 1951). See also, note 10 above.

101. If the policyowner owns a policy on the life of another, at the policyowner's death prior to the death of the insured or the lifetime maturity of the contract, the policy (absent specific provision in the contract regarding successive ownership) will pass into the policyowner's estate and therefore be disposed of according to his or her will or, if there is no valid will, according to the intestate law (i.e., the statutory provisions that direct the disposition of assets of a decedent who dies without a valid will) of the state of domicile.

102. It is best and most convenient to use the insurer's forms where available.

103. If the insurer discovered the first spouse's claim prior to paying the proceeds, the insurer would pay the proceeds into a court in a process called "interpleader" in which the court would decide the proper payee. It is the process used when two or more parties claim property held by a third party who does not claim to own the property but cannot determine who the legal owner is. The court decides the identity of the proper owner. This is, of course, an expensive process.

104. Keep in mind that this presumes the policy is usually not required to be submitted in conjunction with a policy loan. See, e.g., *Elledge v. Aetna Life Ins. Co.*, 406 S.W.2d 374 (Ark. 1966).

105. Planners should thoroughly read Appendix G before allowing any sale of a life insurance policy. Appendix B should be considered before allowing a client to make a gift of a policy. A valid gift requires that the donor have contractual capacity and an intent to make a voluntary gratuitous transfer, and the gift must be delivered to and accepted by the donee (assignee).

106. Planners should beware of "unholy trinity" situations where the policy on the life of the insured is owned by a second party and made payable to a third party. This almost invariably leads to adverse income or gift tax results (and potentially a malpractice suit against the planners who failed to spot the issue).

107. The American Bankers Association Collateral Assignment Form No. 10 is the most commonly used collateral assignment form.

108. In order to avoid litigation, the collateral assignment form will typically require the signature of the policyowner's beneficiary. This puts the beneficiary on notice that there has been a collateral assignment and that he or she may not be receiving the entire death benefit. It also makes it more convenient for the lender to exercise any policy rights while the insured is still alive. Most importantly, because the beneficiary is consenting to the collateral assignment when he or she signs the form, he or she cannot later object if the proceeds must be used to pay off the loan.

109. A collateral assignment does not bind the transferee lender to pay life insurance premiums even if the policyowner defaults. If the lender does so, the amount of those premiums can be added to the total debt owed to the lender.

110. An insurer is typically presumed to know the rights it holds under the life insurance contract. However, if pertinent (i.e., material) facts are unknown or deliberately withheld from the insurer, the insurer's actions in ignorance of these facts will not constitute a waiver of its rights. So if a premium payment were accepted on a policy applied for on a "nonsmoking" basis, the insurer's right to deny a claim would not be forfeited if the insured was in fact a heavy and long term smoker. The insurer did not have knowledge of this material fact.

Harsh as it may sometimes seem, most courts hold that "an applicant is responsible for the truth of statements in an application he or she signs" – even if the agent (or medical examiner) knew of a misstatement and filled in an answer accidentally – or on purpose – falsely. In other words, the knowledge of the agent is not universally imputed to the insurer. Nor will knowledge of the agent be imputed to the client—even in those courts which do not hold the applicant responsible for reading the contract and the copy of the attached application – if the client colluded with the agent to defraud the insurer. See, e.g. *Aetna Life Ins. Co. v. Routon*, 179 S.W.2d 862 (Ark. 1944). Since the insurer has neither actual nor imputed knowledge, it cannot "knowingly" waive its rights to cancel the policy.

Most courts hold the insured responsible for reading the application – before signing it! That also binds the policyowner's beneficiaries. Obviously, this rule would not be applied if the agent lied on the application in order to make a sale and ripped out the copy before giving the policy to the policyowner. See, *Hart v. Prudential Ins. Co.*, 117 P.2d 930 (Cal. 1941).

111. Any party to the life insurance contract can waive a right or be estopped from asserting a right. For simplicity, the authors will explain these two terms using the insurer as the violator and the policyowner or beneficiary as the injured party even though in many cases the reverse is true.

112. Crawford, note 1 above, p. 116.

113. These forbidden waivers also apply to the doctrine of estoppel.

114. See, e.g., *Fayman v. Franklin Life Ins. Co.*, 386 S.W.2d 52, 58 (Mo. 1965).

115. See, e.g., *Pierce v. Homesteaders Life Ins. Assoc.*, 272 N.W. 543 (Iowa 1937).

116. Crawford, note 1 above, at p. 123.

117. Here the term "agent" is used in the more narrow sense of a soliciting agent only. Decisions as to whether to allow a waiver would be submitted in writing by the soliciting agent to the appropriate home office agent.

118. See, e.g., *Hoffman v. Aetna Life Ins. Co.*, 22 N.E.2d 88 (Ohio Ct. App. 1938).

119. Silence will not generally operate to change a legal relationship unless particular circumstances impose a duty to speak, i.e., when remaining silent would prove inequitable to the other party.

Anderson, note 1 above, at p. 413, states general rules which have evolved in this area:

(a) Mere nonaction is not enough to bar an insurer from declaring a policy is lapsed where the cause is nonpayment of premiums – unless the insurer had habitually kept the policy in force after the policyholder's default or unless the insurer failed to give adequate notice that premiums were due.

(b) The insurer must notify the insured within a reasonable time when it learns of a ground of forfeiture (other than nonpayment of premiums) or lose the right.

(c) Where the insured dies before the insurer learns of a ground for forfeiture, the insurer by its silence after the loss is not considered to have waived its rights since the policyowner or beneficiaries are not prejudiced by the insurer's silence.

120. Crawford, note 1 above, p. 116, states that estoppel (technically equitable estoppel) can only be raised as a defense if three elements are present:

(a) words or conduct of one party (typically the insurer) mislead the other party (usually the policyowner or beneficiary) into believing that facts which were untrue were true,

(b) the injured party had no knowledge of the true facts, and

(c) the party requesting that the other be "estopped" was reasonable in relying on the untrue words or conduct and was consequently injured.

121. But see Anderson, note 1 above, at p. 402, who disagrees with the opinion of the authors and states, "cases frequently arise in which the distinction between the two concepts is vital to the sound disposition of the cause [sic]."

Chapter 6

SPECIAL POLICY PROVISIONS AND RIDERS

INTRODUCTION

In addition to the many required legal provisions of a life insurance contract (as described in Chapter 5), many life insurance contracts include special provisions, permit special endorsements, and/or allow special riders to be attached to the basic contract. The purpose of these provisions and riders is often to enhance the flexibility and "fit" of the policy to the policyowner's needs. However, in some cases, they serve to restrict the policyowner's options and to limit the insurer's exposure. Also, some of the standard policy provisions, such as the dividend provision, the nonforfeiture provision, the policy loan provisions, and the settlement provisions, usually include default options that may be replaced with other options but only if requested by the policyowner. However, the options are not uniform among contracts; some companies offer a more restrictive list of choices than others or include other limiting features or provisions.

To select the policy or insurance "package" with the most favorable combination of features it is important not only to know the options, but also to know something about how options may differ among contracts.

Topics discussed in this chapter include:

1. term riders;

2. limitation riders;

3. cost-of-living riders;

4. accidental death benefit riders;

5. waiver of premium rider;

6. disability income rider;

7. additional purchase options (guaranteed insurability riders);

8. accelerated death benefit riders;

9. automatic premium loan provision;

10. policy loan interest rate;

11. dividend options;

12. bailout provisions;

13. change of plan provisions;

14. change of insured provisions;

15. additional insured riders;

16. common accident provision (survivorship clause); and

17. settlement options.

TERM RIDERS

The most common and familiar rider is the term insurance rider. Virtually any form of term insurance – increasing, decreasing, or level – may be added to a base permanent policy. The principal advantage to the insured of using a term rider is that no separate policy is issued with additional fees. In other words, the additional insurance is issued on a net cost basis, without some of the fees typical of new issues. Such riders are frequently used when there is a temporary need above the long-term base need or when the policyowner is unable to pay the premium for a permanent policy for the full amount of insurance needed but wishes to assure coverage.

Term riders normally provide that the rider may be changed to a separate policy or converted into a permanent form of coverage within a specified period or before a specified age without evidence of insurability. Companies differ with respect to the length of the period of coverage they will permit under the term rider. For instance, some companies limit both the coverage period and the conversion period to the insured's age 65 or younger; others will permit coverage and conversion to later ages, such as age 75 or older.

One of the critical elements to investigate is the current term rates charged by the company as well as the maximum guaranteed term rates. Some companies guarantee that current term rates will never increase. However, their current rates may be higher than those of companies who reserve the right to increase term rates, subject to a maximum, if their experience so dictates. Also, if future conversion is anticipated, check the conversion charges, which may vary widely among companies.

LIMITATION RIDERS

Certain riders or endorsements may be added to the base contract to limit the liability of the insurance company under the base policy. The most common forms of limitations are the war rider, the aviation rider, the hazardous occupation or avocation rider, and the limited-benefit-period rider.

War Rider

The war rider provides that insurance will not be paid in the event of death due to war or acts of war. As a result of the Korean and Vietnam "conflicts," this rider has generally been broadened to cover what are now described as military "police actions" as well.

Aviation Rider

The aviation rider excludes payment of death benefits in the event of death as a result of an airplane crash unless on a regularly scheduled commercial airline flight. This limitation is less frequently encountered today, because aviation is much safer and the hazards more predictable than in the past. In most cases now, companies will charge an additional premium, which varies according to the experience of the pilot, the type of aircraft, and other factors such as the general nature of the flights, common destinations, and types of cargo. Most commercial pilots can be covered by standard insurance. Some insurers specialize in offering policies to noncommercial pilots. Some nonpilots, such as business executives, may be underwritten similarly to noncommercial pilots if they frequently use noncommercial flights to conduct business and travel to what are considered hazardous landing facilities, such as small foreign landing fields. In some cases, the rider may exclude coverage for death in an airplane accident that occurs in a foreign country.

Hazardous Occupation or Avocation Rider

Many companies either will not issue policies on persons in hazardous occupations or who practice hazardous avocations or will exclude death benefits if death occurs as a direct result of practicing the occupation or engaging in the avocation. The hazardous occupation classification varies by company and may cover dozens of jobs from astronaut to lumberjack to skyscraper window cleaner. High risk avocations normally include such things as skydiving, scuba diving, hang-gliding, mountain climbing, spelunking, race car driving, motocross racing and similar high risk activities. However, for almost any hazardous occupation or avocation there is an insurer who specializes in writing insurance on such risks.

Limited-Benefit-Period Rider

Policies with limited-benefit-period riders are a form of modified death benefit policy. Generally, death benefits are limited to a return of premiums if death occurs within a specified period after policy issue, typically two years. After the limitation period, the face amount jumps up to a higher level or the death benefit may increase gradually over time. Policies are often issued with this rider when the insured has a pre-existing health condition that would otherwise make him or her uninsurable. For example, someone who recently underwent cancer surgery might not otherwise qualify for coverage. However, if the person survives for a certain period of time after surgery, the probability of long-term survival increases. Consequently, after a certain limited benefit period, the insurer can be relatively assured that the risk of imminent death has decreased and can increase the face amount of coverage. In general, these policies are still highly rated with much higher than standard premiums relative to the face amount of coverage.

Similar to the case with hazardous occupations and avocations, there are companies that specialize in writing coverage on various forms of substandard health or unusual disease cases.

COST-OF-LIVING (COL) RIDERS

The COL rider is typically a term insurance rider that provides automatically increasing coverage each year, or every few years, equal to the increase in the cost of living as measured, normally, by the consumer price index (CPI). The policyowner is billed for the additional coverage with the regular notice for the base policy. No evidence of insurability is required. However, if the additional coverage is rejected by the policyowner at any time by nonpayment of the additional premium, future COL adjustments will usually be available only by providing evidence of insurability. Once coverage is increased, the new level of coverage remains in effect, even if later increases are rejected or the CPI declines.

Some companies guarantee the term rates, while others do not.

In the case of adjustable life products, the COL increases typically are part of the readjusted base policy, rather than term additions, and premiums are adjusted accordingly. In universal life policies, the face amount of coverage may be increased for COL adjustments without the need to pay additional premiums if there is sufficient cash value in the policy to support the higher death benefit at the current premium level.

ACCIDENTAL–DEATH–BENEFIT (ADB) RIDERS

Many insurers offer an accidental-death, or double-indemnity, rider that, for a small additional premium, provides some multiple of the base face amount (typically double) if death is "accidental." Most experts feel there is little use for this coverage, since the insurance need is rarely tied to the means of death. In fact, a *nonaccidental* death rider, if it were available, would be a better option, since death benefit needs are likely to be higher if death occurred after a prolonged and expensive illness than if it occurred suddenly as a result of an accident.

If such a rider is purchased, care must be taken to determine what is meant by "accidental" death. Two different clauses are used: the accidental-means and the accidental-death type clauses. Most companies now use the accidental-death clause which provides that when death occurs as a result of accidental bodily injury, the accidental death benefit is paid.

If the contract uses the accidental-means clause, both cause and result must have been accidental. The ADB will not be paid if death is "accidental" but did not occur as a result of an "accidental" means or cause. For instance, if a person dies as a result of falling down his stairs, it is an accidental death, but it might not qualify for the ADB if the means were not also accidental (he intended to go down the stairs). Only if the fall resulted from an accidental means (he tripped on his child's roller skate), would the ADB be paid.

Whatever merit an ADB rider may have, it is virtually useless if the accidental-means clause is used to determine when the ADB will be paid. One would be better off taking a chance spending the additional premium on the Irish sweepstakes.

Companies differ with respect to the minimum and maximum ages of coverage under the ADB rider. Some companies do not specify either minimum or maximum ages. Those that do, set age 1 or 5 as the minimum age and most set age 70 as the maximum age, although some set earlier maximum ages, such as age 65 or 60. Companies also differ with respect to the period of time after an accident during which death must occur to be paid the ADB. Most companies limit the period of time to 90 days, but some set the period at 120 or 180 days or 1 year. A few companies allow payment as long as the rider is in force.

Finally, some companies offer a curious limited ADB rider that pays a multiple benefit if death occurs on a common carrier, such as an airline, bus, taxi, or train. Some contracts include school buses and private passenger automobiles and/or will pay the ADB if death occurs as a result of being struck while a pedestrian. Once again, unless one has a gambling nature and spends a lot of time on common carriers in high-risk areas, the premium dollars spent on such an ADB rider would be better spent buying additional coverage that will pay off regardless of the cause or means of death.

WAIVER–OF–PREMIUM RIDER

The waiver-of-premium rider is a form of disability insurance which provides that the basic policy (and often other riders) will continue in force if the insured becomes disabled and incapable of premium payment. Waiver-of-premium riders differ with respect to the period of coverage, the waiting period needed to qualify, and the definition of total disability.

Period of Coverage

In the event of disability, premiums are paid for a specified period of time that varies from company to company. If disability occurs before age 60, most companies will waive premiums for as long as the disability continues or until the policy would otherwise terminate or endow. Some policies become paid up at age 65. If the waiver-of-premium rider is in effect at the time a policy becomes paid up, the insured would not be required to resume premium payments even if he should overcome his disability.

If the insured becomes disabled after age 60, about half the companies' provisions provide no waiver-of-premium benefit. Of those companies that do provide a waiver-of-premium benefit for disabilities occurring after age 60, most will waive premiums only to age 65, although some specify a period equal to the longer of a specified minimum number of years or to age 65 or 70. For example, the rider may specify that if disability occurs after age 60, premiums will be waived for two years or until the insured is age 65, whichever is longer.

Waiting Period

Most companies use a waiting period of 6 months in order to qualify for disability waiver-of-premium benefits. However, some companies use a shorter period of 4 months or less.

Definition of Total Disability

The definition of total disability varies widely and may be more or less liberal. It is therefore critical to determine which definition is used in policies being considered.

A majority of the insurers use what is generally considered the most liberal definition:

Inability to perform one's own job for two years, then any job for which reasonably suited by education, training, and experience.

A sizable minority of insurers use a somewhat less liberal definition:

Inability to perform any job for which reasonably suited by education, training, and experience.

A few insurers use a very limiting definition of total disability:

Inability to perform any job for pay or profit.

Most insurers' definitions also include conditions that are presumptive of total disability. Typically the "loss of use of" or, less liberally, the "loss of" two body members such as an arm and a leg, or of sight, would be presumed to constitute total disability qualifying for waiver of premium. Some companies even include total loss of hearing as a presumptive condition. A minority of insurers include no presumptive conditions in their definition of total disability.

DISABILITY INCOME RIDER (DIR)

The disability income rider provides both a waiver of premium and supplementary income if the insured becomes totally disabled. The definition of total disabil-

ity is the same as that used for purposes of the waiver-of-premium rider. Customarily, the disability income benefit is expressed as a specified percentage of the face amount payable monthly. The common percentage is 1%. For example, if the face amount of the policy is $50,000, the DIR will pay $500 per month in the event the insured becomes totally disabled.

As with regular disability income insurance policies, insurers generally place maximum limits on the amount of disability income they will issue to some stated figure, such as $1,000 per month. Also, through coordination of benefits provisions they may further limit the amount of disability income they will issue and pay based on the total amount of income payable on all other disability income policies on the insured. As a general rule, insurers are reluctant to issue disability income policies when aggregate disability income payments may exceed 65 to 80% of the insured's net earned income.

Commonly, disability must continue for a 6-month waiting or elimination period before benefit payments commence, although a few companies use a 4-month waiting period. As with the waiver-of-premium rider, if the insured overcomes the disability, disability income payments cease and the insured must commence paying premiums on the life insurance policy once again. However, in those cases where the disability ceases after age 65 and when the waiver-of-premium provision pays-up the policy at age 65, no further premium payments would be required.

The additional premium charged for a given disability income benefit varies among companies, but will generally be higher for policies issued by the companies that use the most liberal definition of total disability (as described above for the waiver of premium) and lower for those that use the most restrictive definition. Regardless of the definition used, the DIR generally will only pay if the insured is totally disabled and the disability is presumed to be permanent. Therefore, the DIR is not generally considered the most suitable form of disability income insurance. If the insured needs disability income protection, often a comprehensive disability income policy (independent of the life insurance policy) that can be tailored to his or her needs is a better and more cost effective solution to the disability risk.

ADDITIONAL PURCHASE OPTIONS (GUARANTEED INSURABILITY OPTIONS)

In their most common use, additional purchase options (APOs) or guaranteed insurability options (GIOs) are attached to permanent policies on younger insureds. The APO gives the younger insured who cannot afford the premiums for a large face amount the option to purchase additional insurance without evidence of insurability at specified times in the future or upon the occurrence of certain "life" events. The traditional pattern provides regular options every three years beginning with age 25 and ending at age 40. However, some companies start options earlier and/or may continue the options at regular intervals to age 65.

Most companies also provide alternate purchase options and dates based on the occurrence of certain critical "life" events that would normally warrant additional life insurance coverage. Most companies allow exercise of the option in case of marriage or birth, with multiples for multiple births. Some will also allow exercise if and when the insured adopts a child. In most cases, the exercise of an alternate purchase option will preempt exercise of the next regularly scheduled purchase option.

The option amounts are generally scheduled on the specifications page of the contract and are usually equal to or less than the original face amount of coverage. In some cases, companies also specify a minimum purchase amount, such as $5,000 or $10,000.

A sizable minority of insurers will automatically include a disability waiver-of-premium in the new policies if it was contained in the original policy. Many other insurers will include the waiver-of-premium if requested. However, there is a great diversity in the conditions for the waiver-of-premium benefit in new policies issued under an APO. The waiver may be automatic, but only if the original policy is whole life or premiums are payable to an advanced age, such as age 95. In other cases, the waiver will be included if it is requested and then only if the premium on the new policy is equal to or less than that of the whole life policy. In some cases, the waiver-of-premium benefit is available only if the insured is not already totally disabled at the time the new policy is issued. In other cases the waiver will be included if requested and the company consents.

In virtually all cases, the new policy must be a type of whole life or endowment policy. However, a few companies permit the insured to purchase term insurance.

In addition to the traditional APO for young insureds, some companies now offer special APOs or GIOs in other circumstances. For example, many companies offer a GIO for the survivor to a joint life contract. Also, some companies offer GIOs or APOs to policies issued

to fund business buy/sell agreements. This permits the policyowners to increase necessary coverage as business values increase.

ACCELERATED–DEATH–BENEFIT (ADB) RIDERS[1]

Accelerated-death-benefit riders, also called living-benefit or advanced-death-benefit riders, are a relatively recent innovation with many variations. In general, with this rider part or all of the policy face amount may be paid in advance on the diagnosis of certain dread diseases or in the event of circumstances significantly affecting the insured's longevity and quality of life, such as a major organ transplant or entering a nursing home.

The amount that may be paid in advance varies by company and circumstance. The percentage of the face amount of coverage that may be paid out in advance ranges from 25 to 100%. In those policies with high percentage-of-face payouts, the limits may depend on the reason for payout. For example, about 70 to 85% of the death benefit may be available under the nursing home option and 90 to 98% under the terminal illness option. The advanced death benefit amount is reduced by actuarial computation to reflect the earlier and determinable payout. Among the factors that affect the actual amount available are the face amount of death coverage, the insured's actual future mortality, outstanding policy loans, current interest rates, future scheduled premiums, and administrative charges.

In most cases, once the conditions necessary to trigger accelerated payments have been met, the insured can elect to receive benefits in a single lump sum or as a series of installment payments. However paid under the option, the amount of money the insured may receive is generally more than would be realized by surrendering the policy for cash or by taking a policy loan. Amounts received under the option usually do not have to be used to pay medical or nursing home expenses. Rather, they may generally be used in any manner desired by the insured.

The policyowner may make the ADB election with respect to less than the total available insurance, provided the minimum election is for at least a specified amount, typically $25,000, and at least a specified amount of death benefit, such as $25,000, remains in force. When only a portion of the benefit is elected, the life policy is reduced proportionately as to death benefit, premium, and value.

Events Triggering Early Payout

Some policies permit early payout more liberally than others. The most restrictive policies limit advance payments to cases where life expectancy is diagnosed to be 6 months or less. Other policies are somewhat less restrictive such as requiring confinement to a long-term care facility for a certain period of time, such as six months, and the expectation that such care is permanent before early payouts may begin. The broadest options permit payouts not only for diagnosis of a terminal illness or confinement to a nursing home but also for life-threatening conditions, even if death is not virtually imminent. These conditions may include heart attack, heart surgery, cancer, stroke, major organ transplant, kidney failure, paraplegia, blindness, serious injury, or inability to perform 2 or 3 normal activities of daily living, such as general care, feeding, and bathing.

Closely related to the triggering events is the company's policy with respect to pre-existing conditions. Some companies place no restrictions based on pre-existing conditions. Others institute what is the equivalent of a waiting period of from one to six months before advance benefits may be paid. They may also limit the number of times a benefit may be collected. For example, some companies may permit advance payments only once for illness but more than once for successive internments in a nursing home facility.

Policies ADB Riders May Be Attached To

Virtually any type of policy may include an ADB rider. However, companies vary widely with respect to the age limit on purchase of the ADB option. The maximum age ranges from 50 to 80. They also vary widely with respect to the premium charge. Some companies offer the rider with no charge to any new insured who requests it. Others charge a level premium while still others charge an increasing premium over time. Those companies that charge an additional premium for the ADB rider may or may not provide a waiver-of-premium benefit with respect to the ADB rider. Often the premium is waived during any period in which the insured qualifies for waiver-of-premium under the base policy.

Income Taxation of Accelerated Death Benefit Payments

Amounts received under a life insurance contract on the life of individuals who are terminally ill or chronically ill are excluded from gross income as amounts paid by reason of the death of an insured.[2] A similar exclusion applies to amounts received for the sale or assignment of any portion of a death benefit under a life insurance contract to a viatical settlement provider.[3] However, the exclusion applies only if the insured under the life insurance contract is either terminally ill or chronically ill.[4] Further, excludable amounts paid to a chronically ill individual are subject to a per diem limitation that changes annually, as indexed for inflation. (See Chapter 19.)

A person is terminally ill if he has been certified by a physician as having an illness or physical condition that reasonably can be expected to result in death within 24 months of the date of certification.[5] A person is a chronically ill individual if a licensed health care practitioner has certified within the previous twelve months that the person has met one of three qualifying criteria. These criteria include: (1) being unable to perform without substantial assistance at least two activities of daily living (e.g., eating, toileting) for at least 90 days due to a loss of functional capacity; (2) having a similar level of disability; or (3) requiring substantial supervision to protect him from threats to health and safety due to severe cognitive impairment.[6] The term chronically ill individual does not include a terminally ill individual.

In the case of chronically ill individuals, the exclusion applies only if detailed requirements are met. For example, the payment must be for costs incurred by the payee (not compensated for by insurance or otherwise) for qualified long-term care services provided for the insured for that period. Under the terms of the contract, the payment must not be a payment or reimbursement of expenses reimbursable under Medicare (except where Medicare is a secondary payor, or the arrangement provides for per diem or other periodic payments without regard to expenses for qualified long-term care services).[7]

The income tax exclusion may not apply to amounts paid to a taxpayer other than the insured in certain circumstances. The exclusion is denied if the non-insured payee has an insurable interest in the insured's life because the insured is a director, officer or employee of the payee, or because the insured is financially interested in any trade or business carried on by the payee.[8]

AUTOMATIC PREMIUM LOAN PROVISION

Many companies provide an automatic premium loan provision, but the policyowner must in some states actively elect to make the feature operative. When operative, if a premium is unpaid at the end of the grace period and there is sufficient cash value, a loan will be advanced automatically against the policy to pay the premium and prevent lapse. Most companies place no restrictions or limitations on the use of the automatic policy loan provision. However, some companies permit the provision to be used to pay premiums only a limited number of consecutive times before the policy will lapse, even if the cash value is sufficient to continue using loans to pay premiums.

POLICY LOAN INTEREST RATE

Despite the fact that companies may use a variable policy loan interest rate, the majority of companies still use a fixed rate, which is commonly 8%. This suggests that many consumers prefer the certainty of a fixed rate. Other companies use a variable rate that usually refers to using the *greater* of (1) Moody's corporate bond yield for the month ending two months before, *or* (2) 1% plus the rate being credited to cash values. The impression seems to be widely held that the variable rate cannot exceed 8% or Moody's composite yield. However, this is in fact not generally true. There is no absolute limit in most cases except that which may be specifically imposed under state law.

Another apparently widely held misconception is that most companies using variable policy loan rates also generally permit policyowners to elect to use a fixed rate. Only a subset of the companies using variable rates permit policyowners to elect to use a fixed rate instead.

When market interest rates exceed 8%, most policyowners feel that fixed rates are more attractive than variable rates. However, companies that use a fixed rate typically also use an offset provision that credits cash values backing policy loans with a lower rate than currently being credited to other cash values. In the case of dividend paying policies, the dividend allocation formula will typically take account of loan balances and credit lower dividends to policies with higher loan balances. Consequently, it is not at all clear that the fixed policy loan rate is more economically beneficial than a variable rate.

Given the misconceptions and misunderstandings regarding policy loan rates, offset provisions, and the availability of an election between fixed and variable loan rates, it is important to closely inspect the policy loan interest rate provisions of all policies under consideration.

DIVIDEND OPTIONS

Although most companies provide the "basic four" dividend options – (1) cash, (2) reduced premiums, (3) dividend accumulations at interest, and (4) additional paid-up insurance – some *do not* provide all these options. In fact, one large New York company provides *no* options – dividends are used exclusively to reduce premiums. Many other companies, but certainly not most companies, also permit the policyowner to use dividends to buy one-year term insurance. In most cases, the term amount is limited to either the cash value or the total of premiums paid to date. However, some companies are more liberal and will permit the policyowner to use dividends to buy as much term insurance as the dividends will purchase. Also, many companies permit the policyowner to apply dividends as additional premium to more quickly pay-up the policy and to accelerate the period until the premiums vanish.

Most state laws require insurance policies to clearly indicate which is the default option if the policyowner does not make an election at the time the policy is issued. The paid-up option is most frequently used as the default option, but some states mandate the cash option, reduction-of-premium option, or the accumulation option. Although dividend options are often taken for granted, to assure maximum flexibility it is wise to carefully inspect the dividend options provided in any participating policy considered and to select the desired option when the policy is issued.

BAILOUT PROVISIONS

Most current-assumption and universal life policies use surrender charges rather than front-end loads to recover issuing expenses if the policy is terminated in the early years. Some of these policies provide a bailout provision that reduces or eliminates the surrender charge for early termination if the current rate credited to cash values falls below specified levels. This is an extremely attractive feature since it provides some assurance that the company is not using "inflated" current rates to encourage policy sales, only to lower the rates once the policy is issued.

CHANGE–OF–PLAN PROVISION

Many policies provide a change-of-plan provision that gives the policyowner the privilege of exchanging the policy for some other contract issued by the company. In essence, it is an "in house" IRC Section 1035 exchange provision. In term contracts this is generally the "conversion option" that allows the policyowner to exchange a term contract for some form of permanent cash-value contract. In permanent cash-value contracts, the privilege is normally to change to some other form of cash-value contract. In general, the exchange is permitted without evidence of insurability if the new plan is a higher-premium, higher cash value type of policy. Also, the new policy must generally have the same policy date and the same underwriting class and issue age as the original policy.

Despite these commonalities, there is a great deal of diversity among companies as to how the change-of-plan provision operates. In some contracts, certain types of exchanges are allowed only with the approval of the company. In a few other companies' contracts, virtually any type of policy may be exchanged for any other type, including permanent for term, with evidence of insurability but otherwise without the need for approval by the company. In many contracts, the change-of-plan clause states that the new policy may not have any riders attached, even if the old policy included certain riders, unless the company agrees. Although in most cases companies permit existing riders to continue in the new policy, some companies' change-of-plan clauses specifically state that riders may continue in the new policy without the need for special approval by the company.

Policy exchange fees also vary widely. In some contracts, the new policy is treated as a new issue with new issue charges and commissions. In other cases, the new policy is issued at net cost, that is, without new issue fees and commissions. Only a minimal charge is levied to cover the administrative and clerical costs of handling the paperwork.

CHANGE–OF–INSURED PROVISION OR RIDER

The change-of-insured provision or rider is an attractive option in business insurance applications such as key person insurance or buy/sell funding. It is a special form of change-of-plan provision that essentially permits the policyowner to exchange a policy on one life for a similar policy on another life with evidence of insurability. The key attraction is that this type of policy exchange is less expensive than terminating the old policy and acquiring a new policy. It avoids surrender charges or fees on termination of the old policy and generally avoids most of the new issue charges and commissions that would otherwise be paid on the new policy. The premium for the new policy is based on the age and underwriting class of the new insured for the same death benefit as in the old policy. In general, the

change-of-insured rider and other riders may be continued in the new policy. The company will usually charge an additional premium for the change-of-insured rider, but if the probability of changing insureds is relatively high, the premium cost is usually much lower than the cost of terminating old policies and acquiring new policies when changing insureds.

ADDITIONAL INSURED RIDERS

Additional insured riders are generally term insurance riders on insureds other than the insured named in the base policy. One of the most common uses of the additional insured rider is in what is called the family policy. The family policy insures all or selected members of the family in one contract. Typically the base policy is some form of permanent cash-value policy on the principal breadwinner with term riders on the spouse and children. Although variations may be created, the usual plan calls for a specified percentage of coverage for the spouse and children for each unit of coverage on the principal breadwinner. For example, for each $10,000 of coverage on the husband, $3,000 of term coverage is provided for the wife and $2,000 of term coverage is provided for each child under a specified age, generally age 18. All children living with the family are covered, even if born or adopted after the policy is issued.

Additional insured riders are also commonly used in first-to-die plans, often in business applications, such as to fund buy/sell agreements. The principal advantages in either case are the economies of one policy issue and administration and the flexibility to structure the plan to meet specific planning needs.

COMMON ACCIDENT PROVISION (SURVIVORSHIP CLAUSE)

Only about one in three contracts issued specifically includes a common accident provision, or what is sometimes called a survivorship clause or common disaster clause. The clause is designed to avoid inclusion of death benefits in the beneficiary's estate if he or she dies within a designated period after the insured. Where found, the provisions provide that the principal beneficiary must survive the insured by anywhere from seven to 30 days to receive the policy death benefits. If the principal beneficiary does not survive for the designated period, death benefits are paid to the contingent beneficiary. At least one company permits the policyowner, if other than the insured, to change the beneficiary for up to 60 days following the death of the insured.

SETTLEMENT OPTIONS

The commonly offered and state mandated settlement options include payments made as follows: (1) in cash; (2) in a fixed amount over some period of time; (3) for a fixed period of time in some amount; or (4) any of the common annuity options. The critical element to examine is not the options, per se, but whether or not the insurer makes age or time adjustments to the settlement options. A relatively small number of companies have provisions that are apparently intended to make an adjustment for anticipated increases in longevity so as to decrease the present value of future benefits for persons who are expected to begin receiving life annuity benefits well into the future. In other words, the annuity rates for annuity settlement options specified in the contract become less favorable the farther in the future the annuity is expected to be paid. Although these reductions may be warranted if life expectancies increase as these companies apparently believe they will, the longevity improvements may not materialize as anticipated. Regardless, companies that have not made adjustments to the future annuity settlement rates in their policies are clearly more attractive than those that have made adjustments.

CHAPTER ENDNOTES

1. See Chapter 19 for a more complete discussion of the features, operations, and planning implications of ADB riders and viatical settlements.

2. IRC Sec. 101(g)(1).

3. A viatical settlement provider is an entity that regularly buys or takes assignments of life insurance contracts on the lives of the terminally ill and that meets detailed standards.

4. IRC Sec. 101(g)(2)(A).

5. IRC Sec. 101(g)(4)(A).

6. IRC Sec. 101(g)(4)(B); IRC Sec. 7702B(c)(2).

7. IRC Sec. 101(g)(3).

8. IRC Sec. 101(g)(5).

Chapter 7

ADJUSTABLE LIFE

WHAT IS IT?

Adjustable life (AL) is a "flexible-premium" "adjustable-death-benefit" type of permanent cash value insurance. It is essentially a hybrid combination of universal life (UL) and ordinary level-premium participating life insurance.

AL has Features of Universal Life

In contrast with ordinary level-premium level-death-benefit policies and similar to UL, AL gives the policyowner the flexibility to change the plan of insurance. That is, within limits, the policyowner may change the premium and/or the level of death benefit. Note that when changes are made to an AL contract, the guarantee period will also change. In general, the policyowner may:

- increase or decrease the premium;

- increase or decrease the face amount;

- lengthen or shorten the guaranteed protection period; and/or

- lengthen or shorten the premium payment period.

Increases in the face amount usually require evidence of insurability. Also, an increase in premiums that requires an increase in the face amount to stay within the definition-of-life-insurance guidelines of Code section 7702 will usually require evidence of insurability.

Despite its similarities, AL should not be confused with universal life (UL), which is often called flexible-premium adjustable life. Direct-recognition current-assumption policies, such as UL, "unbundle" policy elements, explicitly showing mortality and expense charges and interest credits. In addition, they credit interest directly to cash values.

In contrast, most AL policies' elements are "bundled." Like traditional participating policies, the pure protection and savings components are not segregated. However, partial surrenders up to the sum of premiums can be made without surrendering the policy, or paying income tax (assuming the policy is not treated as a modified endowment contract). However, like many participating policies in the market today, most AL policies are "indirect-recognition interest-sensitive" or "indirect-recognition current-assumption" policies. The company's favorable investment, mortality, and expense experience can be indirectly reflected in the level of dividends that is actually paid, or directly reflected as additional credits to cash values.

AL has Features of Ordinary Level–Premium Whole Life Insurance

In addition to the "bundled" nature of its policy elements, AL has all the usual features of ordinary level-premium whole life insurance including:

- a minimum interest guarantee;

- guaranteed maximum mortality charges;

- cash values;

- nonforfeiture values;

- a policy loan provision;

- dividend options;

- a reinstatement period; and

- settlement options.

Similar to other traditional forms of insurance, various options or riders are available including:

- waiver of premium;

- guaranteed purchase or insurability;

- accidental death benefits; and

- cost-of-living adjustments.

Although the policyowner has flexibility in selecting the plan of insurance, changes are generally permitted only at specified intervals and with advance notice to the insurer. Between adjustment periods, the policy is a level-premium, level-death-benefit policy. Depending on the particular premium and death benefit levels chosen, the policy can assume the form of almost any traditional term or whole life policy from low-premium term through ordinary whole life to high-premium limited-pay whole life.

Premiums generally can be set to zero without policy lapse (or without invoking the automatic policy loan provision), although this generally requires notice to the insurer. The minimum annual premium is typically equivalent to the premium for a five-year term policy. In contrast with UL and similar to ordinary level-premium policies, once a policyowner has selected a given plan of insurance, premiums must be paid as scheduled unless the policyowner notifies the insurer of his or her desire to change the plan of insurance. The plan of insurance defines the length of the guarantee at any point in time. The schedule of cash values is computed based on the current program of premium payments, the face value, and the term or duration of coverage. The cash value schedule is recomputed each time the plan of insurance is changed.

WHEN IS THE USE OF THIS TOOL INDICATED?

AL may be considered for any life insurance need. Initially, an AL policy's death benefit and premium level can be configured to resemble virtually any type of life insurance policy from five-year term insurance to single-premium whole life. However, because of policy costs, it is generally best suited for long-term coverage needs. For short-term coverage needs where future insurability is not a factor, a nonrenewable term policy would generally be more cost effective.

1. AL is indicated whenever flexibility in life insurance is desired, guaranteed protection is needed, and the "forced savings" feature of ordinary level-premium whole life insurance is preferred. Policyowners whose circumstances change can later "reconfigure" the policy by changing the schedule of premium payments and/or the face amount or duration of coverage.

2. AL has been marketed as the only policy a person will ever need. The flexibility makes it very useful in the family market. For example, a young parent with a growing family and modest income can acquire an AL policy that is initially configured with low premiums and a high death benefit to resemble a traditional term policy. As the parent's income grows, the scheduled premiums can be increased to build up tax-sheltered cash within the policy. At later times when cash is needed, such as to pay for children's educations, the scheduled premiums can be reduced. Partial surrenders or policy loans can be used to help pay the school expenses. After a time, the scheduled premiums can be increased once again to build cash values that can be used for the policyowner's retirement. Similarly, if the amount of death protection that is needed changes, the death benefit may be decreased or increased or the term of coverage extended or reduced. However, increases in death benefits will usually require evidence of insurability. Each time a change is made the guarantee period is recalculated.

3. The flexibility of AL also makes it suitable for many business life insurance needs. AL offers a conservative and guaranteed vehicle for all sorts of business applications where adjustments in death benefits and/or cash accumulations are frequently required, including split dollar plans, nonqualified deferred compensation plans, death benefit only plans, key person insurance, buy-sell agreements, retiree-benefits funding, and in qualified retirement plans that use insurance.

ADVANTAGES

1. Policyowners have discretion or flexibility in selecting the schedule of premiums that they will pay until they next request a change in the plan of insurance.

2. Similar to ordinary level-premium whole life policies, once a policyowner has chosen a premium payment plan, there is an element of "forced saving" until the policyowner requests a change in the premium payment plan. Many people who lack the discipline to continue a regular savings program will find this feature attractive.

3. The policyowner may change the face amount of coverage or the term of coverage. Decreases in the

face amount are permitted at virtually any time. However, policyowners who reduce death benefits within the first seven years of issue may be subjected to adverse tax consequences under the modified endowment contract (MEC) rules. Increases in face amount are generally permitted, subject to evidence of insurability. Increases in the death benefit may also subject the policy to a new test period under the MEC rules. (See discussion under "Tax Implications" below).

4. Most AL policies offer a cost-of-living agreement that automatically increases the face amount in response to increases in the CPI without evidence of insurability. Commonly, the premium is also correspondingly adjusted upwards.

5. Cash value interest or earnings may accumulate tax-free or tax-deferred, depending on whether gains are distributed at death or during lifetime.

6. The cash values are not subject to the fluctuations in market value characteristic of longer-term municipal bonds and other longer-term fixed income investments when market rates change.

7. Policy cash values can be borrowed at a low net cost. Although policyowners must pay interest on policy loans, cash values continue to grow and are credited with at least the minimum guaranteed rate in the policy. Consequently, the actual net borrowing rate is less than the stated policy loan rate.

DISADVANTAGES

1. Some AL policies, similar to many ordinary whole life policies, use what is called the "direct recognition" method to determine how favorable investment, mortality, and expense experience is allocated to dividends on policies with policy loans. Under this method, the amount of dividends allocated to policies with policy loans is reduced to account for the generally lower yield the company earns on policy loans relative to other investments in their general portfolio. The direct recognition method is most commonly used in policies that have fixed loan rates. Typically, policies with variable loan rates, and some others with fixed loan rates, do not employ the direct recognition method and instead allocate dividends without regard to loans. There are also some AL policies that do not have dividends, but credit current mortality and interest similar to UL.

2. Lifetime distributions or withdrawals of cash values are subject to income tax to the extent attributable to gain in the policy.

3. Surrender of the policy within the first five to ten years may result in considerable loss since cash surrender values reflect the insurance company's recovery of sales commissions and initial policy expenses.

4. Interest paid on policy loans is generally nondeductible.

5. The flexibility with respect to premium payments and death benefits permits policyowners to change the policy in such a way that it may inadvertently become a modified endowment contract (MEC) with adverse tax consequences.

TAX IMPLICATIONS

General Tax Rules

AL policies are generally taxed in the same manner as other types of life insurance policies. Death benefits are usually paid free of any federal income tax. AL policies are subject to the same income tax and estate, gift, and generation-skipping transfer taxation rules as all other types of life insurance policies.

Living benefits from AL policies are also taxed in the same manner as living benefits from other types of life insurance policies. All other types of living benefits are generally taxed under the "cost recovery rule." The cost recovery rule, which is sometimes called the FIFO (first-in-first-out) rule, treats amounts received as nontaxable recovery of the policyowner's investment in the contract. Only after the policyowner's investment is fully recovered are additional amounts received treated as taxable interest or gain in the policy. Included in this category of living benefits are policy dividends, lump-sum cash settlements of cash surrender values, cash withdrawals, and amounts received on partial surrender. Such amounts are included in gross income only to the extent they exceed the investment in the contract (as reduced by any prior excludable distributions received from the contract). In other words, nonannuity distributions during life are generally first treated as a return of the policyowner's investment in the contract, and then as taxable interest or gain. Interest paid on or credited to living benefits held by the insurer under an agreement to pay interest is immediately taxable in full.

Exception to the Cost Recovery Rule

There is an important exception to the general cost recovery rule for withdrawals within the first 15 years after the policy issue date that are coupled with reductions in death benefits. In general, withdrawals from AL policies are not permitted without a complete or partial surrender of the policy. In other words, to the extent permitted, withdrawals will be accompanied by reductions in the amount or term of death benefits. Reductions of the face amount or term of coverage could "force out" some of the cash value under the rules of Section 7702. If such withdrawals or distributions take place within the first 15 contract years, they will generally be fully or partially taxable to the extent of gain in the policy.

Such withdrawals or distributions are taxed in whole or in part as ordinary income to the extent "forced out" of the policy as a result of the reduction in the death benefits. The taxable amount depends on when the withdrawal is made:

- *Within first five years* – If the distribution takes place within the first five years after policy issue, a very stringent and complex set of tests apply.[1] Potentially, a larger portion, or perhaps all, of any withdrawal within the first five years will be taxable if there is gain in the policy.

- *Fifth to fifteenth years* – For distributions between the end of the fifth year and the end of the fifteenth year from the issue date, a mathematical test applies. Essentially, the policyowner is taxed on an income-first basis to the extent the cash value before the withdrawal exceeds the maximum allowable cash value under the cash value corridor test for the reduced death benefit after the withdrawal.[2] Frequently, only a portion or none of the withdrawal will be taxable in these cases.

Caveat: Potential Taxation under the MEC Rules

The flexibility inherent in AL policies with respect to changes in premiums and face amounts raises the possibility that the policy could become a modified endowment contract (MEC).[3] The penalty for classification as a MEC relates to distributions. If a policy is classified as a MEC, "distributions under the contract" are taxed under the interest-first rule rather than the cost recovery rule. In addition, to the extent taxable, these distributions are subject to a 10% penalty if they occur before the policyowner reaches age 59½, dies, or becomes disabled. So MEC classification of an AL contract means both faster taxation of investment gains and a possible penalty tax for "early" receipt of that growth.

"Distributions under the contract" include living benefits (as described above), partial surrenders, policy loans, loans secured by the policy, loans used to pay premiums, and dividends taken in cash. "Distributions under the contract" generally do *not* include dividends used to pay premiums, dividends used to purchase paid-up additions, dividends used to purchase one year term insurance, or the surrender of paid-up additions to pay premiums.

Changes in premiums or death benefits may inadvertently cause an AL policy to run afoul of the MEC rules in basically three ways:

1. An increase in premium payments during the first seven contract years may push the cumulative premiums above the amount permitted under the "seven-pay test."[4]

2. A reduction in the death benefit during the first seven contract years triggers a re-computation of the seven-pay test. The seven-pay test is applied retroactively as of the original issue date as if the policy had been issued at the reduced death benefit.

3. A "material" increase of the death benefit at any time triggers a new seven-pay test which is applied prospectively as of the date of the material change.

When issued, AL policy illustrations show the maximum amount (the seven-pay guideline annual premium limit) that may be paid within the first seven years without having the policy classified as a MEC. If a policyowner inadvertently exceeds that maximum, MEC status can be avoided if excess premiums are returned to the policyowner with interest within 60 days after the end of the contract year in which the excess occurs. The interest will be subject to taxation.[5]

A policy will fail the seven-pay test if, in any year, the cumulative premiums paid to that year exceed the sum of the seven-pay guideline annual premiums to that year. For example, assume the guideline annual premium is $10,000 based on the original death benefit. The policyowner pays $9,000 each year for the first six years. In year seven, the policyowner reduces the face amount which "forces out" $18,000 of the cash value. The recomputed guideline premium is $8,000. The policy now fails the seven-pay test and is a MEC since cumulative premiums paid in just the first year, $9,000, (and through year six as well) exceed the sum of the recomputed guideline annual premiums of $8,000. The $18,000 will be taxable to the extent of any gain in the policy. In addition, unless the policyowner is over age 59 _ or disabled, a 10% penalty will be imposed on the taxable portion of the distribution.

Any reduction in death benefits attributable to the nonpayment of premiums due under the contract will not trigger a re-computation of the seven-pay test if the benefits are reinstated within 90 days after being reduced.[6]

The term "material" change is not defined in the statute. However, the statute states that it "includes any increase in death benefit under the contract,"[7] but *not* increases attributable to dividends (for paid-up additions), interest credited to the policy's cash surrender value, increases necessary to maintain the corridor between the death benefit and the cash surrender value required by the definition of life insurance[8] or cost-of-living adjustments. Increases in death benefits that require evidence of insurability will generally be considered material changes that invoke a new seven-pay test. See Appendix D for more information.

ALTERNATIVES

1. Universal life is the principal alternative to adjustable life.

    When AL was introduced, it was promoted as the perfect policy for virtually everyone. It could be adjusted to meet anyone's changing insurance needs throughout life. However, with the introduction of universal life, the popularity of adjustable life has waned for several reasons:

    AL provides somewhat less flexibility to adjust premiums and death benefits than UL policies. Generally, UL policyowners may vary their premiums at will or skip premium payments altogether if the policy has sufficient cash values to cover mortality and expense charges. In contrast, unless an AL policyowner officially requests a change in the premium payment plan, skipping premium payments will either cause the policy to lapse or trigger policy loans under the automatic premium loan provision. In addition to the inconvenience of having to make requests in advance regarding a change in the

premium payment plan or face amount or duration of coverage, such requests may be limited or restricted to specific dates or intervals.

AL policy elements are "bundled" whereas UL policy elements are "unbundled." The annual statements for UL policies report mortality and expense charges and interest credits to cash values separately. This allows policyowners to easily monitor actual versus projected performance. New cash value schedules and schedules of projected dividends are also issued for AL policies when the plan of insurance is changed, but there is no regular and separate accounting for mortality and expense charges and interest credits. (Note, however, that some AL policies are "unbundled.") Although favorable company experience may be reflected in higher than projected dividend payments or lower current mortality and interest charges, most companies do not regularly report how dividends actually paid compare with those projected. This makes it more difficult to monitor actual versus projected performance.

AL has more restrictive withdrawal rules than UL. In general, withdrawals are permitted from AL policies only when accompanied by reductions in the face amount of coverage. Many UL policies permit withdrawals of up to 10%, and sometimes more, of the cash value without reductions in the face amount of coverage.

UL offers two death benefit options (option I – level total death benefit, and option II – level insurance benefit plus cash value) whereas AL offers only the traditional level total death benefit. Note, however, that AL can be reconfigured to resemble the UL option II program with the purchase of a term rider or by using dividends to purchase paid-up additions. With over a dozen dividend options, this type of AL policy can return benefits to a client by reducing premiums, strengthening the plan of insurance, or growing cash value.

Despite these relative disadvantages, AL may be preferred to UL for several reasons:

AL offers more certainty regarding cash value accumulations than UL. Like ordinary level-premium whole life policies, an AL policy's cash value schedule is guaranteed for as long as the selected plan of insurance is maintained. When a new premium payment plan or a new face amount is arranged, a new guaranteed cash value schedule is produced. In contrast, illustrations of UL policy cash values are just that – projected, non-guaranteed illustrations.

AL dividends give the policyowner more options as to how to use or apply the favorable investment experience of the company than UL policies. UL policies reflect favorable investment performance directly in the amounts credited to cash values. In virtually all AL policies, favorable investment performance is reflected in the level of dividends paid, which can be used in several ways. Dividends can be paid in cash, used to reduce premiums, accumulated at interest, used to purchase additional term insurance (with a rider), or added to policy cash values.

The requirement to pay scheduled premiums under the selected plan of insurance with AL provides a "forced saving" feature that is absent with UL. AL policyowners have a strong incentive to continue scheduled premiums since failure to do so will often have adverse consequences. If an AL policyowner fails to pay scheduled premiums under the selected plan of insurance without requesting a change in the plan, the policy may lapse and be put on either the extended term or the paid-up nonforfeiture option, depending on the default option under the contract. AL policies typically have very liberal reinstatement provisions, but they do normally require evidence of insurability. Lapse can be avoided with the automatic premium loan provision, but then each failure to pay premiums will incur a loan against the policy.

2. Pre-programmed combinations of differing life insurance policies.

   To the extent future life insurance needs and premium paying ability can be anticipated, a program combining various cash value and term insurance products may meet an insured's needs. However, most people cannot anticipate all the ways their insurance needs may change over time. Therefore, they must rely on the possibility of buying new insurance and their rights to lapse, change, or surrender old policies, to keep their programs up-to-date. The Code section 1035 exchange provisions provide some flexibility to change the plan of insurance. Also, some companies include "change" provisions that permit limited changes to the face amount of coverage. To some extent the right to buy

additional insurance can be assured with guaranteed purchase options, but the amounts guaranteed may turn out to be insufficient. Policy loan provisions, the dividend options on participating policies, and the renewable and convertible features of term insurance all give policyowners some flexibility in their overall plan of insurance. Although these features and provisions are useful for limited adjustments in the plan of insurance, major changes are difficult to arrange within these somewhat constrained options.

WHERE AND HOW DO I GET IT?

Very few companies continue to develop, distribute, and market true Adjustable Life products.

WHAT FEES OR OTHER ACQUISITION COSTS ARE INVOLVED?

Life insurance companies are free to set their premiums according to their own marketing strategies. Almost all states have statutes prohibiting any form of rebating (sharing the commission with the purchaser) by the agent. The premium includes a "loading" to cover such things as commissions to agents, premium taxes payable to the state government, operating expenses of the insurance company such as rent or mortgage payments and salaries, and any other applicable expenses.

A few companies offer "no-load" or "low-load" life insurance policies. These policies are not really no-load, since certain expenses are unavoidable (e.g., the premium tax), but rather pay either no sales commission or a very low sales commission. Consequently, the cash value buildup tends to be larger in the early years. Although commissions are lower, these companies typically must spend somewhat more money on alternative methods of marketing and may therefore incur generally higher expenses in this area than companies that pay commissions to agents.

The bulk of an insurance company's expenses for a policy are incurred when the policy is issued. It may take the company five to nine years or longer to recover all its front-end costs. The state premium tax is an ongoing expense that averages about 2% of each premium payment. Many companies pay 55% first year commissions when the plan of insurance is similar to an ordinary whole life policy. They will typically pay somewhat lower rates on low-premium and high-premium plans. Under most plans, the aggregate commissions paid to the selling agent over the years is approximately equal to the first year premium on the policy configured as an ordinary whole life policy. Commissions are typically paid on a renewal basis over a period of three to nine years. When a new plan of insurance requires additional premiums, the change is usually treated as a new sale for commission purposes as it would be with other policies.

Most adjustable life policies have no explicit surrender charges. However, many will pay a terminal dividend when the policy is surrendered. The terminal dividend is typically higher the longer the policy has remained in force. In essence, this is a form of surrender charge since the company is essentially holding back dividends it could otherwise pay currently and rewarding those policyholders who maintain their policy longer with a greater terminal dividend.

The costs of administration, record-keeping, and service are generally somewhat higher with adjustable policies than with traditional fixed-premium, fixed-benefit policies. In addition, the company faces greater risk of adverse selection. Policyowners are more likely to exercise their rights to increase face amounts within the limits not requiring evidence of insurability and/or to reduce premium payments without reducing the face amount if the insured's health declines. Consequently, expense charges and mortality charges tend to be somewhat higher in these policies than in otherwise comparable fixed-premium, fixed-benefit policies.

HOW DO I SELECT THE BEST OF ITS TYPE?

Although the plan of insurance can be changed, AL is essentially a traditional fixed-premium, fixed-benefit policy at any given point in time. Some of the key considerations are the policy loan provisions, the policy loan interest rate, whether or not the company uses a direct-recognition method to determine the dividend paid on policies with policy loans, the dividend interest rate (the rate that must be earned on the company's investments to justify the projected dividends), the current crediting rate, the method used to determine the amount of investment income allocable to the policy (portfolio method, new money method, or some weighted average), and, of course, the financial stability and strength of the company. Each of these items is discussed, where appropriate, in Chapter 13 "Ordinary Level-Premium Whole Life Insurance," Chapter 12, "Limited-Pay Life Insurance" and Chapter 16, "Single Premium Life Insurance." What to look for in a policy illustration or ledger statement is similar to that discussed in Chapter 12, "Limited-Pay Life Insurance."

The items that are of special importance when evaluating AL policies are the adjustment provisions and the commonly-offered guaranteed insurability options. Look for policies with the more liberal adjustment provisions. All else being equal, policies that permit more frequent changes in the plan of insurance and that permit them sooner after the policy issue date should be favored. Similarly, policies that permit larger and more frequent face amount increases without evidence of insurability should be favored. However, all else is never quite equal. More liberal adjustment provisions may involve higher expense charges. More liberal guaranteed insurability provisions will generally require higher premium charges.

Another key consideration is the quality of service. Changes in the plan of insurance require re-computation of the premium payment plan, cash value schedules, and projected dividend schedules and may involve a new underwriting evaluation if evidence of insurability is required. This service generally comes from a combination of the insurer and the agent. If either the agent or the insurer is slow to perform his or its part, desired changes may not take effect for months.

QUESTIONS AND ANSWERS

Question – How does the adjustments provision of AL differ from the "change" provision often found in ordinary whole life insurance policies?

Answer – Adjustments in AL policies are made prospectively only, affecting the future but in no way amending the past. The change provisions in traditional policies typically require payment of back premiums and/or other retroactive adjustments that may affect cash values. Such changes typically become increasingly and prohibitively expensive the longer the policy has been in force.

Question – Do AL policies offer dividend options that are not available with ordinary whole life policies?

Answer – AL policies offer the conventional dividend options – cash, premium reduction, accumulate at interest, and paid-up additions. Some AL policies offer what is called a "policy improvement" dividend option. With this option dividends become a part of the cash value and thereafter lose their separate identity. If the current plan of insurance is equivalent to some form of whole life insurance, this option causes the face amount to increase without an increase in premiums or without changing the premium paying period. The effect is essentially the same as buying paid-up additions, except that these amounts cannot be surrendered without surrendering the policy as a whole. Generally, regular paid-up additions may be surrendered separately. If the current plan of insurance is of a term nature, this option will increase the term of coverage.

Question – Can unscheduled additional premiums be paid on AL policies similar to universal life?

Answer – Most AL policies permit unscheduled additional premium payments. Such payments will lengthen the term of coverage or shorten the premium-paying period depending on whether the current plan of insurance is in a term mode or a whole life mode. For example, a large enough payment might change a plan from term to age 50 to term to age 65, or from a life paid-up at age 75 to a life paid-up at age 65. Some companies restrict the availability of this feature in the first few policy years.

Question – Will a change in the plan of insurance cause an AL policy to become a modified endowment contract (MEC)?

Answer – Generally, a change in the plan of insurance that either lengthens the period of coverage or increases the face amount of coverage will be treated as a material change in the policy that triggers a new seven-pay test. However, the reconfigured policy will be treated as a MEC only if it fails the seven-pay test in its new configuration. In general, the insurance company will inform the policyowner if the desired change may cause the policy to fail the seven-pay test.

Also, a reduction of the face amount of coverage (or, in the authors' opinion, a shortening of the term of coverage) within the first seven policy years triggers a re-computation of the seven-pay test that is based on the reduced death benefit level and retroactive to the original policy issue date. The closer earlier premium payments were to the original seven-pay premium limit, the more likely is a reduction of death benefits within the first seven years to cause the policy to be reclassified as a MEC.

In the authors' opinion, a change in the premium payment plan that does not change the level of benefits, such as a change from a whole life level-premium payment plan to a paid-up at age 65 plan, should not be treated as a material change and should not require new seven-pay testing. However, if the change in premiums requires a change in the face amount to meet the requirements of life insurance under Code section 7702, the change should be considered material and require new seven-pay testing. See Appendix D for a more complete discussion of the material change rules and the seven-pay test.

Question – If the option to increase the face amount of coverage requires new evidence of insurability, of what benefit is this option if a person becomes uninsurable?

Answer – The companies that offer AL policies realize that the flexibility to increase the face amount is not that significant if increases require evidence of insurability. Consequently, most AL policies are issued with guaranteed purchase or insurability riders. This provision allows the policyowner to periodically purchase (e.g., every three to five years) a limited amount of additional coverage without proving insurability. In general, a purchase option expires if it is not exercised when it matures, but the later options remain open without proof of insurability. Any desired increase in face amount beyond the limits set in the guaranteed insurability option will require evidence of insurability.

The guaranteed insurability option should not be confused with the cost-of-living adjustment (COLA) provision that is also generally offered in AL policies. COLAs are generally similarly granted without proof of insurability. In some cases, the policy face amount is increased automatically each year by the increase in the consumer price index (CPI) unless the policyowner elects otherwise. The premium payment plan is also correspondingly adjusted upwards. In other policies, the insured has the option to periodically (e.g., every three years) increase the face amount by the change in the CPI since the last adjustment period. In contrast with the guaranteed insurability option, if the policyowner declines the additional coverage at any time, future COLA increases will be available only after proving insurability.

CHAPTER ENDNOTES

1. IRC Secs. 7702(f)(7)(B), 7702(f)(7)(C).

2. IRC Secs. 7702(f)(7)(B), 7702(f)(7)(D). The cash value corridor test is discussed in Appendix F.

3. In cases where there are extreme reductions in the death benefit or very large premium payments, it is even possible for a policy to fail the tests for life insurance under IRC Section 7702 with

much more disastrous tax consequences. See the discussion of the definition of life insurance in Appendix F.

4. IRC Sec. 7702A(a)(1)(B). Classification as a MEC occurs in the year when the seven-pay test is first violated and for each year thereafter. See Appendix D for a more complete discussion of the seven-pay test.

5. IRC Sec. 7702A(e)(1).

6. IRC Sec. 7702A(c)(2)(B).

7. IRC Sec. 7702A(c)(3).

8. IRC Sec. 7702. See Appendix F.

Chapter 8

ANNUITIES

WHAT IS IT?

Annuities are the only investment vehicles that can guarantee investors that they will not outlive their income, and they do this in a tax-favored manner. In addition, annuities are available with a host of features to meet a wide variety of investor needs. The taxation of annuities is governed by Internal Revenue Code section 72.

Technically, annuities are contracts providing for the systematic liquidation of principal and interest in the form of a series of payments over time.[1] However, this really refers to the "payout" phase of an annuity; in point of fact, annuities can (and often do) have an accumulation phase that also lasts for a substantial period of time.

An annuity is established when an investor makes a cash payment to an insurance company, which invests the money – this may be a single large cash payment or a series of periodic payments over time. The money remains invested with the insurance company and is periodically credited with some growth factor – this is the accumulation phase of the annuity. In return for making a deposit into an annuity, the insurance company ultimately agrees to pay the owner (or owners) a specified amount (the annuity payments) periodically, beginning on a specified date – this is the payout phase of the annuity.

If the specified date for payouts to begin is within one year of the date the contract is established (i.e., a single cash payment is made and the insurance company begins a systematic liquidation of the payment back to the owner within one year), the annuity is called an "immediate annuity". If, alternatively, the specified date for payouts to begin is later than one year, the annuity is called a "deferred annuity" (because deposits are made now, but the payout is deferred). An immediate annuity only has a payout phase; a deferred annuity has both an accumulation and a payout phase.

If the payout phase of the annuity is a *life annuity*, the company promises that payouts will continue for as long as the annuitant (or annuitants) live; the income stream can never be outlived (NOTE: although often the same, technically the owner of the annuity does not necessarily need to be the annuitant as well; occasionally these *are* different individuals). If the payout phase is a *fixed period annuity* (also called a *term-certain annuity*), the company promises to pay stipulated amounts for a fixed or guaranteed period of time independent of the survival of the annuitant. An annuity payout can also utilize a combination of the life and fixed period options, such as "for the greater of 10 years or the life of the annuitant(s)."

In addition to differentiating between immediate and deferred annuities, and fixed and term-certain payouts, annuities are also categorized as to whether they are fixed or variable (be careful not to confuse a "fixed annuity" with a "fixed period payout"). Classification as a fixed or variable annuity refers to the underlying investments during the accumulation phase of the annuity; a fixed annuity is invested in the general fixed account of the insurance company, while a variable annuity is invested in separately managed sub-accounts (that function similarly to mutual funds) selected by the annuity owner. Variable annuities often have additional features to help manage the risk of their underlying investments, such as guaranteed death benefits or newer "living benefits" that provide company-guaranteed payments for owners or beneficiaries even if (or especially if) they would be higher than actual investment performance would provide for.

Newer annuities may also offer a variable option during the payout phase (whether for a fixed or term-certain period). A "variable annuitization" has payments that may fluctuate up or down depending upon the performance of the underlying sub-account investments; a "fixed annuitization" has payments that remain the same through the payout phase (or occasionally increase by some set rate to keep pace with inflation; however, this rate is pre-determined and contractual, is still invested in the insurance company's general account, and is thus still considered a "fixed payout").

Annuities purchased from an insurance company are called "commercial annuities" while those purchased from a person or entity that is not in the business of selling annuities are called "private annuities."[2] Technically, the living proceeds received from a life insurance contract are also considered annuities if they consist of periodic payments of both principal and interest.

Annuities grow tax-deferred during the accumulation phase, although withdrawals during this phase are taxed on a LIFO (last in, first out) basis – meaning that withdrawals during the accumulation phase are considered to be withdrawals of growth first (fully taxable) and principal second.[3] Payouts during the annuitization phase are split; a portion of each payment is considered principal, and a portion is deemed interest/growth. The proportion of each is determined at the annuity's beginning payment date and is based upon the already-accumulated growth, an assumed internal growth factor for the payout period, and the expected length of the payout period. All amounts distributed that are considered interest/growth are taxed as ordinary income, regardless of the phase or timing of the withdrawal. In addition, certain withdrawals before the age of 59½ may be subject to an additional 10% tax penalty.

Although annuities have tax-deferral features that can be quite advantageous, the primary reason annuities should be purchased are for their risk management features. Annuities can provide a variety of guarantees, whether protecting against interest rate risk, reinvestment risk, superannuation (living too long, such as outliving one's assets), or certain market volatility risks. Annuities are first and foremost a risk management tool.

WHEN IS THE USE OF THIS TOOL INDICATED?

There is such a fundamental difference in the risk and return characteristics of fixed and variable annuities that each type is more or less suitable for various purposes. However, some form of annuity would be indicated in the following circumstances:

1. When a person wants a retirement income that can never be outlived.

2. When an individual (often retired) wants a monthly income equal to or higher than other conservative investments and is willing to (or especially if he/she *wants* to) have principal liquidated.

3. When the person would like to avoid probate and pass a large sum of money by contract to an heir to reduce the possibility of a will contest.[4]

4. When a tax-deferred accumulation of interest is desired. The interest earned inside an annuity owned by an individual grows income-tax free and is not taxed until it is withdrawn.[5]

5. When an investor wants to be free of the responsibility of investing and managing assets (in the case of a fixed annuity or an annuity payout; this is not applicable to a variable deferred annuity, as the owner still retains the burden of making all investment selections).

6. As a supplement to an IRA. With limited opportunity for pre-tax contributions to IRAs, many clients are seeking opportunities of making regular after-tax contributions to an investment vehicle after reaching the IRA contribution limits. The annuity may be a good choice because contributions are not limited.

7. Fixed annuities, in particular, would be indicated: (1) when safety of principal is a paramount consideration (this can be particularly important in some retirement planning scenarios); (2) when an investor wants a guarantee that a given level of interest will be credited to his investment for a long period of time; or (3) when a conservative complement to other investment vehicles is desired.

8. Variable annuities, in particular, would be indicated: (1) when an investor wants more control over his or her investment and is willing to bear the risk associated with his or her investment selections; or (2) when a person is looking for potentially increasing retirement income.

9. When an individual would like to be invested in variable sub-accounts, but desires some aspect of risk management, such as the guaranteed death benefits or living benefits offered by most insurance companies.

ADVANTAGES

1. The guarantees of safety, interest rates, and particularly lifelong income (if selected) give the purchaser peace of mind and psychological security.

2. An annuity protects and builds a person's cash reserve. The insurer guarantees principal and interest (in the case of a fixed annuity; a variable

annuity is subject to the performance of the underlying selected sub-accounts), and the promise (if purchased) that the annuity can never be outlived. This makes the annuity particularly attractive to those who have retired and desire, or require, fixed monthly income and lifetime guarantees.

3. An annuity allows a client to invest in the market while moderating risk. The insurer may provide guarantees of death proceeds or a certain annuitization amount (if purchased) within a variable annuity, thus providing guarantees that would otherwise be unavailable to a client that purchased the underlying investments directly. This makes a variable annuity particularly attractive to those who have retired or are nearing retirement and need (or want) to hold risky investments while trying to moderate risk.

4. A client can "time" the receipt of income and shift it into lower bracket years. This ability to decide when to be taxed allows the annuitant to compound the advantage of deferral.

5. Because the interest on an annuity is tax-deferred, an annuity paying the same rate of interest (after expenses) as a taxable investment will result in a higher effective yield.

6. Because of the risk-management factors available, especially in variable annuities, a client may be able to take on greater risk in the underlying investment options (e.g., equities, smaller-capitalization equities, high-yield bonds, etc.) while still maintaining a reasonable overall risk exposure due to the underlying guarantees.

7. Adjusted Gross Income (AGI) may be reduced in years where the annuity is held with no withdrawals (thanks to the tax-deferral features of the accumulation phase). In addition, lower taxable income may be recognized during the payout phase, due to the partial recovery of basis associated with each payment. A reduced AGI can bring tax savings, as many other income tax rules are calculated based upon AGI and generally a lower AGI results in lower taxation (and vice versa). A reduced AGI can create tax savings by lowering the amount of Social Security includable in income, reducing the floor threshold for deduction of medical expenses (7.5% of AGI) or miscellaneous itemized deductions (2% of AGI), and avoiding the threshold for phase-out of exemptions and itemized deductions.

DISADVANTAGES

1. Receipt of a lump sum (either at retirement, or to a beneficiary at death) could result in a significant tax burden because income averaging is not available (however, this can be moderated if the proceeds are annuitized).

2. The cash flow stream of a fixed payout may not keep pace with inflation, particularly for longer-term payout phases such as a life annuitization.

3. A 10% penalty tax is generally imposed on withdrawals of accumulated interest during the accumulation phase prior to age 59½ or disability (this may also apply to the annuitization phase if the annuity was not an immediate annuity and certain short payout terms are selected).[6]

4. With a few limited exceptions, if an annuity contract is held by a corporation or other entity that is not a natural person, the contract is not treated as an annuity contract for federal income tax purposes. This means that income on the contract for any taxable year is treated as current taxable ordinary income to the owner of the contract regardless of whether or not withdrawals are made.

5. If the client is forced to liquidate the investment in the early years of an annuity, management and maintenance fees and sales costs could prove expensive. Total management fees and mortality charges can run from 1% to 2½% of the value of the contract (occasionally as high as 3% in the case of variable annuities with a number of underlying guarantees). There may be a "back end" surrender charge if the contract is terminated within the first few years to compensate the insurer for the sales charges that are not typically levied "up front."

6. Investment earnings are taxed at the owner's ordinary income tax rate when the owner receives payments, regardless of the source or nature of the return. Consequently, investment earnings attributable to long-term capital appreciation (typically in variable annuities) do not enjoy the more favorable long-term capital-gain tax rate that would otherwise generally apply. This has become even more disadvantageous with the reduction of the maximum long-term capital-gain rate to 15% (or even 5% for lower-income taxpayers). Furthermore, investment earnings attributable to dividends on stocks that would qualify for the 15% maximum tax rate if the stocks were held outside an annuity will also be

taxed at the owner's ordinary income tax rate (although these dividends will not be taxed until withdrawal). Consequently, variable annuities where the annuity owner is inclined to invest in equities are much less attractive than previously. (See the question and answer section for a discussion of mutual funds versus variable annuities.)

TAX IMPLICATIONS

1. A client's investment in an annuity is returned in equal tax-free (return of capital) amounts during the payout phase. Any additional amount received is taxed at ordinary income rates. This means each payment consists of two parts – the first is considered return of capital and is therefore nontaxable, while the second part of each payment is considered return on capital (income) and is therefore taxable at ordinary rates.

The amount of each period's payment that will be considered nontaxable is determined by the following ratio, called the "exclusion ratio":[7]

$$\frac{\text{Investment in Contract}^8}{\text{Expected Return}^9}$$

The "exclusion ratio" is expressed as a percentage[10] and applies to each annuity payment equally through the payout phase. For instance, assume a 70-year-old purchases an annuity. He pays (the investment in the contract is) $12,000 for the annuity. Assume his expected return through the payout phase is $19,200.

The exclusion ratio is $12,000 / $19,200, or 62.5%. If the monthly payment he receives is $100, the portion that can be excluded from gross income is $62.50 (62.5% of $100). The $37.50 balance of each $100 monthly payment is ordinary income.

The full amount of each annuity payment received would be tax free if the investment in the contract exceeds the expected return (i.e., when the exclusion ratio would be greater than or equal to 100%).[11]

The excludable portion of any annuity payment may not exceed the unrecovered investment in the contract (unless the annuity started before January 1, 1987).[12] The "unrecovered investment in the contract" is the policyowner's premium cost, reduced by any dividends received in cash or used to reduce

premiums, and by the aggregate amount received under the contract on or after the annuity starting date to the extent it was excludable from income. Thus, the unrecovered investment in the contract is reduced each time an annuity payment is made, by the amount of the payment that is excluded from income by the exclusion ratio. This rule limits the total amount the policyowner can exclude from income to the total amount of his contribution. Once an annuitant has fully recovered his investment in the contract (which generally occurs at the end of the *expected* payout term), 100% of each subsequent payment will be taxable. Payments can continue beyond the expected payout term when the annuitant actually lives longer than his or her actuarial (expected) life expectancy.

Some annuities provide a refund if the annuitant dies before recovering his entire cost. The present value of the refund option must be ascertained by government tables and subtracted from the investment in the contract.[13] This would also apply if the annuity payout phase incorporated a combined life expectancy and term-certain structure.

The "expected return" is the total amount that the owner (or owners) should receive given the payments specified (which include an assumed internal growth rate) multiplied by the certain term or life expectancy according to the government's tables (currently Table V for single lives and Table VI for joint and survivor annuities). For instance, under Table V, a 70-year-old has a life expectancy of 16 years. If he (or she, since the life expectancy tables are unisex) receives $100 a month, the expected return would be $19,200 ($1,200 a year x 16 years).

2. When an annuitant dies before receiving the full amount guaranteed under a refund or period certain life annuity, the owner or beneficiary receiving the balance of the guaranteed amount will have no taxable income (unless the amount received by the beneficiary plus the amount that had been received tax free by the annuitant exceeds the investment in the contract).

If the refund or commuted (present) value of the remaining installments is applied by the owner or beneficiary to purchase a new annuity, payments received will be taxed under the annuity rules to the beneficiary. The refund amount will be considered the beneficiary's investment in the new contract and a new exclusion ratio must be determined. This option is often selected if the guaranteed refund amount will exceed the unrecovered investment in the contract and would otherwise create a partially taxable lump sum payment.

3. If the owner was receiving payments under a joint and survivor annuity, the surviving owner excludes from income the same percentage of each payment that was excludable by the first annuitant (assuming that the joint annuitants were joint owners). An income tax deduction may be available to the survivor owner/annuitant to the extent inclusion of the annuity in the estate of the first to die generated an estate tax (under the rules for income in respect of a decedent).

4. When an owner makes a partial withdrawal from the contract and takes a reduced annuity for the same term, a portion of the amount withdrawn will be subject to income tax.

5. When an owner makes a partial withdrawal from the contract (allocable to an investment in the contract made after August 13, 1982) and chooses to take the same payments for a different term, to the extent the cash surrender value of the contract exceeds the investment in the contract, gain will be realized in the form of a taxable withdrawal of interest.

6. The purchase of a variable annuity (see Questions and Answers below) is not taxed on income during the accumulation period. No tax will be payable until the earlier of: (a) the surrender of the contract; (b) withdrawal from the contract; or (c) the time payments under the annuity begin (annuitization). To obtain annuity treatment, however, the underlying investments of the segregated asset account must be "adequately diversified" according to IRS regulations.[14]

Payments made as an annuity under a variable annuity are not subject to the same exclusion ratio as is a regular fixed annuity. This is because it is impossible to determine the expected return. Instead, the following formula is used:[15]

$$\frac{\text{Investment in Contract}}{\text{Number of Years of Expected Return}}$$

If there is a period certain or refund guarantee, the investment in the contract is adjusted accordingly. If payments are made for a fixed number of years without regard to life expectancy, the divisor is that fixed number of years. If payments are made for a single life, use IRS Table V. If payments are to be made on a joint and survivor basis, use Table VI. As in the case of a fixed annuitization, the exclusion ratio no longer applies once an annuitant reaches his life expectancy and has fully recovered his investment in the contract.

If payments drop below the excludable amount in any given year, the annuitant can elect to redetermine the excludable amount in the next tax year in which he receives an annuity payment. The loss in exclusions is divided by the number of years remaining (in the case of a fixed period annuity). In the case of a life annuity the loss is divided by the annuitant's life expectancy computed as of the first day of the first period for which an amount is received as an annuity.[16]

For instance, assume a 65-year-old taxpayer purchased an annuity for $20,000. The contract provides variable monthly payments for life. Since his life expectancy is 20 years (Table V), he may exclude $1,000 of each annuity payment from income ($20,000/20). Assume on his 70th birthday he receives only $200, $800 less than his excludable amount. At age 70 his life expectancy is 16 years. He may elect to add $50 ($800/16) to his $1,000 exclusion, a total of $1,050 which he may exclude that year and in subsequent years.

7. If an annuitant dies before payments received equal cost, a loss deduction can be taken by the owner for the amount of the unrecovered investment, provided the annuity starting date was after July 1, 1986. So if a wife purchases a single premium nonrefundable annuity (whether on her own life, or alternatively on the life of her husband), and the annuitant dies before all costs have been recovered, a loss deduction will be allowed.

The deduction for the unrecovered investment in the contract is an itemized deduction, but not a miscellaneous deduction.[17] Therefore, it is not subject to the 2% floor. It is taken on the decedent's final return, and will be treated as a business loss, eligible to be carried back if the loss exceeds the income shown on the decedent's final return. In addition, these deductions can ultimately be taken by the estate or any other beneficiary that receives post-death payments.[18]

8. Amounts payable under a deferred annuity contract at the death of an annuitant (prior to the contract's maturity) will be partially taxable as ordinary income to the beneficiary. The taxable amount

is equal to the excess of (a) the death benefit (plus aggregate dividends and any other amounts that were received tax free) over (b) total gross premiums.

Beneficiaries can elect to delay reporting of the gain in the year of the annuitant's death if the beneficiary applies the death benefit under a life income or installment option within 60 days of the annuitant's death. The beneficiary will then report income according to an exclusion ratio. The beneficiary's investment in the contract will be the same as the annuitant's investment in the contract. The expected return is based on the income the beneficiary will receive and the beneficiary's life expectancy.[19]

9. The owner of an annuity often takes dividends, makes cash withdrawals, or takes other amounts out of the annuity contract before the annuity starting date. Such amounts are taxable as income to the extent that the policy cash value exceeds the investment in the contract – this results in a LIFO (last in, first out) type of treatment where all interest/growth is taxed before any tax-free return-of-capital payments can occur.[20]

This "interest-first" rule was imposed to discourage the use of annuity contracts as short term investment vehicles. Under this rule, a loan is considered a cash withdrawal.

Likewise, to the extent the contract is used as collateral for a loan, amounts borrowed will be taxable (to the extent that the amount received is less than or equal to the gain inherent in the contract). If the amount received exceeds the built-in gain, the excess of what was borrowed over potential gain is considered a tax free return of the contract owner's investment. With respect to contracts entered into after October 21, 1988, amounts borrowed increase investment in the contract to the extent they are includible in income under these rules.

In applying the interest-first rule, all contracts entered into after October 21, 1988 and issued by the same company to the same policyholder during any 12-month period are treated as one contract.

10. "Premature" distributions (those made before certain dates listed below) are subject not only to the normal tax on ordinary income but also to a penalty tax of 10%. The 10% penalty applies only to the amount of the distribution that is included in income.

The penalty for premature distributions will not apply to any of the following:[21]

a) Payments that are part of a series of substantially equal periodic payments made for the life (or life expectancy) of the taxpayer or the joint lives (or joint life expectancies) of the taxpayer and his beneficiary (unless the series of payments is modified under certain circumstances);

b) Payments made on or after the time the contract owner reaches age 59½;

c) Payments made on account of the contract owner's disability;

d) Payments made from qualified retirement plans and IRAs (but these are subject to other similar premature distribution requirements);

e) Payments made to a beneficiary (or annuitant's estate) on or after the death of an annuitant;

f) Distributions under an immediate annuity contract;

g) An annuity contract purchased on the termination of certain qualified employer retirement plans and held until the employee separates from service;

h) Payments allocable to investment in the contract before August 14, 1982.

11. If an annuity owner dies before the starting date of the annuity payments, the cash value of the contract must either be distributed within 5 years of death or used within one year of death to provide a life annuity or installment payments payable over a period not longer than the beneficiary's life expectancy. However, if the surviving spouse is the beneficiary; the spouse can elect to become the new owner of the contract instead of selecting one of the above options.[22]

The 10% premature distribution penalty tax does not apply to required after-death distributions.

If the annuity contract is transferred by gift, the tax deferral on the inside build up that was allowed to the original contract owner is terminated. The donor of the gift is treated as having received non-annuity income in an amount equal to the excess of the cash surrender value of the contract over the investment in the contract at the time of the transfer. The recipient of the gift will take a new basis in the contract equal to the donor's investment in the contract, plus the amount of gain recognized on the gift (note that the new basis, the sum of the donor's basis and the donor's investment in the contract, is generally equal to the fair market value of the contract).

12. Tax free build-up within the contract is allowed only to "natural persons."[23] If an annuity contract is held by a person who is not a natural person, then the annuity contract is not treated as an annuity and the income on the contract is treated as ordinary income received or accrued by the owner during that taxable year.

Corporations are not "natural persons." Neither is the typical trust, although a trust acting as the agent for a natural person would itself be considered a natural person. But if an employer is the agent for its employees, the contract will be considered as if owned by the employer. The employer will therefore be taxed on the inside build up. This means annuities are no longer appropriate tax advantaged investments for nonqualified deferred compensation agreements. Exceptions from the "natural persons" rules allow tax-free build up of the following annuities:[24]

a) Annuities received by the executor of a decedent at the decedent's death,

b) Annuities held by a qualified retirement plan or IRA,

c) Annuities considered "qualifying funding assets" (used to provide funding for structured settlements and by property and casualty insurance companies to fund periodic payments for damages),

d) Annuities purchased by an employer on termination of a qualified plan and held until all amounts under the plan are distributed to the employee or his beneficiary,

e) Annuities which are "immediate," i.e., those which have a starting date no more than one year from the date the annuity was purchased and provide for a series of substantially equal periodic payments to be made at least annually over the annuity period.

ALTERNATIVES

1. *Municipal bond funds* – These funds are an attractive option for retirement savings. The income they produce is exempt from federal and in many cases state income tax (although the sale of the bonds may result in taxable capital gains or losses, and some municipal bonds may be subject to the alternative minimum tax).

If a municipal bond fund's average yield is 6%, the equivalent taxable yield is almost 8.6% if the investor is in the 30% personal tax bracket. Money can be withdrawn from a municipal bond fund at any time without a tax penalty. A drawback of municipal bond funds as compared with annuities is the lack of a guaranteed return (bond rates may go down in future years, resulting in a lower yield on reinvestments of interest and matured bonds), and the potential for capital losses (if interest rates rise and bonds must be sold before maturity).

2. *Single premium life insurance (SPLI)* – This type of life insurance offers many of the same advantages of annuities, but incorporates a death benefit at issuance that is higher than the cash deposit (whereas, for annuities that contain a death benefit feature, the guarantee is usually *equal* to the amount of the cash deposit). However, there are important differences between an SPLI policy and other types of life insurance.

Generally, no income tax or penalties are payable until or unless the policy is surrendered. However, single premium life insurance policies issued after June 21, 1988 are generally modified endowment contracts (MECs). Distributions from MECs are taxed under essentially the same rules as annuity contracts. This means that any policy distributions, including loans, will be taxed at the time received to the extent that the cash value of the contract immediately before the payment exceeds the investment in the contract. Additionally, a 10% penalty tax may apply to certain distributions. In effect, the MEC rules remove the tax-free borrowing possibilities otherwise associated with life insurance policies.

A client should not be directed to a product – any product – merely for its tax advantages, since these are at the mercy of a voter-conscious Congress, as demonstrated by the effect of legislation passed in 1988 on SPLI, discussed above (although Congress generally provides some level of grandfathering provisions for most tax law changes, as it did for the new MEC rules in 1988). Certainly, if a client doesn't need the leverage that life insurance provides, the costs and restrictions make SPLI less attractive as there is a cost for the death benefit which, in turn, leaves less capital available for investment growth.

3. *Mutual funds* – During the accumulation period, variable annuities offer investment options that are essentially the same as mutual funds. Mutual funds do not enjoy the tax-deferred accumulation associated with variable annuities. However, tax on the capital appreciation of the assets in a mutual fund is deferred until the gains are realized. In addition, the realized gains are taxed as either long- or short-term capital gains, depending on the holding period. In contrast, all gains and income on the assets in the separate accounts of a variable annuity are taxed at ordinary income tax rates when paid. Also, mutual funds receive a step-up in basis at death in the hands of the heir.[25] There is no step-up in basis in annuity values in the hands of the beneficiary when the annuity contract owner dies.

WHERE AND HOW TO GET IT

Almost all life insurance companies offer annuities, and these companies distribute annuities to customers through life insurance agencies, many stock brokerage firms, independent insurance agents and financial planners, independent insurance brokerage firms, and direct to consumers through the mail and the internet. In addition, many banks now offer annuities (often through internal broker-dealers).

Variable annuities are considered securities under the federal securities laws. Consequently, they may be offered only by agents who are licensed and who have passed the applicable securities examinations. In addition, prospective buyers must be given a prospectus. The prospectus must describe the product and its features and the company offering the product. The prospectus must also explain and detail expense charges, contract options, investment options, and related information.

WHAT FEES OR OTHER ACQUISITION COSTS ARE INVOLVED?

There are five typical fees or charges that are usually incurred when purchasing annuities, particularly variable annuities. These include:

1. *Investment management fees* – These fees run from a low of about 0.25% to a high of about 1%.

2. *Administration expense and mortality risk charge* – This charge ranges from a low of about 0.5% to a high of about 1.3%. However, additional riders and features can increase this cost as high as nearly 2.0%.

3. *Annual maintenance charge* – This charge typically ranges from $25 to $100. However, it is often waived once total investments exceed a specified amount, such as $25,000.

4. *Charge per fund exchange* – This charge generally ranges from $0 to $10, but most funds will permit a limited number of charge-free exchanges per year. In addition, automatic rebalancing programs usually do not count towards this limit.

5. *Maximum surrender charge* – Surrender charges vary by company and policy and generally phase-out over a number of years. If the charge is lower, the phase-out range tends to be longer. For example, typical charges and phase-out periods are 5% of premium decreasing to 0% over 10 years or 8% of premium decreasing to 0% over 7 years.

Items 1 through 4 in the above list must be explicitly stated in the prospectus for a variable annuity. In a fixed annuity, these costs are generally incorporated into the management of the insurance company's general account and are simply netted out of the return credited to annuity-holders. Thus, when comparing fixed annuities, cost comparisons (although other non-cost aspects are also analyzed) are generally restricted to an evaluation of the comparable crediting rates of the general account and the surrender charges.

HOW DO I SELECT THE BEST OF ITS TYPE?

1. Compare, on a spreadsheet, the costs and features of selected annuities. Consider all of the five costs discussed above as well as how much can be withdrawn from the contract each year without fee. Be certain to fully read through the *full* details of costs/charges, guarantees, riders, and special features in the prospectus of a variable annuity.

2. Compare the total outlay with the total annual annuity payment in the case of fixed annuities. Be

certain to incorporate the time value of money if the payment schedules are different.

3. In an analysis of variable annuities, evaluate the total return for the variable annuity sub-accounts over multiple time periods (Lipper Analytical Services, Inc., and Morningstar, Inc., both have information to help assess this).

4. Compare the relative financial strength of the companies through services such as A.M. Best. Insist on a credit rating of A+ (or at the very least, thoroughly discuss with the prospective buyer the risks involved in purchasing from a company with a lesser rating).

WHERE CAN I FIND OUT MORE ABOUT IT?

Information on annuities can be obtained in newspapers (especially the *Wall Street Journal's* quarterly report on mutual funds and variable annuities) and in three major statistical sources: (a) A.M. Best Co., (b) Lipper Analytical Services Inc., and (c) Barron's. Substantial comparative information, particularly for fixed annuities, can often be obtained from insurance brokerage firms that deal with multiple annuity product providers.

QUESTIONS AND ANSWERS

Question – What are the different ways that annuities can be categorized?

Answer – Annuities are classified according to: (1) How premiums are paid; (2) What residual values, if any, are paid upon the death of the annuitant; (3) When benefit payments begin; (4) How many lives are covered; (5) What investment options are available to the owner of the annuity contract; and (6) How benefits are calculated. It is important to bear in mind that a change in almost any of the above classifications results in an adjustment in the payout the annuity provides to maintain an actuarially equivalent benefit.

Figure 8.1 shows how annuities are classified.

1. *Premium paying method – Single premium annuities* are often the ideal vehicles for people who have come into large cash sums. A single premium annuity will convert such amounts, for example, from an inheritance, from the sale of a business or a large piece of real estate, or from a qualified pension or profit-sharing plan lump-sum distribution, into a lifetime or certain fixed period stream of payments. Immediate annuities are virtually always single-premium annuities (clients with subsequent investment amounts would simply purchase another immediate annuity). Single premium structures also occur sometimes with deferred fixed annuities that provide for guaranteed interest crediting rates for a specified period (to prevent subsequent investments at these guaranteed rates if general interest rates decline in the future). Single premium structures are fairly rare amongst deferred variable annuities.

    Fixed premium annuities are favored by investors who do not have large cash sums to invest but who desire a regular investment program with a "forced saving" feature. Typically, fixed annual (semiannual, quarterly, monthly or even weekly) premium payments are required and continue until the desired annuity starting date (the date when payouts begin). Since the periodic premiums are fixed, the total accumulation, and therefore the ultimate annuity payout, is very predictable. Fixed premium annuities are now fairly rare, having been replaced instead by flexible-premium annuities.

    Flexible-premium annuities allow the contract owner to invest (make premium contributions) at any time and in any amount desired. In rare instances, the insurance company requires certain minimum annual contributions within the first few years, but after this initial period (or from the start in most cases) there are generally no restrictions or requirements that apply with regard to the timing or amount of further contributions.

2. *Disposition of poceeds* – A *life annuity* with no refund feature continues annuity payouts only as long as the annuitant (or one of the annuitants) survive, with no final payment or refund at the death of the last annuitant, even if the total paid out of the annuity is less than the amount invested in the contract. This can involve a high amount of risk, as the death of a lone annuitant shortly after contract issuance could result in a forfeiture of virtually the entire original deposit.

    For example, if Mr. Smith purchases an immediately annuity for $50,000 that provides for payments of $300/month for life, and dies after only receiving two payments, his total return out of the contract will be only $600. The remaining $49,400 of his original deposit will be forfeited to the insurance company, which will use the proceeds to help offset the payments due to annuity-holders that outlive their life expectancies.

Insurance companies also offer annuity contracts with minimum payback guarantees, since many investors are reluctant to forfeit a portion of their investment in the event of the premature death of the annuitant – particularly if there are heirs that will ultimately inherit all assets not consumed by the individual during his/her life. These guarantees take two forms.

Refund annuities promise to pay the difference between the amount invested in the contract (generally the total of the premiums paid) and the annuity payments actually paid out before the death of the annuitant. This refund takes the form either of lump-sum cash payments or of installment payouts. *Period certain annuities* promise to make payments for a stipulated period, such as 5, 10, or 20 years, or for the annuitant's life, whichever is longer. It is important to bear in mind that, due to the time value of money, this guarantee still does not make the annuity-holder entirely "whole" in comparison to having invested the assets in an alternative to begin with (where they would have ostensibly been *growing* during this time period, not merely preserving the original principal amount).

The payout period may also be short term - that is, for a specified period generally shorter than the expected life (or lives) of the annuitant(s). *Term-certain annuities* operate similarly to the amortization of a loan. Payments continue for a specified term only, regardless of when the annuitant dies. A *temporary annuity* is a variation on the period certain annuity concept. However, rather than paying a specified amount for the *longer* of the annuitant's life or the specified term, a temporary annuity continues payments only for the *shorter* of the annuitant's life or the specified term.

3. *Date benefits begin* – An *immediate annuity* begins annuity payments within one year after all premiums are contributed. Immediate annuities are commonly used when a person wishes to

convert a large lump-sum amount, such as a substantial distribution from a qualified pension or profit-sharing plan, the settlement proceeds of a lawsuit, or simply a sizeable amount of cash, into an immediate income stream. As the name suggests, payments from *deferred annuities* are delayed or deferred for a period of time (the 'accumulation phase') after the premiums or contributions have been completed. Deferred annuities are frequently used when a person has cash to invest before retirement and wishes to postpone the beginning of the annuity payments until retirement or later.

4. *Number of lives covered* – The annuity payout period may depend on one or two lives, or, less commonly, more lives. A *single life annuity* (with no refund feature) makes payments until the single covered life (the sole annuitant) dies. In the case of annuities based on two or more lives, payouts may continue until the last annuitant dies or only until the first annuitant dies (depending upon the exact terms of the contract). Annuities whose payments continue until the last death of the covered lives are called *joint and last survivor annuities*, or just joint and survivor annuities. Those annuities whose payments cease upon the first death are called *joint life annuities*. Currently, joint and survivor annuities are more common than joint life annuities.

A joint and survivor annuity may pay one amount while both annuitants are alive and the same, or another (lesser) amount, after the first death. The surviving annuitant often receives some specified percentage (called the survivor benefit ratio) of the amount payable before the first death. Survivor benefit ratios typically range from 50% to 100%, with 50, 66, 75, and 100% being the most common. For example, a joint and 75% survivor annuity paying a $50,000 annual joint benefit would pay $37,500 per year to the survivor after the first death. The amount of the survivor benefit ratio is generally selected at the inception of the payout phase (annuitization) of the contract.

The benefit payable to the survivor may also depend on which annuitant dies first. The *traditional joint and survivor annuity* has a principal annuitant and a secondary annuitant or beneficiary. The survivor benefit ratio applies only to the benefit payable to the surviving secondary annuitant after the principal annuitant's death.

Figure 8.1

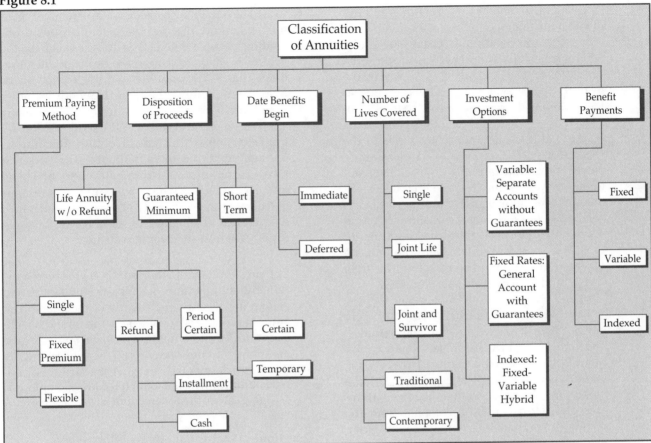

If the principal annuitant outlives the secondary annuitant, the benefit payments are not reduced. These types of payment structures are particularly common in joint and survivor annuity payments from defined benefit pension plans (where the former employee is the principal annuitant). In recent years an alternative form of the joint and survivor annuity has become popular. This *contemporary joint and survivor annuity* pays the reduced benefit to the survivor regardless of which annuitant dies first. These types of payment structures are most common from commercially available joint and survivor annuities. For a given total investment, insurance companies can afford to pay relatively higher joint and survivor benefits on these annuities than on traditional joint and survivor annuities.

5. *Investment options* – Fixed rate annuities are similar to universal life policies in that amounts credited to cash values are based on the insurer's current declared rate, subject to a minimum guarantee of about 3% to 4.5% (varying by annuity contract and insurance company). Rates paid on new money (current contributions) may be guaranteed for one to five years (or occasion-

ally as long as ten years). The currently declared rate depends on the performance of the insurer's general investment portfolio or general account, which is largely invested in fixed income investments such as bonds and mortgages. Although interest credits to the annuity depend on market rates on these types of fixed-income investments, the cash value itself is not market valued. Similar to a savings account, once interest is credited, the cash value will not decline if the market value of the underlying assets in the insurer's general account declines (however, some annuities levy a market-adjustment to the contract value based upon interest rate changes in the event of early surrender). The insurer bears the market risk.

Analogously, variable annuities are similar to variable insurance policies. The annuity owner may choose to invest contributions and cash values in a broad spectrum of investment options or separate accounts, which are similar to mutual funds (although the investor is limited to the selection of investment choices that are offered within the annuity contract). The investment options usually include diversified stock, bond, and money market funds and frequently include specialized stock funds, foreign stock and bond funds, real estate equity and mortgage funds, and even asset allocation funds (a type of balanced fund where the insurer's investment manager allocates investments among the other funds). In contrast with fixed rate annuities, cash values depend on the market value of the underlying assets in the selected separate accounts. Variable annuity owners bear the market risk of investment and forego minimum interest rate guarantees (although some limited guarantees may be available, subject to additional costs and substantial restrictions). However, they have the flexibility to choose their investment portfolio and the potential to earn far greater total returns than they would earn on fixed rate annuities.

Equity-index annuities (EIAs) are a recently devised hybrid of fixed and variable annuities. The returns on EIAs are linked to an equity index, such as the S&P 500 index. However, the annuity is not actually invested in the stocks making up the index. Rather, like fixed annuities, the returns to EIAs are paid from the insurance company's general account. However, the amount allocated to the EIA is based on some percentage, for example, 85%, of the appreciation in the reference index (often subject to annual caps and/or interest spreads). If the index declines in value, a minimum guaranteed amount (which may be 0%, but is generally never negative) is credited to the EIA. In this way, EIAs attempt to provide investors with some of the upside potential of the equity markets with the downside protection of more conservative general account investments.

6. *Benefit payments* – The annuity benefit may be fixed or variable. Fixed benefit annuities guarantee a minimum annuity benefit payment per dollar of accumulated value, similar to settlement options under life insurance policies. Variable benefit annuities make no guarantees. Annuity benefit payments depend on the market value of the assets in the separate accounts.

Question – What happens to the money paid to the insurance company when the annuitant dies?

Answer –A "pure life annuity" is one in which the continuation of payments by the insurer is contingent upon the continuing survival of one or more lives. The remaining consideration (premium) paid for the annuity that has not been distributed (including accrued interest) is fully earned by the insurer immediately upon the death of the annuitant. This is why annuities payable for the life or lives of one or more annuitants frequently include a minimum payment guarantee. In other words, many annuities include both life and fixed period or refund elements so that if death occurs prematurely, the annuitant and the annuitant's survivors will recover a total of at least a minimum amount. Therefore, each annuity payment where a minimum guarantee has been purchased is composed of (a) return of principal, (b) interest or earnings on invested funds, and (c) a survivorship element.

If an annuitant dies before having recovered the full amount guaranteed under a refund or period certain life annuity, the balance of the guaranteed amount is not taxable income to the refund beneficiary - until the total amount received tax free by the annuitant plus the total amount received tax free by the beneficiary equals the investment in the contract. From that point on, all additional amounts received are ordinary income.[26]

Question – What is the difference between a "fixed" annuity and a "variable" annuity?

Answer – Although annuities have many other ways of being classified, the major distinguishing factor of annuities being sold today is whether they are fixed or variable. About 90% of all outstanding annuity contracts fall into the fixed rate category, but variable annuities are becoming increasingly popular (variable annuities are also fairly *new* compared to the long history of fixed annuities). The investment account in a fixed rate contract operates much like the cash value account of a universal life policy. The annuity investment earns a fixed rate, which is often guaranteed for the first one to five (occasionally as many as ten) years of the contract. After that time, the rate depends on the investment success of the insurer's general portfolio (subject to a guaranteed floor, typically about 3 to 4.5%). The fixed rate contract gives the contract owner no choice or say in the underlying investments.

In some fixed rate contracts, there is a "bailout" provision. If the contract return falls below a certain rate (the "bailout rate"), the contract owner can terminate the contract without cost (i.e., without surrender charges).

Variable annuities are becoming increasingly popular because, in return for the assumption of greater risk, the contract owner may obtain both greater investment flexibility and a (potentially) higher return. The contract owner can select from among a number of separate accounts that are similar to mutual fund investments. The investment options typically include diversified stock, bond, and money market funds. Most insurers also now offer a broad array of alternative funds such as specialized stock funds (sector funds, small-capitalization stock funds, index funds), foreign stock and bond funds, junk bond funds, real estate equity and mortgage funds, GNMA-type funds, and asset-allocation funds (where the company's investment manager selects portfolio weights allocating investments among the other funds). It is important to note that although there is a great deal of latitude in investment selection, the investor is limited exclusively to the selection of investment choices that are offered within the annuity contract.

Question – What is the difference between a joint annuity and a joint and last survivor annuity?

Answer – A joint life annuity is a contract that provides a specified amount of income for two or more persons named in the contract. Income ends upon the first death. A joint and last survivor contract is much more popular because payments continue until the last death among the covered lives. Obviously, this form of annuity is more expensive than other forms because, on average, it will pay income for a longer time. This increased cost is reflected in a lower annuity payment than would be paid under a single life annuity at either of the two ages, or under the joint life annuity structure.

Clients can purchase the joint and survivor annuity on either a pure life basis (ending at the later death) or with a certain number of payments guaranteed. Most insurers offer a form of joint and survivor annuity that pays the full amount while both annuitants are alive and then two-thirds or one-half of that income when the first annuitant dies. This is called a "joint and two-thirds" or "joint and one-half annuity."

Question – How does the variable annuity work?

Answer – The variable annuity was the product of a search for a tool that would provide a guaranteed lifetime income that could never be outlived and also provide a relatively stable purchasing power in times of inflation by allowing for returns that may keep pace with (or even exceed) inflation. This can be contrasted with the level payments generally received from fixed annuities, whose purchasing power will be eroded over time by inflation.

The variable annuity is based on equity investments. Premiums are paid to the insurance company during the "accumulation phase." That money is placed into one or more separate accounts. The funds in these accounts are invested separately from the other assets of the insurer. Each year, some money is taken out of the contract owner's premium (or deducted from the account value) for expenses. The balance is applied to purchase "units of credit" in the separate accounts.

The number of credits purchased depends on the current valuation of a unit in terms of dollars. For example, if each unit was valued at $10 a unit based on current investment results, a $100 level premium (after expenses) would purchase 10 units. If the value of a unit dropped because of investment experience, the premium would purchase more units. If the value of a unit increased, the same premium would buy fewer units. The price of a unit of a separate account is analogous to the NAV price of a share of a mutual fund. This unit purchasing continues until the "maturity" of the contract.

At the transition to the payout phase (annuitization) of the contract, the insurer credits the value of the contract owner's total accumulation units to a retirement fund. A value of a given number of accumulation units will purchase so many retirement income units (based on actuarial principles). Note that a variable annuitization does not promise to pay a fixed number of dollars each month but rather a fixed number of retirement income units. In other words, the dollar amount of each payment depends on the dollar value of a retirement income unit (also called an annuity unit) when the payment is made. The dollar value of an annuity unit is in turn based on the investment results of the separate accounts. For example, assume an annuitant was entitled to a payment based on 10 annuity units each month. If the dollar value of an annuity unit varied from $12.10 to $12.50 to $12.80, the annuitant would be paid $121, $125, and $128, respectively.

Question – What are the risks assumed by the contract owner under a variable annuity?

Answer – Under a variable annuity, the insurer assumes only the risk of fluctuations due to mortality and expenses (guaranteeing that the annuitant will not outlive his or her income and that internal expense fluctuations will be absorbed). This means the contract owner is assuming the entire investment risk. If the separate accounts are invested poorly or in the wrong investments, the annuitant could receive fewer dollars of income than would have been paid under a fixed annuity.

Question – Why, if payments from variable annuities depend on the market value of the underlying assets, do variable annuities have an assumed investment rate (AIR)?

Answer – Under most variable annuity contracts there is an assumed investment rate (AIR) that the investment portfolio must earn in order for benefit payments to remain level. If the investment performance exceeds the AIR, the level of benefit payments will increase. On the other hand, if the selected investments underperform the AIR, the level of benefit payments will decrease.

For example, assume a variable annuity contract is issued with a 6% AIR and a beginning unit value of $20. The contract is issued with a payout of 100 units per month (providing an initial monthly payment of $20/unit x 100 units/month = $2,000/month). The investment yield during the first month of the contract was 10%; during the second month the investment yield was 4%. The monthly benefit can be calculated by monitoring the changes in the unit value and by comparing the actual performance with the assumed 6% interest rate. During the first month, the 10% return on the portfolio exceeds the assumed 6% AIR by 4% – which leads to a 4% increase in the $20 unit value. The new unit value is now $20.80 ($2,080 per month). During the subsequent month, because the actual return is only 4%, which is 2% less than the AIR, there will be a 2% reduction in the unit value to $20.38 ($2,038 per month). The unit value could actually drop below the beginning $20 value ($2,000 per month) if investment performance remains below the assumed 6% level for an extended period of time. However, for an increased cost, some annuities provide a guarantee that the monthly payment will never drop below the initial monthly payment, regardless of adverse investment performance.

Question – Can a person select the assumed interest rate (AIR) used to determine the payments from a vari-

able annuity and, if so, what impact will it have on the level of benefit payments?

Answer – Under some contracts, the purchaser is able to select the AIR from a narrow range of possible rates (such as 3, 5, or 7%). It is much easier to receive an increasing stream of benefit payments by selecting a lower AIR – however, this can be initially more expensive (meaning the starting monthly payment will be reduced). The effect of choosing a different AIR can be demonstrated by returning to the example of the previous question.

If an AIR of 8% rather than 6% is chosen, the benefit increase in the first month will be 2% instead of 4%. The unit value changes to $20.40 instead of $20.80. The next month's decrease in benefits is more drastic, a 4% reduction rather than the 2% reduction. The unit value decreases to $19.58 instead of $20.38 from the lower AIR. Choosing the less costly higher AIR will start with a higher initial benefit (i.e., with an 8% AIR, the starting payment in the above example would likely have been higher than $2,000) but will increase the likelihood that benefit payments increase less rapidly and decrease more rapidly.

Keep in mind that although variable annuity contracts are intended to provide a hedge against inflation and protect the purchasing power of the benefits through positive market returns, the increases in market value have not always occurred at exactly the same time that prices increase. Often prices go up significantly before the market provides high returns and increases the level of benefits. These temporary mismatches between price increases and benefit increases are inevitable and can lead to a temporary loss of purchasing power.

Question – Although the investment options in variable annuities are similar to mutual funds, mutual funds are taxed differently than annuities and annuities charge higher fees and loads to cover various guarantees within the annuity contract. How can one determine if and when a variable annuity is a better investment than a mutual fund?

Answer – Conceptually, variable annuities are simply mutual funds wrapped in an instrument that permits tax on all income, whether ordinary or capital gain, to be deferred until monies are distributed. If annuitized, distributions are taxed under the rules of Internal Revenue Code section 72, which essentially prorates the recovery of basis over the distribution period. In addition, and *more importantly*, the investor may enjoy any number of a myriad of contractual guarantees in a variable annuity contract (although the details of these guarantees are *highly* variable across various contracts). However, an investor must pay a price for these advantages.

First, the amount of each annuity payment in excess of the amount of basis recovery is taxed at ordinary income tax rates, regardless of whether it is attributable to ordinary investment income (i.e., interest or dividends, including the potentially tax-favored qualifying dividends) or capital appreciation. Since an investor's marginal ordinary income tax rate always equals or exceeds the applicable capital gains rate (depending upon whether the gains are short-term or long-term), he/she will forfeit the favorable lower tax treatment on the portion of payments that is attributable to previously unrecognized capital gains. In addition, the taxpayer will be unable to take advantage of capital losses as they accrued (although capital losses will still offset gains within the contract, ultimately reducing the amount of growth taxed as ordinary income at withdrawal).

Second, variable annuities incur mortality and expense (M&E) charges (for other various riders and guarantees) that range from about 0.5%, up to 1.25% (occasionally as high as 2.0% with additional riders, features, and guarantees) in addition to the usual fund expenses which average from about 0.6% to 1.25% on equity funds (occasionally as high as 2.25% for small-cap equity or international equity funds), depending on the type of fund.

Third, most variable annuities impose surrender charges if money is withdrawn within the first five to nine years. The charge typically declines to zero in steps of 1% per year. As a general rule, variable annuities are less attractive than mutual funds if there is any possibility the contract will be surrendered within the first five to seven years. The period of tax deferral will generally be insufficient to overcome the additional fees and surrender charges. It is notable that in recent years, an increasing assortment of variable annuities are being offered to the public that allow for substantially reduced periods of surrender charges (as short as three years, or even one year) or no surrender charges. However, these contracts have increased M&E charges to compensate for the higher risk (to the insurance company) of an early liquidation.

Fourth, and potentially more problematic, is the 10% early withdrawal penalty on distributions from annuities before age 59½. Distributions that are not part of a series of substantially equal periodic payments for the life (or joint life) expectancy of the annuitant(s) are in most cases subject to a 10% penalty tax on the taxable amount withdrawn from the annuity, in addition to the ordinary income tax due.

Keep in mind that, although equity mutual funds do not enjoy the same degree of tax deferral as variable annuities, they are, nonetheless, tax-favored investments. Although the tax on ordinary dividend and interest income earned by a fund is paid by the shareholders in the year the income is earned, the tax on capital gains is deferred until the gains are recognized, either through buy and sell transactions within the mutual fund portfolio or when the investor sells his shares in the fund.

Therefore, when trying to decide whether variable annuities or mutual funds are more appropriate for a particular client situation, the results (particularly the analysis of comparable returns) depend on certain critical assumptions regarding the size of the differential in fees and loads, the rate of return, tax rates on ordinary income, qualifying dividends, and long-term capital gains, the turnover rate of the underlying investments, the length of accumulation period, and whether annuity distributions will be subject to a 10% penalty. In addition, the relative merit depends on how the variable annuity will be liquidated. Variable annuities are relatively more attractive if proceeds will be annuitized rather than taken in a lump-sum (because longer time periods generally favor the annuity's tax-deferral benefits).

For any combination of assumptions regarding the fee differential, tax rates, and rates of return and distribution options, there is a "break-even holding period" after which an investor can withdraw the accumulated value in a variable annuity, pay the regular income tax and, if applicable, the 10% penalty, and still be left with at least as much as he would have accumulated in a taxable mutual fund.

Figure 8.2 compares the effective after-tax rates of return of a variable annuity with a no-load mutual fund over various accumulation periods and a range of assumed pre-tax and before-expense rates of return. Since the maximum tax rate of 15% for long-term capital gains and qualifying dividends is scheduled to expire after 2009, the break-even periods are first computed as if they have already expired. This places the variable annuities in the most favorable light possible at this time. Subsequent analyses apply the current law rates for long-term gains and qualifying dividends assuming instead that the current law rates are extended indefinitely beyond 2009. Additional assumptions include that:

- Both the mutual fund and variable annuity are invested in common stocks;

- There are no front-end loads on either the mutual fund or the variable annuity;

- The variable annuity has surrender charges that grade to zero after year seven;

- The investor's marginal tax rate for current taxable (ordinary) income is 35% and for deferred gains is 20% (applicable state and local taxes are ignored);

- Regarding the mutual fund, 40% of the total returns are attributable to dividends and 60% to capital gains;

- The investor will be age 59½ or older at the end of the investor's variable annuity holding period (i.e., withdrawals from the variable annuity will not be subject to the 10% early-withdrawal penalty);

- All of the earnings from the variable annuity will be deferred until distributions are made;

- Total annual expense charges for administration and management of the mutual fund are 1%;

- Total annual expense charges for the variable annuity are 2% (1%, comparable to the administrative and management charges for the mutual fund, plus a 1% annual mortality charge); and

- The average annual turnover rate (for the calculation of taxes on gains recognized when the fund buys and sells securities) for the mutual fund is 20% (i.e., the average holding period for securities within the mutual fund is five years).

Figure 8.2 shows the effective after-tax and after-expense rate of return for the investment in the mutual fund and the variable annuity for the as-

sortment of accumulation periods and the various assumed pre-tax and before-expense rates of return. The values are computed by assuming that both the mutual fund and the variable annuity are liquidated at the end of the specified accumulation period and that all taxes on the tax-deferred gains and tax-deferred income, respectively, are paid at that time. The vehicle with the largest effective return is the better performing investment; that is, it is the one that would provide the investor with the greatest after-tax balance at the end of the accumulation period.

Figure 8.2 shows that even if the total pre-tax and before-expense average annual compound rate of return on the investment is as great as 12%, the variable annuity becomes the better accumulation vehicle only if the accumulation period approaches 20 years. That is, under the assumptions listed above, if an investor is planning to accumulate funds for a period shorter than about 20 years, the mutual fund would be the better accumulation vehicle.

The period of years until the variable annuity becomes the better accumulation vehicle is even longer for lower assumed total rates of return. For instance, the average annual compound rate of return on the S&P 500 index since 1926 has been just slightly over 10%. Using this rate of return as a general guideline for a broadly diversified portfolio of stocks, an investor would have to wait almost 27 years before the variable annuity would provide the greater after-tax accumulation. If the rate of return is expected to be 8% or less, even 40 years is not a sufficient accumulation period for the variable annuity to outperform the mutual fund after taxes and expenses. In addition, it is important to note that most of the assumptions used in this exercise favor the variable annuity, and alternative assumptions could extend the break-even period even further.

In most cases, investors who accumulate substantial sums for retirement, either inside or outside of an annuity, do not take a lump-sum distribution, which would then trigger the immediate recognition and taxation of all deferred income or accumulated gains. Instead, they make periodic withdrawals (and/or outright annuitize the contract) which enables them to continue to enjoy the benefits of tax deferral on the remaining balance over the distribution years. This continuation of tax deferral increases the relative benefit of the variable annuity as compared to the mutual fund.

Figure 8.2

	EFFECTIVE AFTERTAX RATE OF RETURN Mutual Fund v. Variable Annuity					
	Lump-Sum Distribution at End of Accumulation Period					

Accum Period		Total Before-Tax and Before-Expense Rate of Return					
		12%	11%	10%	9%	8%	7%
5	MF	7.82	7.09	6.37	5.65	4.93	4.22
	VA	6.91	6.19	5.47	4.76	4.05	3.36
	Dif	0.91	0.90	0.90	0.89	0.88	0.86
10	MF	7.94	7.20	6.46	5.72	4.99	4.26
	VA	7.37	6.57	5.78	5.00	4.24	3.49
	Dif	0.57	0.63	0.68	0.72	0.75	0.77
15	MF	8.00	7.25	6.50	5.75	5.01	4.28
	VA	7.50	6.89	6.05	5.21	4.40	3.61
	Dif	0.50	0.36	0.45	0.54	0.61	0.67
19	MF	8.03	7.27	6.52	5.77	5.03	4.29
	VA	8.01	7.12	6.23	5.37	4.52	3.70
	Dif	0.02	0.15	0.29	0.40	0.51	0.59
20	MF	8.04	7.28	6.52	5.77	5.03	4.29
	VA	8.07	7.17	6.28	5.40	4.55	3.72
	Dif	-0.03	0.11	0.24	0.37	0.48	0.57
22	MF	8.05	7.29	6.53	5.78	5.04	4.30
	VA	8.18	7.26	6.36	5.47	4.60	3.76
	Dif	-0.13	0.03	0.17	0.31	0.44	0.54
23	MF	8.05	7.29	6.53	5.78	5.04	4.30
	VA	8.23	7.31	6.40	5.51	4.63	3.78
	Dif	-0.18	-0.02	0.13	0.27	0.41	0.52
26	MF	8.06	7.30	6.54	5.79	5.04	4.30
	VA	8.38	7.44	6.51	5.60	4.71	3.84
	Dif	-0.32	-0.14	0.03	0.19	0.33	0.46
27	MF	8.07	7.30	6.54	5.79	5.04	4.30
	VA	8.42	7.48	6.55	5.63	4.73	3.85
	Dif	-0.35	-0.18	-0.01	0.16	0.31	0.45
33	MF	8.08	7.32	6.56	5.80	5.05	4.31
	VA	8.65	7.69	6.73	5.79	4.87	3.96
	Dif	-0.57	-0.37	-0.17	0.01	0.18	0.35
34	MF	8.08	7.32	6.56	5.80	5.05	4.31
	VA	8.68	7.72	6.76	5.82	4.89	3.98
	Dif	-0.60	-0.40	-0.20	-0.02	0.16	0.33
40	MF	8.09	7.33	6.56	5.81	5.06	4.31
	VA	8.85	7.88	6.91	5.95	5.00	4.07
	Dif	-0.76	-0.55	-0.35	-0.14	0.06	0.24
Crossover Yr.		19.4	22.5	26.9	33.3	43.6	62.2

Assuming a distribution period of 20 years, Figure 8.3 shows the effective annual compound after-tax and after-expense rates of return for the entire accumulation and distribution period and the number of years in the accumulation period (the crossover year) until the variable annuity would outperform (provide greater annual after-tax distributions than) the mutual fund. These crossover years were calculated using the same assumptions as listed above plus the following assumptions with regard to the taxation of distributions during the 20-year distribution period:

- Distributions from the annuity are assumed to be level and taxed under the rules of IRC Section 72. Under these rules, basis is recovered in a pro rata fashion over the distribution period. For example, if the basis is $100,000 and the distribution period is 20 years, 1/20 of the basis, or $5,000 of each annual payment is treated as a nontaxable recovery of basis. The remaining portion of each annual payment is taxable as ordinary income. Given the assumptions of a level 35% tax rate on ordinary income and level annual distributions, the after-tax payments from the annuity will also be level each year over the distribution period;

- The amount withdrawn in any given year from the mutual fund is the amount necessary to provide equal after-tax annual distributions over the 20-year distribution period. It is assumed that the after-tax dividend income each year is the first money withdrawn. If, in a given year, the after-tax dividend income is less than the desired after-tax distribution, shares in the mutual fund must be sold to make up the difference. It is assumed that gain is recognized

and taxed on the sale of such shares in the same proportion as the ratio of the total accumulated gains within the portfolio to the total value of the portfolio. For example, if the total value of the portfolio is $100,000 and the built-in gain is $40,000, a sale of $5,000 worth of securities would result in the recognition and taxation of $2,000 of gains. The remaining $3,000 would be tax-free recovery of basis.

The variable annuity becomes relatively more advantageous when the continuing benefits of tax deferral over an extended payout period are also included in the analysis. However, even if funds are to be liquidated over a 20-year period, the variable annuity becomes the better alternative (under the listed assumptions) only if the accumulation period is still quite long.

For example, assume an investor expects to invest at a total pre-tax and before-expense rate of return of about 10% (matching the long-term compound average annual rate of return on the S&P 500 index). The investor can expect the variable annuity to outperform a mutual fund only if the investor plans to accumulate money in the variable annuity for about 20.4 years before beginning distributions over a 20-year payout period. Stated another way, an investor who plans to retire at age 65, for instance, would gain by making contributions to a variable annuity before age 45. However, any further investments made after age 44 would be better invested in the mutual fund outside the variable annuity. The after-tax payments associated with a systematic liquidation of the mutual fund for a twenty year period starting at age 65 for contributions after age 44 would be greater than for comparable contributions to the variable annuity.

Figure 8.3

MUTUAL FUND VERSUS VARIABLE ANNUITY 20-Year Annuitization			
Total ROR	Effective Aftertax ROR		Crossover Year
	MF	VA	
12%	8.0920%	8.0920%	13.8
11%	7.3265%	7.3265%	16.5
10%	6.5683%	6.5683%	20.4
9%	5.8156%	5.8156%	26.4
8%	5.0670%	5.0670%	36.3
7%	4.3235%	4.3235%	54.5

Although the new preferential tax rate provisions for capital gains and dividend income are scheduled to expire in 2009, many experts expect that these provisions may become permanent or be extended beyond 2009. Figures 8.4 through 8.7 show break-even periods assuming the new tax rates for capital gains and qualifying dividend income will continue indefinitely into the future for taxpayers in the 35%, 30%, 25%, and 15% tax brackets, respectively.

Since dividend income is now taxed differently than interest income, the tables compute break-even periods by assuming that the income component of the return on the underlying mutual fund is composed of equal shares of dividend and interest income. Therefore, the preferential dividend income tax rate applies to half of the fund's income and the taxpayer's ordinary tax rate applies to half of the fund's income.

In addition, given the change in tax rates, it is assumed that variable annuities will have to reduce their mortality charges and expenses to have much chance to compete with mutual fund investments. Consequently, the additional variable annuity mortality charge is assumed to be just 0.75% rather than 1% as in the analyses above.

Otherwise, the analysis remains essentially the same, except that the new tax rates are used and the crossovers or break-even periods are computed for a number of different capital-gain proportions. That is, the break-even periods are shown not just for a mutual fund with 60% of the return attributable to capital appreciation but for capital-gain proportions ranging from 0% to 95% of the return. All other assumptions remain the same as those used in computing the values in Figures 8.2 and 8.3. The charts find the number of years that money must be invested in the variable annuity before payouts commence in order for the after-tax payouts from the annuity over the 20-year payout period to exceed the after-tax payments the investor could obtain from the mutual fund.

Not surprisingly, the crossover or break-even period is longer uniformly than under the previous tax regime. For example, Figure 8.4 assumes the taxpayer is in the 35% tax bracket, just as was assumed when computing the values in Figure 8.3. Capital appreciation comprised 60% of the return in Figure 8.3. The grayed cells of Figure 8.4 show the corresponding values using the new tax rates for long-term gains and qualifying dividends for a taxpayer in the 35% bracket. The crossover or break-even period under the new tax rules until an amount invested in the variable annuity could provide the same after-tax payout over a 20-year period as the investment in the mutual fund outside the annuity is over 60 years until the rate of return exceeds 9%. At a 10% rate of return, the crossover occurs after 54

Figure 8.4

MUTUAL FUND VERSUS VARIABLE ANNUITY BREAK-EVEN YEARS FOR TAXPAYER IN 35% BRACKET								
	Assumed Return							
	6%	**7%**	**8%**	**9%**	**10%**	**11%**	**12%**	**13%**
0%	60+	47+	33+	24+	19+	15+	12+	10+
15%	60+	60+	41+	30+	24+	19+	16+	14+
30%	60+	60+	53+	39+	31+	25+	21+	18+
45%	60+	60+	60+	51+	40+	33+	28+	24+
60%	60+	60+	60+	60+	54+	44+	37+	32+
75%	60+	60+	60+	60+	60+	60+	52+	45+
90%	60+	60+	60+	60+	60+	60+	60+	60+
95%	60+	60+	60+	60+	60+	60+	60+	60+

Assumptions: 0.75% variable annuity mortality charge; 1.00% management and operating expense rate of both mutual fund and VA; 35% tax rate on ordinary income; 15% tax rate on long-term capital gain; 15% tax rate on dividend income; 25.0% averaged tax rate on mutual fund dividend and interest income; 20% portfolio turnover rate (portion of built-up gain taxed each year as a result of portfolio turnover); 50% dividend income portion of mutual fund income; 20-year payout period; **Capital Gain Portion**: the proportion of the fund's total return attributable to capital appreciation

Figure 8.5

MUTUAL FUND VERSUS VARIABLE ANNUITY BREAK-EVEN YEARS FOR TAXPAYER IN 30% BRACKET								
	Assumed Return							
	6%	7%	8%	9%	10%	11%	12%	13%
0%	60+	50+	32+	24+	18+	14+	12+	9+
15%	60+	60+	41+	30+	23+	18+	15+	13+
30%	60+	60+	52+	38+	29+	24+	20+	17+
45%	60+	60+	60+	49+	38+	31+	25+	22+
60%	60+	60+	60+	60+	50+	40+	34+	29+
75%	60+	60+	60+	60+	60+	55+	46+	40+
90%	60+	60+	60+	60+	60+	60+	60+	59+
95%	60+	60+	60+	60+	60+	60+	60+	60+

Key: 0.75%: variable annuity mortality charge; 1.00%: management and operating expense rate of both mutual fund and VA; 30%: tax rate on ordinary income; 15%: tax rate on long-term capital gain; 15%: tax rate on dividend income; 22.5%: averaged tax rate on mutual fund dividend and interest income; 20%: portfolio turnover rate (portion of built-up gain taxed each year as a result of portfolio turnover); 50%: dividend income portion of mutual fund income; 20-year payout period; **Capital Gain Portion**: the proportion of the fund's total return attributable to capital appreciation.

Figure 8.6

MUTUAL FUND VERSUS VARIABLE ANNUITY BREAK-EVEN YEARS FOR TAXPAYER IN 25% BRACKET								
	Assumed Return							
	6%	7%	8%	9%	10%	11%	12%	13%
0%	60+	56+	35+	24+	17+	13+	10+	8+
15%	60+	60+	43+	30+	22+	18+	14+	11+
30%	60+	60+	54+	37+	28+	22+	18+	15+
45%	60+	60+	60+	47+	35+	28+	23+	19+
60%	60+	60+	60+	60+	46+	36+	30+	25+
75%	60+	60+	60+	60+	60+	49+	40+	34+
90%	60+	60+	60+	60+	60+	60+	57+	48+
95%	60+	60+	60+	60+	60+	60+	60+	55+

Key: 0.75%: variable annuity mortality charge; 1.00%: management and operating expense rate of both mutual fund and VA; 25%: tax rate on ordinary income; 15%: tax rate on long-term capital gain; 15%: tax rate on dividend income; 20%: averaged tax rate on mutual fund dividend and interest income; 20%: portfolio turnover rate (portion of built-up gain taxed each year as a result of portfolio turnover); 50%: dividend income portion of mutual fund income; 20-year payout period; **Capital Gain Portion**: the proportion of the fund's total return attributable to capital appreciation.

Figure 8.7

MUTUAL FUND VERSUS VARIABLE ANNUITY BREAK-EVEN YEARS FOR TAXPAYER IN 15% BRACKET								
	Assumed Return							
	6%	7%	8%	9%	10%	11%	12%	13%
0%	60+	60+	60+	60+	60+	60+	44+	33+
15%	60+	60+	60+	60+	60+	60+	60+	49+
30%	60+	60+	60+	60+	60+	60+	60+	60+
45%	60+	60+	60+	60+	60+	60+	60+	60+
60%	60+	60+	60+	60+	60+	60+	60+	60+
75%	60+	60+	60+	60+	60+	60+	60+	60+
90%	60+	60+	60+	60+	60+	60+	60+	60+
95%	60+	60+	60+	60+	60+	60+	60+	60+

Key: 0.75%: variable annuity mortality charge; 1.00%: management and operating expense rate of both mutual fund and VA; 15%: tax rate on ordinary income; 5%: tax rate on long-term capital gain; 5%: tax rate on dividend income; 10%: averaged tax rate on mutual fund dividend and interest income; 20%: portfolio turnover rate (portion of built-up gain taxed each year as a result of portfolio turnover); 50%: dividend income portion of mutual fund income; 20-year payout period; **Capital Gain Portion**: the proportion of the fund's total return attributable to capital appreciation.

years. This is about 24 years longer, or more than twice as long, as the crossover period of 20.4 years under the old tax rules. If the investment earns 12%, the crossover occurs under the new rules after 37 years, or about 23 years longer than under the previous tax rules.

As Figure 8.7 shows, the crossover point is over 60 years in almost all circumstances for taxpayers in the 15% bracket. This is primarily because taxpayers in the 15% tax bracket pay long-term capital gains tax rates of only 5% (rather than 15% in all prior scenarios).

Figures 8.4 through 8.7 also show the crossovers if it is assumed no portion of the return (0%) is attributable to capital gains. This could conceivably be the case if the portfolio were invested in preferred stocks and bonds (it would also be applicable in a high-turnover portfolio, where all capital gains are taxed as short-term capital gains). Even if a taxpayer in the 35% bracket could earn 10% on such a portfolio, the crossover still does not occur for 19 years. For taxpayers in the 30% or 25% tax brackets, the crossover is only a year shorter for each step down in the tax bracket.

Figure 8.8 presents the results for a taxpayer in the 35% tax bracket assuming that the variable annuity assesses **no mortality** charge at all. In other words, it assumes the variable annuity and the mutual fund have exactly the same expenses. The table shows that if investors can find annuities with very low mortality charges, and the investors are planning to invest in assets with low appreciation potential, the annuities could be viable alternatives. However, based upon current rates of return for fixed-income investments, a 6% return would probably be an aggressive assumption, at least for the first few years of the investment. At 6%, investors still need to invest in the annuities for at least 14 years before they plan to start taking distributions to make the investment profitable compared to investing outside the annuity.

Basically, what all of this means is that if investors anticipate that the new tax regime for dividends and capital gains are more likely than not to remain in effect beyond their current sunset date of 2009, then it appears that it is hard to justify any investment in variable annuities *on the basis of returns alone*. Even if the tax rates revert to the pre-2003 rules in 2009, taxpayers investing in variable annuities now will still find their break-even periods for investments in variable annuities considerably longer than under the prior rules. **However, the above charts have not taken into account the value provided by the annuity guarantees.**

Our entire analysis up to this point has assumed a level annual return. However, in point of fact, we know that annual returns are *not* level. Although the S&P 500 index has had a long-term compound average annual rate of return of approximately 10%

Figure 8.8

MUTUAL FUND VERSUS VARIABLE ANNUITY BREAK-EVEN YEARS FOR TAXPAYER IN 35% BRACKET								
No Variable Annuity Mortality Charge								
				Assumed Return				
	6%	7%	8%	9%	10%	11%	12%	13%
0%	14+	12+	10+	8+	7+	6+	5+	5+
15%	19+	15+	13+	11+	10+	8+	7+	7+
30%	23+	20+	17+	14+	13+	12+	10+	10+
45%	30+	25+	21+	17+	16+	15+	14+	13+
60%	36+	30+	26+	23+	21+	19+	17+	17+
75%	44+	38+	33+	29+	27+	24+	22+	21+
90%	54+	46+	41+	36+	33+	31+	29+	27+
95%	58+	49+	44+	39+	36+	34+	33+	30+

Key: 0.00%: variable annuity mortality charge; 1.00%: management and operating expense rate of both mutual fund and VA; 35%: tax rate on ordinary income; 15%: tax rate on long-term capital gain; 15%: tax rate on dividend income; 25%: averaged tax rate on mutual fund dividend and interest income; 20%: portfolio turnover rate (portion of built-up gain taxed each year as a result of portfolio turnover); 50%: dividend income portion of mutual fund income; 20-year payout period; **Capital Gain Portion**: the proportion of the fund's total return attributable to capital appreciation

over the past 75 years or so, individual year returns have ranged dramatically, and substantial losses in a particular year are possible. If withdrawals need to be made from the investment, either on account of retirement (or other) spending needs, or because of a death of the account-holder, the guarantees provided by the annuity may become highly relevant. A severe market downturn shortly before a substantial withdrawal can provide an *immense* savings to the annuity-holder as the contractual guarantees are exercised. Over the long run, if the annuity is properly priced, individual fluctuations will average out and will approach the long-term averages (and concomitant long-term-based results) shown in the charts contained herein. However, on an individual basis, the guarantees may be vitally important to an individual client.

In addition, the provision of underlying guarantees may allow an investor to otherwise take a higher level of risk than he/she may otherwise be comfortable with. Consequently, an annuity investor might potentially earn an average rate of return of 10% in an S&P 500-like investment, while the mutual fund holder might only earn an average rate of return of 8%, due to a more conservative investment in light of the lack of underlying guarantees. The potential for a higher rate of return to an annuity-holder in light of higher investment risk taken on (mitigated by reduced total risk due to annuity

contractual guarantees) can substantially shorten the break-even period necessary.

Because the appropriate amount of risk can vary tremendously on an individual basis, and risk characteristics can change over time, the primary factor in the decision to select a variable annuity should be its value as a *risk management* tool, not merely as a tax-deferral method. Because of the tremendous variety of contractual guarantees, with varying costs, available through commercial variable annuity providers, full analysis of the relevant options, and the client's needs and concerns, is *vital* to the decision to utilize a variable annuity and the appropriate selection of a particular contract.

Question – What is an FPDA?

Answer – An FPDA is a flexible premium deferred annuity. As the last two words indicate, the contract provides for the accumulation of funds to be applied at some future time designated by the contract owner to provide an income based upon the life of the annuitant(s) (or for a certain term). Premium payments are flexible – they can be paid as frequently or infrequently as the owner desires. They can be paid monthly, annually, or one or more years can be skipped as there is no specified contribution amount or required payment frequency. Most insurers do set a minimum payment level for administrative purposes – typically this runs from $25 to $50 for most companies.

Most FPDA contracts have no "front-end" load. Annual loads vary but many are under $50 a year. Some companies charge loads based on a percentage of each contribution, as a percentage of the annuity fund balance, or as a percentage of both. The insurer often does charge a "back-end" load (a surrender charge) when a cash withdrawal in a year exceeds a stipulated percentage of the fund balance – typically the annual "free withdrawal" amount is 10% of the premium deposits or contract value. The surrender charge will typically reduce year by year to 0 % by the 7th or 8th contract year.

With fixed FPDAs, insurers guarantee minimum interest rates (typically 3 to 4.5%) but usually pay much higher rates. The actual rate will depend on the earnings rate of the insurer. Current rates have ranged from 5 to 11% in recent years but are subject to rapid change as interest rates trend upward or downward (although the crediting rate is often set on the contract anniversary date and is valid for the entire year). Focus should be placed on the net (after loads and charges) return earned, over the entire expected holding period, when comparing fixed annuities.

Most variable annuities are FPDAs. Fixed annuities are often FPDAs, but some types do not have flexible premiums, or are immediate annuities. Equity-indexed annuities are virtually always deferred annuities, but often do not have flexible premiums.

Question – What is an SPDA?

Answer – An SPDA is a single premium deferred annuity. It provides, as its name implies, a promise that an annuity will begin at some time in the future in return for a single premium.

For fixed annuities (variable annuities are rarely single-premium contracts), a minimum stated rate of interest is guaranteed but most insurers pay competitive market rates. The actual rate paid is a function of: (a) the current investment earnings of the insurer, and (b) how competitive the insurer is determined to be. The rate is subject to change by the insurer.

The SPDA, like the FPDA, is back end loaded. No front-end charges are imposed. Surrender charges are graded and partial withdrawals are often allowed without charge. Bailout provisions allow the contract owner to withdraw all funds without the imposition of a surrender charge if the interest rate actually credited falls below the "bailout rate" (typically set at the inception of the contract as 1 to 3% below the rate being credited at that time). Keep in mind that on any withdrawal both an ordinary income tax and a penalty tax may apply.

Question – What is a "temporary life annuity"?

Answer – A temporary life annuity is one which provides for fixed payments until the earlier of the death of the annuitant(s) or the end of a specified number of years. To compute the annuity exclusion ratio, expected return is found by multiplying one year's annuity payments by a multiple from the appropriate IRS annuity table.[27]

Question – In recent years, a new product, called an "equity-indexed annuity" has burst on the scene. What is it and what is the attraction?

Answer – Equity-indexed annuities (EIAs) are annuities with a crediting rate (return) that is tied to an index such as the S&P 500 stock index. But they are not the same as a variable annuity that invests directly in the securities of a market index (such as the S&P 500) through the use of sub-accounts. Rather, the assets deposited under an EIA are held directly by the insurance company, which invests the funds as necessary to apply a certain unique, formulaic crediting rate. EIAs promise to credit to the annuity-holder some percentage of the amount by which the underlying index has increased, subject to annual caps, if the index goes up, and to cut the investor's losses at zero (or even guarantee a slight positive return), if the index goes down.

The fundamental point is this: If the market goes up, the investor is happy because the value of the annuity will increase by some partial amount of the market increase. If the market goes down, the investor is happy because the annuity still has an underlying guarantee against loss.

However, the gain on the index does not include dividends, if any, earned by the companies making up the index. The loss of dividend income, a cap on market gains, and the possibility that the investor will only receive a percentage (such as 40, 60, or 80%) of the market return, can be a major drag on performance.

Figure 8.9

THE VANGUARD INDEX TRUST RETURNS AND FIXED ANNUITY RATES: 1976-1995				
Vanguard Index Trust 500*				
Year Ended (%)	Capital Return (%)	Income Return (%)	Total Return (%)	Fixed Annuity Rates**
1976	4.1	1.2	5.3	2.1
1977	-11.7	3.7	-8.0	7.0
1978	0.8	5.0	5.8	7.3
1979	12.1	5.9	18.0	7.8
1980	25.5	6.4	31.9	8.4
1981	-9.8	4.6	-5.2	9.5
1982	14.8	6.1	20.9	11.0
1983	16.2	5.1	21.3	11.5
1984	1.5	4.7	6.2	12.0
1985	26.1	5.1	31.2	12.1
1986	14.0	4.0	18.0	11.2
1987	2.3	2.4	4.7	9.8
1988	11.6	4.6	16.2	9.5
1989	26.7	4.6	31.3	9.0
1990	-6.8	3.4	-3.4	8.4
1991	26.3	3.9	30.2	7.8
1992	4.4	3.0	7.4	7.5
1993	7.1	2.7	9.8	6.5
1994	-1.5	2.6	1.1	6.2
1995	34.4	3.0	37.4	6.1

* Vanguard Index Trust - 500 portfolio data from its inception August 1, 1976, to December 1995. Includes reinvestment of income dividends and any capital gains distributions and is adjusted for account maintenance fees.

** Representative fixed annuity rates for the period August 1, 1976, to December 1995.

Question – Are equity-indexed annuities (EIAs) a good buy for astute individual investors?

Answer – EIAs issued by one company will differ (possibly quite dramatically) from EIAs issued by another company, but the annual investment returns generally are tied to a percentage (which could easily range from 40% to 80% or higher, and may be subject to periodic adjustments) of the S&P 500's gains (or occasionally other indexes such as the NASDAQ 100), not including dividends. The percentage (usually less-than-100%) of market returns

and cap on gains is offset by protection against market losses.

It is not possible to compare historical fixed annuity, variable annuity, and EIA results because EIAs have only been available for several years. But, it is possible to construct a theoretical comparison by using the Vanguard Index Trust 500 portfolio and fixed annuity yields from August 1, 1976, to December 31, 1995. The results are shown in Figure 8.9.

As suggested by the data in Figure 8.9, "does not include dividends" can be a drag on an EIA's perfor-

Figure 8.10

VARIABLE VS. FIXED VS. INDEXED ANNUITIES: A THEORETICAL HISTORICAL COMPARISON (BASED ON A $100,000 INVESTMENT, AUGUST 1976 - DECEMBER 1995)								
Time Period	Variable Annuity Vanguard 500* Projected		Fixed Annuity Projected		Company A Indexed** Projected		Company B Indexed** Projected	
	Value ($)	Return (%)	Value ($)	Return (%)	Value ($)	Return (%)	Value ($)	Return (%)
8/76-12/80	152,340	10.3	136,980	7.6	125,190	5.4	131,050	6.5
8/76-12/85	282,310	11.8	233,073	9.5	181,310	6.6	193,930	7.4
8/76-12/90	491,520	11.8	368,187	9.5	278,980	7.4	273,320	7.4
8/76-12/95	1,005,300	12.7	512,018	8.8	480,320	8.5	396,170	7.4

* Vanguard Index Trust-500 portfolio total returns reduced by 100 basis points to simulate variable annuity expenses.

** Company A computes the cash value every five years by taking 83% of the highest S&P 500 market value, not including dividends, during the five-year period. For example, if the starting investment is $100,000 and the five-year high point is $130,353, the fifth-year cash value is $125,190 — 83% of the highest capital gain for the five years. Each five years the equity-indexed annuity policyowner can decide to cash it in, convert to a traditional fixed annuity or lock into the equity-indexed annuity for another five years. Company B allows for 85% of the S&P 500 market gain (not including dividends), capped at 14% in any one year, but treats market losses as zero. For example, if the S&P 500 (without dividends) went up 10% in year one, Company B would recognize 8.5%; if it went up 20% in the second year Company B would recognize 14%; and if the index went down 5% in year three, Company B would recognize 0%.

mance. Dividends accounted for about 29% of the total return for the Vanguard Index Trust 500 (an S&P 500 index fund), over the 20 years from 1976 to 1995. Giving up dividends plus imposing a cap on market capital gains can be a severe penalty to pay for protection against periodic market losses, as will be shown below. In many cases, consumers may not even realize that dividends are not included in the index performance measure used by EIAs.

Figure 8.10 simulates the results for a fixed annuity, variable annuity, and indexed annuity, had they been purchased August 1, 1976. The table shows results through the end of 1995, in five-year increments, using the data from Figure 8.9.

Figure 8.11 shows the same simulation, but for the period January 1991 through the end of 1995. Isolating these five years is interesting because fixed annuity rates were much lower, while equity returns were robust, which are the market results that motivated insurance companies to develop the hybrid EIA.

Please note that Figures 8.10 and 8.11 are not an attempt to predict possible future results for fixed, variable, or indexed annuities. The only purpose of these tables is to show how the EIA formulas affect results relative to fixed and variable annuities.

If these 20 years offer any guidance (as shown in Figures 8.10 and 8.11), EIAs are a poor substitute for a variable annuity invested in the S&P 500 index. The benefit of eliminating periodic market losses is simply overwhelmed by the deficits of giving up reinvested dividend income and placing a limit on the capital gains in figuring the index. When the proper choices are identified, most astute investors will conclude that variable annuities are a better choice than EIAs.

However, these conclusions do not mean to imply that EIAs have no use whatsoever. In certain circumstances, investors in their 50s and 60s who are making their final investment push to retirement may wish to consider EIAs because their investment time horizon might be just five to 10 years.

Figure 8.11

VARIABLE VS. FIXED VS. INDEXED ANNUITIES: THE LAST 5 YEARS (BASED ON A $100,000 INVESTMENT, JANUARY 1991 - DECEMBER 1995)								
Time Period	Variable Annuity Vanguard 500* Projected		Fixed Annuity Projected		Company A Indexed** Projected		Company B Indexed** Projected	
	Value ($)	Return (%)	Value ($)	Return (%)	Value ($)	Return (%)	Value ($)	Return (%)
1/91-12/95	213,283	16.4	139,065	6.8	172,169	11.5	140,712	7.1

As they have so little time to earn back any losses caused by market setbacks or investment mistakes, new investments and the repositioning of equity-invested assets might now be considered with an eye on conservation. If fixed-income yields are low and expected to remain so, an EIA can be a reasonable investment product for this investor. It will allow for the potential of outperforming fixed-income returns while not being fully exposed to market risk.

Question – What is the difference between an owner-driven and annuitant-driven contract?

Answer – The differentiation between owner-driven versus annuitant-driven contracts addresses the consequences of the death of an annuitant during the accumulation phase of a deferred annuity.

In the past, almost all contracts were annuitant-driven, but recently some contracts are occasionally owner-driven. It is important to read the details of the annuity contract to determine which type of contract is being evaluated or is in force.

Under the classic model of an annuitant-driven contract, if the annuitant were to pass away during the accumulation phase, the contract would pay the death benefit to the primary beneficiary of the contract. Any special death benefit provisions of the contract apply at the death of the annuitant. In situations where the owner and annuitant of the contract are the same person, this is not consequential. However, this can have substantial impact if the owner and annuitant are different people.

For example, let us assume that John Doe owns an annuitant-driven contract on his wife, Jane Doe. John Doe is the primary beneficiary, and John's son Daniel is the contingent beneficiary. The annuity contract has a current value of $120,000, and the death benefit is $150,000. In the event that Jane dies, the enhanced death benefit of $150,000 will be paid

to John. However, it is important to remember that all annuities, whether owner- or annuitant-driven, must pay out at the death of the owner.[28] Therefore, we must contrast this with the result in the event that John Doe dies. If John Doe were to pass away, under an annuitant-driven contract, the enhanced death benefit would not be paid; the current value would be paid out, and Daniel would receive $120,000, *not* $150,000.

Alternatively, the results of an owner-driven contract reverse these results. Under an owner-driven contract, the death of the owner, John Doe, will cause a payout of the enhanced death benefit. A death of the annuitant, Jane Doe, simply creates an annuitant-less contract, and the owner will have the option of assigning a new annuitant.

Because of the radical differences in potential payouts at the death of the owner or annuitant, it is critical to understand whether a contract is owner-driven or annuitant-driven when structuring the setup of owners, annuitants, and beneficiaries.

Question – Where can I obtain additional information?

Answer – This chapter has still only lightly covered some of the complexities of annuities. The broad range of choices, and the numerous changes in tax law as applied to annuities necessitates a thorough understanding for anyone wishing to seriously delve into this investment tool. For further reading on annuities, see *The Annuity Handbook: A Guide to Non-Qualified Annuities*, by Darlene Chandler (Cincinnati, OH: The National Underwriter Company).

CHAPTER ENDNOTES

1. The term "annuity" encompasses all periodic payments resulting from the systematic liquidation of principal. A payment of interest only would not be an annuity payment. See Treas. Reg. §1.72-1.

2. See Leimberg, Stephan R., et al., *The Tools and Techniques of Estate Planning*, 13th ed. (Cincinnati, OH: The National Underwriter Company, 2004).

3. Except for FIFO for withdrawals from contracts that have not been substantially modified and were entered into prior to August 14, 1982.

4. This only applies to annuities purchased *outside* a retirement plan; investments purchased *inside* a retirement plan already pass by beneficiary designation and are not subject to probate. Annuities provide no additional probate avoidance benefits *inside* a retirement plan that are not already provided by the underlying plan.

5. This only applies to annuities purchased *outside* a retirement plan; investments purchased *inside* a retirement plan are already tax-deferred by virtue of the retirement plan. Annuities provide no additional tax-deferral benefits *inside* a retirement plan, and thus should be purchased for other reasons, such as risk management.

6. Annuitization of a deferred annuity during the accumulation phase will be subject to the pre-59½ penalty unless the IRC Section 72(q)(2)(D) requirements for substantially equal periodic payments are met.

7. IRC Sec. 72(b)(1).

8. Investment in the contract is defined as the consideration paid for the contract (i.e., the premium) less any amounts received back from the insurer that were income tax free. IRC Sec. 72(c). Premium cost does not include any premiums paid for (1) waiver of premiums, (2) disability income, or (3) accidental death ("double indemnity"). Rev. Rul. 55-349, 1955-1 CB 232.

9. Expected Return is defined as the aggregate payments the annuitant can be expected to receive under the annuity contract. In other words expected return is:

*	If payments are for a fixed period:	The sum of the guaranteed payments. IRC Sec. 72(c)(3)(B). See also Treas. Reg. §1.72-5(c).
*	If payments are of a fixed amount (with no life expectancy):	The sum of the guaranteed payments. IRC Sec. 72(c)(3)(B). See also Treas. Reg. §1.72-5(d).
*	If payments are for the life (or lives) of the annuitant(s):	Sum of one year's annuity payments multiplied by the life expectancy of the live or lives involved. IRC Sec. 72(c)(3)(A).

10. Round the quotient to 3 decimal places. See Treas. Reg. §1.72-4(a)(2).

11. Treas. Reg. §1.72-4(d)(2).

12. If the "annuity starting date" (first day of first period for which an amount is received as an annuity) is after December 31, 1986, the exclusion ratio applies to all payments received until the annuitant has fully recovered his or her investment in the contract. Once the annuitant's investment is fully recovered, further payments are subject in full to ordinary income tax. IRC Sec. 72(b)(2). But if the annuity starting date was prior to January 1, 1987, the amount tax free under the annuity exclusion ratio remains income-tax-free for as long as the annuitant receives payments, no matter how long he or she lives. IRC Sec. 72(b)(4)(A), before amendment by Sec. 1704(I)(1), PL 104-188, 8/20/1996.

13. See IRC Sec. 72(c)(2).

14. Rev. Rul. 2003-91, 2003-33 IRB 347.

15. Treas. Regs. §§ 1.72-2(b)(3), 1.72-4(d)(3).

16. Treas. Reg. § 1.72-4(d)(3)(ii).

17. IRC Sec. 72(b)(3)(A).

18. IRC Sec. 72(b)(3)(B).

19. IRC Sec. 72(h).

20. Different rules apply to contracts purchased on or before August 13, 1982, allowing withdrawal of principal first and interest/growth second. IRC Sec. 72(e)(5).

21. IRC Sec. 72(q)(2).

22. IRC Sec. 72(s)(3).

23. IRC Sec. 72(u).

24. IRC Sec. 72(u)(3).

25. This is true until 2009, and then in 2011 and thereafter. In 2010, under EGTRRA 2001, new rules repeal the current estate tax system, but also remove the across-the-board, step-up-in-basis rules at death, replacing them with a new set of rules for basis increase at death with limitations. Then in 2011, these new rules "sunset" and the pre-2010 rules will again be in effect.

26. IRC Sec. 72(e)(2).

27. Table IV or VIII of Treas. Reg. §1.72-9. See also Treas. Reg. §1.72-5(a)(3).

28. IRC Sec. 72(s)(1).

Chapter 9

CURRENT–ASSUMPTION WHOLE LIFE

WHAT IS IT?

Current-assumption whole life insurance (CAWL) is essentially a hybrid of traditional cash-value whole life insurance and universal life insurance (UL). At the time of issue, the premium and death benefit levels are fixed, similar to traditional whole life policies. However, similar to UL, the insurer credits separately identifiable interest and charges separately identifiable mortality and expense charges to an accumulation account.

As a result of this combination of features of both ordinary whole and universal life, CAWL is sometimes called interest-sensitive whole life or fixed-premium universal life. But neither of these terms is quite accurate.[1] The term "fixed premium" is not apt because premium and death benefit levels generally remain fixed only for a certain period of time, such as five years, based on anticipated interest, mortality, and expenses. At the end of each period, the premium level and sometimes the death benefit level are recalculated taking into account the actual accumulation account value and new experience assumptions. Also the term "interest sensitive" is not correct since most CAWL policies are "sensitive" not only to interest or investment performance on the underlying assets but also to the mortality and expense experience of the company.

Features of universal life possessed by CAWL include:

1. In contrast with traditional whole life and similar to UL, CAWL policy elements are "unbundled," or separately reported, and the actual cash value accumulation is prospectively indeterminate.

    An accumulation account is used to track cash values. Each year the premium less annual expense charges is added to the preceding year's accumulated account balance. Interest is credited to the balance in the cash value accumulation account based on the company's current rate. The policy promises to pay a rate not less than the contract guaranteed rate, which varies from 4 to 6%, but is typically 4 or 4½%. Finally, mortality charges, which are based on the net

amount at risk (face amount less cash value), are deducted from the account. The maximum mortality rate the company may charge is also specified in the contract. Since the interest rates that will be credited and the mortality charges that will be debited to the cash accumulation account balance in future years are uncertain, the future accumulation account balance cannot be known with certainty.

Some CAWL policies have no explicit expense charges. Instead, expense charges may be wrapped into the mortality charges or included as an adjustment to the current rate that is credited to cash values. Also, a few CAWL policies are truly interest-sensitive policies only. Similar to many traditional whole life policies, the mortality charge is fixed and guaranteed.

2. Most CAWL policies have very low or no front-end loads and, instead, impose back-end surrender charges.

    Typically, the entire first-year premium, less the usual yearly expense charge, is added to the accumulation account. Therefore, most of the policyowner's premium payment immediately begins to earn interest. The back-end charge is levied when and if the policy is lapsed or surrendered. The surrender charge is usually specified as a percentage of the premium or cash accumulation account. The surrender charge rate typically declines each year until it reaches zero in 9 to 15 years.

3. Some insurers offer CAWL policies that provide a death benefit similar to UL option II. Thus, the death benefit of these policies is equal to a level face amount plus the balance in the cash accumulation account.

4. The current interest rate on some CAWL policies is linked to a specific index, such as the yield on Treasury bills or an index of high-grade corporate or government bonds.

5. Policyowners may usually withdraw the excess in the cash accumulation account, subject to any surrender charges, without impairing the base policy.

Features of traditional level-premium life insurance possessed by CAWL include:

- level premiums and a level face amount between each "redetermination period;"

- a minimum interest guarantee;

- guaranteed maximum mortality charges;

- minimum guaranteed cash values;

- nonforfeiture values;

- a policy loan provision;

- a reinstatement period; and

- settlement options.

Contract provisions similar to traditional forms of insurance that are or can be obtained as options in CAWL include:

- waiver of premium;

- guaranteed purchase of insurability;

- accidental death benefits; and

- cost-of-living adjustments.

WHEN IS THE USE OF THIS TOOL INDICATED?

CAWL is indicated when a person wants the fixed-premium, "forced-savings" feature of traditional whole life and the potential for better investment results than those guaranteed in traditional policies. CAWL has a minimum guaranteed cash value accumulation but the policyowner bears the risk that the investment performance and mortality experience of the company will be less favorable than originally assumed. Required premiums may have to be periodically increased or the face amount of coverage decreased if performance does not meet expectations.

ADVANTAGES

1. Premiums are level and fixed between each redetermination period.

2. Cash value interest or earnings accumulate tax-free or tax-deferred, depending on whether gains are distributed at death or during lifetime.

3. CAWL frequently pays a higher effective interest rate on cash values than the rate available with tax-free municipal bonds.

4. Cash values are not subject to the market risk associated with longer-term municipal bonds and other longer-term fixed income investments.

5. Policy cash values can be borrowed at a low net cost. Although policyowners must pay interest on policy loans, cash values continue to grow and are credited with at least the minimum guaranteed rate in the policy. Consequently, the actual net borrowing rate is less than the stated policy loan rate.

6. The policy is "transparent." That is, policy illustrations and annual reports explain each of the policy elements separately. This "unbundling" of the policy allows the policyowner to specifically identify and track premiums, death benefits, interest credits, mortality charges, expenses, and cash values. Further, the policyowner can compare projections with actual performance over time.

7. Many polices have cost-of-living riders that, without evidence of insurability, automatically increase the policy death benefit periodically by the increase in the CPI (Consumer Price Index).

8. In contrast with most traditional whole life policies, most CAWL policies use "back-end loads," or surrender charges, rather than "front-end loads." (A load is the charge imposed by an insurer to recover the initial policy expenses. The terms front end and back end refer to when the charge is imposed.) Consequently, most of the policyowner's initial premiums go into cash values, subject, of course to regular annual expense and mortality charges. Therefore, cash values build more quickly than with traditional whole life policies.

9. Many CAWL policies permit policyowners to withdraw excess cash value accumulations without impairing the policy or changing the death benefit.

DISADVANTAGES

1. In the early years, the amount of protection is lower relative to the premium spent with CAWL than with term insurance. However, later, as term rates rise while the premium for CAWL remains relatively level, the reverse will typically be true.

2. Surrender of the policy within the first 5 to 10 years may result in considerable loss since surrender values reflect the insurance company's recovery of sales commissions and initial policy expenses. In addition, most CAWL policies levy surrender charges rather than up-front fees or loads. These surrender charges generally decline each year the policy is held. After approximately 9 to 15 years, no explicit charges are assessed if the policy is surrendered.

3. Although traditional participating whole life policies are indirectly "interest-sensitive," mortality and expense charges are guaranteed. In contrast, current-assumption policies only guarantee that mortality charges and expense rates will not exceed certain maximums. Consequently, policyowners bear more of the risk of adverse trends in mortality or expenses than if they owned traditional whole life policies. Also, if the trend of mortality costs and expenses improves, CAWL policyowners may participate in the improvement through lower charges.

4. Some CAWL policies, similar to many traditional whole life policies, use what is called the "direct recognition" method to determine the amounts credited to cash values that are subject to policy loans. Under this method, only the portion of the cash value that is not used to secure a loan is credited with the current rate. Amounts backing the loan are credited with the minimum guaranteed rate or a rate usually 1 to 2 percentage points lower than the loan rate. The direct recognition method is most commonly used in policies that have fixed loan rates. Typically, policies with variable loan rates, (and some with fixed loan rates) do not employ the direct recognition method and instead credit current rates on the entire cash value without regard to loans.

5. A CAWL policy will lapse if the premium is not paid. However, some policyowners may view this feature as an advantage since it forces them to pay the premiums regularly. CAWL differs from universal life in this respect since a UL policy will not necessarily lapse if a premium payment is missed.

TAX IMPLICATIONS

General Tax Rules

CAWL policies are taxed in the same manner as other types of life insurance policies. Death benefits are usually paid free of any federal income tax. CAWL policies are subject to the same income, estate, gift, and generation-skipping transfer taxation rules as all other types of life insurance policies. See Appendices A through G for a complete discussion of the taxation of life insurance.

Living benefits from CAWL policies are also taxed in the same manner as living benefits from other types of life insurance policies. Annuity-type distributions are taxed under the cost-recovery rules of Section 72 which states that the policyowner's investment in the contract (generally, total premiums paid less prior nontaxable distributions) is recovered ratably over the expected payout period. Interest paid on or credited to living benefits held by the insurer under an agreement to pay interest is immediately taxable in full.

All other types of living benefits are generally taxed under the "cost-recovery rule." The cost-recovery rule, which is sometimes called the FIFO (First-In-First-Out) rule, treats amounts received as nontaxable recovery of the policyowner's investment in the contract. Only after the policyowner's investment is fully recovered are additional amounts received treated as taxable interest or gain in the policy. Included in this category of living benefits are policy dividends, lump-sum cash settlements of cash surrender values, cash withdrawals, and amounts received on partial surrender. Such amounts are included in gross income only to the extent they exceed the investment in the contract (as reduced by any prior excludable distributions received from the contract). In other words, nonannuity distributions during life are generally first treated as a return of the policyowner's investment in the contract, and then as taxable interest or gain.

Exception to the Cost–Recovery Rule

There is an important exception to the general cost-recovery rule for withdrawals within the first fifteen years after the policy issue date that are coupled with reductions in death benefits. Since death benefits are generally reduced in an amount equal to any withdrawal of cash values, these withdrawals will generally be fully or partially taxable to the extent of gain in the policy.

Such withdrawals are taxed in whole or in part as ordinary income to the extent "forced out" of the policy as a result of the reduction in the death benefits. The taxable amount depends on when the withdrawal is made.

- *Within first five years* – If the withdrawal takes place within the first five years after policy issue, a very stringent and complex set of tests applies.[2] Potentially, a larger portion, or perhaps all, of any withdrawal within the first five years will be taxable if there is gain in the policy.

- *Fifth to fifteenth years* – For withdrawals between the end of the fifth year and the end of the fifteenth year from the issue date, a mathematical test applies. Essentially, the policyowner is taxed on an income-first basis to the extent the cash value before the withdrawal exceeds the maximum allowable cash value under the cash value corridor test for the reduced death benefit after the withdrawal.[3] Frequently, only a portion or none of the withdrawal will be taxable in these cases.

ALTERNATIVES

1. *Traditional Participating Whole Life Insurance* – CAWL has many of the features of traditional whole life. Also, many participating whole life policies now offered are essentially a type of current-assumption policy, with current mortality and expense experience as well as interest reflected in the level of dividends paid.

2. *Universal Life* – UL and CAWL are both "unbundled" current-assumption policies. In most respects, CAWL can be described as a form of fixed-premium universal life.

3. *Variable Life (VL)* – If a VL policyowner selects a portfolio of investments within the policy that is similar to the general investment portfolio of the insurance company (mostly long-term bonds and mortgages), investment performance and cash value accumulations can be expected to be similar to that of CAWL.

4. *A combination of a level-premium deferred annuity and decreasing term insurance* – Cash values accumulate in both annuities and CAWL policies on a tax-deferred basis. Therefore, a combination of a level-premium deferred annuity and a

decreasing term policy can provide levels of tax-preferred cash accumulation and death benefits similar to a CAWL policy.

There are some important differences, however. Withdrawals, lifetime distributions, or loans from each are treated differently for tax purposes. Although most CAWL policies do not permit withdrawals, as such, except to the extent of excess cash values, amounts withdrawn or partial surrenders are taxed under the cost-recovery rule. That is, the amounts are included in taxable income only to the extent they exceed the investment in the contract. In contrast, such distributions from annuities are taxed under the interest-first rule. In other words, the amounts are fully taxable until the excess over the investment in the contract has been recovered.

Nonannuity distributions from an annuity contract received before age 59½ may be subject to a 10% penalty tax. Also, while loans from life insurance policies are not subject to tax, loans from annuities, if permitted, are treated as distributions and taxed under the interest-first rule. That is, loan proceeds are subject to regular income tax and may be subject to the 10% penalty tax. Also, loan provisions of deferred annuity contracts are generally more restrictive than those of life insurance policies.

The annuity/term combination will require increasing premiums over the years for the term coverage. In addition, the mortality charges for term insurance coverage are typically higher than the mortality charges in a CAWL policy. Finally, the death proceeds from the insurance policy generally may pass to the beneficiary entirely income and estate tax free, regardless of who the beneficiary is, if the policyowner has no incidents of ownership in the policy. The gains on the annuity contract will still be taxable income to the beneficiary and will avoid estate taxation only if the annuitant's spouse is the beneficiary and can take advantage of the estate tax marital deduction.

5. *A combination of investments in tax-free municipal bonds and decreasing term insurance* – This combination can create a cash accumulation and death benefit similar to a level-death benefit CAWL policy. Similar to the cash values in a life insurance policy, municipal bonds may be used as collateral for loans without any adverse income tax consequences. However, interest paid on debt secured by municipal bonds is generally not tax deductible. Although not the general rule, in some cases, the interest paid

on life insurance policy loans may be tax deductible. (See Appendix F for a further discussion of policy loans.) The life insurance policy allows the death benefits to be transferred by operation of the contract and avoids probate. Municipal bonds are part of the probate estate and must be distributed by will. Once again, if the policyowner has no incidents of ownership, the death proceeds are paid estate tax free. The municipal bonds will escape estate tax only if they are left to the spouse who takes advantage of the estate tax marital deduction.

WHERE AND HOW DO I GET IT?

Over 80 life insurance companies in the United States offer some form of current-assumption or interest-sensitive whole life policies. Most of these companies are stock, rather than mutual, life insurance companies.

WHAT FEES OR OTHER ACQUISITION COSTS ARE INVOLVED?

Most CAWL policies have low or no initial charges or front-end fees. Rather, most or all the first year premium is added to the cash accumulation account and begins to earn interest immediately. However, the commission and other start-up costs of issuing new policies are substantial and must be recovered somehow. These costs are generally recovered through a combination of annual expense charges and surrender charges.

The surrender charge in the first year may be as high as 100% of the first year premium. After the first year, the surrender charge is usually computed as a declining percentage of the cash accumulation account. The rate will usually reach zero in 9 to 15 years. As a result of competition in the industry, shorter phaseout periods have been the general trend.

The surrender charge can be determined explicitly by looking at the policy illustration or ledger statement. This statement shows both a cash value figure and a net cash value figure for each policy year. The cash value is the amount on which interest credits are based. The net cash value is the amount that the company would pay if the policy was surrendered. The difference is the surrender charge.

Commissions paid to agents are one of the principal components of the total issue costs. Commissions are commonly 50% or more of the first year premium for an ordinary whole life design policy. If the policy is of a limited-pay type, a lower commission rate ranging from 3 to 20% is effectively paid on the amount of premium in excess of the ordinary whole life premium. Commissions on renewal premiums are lower. Total initial and renewal commissions generally equal about one year's level premium if the original plan of insurance remains the same.

The company must also charge for ongoing administrative and state premium tax expenses. Companies also typically include an allowance for contingencies and a margin for contribution to the company's surplus or profit. Premium taxes average about 2½% of the premium paid. The ongoing expenses vary by company but are reflected in their expense charges. Allowances for contingencies and profit are often included by grossing-up mortality charges and / or grossing-down the current interest rate from the net rate actually earned on company funds.

Policy expenses and commissions may be recouped in a number of ways including a flat policy assessment charge, a percentage of premium charge, a fee based on each $1,000 of face amount, or some combination of each. The trend has been towards lower policy assessment charges and level percentage of premium charges. Many insurers now charge about $25 to $50 per year plus 2½ to 20% of each premium. The percentage of premium charge is generally lower for higher-premium, higher-death-benefit policies than for lower-premium, lower-death-benefit policies.

HOW DO I SELECT THE BEST OF ITS TYPE?

Selecting the best cash value life insurance policy is a difficult task involving a number of complicated concepts and analyses. (See Chapter 4 for further discussion.) However, since the amount credited to cash values on CAWL policies is a critical element of the overall cost of the protection, one primary area of focus should be how the company determines the amount credited to the cash accumulation account.

The amount credited to the accumulation account each year depends on four factors:

1. the expenses charged against the policy;

2. the mortality charges assessed against the policy;

3. the net investment yield earned by the insurer on its portfolio of investments; and

4. the method used to allocate interest to various blocks of policies.

The cash value at the end of any given year is equal to the cash value from the end of the prior year plus premiums (or less withdrawals) paid during the year less expense and mortality charges and plus interest credited. The annual report should usually explicitly show the expense and mortality charges and the amount of interest that is credited each year.

Expense Charges

As described above, the expense charge is usually composed of two elements, a fixed annual fee plus a percentage of premiums paid. The company may or may not reveal these fees in its original policy illustration. However, even if it does, the company usually does not guarantee that the expense charges will not change. Actual expense charges may increase or decrease in future years.

Mortality Charges

A CAWL contract explicitly states the maximum mortality rates it will charge for all ages and guarantees that mortality rates will not exceed those maximums. Many companies now use the 2001 Commissioner's Standard Mortality (CSO) table as the basis for their contractually guaranteed maximum rates on newly issued policies, but some companies still use the older 1980 CSO mortality table for their new policies. In addition, all policies issued before about 2002 used the 1980 CSO mortality table or even the 1958 CSO mortality table. All three tables are very conservative – that is, they assume mortality rates that are considerably higher than what is actually expected – but the 1980 CSO table and, even more so, the 1958 CSO table are considerably more conservative than the 2001 CSO table. Virtually every company currently charges less than the stated maximums, but those using the more conservative 1980 or 1958 CSO tables have even more room to increase mortality charges in future years if their mortality experience is poor.

Although annual statements explicitly show actual mortality charges, many policy illustrations do not. In fact, some illustrations assume very low or no mortality charges, which tends to show projected cash values that are overstated relative to what can actually be expected. Other illustrations include mortality charges based on rates the company is currently assessing, but they may also assume that there will be improvements in mortality experience in future years. If the mortality improvements do not materialize as anticipated, actual cash values are unlikely to match the projected cash values.

Net Investment Yield on Investment Portfolio

Over the long run, insurance companies cannot credit more interest to policy cash values than they earn on their general investment portfolios. To assess a company's long-run interest-crediting ability, one should evaluate the insurer's current portfolio and its investment philosophy.

As a general rule, insurance company portfolios are invested predominantly in long-term corporate and government bonds and mortgages. However, there are differences in the proportions invested in each type of asset and in the quality, duration, yields, and risk. In the past, some companies were pushed to insolvency because of overly aggressive investments in high-yield and high-risk junk bonds and developmental mortgage loans. Therefore, the objective should be to select companies with investment portfolios and investment philosophies that show a reasonable and acceptable combination of risk and return. What is reasonable and acceptable, of course, depends on the level of risk and the certainty of return desired by the policyowner.

Procedures for evaluating the investment portfolios of insurance companies are discussed in Chapter 3, "How to Determine the Right Company."

Interest–Crediting Methods

All CAWL policies, just like all other types of cash-value policies, have a guaranteed minimum interest rate. The guaranteed rates range from 4 to 6%. The rate actually being credited to cash values, called the current rate, is (or has historically been) higher than the guaranteed rate.

Companies use various methods to determine the current rate they credit to cash values. Included in a list of such methods are:

- linked rates method;

- discretionary method;

- portfolio method;

- new money method;

- blending method;

- modified portfolio method;

168

- direct recognition method; and

- bonus for persistency method.

Chapter 17, "Universal Life Insurance," contains an extended discussion of these methods.

How to Navigate Through a Ledger Statement for Current-Assumption Whole Life

The principal source of information regarding a new policy is the policy illustration or ledger. Figure 9.1 shows an annotated policy illustration with the following commentary.[4]

1. Base mandatory premium combined with a rider (similar to a paid-up additions rider for a traditional whole life policy) which accommodates additional money, resulting in an annual payment of $2,001.

2. Insurability classification for this company. Preferred means nonsmoker and not rated extra because of medical and occupational reasons.

3. Gender and issue age–male, age 45.

4. This is an end-of-year ledger statement.

5. Base premium of $732.94 that must be paid each and every year that the policy is in force.

6. Rider premium of $1,268.06 in addition to the mandatory base premium of $732.94. In year 21 and for every year thereafter, $732.94 is withdrawn [minus sign (-)] from the rider to pay the base premium of $732.94.

7. Total premium is $2,001, consisting of $732.94 base premium and $1,268 paid into the rider. $2,001 is paid each year for 20 years. Starting in year 21 and every year thereafter, the premium outlay is 0. Base mandatory premium of $732.94 is paid by withdrawing $732.94 each year from the rider.

8. Total death benefit.

9. Accumulation account money.

10. Total cash value.

11. Life expectancy is 29 years for a 45-year-old, or to age 74.

Ledger Statements Do Not Tell All

Purchasers of life insurance should be told either verbally or in writing the following additional information:

1. The investment strategy employed by the life insurance company, (e.g., pure portfolio rate, modified portfolio rate, weighted-average portfolio rate, old money or new money) in order to warrant the current interest-rate assumption. Although not reflected in the ledger statement of Figure 9.1, the current interest-rate assumption is 10.25% for 1 year and 9.5% thereafter. The guaranteed rate at all times is 5.5%.

2. In addition to asking for the investment strategy employed, a definitive explanation of mortality charges as to the ratio of current charges to the maximum charges that can be imposed should be requested.

3. Another item of importance is the interest rate on any loan against the cash value. More specifically, it should be disclosed how much interest the insurance company charges on the loan and how much interest the insurance company pays on the cash value equal to the amount borrowed. For this ledger statement, the rate charged for the loan is 7.41% in advance (most companies charge interest in arrears) and the rate paid on the amount of cash value equal to the loan is 6%.

4. Another figure that should be made clear is the total accumulation account value which is the amount of money that is earning interest based on the current interest-rate assumption. This amount is not, however, the amount of money that would be received on surrender of the policy. It is also not the amount of money that can be borrowed against.

5. In Figure 9.1, note that the total cash value includes the value of the rider plus the guaranteed reserve (cash value) of the policy. This is the amount of money that would be received on surrender of the policy and the amount of money that can be borrowed against. For balance sheet purposes, this value must be used, not the total accumulation account value. These respective values become the same in year 20. They differ before year 20 because this policy is a 20-year

Figure 9.1

CURRENT ASSUMPTION WHOLE LIFE					
Annual Premium Save Plus Rider **1**					
Preferred Classes **2**					
Male, Age 45 **3**					
4 Policy Year	**5** Base Premium	**6** Rider Premium	**7** Total Premium	**8** Total Death Benefit	**9** Total Accumulation Account	**10** Total Cash Value
---	---	---	---	---	---	---
1	$732.94	$1,268.06	$2,001.00	$103,674	$ 2,079	$ 1,298
2	732.94	1,268.06	2,001.00	107,435	4,310	3,282
3	732.94	1,268.06	2,001.00	111,317	6,441	5,359
4	732.94	1,268.06	2,001.00	115,331	8,744	7,700
5	732.94	1,268.06	2,001.00	119,490	11,237	10,300
6	732.94	1,268.06	2,001.00	123,807	13,938	13,119
7	732.94	1,268.06	2,001.00	128,297	16,862	16,078
8	732.94	1,268.06	2,001.00	132,978	20,029	19,279
9	732.94	1,268.06	2,001.00	137,867	23,456	22,740
10	732.94	1,268.06	2,001.00	142,977	27,153	26,470
11	732.94	1,268.06	2,001.00	148,325	31,136	30,522
12	732.94	1,268.06	2,001.00	153,927	35,426	34,880
13	732.94	1,268.06	2,001.00	159,797	40,038	39,561
14	732.94	1,268.06	2,001.00	165,951	44,991	44,582
15	732.94	1,268.06	2,001.00	172,404	50,299	49,958
16	732.94	1,268.06	2,001.00	179,170	55,973	55,700
17	732.94	1,268.06	2,001.00	186,305	62,081	61,877
18	732.94	1,268.06	2,001.00	193,838	68,650	68,514
19	732.94	1,268.06	2,001.00	201,800	76,707	75,639
20	732.94	1,268.06	2,001.00	210,226	83,281	83,282
21	732.94	-732.94	0.00	215,755	89,472	89,472
22	732.94	-732.94	0.00	221,679	96,098	96,098
23	732.94	-732.94	0.00	228,022	103,194	103,195
24	732.94	-732.94	0.00	234,818	110,804	110,804
25	732.94	-732.94	0.00	242,105	118,974	118,974
26	732.94	-732.94	0.00	249,924	127,739	127,740
27	732.94	-732.94	0.00	258,313	137,128	137,128
28	732.94	-732.94	0.00	267,331	147,179	147,180
29 **11**	732.94	-732.94	0.00	277,039	157,940	157,941
30	732.94	-732.94	0.00	287,491	169,455	169,455

rear-end-loaded contract. Thus, there are penalties imposed if the policy is terminated before 20 years.

6. The rate of return expressed in terms of compound interest should be given either on the ledger statement or by the life insurance agent. Ideally, it should be provided for each year.

7. The rate of return upon death for this policy for sequential years is as follows:

Year	Rate of Return
1	5,081.11%
5	98.20
10	34.46
20	14.10
29 (life expectancy)	9.66

8. Once the rate of return upon death is known, it can then be determined what would have to be earned before taxes (it is assumed that the death benefit is considered life insurance proceeds and as such not subject to federal or state in-

come taxes) in other financial services products (e.g., mutual funds, certificates of deposit, real estate, or commodities) to duplicate the tax-exempt rate of return provided by life insurance. The before-tax rate of return is determined by dividing the life insurance rate of return by the marginal tax bracket subtracted from 100% – for 15%, the factor is 0.85; for 25%, 0.75; for 28%, 0.72; for 33%, 0.67; and for 35%, 0.65. The results are shown in Figure 9.2.

9. The rate of return upon surrender should also be provided. When the rate of return upon surrender is positive, it means that taxes are due. Taxes are due on the difference between the cash surrender value and the premiums paid.

10. Generally, the rate of return upon surrender even before taxes never equals the interest assumption of 10.25% for 1 year and 9.5% thereafter.

11. The ledger statement is the official ledger statement produced by the computer service of the life insurance company. It should be "bug-free." In addition, the ledger statement should contain the following information: guaranteed interest rate to be paid on the cash value, the current interest rate, mortality charges statement, interest-adjusted index, guaranteed fixed loan rate charged for loans made against the cash value, and interest paid on borrowed money.

WHERE CAN I FIND OUT MORE?

The following references include authoritative discussions of various types of life insurance including CAWL:

1. B. Anderson, *Anderson on Life Insurance* (Waltham, MA: Little, Brown and Company, 1991).

2. B. Baldwin, *New Life Insurance Investment Advisor: Achieving Financial Security for You and Your Family Through Today's Insurance Products*, 2nd ed. (Hightstown, NJ: McGraw-Hill Trade, 2001).

3. J. Belth, Life Insurance: A Consumer's Handbook, 2nd ed. (Bloomington, IN: Indiana University Press, 1985).

4. K. Black, Jr. and H. Skipper, Jr., *Life Insurance*, 13th ed. (Old Tappan, NJ: Prentice Hall Inc., 1999).

5. E. Graves, Editor, *McGill's Life Insurance*, 5th ed. (Bryn Mawr, PA: The American College, 2004).

The following references are useful guides for policy and company rating information:

1. *Best Insurance Reports* (Oldwick, NJ: A. M. Best Company, published annually).

2. *Best's Review – Life/Health Edition* (Oldwick, NJ: A. M. Best Company, published monthly).

QUESTIONS AND ANSWERS

Question – What is meant by the term, "redetermination period?"

Answer – CAWL may initially be configured to resemble a traditional whole life policy with level premiums payable for life or as a limited-pay policy where higher level premiums are paid for some specified period, such as 10, 15, or 20 years, or until age 65. At the time of issue, the premium and death benefit levels are fixed, just as with traditional whole life policies. However, after a time, called the "redetermination period," the company recalculates the premium and sometimes the face amount using the same or new assumptions as to future interest and/or mortality. The redetermination period is commonly 5 years, but there is some variation. Some companies redetermine premiums every three years or even annually.

Periodic redetermination is required because of the uncertainty of the value of the cash accumulation account. The new premium is determined such that, together with the current cash accumulation account value, the new premium payment schedule will be able to maintain a level death benefit to the end of life under the current interest and mortality assumptions. The premium is guaranteed never to exceed a certain maximum that is the premium computed using the minimum interest guarantee and the maximum mortality charges stated in the contract.

If the redetermined premium is *lower* than before, the policyowner may usually choose one of three options:

1. Continue to pay premiums at the old higher level, maintain the old face amount, and add excess premiums to the cash accumulation account. This option effectively short-

Figure 9.2

	BEFORE TAX RATE OF RETURN				
Year	15% taxpayer	25% taxpayer	28% taxpayer	33% taxpayer	35% taxpayer
1	5,977.78%	6,774.81%	7,057.10%	7,583.75%	7,817.09%
5	115.53	130.93	136.39	146.57	151.08
10	40.54	45.95	47.86	51.43	53.02
20	16.59	18.88	19.58	21.04	21.69
29 (life expectancy)	11.36	12.88	13.42	14.42	14.86

ens the premium-paying period until the policy reaches paid-up status.

2. Pay the new lower premium and maintain the old face amount.

3. Continue to pay premiums at the old higher level and use the excess premiums to pay for an increased death benefit, subject to proof of insurability.

If the redetermined premium is *higher* than before, the policyowner may usually choose one of three options:

1. Continue to pay premiums at the old lower level with the face amount reduced to the level supportable at that premium level.

2. Pay the new higher premium and maintain the old face amount.

3. Continue to pay premiums at the old lower level, maintain the old face amount, and draw down the cash accumulation account to pay the premium deficiency. To elect this option, the cash accumulation account value must exceed certain minimums necessary to assure the policy can be maintained until the next readjustment period.

When and if the policy's cash accumulation account exceeds the amount necessary to fully fund the current death benefit for life (that is, it equals or exceeds the net single premium based on current interest and mortality assumptions), the policy may be treated as a paid-up policy. However, it is not quite like a traditional paid-up policy. The policyowner may discontinue paying premiums only for as long as the cash accumulation account continues to exceed the net single premium at each redetermination period. If the accumulation account falls below this amount, additional premiums are required. The policyowner may proceed under one of the three options described above when the redetermined premium increases.

CHAPTER ENDNOTES

1. What is otherwise considered a traditional dividend-paying whole life policy may also be properly described as a type of current-assumption policy if the dividend formula reflects the insurer's current mortality and expense experience as well as its current investment performance. Many participating whole life policies now use current experience for interest, mortality, and expenses in their dividend formulas. However, these policies are not what are currently known generically as current-assumption whole life policies. See Chapter 12, "Limited Pay Life," Chapter 13, "Ordinary Level-Premium Whole Life Insurance," and Chapter 14, "Single Premium Life Insurance," for discussions of these traditional, yet often current-assumption-type, policies.

2. IRC Secs. 7702(f)(7)(B), 7702(f)(7)(C).

3. IRC Secs. 7702(f)(7)(B), 7702(f)(7)(D). The cash value corridor test is discussed in Appendix F, "Taxation of Benefits."

4. This analysis is adapted from the excellent discussion on this topic in *The Life Insurance Buyer's Guide,* by William D. Brownlie with Jeffrey L. Seglin, published by McGraw-Hill Publishing Company (1989).

Chapter 10

GROUP LIFE INSURANCE

WHAT IS IT?

Group life insurance, as its name implies, provides insurance for a group – typically but not necessarily 10 or more employees – under a master contract between the insurer and the employer. Technically, the insured individuals are not part of that contract. Planners should note that almost 40% of all life insurance in force in this country is issued on a group basis.

Group insurance is almost always issued as yearly renewable (one year) term insurance. This means that the coverage expires at the end of each year but is renewed automatically without a medical examination and without further evidence of insurability. The premium rate per $1,000 of protection increases from year to year. Death benefits are paid upon the insured's death from any cause.

WHEN IS THE USE OF THIS TOOL INDICATED?

1. When an employer wants a means of acquiring an employee benefit that most employees appreciate, and even expect.

2. When insurance is difficult to obtain at standard rates because a key employee has a health condition or a dangerous avocation.

3. When an employer would like to provide life insurance protection in amounts up to $50,000 in a cost effective manner for shareholder-employees as well as others.

ADVANTAGES

1. Helps to satisfy an employer's moral obligation to the dependents of employees.

2. Contributes to employee morale and productivity.

3. Provides a before-tax benefit to employees that they otherwise would have to pay for with personal after-tax dollars.

4. Is expected in most firms as part of the employee benefit package. Its absence would put an employer at a competitive disadvantage in hiring and retaining employees.

5. Costs less for the employee than an individual policy, even though the plan may be contributory. From the employee's perspective, group life insurance (especially with respect to the first $50,000) is a bargain since, in most cases, the employer pays all or most of the premium.

6. Provides insurance for those who otherwise might be uninsurable and provides insurance at standard rates for those who might be insurable only at an increased premium.

7. Enables terminated employees, through the conversion privilege, to convert to individual policies without submitting evidence of insurability.

8. Forms a base on which an employee can build a personal financial program.

9. Allows an employer to deduct the premiums for group life insurance.

DISADVANTAGES

1. Group life insurance is temporary in nature – it runs out or is significantly reduced at the very time it is needed by most clients. This drop-off particularly impacts wealthy clients with high post-retirement living standards.

2. The Table I cost (reportable income for tax purposes as discussed below) increases significantly as insured individuals grow older. Ironically, in the post-retirement years when medical and other expenses are high but income is low, the reportable income from group term life – and therefore the tax payable – is highest.

3. Because group life insurance is a "welfare benefit plan" it is subject to certain ERISA (Employee

Retirement Income Security Act) limitations and requirements, including certain reporting obligations.

4. Group life insurance coverage must be provided for a number of employees. This increases the employer's cost significantly over nondeductible plans that allow the employer to "pick and choose" who will be covered, and on what terms.

5. The employer's out-of-pocket cost can skyrocket if no new employees enter the plan. This is due to the yearly renewable term aspect of group insurance. As the pool of employees grows older, the average age increases and, consequently, premiums also increase. This problem is particularly acute in professional corporations with little employee turnover.

6. A group term life plan cannot cover shareholders who are not employees. Further, the employer is not free to pick and choose who will be covered, the amount of coverage, or the terms and conditions of coverage. This is because certain design features must be built into the plan in order to insure that the plan meets certain tax law requirements listed in Section 79 of the Internal Revenue Code.

7. Employees have no guarantee that group coverage will be continued by the employer since a group policy is a contract solely between the employer and the insurer and may, therefore, be discontinued or changed without employee approval. Post-retirement coverage may be lost if an employer files for bankruptcy.

8. When an employee is terminated, the group insurance protection is lost. Although a conversion option is usually available, relatively few persons ever execute this privilege because of the high premiums at the attained age. Furthermore, if many employees did, in fact, exercise the right to convert, group insurance would become highly expensive for the employer since the insurance company typically imposes a "conversion charge" on the employer when an employee chooses to exercise the conversion feature.

9. By design and formula, group protection generally ceases, or is significantly reduced, at retirement.

10. Employees may be lulled into complacency, being under the misconception that the group term provided by their employer provides adequate benefits, and therefore not utilize the services of a professional insurance agent. Adequacy of coverage does not necessarily equate to the proper arrangement or ownership, nor does group term provide the collateral planning advice found only through competent financial services professionals.

WHAT ARE THE TAX IMPLICATIONS?

1. An employee does not have to report any income with respect to the first $50,000 of life insurance coverage provided by the group plan. But although term insurance protection provided by an employer to an employee is income tax free for amounts of insurance up to $50,000, an employee must report and pay income tax on the economic benefit (i.e., the term insurance cost) of coverage in excess of $50,000.[1]

The amount reportable is computed by multiplying the "Table I" rates shown in Figure 10.1 by the amount of coverage in excess of $50,000. These monthly rates are added together to determine the total annual economic benefit received and reportable by the employee.

For purposes of Table I, the age of the employee is the employee's "attained age" on the last day of the employee's taxable year (generally December 31st).

In the case of a "contributory" plan (i.e., the employee pays a portion of each month's premium), the employee may reduce the reportable amount by the amount the employee has paid.[2]

The steps in the computation process are:

1. Find the total amount of group term life insurance coverage in each calendar month of the taxable year. (If the employee was covered with different amounts of group term life during the coverage period, average the amount payable at the beginning and the end of the period to find the proceeds payable.)

2. Subtract $50,000 from each month's coverage.

3. Apply the appropriate rate from Table I.

4. From the sum of the monthly costs, subtract total employee contributions for the year. (The employee's contributions can be allocated entirely to the cost of the excess coverage over $50,000 to reduce or eliminate cur-

Figure 10.1

TABLE I. UNIFORM PREMIUMS FOR $1,000 OF GROUP TERM LIFE INSURANCE PROTECTION	
Rates Applicable to Cost of Group Term Life Insurance	
5-Year Age Bracket	Cost per $1,000 of Protection for One-Month Period
Under 25	$0.05
25 to 29	.06
30 to 34	.08
35 to 39	.09
40 to 44	.10
45 to 49	.15
50 to 54	.23
55 to 59	.43
60 to 64	.66
65 to 69	1.27
70 and above	2.06

rent tax cost to the employee. However, any unused portion of the employee's contributions may not be carried over into later years.)

For example, assume your client is age 56. The employer provides her with $150,000 of group term life insurance. She makes no contribution to the coverage. The "excess amount" over $50,000 is $100,000. The monthly rate, $.43 per $1,000, is multiplied by 100 (000) to arrive at $43 per month. If she was covered for 12 months, the yearly income reportable by her would be $516. Had she made a contribution of $200, her taxable economic benefit would be reduced to $316.

It is obvious that Table I costs will increase dramatically once the client reaches his early 60s. Group coverage at retirement, if it is still available, becomes extremely expensive in terms of reportable income. This problem is particularly acute with respect to shareholder-employees with group life insurance significantly in excess of $50,000.

The economic benefit generated by coverage in excess of $50,000 will *not* be taxed to the employee to the extent:

- the employer is the beneficiary;

- a qualified charity is the sole beneficiary for the entire period for which the cost otherwise would be taxed to the employee; or

- the employee has terminated employment with the employer because of disability.[3]

None of the $50,000 exclusion is available for group term insurance provided through an IRC Section 401(a) qualified retirement plan, such as a pension, profit sharing, stock bonus, or qualified annuity plan.[4] Generally, this means the employer premium for the entire amount of protection afforded with employer contributions is taxable to the covered employee. Table I rates may not be used.

2. Special tax treatment applies to "small groups" (i.e., groups insuring under 10 lives). In under-10 group term life plans, premiums are tax deductible for the employer and not taxable income up to the $50,000 limit only if the following conditions are met:[5]

a) Group coverage must be provided for either (1) all full-time employees, or (2) all full-time employees who can prove, to the insurer's satisfaction, insurability assuming that evidence of insurability affects eligibility.[6]

b) The amount of insurance must be computed (1) as a uniform percentage of compensation, or (2) on the basis of coverage brackets established by the insurer.

- The amount computed under either method may be reduced for employees who do not provide satisfactory evidence of insurability.

- No bracket may exceed two and a half times the next lower bracket.

- The lowest bracket must be at least 10% of the highest bracket.

- A separate schedule of coverage may be established within similar guidelines for employees who are over age 65.

c) Evidence of insurability, if required, is limited to a medical questionnaire completed by the employee and no physical examination is required.

Even if all three of these requirements are not met, an under-10 lives group term plan will still qualify for favorable tax treatment if it meets the following requirements:

- Coverage is available under a common plan to employees of two or more related employers.

- Coverage is restricted to, but must be provided for, all employees who belong to an organization (such as a union) that carries on other substantial activities on behalf of the employer.

- Evidence of insurability is not required, and in no way does that affect the amount of insurance available to individual employees.

3. To satisfy nondiscrimination rules, a group insurance plan must not discriminate in favor of key employees in terms of (a) eligibility to participate and (b) benefits provided.[7]

To meet "eligibility" nondiscrimination rules, a plan must meet at least one of the following three tests:

a) the plan benefits 70% or more of all of the employer's employees; or

b) at least 85% of plan participants are not "key" employees; or

c) the plan benefits employees under an employer-specified classification that is approved by the IRS as nondiscriminatory.

To meet "benefit" nondiscrimination rules, a plan must provide all participants with benefits at least

as great as those provided to key employees. It is permissible, under this rule, to base benefits on a uniform percentage of compensation.

If a plan discriminates in favor of "key employees," either as to eligibility or with respect to the kind or amount of benefits, the cost of the entire amount of life insurance coverage becomes taxable to key employees. Thus, the exclusion for the cost of the first $50,000 of coverage is lost.[8]

If a plan is discriminatory, key employees (and only key employees) must include as taxable income the higher of (a) the actual cost, or (b) the Table I cost of all insurance provided on their behalf.

A key employee is defined as a person who, during the plan year or any one of the four preceding plan years, was:

- an officer whose compensation exceeds a certain limitation;[9] or

- an employee owning both more than a ½% interest and one of the 10 largest interests in the employer; or

- a more-than-5% owner of the employer firm; or

- a more-than-1% owner of the employer receiving compensation of $150,000 or more.

If a person is a key employee at retirement, that person remains a key employee indefinitely.[10]

4. The amounts reportable as income by the employee are also treated as additional salary for purposes of FICA and FUTA.[11] State unemployment and workers' compensation taxes may also apply in some states.

5. A beneficiary of group life insurance receives the death benefit income tax free.[12]

6. Premiums paid by the employer for group term life insurance are income tax deductible as ordinary and necessary business expenses (unless the employer is directly or indirectly the beneficiary of the coverage).[13] No deduction is allowed for premiums paid for the coverage on partners or sole proprietors since the premiums would be considered in payment of personal coverage. However, premiums paid to cover the partners' or sole proprietor's common law employees are typically deductible.

Shareholder-employees of S corporations who own more than 2% of the stock of the business are treated in the same way as a partner.

7. Proceeds of group term life insurance are includable in the insured's estate if they are payable to or for the benefit of the insured's estate, or if at death the insured holds any "incident of ownership" regardless of who is named as beneficiary.[14] "Incidents of ownership" include the right to change the beneficiary and the right to assign the policy or revoke an assignment. The proceeds of group term life may be removed from an employee's estate if certain requirements are met.[15]

8. A gift is made from the covered employee to the assignee when an absolute assignment is made of the employee's rights under group term insurance.[16] A further series of gifts is made by the covered employee to the third party assignee when the employer makes each additional premium payment.[17] Table I rates are used if the group term plan was nondiscriminatory or if the covered employee was not a key employee. If the plan is discriminatory and the covered employee is a key employee, the actual cost allocable to the employee's entire insurance coverage must be used (unless Table I costs are higher).[18] Depending on the facts and circumstances, those gifts may or may not be present interest gifts qualifying for the gift tax annual exclusion.[19]

Group term life insurance may result in a taxable gift where it passes to someone other than the primary beneficiary and it was not disclaimed in a timely manner.[20]

WHAT ARE THE REQUIREMENTS?

1. The Employee Retirement Income Security Act (ERISA) requires that any employee benefit plan (including group life insurance) meet certain requirements.[21] Among these requirements are that the plan must be established and maintained in writing, plan documents must provide for one or more "named fiduciaries" who administer the plan, and the plan document must provide a procedure for amending the plan and specify the basis on which payments are to be made to and from the plan. Additionally, the plan must provide a claims review procedure.

2. A group term life plan must meet the following IRC Section 79 requirements[22]:

a) The plan must provide a death benefit that meets the definition of a "life insurance contract."

b) The plan's benefits must be provided to a group of employees as compensation for services.

c) Benefits must be provided under a policy carried directly or indirectly by the employer.

d) The amount of insurance provided to each employee must be computed under a formula that precludes individual selection.

WHERE CAN I FIND OUT MORE?

The discussions of group life insurance contained in the following publications can be helpful:

1. *Introduction to Group Insurance*, 5th ed. (Chicago, IL: Dearborn Financial Publishing, Inc., 2001).

2. *Advanced Sales Reference Service*, Sec. 66, (Cincinnati, OH: The National Underwriter Company, updated monthly).

3. *The Group Life Insurance Handbook* (Cincinnati, OH: The National Underwriter Company, 1997).

QUESTIONS AND ANSWERS

Question – May an employee name anyone he wants as beneficiary of a group term life contract?

Answer – Yes. Basically, each covered employee has absolute freedom to name any beneficiary he wants, although some states prohibit the naming of the employer as a beneficiary. Also, the employee may change the beneficiary as often as he wants. If the named beneficiary does not survive the insured, and there is no secondary beneficiary named, the death benefit will be paid to the estate of the covered employee or to a "successive beneficiary" specified in the master contract. In other words, the master contract may give the insurer the option of paying the proceeds to one or more of the following survivors: spouse, parents, children, brothers and sisters, or the estate's executor.

A "facility of payment" clause in the master contract allows the insurer to pay part of the proceeds (typically up to $500) to any person who has incurred funeral or last illness expenses for the covered employee (even though the named beneficiary may still be alive). Furthermore, the facility of payment clause may allow the insurer to make payments on behalf of a minor beneficiary or legal incompetent to a relative assumed to have "custody and principal support" of the beneficiary until a guardian is appointed.

The recipient of the proceeds can elect an optional method of settlement in place of a lump sum. See Chapter 5 for a discussion of settlement options.

Question – What is "Dependent Life"?

Answer – Dependent life is optional coverage for the spouse and/or dependent children of covered employees. Generally, this coverage is limited to no more than 50% of the employee's coverage and is almost always further limited by insurers to $5,000 or $10,000. For tax reasons, most coverage for dependents is $2,000, or less. Coverage on the lives of children is usually $1,000 or $2,000. Not all states permit dependent life.

Employer-paid premiums for dependent life are tax deductible by the employer and tax free to the employee only to the extent the coverage is considered "incidental." Incidental is defined as "not exceeding $2,000," so the premiums paid by an employer on $2,000 or less of coverage for a spouse and each dependent child can be totally excluded from a covered employee's gross income.[23] If the coverage exceeds $2,000 per individual dependent, it is not incidental. In that case, the Table I costs of the excess dependent coverage (less any employee contribution) must be included in the gross income of the employee.

Where there are less than 10 employees in the group, dependent coverage should be provided to all employees if provided at all. A safe way to determine the amount of benefits would be to provide coverage as a uniform percentage of each employee's compensation or perhaps as a percentage of the coverage provided on the life of each employee.

Question – Can group insurance be used to fund a buy-sell agreement?

Answer – The use of group insurance to fund a buy-sell is generally not a sound idea. First, if the buyout price is artificially reduced in return for a corresponding increase in the group term coverage (un-

der the pretext that "This makes your buy-sell partially tax deductible. What's the difference where the family gets the money as long as they get the same number of dollars?"), the family is cheated; it does not receive a fair price for the business interest held by the estate plus the group insurance to which it is entitled. Furthermore, since the IRS is likely to claim that the corporation is an indirect beneficiary of the group term insurance (by virtue of the reduction in the buy-sell price) the premium for the additional life insurance may not be deductible.[24] Furthermore, the price set in the agreement will not be binding on the IRS or on the courts, and the estate could conceivably pay an estate tax greater than the money it "receives" for the stock.[25]

Another ploy that will be unsuccessful (and is dangerous from a tax viewpoint as well) is for two shareholders to sign a cross purchase buy-sell agreement and name each other the beneficiary of the coverage on their respective lives. In return, they lower the price of a decedent's interest in a buy-sell. Under these circumstances, there has been a transfer of an interest in a policy (i.e., when one shareholder named the other as beneficiary), and that transfer of an interest has been made for valuable consideration (i.e., reciprocity of the other's action). This is clearly a "transfer for value" and it will cause the proceeds to be income taxable.[26]

Yet another trick that is periodically suggested is to name one's own family as the beneficiary of an increased amount of group term life, but agree that the increase will in turn be considered payment made to the family of the deceased insured in return for a full or partial payment for his or her stock. Mechanically, it is almost impossible to match insurance needs with the group schedules of benefits because of the nondiscrimination rules. Furthermore, once the family has received the proceeds, but still holds the stock, if they decide not to transfer the shares, how (aside from an expensive and aggravating lawsuit) will the surviving shareholder obtain the stock?

Question – When an employee becomes older, the reportable income tax cost of very large amounts of group term life insurance tends to increase very rapidly. What are the techniques available to solve this problem?

Answer – It is true that a very substantial amount of income can be generated by group term life as the employee ages. For ages 65 to 69, the reportable cost per thousand per month is $1.27, while for ages 70 and over, the reportable cost per thousand per month is $2.06.[27]

One solution is the "executive bonus carve-out," a simple arrangement that provides up to $50,000 of coverage for all employees (including retired employees) through the group insurance plan, but "carves out" selected employees for special treatment.

Specifically, the chosen individuals are provided with amounts of individual term and/or whole life insurance by the employer. Premiums are paid by the employer, but reportable by the employee as income. To make up for the income tax burden, an additional bonus is paid in cash to the employee. This is particularly appealing when the corporation is in a higher bracket than the executive.

Permanent insurance is often preferable in a group carve-out since the goal is to reduce or eliminate the out-of-pocket cost and reportable income of retired executives. This can be accomplished by using "vanishing premiums."

Since the shareholder-employees and other key executives generally want substantial and permanent coverage, one solution is the executive bonus carve-out life insurance plan. The characteristics that make this approach appealing include:

- The plan is simple and easy to present to corporate officers.

- The corporation can be used as a vehicle to provide individually owned permanent life insurance for shareholder-employees and key executives.

- The plan avoids the complex and costly nondiscrimination rules for excess coverage.

- The plan is flexible and the additional insurance amounts can be provided through IRC Section 162 bonus or split dollar coverage.

- Leveraging may be possible since the corporate deduction may be greater than the taxable income incurred by the participants in the plan.

See Chapter 29 for a more complete discussion of Section 162 Bonus Plans.

Question – Does the substantial individual insurance benefit available under an IRC Section 162 plan render the Section 79 group term plan obsolete?

Answer – The answer to this question depends on many factors:

1. Does the corporation already have a group insurance plan in place that benefits employees?

2. Does the current plan meet the nondiscrimination rules?

3. Does the corporation wish to continue to provide group term life insurance coverage to non-highly compensated rank-and-file employees?

Generally the group term life insurance plan is still favorable on a nondiscriminatory basis. The corporation is allowed an ordinary business-expense deduction for contributions to the plan. Employees, including the shareholder-employees and other key executives, receive the first $50,000 of coverage income tax free.

There are, therefore, many reasons to continue an existing group term plan. The corporation may also want to avoid the adverse morale consequences of terminating a popular fringe benefit plan covering a broad cross-section of employees and replacing it with a highly discriminatory life insurance plan covering only a few key employees.

What is generally recommended is that the shareholder-employees and other key executives who require (and for whom the corporation wishes to provide) more substantial life insurance coverage participate in either an IRC Section 162 bonus or split dollar life insurance plan to supplement an IRC Section 79 plan. The group term plan can still provide the key employees with the $50,000 of tax-free coverage. Coverage in excess can instead be "carved out" of the group term life insurance plan and provided through a discriminatory arrangement.

Generally, the IRC Section 162 bonus plan makes more sense when the corporation is in a higher bracket than the participant and the plan is limited to shareholder-employees. Under the Section 162 plan, the corporation pays the entire cost as deductible compensation and the participant is taxed on the full amount of the premium bonus. No reimbursement of corporate contributions will be available.

The split dollar approach is favored when the size and permanency of the corporation's outlay is a concern and the corporation is in a lower bracket than the participant. Split dollar becomes more favorable if coverage extends beyond the shareholders. But since the employer's share of the premium is nondeductible, the higher-bracket corporation should generally avoid the substantial nondeductible outlays in a split dollar plan and instead provide deductible bonuses through an IRC Section 162 bonus life insurance plan.

Question – What is the role of the "master policy"?

Answer – The only contract issued in a group term life plan is between the employer and the insurer. This is called the master policy and it is the only contract required regardless of how many employees are covered by the plan. The master policy states the contractual relationship between the policyholder (the employer) and the insurance company.

Each employee, the "individual insured," is issued a certificate that provides essential information such as who is covered, when the coverage takes effect, how long it lasts, the amount of insurance provided, the claims procedures, etc. Typically, the certificates are included in the announcement booklet distributed to the insureds at the time that a group insurance plan is installed.

The master contract will usually provide that the insurer cannot refuse to renew the contract as long as the employer wishes to continue coverage and pays premiums. (However, it is true that the insurer may increase premium rates to the point where, for all practical purposes, the right to renew is not of any value.) The insurer will also provide in the master contract that if the number of employees drops below a specified amount (e.g., 10 employees), the plan may be canceled.

Typical clauses found in master contracts also include:

1. *Adjustment in premiums clause* – If an employee's age is overstated, the employer will receive a refund. If the age is understated, there is no change in coverage, but the employer must make up the difference in premiums.

2. *Incontestability clause* – The policy is incontestable, except for fraud.

3. *Grace period* –Coverage continues for 31 days after the premium is due.

4. *Claims limitation* – The death benefit claim must be made within one year of the last premium paid for a deceased employee.

Question – When does an individual's coverage begin?

Answer – Employees are required to meet certain requirements before their coverage becomes effective. For instance, an employee must be actively at work on the date he becomes eligible for initial coverage or for subsequent increases in benefits.

Once the group insurance is in effect, new employees must satisfy a "probationary period" before they can enroll. This typically runs 30 to 90 days. From the time the probationary period has been satisfied, employees have 31 days to enroll. If an employee does not sign up during the enrollment period, generally he must submit evidence of insurability when applying at a later date.

Question – What is a "benefit schedule"?

Answer – A benefit schedule is a predetermined statement of the formula under which benefits will be provided. Benefit schedules generally base coverage amounts on:

1. *Earnings* – Proponents of an earnings basis schedule point out that this type of formula benefits survivors by providing an amount equal to full salary for a limited time after death and because it is tied to salary, will tend to increase with inflation. More productive employees who presumably are paid more are rewarded appropriately and if the plan requires contributions, cost is directly related to the employee's ability to pay.

2. *Occupational classifications* – Uniform amounts of coverage are provided within each classification. The advantage of this type of formula is that it is easy to administer and is somewhat related to the employee's survivors' needs, the employer's

assessment of the employee's worth to the business, and the employee's ability to pay in the case of a contributory plan.

3. *Flat benefit* – This type of schedule provides a flat benefit amount for all participants. Giving everyone the same benefit is, of course, the easiest formula to administer and to the extent wage rates within the group are relatively uniform, coverage bears a close relationship to needs and abilities to pay. This is obviously not the correct formula to use in a multi-level business, but would be appropriate for very large multiple-employer groups providing coverage under collective bargaining agreements.

4. *Length of service* – This formula rewards long term employees (some call this rewarding loyalty) and may tend to decrease an employee's incentive to leave the firm. In reality, few employees would stay with a firm merely because of the group coverage or its formula, and the insurance coverage provided to employees under this method bears no relationship to their needs or ability to pay in the case of contributory coverage.

5. *A combination of these factors* – The most common formula bases the amount of insurance on a multiple of the employee's income – from one to three times earnings. Most insurers require a minimum of $5,000 on each covered employee or even $10,000 in the case of smaller groups. Some insurers require a minimum coverage for the entire group. Maximum coverage depends on the total volume of the group and state law ceilings, if any. Most companies will issue up to $500,000 or more on a given life although to protect themselves for ultra large amounts, group insurers use medical examinations, reinsure at least a portion of the coverage, and sometimes establish special reserves.

Question – What is meant by "experience rating"?

Answer – Insurance companies renew group term life year by year and may adjust premiums up or down at that time or guarantee an upper limit for a specific period of time, such as for two or three years. Experience rating means that premiums (and/or

dividends) in the future are based at least in part on the number of deaths and administrative costs in administering the specific employer's actual group rather than by the experience of a larger pool of employers. Experience rating should be considered where the group is large, the employees covered in the group are young, and a steady number of young healthy individuals come into the plan, leading to below-average claims.

Competition for group sales may have some effect on the size of employer that is experience rated and the amount of the ratings. Group term premiums are recalculated annually and based on the average age of the group, which is then adjusted for the aggregate experience. Usually, experience ratings are based on claims and expense experience of groups of 200 or more employees. Premiums of smaller employers will typically be based on the experience of a large pool of employers covered by similar master contracts. In a "pooled rate" situation, a uniform rate is applied to all the groups in the pool.

Question – What rights does an employee have upon termination of coverage?

Answer – When an employee is terminated or retires, a legal right (subject to certain conditions) called a "conversion privilege" comes into play. This conversion privilege allows the employee to convert what was group term life insurance into individual protection through the issuance of a personal contract.

When an employee quits or is fired or the employee continues working but the master contract is terminated, he generally has 31 days in which to apply for a converted policy without submitting evidence of insurability. That new individual policy may be any of the insurer's permanent life policies in an amount up to but not exceeding the term coverage. The insurer is not allowed to apply a rating (an extra premium charge for impaired health or avocation), and must issue the policy at its standard premium. The premium will be at the insured's "attained-age" (nearest birthday) rates for up to a specified maximum face amount.

Question – What happens to group life insurance coverage if an employee is temporarily laid off or granted a leave of absence?

Answer – If an employee is laid off, granted a leave of absence, or is disabled for a short period of time, at the employer's discretion, (but on a nondiscriminatory basis) coverage can be continued for some limited period of time (e.g., six months), but the individual employee will be responsible for payment of the premiums. Coverage will be terminated at the end of that continuation period. At that point, the insured has the right to the extension of benefits as well as the right to convert the term coverage to a permanent individual policy.

Question – Do group term policies provide any type of disability coverage?

Answer – Typically, group master contracts will contain provisions for the protection of disabled employees. Two of these provisions are "waiver of premium" and "maturity value benefit." The waiver of premium provision, as its name implies, relieves the employer of the requirement of paying premiums for any covered employee who becomes totally and continuously disabled prior to a specified age. (Age 60 is common.) The maturity value benefit provides for the payment of the face amount of an employee's group life insurance in a lump sum or in monthly installments when an employee becomes totally and permanently disabled prior to age 60. This provision is much less commonly used than the waiver of premium feature.

Question – How does the use of a "reduction formula" alter the amount of group term insurance coverage for employees who are still employed?

Answer – The master contract will often contain a "reduction formula." This provision reduces the coverage of those insureds who reach a certain age. (Age 70 is typical.) Age discrimination laws (such as The Age Discrimination in Employment Act) have slowed down the reduction so that a common clause might provide that, "Benefits reduce to 65% of original amount at age 70 and 50% of original amount at age 75."

Question – Can a group plan include an owner-employee?

Answer – Yes. The employer may be a sole proprietorship, partnership, or close corporation. "Employees" eligible for coverage may include sole proprietors, partners, and employee-shareholders. (Note, however, that tax rules are different for self-employed individuals and partners than for common law employees.) Some group contracts also cover employees of an employer's subsidiary. Retired employees may also be included.

Question – What is "group survivor income benefit insurance"?

Answer – Group survivor income benefit insurance provides a continuing monthly income benefit to "qualified family survivors" at the death of a covered employee. The benefit is typically a fixed percentage of the covered employee's basic monthly earnings, a flat specified amount applicable to all insureds, or an amount dependent on job classification. Group survivor plans are often designed to supplement group term life, Social Security benefits, and income from other sources. The initial value of these survivor benefits can range from three to ten times an employee's annual salary.

By design, death benefits are made only in the form of monthly payments, paid only when a beneficiary is a qualified member, and only if that family member survives the covered employee. "Qualified family members" are typically a spouse or an unmarried, dependent child.

Payments made to a surviving spouse stop at the earlier of a specified age (e.g., age 62), or the survivor's death. Some benefits cease at the age at which Social Security retirement payments become available or on remarriage of the surviving spouse. Payments made to surviving children usually end when the youngest unmarried child reaches age 19.

For purposes of computing the covered employee's income tax liability under group survivor income benefit insurance, "proceeds payable," (i.e., the amount that is multiplied by the Table I rates) is the present value of the named beneficiary's right to receive payments under the employee's certificate. Likewise, the present value of payments to be made at a covered employee's death would be the amount includable in the decedent's estate.

Question – What is a "Section 79 Plan"?

Answer – All group life insurance is covered under IRC Section 79. Life insurance can provide permanent protection as well as term and still receive the favorable tax treatment afforded to group term if certain requirements are met. Such insurance has come to be called "Section 79" insurance.

The requirements that must be met are: (1) the policy itself, or the employer under a separate document, must state the portion of the death benefit that is group term coverage; and (2) the portion of the death benefit generated by the group term life portion of the coverage must not be less than the difference between the total death benefit provided under the policy and the employee's deemed death benefit at the end of the policy year.[28]

A Section 79 plan is one designed to solve some of the problems inherent in any term vehicle and yet retain some of the cost advantages of group coverage. Group term insurance builds no cash values to keep premiums paid after the covered employee retires. Furthermore, there are no paid-up policy values to carry the coverage into the post-retirement period. So generally, when the employee retires, the coverage terminates (although some employers provide a reduced amount of coverage).

The Section 79 plan employs a permanent product designed to provide tax-favored, post-retirement insurance coverage. Specifically, it is group life insurance that provides a combination of both term and permanent insurance under a master contract, under separate policies, or under a combination of the two. Alternatively, a Section 79 plan may be "superimposed" on an existing plan of group term life insurance that covers more than 10 employees.

Question – What is group universal life (GUL)?

Answer – As its name implies, group universal life combines the economy of scale and other advantages of group coverage with the flexibility and potential for gain of a universal life contract. It is a combination of group term life insurance with a cash accumulation feature. The insurer issues a master contract to an employer who in turn makes it available to employees who receive certificates of coverage and who pay the entire premium.

The policy is divided into two separate portions, pure life insurance protection and the cash values. A part of each premium goes toward mortality costs (i.e., the charge for the term insurance) while the balance of the covered employee's premium is placed (after certain expense charges are subtracted) into the cash value portion of the policy. Premiums are flexible, not fixed. Each insured can, at his discretion, increase or decrease the premium, increase or decrease the benefits, or borrow against the cash value. (All of these flexible options are subject to some limit on frequency to keep administrative costs down.) As is the case with individual policy universal life, an employee's premium payments can be suspended, and coverage will continue as long as the cash value is high enough to meet the insurer's mortality and expense charges.

The typical group universal life contract is held by a large group of 1,000 or more employees. Employees pay the entire premium for the coverage and the employer's only outlay is for indirect costs such as installation and administration.

A GUL contract can be purchased as a stand alone employee benefit or it may be combined with group term. An employee may participate in either or both plans. An employee who participates in the GUL plan must pay premiums high enough to build some cash value. An employee who begins in the term insurance plan may later switch to the GUL plan, or vice versa.

Death benefits are usually pegged to some multiple of salary (e.g., one to five times earnings). Some plans of smaller employers limit the salary multiple to some lower amount, such as three times salary, or provide for specific dollar limits such as $25,000 or $50,000. For administrative simplicity, the plan will offer either level or the more popular increasing death benefits but once the employer makes the decision, all employees must use the same option.

GUL plans usually guarantee the initial interest rate on cash value accumulations for one year. The rate is then adjusted every three to six months, subject to some guaranteed minimum. This rate adjustment is made at the sole discretion of the insurer.

Taxation is the same as under an individual universal life policy. Thus, premiums are nondeductible, cash values accumulate tax free, and death proceeds are generally income tax free.

Question – What are the advantages of group universal life (GUL)?

Answer – Advantages to GUL are enjoyed by both the employer and employee. Some of these include:

1. The employer's direct costs are limited to the expenses of installation, payroll deductions, and ongoing administration.

2. Although the plan entails no direct employer out-of-pocket cost for premiums, the existence of the plan has the psychological effect of reducing the pressure for employer-provided post-retirement benefits.

3. Employees who participate in a group universal life plan receive universal life insurance at group rates.

4. Covered employees can continue coverage into retirement.

5. Employees can purchase coverage based on their individual needs.

6. Policy cash values of the plan are available to employees through either a withdrawal or loan.

Question – Can withdrawals or loans be made from a group universal life (GUL) policy?

Answer – Yes. Withdrawals or loans may be made against cash values of a GUL, subject to restrictions on frequency and subject to minimum amounts in order to control costs. As is the case with all universal life contracts, sufficient cash must be left in the cash value portion to pay mortality and expense charges for some specified period.

Loans and withdrawals decrease the death benefit under the increasing death benefit option (but do not reduce the benefit if the employer has selected the level death benefit option). When money is borrowed out of a GUL, a reduced interest rate is credited on the cash value equal to the loan amount.

Question – What happens when an employee covered by a GUL retires or is terminated?

Answer – An employee has a number of choices including:

1. The coverage may be continued.

2. The policy can be cashed in for its cash value.

3. Policy cash values can be taken under a settlement option.

4. In some cases, the insurance can be continued under a "reduced paid-up" policy.

Question – Can a trade association offer life insurance to its members?

Answer – Yes. Employers in the same type of business or industry can sponsor voluntary insurance plans for their members. For instance, a national associa-tion or state association of teachers, doctors, law-yers, or CPAs might sponsor such a plan. Generally, a trust acts as the master policyholder for trade association plans.

Question – What is group creditor life?

Answer – Banks, finance companies, credit unions, retail-ers, and others may qualify for group life insurance on the lives of individuals who borrow money from the creditor. Although one purpose of group credi-tor life is to protect lenders against possible financial loss due to the death of a debtor, these companies are often in the business of selling the insurance and, therefore, profit from the sales directly.

CHAPTER ENDNOTES

1. IRC Sec. 79(a). This $50,000 exemption must be reduced if the applicable state law imposes a lower maximum on group cover-age on one life. Treas. Reg. §1.79-1(e). Most states, however, no longer have such limits.

2. IRC Sec. 79(a).

3. IRC Sec. 79(b).

4. IRC Sec. 79(b)(3); Treas. Reg. §1.79-2(d); See also IRC Sec. 72(m)(3).

5. Treas. Reg. §1.79-1(c).

6. See Treas. Reg. §1.79-1(c)(2)(i). Generally, an employer can ex-clude employees over a certain age, employees who work less than full-time, and employees who waive their right to partici-pate.

7. Church and synagogue plans are exempt from the IRC Section 79 nondiscrimination rules under IRC Section 79(d)(7).

8. IRC Sec. 79(d)(1).

9. At most, only 50 employees of an employer can be treated as "officers" for purposes of the key employee test. If the firm employs less than 50 officers, the maximum number is the greater of (a) three employees or (b) 10% of all employees.

10. IRC Sec. 79(d)(6).

11. See IRC Secs. 3121(a)(2)(C), 3102(d). Only the cost of coverage in excess of $50,000 is generally subject to the Social Security tax.

12. Proceeds of life insurance are generally excludable from income under IRC Section 101(a).

13. IRC Secs. 162(a), 264(a). Deductibility assumes that amounts paid are compensation for services actually rendered and that the total compensation paid to the employee is reasonable when viewed with respect to the services actually performed for the employer.

14. IRC Sec. 2042.

15. See Rev. Rul. 72-307, 1972-1 CB 307 which modified Rev. Rul. 69-54, 1969-1 CB 221. See also *Estate of Max J. Gorby v. Comm.*, 53 TC 80, acq. 1970-1 CB xvi; *Landorf v. U.S.*, 408 F.2nd 461 (1969).

16. See Rev. Rul. 76-490, 1976-2 CB 300.

17. See Rev. Rul. 79-47, 1979-1 CB 312.

18. IRC Sec. 79(d)(1).

19. The employer's premium payments were considered present interest gifts and therefore did qualify for the gift tax annual exclusion in Revenue Ruling 76-490, 1976-2 CB 300, where the assignment was to an irrevocable trust the employee had created and the trust terms fortuitously provided that, immediately upon the insured's death, the entire proceeds were to be distributed to the beneficiary or the beneficiary's estate. Most trust instruments will not provide beneficiaries with immediate distribution of or access to proceeds and are, therefore, not likely to qualify for the annual exclusion. See Rev. Rul. 79-47, 1979-1 CB 312.

20. See Let. Rul. 8702024.

21. ERISA Secs. 402, 403, 503.

22. Treas. Reg. §1.79-1.

23. Notice 89-110, 1989-2 CB 447. See also Treas. Reg. §1.61-2(d)(2).

24. IRC Sec. 264(a).

25. IRC Sec. 2703.

26. IRC Sec. 101(a)(2). See Appendix G, "The Transfer for Value Rule."

27. Treas. Reg. §1.79-3(d).

28. Treas. Reg. §1.79-1(b).

Chapter 11

JOINT LIFE (FIRST–TO–DIE) INSURANCE

WHAT IS IT?

Joint life (JL) insurance, which is sometimes called multi-life insurance, is first-to-die coverage on two or more insureds. Joint life coverage is offered in many forms, including base policies of permanent or term insurance or additional-insured riders (AIRs) to single-life policies. The permanent plans may use traditional whole life, current-assumption life, or universal life. The AIRs are usually term riders.

WHEN IS THE USE OF THIS TOOL INDICATED?

1. *In the dual-income family market* – JL may provide a cost effective means of replacing income at the first spouse's death. Since the family frequently needs insurance at the second death even more than at the first death, JL is often used to fund specific goals and objectives that depend on the presence of the second of two incomes. For example, a JL policy might be used to pay off a mortgage or to fund a child's education in the event one spouse dies. Since the liquidity needs of the family often depend more on when the first death occurs than on which spouse dies first, JL is often a useful tool in conjunction with survivorship life (SL).

   The JL/SL combination is often a better plan than two single-life policies. For example, assume a husband and wife are each making about the same income and their estate plan calls for maximum use of the marital deduction to defer the bulk of their estate tax until the second death. Assume, as well, that they wish to assure certain benefits for their children, such as funding for educations, in the event of either spouse's premature death and regardless of who dies first. Just for illustration, assume they will need about $1 million at the first death and $3 million at the second death, regardless of who dies first. It would be difficult to determine just what amount of single-life insurance coverage would be needed on each spouse to assure their goals are met, since they do not know who will die first. However, a JL policy with $1 million of coverage and a SL policy with $3 million would exactly meet their needs.

2. *In the key employee business insurance market* – Purchase of separate single-life policies on all key employees can be costly and at times unnecessary. The cost of a multi-life policy on several key persons will be less than the total cost of separate policies on all insureds. In these cases, the base policy often includes, for additional cost, a guaranteed insurability option that permits all, or selected, remaining key employees to be insured under a new JL policy after the first death without evidence of insurability. Some companies also offer a substitute-insured rider that permits the owner of the policy to replace one insured with another, with evidence of insurability. This is an attractive feature if employees in key positions may leave and be replaced by others.[1]

3. *For use in business buy-sell funding* – Perhaps the principal use of JL to date has been to fund buy-sell agreements in closely-held businesses. Since it is the first death among the owners that triggers the need, JL is perfectly designed to meet the need. Similar to key employee cases, guaranteed insurability riders and substitute-insured riders are frequently attractive options.

ADVANTAGES

1. In the family market, a JL/SL combination may provide a more cost effective match with insurance needs than two separate single-life policies on the spouses.

2. In the business insurance market, JL may eliminate the need for redundant coverage when the need is simply to insure the first death among several lives.

DISADVANTAGES

1. Unless the JL policy is coupled with a guaranteed insurability rider, all coverage ceases upon the first death.

2. The cost of a JL policy is greater than the cost of a single-life policy with the same face amount since the insurer must pay the benefit at the first death of

two insureds. The expected time until the first death of two insureds is less than the expected time to the death of either insured separately. For example, assume that the life expectancy of a 55-year-old is 23.8 years. However, note that the expected time until the first death of two 55-year-olds would be less, approximately 17.6 years. Therefore, all else being equal, an insurance company would have to charge roughly 60% more for the joint life coverage than for a single-life policy with the same death benefit. However, if the alternative is to insure *both* lives for the same face amount as the joint life policy, the premium cost should be about 20% *less* than the combined cost of the two single-life policies.

3. There are a number of important ownership issues and tax traps for the unwary. Failure to adhere to certain guidelines can have adverse tax consequences.

TAX IMPLICATIONS

General Income Taxation

JL is taxed in the same manner as other life insurance for income tax purposes. Death benefits are generally received income-tax free. As long as the policy is not classified as a modified endowment contract (MEC), cash values build without current taxation. Withdrawals or distributions during the insured's lifetime are generally taxed under the "cost recovery" rule. That is, amounts are treated as tax-free recovery of principal or basis (generally, net premiums paid) until basis has been fully recovered and only then as taxable gain on the policy. However, also similar to other types of insurance, withdrawals or distributions within the first 15 policy years that are coupled with a reduction in the policy's death benefits trigger income. Subject to a statutory ceiling, all income or growth in the cash surrender value may be deemed to have been received by the policyowner if such withdrawals or distributions occur within the first 15 years.[2]

Income Taxation of Split Dollar Arrangements

In a pure vanilla split-dollar arrangement, the economic benefit of a single-life policy generally is measured by the cost of the pure insurance element of the policy (the difference between the face amount of coverage and the cash surrender value). This cost generally is based upon the lesser of the Table 2001 rates or the term

rates actually used by the company, if clearly identifiable. If the company pays the entire premium, the economic benefit so measured is taxable income to the policyowner. In theory, the economic benefit should be measured in a similar way for JL policies using joint life first-to-die rates rather than single Table 2001 rates or term rates, but the matter has not yet been resolved. For example, is the economic benefit for each insured in a two-life JL policy where each insured is the beneficiary if the other dies first the other insured's single-life Table 2001 or term cost? This is not an unreasonable assumption since the insurance company will have to pay the benefit if either or both die within the year. Therefore, the insurer's term cost should be equal to the sum of the individual term costs.

In the case of JL policies with three or more insureds, the argument is that the economic benefit of each insured would be equal to the sum of the term rates for the other insureds times his or her respective share of the pure death benefit.

Corporate Owned Life Insurance

Since JL is frequently owned by corporations and used for business purposes such as key person insurance or stock redemption buy-sell plans, the corporate alternative minimum tax may be a consideration in its use. A corporation's tax base must be adjusted to take into account certain items. The net death proceeds from a life insurance contract are one such adjustment. The maximum effective alternative minimum tax rate is 15%.[3] In some cases, the strategy is to gross up the amount of insurance to pay the expected AMT. In any event, any payment of AMT becomes a credit available in future years to offset a portion of a corporation's regular tax liability.

Estate and Gift Taxation

Similar to other life insurance, issues of ownership are critical in determining how the policy will be treated for estate and gift tax purposes. When JL is used in a business application, great care should be exercised to avoid adverse estate and gift tax consequences. This issue is addressed in the question and answer section below.

Estate Inclusion When Policy Owned By Corporation

If a key employee / controlling stockholder of a corporation dies and the corporation has complete control over the policy or at least the right to borrow against the policy, the employee/stockholder will be treated as having sufficient incidents of ownership for the policy to be included in his or her estate.[4]

ALTERNATIVES

The principal alternative for a JL policy is separate single-life policies on each insured. If the need for insurance terminates at the first death, JL is the more cost effective method of insuring the risk. If the need for insurance on the survivors will continue after the first death, often separate policies on each insured or some combination of JL and survivorship life might be a better alternative. If the need for insurance on the survivors is uncertain or the amount of coverage required on the survivors is uncertain, JL policies may be acquired with guaranteed insurability options that provide "wait-and-see" flexibility in determining whether to exercise the full option on each insured after the first death.

WHERE AND HOW DO I GET IT?

JL is becoming less a "specialty" item than in the past and is now offered in a variety of forms by a number of insurance companies. A fair number of insurance companies offer some form of term or permanent JL plan insuring two lives. Fewer companies offer JL products insuring three or more lives.

WHAT FEES OR OTHER ACQUISITION COSTS ARE INVOLVED?

JL policies are offered in a number of configurations including annually renewable term, level term, ordinary life, current-assumption life, universal life, and as additional insured riders to single-life policies. The various policy fees, charges, expenses, and commissions associated with JL policies are similar to those of comparable single-life policies relative to the premium. However, since JL policies usually require evidence of insurability for each named insured, the issue expenses associated with underwriting the policy will be proportionally higher than for single-life policies with comparable death benefits. Premiums, of course, will also be correspondingly higher, since the insurer must assess yearly mortality charges that are essentially equivalent to single life mortality charges on each insured.

HOW DO I SELECT THE BEST OF ITS TYPE?

As with any type of insurance policy, the insurer's ability to pay as measured by its financial strength and stability is a critical element in the selection process. See Chapter 3 for a discussion of this issue.

Otherwise, the best policy is the one that has the combination of features desired at the lowest overall cost. See Chapter 4 for a discussion of cost comparison methods.

The basic plan of insurance will greatly affect the schedule of premiums and the availability, if any, of cash values. Annually renewable term JL will offer the lowest initial premiums, but premiums will escalate extremely rapidly as the named insureds age. Level-premium term JL will offer lower annual premiums than permanent plans, but will provide little, if any, cash value accumulations. If the need for insurance is short term as, for example, may be the case with certain key employees who will retire at a specified age, level-premium JL may be the best plan. Permanent types of insurance will require larger premium outlays, but will assure coverage at a known maximum premium outlay for an extended term in the event the insureds live longer than expected. If tax-preferred cash value accumulations are also desirable, some type of permanent plan would be recommended. Permanent plans, and especially universal life plans under option B, offer increasing death benefits if the insurance need is expected to increase over time.

The availability of other policy features and riders should also be considered. Among the options are:

- *Substitute-insured options* – Some insurers offer riders that permit substitution of insureds with evidence of insurability. This is an attractive feature in buy-sell plans or key person plans where there is a potential for change of partners or stockholders or in personnel in key positions.

- *Guaranteed-purchase riders* – Some insurers also offer guaranteed purchase riders that permit surviving insureds to buy insurance on themselves or other surviving insureds without evidence of insurability that may be critical in buy-sell arrangements.

- *Joint premium waiver* – Several companies offer a joint disability premium waiver that is designed principally for the family market.

- *Split option* – Some companies permit insureds to split the policy into two separate policies on each insured, each with a face amount of coverage equal to the JL face amount. Evidence of insurability is usually required.

- *Graded-premium plans* – Graded-premium plans may be attractive if resources to pay premiums are initially low but are expected to increase over time. A graded-premium plan permits policyowners to pay lower initial premiums comparable to term premiums that increase over time to a level somewhat above what the level premium would be with traditional whole life.

- *Common-disaster clause* – Some policies include a provision that if both insureds die in a common disaster, the insurer will pay the face amount on each death. In such cases, it is imperative to name contingent beneficiaries.

WHERE CAN I FIND OUT MORE?

Since joint life is somewhat of a "specialty" product, most life insurance texts give it little coverage. Perhaps the best source of information is the insurers' product informational brochures.[5]

QUESTIONS AND ANSWERS

Question – What problems may arise in using JL in business insurance situations?

Answer – Proper planning of ownership and other policy rights is always an important concern with any life insurance policy to insure the most advantageous treatment for income, gift, and estate tax purposes. Ownership issues are generally not problematic in family situations as long as the husband and wife are the insureds and beneficiaries of the other's death benefit. The major ownership concern arises when three distinct parties are involved as insured, owner, and beneficiary. For example, assume a wife owns a JL policy with herself and her husband as insureds. Their son is named as beneficiary. If the husband dies first, the wife will have made a taxable gift of the death benefit to her son.[6] This adverse result may be eliminated by having the son own the policy.

The planning is also relatively easy in the typical key person business situation. The key person policy is usually owned by and payable to the company. If the company owns the policy and names itself as beneficiary of all death benefits, no special problems exist when using JL as compared with any other type of insurance to insure key persons. The one potential tax problem with any corporate-owned life insurance is the alternative minimum tax (AMT). Since life insurance death proceeds are an item of corporate tax preference, the proceeds could become subject to AMT. The maximum effective AMT rate is generally 15% of any amount so included in AMT income.

Ownership issues become more complicated when JL is used to fund business buy-sell agreements. Stock redemption buy-sell agreements present no special ownership planning problems when JL is used as the funding instrument. In fact, JL is uniquely suited to stock redemption agreements in small closely-held businesses because one policy owned by the corporation on many lives is less expensive than many polices on each owner. Plus, the policy matures when the first owner dies, exactly when it is needed. For other reasons, however, entity buyout plans are often considered less favorable than cross-purchase agreements because of AMT, family attribution, and tax basis issues. See Chapter 20 for further discussion of life insurance in buy-sell agreements.

Although cross-purchase buy-sell plans avoid the corporate AMT and provide survivors with an increased basis, they also require, in the absence of some other funding mechanism, that each owner own life insurance on each other owner. The number of separate single-life policies required can add up quickly as the number of owners increase. For example, if there are five owners, each owner would need to acquire four policies covering each of the other owners, a total of 20 policies. If JL is used, the number of policies required can be reduced to just five, one owned by each owner covering the lives of the remaining four owners. If a trust is used, it is feasible that a single JL policy on all owners could fund the buy-sell agreement.

Question – What special ownership issues arise when JL is used to fund cross-purchase buy-sell agreements?

Answer – Although joint ownership by both insureds of a JL policy in a case with two business owners might seem to be the natural choice, it would be extremely unwise. As a joint owner of the policy, the death proceeds, as well as the deceased's share of the business value would be included in the estate, effectively causing double taxation. Even if the policy is owned by just one of the business owners, there is still a chance the policyowner will die first, with exactly the same double taxation as with joint policy ownership. Only if the business owner who does not own the policy dies first is the double taxation avoided. However, if the business owners knew who would die first, a JL policy wouldn't be necessary.

The key is to keep death proceeds out of the deceased's estate through third-party ownership of the JL policy. In the case of two business owners, this is traditionally accomplished through a trusteed plan. In the case of three or more owners, there are several alternatives: (1) a trusteed plan using a single JL policy on all owners; (2) ownership by each business owner of a separate JL policy on all the other business owners' lives; or (3) a partnership organized to facilitate business continuity.

Question – How would a trusteed plan operate?

Answer – A trust would be set up by the corporation for the benefit of the shareholders. The trust would then apply for and own the JL policy insuring all the owners. Each business owner would have a specific and limited interest in the trust equal to his or her ownership interest less the interest of the decedent. The shareholders would have no other rights to the insurance policy, cash values, or the trust. For example, in a business with five equal owners, each survivor would be entitled to ¼ of any insurance proceeds on the decedent.[7]

If premiums are paid by corporate contributions to the trust, they would be taxable either as income or dividends to the shareholders.[8] Alternatively, shareholders could make nondeductible contributions to the trust in proportion to their ownership interests. The trust would actually pay the premiums.

When the first shareholder dies, the death proceeds will pass to the surviving shareholders who can then use the proceeds to purchase their respective portions of the deceased's interest in the corporation.[9]

Question – In a trusteed plan, is there a potential transfer for value problem after the first death?

Answer – The transfer for value rule essentially says that death benefits will be subject to income tax to the extent they exceed the consideration paid for the

policy if the policy has been transferred for valuable consideration.[10] The question arises after the first death whether the increase each shareholder now has in the death benefit payable on the next to die (assuming, of course, that the trust exercises options to keep an equivalent JL coverage on the surviving shareholders) is an indirect transfer from the first deceased (upon his or her death) which violates the transfer for value rule. The value in this case would be the consideration on the part of all shareholders for entering into the agreement.[11] If the transfer for value rule applies, the increase in the death benefit after the first death would be subject to tax to the extent it exceeds consideration paid.

Experts are divided on the question, but some have argued that a properly designed trust will avoid the problem. The key, it is argued, is to draft the trust instrument so that the shareholders only have an interest in a trust and not an interest in an insurance policy. With the trust as the owner and beneficiary and with each shareholder's interest in the trust limited to a life interest only, there is nothing transferred at death and, consequently, no transfer for value.[12]

Also, if each shareholder owns a JL policy insuring the other shareholders, the transfer for value problem can be avoided. However, after the first death, the face value on the policies owned by each survivor on the lives of the remaining survivors would generally be inadequate to buy out the second-to-die shareholder's ownership interest (which would typically increase after the first death). Also, the value of the policy owned by the first shareholder to die on the other shareholders would be included in the deceased's estate. Since transfer of the deceased's policy to the surviving shareholders would represent a transfer for value, the recommended plan of action is to transfer the policy to the corporation. The transfer of policies on the lives of shareholders to a corporation is an exception to the transfer for value rule.[13] The buy-sell agreement could be amended to effect a combination cross-purchase-entity-buyout plan.

Question – Is JL suitable for S corporations and partnerships?

Answer – S corporations and partnerships are flow-through entities. Consequently, unlike regular corporations, there are no items such as the AMT or increased basis favoring the cross-purchase plan over the entity buyout plan. As discussed above, JL is especially well suited to stock redemption plans if transfer for value problems can be avoided. In general, there should be no transfer for value problems if JL is used in these business forms.

CHAPTER ENDNOTES

1. It should be noted that the exercise of a substitute insured or exchange-of-insured option may bring unanticipated income tax results. In Revenue Ruling 90-109, 1990-2 CB 191, the substitution of one insured for another was treated as a sale rather than a tax-free exchange under Section 1035.

2. IRC Sec. 7702(f)(7). See Appendix F for a further discussion of the 15 year rules.

3. Over the range of corporate alternative minimum taxable income (AMTI) from $150,000 to $310,000, the maximum effective AMT rate is actually 18.75%, because of the phase out of the $40,000 exemption at $0.25 on the dollar. Otherwise, the 20% AMT rate applies to 75% of the net proceeds, thus the 15% maximum rate, if the entire amount is subject to the AMT.

4. Treas. Reg. §20.2042-1(c)(6); Rev. Rul. 82-145, 1982-2 CB 213.

5 See for example *First-To-Die Life Insurance: An Analysis of Ownership Issues* by Keith Staudt, Fidelity Union Life Insurance Company, Dallas, Texas. The discussion in the following questions and answers on the use of JL in business applications is adapted from this treatise.

6. *Goodman v. Comm.*, 156 F.2d 218 (2nd Cir. 1946).

7. The formula in the trust agreement should state that each shareholder during lifetime is entitled to a portion of the death proceeds paid on account of the death of any shareholder who is party to the agreement.

8. As long as premiums are being paid as part of the owner/employee's compensation, and compensation is "reasonable" within the guidelines of IRC Section 162, they should be taxable compensation to the owner/employees and deductible by the company. If an owner is not also an employee or compensation does not fall within "reasonable" limits, the premiums will be treated as nondeductible dividend payments and would be included in each such shareholder's income based on his or her proportionate ownership of the corporation.

9. IRC Secs. 101(a), 641(a)(1).

10. IRC Sec. 101(a)(2).

11. *Monroe v. Patterson*, 197 F. Supp. 146 (N.D. Ala. 1961).

12. See "Meet Closely Held Business Buy/Sell Needs with an OPPO Plan," Chasman, *Life Association News*, October 1990. Chapter 29 and Appendix F also address the transfer for value rule.

13. IRC Sec. 101(a)(2)(B).

Chapter 12

LIMITED–PAY WHOLE LIFE INSURANCE

WHAT IS IT?

Whole life insurance, as the name implies, is designed to provide protection over the insured's entire lifetime. Although coverage continues throughout life, the policy may be designed to allow the owner to pay for the coverage over virtually any duration. At one extreme is the ordinary level-premium whole life policy where the owner pays level premiums each year for as long as the insured lives (or generally to a maximum age of 100). At the other extreme is the single premium life policy where just one large premium payment is sufficient to purchase lifetime coverage. See Chapter 14 for more on single premium life insurance.

The principal characteristics of ordinary limited-pay whole life are:

1. level or fixed periodic premiums payable for a specified number of years;

2. a level or fixed death benefit; and

3. a fixed schedule of minimum cash surrender values that increase over time.

The policy owner agrees to pay a fixed or level premium at regular intervals for the specified period, or until the insured dies, if sooner. Once the policy owner has paid premiums for the stipulated number of years, the policy is "paid up" for its full face amount. In other words, no premiums need to be paid past that point to keep the policy in force for as long as the client lives. In return, the insurance company agrees to pay a fixed death benefit when the insured dies even if the death occurs after the premium-paying period.

As the length of the premium payment period increases, limited-pay policies more closely resemble ordinary level-premium whole life policies. However, since limited-pay policies require premium payments for a term that is less than the term of the contract, the annual premiums must be larger than for ordinary level-premium whole life, and become increasingly larger as the specified premium-paying period grows shorter. Correspondingly, policy cash values grow more

quickly for policies with shorter premium payment periods than for policies with longer payment periods.

Limited-pay policies are commonly offered with 10, 15, 20, 30 years, or longer premium-payment periods. Most companies also offer policies that set the payment period based on the insured's age. The most common form is the life-paid-up-at-age-65 (LP65) policy which allows the insured to discontinue premium payments at retirement (age 65) while the policy remains in force for the rest of the insured's life.

In almost all respects other than the premium-paying period, limited-pay policies have the contract features and characteristics of ordinary level-premium whole life insurance policies. All limited-pay policies contain the same nonforfeiture, settlement, dividend options, rider availability, loan provisions, mortality, expense, interest guarantees, and other features as ordinary life policies. However, limited-pay policies with short premium-payment periods (generally seven years, or less) may be classified as modified endowment contracts (MECs), which are subject to less favorable tax treatment than ordinary life policies, if they fail the seven-pay test. See Appendix D for a discussion of the MEC rules.

WHEN IS THE USE OF THIS TOOL INDICATED?

Limited-pay policies may be indicated in any circumstance where whole life coverage is desired and the policy owner has the financial resources to pay the higher premiums necessary for less than the full term of the coverage. Limited-pay policies are generally not well suited to persons whose need for coverage is great and whose income is limited. In particular, limited-pay policies are often preferred in the following situations:

1. *To acquire insurance protection for juveniles* – Parents often wish to acquire a minimum amount of insurance protection for their children and to pay for the coverage before the children leave the nest, typically at age 21. In the unfortunate event of a child's death, the insurance may provide a fund for funeral and other expenses.

In the more common case where the child survives to adulthood, the policy cash values can serve as part of a nest egg to start him or her on his or her way. In addition, if a child should become uninsurable, he or she will have some life insurance protection, even if he or she is not able to pay the premiums.

2. *To assure insurance protection after retirement without the need for additional premium payments* – Many people wish to keep insurance protection in force after they retire to pay estate tax bills, provide estate liquidity, fund charitable bequests, and provide for dependents. A limited-pay policy whose premium-payment period terminates when an individual retires assures that person that the policy will remain in force even if the individual no longer has the income for ongoing premium payments.

3. *For many business life insurance applications* – Perhaps the most common use of limited-pay policies is in business insurance applications. Businesses typically want to know exactly what their financial commitment is to the insurance and want to fund obligations over fixed periods. Limited-pay policies are frequently used for key employee insurance and for nonqualified deferred compensation funding. For example, limited-pay policies with payment periods equal to the time until executives are scheduled to retire are often used with nonqualified deferred compensation arrangements. If an executive participating in the plan dies before retirement, the policy proceeds can be used to pay survivor benefits under the plan. If the executive survives to retirement, cash values can be used to pay part or all of the obligations to the executive under the plan. In the meantime, cash values have grown without any current tax, and life insurance proceeds can ultimately repay the company for earlier premium outlays.

4. *When the client's working lifetime or high income period is limited* – For instance, a professional athlete such as a football player has high income, but for a relatively short period of time. By compressing payments into a relatively short period that coincides with his or her expected high income years, the policy terms are matched to the client's circumstances more appropriately than if the premium payment period were extended beyond the professional's career.

ADVANTAGES

In addition to all the advantages attributable to life insurance in general and whole life insurance in particular (see Chapter 13), limited-pay policies have three distinct advantages:

1. It is easier to forecast the total dollar outlay for the coverage than for ordinary level-premium whole life insurance. Since premiums on ordinary life continue throughout the insured's lifetime, the total premium outlay for a person who enjoys a longer than average life will be considerably greater (both in total dollars and in present value terms) than the outlay for a limited-pay policy.

2. Limited-pay policies build tax-favored cash values more quickly than ordinary life policies. Therefore, policy owners enjoy greater tax-deferred earnings in the policy. This faster growth makes policy cash values available more quickly and in larger amounts in a given year than with a whole life policy of a comparable amount.

3. Once the policy owner has paid all required premiums, the policy will remain in force for the remainder of his or her life. Therefore, there is less risk that the policy may lapse for failure to pay premiums if the policy owner faces financial difficulties in the future.

DISADVANTAGES

The disadvantages of limited-pay policies are similar to those of ordinary level-premium whole life policies. Since premium payments are necessarily greater than for level-premium policies, these policies are even less affordable for persons of limited income than level-premium policies. In addition, since limited-pay policies build cash values more quickly than level-premium policies, in the early years the amount of protection (the difference between the face amount of coverage and the cash value) is lower relative to the premium spent than with level-premium policies or term policies.

TAX IMPLICATIONS

Non–MEC Policies

Limited-pay policies that are not classified as modified endowment contracts (MECs) are taxed in the same manner as ordinary level-premium whole life insurance. In general, death benefits are subject to the same income, estate, gift, and generation-skipping transfer taxation rules as all other types of life insurance policies. See Appendices A through G for a complete discussion of the taxation of life insurance.

In summary, life insurance death proceeds are generally paid free of any federal income tax.[1] Living benefits are taxed under the rules of Section 72 of the Internal Revenue Code. Under the IRC Section 72 rules, annuity payments are treated as part taxable income or gain and part nontaxable recovery of the investment in the contract until the entire investment in the contract has been recovered. After the investment in the contract has been fully recovered, additional annuity payments are entirely taxable as income.

Payments of interest only are generally taxable in full when paid.[2] Other amounts not received as an annuity, such as dividend payments, lump-sum cash settlements of cash surrender values, cash withdrawals (if permitted), and amounts received on partial surrender are taxed under the cost-recovery rule. That is, these amounts are initially treated as nontaxable recovery of investment in the contract, and, only after the entire investment has been recovered, taxable income or gain.[3]

Policy loans are not treated as distributions. If a policy loan is still outstanding when a policy is surrendered, the borrowed amount becomes taxable at the time of surrender to the extent of gain in the contract.[4]

MEC Policies

Policies that fail the seven-pay test will be treated as modified endowment contracts (MECs).[5] In summary, similar to non-MEC policies, death benefits will generally be paid free of federal income taxation[6] and the cash value buildup is not subject to current taxation. However, in contrast with non-MEC policies, distributions, including loans (even if the loan proceeds are retained by the company to pay premiums) and dividends that are either paid in cash or retained by the insurer to pay either interest or principal on a policy loan, will generally be taxed under the nterest-first rule rather than the cost-recovery rule. That is, amounts received are treated first as taxable income to the extent the cash value exceeds premiums paid, and only then as nontaxable recovery of investment in the contract.[7] In addition, taxable amounts are subject to a 10% penalty tax unless the distribution is made after the taxpayer becomes disabled, attains age 59½, or the distribution is part of a

series of substantially equal periodic payments made for the taxpayer's life or life expectancy, or the joint lives or life expectancies of the taxpayer and his or her beneficiary.[8] Dividends that are retained by the insurer for the purpose of purchasing paid-up additions are not treated as taxable amounts received under the contract.[9]

ALTERNATIVES

There is no substitute for life insurance of some type if an individual desires to provide an immediate estate upon his or her death. All types of life insurance policies can provide income-tax-free cash upon death. The unique features of limited-pay life insurance are its predictable total premium outlay and accelerated, tax-favored cash buildup. It provides lifetime coverage even though premiums cease at the end of the specified premium-paying period. As a by-product of the limited-premium-payment financing, the policy creates a tax-free, or tax-deferred, cash buildup.

If a combination of tax-preferred cash accumulation and life insurance is desired, several other alternatives may be explored:

1. *A combination of a limited-payment-premium deferred annuity and decreasing term insurance –* Cash values accumulate in both annuities and limited-pay life insurance policies on a tax-deferred basis. Therefore, a combination of a limited-premium-payment deferred annuity and a decreasing term policy can provide levels of tax-preferred cash accumulation and death benefits similar to a level-premium policy.

    There are some important differences, however. Withdrawals, lifetime distributions, or loans from each are treated differently for tax purposes. Although most ordinary life policies do not permit withdrawals, as such, if a withdrawal of cash values is permitted or the policy is partially surrendered, the amount distributed is taxed under the "cost recovery rule." That is, the amounts are included in taxable income only to the extent they exceed the investment in the contract. In contrast, distributions from annuities are taxed under the interest-first rule. In other words, the amounts are fully taxable until all of the excess over the investment in the contract has been recovered. In addition, nonannuity distributions from an annuity contract before age 59½ may be subject to a 10% penalty tax. Also, loans from life insurance policies are not subject to tax; loans from annuities, if permitted, are treated as distributions and taxed under the interest-first rule. That is, loan proceeds are subject to the regular income tax and may be subject to the 10% penalty tax. Also, loan provisions of deferred annuity contracts are generally more restrictive than those of life insurance policies.

The annuity/decreasing term combination will require some additional and increasing premiums over the years for the term coverage. In addition, the mortality charges for term insurance coverage are typically higher than the mortality charges in a whole life policy. Finally, the death proceeds from the insurance policy generally may pass to the beneficiary entirely income and estate tax free, regardless of who the beneficiary is, if the policy owner has no incidents of ownership in the policy. The gains on the annuity contract will still be taxable income to the beneficiary and will avoid estate taxation only if the annuitant's spouse is the beneficiary and certain conditions are met.

2. *A combination of investments in tax-free municipal bonds and decreasing term insurance* – This combination can create a cash accumulation and death benefit similar to a limited-pay policy. Similar to the cash values in a life insurance policy, municipal bonds may be used as collateral for loans without any adverse income tax consequences. However, interest paid on debt secured by municipal bonds is generally not deductible. Similarly, interest paid on life insurance policy loans is rarely deductible. The life insurance policy allows the death benefits to be transferred by operation of the contract and avoids probate. Municipal bonds are part of the probate estate and must be distributed by will. Once again, if the policy owner has no incidents of ownership, the life insurance death proceeds are paid estate tax free. The municipal bonds will escape estate tax only if they are left to the spouse.

3. *A universal life policy configured as a limited-pay policy.* A universal life policy can be initially configured to resemble a limited-pay life policy. However, in contrast with "true" limited-pay ordinary life policies, charges for mortality and expenses can change in the universal life policy in such a way that additional premiums could be required in the future to maintain the face value of coverage.

WHERE AND HOW DO I GET IT?

There are nearly 2,000 life insurance companies actively marketing coverage in the United States. Most of these companies offer limited-pay whole life policies as well as other permanent forms of life insurance. In addition to commercial insurance companies, some fraternal organizations, savings banks, professional associations, membership organizations, and stock brokerage houses offer limited-pay whole life policies. Policies can be purchased through many agents representing a licensed insurance company.

WHAT FEES OR OTHER ACQUISITION COSTS ARE INVOLVED?

Life insurance companies are free to set premiums according to their own marketing strategies. The premium includes a "loading" to cover such things as commissions to agents, premium taxes payable to the state government, operating expenses of the insurance company, such as rent or mortgage payments and salaries, and any other expenses.

A few companies offer "no-load" or "low-load" life insurance policies. These policies are not really no-load, since certain expenses are unavoidable (e.g., the premium tax), but rather pay either no sales commission or a very low sales commission. Consequently, the cash value buildup tends to be larger in the early years. Although commissions are lower, these companies typically must spend somewhat more money on alternative methods of marketing and may, therefore, incur generally higher expenses in this area than companies that pay commissions to agents.

The bulk of an insurance company's expenses for a policy are incurred when the policy is issued. It may take the company five to nine years or even longer to recover all its front-end costs. The state premium tax is an ongoing expense that averages about 2% of each premium payment. With most cash value policies, the aggregate commissions paid to the selling agent are approximately equal to the first year's premium on the policy. About half (often 55%) is payable in the year of sale and the other half is paid on a renewal basis over a period of three to nine years.

Most ordinary whole life insurance policies have no explicit surrender charges. However, most participating policies will pay a terminal dividend. The terminal dividend is typically higher the longer the policy has remained in force. In essence, this is a form of surrender charge since the company is essentially holding back dividends it could otherwise pay currently and rewarding those policy holders who maintain their policies longer with a greater terminal dividend.

HOW DO I SELECT THE BEST OF ITS TYPE?

Selecting the best cash-value life insurance policy is a difficult task involving a number of complicated concepts and analyses. (See Chapters 2 through 4 for a further discussion of the basic principles.) However, since the level of dividend payments on participating ordinary limited-pay life insurance is a critical element of the overall cost of the protection, one primary area of focus should be how the company determines the dividends it pays.

What to Look for in the Ledger Statements of Whole Life Policies Paying Dividends as Declared[10]

The ledger statement or policy illustration in Figure 12.1 is for a traditional ordinary level-premium whole life policy that is configured to operate like a 20-pay life policy. This is accomplished by using dividends as projected to buy paid-up additions until the 20th policy year. After year 20, dividends are used first to pay the annual premium with any remainder applied to the purchase of paid-up additions. A true 20-pay life policy would have higher annual premiums that would terminate after 20 years with no need to apply dividends to pay premiums. Each of the numbers in the ledger corresponds to the following notes:

1. The length of time in years that the gross premium is to be paid.

2. The plan of life insurance. In this case, it is 20-pay whole life paying dividends as declared.

3. The insurability status (e.g., nonsmoker, smoker (would be standard)) or rated (extra charge because of being a higher risk for medical or occupational reasons). For this life insurance company, "preferred" risk means the insured is a nonsmoker and is not rated.

4. The gender is male, and the issue age is 45.

5. The gross premium (i.e., the premium charged not taking dividends into consideration) not including any additional benefits provided by any riders (e.g., waiver of premium).

6. The initial amount of life insurance that will be payable to the named beneficiary upon the death of the insured.

7. The beginning-of-the-year ledger statement versus the end-of-the-year ledger statement. Dividends, when paid, are not paid until the end of a specific year. If an end-of-the-year ledger statement is used, it would show dividends paid during the first year, which would be inaccurate.

8. The amount of premium to be paid each year.

9. The cash amount of premium to be paid each year. In this case it is $2,001 for the first 20 years, and $0 thereafter.

10. The cumulative guaranteed amount of reserve (i.e., the guaranteed cash value) that has accumulated for each year.

11. The cumulative total amount of reserve (i.e., the guaranteed cash value), including the nonguaranteed cash value of the additional paid-up life insurance purchased each year, starting at the beginning of year two, with the yearly declared paid dividend.

12. The yearly amount of increase in the total reserve (i.e., the guaranteed cash value and the nonguaranteed cash value of the additional paid-up insurance purchased each year).

13. The yearly difference between the gross premium of $2,001 and the yearly guaranteed cash-value increase and the yearly increase of the nonguaranteed cash value of the additional paid-up life insurance purchased by the yearly declared paid dividend. A minus sign (-) means the combined yearly increase is less than the gross premium of $2,001. The figures do not reflect the time value of money.

14. The amount of additional paid-up life insurance purchased by the declared paid dividend.

15. The yearly total death benefit including the projected additional paid-up life insurance purchased through the projected dividends. From year 16 on, the projected terminal dividend is included.

16. The life expectancy of a 45-year-old male is 29.1 years – age 74 – based on life expectancies for males of all races from *Vital Statistics of the United States*, for the year 1980.

Figure 12.1

LEDGER STATEMENT FOR WHOLE LIFE PAYING DIVIDENDS AS DECLARED

1   20-PAY LIFE ILLUSTRATION

+Plan: Ordinary Life **2**

Class: Preferred Standard **3**

Male Age 45 **4**

5 Basic Annual Premium: $2,001.00

6 Face Amount: $100,000

7 Beg. Pol. Year	8 Pre- mium Payable*	9 Cash Pre- mium Pmt.*	10 Guar. Cash Value	11 Total Cash Value*	12 Ann. Incr. in Total Cash Value*	13 Total Cash Value Incr.(-) Cash Prem.*	14 Div. Adds Death Benefit*	15 Total Death Benefit*
1	$ 2,001	$2,001	$ 0	$ 0	$ 0	-$ 2,001	0	$100,000
2	2,001	2,001	1,026	1,058	1,058	-943	113	100,113
3	2,001	2,001	2,938	3,043	1,985	-16	354	100,354
4	2,001	2,001	4,890	5,130	2,087	86	780	100,780
5	2,001	2,001	6,881	7,347	2,217	216	1,460	101,460
6	2,001	2,001	8,909	9,724	2,377	376	2,456	102,456
7	2,001	2,001	10,971	12,289	2,565	564	3,830	103,830
8	2,001	2,001	13,069	15,085	2,796	795	5,646	105,646
9	2,001	2,001	15,202	18,150	3,065	1,064	7,965	107,965
10	2,001	2,001	17,366	21,526	3,376	1,375	10,848	110,848
11	2,001	2,001	19,432	25,135	3,609	1,608	14,362	114,362
12	2,001	2,001	21,520	29,152	4,017	2,016	18,573	118,573
13	2,001	2,001	23,626	33,632	4,480	2,479	23,544	123,544
14	2,001	2,001	25,746	38,531	4,899	2,898	29,109	129,109
15	2,001	2,001	27,878	43,890	5,359	3,358	35,297	135,297
16	2,001	2,001	30,016	49,735	5,845	3,844	42,119	142,467
17	2,001	2,001	32,160	56,220	6,485	4,484	49,829	150,519
18	2,001	2,001	34,304	63,404	7,184	5,183	58,476	159,553
19	2,001	2,001	36,445	71,235	7,831	5,830	67,884	169,393
20	2,001	2,001	38,580	79,762	8,527	6,526	78,085	180,071
21	-3,984	0	40,702	87,033	7,271	7,271	85,431	187,939
22	-4,544	0	42,805	94,954	7,921	7,921	93,586	196,232
23	-5,178	0	44,882	103,597	8,643	8,643	102,638	205,420
24	-5,878	0	46,925	113,028	9,431	9,431	112,655	215,572
25	-6,655	0	48,929	123,322	10,294	10,294	123,723	226,773
26	-7,510	0	50,892	134,563	11,241	11,241	135,923	239,103
27	-8,445	0	52,820	146,848	12,285	12,285	149,336	252,644
28	-9,458	0	54,718	160,272	13,424	13,424	164,033	267,466
29 **16**	-10,551	0	56,596	174,946	14,674	14,674	180,088	283,645
30	-11,723	0	58,458	190,978	16,032	16,032	197,564	301,243
31	-12,993	0	60,303	208,489	17,511	17,511	216,551	320,351
32	-14,389	0	62,124	227,616	19,127	19,127	237,172	341,092
33	-15,963	0	63,912	248,530	20,914	20,914	259,620	363,658
34	-17,699	0	65,651	271,379	22,849	22,849	284,057	388,211
35	-19,613	0	67,331	296,317	24,938	24,938	310,667	414,934

Figure 12.1 (cont'd)

Beg. Pol. Year	Premium Payable*	Cash Premium Pmt.*	Guar. Cash Value	Total Cash Value*	Ann. Incr. in Total Cash Value*	Total Cash Value Incr.(-) Cash Prem.*	Div. Adds Death Benefit*	Total Death Benefit*
36	-21,690	0	68,947	323,488	27,171	27,171	339,605	443,982
37	-23,913	0	70,499	353,028	29,540	29,540	371,007	475,489
38	-26,277	0	71,989	385,977	32,049	32,049	404,998	509,580
39	-28,780	0	73,426	419,802	34,725	34,725	441,699	546,378
40	-31,441	0	74,818	457,379	37,577	37,577	481,251	586,024

17   *Dividends are used to purchase paid-up insurance in years 1 through 20. Thereafter, dividends are used to reduce premiums, and if necessary, a portion of the paid-up insurance is surrendered to pay the balance of the premium.

Summary # Page   **18**

	19 Guar. Cash Value	20 Total Cash Value*	21 Cash Premium Payments	22 Total Cash Value Less Prem. Payments	23 Guar. Paid-up Insurance	24 Total Paid-up Insurance*
5 Years	$ 6,881	$ 7,696	$10,005	$ 2,309 -	$17,453	$ 19,519
10 Years	17,366	23,069	20,010	3,059	37,811	50,228
15 Years	27,878	47,945	30,015	17,930	52,791	90,792
20 Years	38,580	89,420	40,020	49,400	64,503	149,504
Age 65	38,580	89,420	40,020	49,400	64,503	149,504

25   Terminal dividend*

     Interest-adjusted indexes* based on a 5.00% interest rate, for basic policy only:

26   Life insurance net payment cost index   10 years: $16.24   20 years: $ 9.89   Age 65: $ 9.89

     Life insurance surrender cost index   10 years: 3.09   20 years: 1.95-   Age 65:   1.95-

     Equivalent level annual dividend   10 years: 3.77   20 years: 10.12   Age 65:   10.12

27   Premium information: Annual   Semiannual   Quarterly   Pac.
     Ordinary Life $2,001.00 $1,025.70 $520.56 $173.20

Figure 12.1 (cont'd)

20-PAY LIFE ILLUSTRATION
Explanatory Notes

*Includes dividend values. Dividends are not guaranteed. **28**

Illustrated dividends are based on the company's current mortality, expense, and investment experience. Actual dividends may be higher or lower than shown as a result of future changes in the company's experience, especially the interest rates earned on investments. A terminal dividend is payable upon surrender, lapse, or death, after at least 15 policy years, but only if declared by the company at such time, and is included in the total death benefit, in summary values for total cash value and total paid-up insurance, and in the interest-adjusted surrender cost index.

*Illustrated dividends assume no loans on policy. Policy loans will affect dividends. **29**

30 +The values shown in the ledger assume an annual mode of premium payment and a fixed policy loan interest rate of 8.00% applied in arrears, except in the case of a partial cash premium payment; then, a change to the automatic monthly premium modes has been assumed. The issuance of any policies or riders is subject to the company's regular underwriting practices. The amounts of coverage and premiums for any policies or riders, if issued, may differ from those illustrated.

#Summary values are calculated as of the end of the year. **31**

17. A statement indicating that dividends are used to purchase paid-up insurance. The gross premium of $2,001 is paid during the first 20 years. Thereafter, dividends are used to reduce the gross premium of $2,001 and, if necessary, a portion of the paid-up insurance is surrendered to pay the balance of the gross premium. Looking at column 8 in year 21 reveals that this is unnecessary. The projected dividend in year 21 is $3,984, more than the gross premium of $2,001. A minus sign (-) in this column means that the projected dividends exceed the gross premium. Finally, from year 21 on, the dividend in excess of the gross premium is used to purchase additional paid-up life insurance. If desired, the death benefit could be frozen at $180,071 (year 20), and the dividend amount in excess of the gross premium could then be paid in cash.

18. The summary page values for this insurance company's ledger statement are different from the values shown on the non-summary pages for two reasons. First, the yearly declared dividend is assumed to be paid at the end of the year. Second, the terminal dividend is included. The insurance company assumes for the summary page that the policy is surrendered for the years shown.

19. The cumulative amount of guaranteed cash value for the years shown.

20. The cumulative amount of total cash value for the years shown including the nonguaranteed cash value of additional paid-up insurance purchased through the dividends.

21. Each figure represents $2,001 times the number of years shown.

22. The difference between columns 21 and 20. Although mathematically correct, it does not take into consideration the time value of money.

23. The amount of paid-up life insurance for the years shown that can be purchased by the guaranteed cash value. Once purchased, no additional premiums are required and the insurance company pays a paid-up dividend per $1,000 of paid-up insurance.

24. The amount of paid-up life insurance for the years shown that can be purchased by the total cash value.

25. The terminal dividend may be payable after the policy has been in force 15 years or longer.

26. The interest adjusted index.

27. The premium information for various payment options (i.e., annual (once a year), semiannual (twice a year), quarterly (four times a year), and preauthorized monthly payment through checking account (PAC)). The cost is higher if paid more

frequently than annually. This is because of the expenses incurred to send a premium notice more than once a year and the time value of money (the insurance company does not have the use of your money all at once). The company is implicitly charging 10.34% interest for semiannual payments, 10.88% for quarterly payments, and 8.37% for monthly payments of the premiums.

28. A statement that dividends in any form are not guaranteed.

29. A statement that a loan against the reserve (i.e., cash value) will affect dividends.

30. A statement that the guaranteed fixed contractual interest rate charged for loans against the reserve is 8% payable in arrears, meaning that interest is due one year from the date of the loan.

31. A statement about the summary page calculations.

Ledger Statements Do Not Tell All

In addition to the ledger statement, the following additional information should be available, either verbally or in writing:

1. The rate of return the insurance company assumes it must earn on premium payments to warrant the dividends it projects. In this case the dividend interest assumption rate is 11.57% for the first year, graded up over a 20-year period to 11.73%.

2. The investment strategy employed by the insurance company, which dictates the dividend interest assumption rate. In this case the investment strategy is a *weighted-average portfolio rate*. This means that 40% is weighted toward old money and 60% is weighted toward new money. The insurance company, as part of its investment strategy, anticipates gains from real estate and common stock investments.

3. The conditions in which dividends will be reduced if a loan is taken against the reserve (i.e., guaranteed cash value) of the policy. As stated in the ledger statement, the fixed guaranteed interest rate charged for loans against the reserve is 8%. Because the insurance company assumed that it must earn from 11.57% to 11.73% on money coming in to pay the projected dividend, the dividend will be reduced if the policy owner borrows money from the policy because

the insurance company is earning 3.57 to 3.73% less than it assumed.

4. Although not stated on the ledger statement, this particular insurance company gives the option of electing a variable loan rate versus the fixed loan rate. If the variable loan rate is equal to the dividend interest assumption rate, the dividend should not be reduced. If the variable loan rate exceeds the dividend interest assumption rate, the dividend may be increased. Variable loan rates change with market rates and are often explicitly linked to an index, such as the average yield on government bonds with five years to maturity. The information should also be included on the ledger statement.

5. The rate of return expressed in terms of compound interest should be given either on the ledger statement or by the life insurance agent. Ideally, it should be provided for each year. If the agent does not have the proper financial decisions software, it will be economically impossible to provide yearly rates of return. A financial decisions calculator can be used, however, on an economical basis to provided rates of return for various years (year 1, year 5, year 10, year 20, and to life expectancy).

6. The rate of return upon death for this policy for sequential years is as follows:

Year	Rate of Return
1	4,897.50%
5	90.50
10	30.00
20	12.87
29 (life expectancy)	9.77

7. Once the rate of return upon death is known, then it can be determined what would have to be earned before taxes (it is assumed that the death benefit is considered life insurance proceeds and, as such, not subject to federal or state income taxes) in other financial services products (e.g., mutual funds, certificates of deposit, real estate, or commodities) to duplicate the tax-exempt rate of return provided by life insurance. The before-tax rate of return is determined by dividing the life insurance rate of return by the marginal tax bracket subtracted from 100% (for 15%, the factor is 0.85; for 25%, 0.75; for 28%, 0.72; for 33%, 0.67; and for 35%, 0.65). The result is shown in Figure 12.2.

Figure 12.2

	BEFORE TAX RATE OF RETURN				
Year	15% taxpayer	25% taxpayer	28% taxpayer	33% taxpayer	35% taxpayer
1	5,761.76%	6,530.00%	6,802.08%	7,309.70%	7,534.62%
5	106.47	120.67	125.69	135.07	139.23
10	35.29	40.00	41.67	44.78	46.15
20	15.14	17.16	17.88	19.21	19.80
29 (life expectancy)	11.49	13.03	13.57	14.58	15.03

8. The rate of return upon surrender should also be provided. When the rate of return upon surrender is positive, it means that taxes are due. Generally, taxes are due on the difference between the cash-surrender value and the premiums paid. The result before taxes is as follows:

Year	Rate of Return
1	-100.00%
5	-8.62
10	2.57
20	7.16
29 (life expectancy)	7.40

9. The ledger statement should be the official ledger statement produced by the computer service of the life insurance company. If it is not "bug-free," the bugs should be revealed.

WHERE CAN I FIND OUT MORE?

See the list of references in Chapter 13, "Ordinary Level-Premium Whole Life Insurance."

QUESTIONS AND ANSWERS

Question – What is the difference between a "paid-up" policy and a "matured" policy?

Answer – A policy that is "paid-up" requires no further premium payments to keep the policy's full face amount of coverage in force for the remaining term of the contract (generally to age 100). This results when premium payments have been sufficiently large to build the reserve necessary to support the policy for the remaining term. However, the reserve, which is closely tied to the cash surrender value of the policy, will always be less than the face value of the policy until the end of the term of the contract. At the time when the reserve equals the face value of the contract, the policy has "matured."

In other words, the face value (death benefit) and the cash value of a matured policy are equal (or nearly so). In a paid-up policy, the cash value is less than the face value until the end of the term of the contract when it matures.

Question – Can a limited-pay policy with scheduled premium payments for more than seven years still fail the seven-pay test and be treated as a modified endowment contract (MEC)?

Answer – In general, insurance companies are careful to design limited-pay policies so that they pass the seven-pay test under the MEC rules. If the policy initially fails the seven-pay test, the policy illustration or ledger statement should clearly say so. However, even if the policy initially satisfies the seven-pay test, it may later fail the test if dividends are applied as additional premiums. It is conceivable that a 10-pay policy, for example, may fail the seven-pay test if the insured continues to pay the full annual premiums and dividends are applied as additional premiums. See Appendix D for a full discussion of the MEC rules (including the procedure allowing life insurance companies to correct the payment of excess premiums).

CHAPTER ENDNOTES

1. IRC Sec. 101(a).
2. IRC Sec. 72(j); Treas. Reg. §1.72-14(a).
3. IRC Sec. 72(e).
4. IRC Sec. 72(e).
5. IRC Sec. 7702A(a).
6. IRC Sec. 101(a).
7. IRC Sec. 72(e).
8. IRC Sec. 72(v).
9. H.R. Conf. Rep. No. 100-1104, (TAMRA '88) *reprinted in* 1988-3 CB 592.
10. This analysis is adapted from the excellent discussion on this topic in *The Life Insurance Buyer's Guide* by William D. Brownlie with Jeffrey L. Seglin published by McGraw-Hill Publishing Company (1989).

Chapter 13

ORDINARY LEVEL–PREMIUM WHOLE LIFE INSURANCE

WHAT IS IT?

Whole life insurance, as the name implies, is a contract designed to provide protection over the insured's entire lifetime. There are many types of whole life policies, but the oldest and still the most common type of whole life policy is ordinary level-premium whole life insurance, or simply ordinary life. This form of insurance is also known as "straight life," "traditional whole life," or "continuous-premium whole life." If the term "whole life" is used alone, it is generally accepted that the reference is to ordinary level-premium whole life as opposed to any other type of life long policy.

This type of contract features level or fixed periodic premiums computed on the assumption that the policy can be retained by the policyowner for the life of the insured. The death benefit remains level throughout the lifetime of the contract. The level premium was created to make the whole life contract affordable for as long as the policyowner decided to keep it.

As an outgrowth and natural byproduct of the fixed and level premium, the whole life contract develops cash values. These are values that result from the reserve the insurer needs to accumulate in the early years of the policy's life so that there will be sufficient money (together with interest earned on the reserve) in later years to pay the promised death benefit while keeping premiums level. Absent this reserve, the level premium would be insufficient to pay the increasing mortality costs. The policy contains a fixed and guaranteed schedule of the cash values that can be borrowed by the policyowner for any reason (such as an emergency or opportunity) at any time or taken upon the surrender of the contract.

The policyowner agrees to pay a fixed or level premium at regular intervals for the rest of the insured's life (generally only up to age 100, if the insured lives that long, or in some cases, to age 95). In return, the insurance company agrees to pay a fixed death benefit when the insured dies if the policyowner has continued to pay the premiums. Policyowners who discontinue paying premiums and terminate their policies are entitled to the scheduled cash surrender value.

WHEN IS THE USE OF THIS TOOL INDICATED?

In general, some type of life insurance is indicated when a person needs or wants to provide an immediate estate upon his or her death. This need or desire typically stems from one or more of the following reasons.

1. To provide income for dependent family members until they become self-supporting after the head of household dies.

2. To liquidate consumer or business debts or mortgages, or to create a fund that would enable the surviving family members to do so when the head of household dies.

3. To provide large amounts of cash at death for children's college expenses or other capital needs.

4. To provide cash for federal estate and state inheritance taxes, funeral expenses, and administration costs.

5. To provide funds for the continuation of a business through a "buy-sell" agreement.

6. To indemnify a business for the loss of a key employee.

7. To help recruit, retain, retire, or reward one or more key employees through a salary continuation plan and finance the company's obligations under that plan to the dependents of a deceased key employee.

8. To fund bequests of capital to children, grandchildren, or others without the erosion often caused by probate costs, inheritance taxes, income taxes, federal estate taxes, transfer fees, or the generation-skipping transfer tax.

9. To fund charitable bequests.

10. To preserve confidentiality of financial affairs. Life insurance proceeds payable to someone

other than the deceased's estate are not part of the probate estate and are not a matter of public record. It is not unusual for a beneficiary to be a lover, illegitimate child, or to have some other relationship to the insured that the insured may not want to publicly acknowledge. Likewise, the insured may not want the amount payable to the beneficiary to become a matter of public record.

11. To assure nearly instant access to cash for surviving dependents. Life insurance proceeds are generally paid to beneficiaries within days of the claim. There is no delay, as might be the case with other types of assets, because of the intervention of state or other governmental bodies due to settlement of tax issues, or because of claims by the decedent's creditors.

12. To direct family assets to family members in a way that minimizes state, local, and federal taxes.

13. Level-premium whole life, in particular, is the preferred type of policy when the need is long term and there is a desire to maintain a relatively fixed annual premium cost. For many families, it is the most "affordable" form of long-term coverage on the principal breadwinners.

14. Level-premium whole life may satisfy various business life insurance needs, such as financing vehicles for buy-sell agreements, key person insurance, and nonqualified deferred compensation arrangements. It is especially suitable if the objective is also to receive tax sheltered returns and the company has accumulated earnings problems. The cash buildup in life insurance policies held for legitimate business purposes is not counted towards the accumulated earnings limitation.

15. Level-premium whole life insurance is often the preferred type of insurance for split dollar arrangements. (See Chapter 30 for a further discussion.)

16. Level-premium whole life is a tax-sheltered way to finance post-retirement health insurance for a selected group of executives or key employees by using life insurance policies on their lives. Cash values are available to the corporation to help meet future cash needs for health insurance premium payments for retirees. When the employee dies, the corporation receives the death proceeds free from federal income tax (except for some potential alterna-

tive minimum tax liability). The corporation is reimbursed for part or all of its costs for the post-retirement health insurance. Corporate owned life insurance (COLI) offers certain advantages over other methods for recovering post-retirement health insurance liabilities.

ADVANTAGES

1. A fixed and known annual premium. Although, it should be noted that net premiums (fixed premiums minus dividends) for par policies will generally decline over the years.

2. Guaranteed ceiling on mortality and expense charges and guaranteed floor on interest credited to cash values.

3. Cash value interest or earnings accumulate tax-free or tax-deferred, depending on whether gains are distributed at death or during lifetime.

4. Ordinary life, through the combination of guaranteed cash values and dividend formulas, frequently pays higher effective interest on cash values than is available from tax-free municipal bonds.

5. Cash values are not subject to the market risk associated with longer-term municipal bonds and other longer-term fixed income investments.

6. Policy cash values can be borrowed at a low net cost. Although policyowners must pay interest on policy loans, cash values continue to grow and are credited with at least the minimum guaranteed rate in the policy. Consequently, the actual net borrowing rate is less than the stated policy loan rate.

7. Life insurance proceeds are not part of the probate estate, unless the estate is named as the beneficiary of the policy. Therefore, the proceeds can be paid to the beneficiary without the expense, delay, or uncertainty caused by administration of the estate.

8. There is no public record of the death benefit amount or to whom it is payable.

9. In most cases, the death benefit proceeds are not subject to federal income taxes.

10. The death benefit proceeds are often fully or partially exempt from state inheritance taxes unless payable to the insured's estate.

11. Life insurance policies can be used as collateral or security for personal loans.

DISADVANTAGES

1. Lifetime distributions of cash values are subject to income tax to the extent attributable to gain in the policy.

2. The premium may be unaffordable for persons of limited financial resources.

3. In the early years, the amount of protection is lower relative to the premium spent than with term insurance. However, later, as term rates rise while the premium for ordinary life remains level, the reverse will typically be true.

4. Surrender of the policy within the first 5 to 10 years may result in considerable loss since surrender values reflect the insurance company's recovery of sales commissions and initial policy expenses.

5. Interest paid on policy loans is generally not tax deductible.

6. Cash values accumulating in the contract are subject to inflation. Whole life insurance is by definition a long-term purchase and the guaranteed return on this type of policy provides little inflation protection. However, a partial hedge against inflation is provided by the dividends paid on participating policies which reflect the favorable mortality, investment, and business expense results of the insurer.

7. The overall rate of return on the cash values inside this traditional whole life contract has not always been competitive in a before tax comparison with alternative investments. However, when safety of principal, contractually guaranteed liquidity, and the cost of term insurance if purchased outside the policy are factored into the analysis, whole life often compares favorably to alternative types of policies as well as non-life insurance investments.

TAX IMPLICATIONS

General Tax Rules

Death benefits are usually paid free of any federal income tax. In general, death benefits paid under these policies are subject to the same income, estate, gift, and generation-skipping transfer taxation rules as all other types of life insurance policies. See Appendices A through G for a complete discussion of the taxation of life insurance.

Taxation of Living Proceeds

Section 72 of the Internal Revenue Code governs the taxation of living proceeds from life insurance policies. Living proceeds are generally any amounts received during the policyowner's lifetime. For tax purposes, payments are separated into three classes: (1) annuity payments; (2) payments of interest only; and (3) amounts not received as an annuity.

Annuity payments – Annuities include all periodic payments received from the contract in a systematic liquidation of the cash value. This includes both life contingent annuities and fixed term or fixed amount annuities. The rules of IRC Section 72 determine what portion of each payment is treated as a tax-free recovery of investment in the contract and what portion is treated as taxable income or gain. To oversimplify, the rules essentially pro-rate the recovery of investment in the contract over the expected payout period. Therefore, each payment is treated partially as recovery of investment and partially as taxable interest until the entire investment in the contract has been recovered. Any further payments are treated entirely as taxable income. (See Chapter 8 for a more in depth discussion of the taxation of annuities.)

Payments of interest only – Payments consisting of interest only, that is, they are not part of the systematic liquidation of a principal sum, are not annuity payments and are not taxed under the annuity rules. In general, if living benefits are held by the insurer under an agreement to pay interest, the interest payments are taxable in full, whether distributed or simply credited to the account.

Amounts not received as an annuity – In general, all living proceeds except for interest and annuity settlements are taxed under the "cost recovery rule." Included in this category are policy dividends, lump-sum cash settlements of cash surrender values, cash withdrawals, and amounts received on partial surrender. These amounts are included in gross income only to the extent they exceed the investment in the contract (as reduced by any prior excludable distributions received from the contract). In other words, nonannuity distributions during life are first treated as a return of the policyowner's investment in the contract (generally premiums paid less dividends received), and then as taxable interest or gain.

The exceptions to this rule are generally unlikely to arise with level-premium policies. The first exception is with respect to policies that initially fail the seven-pay test under the modified endowment contract (MEC) rules. Since level-premium policies are designed to have premiums payable for the life of the insured, they are not likely to fail the seven-pay test. The second exception is with respect to policies that originally satisfied the tests to avoid MEC treatment, but that as a result of certain changes in the benefits of the contract, subsequently fail the tests. Once again, the types of changes that would jeopardize favorable MEC status are unlikely to arise with ordinary level-premium whole life policies. Problems are more likely to arise with limited-pay policies and universal life policies. If any life insurance contract is treated as a MEC, cash distributions are generally taxed under the interest-first rule. Under this rule, distributions are first attributed to interest or gain in the contract and are fully taxable. Only when the interest or gain is exhausted are distributions treated as a nontaxable recovery of investment in the contract.

Loan proceeds – Policy loans under non-MEC life insurance policies are not treated as distributions. If a policy loan is still outstanding when a policy is surrendered, the borrowed amount becomes taxable at the time of surrender to the extent the cash value exceeds the policyowner's investment in the contract. Loans are essentially treated as if the borrowed amount was actually received at the time of surrender and used to pay off the loan.

ALTERNATIVES

There is no substitute for life insurance that provides an immediate estate upon a person's death. All types of life insurance policies can provide tax-free cash upon death. The unique feature of level-premium life insurance is its "affordability." It provides lifetime coverage at the lowest level annual cost relative to other types of whole life policies. As a byproduct of level-premium financing, the policy creates a tax-free or tax-deferred cash buildup. If a combination of tax-preferred cash accumulation and life insurance is desired, several other alternatives may be explored:

1. *A combination of a level-premium deferred annuity and decreasing term insurance* – Cash values accumulate in both annuities and level-premium life insurance policies on a tax-deferred basis. Therefore, a combination of a level-premium

deferred annuity and a decreasing term policy can provide levels of tax-preferred cash accumulation and death benefits similar to a level-premium policy.

There are some important differences, however. Withdrawals, lifetime distributions, or loans from each are treated differently for tax purposes. Although most ordinary life policies do not permit withdrawals, as such, if a withdrawal of cash values is permitted or the policy is partially surrendered, the amount distributed is taxed under the cost-recovery rule. That is, the amounts are included in taxable income only to the extent they exceed the investment in the contract. In contrast, distributions from annuities are taxed under the interest-first rule. In other words, the amounts are fully taxable until all of the excess over the investment in the contract has been recovered. In addition, nonannuity distributions from an annuity contract before age 59½ may be subject to a 10% penalty tax. Also, loans from life insurance policies are not subject to tax; loans from annuities, if permitted, are treated as distributions and taxed under the interest-first rule. That is, loan proceeds are subject to the regular income tax and may be subject to the 10% penalty tax. Also, loan provisions of deferred annuity contracts are generally more restrictive than those of life insurance policies.

The annuity/term combination will require some additional and increasing premiums over the years for the term coverage. In addition, the mortality charges for term insurance coverage are typically higher than the mortality charges in a level-premium policy. Finally, the death proceeds from the insurance policy generally may pass to the beneficiary entirely income and estate tax free, regardless of who the beneficiary is, if the policyowner has no incidents of ownership in the policy. The gains on the annuity contract will still be income-taxable to the beneficiary and will avoid estate taxation only if the annuitant's spouse is the beneficiary and is a United States citizen.

2. *A combination of investments in tax-free municipal bonds and decreasing term insurance* – This combination can create a cash accumulation and death benefit similar to a level-premium policy. Similar to the cash values in a life insurance policy, municipal bonds may be used as collateral for loans without any adverse income tax conse-

quences. However, interest paid on debt secured by municipal bonds is not deductible. Although not the general rule, in some cases, the interest paid on life insurance policy loans may be tax deductible. The life insurance policy allows the death benefits to be transferred by operation of the contract and avoids probate. Municipal bonds are part of the probate estate and must be distributed by will. Once again, if the policyowner has no incidents of ownership, the death proceeds are paid estate tax free. The municipal bonds will escape estate tax only if they are left to the spouse.

3. *A universal life policy configured as a level-premium policy* – A universal life policy can be initially configured to resemble a level-premium life policy. However, in contrast with "true" level-premium life policies, charges for mortality and expenses can change in the universal life policy in such a way that additional premiums could be required in the future to maintain the death benefit coverage.

WHERE AND HOW DO I GET IT?

There are nearly 2,000 life insurance companies actively marketing life insurance coverage in the United States. Most of these companies offer level-premium whole life policies as well as other permanent forms of life insurance. In addition to commercial insurance companies, some fraternal organizations, savings banks, professional associations, membership organizations, and stock-brokerage houses offer level-premium whole life policies. Policies can be purchased through many agents representing licensed insurance companies.

WHAT FEES OR OTHER ACQUISITION COSTS ARE INVOLVED?

Life insurance companies are free to set premiums according to their own marketing strategies. Almost all states have statutes prohibiting any form of rebating (sharing the commission with the purchaser) by the agent. The premium includes a "loading" to cover such things as commissions to agents, premium taxes payable to the state government, operating expenses of the insurance company such as rent, mortgage payments and salaries, and other company expenses.

A few companies offer "no-load" or "low-load" life insurance policies. These policies are not really no-load,

since certain expenses are unavoidable (e.g., the premium tax), but rather pay either no sales commission or a very low sales commission. Consequently, the cash value buildup tends to be larger in the early years. Although commissions are lower, these companies typically must spend somewhat more money on alternative methods of marketing and may therefore incur generally higher expenses in this area than companies that pay commissions to agents.

The bulk of an insurance company's expenses for a policy are incurred when the policy is issued. It may take the company five years or longer to recover all its front-end costs. The state premium tax is an ongoing expense that averages about 2% of each premium payment. With most cash value policies the aggregate commission paid to the selling agent is approximately equal to the first year premium on the policy. About half (often 55%) is payable in the year of sale and the other half is paid on a renewal basis over a period of three to nine years.

Most ordinary level-premium life insurance policies have no explicit surrender charges. However, most participating policies will pay a terminal dividend. The terminal dividend is typically higher the longer the policy has remained in force. In essence, this is a form of surrender charge since the company is essentially holding back dividends it could otherwise pay currently and rewarding those policyholders who maintain their policy longer with a greater terminal dividend.

HOW DO I SELECT THE BEST OF ITS TYPE?

Selecting the best cash value life insurance policy is a difficult task involving a number of complicated concepts and analyses. (See Chapter 4, "How to Determine the Right Policy" for a further discussion.) However, since the level of dividend payments on participating ordinary level-premium life insurance is a critical element of the overall cost of the protection, one primary area of focus should be how the company determines the dividends it pays.

How to Evaluate the Dividends Paid on Par Policies

1. Compare the current rate credited to policy cash values and the length of the guarantees. All else being equal, policies with higher current rates and longer guarantee periods will be better than those with lower current rates and shorter guarantees.

2. Check to see how the company will determine the rate credited to policy cash values after the guarantee period. Policies that determine the rate based on a specific money rate or bond index leave the company with little room to manipulate the amount credited in an adverse way.

3. Look at the current mortality and expense factors and compare them with the guaranteed maximum mortality and expense factors. The mortality factors currently used should be competitive. If the difference between the current mortality rates and the maximum rates is small, the company has little room to use higher mortality charges as a means of reducing the effective rate credited to cash values.

4. Look for a bailout provision that reduces or eliminates surrender charges if investment performance does not meet reasonable guidelines.

5. Check the policy loan provision to see if the company uses an "offset" provision to credit borrowed amounts with a lower rate than non-borrowed amounts. If the insured anticipates borrowing from the policy, a company that does not use the offset method is preferable. If borrowing is not anticipated, a company that uses the offset method may be more desirable because the company should in theory be able to credit higher interest to policies without borrowing than they otherwise would be able to without the offset provision.

6. Check the financial soundness of the company using the criteria in Chapter 3, "How to Determine the Right Company." In the past, some insurance companies attempted to increase their portfolio yield by investing a substantial portion of their assets in relatively high yield but also high risk "junk" bonds. As a result of adverse market conditions and increased defaults on these bonds, some of these companies experienced serious financial stress and reduced portfolio yields.

What to Look for in the Ledger Statement of an Ordinary Life Policy

What to look for in the ledger statement of an ordinary level-premium policy is similar to the items that should be evaluated in relation to any whole life policy. See Figure 12.1 in Chapter 12, "Limited-Pay Whole Life Insurance" for a discussion of what to look for in whole life policy illustrations.

WHERE CAN I FIND OUT MORE?

The following references include authoritative discussions of various types of life insurance including ordinary level-premium whole life insurance:

1. B. Anderson, *Anderson on Life Insurance* (Waltham, MA: Little, Brown and Company, 1991).

2. B. Baldwin, *New Life Insurance Investment Advisor: Achieving Financial Security for You and Your Family Through Today's Insurance Products,* 2nd ed. (Hightstown, NJ: McGraw-Hill Trade, 2001).

3. J. Belth, Life Insurance: A Consumer's Handbook, 2nd ed. (Bloomington, IN: Indiana University Press, 1985).

4. K. Black, Jr. and H. Skipper, Jr., *Life Insurance,* 13th ed. (Old Tappan, NJ: Prentice Hall Inc., 1999).

5. E. Graves, Editor, *McGill's Life Insurance,* 5th ed. (Bryn Mawr, PA: The American College, 2004).

The following references are useful guides for policy and company rating information:

1. *Best Insurance Reports* (Oldwick, NJ: A. M. Best Company, published annually).

2. *Best's Review – Life/Health Edition* (Oldwick, NJ: A. M. Best Company, published monthly).

QUESTIONS AND ANSWERS

Question – What is the difference between "par" and "nonpar" ordinary level-premium whole life?

Answer – The premiums, the death benefit, and the minimum cash surrender value schedule are initially fixed in ordinary level-premium whole life policies. However, if the policy is a dividend-paying, or "participating" (par) policy, the premiums may effectively decrease and the death benefit and the scheduled cash surrender values may increase. Only if the policy is a "guaranteed-cost, nonparticipating" (nonpar) policy that does not pay dividends will each of these features truly remain fixed for the life of the insured. See Chapter 1, "Introduction to Life Insurance" for a general discussion of the differences between par and nonpar policies.

Question – In a policy that pays dividends (a par policy) what choices does the policyowner have when dividends are paid?

Answer – Policyowners have considerable flexibility in choosing how dividends paid on par policies are used. Usually they may elect to have dividends paid in cash, allocated to pay premiums, accumulate at interest, used to purchase paid-up additional amounts of insurance, used to purchase one-year term insurance, applied against policy loans and/ or interest on policy loans, or in some cases, treated as additional premium payments. In addition, policyowners may change these options at any time in most policies.

Cash option – Under this option, the company pays dividends to the policyowner in cash. The cash option is infrequently used since most policyowners find one of the other options more attractive.

Premium reduction option – One of the more frequently used options is to apply dividends against required premium payments. This option is really just an administratively convenient cash option, since, in either case, dividends effectively serve to reduce premiums. In general, the amount of dividends paid increases over time, ever reducing the policyowner's net premium outlay (premiums less dividend payments), sometimes to zero or less after the policy has been in force for a long period of time. At this point, the policyowner usually must elect another option for the excess dividend payments.

Under the cash option or the premium reduction option, the policyowner's net premiums effectively decline over time (since the dividend level – generally – increases) while the death benefit remains level and the cash surrender schedule remains fixed.

Accumulate at interest option – Policyowners may elect to leave their dividend payments with the insurance company to accumulate in a fund appended to the policy. In other words, the insurance company will provide a savings-type account for dividends. The interest rate payable on the fund is guaranteed to equal or exceed a specified minimum (typically 4.5 to 6%), but most companies have historically credited rates higher than the guaranteed minimum. Policyowners may withdraw cash from the fund at any time. If the insured dies the policy pays the face value. If the policy is surrendered, it pays the net cash surrender value plus the value of the dividend accumulation account.

Paid-up additions option – Under this option, each dividend payment is used to buy as much paid-up single-premium whole life insurance as the dividend will allow at the insured's attained age. Consequently, under this option the premiums payable by the policyowner remain level while the total death benefit and the schedule of total cash values increases over time.

The paid-up additions are available without evidence of insurability. The insurance is purchased at net rates, that is, without any of the commissions and other front-end charges associated with new sales of insurance. Therefore, this is a low-cost method of acquiring additional insurance without proving insurability.

The paid-up additions are usually (but not always) participating. This means the annual dividends paid on the paid-up additions further escalate overall dividend payments and further supplement the policy's total death benefit and cash values. Similar to cash values under the base policy, the policyowner may borrow against the cash values of the paid-up additions. As described above, some companies will permit policyowners to surrender paid-up additions for the net surrender values while keeping the underlying policy in force.

One-year term insurance option – Under the general form of this option, each year's dividend is used to purchase as much one-year term insurance as the dividend will allow at the insured's attained age. Similar to the paid-up option, the term insurance is acquired at net rates and without the need to prove insurability.

Under a second form of this option, the dividend is used to buy one-year term insurance in an amount up to the cash value of the policy. Any excess dividends may be applied under one of the other options. This form of the option is frequently used with split dollar insurance which is commonly used in key person and other business life insurance applications. (See Chapter 30 for a further discussion of split dollar life insurance arrangements.) With the split dollar arrangement, the premium payer, generally the insured's company, is entitled to the cash value or an amount equal to the cash value from the death proceeds. The net amount at risk (the difference between the face amount and the cash value) is generally payable to whomever the insured so designates, often the spouse or child of the insured. Under this form of the one-year term option, the insured's designated beneficiary can receive a death benefit equal to the full face value of the underlying policy.

Question – How does the "savings component" of ordinary life work?

Answer – Ordinary level-premium whole life can be viewed mathematically (but not legally) as a combination of decreasing term insurance and increasing "savings fund." Although the level-premium payment method permits the policyowner to pay the lowest up-front outlay necessary to acquire lifetime coverage, the premiums are still greater than the mortality costs in the early years. Since premiums remain level while mortality costs increase at later ages, the premiums in the early years must be set high enough to pre-fund the excess of mortality costs over premiums in the later years. Consequently, ordinary level-premium whole life policies build reserves to pay the future excess mortality costs and to serve as the basis for determining the policyowner's cash surrender values.

The cash value normally increases each year until it reaches the face value at age 100. The cash value grows more slowly in the early years and more swiftly in the later years because the company typically recovers the expenses associated with the sale of the policy over the early years.

Policyowners may directly access cash values in ordinary life policies in two ways. First, policies permit policyowners to borrow cash values. As long as the policyowner continues to pay premiums, the policy remains in force, but the death benefit is reduced by any outstanding policy loans and unpaid interest on the policy loans.

Alternatively, policyowners may terminate or surrender their policies and receive the net cash surrender value shown in the policy as of the date of surrender. The net surrender value is the gross cash value shown in the policy *minus* any identifiable surrender charges, outstanding policy loans, and unpaid interest on policy loans *plus* any prepaid premiums, dividends accumulated at interest, cash values attributable to paid-up additions, and any additional terminal dividends. In this case, however, the policyowner must give up the insurance protection.

Since virtually the same amount of cash may be accessed through policy loans as through surrender of the policy, loans are generally the better alternative if the need for protection is expected to continue.

In some cases, partial surrenders are permitted. Some participating policies permit policyowners to surrender paid-up additions without surrendering the base policy. Although it is not a matter of legal right, in practice some companies will also allow partial surrenders of ordinary life policies. In these cases, the death benefit and premiums are reduced in proportion to the reduction in the cash value.

One additional method to access cash values without giving up coverage entirely may be to exchange a policy for another policy with a lower cash value under the exchange rules of IRC Section 1035. These rules are discussed in Appendix E.

Question – What is the "policy loan repayment option?"

Answer – Similar to the premium reduction option, this option is really just an administrative convenience variation on the cash option. Rather than having the company pay the dividends in cash to the policyowner and then have the policyowner turn around and write a check to the insurance company to pay policy loans or interest on loans, the policyowner may have the dividends applied directly against the policy loans and/or interest on loans.

Question – What is meant by the "vanishing premium" option?

Answer – This option is similar to the premium reduction option except that the dividends are applied as additional premiums while the policyowner continues to pay the full annual premium. Under this option, the policyowner is essentially converting what is an ordinary level-premium whole life policy into a form of increasing premium limited-pay policy. After a number of years, the policy will be entirely paid-up and no further premiums will be required to keep the full face amount in force for the remainder of the insured's life. In other words, if the assumptions are met the premium "vanishes." (Of course, if the level of dividends projected is not met, it will take longer than anticipated for this to occur.) Once the policy reaches paid-up status, additional dividends are typically used to buy paid-up additions, but may generally be applied under any of the other dividend options.

Although it would be unusual for dividend payments to reach a sufficiently high level soon enough to violate the modified endowment contract (MEC) rules if dividends are applied as additional premiums, it is theoretically possible. Since having the policy classified as a MEC would have adverse tax consequences, some care should be taken if this dividend option is selected to assure that premiums do not exceed the MEC levels. (See Appendix D for a further discussion of the MEC rules.)

Question – Do all policies allow a policyowner to borrow on the policy?

Answer – All cash value policies must allow policyowners to borrow cash values from the policy. For many policyowners, the cash values in their life insurance policies represent an important source of emergency funds. The loan provision typically has the following features:

1. In general, policyowners may borrow up to the cash value less interest on the loan as of the subsequent policy anniversary.

2. The interest rate may be fixed or variable, depending on the policy and, sometimes, on the election of the insured.

3. Policyowners generally have no obligation to repay loans and interest on any fixed schedule; they may repay in whole or in part at any time. However, if the policy is terminated or if the insured dies, the cash surrender value or the death benefit is reduced by any outstanding policy loans and unpaid interest. Also, if policy loans equal or exceed the cash value, the policyowner generally must repay the loan in full or in part within 31 days of being notified by the company or the policy will terminate.

4. If interest is not paid when due, the company usually automatically charges an additional loan against the policy equal to the unpaid interest.

5. Policy loans require no approval and are confidential.

6. The amount of loan available generally includes the cash value of any paid-up additions.

Question – What interest rates are charged on loans made by policyholders?

Answer – At one time, virtually all policies were issued with fixed policy loan rates, often as low as 5 or 6%. However, when market interest rates were higher than policy loan rates, insurance companies found themselves squeezed by disintermediation – the process whereby policyowners borrow their cash values at low rates and invest outside their policies in higher-yielding market investments. The insurance companies found themselves with an ever-increasing portion of the investment portfolio in low-yielding policy loans and their investment performance suffered. As a result, dividends paid on many participating ordinary life policies were not competitive with the interest being credited to current-assumption and universal life policies.

The insurance companies took three steps to counter this trend. First, new policies were offered with variable or adjustable loan rates. In these policies, the variable loan rate is tied to an index of corporate bonds, must be adjusted at least once a year, and may be adjusted as frequently as quarterly. Some policies are still issued with fixed rates, but at generally higher rates, ranging from 7 to 10%. Many new policies allow policyowners to choose either a fixed or variable loan rate. However, in most cases, policyowners are offered potentially higher dividends if they are willing to accept the adjustable loan rate.

Second, insurance companies offered incentives for policyowners of existing policies with low fixed loan rates to either agree to a higher fixed loan rate (usually 8%) or to an adjustable loan rate. In return, the company promised to move the policy into a higher dividend rating class. Many companies allow existing policyowners to exchange their existing low-loan-rate policies for new adjustable-loan-rate policies with favorable terms or conditions such as enhanced cash value schedules, higher face amounts, a higher dividend classification, and lower-than-normal upfront exchange fees.

Third, many new policies have "direct recognition" provisions that permit the insurer to adjust dividends within a class of policies based on policy loan activity. Dividends paid on policies with loans outstanding may be lower than those paid on similar policies without policy loans. This is an important concept since it is essentially an indirect method of increasing the policy loan rate. For example, assume the policy loan rate is fixed at 8%. The policyowner would pay $80 interest per year on each $1,000 borrowed from the policy. However, assume that for this class of policies dividends paid on policies with loans are $10 less for each $1,000 of borrowing than on policies without any loans. The policyowner is actually paying an effective rate of 9% on the amount borrowed, not the stated 8% policy loan rate. This can have even further implications if, for instance, dividends are used to purchase paid-up additions. The additional paid-up face amount and the additional cash value will be less than it otherwise would be. Also, if the paid-up additions are participating, future dividends will be less than they would otherwise be as a result of the lower cash values in the paid-up additions, even if the policy loan is later repaid.

Question – What is the "automatic premium loan" provision?

Answer – Most ordinary life policies are issued with an automatic premium loan provision that authorizes the company to automatically pay the premium by borrowing against the cash value if the premium remains unpaid at the end of the 31-day grace period. This provision prevents the policy from lapsing if the policyowner inadvertently misses a premium payment. In most states, the provision is operative unless the policyowner specifically indicates that it should not be operative. In some other states, the provision becomes operative only if the policyowner specifically elects to make it operative.

The automatic premium loan is generally a "no charge" provision that policyowners should look for to avoid unintentional lapses. In most cases, the policy may be reinstated if it inadvertently lapses, but the insured must usually show evidence of insurability.

Question – Is it better to pay premiums annually, quarterly, or monthly?

Answer – Insurance premiums are usually quoted on an annual basis but can be converted to monthly or quarterly payments if desired. When premiums are converted to monthly or quarterly payments, the insurance company typically charges an implicit interest rate on the payments that are deferred until later in the year. In other words, the insurance company is essentially loaning the policyowner a portion of the annual premium that is then repaid over the term of the year with a "borrowing" rate equal to the implicit rate. If the implicit rate is greater than the policyowner's after tax opportunity cost of funds (the policyowner's potential after tax investment rate), he or she should pay the premium annually, if possible. Conversely, if the implicit rate is less than the policyowner's potential after tax investment rate, the policyowner will be better off deferring payments by electing to pay monthly or quarterly.

If, for cash flow reasons, the policyowner cannot pay the premiums annually, the issue is whether the insurance company's implicit rate is greater than or less than the after tax rate at which the policyowner could otherwise borrow money to pay the annual premium. If the implicit rate is higher than the policyowner's after tax borrowing rate, he or she should borrow the money elsewhere and pay the premium annually. Conversely, if the implicit rate is lower than the after tax borrowing rate, the policyowner should elect to pay premiums quarterly or monthly.

The decision as to which payment plan to elect depends on the insurance company's implicit rate. The implicit rate may be determined in the following manner. The ratio of the monthly (or quarterly) premium to the annual premium is called the monthly (or quarterly) conversion factor. Once the conversion factor is known (or computed), the interest rate that the insurance company is implicitly charging for the monthly or quarterly payment plan can be determined. For example, if the monthly payment is equal to 1/12 (.083333) of the annual premium, the insurance company is charging 0% interest on the premium payment plan.

In virtually all cases, however, the monthly payment is greater than 1/12 (.083333) of the annual premium because of an implicit interest charge. Figure 13.1 shows the interest rate the insurance company is implicitly charging for various monthly and quarterly conversion factors. For example, assume the premium for a policy is $1,000 if paid annually or $88.75 if paid monthly. The monthly conversion factor is the ratio of the monthly premium to the annual premium, $88.75/$1,000, or 0.08875. According to the table, the implicit interest rate for this monthly conversion factor is about 14%.

Figure 13.1

	IMPLICIT INTEREST RATES FOR CONVERTING ANNUAL PREMIUMS TO QUARTERLY OR MONTHLY PREMIUMS	
Quarterly Conversion Factor*	Monthly Conversion Factor*	Implicit Interest Rate
0.25000	0.083333	0%
0.25467	0.085250	5
0.25560	0.085638	6
0.25747	0.086412	8
0.25933	0.087189	10
0.26119	0.087969	12
0.26304	0.088752	14
0.26397	0.089144	15
0.26489	0.089537	16
0.26674	0.090325	18
0.26858	0.091115	20
0.27317	0.093104	25
0.27773	0.095109	30

*Ratio of monthly or quarterly premium to annual premium.

Chapter 14

SINGLE PREMIUM LIFE INSURANCE

WHAT IS IT?

Single premium life insurance is permanent cash value whole life insurance that is purchased with a single large premium. As its name implies, it requires no further premiums to keep the coverage in force for the life of the insured.

Single premium life insurance represents one end of the spectrum in terms of the payment schedules policyholders may chose to purchase lifetime coverage. Ordinary level-premium whole life insurance represents the other extreme. Limited-pay policies (for example, where premiums are paid for 10 or 20 years or until the insured reaches age 65) represent the middle ground.

In each case, the premiums charged by the insurance company must be sufficient to pay all anticipated death benefits from the group of similar policies issued by the company over the lives of all the insureds. All other things remaining the same, as the number of payments decreases, the annual premium, and consequently, the rate of growth of policy cash values, becomes correspondingly larger. Therefore, single premium life insurance, for those who can afford the premium, provides the maximum allowable tax-free investment buildup permitted in a life insurance policy (or tax-deferred buildup, depending on how the proceeds are received).

These policies are designed so that the cash value invested in the policy earns a rate of interest that is competitive with other investments of comparable risk. The initial interest rate is typically guaranteed for one year, although there are some three-year and even five-year guarantees available. These policies also provide a long-term guarantee that the rate credited to cash values in later years will not fall below a certain minimum. Some policies guarantee a rate of 6%, while others guarantee rates ranging up from 4%.

Single premium life insurance has been in existence for many years. However, it increased in popularity after the Tax Reform Act of 1986, which severely limited the tax benefits associated with many other popular tax-sheltered investments. At that time, single premium life insurance was treated and taxed just like any other life insurance contract. Cash values accumulated with no current taxation, death proceeds were paid income tax free, and the policyholder was permitted to borrow against the policy cash values without taxation.

This special tax-shelter-like status was diminished by subsequent legislation. In 1988, congress passed the Tax and Miscellaneous Revenue Act (TAMRA) which created a new class of life insurance contracts called modified endowment contracts (MECs)[1]. MECs enjoy fewer tax benefits than other types of life insurance contracts. (See Appendix D.) Generally, all single premium life insurance contracts issued on or after June 21, 1988 are likely to be MECs. Single premium life insurance contracts issued before June 21, 1988 were grandfathered from the provisions of the new law. However, they can become MECs and lose their favorable tax status under certain circumstances, which are discussed below.

Types of Single Premium Life Insurance Policies

There are generally three types of single premium life insurance policies, with many slight variations, that are available:

1. single premium ordinary whole life;

2. single premium current-assumption (interest-sensitive) whole life, and;

3. single premium variable life.

(Chapters 9, 13, and 18 discuss the features of current-assumption whole life insurance, ordinary whole life insurance, and variable life insurance, respectively.)

Although universal life insurance policies can be configured to initially mimic single premium policies, policyholders have no assurance that additional premiums will not be required at a later date to maintain the face value of the coverage. (See Chapter 17 for a discussion of the features of universal life insurance.) Therefore, single-payment universal life insurance is not technically single premium life insurance.

Single premium ordinary whole life – When participating ordinary whole life insurance is configured as a single-payment policy, the policyholder is guaranteed that:

1. No further premiums will be required to keep the policy in force.

2. The face value of the policy will never decline.

3. The cash values will grow exactly as shown in the schedule in the contract. The cash value schedule is based on a guaranteed minimum rate of interest of between 4 and 6%. These guaranteed rates are generally higher than those guaranteed on policies with continuous premiums.

The policy will also generally show a schedule of projected dividends. The dividend schedule is not guaranteed. If the company's investment and mortality experience is favorable, dividends paid on the policy may be higher than projected; if experience is unfavorable, dividends may fall below projections.

Dividends paid on participating single premium ordinary whole life policies are typically used to buy "paid-up additions," which are essentially just small additional single premium policies. In general, the policyholder can expect the total face amount of coverage to increase over time. Also, the paid-up additions build additional cash values that increase the total cash value above that originally projected in the basic policy. In some cases the dividends can be used to buy additional term insurance without evidence of insurability that, over the years, can substantially increase the face amount of coverage.

Since all newly-purchased single premium policies are likely to be MECs, if dividends are paid to the policyholder in cash or if they are retained by the insurer to pay principal or interest on a policy loan, they are treated as payments received under a contract and may be subject to income tax. (See Appendix D.)

Although some stock companies have offered nonparticipating single premium policies in the past, these policies are virtually nonexistent today, having been replaced in most instances by single premium current-assumption whole life policies.

Single premium current-assumption whole life – Most single premium policies are "current-assumption whole life," which is also (somewhat misleadingly) called "interest-sensitive whole life." The interest-sensitive

label is understandable, however, since these policies are marketed by focusing on the interest rate that is credited to cash values. They generally guarantee a very competitive rate for at least one year after the policy issue date and sometimes for up to five (and even 10) years. After that, the rate generally depends on the company's investment and mortality experience.

Actually, current-assumption whole life insurance is a type of participating policy where the company's favorable investment and mortality experience is reflected directly in the interest rate credited to cash values rather than through dividends.

Similar to ordinary whole life policies (and in contrast to universal life policies), current-assumption whole life policies usually guarantee that mortality charges will not exceed certain maximums. However, usually the interest rate credited to cash values is quoted net of mortality and other expenses. In other words, in contrast with universal life policies, the policy illustrations make no explicit recognition of mortality charges. In other words mortality charges are not broken out and separately stated. As a result, it is difficult to tell whether any reductions in the interest rate credited to cash values are attributable to poor investment performance or excess mortality.

To counter this problem, some policies provide that the rate credited to cash values will never be less than a specified percentage of the rate earned on the investment assets backing the policy or on a specified index, such as the government long-term bond index. But this too presents problems, since companies' practices vary with respect to how they determine the return on their assets and how they allocate investment performance to various blocks of policies.

Similar to single premium ordinary life policies, single premium current-assumption policies generally guarantee that:

1. No further premiums will be required to keep the coverage in force.

2. The face value will never decline.

3. The cash values will never fall below a fixed schedule of minimum values based on a guaranteed minimum interest rate of between 4 and 6%.

In contrast with single premium ordinary policies, single premium current-assumption policies typically specify current and maximum allowable mortality charges. However, this is really a distinction with little practical value since companies will adjust dividends on participating single premium ordinary policies to reflect changing mortality (and expense) experience.

If the investment and mortality experience is favorable, the cash values may grow enough to exceed the amount permissible under the IRC Section 7702 definition of life insurance for the original face amount of coverage. When this happens, the company automatically increases the face amount to keep the policy in compliance with the requirements. Consequently, similar to single premium ordinary whole life, policyholders can generally expect the total face amount of coverage for single premium current-assumption whole life to increase over time.

Single premium variable life – Only a relatively few companies offer single premium variable life policies. This product is very similar to single premium current-assumption life, with one important difference. The similarities include guarantees that:

1. No further premiums will be required to keep the coverage in force.

2. The face value will never fall below the initial face amount of coverage.

3. Mortality charges will never exceed specified maximums.

4. The growth of the cash value will depend on the investment performance of the assets backing the policy.

The key distinction is that the single premium variable life policy does not guarantee that at least a minimum rate of interest will be credited to cash values; in fact, it does not guarantee *any* level of cash value. In other words, the policyholder who purchases a single premium variable life contract bears virtually all of the investment risk associated with the policy.

The lack of a minimum interest rate guarantee has several corresponding consequences. First, since the company does not have to earn a minimum rate on the investments backing the policy, policyholders can be given wide latitude in choosing the types of investments that will be made with the cash in their policies.

Policyholders can choose to allocate the premium to a number of mutual fund-type accounts that typically include a:

1. diversified common stock account;

2. fixed-income (bond-type) account; or

3. money-market account.

Some companies offer a wider range of specialized accounts that are invested in such vehicles as zero-coupon bonds, mortgage-backed securities, non-diversified (industry sector) common stocks, gold, real estate, and foreign equities or bonds.

Second, generally policyholders are also given considerable flexibility to transfer funds between accounts. Some companies allow virtually unlimited shifts between accounts without charge, but most companies limit free transfers to between two and five times per year. A transaction fee is usually imposed for transfers in excess of the specified number per year.

Third, variable life is considered a security and, as such, is subject to regulation by the Securities and Exchange Commission (SEC) as well as by the state insurance regulators. This means that prospective policyholders must be given a current prospectus describing the investment characteristics of the product, similar to that which is given to mutual fund investors. A single premium variable life contract can only be sold by persons who have passed a specific securities examination. Also, the SEC requires that policy illustrations include projections based on several specified rates of return. The illustration may include additional projections, but the assumed rate of return may not exceed an upper limit.

The assumed rate of return in policy projections is extremely important and should be kept in perspective. Although market rates of returns on bonds and equities vary and may be extremely high for some relatively short periods of time, projections should be based on realistic long-term trends.

What is a reasonable and realistic long term rate? The long-term average compound annual rate of return on the S&P 500 stock index (which is considered by many experts as the "best indicator" of the U.S. equity market performance overall) for the period from 1974 to 2003 was about 12.2%. The average for 10-year government bonds was about 9.03% and for Treasury bills was about 6.48%. So, depending on the asset mix selected by the policyowner, long-term projections using rates exceeding 10% and, certainly, exceeding 12%, would appear overly aggressive and unrealistic.

Similar to single premium current-assumption policies, the company will automatically increase the face value of variable life coverage to remain within the IRC Section 7702 definition of life insurance if the investment performance of the policyholder's account(s) exceeds that assumed when the company set the premium. However, if the investment value of the policyholder's account(s) later declines, the face value of coverage will also decline, but never below the initial face amount.

Contract Provisions of Single Premium Life Insurance Policies

All life insurance policies have certain contract provisions that may be applied somewhat differently depending on the type of policy. (See Chapter 5 for a general discussion of contract provisions.) Those that need special attention when purchasing single premium life insurance include the following:

Loan provision – Many single premium policies allow the policyholder to borrow against the interest accumulated in the policy at what the companies call a "0% net cost." That is, the interest rate on borrowed funds equals the rate credited to the funds in the policy. The borrowing interest rate for principal amounts (the original premium) is generally 1 to 2% higher than the rate credited to policy cash values.

From a quick reading of the paragraph above, it would appear that the cost of borrowing would be offset dollar for dollar with the earnings of the fund. This may be misleading. Policy loan provisions should be checked carefully because the net borrowing rate may be effectively higher than the stated rate in many cases. Frequently, in current-assumption policies the company sets aside an amount of the remaining cash value as collateral for the loan. This "set aside" may be credited with interest at the minimum guaranteed rate in the policy (or some higher rate that is still less than that credited to non-borrowed amounts), while non-borrowed cash values that are not subject to the set aside provision are credited with a higher current rate.

For example, assume non-borrowed funds are being credited with 9% interest and the loan rate on interest accumulations is also 9%, while the guaranteed rate is 6%. If the company sets aside an amount equal to the debt balance and credits it with only 6% interest, the effective interest on borrowed funds is 12%; 9% on the loan and 3% in foregone interest on the amount set aside.

Similarly, in participating single premium ordinary policies, many companies "adjust" dividends to reflect borrowing activity. In other words they pay lower dividends on policies with policy loans. Although the loan rate may be equal to (or only slightly higher than) the interest rate credited to the policy, the actual cost of borrowing is equal to the borrowing rate plus any decrease in dividends relative to that which is paid to policies without loans.

Surrender charges – Most single premium policies charge a "back-end" fee if the policy is surrendered within the first five to 10 years. The charge usually starts at 7 to 10% of the initial premium and declines each year the policy is in force. For example, for a $10,000 single premium policy, the surrender charge might be $700 the first year, $600 the second year, $500 the third year, and so on until the eighth and later years when no surrender fees are charged.

Other policies charge a declining percentage of the cash value. For instance, the charge may be 7% of the first-year's cash value the first year, 6% of the second-year's cash value the second year, and so on. Since cash values grow each year, surrender charges will generally be higher on those policies that charge a declining percentage of the cash value than on those that charge a declining dollar fee each year or a declining percentage of premium.

Bailout provisions – Some companies have "bailout plans," which are money-back guarantees that enable the policyholder to cash in the policy without penalty if interest rates drop a percentage point or two below the initial guaranteed rate. (Any surrender charge is waived by the insurer.) The bailout provision may have a limited duration, such as the first two to seven years, depending on the length of the original interest-rate guarantee.

A bailout feature allows policyholders to change their minds after the policy is issued and still obtain a refund of their entire original investment if the specified conditions are met. But keep in mind that the bailout provision applies only to the insurance company surrender charges, not to any income tax or income tax penalties that may be payable on amounts received upon surrender.

Interest crediting method – How the insurance company determines the amount of interest to credit to single premium current-assumption policies (and indirectly to ordinary life policies through the dividends) is extremely important. Some policies make this very clear by indexing the policy's current interest rate to interest rates on third party money instruments, such as Treasury bills or certain bond indexes. In other cases, insurance companies credit interest to individual policies using one of two distinct methods – "portfolio rates" or "new money" rates.

If the company uses the portfolio method, all non-borrowed values within all contracts receive the same rate, regardless of when the premium is received. In other words, all policyowners share equally in the company's overall portfolio performance, including both old and new investments.

New money methods, in contrast, credit to new premiums an interest rate that reflects current investment conditions. If current market investment rates are higher than previous rates (and therefore, higher than the overall rate on the company's investment portfolio), cash values attributable to new premiums are credited with higher rates than cash values attributable to previous premiums. Conversely, if market rates are down, new money is credited with a rate that is lower than the company's overall portfolio rate.

Renewal values receive some form of "aged" portfolio rate depending on how the contracts are grouped. Contracts may be grouped by issue year or by contract type. Assets and liabilities are segmented for each group or block of policies, with each block thus developing its own portfolio rate.

Since single premium policyowners make just one payment, the trend of market rates will determine whether the portfolio method or the new money method is more favorable. If market rates are historically high, the new money method will give the most favorable performance. In contrast, if market rates are historically low, the portfolio method will be most favorable. Over a decade or more, the initial advantage will vanish and the differences will be small, or perhaps even nonexistent.

In the late 1970's and early 1980's, market rates of interest were historically high, and most single premium policies were issued using new money rates and an "aging" formula that gradually shifted to the portfolio method. As interest rates began to fall in the late 1980's and early 1990's, the new money rates were not as high and single premium policies using new money rates became less attractive. As a result, some companies shifted to using the portfolio method for new single premium policies to make them more attractive.

Since variable life policy cash values are invested in separate accounts similar to mutual funds, the issue of how interest is credited to cash values is essentially moot. Investment earnings in separate accounts are allocated to all policyowners essentially in proportion to their ownership of the fund in much the same way as earnings are allocated to mutual fund shareholders.

WHEN IS THE USE OF THIS TOOL INDICATED?

In general, some type of life insurance is indicated when a person needs or wants to provide an immediate estate upon his or her death. This need or desire typically stems from one or more of the reasons discussed in detail in Chapter 13. Single premium life insurance may be appropriate for any of these purposes, but is more appropriate for some and is uniquely suited for other purposes. Single premium life, in contrast with term insurance which provides the highest possible death benefit for the lowest initial premium outlay, provides the lowest initial death benefit for the level of premium paid. Consequently, the single most important reason for buying a single premium policy is the desire for maximum tax-deferred or tax-free investment in conjunction with life insurance. If the investment objective is not present, or at least, not highly important, some other form of insurance will typically be more suitable.

If the need for at least some insurance is not present, typically annuities or some form of investment will be more suitable. However, if both life insurance and tax-deferred investment objectives are present, single premium life provides a unique combination of attractive features.

Since all new single premium policies are likely to be MECs, the limitations applying to MECs (discussed below under "Tax Implications") must be fully considered when assessing whether a single premium policy or some other form of life insurance is most appropriate for the intended use.

Single premium life insurance in particular is indicated in the following circumstances:

1. *When the objective is to entirely pre-fund a specified minimum death benefit for a specific purpose, such as a charitable bequest or a legacy for children* – The single premium policy permits the policyowner to assure the bequest with no further concern about possible lapse due to failure to pay premiums. Further, the premium payment is deter-

mined based on competitive tax-free rates of return. In addition, in most cases if the investment and mortality experience of the company is favorable, the face value of coverage will increase in order to continue to satisfy the IRC Section 7702 tests to qualify as life insurance.

2. *As a vehicle for gifts* – For example, a grandparent can give up to $11,000 (the gift-tax annual exclusion in 2004, as indexed) a year gift-tax free to a child as custodian for a grandchild. The parent can then use the cash to purchase a single premium policy with an $11,000 premium on the life of the grandparent for the grandchild's benefit. The $11,000 is removed from the estate of the grandparent without federal gift tax cost, and can provide an income and estate tax free transfer to the child greatly in excess of the original $11,000.

3. *In exchange for ordinary whole life policies at retirement* – Under the Section 1035 exchange provisions, an existing ordinary whole life policy that has substantial cash values and continuing premium payments may be exchanged for a single premium policy. The exchange would eliminate future premium payments, provide a relatively high tax-free rate of earnings on the underlying cash values, and may provide a higher death benefit. Such possible exchanges should be compared to the reduced amount paid-up nonforfeiture option available with all cash value policies.

4. *As a substitute for tax-free municipal bonds and other investments so as to reduce exposure to income tax on Social Security benefits* – Both single and married persons with adjusted gross incomes exceeding certain levels are subject to income tax on up to 85% of their Social Security benefits. Taxable income from certificates of deposit, money market funds, and other taxable investments as well as what is otherwise tax-free municipal bond interest is included in determining the amount of Social Security benefits subject to income tax. The interest earned on cash values of life insurance policies is not included. Therefore, investment funds could be converted into a single premium policy, thereby reducing taxable income and the taxpayer's tax base, and eliminating the tax on Social Security benefits.

5. *As an emergency fund reserve* – Although proceeds from MEC policy loans are taxable to the extent attributable to earnings in the policy, after age 59½ there is no 10% penalty on the taxable income portion of policy loan proceeds.[2] Since interest on investments of comparable risk, such as Treasury bills, is taxable as earned, the total tax-deferred return on cash values often exceeds that on such comparable investments. With the single premium policy, the only portion subject to taxation is the income portion of proceeds actually withdrawn as a loan.

6. *As a safe haven from future potential creditors* – In many cases life insurance cash values are afforded significant protection under state law from the claims of creditors. The amount that is exempt from creditor claims varies from state to state. Since single premium policies permit the highest potential cash values, they also provide the greatest potential safe-haven from creditors.

7. *To build a fund for retirement income* – Similar to deferred annuities, cash values in single premium policies accumulate on a tax-deferred basis. Also, distributions or loans from single premium policies that are classified as MECs are taxed similarly to distributions from annuities (see Chapter 8 and Appendix D). The nonforfeiture options under a single premium policy are essentially identical to the payout options for annuities. Therefore, a single premium policy can be used to build a tax-deferred fund for retirement, similar to a deferred annuity, while also guaranteeing a death benefit in excess of that paid from an annuity if the insured dies before retirement.

8. *As a means of eliminating the tax liabilities on corporate retained earnings* – If used in conjunction with some other bona fide corporate purpose, such as key employee insurance, the company can contribute substantial amounts to single premium policies and reduce exposure to the tax on excess retained earnings. This may still give the company flexibility to use the cash values at some later date for other corporate purposes.

9. *As a vehicle for financing an employer's obligation under nonqualified deferred compensation plans* – Although cash values in single premium policies cannot be assigned to employees without such amounts being currently taxable as compensation to the employees, employees generally feel more secure if promises under a deferred compensation plan are financed with earmarked as-

sets. A single premium policy can provide reasonable tax-deferred earnings to pay deferred compensation benefits at retirement and tax-free death proceeds to pay benefits for a deceased employee's family under the agreement.

10. *As an investment vehicle for a net rollover that is not tax free* – Generally, a tax-free rollover to an IRA is the preferred rollover vehicle for distributions from qualified plans that would otherwise be subject to tax. However, any nontaxable portions of such distributions, such as amounts attributable to after-tax employee contributions, may not be rolled over to an IRA. The after-tax portions may be invested in a single premium life policy and continue to enjoy tax-deferred growth. Also, single premium policies could be suitable investments for other types of large after-tax or tax-free dollar receipts such as after-tax proceeds from the sale of a business, tax-free proceeds from a life insurance policy, or the proceeds from a maturing tax-free bond issue.

ADVANTAGES

1. The initial guaranteed rate in a single premium policy is generally quoted "net" of commissions and other fees. Therefore, the policyowner's entire premium goes into the cash value.

2. Cash value interest or earnings accumulate tax-free or tax-deferred, depending on whether gains are distributed at death or during lifetime.

3. Single premium current-assumption life insurance (and ordinary life, through dividend formulas) frequently pays higher interest on cash values than are available from tax-free municipal bonds.

4. Variable policies give the policyowners wide discretion to direct the investments that back the cash values by selecting among various types of investment assets.

5. In current-assumption policies and ordinary policies, cash values are not subject to the market risk associated with longer-term municipal bonds and other longer-term fixed income investments. Although the interest credited to cash values can be expected to vary with market conditions, the cash value itself will not be subjected to the market value swings associated with market prices of longer-term fixed income investments.

6. Policy cash values can be borrowed at a low or zero net interest rate cost.

7. Life insurance policies can be used as collateral or security for personal loans. Note, however, that since single premium policies issued after June 20, 1988 are likely to be MECs, loans or amounts received through collateral assignments of these policies will be treated as "amounts received under the contract." Therefore, the amounts received will generally be subject to the ordinary income tax and, if received prior to age 59½, subject to an additional 10% penalty tax. Income and penalty taxes apply only to the gain in the policy.

8. Policies issued before June 21, 1988 are "grandfathered" from the MEC rules. (See the discussion under "Tax Implications.")

DISADVANTAGES

1. Lifetime distributions or loans of cash values may be subject to income tax and, if received before age 59½, a 10% penalty tax.

2. The premium may be unaffordable.

3. The amount of protection is low relative to the premium paid.

4. Surrender of the policy within the first five to 10 years may result in substantial surrender charges.

TAX IMPLICATIONS

General Tax Rules

Death benefits under single premium life policies are usually paid free of any federal income tax. In general death benefits paid under these policies are subject to the same federal and state income, estate, gift, and generation-skipping transfer taxation rules as all other types of life insurance policies. See Appendices A through G for a complete discussion of the taxation of life insurance.

Taxation of Lifetime Distributions and the MEC Rules

Taxation of lifetime distributions and loans from single premium policies generally depends on when the policy was acquired. Policies issued after June 20, 1988 are likely to be MECs; polices issued before June 21, 1988 were "grandfathered," and are generally not subject to the MEC rules.

Policies issued after June 20, 1988 – Single premium life policies issued after June 20, 1988 are modified endowment contracts (MECs). Under the MEC rules, amounts received under the policy because of surrender or lapse of the policy or as loans from the policy are subject to income tax – to the extent of "gain" in the policy.[3]

Gain in the policy is determined by subtracting the adjusted premium from the policy cash value. In single premium policies, the adjusted premium is generally simply the initial premium paid. The last-in first-out (LIFO) method is used to determine whether amounts distributed are gain or return of principal (premium). This means that amounts received under the contract are treated as first coming from income or gain and only when the gain is exhausted are they treated as a return of principal or premium.

Loans secured by the collateral assignment of a single premium policy as well as interest accrued on policy loans are also generally treated as potentially taxable amounts received under the policy. The policyowner will receive an increase in the basis in the policy to the extent that any loan or pledge is taxable.

Dividends paid in cash, as well as dividends retained by the insurance company as principal or interest on a policy loan, are amounts received under the contract and are potentially taxable. Amounts not treated as received under the contract (and, therefore, not subject to tax) include dividends retained by the insurer to purchase paid-up additions or contractually mandated additional term insurance, to acquire other qualified additional benefits, or which are treated as other consideration for the contract.

Any amounts received under a contract that are taxable are also subject to an additional 10% tax *unless*:

1. made on or after a taxpayer attains age 59½;

2. attributable to a taxpayer becoming disabled; or

3. part of a series of substantially equal periodic payments (not less frequently than annually) made for the life (or life expectancy) of the taxpayer or for the joint lives (or joint life expectancies) of the taxpayer and beneficiary.[4]

Generally, contracts owned by "non-natural persons," such as corporations, are not eligible for these penalty exceptions.

Policies issued before June 21, 1988 – Policies issued prior to June 21, 1988 are "grandfathered" and avoid the MEC rules unless there is a "material change" in the policy.[5] In particular, this means that proceeds from policy loans will not be subject to income tax and that other withdrawals or distributions of cash values before age 59½ will not be subject to the additional 10% tax.

A material change is any increase in the future benefits under the contract, with the following exceptions:

1. cost-of-living increases that are based on a broad-based index, such as the Consumer Price Index;

2. death benefit increases inherent in the policy design due to the crediting of interest or other earnings; or

3. death benefit increases necessary to keep the relationship between the death benefit and cash values required to maintain the tax code definition of life insurance under IRC Section 7702.[6]

In general, grandfathered single premium policies should meet the second or third exception. Therefore, policyowners who own grandfathered policies enjoy a special tax privilege allowing them to borrow from their policies without being subject to LIFO-based income taxes. However, their grandfathered status can be lost if a policy is exchanged for a new policy or if the face value of the policy is increased in such a way that it is treated as a material change.

A warning is in order regarding the future taxation of single premium policies. Congress has been looking at the tax-deferred cash accumulation feature of life insurance as a potential source of additional tax revenues. Although many experts believe cash value life insurance will retain its tax-deferred accumulation feature, if Congress acts to discontinue or limit this tax deferral feature, it will be single premium and other limited-premium-payment, high cash value policies that will be the most likely targets. In the event of tax changes in this area, the likelihood of a grandfather provision for existing policies is uncertain. In the authors' opinion, existing policies will have possibly only very limited protection. Amounts already accumulated in these types of policies may be grandfathered if and when reforms are enacted, but future accumulations will probably not be sheltered.

ALTERNATIVES

All life insurance policies can provide tax-free cash upon death. The unique feature of single premium life insurance is its large tax-free or tax-deferred cash buildup. If a combination of high tax-preferred cash accumulation and life insurance coverage is desired, several other alternatives may be explored:

1. *The combination of a single premium deferred annuity and decreasing term insurance* – Cash values accumulate in both annuities and single premium life insurance policies on a tax-deferred basis. Withdrawals, lifetime distributions, or loans from each are treated similarly for tax purposes (assuming the life insurance policy is treated as a MEC). Therefore, the combination of a single premium deferred annuity and a decreasing term policy can provide levels of tax-preferred cash accumulation and death benefits similar to a single premium policy.

   There are some important differences, however. The annuity/term combination will require some additional and increasing premiums over the years for the term coverage. In addition, the mortality charges for term insurance coverage are typically higher than the mortality charges in a single premium policy. Also, loan provisions of deferred annuity contracts are generally more restrictive than those of single premium life policies. Finally, the death proceeds from the single premium policy generally may pass to the beneficiary entirely income and estate tax free, regardless of who the beneficiary is, if the policyowner has no incidents of ownership in the policy. The gains on the annuity contract will still be taxable income to the beneficiary.

2. *A combination of tax-free municipal bonds and decreasing term insurance* – This combination can create a cash accumulation and death benefit similar to a single premium policy. In contrast with the cash values in a single premium policy, the municipal bonds may be used as collateral for loans without any income tax consequences. Similar to life insurance policy loans, the interest paid on the borrowed funds generally is not deductible. The single premium policy allows the death benefits to be transferred by operation of the contract and avoids probate. Municipal bonds are part of the probate estate and must be distributed by will. Once again, if the policyowner has no incidents of ownership, the life insurance death proceeds are paid estate tax free. The municipal bonds will escape estate tax only if they are left to the spouse and, thus, qualify for the estate tax marital deduction.

3. *A single-payment universal life policy* – A universal life policy can be initially configured to resemble a single premium life policy. However, in contrast with "true" single premium life policies, charges for mortality and expenses can change in the universal life policy in such a way that additional premiums could be required in the future to maintain the face value of coverage.

WHERE AND HOW DO I GET IT?

There are nearly 2,000 life insurance companies actively marketing life insurance coverage in the United States. Many of these companies offer single premium life policies as well as other permanent forms of life insurance. In addition to commercial insurance companies, some fraternal organizations, savings banks, professional associations, membership organizations, and stock brokerage houses offer single premium policies. Policies can be purchased through many agents representing licensed insurance companies.

Most insurance companies that offer single premium life insurance will issue policies only up to certain ages, typically about age 75 or less, although some companies may issue policies to age 80 in special circumstances.

Universal life policies, because of their flexibility, have become more popular than single premium life insurance in recent years. Consequently, agents may be inclined to offer a universal life policy that is configured to resemble a single premium life contract if the insured's objective is to build high cash values in a life insurance policy. In general, therefore, unless the flexibility inherent in universal life is desired or needed, a single premium policy, where the policyowner is guaranteed that no further premiums will ever be required, may be more suitable.

WHAT FEES OR OTHER ACQUISITION COSTS ARE INVOLVED?

The sales commission is generally about 3 to 10% on these products. In addition, the insurance company typically pays a premium tax of about 2½%. However, these fees are generally taken into account when the company quotes the short-term guaranteed net rate that will be credited to the policy in the first or first few years. For example, a policy might be subject to an 8% surrender charge in the first year with the charge declining each year thereafter by 1% until it reaches 0% after the eighth policy year. Therefore, the entire premium usually goes into the cash value.

If the policy is surrendered in the first five to 10 years, there is generally a surrender charge ranging from 7 to 10% of the initial premium, declining each year for the first five to 10 years. In subsequent years, there is no surrender charge.

In current-assumption policies, the interest credited to the policy each year is usually net of mortality charges and expenses. In ordinary life policies, the dividends reflect the mortality, investment, and expense experience and, therefore, the amount of the paid-up additions that are credited to the policy.

HOW DO I SELECT THE BEST OF ITS TYPE?

Selecting the best cash value life insurance policy is a difficult task involving a number of complicated concepts and analyses. (See Chapter 4 for a further discussion of the basic principles.) However, since the investment element of single premium life insurance is a paramount concern, focus should center on the following factors:

1. Compare the current rate being credited to policy cash values and the length of the guarantees. All else being equal, policies with higher current rates and longer guarantee periods will be better than those with lower current rates and shorter guarantees.

2. Check to see how the company will determine the rate credited to policy cash values after the guarantee period. Policies that determine the rate based on a specific money rate or bond index leave the company with little room to manipulate the amount credited in an adverse way.

3. Look at the current mortality and expense factors and compare them with the guaranteed maximum mortality and expense factors. The mortality factors currently being used should be competitive. If the difference between the current mortality rates and the maximum rates is small, the company has little room to use higher mortality charges as a means of reducing the effective rate credited to cash values.

4. Look for a bailout provision that reduces or eliminates surrender charges if investment performance does not meet reasonable guidelines.

5. Check the policy loan provision to see if the company uses an "offset" provision to credit borrowed amounts with a lower rate than non-borrowed amounts. If the insured anticipates borrowing from the policy, a company that does not use the offset method is preferable. If borrowing is not anticipated, a company that uses the offset method may be more desirable since the company should, in theory, be able to credit higher interest to policies without borrowing than they otherwise would be able to without the offset provision.

6. Check the financial soundness of the company using the criteria in Chapter 3.

WHERE CAN I FIND OUT MORE?

The following references include authoritative discussions of various types of life insurance including single premium life insurance:

1. B. Anderson, *Anderson on Life Insurance* (Waltham, MA: Little, Brown and Company, 1991).

2. B. Baldwin, *New Life Insurance Investment Advisor: Achieving Financial Security for You and Your Family Through Today's Insurance Products*, 2nd ed. (Hightstown, NJ: McGraw-Hill Trade, 2001).

3. J. Belth, Life Insurance: A Consumer's Handbook, 2nd ed. (Bloomington, IN: Indiana University Press, 1985).

4. K. Black, Jr. and H. Skipper, Jr., *Life Insurance*, 13th ed. (Old Tappan, NJ: Prentice Hall Inc., 1999).

5. E. Graves, Editor, *McGill's Life Insurance*, 5th ed. (Bryn Mawr, PA: The American College, 2004).

The following references are useful guides for policy and company rating information:

1. *Best Insurance Reports* (Oldwick, NJ: A. M. Best Company, published annually).

2. *Best's Review – Life/Health Edition* (Oldwick, NJ: A. M. Best Company, published monthly).

QUESTIONS AND ANSWERS

Question – Is single premium whole life a good idea for an individual who does not need death benefit coverage?

Answer – Probably not. A single premium policy does provide a death benefit, which means the client is paying mortality charges. If the client does not need or want life insurance protection, a single premium deferred annuity can provide similar tax sheltered cash buildup benefits without the mortality charges.

Question – How can insurance companies guarantee higher rates of interest on single premium policies than on other life insurance policies?

Answer – The insurance company receives the full premium that will be paid under the policy at the beginning of the contract. This permits it to invest the money in long-term assets with fairly certain or predictable long-term returns. These longer term assets generally pay a higher yield than shorter term investments. In addition, the insurance company is allowed by regulation to base its reserve calculations on rates as high as 6% annually for single premium policies. The upper limit on assumed interest rates for reserve calculations is lower for policies with periodic premium payments.

Question – Is a single premium life insurance policy a good short-term investment?

Answer – Not generally. There are generally significant surrender charges in the early years. Also, since newly-issued policies are likely to be MECs, if the policy is terminated before age 59½, there is a 10% penalty tax in addition to income tax payable on any taxable gain from the terminated policy.

Question – Do the bailout provisions found in some single premium life insurance policies make them good short-term investments?

Answer – Bailout provisions may eliminate or reduce surrender charges imposed by the insurer, but they cannot waive the penalty tax applicable to persons under age 59½. Generally, there are better short-term investments available without the mortality charges and the potential penalty tax.

Question – Does MEC status of a single premium policy affect the taxation of the policy death benefit?

Answer – The MEC rules have essentially no effect on the taxation of death benefits. The death benefits are generally exempt from federal income tax, and federal estate and gift taxes are applied in the same manner as for policies that are not classified as MECs.

Question – Is a single premium policy with an interest rate guarantee that is for a longer period than competing policies necessarily the "best buy" of those available?

Answer – No. The long-term performance is most important. Insurers have wide discretion in setting the interest rates they credit to policies after the guarantee period expires. It is possible to promise high rates for the initial guarantee period and then compensate for that early promise by lowering the rates credited after the guarantee period expires.

CHAPTER ENDNOTES

1. IRC Sec. 7702A.
2. IRC Sec. 72(v).
3. IRC Secs. 72(e), 7702A.
4. IRC Sec. 72(v).
5. Section 5012(e)(1) of P.L. 100-647, Technical and Miscellaneous Revenue Act of 1988.
6. IRC Sec. 7702A(c)(3)(B).

Chapter 15

SURVIVORSHIP LIFE

WHAT IS IT?

In its pure form, survivorship life (SL), which is also called second-to-die or last-to-die life insurance, is a life insurance policy or, often, a combination of policies and riders that pays a death benefit only when the last of two or more named insureds dies. It is most frequently used to insure two lives, typically a husband and wife, but some companies offer products that will insure three or more lives.

The three-or-more-insureds policies offer some variation on the last-to-die concept. In some policies, the policyowner may choose at the time of issue at which death policy proceeds will be paid. For example, if the policy covers four lives, the policyowner could elect to have the proceeds paid after the third death, rather than the last death. In addition, some of the three-or-more-lives policies allow the policyowner to choose to have multiple payouts. For instance, the policyowner might elect to have the face amount paid when the first and last, but not the second and third, of four named insureds dies.

The basic policy in a survivorship life plan is generally a permanent form of life insurance – traditional whole life, current-assumption whole life, or universal life – but some companies offer term survivorship life. As a result of competitive pressures in the industry to keep premium costs down, many survivorship life plans now involve a combination of permanent and term life elements.

WHEN IS THE USE OF THIS TOOL INDICATED?

1. *To provide estate liquidity at the second death of a married couple* – SL is most often used where there is a substantial estate and heavy use will be made of the marital deduction. Use of the unlimited marital deduction, either outright or in conjunction with some form of marital trust, permits deferral of all or most federal estate taxes until the second death. SL provides liquidity when it is most needed, upon the second death, often at the lowest possible outlay.

2. *To protect two-career families* – If both husband and wife have successful careers, the loss of one income may be tolerable, but the loss of both incomes would leave remaining dependents with no support. SL provides a relatively low cost method of protecting the family against the loss of the income of both parents.

3. *To provide key person business insurance* – In many cases, the loss of a single employee in a key area may present some transitional inconvenience, but it is not insurmountable. Often, companies cross-train employees or assign some overlap of responsibility among key executives to minimize the risk of loss of just one key employee. However, the loss of two key employees in a sensitive area may cause serious disruption in a development effort. Similarly, the loss of one key financial backer may be acceptable, but the loss of two could seriously jeopardize a company. In these types of situations, survivorship life may provide the most economical means of protecting the company.

4. *In split dollar plans* – The same rationale used to justify the use of a split dollar single life applies to survivorship life. The annual taxable cost of insurance should be calculated by taking into account the probability of both insureds dying in a given year, rather than the costs that are used for single life insurance policies. Consequently the tax cost to the employee is many times lower than what the cost would be on separate policies at the same ages.

5. *To help fund charitable bequests* – The use of survivorship life can provide the resources necessary to fund charitable bequests after both husband and wife have died. Also, when properly used in combination with contributions of appreciated assets to charitable remainder trusts, all or most of the assets passing to the charity can be replaced by insurance proceeds at a low overall premium cost. In many instances, the combined income and estate tax savings will be more than the total premiums paid on the insurance.

ADVANTAGES

1. If used in conjunction with the unlimited marital deduction, proceeds are payable when needed – at the second death.

2. Premiums are lower than for equivalent coverage in two separate policies.

3. There are a number of alternative term / permanent life combinations available that provide wide latitude and flexibility in premium payment and death benefit arrangements.

4. A lower taxable "economic benefit" is reportable in split dollar plans.

5. Medical underwriting standards are often eased (at least for one of the two insureds) due to the fact that death benefits are not paid until the last death.

DISADVANTAGES

1. SL provides no benefits at the first death if needed, without the addition of a special rider.

2. In term / permanent plans, there is a risk that premiums could escalate prohibitively if dividends are lower than projected and / or term rates increase.

TAX IMPLICATIONS

General Income Taxation

SL is treated in the same manner as other types of life insurance for income tax purposes. Death benefits are paid tax free. If the policy is not classified as a modified endowment contract (MEC), nonannuity distributions or withdrawals will be taxed on the "cost recovery" or first-in first-out basis. That is, amounts received will be treated as a tax-free recovery of investment in the contract until the entire cost basis is recovered. Once basis is recovered, any further amounts will be taxed at ordinary rates as gain in the policy. Annuity distributions will be taxed as a combination of tax-free recovery of cost basis and taxable interest or gain as described in IRC Section 72. Loan proceeds are not taxable and, in general, interest paid on policy loans will be treated as nondeductible consumer interest.[1]

If an SL policy is treated as a MEC, lifetime distributions and loans are essentially taxed under the "interest-first" rules applicable to annuities.[2] In addition, if amounts are received prior to age 59½, a 10% penalty is imposed on the taxable portion of the distribution. However, in the typical case where an SL policy is part of an estate plan that makes maximum use of the unlim-ited marital deduction to defer estate taxes until the second death, MEC status may be almost immaterial. In these cases, there is little incentive to withdraw cash values since it could jeopardize the plan. In cases where it is unlikely cash values will be withdrawn prior to the second death, tax treatment of the SL policy as a MEC will be of little consequence.

Consequently, it may be advantageous if sufficient cash is available to pay up the policy as quickly as possible, even if it will result in the policy being treated as a MEC. However, care should be taken to avoid MEC status if the plan contemplates borrowing from the policy to pay premiums. Also, MEC status could lead to adverse consequences if borrowing becomes necessary to finance premiums because dividends are lower than projected and / or term rates are higher than projected in a plan using a large portion of term insurance.

Income Tax Implications in Split Dollar Plans

SL policies provide a significant income tax advantage while both insureds are alive when the policy is used in a split dollar arrangement with an employer. In a basic endorsement split dollar plan with a single-life policy, the employee is generally taxed on the term cost of the insurance as measured by the lesser of the P.S. 58 costs or Table 2001 rates (for plans entered into after January 28, 2002) or the actual term rates used.

If a SL policy is used (typically naming the employee and his or her spouse as the insureds), joint and survivor rates based on U.S. Table 38 or the joint and survivor life mortality factors underlying Table 2001 (for plans entered into after January 28, 2002) are typically used to measure the pure term cost. The joint and survivor rates are significantly lower than the single life rates. At younger ages, for a spouse 5 years younger than the insured, the joint and survivor rates can be 1/200 of the corresponding single life rates. This differential declines at older ages but still may be as much as 1/20 the single life rates at age 75.

After the first death, the single-life rates apply with respect to the survivor, not the joint-life rates.

Estate Taxation

SL is treated in the same manner as other types of insurance for estate tax purposes, with certain special consideration because there are two insureds and death proceeds are paid only upon the second death. There may or may not be estate tax consequences as of the first death depending on who owns the policy. (Throughout the following discussion, it should be kept in mind that insurance proceeds received by an insured's estate are also generally included in the insured's estate under IRC Section 2042 even if the insured is not the policyowner.) Basically, the policy may be owned in one of three ways:

1. A third party may own the policy.

2. The policy may be owned exclusively by one or the other insured.

3. The policy may be owned jointly by both insureds.

Similar to any other insurance policy, if neither insured has any incidents of ownership in the policy and they have not transferred ownership within three years of death, it will not be included in the gross estate of either insured. However, under the three-year rule of IRC Section 2035, the policy will be included in the estate of the second to die if, and only if, both spouses die within the three-year period after the policy is transferred and the transferor spouse is the last to die. If both spouses die within the three-year period and the transferor spouse is the first to die, there should be no inclusion of the proceeds under IRC Section 2035.[3] If the transferor is the first to die, the policy would not have been included in his gross estate under IRC Section 2042 or any of the other specified code sections had the transfer not been made. Therefore, the policy proceeds do not fall within the scope of IRC Section 2035 and should not be included in the gross estate of either insured if the transferor is the first to die within the three-year period following a transfer of the policy.

Under IRC Section 2033, an insurance policy owned by the decedent on the life of another is included in his gross estate at the replacement cost of comparable policies of the issuing company or the interpolated terminal reserve.[4] If the policy is owned jointly by both insureds, the deceased's portion of the policy's value (which is arguably best determined as the actuarial value of his probable survivorship benefits estimated as if he had not died) is included in his gross estate. If the policy is transferred by will to the surviving insured who is the decedent's spouse, the transfer qualifies for the marital deduction. In this case, there will be no estate tax at the first death. If the surviving insured becomes the owner of the policy when the first insured dies and continues to own the policy until the second

insured's death, the proceeds of the policy will be included in the second insured's gross estate. However, if the first-to-die policyowner transfers the policy by will to someone other than the surviving insured, the proceeds will generally not be included in the gross estate of the surviving insured when the surviving insured dies. The proceeds would be included only if the three-year rule of IRC Section 2035 discussed above applied or if the surviving insured retained an incident of ownership in the policy.

If the second insured dies within 6 months after the policyowner dies, and the policyowner's executor elects to have the assets of the estate valued as of the alternate valuation date, the proceeds of the policy will be included in the policyowner's estate. The death benefits will not be included in the estate of the second to die (assuming he was not the policyowner at any time within three years of his death and proceeds are not received by his estate).

If the insured who does not have any incidents of ownership in the policy dies first, nothing will be included in his estate since the policy proceeds are not payable at his death and such insured has no ownership rights in the policy. At the owner-insured's later death, the proceeds will be includable in the owner-insured's gross estate, unless he has transferred the policy more than three years before his death and has retained no incidents of ownership.

Estate Inclusion When Policy Owned by Corporation

If a key employee/controlling stockholder of a corporation dies and the corporation has complete control over the policy or at least the right to borrow against the policy, the employee/stockholder will be treated as having sufficient incidents of ownership for the policy to be included in his estate.[5]

Gift Taxation

Gift taxation becomes an important planning issue when a married couple wants a very large policy to be owned by a third party so it will not be included in their estates and also wants to make gifts of premiums at minimal gift tax cost. If the policy is owned outright by a son or daughter for instance, the parents may make tax-free joint gifts of up to $22,000 (as indexed for inflation in 2004) each year under the annual gift tax exclusion. If annual gifts in excess of the annual gift tax exclusion amount are necessary, the parents will have to use up part of their unified gift and estate tax credit.

The amount qualifying for the annual gift-tax exclusion can be leveraged by making gifts to multiple beneficiaries, which is most appropriate if the parents have several children. However, as more independent donees are included in the arrangement, the risk increases that the gifts will not be used as intended to pay the required premiums. Also, outright ownership of the policy by the parents' children presents other related problems. The parents have no assurance that the children will not raid cash values and essentially undermine their not-so-well-laid-out plans.

These problems are often avoided by using an irrevocable life insurance trust to own the policy. Through proper planning and use of the Crummey withdrawal rights[6], the parents can provide up to $22,000 (as indexed for inflation in 2004) of annual premium gift-tax free to the trust for each primary and contingent beneficiary of the trust.[7] In addition, they can put certain restrictions on how trust assets are used for the benefit of the beneficiaries and when principal passes to the beneficiaries.

ALTERNATIVES

Survivorship life is a unique life insurance product for its intended purpose: to provide death benefits only when the last covered insured dies. The closest alternative strategy is to insure each life separately, but that strategy may often be a relatively poor solution.

Typically, after a death, the estate's personal representative has three principal alternatives if estate taxes must be paid: (1) to sell estate assets; (2) to borrow money; or (3) to have cash available.

Selling estate assets may result in an economic loss to the heirs because of adverse economic conditions at the time assets must be sold. Also, forced sales of illiquid assets may in fact become fire sales, where the amount received is only a fraction of the real value.

Borrowing may only delay the day of reckoning, while incurring additional interest expense to further deplete the estate. Cash will be available in the absence of life insurance only if assets were converted to cash before death. Since most people do not know when they will die, this implies they must keep a large portion of their assets in low-yielding liquid instruments at all times.

The opportunity cost of foregoing more lucrative but less liquid investments can be sizable over time. If preservation of wealth for heirs is a major objective, life insurance is frequently the best way to reach this goal. If the goal of the estate plan is also to defer much of the estate tax until the second death, survivorship life is frequently the best choice.

WHERE AND HOW DO I GET IT?

Many U.S. insurers offer survivorship life products. Since the market for survivorship life is dynamic and competitive, with new product innovations, riders, and package plans being introduced at a rapid pace, it is probably wise to consider products from several companies as well as alternative plans offered by the same company.

WHAT FEES OR OTHER ACQUISITION COSTS ARE INVOLVED?

There are many different survivorship life plans that use the various types of permanent policies as the base policy and a host of riders and premium-payment plans. The fees, charges, and commission rates are similar to those charged for similar types of single-life policies with similar riders and premium-payment plans, relative, of course, to the generally lower premium level for survivorship life for any given level of coverage. There will generally be additional charges for riders or options that are unique to survivorship life such as the split options available with many plans.

HOW DO I SELECT THE BEST OF ITS TYPE?

Survivorship life policies may require more careful scrutiny and analysis than other life insurance products both because of the extended expected period of coverage and because of the many options and policy features. A key consideration when selecting any insurance policy, but especially survivorship life because of the relatively long term of coverage, is the financial strength and stability of the insurance carrier. See Chapter 3, "How to Determine the Right Company," for a discussion of this issue. The following discussion outlines the key issues and questions concerning the selection of a SL policy.

What is the Composition of the Base Policy?

The base policy is typically a permanent type of insurance – traditional whole life, current-assumption whole life, or universal life. Whole life is generally preferable in the simpler situation where a vanishing premium is desired that will endow the policy. Universal life is usually more desirable for older insureds who are looking for a low premium and more flexibility. For example, using current (non-guaranteed) assumptions to determine the premium can produce a premium that is as little as half that for a traditional whole life policy. However, the low-premium universal life plan will usually require premium payments each year until the second death. Premium payments under the whole life plan may vanish well before the expected time until the second death. In general, the present value of the premium payments can be expected to be about the same under each policy. Therefore, the critical element is the desire for flexibility versus relative certainty. Although the performance of each type of policy is uncertain, since both dividends and interest credits are not guaranteed, the whole life plan typically involves more advanced and "forced" funding. Therefore, the policyowner has more assurance the plan will be completed as originally contemplated, even if the premium payment period must be extended beyond that originally planned if dividends are lower than projected.

If a growing benefit is desired to cover a potentially increasing estate tax liability, a whole life policy without a vanishing premium (and without term insurance blends) where dividends are used to buy paid-up additions or a universal life policy under option B (net level death benefit plus cash value) is often the preferred plan of insurance. Assuming premium payments and other elements are similar, in most cases the UL plan will provide a faster growing benefit. However, at longer durations the whole life plan may surpass the benefits provided under the UL plan.

How Much Term Insurance is Included in the Recommended Plan?

Many survivorship life plans involve combinations or blends of permanent and term insurance. Critical questions include what are the proportions of term and permanent insurance and what term cost is built into the sales illustration. What is the difference between the illustrated term cost and the maximum cost the company *may* charge in the future under the contract?

The objective of the term/perm blending technique is to reduce the required premiums. Since term insurance generally builds no cash values and premium costs increase with age, the initial term premium is typically only a fraction of the premium cost of the permanent insurance. In theory, dividends on the permanent insurance should be sufficient to buy paid-up additions that reduce the amount of term insurance required over time before the escalating cost of the term insurance explodes. The death benefit of a term/perm plan will generally remain level until the term insurance is entirely replaced by paid-up additions.

The period until the term insurance is phased-out depends on the proportion of term to permanent insurance, the design of the term rider, the dividend performance of the permanent insurance, and the term rates. Insurers use variations on essentially three types of term riders in their term/perm plans, which involve varying degrees of risk to the policyowner.

Term rider cost paid by dividends – The riskiest plan, but also, all else being equal, the lowest premium plan, is where the term insurance cost is paid entirely by policy dividends. Excess dividends are used to buy paid-up additions that theoretically will ultimately entirely replace the term insurance.

This type of plan is the riskiest because its performance depends on two variable and non-guaranteed factors: (1) the dividends that will actually be paid on the underlying permanent policy; and (2) the term rates actually charged for the term coverage. Although term rates may not exceed guaranteed maximums, most illustrations use current term rates that are below the guaranteed maximum. If dividends fall short of projections and/or term rates increase, the dividends available to purchase paid-up additions will fall short of projections. If the paid-up additions grow too slowly, the ever increasing cost of the term at each advancing age may ultimately exceed the dividends available to pay for the term coverage and the policy will "explode." The policyowner is then left with the choice of paying significantly higher premiums or reducing the amount of coverage.

Most experts suggest that the risk of an exploding policy can be minimized if this type of term insurance does not exceed 50% of the total coverage.

Term rider cost paid by additional premium – The risk of an exploding policy is reduced but not entirely eliminated, depending on the term/perm blend, if an additional premium is charged for the term rider. In the typical additional-premium plan, the additional premium is a level annual amount that vanishes once paid-up additions entirely replace the term coverage. Since the premium is level, it initially exceeds the actual term cost. The excess term premium in the early years and policy dividends are used to buy paid-up additions that grow more quickly than in the dividend-only-pay-term/perm plan. Since the term rates may increase to guaranteed maximums and dividends on the permanent insurance are not guaranteed, the policyowner still may bear some risk that the policy will explode. However, for term/perm blends of about 50/50 or less, this risk is virtually eliminated. The only risk is that the premium vanish may take longer than projected.

Convertible term rider – A convertible term rider is the least risky, but generally the highest premium alternative, all else being equal. Dividends are generally used to buy paid-up additions and to increase the total face amount of coverage, but they may be applied against premiums to keep the face amount of coverage level while net premiums decline over time. The principal risk with this plan is that the conversion right may expire before the second death. To keep the coverage in place, the policyowner must convert, which will require an increase in premiums. Also, often there are charges associated with the conversion.

How is the Policy Affected by the First Death?

Originally, survivorship life policies were designed to revert to single life pricing after the first death. As a result, the mortality charges for the pure insurance protection jumped significantly after the first death. However, reserves and cash values also increased substantially after the first death, reducing the pure insurance protection. Depending on when the first death occurred and whether the older or younger insured died first, there could be a sizable increase in the premiums required to keep the level of coverage in place. To avoid the possibility of a premium increase after the first death, some policies were essentially priced to include a first death element that would provide enough additional cash value to keep premiums level after the first death. Most permanent policies are now designed to avoid a premium increase after the first death. Some companies even offer a rider (what is essentially a joint life – first death – rider) for additional premium that pays up the policy and eliminates the need to pay premiums after the first death.

However, term/perm plans are still often subject to the risk of a premium increase after the first death. Companies use one of two term pricing strategies. Some companies have two schedules of term rates. The rates used when both insureds are living are the low second-death rates. This keeps premiums to the absolute minimum while both insureds live. However, after the first death, the term rates jump up to the single life mortality rates, which can be a sizable increase. Other companies use a blended rate both before and after the first death. All else being equal, the required premium for a plan using blended rates will be higher than for a plan using two schedules of rates while both insureds live, but the premium will not increase after the first death.

What Yields or Interest Rates are Assumed?

Are illustrated yield values based on the company's "portfolio rate" or a "new money" rate? Policy illustrations with new money rates will tend to look more favorable than those using portfolio rates when market rates are currently high. Similarly, policies using portfolio rates may look more favorable than those using new money rates when market rates are currently down.

Is the Level of Projected Yields or Interest Rates Reasonable?

If one company's illustration uses higher yields than another, are they justified based on the portfolio compositions of the insurers? If not, illustrations should be based on similar yield assumptions. If a higher yield assumption is warranted based on differences in the insurers' portfolios, are the investments of the higher-yielding company riskier and is the additional risk justified?

What is the Sensitivity of the Plan to Changes in Yields or Interest Rates?

Typically, plans that employ a greater proportion of term insurance are more sensitive to changes in the interest rate. Survivorship plans that combine participating whole life and term insurance often use dividends to buy paid-up additions to reduce the term component over time. If interest rates fall below the yield assumed with projected dividends, the actual dividend payments will be insufficient to reduce the term component as projected. Since term rates escalate rapidly as age increases, the term cost can explode.

The interest rate sensitivity is also significant if the insurance is designed as a vanishing premium plan. Under a vanishing premium plan, no further premiums are required after a specified period if interest credits accrue as assumed and cash values reach the equivalent of the paid-up level. However, if interest rates are not maintained at the assumed level, the vanishing point will lengthen, perhaps substantially. With some products, a 2% decrease in a dividend interest rate may double the number of years needed for premiums to vanish. The premium-paying period will tend to lengthen more for a given deficiency in the interest rate for plans that are more heavily weighted with term insurance. Even if the premium vanishes at one point, it may reappear later at a substantially higher rate than the original premium. In some cases, policyowners may be faced with the unpleasant choice of paying substantially increased premiums or reducing the face amount of coverage.

To determine the sensitivity of the plan to changes in interest rates and to avoid unpleasant surprises, illustrations should be prepared showing how the plan plays out with the initial premium based on current rates but with future projections based on lower assumed dividend rates or cash value credit rates.

Do the Illustrations Assume Bonus Credits or Terminal Dividends?

Bonus credits, which are designed to reward persistency, usually take the form of an extra crediting rate to policies in force for a specified period of years. Often the illustrations will show higher rates being credited to policies after the 10th year, even higher rates after the 15th year, and even higher rates after the 20th year. These bonus credits are usually not guaranteed, so there is a potential that excessive illustrated bonus credits could be used to enhance the illustrated performance relative to competitive policies that do not project bonus credits.

Terminal dividends, which are paid at death or when a policy is surrendered are similarly used to reward persistency. They are typically greater the longer the policy remains in force. Although many companies provide some form of guarantee with respect to bonus credits (although it generally is a relative guarantee that dividends or cash value credits will be relatively higher on policies that have been in force longer, not an absolute guarantee as to the actual dollar level of credits), terminal dividends are not generally guaranteed.

If bonus credits and terminal dividends are not guaranteed, the results should be illustrated in 3 ways: (1) with the projected bonus credits and terminal dividends; (2) without these credits; and (3) with an intermediate assumption such as at two-thirds the projected rates.

Are Mortality Assumptions Realistic?

Both dividend illustrations on participating policies and the interest credited on "excess" premiums and cash values in current-assumption and universal life policies depend on the assumed mortality charges. Lower assumed mortality charges allow an illustration to show favorable results at a lower premium cost. In addition, some companies show illustrations that assume mortality will improve in the future. However, if actual mortality experience is worse than assumed, the long-term cost of the policy will increase either because dividends are lower than projected or because direct charges to cash values are greater than assumed. In either case, net premiums effectively will have to increase from the level projected to maintain benefits as projected.

Care should be exercised in selecting policies with lower than average assumed mortality charges. Is it reasonable to assume a company may be so much more selective in its underwriting that it can maintain lower than average mortality costs even well beyond the 10 to 15-year period when the benefit of selective underwriting is usually assumed to completely "wear off"? If a company that has used aggressive mortality assumptions or has projected mortality improvements turns out to be correct, it is also quite likely other companies that have used more conservative assumptions will also experience better than projected mortality. These companies will be able to pass on substantially better results in future years than are currently being illustrated. All else being equal, it may be better to select companies using more conservative mortality assumptions. This may reduce the risk of having to pay additional premiums in the future to maintain the level of benefits when such payments may be most difficult to sustain. The alternative may be a decrease in benefit levels. If mortality experience is better than assumed, few policyowners will complain if their premium costs decline or vanish sooner than projected.

Does the Policy Illustration Use Loans to Finance any Premium Outlays?

Some plans show very quick premium vanishes based on borrowing the required premium from the cash values. These illustrations assume that dividends will be sufficient to pay interest on the loans. If dividends are lower than projected, the policyowner will have to pay more into the policy than projected to pay interest or borrow more each year to cover the shortage. Since loans are netted against the death benefit, this could lead to substantially lower net death benefits than projected.

Are Assumed Lapse Rates Realistic?

Another component of policy pricing and illustrations is the assumed lapse rate for blocks of similar policies. The lapse rate assumption is a two-edged sword that can have adverse effects if it is either over-estimated or under-estimated. Although most experts expect lapse rates for survivorship policies to be 2 to 4 times lower than for single-life policies, there has not yet been enough experience to know for sure. If a product is priced for a number of early lapses, the company may have a problem if the lapses do not occur as expected. The company will have to pay higher death benefits than assumed and higher cash values on later lapses. However, if more policies are lapsed and they are lapsed sooner than assumed, the company pricing will not include sufficient loadings to recover initial policy issue expenses and commissions. In either case, remaining policyowners ultimately must pay the cost of incorrectly estimating the number and timing of policy lapses.

It is generally not easy to discover what lapse rate assumptions a company uses. General information may be acquired from the state department of insurance or the company may be asked to provide the assumptions in writing.

What Split Options are Offered?

The policy split option is a desirable feature, since it permits the policy to be split into two individual policies. Most split options may be exercised if a married couple becomes divorced. Others also permit the policy to be split if the tax law changes in such a way that the survivorship life policy would no longer be an effective estate planning tool, such as if the unlimited marital deduction was repealed. In some cases the split option may be exercised only if both insureds show evidence of insurability. In general, the split option allows each insured to acquire individual coverage equal to half the face amount of the survivorship policy. However, some companies allow the policyowner to elect unequal splits at the time the survivorship policy is issued. If a couple's assets are not split 50/50, as is generally the case, this feature is attractive.

What are the Underwriting Standards?

Most companies will issue policies on highly rated lives if the other life is within the standard rating class or only slightly rated. Some companies will even issue policies if one of the insureds is otherwise uninsurable if the second life is insurable. In these cases, the premium is usually about equal to that for a single life policy on the insurable life alone. Since there is always some probability that the insurable person will die before the highly rated or uninsurable person, a survivorship life policy can be of immense benefit in providing protection where there would otherwise be none.

What is the Death Benefit Internal Rate of Return?

Given the broad array of plan designs and options, comparisons of SL plans for a given case are difficult. A method frequently used to evaluate SL plans is the "death benefit internal rate of return" (IRR). First, each potential policy's illustration is inspected to assure that the assumptions used and the projected premiums are reasonable. Then the IRR method basically answers the question of what rate of return a person would have to earn to equal the benefit payable after the second death if net premiums were invested outside the life insurance policy. Typically, the second death is assumed to occur, for instance, in 15, 20, 30 years, at the insureds' joint and survivor life expectancy and 5 years before and after the insureds' joint and survivor life expectancy. The plan with the highest IRR is the "best" buy.

Although the IRR method ignores intermediate cash values, they are usually irrelevant in the typical survivorship life plan where the principle objective is to assure payments of benefits at the second death. The IRR method puts all policies on a common base, regardless of whether premiums are high or low, whether plans are current-assumption or not, whether the insurance plan includes term coverage or not, whether premiums are level or changing, or whether premiums are to be paid until death or are expected to vanish at some specified time.

However, if access to cash values in the intermediate term is an important consideration, the death benefit IRR method would be a less satisfactory method of plan comparison unless all the plans being considered had similar projected cash value buildups. To overcome this limitation, the IRR method can also be applied to cash values at various durations, in addition to death benefits. To compare policies one would apply a weighting factor to the cash value IRR ranking and the death benefit IRR ranking. For example, if the death benefit IRR is considered three times more important than the cash value IRR, a plan's composite "score" at any specified duration for comparison purposes among policies would be .75 multiplied by the death benefit IRR plus .25 multiplied by the cash value IRR. Or if the cash value return is considered just as important as the death benefit return, the score would be computed by dividing each IRR by two and adding the results together.

WHERE CAN I FIND OUT MORE?

Although the references cited in the other chapters contain discussions of survivorship life, the dynamic nature of this relatively new product market makes any discussion dated relatively quickly. Perhaps the best and most up-to-date source is the product information brochures prepared by the various insurers. In addition, the following articles may be informative:

1. "Factors to Analyze in Selecting a Second-To-Die Life Insurance Policy," Philip J. Lyons, *Estate Planning*, May/June 1991, pp. 166-171.

2. "Survivor Life Insurance and The Gatewood Endorsement: An Update," Robert P. Gatewood, *Journal of the American Society of CLU & ChFC*, July 1991, pp. 42-46.

3. "Survivorship Riders: Funding Estate and Buy/Sell Plans," Timothy J. Archbold, *Life Insurance Selling*, October 1991, pp. 164-169.

4. "Due Diligence and Product Design Considerations in Purchasing Survivor Life Insurance," Robert D. Stuchner, *CCH Financial and Estate Planning*, Vol. 3, 1991, ¶29,551, pp. 24,945-24,950.

5. "Evaluating A Survivorship Life Insurance Plan for Clients," James Brogan, *Trusts and Estates*, January 1991, pp. 35-38.

6. "Survivorship Life Insurance: Providing The Liquidity to Preserve Family Wealth," Thomas J. Hakala and David S. Dauman, *The Journal of Taxation of Trusts and Estates*, Winter 1990, pp. 47-51.

7. "New Developments Affect Second-To-Die Insurance Policy Products and Planning," Howard Saks, *Estate Planning*, November/December 1990, pp. 372-374.

8. "An Agent's Guide to Last Survivor Plans 1991," *Life Insurance Selling*, October 1991, pp. 90-144.

QUESTIONS AND ANSWERS

Question – Why is the premium for survivorship life insurance so low relative to two single life insurance policies on the same insureds?

Answer – One of the key attractions of SL is that the premium cost for a SL policy is less than the combined premium cost to purchase separate policies on each named insured. This is possible because the premium is based on the probability of paying benefits on someone other than the first to die. To illustrate, based on the IRS' most recent mortality table in 9 out of 10 cases involving two people of average health who are age 55 and 52, at least one will die within 31.3 years. However, the probability that *both* people will die within 31.3 years is only 46%. In other words, an insurer would be almost twice as likely to pay a death claim within 31.3 years if it issued two separate policies rather than a single survivorship life policy.

Premiums normally continue after the first death, and in some plans may increase dramatically. Other plans provide that premiums cease after the first death. The premium schedule depends on how the plan is designed, the relative proportions of permanent and term coverage, as well as other factors. Since the insurer's reserve requirements are low while both insureds live, even relatively modest premiums (compared to the total payments that would be necessary for two separate policies) may build substantial cash values. However, after the first death, the policy essentially becomes a traditional single life policy. As a result, the company's reserves generally must increase substantially after the first death. If earlier premium payments were not sufficiently high to build the cash value necessary to support the higher required reserve, the policyowner may have to pay higher premiums or suffer a reduction in the face amount of coverage.

Question – What is the difference between survivorship life and joint life insurance?

Answer – Timing! SL and joint life are at opposite ends of the spectrum. SL is last-to-die insurance and joint life is first-to-die insurance. They are designed to satisfy entirely different estate and financial planning needs. SL provides cash to meet the costs resulting from the last death among the covered insureds and is typically used to provide estate liquidity. Joint life provides cash to meet the costs resulting when the first of the covered insureds dies and is more frequently used in business applications, such as to fund buy-sell agreements.

Question – How does SL fit into an estate plan?

Answer – SL is uniquely designed to provide for a married couple's estate planning needs. The demand for this popular product has grown in recent years because of several distinct needs created by the *second* death of two spouses. First, the number of two-income families has increased which means that significant income will continue to be available to the family after the death of the first spouse to die in a two-income family. The need for death benefits to protect dependents is often greatest at the second death of two income-earning parents. SL exactly matches the maturity of the need with the maturity of the policy should both parents die prematurely with young children still dependent upon the parents' income. In addition, SL is generally a less expensive method to provide this coverage for young two-income parents on a tight budget.

Second, estate plans typically are designed to take advantage of the current tax laws and the unlimited marital deduction to defer most or all estate tax until the surviving spouse dies. The unlimited marital deduction permits most or all of the couple's assets to pass to the surviving spouse without estate tax. As a result, the typical estate plan defers the most significant death taxes until the second death of the two spouses. Once again, the timing of SL's death benefit perfectly matches the timing of the need.

Finally, SL is appropriate for even the most rudimentary estate plan. Many married individuals own much of their property jointly in the form of tenancy by the entireties. This means the surviving spouse automatically has survivorship rights in the property that passes by operation of law when the first spouse dies. This automatic transfer avoids probate costs and qualifies for the unlimited marital deduction from estate taxes. All probate costs and federal estate taxes associated with property held jointly by the spouses will be incurred at the second death–the exact time when SL will provide its cash benefit.

Question – Should single-life insurance be considered as an adjunct to survivorship life?

Answer – Survivorship life, although a useful tool, is not a panacea for all estate planning needs. In many cases there are complicating factors that make survivorship life alone an insufficient tool to meet estate liquidity needs and asset transfer objectives. Single-life insurance is often needed when use of the maximum marital deduction is inconsistent with wealth transfer objectives. For instance, if a significant estate tax liability is anticipated at the first death, it is obviously important to continue to hold individual insurance on the life of each spouse. If first death costs are anticipated to be minor, the cash surrender value on the SL policy may be available to provide liquidity to the surviving spouse to handle these costs. In many SL plans, the cash surrender value under the SL policy increases dramatically at the death of the first spouse. This substantial cash surrender value may alleviate any liquidity problems caused by first death costs.

Single-life insurance may also be advisable in other circumstances. For example, in some cases one spouse has children from a prior marriage that he or she wishes to provide for at his or her death without having to wait until the subsequent death of the spouse. In these cases amounts transferred outright to children are included in the deceased's estate. Single-life insurance can provide the necessary cash to pay estate taxes without the need to liquidate estate assets, thus preserving the assets for the children.

It may also be advisable to consider keeping assets with substantial appreciation potential out of the surviving spouse's estate. Life insurance on the first to die (payable to an irrevocable trust or a family partnership) could be used to purchase the assets. Under current law, the income tax on any unrealized gain at the time of the first death is avoided because the assets receive a step-up in basis. If, as is commonly the case, the insurance proceeds are invested to provide income for the surviving spouse and the appreciation potential of the assets is substantially greater than any accumulated income on the insurance proceeds, the differential in value avoids estate taxation at the second death.

Question – Would not individual policies on each spouse meet their estate planning needs as well as a SL policy?

Answer – Individual policies on the life of each spouse certainly would provide benefits to fund the costs of the death of either spouse. However, if the insurance programming is designed to provide for the costs of the second death, the SL policy is substantially more cost-effective. As described earlier, the addition of a second life in a SL policy dramatically reduces the cost for a given level of coverage.

In cases where the estate plan is designed to defer most or all of the potential estate tax liability to the time of the second death, the use of single-life policies on each spouse will provide benefits at the first death, which is earlier than needed. If the deceased has any incidents of ownership in the policy these benefits will be included in his or her estate and generally *added to* the assets included in the estate of the surviving spouse. Although these benefits will provide liquidity for the costs of settling the second estate, they unnecessarily increase the tax base of that estate. It is easy to demonstrate that SL is the most cost-effective method to provide life insurance benefits to handle the liquidity needs caused by the second death of two spouses.

Question – Why not simply insure the spouse with the longest life expectancy (generally the younger spouse)?

Answer – In some instances, one spouse is much younger than the other. Under these circumstances, the younger spouse is quite likely to be the last to die. A single-life policy on the younger spouse would provide the necessary liquidity for the second death costs in most cases. This approach, however, has some inherent flaws. First, despite any differences that exist between the age and health of the two spouses, it is never a certainty that one particular spouse will die first. Most people underestimate the probability of the younger spouse predeceasing the older spouse. The probability remains quite significant even for sizable differences in ages.

For example, the probability that a 40 year old will predecease a 65 year old is 11%, or more than one in ten, based on mortality factors in the IRS Table 80CNSMT. If the older spouse should survive, the single-life policy on the younger spouse will pay the benefits at an inappropriate time and further increase the settlement costs of the older spouse's eventual estate. Also, as described earlier, an individual policy covering the younger spouse will be more costly than a SL policy covering both spouses. In all events, the addition of this life will cause a decrease in the required premium for a given face amount if all other factors are equal.

Question – But isn't a single-life policy on the younger spouse the only option if the older spouse has impaired health or is uninsurable?

Answer – No! Most insurers will issue SL policies even if one of the insureds is highly rated or otherwise uninsurable. The insurance company is never at greater risk on a SL policy where one spouse is highly rated or otherwise uninsurable than they would be on a single-life policy issued on the healthy insurable spouse. There is always some probability

that the healthy spouse will die first, regardless of the severity of the second spouse's health impairment. Although the premium for the SL policy may be almost as great as the premium for the single-life policy on the healthy spouse, it will never be more.

Therefore, a SL policy can be obtained that should always cost less than the single-life policy and that will provide the necessary coverage for the surviving impaired-health spouse in the event the healthy spouse dies first. In other words, the single-life policy will always provide less advantageous coverage for greater cost in these circumstances. A SL policy is an especially attractive plan of insurance in these cases.

Question – Can a SL policy be used with an irrevocable life insurance trust to keep policy proceeds out of the estate of the second to die?

Answer – A SL policy may be transferred to an irrevocable life insurance trust and is often the solution for many estate planning problems. First, if the SL policy is owned by the trustee of an irrevocable life insurance trust, death proceeds will not be included in the estates of the insured spouses (assuming the spouses held no incidents of ownership within three years of death). The SL trust will pass the substantial death benefits to the heirs of the insured spouses outside of their estate tax base. Therefore, the SL trust will avoid compounding estate settlement costs facing the usual estate. A SL trust will also avoid the risks associated with using the children as individual third party owners. The assets of the SL trust will generally be protected from the creditors of both the insureds and the beneficiaries.

Question – Can SL be used to meet the insurance needs of a closely-held family business owner?

Answer – SL can be an effective tool in the estate plan of the family business owner. Often the parents will retain majority ownership of a family business until the death of the second spouse. To avoid estate tax upon the first death, much of the deceased parent's ownership interest will be transferred to the surviving spouse, which qualifies for the marital deduction. As a result, most of the business value will be included in the surviving spouse's estate for estate tax purposes and death taxes could be significant. Frequently the family business, which is usually highly illiquid, is the major estate asset. In addition, the family heirs often desire to continue the business. If the liquidity needs cannot be met out of other estate assets, the family business may have to be liquidated or sold to outsiders to pay these costs.

SL coverage on the lives of parents who own a family business is designed to provide for these liquidity needs. A SL policy will provide benefits at the exact time they are needed – when the surviving spouse dies. The SL benefits can be used to provide the needed liquidity to the estate and provide distributable cash for family members who will not inherit the business interest. The use of a SL policy in these circumstances will both preserve the business of the family heirs and provide family harmony for the next generation.

Question – How can SL be used in split dollar plans?

Answer – Like single-life policies, SL can be used in split dollar plans, permitting business funds to finance the purchase of insurance coverage. This is particularly attractive if the retained corporate dollars used to finance the premium payments are taxed at a corporate rate that is lower than that of the stockholder-employee. Since the premium payments are nondeductible, it will be tax cost effective to use lower-taxed corporate dollars to finance this insurance.

The stockholder-employees share of the split dollar SL proceeds can provide estate liquidity to solve the problems discussed earlier for the family-owned business. The corporation can retain a share of the proceeds through a collateral assignment split dollar arrangement and be repaid fully for its entire contribution. Alternatively, the corporation share can be rolled-out or bonused to the stockholder-employee at a later date.

The split dollar SL plan can be designed favorably for both income and estate tax purposes. All estate tax consequences to the insured stockholders can be avoided if a SL trust enters into the split dollar agreement with the employer. The insureds should obtain no incidents of ownership in the policy if the SL trust is the policyowner and applicant. In addition, the corporation should avoid obtaining incidents of ownership (e.g., access to the cash surrender value) if an insured is a majority shareholder. Any incidents of ownership held by the corporation will be attributed to the majority shareholder if the proceeds are not payable to or for the benefit of the corporation.

The design of the plan controls the income tax consequences of the split dollar SL plan. If the

employer pays the entire premium, the stockholder-employee is taxed annually on the economic benefit of the coverage.

The SL split dollar plan works the same way as the single-life split dollar plan except that very low rates are likely to be used to measure the pure term insurance cost while both insureds under the SL policy are alive. Depending on the age of the insureds, the premium rates may be dozens or even hundreds of times lower than the single life rates. What this means is that the taxable benefit in the employer-pay-all SL split dollar plan is only a fraction of what it would be if the plan used a single-life policy.

Question – What happens if a married couple insured under a survivorship life policy becomes divorced?

Answer – Almost all currently available survivorship contracts allow policy splits between divorced spouses. However, some policies force the husband and wife to prove evidence of insurability at the time of the split, which is a major disadvantage, especially at older ages, when a person is more likely to be rated and it is more difficult to find coverage for substandard risks. In addition, some split-option riders or exchange riders add significant costs to the contract each year the policy is in force or allow the company to charge a split or exchange fee that can further erode cash values. Also, survivorship plans that use term riders often exclude them from the split option.

Usually two new single-life policies are offered with premiums based on the insureds' ages when the survivorship life policy was issued. The cash value is generally evenly split into the new policies. A problem may arise if the premium on the new policy and the divisible share of the cash value from the survivorship policy are insufficient to cover the necessary reserves on the new policy. If a policy split occurs many years after issue of the survivorship policy and dividends have been sizable, the probability that this problem will arise is negligible. However, the likelihood of a problem increases if the split occurs soon after issue or if dividends have been low, especially in the male's policy. A lump-sum payment may be required to cover the shortfall or the benefit may be reduced. Some companies offer the option of paying higher premiums to fund the shortfall over time. Other companies avoid this problem by issuing new policies at attained ages. In these cases the premiums are based on higher mortality charges and the policyowners must pay full commissions and other new policy costs once again. If the split occurs at later ages, many insureds may find the premium cost prohibitive.

Other companies issue survivorship policies that allow splits without evidence of insurability and without new policy charges. However premium costs may be somewhat higher on the survivorship policy to compensate the company for these potential costs.

Question – What are some of the unique characteristics of the SL product that should be considered?

Answer – Competition and special needs have fostered the development of a number of new SL product innovations including:

- *Graduated premiums* – Graduated premium policies that start with lower premiums which increase over time may make an SL plan more affordable for couples who expect to have a greater premium-paying capacity over time. Care must be exercised in selecting these policies, however, since they may fail if the policyowner(s) are unable to pay the increasing premiums. Also, if the policy is put in trust, as the premiums increase they may exceed the amount the policyowner(s) can give the beneficiary without adverse gift tax consequences.

- *Substitute insured* – Some companies will permit substitutions of insureds, with evidence of insurability. This feature is attractive when SL is used in business insurance applications such as when used to fund partnership buy-sell agreements where partners may change and in key person insurance situations.

- *Enhanced death benefit* – Death benefits payable to an irrevocable trust on a policy transferred by the deceased within three years of death are included in the estate. To cover this contingency some companies will increase the death benefit during the policy's first three years to cover the additional estate tax.

- *Guaranteed death benefit* – Universal life SL policies typically do not guarantee the death benefit. Some companies, however, provide death benefit guarantees on their universal life SL policies.

- *First-death rider* – SL policies with this rider provide a specified death benefit to the surviving insured to cover probate, funeral, and other expenses associated with the first death.

- *Survivorship riders* – These riders, which are attached to single-life policies on a husband or wife, can be tailored to mimic a SL policy while providing important additional flexibility.

Question – How do survivorship riders work?

Answer – Survivorship riders are a form of guaranteed purchase option. A survivorship rider naming someone other than the insured as the "designated life" is attached to a single-life policy. If the designated life dies before the insured, the policyowner has the right to increase coverage on the insured without evidence of insurability. The rider provides "wait-and-see" flexibility since the policyowner may exercise the right to the full amount of additional insurance or any portion thereof.

Use of survivorship riders with single-life policies on a husband and wife can be designed to mimic a SL plan. Each spouse names the other spouse as the designated life. This arrangement is essentially equivalent to a three-policy survivorship life plan where there is a single-life policy on each spouse and a SL policy on both spouses. In contrast with many SL plans, the survivorship rider plan will require additional premiums to pay for the added coverage after the first death. However, premium payments will cease (if they have not already ceased under a vanishing premium plan) on the policy of the deceased. Also, depending on how ownership and beneficiary designations are selected, the death proceeds from the single-life policy on the first to die may be available to pay premiums on the survivor's policy or as a lump-sum payment into the survivor's policy. Similar to SL, the policies may be held in an irrevocable life insurance trust. Because the additional coverage is optional, the trustee has the flexibility to select only that amount of additional coverage that is deemed necessary after the first death.

Survivorship riders can also provide great versatility in business insurance planning, such as in cross-purchase buy-sell arrangements. For example, assume each of three shareholders (A, B, C) purchases policies on the other two shareholders equal to one-sixth of the company's value. They also attach survivorship riders to the policies allowing them to purchase additional insurance on the survivors equal to one-third of the business value. In specific dollar terms, if the company is worth $6 million, A would purchase policies on B and C with base amounts of $1 million. The policy on B would name C as the designated life and vice versa. The survivorship riders would permit A to buy an additional $2 million of coverage on B if C died first or on C if B died first. B and C would make analogous arrangements.

Now assume C dies. A and B would receive $1 million each in insurance proceeds, which together is enough to buy out C's $2 million interest in the company. A and B now each own 50% of the $6 million company, but the face value on the base policies each owns on the other is only $1 million. However, the survivorship rider permits them to purchase an additional $2 million of coverage on each other for a total of $3 million. They each will then have sufficient insurance in the event of the other's death to buy out the other's $3 million interest in the company.

CHAPTER ENDNOTES

1. Deductibility of interest on policy loans may depend on how the loan proceeds are used as described in IRC Section 163. See Appendix F, *Taxation of Benefits*, for a complete discussion of the taxation of policy loan interest.

2. For a complete discussion of the MEC rules, see Appendix D, *Modified Endowment Contracts*.

3. This conclusion is based on the language of IRC Section 2035(a)(2), which provides that transfers made within the three-year period prior to death will be included in the gross estate of the transferor only if "the value of such property (or an interest therein) would have been included in the decedent's gross estate under section 2036, 2037, 2038, or 2042 if such transferred interest or relinquished power had been retained by the decedent."

4. The interpolated terminal reserve is essentially the cash value of the policy adjusted for any unearned premiums, earned dividend credits, partial mortality charges, and other expense adjustments.

5. Treas. Reg. §20.2042-1(c)(6); Rev. Rul. 82-145, 1982-2 CB 213.

6. See Chapter 23, *Irrevocable Life Insurance Trusts*, for a thorough discussion of irrevocable life insurance trusts and Crummey powers.

7. The Tax Court's decision in *Est. of Maria Cristofani v. Comm.*, 97 TC 74 (1991), acq. in result, 1992-2 CB 1, held that Crummey powers granted to minors who were contingent remainder beneficiaries of a trust created gifts of a present interest qualifying for the annual exclusion. The IRS argued that holders of such Crummey withdrawal powers must have current beneficial interests in the trust for gifts to be present interests qualifying for the annual exclusion.

Chapter 16

TERM INSURANCE

WHAT IS IT?

The two principal characteristics of term insurance are: (1) the insured must die for any payments to be made; and (2) by definition, the contract expires at the end of the term. Stated more specifically, a term life insurance policy promises to pay a death benefit to a beneficiary only if the insured dies during a specified term.

The contract makes no promise to pay anything if the insured lives beyond the specified term. Generally, no cash values are payable under a term life insurance contract. If the insured survives the specified term, the contract expires and provides no payment of any kind to the policyowner.

WHEN IS THE USE OF THIS TOOL INDICATED?

In general, some type of life insurance is indicated when a person needs or wants to provide an immediate estate upon his or her death. This need or desire typically stems from one or more of the following reasons:

1. To provide income for dependent family members until they become self-supporting after the head of household dies.

2. To liquidate consumer or business debts, or to create a fund, that would enable the surviving family members to do so when the head of household dies.

3. To provide large amounts of cash at death for children's college expenses or other capital needs.

4. To provide cash for federal estate and state inheritance taxes, funeral expenses, and administration costs.

5. To provide funds for the continuation of a business through a "buy-sell" agreement.

6. To indemnify a business for the loss of a key employee.

7. To help recruit, retain, or retire one or more key employees through a salary continuation plan, and finance the company's obligations to the dependents of a deceased key employee under that plan.

8. To fund bequests of capital to children, grandchildren, or others without the erosion often caused by probate costs, inheritance taxes, income taxes, federal estate taxes, transfer fees, or the generation-skipping tax.

9. To fund charitable bequests.

10. To preserve confidentiality of financial affairs. Life insurance proceeds payable to someone other than the deceased's estate are not part of the probate estate and are not a matter of public record. It is not unusual for a beneficiary to be a lover, illegitimate child, faithful domestic servant, or have some other type of relationship with the insured that he or she may not want to be publicly acknowledged.

11. To assure nearly instant access to cash for surviving dependents. Life insurance proceeds are generally paid to beneficiaries within days of the claim. There is no delay, as might be the case with other types of assets, because of the intervention of state or other governmental bodies due to settlement of tax issues, or because of claims by the decedent's creditors.

12. To direct family assets to family members in a way that minimizes state, local, and federal taxes.

Generally, term insurance is not the most effective type of life insurance for all of these death benefit needs. However, term insurance may be indicated in many circumstances. Since term insurance is not just one product, but rather many variations on a general theme, different types of term insurance are indicated for different types of needs.

Keep in mind, term insurance, more than any other type of insurance, is pure death protection with little or no ancillary or lifetime benefits. Therefore, the two overriding considerations in the use of term insurance, regardless of the specific application, are (1) "Will death protection alone meet the need?" and (2) "Will the coverage last as long as the need?" In short, with term – as with any other decision about the appropriate type of coverage – *the product must match the problem.*

With these thoughts in mind, term insurance would be indicated in the following circumstances:

1. *When the need for life insurance is temporary.* – For example, assuming a parent has adequate income to pay college expenses on a pay-as-you-go basis and adequate life insurance for other purposes, the parent might use term insurance to assure payment of a child's college education expenses in the event of the parent's death during the child's college years. For this type of need, a five-year nonrenewable term policy might offer the best cost/benefit relationship. Similarly, decreasing term policies are often used to pay off the mortgage on the family's principal residence in the event of the breadwinner's death.

2. *When the need is long term but cash flow; is currently insufficient to buy the needed coverage using higher premium ordinary whole life* – Parents in younger families often have major long-term support obligations for their young children and spouses, have committed expenses that already strain the family's budget and, therefore, simply cannot afford the premiums necessary to buy the amount of coverage they need to protect their families using ordinary whole life insurance.

    Term insurance, especially at the younger ages, provides the greatest possible coverage for the lowest premium outlay. In these circumstances, one-year or five-year renewable and convertible term insurance is generally recommended. As the family breadwinner moves into his or her higher earning years and can afford the higher premium outlay, it is often advisable to convert to ordinary whole life insurance. Upon conversion there will be a one time premium increase. But premiums will remain level from then on.

3. *When the policyholder has better investment opportunities outside the insurance policy than inside the policy* – If the policyholder has investment op-

portunities that will pay a higher tax-free or after-tax yield with the same level of safety as the insurance policy, it may be better to buy renewable term insurance and to invest the early years' premium savings outside the insurance contract. However, this "buy-term-and-invest-the-difference" choice should not be based solely on differentials in potential yields inside and outside the policy. The cash value policy may offer many features not available on the outside investment including: (a) creditor protection; (b) a minimum rate guarantee; (c) waiver of premium in the event of disability; (d) loan provisions, and (e) a host of flexible non-forfeiture and settlement options.

4. *To guarantee a savings fund* – Many parents set up a savings program for their children's college educations well before their children start college. A decreasing term policy is often a perfect vehicle to assure the necessary savings fund if the parent dies before the funding is completed. There are many other similar types of applications where term insurance can be used to assure an adequate savings fund.

5. *For liquidity in the event of death* – One major life insurance application is to provide estate liquidity and to pay estate and inheritance taxes. Because of the ages typically involved, term insurance applications for estate planning and estate liquidity purposes are rather limited (and discussed further in Appendix A).

    However, the need for liquidity may stem from temporary special or extenuating circumstances not directly associated with payment of death taxes. New business startups are a case in point. The cash-flow needs of starting a new family business preclude the higher premiums of cash value policies until the business passes a critical break-even point or attains minimum profitability. Similarly, it is not uncommon for a successful small business owner to tie up virtually all of his or her assets in the business. This general lack of liquidity becomes even more severe when the business is expanding and engaging in capital improvement projects, such as building a new warehouse or plant, or starting new projects, such as developing and marketing a new product line. If the business owner should die while the expansion project is in process, it might jeopardize not only the expansion project, but also the entire business.

Although liquidity in the event of death will always be a problem (which might best be solved using a whole life policy), the temporary added liquidity risk during these expansion periods can often best be hedged using a term policy. Similar logic may be applied in dealing with any potential liquidity squeeze. Instances would include an executive who has received sizable bonuses of restricted stock in his or her company, an investor who has committed a significant portion of his or her portfolio to a temporarily illiquid position, and a real estate developer who is in the process of subdividing and developing a large tract of land.

6. *For business purposes* – Term insurance may be the most suitable form of insurance for business purposes in many circumstances. For example, one problem of funding buy-sell agreements with a cross-purchase arrangement when the ages of the business owners are disparate is the relatively high premium cost that the younger business owner must pay for coverage on the older owner. Initially, at least, term insurance or some combination of term insurance and ordinary life insurance may provide an affordable alternative.

    Similarly, often term insurance may be the most affordable alternative when insuring key employees, especially when these employees are engaged in special projects where their expertise is critical to the successful completion of the particular task or project. (These and other business uses of term insurance and other forms of life insurance are discussed in more detail in Chapter 20, "Life Insurance in Buy-Sell Agreements," Chapter 26, "Nonqualified Deferred Compensation," Chapter 24, "Key Employee Life Insurance," and Chapter 30, "Split Dollar Life Insurance".)

7. *When additional death benefits are desired in conjunction with other permanent forms of life insurance or "packages" of policies* – Level, increasing, or decreasing term riders are often packaged with permanent forms of life insurance to create a combination of death benefits and living benefits that fit a person's particular needs and resources. For instance, a participating whole life policy combined with a decreasing term rider can often be used when a person cannot afford the premiums necessary to fully insure using whole life insurance alone. The package can be designed so that dividends on the whole life policy will be used to buy paid-up additions that replace the term insurance as its face amount declines over time.

    Family policies are another example. The family package policy consists generally of some level of ordinary whole life insurance on the principal breadwinner, half that amount in term insurance on the spouse, and about half that amount, again, of term insurance on each of the children. It is less expensive for the insurance company to cover several persons in one policy than to issue separate policies for each person. The savings help to reduce the overall cost of the coverage to the family.

8. *To assure coverage in the event of unemployment or loss of employer-provided coverage* – Renewable and convertible term insurance provides a relatively low-cost method to cover the contingency of continuing protection in the event of unemployment or discontinuation of employer-provided coverage.

ADVANTAGES

1. Term insurance allows a person to acquire the greatest death benefit for the lowest premium outlay when the policy is first issued. However, this does not mean that term insurance is necessarily the least expensive form of insurance over the full duration of needed coverage. Since term premiums increase at each renewal, at the later ages the premium cost will far exceed the level premium that would have been charged for an ordinary whole life policy issued at the same age as the original term policy.

2. Term insurance is the best alternative for temporary life insurance needs. Usually term insurance is the best alternative if protection is needed for less than 10 years. Conversely, some form of cash value life insurance will generally be the best alternative if protection must continue for 15 or more years. If the duration of the needed protection is between 10 and 15 years, the best alternative depends upon the facts and circumstances of the case. As a general rule of thumb, term insurance will tend to be better than cash value insurance at issue ages below age 45, and worse at older issue ages if the length of the need for protection is between 10 and 15 years.

3. Younger persons may acquire substantial face amounts of coverage at relatively low immediate

cost, perhaps more than their immediate needs, and thereby guarantee that they will have the necessary level of coverage when their needs and family obligations later increase, even if they are then uninsurable.

4. The conversion feature of renewable and convertible term allows policyholders to enjoy higher death protection than they could otherwise afford and later allows them to "lock-in" their premiums and build cash values when their ability to pay premiums increases.

5. Various types of term insurance – level, decreasing, and increasing – can be combined as riders with other types of permanent insurance to create a package that meets a person's special death protection, savings, and affordability needs.

6. Life insurance proceeds are not part of the probate estate, unless the estate is named as the beneficiary of the policy. Therefore, the proceeds can be paid to the beneficiary without any delay caused by administration of the estate.

7. There is no public record of the death benefit amount or to whom the death benefit is payable (if paid to someone other than the deceased's estate).

8. The death benefit proceeds are generally not subject to federal income taxes.

9. The death benefit proceeds are often exempt from state inheritance taxes.

10. Life insurance policies can be used as collateral or security for personal loans. Although lenders generally prefer permanent types of policies because of the cash values, a term policy is often sufficient if the borrower is a good credit risk and the loan is very likely to be repaid unless he or she dies.

DISADVANTAGES

1. Term insurance has no tax-free, automatic savings feature as does permanent coverage.

2. The premiums increase until payment becomes prohibitive at later ages. This is one of the main reasons for the purchase of whole life insurance since coverage is useless if it cannot be held until the date it is needed most.

3. Term insurance generally has no loan values and no living benefits.

4. Term insurance only provides coverage for the term of the contract, not for the insured's entire life. In other words the term coverage may expire before the need does. A person may become uninsurable at a later age when the need for insurance still exists.

5. Life insurance of any kind is generally not available to persons in extremely poor health. However, persons in moderately poor health can often obtain insurance at "substandard" rates (a reference to the insured person's health, not to the quality or strength of the insurance company), which means higher premiums. It is easier to find ordinary whole life policies than term policies for persons who fall into the substandard rating category.

TAX IMPLICATIONS

Term insurance is subject to the same income, estate, gift, and generation-skipping transfer taxation rules as all other types of insurance policies. See Appendices A through G for a complete discussion of the taxation of life insurance.

ALTERNATIVES

There are no good alternatives to life insurance for providing tax-free cash upon death. The alternative forms of life insurance discussed in the other chapters of this book may be better than term insurance for many life insurance needs. If an individual is uninsurable and, therefore, cannot obtain life insurance of any kind, the best alternatives are accumulation funds and tax-deferred investments.

The most important thing is to *match the product to the problem!*

WHERE AND HOW DO I GET IT?

There are nearly 2,000 life insurance companies actively marketing coverage in the United States. Many, but not all, of these companies offer term insurance policies as well as other permanent forms of life insurance. In addition to commercial insurance companies, coverage is also available through fraternal organizations, certain savings banks in some states, professional associations, membership organizations, employer group benefit packages, and insurance purchasing groups. Policies can be purchased through many licensed agents representing a licensed insurance company.

For persons having difficulty finding coverage because of health problems, there are agents who specialize in what is called the "substandard" market. They know which insurance companies are likely to write coverage for people with specific problems.

Life insurance coverage can be acquired by people who cannot obtain it in any other way through "credit life insurance." This is a form of "group insurance" associated with lenders for the purchase of automobiles, furniture and other consumer durables, and even homes. This coverage is generally extremely expensive because it is priced to cover all ages and health conditions for the same premium, but it is available to anyone who qualifies for the loan at the same premium rate.

Some insurance companies offer "limited benefit" policies that repay all premiums in the event the insured dies within the first few years (usually two) after the policy is issued, but pay no death benefit. If the insured survives the first few years of the policy, the death benefit amount becomes the face amount. These policies often are offered during "open-enrollment" periods when the insurance company agrees to issue a policy to anyone who applies. Typically, the offer is restricted to persons within specified ages, such as between ages 40 and 65. Since the company is accepting any applicants and it knows many of these applicants are not otherwise insurable, the premium rates are extremely high. This type of coverage is often marketed through television advertisements which emphasize that no one can be rejected for coverage.

WHAT FEES OR OTHER ACQUISITION COSTS ARE INVOLVED?

Life insurance is generally sold on a specified price basis. Life insurance companies are free to set their premiums according to their own marketing strategies and classifications. The premium set by the insurance company includes a "loading" (a specified part of each premium payment). Typically, loading will cover such things as: (1) commission payments to agents; (2) premium taxes payable to the state government; (3) operating expenses of the insurance company, such as rent or mortgage payments and salaries; (4) federal income taxes; and (5) other applicable expenses, such as claims handling and policy change services.

The bulk of an insurance company's expenses are incurred when the policy is issued. It may take an insurance company five to nine years, or even longer, to recover all of its front-end costs. The state premium tax applicable to all life insurance premium payments is an ongoing expense. The average level of this tax is about 2% of each premium payment.

The aggregate commission payable to the selling agent on term insurance policies is generally less than on cash value policies. This is due to two factors. First, initial premiums for term insurance policies are lower than for permanent forms of life insurance. Therefore, even if the commission rates were equal, the amount paid would be lower. Second, the commission rate on term policies is generally lower than the rate on permanent forms of insurance. Whereas the total commission on a permanent policy typically is equal to about one year's premium with about 55 to 80% generally being paid in the first year, commission rates on term insurance policies tend to run about 40 to 60% of the first year's premium, and about 5 to 8% of each successive premium.

Some life insurance companies sell "no-load" life insurance policies. That is, they do not pay a commission to the selling agent. However, the premiums charged by these companies tend to be as high as those charged by companies that pay commissions to agents. Although there are no commission costs on these no-load policies, these companies apparently tend to incur, in the aggregate, about the same level of direct mail and other marketing costs to sell their policies as other companies pay in commissions to agents to market their policies.

HOW DO I SELECT THE BEST OF ITS TYPE?

In contrast with permanent cash value types of insurance, the term insurance policy, with the lowest premium among all identical term insurance policies, is generally the least expensive policy. This would seem to indicate that term insurance can be purchased as a commodity with the lowest price being the indicator of the "best" policy among insurers of acceptable quality and financial strength.

Comparing Term Policies

All of the policy provisions must be checked to see if the policies provide identical benefits. In most cases, the policies available from different companies will not be identical. Therefore, the slight differences in the policy provisions will need to be weighed against the differences in the premiums.

Here are some factors to consider:

1. In the case of renewable term policies, check the schedule of future renewal premiums. A policy with the lowest initial premiums may have higher renewal premiums than other policies.

2. Check the age to which coverage may be continued without evidence of insurability. A policy with a lower premium may discontinue the automatic renewal right before other higher premium policies.

3. Check the grace period provision to see if the policy remains in effect for 31 days after the expiration of the term of the policy. A policy that does not provide the grace period may leave the client uninsured if he or she happens to be late with a renewal premium.

4. Check the age to which a convertible policy may be converted to ordinary whole life at attained age without evidence of insurability. It may be worth some additional premium dollars to guarantee this conversion right for additional years.

5. Check whether the incontestability and suicide clauses of the conversion policy will be modified to provide that the two-year qualifying periods will run from the issue date of the term policy if the term policy is converted to whole life.

6. Check whether the conversion clause permits the client to convert the policy to an ordinary whole life policy with the waiver of premium rider without evidence of insurability. If it does, check whether there are any limitations due to preexisting conditions.

The right to include the waiver of premium rider in the converted policy can be an important feature, particularly if the conversion to a policy with a waiver of premium rider can be made even if the insured is already disabled. Also, in those policies that permit conversion to a policy with a waiver of premium rider, check to see if there is a minimum age to convert (such as age 55) if the insured individual is already disabled. In general, it is worth it to pay higher premiums to acquire a policy with more liberal

rules regarding conversion to an ordinary whole life policy with the waiver of premium rider.

7. Check the soundness of the company using the criteria in Chapter 3.

What to Look for in Ledger Statements of Yearly Renewable Term[1]

Policy illustrations or ledger statements are typically presented to potential purchasers to describe the financial aspects of the policy being considered under various assumptions regarding credited interest rates, dividend payments, and premium payment plans. Figure 16.1 shows a sample ledger statement for yearly renewable and convertible reissue term. Each of the numbers in the ledger corresponds to the following notes:

1. The death benefit is "level," in this case, $100,000.

2. The plan of term insurance is yearly renewable to age 95.

3. The gender is male, and the issue age is 45.

4. The insurability status (e.g., smoker or nonsmoker), or rated (extra charge because the insured is a higher risk for medical or occupational reasons). The "preferred" risk for this life insurance company refers to a nonsmoker, nonrated policyholder – the company's best insurability category.

5. The face amount of life insurance is $100,000.

6. The ledger statement shows values at the beginning of each year, rather than at the end of each year.

7. The gross premium charged (not taking dividends into consideration) on a non-reissue basis.

8. The projected dividend payable at the end of the prior year (i.e., at the beginning of the following year). In this case, the first projected dividend is to be paid at the beginning of year 6.

9. The net annual premium (gross premium charged on a non-reissue basis taking projected dividends into consideration).

10. A column showing premiums on a reissue basis for the first reissue period. Each successive

Figure 16.1

LEDGER STATEMENT FOR YEARLY RENEWABLE TERM

LEVEL TERM LEDGER STATEMENT **1**
+Plan: Yearly Renewable Term to Age 95 **2**   Male: Issue Age 45 **3**
CLASS: Preferred Standard **4**   Face Amount: $100,000 **5**

6	7	8	9	10	See 14	See 17	See 20
Beg. Pol. Year	Basic Ann. Prem#	Div. End of Prior Year*	Net Ann. Prem*	Reissue Premiums@ 1	Reissue Premiums@ 2	Reissue Premiums@ 3	Reissue Premiums@ 4
1	$ 238	$ 0	$ 238				
2	314	0	314				
3	395	0	395				
4	479	0	479				
5	568	0	568	**11** $286			
6	842	171	671	388			
7	898	178	720	497			
8	984	183	801	614			
9	1,042	189	853	**12** 738	**14** $378		
10	1,126	224	902 **13**		449		
11	1,244	245	999		592		
12	1,319	266	1,053		742		
13	1,421	317	1,104		**15** $900	**17** $498	
14	1,531	377	1,154 **16**			585	
15	1,689	417	1,272			773	
16	1,781	460	1,321			964	
17	1,929	471	1,458			**18** $1,164	**20** $ 700
18	2,097	487	1,610 **19**				902
19	2,287	508	1,779				1,166
20	2,498	536	1,962	Reissue Premiums@ 5			1,418
21	2,830	668	2,162	**23** $1,034			**21** $1,665
22	3,072	733	2,339 **22**	1,405			
23	3,372	860	2,512	1,758	Reissue Premium@ 6		
24	3,665	1,010	2,655	2,083			
25	3,920	1,125	2,795	**24** $2,380	**26** $1,580		
26	4,342	1,293	3,049 **25**		2,231		
27	4,674	1,309	3,365		2,720		
28	5,289	1,486	3,803		3,159		
29	5,692	1,625	4,067 **28**		**27** $3,567		
30	6,035	1,675	4,360				
31	6,480	1,725	4,755				
32	7,110	1,797	5,313				
33	7,867	1,992	5,873				
34	8,775	2,062	6,713				
35	10,280	2,130	8,150				
36	11,116	2,192	8,924				

Dividends used to reduce premiums.*
Dividends are not guaranteed and will vary.

Figure 16.1 (cont'd)

LEVEL TERM LEDGER STATEMENT

Summary and Explanatory Notes

Summary: 29	Total Annual Premiums⁺	Total Annual Dividends*	Total Net Premiums*	Total Reissue Premiums@
5 years	$ 1,994	$ 171	$ 1,823	$ 1,712
10 years	6,886	1,190	5,696	4,038
15 years	14,090	3,027	11,063	7,228
20 years	24,682	5,697	18,985	12,378
Age 60	14,090	31 3,027	32 11,063	33 7,228
Age 65	24,682	5,697	18,985	12,378
Age 70	30 41,541	10,718	30,823	20,238

Interest-adjusted indexes* based on a 5.00% interest rate, for basic policy only without reissue.

	10 years:	20 years:	Age 65:
Net payment cost index	$5.45	$8.36	$8.36
34 Surrender cost index	$5.45	$8.36	$8.36
Equivalent level annual dividend	$1.01	$2.21	$2.21

35 ⁺Plan renews automatically each year on payment of a renewal premium, but not beyond insured's age 95. Convertible to any life or endowment policy with a level face amount prior to the insured's age 90.

36 @If satisfactory evidence of insurability is submitted at the end of each 4-year period, but not beyond age 69, the lower premium rates may apply. Otherwise the original rates apply.

37 *Includes dividend values. The dividend levels in this illustration are based on the company's current experience with respect to mortality, persistency, taxes, expenses, and investments. They are not guaranteed. The dividends actually paid will be determined by the company's future experience in these factors and will likely differ from those illustrated, being either higher or lower.

38 Among these dividend factors, investment earnings are of major significance. The illustrated dividends assume continuation of the company's current investments experience. If all other dividend factors were to remain at current experience levels, future dividends would be higher or lower than those illustrated, depending upon future investment earnings. To demonstrate this, dividend levels resulting from future investments that are 2% higher and 2% lower than the illustrated scale are also available.

39 #Summary values are calculated as of the end of the year and, because of rounding, may differ slightly from values shown on the ledger page.

40 ⁺Issuance of this plan for the values shown is subject to underwriting approval.

column shows reissue premiums at subsequent reissue dates.

11. At the beginning of year 5, the insured may apply for reissue rates. If the insured satisfies the underwriting requirements of the insurance company (just as though applying for new insurance), the premium for year 5 will be $286, not $568. If underwriting requirements are not met, the net projected premiums in column 9 will apply.

12. At the beginning of year 9, those who qualified for reissue rates at the beginning of year 5 apply

again. If their application is denied, their year 9 premium will be $738, and then the non-reissue rates (column 9) apply. If they qualify for reissue rates, their premium in year 9 will be $378.

13. The net projected premium in year 10 is $902 for those who did not qualify for reissue.

14. The premium is $378 in year 9 for those who did qualify for reissue.

15. At the beginning of year 13, those who qualified for reissue rates at the beginning of year 9 apply again. If denied, their premium in year 13 will be $900, and then the non-reissue rates (column 9) apply. If they qualify for reissue rates, their premium in year 13 will be $498.

16. The net projected premium is $1,154 in year 14 for those who do not qualify for reissue.

17. The premium is $498 in year 13 for those who do qualify for reissue.

18. At the beginning of year 17, those who qualified for reissue rates at the beginning of year 13 apply again. If denied, their year 17 premium will be $1,164; and then the non-reissue rates (column 9) apply. If they qualify for reissue rates, their premium in year 17 will be $700.

19. The net projected premium in year 18 for those who do not qualify for reissue is $1,610.

20. The premium is $700 in year 17 for those who do qualify for reissue.

21. At the beginning of year 21, those who qualified for reissue rates at the beginning of year 17 apply again. If they are denied, their year 21 premium will be $1,665, and then the non-reissue rates (column 9) apply. If they qualify for reissue rates, their premium in year 21 will be $1,034.

22. The net projected premium in year 22 for those who do not qualify for reissue is $2,339.

23. The premium is $1,034 in year 21 for those who do qualify for reissue.

24. At the beginning of year 25, those who qualified for reissue rates at the beginning of year 21 apply again. If they are denied, their year 25 premium will be $2,380, and then the non-reissue rates (column 9) apply. If they qualify for reissue rates, their premium in year 25 will be $1,580.

25. The net projected premium in year 26 for those who do not qualify for reissue is $3,049.

26. The premium is $1,580 in year 25 for those who do qualify for reissue.

27. The premium in year 29 for those who do qualify for reissue rates at the beginning of year 25. In year 29, the insured is beyond age 69; therefore, reissue rates no longer are available.

28. The net projected premium in year 29 (based on the life expectancy for a 45-year-old male) for those who do not qualify for reissue is $4,067. For those still alive after age 74 who want to have their insurance continue in force, the net projected premiums in column 9 will apply.

29. This is a summary page.

30. The total gross non-reissue premiums for the years shown without adjustment for dividends. These sums do not adjust for the time value or opportunity cost of money.

31. The total projected dividends for the years shown. Projected dividends are not guaranteed. These sums do not adjust for the time value or opportunity cost of money.

32. The total net projected premiums on a non-reissue basis (gross premium minus projected dividends) for the years shown. The sums do not adjust for the time value or opportunity cost of money.

33. The total premiums on a reissue basis. These sums do not adjust for the time value or opportunity cost of money.

34. The interest-adjusted indexes for the years are shown on a non-reissue basis.

35. A statement about the renewability as term insurance and convertibility to a non-term plan.

36. A description of the reissue rules.

37. The dividend statement explaining that dividends are not guaranteed.

38. A statement explaining that dividends are related to the company's investment experience and that illustrations with higher or lower assumed dividend interest rates are available.

39. A statement about summary values which are based on the end of the year, not the beginning of the year.

40. A statement explaining that the illustrated values are only applicable if the insured meets the company's underwriting standards.

Information the Ledger Statements Do Not Provide

Although ledger statements are the principal source of information about the economic aspects of the policy, they generally do not provide all of the information necessary to properly and fully evaluate and understand the policy. The following additional information should also be provided, preferably in writing:

1. A full explanation of the *reissue* rules. The company will reissue the policy on its terms, which may mean the insured will have to undergo an entirely new medical checkup or provide other evidence of good health. In general, the actual reentry premium will be what the insurance company deems proper at the time. Depending on the company's experience on its block of similar policies, premiums may be higher or lower than the reissue premiums shown on the current ledger statement.

2. The compound rate of return upon death on both a non-reissue basis and a reissue basis. Although it would be best to know rates for each year, it is generally satisfactory to know rates for each five-year period for up to 25 years and for the insured's life expectancy.[2]

   The rate of return upon death on a non-reissue basis is:

Year	Rate of Return
1	41,916.81%
5	200.04
10	58.83
20	17.45
29 (life expectancy)	6.85

   The rate of return upon death on a reissue basis is:

Year	Rate of Return
1	41,916.81%
5	200.62
10	61.26
20	20.53
29 (life expectancy)	9.78

3. The rate of return upon death should then be compared with the before-tax rate of return one would have to earn in another non-insurance investment such as mutual funds, bonds, or certificates of deposit to duplicate the tax-exempt rate of return provided by life insurance. The before-tax rate of return may be determined by dividing the life insurance rate of return by the insured's marginal tax bracket subtracted from 100% (e.g., for 15%, the factor is 0.85; for 28%, 0.72; for 33%, 0.67; and for 34%, 0.66).

   The before-tax rate of return required in another non-insurance investment to duplicate the rate of return upon death on a non-reissue basis is shown in Figure 16.2.

   The before-tax rate of return required in another non-insurance investment to duplicate the rate of return upon death on a reissue basis is shown in Figure 16.3.

4. Since annually renewable term policies generally provide no surrender cash value, the rate of return upon surrender is always 100% compound.

WHERE CAN I FIND OUT MORE?

The following references include authoritative discussions of various types of life insurance including term insurance:

1. B. Anderson, *Anderson on Life Insurance* (Waltham, MA: Little, Brown and Company, 1991).

2. B. Baldwin, *New Life Insurance Investment Advisor: Achieving Financial Security for You and Your Family Through Today's Insurance Products*, 2nd ed. (Hightstown, NJ: McGraw-Hill Trade, 2001).

Figure 16.2

	15% taxpayer	28% taxpayer	33% taxpayer	34% taxpayer
BEFORE TAX RATE OF RETURN TO DUPLICATE TERM INSURANCE RATE OF RETURN ON A NON-REISSUE BASIS				
Year	**15% taxpayer**	**28% taxpayer**	**33% taxpayer**	**34% taxpayer**
1	49,313.89%	58,217.79%	62,562.40%	63,510.20%
5	235.34	277.83	298.57	303.09
10	69.21	81.71	87.81	89.14
20	20.53	24.24	26.04	26.44
29 (life expectancy)	8.06	9.51	10.22	10.38

Figure 16.3

	15% taxpayer	28% taxpayer	33% taxpayer	34% taxpayer
BEFORE TAX RATE OF RETURN TO DUPLICATE TERM INSURANCE RATE OF RETURN ON A REISSUE BASIS				
Year	**15% taxpayer**	**28% taxpayer**	**33% taxpayer**	**34% taxpayer**
1	49,313.89%	58,217.79%	62,562.40%	63,510.20%
5	236.02	278.64	299.43	303.97
10	72.07	85.08	91.43	92.82
20	24.15	28.51	30.64	31.11
29 (life expectancy)	11.51	13.58	14.60	14.82

3. J. Belth, Life Insurance: A Consumer's Handbook, 2nd ed. (Bloomington, IN: Indiana University Press, 1985).

4. K. Black, Jr. and H. Skipper, Jr., *Life Insurance*, 13th ed. (Old Tappan, NJ: Prentice Hall Inc., 1999).

5. E. Graves, Editor, *McGill's Life Insurance*, 5th ed. (Bryn Mawr, PA: The American College, 2004).

The following references are useful guides for policy and company rating information:

1. *Best Insurance Reports* (Oldwick, NJ: A. M. Best Company, published annually).

2. *Best's Review – Life/Health Edition* (Oldwick, NJ: A. M. Best Company, published monthly).

QUESTIONS AND ANSWERS

Question – How long do term insurance policies usually last?

Answer – Term policies are generally issued with one-year or five-year durations or terms. Some companies issue 10-year, 20-year, or longer term policies, or term to age 65 or 70. The premium charges for longer term contracts are generally level over the life of the policy.

As the term of the policy increases it tends to take on more of the characteristics of permanent or ordinary cash value whole life policies. In fact, level-premium term insurance to age 100 is, by definition, ordinary whole life insurance. Specifically, since premiums are level over the term of the policy, longer term policies will begin to generate some cash values because the company must "overcharge" in the early years to build a reserve to cover the "undercharge" in the later years as mortality costs increase. If a level term policy is surrendered before the end of the term, the owner may be entitled to a return of a portion of the reserve.

Question – What is a "renewable" term policy?

Answer – Term policies are either renewable or nonrenewable. This means, for a small additional premium, the policyowner has the contractual right to continue the contract. If a policy is renewable, the policyholder may unconditionally renew the coverage for successive terms at higher premiums (appropriate for the given renewal age) merely by

Chapter 16 – Term Insurance

paying the indicated premium. No forms must be signed or evidence of good health must be given at each renewal period.

If the policy is nonrenewable, at the end of the term of coverage the policyholder has no legal right to continue the insurance. This means the policyowner must apply for new insurance. If the insured's health has deteriorated, he or she may no longer qualify for coverage, or coverage may be obtainable only at a significantly higher rate.

Although premiums are typically higher for renewable policies than for nonrenewable policies, the added cost is generally worth it if the policyholder expects the need for insurance to continue beyond the initial term of the policy. In many cases what was thought to be a temporary need continues far longer than was originally anticipated.

Some term policies are renewable to age 100. However, many policies restrict renewability after certain ages, typically between ages 75 and 85. In addition, most insurance companies do not offer renewable term policies to new applicants after a certain age, typically between age 60 and 70.

Question – What is a convertible policy?

Answer – This is one of the most important options a policyholder should consider in purchasing term insurance. In return for a slightly larger premium (to compensate the insurer for the extra risk it is assuming), most renewable term policies give the policyholder a contractual right to exchange the term policy for some other type of life insurance policy without evidence of insurability. Typically, the conversion privilege gives the policyholder an absolute contractual right to convert the term insurance into some form of permanent insurance that builds cash values, typically ordinary whole life.

The conversion feature is often attractive when a person's circumstances change and there is a need for lifetime coverage. Conversion allows the policyholder to lock-in the premiums, albeit at a higher rate than the current renewal term rates, and avoid the ever increasing term premiums at later ages. For the client who becomes ill or permanently disabled on a long term basis, conversion to a whole life contract will represent the best means of continuing insurance coverage beyond the originally anticipated term.

The conversion privilege often expires after a specified number of years or after the insured reaches

a certain age. Typical examples would be one-year renewable term policies that are convertible for 20 years or that may be converted until the insured reaches age 60. The upper age limit on conversion is usually lower than the renewability limitation. A policy renewable to age 60 may only be convertible to age 55 or 59. This limitation helps to prevent extreme cases of adverse selection against the insurance company whereby persons in poor health convert their policies just before the expiration of their rights to renew coverage without evidence of insurability.

All convertible term policies allow what is called "attained age conversion." The company issues a new policy based upon the insured's attained age in the year of conversion. In other words, the new policy is issued and the policyholder pays premiums as if the policy were based on an entirely new application, except that there is no need to prove insurability.

Some company's term policies allow the policyholder to elect to convert in another way called "original age conversion." In this case, the new policy is written as if it had been issued as of the issue date of the term policy that is being converted. The premium is based on the insured's age when the term policy was issued, not the insured's attained age. Consequently, when the original age conversion method is used, the premiums for the converted policy will generally be less than when the attained age method is used.

However, since the new policy is usually some form of permanent cash value insurance, an adjustment must be made for the fact that the policyholder has not been paying the higher premiums associated with the new permanent form of insurance. Typically, the policyholder must pay the difference in premiums since the issue date of the term policy, along with 5 or 6% interest compounded annually on these differences. Because the adjustment factor becomes quite large and, in most cases, unaffordable, unless the term policy is converted within a few years, this type of conversion is often offered only for a limited period, such as only within five years of the issue date of the term policy.

Question – What is level term insurance?

Answer – As its name implies, level term means that the death benefit remains level throughout the selected term of coverage. Term policies may be issued with virtually any initial face amount (i.e., the amount payable at death). However, they are generally issued only in increments of $5,000 or $10,000. Generally, premiums for level term increase each time the contract is renewed even though the face amount remains the same.

Question – What is increasing term insurance?

Answer – Increasing term is typically only offered as a rider (i.e., a low cost "add-on") to another basic policy, such as ordinary whole life, or as part of a package of policies. This type of coverage is commonly called a "return-of-premium" benefit or a "return-of-cash-value" benefit. The basic idea is that in the event of the insured's death while the increasing term policy is in effect, the beneficiaries receive the entire face amount on the basic policy plus a return of the premiums paid or the cash value. In essence, it is equivalent to owning a level term policy plus a savings account equal to the cash value of the basic policy. Increasing term riders typically do not extend for a period of more than 20 years.

Question – What is decreasing term insurance?

Answer – Decreasing term is a popular form of term coverage frequently used to assure that a family will have the resources to pay-off a home mortgage and/or other loans in the event the family's primary breadwinner dies. For this reason, it is often called "mortgage insurance."

The policyowner selects an amount of initial coverage. Then, over a specified period, the death benefit declines steadily until it reaches zero at the end of the term. This decrease in face value may occur monthly or annually. Premiums typically remain constant and are payable for the duration of coverage or for a shorter term. Because the coverage is decreasing while the premiums remain level, as the insured ages each dollar of outlay buys less insurance.

The coverage may continue for a specified term of years, typically 10, 15, 20 or 30 years, or until the insured reaches a certain age, often age 65. The duration is usually selected to coincide with the time normally required to repay the loan.

Question – What is an increasing premium, level death benefit term policy to age 65?

Answer – Term policies with level death benefits and annually increasing premiums are simply one-year renewable term policies. An increasing premium, level death benefit term policy to age 65 is simply a one-year term policy renewable to age 65. One-year renewable term policies, which are also known as yearly renewable term (YRT) policies or annually renewable term (ART) policies, are the most common form of term insurance sold today.

Question – Do term policies carry a waiver of premium provision?

Answer – The waiver of premium rider, which is a common rider to most permanent or ordinary whole life policies, provides that premiums are waived if the insured becomes totally and permanently disabled. This rider is available on many renewable term policies.

Company practice is not uniform with respect to the inclusion of the waiver of premium rider in a new policy obtained by converting a term policy that includes a waiver of premium rider. Some companies do not allow a waiver of premium rider in the converted policy unless the insured shows evidence of insurability. Some companies will permit the converted policy to include a waiver of premium rider without evidence of insurability, but will restrict its operation to disabilities that are the result of injuries sustained or of diseases contracted after the date of conversion.

Question – If a person is in good health, does it pay to apply for new insurance rather than to continue to renew a YRT policy?

Answer – The hassle and inconvenience of applying for new insurance every year while one maintains his or her health is not worth it. However, it may pay to purchase new insurance every ten years or so if the individual is still healthy.

Insurance companies can afford to charge relatively low premiums in the first few years after issue because they have had the opportunity to screen their applicants and select only those who are in good health. Insureds tend to remain in good health for the first few years after the policy is issued. However, over the years, the pattern is for some of the policyholders who are in the best health to drop the coverage and for those with the worst health to continue their coverage. This is known as "adverse selection" since the worst (most likely to die early) risks remain and the best (the most likely to survive to older ages) risks no longer support the pool of dollars available to pay claims.

Consequently, the insurers must build additional renewal premium charges into the policy in later years to cover the additional mortality costs associated with this adverse selection against the insurance company. If an individual is in good health, he can apply for new insurance by showing evidence of insurability and once again enjoy the lower "select" mortality charges associated with new policy issues.

This process of adverse selection against the insurance companies is what has led many companies to offer reentry term policies, which are also sometimes called "select" and "ultimate" term policies. As long as the insured continues to show evidence of insurability at periodic intervals (typically every two, three, or five years) the renewal premiums, which are based on the lower "select" mortality charges, remain comparable to the premiums for newly-issued policies.

If the insured's health deteriorates, the renewal premiums increase and reflect what is called "ultimate" mortality charges. In general, if the insured fails to show evidence of satisfactory health, the renewal premiums are higher than the renewal premiums for regular renewable term, which are based on data from both select and ultimate mortality experience.

Question – What is "universal term" insurance?

Answer – Universal term is a type of flexible term insurance contract. Similar to, and actually a variation of, universal life insurance, it allows the policyholder to set up a customized pattern of premiums and face amounts. Changes may also be allowed after issue, within limits.

Question – Is the cost per $1,000 of face value on term policies lower for higher total face amounts?

Answer – Yes, most companies charge a lower rate per $1,000 for greater amounts of coverage. The break points vary by company. Term, like whole life or any other form of permanent coverage, is "cheaper by the dozen."

CHAPTER ENDNOTES

1. Adapted from the excellent book by William D. Brownlie with Jeffrey L. Seglin, *The Life Insurance Buyer's Guide* (McGraw Hill Publishing Company, Inc., 1989).

2. The compound rate of return upon death is an internal rate of return calculation that requires the use of a computer or a financial calculator. The internal rate of return is computed finding the discount rate that equates the present value of the net premium payments with the present value of the death benefits. For simplicity, it is usually assumed that premiums are paid at the beginning of each year and death benefits are paid at the end of the year of death.

Chapter 17

UNIVERSAL LIFE

WHAT IS IT?

Universal life (UL) is a "flexible-premium" "current-assumption" "adjustable-death-benefit" type of cash value life insurance. The term flexible premium means the policyowner is permitted to select whatever premium he or she wishes to pay, within limits, and later to adjust or change the premium. Policyowners may even skip premium payments as long as the cash value is sufficient to cover policy charges. The term current assumption means that current interest rates, as well as current mortality and expense charges, are used to determine additions to cash values. The term adjustable death benefit means that policyowners are permitted to raise or lower their policy death benefits. However, increases may require evidence of insurability.

As a result of this tremendous flexibility, UL has captured a major share of the new insurance market since its introduction in the late 1970's. Some insurance companies use the term flexible-premium adjustable life to describe their UL policies.

WHEN IS THE USE OF THIS TOOL INDICATED?

UL may be considered for any life insurance need. Initially, a UL policy's death benefit and target premium level can be configured to resemble virtually any type of life insurance policy from annually renewable term insurance to single premium whole life. However, because of policy costs, it is generally best suited for long-term coverage needs. For short-term (less than five years) needs, a nonrenewable term policy will generally be more cost effective.

1. UL is indicated whenever the ultimate in flexibility in life insurance is desired. Policyowners whose circumstances change can later "reconfigure" the policy by changing their premium payments and/or the death benefit.

2. UL is extremely popular in the family market. For example, a young parent with a growing

family and modest income can acquire a UL policy that is initially configured with low premiums and a high death benefit to resemble a traditional renewable term policy. As the parent's income grows, premiums can be increased to build tax-sheltered cash within the policy. At later times when cash is needed, such as to pay for a child's education, premium payments can be reduced or stopped altogether and cash values can be used to help pay the school expenses. After a time, the premiums can be increased once again to build cash values. Similarly, if the amount of death protection that is needed changes, the death benefit may be decreased or increased. However, increases in death benefits will usually require evidence of insurability.

3. UL has also become extremely popular in the business market where flexibility is often essential. UL has become the preferred vehicle in all sorts of business applications including split dollar plans, funding for nonqualified deferred compensation plans, key person insurance, funding vehicles for buy-sell agreements, and even in insured qualified retirement plans.

ADVANTAGES

1. The policyowner has wide discretion or flexibility in selecting the premiums that are paid. Provided that there is enough cash value to cover mortality charges, the policyowner may even skip premium payments. In contrast with other types of policies, skipping premiums does not result in the creation of policy loans.

2. The policyowner may change the level of death benefits. Decreases in the death benefit are permitted at virtually any time. However, policyowners who reduce death benefits within the first seven years of issue may be subjected to adverse tax consequences under the modified endowment contract (MEC) rules. Increases in face amount are generally permitted, subject to evidence of insurability. Increases in the death benefit may also subject the

policy to a new test period under the MEC rules. (See Appendix D, "Modified Endowment Contracts.")

3. The policy is "transparent." That is, policy illustrations and annual reports break out and report each of the policy elements separately. This "unbundling" of the policy allows the policyowner to specifically identify and track premiums, death benefits, interest credits, mortality charges, expenses, and cash values and to check projections against actual performance over time.

4. Most UL policies offer two death benefit patterns, called option A and option B, or option I and option II.

   • *Option A* – This option, which is similar to a traditional whole life policy, offers a fixed (level) death benefit. As cash values grow larger, the net amount at risk (or pure insurance) is reduced to keep the total death benefit constant (unless the cash value grows to an amount where the death benefit must be increased to avoid classification as a modified endowment contract).

   • *Option B* – This option operates in a manner similar to the death benefit one would receive from a traditional whole life policy with a term insurance rider that is equal to the current cash value. Under option B, the death benefit at any time is equal to a specified level of pure insurance, plus the policy's cash value at the time of death. Therefore, the death benefit increases as the cash value grows.

5. Many companies permit policyowners to attach a "cost-of-living" rider to UL policies that, without evidence of insurability, automatically increases the policy death benefit each year by the increase in the Consumer Price Index.

6. In contrast with most traditional whole life policies, many UL policies use "back-end loads," rather than "front-end loads." (A load is the charge imposed by an insurer to recover the initial policy expenses. The terms front-end and back-end refer to when the charge is imposed.) Consequently, most or all of the policyowner's initial premiums go into cash values, subject of course to regular annual expense and mortality charges. Therefore, cash values build more quickly than with traditional whole life policies.

7. UL, as a current-assumption policy, allows policyowners to directly participate in the favorable investment, mortality, and expense experience of the company. Although a traditional participating whole life insurance policy is essentially a type of "interest-sensitive" current-assumption policy, as reflected in dividend payments, the connection is indirect and difficult to measure. The annual UL policy statements explicitly show the amount of credited interest and expense and mortality charges for the year.

8. Cash value interest or earnings may accumulate tax-free or tax-deferred, depending on whether gains are distributed at death or during lifetime.

9. UL policies have historically paid a higher effective rate of interest on cash values than have tax-free municipal bonds. Rates credited to UL policies have more closely tracked rates paid on high-grade corporate and government bonds and mortgages.

10. Although the interest credited to cash values will vary with market rates, the cash values are not subject to the fluctuations in market value characteristic of longer-term municipal bonds and other longer-term fixed income investments when market rates change.

11. Policy cash values can be borrowed at a low net cost. Although policyowners must pay interest on policy loans, cash values continue to grow and are credited with at least the minimum guaranteed rate in the policy. Consequently, the actual net borrowing rate is less than the stated policy loan rate.

12. In most UL policies, policyowners may withdraw a portion of their cash value without surrendering the policy. However, if money is withdrawn, the pure life insurance portion of the death benefit is typically reduced by the amount of the withdrawal. In addition, withdrawals may be subject to income tax.

DISADVANTAGES

1. The flexibility associated with premium payments can be a disadvantage since policyowners can too easily allow their policies to lapse. There is no forced savings feature, since premium payments are not required as long as there is sufficient cash value to carry the policy. To reduce the likelihood of lapse, most companies "bill" policyowners for a target premium set by the policyowner.

2. Although traditional participating whole life policies are indirectly "interest-sensitive," mortality and

expense charges are guaranteed. In contrast, current-assumption policies, including UL, only guarantee that mortality charges and expense rates will not exceed certain maximums. Consequently, policyowners bear more of the risk of adverse trends in mortality or expenses than if they owned traditional whole life policies. The converse is also true. If the trend of mortality costs and expenses improves, UL policyowners may participate in the improvement through lower charges.

3. Although most new UL policies do not use a two-tiered interest crediting approach, some new and most older policies do. The two-tiered method credits interest on the first $1,000 or so of cash value at the minimum rate guaranteed in the contract, typically 4 to 4.5%. Cash value amounts in excess of $1,000 are credited with the current rate. Consequently, on policies that credit interest in this manner the current rate is not earned on the entire cash value.

4. Some UL policies, similar to many traditional whole life policies, use what is called the "direct recognition" method to determine the amounts credited to cash values that are subject to policy loans. Under this method, only the portion of the cash value that is not used to secure a loan is credited with the current rate; amounts backing the loan are credited with the minimum guaranteed rate or a rate usually 1 to 2 percentage points lower than the loan rate. The direct recognition method is most commonly used in policies that have fixed loan rates. Typically, policies with variable loan rates, and some others with fixed loan rates, do not employ the direct recognition method and instead credit current rates on the entire cash value without regard to loans.

5. Surrender of the policy within the first five to ten years may result in considerable loss since surrender values reflect the insurance company's recovery of sales commissions and initial policy expenses. In addition, most UL policies now assess surrender charges rather than up-front fees or loads. These surrender charges generally decline each year the policy is held. Generally, after about seven to fifteen years no explicit charges are assessed if the policy is surrendered.

6. The flexibility with respect to premium payments and death benefits permits policyowners to change the policy in such a way that it may inadvertently become a modified endowment contract (MEC) with adverse tax consequences.

TAX IMPLICATIONS

General Tax Rules

UL policies that do not run afoul of the modified endowment contract (MEC) rules are taxed in the same manner as other types of life insurance policies. Death benefits are usually paid free of any federal income tax. UL policies are subject to the same income, estate, gift, and generation-skipping transfer taxation rules as all other types of life insurance policies.

Living benefits from UL policies are also taxed in the same manner as living benefits from other types of life insurance policies. These living benefits are generally taxed under the cost-recovery rule. The cost recovery rule, which is sometimes called the FIFO (first-in first-out) rule, treats amounts received as nontaxable recovery of the policyowner's investment in the contract. Only after the policyowner's investment in the contract is fully recovered are additional amounts that are received treated as taxable interest or gain in the policy. Included in this category of living benefits are policy dividends, lump-sum cash settlements of cash surrender values, cash withdrawals, and amounts received on partial surrender. These amounts are included in gross income only to the extent they exceed the investment in the contract (as reduced by any prior excludable distributions received from the contract). In other words, nonannuity distributions during life are generally first treated as a return of the policyowner's investment in the contract, and then as taxable interest or gain.

Exception to the Cost Recovery Rule

There is an important exception to the general cost recovery rule for withdrawals within the first 15 years after the policy issue date that are coupled with reductions in death benefits. Since death benefits are generally reduced in an amount equal to any withdrawal of cash values, these withdrawals will generally be fully or partially taxable to the extent of gain in the policy.

Such withdrawals are taxed in whole or in part as ordinary income to the extent "forced out" of the policy as a result of the reduction in the death benefits. The taxable amount depends on when the withdrawal is made:

- *Within first five years* – If the withdrawal takes place within the first five years after policy issue, a very stringent and complex set of tests applies.[1] Potentially, a larger portion, or perhaps all, of any withdrawal within the first five years will be taxable if there is gain in the policy.

- *Fifth to fifteenth years* – For withdrawals between the end of the fifth year and the end of the fifteenth year from the issue date, a mathematical test applies. Essentially, the policyowner is taxed on an income-first basis to the extent the cash value before the withdrawal exceeds the maximum allowable cash value under the cash value corridor test for the reduced death benefit after the withdrawal.[2] Frequently, only a portion or none of the withdrawal will be taxable in these cases.

Changing from option B (increasing death benefit) to option A (level death benefit) will trigger a test to see whether any amount must be forced out of the policy. In general, option B contracts allow for greater cash accumulations within the policy than option A contracts. Consequently, if a policy with option B has close to the maximum permitted cash value, a switch to option A will generally trigger a taxable distribution. (See Appendices A through G for a complete discussion of the taxation of life insurance.)

Caveat: Potential Taxation under the Modified Endowment Contract Rules

The flexibility inherent in UL policies with respect to changes in premiums and death benefits raises the possibility that the policy could become a modified endowment contract (MEC).[3] The penalty for classification as a MEC relates to distributions. If a policy is classified as a MEC, "distributions under the contract" are taxed under the interest-first rule rather than the cost recovery rule. In addition, to the extent taxable, these distributions are subject to a 10% penalty if they occur before the policyowner reaches age 59½, dies, or becomes disabled. So MEC categorization of a UL contract means both faster taxation of investment gains and a possible penalty tax for "early" receipt of that growth.

"Distributions under the contract" include nonannuity living benefits (as described above), policy loans, loans secured by the policy, loans used to pay premiums, and dividends taken in cash. "Distributions under the contract" generally do *not* include dividends used to pay premiums, dividends used to purchase paid-up additions, dividends used to purchase one year term insurance, or the surrender of paid-up additions to pay premiums.

Changes in premiums or death benefits may inadvertently cause a UL policy to run afoul of the MEC rules in basically three ways:

1. An increase in premium payments during the first seven contract years may push the cumulative premiums above the amount permitted under the "seven-pay test."[4]

2. A reduction in the death benefit during the first seven contract years triggers a recomputation of the seven-pay test. The seven-pay test is applied retroactively as of the original issue date as if the policy had been issued at the reduced death benefit.

3. A "material" increase of the death benefit at any time triggers a new seven-pay test which is applied prospectively as of the date of the material change.

When issued, most UL policy illustrations show the maximum amount (the seven-pay guideline annual premium limit) that may be paid within the first seven years without having the policy classified as a MEC. If a policyowner inadvertently exceeds that maximum, MEC status can be avoided if excess premiums are returned to the policyowner with interest within 60 days after the end of the contract year in which the excess occurs. The interest will be subject to taxation.[5]

In general, a reduction in death benefit within the first seven contract years that is caused by and equal in amount to a withdrawal is less likely to cause the policy to fail the recomputed seven-pay test than a death benefit reduction without a withdrawal. However, a policy will fail the seven-pay test if in any year the cumulative premiums paid to that year exceed the sum of the seven-pay guideline annual premiums to that year.

Example. Assume the guideline annual premium is $10,000 based on the original death benefit. The policyowner pays $9,000 each year for the first 6 years. In year seven, the policyowner withdraws $36,000, with a corresponding decrease in the death benefit. The recomputed guideline premium is $8,000. The policy now fails the seven-pay test and is a MEC since cumulative premiums paid in just the first year, $9,000, (and through year 6 as well) exceed the sum of the recomputed guideline annual premiums of $8,000.

Any reduction in death benefits attributable to the nonpayment of premiums due under the contract will not trigger a recomputation of the seven-pay test if the benefits are reinstated within 90 days after being reduced.[6]

A change from option B (face amount plus cash value) to option A (face amount) appears to be a decrease that triggers the look-back rule and a retroactive reapplication of the seven-pay test. In general, one would not expect the switch in options to result in a lower seven-pay limit unless the face amount of insurance was also reduced to less than the face amount at the time of issue. Therefore, switching from option B to option A should not, in general, cause the policy to be reclassified as a MEC.

The term "material" change is not defined in the statute. However, the statute states that it "includes any increase in death benefit under the contract,"[7] but *not* increases attributable to dividends (for paid-up additions), interest credited to the policy's cash surrender value, increases necessary to maintain the corridor between the death benefit and the cash surrender value required by the definition of life insurance,[8] or cost-of-living adjustments. Whether changing from option A to option B constitutes a material change in death benefit is unclear. Other increases in death benefits that require evidence of insurability will be considered material changes that invoke a new seven-pay test. See Appendix D, "Modified Endowment Contracts" for more information.

ALTERNATIVES

A UL policy's premium payments and death benefits can be configured to resemble virtually any type of life insurance policy, from annually-renewable term to single premium whole life. Consequently, any other type of policy that meets a policyowner's needs is a suitable and, perhaps, preferable alternative if the UL's flexibility is not desired. However, a number of other types of policies or strategies offer some of the features of UL and not others, if only certain features are desired.

1. *Current-assumption whole life (CAWL)* – Sometimes called interest-sensitive whole life, CAWL is essentially UL without the adjustability features. CAWL, similar to UL, uses current interest rates in determining additions to cash values. However, similar to traditional ordinary whole life and in contrast with UL, CAWL generally offers the policyowner little flexibility with respect to changing premium payments or death benefits.

2. *Adjustable life (AL)* – AL combines elements of traditional, fixed-premium ordinary life insurance and the ability, within limits, to alter the policy plan, premium payments, and the face amount. AL can be viewed as UL without the current-assumption feature.

3. *Variable life (VL) and variable universal life (VUL)* – If a VL policyowner selects a portfolio of investments within the policy that is similar to the general investment portfolio of the insurance company (mostly long-term bonds and mortgages), investment performance and cash value accumulations can be expected to be similar to those with UL.

4. *Flexible premium deferred annuity (FPDA) combined with term insurance* – A combination of a FPDA with level term can generate cash value accumulations and death benefit levels similar to UL under option B. A FPDA combined with a decreasing term policy is similar to UL under option A. The FPDA, however, has less favorable tax treatment for withdrawals and loans than a UL policy.

5. IRC *Section 1035 exchanges* – The exchange provisions under Internal Revenue Code section 1035 allow certain types of exchanges from one policy type to another without adverse tax consequences. Clearly, these exchange provisions provide nowhere near the flexibility or convenience that a UL policy does to change premium levels or death benefits. However, the existence of these exchange provisions means that other types of policies are not quite as inflexible as they might otherwise seem.

WHERE AND HOW DO I GET IT?

There are nearly 2000 life insurance companies actively marketing coverage in the United States. The majority of these companies offer UL policies as well as other forms of permanent life insurance. In addition to commercial insurance companies, some fraternal organizations, savings banks, professional associations, membership organizations, and stock-brokerage houses offer UL policies. A policy can be purchased through one of many agents that represent a licensed insurance company.

Most companies have minimum death benefit requirements, ranging from $25,000 to $100,000, depending on age and policy form.

WHAT FEES OR OTHER ACQUISITION COSTS ARE INVOLVED?

UL policies charge front-end and/or back-end loads or surrender charges to recoup commissions paid to the selling agent and the expense of issuing the policy. Originally, UL policies were front-end loaded, but now most policies are issued with little or no front-end load. In other words, the policyowner's entire premium is credited to the cash value. Instead, companies assess a surrender charge that generally declines with longer durations. Surrender charges often start declining yearly after about the fifth policy year or sooner and reach zero in from seven to fifteen years. As a result of competition in the industry the trend has been towards starting the phase out of surrender charges sooner and more quickly.

The surrender charge can be determined explicitly by looking at the policy illustration or ledger statement. This statement shows both a cash value figure and a net cash value figure for each policy year. The cash value is the amount on which interest credits are based. The net cash value is the amount that the company would pay if the policy was surrendered. The difference is the surrender charge.

Commissions paid to agents depend on the size and timing of premium payments and how the policy is initially configured. They typically range from 20% to 55% (or higher) of the first year premium for premium amounts up to the "target level premium." The target level premium is generally the level annual premium the policyowner would have to pay if the policy was configured as a level-premium whole life policy. The commission on the portion of any premium payment that is in excess of the target level premium is lower, often about 3% to 8%. Commissions on subsequent premiums are usually lower. Total initial and renewal commissions generally equal about one year's target level premium if the original plan of insurance remains the same.

Policy issue expenses and commissions may be recouped in a number of ways including a flat policy assessment charge, a percentage of premium charge, a fee based on each $1,000 of face amount, or some combination of each. The trend has been towards lower policy assessment charges and level percentage of premium charges. Many insurers now charge about $25 to $50 per year plus 2½ to 20% of each premium. The percentage of premium charge is generally lower for higher-premium, higher-death-benefit policies than for lower-premium, lower-death-benefit policies.

HOW DO I SELECT THE BEST OF ITS TYPE?

Selecting the best cash value life insurance policy is a difficult task involving a number of complicated concepts. (See Chapter 4, "How to Determine the Right Policy," for a further discussion of the basic principles.) However, since the amount credited to cash values on UL policies is a critical element of the overall cost of the protection, one primary area of focus should be how the company determines the amount credited to cash values.

The amount credited to cash values each year depends on four factors:

1. the expenses charged against the policy;

2. the mortality charges assessed against the policy;

3. the net investment yield earned by the insurer on its portfolio of investments; and

4. the method used to allocate interest to various blocks of policies.

The cash value at the end of any given year is equal to the cash value from the end of the prior year plus premiums (or less withdrawals) paid during the year less expense and mortality charges and plus interest credited. The annual report will usually explicitly show the expense and mortality charges and the amount of interest that is credited each year.

Expense Charges

As described above, the expense charge is usually composed of two elements, a fixed annual fee plus a percentage of premiums paid. The company may or may not reveal these fees in its original policy illustration. However, even if it does, the company usually does not guarantee that the expense charges will not change. Actual expense charges may increase or decrease in future years.

Mortality Charges

Every UL contract explicitly states the maximum mortality rates it will charge for all ages and guarantees that mortality rates will not exceed those maximums.

Many companies now use the 2001 Commissioner's Standard Mortality (CSO) table as the basis for their contractually guaranteed maximum rates, but some companies still use the older 1980 CSO mortality table for their new policies. In addition, all policies issued before 2002 used the 1980 CSO mortality table or, possibly, the 1958 CSO mortality table. All three tables are very conservative – that is, they assume mortality rates that are considerably higher than what is actually expected – but the 1980 CSO table and, even more so, the 1958 CSO table are considerably more conservative than the 2001 CSO table. Virtually every company currently charges less than the stated maximums, but those using the more conservative 1980 or 1958 CSO tables have more room to increase mortality charges in future years if their mortality experience is poor.

Although annual statements explicitly show actual mortality charges, many policy illustrations do not. In fact, some illustrations assume very low or no mortality charges, which tend to show projected cash values that are overstated relative to what can actually be expected. Other illustrations include mortality charges based on rates the company is currently assessing, but they may also assume that there will be improvements in mortality experience in future years. If the mortality improvements do not materialize as anticipated, actual cash values are unlikely to match the projected cash values.

Net Investment Yield on Investment Portfolio

Over the long run, insurance companies cannot credit more interest to policy cash values than they earn on their general investment portfolios. To assess a company's long-run interest-crediting ability, one should evaluate the insurer's current portfolio and its investment philosophy.

As a general rule, insurance company portfolios are invested predominantly in long-term corporate and government bonds and mortgages. However, there are differences in the proportions invested in each type of asset and in the quality, duration, yields, and risk. In the past, some companies were pushed to insolvency because of overly aggressive investments in high-yield and high-risk junk bonds and developmental mortgage loans. Therefore, the objective should be to select companies with investment portfolios and investment philosophies that show a reasonable and acceptable combination of risk and return. What is reasonable and acceptable, of course, depends on the level of risk and the certainty of return desired by the policyowner.

Procedures for evaluating the investment portfolios of insurance companies are discussed in Chapter 3, "How to Determine the Right Company."

Interest–Crediting Methods

All UL policies, just like all other types of cash value policies, have a guaranteed minimum interest rate. The guaranteed rates range from 4 to 6%. The rate actually credited to cash values, called the current rate, is (or has historically been) higher than the guaranteed rate. Companies use various methods to determine the current rate they credit to cash values:

- *Linked rates* – Some companies link their current rates to some specified external, well-known index of yields, such as one-year T-bill rates or an index of intermediate-term high-quality corporate or government bond yields. For example, the current rate might be set at ½ of 1% less than the yield on the specified index.

- *Discretionary* – Many UL policies provide that the insurance company may use its discretion to determine the current rate. In other words, other than the upper limit set by the investment performance of its general portfolio, the insurance company may credit any rate it wishes. There is no guaranteed link between the rate earned by the company and the rate credited to policies. However, competitive pressures prevent companies from abusing their discretion and most companies use formulas related to their investment performance to allocate interest to policies.

- *Portfolio* – The formulas used by companies to determine their current rates on non-indexed UL policies may be based on "new money" rates or "portfolio" rates or, more commonly, some weighted average of new money and portfolio rates. The new money rate is the rate of return being earned on the new investments the company acquires with current premium dollars. It is essentially the average current market rate of return on the company's new investments. The portfolio rate is the rate of return on the company's general investment portfolio (or the portfolio of investments backing the block of policies). The portfolio rate is actually a blend of the rates earned on new and old money.

- *New money* – Since insurers invest principally in long-term fixed-income types of investments, new money rates are clearly more responsive to changing market interest rates than portfolio rates. This can work for or against the policyowner. If market rates are generally rising, UL cash values credited with new money rates will grow faster than those credited with portfolio rates. Conversely, if market rates are falling, UL policies credited with portfolio rates will have faster growing cash values.

- *Blending* – Most companies use a weighting scheme to produce a current rate that is a blend of new and old money rates somewhere between the portfolio rate and the new money rate. One method, called the "weighted-average portfolio" method, computes the current rate by blending new and old money rates in a specified proportion. For example, the current rate may be set at 20% of the new money rate and 80% of the old money rate. If the new money rate is 10% and the old money rate is 8%, the current rate would be set at 8.4%.

- *Modified portfolio* – Another method, which has been called the "modified portfolio" method, is the weighted-average percentage rollover method. This method credits a specified proportion (the rollover percentage) of the cash value and current premium payments with the new money rate each year. The rest of the cash value continues to be credited with the "old" new money rates that applied in previous years. That is, the specified percent of previously invested money plus interest on the cash value is rolled over each and every year into a new money rate. For example, (ignoring mortality and expense charges) assume the rollover percentage is 20% and the annual premium is $1,000.

Year 1: New money rate = 9%. The first year premium would be credited with 9%. End of year value, $1,090.

Year 2: New money rate = 8%. Second year premium, $1,000, plus 20% of the first year premium and interest, $218 (0.2 x $1,090), is credited with 8%. The remaining portion of the first year premium plus interest, $872, is credited with 9%. Total end of second year value, $2,265.92 [($1,218 x 1.08) + ($872 x 1.09)]. End of year second year money, $1,315.44. End of year remaining first year money, $950.48.

Year 3: New money rate = 10%. Third year premium, $1,000, plus 20% of remaining first year's money plus interest, $190.10 (0.2 x $950.48), plus 20% of second year's money plus interest, $263.09 (0.2 x $1,315.44), which totals $1,453.19, is credited with 10% interest. The remaining first year money plus interest, $760.38 (0.8 x $950.48), continues to get 9%. The remaining second year money plus interest, $1,052.35 (0.8 x $1,315.44), is credited with 8%. Total end of third year value, $3,563.86 [($1,453.19 x 1.10) + ($1,052.35 x 1.08) + ($760.38 x 1.09)]. End of year third year money, $1,598.51. End of year remaining second year money, $1,136.54. End of year remaining first year money, $828.81.

The process continues each year. After a number of years, each year's remaining money will be entirely absorbed or rolled over into later year's new money classes.

The amount of interest that is actually credited to any policy depends on the timing and size of premium payments. If large premium payments are made in years when the new money rate is high and no premium payments are made in years when new money rates are low, cash values will grow more rapidly. However, even if no premium payments are made in years when new money rates are low, the amount credited to cash values will reflect the low new money rates because the specified percentage of each prior year's money is always rolled over to the new money rate of the current year.

With either the weighted-average portfolio method or the modified portfolio method, the rate credited to cash values will be more responsive to changes in new money rates if the new money percentage or the rollover percentage is higher. If market rates are currently low by historical standards and market rates are expected to increase, one should look for companies with high new market or rollover percentages. Conversely, if market rates are currently high by historical standards and are expected to fall, one should look for companies that use lower new money or rollover percentages.

- *Direct recognition* – Some companies use the direct recognition method to determine the rate credited to the portion of the cash value that is secured by policy loans. Companies that use this method typically credit interest on the portion of the cash value that secures policy loans at the minimum guaranteed rate or 2 percentage points lower than the policy loan rate, whichever is higher.

- *Persistency bonus* – Some companies also pay periodic bonuses for persistency, that is, to reward long-term policyowners. These bonuses may be paid either as retrospective increases in the general interest rate or as lump-sum additions to the policy cash value. However, projected persistency bonuses that are not guaranteed should be viewed with caution. Bonuses that are not guaranteed may, in some cases, merely be a way to make illustrated values appear higher, without any requirement that the company actually pay the bonuses as illustrated.

How to Navigate through a Universal Life Ledger Statement

The principal source of information regarding a new policy is the policy illustration or ledger. Figure 17.1 shows an annotated UL policy illustration. Each of the numbers in the ledger corresponds to the following notes:[9]

1. Universal life is the type of insurance.

2. The premium is $2,001.

3. The initial death benefit of $100,000 is increased each and every year by the cash value amount of the policy. This is referred to as universal life option B or option II.

4. Insurability status – e.g., nonsmoker or smoker (would be standard), or rated (extra charge because of a higher risk for medical or occupational reasons). The preferred risk for this company means nonsmoker, nonrated. It is the company's best insurability classification.

5. Gender and issue age – male, age 45.

6. A premium of $2,001 is paid each year for 20 years. Starting in year 21, the premium is 0.

7. The initial face amount of life insurance payable to the named beneficiary is $100,000.

8. The premium is to be paid annually (once a year).

9. This is an end-of-the-year ledger statement.

10. A yearly premium of $2,001 is paid once a year each and every year for the first 20 years.

11. The amount withdrawn from the cash value as a living benefit. For this ledger statement, there are no withdrawals.

12. Guaranteed interest of 4.5% column. This is the minimum percentage rate at which the insurance company will accumulate the reserve. Under this column are cash value, net cash value, and death benefit. The cash value is the amount of reserve earning interest. It is not, however, available to borrow against nor is it the amount received if the policy is surrendered. The net cash value is the amount of money in any given year that is available to borrow against and is the amount of money payable if the policy is surrendered. It is also the amount that must appear on the balance sheet when necessary. The death benefit is based on the current interest rate of 8.5% for the first year only. Thereafter, the guaranteed minimum rate of 4.5% applies. The current mortality charges are for the first year only. Thereafter, the maximum mortality charges can be imposed. Under these assumptions, if no further premiums are paid, the insurance will lapse at age 72. For assumption purposes, the guaranteed section is the worst possible scenario.

13. Assumed interest rate of 8% column (the current interest rate is 8.5% for the first 10 years and 9.1% thereafter) is 50 basis points (0.50%) for the first 10 years and 110 basis points (1.1%) *less* than the current rate. Cash value is predicated on an 8% interest assumption. This is also true for the net cash value and the death benefit.

14. Life expectancy of a 45-year-old male is 29 years, or age 74.

15. Summary page indicates values based on the current interest rate, not the assumed rate. The assumed rate of 8% is less than the current rate, i.e., 8.5% for the first 10 years and 9.1% thereafter.

16. Interest adjusted index: guaranteed interest rate, current interest rate, and assumed rate. (See Chapter 4, "How to Determine the Right Policy.")

17. Explanatory notes page.

Figure 17.1

UNIVERSAL LIFE

1 UNIVERSAL LIFE

Premiums: First Year: $2,001.00 **2**
Increasing Death benefit Option **3**
Classification: Preferred   **4**

Insurance Age: 45 Sex: Male **5**
Thereafter: Varying **6**
Initial Face Amount: $100,000 **7**
Payment Mode: Annual **8**

9 End of Year	Age	**10** Yearly Premium	**11** Annual Withdrawal	**12** Guaranteed Interest of 4.5%			**13** Assumed Interest of 8.00%		
				Cash Value	Net Cash Value	Death Benefit	Cash Value	Net Cash Value	Death Benefit
1	46	$2,001.00	$0	$ 1,749	$ 809	$101,749	$ 1,749	$ 809	$101,749
2	47	2,001.00	0	3,198	2,362	103,198	3,615	2,779	103,615
3	48	2,001.00	0	4,658	3,927	104,658	5,606	4,874	105,606
4	49	2,001.00	0	6,124	5,497	106,124	7,731	7,104	107,731
5	50	2,001.00	0	7,589	7,067	107,589	9,999	9,476	109,999
6	51	2,001.00	0	9,047	8,629	109,047	12,416	11,998	112,416
7	52	2,001.00	0	10,490	10,177	110,490	14,994	14,681	114,994
8	53	2,001.00	0	11,911	11,702	111,911	17,744	17,536	117,744
9	54	2,001.00	0	13,301	13,196	113,301	20,678	20,574	120,678
10	55	2,001.00	0	14,650	14,650	114,650	23,810	23,810	123,810
11	56	2,001.00	0	15,948	15,948	115,948	27,155	27,155	127,155
12	57	2,001.00	0	17,180	17,180	117,180	30,724	30,724	130,724
13	58	2,001.00	0	18,332	18,332	118,332	34,533	34,533	134,533
14	59	2,001.00	0	19,386	19,386	119,386	38,596	38,596	138,596
15	60	2,001.00	0	20,326	20,326	120,326	42,925	42,925	142,925
16	61	2,001.00	0	21,129	21,129	121,129	47,538	47,538	147,538
17	62	2,001.00	0	21,773	21,773	121,773	52,444	52,444	152,444
18	63	2,001.00	0	22,235	22,235	122,235	57,658	57,658	157,658
19	64	2,001.00	0	22,486	22,486	122,486	63,189	63,189	163,189
20	65	2,001.00	0	22,495	22,495	122,495	69,052	69,052	169,052
21	66	0	0	20,262	20,262	120,262	73,226	73,226	173,226
22	67	0	0	17,621	17,621	117,621	77,590	77,590	177,590
23	68	0	0	14,522	14,522	114,522	82,149	82,149	182,149
24	69	0	0	10,909	10,909	110,909	86,907	86,907	186,907
25	70	0	0	6,730	6,730	106,730	91,866	91,866	191,866
26	71	0	0	1,931	1,931	101,931	97,027	97,027	197,027
27	72	0	0	*******	*******	*******	102,393	102,393	202,393
28	73	0	0				107,962	107,962	207,962
14 29	74	0	0				113,730	113,730	213,730
30	75	0	0				119,691	119,691	219,691
31	76	0	0				125,835	125,835	225,835
32	77	0	0				132,128	132,128	232,128
33	78	0	0				138,495	138,495	238,495
34	79	0	0				144,836	144,836	244,836
35	80	0	0				150,981	150,981	250,981

Figure 17.1 (cont'd)

End of Year	Age	Yearly Premium	Annual Withdrawal	Guaranteed Interest of 4.5%			Assumed Interest of 8.00%		
				Net Cash Value	Net Cash Value	Death Benefit	Cash Value	Cash Value	Death Benefit
36	81	0	0				156,756	156,756	256,756
37	82	0	0				162,020	162,020	262,020
38	83	0	0				166,526	166,526	266,526
39	84	0	0				170,032	170,032	270,032
40	85	0	0				172,170	172,170	272,170

Assumed interest rates are for illustrative purposes only; actual rates may be more or less than those shown.

UNIVERSAL LIFE

Plan Summary Page   **15**

Based on the Current Interest Rate

End of Year	(1) Total Premiums	(2) Total Withdrawals	(3) Net Cash Value	(4) Difference (1) - [(2) + (3)]	(5) Cash Value	(6) Death Benefit
5	$10,005	$0	$ 9,593	$ 411	$10,116	$110,116
10	20,010	0	24,450	4,440-	24,450	124,450
15	30,015	0	45,445	15,430-	45,445	145,445
20	40,020	0	76,137	36,117-	76,137	176,137
Age 65	40,020	0	76,137	36,117-	76,137	176,137

Interest-adjusted Indexes Based on a 5.00% Interest Rate for Basic Policy Only   **16**

	Guaranteed Interest of 4.5%		Current Interest of 8.5%		Assumed Interest of 8.00%	
	10 Years	20 Years	10 Years	20 Years	10 Years	20 Years
Surrender Cost	$ 8.39	$12.18	$ 1.38	$ 1.58-	$ 1.82	$ .60
Net Payment	18.84	18.01	18.41	16.46	18.44	16.60

Figure 17.1 (cont'd)

FLEXIBLE PREMIUM ADJUSTABLE LIFE
Explanatory Notes Page   17

The current rate is 8.50% for the first 10 years and 9.10% thereafter.   **18**

Each premium is credited with interest at the current rate of the company. The rate for the policy reflects the weighted average of the rate on each premium. A portion of the cash value is reinvested at the end of each year at the then-current rate.   **19**

The interest rates shown are effective annual rates. Interest is credited after deduction of expense and cost of insurance charges.   **20**

A policy loan balance may not be credited with the full current interest rate, but the rate applied will not be less than the greater of 4.5% and 2% less than the policy loan interest rate.   **21**

The net cash value equals the cash value minus any policy loan balance minus any surrender charge.   **22**

Actual amounts may differ from those shown due to changes in: current interest rate, cost of insurance rate, face amount, timing or amount of premiums, or death benefit option.   **23**

It is unlikely that dividends will be paid on this policy. Dividends, if any, will be small and paid only in later policy years.   **24**

This illustration incorporates the company's interpretation of the Tax Reform Act of 1984 as it pertains to the definition of life insurance in general and universal life in particular. The company will comply with any IRS regulations issued regarding its interpretation of the definition of life insurance.   **25**

The "Current" column uses current mortality costs and current interest rate, which are not guaranteed beyond the first year.   **26**

The "Guaranteed" column uses the current mortality costs for the first year and the current interest rate guaranteed for the initial premium. Thereafter, this column uses the guaranteed minimum interest rate and guaranteed maximum mortality costs.   **27**

28   A fixed policy loan interest rate of 8% applied against the net cash value.

18. Statement about the current interest rate at the time the ledger statement was printed.

19. Investment strategy of the insurance company.

20. Statement about how interest is credited.

21. Borrowed money does not earn the current interest rate of 8.5%. It will earn either 4.5% or 2% less than the current rate, whichever is greater.

22. The net cash value and the cash value are different up to year 10. Prior to year 10, the cash value is less than the net cash value because of a rear-end load. There are penalties if the policy is surrendered prior to the end of year 10.

23. Variables due to changes in interest rates, mortality charges, how premiums are paid, or changes in the death benefit option, e.g., going from option II to option I.

24. Dividend statement.

25. Insurance company statement that the ledger statement conforms to the Tax Reform Act of 1984 and meets the various tests, i.e., the net single premium, cash value accumulation, and corridor tests, as well as the guideline on annual premium for all policies issued on or after December 31, 1984.

26. Current column not used for this ledger statement. Guaranteed and assumed columns are used.

27. Guaranteed interest rate column statement.

28. Fixed contractual loan interest rate on loans against the reserve (net cash value) is 8 percent.

What Ledger Statements Do Not Tell

You should be told either verbally or in writing the following additional information:

- The investment strategy employed by the life insurance company is a modified portfolio rate, using a percentage rollover concept with investments having a maturity date of six to eight years. Percentage rollover means that X% of previously invested money plus interest earned on the reserve (the cash value) is rolled over each and every year into a new money rate.

- The ratio of current mortality charges as used in the ledger statement to the maximum charges that can be imposed should be revealed. For this ledger statement, the ratio of current charges to maximum charges for sequential years is as follows. The charges are shown on an annual basis (the actual mortality charges are deducted monthly) per $1,000 of insurance at risk.

Year	Age	Current	Maximum	Ratio
1	45	2.80	5.35	52%
5	50	3.72	7.60	49
10	55	5.37	11.91	45
15	60	7.69	18.62	41
20	65	11.93	29.11	41

- This reveals that there is ample margin for the insurance company to increase its mortality charges to protect itself against unduly high rates of mortality (such as among AIDS sufferers), changes in current tax law that govern how life insurance companies pay taxes, and just about any other area that may increase the cost of doing business.

- This particular universal life product has been priced by the insurance company to make a profit or a contribution to surplus, essentially through the investment spread.

- If necessary, the insurance company by contract can and will decrease the current interest rate to as low as 4.5% and increase the mortality charges to their maximum – if the cost of doing business so dictates.

- The rate of return expressed in terms of compound interest should be given either on the ledger statement or by the life insurance agent. Ideally, it should be provided for each year.

- The rate of return upon death for this policy for sequential years is as follows:

Year	Rate of Return
1	4,984.91%
5	94.28
10	31.93
20	12.37
29 (life expectancy)	8.38

- Once the rate of return upon death is known, then it can be determined what would have to be earned before taxes in other financial services products such as mutual funds, certificates of deposit, real estate, or commodities to duplicate the tax-exempt rate of return provided by life insurance. (For this purpose, it is assumed that the death benefit is considered life insurance proceeds and as such not subject to federal or state income taxes.) The before-tax rate of return is determined by dividing the life insurance rate of return by the marginal tax bracket subtracted from 100% (for 15%, the factor is 0.85; for 25%, 0.75; for 28%, 0.72; for 33%, 0.67; and for 35%, 0.65). The result is shown in Figure 17.2.

- The rate of return upon surrender should also be provided. When the rate of return upon surrender is positive, it means that taxes are due. Taxes are due on the difference between the cash surrender value and the premiums paid. The result before taxes is as follows:

Year	Rate of Return
1	-59.57%
5	-1.81
10	3.14
20	4.95
29 (life expectancy)	5.27

- The rate of return upon surrender even before taxes never equals the interest assumption of 8%.

- The ledger statement should be the official ledger statement produced by the computer

Figure 17.2

	BEFORE TAX RATE OF RETURN				
Year	15% taxpayer	25% taxpayer	28% taxpayer	33% taxpayer	35% taxpayer
1	5,864.60%	6,646.55%	6,923.49%	7,440.16%	7,669.09%
5	110.92	125.71	130.94	140.72	145.05
10	37.56	42.57	44.35	47.66	49.12
20	14.55	16.49	17.18	18.46	19.03
29 (life expectancy)	9.86	11.17	11.64	12.51	12.89

service of the life insurance company. It should be "bug-free."

WHERE CAN I FIND OUT MORE?

The following references include authoritative discussions of various types of life insurance including universal life insurance:

1. B. Anderson, *Anderson on Life Insurance* (Waltham, MA: Little, Brown and Company, 1991).

2. B. Baldwin, *New Life Insurance Investment Advisor: Achieving Financial Security for You and Your Family Through Today's Insurance Products*, 2nd ed. (Hightstown, NJ: McGraw-Hill Trade, 2001).

3. J. Belth, Life Insurance: A Consumer's Handbook, 2nd ed. (Bloomington, IN: Indiana University Press, 1985).

4. K. Black, Jr. and H. Skipper, Jr., *Life Insurance*, 13th ed. (Old Tappan, NJ: Prentice Hall Inc., 1999).

5. E. Graves, Editor, *McGill's Life Insurance*, 5th ed. (Bryn Mawr, PA: The American College, 2004).

The following references are useful guides for policy and company rating information:

1. *Best Insurance Reports* (Oldwick, NJ: A. M. Best Company, published annually).

2. *Best's Review – Life/Health Edition* (Oldwick, NJ: A. M. Best Company, published monthly).

CHAPTER ENDNOTES

1. IRC Secs. 7702(f)(7)(B), 7702(f)(7) (C).

2. IRC Secs. 7702(f)(7)(B), 7702(f)(7) (D). The cash value corridor test is discussed in Appendix F, "Taxation of Benefits."

3. In cases where there are extreme reductions in the death benefit or very large premium payments, it is even possible for a policy to fail the tests for life insurance under IRC Section 7702 with much more disastrous tax consequences. See the discussion of the definition of life insurance in Appendix F, "Taxation of Benefits."

4. IRC Sec. 7702A(a)(1)(B). Classification as a MEC occurs in the year when the seven-pay test is first violated and for each year thereafter. See Appendix D, "Modified Endowment Contracts," for a more complete discussion of the seven-pay test.

5. IRC Sec. 7702A(e)(1).

6. IRC Sec. 7702A(c)(2)(B).

7. IRC Sec. 7702A(c)(3).

8. IRC Sec. 7702. See Appendix F "Taxation of Benefits."

9. This illustration is adapted from William D. Brownlie's treatise, *The Life Insurance Buyer's Guide*, McGraw-Hill Publishing Company, 1989.

Chapter 18

VARIABLE AND VARIABLE UNIVERSAL LIFE

WHAT IS IT?

Variable Life

Variable life (VL) insurance combines traditional whole life insurance with mutual-fund type investments. Basically, it is a whole life policy where the policyowner may direct the investment of cash values among a variety of different investments.

VL has a guaranteed minimum face amount and a level premium like traditional life insurance, but it differs in three respects:

1. The policyowner's funds are placed in separate accounts that are distinct and separate from the company's general investment fund.

    Premiums less an expense or sales load and a mortality charge are paid into a separate investment account. The policyowner may choose to invest premiums and cash values among several mutual-fund type alternatives, typically including stock funds, bond funds, and money-market funds. Many companies that market VL offer a broad array of investment options such as foreign stock funds, bond funds, GNMA funds, real estate funds, zero-coupon bond funds, and specialized funds such as small-capitalization stock funds, market index funds, and funds that focus on specific sectors of the economy or industries (medical, high-tech, gold, leisure, utilities, etc.). Some companies offer a managed fund option where the company's investment manager assumes the responsibility for apportioning investments among the various alternative funds. Some VL policies also offer a guaranteed interest option similar to the declared interest rate on universal life policies. Policyowners may typically switch or rebalance their investments among the funds one or more times per year.

2. There is no guaranteed minimum cash value.

The cash value at any point in time is based on the market value of the assets in the separate account. VL policyowners bear *all* the investment risk associated with the policy.

3. The death benefit is variable.

    The face value may increase or decrease, but not below the guaranteed minimum, based on a formula that relates the investment performance of the separate account to the face value. Companies use two methods to establish the relationship between the investment performance and the face amount. Under what is called the corridor percentage approach, the death benefit is periodically adjusted so that it is at least equal to a specified percentage of the cash value, as required by current tax law.[1] The mandated corridor percentage is 250% until the insured reaches age 40 and then gradually declines to 100% by age 95.

    Example. Assume the cash value is $40,000 at the beginning of the period and $50,000 at the end of the period. The insured is 60 years old. The initial death benefit is $52,000 and the corridor percentage factor is 130%. At the end of the period, the death benefit will be $65,000, or 130% of $50,000.

    The death benefit under what is called the net single premium approach is periodically adjusted so that it matches the amount of insurance that could be purchased with a single premium equal to the cash value, assuming guaranteed mortality rates and a low rate of return, typically 4%.

    Example. Assume the net single premium factor in the example above is 0.65374. That is, it takes $0.65374 to buy $1 of insurance for life. At the end of the period, the death benefit will be $50,000/0.65374, or $76,483.

Although both methods are equally valid, most policyowners find the corridor percentage method easier to understand.

VL has most of the usual features of traditional level-premium life insurance including guaranteed maximum mortality charges, nonforfeiture values, a policy loan provision, a reinstatement period, and settlement options.

Also, VL policies may be participating or nonparticipating. In contrast to traditional par policies, dividends paid on par VL policies depend only on possible mortality and expense savings and include no element of excess investment earnings. Excess investment earnings, less an asset management fee, are reflected in the value of the separate account.

Similar to other traditional forms of insurance, various options or riders are available including waiver of premium, guaranteed purchase or insurability, and accidental death benefits.

Insurers that market VL often offer a number of premium payment plans including single-premium, limited-pay (for a specified number of years or until a specified age), and lifetime-pay plans.

Variable Universal Life

Variable universal life (VUL), which is also called flexible-premium variable life or universal life II, is a combination of universal life and variable life. VUL offers policyowners the flexibility of universal life (UL) with respect to premium payments and death benefits. Specifically, VUL owners can:

1. Determine the timing and amount of premium payments (within limits);

2. Skip a premium payment if the cash value is sufficient to cover the mortality and expense charges;

3. Adjust the amount of the death benefit in response to inflation or changing needs (subject, generally, to policy minimums and, with respect to increases, evidence of insurability requirements);

4. Withdraw money without creating a policy loan and without an interest charge if there is sufficient cash value to cover mortality and expense charges; and

5. Choose between two death benefit options similar to options A (or I) and B (or II) for UL policies. Under option A, the death benefit remains level, similar to a traditional policy. Under option B, the death benefit is equal to a level pure insurance amount plus the cash value.

The death benefit of a VUL policy is not "variable" in the same sense as the death benefit of a VL policy. Under option B, the death benefit will vary directly, not indirectly by formula, with changes in the cash value. Under option A, the death benefit is level. However, the death benefit of VUL policies is flexible or adjustable, within limits and subject to insurability requirements, at the discretion of the insured.

VUL policyowners receive periodic reports that explicitly show mortality and expense charges and changes in the investment value of their accounts.

Since variable life products are considered securities, prospective purchasers must be given a prospectus. The prospectus contains the identity and nature of the insurer's business, the use to which the insurer will put the premiums, financial information on the insurer, and the investment characteristics of the product, as well as the policy's expenses, fees, loads, and policyowner rights. In addition, the agent must be properly licensed to sell security products.

WHEN IS THE USE OF THIS TOOL INDICATED?

Variable life products are most suitable for those individuals who want control over their cash values and need or desire increasing life insurance protection. They should have a basic understanding of investments and believe they are capable of making good investment decisions. They must be willing to bear the entire risk of their investments, since cash values are not guaranteed. If the need for death protection is expected to grow, VL death benefit levels will increase with favorable investment experience on the underlying assets. However, there is no assurance that this growth will be consistent. There is a risk that the market value of the underlying assets, and therefore the death benefit level, will be depressed when the insured dies.

VUL offers greater certainty of death benefit levels than VL as long as premiums continue to be paid at the level necessary to maintain the death benefit. Under option B, death benefit levels are more certain to increase. VUL also permits the policyowner to increase the face amount of coverage with evidence of insurability.

Given the risks and uncertainties associated with both cash values and death benefit levels, variable life products can be attractive supplements to an existing life insurance plan that assures a minimum required base level of coverage. It is less suitable as the means of providing the minimum basic level of coverage.

VL and, more particularly, VUL are especially suitable for many business insurance needs where flexibility and growth of cash values and death benefits are necessary or attractive features. It can be used to provide potentially higher tax-deferred cash value accumulations in nonqualified deferred compensation plans than traditional policies or UL. With successful investment of cash values, the death benefit levels of variable products are more likely than those of traditional products to keep pace with increases in the values of closely-held business interests when a variable product funds a buy-sell agreement. VL and VUL may be equally attractive for key person insurance and other business applications or in insured pension plans.

ADVANTAGES

1. Policyowners have control over how premiums and cash values are invested. They may generally allocate their investments as desired among a variety of mutual-fund type investment accounts.

2. Switches or transfers between funds are permitted at least once and usually more times per year, usually with no charge.

3. Switches or transfers between funds are tax-free.

4. Cash values of VL and VUL policies are more secure in the event of insurer insolvency than cash values of other types of policies. Assets backing VL and VUL policies are in separate accounts that are segregated from the general investment portfolio of the insurer. Cash values are also based on the market value of the assets in the separate accounts. Therefore, cash values are readily available in the event of insurer insolvency. In contrast, since cash values in other types of policies are not adjusted to the market value of the assets in the insurer's general portfolio, in the event of insolvency, the general portfolio may not have sufficient assets to cover cash values.

5. Earnings on the assets underlying the policy cash values accumulate tax-free or tax-deferred, depending on whether gains are distributed at death or during lifetime.

6. VL provides some measure of automatic increases in death benefits that may keep pace with inflation. Death benefits of VL policies are tied to changes in the underlying value of the assets backing the policy. Since the rate of return assumed when setting the guaranteed minimum death benefit is relatively low, death benefits should generally trend upward and provide some measure of inflation protection.

7. A VUL policyowner has wide discretion or flexibility in selecting the timing and amount of premium payments. Provided that there is enough cash value to cover mortality and other account charges, the policyowner may even skip premium payments. In contrast with other types of policies, skipping premiums does not result in the creation of policy loans.

8. VUL permits the policyowner to change the level of death benefits. Decreases in the death benefit are permitted at virtually any time. However, policyowners who reduce death benefits within the first seven years of issue may be subjected to adverse tax consequences under the modified endowment contract (MEC) rules. Increases in face amount are generally permitted, subject to evidence of insurability. Increases in the death benefit may also subject the policy to a new test period under the MEC rules. (See discussion under "Tax Implications," below.)

9. VUL policies are transparent. Annual reports break out and report each of the policy elements separately. This unbundling allows the policyowner to specifically identify and track premiums, death benefits, interest credits, mortality charges, expenses, and cash values and to check projections with actual performance over time.

10. Most VUL policies offer two death benefit patterns, called option A (or I) and option B (or II). Option A, similar to a traditional whole life policy, offers a fixed or level death benefit. As cash values grow larger, the net amount at risk, the pure insurance, is reduced to keep the total death benefit constant (unless the cash value grows to an amount where the death benefit must be increased to avoid classification as a MEC). Option B operates in a manner similar to the death benefit one would receive from a traditional whole life policy with a term insurance rider that is equal to the current cash value. Under option B, the death benefit at any time is equal to a specified level of pure insurance plus the policy's cash value at the time of death. Therefore, the death benefit increases as the cash value grows.

11. Some companies offer cost-of-living riders to VUL option A policies that, without evidence of insurability, automatically increase the policy death benefit periodically by the increase in the CPI. The increasing death benefit associated with option B generally makes the need for a cost-of-living rider under this option moot.

12. In contrast with most traditional whole life policies, many VUL policies use back-end loads, rather than front-end loads, to recover the initial policy expenses. Consequently, most or all of the policyowner's initial premiums go into cash values subject, of course, to regular annual expense and mortality charges. Therefore, cash values build more quickly than with traditional whole life policies.

13. Policy cash values can be borrowed at a low net cost. Although policyowners must pay interest on policy loans, the cash value backing the loan is credited with an interest rate slightly lower than that paid by the policyowner on the loan. Consequently, the actual net borrowing rate is less than the stated policy loan rate.

14. In most VUL policies policyowners may withdraw a substantial portion of their cash value without surrendering the policy. However, if money is withdrawn, the pure life insurance portion of the death benefit is often reduced by the amount of the withdrawal. In addition, withdrawals may be subject to income tax. (See discussion under "Tax Implications," below.)

15. Life insurance proceeds are not part of the probate estate, unless the estate is named as the beneficiary of the policy. Therefore, the proceeds can be paid to the beneficiary without the expense, delay, or uncertainty caused by administration of the estate.

DISADVANTAGES

1. The policyowner bears all investment risk. There is no minimum schedule of cash values as with UL or traditional whole life policies. Instead, cash values are equal to the market value of the policy assets in the separate accounts.

2. VL death benefits depend on the investment performance of the assets underlying the policy. If market values are down when the insured dies, the death benefit may be less than anticipated, but not less than the guaranteed minimum benefit.

3. If the investment performance of a VUL policy is poor, the policyowner may be required to pay additional premiums to maintain the face amount of coverage.

4. VUL policyowners must accept all responsibility for premium payments. This can be a disadvantage since policyowners can too easily allow their policies to lapse. There is no forced savings feature, since premium payments are not required as long as there is sufficient cash value to carry the policy. To reduce the likelihood of lapse, most companies "bill" policyowners for a target premium set by the policyowner.

5. VL and VUL policyowners bear some mortality and expense risk since these policies are "current-assumption" policies with respect to mortality and expenses. VL and VUL only guarantee that mortality charges and expense rates will not exceed certain maximums. In contrast, traditional participating whole life policies guarantee mortality and expense charges. Consequently, policyowners bear more of the risk of adverse trends in mortality or expenses than if they owned traditional whole life policies. However, is also true that if the trend of mortality costs and expenses improves, policyowners may participate in the improvement through lower charges.

6. Lifetime distributions or withdrawals of cash values are subject to income tax to the extent attributable to gain in the policy.

7. Realized capital gains on the underlying assets when taking withdrawals or surrendering the policy are taxed as ordinary income. Effective federal income tax rates on ordinary income may be as high as 35% or higher (depending on phase outs of personal exemptions and itemized deductions). In contrast, capital gains recognized on sales of similar mutual fund shares are treated as capital gains generally taxed at a maximum federal tax rate of 15%. In addition, capital gains can be used to offset other capital losses if from a mutual fund but not if from a life insurance policy.

8. Surrender of the policy within the first 5 to 10 years may result in considerable loss since surrender values reflect the insurance company's recovery of sales commissions and initial policy expenses. In addition, most VUL policies levy surrender charges rather than up-front fees or loads. These surrender charges generally decline each year the policy is

held. Generally, after about 7 to 10 years no explicit charges are assessed if the policy is surrendered.

9. The flexibility with respect to premium payments and death benefits in VUL permits policyowners to change the policy in such a way that it may inadvertently become a modified endowment contract with adverse tax consequences.

10. Expense loadings are generally greater than with other types of policies.

TAX IMPLICATIONS

General Tax Rules

VL products that do not violate the modified endowment contract rules are taxed in the same manner as other types of life insurance policies. Death benefits are usually paid free of any federal income tax. Variable life insurance policies are subject to the same income, estate, gift, and generation-skipping transfer taxation rules as all other types of life insurance policies.

Living benefits from VL products are also taxed in the same manner as living benefits from other types of life insurance policies. Annuity-type distributions are taxed under the cost recovery rules of Internal Revenue Code section 72, which states that the policyowner's investment in the contract (generally, total premiums paid less prior nontaxable distributions) is recovered ratably over the expected payout period.

Interest paid on or credited to living benefits held by the insurer under an agreement to pay interest is immediately taxable in full. All other types of living benefits are generally taxed under the cost-recovery rule. The cost-recovery rule, which is sometimes called the FIFO (first-in first-out) rule, treats amounts received as nontaxable recovery of the policyowner's investment in the contract. Only after the policyowner's investment is fully recovered are additional amounts received treated as taxable interest or gain in the policy. Included in this category of living benefits are policy dividends, lump-sum cash settlements of cash surrender values, cash withdrawals and amounts received on partial surrender. Such amounts are included in gross income only to the extent they exceed the investment in the contract (as reduced by any prior excludable distributions received from the contract). In other words, nonannuity distributions during life are generally first treated as a return of the policyowner's investment in the contract, and then as taxable interest or gain.

Exception to the Cost–Recovery Rule

There is an important exception to the general cost-recovery rule for withdrawals within the first 15 years after the policy issue date that are coupled with reductions in death benefits. Since death benefits are generally reduced in an amount equal to any withdrawal of cash values, these withdrawals will generally be fully or partially taxable to the extent of gain in the policy.

Such withdrawals are taxed in whole or in part as ordinary income to the extent "forced out" of the policy as a result of the reduction in the death benefits. The taxable amount depends on when the withdrawal is made:

- *Within first five years* – If the withdrawal takes place within the first five years after policy issue, a very stringent and complex set of tests applies.[2] Potentially, a larger portion, or perhaps all, of any withdrawal within the first five years will be taxable if there is gain in the policy.

- *Fifth to fifteenth years* – For withdrawals between the end of the fifth year and the end of the fifteenth year from the issue date, a mathematical test applies. Essentially, the policyowner is taxed on an income-first basis to the extent the cash value before the withdrawal exceeds the maximum allowable cash value under the cash value corridor test for the reduced death benefit after the withdrawal.[3] Frequently, only a portion or none of the withdrawal will be taxable in these cases.

Changing from option B (increasing death benefit) to option A (level death benefit) will trigger a test to see whether any amount must be forced out of the policy. In general, option B contracts allow for greater cash accumulations within the policy than option A contracts. Consequently, if a policy with option B has close to the maximum permitted cash value, a switch to option A will generally trigger a taxable distribution. (See Appendices A through F for a complete discussion of the taxation of life insurance.)

Caveat: Potential Taxation under the MEC Rules

The flexibility inherent in VUL policies with respect to changes in premiums and death benefits raises the possibility that the policy could become a modified endowment contract (MEC).[4] The penalty for classification as a MEC relates to distributions. If a policy is classified as a MEC, "distributions under the contract" are taxed under the interest-first rule rather than the cost-recovery rule. In addition, to the extent taxable, these distributions are subject to a 10% penalty if they occur before the policyowner reaches age 59½, dies, or becomes disabled. So MEC categorization of a VUL contract means both faster taxation of investment gains and a possible penalty tax for "early" receipt of that growth.

"Distributions under the contract" include nonannuity living benefits (as described above), policy loans, loans secured by the policy, loans used to pay premiums, and dividends taken in cash. "Distributions under the contract" do *not* include dividends used to pay premiums, dividends used to purchase paid-up additions, dividends used to purchase one year term insurance, or the surrender of paid-up additions to pay premiums.

Changes in premiums or death benefits may inadvertently cause a VUL policy to run afoul of the MEC rules in basically three ways:

1. An increase in premium payments during the first seven contract years may push the cumulative premiums above the amount permitted under the seven-pay test.[5]

2. A reduction in the death benefit during the first seven contract years triggers a recomputation of the seven-pay test. The seven-pay test is applied retroactively as of the original issue date as if the policy had been issued at the reduced death benefit.

3. A "material" increase of the death benefit at any time triggers a new seven-pay test which is applied prospectively as of the date of the material change.

When issued, most VUL policy illustrations show the maximum amount (the seven-pay guideline annual premium limit) that may be paid within the first seven years without having the policy classified as a MEC. If a policyowner inadvertently exceeds that maximum, MEC status can be avoided if excess premiums are returned to the policyowner with interest within 60 days after the end of the contract year in which the excess occurs. The interest will be subject to taxation.[6]

In general, a reduction in death benefit within the first seven contract years that is caused by and equal in amount to a withdrawal is less likely to cause the policy to fail the recomputed seven-pay test than a death benefit reduction without a withdrawal. However, a policy will fail the seven-pay test if, in any year, the cumulative premiums paid to that year exceed the sum of the seven-pay guideline annual premiums to that year.

Example. Assume the guideline annual premium is $10,000 based on the original death benefit. The policyowner pays $9,000 each year for the first 6 years. In year seven, the policyowner withdraws $36,000, with a corresponding decrease in the death benefit. The recomputed guideline premium is $8,000. The policy now fails the seven-pay test and is a MEC since cumulative premiums paid in just the first year, $9,000, (and through year 6 as well) exceed the sum of the recomputed guideline annual premiums of $8,000.

Any reduction in death benefits attributable to the nonpayment of premiums due under the contract will not trigger a recomputation of the seven-pay test if the benefits are reinstated within 90 days after being reduced.[7]

A change from option B (face amount plus cash value) to option A (face amount) appears to be a decrease that triggers the look-back rule and a retroactive reapplication of the seven-pay test. In general, one would not expect the switch in options to result in a lower seven-pay limit unless the face amount of insurance was also reduced to less than the face amount at the time of issue. Therefore, switching from option B to option A should not, in general, cause the policy to be reclassified as a MEC.

The term "material" change is not defined in the statute. However, the statute states that it "includes any increase in future benefits under the contract,"[8] but *not* increases attributable to dividends (for paid-up additions), increases in the policy's cash surrender value attributable to the investment performance of assets underlying the policy, increases necessary to maintain the corridor between the death benefit and the cash surrender value required by the definition of life insurance,[9] or cost-of-living adjustments.

Clearly, increases in death benefits attributable to cash value increases from favorable investment performance will not trigger testing under the material change rules. Whether changing from option A to option B constitutes a material change in death benefit is unclear. Other increases in death benefits that require evidence of insurability will be considered material changes that invoke a new seven-pay test. See Appendix D for more information.

Taxation of Capital Gains on the Underlying Assets

Capital appreciation on the assets underlying a VL or VUL policy loses its character as capital gain. To the extent taxable, withdrawals or surrenders are taxed at ordinary income tax rates. The maximum federal tax table rate on ordinary income is 35%, but effective tax rates can be even higher due to the phaseout of personal exemptions and itemized deductions. In contrast, capital appreciation recognized on the sale of similar mutual fund investments is treated as capital gains. The maximum federal tax rate on long-term capital gains is 15%. In addition, capital gains may be used to offset capital losses.

Taxation of Transfers between Investment Funds

Transfers or switches between one fund and another offered by an insurer under a VL or VUL policy are tax free. In contrast, similar switches between funds in a family of mutual funds are treated as taxable sales and repurchases. However, in recent years, legislation has been proposed to tax transfers or switches between one fund and another under a VL or VUL life policy or annuity in a manner similar to switches between funds in a mutual fund family. Although these proposals have never survived legislative debate, the possibility clearly exists that such proposals could be enacted in the future.

ALTERNATIVES

VL is the insurance industry's answer to the buy-term-and-invest-the-difference strategy. It provides investment options similar to those available from mutual funds, but wrapped within the insurance policy. The loadings and expense charges in the VL policy typically exceed the combined loadings and expense charges of a buy-term-and-invest-in-a-mutual-fund strategy. However, investment earnings within the policy are tax-deferred and death proceeds are received tax free. In contrast, mutual fund dividends and realized capital gains are taxable when received or recognized. For long-term insurance/investment needs, the benefit of a VL policy's tax-deferred accumulation will typically overcome the cost of the higher loadings and fees.

A VUL policy's premium payments and death benefits can be theoretically configured to resemble virtually any type of life insurance policy, from annually-renewable term life to single-premium whole life. As a practical matter, most VUL policies are issued with target premiums at least equal to a lifetime-payment plan of insurance. Consequently, any other type of policy that meets a policyowner's needs may be a suitable, and perhaps preferable, alternative if the VUL's premium and death benefit flexibility is not desired or the policyowner does not wish to bear all the investment risk. However, a number of other types of policies or strategies offer some of the features of VUL and not others, if only certain features are desired.

1. *Traditional universal life* – UL offers the same premium and death benefit flexibility as VUL, but it also provides a minimum cash value guarantee. If the insurer's general portfolio has the risk and return characteristics desired by the policyowner, UL may be a better alternative than VUL. Policy loadings and expenses are generally lower on UL policies than on VUL policies.

2. *Adjustable life (AL)* – AL combines elements of traditional, fixed-premium ordinary life insurance and the ability, within limits, to alter the policy plan, premium payments, and the face amount. AL can be viewed as VUL without the investment options.

3. *Flexible-premium variable annuity (FPVA) combined with term insurance* – A combination of a FPVA with level term can generate cash value accumulations and death benefit levels similar to VUL under option B. A FPVA combined with a decreasing term policy is similar to VUL under option A. The FPVA, however, has less favorable tax treatment for withdrawals and loans than a VUL policy.

WHERE AND HOW DO I GET IT?

Many life insurance companies, including some of the largest, are marketing variable life products. Variable life products are also marketed by most of the major stock brokerage firms. Agents who sell variable life products must be properly licensed to sell security products.

WHAT FEES OR OTHER ACQUISITION COSTS ARE INVOLVED?

Fees and charges on variable products tend to be somewhat higher than on traditional products because of the additional expenses of registering the contracts with the Securities and Exchange Commission and the additional administration, record keeping, and reporting responsibilities associated with the products. In contrast with traditional life products, the securities laws require extensive disclosure of fees and charges in the offering prospectus. VL and VUL policies have two broad classes of fees – charges to the policy and charges to the cash value account. Because of differences in the way premiums and face amounts are handled in VL and VUL policies, some of these fees and charges are treated differently in each type of policy.

Charges to VL Policies

Charges to VL policies include sales loads, a one-time policy fee, annual administration charges, a state premium tax charge, a risk charge and, in some cases, switching fees.

Most companies levy sales loads (principally to pay commissions) in the first year of not more than 30% of the premium. The percentage is generally lower on higher-premium limited-pay policies than on lifetime-pay policies. The sales load on premiums in the subsequent years typically grades down from a maximum of 10% in the second year to 7.5% or lower in later years. In general, SEC rules prohibit aggregate fees and charges from exceeding a reasonable amount in relation to the services provided and the risks assumed.

Policy fees generally range from $3 to $10 per $1,000 of guaranteed face amount. Annual administrative charges typically range from $5 to $70, often with a higher charge in the first year and lower charges in subsequent years. The premium tax charge varies by state but is usually about 2 to 2½% of each premium. Risk charges, which are assessed to compensate the company for the risk that the insured may die when the death benefits are below the guaranteed amount, are often specified as a percentage of the premium ranging from 1 to 3%. Alternatively, some companies compute the risk charge as a dollar amount per $1,000 of guaranteed face amount with charges generally ranging from $0.50 to $1.50 per thousand of face amount. Most companies permit one or more switches or transfers of money among the various accounts each year without fees. Additional switches are generally permitted but the company usually charges from $5 to $30 for this service.

Charges to the VL Cash Value Accounts

Charges to the cash value account include the cost of insurance (mortality charges), mortality and risk expense, and investment management fees and expenses.

Mortality charges are based on the company's current mortality rate as applied to the net amount at risk (the difference between the death benefit and the cash value). Current mortality rates will vary depending on the company's experience but are guaranteed not to exceed certain maximums at each age as specified in the contract. The mortality and risk expense charge is taken against each account within a policy for the risk that the insureds as a group will live for a shorter period of time than estimated and the risk that the administrative expenses will be greater than estimated. This charge usually ranges from 0.1 to 0.9% of the assets in the account. Management fees and expenses vary by the type of fund and the investment activity within the fund and are similar to those fees and expenses associated with mutual funds. For instance, money market funds, bond funds, and stock index funds have lower management fees and expenses than general stock funds, which also have lower fees and expenses than real estate funds and foreign stock and bond funds. Management fees typically range from 0.25 to 2% of the assets in the fund. Expenses, expressed as a percent of assets in the fund, similarly range from about 0.25 to 2%.

Charges to VUL Policies

Policy and account charges on VUL policies are similar to those on VL policies with the exception of the sales loads. Similar to regular universal life, VUL policies charge front-end and/or back-end loads or surrender charges to recoup commissions paid to the selling agent and the expense of issuing the policy. Most companies levy a surrender charge of up to 25% if money is withdrawn in the first year. The surrender charge generally declines in later years. Surrender charges often start declining yearly after about the fifth policy year or sooner and reach zero in from 10 to 20 years. As a result of competition in the industry, the trend has been towards starting the phaseout of surrender charges sooner and more quickly.

HOW DO I SELECT THE BEST OF ITS TYPE?

The key factors in choosing the best VL or VUL policy are the policy loadings and expenses, the suitability and variety of the investment options, and the relative performance of the company's alternative investment accounts. The prospectus must list and explain the various loadings and charges. However, since there is a great deal of variability in these loadings and expenses, it is difficult to determine which policy provides the lowest effective "package" of fees over the long term. The best procedure is to ask for policy illustrations with equal face amount and rate of return assumptions and to compare future cash value accumulations. This is not without its problems, however, since the companies may have different current mortality assumptions and may or may not be assuming future improvements in their mortality experience.

Some companies offer a broader array of investment options than others. All else being equal, the company with the broadest array of offerings should be preferred.

The relative performance of the various investment accounts can be evaluated in much the same manner as one would evaluate mutual funds. The prospectus provides historical information about total returns, expense ratios, and turnover rates. In addition, it must describe the investment management fees. One should compare similar types of funds offered by each company to control for risk. For example, only compare long-term bond funds with long-term bond funds or diversified stock funds with diversified stock funds. A sophisticated analysis would compare risk-adjusted returns, but that can be a daunting task for less knowledgeable investors.[10]

All else being equal, look for companies offering funds with the lowest management fees, the lowest turnover rates, the lowest investment expense ratios, and the highest total returns (or best risk-adjusted return).

How to Navigate Through a Variable Life Ledger Statement

The principal source of information regarding a new policy is the policy illustration or ledger. Figure 18.1 shows an annotated policy illustration with the following commentary.[11]

1. Initial death benefit is $100,000; plan of life insurance is variable life.

2. Gender and issue age–male, age 45.

3. $2,394 is the annual premium.

4. Projected dividends are determined by mortality and expense factors used to purchase variable benefit paid-up life insurance. The projected dividends are small (e.g., at the beginning of the second year - $490; at the beginning of the fifth year - $592; at the beginning of the tenth year - $652; and at the beginning of the twentieth year - $453).

5. End-of-year ledger statement. This means the initial death benefit of $100,000 is assumed to be paid at the beginning of the year. Subsequent death benefit, depending upon the interest assumption (e.g., 0%, 6%, and 12%), is assumed to be paid at the end of the year. Cash values (the assumed values of the separate investment account–0, 6, and 12%) are calculated as of the end of the year.

6. Out-of-pocket cash payment is $2,394 each year, paid on an annual basis.

7. 5% interest assumption column. The value of $2,394 compounded at 5% if not used to purchase life insurance.

8. Death benefit increase because of the projected dividends purchasing additional paid-up life insurance. In the absence of dividends, the death benefit would not increase because the separate investment account must produce a rate of return in excess of 4 percent in order for the death benefit to increase.

9. Death benefit increases due to the projected dividends purchasing additional paid-up life insurance and the 6% interest assumption.

10. Death benefit increases due to projected dividends purchasing additional paid-up life insurance and 12% interest assumption.

11. This column has a value even at 0% interest assumption because not all of the premiums paid were required to meet the insurance company's expenses.

12. The projected value of the separate investment account (cash value) based on a net investment return (after expenses and deductions) of 6%.

13. The projected value of the separate investment account (cash value) based on a net investment return (after expenses and deductions) of 12%.

14. Annual premium for $100,000 variable life is $2,394. The monthly premium by automatic deduction from checking account is $211.10.

15. The underwriting requirements (medical, social, and economic) of the insurance company must be met, in order for the insurance to be issued.

16. Insurability status – e.g., nonsmoker or smoker, or rated (extra charge because of being a higher risk for medical or occupational reasons). Select for this company means nonsmoker, nonrated. It is the company's best insurability classification.

Figure 18.1

LEDGER STATEMENT FOR VARIABLE LIFE

$100,000 Variable Whole Life Plan **1**
For Age 45 Male **2**
Annual Premium $2,394 **3**

4
Dividends Used to Purchase Paid-up Additions

5	6	7	8	9	10	11	12	13
			Death Benefit* Assumed Investment Returns			Cash Value* Assumed Investment Returns		
End of Year	Annual Premium	Premiums Accumulated at 5%	0%	6%	12%	0%	6%	12%
1	$2,394	$ 2,514	$101,367	$101,391	$101,532	$ 1,103	$ 1,154	$ 1,205
2	2,394	5,153	102,707	103,880	103,510	3,145	3,372	3,606
3	2,394	7,924	104,024	104,471	105,962	5,164	5,700	6,268
4	2,394	10,834	105,304	106,157	108,904	7,156	8,137	9,216
5	2,394	13,890	106,549	197,941	112,382	9,201	10,776	12,572
6	2,394	17,098	107,749	109,818	116,420	11,214	13,536	16,286
7	2,394	20,467	108,910	111,797	121,060	13,190	16,422	20,395
8	2,394	24,004	110,023	113,872	126,335	15,126	19,434	24,935
9	2,394	27,717	111,088	116,046	132,287	17,013	22,573	29,949
10	2,394	31,617	112,107	118,327	138,968	18,853	25,845	35,485
11	2,394	35,712	113,068	120,705	146,416	20,634	29,248	41,591
12	2,394	40,011	113,961	123,176	154,678	22,351	32,782	48,320
13	2,394	44,525	114,772	125,729	163,796	23,999	36,451	55,733
14	2,394	49,265	115,490	128,357	173,818	25,570	40,255	63,896
15	2,394	54,242	116,104	131,052	184,800	27,055	44,192	72,874
16	2,394	59,468	116,604	133,808	196,801	28,444	48,262	82,743
17	2,394	64,955	116,984	136,624	209,890	39,727	52,460	93,580
18	2,394	70,716	117,238	139,502	224,146	30,891	56,784	105,469
19	2,394	76,766	117,359	142,443	239,654	31,923	61,230	118,496
20	2,394	83,118	117,334	145,442	256,496	32,806	65,790	132,756
60@	2,394	54,242	116,104	131,052	184,800	27,055	44,192	72,874
65@	2,394	83,118	117,334	145,442	256,496	32,806	65,790	132,756
75@	2,394	167,007	112,535	180,166	527,026	34,997	118,565	74,646

14 Insurance Premiums   Annual   Mo. ISA
                                   2394.00   211.10

Subject to Underwriting Limits **15**
Select **16**

17 *Dividends based on current scale—1988 issue. Not an estimate or guarantee of future results. Hypothetical investment results are illustrations only and should not be deemed representative of past or future investment results. Results illustrated assume no loans. 8% loan provision. The illustration must be preceded or accompanied by a current prospectus.

17. Statement about dividends, assumed investment returns (e.g., 6% and 12%) and loan interest of 8%. In addition, there is a statement pertaining to the prospectus which clearly indicates that variable life is considered a security and as such must be registered with the Securities and Exchange Commission (SEC).

What Ledger Statements Do Not Tell

You should be told either verbally or in writing the following additional information:

- The separate investment account, which is analogous to the reserve (cash value) of traditional whole life, graded premium life, interest sensitive, and universal life, is made up of four divisions: stock, bond, money market, and master portfolio. The master portion typically consists of common stock, other equity securities, bonds, and money market instruments. Inquire about what percentage of your net premium can go into each. In addition, find out how often you can change from one to the other.

- Note whether the various expenses and deductions are contractually guaranteed not to increase. For this company, variable life policy charges to the policy are: sales loads, policy fees, annual administration charges, state premium tax, and risk charge. Charges to the separate investment account are: cost of insurance (mortality charges), mortality and risk expense, and management fees and expenses. Ask for a total disclosure of each.

- The rate of return expressed in terms of compound interest should be given either on the ledger statement or by the life insurance agent. Ideally, it should be provided for each year.

- The rate of return upon death for this policy for sequential years is as follows:

Year	Rate of Return
1	4,141.10%
5	86.94
10	30.81
20	14.25

- The above rates are based on a 12% interest assumption death benefit.

- The rate of return upon death can be used when comparing various variable life policies among respected companies. (It can also be used for any life insurance policy.) Consider the following example:

Rate of return upon death in year 20	Cost per $1,000 of life insurance per year for 20 years
14.25%	$ 9.34
14.23	9.36
13.25	10.59
13.00	10.93

- How were these numbers determined? $1,000 is the future value (death benefit) to be paid, 20 years is the time. Interest is known (14.25%, 14.23%, 13.25%, 13%). You then solve for payment – how much must be spent each year to accumulate $1,000 in 20 years at the various interest rates?

- Once the rate of return upon death is known, then it can be determined what would have to be earned before taxes in other financial services products such as mutual funds, certificates of deposit, real estate, or commodities to duplicate the tax-exempt rate of return provided by life insurance. (For this purpose, it is assumed that the death benefit is considered life insurance proceeds and as such not subject to federal or state income taxes.) The before-tax rate of return is determined by dividing the life insurance rate of return by the marginal tax bracket subtracted

Figure 18.2

Year	15% taxpayer	25% taxpayer	28% taxpayer	33% taxpayer	35% taxpayer
1	4,871.88%	5,521.47%	5,751.53%	6,180.75%	6,370.92%
5	102.28	115.92	120.75	129.76	133.75
10	36.25	41.08	42.79	45.99	47.40
20	16.76	19.00	19.79	21.27	21.90

from 100% (for 15%, the factor is 0.85; for 25%, 0.75; for 28%, 0.72; for 33%, 0.67; and for 35%, 0.65). The result is shown in Figure 18.2.

- The rate of return upon surrender should also be provided. When the rate of return upon surrender is positive, it means that taxes are due. Taxes are due on the difference between the cash-surrender value and the premiums paid. The result before taxes is as follows:

Year	Rate of Return
1	-49.67%
5	1.64
10	7.05
20	8.95

- The above rates of return are based on a 12% interest assumption separate investment account performance. The rate of return upon surrender even before taxes never equals the separate investment account investment performance of 12%.

- The Premiums Accumulated at 5 Percent column on the ledger statement replaces the Interest Adjusted Index. This is what your money would be worth at 5 percent net after taxes if not used to purchase life insurance. In order to net 5% after taxes, the before-tax rates of return in the following tax brackets are:

15% taxpayer	25% taxpayer	28% taxpayer	33% taxpayer	35% taxpayer
5.88%	6.67%	6.94%	7.46%	7.69%

- The ledger statement should be the official ledger statement produced by the computer service of the life insurance company. It should be "bug-free."

WHERE CAN I FIND OUT MORE?

The following references may be useful:

1. Lawrence J. Rybka, "A Case for Variable Life," *The Journal of the American Society of CLU & ChFC* (May, 1997).

2. Ben G. Baldwin, "Understanding and Managing VUL," *The Journal of the American Society of CLU & ChFC* (September, 1996).

3. Gary Snouffer, *Variable Life Essentials* (Cincinnati, OH: The National Underwriter Company, 1998).

4. Carl E. Anderson and James B. Ross, *Modern Mutual Fund Families & Variable Life: Tools for Investment Growth and Tax Benefits* (Homewood, IL: Dow Jones-Irwin, 1988).

QUESTIONS AND ANSWERS

Question – What are the mechanics of the VL contract? How does it actually work when a client pays a premium?

Answer – The VL contract works like this:

1. Premiums (less an investment expense and/or sales load, state premium tax, and a mortality charge) are paid into separate investment accounts.

2. The policyowner selects among several "separate accounts." These include mutual-fund type alternatives such as stock funds, bond funds, and money-market funds to invest the remaining premium.

3. Policyowners may typically switch or rebalance their investments among the funds one or more times per year. The insurer may or may not charge a fee for each such movement of cash.

Question – What is the single most important way a VL contract differs from the traditional life policy?

Answer – The single most important distinction between variable life and traditional whole life is in the investment flexibility and the consequent shifting of the investment risk from the insurer (with classic whole life) to the policyowner (with variable life). In the variable life contract the policyowner's funds are segregated, since they are placed in accounts that are distinct and separate from the company's general investment fund.

Question – Exactly how does the insurer determine the death benefit increase or decrease?

Answer – In a very general sense there are two death benefits under a VL contract. One provides for a minimum payment and is guaranteed. The second will be paid if and only if the actual investment return on the separate account exceeds the assumed rate of return. Excess interest credits are used to buy additional "blocks" of insurance under this "second" death benefit.[12]

Technically, the face value may increase or decrease based on a formula that relates the investment performance of the separate account to the face value. Companies use two methods to establish the relationship between the investment performance and the face amount. Under what is called the corridor percentage approach, the death benefit is periodically adjusted so that it is at least equal to a specified percentage of the cash value, as required by current tax law.[13] The mandated corridor percentage is 250% until the insured reaches age 40 and then gradually declines to 100% by age 95.

The death benefit under what is called the net single premium approach is periodically adjusted so that it matches the amount of insurance that could be purchased with a single premium equal to the cash value, assuming guaranteed mortality rates and a low rate of return, typically 4%.

Although both methods are equally valid, most policyowners find the corridor percentage method easier to understand.

As mentioned above, there is a floor that protects the beneficiary of a variable life contract. The death benefit cannot fall below a guaranteed minimum, the initial face amount of the policy. If the return on the selected portfolio called a "separate account" is greater than the rate of interest assumed at the inception of the contract, the actual death benefit may increase beyond the policy's scheduled face amount.

Question – How does a VL contract compare with a traditional plan with respect to the typical legal protections afforded policyowners?

Answer – Of course, there is no schedule of guaranteed cash values. But otherwise, the VL policyowner is provided with most of the usual features of traditional level-premium life insurance including guaranteed maximum mortality charges, nonforfeiture values, a reinstatement period, and settlement options.

Options or riders available under VL contracts include waiver of premium, guaranteed purchase or insurability, accidental death benefits, and disability income.

Question – Do variable life contracts pay dividends?

Answer – VL policies are issued in both participating and nonparticipating forms. But dividends paid on par

VL policies are based solely on favorable mortality and loading experience and include no element of excess investment earnings. Excess investment earnings, less an asset management fee, are reflected in the value of the separate account.

Question – Do variable life contracts allow policy loans?

Answer – Loans are allowed from VL contracts. But policy loan provisions are not, however, the same as in the traditional insurance policy. This is because a loan equal to the full cash value could leave the insurer with less than complete security for the debt if the value of the underlying portfolio dropped after the loan was made. For this reason, most insurers limit loans on VL products to about 75% of the policy's cash values (compared with about 92% on traditional contracts). If a policyowner makes a loan, the insurer will credit the loan with a lower rate than the full portfolio investment rate, usually a percent specified in the policy.

Question – VL and VUL are sometimes described as life insurance wrapped around a mutual fund investment and as better alternatives than a buy-term-and-invest-the-difference strategy. How does the investment performance of the funds offered by life insurance companies compare with the performance of mutual funds?

Answer – There have been numerous studies measuring the investment performance of mutual funds, but far fewer studies have assessed the performance of other institutional investors, such as the separate accounts of life insurance companies. However, one study examined the attractiveness of the stock portfolios of life insurance companies as an alternative investment to mutual funds.[14] Using testing methods similar to those used to evaluate mutual funds, the study concluded that on the basis of risk-adjusted investment performance alone, both life insurance and mutual fund portfolios yield similar returns. However, as life insurance contracts offer the opportunity for individual investors to defer taxes, these investment vehicles offer an edge over mutual funds when performance is considered on an after-tax basis.

Question – What investments other than the normal stock, bond, and money market separate accounts are available?

Answer – For the more aggressive or knowledgeable investor, some companies now offer GNMA funds, real estate funds, and zero-coupon bond funds. Some specialized funds such as small-capitalization stock funds, market index funds, and funds that focus on specific sectors of the economy or industries (i.e., medical, high-tech, gold, leisure, and utilities) are also available.

Some companies offer a managed fund option where the company's investment manager assumes the responsibility for apportioning investments among the various alternative funds. Some VL policies also offer a guaranteed interest option similar to the declared interest rate on universal life policies. Recently, some insurance companies have offered investments in "hedge funds" for policyowners who meet certain income and net worth requirements. Hedge funds are investment companies that are generally unregulated by the SEC; hedge funds may use high-risk techniques, such as borrowing and short selling, to make higher returns for their investors.

Question – Is there a fixed and increasing schedule of cash values in the variable life contract?

Answer – Unlike the traditional whole life policy, in the variable contract there is no guaranteed minimum cash value. The cash value at any point in time is based on the market value of the assets in the separate account. VL policyowners bear *all* the investment risk associated with policy. So cash values can grow well beyond the assumed rate or not at all. There can even be negative growth. That is to say that it is possible in a variable life contract for the policyowner to lose the entire amount in the selected portfolio.

Question – How do the key features of universal, variable, and variable universal life compare?

Answer – Figure 18.3 compares and contrasts the key features of universal, variable, and variable universal life. As the table shows, variable universal life combines most of the advantages of universal and variable life.

Question – How does one properly compare a variable universal life product with a universal life product?

Answer – A VUL prospectus generally discloses more about expense charges than is disclosed in a UL policy illustration and contract. VUL has higher expenses resulting from the need to prepare prospectuses, to register with the SEC, and to provide investment flexibility. These additional costs are offset somewhat by lower profit requirements on VUL, where the investment risk is assumed by the policyowner.

Front-end sales loads, premium tax loads, and administrative charges on VUL and UL do not differ materially. Surrender charges on VUL policies are generally lower than those on UL to enable the VUL to comply with SEC limits on sales loads. Investment expenses are higher on VUL because the fee paid to the investment manager is usually higher than the typical investment expense for a UL policy. Profit margins are slightly less for VUL than for UL.

Figure 18.4 shows how VUL and UL compare from an investor's perspective.

Question – Why must a prospectus accompany information on variable and variable universal products?

Answer – Since variable life products are considered securities, prospective purchasers must be given a prospectus. It contains the identity and nature of the insurer's business, the use to which the insurer will put the premiums, financial information on the insurer, the investment characteristics of the product, expenses, fees, loads, and policyowner rights. In addition, the agent must be properly licensed to sell securities.

CHAPTER ENDNOTES

1.   IRC Sec. 7702(d).

2.   IRC Secs. 7702(f)(7)(B), 7702(f)(7)(C).

3.   IRC Secs. 7702(f)(7)(B), 7702(f)(7)(D). The cash value corridor test is discussed in Appendix F.

4.   In cases where there are extreme reductions in the death benefit or very large premium payments, it is even possible for a policy to fail the tests for life insurance under IRC Section 7702 with much more disastrous tax consequences. See the discussion of the definition of life insurance in Appendix F.

5   IRC Sec. 7702A(a)(1)(B). Classification as a MEC occurs in the year when seven-pay test is first violated and for each year thereafter. See Appendix D for a more complete discussion of the seven-pay test.

6.   IRC Sec. 7702A(e)(1).

7.   IRC Sec. 7702A(c)(2)(B).

8.   IRC Sec. 7702A(c)(3).

9.   IRC Sec. 7702. See Appendix F.

10. An excellent book on this subject is *Modern Mutual Fund Families & Variable Life: Tools for Investment Growth and Tax Benefits*, by Carl E. Anderson and James B. Ross (Homewood, IL: Dow Jones-Irwin, 1988).

Figure 18.3

KEY FEATURES OF UNIVERSAL, VARIABLE, AND VARIABLE UNIVERSAL LIFE			
Feature	UL	VL	VUL
Death benefit guaranteed while the policy is in force	Yes	Yes	Yes
Premium amounts are flexible	Yes	No	Yes
Policyowner chooses how premiums are invested	No	Yes	Yes
Policyowner may vary frequency or amount of premiums paid	Yes	No	Yes
Policyowner may use cash values to pay monthly deductions	Yes	No	Yes
Policyowner may increase or decrease death benefit	Yes	No	Yes
Death benefit options A and B available	Yes	No	Yes
Cash values fluctuate depending on performance of underlying investment	No*	Yes	Yes
Guaranteed minimum interest rate on cash values	Yes	No	No
Partial withdrawals from cash value allowed	Yes	No	Yes
Cash value grows on tax-deferred basis	Yes	Yes	Yes
Annual statements detailing monthly deductions and cash value growth	Yes	No	Yes
Considered a security	No	Yes	Yes

* The current interest credited to cash values of UL policies fluctuates with the performance of the insurer's general portfolio, but cash values, once accumulated, do not fluctuate in value with fluctuations in the market value of the assets in the general portfolio.

11. This illustration is adapted from William D. Brownlie and Jeffery L. Seglin's treatise, *The Life Insurance Buyer's Guide* (new York, NY: McGraw-Hill Publishing Company, 1989).

12. Black and Skipper, *Life Insurance*, 12th ed. (Englewood Cliffs, NJ: Prentice-Hall, 1994), pp. 114-115.

13. IRC Sec. 7702(d).

14. Robert T. Kleiman and Anandi P. Sahu, "Life Insurance Companies as Investment Managers: New Implications for Consumers," *Financial Services Review: The Journal of Individual Financial Management*, Vol. 1, No. 1, 1991.

Figure 18.4

VUL COMPARED WITH UL FROM THE INVESTOR'S PERSPECTIVE		
Characteristic	**Universal Life**	**Variable Universal Life**
Investment Control	Generally intermediate maturity fixed income assets. Control is with the insurance company.	Choice of investment vehicle (equities, fixed income) left to policyowner.
Asset Security	Assets are part of general account and, as such, are chargeable with all liabilities arising out of the general account. Liabilities also are part of the general account and therefore are backed by all the assets of the general account.	Separate account assets are not chargeable with liabilities arising out of any other business the insurer may conduct. Separate account cash value liabilities are backed by separate account assets only. Separate account death benefits in excess of the cash value are backed by the assets in the general account.
Market Value of Assets	Principal is guaranteed and cash value is not marked to market. Interest guarantee is at 4% to 5%. Credits once earned are not forfeitable.	Assets are marked to market daily, thus creating volatility. No cash value guarantees.
Variations in Charges		
Mortality Charges	Charges are subject to modification up to guaranteed maximum, now generally the 1980 CSO table.	Charges are subject to modification up to guaranteed maximum, now generally the 1980 CSO table.
Expense Charges	Current and guaranteed expense loads sometimes identical.	Current and guaranteed expense loads sometimes identical.
Investment Return	Generally, all earnings above a guaranteed rate of 4% - 5% are declared at the insurer's discretion.	The return on the assets in the fund net of expenses is the policy's investment return. Therefore, while greater investment risk is present on VUL for the policyowner, the risk is entirely with the performance of the fund and not controlled by the insurer's declarations.

Chapter 19

ACCELERATED DEATH BENEFITS AND VIATICAL SETTLEMENTS

WHAT IS IT?

The emotional stress of dealing with one's own impending death due to an illness such as cancer or AIDS is further compounded by the customary increase in medical bills and the additional costs of special care in conjunction with a likely reduction in earning capacity. A similar increase in stress levels is likely to afflict an individual with a seriously debilitating chronic illness as well. A person owning life insurance policies may have several options for essentially accelerating payment of death benefits to ameliorate some of these financial concerns.

Tax legislation, as discussed is detail below, and insurance industry innovation in response to growing demand has made two options much more attractive:

1. Viatical settlements with independent third parties; and

2. Accelerated death benefit payments from the insurance companies issuing the policies.

Before life insurance companies offered accelerated benefits, entrepreneurs formed viatical settlement companies to provide accelerated payments to insureds.[1] In a *viatical settlement*, a third party purchases the life insurance policy of an insured (the *viator*) who has a life-threatening disease or illness. The term "viatical settlement" originated from the Latin "viaticum" which means provision for a journey. The insured receives a one-time payment that usually ranges from 50% to 80% of the policy's face value or the insured can elect to receive periodic payments. The purchaser then becomes the owner of the policy and typically names itself as the beneficiary. The purchaser continues to pay any required premiums and receives the policy's entire face value when the insured dies.

Most purchasers require the insured to have two years or less to live. The shorter the insured's life expectancy, the greater, generally, the purchase price will be.

As the desire for accelerated benefits increased, particularly from AIDS and cancer patients, the life insurance industry quickly reacted to meet the growing demand by including accelerated death benefit provisions in their policies. These provisions require the insurer to prepay all or a portion of the death benefit to the insured when the insured has a disabling or life-threatening condition that doctors predict will cause death within a relatively short period of time. Life insurance companies and insurance regulation may use several different terms to refer to this type of provision, including:

1. accelerated death benefit;

2. living needs benefit;

3. acceleration-of-life insurance benefit; or

4. living payout option.

Accelerated benefits have been available from some insurers in the United States since 1965.[2] Today, hundreds of insurance companies offer living benefits riders in a variety of formats.

State governments have been quick to authorize insurance companies to offer policies that contain accelerated benefits. By the end of 1991, the insurance commissions of most states had authorized accelerated benefits. In addition, many states have extensive provisions regulating viatical settlements.

WHEN IS THE USE OF SUCH A DEVICE INDICATED?

Accelerating death benefits or entering into a viatical settlement generally is indicated only when a person is terminally ill or seriously and chronically ill, in need of cash, and other options to meet those cash needs are not available. In certain cases (see "Questions and Answers," below), estate and income tax planning considerations may prompt the use of these devices for terminally ill policyowners, even if they do not necessarily "need" the cash immediately.

ADVANTAGES

The principal advantage is that terminally ill or seriously chronically ill insureds can receive advance payments on policy death benefits free of income tax. If the insured is terminally ill, he can use the proceeds for virtually any purpose desired. For example, insureds may desire to use the proceeds to:

- cover out-of-pocket medical expenses;

- finance alternative treatments not covered by existing medical insurance;

- purchase a new car or finance a dream vacation before he or she cannot enjoy such things;

- personally distribute cash to loved ones;

- maintain his or her dignity by not dying destitute; and/or

- pay off loans.

DISADVANTAGES

Reduced Total Payout

Accepting accelerated benefits reduces the face amount of the insured's policy, thereby reducing or eliminating death benefits payable to the beneficiary when the insured dies. An insured may not wish to sacrifice the financial security of a spouse or children in exchange for receiving accelerated benefits. Accordingly, the type of individual who would most benefit from taking an accelerated benefit or a viatical settlement is a financially independent person without a financially dependent spouse or children who is unable to work and who has no long-term care or disability insurance.

Eligibility for Governmental Assistance Programs

If the insured's contract is designed with a voluntary election provision, it is uncertain whether a local, state, or federal government agency could force the insured to take accelerated benefits. In other words, is the availability of the benefit deemed property of or potential income to the insured when computing eligibility for benefits? Several bills introduced into Congress over the past years have expressly dealt with this issue.[3]

When life insurance proceeds are paid to the designated beneficiary, most states exempt them from the claims of the insured/deceased's creditors. Once these proceeds are paid to a living insured, however, the insured's creditors may be able to reach them, unless state law has extended creditor protection to accelerated benefits and viatical settlements.

A problem may arise even if the insured does not claim the proceeds but merely has the ability to demand the benefits. In this situation, would the benefits be within the reach of the insured's creditors? Could the creditors force the insured to accept benefits so that they could then attach them? These issues have not been resolved in many jurisdictions.

A life insurance policy containing accelerated benefits should not be considered as a replacement for comprehensive health insurance or long-term care insurance. In fact, many state regulations prohibit insurers and insurance agents from mentioning, illustrating, or referring to the accelerated benefit provision as an alternative or substitute for catastrophic major medical health insurance. Insureds must be strongly advised to obtain appropriate health and long-term care insurance because life insurance policies only benefit individuals who have terminal illnesses.

It is possible for dishonest individuals to take advantage of a terminally or chronically ill person who receives a large sum of money under stressful conditions. An insured may be vulnerable to charlatans claiming that they can cure the insured's ailment or to scam artists who claim that they can earn large returns on the insured's newly-gained wealth.

WHAT ARE THE REQUIREMENTS?

The insured must either be a *terminally ill individual* or a *chronically ill individual* in order for amounts received to be treated as tax-free death benefits. A terminally ill individual is one "who has been certified by a physician as having an illness or physical condition which can reasonably be expected to result in death in 24 months or less after the date of the certification."[4]

Once the insured obtains this certification based upon the doctor's reasonable medical opinion, the reality of what later happens does not matter. In other words, the statute does not contain a "look-back" rule.[5] If the insured actually lives months, years, or decades longer than expected, the accelerated benefits or viatical settlement continue to be excluded from income. The statute does not place any upper limit on the amount of proceeds that a terminally ill insured may exclude from income.

A chronically ill individual is defined as a person "who has been certified by a licensed health care practitioner as (i) being unable to perform (without substantial assistance from another individual) at least 2 activities of daily living [i.e., eating, toileting, transferring, bathing, dressing, and continence] for a period of at least 90 days due to a loss of functional capacity, (ii) having a level of disability similar (as determined under regulations prescribed by the Secretary in consultation with the Secretary of Health and Human Services) to the level of disability described in clause (i), or (iii) requiring substantial supervision to protect such individual from threats to health and safety due to severe cognitive impairment. Such term shall not include any individual otherwise meeting the requirements of the preceding sentence unless within the preceding 12-month period a licensed health care practitioner has certified that such individual meets such requirements."[6]

Note that a person cannot be both terminally ill and chronically ill. A person cannot qualify as chronically ill if he or she can be classified as terminally ill.[7]

Types of Life Insurance Policies

Not all life insurance policies will qualify for preferred treatment of their accelerated benefits. Under IRC Section 7702, the contract must meet either a cash value accumulation test or a two-pronged test consisting of guideline premium requirements coupled with a cash value corridor requirement. The purpose of limiting the tax-favored status of accelerated benefits to distributions from these types of policies is to make certain that the contracts are true life insurance rather than some type of investment-oriented product that the insured is attempting to use to shelter income.

Also, accelerated death benefit payments made to someone other than the taxpayer under a key person and other business policies are not protected. "… any amount paid to any taxpayer other than the insured if such taxpayer has an insurable interest with respect to the life of the insured by reason of the insured being a director, officer, or employee of the taxpayer or by reason of the insured being financially interested in any trade or business carried on by the taxpayer,"[8] is not treated as being paid by reason of the death of an insured.

Limitations on Payments to Chronically Ill Individuals

In order to qualify for the income exclusion, payments to chronically ill individuals must be reim-

bursements for the costs of qualified long-term care services provided for the insured that are not compensated for by insurance or otherwise.[9] Qualified long-term care services include "… necessary diagnostic, preventive, therapeutic, curing, treating, mitigating, and rehabilitative services, and maintenance or personal care services which (A) are required by a chronically ill individual, and (B) are provided pursuant to a plan of care prescribed by a licensed health care practitioner."[10]

In other words, unlike terminally ill insureds, chronically ill individuals do not have the discretion to use accelerated benefits or viatical settlements in whatever manner they desire. Despite the limitation to long-term care costs, the Internal Revenue Code protects periodic payments by providing that a payment will not fail to qualify "… by reason of being made on a per diem or other periodic basis without regard to the expenses incurred during the period to which the payment relates."[11] These payments, however, are generally subject to the cap on excludable benefits that applies under per diem type long-term care insurance contracts.

Also, to qualify for the favorable tax treatment, the life insurance or viatical settlement contract may not "… pay or reimburse expenses incurred for services or items to the extent that such expenses are reimbursable under the title XVIII of the Social Security Act [Medicare] or would be so reimbursable but for the application of a deductible or coinsurance amount."[12]

Additional Rules

In addition to the limitations on the use of the proceeds, the terms of the contract giving rise to the payments to the chronically ill individual must meet specified requirements designed to protect consumers from seeking accelerated payments or viatical settlements without first having the information necessary to make an informed decision and preserving the insured's right to rescind the arrangement within 30 days. Some of these detailed requirements are in IRC Section 101, while others are incorporated from various provisions of the Internal Revenue Code as well as standards adopted by the National Association of Insurance Commissioners that apply to chronically ill individuals.[13]

The Code limits the exclusion for certain periodic payments that are made to chronically ill individuals. For 2004, the maximum is $230 per day, which works out to $84,180 per year in periodic payments. These amounts are indexed for inflation.[14]

Viatical settlements must comply with additional requirements for the proceeds of the sale or assignment in order to be excluded from income tax. First, the payments must be made by a viatical settlement provider. To qualify as a viatical settlement provider, the purchaser must be "… regularly engaged in the trade or business of purchasing, or taking assignments of, life insurance contracts on the lives of insureds…"[15] who are terminally or chronically ill.

Second, the provider must either be licensed to provide viatical settlements under the laws of the state in which the insured resides, or if the insured's state does not require licensing of viatical settlement providers, the provider must meet the requirements specified in the Internal Revenue Code. With regard to terminally ill individuals, the viatical settlement provider must meet the requirement of: (1) Sections 8 and 9 of the Viatical Settlements Model Act prepared by the National Association of Insurance Commissioners; and (2) the Model Regulations of the National Association of Insurance Commissioners relating to standards for evaluation of reasonable payments in determining amounts paid by the viatical settlement provider in connection with the purchase or assignment of life insurance contracts.[16]

With respect to chronically ill insureds, the provider must meet requirements similar to those contained in Sections 8 and 9 of the Viatical Settlements Model Act along with the standards of the National Association of Insurance Commissioners, if any exist at the time of the settlement, for evaluating the reasonableness of the amounts paid by the provider in connection with viatical settlements for chronically ill individuals.[17]

HOW DO I SELECT THE BEST OF ITS TYPE?

"Life insurance continues to be the central source of financial security for most families in this country."[18] Because so many people place their trust and financial future in the hands of insurance companies, it is crucial that consumers ascertain the financial stability of a particular insurance company prior to purchasing any insurance policy, especially one that provides a living needs benefit.

A planner who wants to recommend that a client obtain a policy providing for accelerated benefits should first investigate prospective insurers. Information about insurance policies and insurers can be gathered from organizations such as the Health Insurance Association of America, the American Council of Life Insurers,

National Council on Aging, and individual state insurance boards. It is important to deal with a company with an established track record so that the chances are good that the company will still be in existence to pay the accelerated benefits if the time comes.

Several sources are available to ascertain insurer solvency. The National Association of Insurance Commissioners (NAIC) developed a solvency-policing agenda to improve the ability of state regulators to monitor and regulate industry solvency.[19] Alternately, A.M. Best Company, Standard & Poor's Corporation (S&P), Moody's, and Fitch publish ratings of insurance companies. See Chapter 3 for more detailed information on company ratings.

Eligibility requirements for accelerated benefits vary among insurance companies. While some companies include a living needs benefits rider in both their new and existing life insurance policies, other companies add the rider only to new policies. The purchaser should inquire as to cost, if any, for an accelerated benefit provision. In many instances, there is no additional cost for including such a rider. However, the purchaser may be required to purchase a specified minimum amount of coverage. In addition, most insurance companies restrict the use of living needs benefits riders to permanent and universal life insurance policies.

Every insurance company requires that the purchaser generally be in good health and pass a physical examination at the time the policy is purchased. An accelerated benefit policy is not available to a purchaser diagnosed as terminally ill prior to the purchase. In addition, no two life benefits riders will be identical. Insurance companies can set their own requirements regarding many aspects of these plans, so it is wise to shop around.

In a similar manner, viatical settlement companies may apply different criteria in deciding whether to purchase a policy, as well as the percentage of the face value that they are willing to pay.

The insured should determine how the accelerated payments or viatical settlement will affect the policy's overall death benefit. For instance, will the accelerated payments reduce or eliminate the death benefit? If the death benefit is reduced, is the reduction based upon the amount paid to the insured, or is there an additional processing fee or other penalty that will be deducted from the death benefit? With most viatical settlements, the insured has no control over the death benefit because the policy belongs to the viatical settlement company after the transaction is completed.

Insurance companies vary as to which illnesses trigger the payment of accelerated benefits under their living benefits rider. While some insurance companies include any type of terminal illness for which the insured has only a short time to live, other companies restrict coverage to specified diseases. Generally, the following medical conditions are covered under all insurance plans: AIDS, heart attack, stroke, Alzheimer's disease, renal failure, liver transplant, life-threatening cancer, and coronary artery bypass. Most insurance companies further restrict availability of accelerated benefits to persons with 12 months or less to live.

The amount payable to the insured under a life benefits rider varies between 2% and 95% of the death benefit, depending upon the insurer.[20]

Generally, the insured may receive the accelerated benefits in one of three ways:

1. one lump sum payment;

2. regular installments; or

3. installments based on the insured's expenses.

If the installment option is selected, the insured should inquire as to whether accelerated payments can be canceled once the benefits start. It is important to remember that a benefit received during life reduces the amount payable to the beneficiary. Under certain circumstances, the insured may wish to cancel accelerated payments and retain the remaining value of the life insurance proceeds for the beneficiary. Another concern with installment payments is what happens if the benefits cease before the insured dies. If the accelerated payments are likely to be depleted prior to death, the insured should consider seeking alternative methods of financing for medical and personal expenses.

Insurance companies may also vary on the restrictive uses of benefits received by the insured. Some companies may require that the funds be used strictly for medical care while others may have no limitation on the expenditure of the funds. Though some policyholders may view accelerated benefits as a means of "making dreams come true," these riders are generally designed for health care and medical expenses.

If an installment payout option is available, the insured should ascertain what will happen to the remaining payments if he or she dies before the payments are completed. Some possible consequences may be:

1. The remaining payments are forfeited;

2. The beneficiary receives the remaining payments in installments; or

3. The beneficiary receives a death benefit after adjustment for the accelerated payments.

An insured may have a choice between electing to take accelerated payments from the insurance company or to enter into a viatical settlement with a third party. He or she should "take advantage of competitive forces and the free market to obtain the highest payment for the life insurance contract."[21] The general rule is that accelerated death benefits provide a higher payout than viatical settlements but typically impose a great number of restrictions on medical conditions.

TAX IMPLICATIONS

Income Taxation of Accelerated Death Benefits or Viatical Settlements

As a general rule, the proceeds of a life insurance policy are excluded from the recipient's gross income under IRC Section 101(a). To secure this exclusion, the proceeds must be payable "by reason of the death of the insured." Since accelerated benefits are paid when the insured individual is living, they are not payable by reason of the insured's death. Thus, when the question first arose it appeared likely that the proceeds would be subject to income tax.

The same was true for viatical settlements. In a private letter ruling, the Service indicated that the amount received by the insured under a viatical settlement, to the extent that the amount exceeded the insured's adjusted basis in the life insurance contract, was includable in the insured's gross income.[22]

In response to these questions of taxation, numerous bills were introduced into Congress to exclude accelerated benefits and viatical settlements from the insured's income. At the same time Congress was debating these bills, the Treasury proposed regulations in December of 1992 that would allow certain accelerated benefits to be considered as being paid by reason of the insured's death so that they would escape taxation.[23] Despite predictions that these regulations would be approved as early as 1993, they were not. The taxability of the payments continued to be the subject of rulings and litigation with mixed results. In 1996 the issue was finally resolved.

In 1996, the Health Insurance Portability and Accountability Act of 1996 (HIPAA 96)[24] was enacted. This legislation included an express provision excluding most accelerated payments, as well as viatical settlements, from gross income by deeming them to be "paid by reason of the death" of the insured.[25] The payments must meet the requirements described below to escape taxation.[26]

A person is deemed to be terminally ill if he has been certified by a physician as having an illness or physical condition that reasonably can be expected to result in death within 24 months of the date of certification.[27] A person qualifies as chronically ill if he has met one of three criteria: he has been certified within the previous 12 months by a licensed health care practitioner as being unable to perform without substantial assistance at least two activities of daily living (e.g., eating, toileting) for at least 90 days due to a loss of functional capacity; he has a similar level of disability; or he requires substantial supervision to protect him from threats to health and safety due to severe cognitive impairment. People who are terminally ill are not included within the class of people who qualify as chronically ill.[28]

In the case of chronically ill individuals, the income tax exclusion applies only if detailed requirements are met.[29] For example, the payment must be for costs incurred by the payee (not compensated for by insurance or otherwise) for qualified long-term care services provided for the insured for that period. Under the terms of the contract, the payment must not be a payment or reimbursement of expenses reimbursable under Medicare (except where Medicare is a secondary payor, or the arrangement provides for per diem or other periodic payments without regard to expenses for qualified long-term care services).

A payment to a chronically ill individual will not fail to qualify for the exclusion because it is made on a per diem or other periodic basis without regard to the expenses incurred during the period to which the payment relates.[30] However, the amount of periodic payments that may be excluded is subject to a dollar limit that is adjusted annually. In 2004, the per diem limitation amount is $230 ($84,180 per year).[31]

The income tax exclusion does not apply to amounts paid to any taxpayer other than the insured in certain circumstances. If the payee has an insurable interest in the insured's life because the insured is a director, officer or employee of the payee, or because the insured is financially interested in any trade or business carried on by the payee, the exclusion does not apply.[32]

Unanswered Questions

Although HIPAA 96 addressed many issues that were previously unresolved, unanswered questions still remain. For example, how will payments made to an insured who is chronically ill be treated if that person becomes terminally ill in a subsequent year?[33] If excess payments are made to a chronically ill insured, will those payments be treated as ordinary income or as capital gains?[34]

Transfer for Value Rule

The transfer for value rule, contained in IRC Section 101(a)(2), provides:

In the case of a transfer for a valuable consideration, by assignment or otherwise, of a life insurance contract or any interest therein, the amount excluded from gross income .... shall not exceed an amount equal to the sum of the actual value of such consideration and the premiums and other amounts, subsequently paid by the transferee.

So virtually all transfers of life insurance policies to viatical settlement companies fall within the transfer for value rule. With the exceptions listed below, transferees for value of life insurance policies are taxable at ordinary income rates on receipt of the policy proceeds less the sum of (1) amounts paid by them to acquire the policy and (2) later premiums and other payments.

Since the purchasers make their profit in the transaction on the difference between what they pay and what they receive, the taxation of the differential requires them to pay less for the policies than they would otherwise pay if the death benefits were received tax free.

Planners should explore the possibility of obtaining loans from parties who qualify under one of the exceptions to the transfer for value rule. In this case, by collaterally assigning the policy, or by naming the lender as the beneficiary under the policy, they may be able to receive more than they could from a viatical settlement company, since the death proceeds would escape income taxation.

The transfers that qualify as exceptions to the transfer for value rule include transfers to:

- a partner of the insured;

- a partnership in which the insured is a partner; and

- a corporation in which the insured is a shareholder or officer.[35]

ETHICS[36]

The viatical settlement process has become controversial in recent years. It is important for insurance planners to do all they can to protect their clients who may be contemplating entering into a viatical settlement or filing for accelerated death benefits. First, however, there needs to be a decision about whether or not the policy needs to be sold and whether or not taking accelerated death benefits might be a better idea. It is generally harder to qualify for accelerated death benefits than to engage in a viatical settlement.

If the client decides to viaticate a policy, it is imperative that a reputable viatical broker is used. The broker will shop the policy to the investors who will ultimately purchase the policy. The broker will generally charge from 3 to 6% of the payout. Many states require that a viatical settlement provider have a license, so it is also important that the provider is licensed in the state of the insured. It is important that clients are asked whether they are receiving public assistance, such as Medicaid, because a viatical settlement may cause those benefits to be lost. The insured should also be provided with written assurance from both the viatical broker and the viatical settlement provider that the insured's medical records will remain confidential and will not be shared with anyone without the insured's written permission.

ALTERNATIVES

1. *Borrow against cash values –*

   Permanent type policies such as whole life, variable life, universal life, etc., build up cash values over the years. The owner of the policy is usually able to borrow money from the insurance company, typically at favorable interest rates. When death occurs, the policy loans are subtracted from the face amount of the policy before payment is made to the beneficiary. If there is also a "waiver of premium" provision, the insured will be relieved of the monthly premium payments.

   The advantages of borrowing are that, first, the policy will still pay the full face amount at death, less the amount borrowed, to the beneficiary named by the policyowner. In other words, the policyowner does not have to settle for less than the full amount of insurance. Second, generally, the policyowner will not need to repay the loans while living. In essence, borrowing is a form of advanced death benefit payment. Third, generally loan proceeds will be received free of income tax, similar to death benefits.

   The major disadvantage is that the amount one can borrow, even from a fully paid-up policy, generally will be considerably less than the amount a terminally ill policyowner could get in accelerated benefits or a viatical settlement. If the owner needs more cash than is available from policy loans, he or she may enter into a viatical settlement. However, the policyowner will generally be required to use part of the viatical settlement to repay all policy loans.

2. *Surrender the policy –*

   Policies with cash value buildup can be surrendered to the insurance company. However, this would generally not be desirable, since the face amount of the policy is usually much higher than the surrender value and the time of death is close. In addition, amounts received in excess of the policyowner's basis (paid in premiums less dividends received less amounts previously withdrawn, if any) are subject to income tax. The policyowner would almost always be better off borrowing against the policy or entering into a viatical settlement.

3. *Borrow funds from a third party –*

   Other friends, family members, and possibly the beneficiary of the policy may be willing to lend money to the person who is terminally ill and then receive repayment from the insurance proceeds. Although insurance companies and institutional lenders generally will not lend money in excess of the cash value in the policy, friends and family may be willing to do so.

   Depending on how the loan is secured, lenders run some risk in lending money to the policyowner. For example, if the policyowner issues an unsecured note, the lender runs the risk that other claimants against the policyowner's estate may have a higher priority and there may be insufficient assets to repay the note. Consequently, the note should be secured with specific collateral.

   However, if the policy itself or any interest in the policy (e.g., the cash value or the death benefit) is assigned to the lender as collateral, it may trigger the transfer for value rule with potentially adverse tax consequences for the lender.[37] The best opportunities involve transactions with parties who qualify under one of the exceptions to the transfer for value rule: partners of the insured, partnerships of the insured, or a corporation in which the insured is a shareholder or officer.

QUESTIONS AND ANSWERS

Question – What factors will determine the amount of settlement?

Answer – The following factors will affect the amount of settlement received:

1. *The insured's life expectancy* – The shorter the period until the insured is expected to die, the more the company will pay. Some companies will accept up to a five-year life expectancy, but many prefer a shorter term of years.

2. *The period in which the company can contest the existence of a valid contract must have passed* – The incontestable period, as well as the "suicide provision" (typically two years), generally must have expired. This period may begin again for policies that have been reinstated after a lapse for non-payment of premium.

3. *Company's financial rating* – The company that issued the policy must have a high financial rating.

4. *The amount of the premiums* – The premium level is important, since the buyer of the policy must continue making the payments for the remainder of the insured's lifetime.

5. *The size of the policy* – Most settlement companies have upper and lower limits. For example, a top limit of $1,000,000 scaling down to a minimum of $10,000 is typical.

6. *The current prime interest rate* – The prime rate is important, since the buyer will compare the settlement agreement to other types of investments.

After examining the above factors, a settlement company will generally offer the owner of the policy between 25% and 85% of the policy's face amount. The settlement amount may be received income-tax-free under the same conditions described.

7. *Time of payment* – The time between applying for the settlement and having the cash is generally three to eight weeks. However, this will depend on how quickly the medical information and beneficiary release forms are in the hands of the settlement company.

Question – What other considerations are involved in deciding whether or not to enter into a viatical settlement?

Answer – Planners and those insureds who are considering viatical settlements or accelerating death benefits should also consider the following factors:

1. *Potential impact on other public benefits* – If the terminally ill or qualifying chronically ill person is presently receiving benefits that are contingent upon his or her "means" (income or assets), such as Medicaid, food stamps, etc., he or she must weigh the effect of a viatical settlement on these benefits which may be terminated or reduced until the settlement amount is "spent down."

2. *Policy riders* – If the policy has an accidental death or dismemberment rider, those rights should be specifically retained by the insured.

3. *Confidentiality and beneficiaries* – Most companies stress the confidential nature of the transaction but they require the named beneficiary to release any possible claim to the proceeds. If the insured does not want the beneficiary to know of the illness, he or she may change beneficiaries just prior to completing the settlement. If the estate is named as beneficiary, the insured (owner) would be the only one who would need to sign the release forms. However, if death occurred after the time the beneficiary was changed, but before the settlement was completed, the insurance proceeds would be paid to the estate and would, therefore, be subject to probate administration.

4. *Group insurance* – Group insurance policies can be sold in viatical settlements. Group insurance policies will usually require that one's employer is notified.

5. *Resale of policies* – Confidentiality may be lost if the policy is sold by the settlement company in the "secondary market" to individual investors, since a new investor would want to know the health status of the insured.

6. *Escrow accounts* – An escrow account is generally used to make certain that the payment of the agreed upon amount is made to the insured shortly after the insurance company notifies the escrow company that the ownership of the policy has been transferred.

7. *Shop and negotiate* – Several companies should be investigated in order to negotiate the best offer.

Question – Can a viatical settlement be used as a means of getting a life insurance policy out of one's estate for estate tax purposes?

Answer – For the individual who will not live more than three years, a transfer of an existing policy to an irrevocable trust or a third person will be ineffective to avoid inclusion of the policy in the gross estate at death. For example, an individual who owns a $500,000 life insurance policy on his life and whose estate is in the 55% estate tax bracket will only pass on $225,000 to the beneficiaries of the policy (.55 x $500,000 = $275,000; $500,000 - $275,000 = $225,000).

A sale of the policy avoids the three-year rule because the viatication is a sale for fair market value in money or money's worth. This could provide additional value to the insured's family and reduce estate taxes because the conversion into cash converts the intangible asset into cash that can be given to family members in the form of tax-free annual exclusion gifts, "spent down" by the individual, or a combination of the two.

For example, the same individual who owns a $500,000 policy on his life will leave his beneficiaries only $225,000 if he dies owning the policy. Instead, the individual sells the policy and receives $350,000 (70% of the face amount). The individual can make annual exclusion gifts of the $350,000 to his four children, their spouses, and ten grandchildren over his remaining assumed life expectancy of two years. Under the viatical settlement, the individual has transferred $350,000 to his family tax-free, providing them an additional $125,000 ($350,000 - $225,000). (In addition, the estate can pass the after-estate tax value of the premiums not spent in maintaining the policy as well as the after-income-and-estate tax on the earnings on the declining balance of the $350,000 viatical proceeds over his remaining life.)

Getting a life insurance policy out of the insured's estate can sometimes save the estate administration costs of having to file an estate tax return.

Question – Can an owner of a policy who is not the insured enter into a viatical settlement?

Answer – Yes. Any person who owns an insurance policy, not just the insured, can viaticate an insurance policy.

Question – Why might a person who owns a policy, but is not the insured, enter into a viatical settlement?

Answer – A third party, for example, the trustee of an irrevocable trust, may sell the policy and receive the proceeds free of federal income tax. The third-party individual or trustee entering into the settlement can use the proceeds to purchase assets from the estate at a discount. This technique is especially advantageous where the insured has an ownership interest in a closely held business or partnership, as discounts for such interests (for lack of marketability, lack of control, minority interest, etc.) are typically between 30 and 40%. In addition, such transactions are not subject to the three-year rule since they are transfers for value.

For example, assume a terminally ill individual owns 100% of a closely held business valued at $2,000,000. The estate tax on the stock if included in the gross estate is $1,100,000 ($2,000,000 x .55). The trustee of an irrevocable life insurance trust owns a $1,000,000 face value policy on the life of the individual. If the trustee viaticates the policy and $1,122,000 ($1,020,000 x 1.1). The estate also has $637,000 in cash. Even if the individual makes no annual exclusion gifts before dying, the estate is reduced by $241,000 ($2,000,000 - $1,759,000), resulting in estate tax savings of $132,550 ($241,000 x .55).

Suppose now that the individual makes a gift of a 2% interest in the company (gift tax value of $16,000 = $2,000,000 x .02 x.0.65 - $10,000 annual exclusion). As a result the estate now includes only a 49% minority interest in the company with an estate tax value of $637,000 ($2,000,000 x 0.49 x 0.65), rather than $1,122,000, a reduction in the estate tax base of $485,000 while an increase in the adjusted taxable gifts of $16,000. The net reduction of $469,000 creates an additional savings of $257,950 ($469,000 x 0.55). In all, the estate planning technique triggered by the viatical settlement reduces the estate taxes that would have been paid by $390,500 ($132,550 + $257,950). Thus, by giving up $200,000 through viatical rather than death settlement of the insurance policy, the beneficiaries in the aggregate have saved $190,500 ($390,500 - $200,000).

Please note that this analysis does not take into account savings arising from: (1) the ability to make annual exclusion gifts in addition to spending down the cash received; (2) the saving of future premium payments; (3) the removal of the appreciation in the business sold to the insurance trust from that date to the date of death from the insured's gross estate; and (4) the net earnings on the declining balance of the viatical proceeds. Further, additional discounts may be available by wrapping the stock into a family limited partnership/liability company.

Question – What estate planning opportunities do viatical settlements provide for clients with chronic illnesses or for those over the age of 75?

Answer – Clients with chronic conditions or those over the age of 75 who meet certain underwriting criteria will likely have longer life expectancies (e.g. 4-10 years) than a terminally ill client. For such individuals, viatical settlements may also be an invaluable estate planning tool. In the above example involving a minority discount, an insured with a longer life expectancy would undoubtedly receive considerably less than $800,000 for the sale of a $1 million policy, due to the time value of money over the longer remaining life. However, this is offset to some extent by the greater earnings on the declining balance due to the longer survival period, the greater amount of premiums not paid, and sometimes most importantly, the greater appreciation removed from the client's gross estate in reference to the business interest sold to the life insurance trust. The viability of this option depends in large part on the current valuation of the policy on a viatical basis.

Question – Are there any charitable giving planning opportunities with viatical settlements?

Answer – It is advantageous to donate highly appreciated assets to charity because the donor receives a current income tax deduction equal to the fair market value of the asset, rather than the donor's basis in the asset. Often, however, such assets are income-producing assets (i.e., securities, real estate) and the donor may not be able or willing to part with the income generated by them. Selling an existing policy may free these highly-appreciated assets to satisfy the donor's charitable goals.

For example, X owns securities with a fair market value of $70,000, a tax basis of $20,000 and also owns a $100,000 policy. If X does nothing, the net amount passing to the beneficiaries is $76,500 ($170,000 x

0.45). Assume X can sell the policy for $70,000, which "replaces" the securities to be donated to charity. As a result of donating the appreciated securities, the individual receives a $70,000 income tax deduction, saving $27,720 in income taxes. The tax saving, plus the settlement proceeds, equals $97,720. If the donor's goal is to maximize estate tax savings, he can make annual exclusion gifts and/or spend down the $97,720. In other situations, it might make sense to sell a policy and donate the cash generated from the sale to charity. This would provide a greatly increased charitable deduction versus the donation of the policy itself, and most charities would rather have cash than a policy.

Question – What is a "Life Settlement?"

Answer – A life settlement is also a sale of a policy to a third party, much like a viatical settlement, but the insured is not terminally or chronically ill. While the insured will generally receive less than would be received in a viatical settlement, he or she will generally receive more than the policy's surrender value. A life settlement might be appropriate if the life insurance is not needed anymore, the insured's health has changed, or the insured has a need for cash.

CHAPTER ENDNOTES

1. Martha Groves, "Terminally Ill Cash in on Insurance Policies; For AIDS Patients, Money Helps Buy Medications," *Washington Post*, October 30, 1990, at p. Z9 (discussing BGR International, Inc., of Brooklyn, New York; "BGR" is an abbreviation for "beat the grim reaper").

2. The first large insurance company to enter the accelerated benefits arena was the Prudential Insurance Company, which introduced the "living needs benefits" rider as an option to its life insurance policies in 1990. Connecticut Mutual Life Insurance Company entered the field shortly thereafter. See Jennifer Landes, "Pru Unveils Plan to Pay Living Benefits," *National Underwriter*, Life and Health/Financial Services edition, February 5, 1990, p. 1. (living needs benefit introduced in Canada in 1989 and in the United States in 1990). Smaller insurance companies offered living needs benefits as early as 1987. See Linda Koco, "Small Cos. Need Big Cos. To Help Promote Product," *National Underwriter*, Life and Health/Financial Services edition, May 7, 1990, p. 29; See Linda Koco, "Conn. Mut'l to Add Living Benefits to New Policies," *National Underwriter*, Life and Health/Financial Services edition, July 9, 1990, p. 7.

3. For example, the Living Benefits Act of 1991 was drafted with the assumption that it "would not be fair to force the terminally ill to choose between their own welfare and the future welfare of their survivors." The bill would have amended "the Social Security Act to ensure that policyholders are not compelled to elect prepayment of death benefits in order to become eligible or

remain eligible for federal means-tested programs such as Medicaid." 137 Cong. Rec. S1294-02 (Jan. 30, 1991) (S. 284).

4. IRC Sec. 101(g)(4)(A). The term "physician" is broadly defined to include a medical doctor or a doctor or osteopathy who is legally authorized to practice medicine and perform surgery by the state in which the doctor practices. See IRC Sec. 101(g)(4)(D) and 42 USC Sec. 1395x(r)(1).

5. Gary J. Gasper, "Viatical Settlements-Cashing Out Life Insurance," *Probate & Property*, March/April 1997, at p. 21.

6. IRC Secs. 101(g)(4)(B), 7702B(c)(2). The legislative history for this provision reflects an intent to include individuals who have Alzheimer's disease, Parkinson's disease, and AIDS. See H.R. Conf. Rep. No. 104-350 (1995) and Gary J. Gasper, "Viatical Settlements-Cashing Out Life Insurance," *Probate & Property*, March/April 1997, at p. 21.

7. IRC Sec. 101(g)(4)(B).

8. IRC Sec. 101(g)(5).

9. IRC Sec. 101(g)(3)(A)(i).

10. IRC Secs. 101(g)(4)(C), 7702B(c)(1).

11. IRC Sec. 101(g)(3)(C).

12. IRC Secs. 101(g)(3)(A)(ii)(I), 7702B(b)(1)(B).

13. IRC Secs. 101(g)(3)(A)(ii)(II), 101(g)(3)(B), 7702B(g).

14. IRC Secs. 101(g)(3), 7702B(d); Rev. Proc. 2003-85, 2003-49 IRB 1184.

15. IRC Sec. 101(g)(2)(B)(i).

16. IRC Sec. 101(g)(2)(B)(ii).

17. IRC Sec. 101(g)(2)(B)(iii).

18. "Association Leaders Speak Out; Life Insurance History," *Best's Review*, Life/Health edition, June, 1990, at p. 76.

19. "Association Leaders Speak Out; Life Insurance History," *Best's Review*, Life/Health edition, June, 1990, at p. 76.

20. See, e.g., Linda Koco, "Living Benefit Rider Has Monthly 'Graded' Benefit," *National Underwriter*, Life and Health/Financial Services edition, May 14, 1990, p. 15; "Principal Adds Benefits Advance Rider at No Cost," *National Underwriter*, Life and Health/Financial Services edition, August 13, 1990, p. 21.

21. Gary J. Gasper, "Viatical Settlements-Cashing Out Life Insurance," *Probate & Property*, March/April 1997, at p. 20.

22. Let. Rul. 9443020. This ruling analyzed the transaction under IRC Section 1001 and thus "implicitly allow[ed] taxpayers to claim capital gains treatment for viatical settlement proceeds, assuming that the life insurance contract [was] a capital asset under §1221." See Gary J. Gasper, "Viatical Settlements-Cashing Out Life Insurance," *Probate & Property*, March/April 1997, at p. 20.

23. Prop. Treas. Reg. §§1.101-8, 1.7702-2, as then in effect.

24. Health Insurance Portability and Accountability Act of 1996 (HIPAA 96), P.L. 104-191.

25. IRC Sec. 101(g). This provision applies to payments made after December 31, 1996. For a discussion of this exclusion, see generally Gary J. Gasper, "Viatical Settlements-Cashing Out Life Insurance," *Probate & Property*, March/April 1997, at p. 20.

26. The requirements are presented in this section in summary form. Be certain to consult the complete text of the Internal Revenue Code section before making a definitive decision regarding whether any accelerated payment or viatical settlement will qualify for income tax exclusion.

27. IRC Sec. 101(g)(4)(A).

28. IRC Secs. 101(g)(4)(B), 7702B(c)(2)(A).

29. IRC Sec. 101(g)(3).

30. IRC Sec. 101(g)(3)(C).

31. Rev. Proc. 2003-85, 2003-49 IRB 1184.

32. IRC Sec. 101(g)(5).

33. See Gary J. Gasper, "Viatical Settlements-Cashing Out Life Insurance," *Probate & Property*, March/April 1997, at p. 22.

34. Gary J. Gasper, "Viatical Settlements-Cashing Out Life Insurance," *Probate & Property*, March/April 1997, at p. 22.

35. For further discussion of the transfer for value rule, see Appendix G.

36. See Hal Stucker, "Viatical Settlement: What's a Good Fit," *National Underwriter*, Life and Health/Financial Services edition, February 1, 1999.

37. See "Tax Implications" above and Appendix G for further discussion of the implications of the transfer for value rule.

Chapter 20

BUY–SELL AGREEMENTS

WHAT IS IT?

A buy-sell agreement is a legal contract restricting the right to dispose of a business interest to specified parties according to specified terms. Typically, this arrangement requires a sale of the business interest, at a formula-determined price, upon one or more of the following triggering events:

- death;

- disability;

- retirement;

- withdrawal from the business at some earlier time; or

- in some cases upon attachment of the owner's property by creditors or in a divorce.

These "triggering events" will vary depending on the needs, desires, and circumstances of the parties.

WHEN IS THE USE OF SUCH A DEVICE INDICATED?

1. When it is essential or desirable to create a market for a business interest upon the death, long-term disability, retirement, divorce, or bankruptcy of an owner.

2. When a shareholder is unwilling or unable to continue running a business with the family of a deceased co-stockholder or someone outside the business.

3. When the continuation of a business at an owner's death involves a high amount of financial risk and it is desirable or necessary to convert the business into cash at that time. For example, if the client's estate is large and will not qualify for the estate tax marital deduction, a means to turn the business interest into cash at a fair price must be found so that taxes can be paid.

4. When a highly-paid owner-employee dies, his or her salary often dies too. Proceeds from the buy-sell help replace this salary.

5. When federal or state law make it imperative that the "closeness" of a close corporation be maintained. For example, too many shareholders or the wrong type of shareholder could result in an involuntary termination of "S" corporation status. Likewise, in most states, non-professionals may not be stockholders in a professional corporation. In at least one state, if no buy-back occurs within 13 months of a shareholder's death, the attorney general of the state could remove the corporation's charter, a potentially disastrous result.

WHAT ARE THE REQUIREMENTS?

1. Restraints on the transferability of stock must be placed in the charter of the corporation. Absent these provisions, a disposition of stock may be effective to transfer the shares even if that gift or sale violates the buy-sell agreement. Even though the parties may successfully sue the person who breaches the buy-sell contract, the damages received will probably be in the form of cash rather than a restoration of the status quo, certainly an inadequate remedy.

   Furthermore, absent a "legend" (warning of the existence of the buy-sell agreement) on the stock certificates, restrictions based solely on the buy-sell itself may be considered "personal to the parties" to the agreement. Subsequent shareholders may not have either the prohibitions or protections of the buy-sell agreement.

2. Stock certificates in the corporation must be marked with a "legend." This is a note that clearly states that the stock is subject to restrictions and specifies where those restrictions can be found. Generally, unless the stock certificate states there is a restriction on the transferability, that restriction will not be effective against a transferee. State law will determine the degree of detail necessary. The buy-sell

should itself require that each stock certificate be marked with this legend.

3. A written document between the parties to the agreement should be drawn up and properly executed. This legal agreement should:

    a) state the business purpose to be served for the agreement;

    b) refer to the events which will trigger a buy-out;

    c) provide a formula for determining the price at which shares are to be exchanged;

    d) explain how and when the purchased stock is to be delivered;

    e) list any restrictions on lifetime transfers;

    f) state any exceptions to the general terms (for instance, to allow a gift or sale to immediate family members);

    g) explain how funding is to be arranged with specific reference to life insurance (a schedule of policies should be appended to the agreement or listed within it);

    h) specifically provide for the purchase of additional insurance as the value of the stock increases;

    i) state how funding of any sales price in excess of insurance proceeds is to be made including interest on the unpaid balance;

    j) explain what is to happen in the event of bankruptcy, receivership, or dissolution of the corporation, the purchase or disposal during lifetime or death of all the stock of a shareholder, or termination of the agreement by a voluntary action of the parties; and

    k) state the applicable jurisdiction under whose laws the document is to be construed.

HOW IS IT DONE – AN EXAMPLE

Joe and Paul, two brothers, have operated a highly successful auto repair and parts business. Joe runs the day-to-day operation of the business and makes the long-run hiring and firing decisions. Paul, the younger brother, is the super salesman who "makes things happen."

Joe knows that either brother would have a difficult time continuing to run the business at its present level if the other brother died (or became permanently disabled). Furthermore, both brothers know their stock is worth in excess of $2 million and will therefore generate considerable federal estate tax when added to their other assets. Both brothers realize their families are dependent on their annual salaries of $300,000 a year, salaries which would stop at their deaths.

Joe and Paul have their attorney draft a "wait and see" buy-sell agreement that provides that if either brother dies, either the corporation or the surviving shareholder will purchase the stock of the decedent and in return pay the estate the full fair market value of the stock in cash.

To finance the purchase upon either brother's death, each brother purchases a life insurance policy on the life of the other. To help them with the premiums, the corporation can agree to pay each brother a bonus sufficient so that, after taxes, each will net an amount large enough to pay policy premiums. (See Chapter 29, "Section 162 Plans.") Alternatively, the corporation might enter into a split dollar agreement with the brothers to help them pay the premiums. (See Chapter 30, "Split Dollar Life Insurance.")

The decedent's family will no longer be tied to the economic success of the business, will not need to bother the surviving brother, and will not be able to interfere in the operation of the business. The surviving brother will have no debt to his late brother's family and will enjoy 100% of the financial rewards for his increased burdens.

WHAT ARE THE TAX IMPLICATIONS?

1. Premiums used to fund a buy-sell agreement are not deductible regardless of who (the corporation, shareholders, or a third party) owns the policy.[1] Planners should therefore consider the comparative tax brackets involved in deciding whether to use the stock redemption or cross purchase approaches to funding a buy-sell agreement.

    If the corporation is in a higher income tax bracket than the shareholders, it may be wise to make tax-deductible salary payments or bonuses to the shareholders and have them buy and own the insurance on a cross purchase basis. If the corporation is the lower bracket, it may make more sense (other things being equal) to use a stock redemption plan.

2. Death proceeds will be received income-tax free regardless of who (the corporation, shareholders, or a third party) owns the policy.[2] However, this favorable general rule is modified where the amount of life insurance is large, the business has substantial revenue, and the proceeds are payable to certain C corporations. Life insurance proceeds received by a C corporation may generate an alternative minimum tax (AMT) liability of up to 15% of the amount of the proceeds. (See the discussion of the AMT in Chapter 24, "Key Employee Life Insurance.")

   The corporate AMT is not a problem where the policy proceeds are received by an S corporation, a partnership, or the individual co-shareholders or partners of the insured. Thus, there is no AMT concern with a cross purchase type agreement.

3. The general rule that life insurance proceeds are income-tax free may not apply where there has been a transfer for valuable consideration. If a life insurance policy or an interest in a policy is transferred for valuable consideration, proceeds exceeding the consideration paid plus any premiums paid after the transfer may be subject to income tax at ordinary rates. (See Appendix G, "The Transfer for Value Rule.")

4. The payment of premiums by a corporation that is the beneficiary of a policy on the life of a shareholder will not be taxed to the shareholder as either a constructive dividend or as salary.[3]

   But if the corporation pays premiums for a policy owned by one shareholder on the life of another, that payment is likely to be considered a distribution of dividends to the policyowner-shareholder.[4] Likewise, if a corporation pays premiums on the life of an insured employee and the proceeds are payable to the estate or personal beneficiary of the employee, the premiums will be includable in the employee's income.[5]

5. Typically, there will be no accumulated earnings tax problem where cash values accumulate in policies that will be used to fund a stock redemption. Amounts accumulated to fund life insurance for stock redemptions are considered to satisfy a reasonable business need and, thus, are not subject to the accumulated earnings penalty tax.[6] But planners should take care to document the business (as contrasted with shareholder) purposes served by the accumulation. The accumulated earnings tax is not a problem when life insurance is owned on a cross purchase basis because no corporate funds are involved.

6. Where shareholders own insurance on the life or lives of other shareholders (a cross purchase plan), at the death of one shareholder, the policy or policies owned by the other shareholders on his life will not be includable in his estate.[7] But the cash values (plus premiums paid but unearned on the date of his death) of the policies the decedent owned on the surviving shareholders' lives will be included in his estate.[8]

   There should be no estate tax inclusion of the life insurance proceeds if the corporation (in the case of a stock redemption) is the owner and beneficiary of the policies.[9] However, planners should check the terms of the buy-sell agreement to determine the degree to which policy proceeds are excluded from the price paid to the deceased shareholder's estate. This is a major decision in drafting a buy-sell plan: if the value of insurance proceeds received under a stock redemption plan is ignored, it can be argued that the surviving shareholders receive a windfall at the expense of the decedent shareholder's family.

   Perhaps the best solution is for the purchase price to include the cash values (but not the death benefits) of the policies on the lives of all shareholders. This is appropriate because the cash values represent a corporate asset to which the insured shareholder had indirectly contributed.

7. Where shareholders own insurance on the life or lives of other shareholders (a cross purchase plan), at the death of one shareholder, the policy or policies owned by the other shareholders on his life will not be includable in his estate.[10] But the value (generally, equals cash surrender value plus premiums paid but unearned on the date of his death) of the policies the decedent owned on the surviving shareholders' lives will be included in his estate.[11]

   There should be no estate tax inclusion of the life insurance proceeds if the corporation (in the case of a stock redemption) is the owner and beneficiary of the policies.[12] However, planners should check the terms of the buy-sell agreement to determine the degree to which policy proceeds are excluded from the price paid to the deceased shareholder's estate. This is a major decision in drafting a buy-sell plan: if the value of insurance proceeds received under a stock redemption plan is ignored, it can be argued that the surviving shareholders receive a windfall at the expense of the decedent shareholder's family.

   Perhaps the best solution is for the purchase price to include the cash values (but not the death benefits) of the policies on the lives of all shareholders. This is appropriate because the cash values represent a corporate asset to which the insured shareholder had indirectly contributed.

8. There appear to be two sets of tests for determining whether the formula price for the stock set forth in a buy-sell agreement will fix the value of the stock for estate tax purposes. The first applies where the buy-sell is between parties other than the "natural objects of the others' bounty." The second, more difficult set of tests, applies when the buyer and seller are either family members or the natural objects of each others' bounty.

When the buyer and seller are not the natural objects of the others' bounty, courts will generally accept the formula price as the value of stock for estate tax purposes if the sales price in the buy-sell agreement meets the following requirements:[13]

a) The estate must be obligated to sell the stock at a shareholder's death,

b) The price must be fixed by the terms of the agreement or the agreement must contain a formula or method for determining the price,

c) The agreement must prohibit the owner from selling the stock during lifetime without first offering it to the other party or parties at a price that does not exceed the "death time" price, and

d) The price must be fair at the time the agreement is entered into.

When the buyer and seller are natural objects of the others' bounty, courts will generally accept the formula price as the value of stock for estate tax purposes only if the sales price in the buy-sell agreement meets the requirements above and, in addition:[14]

a) The document must represent a bona fide business agreement,

b) The agreement must not be a device to transfer the stock to the family or other natural objects of the transferor's bounty for less than full and adequate consideration in money or money's worth, and

c) The agreement's terms must be comparable to terms that similar businesses would agree to in a similar arm's length transaction.

As a practical matter, these rules imply that the buy-sell price must be determined by formula, the formula must be based on currently accepted valuation techniques, and the formula price must approximate the fair market value of the business interest at the date of the triggering event. Further, the formula must be generally recognized as suitable to valuing the type of business involved, and at the time the buy-sell is signed, it must be the result of good faith arm's length bargaining.

If all of the requirements above are met, the price at which a deceased stockholder's shares must be sold under a buy-sell agreement will bind the IRS and the courts as the estate tax value of the stock.

9. No taxable gift occurs upon the execution of a buy-sell agreement. Likewise, sales required under the agreement should not be taxable gifts because adequate consideration is given to all parties through their mutual promises, and because the agreement and sales are transactions in the ordinary course of business.

10. A buy-sell agreement will not usually fix the gift tax value of stock because most agreements either prohibit gifts without the written consent of the other shareholders or permit gifts only after the shareholder first offers to sell the shares to the other shareholders.[15] But, in the authors' opinion, a well drafted buy-sell agreement, i.e., one which meets the requirements for binding the IRS to the value set where the parties are the natural objects of the others' bounty, should be considered highly relevant and will probably succeed in establishing a gift tax value.

11. The nonexcercise of a favorable purchase right under a buy-sell may have gift tax implications. It is possible that the IRS could argue that the waiver of an option to buy stock under a buy-sell agreement is, itself, a taxable gift to the extent the holder of the right to buy chooses not to require the sale and a family member benefits by this inaction.

QUESTIONS AND ANSWERS

Question – What are the various forms of buy-sell agreements and what are the differences among them?

Answer – Buy-sell agreements can take a number of forms based on the tax and other objectives and circumstances of the parties to the contract:

1. *Stock redemption* – In this type of buy-sell arrangement, the business itself purchases the shareholder's interest upon the triggering event, preferably according to a formula-determined price. With respect to any insurance, the corporation should be the applicant, owner, beneficiary, and premium payor. This arrangement is sometimes called an "entity purchase."

2. *Cross purchase* – In this type of arrangement, the remaining business owners buy the business interest upon the triggering event, preferably under a formula-determined price. With respect to any insurance, the shareholders should be the applicants, owners, beneficiaries, and premium payors. This arrangement is sometimes called a "criss cross."

3. *Wait and see* – This highly flexible approach allows planners to defer the decision regarding the eventual purchaser until a triggering event occurs. It is appropriate when the corporation or surviving shareholders may not have sufficient funds to purchase a decedent shareholder's stock alone, when the client's advisers seek more flexibility in light of rapidly-changing tax laws and client circumstances, or when the client's advisers seek an escape hatch to avoid adverse income tax consequences. Mechanically, the wait and see buy-sell works as follows:

   a) The corporation is given a first option to purchase any or all of the exiting shareholder's stock. At this stage, the wait and see buy-sell takes the form of a stock redemption plan. To the extent that option is not exercised within a designated period, the parties enter Stage B.

   b) At this stage, the remaining shareholders are given an option to purchase the stock. Here, the arrangement is similar to a cross purchase plan.

   c) Any stock remaining at the expiration of the second option must be purchased by the corporation. In this final stage, the purchase takes the form of a stock redemption.

The order of the three stages is important. If the parties were reversed and the corporation were to purchase shares under option (b), relieving shareholders of an obligation to purchase stock under option (c), the IRS would classify the payment by the corporation as a constructive dividend.

The insurance policies that fund the wait and see can be arranged in a number of ways. The corporation could purchase a policy on the life of each shareholder and use the proceeds to finance its purchase of stock from a decedent-shareholder's estate, to effect an IRC Section 303 partial stock redemption, or to loan the proceeds to the surviving shareholders in order that they might purchase the decedent's shares under option (b). The shareholders could purchase the insurance as under a cross purchase plan and, if they choose not to purchase the decedent's shares themselves, loan the proceeds to the corporation or make additional capital contributions to the corporation, thus increasing their basis in their own stock. Finally, a third party, such as an irrevocable trust, could purchase the insurance as a means of keeping the proceeds out of the decedent's estate.

4. *Third party buy-out* – A third party agrees contractually to purchase the business interest upon a triggering event.

Question – What is the purpose or impetus for a buy-sell?

Answer – Buy-sell agreements are used to accomplish many important estate planning objectives, the four most important of which are:

1. To create a market for a shareholder's stock which in turn reduces or eliminates the liquidity problems created by the ownership of closely-held stock and helps the owner "harvest" the fruit of his or her labor.

2. To help establish the value of the stock of a closely-held enterprise for both federal and state death tax purposes and between the parties and their heirs.

3. To prevent the sale or other transfer of stock or other equity interests beyond the current owners and therefore maintain the "closeness" of the closely-held business. Remaining shareholders are assured that they are protected against inactive and

potentially dissident shareholders who often cause conflict over management policies such as the size of dividends relative to salaries or risks the corporation should take for growth.

4. To preserve the tax status of an S corporation or the professional status of a professional corporation.

Question – There are three ways other than life insurance to fund a buy-sell: (1) cash; (2) installment payments; and (3) borrowing. Why is life insurance almost always the preferable choice?

Answer – The best answer to that question is for all the client's advisers to ask (and answer) a number of further questions. If the buy-out is to depend on cash:

1. How much will be needed?

2. Will after-tax dollars be kept on hand to finance the purchase?

3. Will a higher rate of return have to be sacrificed in order to have adequate cash on hand?

If the buy-out is to depend on borrowing from a bank or other third party:

1. Will the firm or the surviving shareholders be able to borrow money after the death or long-term disability of a shareholder-employee?

2. What rate of interest will be required on the unpaid balance – and will that interest be deductible?

3. How seriously will the cash drain effect corporate and personal reserves?

If the buy-out is to depend on installment payments from the buyer to the seller:

1. Can the decedent-shareholder's family afford to leave large sums of money at the risk of the business?

2. Where will the deceased shareholder's family obtain cash to pay taxes, debts, and other immediate estate settlement costs?

3. What rate of interest will the decedent's family need to charge on the unpaid balance?

4. Will the interest paid by the buyer be deductible?

5. What will the total cost of payments be in terms of sales necessary to generate the cash to pay both principal and interest?

Question – What are some of the advantages of using life insurance in a buy-sell agreement?

Answer – There are a number of advantages. Some of these include:

1. Life insurance funding has a relatively low cost, is simple to explain and implement, and will not adversely affect the working capital or credit position of the business.

2. Life insurance is the only means of guaranteeing that death, the event that creates the need for cash, also "creates the cash" to satisfy that need.

3. Survivors of the deceased shareholder are freed from financial dependence on a business that has just lost a key individual.

4. Survivors of the deceased shareholder are assured of a fair (and hopefully sufficient) amount of both capital and income.

5. The insurance proceeds are paid quickly after the insured's death, making it easy to close the sale quickly.

Question – What are the disadvantages or downside costs to funding a buy-sell with life insurance?

Answer – There are, of course, costs associated with a life insurance funded buy-sell. Some of these costs include:

1. Premiums must be paid with after-tax dollars.

2. Uninsurable shareholders present a problem. Planners should note, however, that very few individuals are refused insurance because of age or physical health. Most insurers will agree to cover almost

any age (up to the mid-70s) and will insure illnesses by adding a "rating," which is a charge that equates the total premium to the appropriate level of additional risk the insurer is assuming.

3. With a stock redemption plan, the corporation needs only one policy on each shareholder's life. But in the case of a cross purchase plan, especially one that involves more than 3 shareholders, where each shareholder owns a policy on each other shareholder's life, the number of policies (and therefore the administrative complexity, cost, and potential for error) multiplies each time new insurance is added because of an increase in the valuation of a stock interest.

To ascertain the number of policies needed where a cross purchase agreement is used, multiply the number of shareholders by that same number less one. In other words, the formula for determining the number of policies is N x (N - 1) with N being the number of shareholders. So if there were four shareholders, 12 new policies would be needed each time the business interest was revalued.

Question – Can a trustee be used to solve the "multiple policy problem" when funding a cross purchase buy-sell?

Answer – Planners should beware of an often mentioned "solution" to the multiple policy problem in a cross purchase arrangement: the use of a trustee. It has been suggested that if the shareholders in a cross purchase agreement give cash to a trustee who will purchase insurance on each shareholder's life on behalf of the others, only one policy is necessary on each shareholder's life.

While this statement is correct, when the first shareholder dies, his estate still owns an interest in the policies he owned on the other shareholders' lives. When that interest is transferred to the other shareholders (regardless of the form of the transfer) who have beneficial interests in the trust, the surviving shareholders now have a right to insurance proceeds they did not have before. This could easily trigger an adverse income tax consequence under the transfer for value rule, as discussed in Appendix G.

Question – How much life insurance should be purchased?

Answer – It is highly recommended that if at all possible the buy-sell be fully funded from inception. This is because the value of a business interest (and therefore the need for cash to buy that interest) increases because of the real value increases in the interest itself as well as because of inflationary growth. For instance, a business interest worth $500,000 today enjoying a 6% real growth and a 4% inflationary growth will be worth almost $1,300,000 just 10 years from now and over $3,000,000 in 20 years.

Another reason full funding is imperative is that at the death of one owner, the value of the survivor's stock increases significantly. When there are three or more owners, this entails the purchase of more insurance at future dates.

To help meet future needs, it is strongly suggested that life insurance used to fund a buy-sell be purchased using dividends to buy "paid up additions" (blocks of additional permanent insurance purchased with no commissions or acquisition cost) and/or "one year term insurance" (pure term insurance with no commissions or acquisition cost).

Question – In general terms what are the tax implications when a cross purchase buy-sell approach is used?

Answer – When a cross purchase form of buy-sell is used, upon a "sale triggering" event (such as death, long-term disability, or retirement), the seller is required to sell shares to the other shareholders at the price and conditions set in the agreement. Any gain on the sale is a capital gain (regardless of the character of the corporation's underlying assets).[16]

If the seller is the shareholder's estate, and the stock is sold shortly after the shareholder's death, there is usually little or no gain realized by the estate. This is because the estate's income tax basis is the federal estate tax (fair market) value of the stock on the date of death.[17] If the buy-sell meets the Chapter 14 requirements discussed under Tax Implications, the formula price should peg the stock's estate tax value and no gain should be realized.

A cross purchase is advantageous from the perspective of the purchasing shareholders. They increase the income tax basis in their total stock interests by the price they pay for the stock bought under the agreement (even if tax-free life insurance proceeds provided the cash for the purchase). So if a surviving shareholder decides at some later date to sell his interest, because of the increase in basis, his gain on the sale will be lower.

For instance, if a shareholder paid $500,000 to the estate of a deceased co-shareholder, the stock he just purchased would now have a $500,000 basis. If that stock was later sold by the surviving shareholder for $700,000, only the $200,000 gain would be taxable. Contrast this with a stock redemption where the survivor gets no increase in basis no matter how much the corporation pays for the deceased shareholder's stock.

Question – In general terms, what are the income tax implications of a stock redemption arrangement where the corporation buys back its own stock?

Answer – A stock redemption can be a much more complicated transaction than a cross purchase for a number of reasons. The main problem is the danger that the IRS will treat the redemption price amount as a dividend to the shareholder selling the stock. Unless the transaction meets certain tests, a corporate distribution in redemption of its stock is classified and taxed as a dividend.[18] That means every cent paid to the seller (not just the gain) is taxable in full, generally at capital gains rates, to the extent of the shareholder's share of corporate current and accumulated earnings and profits. No credit or offset is allowed for the selling shareholder's basis, no matter how large it may have been or how that basis was obtained.[19] The result when the redemption occurs during lifetime may not be so dramatic but in comparison to the typically favorable tax implications when the sale occurs after a shareholder's death, dividend treatment is a tax misfortune.

For instance, assume the following facts:

1. The client's stock is to be purchased at his death for $1,000,000 ($1,000 per share for 1,000 shares).

2. The buy-sell meets Chapter 14 tests and the price paid by the corporation will also be recognized by the IRS as the estate tax value of the stock.

3. The corporation has accumulated earnings and profits far in excess of the distribution.

At the client's death, if the redemption is taxed under "sale or exchange" rules, the estate realizes

$1,000,000, its income tax basis is $1,000,000, and it recognizes no gain because the amount it has realized does not exceed its basis. So the tax is zero.

But if the redemption is taxed as a dividend, the estate realizes $1,000,000 of ordinary income and its basis does not reduce that income. State and federal taxes would likely exceed $150,000.

Question – Internal Revenue Code (IRC) section 302 provides three "safe harbor" tests that, if met, will result in sale or exchange, rather than dividend, treatment upon the sale of stock to a corporation. What are these tests?

Answer – IRC Section 302 provides that a redemption will be treated as a sale or exchange if the redemption meets any of the three following tests:

1. The redemption is not equivalent to a dividend;

2. The redemption is "substantially disproportionate" with respect to the shareholder (the shareholder's interest in the corporation after the redemption is less than 80% of his or her interest before the redemption, and the shareholder's interest after the redemption is less than 50% of the total combined voting power of all shares), or

3. The redemption completely terminates the shareholder's interest in the corporation.

Planners cannot rely on the first test because it is one that can be determined only after the fact. And, as with much of the tax law, neither the substantially disproportionate nor the complete termination test is as easily met as it would appear when there are certain relationships between the seller and other parties who own (or who are deemed to own) stock.

Meeting either of these tests when the corporation is family-owned is extremely difficult because of the attribution (constructive ownership) rules of IRC Section 318. In a nutshell, stock is owned constructively by (treated as if owned by) the seller if it is actually owned by certain family members or entities in which the shareholder holds an interest.

So in the typical family-owned business in which all stock is held by parents and their children, the sale of stock back to the corporation – even if it is all the stock the seller actually owns – may be neither substantially disproportionate nor a complete termination of the selling shareholder's interest because the seller is deemed to own stock actually owned by others.

For instance, assume these facts:

1. Out of 1,000 shares outstanding, the client and his wife each own 250 shares of their family corporation's stock.

2. The client's son and daughter each own 250 shares.

3. At the death of a shareholder, the buy-sell agreement requires the corporation to purchase all the shares the decedent owned from his estate.

4. The purchase price is $1,000 a share.

5. The client dies and leaves his entire estate to his wife.

6. His executor receives the 250 shares at the client's death and under the agreement sells the stock to the corporation which pays the estate $250,000 in return.

The $250,000 payment the corporation makes to the executor in return for the stock is treated as a dividend rather than a sale or exchange. Why? Because the estate is deemed to own – both before and after the transaction – 100% of the corporation's stock.

Under the attribution rules, the client's widow is deemed to own the 500 shares of stock actually owned by her two children. Of course, the widow also actually owns her own 250 shares. The client's estate is deemed to own the stock owned by its beneficiary, the client's widow. So, due to the attribution rules, before the redemption the estate is deemed to own 100% (1,000) of the 1,000 outstanding shares of the corporation. After the redemption, the estate is still deemed to own 100% of the 750 shares still outstanding.

There is a limited way to break this link between family members called a "waiver of family attribution."[20] The selling shareholder can waive (cut the string on) the family attribution rules and treat the transaction as a substantially dispropor-

tionate or complete termination of interest – but only if all three of the following additional requirements are met:

1. During ten years prior to the redemption, the selling shareholder must not have transferred any stock to or received any stock from someone from whom the stock would have been attributed to the seller (unless the seller can prove that the transfer did not have avoiding federal income taxes as one of its principal purposes).

2. Immediately after the redemption, the seller must have no interest in the corporation (other than as a creditor), including interests as an employee, officer, or director.

3. The seller must agree not to acquire any interest in the corporation (other than as a creditor) during the next ten years and to notify the IRS if a prohibited interest is acquired during this period.

Question – Even if the rules of IRC Section 302 are not met, is there a way to qualify a corporation's purchase of its own stock as a sale or exchange by the selling shareholder?

Answer – Yes. This last resort safe harbor is known as IRC Section 303. It applies only if the sale of stock occurs after a shareholder's death and thus will not protect the seller in a lifetime redemption. In general terms, to qualify for an IRC Section 303 redemption and its protection against dividend treatment, the stock owned by the deceased shareholder must have comprised a substantial portion of his or her estate.

More specifically, IRC Section 303 allows sale or exchange treatment on the redemption of closely-held stock to the extent of the estate's federal and state death taxes, administrative expenses, funeral expenses and generation-skipping transfer taxes.

To qualify for this favorable treatment, the stock owned by the decedent must comprise more than 35% of the adjusted gross estate (defined as the decedent's gross estate less deductible losses and expenses).

Stock can be redeemed under the umbrella of IRC Section 303 only to the extent it generates an estate tax. So in many clients' estates, because of the unlimited marital deduction and the unified credit, the amount of stock that can be redeemed is minimal. Further limiting the usefulness of IRC Section 303 is the requirement that it applies only to the extent that the redeemed shareholder's interest is reduced "directly" (or through a binding obligation to contribute to the tax) by any payment of estate taxes or expenses. This makes it impossible for the trustee of the client's marital trust to safely sell stock back to the corporation under IRC Section 303 because such trusts specifically forbid the payment of taxes.

Question – What should be done with existing life insurance where a corporation changes from a stock redemption to a cross purchase agreement?

Answer – In the case of a corporation that switches to a cross purchase from a stock redemption (perhaps to avoid or minimize the impact of any corporate AMT), planners should consider leaving currently owned corporate insurance on a reduced paid up basis (the cash values in the policies pay future premiums but the death benefit is reduced) and using that corporate coverage as key employee insurance. Parties to the agreement can then purchase new coverage without fear of violating the transfer for value rule. See Appendix G for further discussion of this rule.

Question – How can a split dollar arrangement be used to help one shareholder afford the insurance on another shareholder's life?

Answer – The split dollar technique is explained in detail in Chapter 30. Essentially, the corporation pays all or the bulk of the premium necessary to finance the insurance that one shareholder buys on the life of another. To secure the repayment of its outlays, the corporation requires the policyowner to collaterally assign his interest to the firm. Under regulations issued in September 2003, payments by the corporation will be treated as loans to the policyowner. If the policyowner pays market interest rates on these "loans," there should be no additional tax consequences. However, if the policyowner pays less than market interest rates, the split dollar arrangement will be subject to the below market loan rules, which are discussed in detail in Chapter 30.

Question – If the shareholders of a corporation have fully funded a cross purchase agreement by purchasing life insurance policies on each others' lives, what are the problems, if any, upon a sale by a deceased shareholder's estate of policies that the shareholder owned on the lives of co-shareholders?

Answer – A transfer for value problem can exist when a deceased shareholder's executor or administrator sells policies on the lives of the surviving stockholders. (See Appendix G, "The Transfer for Value Rule.") There is both a transfer of a policy and consideration paid for the transfer – the two crucial elements required for the transfer for value rule to be invoked at the death of the insured.

Possible solutions include:

1. The estate can sell the policies it owns on the lives of surviving shareholders to the corporation, which can then establish a stock redemption plan, IRC Section 303 partial redemption, or a wait and see buy-sell agreement that integrates properly with the existing cross purchase agreement.

2. The estate can surrender each policy to the insurer for cash. Surviving shareholders can then purchase additional life insurance on each other's life (assuming they are insurable). Premiums will be higher because the insureds will be older than when the surrendered policies were purchased. Poor health of the survivors or risk-taking avocations may result in rated premiums.

3. The survivors can purchase the policies on their own lives from the decedent shareholder's executor and continue them as personal insurance. The proceeds will be received by the insured's beneficiaries income-tax free because a transfer of a policy to the insured is one of the exceptions to the transfer for value rule.

4. Perhaps the safest approach, if the circumstances are appropriate, is for a partnership consisting of the surviving partners to purchase the policies.

Question – What problems, if any, are entailed where a trust owns policies on the lives of shareholders?

Answer – Some buy-sell agreements use an independent trustee to hold the stock of the various shareholders and the life insurance policies on the lives of each of them. This expedites the buy-sell exchange and gives the parties assurance that the terms of the buy-sell will be carried out. There are relatively few problems when a trusteed approach is used in a stock redemption context.

However, when the trusteed approach is used to reduce the number of policies necessary in a cross purchase plan, there may be a serious problem. At the death of one shareholder, the interest he or she had in the policy on the lives of the other shareholders "terminates" and the surviving shareholders gain an interest (through their beneficial interest in the trust) in the policies on the lives of the other surviving shareholders. On the first shareholder's death, there is no transfer of ownership within the trust. But the transfer for value rule does not require such a transfer. It requires merely a transfer of an interest in a policy. Here, although legal title to the policies on the lives of the survivors does not change, the beneficial interest in the decedent's share of the policies on his co-shareholders' lives does.

Each portion of each policy the deceased shareholder owned during his life has now shifted to the survivors. On each shareholder's death, there would be some transfer of equitable ownership within the trust to the surviving co-shareholders. The valuable consideration is the reciprocity. No policyowner would allow the beneficial interest in a policy he or she owned on another shareholder's life to pass through the legal ownership held by the trustee to the other shareholders unless each of the other shareholders did the same.

A possible solution is for the corporation to purchase the policies on the lives of the surviving shareholders from the estate of the deceased but have the trustee hold those policies within the trust on behalf of the corporation as a new grantor of the trust. Using a wait and see approach, the purchase of a deceased shareholder's stock in the future could be part stock redemption (perhaps under the protection of IRC Section 303) and part cross purchase (using the policies held by the trust that were not part of the corporation's interest).

Question – What are the problems, if any, in using group term insurance to fund the promises under a buy-sell agreement?

Answer – The potential for a transfer for value problem exists where group term life insurance is used to fund a cross purchase agreement. Assume, for example, that Marcy S and Marsha R are two shareholder executives of the S&R corporation. Each is covered for $500,000 under their company's group term life plan. Marcy S names Marsha R as her beneficiary and Marsha R names Marcy S as her beneficiary. Although no money changes hands

between the two and even though the policies are term insurance, there is a transfer for valuable consideration. Their reciprocal promises to name each other as beneficiary provides the requisite valuable consideration. At the death of either, proceeds will be subject to ordinary income taxation.

Question – Is there a simplified way to explain Chapter 14's IRC Section 2703 and its implications to my clients?

Answer – Yes. In a nutshell, neither the IRS nor the courts will be bound for estate tax purposes to the price established in a buy-sell agreement unless the seller would in fact sell the interest to a totally independent non-family member for that price and that party (assuming reasonable knowledge of the relevant facts) would reasonably and without coercion pay that price.

Buy-sell agreements among related parties must now use an appraisal or a reasonable formula. Fixed prices set in buy-sells will probably not be accepted by the IRS or the courts as determinative of estate tax value no matter how reasonable when drafted.

Planners should review all buy-sell arrangements for compliance with the latest estate freeze rules and safe harbor requirements for buy-sell agreements. Many of these agreements should be revised to provide a more realistic price.

CHAPTER ENDNOTES

1. IRC Secs. 264(a)(1), 265(a)(1).
2. IRC Sec. 101(a).
3. *Casale v. Comm.*, 247 F.2d 440 (2d Cir., 1957); Rev. Rul. 59-184, 1959-1 CB 65.
4. *Doran v. Comm.*, 246 F.2d 934 (9th Cir. 1957); Rev. Rul. 59-184, 1959-1 CB 65.
5. Treas. Reg. §1.61-2(d)(2).
6. *Mountain State Steel Foundries, Inc. v. Comm.*, 284 F.2d 737 (4th Cir. 1960); *Oman Constr. Co. v. Comm.*, TC Memo 1965-325. But see also *John B. Lambert & Assoc. v. U.S.*, 76-1 USTC ¶9466 (Ct. Cl. 1976).
7. IRC Sec. 2042.
8. IRC Sec. 2033.
9. IRC Sec. 2042.
10. IRC Sec. 2042.
11. IRC Sec. 2033.
12. IRC Sec. 2042.

13. *May v. McGowan,* 194 F.2d 396 (2nd Cir. 1952); *Comm. v. Child's Est.,* 147 F.2d 368 (3rd Cir 1945); *Comm. v. Bensel,* 100 F.2d 639 (3rd Cir. 1938); *Est. of Seltzer v. Comm.,* TC Memo 1985-519.

14. IRC Sec. 2703.

15. *Est. of James v. Comm.,* 148 F.2d 236 (2nd Cir. 1945); *Kline v. Comm.,* 130 F.2d 742 (3rd Cir. 1942).

16. IRC Sec. 1221.

17. IRC Sec. 1014.

18. IRC Sec. 301(a).

19. IRC Sec. 316(a).

20. IRC Sec. 302(c)(2).

Chapter 21

CHARITABLE USES OF LIFE INSURANCE

WHAT IS IT?

A transfer of cash or other property to certain charitable, religious, scientific, educational, or other organizations may result in favorable income, gift, and estate tax results for the donor.[1] Income taxes can be reduced and estate taxes can be saved. More importantly, a gift to charity serves to reward the donor in significant psychological and moral ways. Charitable giving is one of the most important of all estate and financial planning considerations.

Life insurance is an important vehicle for accomplishing these tax and non-tax objectives. It is used in one of two ways:

1. as a direct means of benefiting the charity; or

2. as a way to allow the donor to give other assets during lifetime or at death to charity without denying or reducing the financial security of his family. It may even serve as a form of wealth enhancement.

Life insurance can be used both during the client's lifetime and at death to make meaningful gifts to charity. Some of the strategies used to provide direct gifts of life insurance to charity include:

• Donation of existing insurance policies on the life of a client to a qualified charity.

• Purchase and donation to a charity of new insurance on the life of the client, the client's spouse, or both.

• Disposition by will of a policy on another's life to a charity. The value of the policy at the policy owner's death will be includable in his estate, but an equal and offsetting deduction will be allowed for the gift to the charity by will.

• Contribution of cash directly to a charity, which in turn uses that cash to purchase a new (or existing) policy on the life of the donor (or other supporter).

• Naming the charity revocable or irrevocable beneficiary of one or more life insurance contracts (individual or group).

• Contribution of an asset other than life insurance in order to generate an income tax deduction, which in turn can save the client money otherwise payable in tax. This tax savings can then be gifted to the client's children or other beneficiary (or to an irrevocable trust for their benefit) who could use that cash to purchase life insurance on the client's life, or on the life of the client's spouse. The charity receives an immediate and certain gift and the client's beneficiary receives what he would have received (or, in many cases, even more) after taxes had there been no charitable gift. This use of life insurance is often called "wealth replacement."

WHEN IS THE USE OF SUCH A DEVICE INDICATED?

1. When the client would like to benefit one or more charities for reasons other than tax savings.

2. When the client would like to benefit himself and/or his family through tax savings and create more income and capital at the same time a charity is benefited.

3. When a client would like to achieve the first and second objectives and is willing to incur expense to accomplish both. Planners and clients should both be aware that tax advantages do not mean a charitable gift is without cost. Charitable tax incentives may reduce the overall cost of the gift, and the achievement of noncharitable financial security goals may be facilitated through charitable giving techniques. But charitable giving should be considered as a planning tool only if the client has genuine charitable motives and has examined more direct alternatives for the accomplishment of noncharitable objectives.

WHAT ARE THE REQUIREMENTS?

1. The gift of the policy or other property must be made to a qualified charity such as a nonprofit school or hospital, a church or synagogue, or a local or civic organization such as the Boy Scouts or Girl Scouts of America. "Qualified" means that the charity meets three conditions:

   a) the organization is operated exclusively for religious, charitable, scientific, literary, or educational purposes, or to foster national or international amateur sports competition, or to prevent cruelty to children or animals;

   b) no part of the earnings of the organization can be used to benefit any private shareholder or similar individual; and

   c) the organization cannot be one disqualified for tax exemption because it attempts to influence legislation or participates in, publishes, or distributes statements for, or intervenes in, any political campaign on behalf of any candidate seeking public office.

2. The gift of the policy or other property must be made before the end of the taxable year, even if the client is an accrual basis taxpayer. (Corporations reporting income on the accrual basis are subject to a less stringent standard.[2])

3. The gift must be of the donor's entire interest; generally, no deduction will be allowed for a gift of a "partial interest" (unless strict and narrow rules are met). So in most cases where a policy will be co-owned, or the death proceeds, cash values, or dividends will be split between noncharitable and charitable beneficiaries, no deduction will be allowed.[3]

4. Records must be kept, preferably in the form of canceled checks payable to the charity and/or a receipt from the charity showing the date, amount, and identity of the donor and donee.

5. The gift must exceed any benefit the client receives from the charity. If the client receives a benefit from the charity in conjunction with his gift, the deduction will be limited to the excess of the amount donated over the value of the benefit received from the charity.

HOW IS IT DONE – AN EXAMPLE

Life insurance creates an instant "expanded estate," and in many cases the proceeds can be transferred free of estate tax. If arranged properly, all parties could end up with a greater economic benefit than if life insurance were not used. Below is a more detailed explanation of some of the strategies used to provide for charity through indirect uses of life insurance:

1. A charity can be named as the annual recipient of any dividends received from life insurance. As dividends are paid to the charity, the client receives a current income tax deduction.

2. Dividends from an existing policy can be used to purchase a new policy. The client can name the charity as the owner and beneficiary of the new policy. An income tax deduction is allowed for the premiums paid by the client.

3. A charity can be named as contingent (backup) beneficiary or final beneficiary under a life insurance policy protecting dependents of a client. Should a primary beneficiary predecease the client, the charity will receive the proceeds, assuming the client does not have the opportunity or desire to change the beneficiary. Because the policy itself is never transferred to charity the proceeds are subject to estate tax. However, the proceeds will qualify for the unlimited federal estate tax charitable deduction and will offset the estate tax liability.

4. A charity can be named as the beneficiary of a currently owned or a newly acquired life insurance policy. Although this strategy will not yield a current income tax deduction and the proceeds will be included in the client's gross estate, it will result in a federal estate tax deduction for the full amount of the proceeds payable to charity, regardless of how large the policy.

5. An absolute assignment (gift) of a currently owned life insurance policy can be made to a charity. Alternatively, a new life insurance policy can be purchased and immediately transferred to the charity. Either strategy will yield a current income tax deduction.

6. Group term life insurance can be used to meet charitable objectives. By naming a charity as the (revocable) beneficiary of group term life insur-

ance for coverage over $50,000, a client can make a significant gift to charity while avoiding any income tax on the economic benefit. For example, a 66-year-old executive with an average top tax bracket of 40% who had $1,050,000 of coverage would save $6,096 each year, 40% of the $15,240 annual "Table I cost" (the amount reportable as income). The advantage of this technique was significantly enhanced by the introduction of higher group term rates for individuals over age 65 who receive group term insurance. So the client saves income taxes every year the charity is named as beneficiary. In a later year if the client changes his mind, he can change the beneficiary designation and name a new charity or even a personal beneficiary. Note that the charity must be the sole beneficiary for the entire tax year.

7. Property can be donated directly to a charity and life insurance can be used to replace the wealth that might otherwise have been received by the client's children. For instance, the client, a widow in a 40% combined state and federal income tax bracket, contributes property worth $100,000 to a tax-exempt charitable entity such as Temple University. Assuming the client is entitled to a deduction on the full value of the gift, the $40,000 that she otherwise would have paid in income taxes is instead still available to her. She can choose to give the tax savings from the charitable gift to her child or grandchild who can, in turn, purchase and maintain insurance on her life.

Assume the amount of the insurance is at least enough to make up for the property the heirs would have received had no gift been made to charity. Life insurance takes the place of the net after-tax (and other cost) assets the heirs would have received had no planning been accomplished and had no gift to charity been made. In some cases the heirs will be able to take the tax savings realized by the client and purchase insurance to cover the value of the assets they would have received (after federal and state death taxes) had no gift been made. Here, life insurance is used to guarantee wealth replacement. Alternatively, they could purchase enough insurance to receive what they would have been left by the client had there been no estate tax on the property that was given to charity. In this case, life insurance provides wealth enhancement.

"Wealth Replacement" or "Wealth Enhancement" are concepts that can be realized in many ways, either during lifetime or at death, and either directly or coupled with a transfer to a charitable trust as illustrated below.

WHAT ARE THE TAX IMPLICATIONS?

The tax implications of using life insurance to benefit a charity include the following:

1. A current income tax deduction is allowed for the transfer of a cash value life insurance policy to a qualified charity. The client will save an amount equal to the value of the deductible gift multiplied by the client's effective tax bracket. For example, a $10,000 gift by a client in a 40% combined federal and state income tax bracket will yield a $4,000 tax savings. This means the cost of the gift is lowered to the amount contributed less the tax savings. In this example, the gift cost $6,000 ($10,000 - $4,000).

The deduction for a charitable gift of a life insurance policy is subject to the same limitations as other charitable gifts.[4] One such limitation relates to the amount of a current deduction allowed based on a percentage of the donor's adjusted gross income in that year.[5]

A second limitation is that to be deductible the gift must be total and absolute. An outright gift of all of the incidents of ownership and all rights and benefits in a life insurance policy will be deductible up to the allowable percentage of the donor's income. A gift of less than the client's entire interest in a life insurance policy (or any other asset) will be deductible only if it constitutes one of the following interests:[6]

a) a remainder interest in a qualified charitable remainder unitrust or annuity trust;

b) a remainder interest in a pooled income fund;

c) a charitable gift annuity;

d) a remainder interest in a personal residence or farm;

e) a qualified conservation easement;

f) an undivided portion of the taxpayer's entire interest in property; or

g) a guaranteed annuity interest or unitrust interest in a charitable lead trust.

In other words, a client can usually deduct the value (as defined below) of a life insurance policy given to charity (or to an irrevocable charitable trust). Furthermore, after a complete and irrevocable gift of the policy, the client can deduct any premiums paid after the transfer of the policy to the charity (or to an irrevocable charitable trust).[7] However, no deduction will be allowed for any portion of the gift unless the client donates to the charity either his entire interest or an undivided portion of his entire interest in the policy. A gift of an "undivided portion" of a policy would include a fraction or percentage of each and every substantial right in the policy. Alternatively, a deduction for a gift of a partial interest in property will be permitted if the partial interest is the client's entire interest in the property.[8]

A gift of the cash value will be considered a transfer of less than the client's entire interest regardless of whether the client (a) retains a continuing right to name some other party as the recipient of the "net amount at risk" (i.e., the pure death benefit) or (b) irrevocably designated the recipient of the death benefit before making the gift of the cash value to charity.[9]

If a client creates a "split-dollar" plan with a qualified charity, under which he contributes to the charity the policy's cash surrender value but designates a noncharitable beneficiary as owner of the death benefit, the IRS will not allow an income tax deduction.[10]

Some flexibility is allowed where the client retains a very limited right that cannot be used for the client's personal benefit. For instance, it appears a client can make a gift of a life insurance policy and reserve the right, exercisable only in conjunction with the donee charity, to add another qualified charity as beneficiary, change the portion of the proceeds one or more qualified charities will receive, or even shift all of the proceeds to another qualified charity. Technically, the IRS has reasoned in such situations that even though the donor shares with the charitable owner of the insurance policy the right to designate other qualified charitable recipients, the donor has still made a charitable gift of any rights he held in the policy and, therefore, the gift is not considered a gift of a partial interest.[11]

Merely naming a charity as the beneficiary of a life insurance policy will not result in an income tax deduction, even if the designation is irrevocable. This follows the rule discussed above that the charity must be given the client's entire interest in the policy. If the charity is named only as beneficiary, regardless of whether that designation is revocable or irrevocable, the policy proceeds will be includable in the client's gross estate. But when the death benefit is paid to the charity, the client's estate will be allowed an offsetting charitable deduction.

There is an important exception to this "all or nothing" rule: an employee who names a charity as the beneficiary of the total death benefit (or at least the entire amount in excess of the first $50,000) under a group term life insurance policy on his life for the entire tax year can exclude from income the value of the otherwise taxable coverage attributable to the charitable portion of the proceeds.[12] This charitable technique can shield considerable amounts from income tax; yet, the client can retain the flexibility to change his mind the following year and name a personal beneficiary. The cost of this exclusion from income taxation is that the term coverage will remain in the client's estate and, unless actually paid at death to the designated charity, will generate federal estate tax.

2. When all incidents of ownership in an existing life insurance policy are donated to charity, the transfer is treated as a gift of "ordinary income" property in the year it is assigned absolutely to the charity. This means the donor must reduce his contribution amount by the gain that would have been realized had he cashed in the policy or sold it.[13] The policy owner will be entitled to a current income tax deduction.

The amount of the deduction for a charitable gift of a life insurance policy is generally the lower of (a) the fair market value of the policy, or (b) the donor's cost basis.[14] Stated another way, where the policy's value at the date of the gift is greater than the net premiums the client has paid, the deduction will be limited to the client's net premiums so in most cases, the donor's deduction will be limited to basis.

Fair market value is dependent on the "replacement cost" of the policy. This depends on which of the following is involved:

Newly Issued Policy – Typically, the deduction for a policy transferred immediately after its issue or within its first year is based on the net (gross premium less dividends, if any) premium payments made by the date of the transfer.

Premium Paying Policy – The deduction value is for the sum of the "interpolated terminal reserve" plus any unearned premium at the date of the gift. The term "unearned premium" is defined as the unexpired payment to the insurer between the date of the gift and the premium due date after the gift. Dividends accrued to the date of the gift are also added. Any loans against the policy are subtracted.

Paid-up or Single Premium Policy – The deduction is based on the single premium the same insurer would charge for a policy of the same amount at the insured's attained age.[15]

If the insured is in impaired health, it could be argued (by both the taxpayer in charitable giving cases and the IRS in non-charitable situations) that adverse health increases the value of the gift to charity. This argument is logical since impaired health to some extent must affect life expectancy. To this point, however, there are no rulings, nor is there a formal IRS position on the subject.

3. Premiums are generally deductible on policies contributed to or owned by charity. Once a policy is donated to or purchased on the donor's life by the charity, subsequent premiums are deductible if (a) paid in cash to the charity or (b) paid directly to the insurer. Cash payments made directly "to" a qualified charity will qualify for a current deduction of up to 50% of the donor's adjusted gross income. The current deduction for premium payments made to the insurer (but "for the use of" charity) may be limited to 30% of the donor's adjusted gross income. The charity could, of course, use other money to pay premiums if the client decided to discontinue contributions.

It makes no difference whether premiums are paid all at once (such as in a single premium policy) or over just a few years (such as in a "vanishing payment" arrangement). The deduction will, nevertheless, be allowed in the year the donor parts with dominion and control over the cash. Note that if the client merely collaterally assigns the policy to the charity as security for a note, premiums he pays on the policy will not be deductible. This makes sense because the charity is not the absolute owner of the policy and the policy could easily end up in the client's hands if he pays off the note.

4. Regardless of the size of the gift of life insurance, no federal gift taxes are payable on transfers to qualified charities, but there is an important qualification, especially where life insurance policies are involved. A gift tax charitable deduction is allowed without limit for an outright transfer of a new or existing life insurance contract but, except in certain defined situations, any deduction will be denied if the transfer is "of less than an entire interest" in the policy.[16]

For instance, your client would not be allowed a gift tax charitable deduction for a gift of a "split-dollar" policy between an individual and a charity. In such situations, the insured's gift of the right to the cash surrender value of the policy is a gift of a "partial interest," less than the donor's entire interest in the property and, consequently, does not meet one of the exceptions that will qualify the gift for a charitable deduction. Note that this disallowance cannot be avoided by having the client make an irrevocable designation of a personal beneficiary before making the gift to the charity.

In addition, if a policy is donated to a charity in a state where the charity has no insurable interest in the insured's life, and the lack of such an interest is deemed to give the insured's estate some rights to control the ultimate disposition of the proceeds, the IRS will disallow the deduction on the grounds that the insured retained an incident of ownership.[17] It would seem that if the charity was the original policy purchaser, even where statutory law gives the insured's estate some right over the ultimate disposition of the proceeds, it could not be said that the insured retained some right since he never had it. But smart planners will avoid the issue and check state law to be sure that insurable interest in the life of the insured is not a problem.

5. If a client holds any incident of ownership in the policy at death, regardless of whether the charity owns the policy or whether a charity has been irrevocably named as the beneficiary of the proceeds, the entire amount of the payment made by the insurer at the insured's death will be subject to federal estate tax in the insured's gross estate.[18] (See Appendix A for a discussion of what constitutes an incident of ownership.)

Gifts of life insurance made at death to a qualified charity (as well as those made prior to death to charity that for some reason were brought back into the client's gross estate) are includable in a client's estate, but will receive a federal estate tax charitable deduction. This deduction is unlimited. The policy proceeds could amount to millions of dollars or more and, regardless of how large, could be left to a qualified charity and the estate tax charitable deduction would eliminate the federal estate tax the proceeds would otherwise have generated.[19]

However, even though the estate tax on the insurance paid to charity may be entirely eliminated, there may be a cost. The inclusion of the life insurance may adversely affect the estate's ability to qualify for the benefits of IRC Section 303 (partial stock redemptions), IRC Section 6166 (installment payments of estate tax), and IRC Section 2057 (deduction for qualified family-owned business interest, "QFOBI").

Once again, however, there is an important qualification. As is the case with both the income and gift tax laws, for estate tax purposes the deduction will be disallowed if the entire interest in property is not transferred to the charity. This is due to the fact that if the insured has not given up each and every incident of ownership he owns, he continues to hold a property interest in the policy. This is sufficient to cause estate tax inclusion of the entire proceeds no matter how seemingly small that incident is.

6. If a client assigns all incidents of ownership in a life insurance contract to a charity, and survives for more than three years after the transfer, the policy should be excludable from the donor's estate for federal estate tax purposes.

7. No tax is paid by the charity upon receipt of either a lifetime gift of a life insurance policy or a bequest of a policy at death. Likewise, the payment of premiums by a charity on a policy it owns and is the beneficiary of will not generate a gift tax to the original donor of the policy.

8. Income earned by a charity on assets it owns generally will not be subject to income tax. But as noted below, if a charity borrows policy cash values to finance the purchase of income producing investments, the income produced by these investments may be considered unrelated business taxable income and result in a tax to the otherwise tax-exempt charity.[20]

QUESTIONS AND ANSWERS

Question – What are the advantages of using life insurance as a means of charitable giving?

Answer – There are a number of reasons for using life insurance for charitable giving. These reasons include:

1. The death benefit of a life insurance contract owned by or payable to a charity is a guaranteed, self-completing gift; as long as the insurance is maintained in force by the payment of premiums the charity is assured of the gift. If the client lives, cash values can be used as soon as they are available by the charity for an emergency or opportunity. These cash values will grow constantly year after year. If the client becomes disabled, the policy will remain in full force through the "Waiver of Premium" feature. This guarantees the ultimate death benefit to the charity, as well as the same cash values and dividend buildup that would have been earned had the client not become disabled. Even if the client were to die after only one premium payment, the charity is assured of the full-intended gift. This distinguishes life insurance from other intended gifts through which the charity may or may not be the beneficiary, or may or may not receive what has been promised. So, the life insurance gift to the charity provides an immediate certainty rather than a mere expectation.

2. The life insurance gift is fixed in value and is not subject to the risks and price variations of the securities or real estate markets.

3. A client who might not otherwise be able to afford a significant gift can magnify the utility of a given number of dollars by leveraging them through life insurance. Through a relatively small fixed and budgetable annual cost (the premium), a significant benefit can be provided for the charity of the client's choice. Furthermore, premiums can be spread out over the client's lifetime, making the payment of the gift less burdensome.

4. Life insurance makes it possible to create a sizable gift without impairing or diluting a family's control over its other investments. Other assets earmarked for the client's family can be kept intact. The charity is benefited while the

314

family's financial security is maintained and, perhaps, enhanced.

5. Life insurance is a cost effective means of making large charitable gifts. Life insurance is transferred free of probate, administrative fees, delays, or any other transfer costs. It is not subject to the claims of present or former spouses, or creditors. The charity, therefore, receives 100% of the money and is more certain of that receipt. This prompt and certain payment should be compared with the payment of a gift to the same charity by will.

6. A gift to charity through life insurance can be completely confidential. Conversely, if publicity is desired, it can be arranged very effectively. The amplified gift can lead to public recognition, if desired. For instance, a charitable organization could establish a Millionaires Club consisting of individuals who donated a policy amounting to $1,000,000 or more.

7. Because of the contractual nature of the life insurance contract, large gifts to charity are seldom subjected to attack by disgruntled heirs.

Question – What are the disadvantages or costs of using life insurance in charitable giving?

Answer – There are certain costs involved in using life insurance for charitable giving. These include:

1. Life insurance requires the payment of a stream of dollars in the form of premiums. Fortunately, if unrestricted cash is given to a charity, which then uses those dollars to pay premiums on a policy insuring the donor (or some other individual), the client will receive a current income tax deduction.

2. Life insurance is typically a gift that will not benefit the charity until some future date. This is particularly true if the policy has not been assigned to or purchased and owned by the charity. Life insurance is not, therefore, the indicated means of providing for a charity that is desperate for cash to meet current operating expenses. (However, any charity that seeks to grow must eventually think of its long-term needs, and the use of life insurance in an effective planned giving program will help to insure the long-term financial stability of the organization.)

Question – Why is the existence of insurable interest important when a client makes a gift of life insurance to a charity?

Answer – Assume your client purchases a policy on her life and donates it to a charity in a state in which the charity has no insurable interest in the client's life. The IRS could argue that under state law the decedent's estate (and therefore her heirs) could claim the policy proceeds in spite of the charity's ownership because the charity has no insurable interest. The IRS could then argue that the client's ostensible transfer of all her rights really gave the charity less than her entire interest in the policy. The IRS would state that even though the donor clearly thought she gave all the interest she actually had, because her estate could claim an interest in the proceeds, she was actually in control of the proceeds. The IRS would then seek to disallow income, gift, and estate tax deductions and include the proceeds in the insured's estate, which would be the worst of all possible tax consequences.[21]

Practitioners must carefully read the precise wording of applicable state law. Under New York law, for example, a charity has an insurable interest only if the insured is the policy purchaser and transferor.[22] The statute does not appear to apply to a transfer where one spouse purchases a contract on the other spouse's life and then assigns it to the charity, nor where the charity itself is the purchaser. Other states (Georgia, for example) provide that any institution that meets the Internal Revenue Code definition of a qualified charity has an insurable interest in the life of any donor.

Question – What is the difference between a gift of a policy directly "to" a charity and a gift of a policy "for the use of" a charity?

Answer – The mechanics of a gift of life insurance to a charity can determine how much is deductible by a client in a given year. Gifts of life insurance are more valuable when they are made directly "to" rather than "for the use of" a charity. For instance, if a client pays premiums to the insurance company on a policy owned by a charity on his life, it is true that he is indirectly helping the charity, but this form of payment of the premiums is deductible as a gift "for the use of" the charity and the deduction in a given year, maximum, will thus be limited to only 30% of the client's adjusted gross income. If the client makes a direct cash gift to the charity, the gift will certainly be deductible up to 50% of his adjusted gross income (assuming the gift is to a public charity).[23]

Direct cash gifts to charity in the form of checks also make it easier for the client to substantiate (a) the fact of the gift, (b) the identity of the charitable donee, (c) the timing of the gift, and (d) that the donee did in fact receive the gift. Direct gifts are therefore less likely to cause an audit or generate litigation, and are the recommended way to secure a deduction for gifts to be used to pay premiums.

Question – What are the advantages of using life insurance as a wealth replacement tool?

Answer – Life insurance used as a wealth replacement tool enables a client to meet both charitable and personal objectives by assuring an immediate and certain gift to charity while also assuring his family that they will receive as much, if not more, than they would have received had no gift been made to charity. Since a qualified charity can sell assets contributed to it without an income tax liability on any gain, a client who lacks liquid assets can make a charitable gift of illiquid assets, while still affording the charity a source of cash through the sale of the assets.

Consider this technique as a way to enable a business owner to harvest the fruits of a lifetime of labor without the penalty and loss of heavy income tax on any gain. Compare, for instance, the retirement income derived, net after taxes, from the sale of a family business with the income derived if the business is donated to a charitable remainder trust. The trustee of the trust could sell the business and pay the donor client an income for life or a term of years with 100% of the sales proceeds since the trust would pay no income tax on any appreciation inherent in the gift. Likewise, consider this technique as a way to enable a highly successful investor to convert taxable gain on an investment portfolio into retirement income without the income tax "slippage" inevitable upon a direct sale.

There are many ways the wealth replacement technique can be employed. One way is to create a charitable remainder trust funded with highly appreciated property that generates a low-income yield. The client receives an annuity from the trust (a fixed annuity if the remainder trust is an annuity trust, or a variable annuity if the trust is a unitrust), with the remaining principal going to the qualified charity upon termination of the trust.[24] The advantages of this technique are:

1. The present value of the charity's right to receive the property when the noncharitable

beneficiary's interest ends is currently deductible by the client.

2. Even if the property contributed to the trust has built-in gain, no tax on that appreciation is imposed on the client.

3. If, and when, the trustee sells the property, neither the client nor the trust must report any capital gains. However, part of the noncharitable beneficiary's distributions from the trust may be treated as a distribution of capital gain and taxed at the time of distribution.

4. In many cases the client's income from the donated property will be significantly increased because the trustee will have been able to sell the property (at no tax to the trust) and use the net proceeds to invest in higher yielding securities. Had the client sold the property, his net investable amount would have been reduced by the tax on the gain. So, the tax savings as well as the higher return from the new investment enhance the yield from the trust.

A portion of the cash generated by both the client's immediate income tax deduction and from the increased return from the property can be given to the client's intended heirs. The heirs can choose to use that money to purchase insurance on the life of the client (and/or the client's spouse) so that, at the client's death, the wealth passing to charity through the trust is replaced. Note that replacement requires only the net amount that the intended heirs would have received had the client retained the asset, and had that property been subjected to state and federal death taxes and other transfer costs.

Question – How can life insurance combined with gifts of stock to charity help a client keep a family business in the family?

Answer – Life insurance can be used creatively to combine business continuity objectives and charitable goals in a number of ways. For instance, suppose your client wants to benefit charity, provide liquidity for her own estate, and guarantee that no one but her son can obtain the stock. One possible solution is for her to transfer stock to the charity directly. She could make a gift to her son of the income tax savings that the donation of stock generates. He could use those tax savings to purchase insurance on his mother's life and enter into a buy-sell agreement to assure him that at her death he will have the money to buy her out. At some time in the future, the corporation could purchase the stock from the charity after an arm's-length valuation. This provides the charity with cash and returns the stock to the corporation.

Question – Suppose a client has a very large estate and believes that if he gives his children too much when he dies, he will limit their personal growth incentives. Also, he is charitably inclined. If he leaves his entire estate to his children, his charitable objectives will not have been met and estate taxes will consume a large portion of his estate. He also knows that if he leaves his entire estate to charity, his children will have no financial security. How can life insurance be used to solve this problem?

Answer – Life insurance can serve as a partial wealth replacement vehicle to accomplish many or even all of the client's planning goals. Suppose, for example, that the client is in his middle fifties and is extremely wealthy, but has a spouse with a relatively small estate. He would like to leave most of his estate to a charity, but would also like to provide his wife with income for life and to provide each of his four children with roughly $1,000,000 after taxes to help them build their own fortunes.

Here's one way the client can accomplish his objectives using life insurance:

Step 1: The client and his spouse can give as much as $2,000,000 ($1,000,000 unified credit equivalent for each spouse) away immediately in the form of $500,000 cash gifts to each of their four children. No gift tax is payable on the transfers, assuming the couple has made no taxable gifts in the past. This money is used by each child to purchase a large policy either on the client's life, his spouse's life, on the survivor of the two, or a combination of these. The children own and are beneficiaries of the insurance, none of which will be in the client's estate, and none of which is subject to the claims of the client's (or his spouse's) creditors.

Step 2: Simultaneous with the large cash gifts, the client establishes a testamentary charitable remainder trust that provides that at the client's death prior to his wife, she will

receive all the income from the trust for as long as she lives. At her death, all the assets in the trust will pass to her alma mater. The entire estate remaining at the client's death passes into this trust, which entirely eliminates the federal estate tax at his death and provides his wife with significant income for as long as she lives. This technique provides a substantial benefit to the charity as well.

The wealth replacement concept is supported by two factors. First, the four children purchase life insurance for pennies on the dollar. Second, some or all of the premiums are financed by money that otherwise would have been paid in taxes or by income that would not have been enjoyed by the client had he done nothing. In the case of a testamentary charitable gift such as the one in the example directly above, the income of the client's spouse is enhanced by income earned on money that otherwise would have been paid in death taxes.

Question – Why do some professionals refer to the combination of life insurance and a charitable remainder trust as a "Wealth Enhancement Trust"?

Answer – Through a combination of charitable trust planning and life insurance replacement of wealth, beneficiaries may receive more wealth than if no charitable gift were made. This is sometimes referred to as "wealth enhancement" rather than mere "wealth replacement."

Charitable remainder trusts are generally exempt from income taxes. This enables a client to convert highly appreciated property such as stock, real estate, or even a business interest into income-producing assets without the amount of capital being used to produce income being reduced by any capital gains taxes. Thus, the entire value of the property, undiminished by federal or state taxes, is available for investment. The increased income produced (over that which would have been produced had the contributed asset been sold and the after-tax proceeds reinvested) can then be used to pay for wealth replacement life insurance.

For instance, suppose a client is a 60-year-old widow with five children. Assume she is in the 40% combined state and federal income tax bracket and in a 48% estate tax bracket. One of her assets is a $1,000,000 parcel of undeveloped land she bought for $100,000 many years ago. She wants to perpetuate the memory of her late father. However, she needs additional income for retirement and wants to be sure her children, one of whom is handicapped, have sufficient financial security at her death.

If she does nothing, the client's five children will receive only $520,000 of her $1,000,000 parcel of land. Federal death taxes alone will consume the other $480,000 of the asset. Under this scenario, the charity will receive nothing. Alternatively, the client could transfer the land to a charitable remainder annuity trust or unitrust (a CRAT or CRUT). Assume she retains an annuity or unitrust interest for life with an annual percentage payout of 5.3%. In the case of a CRAT, she will receive a fixed annuity of $53,000 per year (.053 x $1,000,000) for life. In the case of a CRUT, she will be paid $53,000 in the first year and a future annuity of 5.3% of the value of the trust funds as revalued at the beginning of each year, with payments continuing for as long as she lives.

Assume that the most favorable IRC Section 7520 rate allowable is 5.0%.[25] If she sets up a CRAT, she will receive a $370,620 income tax charitable deduction. See Figure 21.1. If she sets up a CRUT, she will receive a $371,520 deduction. See Figure 21.2.

The charitable gift to the CRAT would result in an income tax savings of $148,248 (.40 x $370,620). This is about 14.8% of the transfer to trust ($148,248 ÷ $1,000,000). The charitable gift to a CRUT would result in an income tax savings of $148,608 (.40 x $371,520). This is about 14.9% of the transfer to trust ($148,609 ÷ $1,000,000).

Note that the client's return in either case is based on the entire value of the capital contributed to the charitable trust ($1,000,000), rather than what it would have been if she sold the land for $1,000,000, paid income taxes of $135,000 [15% capital gain tax rate on the $900,000 ($1,000,000 amount realized - $100,000 basis)] of gain on the land], and invested the $865,000 ($1,000,000 sales proceeds - $135,000 tax) difference. The result can be a significantly higher return.

The client then transfers (a) income tax deduction generated savings[26] and/or (b) a portion of the income retained from the charitable remainder trust as a gift to one or more individuals. They, in turn, could use that money to purchase insurance on her life to replace the wealth transferred to the charitable trust and enhance the net after-tax wealth they would have received.

The major advantage is that the client receives an immediate income tax deduction for the present value of what the charity will someday receive. The tax savings is then given to a personal beneficiary who purchases life insurance on the life of the client, the client's spouse, or the survivor of the two, in order to replace the wealth provided to charity. Because the insurance is not in the client's estate, it is not subject to state and federal death taxes and is exempt from the claims of the client's creditors.

Question – How high a payout can be taken from a CRAT or CRUT?

Answer – Note that The Taxpayer Relief Act of 1997 amended the requirements for a charitable remainder trust. Effective for transfers in trust made after June 18, 1997, the annual payout to the noncharitable beneficiary may not exceed 50% of (a) the initial fair market value of the property contributed to the trust (in the case of a charitable remainder annuity trust), *or* (b) the net fair market value of the trust's assets determined at least annually (in the case of a charitable remainder unitrust). Under preexisting law, the only restriction on the amount of the annual payout was that it had to be at least 5% of (a) or (b), respectively. (The 5% restriction remains in effect.)

In addition, a requirement has been enacted that provides that the value of the remainder interest in a charitable remainder trust must be a least 10% of the value of assets contributed in the trust. In the case of a CRAT, the value of the remainder interest must be at least 10% of the initial fair market value of all property placed in the trust; in the case of a CRUT, the 10% requirement applies to each contribution of property to the trust. The value of the remainder interest in either event is calculated using the IRC Section 7520 interest rate, which is published monthly by the IRS.

In the event that an additional contribution is made to an existing CRUT that does not meet the 10% remainder interest requirement, it will not cause the trust to cease being treated as a CRUT, but it will be treated as a transfer to a separate trust that is not a CRUT.

The 10% remainder interest rule applies, in general, to transfers in trust made after July 28, 1997; however, certain exceptions may apply to wills executed on or before July 28, 1997.[27]

Figure 21.1

CHARITABLE REMAINDER ANNUITY TRUST
(One Life - Table 90CM)

Transfer to Trust:	$1,000,000	Annuity Payment:	$53,000
Age:	60	Frequency of Payments:	Annual
Payments:	End of Period	Section 7520 Interest Rate:	5.0%

Check Possibility Charity Will Not Receive Interest			
Annuity Factor Exhaustion:	18.8679	Years to Exhaust Trust:	59
Mortality L(119):	0	Mortality L(60):	85537
Possibility:	0.0%	5% or Less Possibility Test Passed	

Check Exhaustion of Trust Fund			
Ann. Factor (50 years, 5.0%):	18.2559	Adj. Factor (Annual, 5.0%):	1.0000
Annuity Test Value:	$967,563	Special Factors:	Not Required

Valuation			
Ann. Factor (Age 60, 5.0%):	11.8751	Adj. Factor (Annual, 5.0%):	1.0000
Annuity Value:	$629,380	Charitable Contribution:	$370,620

Source: Trust Calculator (part of *The Ultimate Trust Resource*, a National Underwriter Company publication)

Figure 21.2

CHARITABLE REMAINDER UNITRUST
(One Life - Table 90CM)

Transfer to Trust:	$1,000,000	Unitrust Payout Rate:	5.3%
Age:	60	Frequency of Payments:	Annual
Months Until First Payment:	0	Section 7520 Interest Rate:	5.0%

Adjusted Payout Rate Factor (Annual, 0 months, 5.0%): 1.000000

Adjusted Payout Rate [5.3% x 1.000000]: 5.300%

One Life Unitrust Remainder Factor (Age 60, 5.2%): .... .37761

One Life Unitrust Remainder Factor (Age 60, 5.4%): .... .36542

Difference [.37761 - .36542]: .... .01219

Interpolation Adjustment (5.300%): .... .00609

Unitrust Remainder Factor [.37761 - .00609]: .... .37152

Charitable Contribution [$1,000,000 x .37152]: $371,520

Unitrust Value [$1,000,000 - $371,520]: $628,480

Source: Trust Calculator (part of *The Ultimate Trust Resource*, a National Underwriter Company publication)

Figure 21.3

CHARITABLE REMAINDER ANNUITY TRUST
(Two Lives - Table 90CM)

Transfer to Trust:	$1,000,000	Annuity Payment:	$53,000
First Age:	60	Second Age:	58
Frequency of Payments:	Annual	Payments:	End of Period
Section 7520 Interest Rate:	5.0%		

Check Possibility Charity Will Not Receive Interest

Annuity Factor Exhaustion:	18.8679	Years to Exhaust Trust:	59
Mortality L(119):	0	Mortality L(60):	85537
Mortality L(117):	0	Mortality L(58):	87397
Possibility:	0.0%	5% Possibility Test Passed	

Check Exhaustion of Trust Fund

Ann. Factor (52 years, 5.0%):	18.4181	Adj. Factor (Annual, 5.0%):	1.0000
Annuity Test Value:	$976,159	Special Factors:	Not Required

Valuation

Ann. Factor (60, 58, 5.0%):	14.3346	Adj. Factor (Annual, 5.0%):	1.0000
Annuity Value:	$759,734	Charitable Contribution:	$240,266

Source: Trust Calculator (part of *The Ultimate Trust Resource*, a National Underwriter Company publication)

Figure 21.4

CHARITABLE REMAINDER UNITRUST
(Two Lives - Table 90CM)

Transfer to Trust:	$1,000,000	Unitrust Payout Rate	5.3%
First Age:	60	Second Age:	58
Frequency of Payments:	Annual	Months Until First Payment:	0
Section 7520 Interest Rate:	5.0%		

Adjusted Payout Rate Factor (Annual, 0 months, 5.0%): 1.000000
Adjusted Payout Rate [5.3% x 1.000000]: 5.300%

Two Life Unitrust Remainder Factor (Age 60, Age 58, 5.2%): .... .25364
Two Life Unitrust Remainder Factor (Age 60, Age 58, 5.4%): .... .24125

Difference [.25364 - .24125]: .... .01239
Interpolation Adjustment (5.300%): .... .00619
Unitrust Remainder Factor [.25364 - .00619]: .... .24745

Charitable Contribution [$1,000,000 x .24745]: $247,450

Unitrust Value [$1,000,000 - $247,450]: $752,550

Source: Trust Calculator (part of *The Ultimate Trust Resource*, a National Underwriter Company publication)

Question – How can a "last-to-die" policy be used in conjunction with a joint and survivor charitable remainder trust?

Answer – In many cases the client will be married and will wish to provide financial security beyond his death for his surviving spouse's life. Here, planners should consider a joint and survivor charitable remainder trust that provides an annuity or unitrust amount to the client and his spouse for life. After the death of one spouse, the annuity or unitrust amount will continue to be paid to the surviving spouse. Upon the death of the surviving spouse, the trust assets will then be paid to the charity. Because of the federal estate tax marital deduction, at the first spouse's death, there should be no federal estate tax imposed on the present value of the annuity that continues for the surviving spouse's life. Using the same annuity trust and unitrust examples as presented above, and assuming the client is 60-years-old and has a 58-year-old spouse, the calculations would be as shown in Figure 21.3 for a CRAT and Figure 21.4 for a CRUT.

Note that the charitable deduction is reduced when the value of the noncharitable payout is increased by making payouts for two lives, rather than just for one life. In the case of a CRAT, the deduction is reduced from $370,620 (one life) to $240,266 (two lives). In the case of a CRUT, the deduction is reduced from $371,520 (one life) to $247,450 (two lives).

Since the client's federal estate tax liability on assets not in the charitable remainder trust will not be triggered until the second spouse's death, insurance placement can be more flexible. A policy can be purchased on the client's life, his spouse's life, or a last-to-die policy can be purchased on the lives of the couple since it will not be until the proceeds are payable under this latter policy that estate taxes will be due and the income from the charitable remainder trust will stop.

Question – What are the income tax consequences of a charitable gift of an annuity?

Answer – A charitable gift of an annuity issued after April 22, 1987, whether the gift occurs in the year of maturity or before it matures, will result in the immediate recognition of gain. When the donor gives the contract to charity, it is treated for income tax purposes as if he surrendered it. Reportable gain is equal to the excess of (a) the cash surrender value at the time of the gift over (b) the client's investment in the contract. But in return, since the client must currently recognize the gain as ordinary income, that amount becomes part of the client's basis and so the entire value of the annuity given to charity is fully deductible.[28]

Question - If a policy subject to a loan is donated to a charity, what problems arise as a result of the contribution?

Answer – A gift of a life insurance policy subject to a loan may, in certain circumstances, cause significant tax problems including: (1) generating taxable income to the donor under the bargain sale rules; (2) generating taxable income to the charity under rules relating to charitable unrelated business taxable income; and (3) imposing excise tax penalties under the charitable prohibited transaction rules.

1. *Bargain Sale Problem* – When encumbered property is contributed to a charity, the donor is treated as if he cashed in the policy, received an amount equal to the loan as reportable income, and made a gift of the difference.[29] Technically, bargain sale rules apply and treat the contribution as two separate transactions: (a) the client is treated as if he sold part of the policy to the charity with the charity paying him an amount equal to the loan, and (b) the client is then treated as if he made a gift of the net value of the policy to the charity.

2. *Unrelated Business Taxable Income (UBTI) Problem* – All tax-exempt organizations, including charities, are treated as if they are taxable to the extent they receive UBTI. Essentially, UBTI is income received by the tax-exempt organization or entity that is unrelated to its tax-exempt purpose.[30] However, the definition of UBTI also includes debt-financed income. This is income generated through borrowing on a charity owned asset to finance the purchase of another income-producing asset.[31] If a charity borrows against the cash values of a life insurance policy in order to buy income-producing assets, the IRS may classify the income produced by the new investment as debt-financed income. The income produced by the new investment may be considered unrelated business taxable income and taxed to the charity at corporate tax rates.

    For instance, assume a private foundation owned and was the beneficiary of life insurance policies with cash values in excess of $2,000,000. Assume further that the foundation borrows against the cash surrender at about 5% and finds a way to invest the borrowed funds in marketable government securities yielding more than 10%. The IRS, in such a situation, would argue that the income from the newly purchased marketable securities was passive income generated from debt-financed property and, thus, UBTI.

The solution is simple: charities should borrow against the cash surrender values of life insurance policies only for cash needs of the charity, and not to invest in other income-producing assets. For instance, there should be no problem if the charity in the example above borrowed $2,000,000 from policies it owned to finance the purchase of a new building to provide care for crippled children.

With the advent of interest-sensitive, variable, and universal life contracts, borrowing from a life insurance policy by a charity to achieve current rates of return is no longer necessary. Most importantly, life insurance owned on many lives by a charity can serve as a "money pump" to deliver millions of dollars to an important charity.

3. *Prohibited Transaction Problem* – This problem relates only to transfers of encumbered policies to private foundations (organizations that receive a significant part of their support from one or more specific sources, rather than from the general public). Gifts to private foundations are subject to harsh and complex "prohibited transaction" rules intended to prevent the abuse of their tax-exempt status by related parties.

These abuses include:

a) self-dealing between the entity and certain disqualified persons (including the donor);[32]

b) holding more control of a closely-held corporation or unincorporated business than a Code specified maximum;[33] and

c) the purchase and maintenance of investments that jeopardize the exempt purpose of the charity (so-called "jeopardy" investments).[34] (Unfortunately, many of these same rules may also apply to transactions between related parties and charitable lead trusts or charitable remainder trusts.)

Certain gifts to a private foundation of life insurance subject to a policy loan have been held to violate the prohibitions against self-dealing and jeopardy investments. Prohibitions against self-dealing, particularly where the client who sets up the foundation gains an unfair advantage from his dealing with the trust at taxpayers' (federal treasury) expense, can result in severe tax consequences. Any lending of money from the foundation to the donor, and most sales or exchanges of property as well as transfers of mortgaged property, could trigger a self-dealing excise tax penalty.

Where does a life insurance policy subject to a loan fit into this set of rules? Assume the client gives a life insurance policy on his life to a private foundation. Assume further that the policy was subject to a loan. The client, as a donor, would be considered a "disqualified person" by the IRS. This means he is prohibited from engaging in certain related-party transactions with the foundation. According to the IRS, a private foundation commits a prohibited act of self-dealing if it takes an asset subject to a mortgage or similar lien that a disqualified person placed on the property within the 10-year period ending on the date of the transfer. So in the example, the IRS could treat the policy loan as a mortgage or similar lien for purposes of applying the excise tax on acts of self-dealing in private foundations. The IRS might characterize the client's relief from the loan by the foundation as an act of self-dealing and impose prohibited transaction penalty taxes.

Generally, the problems described in this question will rarely occur when competent counsel is present and the policy in question is financially sound. Note also that it is not life insurance, per se, which causes the problem, but rather the acceptance and payment by the foundation or trust of the donor's debt and obligation to pay interest and principal on the policy loan. If there is no policy loan and the insurer is financially sound, there should be no problem with life insurance.

Question – What is a DAG?

Answer – DAGs (Directors' Amplified Gifts) are a way that a responsible, charitable-minded corporation can meet multiple objectives with a single estate planning technique. Suppose a client owns the Financial Data Center (FDC), a highly successful firm marketing financial and estate planning software and brochures. The FDC is in a combined federal and state tax bracket of 40%. Assume that the FDC has actively sought out some of the brightest and most creative minds in the country to serve on its board of directors. Their insight and guidance has helped the FDC grow even faster and more soundly than its competitors. The client would like to solve a recruiting problem with respect to new board members. There are several problems the client has discussed with you and asked you to consider:

a) Small cash payments to directors are almost meaningless after taxes are considered.

b) Large cash payments may be frowned upon by shareholders.

A potential solution, the DAG, works like this:

a) The FDC corporation sets up a DAG. Each director, in addition to normal director's fees and perks, is allowed to select the charity of his choice as the recipient of between $250,000 and $1,000,000 to be paid to a designated charity in honor of the director at death.

b) To finance the employer's obligation under the plan, the corporation becomes owner and beneficiary of life insurance on the life of each covered director. The policy could be regular whole life or a second-to-die policy in order to lower outlay or cover unhealthy directors more easily. Premiums are designed to vanish before the director's term of service expires.

c) At a director's death, the corporation receives the proceeds free of income tax (except for any possible corporate level AMT).

d) The corporation then leverages the cash by making a deductible corporate contribution to the charity of the director's choice. A corporation in a 30% combined federal and state income tax bracket, for example, could take in $100,000 and pay out $142,857 using the formula below

BEFORE DEDUCTION PROCEEDS / (1 - Combined Tax Bracket)

If the FDC is in a combined state and federal income tax bracket of 40%, and if it receives a net of $100,000 of life insurance proceeds, it could afford to pay out about $166,666 to charity. ($100,000/(1-.40)). This $66,666 amount in excess of the $100,000 of insurance proceeds is the amplified portion of the DAG. Alternatively, the proceeds could be used to reimburse the corporation for an accelerated charitable contribution made on a prior date.

There are a number of advantages to the DAG:

1. The size of the amplified gift is so large that it has appeal even to the most successful and well-paid directors. It makes possible a truly significant statement and carries a large psychological benefit.

2. Despite the size of the gift to charity and the great honor and memorial it will provide after death, as well as the continuing psychological benefit during lifetime, the director so honored is at no time taxable on the corporation's payment of premiums, nor is the director's estate taxable on the actual payment.

3. There is no out-of-pocket cost to the director.

4. The director has great flexibility and can change the charitable recommendation at any time since the charity is given no direct interest in the corporate-owned insurance, or in any other assets the employer may use to support the plan.

5. The corporation can deduct (up to the corporate limits for charitable contributions) payments it makes to the charity. This can be used to lower the cost of the plan or increase the amount going to charity. If corporate tax rates rise in later years, the leverage of the plan increases.

6. In the authors' opinion, the program does not require disclosure under current SEC regulations.

7. A DAG tremendously enhances the corporation's charitable image and multiplies the utility of corporate dollars. It receives a large return in the form of favorable public relations, even before it makes

the first payment to charity, through the charity's anticipation of the gift.

8. This technique may be more cost efficient in recruiting and retaining top-level directors than a less affordable pay increase to directors. Under a DAG, if a director leaves before the expiration of his term, no payment need be made and the corporation can retain the insurance coverage and apply it against future charitable contributions on behalf of other directors.

9. A DAG can be used not only by a large public corporation but, because it is simple and inexpensive to establish and maintain, even small firms can use the concept to achieve the same goals as corporate giants.

Life insurance financing is so essential because it is not possible to accurately predict the timing of the donations (i.e., date of deaths of directors), and a nonfinanced plan could have a significant negative impact on earnings if more than one director died in a single year. Life insurance enables a corporation to favorably describe the arrangement in the firm's financial (and/or proxy) statement and plan for payment through predictable and relatively small corporate outflows in the form of premium payments.

Question – Is it appropriate to contribute a life insurance policy to a charitable remainder annuity trust (CRAT) or a charitable remainder unitrust (CRUT) rather than directly to a charity?

Answer – In the opinion of the authors, generally, neither a CRAT nor a CRUT should be the transferee of a life insurance policy. One reason that a client should not contribute life insurance to such a trust is that both trusts are required to make steady payouts of annuities to the client (and/or some other party in many cases). Adding life insurance to the trust will further drain the trust's cash flow and leave less money for the required annuity payouts.

It is clear that a charitable remainder trust can be named recipient of a life insurance policy's proceeds if the trust is a unitrust created during either the client's lifetime or under the client's will. But because charitable remainder annuity trust rules do not allow contributions after the date the trust is originally created and funded, a CRAT cannot be named as recipient of life insurance proceeds.

Question – What is the alternative minimum tax (AMT) and how does it impact on charitable giving?

Answer – The AMT is a tax designed to assure that individuals who pay little or no regular income tax, because they have taken advantage of certain exclusion, deduction, and credit obtaining techniques called "preferences," will pay at least this minimum tax. Ironically, many of these preferences are in reality tax incentives designed to encourage taxpayers to take certain risks or make certain investments or contributions that are deemed to be in the public interest. So, on the one hand, Congress encourages the action and, on the other hand, it seeks to discourage the same pattern of behavior by diminishing the tax benefits for the same action.

For tax years beginning before 1993, the major preference item in terms of charitable giving was a contribution of appreciated property. Specifically, the unrealized gain inherent in a gift of long-term capital gain property was considered a preference item for purposes of the AMT. However, for taxable years beginning after 1992, a charitable contribution of appreciated property is no longer treated as a tax preference. As a result, if a taxpayer makes a gift to charity of long-term capital gain property that is real property, intangible property, or tangible personal property, the use of which is related to the donee's tax-exempt purpose, the taxpayer is allowed to claim a deduction for both regular tax and AMT purposes in the amount of the property's fair market value (subject to applicable percentage limitations).[35]

Since life insurance is an ordinary income type asset and a donation of life insurance is not considered a preference item, and since the receipt of insurance proceeds will not be taxable in any way to the charity, it does not present AMT problems in and of itself.

Question – What is charitable split dollar (and charitable reverse split dollar)?[36]

Answer – In both of these arrangements, donors use a charity as a conduit to purchase large amounts of life insurance on a tax-deductible basis. The plans mimicked a similar corporate split dollar technique and while the strategy may or may not have worked under insurance law, it violated several aspects of charity law, in particular private benefit rules.

The IRS effectively shut down this technique with IRS Notice 99-36, and Congress imposed harsh penalties for becoming involved in such plans by enacting legislation in December, 1999 that makes it clear that no deduction is (or was) allowed for the donation of a personal benefit contract.[37] Current law defines a "personal benefit contract" as "any life insurance, annuity, or endowment contract if any direct or indirect beneficiary under such contract is the transferor, any member of the transferor's family, or any other person (other than [certain charitable organizations]) designated by the transferor." Charities that continue to pay premiums on personal benefit contracts must report all payments made after February 8, 1999 to the IRS on Form 8870 and must pay a 100% excise tax on all premiums paid after December 17, 1999.

Because the legislation that was passed in December 1999 made it clear that charitable split dollar and charitable reverse split dollar never did give rise to an income tax deduction, it is possible that some of the charities involved will face legal suits and may even lose their tax-exempt status as a result of their participation in promoting or agreeing to implement these programs.

Question – What is "financed" charitable life insurance?[38]

Answer – This is a technique that is also growing in popularity in the non-charitable marketplace. To summarize, the charity takes out a loan from a bank to pay premiums on a pool of insurance contracts. The death benefits, or in some cases other assets of the charity, are used as collateral for the cumulative loan. This planning is problematic in several ways. Depending on the circumstances, it may trigger unrelated business taxable income, and if the policy does not perform as well as projected, the underlying contract could lapse and the charity would be forced to repay a substantial cumulative loan plus interest with nothing to show in return. Such planning should be considered highly speculative and be scrutinized carefully by legal counsel.

Practitioners are cautioned to carefully evaluate the actual performance of the policies and the economic viability of the overall strategies. The more money borrowed, the greater the risk the client is taking and the higher the cost – because the ultimate loan balance must be paid either out-of-pocket during the insured's lifetime or from death proceeds. If the intent is to pay the loan off at death, then sufficient additional death proceeds must be purchased to satisfy the obligation and still have enough proceeds to accomplish the objective of the insur-

ance. If premium financing is used to support a large life insurance contract, it is suggested that advisors borrow as little as possible, keep the duration of the loan relatively short, consider worst case scenarios, and develop an "exit strategy" before implementing the plan. Constant monitoring of policy performance and disclosure of the cost and risk to the client are essential.[39]

Question – What are the substantiation rules for a charitable gift of life insurance?

Answer – The rules are explained as follows:

Value and Form of Gift

Deduction Disallowed Unless

$250 or greater:

The charity provides the donor with a contemporaneous written acknowledgement of the contribution stating the amount of cash or non-cash property received and the value of any consideration provided by the charity to the donor in return for the gift.

More than $250, but less than $5,000:

Same as above, plus the donor must complete IRS Form 8323, which provides the charity's name, address, description of property, how and when the donor acquired the property, basis, FMV, and method by which the property was valued.

$5,000 or more

A "qualified appraisal" must be obtained. Treasury regulation section 1.170A-13(c) provides that neither the donor nor the insurance agent (or insurer who issued the policy) can perform this appraisal.

CHAPTER ENDNOTES

1. See Stephan R. Leimberg, *Tools & Techniques of Charitable Planning* (The National Underwriter Company, 2001), Ch. 2.; Stephan R. Leimberg, *Tools & Techniques of Estate Planning* (The National Underwriter Company, 13th ed. 2004), Ch. 32.

2. A corporate charitable contribution paid on or before March 15 will be treated as paid in the prior taxable year if the corporation's board authorizes the contribution in that prior year and makes an appropriate election. IRC Sec. 170(a)(2).

3. IRC Sec. 170(f)(10); Tax Relief Extension Act of 1999 (P.L. 106-170); Notice 99-36, 1999-1 CB 1284. See also *Addis v. Comm.*, No.

02-73628 (9th Cir. 2004), *aff'g.*, 118 TC 528 (2002), and *Weiner v. Comm.*, TC Memo 2002-153 (involving deductions taken in 1997 and 1998 – before the enactment of IRC Sec. 170(f)(10) on December 17, 1999 – and denying the charitable income tax deduction on the basis of failure to meet the substantiation requirements of IRC Section 170(f)(3)).

4. See IRC Sec. 170.

5. IRC Sec. 170(b). The amount of charitable contributions that can be deducted for federal income tax purposes in a given year is limited by the Code. Technically, there exist percentage limitations of 30% and 50% of the donor's "contribution base", essentially adjusted gross income without considering loss carrybacks. The 50% limit is reserved for cash type gifts to hospitals, schools, mosques, synagogues, and churches, and other publicly supported charities. Most gifts of property to public charities as well as contributions "for the use of" charity are subject to a 30% limit. A 20% limitation is imposed where the contribution consists of appreciated capital gain property donated to private foundations.

6. IRC Secs. 170(f)(2), 170(f)(3).

7. See *Eppa Hunton IV v. Comm.*, 1 TC 821 (1943); *Behrend v. Comm.*, 23 BTA 1037 (1931).

8. Treas. Regs. §§1.170A-7(a)(2)(i); 1.170A-7(b)(1).

9. Rev. Rul. 76-143, 1976-1 CB 63.

10. IRC Sec. 170(f)(10); Tax Relief Extension Act of 1999 (P.L. 106-170); Notice 99-36, 1999-1 CB 1284. See also *Addis v. Comm.*, No. 02-73628 (9th Cir. 2004), *aff'g.*, 118 TC 528 (2002), and *Weiner v. Comm.*, TC Memo 2002-153 (involving deductions taken in 1997 and 1998 – before the enactment of IRC Sec. 170(f)(10) on December 17, 1999 – and denying the charitable income tax deduction on the basis of failure to meet the substantiation requirements of IRC Section 170(f)(3)).

11. See Let. Rul. 8030043.

12. IRC Sec. 79(b)(2)(B).

13. IRC Sec. 170(e)(1)(A).

14. See *Behrend v. Comm.*, 23 BTA 1037 (1931); *Tuttle v. U.S.*, 305 F. Supp. 484 (1969), *rev'd on other grounds*, 436 F.2d 69 (2nd. Cir. 1970).

15. See Treas. Reg. §25.2512-6.

16. IRC Secs. 2522(a), 2522(c).

17. See Let. Rul. 9110016, which was revoked by Let. Rul. 9147040 because of a retroactive change in the statutory law of the taxpayer's state of residence.

18. IRC Sec. 2042.

19. IRC Sec. 2055.

20. See IRC Sec. 511(a).

21. See Let. Rul. 9110016 for a description of the adverse tax consequences associated with such gifts in states where charities do not have an insurable interest in donors' lives. Letter Ruling 9110016 was revoked by Let. Rul. 9147040 after legislation was passed granting charities insurable interests by the state in which the gift occurred.

22. Note that some states are currently considering modifying their insurable interest statues to permit charities to assign their insurable interest to outside investors. For more information, see the testimony of JJ McNab, CFP, CLU, QFP, before the Senate Finance Committee in the hearing, "Charity Oversight & Reform: Keeping Bad Things from Happening to Good Charities," held on June 22, 2004, at: http://finance.senate.gov/hearings/testimony/2004test/062204jmtest.pdf.

23. IRC Sec. 170(b)(1). There are cases that seem to imply that even payments made directly to the insurer on the charity's behalf

will qualify for the larger current deduction. The authors suggest the more conservative and certain approach of the donor writing a check to the charity, and the charity writing its check to the insurer. This approach makes an IRS audit less likely, especially if the amount of the check is rounded upward (e.g., an $1,895 premium is rounded to $2,000), and makes compliance with an IRS audit a much easier process.

24. See Stephan R. Leimberg, *Tools & Techniques of Estate Planning* (The National Underwriter Company, 13th ed. 2004), Ch. 33.

25. In the case of charitable deductions, the client can choose either the current month's IRC Section 7520 rate, or look back to either of the two prior months' rates and select the most favorable of the three. By waiting until the date the IRC Section 7520 rate is announced by the IRS (usually between the 18th and 21st of the month), the client can determine which of four months' rates is most favorable. The IRC Section 7520 interest rate is published at www.national underwriter.com/taxfactsfx as it becomes available.

26. An income and gift tax charitable deduction is allowed for the present value (measured actuarially) of the charity's right to someday receive what remains in the trust (i.e., the donor is given an immediate deduction for the value of the charity's remainder interest in the trust). That present value is computed using the monthly varying federal discount rates under IRC Section 7520.

27. Taxpayer Relief Act of 1997, Sec. 1089; IRC Sec. 664(d). More extensive information on charitable trusts can be found in Stephan R. Leimberg, *Tools & Techniques of Charitable Planning* (The National Underwriter Company, 2001).

28. See Treas. Reg. §1.170A-4(a).

29. See Treas. Reg. §1.1011-2(a)(3).

30. See IRC Secs. 511, 512.

31. See IRC Sec. 514.

32. See IRC Sec. 4941.

33. See IRC Sec. 4943.

34. See IRC Sec. 4944.

35. See, generally, IRC Sec. 57(a)(6).

36. Adapted from Stephan R. Leimberg, *Tools & Techniques of Charitable Planning* (The National Underwriter Company, 2001), p. 114.

37. IRC Sec. 170(f)(10); Tax Relief Extension Act of 1999 (P.L. 106-170); Notice 99-36, 1999-1 CB 1284. See also *Addis v. Comm.*, No. 02-73628 (9th Cir. 2004), *aff'g.*, 118 TC 528 (2002), and *Weiner v. Comm.*, TC Memo 2002-153 (involving deductions taken in 1997 and 1998 – before the enactment of IRC Sec. 170(f)(10) on December 17, 1999 – and denying the charitable income tax deduction on the basis of failure to meet the substantiation requirements of IRC Section 170(f)(3)). For commentary on charitable split dollar, see www.leimbergservices.com.

38. Adapted from Stephan R. Leimberg, *Tools & Techniques of Charitable Planning* (The National Underwriter Company, 2001), pp. 114-115.

39. For more information, see Lawrence L. Bell, "Charities and Insurance: The Next Big Thing," Steve Leimberg's Estate Planning Newsletter No. 671 at: http://www.leimbergservices.com; Michel Nelson, "Insurance Interest Under Siege, Steve Leimberg's Estate Planning Newsletter No. 670 at: http://www.leimbergservices.com; Stephan Leimberg and Albert Gibbons, "TOLI, COLI, BOLI, and Insurable Interests – an Interview with Michel Nelson, *Estate* Planning (July 2001), p. 333; Stephan Leimberg and Albert Gibbons, "Premium Financing: The Last Choice – Not the First Choice," *Estate Planning* (January 2001), p. 35. See also the testimony of JJ McNab, CFP, CLU, QFP, before the Senate Finance Committee in the hearing, "Charity Oversight & Reform: Keeping Bad Things from Happening to Good Charities," held on June 22, 2004, at: http://finance.senate.gov/hearings/testimony/2004test/062204jmtest.pdf.

Chapter 22

DEATH BENEFIT ONLY (DBO) PLAN

WHAT IS IT?

A DBO plan (sometimes called a survivors' income benefit plan) is an executive benefit that promises payments from the employer to the survivors of an eligible employee at the employee's death. As its name implies, a DBO plan provides only death benefits and promises no payments to the employee during his lifetime. In essence, the DBO plan is a form of deferred compensation plan that provides no retirement benefit for the covered employee and defers payments until the employee dies. Payment of DBO benefits is typically conditioned upon (a) the survival of the employee by an employer-designated beneficiary and (b) the employee's continued employment with the employer until the time of his death.

The key goals of a DBO are to provide a significant (and often estate tax free) death benefit, generate substantial amounts of income and/or capital to an employee's family, and help recruit, retain, and reward employees while acting as a counterbalance to the limitations upon highly compensated employees found in qualified retirement plans.

Although payments can take the form of a lump sum, in most cases, benefits will be payable in monthly installments over a fixed period of time (such as five years) or as a lifetime annuity. The death benefit can be a set, predetermined amount, a multiple of the participant's final salary, or a multiple of the covered employee's final average compensation (an average of the covered employee's three final years of compensation is common).

WHEN IS THE USE OF SUCH A DEVICE INDICATED?

1. When the employer client seeks an employee benefit to recruit, retain, reward, and counterbalance the limitations upon key employees found in qualified retirement plans.

2. When the employer client wants an employee benefit that is simple, cost effective, and free from administrative burdens. Cost effective, in this sense, means the employer pays nothing if the plan does not achieve its goals and pays a minimal amount if the plan is successful. No payments are required under a DBO program if the employee leaves the employer, for any reason, before his death–all benefits are forfeited. This is a strong incentive for an employee to remain with the employer. The employee also becomes aware of the fact that the after-tax personal cost of a death benefit (such as $100,000 per year for 10 years) is significant, even if term insurance is used. This enhances the employee's appreciation of the employer and increases employee loyalty and makes it less likely that an employee will leave the employer. Additionally, should an employee leave, the employer may still maintain the life insurance on the employee's life and retain 100% of the proceeds (net of premium costs), since there would be no obligation to make payments to the employee's survivor. The net (after any AMT) proceeds would be a direct positive addition to corporate surplus.

3. When the employer wants to pick and choose who will be covered, under what terms and conditions, and at what amounts.

4. When the employer wants a supplement to a qualified retirement plan.

5. When a shareholder-employee wishes to utilize his corporation to provide personal financial security.

6. When a means is sought to supplement payments under a buy-sell agreement. Instead of increasing the valuation of stock to the highest level reasonable minds might agree to, this difference could be made up outside the buy-sell through the DBO plan. This technique might be particularly useful in a large professional corporation.

7. When an employer would like to provide liquidity and income security for a younger employee's surviving family if the employee were to die while employed, and then, if the employee should survive until retirement, convert the DBO plan to a

nonqualified deferred compensation plan in order to provide retirement security. If the employee dies while working but before retirement, payments will be made from the DBO plan. After the employee reaches age 65 (or whatever retirement age is selected), payments can be made from a deferred compensation plan established voluntarily by the employer shortly before the employee's retirement and financed fully or partially with assets (typically policy cash values) that otherwise would have been used in the DBO Plan.

8. When a client is over age 50, is currently providing protection for his family under a split dollar arrangement, and would like to avoid rapidly rising costs of the taxable insurance protection element. Conversion of the split dollar arrangement to a DBO plan provides a way to continue the security without the income tax (but changes tax-free income to taxable income at death).

9. When a client has a large estate subject to federal estate tax, is in a high income tax bracket, has no need for additional retirement income, but wants to provide additional income or estate liquidity for survivors.

10. Where the group term life insurance plan is adequate for rank and file employees but is not sufficient (or is becoming overly expensive in large amounts) for top executives or other key individuals. It is often possible to provide DBO coverage of equivalent value at comparable cost to the employer and reduced cost to the executive.

11. Where an employer is truly and deeply concerned with the well being of the families of company employees but does not want death benefits diverted to someone other than a survivor of a deceased employee. Especially, because widows between the ages of 50 and 65 have a particularly difficult time finding employment and are less likely to remarry, and because many executives have children in college, graduate, or professional school about that same time, covering key employees in this same age range can be particularly important.

WHAT ARE THE ADVANTAGES?

1. Under current law, if the covered employee is a shareholder who owns 50% or less of the stock of the corporation, payments under the DBO plan will be excludable from the covered employee's gross estate.

This avoidance of federal estate tax is particularly valuable to individuals whose estates, for one reason or another, will not qualify for a marital deduction.

2. Large amounts of continuing income can be provided through a business to the beneficiary of a key employee. This significant financial assistance is available to employees without regard to whether they are shareholders.

3. During the employee's lifetime, since the employee has no current right to payments or to the life insurance financing the employer's obligation under the plan, the employee is not taxable on premium payments. Compare this with the taxable income reportable under large amounts of group term life insurance (Table I costs), split dollar life insurance (cost of the pure death benefit), or life insurance maintained inside a qualified retirement plan (cost of the pure death benefit).

4. Employers can pick and choose who will be covered under a DBO plan, the terms of that coverage, and the level of benefit payments to be provided to recipients. There are no government (state or federal) mandated limits. This makes the DBO plan an ideal way to help solve the employer's problem of attracting, retaining, and rewarding employees, as well as counterbalancing the limitations upon highly compensated employees found in qualified retirement plans, without the costs of extending such benefits to the entire work force.

5. When payments are made by the employer, income is taxed at the brackets of the beneficiaries, which are likely to be lower than the covered employee's tax bracket.

6. An employer can leverage payouts with income tax deductions. So if tax rates increase, the amount that can be paid out increases. Conversely, if the employer decides to keep payouts level, the corporation will often receive enough, even after all promised payouts are made, to realize not only a return of all outlays, but, in some cases, net a "profit" that can serve to offset the cost of the use of money expended for premiums.

WHAT ARE THE DISADVANTAGES?

1. The entire payment by the corporation to the beneficiary under a DBO plan is subject to ordinary income tax.

2. No deduction is allowed to the employer until the benefit is paid, and the beneficiary must include payments received in income. Even if the employer sets funds aside in advance to meet promised payments (almost always through the purchase of a life insurance contract), the employer's deduction is deferred until benefits are paid. (But, of course, the total deductions are almost certain to significantly exceed the outlays).

3. To avoid federal estate tax inclusion of payments, the employee can be given no right to name or veto the naming of the beneficiary of death benefit payments. Avoiding federal estate tax requires careful plan design, which, to some degree, limits flexibility in plan design for controlling (i.e., greater than 50%) shareholder-employees.

4. A plan covering a large and broad group of employees may have to comply with ERISA (Employee Retirement Income Security Act) provisions for vesting, funding, reporting, and disclosure.

But, in most cases, a DBO plan will be unfunded and limited to a select group of management or highly compensated employees, and will therefore be exempt from virtually all provisions of ERISA, with the exception of a simple, one page notification of the existence of the plan, which must be filed with the Department of Labor (see next Q&A).

5. Premiums on life insurance used to finance a DBO plan must be paid with after-tax dollars.

6. Formal funding of a DBO plan through a trust, escrow account, or other means by which money, mutual funds, life insurance, or any other asset is placed beyond the claims of the employer's creditors can trigger constructive receipt of the funds, may cause estate tax inclusion, and will probably result in ERISA reporting, disclosure, and funding requirement implications.

If the employer's obligation under a plan of deferred compensation is represented by an unsecured promise, the participants are general creditors of the employer and their claim (or the claims of their heirs) is subordinated to the claims of the employer's secured creditors, and their interests are nontransferable, there should be no reportable income under either the constructive receipt or economic benefit doctrines. Beneficiaries are therefore dependent upon the financial ability and willingness of the employer to make payments as promised.

WHAT ARE THE REQUIREMENTS?

The employer installs a nonvoluntary DBO plan by a written contract between the employer and the selected employee stating the terms of the contract. The employee should have no choice with respect to whether to elect coverage.

The agreement should specify:

1. the amount of the benefit, or the formula upon which the benefit is based;

2. the employee (or employees) covered by the plan;

3. the class of beneficiaries entitled to the benefit;

4. the terms upon which the benefit can be forfeited; and

5. collection procedures.

There is no IRS or Department of Labor guidance or requirement with respect to the formula for determining how much survivors will be paid–the amount is entirely up to the employer. Most will want to keep the formula simple. A common formula uses multiples of $10,000 (such as $30,000, $40,000, $50,000 per year) and combines that with a specified number of years ranging from two to 15. An alternative is to make payments based upon either a percentage of the employee's final salary or an average of the top three or five years of salary prior to death. Some use the same formula as is used in the firm's qualified pension or profit sharing plan.

It is suggested that, instead of specifying the name of the employee's spouse and children, the contract should be drafted to state that benefits are payable to "the covered employee's surviving spouse, if living, otherwise the children of the covered employee, in equal shares." (Some plans also provide benefits to parents of covered employees). No benefit should be payable if the employee is not survived by an eligible beneficiary.

A corporate resolution by the company's board of directors should be adopted in writing well in advance of the time payments are to be made (and preferably before the contract with the employee is signed). Note that:

1. no amounts are set aside beyond the claims of the corporation's creditors in a trust, escrow account, or annuity to meet the employer's obligation (since benefits are unfunded, survi-

vors are general unsecured creditors of the employer), and

2. the obligation of the corporation to make payments is contingent upon both (a) the employee's continued employment with the employer as of his date of death and (b) survival of a beneficiary from among the employer specified eligible class.

Life insurance is almost always used to finance the employer's obligation under a DBO. Although, in most cases, a form of whole life insurance is used, term coverage could be used to minimize employer outlays, if coverage will cease under the DBO contract by age 60 or 65. Life insurance guarantees that adequate amounts will be available to make promised payments, even if the eligible employee dies immediately after being insured (in fact, the employer may want to wait until the employee's insurability is assured and actual coverage is in force before executing the DBO contract).

This life insurance should not be mentioned in the contract with the employee. A linking of the life insurance with the promised benefits could cause unnecessary estate tax inclusion, income taxation on premium payments, and Department of Labor intrusion.

Under a separate corporate resolution, the board of directors should authorize the purchase of the life insurance as "key employee" insurance.

HOW IT IS DONE–AN EXAMPLE

A client, Red Leitz, is an employee of Traffic Jammers, Inc. He enters into an agreement with the corporation. The contract provides, in part:

> In consideration of Red Leitz's past service and continued performance of services, Traffic Jammers, Inc. will pay a death benefit of $100,000 per year for a continuous period of 10 years in equal annual installments to Red's spouse, if living, otherwise to Red's children.

To finance its obligation under the plan, Traffic Jammers purchases a $1,000,000 policy on Red's life. The corporation names itself owner and beneficiary of the life insurance. At Red's death, the corporation receives the proceeds, owes no AMT, and decides to invest the amount received, net of the cost of premiums, in tax-free municipal bonds. Assume the bonds yield $80,000 annually. Each year for 10 years, Traffic Jammers sends

Red's widow or children a check for $100,000. The recipient declares that amount as income.

Since Traffic Jammers is in a combined federal and state tax bracket of 40%, the cost to pay $100,000 per year (classified as a continuation of salary) is $60,000 per year ($100,000 - $40,000 deduction). That amounts to $600,000 over 10 years ($60,000 x 10).

The business receives $80,000 each year from the tax-free bonds. It pays out, after tax deduction, $60,000. So each year, Traffic Jammers has received $20,000 more than it needs to meet its obligation. If Traffic Jammers invests the $20,000 each year at 8% for 10 years, it will grow to $289,731. The corporation also has the tax free municipal bonds. Most importantly, the DBO plan has helped to place "golden handcuffs" on a key executive.

WHAT ARE THE TAX IMPLICATIONS?

1. No income tax is payable by the covered employee on the premiums that the employer pays for key-person insurance, which is used to finance the employer's obligation under a DBO plan. To obtain this result, the promises made by an employer under a DBO plan should not be, and should not appear to be, dependent upon and funded directly by an insurance policy. The facts should indicate that if and when a liability to make payments occurs, the employer is always directly responsible for those payments and has not, at any time, shifted that obligation to an insurer.[1]

2. Premiums on the policy, of which the corporation is both the owner and beneficiary, are not deductible.[2]

3. Except for any alternative minimum tax (AMT), proceeds of the key-person life insurance policy used to finance the employer's obligation under the plan are received income tax free.[3] (AMT is discussed in more detail in the Q&A section of this chapter, below.)

    As a conservative rule of thumb, planners should figure that when more than $1,000,000 of insurance is involved, the corporate AMT will result in a "slippage" of approximately 15% of the face value of the life insurance payable to the corporation. An additional amount of insurance should therefore be purchased in order to assure receipt of the net amount required (or desired). Because the additional insurance may itself generate additional AMT, the formula used to calculate the appropriate coverage is

    Net proceeds desired ÷ (1 - .15)

For instance, if $1,000,000 is the target amount, the employer should purchase $1,176,470 ($1,000,000 ÷ .85). A more simple way to arrive at the approximate amount is to merely multiply the target amount by 118%. In this example the result would be $1,180,000 ($1,000,000 x 1.18).

There is an important "small corporation" exemption that is discussed in detail in the Q&A section of this chapter.

4. Corporate earnings and profits are decreased by the amount of premium payments, but increased by the sum of (a) cash surrender value increases and (b) the excess of death proceeds over cash values in the year received.

5. Cash values should not, per se, trigger an accumulated earnings tax.

6. Benefits paid by a corporation to the employee's beneficiary are taxable in full as ordinary income to the beneficiary, just as if the payments were a continuation of the deceased employee's salary. Even though the employer generally receives the insurance proceeds income tax free, that characterization is lost once the employer pays out the promised continued salary to the beneficiary. So whether the DBO payments are made for a period of years or in the form of a lump sum, payments are taxable to the beneficiary at ordinary income tax rates.

Death benefit payments are considered income in respect of a decedent (IRD, also known as "Section 691 income"). No stepped-up basis is allowed for IRD.[4] However, the beneficiary is allowed to take an income tax deduction for any federal estate taxes paid on that income.[5] In other words, to prevent the beneficiary from paying a tax on a tax (i.e., income taxation on the portion of the death benefit depleted by estate tax), an income tax deduction is allowed on estate taxes paid.

7. When benefits are paid, they are deductible as deferred salary by the employer corporation, to the extent that amounts represent "reasonable compensation" (in amount and duration) for the services actually rendered by the deceased employee. In addition, the plan must serve a valid business purpose. One article has suggested that if an employer purchases key employee life insurance to recover a portion of the costs associated with the plan, payments made by the employer to the beneficiary would not be deductible, on the grounds that

no deduction is allowed for a business expense which is reimbursed by insurance or otherwise.[6] But this reasoning appears flawed because there is no "nexus" between the life insurance and the employer expenses, a connection essential to operation of IRC Section 265(a)(1), which would then block the deduction.

As a practical matter, the issue of nondeductibility seldom arises except when (a) the decedent was a controlling or major shareholder employee, (b) the beneficiary is a stockholder, (c) there was no written agreement to pay the benefit prior to the employee's death, or (d) the facts indicate a lack of arm's length bargaining. In such cases, the IRS may attempt to disallow the corporation's deduction and treat payments as a dividend, rather than as a form of deferred compensation. Careful documentation of the bargaining process and of the employer's need to recruit, retain, or reward a true key employee will minimize the chance for an IRS success.

8. Payments from the corporation to the beneficiaries of the covered employee may be excludable from the employee's gross estate. For instance, if the payment is purely and truly voluntary on the part of the business and is not made under a contract or plan, it should be excludable from the employee's estate because, at death, the covered employee never had a right subject to transfer. But even if the DBO payments are made under a formal and binding contract or plan, estate tax exclusion is possible. To assure estate tax exclusion:

a) Give the employer (rather than the covered employee) sole discretion as to the class of beneficiary to receive the death proceeds (preferably by stating a class of beneficiary such as "the employee's spouse, if living, otherwise the employee's children in equal shares"). No rights over the life insurance policy used to finance the employer's obligation should be given to the employee. If the agreement gives the employee the right to name, change, or veto an employer change of beneficiary, payments will be includable in the employee's estate. The employee's estate should not be named as beneficiary.

b) Give the employee no lifetime postretirement benefit or plan (other than a qualified pension or profit sharing plan). Be sure that the DBO plan provides only death benefits and provides no postretirement lifetime payments to the employee. (Keep in mind that the IRS can also link lifetime payments under other plans to the DBO plan and consider the two as a single plan, even if they are separate plans. So estate tax inclusion cannot be avoided by providing death benefits under the DBO and lifetime postretirement payments under a separate plan.) (See Q&A below for more details.)

c) Give the employee (and the employee's estate) no right to dispose of the payments, should one or more specified beneficiaries die. If the employee is found to hold a reversionary interest (one which could revert back to his estate) and that interest has an actuarial value exceeding 5% of the benefit, the IRS will include the payments in his estate.

d) The employee should be given no right to alter, amend, revoke, or terminate the agreement or change its terms. If the employee had any of these rights (either alone or in conjunction with any other person), the IRS would require inclusion. This inclusion by virtue of the employee's right to make changes to the agreement spurs a number of issues. For instance:

(1) Will the mere possibility of exerting influence upon an employer to make changes to the agreement cause inclusion? What if the covered employee were an officer, director, or shareholder? Can the employee, by terminating employment, terminate the plan? To each of these questions, the courts have held that no inclusion was required.

(2) Will a controlling (more than 50%) shareholder, merely by virtue of such control, have the power to unilaterally make a change to the agreement that would cause estate tax inclusion? It is likely that the IRS will attack any situation where the covered individual owns more than a 50% interest, although, in the authors' opinion, the fiduciary responsibility one owner owes to another, regardless of the size of the other's interest, negates the ability to make unilateral decisions that affect others. (See Q&A below for more details.)

If there is estate tax inclusion and the DBO benefit is paid in a lump sum, the entire lump sum will be taxable. If there is estate tax inclusion and benefits are payable in installments, the present value of payments to be made at the covered employee's

death would be includable in his gross estate. For instance, assuming a 5% federal discount rate, payments of $100,000 per year for 10 years would have a commuted (present) value of about $772,170 ($100,000 x 7.7217).[7]

Payments under a DBO plan, if paid to a surviving spouse outright or to the estate of a surviving spouse or to a general power of appointment or QTIP trust, could qualify for the federal estate tax marital deduction. This would eliminate the federal estate tax at the death of the first spouse.

Planners should note, however, that if payments are subject to contingencies, such as a reduction or cessation of payments upon remarriage, there will be both positive and negative results. A contingency typically reduces the value of the amount includable in the decedent employee's estate. But that same contingency could also cause a forfeiture of the estate tax marital deduction. If the contract provides that after the surviving spouse's interest ends, payments will be made to another beneficiary (other then the surviving spouse's estate), the spouse's interest is terminable (i.e., one which may end or fail upon the lapse of time or on the occurrence or failure to occur of some contingency). Annuities are, by definition, a systematic liquidation of principal and interest over a period of time, and are therefore terminable interests.[8] Since payments to the employee's beneficiary take the form of an annuity from the employer for a given term of time, DBO payments that pass to someone other than the surviving spouse at the employee's death (or for any other reason) are terminable interests.

Some terminable interests are still deductible for federal estate tax purposes. For instance, if payments were for the shorter of 10 years or the life of the employee's surviving spouse, the interest would be deductible. Furthermore, a QTIP (qualified terminable interest property) election could obtain an estate tax deduction for what might otherwise be a nondeductible interest.[9]

9. The IRS will no longer claim that the payment of the death benefit at the employee's death constituted a completed gift at the time of death.[10]

10. Death benefits paid to beneficiaries are not considered "wages" subject to income tax withholding.

11. If a DBO plan covers only a single employee (as opposed to a class or classes of employees), then, for

FICA purposes, only the benefits paid to the beneficiaries in the calendar year of the employee's death will be subject to FICA taxes.[11] Benefits paid after that calendar year should escape FICA taxes.[12] If an entire class or classes of employees are covered under a DBO plan, benefits paid to beneficiaries should be totally exempt from FICA taxes.[13]

WHAT ARE THE ERISA IMPLICATIONS?

A DBO plan is considered to be an employee welfare benefit plan subject to the requirements of Title I of ERISA. Fortunately, most DBO plans are exempt from ERISA's participation, vesting, and funding requirements. Reporting and disclosure is streamlined if the DBO plan is limited to a select group of management or highly compensated employees (generally, less than 5% of total employees should be participants). So, in most cases, no annual ERISA filings need be made with the Department of Labor.

In order to successfully avoid ERISA's funding requirements:

1. Counsel should state in the contract between the employer and employee that employees have no right to any instrument that will be used to finance the employer's potential obligations under the DBO plan.

2. The employer should maintain any life insurance as part of its general unrestricted assets (the employer should be the owner and beneficiary of the insurance). No financing vehicle, especially life insurance, should be tied to the DBO plan in any way. Life insurance should not be mentioned as a financing vehicle in the plan, nor should the phrase "fund" or "informally fund" be used in discussing the use of life insurance in any documents (such as corporate resolutions or SEC annual report disclosure statements) related to the DBO plan.

3. Only a select group of management and highly compensated employees should be covered under a DBO plan.

QUESTIONS AND ANSWERS

Question – How should the corporate resolution authorizing the plan and the purchase of supporting life insurance be phrased?

Answer – Part of the corporate resolution might read as follows:

RESOLVED: In order to insure itself against all financial losses and other economic detriment that the Corporation would incur in the event of a preretirement death of [name of key executive], the vice president of the Corporation is authorized to enter into a contract of [description of type of policy] life insurance with the [name of insurer] life insurance company for coverage in the amount of [$] insuring the following person(s).

Question – How is the amount of insurance necessary to finance a DBO plan determined?

Answer – Most DBO plans promise to make payments over a number of years (e.g., $100,000 per year for 10 years, if death occurs prior to age 65). Assume a plan promised a $10,000 annual death benefit for 10 years to the surviving spouse of a key executive, otherwise to the executive's children. Assume the employer corporation is expected to be in a 40% (or higher) combined state and federal income tax bracket at the time payments are made. After its $4,000 deduction for each payment, the net cost would be only $6,000 per payment. So it could purchase a $60,000 policy on the employee's life, and even if it earned no interest on the unpaid balance, it would have sufficient funds to make the promised annual payments. Actually, when interest earnings are factored in, the policy death benefit could even be less than $60,000.

The corporation would own and be the beneficiary of the policy and pay all premiums. Note that the $60,000 of life insurance would be received by the employer-corporation income tax free (and, in this example, because of the relatively low amount of insurance, would probably not be subject to any AMT). However, in the case of a larger life insurance policy, planners should multiply the target amount that the employer firm needs to net by 118%, in order to find the proper level of insurance to purchase (assuming a worst case scenario and a "large corporation"). For example, if the company needed to net $60,000 in a worst case situation, it should purchase $70,800 ($60,000 x 1.18) worth of insurance coverage.

If the benefit is to be paid to the beneficiary over a period of years, rather than in a lump sum, the amount of life insurance needed by the corporation is further reduced. This is because the corporation can invest the life insurance proceeds received at the date of the employee's death. Since it will pay those funds over a number of years, it can continue to invest any balance and use the net after-tax interest income to help fund the benefit payments. The use of a calculator or software package with discounting tables will quickly show the low cost of providing a large benefit when the employer can use both tax leveraging and the time value of money. Alternatively, the employer could obtain the full amount of insurance needed and use interest earnings as a cost recovery vehicle to reimburse itself for premium outlays. For instance, in the example above, by purchasing $100,000 of coverage, rather than $60,000 or $70,800, the corporation would have much more than necessary to make the promised payments. The excess could serve as an "economic shock absorber" and a way to return to the corporation a significant portion of its premium outlays.

Question – How could IRC Section 2033 be used by the IRS to require inclusion of the DBO plan payments, and how can this result be avoided?

Answer – IRC Section 2033 requires that property in which the decedent has an interest at the time of death be included in his estate. Inclusion is required to the extent of the decedent's interest. The courts have uniformly held that under a properly structured DBO plan, the decedent has completely and irrevocably transferred any interest he may have had to the named recipient and thus, at the time of death, has no interest under IRC Section 2033.

The key to avoiding inclusion under Section 2033 is to avoid giving the employee (and the employee's estate) any vesting or reversion rights. Language specifically stating that neither the employee nor his estate has any interest or rights in the payments to be made to the beneficiary after the employee's death should be included in the plan documents, as well as a statement that under no circumstances will payments be made to the decedent's executor.

Question – How could IRC Section 2036 be used by the IRS to require inclusion of the DBO payments, and how can this result be avoided?

Answer – Section 2036 applies to transfers with a retained life estate and requires that gratuitous transfers, in which the decedent retained the right to the income or property from the gift or the right to say who will possess or enjoy that property or its income, be included in the decedent's estate. Courts

have held that the beneficiary's right to receive a death benefit can be considered an indirect gratuitous lifetime transfer by the covered employee. So if the employee is given and retains the right to name or change the beneficiary of the DBO plan benefit, the IRS could argue that the employee has retained a Section 2036 right. The solution is to state in the DBO plan or agreement that the employee has no right to name or change the beneficiary and that the right to do so vests solely in the employer.

The mere possibility that the employee could negotiate a new contract with the employer or terminate the plan by terminating employment is not considered a retention of Section 2036 powers. Close family relationships or stock holdings are not, in and of themselves, enough to be considered a Section 2036 retained power. However, DBO plan payments could be included in the estate of a controlling shareholder.

Question – How could IRC Section 2037 be used by the IRS to require inclusion of the DBO payments, and how can this result be avoided?

Answer – Section 2037 requires inclusion in the decedent's gross estate only if there is a reversion (i.e., the property given away comes back), either to the decedent or to the decedent's estate and the actuarial value of that reversion right is greater than 5% of the value of the property in question. For instance, if the attorney who drafted the agreement did not specify a contingent beneficiary, then, should the first named beneficiary predecease the covered employee, there could be a Section 2037 inclusion.

For example, if the death benefit is payable to the employee's child, but the child did not survive the employee, payments would revert to the deceased employee's legal representative (in other words, the employee's estate). If the relative ages of the parties were such that the potential payment to the employee's estate (the value of the reversionary interest) was worth more than 5%, the death benefit payable by the corporation would be includable in his taxable estate. So, naming the covered employee's executor or making the benefit payable to the employee's revocable living trust (or testamentary trust) would result in inclusion.[14] If an employer agrees to pay benefits either to the surviving spouse or to the employee's estate, this may create a reversionary interest that, if valued in excess of 5% of the estate, will result in inclusion of the present value of the benefit.

The solution to the potential Section 2037 problem is for the employer to create several levels of beneficiaries, in order to provide for the contingency of one or more beneficiaries predeceasing the covered employee. For example, the DBO contract might provide words to the effect that payments were to be made "to the employee's surviving spouse, if living, otherwise to the employee's surviving children in equal shares, or to the survivor of them, but if no such children survive the employee, then all liability under this agreement ceases." Clearly, the estate of the employee should not be named contingent beneficiary.

Question – How could IRC Section 2038 be used by the IRS to require inclusion of the DBO payments in the employee's estate, and how can this result be avoided?

Answer – Section 2038 provides that if a gratuitous transfer is made coupled with the retention of the right to alter, amend, revoke, or terminate the gift, the value of the property interest given away is brought back into the donor's estate. So, if the covered employee is given any right to change the amounts or terms of the coverage under the plan or the identity of the beneficiaries, inclusion will result under Section 2038. The clearest example of this is where the contract gives the employee a continuing right during employment to change the beneficiary of the death benefit under the DBO plan. Likewise, if a revocable trust established by the employee is named as beneficiary, payments will be included in the beneficiary's estate since, by definition, the employee reserved the right to alter, amend, revoke, and terminate the revocable trust and can therefore change the identity of the DBO plan's beneficiaries.

One solution is to make the designation of the beneficiary irrevocable. But that would involve gift tax implications and loss of control (and create the implication that the employee had the right to make changes up until that time). The preferred solution is for the employer to state in the agreement that the employer reserves total, sole, and unlimited right to name or change the beneficiary. The agreement should specifically provide that the employee has absolutely no power to "alter, amend, revoke, or terminate" the plan or the identity of beneficiaries under the plan in any way, either alone or in conjunction with any other party. It is important not to make the mistake of drafting the DBO contract to provide that the employee can, with the mutual consent of his employer, modify the beneficiary's rights. If such an express power to modify or change the beneficiary's rights should exceed those rights allowable under applicable state law, estate inclusion will result. This adverse impact occurs even though the employer's consent is required to change the DBO beneficiary.

IRC Section 2038 poses a more insidious problem: the "more than 50%" shareholder. Specifically, the question posed is, "Does an individual who owns the controlling voting power in a corporation have, as the mere result of that power over corporate actions, the right to alter, amend, revoke, or terminate the DBO agreement or change the designation of its beneficiary?" In a private letter ruling, payments under a DBO plan escaped estate tax inclusion, even though the decedent owned 85% of the corporation's voting stock. The IRS held that the deceased owner's fiduciary duty and responsibility to the other shareholder (his wife) was enough to prevent his control from resulting in inclusion.[15] However, in facts almost indistinguishable from those in the letter ruling, the IRS successfully argued that if the employee-decedent controlled the corporation, the DBO payments would be includable.[16] This same case seems to confirm that a properly drafted DBO plan covering employees of a publicly held corporation or of a noncontrolling (50% or less) shareholder should not be subject to either estate or gift taxation. The outcome where the covered shareholder owns 51% or more is uncertain.

Question – How could IRC Section 2039 be used by the IRS to require inclusion of the DBO payments, and how can this result be avoided?

Answer – Section 2039 deals with "annuities and other payments." The "annuity or other payment" requirement is satisfied if one or more payments are made over any period of time, regardless of whether those payments are equal or unequal, conditional or unconditional, periodic or sporadic, fixed, or variable. Essentially, it requires estate tax inclusion of amounts received at an individual's death under any form of contract or agreement that provides *both* an annuity or similar payment during lifetime *and* a death benefit.

A pure DBO plan, as its name implies, provides only death benefits and no payments while the employee lives. So standing alone, the properly drafted pure DBO plan should not require inclusion under Section 2039.

Where both postdeath and lifetime postretirement benefits exist in a single plan (or the IRS treats two separate plans that provide such benefits to the same employee as one plan), Section 2039 will require estate tax inclusion of the death benefit. Payments would be treated as though received by the survivor from a joint and survivor annuity (which, in essence, they would be). In such a case, the lump sum paid to the beneficiary or the present value of the stream of payments would be subject to estate tax.

For example, suppose a client has the right to $60,000 per year for 10 years after retirement in one plan. In an entirely separate agreement, executed five years later, the client's employer promises to pay $100,000 per year for 10 years to the client's children. The present value of the children's rights to the stream of income will be includable in the client's estate.

Just what sort of postretirement lifetime payments will be linked to death benefit payments under Section 2039? Does the mere acceptance of wages constitute "postretirement lifetime payments"? The answer is no.[17] What if an employee signs an agreement with his former employer to serve as a consultant for life? Will this be considered an annuity? Again, the answer is negative. Assuming payments are made for services actually rendered after retirement, those salary payments will not be linked to payments under the DBO plan.[18] Likewise, if substantial services are necessary to receive payments, such amounts will be considered salary, rather than retirement benefits. Benefits payable under a short-term sickness and accident income plan or wages paid for a period of illness or other temporary incapacities, after which the employee is expected to return to work, are considered compensation.[19]

On the other hand, if the agreement calls for payments to be made to the employee after he becomes too incapacitated to perform services, or requires only nominal services after the employee reaches a certain age, payments will be treated as postretirement benefits. Also, payments made if an employee becomes "totally incapacitated" before retirement are considered "an annuity or other payment." Benefits payable under a long-term disability plan that, in essence, assumes that the employee will never return to work and "retires" the employee on disability payments are not considered compensation, and will be treated as postretirement payments. Linked constructively with a DBO plan,

the result will be inclusion of the "annuity" under Section 2039.

Note that for linkage to be made, the employee must be receiving (or have the right to receive at the date of death) an annuity or "other payment" for life (or for a stipulated term that does not end before the employee's death). For inclusion to be warranted, payments must continue to a survivor as they do in a normal joint and survivor annuity. For instance, if payments were being made to the disabled employee and the employee died before exhausting the fund, and the remaining payments were made to the next class of beneficiary, the long-term disability plan would be coupled with payments under a DBO plan.

Another key issue in determining whether a deceased employee had the right under the plan to any postretirement lifetime payments is, "What is meant by a plan?" The answer is that all rights and benefits that the employee had by virtue of employment (except those under qualified retirement plans) are considered part of one contract or plan in determining whether Section 2039 applies. So it is not possible to avoid inclusion by providing death benefit payments under one contract and lifetime retirement benefits under another.

What is meant by the term "contract"? The term is applied broadly and includes not only contracts enforceable under state law but also payments made under an agreement, understanding, or plan. For example, a corporate resolution may constitute such an understanding.[20]

Question – How could IRC Section 2041 be used by the IRS to require inclusion of the DBO payments, and how can this result be avoided?

Answer – IRC Section 2041 is concerned with general powers of appointment – the ability to determine who is to receive someone else's property. If a decedent has a general power (i.e., the unlimited ability to reduce property to the possession of himself, his creditors, his estate, or the creditors of his estate), the entire amount subject to that power will be included in the decedent's estate.

Suppose the death benefit was payable to a trust, over which the decedent retained or was given a general power of appointment. If the payments from a DBO plan are made to that trust, they will be includable under IRC Section 2041.

Question – How could IRC Section 2042 be used by the IRS to require inclusion of the DBO payments, and how can this result be avoided?

Answer – IRC Section 2042 requires inclusion where the insured decedent held any significant incident of ownership over the policy or (even where no incident of ownership was held at death or given up within three years of death by the insured) where the proceeds are paid to or for the benefit of the insured's estate. Where life insurance is used as the financing mechanism for the employer to meet its potential obligations under the DBO plan, the IRS would probably claim inclusion under IRC Section 2042 where the employee either owns the policy or is given any right of substance with respect to the policy. For example, if the employee is given veto rights over a change of beneficiary, the IRS would likely argue that this is an incident of ownership, causing inclusion.

It is possible that the IRS would also claim inclusion where the DBO plan or some other employment related agreement gave the covered employee the right to prevent the cancellation of the policy, by providing that the employee could purchase the policy from the corporation. Of course, there would be no inclusion merely because the corporation could voluntarily choose to sell a life insurance policy to a terminating employee for its fair market value.

The safest course of action is for the corporation to name itself owner and beneficiary of the policy and to give the insured employee no rights whatsoever with respect to the policy or its values. The policy should be carried on the company's books as key employee coverage and should not be mentioned in the DBO agreement with the employee.

Question – Why shouldn't DBO payments always be made voluntarily on the employer's part in order to avoid estate tax inclusion?

Answer – It is true that if the death benefit payments are not made under a contract or plan and are completely voluntary on the employer's part, there should be no inclusion in the covered employee's estate for federal estate tax purposes. Such voluntary payments are not includable in the employee's estate, because neither the employee nor the employee's beneficiary ever possessed the right to compel the employer to pay the benefit and the employee made no transfer of property or an interest in property.

But a plan that is completely voluntary on the employer's part fails to achieve the "golden handcuffs" effect that is the goal of many employers (i.e., the employee who is not sure of a benefit is given no incentive to come to a business or stay with the business). Such an employee does not feel rewarded by the firm for his efforts in a way that builds loyalty toward the employer. From the employee's viewpoint, a benefit provided at the whim of the employer provides neither peace of mind nor financial security. The mere possibility of such a benefit does not free up other dollars that the employee has discretion to use during lifetime.

Question – What happens to the interest of an employee (or his beneficiary) if the employer goes bankrupt?

Answer – Both the covered employee and his beneficiaries have only the status of an unsecured creditor. A living employee typically has no rights under a DBO plan, since there are no obligations that become fixed until and unless the employee dies while working for the employer. Beneficiaries, as unsecured creditors, have no priority claim to any employer assets, including life insurance used by the employer to finance potential obligations.[21] The likelihood is that beneficiaries would take a pro rata share of the assets that remain (if any) after any secured creditors and priority unsecured claimants have been satisfied.

Question – How does the corporate exemption from the AMT work?

Answer – Certain "small corporations" will qualify for an exemption from the AMT.[22] In order to initially qualify for the exemption, the corporation's average annual gross receipts for its first three-year period must not exceed $5 million. Thereafter, in order to continue to qualify for the exemption, the corporation's average annual gross receipts must not exceed $7.5 million in subsequent three-year periods. For a corporation that has not been in existence for three full years, its years of existence are substituted for the three-year period (with annualization of any short taxable year). A corporation will generally be exempt from the AMT in its first year of existence. Once a business fails to meet the gross receipts test, it cannot qualify as a small corporation in any later year. If a corporation fails to maintain its small corporation status, it loses the exemption from the AMT.

For example, assume that a calendar-year corporation started its business on January 1, 2003.

The corporation will generally be exempt from the AMT in 2003. It will be exempt in 2004 if its gross receipts in 2003 do not exceed $5 million. It will continue to be exempt in 2005 if its average receipts for 2003 and 2004 do not exceed $7.5 million.

CHAPTER ENDNOTES

1. Compare *Casale v. Comm.*, 247 F.2d 440 (2nd Cir. 1957) with *Goldsmith v. U.S.*, 586 F.2d 810 (Ct. Cl. 1978).

2. IRC Sec. 264(a)(1).

3. IRC Sec. 101(a).

4. IRC Sec. 1014(c).

5. IRC Sec. 691(b).

6. See Roberts, "Tax Traps in Tax-Leveraged Employee Death Benefit Plans; Analysis and Planning," 59 J. Tax. 324 (1983). For a somewhat different analysis, see Swirnoff, "Interplay of Deductions for Non-qualified Compensation and Employee Life Insurance," 62 J. Tax. 130 (1985).

7. See *The Tools and Techniques of Estate Planning* for information on the computation of annuity, life estate, and remainder values and the AFMR. The rates, which vary from month to month, are published monthly in a revenue ruling.

8. IRC Sec. 2056(b).

9. For more information on the marital deduction, see Appendix A.

10. *Est. of DiMarco v. Comm.*, 87 TC 653 (1986), acq. in result, 1990-2 CB 1.

11. IRC Secs. 3121(a)(14), 3121(a)(13)(B).

12. IRC Sec. 3121(a)(14).

13. IRC Sec. 3121(a)(13)(B).

14. See *Est. of Fried v. Comm.*, 445 F.2d 979 (2nd Cir. 1971).

15. Let. Rul. 8701003.

16. *Est. of Levin v. Comm.*, 90 TC 723 (1988).

17. See *Est. of Fusz v. Comm.*, 46 TC 214 (1966), acq. 1967-2 CB 2, which held that "other payment" means postemployment benefits paid or payable to the decedent during his lifetime. Fusz was an employee who signed an employment contract that provided (a) monthly salary payments to him and (b) monthly payments after his death to his surviving spouse. Section 2039 was held to be inapplicable because the only postemployment promise that was made to Fusz was to pay a salary for services rendered.

18. Planners should caution clients that merely stating that a payment is salary will not be sufficient to have it treated as such. For instance, if the IRS can show that services actually (or to be rendered) were not worth the agreed upon payments, or that (in view of close family ties or voting control) it was never intended that services be performed in return for the promised payments, the Service will treat such payments as a retirement arrangement. See *Kramer v. U.S.*, 406 F.2d 1363 (Ct. Cl. 1969), where the IRS used this very argument (but was unsuccessful only because it failed to prove the services to be rendered were nominal or pro forma).

19. Planners must make a distinction between a wage continuation plan, which presumes that the employee will return to work, and a disability plan, which presumes that the employee will not (i.e., benefits are payable only if the disability is expected to be total and permanent and the employee is "retired" on disability). If the employee is never expected to render additional services to the employer after payments begin, benefits are considered "an annuity or other payment" within the scope of Section 2039. See *Est. of Schelberg v. Comm.*, 79-2 USTC ¶13,321 (2d Cir. 1979).

20. In *Neely v. U.S.*, 613 F. 2d 802 (Ct. Cl. 1980), the court held that it was immaterial whether the widow could enforce payment, since she held (individually or as her husband's executrix) 70% of the voting stock of the company after her husband's death.

21. See 11 U.S.C.A. Secs. 724(b), 726(a), 726(b).

22. IRC Sec. 55(e).

Chapter 23

IRREVOCABLE LIFE INSURANCE TRUSTS

This chapter will cover many topics with respect to irrevocable life insurance trusts. These include:

1. Why a Gift of Life Insurance?

2. Advantages of Ownership of Life Insurance by 3rd Party

3. Disadvantages of 3rd Party Ownership of Life Insurance

4. Why Make a Gift of Life Insurance to an Irrevocable Life Insurance Trust?

5. Disadvantages to Ownership of Life Insurance by an Irrevocable Trust

6. Irrevocable Trust – What It Is and How It Works

7. Mechanics

8. Selection of a Trustee

9. Reducing or Eliminating Gift Taxes on Policy Transfers and Premium Payments through Crummey Powers

10. Gift, Estate, and Income Tax Problems Related to Crummey Powers

11. Reducing or Eliminating Gift Taxes on Premium Payments through Methods Other than Crummey Powers

12. What the Attorney Should Consider in Drafting

13. How to Avoid the Transfers within Three Years of Death Rule

14. Structuring the Trust for "What Ifs"

15. Allocation of the Federal Estate Tax

16. Income Tax Implications

17. How to Handle Last to Die (Survivorship) Insurance in an Irrevocable Trust

18. How to Handle Group Term Life Insurance in an Irrevocable Trust

19. Community Property Issues

WHY A GIFT OF LIFE INSURANCE?

Life insurance is an almost magic tool in estate planning. But because its utility is diminished in direct proportion to the taxes imposed on it and the security life insurance provides becomes illusory, it often makes sense for highly successful clients to give it away. Gifts of life insurance offer special planning opportunities that are not available with other assets.

These include:

1. Life insurance proceeds can be removed from a client's estate at a relatively low gift tax cost.[1] Compare this with most other property, which has the same value for gift tax purposes as it does for estate tax calculations.

2. A gift of other assets may result in a loss of a stepped up basis to the client's heirs.[2] But a gift of life insurance does not result in such a loss in income tax savings; there is generally no income tax payable on the proceeds and the loss of a step-up in basis is no concern.

3. Psychologically, life insurance is an easier gift for a client to part with than most other assets since it is not income producing and is generally thought of as a post death security vehicle for others.[3]

ADVANTAGES OF OWNERSHIP OF LIFE INSURANCE BY 3RD PARTY

The benefits of shifting ownership of life insurance to save estate taxes are most easily and certainly obtainable if a party who has an insurable interest in the insured's life purchases the policy and pays all the premiums and is the beneficiary of the proceeds when the insured dies. That party should be someone other than the insured or the insured's estate. Since the proceeds are not paid to or for the benefit of the estate of the insured and because the insured owned no incidents of ownership over the policy and because there was no transfer of the policy within three years of death, there will be no estate tax inclusion.

The second best alternative is to transfer existing policies by gift to the insured's spouse or some other trusted person or, the most preferable method when the combined estates exceed the unified credit exemption equivalent, transfer the policies to an irrevocable life insurance trust. Removing the proceeds from the insured's gross estate in this manner not only lowers the overall tax burden but also provides a means of creating estate liquidity (cash to pay the decedent's debts, taxes and other expenses of estate administration). The recipient of the policy proceeds can make fully secured interest bearing loans to the estate's executor or purchase assets from the estate. This gives the estate cash and helps assure that desired assets remain within the family unit.

Liquidity could be provided by the direct purchase of life insurance by the grantor. However, the incredible advantage of third party ownership of life insurance is that it provides liquidity for the estate without causing inclusion of the life insurance proceeds in the client's estate (or, where the insurance is owned by a 3rd party such as the insured's child or an irrevocable life insurance trust, without causing inclusion in the estate of the client's spouse).

If the policy is originally owned or transferred to the insured's spouse who is also the premium payor and beneficiary, the estate tax will be delayed until the death of the surviving spouse. Assuming the insured's spouse survives the insured, this means that money that otherwise would have been paid in federal estate taxes can instead be used to provide support for the spouse and children. To the extent used by the surviving spouse, those proceeds will never be subject to federal estate tax.

If the policy is originally owned or transferred to the insured's children, then no estate tax is imposed until the next generation and even then only to the extent the children have not used the money.

DISADVANTAGES OF 3RD PARTY OWNERSHIP OF LIFE INSURANCE

Planners must not let the advantages to 3rd party ownership totally obscure the potential risks or costs:

1. To avoid the federal estate tax, at least, the client must give up direct control over the policy. The transfer must be both complete and permanent. An absolute assignment or total change of ownership must be made if a presently existing policy is to be removed from the client's estate. This means the client must forgo the right to name or change the policy beneficiary, veto a change, borrow against the cash values of the policy, and give up every other meaningful and significant incident of ownership.

2. Many events, unpredictable at the time 3rd party ownership is arranged, can drastically change the way or the parties the client would prefer to own coverage on his life. For instance, the insured's marriage could become unstable, the insured may no longer get along with the children who are the owners of a policy on the insured's life, or the insured's spouse or other owner could predecease the insured. The insured may remarry. Tax laws can change. During this time, the insured may become highly rated due to health problems or even become uninsurable or insurable only at prohibitive cost. Business reverses or opportunities may suggest a need for insurance cash values, which are unavailable if the policy is no longer owned by the insured.

WHY MAKE A GIFT OF LIFE INSURANCE TO AN IRREVOCABLE LIFE INSURANCE TRUST?

Incredible federal estate and state death tax savings are possible though an irrevocable trust which has as one of its assets a life insurance policy on the life of the grantor. For the highly successful individual, no means exists under current law to transfer large amounts of wealth and provide financial security that are as certain or as dramatic as the irrevocable life insurance trust.

Reasons for the popularity of this estate planning tool include almost all of the advantages listed for implementing revocable trusts and these important additional reasons:

1. Federal estate taxes on millions of otherwise taxable dollars can be avoided, not only when the client dies, but also when the client's spouse dies. Leveraging life insurance through tax savings in this manner means death taxes bypass both spouses' estates and the amount effectively passing to heirs is substantially increased.

2. State death taxes can be saved in the same manner as federal estate taxes. This advantage becomes particularly important in states that provide limited exemptions for life insurance proceeds and those that have high rates on transfers at death to persons other than spouses.

3. In most cases relatively little (and in many cases no) gift tax is required to create and simultaneously shelter high amounts of life insurance from transfer taxes. At a relatively low gift tax cost (because the gift tax value of life insurance transferred to the trust is valued at its much lower lifetime value, in most cases the interpolated terminal reserve plus any unearned premiums on the date of the gift) the many times larger amount of the policy proceeds is removed from the client's estate. This leverage is impossible to find with any other estate transfer tool or technique under current law.

4. There will be no probate expenses, delays, or uncertainties with respect to the transfer of assets in an irrevocable life insurance trust. Had the surviving spouse owned the coverage on her husband's life, proceeds she didn't exhaust during her life would be subject to both federal and state death taxes and probate costs.

5. By making loans to the client's estate or purchasing assets from the estate, the trustee can use trust assets at the client's death to help provide estate liquidity, prevent a forced sale of a family business, valuable real estate, or a securities portfolio, and keep treasured property in the family. Furthermore, because the life insurance used to make that loan or purchase is not included in either spouse's taxable estate, the irrevocable life insurance trust provides estate liquidity without increasing the liquidity problem. Had some other 3rd party policy ownership arrangement been used, it is possible that such a person, depending on the terms of the insured's will or that person's relationship with the other beneficiaries, may be unwilling to make loans to the estate or purchase assets from the estate with the proceeds.

6. Significant income and capital can be provided for or on behalf of the surviving spouse without causing inclusion of the life insurance proceeds or other trust assets in the surviving spouse's estate.

7. The irrevocability of the trust generally translates into protection from the claims of creditors.

8. Trusts that are irrevocable generally provide protection from a surviving spouse's rights of dower, courtesy, or right of election under state law.

9. A gift of an insurance policy to a life insurance trust gives the insured more control over the ultimate disposition of both the policy and its proceeds than would an outright policy gift. In other words, when an irrevocable trust is the owner of life insurance on the client's life, the client controls the ultimate disposition of the policy after the surviving spouse's death through provisions in the trust. It also resolves the problem of what happens to the policy if the 3rd party owner predeceases the insured. An individual donee policyowner can give or bequeath the policy to third persons, frustrating the insured's planned use of the proceeds. The use of a trust provides greater assurance that the proceeds will be used for the grantor's intended purpose. For instance, if a client transfers a policy to a potential beneficiary, such as a child, and that party predeceases the client, it is possible that the policy would revert back to the client and end up being taxed in the client's estate. The use of an irrevocable trust can prevent this result. The irrevocable trust also reduces the potential that a policy owned by a spouse on the other spouse's life will inadvertently lapse upon the death of the owner prior to the insured.

10. Sprinkle and spray powers (i.e., giving the independent trustee discretion to sprinkle income and spray capital among the trust's beneficiaries in the manner that best meets the client's dispositive objectives and the beneficiaries' needs and minimizes the income taxes of the family unit) are highly advantageous. Most importantly, the trustee can deny payments, when appropriate, on a more objective basis and with less potential for family conflict than if a family member received the insurance proceeds and then attempted to provide family security.

11. When compared to the use of settlement options (an often overlooked alternative to trusts in small estates), the trust offers greater flexibility and, in some cases, an opportunity for increased capital and income. A trust can provide for payments according to the beneficiaries' needs and circumstances by giving the trustee

sprinkle and spray powers and by giving beneficiaries limited powers of appointment. This is particularly important where a primary function of the trust is to fund a large security reserve for beneficiaries who are inexperienced, minor, or disabled. The trustee can be authorized to invest aggressively to maximize income and growth (but in comparing trusts to settlement options, planners should also consider the increased risk).

12. Generation-skipping transfer tax (GSTT) problems can be reduced or eliminated by judicious use of GSTT annual exclusions and the GSTT exemption. Significant leverage can be obtained through the use of life insurance inside the trust.

13. Wealth replacement is another advantage to the use of irrevocable life insurance trusts. A client may want to make a tax deductible gift to a charity during lifetime or at death, yet replace the net after estate tax wealth his heirs would have received had no charitable gift been made. This goal can be accomplished through gifts to an irrevocable trust followed by a purchase by the trustee of life insurance on the client's life in an amount sufficient to replace the (after estate tax) value of the donated land, stock, or other gift made to charity.

14. Clients who establish GRITs, GRATs, or GRUTs[4] or charitable lead trusts and who die during the initial term of the trust will have all or a large portion of the trust's assets included in their estates. If the client survives that term, nothing will be included in the client's gross estate and great wealth can be shifted at a gift tax discount. Many attorneys have suggested that clients insure the estate tax savings by making annual gifts to a trustee who uses the money to purchase insurance on the client's life equal to the potential estate tax savings.

15. An often overlooked advantage of an irrevocable life insurance trust is that through the leverage of life insurance and the flexibility of the trust vehicle, even a person of modest means can be assured that adequate financial security and the achievement of important and costly economic goals such as the education of children or grandchildren can be met.

16. An irrevocable trust provides all the above advantages, in addition to the classic uses for

trusts in general:[5] professional management, protection from creditors, postponement of receipt of inheritance, and avoidance of guardianship for minors or other incompetents.

DISADVANTAGES TO OWNERSHIP OF LIFE INSURANCE BY AN IRREVOCABLE TRUST

1. The client must give up:

   a) the income produced by any income producing trust assets if the trust has been funded;

   b) the use and enjoyment of any property including the life insurance cash values held by the trust or use of the cash values as collateral;

   c) the right to name, add, subtract, or change the size or terms of a beneficiary's interest;

   d) the right to regain assets (including life insurance) placed into the trust; and

   e) the ability to alter, amend, revoke, or terminate the trust.

The psychological cost of losing this control and flexibility should not be underestimated. Many clients should not set up such trusts, in spite of the tremendous potential death tax savings, because of the offsetting lifetime loss of peace of mind and flexibility. Clients who are relatively young will be faced with a long lifetime of rapidly changing personal and financial circumstances.

Planners must make clients aware of the problems inherent in the event the client's objectives, client's or beneficiary's circumstances, or tax laws change. The client may decide at some future date that he does not like the payout provisions and would like them to be longer (or shorter) or provide more (or less) to a given beneficiary. Counsel may find the powers in the trust instrument are tainted in such a manner that trust assets will be included in the client's estate. The client may have failed to name enough backup trustees or there may be a personality conflict between the client and the trustee.

Clients must also be made to understand that there is a certain level of paperwork and record keeping that cannot be safely ignored. "Responsibilities of this nature can seem unduly complex and frustrating to the client, who, unless he has been forewarned, may well become unhappy with his attorney for placing him in the situation in the first place."[6]

Although there are potential solutions to the problems confronted when dealing with an irrevocable trust, there is no free lunch. Tax savings and additional flexibility comes with a cost. Escape hatches are less than perfect. Yet, in weighing these disadvantages, planners should consider:

- The client can discontinue premium payments, let the policy inside the trust lapse (or use policy cash values to purchase extended term insurance for a limited time or a lower amount of paid up insurance for the insured's life) and start over with a new trust with new terms and new insurance (assuming insurability at affordable rates).

- Even an irrevocable trust can be revoked by court action assuming the written consent of all (including guardians for minor) beneficiaries. A trust can be revoked in whole or in part in many states assuming all persons beneficially interested (i.e., who have a vested interest) agree to the revocation in writing and file a notarized copy of the request for revocation in the appropriate county clerk's office. The mere state statutory power enabling such a revocation would not be enough to require inclusion of irrevocable trusts in the estates of such persons. However, when the trust terminates, the property may end up back in the client's estate if there is no specific provision in the trust paying over the assets to beneficiaries named in the event of a premature termination by revocation. The client must then create a new irrevocable trust or make a further disposition of trust assets to remove them from his gross estate.

    Planners should keep in mind that revocation is not automatic and is usually granted only as an escape hatch from unforeseen events occurring subsequent to the creation of a trust. If beneficiaries are below the state age of majority, it will be necessary to have guardians ad litem appointed since the minors cannot consent to the termination or amendment.

- One common objection to the creation of an irrevocable life insurance trust is the loss of the use of life insurance cash values. When a cash value policy is placed in or purchased by an irrevocable trust, the client normally does lose all control over the policy values. The trustee, acting in a fiduciary capacity, is the only party that can utilize those values. But, by giving the trustee the authority to make distributions to the beneficiaries during the grantor's lifetime, the cash value and/or dividends of the policy can be used during the lifetime of the insured client. In other words, it is possible to draft an irrevocable life insurance trust in such a way that distributions could be made to beneficiaries before the client's death.

- The client could purchase the policies from the trust at their fair market value. This gives the trust a relatively small amount of cash but returns the insurance (transfer for value tax free) back to the client, who can then create a new trust with new terms and contribute the old policies into that new trust. If the policy held extensive cash values, the out of pocket cost of the purchase could be reduced by stripping out all or a portion of the cash values prior to the transfer. Of course, the purchase cannot be guaranteed by requiring such a sale in the trust agreement. A call on trust assets would result in estate tax inclusion. The legal right to purchase a policy would clearly be an incident of ownership.

- A special power of appointment could be inserted from inception into the irrevocable life insurance trust. That power would give the insured's spouse, an adult child, or someone else the insured implicitly trusts the ability to appoint (direct ownership of) trust property to herself or her children (or anyone else other than back to the insured-grantor, his estate, his creditors, or the creditors of his estate). The authors suggest that the trust bar the holder of the power from using it to pay for any item that could be considered in satisfaction of either spouse's legal obligation of support. This special power should cause no inclusion in the estate of the holder and unless the policy is in fact transferred back to the insured-grantor, it should not attract estate tax in his estate. A contingent limited powerholder should also be named.

    The disadvantage of this technique is, if the parties divorce or the holder dies before the grantor-insured, the ability to remove trust assets and appoint them in a direction consistent with the client's desires is eliminated. Obviously, if there is marital discord at the time of planning, the spouse should not be considered as the holder of this power.

- Name the grantor's spouse as initial holder of the power to appoint trust assets but provide if (a) the spouse dies first, (b) the spouse is no longer married to the grantor, or (c) for any reason the spouse no longer has the legal or mental capacity to exercise the power, the limited power would automatically pass to the individual named as contingent holder.

- It is possible to name as beneficiary "my wife if I am legally married at the time of my death, otherwise." This designation will eliminate payment to an ex-spouse without causing inclusion of the policy proceeds or any other trust property in the insured's estate.[7] In other words, a client's attorney could question the client exhaustively and attempt to anticipate in drafting the trust document every possible circumstance in which the client might want to change the terms. It is clear, for example, that an irrevocable life insurance trust can now safely provide that "Upon a legal separation or divorce, any and all interest my wife, Sadie may have in this trust shall cease."

- Consider a provision giving the independent trustee sole discretion to terminate the trust in the event that the trust can no longer meet its intended objectives due to unforeseen circumstances. In other words, the trustee (assuming the trustee is a party other than the insured or a beneficiary) can be given a discretionary power to collapse the trust and assign the life insurance or distribute assets to the trust's beneficiaries if the trust should become unworkable because of a tax or other legal change or if funds are no longer available to pay premiums. The trustee may also be given the power to distribute trust assets, including life insurance policies and the right to benefits under group term life, in kind.

  The drawbacks here are: (a) the assets in the trust go to the trust's beneficiaries, perhaps prematurely; and (b) the trustee may be reluctant to exercise this power unless all beneficiaries will sign an agreement that the action is proper and in conformance with the trustee's fiduciary responsibilities to all beneficiaries.

- The trustee (assuming the trustee is a party other than the insured or a beneficiary) can be given a power to sprinkle or spray income and principal among a class of persons and thus add additional flexibility to the dispositive terms of the trust without adverse tax consequences.

- The trust could provide that, if the grantor died within 3 years of transferring life insurance held within the trust or if for any reason life insurance owned by the trust was includable in the grantor's estate, the proceeds would be paid to the insured-grantor's executor. That way, the proceeds could be channeled to the insured's surviving spouse and qualify for the marital deduction. In fact, the trust could contain a marital clause so that if the client doesn't want the trust to end upon his death or doesn't want the proceeds paid to his probate estate, the tax savings objectives can be accomplished within the trust itself.

- The noninsured spouse could create a split dollar arrangement (see Chapter 30) with the trust in which such spouse retains access to policy cash values. This would indirectly give the insured spouse access to policy values without risking estate tax inclusion of the proceeds. The drawback here is the possibility of spousal estrangement.

2. There are up front and continuing cash costs involved with an irrevocable life insurance trust.

   Obviously, there are legal fees for preparing the trust agreement. These costs range from over $1,000 to more than $10,000 depending on the nature and extent of the client's assets and the part the irrevocable trust plays in the overall planning process.

   Accounting costs must also be considered. As long as the trust is unfunded no annual income tax returns will be required because the trust will have no income. But records must be kept and an accounting should still be made to trust beneficiaries and the trust must have a taxpayer identification number (TIP).

   Professional trustees, such as banks operating as trust companies, often charge an acceptance fee and all charge a fee for management and investment services. Although these fees are typically nominal during the insured's lifetime (when the trust has little or no assets and the trustee has few responsibilities other than safeguarding the trust document), they can be significant when the trust is swelled with policy proceeds and other assets poured over into the trust at the death of the insured.

3. There may be a termination fee if the trust is terminated before the insurance policies have matured and the trustee has had the opportunity to recover set up costs.

4. Yet another consideration is the potential loss of the donor's contributions out the back door of the trust. Irrevocable life insurance trusts usually require special provisions (Crummey powers) that enable the client's gifts to the trust to qualify for the gift tax annual exclusion. By definition, these Crummey powers are withdrawal powers. They give the powerholder the legal right to demand specified amounts at given times. If the demand powers are not real, they will not eliminate gift taxes. Yet, if they are real powers, there is always a possibility that money that could and should have been used to pay life insurance premiums will instead be drained off by the power holding beneficiaries. There are techniques and devices to persuade the beneficiary not to exercise this right. But the IRS has been vigorous in attempts to disallow the gift tax annual exclusion in just such situations.

5. To the extent the annual exclusion cannot shield the premium outlays, the client will first have to use up his unified credit and then pay gift taxes on each transfer.

IRREVOCABLE TRUST – WHAT IT IS AND HOW IT WORKS

There are two basic ways an irrevocable trust becomes a life insurance trust. The first way is when a client makes an absolute assignment of one or more life insurance policies to the trust. The obvious disadvantage to this method is the potential for estate tax inclusion under the transfers within three years of death rule of IRC Section 2035. Alternatively, under the preferred approach, the trust is established, cash contributions are made by the grantor to the trust, and then the trustee uses cash or income from funds provided by the grantor or others to purchase new insurance on the life of the grantor. Preferably, the trustee should initiate the purchase of life insurance, own from inception all the incidents of ownership in the policy, be the premium payor, and be named as beneficiary.

An irrevocable life insurance trust may either be "funded" or "unfunded." In the most general sense, the term funding means that assets other than life insurance policies have been placed into the trust. In the narrower and commonly used sense, when applied to irrevocable life insurance trusts, funding means the placement of income producing assets into the trust. These assets typically are placed inside the trust in order to produce sufficient income to pay the insurance premiums. If the trust is funded, the trust agreement should specify: (a) what should happen if the income of the trust is insufficient to pay the entire premium, and (b) what should happen if trust income is more than sufficient and there is an excess of income. Usually, the trust will provide that if trust income will not be sufficient to pay the entire premium, the trustee is responsible for notifying the grantor (or beneficiary or other interested party) of the shortfall. The trust should specifically authorize the trustee to borrow on the policy to keep it in force or to place the policy on extended term or purchase paid up whole life coverage if the grantor fails to pay the balance of the premium.

Most irrevocable trusts are unfunded and contain only life insurance policies. The insured typically pays premiums on policies held by an unfunded life insurance trust, by either making direct payments to the insurer or by the preferred method, annual gifts to the trustee in amounts large enough for the trustee to pay the premiums and have enough cash left over to cover any incidental trust expenses. Here, the trustee typically assumes no obligation to keep the life insurance in force or even the responsibility to notify the client that premiums are due or overdue.

The major tax objectives of many irrevocable life insurance trusts are to (1) make the maximum amount of income and capital available to the surviving spouse and increase both her personal financial security and that of those she loves and feels responsibility toward, and (2) avoid inclusion of the proceeds in both spouses' estates.

To accomplish these goals, the draftsperson of the trust inserts certain provisions that:

1. allow the trustee (and only the trustee) discretion to sprinkle income or spray capital to the spouse and the grantor-insured's children; and/or

2. give the surviving spouse "all of the income for life and as much principal as necessary for her health, education, maintenance, and support" (HEMS); and

3. state "when she dies, my surviving spouse can appoint the remainder of the trust assets among our then living children."

Most irrevocable life insurance trusts are designed to do more than provide food, clothing, and shelter for the grantor's survivors. A major goal of such trusts is to keep assets, such as a family business or real estate, in the family by avoiding the forced (and often fire) sale that results from a lack of liquidity. Properly arranged, an irrevocable trust does just that; provides liquidity for the insured grantor's estate without increasing the estate tax burden.

These twin goals, estate liquidity and exclusion of the life insurance that provides that liquidity, must be carefully planned. If the provisions of a life insurance trust required the trustee to pay to the insured's estate any cash needed to pay debts, expenses, and taxes, such an instruction would result in federal estate tax inclusion of all amounts that could be so expended (as amounts receivable by the executor). This would cause a loss of the estate tax savings objective.

The solution is simple: A provision is placed into the trust document authorizing, but not directing, the trustee to: (1) lend money to the estate at an interest rate equal to or in reasonable excess of the current bank lending rate in the area; or (2) purchase assets at their fair market value from the estate of the insured and the estate of his spouse. Such loans and/or purchases will (to the extent of the life insurance relative to the taxes and other expenses) solve or reduce the decedent's estate's liquidity problem while keeping purchased estate assets within the family unit. If the draftsperson has been careful to frame the wording of the trust in the form of a permission rather than as a command, neither loans by the trust nor purchases from the estate should cause the insurance proceeds to be included in the insured's gross estate. Neither should be interpreted as falling within the scope of the statute dealing with the inclusion of life insurance proceeds.

Furthermore, the estate should realize little or no gain on the sale because appreciated assets in the estate receive a stepped up basis equal to the estate tax value of each piece of property. Best of all, when the trustee pays the executor cash for an appreciated asset, the trustee then takes that asset with a basis that is stepped up to its purchase value. The trustee (or the trust's beneficiaries if the assets are distributed) can then invest the assets, or sell them with relative income tax impunity and diversify their portfolio to achieve higher safety, liquidity, growth, or income.

These clauses must be carefully inserted into an irrevocable life insurance trust so as to accomplish a delicate balancing act. On the one hand, they are designed to enhance the trust's flexibility and usefulness as a means of providing managed financial security for the surviving spouse. Yet, on the other hand, they must not give the surviving spouse powers broad enough to be considered a general power of appointment (i.e., a virtually unlimited right to say who receives the proceeds), since such a power would cause the policy proceeds to be included in the surviving spouse's gross estate. The three standard clauses above are designed to accomplish these two important objectives.

MECHANICS

A policy should be placed into the trust as follows:

1. An attorney drafts and the client signs the irrevocable trust document.

2. The trustee then applies for the policy on the insured's life, under a provision in the document allowing the trustee to purchase a policy and/or pay premiums on a policy insuring the life of the grantor.

Of course, that is the ideal arrangement and, with a lawyer who is expert in estate planning and who has a modern well-automated office, the appropriate speed, accuracy, and efficiency, is possible. But it will not always work so smoothly. More often, the insured wants to put a policy in force immediately, but the trust will not be established until a future date. Here, several alternatives are available.

Under Plan A:

1. The client could apply for the policy as policyowner.

2. After the trust is created, the client could transfer ownership of the policy to the trust by an absolute assignment or ownership form "for love and affection." (Note that if a beneficiary transfers a policy to the trust, he will be considered a grantor of the trust. So, for example, in a community property state, rather than having the insured grantor's spouse transfer an existing policy on his life directly to the trust, the insured should purchase the policy on his life from his wife and then transfer it – in a time separated separate and independent step – to the trust by gift.) A copy of the executed trust is sent to the insurance company together with the absolute assignment form.

3. In a "nonprepaid" case, an informal application could be submitted to the insurer for an informal opinion as to whether the policy will be issued on a select, standard, or rated basis. Once the policy's issue status is known, plans can be made to establish the trust, and then the trust formally applies for the policy.

A second alternative, Plan B, works like this:

1. The client applies for term insurance.

2. When the trust is established, the trustee applies for new whole life coverage. (Some form of permanent protection is almost always indicated as the sole, or the bulk of the, insurance coverage when a major objective of the irrevocable trust is to provide estate liquidity, since a term contract may expire before the client dies and the need for liquidity begins). Once the permanent coverage is issued, the term policy can be lapsed. Some companies treat the two transactions as a policy conversion.

Under Plan C (often called the "substitute application"):

1. The applicant, owner, and policy date of a recently issued policy (less than a year old) are changed to coincide with the effective date of the trust. At this point, the policy may appear to have been originally purchased by the trustee. Under this substitute application procedure, a short term premium is charged to pay for coverage from the date of the original application to the new policy date.

Planners should note that the IRS could claim in Plan A, B, and C that a constructive transfer of a policy occurred and so, if death results within three years of that transfer, inclusion may result. Whenever possible, therefore, the trust should be in existence prior to the purchase of the life insurance and the trustee should apply for and own the policy from inception. A copy of the signed trust document accompanies the policy application and the trustee signs as owner-applicant and the insured signs only as proposed insured.

What about the case where a client wants to transfer existing policies to an irrevocable trust? Existing policies may be transferred to the trust through an absolute (and gratuitous) assignment of ownership from the insured to the trust or through a change of ownership form obtained from each insurer. Again, the client must survive the three year period commencing on the date of the transfer or ownership change in order for the proceeds to be excludable from his gross estate.

It is important that the client transfers all ownership rights to the trustee, not only to divest himself of incidents of ownership and avoid the transfers within three years of death rule, but also to avoid a conflict between the terms of the trust instrument and the terms of the policies. A list and description of all the policies transferred to the irrevocable trust should be attached to the trust document. Included in the description should be the following information:

1. policy number;

2. name of insurer; and

3. face amount of coverage.

There are alternatives to these fairly standard ways to set up an irrevocable trust. For instance, someone other than the insured can establish the trust and one or more persons other than the insured could fund the trust. If some third party sets up the trust and funds it, some or all of the income and estate tax traps common under the classic arrangement can be avoided. For instance, once grandparents set up and fund a trust, the trustee could split the premium dollars with the son or daughter of the clients and insure the son or daughter for the benefit of grandchildren. Arranged this way, it can be shown that the insured never held any incidents of ownership and the proceeds should be excludable from the insured's estate as well as the estate of the insured's spouse.

SELECTION OF A TRUSTEE

A trustee of an irrevocable life insurance trust must review the trust document for efficacy in meeting both tax and dispositive objectives, set up a trust account, purchase the life insurance, receive premiums from the grantor, notify beneficiaries holding demand powers of their rights each year, and pay premiums to the insurance company. Clients, even though charged only a hundred dollars or so each year for this service, often do not perceive the value they are receiving as worth the cost.

For this and other reasons (such as control), many clients will want to be the trustee themselves or name their spouses as trustees. Both choices are contraindicated because of potential adverse estate tax ramifications and both choices would limit the flexibility that should be built into an irrevocable life insurance trust.

1. *Grantor-insured as trustee* – If the grantor-insured is named as trustee, the IRS could argue that even as trustee and in spite of a trustee's definitional fiduciary obligations, the insured has retained an incident of ownership that causes the insurance proceeds to be includable in his estate. For instance, if the insured is named as trustee, it is likely the IRS will argue that the policy proceeds should be included in the insured-trustee's estate, even if he holds no interest in the trust as a beneficiary, because of the control (incidents of ownership) he as trustee holds over trust property (the life insurance).[8] Furthermore, the discretionary and administrative powers of a trustee, if retained by the insured-grantor, could be held to be rights over the trust's assets that cause estate tax inclusion. An independent trustee, one who is not a beneficiary and who is not legally subservient to the grantor is the preferable choice for a trustee.

2. *Spouse of insured-grantor as trustee* – Could the problem be solved and intrafamily control be maintained by naming the insured's spouse as trustee? There are no attribution rules that impute the trustee's incidents of ownership to the insured grantor merely because the two happen to be married. So, it is possible for the insured's spouse to be the trustee of an irrevocable life insurance trust, assuming such spouse hasn't made transfers of property into the trust and thereby become a co-grantor.

Naming the insured's spouse as trustee may not be a bad choice during the insured's lifetime while there are no assets in the trust other than the life insurance policy and the duties of the trustee are practically nonexistent. Then, when the insured dies, the spouse can automatically be removed as trustee and a corporate fiduciary inserted (or added to the surviving spouse who would be prohibited from making the types of decisions which would cause inclusion of the proceeds in her estate). But if the insured's spouse is given a general power of appointment over the policy in the trust document, the proceeds will be in her estate.[9]

Here are some guidelines for safely naming a spouse as trustee:

1. name at least one other (preferably independent) individual or corporate fiduciary as co-trustee;

2. specifically exclude the surviving spouse from all potential exercises of incidents of ownership in the policy(ies) held by the trust insuring her life;

3. allow distributions to the surviving spouse from the irrevocable life insurance trust only if and when the principal of the marital trust is exhausted;

4. forbid any distributions to individuals that would relieve or discharge the spouse from a state legal support obligation (such as the providing of food, clothing, or shelter, or in some states education);

5. limit the surviving spouse to a special power of appointment over trust assets, but specifically exclude from this power the right to dispose of life insurance on her own life; and

6. exclude the surviving spouse as trustee from making any decisions involving the distribution of principal or income to herself as a beneficiary except those limited by a health, education, maintenance, and support ascertainable standard.

The authors' opinion is that the advantages of naming the spouse as trustee are outweighed by the potential tax traps and drafting difficulties. At the least, if a spouse is named, another individual should be named as a co-trustee with the trust wording noted above.

One of the more important issues in a country where there is great geographic mobility (not only of beneficiaries, but also of trust administration personnel) is the question of changing trustees. Can the trust safely provide for replacement of trustees if the beneficiaries move or, for any reason, decide they want a new trustee?

It is clear that the grantor should not be given the power to remove the trustee and become the successor trustee. Even if the grantor never exercises that removal power and even if the removal power is subject to a condition or contingency, such as the trustee's death, resignation, or malfeasance, which has not yet occurred, the mere existence of the right will cause the inclusion of the trust's assets in the grantor's estate.

The IRS claims that a grantor should be considered to hold those powers over a trust that are in fact held by an independent trustee if the grantor has the power to remove the trustee, even if the replacement trustee is legally independent. It is the opinion of the authors that the IRS position is wrong because it imputes to a grantor powers that he can never hold personally. It ignores entirely the independence and fiduciary obligations of the trustee.

As a practical matter, many authorities approach the selection of a trustee by considering the existence of the trust during two time periods: (1) Who should be the trustee during the insured's lifetime? and (2) Who should be the trustee thereafter?

During the insured's lifetime, the trustee must be a person who will cooperate with the grantor and the grantor's family. This criterion may include the attorney, accountant, trusted friend, or adult child of the grantor. Generally, the time commitment (and therefore the trustee's compensation) is minimal during this stage of trusteeship.

But after the grantor's death, the trustee's role changes drastically. At this point, the trustee must invest, safeguard, and manage the insurance proceeds and other funds that may have poured over from the client's estate into the trust. Those assets must now be administered over a long period of time and countless difficult decisions may be required.

So, in many cases, an individual is selected for the predeath period, while a corporate trustee (with or without individual co-trustees) takes over the burdensome task of trust administration after the death of the grantor. Certainly, a bank or other professional trustee should be named in the trust instrument as a contingent trustee in case the individuals named cannot or become unwilling or unable to serve.

A corporate trustee during this second phase of the irrevocable trust's existence avoids all of the potential tax traps, provides continuity of investment, management, and record keeping, and relieves the client's family and other advisors of a myriad of bothersome and time consuming details. Since the trust may remain in existence for several generations, this continuity can be extremely important. A collateral (but not insignificant) advantage to the use of a corporate fiduciary is that the bank or trust company usually will have highly competent counsel to provide a second opinion and review the trust document and its provisions.

REDUCING OR ELIMINATING GIFT TAXES ON POLICY TRANSFERS AND PREMIUM PAYMENTS THROUGH CRUMMEY POWERS

When a client transfers a life insurance policy to an irrevocable trust, a gift is made subject to the gift tax.

The tax, if any, payable on that transfer depends on the value of the policy, the availability of the annual exclusion, and the unified credit. If the annual exclusion is available, then up to $10,000 as indexed ($11,000 in 2004) of the value of the gift is shielded if the client is unmarried and up to $20,000 as indexed ($22,000 in 2004) if the client is married and the spouse consents to split the gift so that each is treated as making a gift of one half of the policy.[10] The value of the transfer in excess of that amount would be taxable to the extent not protected by the client's remaining unified credit. If the annual exclusion is not available, the entire value of the contract on the date of the gift would be a taxable transfer to the extent not protected by the unified credit.[11]

The gift tax valuation rules can be summarized as follows:

Policy Transferred	Gift Tax Value
New policy transferred immediately after issue	Cost (net premiums paid)
Existing policy - no further premiums due	In case of a paid up or single premium policy, cost of replacement
Policy in "premium paying" stage	"Interpolated terminal reserve" plus any unearned premiums paid on the date of death less any policy loans
Group term life insurance	At the client's option, the actual cost or Table I cost
Policy is about to mature on the date of transfer (for instance, client is within a few weeks of death due to cancer)	IRS may value the policy at or near its face amount.

To minimize gift tax exposure upon the contribution of a policy to an irrevocable trust, a client may want to borrow a portion of the cash values out of the policy before making the gift. This reduces the initial gift tax value of the policy itself. When more than one large policy is to be transferred to the trust, they can be transferred over a period of years to fully utilize the annual exclusion and yet stay within the "5 or 5" maximum limitations. Alternatively, one large policy could be split into several smaller ones and staggered gifts could be made to the trust.

Payment of premiums by the client following a transfer of a policy to an irrevocable trust is an additional gift, regardless of whether the client makes the payment directly to the insurer or makes a cash contribution to the trustee who then pays the premium.

If someone other than the person who created the trust pays the premiums, there is a potential gift tax problem if that additional grantor is not a beneficiary of the trust. For instance, the aunt of a beneficiary makes contributions to a trust set up by her brother for her niece. Each premium the aunt pays is a gift to the niece.

If a beneficiary of the trust pays premiums to keep the insurance in force and protect his interest, the portion of the premium equal to the payor's share of the trust would not be considered a gift but the portion of the premium that enriches the other beneficiaries would be treated as a gift from the payor to the others. Suppose, for example, that the client cannot or will not make further contributions and the policy on his life held by the trust is about to lapse. To the extent the beneficiary's contribution will be returned in the form of insurance coverage the beneficiary will receive, he has made a (nontaxable) gift to himself. But to the extent the money paid exceeds his share, the difference would be considered a gift to the other beneficiaries. So if three brothers were three equal beneficiaries of a trust and the oldest gave $12,000 to the trustee who in turn used it to pay a $12,000 premium, he would be deemed to have made a $9,000 (2/3 of $12,000) gift to his siblings.

This gift tax liability is imposed even if there was no donative intent by the premium paying brother. Should the grantor not have the funds (or the will) to pay the premiums, one solution is for the trustee to have the insurer divide the policy up into separate policies for each beneficiary and ask each to contribute his share of the premiums. That way, in the event of a lapse, only the beneficiaries who did not pay premiums will suffer.

In general, since gift tax rates are identical to estate tax rates, in the long run a client would be trading dollars if he incurred gift tax in the attempt to save estate tax. Actually, because gift tax must be paid currently while estate tax can be put off until death, each dollar of gift tax, in essence, costs (time value of money wise) more than each dollar of estate tax. At the least, psychologically, each dollar of gift tax hurts more. Of course, there is no current gift tax cost to the extent gifts are covered by the annual exclusion or unified credit.

The high financial and psychological cost of gift tax on taxable gifts is why planners must use every effort to accomplish the estate tax saving goals of an irrevocable life insurance trust at the least possible gift tax cost (and if possible without using up all or any of the client's available estate and gift tax unified credit).

The major tool for getting the most estate tax savings at the least gift tax cost is the gift tax annual exclusion. As the following calculation shows, a long term systematic use of the annual exclusion, even without life insurance leveraging, can result in amazing federal estate tax savings.

Donor's Age	40
Donor's Life Expectancy	42.5 Years
Annual Exclusion	$11,000
Split Gifts	Yes
Number of Donees	5
Annual Gifts ($11,000 x 2 x 5)	$110,000
Donor's Projected Estate Tax Bracket	48%

No Growth

Total Amount of Gifts ($110,000 x 43)	$4,730,000
Potential Estate Tax Savings (48%)	$2,270,000

With Growth

Annual After-Tax Return on Gifts	4%
Value of Gifts at Life Expectancy	$12,101,362
Potential Estate Tax Savings (48%)	$5,808,654

If the beneficiaries, either inside or outside a trust, used the annual gifts (each of the five donees were given $22,000, a total of $110,000 a year of gifts in the above example) to purchase life insurance on the life of the client, the estate tax leverage in the illustration above could be multiplied many times over.

However, the annual exclusion is available only for gifts of a "present interest." Present interest is defined for gifts of life insurance under the same rules as it is for other gratuitous transfers. Essentially, to be considered a present, as opposed to a future, interest, the donee must receive the immediate, unfettered, and ascertainable right to use, possess, or enjoy the transferred property. No annual exclusion will be allowed if the beneficiary's right to take can possibly be threatened or delayed for even one minute. For instance, if the trustee has the discretion to invade trust corpus for the benefit of non-Crummey beneficiaries, even if that discretionary right is never actually used, the IRS will deny the gift tax exclusion.

If a client gave his intended beneficiary an outright gift of a life insurance policy, the transfer would qualify for the gift tax annual exclusion. The mere fact that the policy will not pay off until the death of the insured at some distant and uncertain date in the future does not cause the transfer to be considered a future interest since the recipient has the immediate, unfettered, and ascertainable right to use, possess, and enjoy all of the incidents of ownership in the contract.

But a gift of an insurance policy to a trust designed, almost by definition, to delay the timing and control the beneficiary's use, possession, and enjoyment of its assets will be a gift of a future interest. Absent a special trust provision creating a present interest in one or more of the trust's beneficiaries, each time a client made a contribution to a trust to enable the trustee to pay life insurance premiums, the client would have to use up more of his unified credit to avoid gift taxes or actually pay gift taxes.

The solution to the problem of the beneficiary's inability to immediately use, possess, and enjoy the client's contribution is to create a "window" through which the beneficiary could reach to take all or a portion of that annual contribution or alternatively use the policy. This window is what practitioners call the "Crummey power" which is named after the successful taxpayer[12] who was able to obtain a gift tax annual exclusion because of his beneficiaries' rights to make a demand of the trustee even though:

1. each beneficiary was a minor and obviously could not exercise the demand power without the appointment of a legal guardian;

2. no guardian was ever in fact appointed on behalf of the children;

3. the demand power was never actually exercised by either the children or by a guardian on their behalf and none of the children had received any payment from the trust fund; and

4. the power had a limited duration of only 13 days (the demand was to be made by the end of the year in which the transfer was made from the gift the donor made that year but most transfers were made about the middle of December).

The key to recognition of this window as an effective gift tax exclusion device is therefore not the actual enjoyment of the right by holders of the Crummey power but rather the reasonable and realistic legal right to enjoy. The trust must therefore specify that each trust beneficiary to whom a Crummey power is to be granted is given an absolute but noncumulative right to withdraw a specified amount from the client's annual contribution. The client may wish to limit this noncumulative right to the lowest of (1) the amount of the annual exclusion per donor/donee per year, (2) the amount actually contributed, or (3) the greater of $5,000 or 5% of the value of the trust's assets at the time of the withdrawal (see below).

Although the IRS has accepted the Crummey power as a means of creating a present interest and has even privately approved the use of Crummey powers to satisfy the present interest requirement with respect to gifts of life insurance policies in trust, it continues to disallow the annual exclusion unless both the letter of the law and good intent are shown by the taxpayer.

When a grantor sets up the Crummey power window through which a beneficiary can reach in and make a withdrawal, the grantor is attempting to qualify each year's transfer to the trust for the gift tax annual exclusion. But the grantor does not want to make the window opening so large and keep it open so long that the beneficiary will actually reach in and take the contribution. If the beneficiary does exercise the right to withdraw, the money will not be available to pay premiums on the life insurance that is meant to provide estate liquidity and provide financial security for the trust's beneficiaries. (It would not be wise to provide for a shutting of the window in the event a holder does take a given year's contribution, since that would be evidence that the power was a sham.)

But the client could maintain some control by providing in the trust agreement that each year's contributions to the trust would be earmarked to specific donees. That way, if a powerholder actually took money in the prior year, the client could decide not to make a contribution subject to that beneficiary's withdrawal right. In other words, the trust could provide that each powerholder had a right to withdraw funds from the trust only if specific contributions were designated as subject to that beneficiary's right of withdrawal. The trust could also provide that if a beneficiary is subject to a bankruptcy proceeding, the right of withdrawal lapses. This would prevent the bankruptcy trustee from exercising the withdrawal right.

The open window (demand period) must be allowed to remain open long enough to give the beneficiary a meaningful interest in the property given to the trust. In other words, the beneficiary must know of his right to make a withdrawal and have a realistic and reasonable opportunity to actually exercise that right. So the trustee should keep sufficient funds in the trust during the open window period so that a demand can be realistically and immediately satisfied. If a client contributed money to the trust but the trustee paid the premiums for trust owned life insurance the very same day, the IRS could argue that, in reality, the Crummey powerholder never had a chance to make a withdrawal. So if the demand period is too short, the IRS will argue that the power was a sham and disallow the exclusion.

Notification should be made by the trustee to all demand powerholders of the right to make withdrawals. In the case of minor beneficiaries, notification should be made to the person who can legally exercise the demand power on the minor's behalf, typically the minor's parent or legal guardian. This notice should take the form of a return receipt requested letter informing the beneficiaries that gifts to the trust can be expected on specified dates (coincident with premium payment dates). The letter should inform them of their demand rights, and promise supplementary information if gifts are not made according to this schedule or if additional gifts are made. An alternative is to request that the beneficiary acknowledge receipt of each year's notice by initialling a copy and returning it to the client or trustee. The safer course would be to provide notice to the powerholder of each contribution with respect to which a withdrawal power is available.

What if no guardian has been appointed for a minor beneficiary? The IRS position is liberal:

> "If there is no impediment under the trust or local law to the appointment of a guardian and the minor donee has a right to demand distribution, the transfer is a gift of a present interest that qualifies for the annual exclusion."[13]

There is no specific number of days during which a demand power can be exercised that assures that a demand power will create a present interest. The number of days within which the beneficiary can exercise the power is measured by both the terms of the trust and the date of the gift. The bottom line is that the trust agreement should give the beneficiary adequate time to realistically make a demand and exercise the right to enjoy the contribution the insured-client has made to the trust.

It is essential that the beneficiary or guardian for the beneficiary to whom the Crummey power is granted be given proper and timely written notice of the right to make a withdrawal. Regardless of the form of the gift, a withdrawal power will not be considered a present interest unless the beneficiary is aware of its existence. In the authors' opinion, 30 days from the date of the notice seems to be the shortest reasonable period. So if the beneficiary's power to make a withdrawal lapses at the end of the year, contributions should be made to the trust before December 1.

On the other hand, if the window is held open too long, there may be adverse tax implications to the Crummey powerholder. So if the beneficiary were to die while the window was open, the assets subject to that power to withdraw would be included in his estate.[14] By limiting the duration of the opening to one month each year, if the beneficiary dies during any other month of the year (during which he had no power to make a withdrawal), there should be no estate tax inclusion.

If the window is opened too high, i.e., if the "5 or 5 power" were not included in the withdrawal limitations, the value of any unexercised demand right existing at the beneficiary's death would be included in his estate. This is because the absolute power to make a withdrawal is technically a general power of appointment, an unlimited right to direct the disposition of the property subject to the power to anyone, including the powerholder, his estate, his creditors, or the creditors of his estate. The mere possession of such a general power is enough to require estate tax inclusion.[15] So if a beneficiary had the right to take an unlimited amount from the trust, the entire value of the trust's principal would be included in his estate.

Furthermore, each year that the beneficiary allowed the right to make a withdrawal lapse, the IRS would claim that by not taking what could have been taken, the beneficiary is making a gift to the trust's remainder person. Allowing a general power to lapse or expire is treated for gift and estate tax purposes as a release (i.e., as if the powerholder made an actual transfer of the property subject to the power). For instance, if the client's wife is to receive income for life and then trust assets are to pass to the client's children, to the extent the client's wife does nothing and allows this year's Crummey power to lapse, she is in essence making a gift to her son of what she could have withdrawn. That would trigger both gift taxes and gift tax filing requirements since the gift would not pass to the son immediately and would therefore be a future interest gift that by definition could not qualify for the annual exclusion. Worse yet, the wife retains for life the income from the gift she is deemed to have made. This is a classic gift with a retained life estate that requires inclusion in the wife's estate of the date of death value of the entire property producing the income.

Here's where the "5 or 5" provision comes in. Under a de minimis rule, the gift/estate tax problem of the powerholder who doesn't exercise the power is avoided to the extent the lapse of the power each year does not exceed the greater of $5,000 or 5% of the value of the trust's assets at the time of the lapse. In other words, the lapse of a Crummey power is considered a release (taxable gift) only to the extent that the value of the property in question exceeds the greater of $5,000 or 5% of the total value of the assets out of which the exercise of the lapsed power could have been satisfied. This is the reason why the familiar "5 or 5" limitation is built into the wording of most irrevocable life insurance trusts.

Planners should note, however, that it may pay in certain cases to use a higher withdrawal limit where it is expected the Crummey powerholder will never have a significant estate or gift tax problem and the major objective is to shield the client's premium payments on a large policy from gift tax.

Many clients, who have discovered the irrevocable life insurance trust's advantages, place sizable policies in such trusts. The large premiums that are generated by those policies quickly exceed the per donee annual exclusion limit. For this reason, clients want to multiply the annual exclusions available by giving many beneficiaries a Crummey withdrawal power.

A trust may grant demand powers to several individuals and therefore multiply the number of available gift tax annual exclusions, which in turn allows the grantor to make larger gifts in the form of policy assignments and/or premium payments without gift tax. It's also good planning for the trust to provide for contingent powerholders, so that if a spouse or child who holds a power dies, another person would take over and the present interest exclusion could be maintained. But there are limitations on the grantor's ability to use multiple Crummey demand powers in this fashion:

First, each beneficiary's interest must be ascertainable at the moment the client's annual contribution is made to the trust. So proper apportionment of demand rights is necessary. If the donee's exact present interest can't be immediately ascertained, no annual exclusion will be allowed since it would be impossible to determine whether the client should be credited with the full amount of the exclusion or some lesser amount. The trick is, therefore, to either: (a) make the number of eventual donees immediately ascertainable at the time of each gift to the trust, or (b) assure that the interest of each Crummey powerholder be immediately capable of valuation.

If a trust does not have sufficient principal to satisfy all of the Crummey demand powers given to its beneficiaries, the IRS could argue that none of the interests are capable of valuation and the gift was one of a future interest since no beneficiary's right can be ascertained on the date of the gift. The solution is for the trust to provide that if any year's contribution is insufficient to meet all the possible Crummey demands, then the contribution must be distributed on a pro rata basis among the powerholders. The trust should further require that if any donee receives an amount greater than his pro rata share of the trust corpus, that donee must immediately reimburse the trustee for the excess amount in the event there are insufficient assets to satisfy the potential demands made by other powerholders.

Second, it remains the IRS position that a demand holder must have a significant beneficial interest in the trust. The IRS believes that the critical test is whether the grantors ever expect that a particular demand power will be exercised. Because remote beneficiaries have little or no reason not to exercise their demand rights, the IRS views the failure of remote beneficiaries to exercise their demand rights as evidence that some understanding exists between them and the grantors that they would not exercise those rights. According to the IRS, this is fatal to the annual exclusion.

However, it has been the author's opinion that it should be immaterial that the donor does not want particular demand powers to be exercised. The statute requires only that the donees are appraised of their rights and legally can exercise those powers. The Tax Court agrees with the authors. It clearly stated in several cases that the sole criteria for allowing an annual exclusion is the existence in the donee's hands of the immediate, unfettered, and ascertainable right to use, possess, and enjoy the subject of the gift on the date the power is issued. The Tax Court expressly rejected the IRS's contention that "evil intent"–even when manifested by a family discussion about how funds transferred to the trust would be used by the trustee–taints the transfer and makes it a future interest. The only relevant test is: "Does the donee have the legal right to make a demand for payment?" and "Is the trustee legally obligated to comply with a demand from a Crummey power-holder?"

Having stated both our opinion and the Tax Court's, we continue to suggest that notices in fact be made in writing on a timely basis. We further suggest that family discussions as to what might or might not happen to the fortunes of a powerholder who made a withdrawal be avoided. Counsel should insert wording into the agreement to the effect that "Trustee shall promptly comply with every demand for payment under the above withdrawal power."[16]

Another solution may be to give all demand powerholders at least a discretionary right to current distributions from a life insurance trust, despite the fact that no such distributions are likely.

Not all authorities agree on how gifts to the irrevocable life insurance trust should be structured or how best to word the trust so that an annual exclusion will be allowed, regardless of what type of gift is made to the trust or how large that gift is.

When a trust is unfunded, the client's contribution may be in the form of: (a) direct payment of the insurance premiums to the insurance company by the insured-grantor; or (b) indirect payments by grantor to a trust, either by check or through his employer (for example, as payments toward group insurance or split dollar premiums).

Where the trust is unfunded, there are only two sources from which the demand right can be satisfied: (1) the cash contributions made by the grantor to the trustee in order to pay premiums, and (2) the life insurance policy itself.

An annual exclusion should be allowed even if the trust holds only term insurance or whole life insurance that has no cash value on the date contributed. However, the trust must give the trustee the authority to make payments in cash or in kind. This ability to satisfy the demand by distributing a fractional interest in individual life insurance policies or group term insurance should enable the grantor to obtain the annual exclusion in exactly the same way that an outright gift of a fractional interest in an insurance policy would qualify.

Conservative planners may protect the insured-grantor's gift tax annual exclusion even further by funding the trust with some assets other than life insurance policies. If the trust has an amount of cash or other liquid assets equal to the annual premiums (the required amount of annual exclusion), the trustee could always distribute that cash to satisfy a beneficiary's demand.

The recommended course of action in most cases is for the insured grantor to give the trustee a cash sum each year that the trustee could hold for the duration of the demand period. Only after the expiration of the demand period would the trustee use this contribution to pay the premiums. This requires that the client grantor make premium payments well ahead of their scheduled due date to avoid a policy lapse.

One conceptually simple alternative approach is for the client to make direct gifts of cash to the trust's adult beneficiaries who then make contributions back to the trust. The amount given to each beneficiary should equal his proportionate share of the trust. Since the gifts are both direct and outright, the client should obtain an annual exclusion gift for each transfer. Then, when the children contribute the gifts back to the trust, they should not be deemed to be making gifts since each should be contributing only his share and that should be going only to his portion of the trust.

This technique may prove more difficult, however, in real life because of the administrative difficulties and the fact that beneficiaries may not co-operate. This technique should pose few problems during the life of the grantor or the grantor's spouse, but may result in a portion of the trust being included in the beneficiary's estate under section 2036(a). This may not be a major problem if the beneficiary does not have a very large estate or is young and likely to exhaust the trust funds.

There are two major reasons why a client may wish to give a spouse Crummey powers:

1. The client may be worried that children or other donees will exercise their demand powers and thus defeat the purpose of the trust by depriving the trustee of funds from which to pay premiums.

2. The client may want to increase the number of available annual exclusions.

In most cases, there is no good reason to deny the client's spouse a demand power, but it should be limited to an annual amount not exceeding the greater of: (a) $5,000, or (b) 5% of the trust fund. To allow a greater right of withdrawal would invite IRS inclusion of the policy proceeds in the spouse's estate. If the grantor's spouse has the requisite beneficial interest in the trust, the IRS could argue that the lapse of the spouse's demand power (i.e., the spouse's failure to exercise the withdrawal right on her own behalf) is equivalent to the release of a general power of appointment. Under IRC Section 2041(a)(2), a decedent's gross estate includes the value of property subject to a general power of appointment that was released or exercised before the decedent's death, if the result of the release or exercise is the creation of a retained interest described in IRC Sections 2035, 2036, 2037, or 2038. If the spouse is also an income beneficiary, therefore, this would create estate tax inclusion. [This problem does not exist, however, if the spouse's interest in the trust (apart from the demand power) is merely a right to principal and income at the discretion of an independent trustee or is limited to an ascertainable standard, such as the right to make withdrawals for health, education, maintenance, or support (HEMS)].

One technique that will not work is the use of reciprocal demand powers. For instance, suppose a client and his brother both want to shelter very large life insurance premiums from gift tax, so both simultaneously create irrevocable life insurance trusts in order to increase the number of available gift tax annual exclusions. Assume, further, that each brother gives his own children and his brother a Crummey power. The reciprocal powers the brothers gave each other will be ignored for purposes of the gift tax annual exclusion. Furthermore, the trusts will be included in each brother's estate as a transfer with a retained life estate under IRC Section 2036.

GIFT, ESTATE, AND INCOME TAX PROBLEMS RELATED TO CRUMMEY POWERS

Unexpected gift tax problems can arise in certain situations upon the lapse (non exercise) of a Crummey power. In most cases, this problem will not occur or, if it does, it will be minor. But planners should be aware of it in cases where the value of a life insurance policy or the subsequent premiums is large.

Specifically, the problem most frequently arises where premium outlays will exceed the greater of $5,000 a year or 5% of the trust's assets in the year of the grantor's contribution. The trap is set when the client, in an attempt to create a larger window through which the beneficiary can make withdrawals in order to take full advantage of the annual exclusion (including the annual exclusion of the client's spouse where the client is married and splits the gift), opens that window too much. This may reduce the grantor's gift tax problems, but increase those of the beneficiary.

Why might opening the window too high create a gift (and possibly estate) tax problem for the beneficiary? The problem stems from the fact that another term for an absolute demand or withdrawal or Crummey power is a general power of appointment (a power the beneficiary has to appoint trust funds to the beneficiary himself). By allowing that general power to lapse, the beneficiary who could have taken the cash, but didn't, is making a taxable gift to anyone who has interests in the trust that are enlarged by the lapse.

Unfortunately, those donees will not receive their gifts immediately. That makes such gifts future interests and, therefore, the gifts are ineligible for the gift tax annual exclusion. This means the Crummey beneficiary

who permits the withdrawal power to lapse would (absent the "5 or 5" de minimis rule) be required to file annual gift tax returns (no matter how small the gift) and may have to use part of his unified credit or pay a gift tax.

In many cases, as a practical matter, the annual right of withdrawal for each Crummey powerholder will be limited to $5,000 each year. That presents a major problem in the large premium situation, i.e., those where the premium significantly exceeds the amount sheltered under the normal Crummey limits. A client who sets up a trust with four Crummey powerholders can safely contribute only $20,000 ($5,000 x 4 beneficiaries) a year before running into gift tax problems. Yet if the premium were $60,000 a year, the $40,000 annual difference would soon exhaust the client's unified credit.

There are ways in which the irrevocable trust can be designed to avoid or minimize this problem:

1. *Use a limited pay type life insurance arrangement* – For instance, a Ten-Pay Life contract would be complete in ten years. The amount saved in estate taxes would be considerable compared to the relatively small gift taxes paid during the ten year period.

2. *Use a vanishing premium type arrangement* – This is a variation on the first theme. However, while premiums may be projected to vanish, they may not actually do so.

3. *Increase the number of legitimate powerholders* – The use of multiple powerholders must be coupled inversely with the client's desire not to have to litigate with the IRS and his fear that such powerholders will exercise their rights. There is no question that success with multiple powerholders requires giving them all legitimate and realistic rights to exercise their powers. There must be no implied or express agreement that they will not exercise their rights.

   The problem can't be solved by creating multiple trusts with multiple demand rights for the same beneficiary. Multiple demand powers held by the same beneficiary over the same or different trusts are aggregated to determine if the grantor has exceeded the $5,000 portion of the "5 or 5" limitation.[17]

4. *Add testamentary control* – Here, the powerholder is given testamentary (by will only) control as a means of preventing a taxable gift when the

power lapses. There are two different ways to utilize this approach, a general testamentary power of appointment and a special testamentary power of appointment.

Under the general testamentary power technique, each beneficiary is given a general ("name anyone you want to receive it") testamentary power of appointment over his share of the trust. So each beneficiary can choose who will receive that share of the trust if he doesn't live to get it. But that right to direct who will receive it can be exercised only at death and only by a specific written provision in his will referring to the general power in the trust. The trust will provide that if the beneficiary doesn't properly exercise the power, the property will pass to the other beneficiaries in the trust. So if the beneficiary dies during minority or at any time before diverting the property to someone other than the client-named remainder person, not only will the property go to the party the client desired but it will pass at the time and in the manner desired.

Using this technique, a client can make gifts equal to the full annual exclusion amount and couple those gifts with equal withdrawal rights. So with five donees, the client could give up to $55,000 a year (in 2004) rather than just $25,000. If the powerholder didn't exercise the right to take the $11,000 in a given year, the lapse would not be considered a completed gift (i.e., it wouldn't be subject to the gift tax) because the powerholder can, at any time, name someone other than the client-specified remainder person as the recipient of the property subject to the power.

There are, of course, costs and downsides to the general power of appointment approach: First, whether or not the powerholder chooses to allow the power to lapse without use, property subject to the power will be in his estate because the power is general.[18] Second, this powerholder controlled ability to shift property rights equates, by definition, to a loss of control by the client.

The second variation on the testamentary Crummey power technique is to grant each beneficiary only a limited (special) power of appointment. Assume the trust provides separate shares for each beneficiary and, if the beneficiary dies, his share will pass to whomever he

provides by will within a client-specified class such as the powerholder's siblings (i.e., the beneficiary is given a special testamentary power of appointment to choose who will take the property if he does not exercise the Crummey power, but the powerholder's choices are limited to parties or classes of individuals selected by the client-grantor). The class of limited takers can, in fact, be quite broad and include anyone other than the powerholder, his estate, his creditors, or the creditors of his estate.

Here again, the trust provides that, if the beneficiary fails to make a withdrawal within the specified time frame, his right to make an immediate withdrawal ends. The window closes. But the cash or other assets he could have taken are earmarked for his exclusive benefit. This avoids the gift tax problem since the cash subject to the power does not pass to anyone else until the beneficiary's death. The lapse of the withdrawal power is therefore not a completed taxable transfer. The powerholder could, at any moment until death, name some new beneficiary or change the size of the interest going to the client-named beneficiaries. Of course, since the cash he could have taken is held in his name, there is an estate tax implication: The proportionate share of the principal of the trust attributable to the lapsed withdrawal powers will be includable in the Crummey holder's estate if the beneficiary dies before the trust ends.[19]

There are, of course, costs and downsides to the limited testamentary power of appointment approach: First, whether or not the powerholder chooses to allow the power to lapse without use, some portion of the property subject to the power will be in his estate if the powerholder dies before the trust ends. So, like the general testamentary power technique, the limited power in someone else's hands in a separate trust means the client can't fully use generation-skipping exclusions to shift wealth without the generation-skipping transfer tax. Second, this powerholder controlled ability to shift property rights equates, by definition, to a loss of control by the client. The Crummey holder has actual dispositive rights that may or may not mesh with the trust grantor's dispositive objectives.

5. *Use a hanging power* – Some authorities claim that this alternative gives the client the best of all worlds by avoiding the gift tax problem

upon the lapse of the power and allows full use of the maximum annual exclusion without creating estate tax or control problems. Is it possible to make maximum annual exclusion gifts and yet avoid inclusion of any portion of the lapsed power in the beneficiary's estate while retaining control in the grantor-client?

The hanging power works like this: The holder is allowed to make a withdrawal each year equal to his share of the client's contribution up to the maximum allowable annual exclusion ($11,000 in 2004). The right to that aliquot share is cumulative. So to the extent no withdrawal (or less than the holder's share is withdrawn) is made in a given year, the balance hangs over and can be used in a following year. Specifically, each year, assuming the power is not used, the right to take the greater of $5,000 or 5% of the trust's principal lapses. But the right to take any amount over that amount continues. It carries over or hangs over to future years.

So if the client contributed $10,000 to the trust and there was only one powerholder, the right to take $5,000 would lapse in the first year but the right to withdraw the remaining $5,000 would continue. In later years, the right to take the first $5,000 (or 5% of trust corpus if greater) continues to lapse while a pot builds up of the excess amounts. By the second year, if no withdrawals were made, $10,000 worth of contributions would have lapsed but $10,000 worth of excess contributions ($5,000 from the first year and $5,000 from the second year) are now available as credits against future years. This pot of credits builds up until the client stops or slows down contributions. Figure 23.1 illustrates this concept. Note that, in the example, premiums are assumed to vanish along with the need to make additional gifts to the trust after 2003. Also, the hanging power is extinguished in 2010.

The hanging power concept assumes that the major premium payments will be made in the early years and then vanish, while at a certain point the beneficiary's right to make withdrawals (and therefore estate and gift tax liability) will be extinguished.

If the beneficiary dies while money is in the pot (i.e., while amounts remain available at the beneficiary's demand), whatever is subject to that general power is includable in the power-holder's estate. Once there is no longer any amount which can be taken, nothing should be includable.

The nontax problem here is one of control; while there are funds that can be taken, the client's dispositive objectives are at risk. The hanging powerholder can legitimately and realistically take a sizable sum. So beneficiaries could frustrate the client's intent by making withdrawals of large amounts. (Of course, minors could only exercise this right through the unlikely course of action of having a guardian appointed to exercise the right.) This should serve as a warning. Clients should be cautioned to carefully select powerholders mature enough to understand the client's objectives and the potential consequences of their actions. Remember, also, that the client can always choose not to make future gifts to a beneficiary.

Yet a further problem is the IRS position on hanging powers. The IRS has equated a hanging power with the following language to a mere tax savings clause that is adverse to public policy and should be disregarded, an invalid condition subsequent that discourages enforcement of federal gift tax provisions.

The clause that triggered the negative IRS response to hanging powers read: "If upon the termination of any power of withdrawal, the person holding the power will be deemed to have made a taxable gift for federal gift tax purposes, then such power of withdrawal will not lapse but will continue to exist with respect to the amount that would have been a taxable gift and will terminate as soon as such termination will not result in a taxable gift."

Many experts feel that the IRS is wrong in its position but suggest that a modification of the hanging power language will counter the IRS argument. They suggest avoiding any reference to the term taxable gifts or to a recharacterization of a gift as an incomplete gift if the IRS finds such a gift. The drafting attorney should clearly delineate the lapse formula including the timing and amount so that it can be shown that all the withdrawal rights could have been determined at the moment granted and the powerholder didn't have to wait until a tax audit or court determination to ascertain his rights to take trust property.

Figure 23.1

			HANGING POWERS		
YEAR	**GIFT**	**CORPUS**	**POWER**	**LAPSE**	**CARRYOVER**
1997	$10,000	$10,000	$10,000	$5,000	$5,000
1998	10,000	20,000	15,000	5,000	10,000
1999	10,000	30,000	20,000	5,000	15,000
2000	10,000	40,000	25,000	5,000	20,000
2001	10,000	50,000	30,000	5,000	25,000
2002	11,000	61,000	36,000	5,000	31,000
2003	5,000	66,000	36,000	5,000	31,000
2004	0	66,000	31,000	5,000	26,000
2005	0	66,000	26,000	5,000	21,000
2006	0	66,000	21,000	5,000	16,000
2007	0	66,000	16,000	5,000	11,000
2008	0	66,000	11,000	5,000	6,000
2009	0	66,000	6,000	5,000	1,000
2010	0	66,000	1,000	1,000	0

It is suggested that the client contribute the full $11,000 (up to $22,000 per married couple, annual exclusion amounts as indexed for 2004) and give each powerholder the right to withdraw an amount equal to the "5 or 5" limits. This right will lapse each year 30 days after each year's contribution has been made and that same amount will lapse each further year. This way, all gifts made by the powerholder are safe gifts in that they fall within the protected "5 or 5" limits. If there are excess gifts, the amount of the excess can't exceed $17,000 ($22,000 maximum annual exclusion limit in 2004 for a married couple less $5,000 protected amount). Even after 20 years of premiums, this would be within the unified credit limits. This relatively small use of the unified credit would be a good investment since it would be leveraged many times over by the shifting of wealth through the use of estate tax free life insurance.

6. *The single beneficiary trust* – Providing separate trusts or separate trust shares may be the simplest way to overcome the "5 or 5" limits if the client is willing to give up flexibility and risk several disadvantages; the trustee will not be able to make discretionary trust distributions to persons other than the beneficiary since there will be only one beneficiary (or one trust with separate "sole benefit" shares for each beneficiary). Furthermore, all the income and principal must be payable to the estate of the beneficiary if he dies before the trust pays out all its principal and each beneficiary must be given a testamentary general power of appointment over his trust share. When a Crummey power lapses, no gift is made to someone else since there are no other beneficiaries. Since the lapse results in a transfer only to the sole beneficiary's estate, there is no taxable gift. So a married parent splitting gifts and who has four children can fund a trust with separate shares for each of her four children, a total of $88,000 (in 2004).

In addition to the loss of flexibility, other disadvantages include: (a) the trust's assets can't be sprinkled or sprayed to the person who needs or deserves it the most or who is in the lowest tax bracket, since there is only one beneficiary; (b) the property will pass as if owned by the beneficiary rather than the client, possibly to a person and in a manner that would be objectionable to the client; (c) the property will be includable in the beneficiary's estate, for tax, probate, and creditor purposes; and (d) the property may be distributed (due to the untimely death of the beneficiary) prior to the date expected by the client.

7. *Grant withdrawal rights to secondary/contingent beneficiaries* – This was the strategy used in the now well known *Cristofani* case.[20] Here, grandchildren who were contingent beneficiaries were given withdrawal rights in addition to those provided to the client's children who were the primary beneficiaries of the trust. These grandchildren were entitled to principal and income

only to the extent the prior level of beneficiaries (their parents) hadn't exhausted trust assets.

The IRS found that this level of powerholders had, as beneficiaries, such a remote chance of actually receiving assets from the trust that there must have been some implied understanding between them and the grantor client that they would not make a withdrawal; why else would they not have exercised their power and taken some of the assets in the trust?

But the Tax Court disagreed with the IRS and focused on the central issue: Did the powerholders (no matter what level or how remote their chance of taking a share of the trust as a beneficiary) have the absolute legal right to make an unfettered withdrawal of property from the trust? The authors suggest, in spite of the court's favorable conclusion, that conservative practitioners will limit Crummey rights to beneficiaries who have a realistic chance to receive something from the trust as beneficiaries rather than merely as powerholders.

Even this tack has its downsides and costs. The most obvious is that the IRS is right in one sense; with nothing to lose, what will stop a remote beneficiary from making a withdrawal? Aside from that, the right to make a withdrawal does carry estate tax inclusion if the powerholder dies while the window is open. Likewise, the lapse of a power will be considered a future interest gift and so there may be gift tax consequences.

REDUCING OR ELIMINATING GIFT TAXES ON PREMIUM PAYMENTS THROUGH METHODS OTHER THAN CRUMMEY POWERS

Split-gifts – A split-gift is yet another way to increase the number of gift tax annual exclusions and unified credits available for each gift to a Crummey trust. A gift can be split by having the nondonor spouse agree to be treated as if he had made one-half of the gifts made by the donor spouse.[21]

The election for a split-gift is made on the gift tax return for the year in which the gift is made. The gift tax return must be filed on or before April 15 of the following year.[22] But the amount or existence of the beneficiary's right to make a withdrawal should not be dependent in any way on the donor's spouse's agreement to split gifts. The reason is that this would make the beneficiary's power contingent on an event that will not yet have occurred by the date of the gift.

The trust should specifically empower the grantor with the right to expand the beneficiary's demand power with respect to future gifts by stating at the time of the gift that it is to be treated for demand purposes as if it had been made equally by the donor and his spouse.

Split-gifts can therefore increase the annual exclusion to $22,000 as indexed ($11,000 per spouse in 2004) per donee. But giving a powerholder the right to withdraw this amount sets up a tax trap in the powerholder's estate; if the right to demand that much is allowed to lapse, the excess over the "5 or 5" maximum will be considered a gift to the remainder person subject to gift tax. That gift, coupled with the retention of a lifetime interest, will cause inclusion of a portion of the trust in the powerholder's estate. Of course, if the beneficiary lives until the trust ends, a great deal of the trust may be in his estate anyway.

Permanent withdrawal rights – An additional way to increase the window is to make the withdrawal rights permanent. However, the powerholders' rights do not lapse and therefore grow each year. The advantage is that a larger premium can be paid and sheltered by the gift tax annual exclusion. The disadvantage is that as the value of the property that can be taken grows, so does the beneficiary's temptation to make a withdrawal. Another downside is the growing estate tax liability in the beneficiary's estate. But, in the right circumstances (for instance if there are many beneficiaries, all of whom can avoid the temptation to make a withdrawal, and all of whom are likely to survive the grantor), this solution may prove quite advantageous.

All out maximum transfers – This method is simple. The client makes a first gift equal to $200,000 (doubled to $400,000 if the client's spouse will be splitting gifts and is not an income or principal beneficiary). The bulk of such a gift (i.e., the excess over $11,000 or $22,000, in the case of split-gifts, in 2004) will not qualify for the annual exclusion, so the client must use his unified credit to avoid a current gift tax liability.

But, once at least $200,000 of assets are in the trust, the greater of $5,000 or 5% of the trust's corpus is $10,000 ($20,000 if $400,000 is placed into the trust). So, from this point on, the client can make gift tax free gifts of the maximum annual exclusion amount. Even if the beneficiary doesn't exercise his withdrawal rights, no taxable gift occurs because the entire contribution is shielded by the de minimis greater of $5,000 or 5% of trust principal rule. A married client with four children could therefore give each child $100,000 ($400,000 total) which would mean $22,000 (in 2004) would qualify for the annual exclusion and $78,000 of the client's unified credit equivalent would be exhausted per child (a total of $312,000). In all of the following years, the client could give up to $22,000 per child ($88,000 total) and there would be no taxable gifts per donee.

The all out maximum transfers technique is simple, easy to implement, and avoids naming an estate as beneficiary, the drafting of Crummey powers, or the uncertainty inherent in some of the more exotic and untested methods of balancing between the client's tax and dispositive objectives.

The two downsides of the technique are equally obvious: First, the client must have a large amount of cash or other easily liquidated assets that he can afford financially and psychologically to permanently part with. Second, the client must be willing to use all or a large portion of his remaining unified credit.

WHAT THE ATTORNEY SHOULD CONSIDER IN DRAFTING

Although life insurance agents and financial planners, by definition, do not draft documents, an understanding of certain drafting tools and techniques is helpful, if for no other reason than, to provide a back-up and a second pair of eyes for the attorney.

An irrevocable life insurance trust should generally contain one or more of the following provisions:

1. The right of the Crummey power beneficiaries to make withdrawals extends to contributions to the trust from all sources. This makes it possible for the gifts of persons other than the grantor to qualify for the annual exclusion.

2. The amount subject to the Crummey power should be limited to the smallest amount that will protect the client's annual contributions. This will reduce or eliminate the gift tax payable and the gift tax return that must be filed by the Crummey powerholder (and the potential federal estate tax payable) if the holder's power extends beyond the de minimis "$5,000 or 5%" protected amount and he lets that excess right of withdrawal lapse.

3. Require the trustee to give return receipt requested notice of any additions to principal and keep the right of withdrawal open for at least 30 days. This gives the beneficiary ample opportunity to realistically exercise his withdrawal rights.

4. Require that the beneficiary exercise the withdrawal right within a period of time well within the policy's grace period for payment. This assures that the trustee will have adequate time either to pay the premiums or to notify the grantor or others that the premiums must be paid from a source outside of the trust.

5. Require that the beneficiary exercise withdrawal rights in writing.

6. Allow any power given to a minor (or otherwise incompetent) beneficiary to be exercised on his behalf by a guardian. It is important to document that the legal right of the minor could, in fact, be exercised on his behalf. But provide that only the named individual or his guardian (or, if incompetent, his conservator) can exercise the power. That way, if the powerholder is declared bankrupt, his trustee cannot make withdrawals.

7. Terminate the power of withdrawal upon the insured's death (except in the case where the trust may hold a survivorship policy, in which case the demand power should continue until the surviving spouse insured dies).

8. Name back up powerholders so that, if a primary Crummey powerholder dies, the annual exclusion is not lost.

9. Have the grantor irrevocably renounce all rights in any policies or other assets in the trust.

10. Be sure the noninsured spouse pays no premiums and contributes no premiums, policies, or any other assets to the trust. If the noninsured spouse pays premiums, she may be considered a co-grantor of the trust. If she is also an income beneficiary of the trust, all or a portion of the proceeds purchased with her contributions may be includable in her estate.

11. The trustee should be given a duty to collect proceeds and indemnification for costs involved in a suit if required. Authority should be given to settle any such suit.

12. Give the trustee the right, if the insurer allows, to take one or more policy death benefits under the settlement options provided by the insurer.

13. In community property states, the grantor should indicate that any insurance contributed to the trust was the separate property of the grantor. If possible, premiums should be paid by the grantor with separate property funds.

Among the "Do Nots" often suggested in setting up these trusts are:

1. Do not require that the trustee purchase life insurance or apply contributions to the trust to be used to buy life insurance or pay life insurance premiums.

2. Do not name the trust the "Lotta Doe Life Insurance Trust," especially, if it is important to document that the trustee acted independently in the purchase of life insurance rather than as the client's agent and at the client's direction.

3. Do not allow the client to sign the policy application as applicant or owner. The client should sign only in the place where it says, "Insured."

4. Do not allow the trustee to merely endorse the client's contribution to the trust each year and send them directly to the insurance company. It is important that the trustee reduce those funds to possession by cashing each check in a separate checking account in the trust's name and writing a check drawn against the trust's account to the insurance company.

HOW TO AVOID THE TRANSFERS WITHIN THREE YEARS OF DEATH RULE

If an insured client dies within three years of a transfer of a life insurance policy to an irrevocable trust, the proceeds will be included in the insured's gross estate.[23] Assuming the insured cooperates in not dying during this danger zone, it is possible to limit or avoid federal estate tax inclusion under this rule.

An incredible amount of trouble is taken by advisors who delay the purchase of life insurance while trying to figure out means of avoiding the three year rule. As the following table, illustrates, the odds of a normally healthy client dying within this period is usually extremely low. For example, a person age 70 has about a 91.3% probability of surviving three years to age 73, and only an 8.7% probability of dying within three years (100% – 91.3%).

Current Age	Probability of Surviving 3 Years (%)
90	58.0
85	71.3
80	80.7
75	87.2
70	91.3
65	94.2
60	96.1
55	97.5
50	98.4
45	99.0
40	99.3
35	99.4
30	99.6

Yet the professional's delay is amusing; if the advisor really thinks there is a chance that the client will in fact die within this period, the client should be told to buy as much coverage as quickly as possible. Unlike the typical advice the planner should give to a client, the client whose advisor feels that he is likely to die within three years of the policy purchase should buy first and shop later.

It is now clear that the three-year rule of IRC Section 2035 applies only if the insured held an incident of ownership in a policy within three years of his death. Thus, a policy should not be subject to the three year rule where an independent trustee applies for the policy and requires of the insured only the verification of the information in the application.

Here are the guidelines for success:

1. Be sure the client never owns the policy.

2. Suggest to the independent trustee (or adult beneficiary) the advantages of owning a policy on the life of the "to be insured" but let that party make the decision and take all the action to put the policy into effect.

3. Authorize, but do not require, the purchase of life insurance. The trust document must provide evidence that the trustee is free to use funds transferred to the trust to purchase any type of investment.

4. Expand the authority for the trustee to purchase life insurance on the life of anyone on whom the trust's beneficiaries have an insurable interest (including but not limited to the client and the client's spouse).

5. Specifically deny the insured the power to reacquire any rights in a policy currently owned or that the trust might purchase in the future.

6. Permit, but do not require, that the trustee pay premiums.

7. If the client is to transfer existing insurance to the trust, make the gift outright with no strings attached.

8. Make sure that the facts indicate that the recipient of cash is not acting mechanically as the insured's agent. Substantiate that the trustee made an independent decision in the best interest of the beneficiaries to purchase the life insurance.

9. If possible, for the first three years, have the trustee pay premiums from a source other than the insured. Consider, if necessary, a loan from a bank or relative other than the insured or the insured's spouse.

10. Be sure that the trustee physically obtains and retains possession of all the policies assigned to the trust. Likewise, the trustee should take physical possession of any policies subsequently issued or assigned to the trust (and, of course, the trustee should take the appropriate steps to name the trust as owner and beneficiary of the coverage).

11. Authorize the trust to enter into a special arrangement with the client's corporation or other business enterprise or a third party for splitting premium dollars and policy ownership.

One possible way to sidestep IRC Section 2035 problems (which apply only if the client makes a gratuitous transfer of a policy on his life) is a sale of the policy to the irrevocable trust. A sale of a policy normally creates a transfer-for-value problem, but it may be possible to meet one of the exceptions to the transfer-for-value rule. For instance, it may be possible to argue that:

1. The transfer was to the insured, if the trust was defective (i.e., for income tax purposes the trust and the grantor-insured are the same and therefore there was no transfer; see discussion of grantor trusts under "Income Tax Implications," below).

2. If an irrevocable trust is a partner of the insured (in a viable partnership), the transfer falls within an exception to the transfer for value rule.

The purchase of the policy solution to the transfers within three years of death problem may be excellent planning when an existing policy is to be transferred to an irrevocable trust, but has one major drawback. The transaction requires the trustee to have cash available with which to purchase the policy or be able to borrow the money (perhaps with an interest bearing note). The loan can be repaid at a future date using policy values or dividends.

Suppose the trustee of an irrevocable trust wants to exchange an existing contract in the trust for a new policy. Assume further that the existing policy has been in the trust for more than three years and is therefore beyond the scope of IRC Section 2035. Will an IRC Section 1035 exchange (see Appendix E) create a new three year period for purposes of Section 2035? If the money in the existing policy has been in the trust for more than three years, a Section 1035 exchange should not cause a new three year period to begin because the exchange (transfer if any) is made by the trustee and is not a transfer by the client. The trustee is the applicant, owner, beneficiary, and premium payor of the new policy. The client merely signs the application as the insured. Because the insured client has not made a transfer, no new three year rule should begin for purposes of Section 2035.

STRUCTURING THE TRUST FOR "WHAT IFs"

In real life it is not always possible to structure the transactions as described above in the preferred approach. For instance, the client may have purchased a policy years before discovering the federal estate tax inclusion problem. It may be transferred into the trust too late to escape federal estate tax inclusion, or some other unforeseen problem may cause the proceeds to be included in the client's estate.

There is an escape or failsafe (or bail-out) contingency provision that can be placed into a trust where the irrevocable trust is to be the recipient of a pre-existing policy. This escape provision can require the trustee to hold any insurance proceeds that are included for any reason in the grantor's gross estate, and to pay them out in a manner that qualifies the proceeds for the estate tax marital deduction, either a general power of appointment or QTIP deduction. So, if the proceeds are for any reason includable in the insured's gross estate, this escape clause will eliminate the tax if the insured is, in fact, survived by a U.S. citizen spouse.

Such failsafe trust clauses are extremely important for most insurance trusts created by married grantors, but must be drafted with considerable care. The reason is that tax law requires that the surviving spouse receive property outright, or in a manner tantamount to outright, to qualify for the marital deduction. Conversely, most life insurance trusts usually limit the powers given to the surviving spouse in order to avoid inclusion in the surviving spouse's estate, rather than to qualify for the estate tax marital deduction. This eliminates the use of QTIP (qualified terminable interest property) planning because the QTIP marital deduction is allowed only at the cost of estate tax inclusion of the trust's assets in the surviving spouse's estate. So, the drafting attorney must walk the tightrope between estate tax exclusion of the life insurance proceeds, if at all possible, and the obtaining of the marital deduction, if all else fails.

The clause could obtain the marital deduction by providing for:

1. outright payment of included insurance proceeds to the surviving spouse;

2. an income interest to the surviving spouse coupled with a general power of appointment; or

3. payment of the proceeds to a trust the surviving spouse can revoke at will.

ALLOCATION OF THE FEDERAL ESTATE TAX

Life insurance proceeds, if includable in the insured's gross estate, will generate federal estate taxes if the insured is not survived by a spouse and/or does not wish to leave the insurance proceeds in a manner that will qualify for the estate tax marital deduction. Who will pay this tax? Should it be paid by the beneficiaries out of the proceeds or by the heirs of the probate estate? Should it be apportioned between them? The answer, of course, should only be given by the client.

The problem can, and should, be addressed by the planner drafting the client's will and irrevocable trust. The insured decedent's executor or administrator has the legal right to recover from the beneficiary of the insurance proceeds any estate taxes attributable to the inclusion of those proceeds in the insured's taxable estate. On the other hand, if the proceeds were not taxable (for example because they passed outright to the insured's surviving spouse or to a charity), the beneficiary has no liability for their payment.[24] The IRC allows the insured to specify, by an allocation clause in his will, who will bear the burden of any estate tax.

INCOME TAX IMPLICATIONS

Typically, an irrevocable life insurance trust will not be funded. Since it holds no income producing assets, generally no income tax problems are created.

In general, if an irrevocable life insurance trust is funded, income it generates is taxed to the trust since it is a separate entity. To the extent income is paid to the trust's beneficiaries, it is taxed to them rather than to the trust.

However, if the trust is treated as a "grantor trust," the income earned by the trust will be taxed to the grantor and any deductions, gains, losses, or credits realized by the trust can be used by the grantor.

The following will cause the trust to be considered a grantor trust:

1. Retention by the client or the client's spouse of a reversionary interest (right to receive property back or determine its disposition) in the income or the principal of any portion of a trust, but only if the actuarial value of the retained reversionary interest is greater than 5% of the value of the income or principal that may revert.[25]

2. Retention of the power by the client or the client's spouse to control the beneficial enjoyment of the income or principal of the trust.[26]

3. Retention of certain administrative powers by the client or the client's spouse. These powers include:[27]

   a) power to purchase, deal with, or dispose of the income or principal of a trust for less than adequate and full consideration;

   b) power to borrow from income or principal without adequate interest or security (an exception is made where a trust authorizes such loans under a general lending power by a trustee who is not the grantor);

   c) if a related or subordinate trustee lends income or principal to the client and the loan is made without adequate collateral or a reasonable rate of interest (and the loan is not repaid before the beginning of the next tax year); or

   d) if someone other than the trustee can vote corporate stock held by the trust, or has the power to control the investment of stock or securities held by the trust, or has the power to reacquire the principal of the trust by substituting property of equal value.

4. Retention of the power by the client or any nonadverse party (including the client's spouse) to revoke the trust.[28]

5. If the income of the trust is, or in the discretion of the client or a non-adverse party, *may be,*[29]

- distributed to the client or his spouse;

- held or accumulated for future distribution to the client or his spouse;

- used to pay premiums on a policy insuring the life of the client or his spouse (since there is little or no income in the typical irrevocable life insurance trust, this should not be a problem); or

- used to discharge a legal obligation of the client or his spouse.

A trustee, beneficiary, or some party other than the grantor-client can be taxed on the income of a funded irrevocable trust if that person has the power to vest (obtain without conditions or risk of forfeiture) the income or principal of all or a portion of the trust in himself.[30]

When a trust beneficiary allows a Crummey power to lapse, there may be income tax consequences. Unfortunately, the income tax consequences of the lapse of the Crummey withdrawal right are far from certain.

HOW TO HANDLE LAST TO DIE (SURVIVORSHIP) INSURANCE IN AN IRREVOCABLE TRUST

Last-to-die (or second to die) policies (see Chapter 15) pay at the second death, regardless of which insured dies first. These survivorship contracts are often used in estate planning with irrevocable trusts for the following reasons:

1. The payment pattern of last to die policies often tracks with the estate's need for cash; by paying proceeds only after the survivor of the insureds (typically, a husband and wife) has died, the event which creates the need for the greatest

amount of federal estate tax creates the cash to solve that liquidity problem. But planners should note that, even with married couples who will eliminate all or much of the federal estate tax at the first death through the marital deduction, not all of the demand for cash is delayed until the second death. In fact, a distressing amount of money is needed to pay off debts, expenses, and state death taxes at the first death. Also, a surviving spouse can, and often will, survive for decades and need hundreds of thousands of dollars to provide food, clothing, and shelter, as well as education for herself and the couple's children.

2. Last to die policies require a lower outlay than if the same amount of coverage were obtained on the older of the two insureds, since: (a) the premium will in many cases be paid for a longer period of time, and/or (b) the insurer will have the use of policy dollars for longer periods of time. (The probability of two people dying in the early years of a contract is much less than the probability of one of those persons dying during such period.)

From a planner's perspective, last-to-die policies placed in an irrevocable trust present potential problems not raised with regular policies because, for tax purposes, both spouses are insureds under a last-to-die policy. Here are some guidelines:

- Do not name either spouse a life beneficiary of the trust. If either spouse is given the right to the income of the trust for life, the proceeds will be includable in that spouse's estate as a retained life interest.[31]

- Do not name either spouse as the trustee of a trust holding a last-to-die policy. Since both spouses are insured, if the spouse who serves as trustee dies second, it is likely the IRS will include the proceeds in the spouse's estate under an argument that "As trustee, the insured held incidents of ownership." Should the insured trustee discover the problem and resign as trustee during the three years prior to death, the proceeds will nevertheless be included in his estate as a transfer within three years of death.[32]

Even if the trustee spouse dies first, the consequences could be severe. The fair market value of the policy at that time (usually, interpolated terminal reserve plus unearned premium on the date of death) is included in his gross estate, since that best reflects the estate tax value of the policy. This may be quite a large amount and can aggravate the first decedent's liquidity problem, since it creates a cash need but the policy's reserve cannot be used to provide cash to satisfy that need.

- How does the three year rule of IRC Section 2035 operate where a survivorship policy is owned by an irrevocable trust (or other third party)? Only if (a) both spouses die within the three year period following the transfer of a second to die policy to an irrevocable trust, and (b) the transferor spouse is the second to die, will the life insurance proceeds be includable under the three year rule. If both spouses died within three years of the transfer but the transferor spouse died first, the policy would have been included, if at all, under IRC Section 2033, as an interest one person held in a policy on another person's life. That IRC section does not apply, however, unless an interest was held at death – which it was not. Furthermore, IRC Section 2035 applies only if, within three years of the transfer, IRC Section 2042 (incidents of ownership) would have applied had there been no transfer.

Planners should note that there are many situations in which survivorship policies are not indicated (or should be used in conjunction with first to die contracts). These include:

- Estates where the client wants to pass significant wealth to someone other than a surviving spouse,

- Estates where there is no surviving spouse,

- Estates where the surviving spouse is not a U.S. citizen and the qualified domestic trust (QDOT) is contra indicated, and

- Estates where the need to provide funds to maintain the survivors' standard of living will require significant capital.

HOW TO HANDLE GROUP TERM LIFE INSURANCE IN AN IRREVOCABLE TRUST

Group insurance is an ideal type of life insurance to transfer to an irrevocable trust for many reasons:

- A transfer of group term life to an irrevocable life insurance trust makes significant estate tax savings possible at minimal gift tax cost.

- There is a considerable psychological advantage to the use of group term life with an irrevocable trust; since the premiums are paid for by the insured's employer, the employee feels the cost is low since "little of current value" is given up.

- In the case of an insured who also controls or influences the employee benefit decisions of the corporation, since the employer controls the ability to cancel the master contract, indirectly at least the employee can terminate the coverage inside of the trust by suggesting that the employer purchase coverage from a new carrier. (However, this control will not be deemed an incident of ownership.) For practical purposes, however, an employee who wishes to remove group insurance from his estate will usually assign all rights in replacement policies, as well as in the original policy (see below).

Virtually all states specifically allow the absolute assignment of group term life insurance. This creates an opportunity to remove huge amounts of insurance from both the estate of the insured employee and the estate of his spouse through a transfer to an irrevocable life insurance trust.

But there are special problems inherent where group term life insurance is contributed to or owned by the irrevocable trust:

1. *Assignability* – The insured must divest himself of all incidents of ownership through an absolute assignment. The insurance company's form should be examined to be sure it transfers all the insured's rights with respect to the coverage. Be sure to obtain an endorsed copy of the form from the insurance company as evidence that the transfer has, in fact, been officially made. If the date or the existence of the transfer becomes an issue, that endorsed copy will prove that the insurer recognized the change of ownership.

   Obviously, the terms of the master contract between the employer and the insurer should allow the assignment. But if there is a prohibition, the master policy should be amended at the employer's request and documentation retained by the firm's counsel. State law must also permit the assignment. As mentioned above, almost all states currently allow an insured under group term coverage to make an absolute assignment of all rights.

Assuming both the terms of the policy and state law permit a client to assign interests in group term coverage to an irrevocable trust (or other third party), the transfer should be effective to avoid federal estate tax. Furthermore, the payment of each premium by the employer is not considered to start a new three year period for purposes of IRC Section 2035 estate tax inclusion.

Planners must beware, however, of events beyond some employee-clients' control (e.g., a change by the employer of the group insurance carrier). An assignment with one company typically doesn't apply to the new coverage with the new insurer.

At first glance, the solution seems obvious; transfer all rights, not only in the current coverage, but also to any future coverage. Assuming the new coverage was purchased without the employee's direction, was necessitated by the change in the master contract, and was identical in all relevant aspects to the old plan, the IRS will recognize the anticipatory assignment, at least in removing the proceeds from the insured's estate. This implies that if the amount or terms of coverage was significantly different, the IRS might not consider itself bound to honor the assignment.

More importantly, what havoc might such an anticipatory assignment play on a client who, after having assigned away all future group term coverage, is divorced from his spouse? Not only must the client report Table I costs[33] (regardless of who owns the contract) as income and report an amount equal to the Table I costs as gifts, but every time his salary is increased, assuming group coverage is a function of salary, the ex-wife is potentially enriched at the client's current expense.

2. *Obtaining the annual exclusion* – Attainment of the annual exclusion is not certain. Although there is no official requirement that the exact property contributed to a trust each year be the property subject to the power, in the opinion of the authors, if the beneficiary can't get what the grantor puts in, the IRS may someday argue that

the withdrawal power is ineffective and the gift tax exclusion should be denied. In the case of an irrevocable trust where there are no assets except group term life coverage contributed to the trust, the employee-insured-grantor is making only a constructive transfer of premium dollars; premiums are in fact actually paid directly to the insurer by the employee-insured-grantor's employer. The employee is deemed to have made a gift to the trust for gift tax purposes. The authors feel it is essential that, in such cases, the initial and annual rights of the beneficiary to make withdrawals be satisfiable by any property held by the trust including, but not limited to, group term coverage.

When a client is covered by a large amount of group term insurance, premiums can be substantial. Absent an annual exclusion, the annual gift the client is deemed to make every time his employer pays a premium on coverage absolutely assigned to an irrevocable trust could be costly. For instance, a 61 year old executive covered by $1,000,000 of taxable group term coverage would be deemed to transfer about $7,920 each year to the donees of his trust. A 65 year old with the same coverage would be considered to be making gifts of $15,240 each year. See Chapter 10 regarding Table I and the cost of group term life insurance.

As mentioned above, a purely tax oriented solution for obtaining the annual exclusion would be to give the donee the right to take the coverage out of the trust and/or give the donee the right to an immediate distribution of the insurance proceeds at the moment of an insured-employee's death. But if this right is exercised, it would defeat some of the tax and personal objectives the client had when establishing the trust. If the beneficiary in fact exercises the power and takes the coverage during the client's lifetime, the client has lost all control. Until the master contract is changed to a new carrier or dropped by the employer, the Crummey powerholder (or the person who buys the coverage from him) owns the insurance on the client's life. If the beneficiary has the right to take the proceeds at the moment of the client's death, again, the dispositive and limiting objectives of the client are defeated.

To avoid these problems, consider giving the beneficiaries, in addition to the normal

Crummey withdrawal right, the right to require the trustee to sell any group term coverage on the insured employee and pay them their share of the sales proceeds. To prevent the policy from ending up in the wrong hands should they in fact exercise this right, the trust would provide that the trustee could sell it only to the insured. The sale price would be an amount exactly equal to the premium paid that year by the employer on the employee's behalf. In essence, this would give the beneficiaries a withdrawal power operative on the amount of the constructive gift made by the employee client; as soon as the employer pays the premium, the beneficiaries can demand the equivalent of that amount from the trust. The grantor must buy if the trustee exercises his put, but the grantor has no right to compel a sale.

3. *Community property issues* – Planners in community property states must remember that one-half of the compensation and, therefore, the assets purchased with or because of that portion of the employee's compensation are considered the property of the nonworking spouse. A retained life estate is held by the nonworking spouse with respect to that one half. Some authorities have suggested that the nonworking spouse should assign his one half of the future premium payments made by the employer to the working spouse or have the working spouse reimburse the nonworking spouse from separate property.

COMMUNITY PROPERTY ISSUES

There are currently ten states subject to community property or marital property (Alaska, Arizona, California, Idaho, Louisiana, Nevada, New Mexico, Texas and Washington are community property; Wisconsin is a quasi-community property state). Life insurance obtained by one or both of the spouses during the marriage while domiciled in any of these states is typically community property. Essentially, this means each spouse, from inception, is the owner of one half of the policy.

This community property treatment can have adverse estate tax consequences. The noninsured spouse's interest in the community's property may be included in her estate. By extension, if community funds are used to pay premiums and the policy purchased with those premiums becomes community property, a noninsured nongrantor has made a gift of her interest. Coupled with the life income so often given to spouses by an insured grantor, the surviving spouse may have made a constructive gift followed by lifetime retention of income. This is a classic estate tax inclusion type tax trap.[34]

The inclusion may be somewhat ameliorated by claiming a consideration offset for the actuarial value of the survivor's life income interest. In other words, it may be possible to argue that the amount of the includable proceeds should be reduced by the consideration paid (i.e., the noninsured spouse gave up a remainder interest in his community share of the proceeds in return for a life income interest in the other share of the proceeds). But to avoid inclusion altogether, do not:

1. give either spouse a life income in the trust; or

2. convert the insurance, prior to its transfer to the trust, to separate property of the insured.

Some attorneys suggest that the couple deliberately classify the life insurance as the separate property of the insured spouse. The reason for this is to make it possible for that spouse to transfer it to the irrevocable trust. Mechanically, this is accomplished by a waiver by the noninsured spouse of his rights. Alternatively, the noninsured spouse's rights can be sold to the insured spouse (in return for a payment from noncommunity funds) or transferred by gift. The insured then (some time later) transfers the insurance to the trust. If this later course of action is taken, the noninsured spouse should not be made a beneficiary of the trust. Otherwise, the IRS could claim that she was a grantor of the trust and that she made a gift with a retained life estate. The result would be estate tax inclusion of the policy proceeds. Likewise, death of the insured within 3 years of the transfer will result in estate tax inclusion.

A similar problem arises with respect to the imputed (Table I) income from large amounts of group-term life insurance and Table 2001 income from noncontributory split dollar plans. In both cases, the imputed income is treated as community property, which is then deemed to be transferred (by the employee receiving that income) to the trust. This deemed transfer will result in the noninsured spouse being treated as a grantor. Again, the solution is to make sure neither spouse is an income beneficiary of the trust.

A sale of the policy to the trustee would solve the transfers within three years of death problem, but create a transfer for value that could cause a loss of the income tax free payment of the proceeds when the insured died.

CHAPTER ENDNOTES

1. The estate tax is repealed for one year in 2010.

2. For instance, if a client gave away a home that cost $200,000 and was worth $2,000,000 on the date of the gift and remained the same until the donor's death, the donees' basis would be only $200,000 (plus an adjustment for gift taxes paid). If it is later sold by the donees for $2,000,000, the gain would be $1,800,000 ($2,000,000 amount realized minus $200,000 basis). Had the home been kept until death, its basis would have been stepped up to its date of death value, $2,000,000. Note that stepped up basis is scheduled to be replaced by a modified carryover basis in 2010.

3. Donors concerned with a loss of the policy's cash values can borrow before the transfer, but should note two things: First, a loan in excess of basis can trigger reportable gain to the donor and, perhaps, set the transfer for value tax trap for the "purchaser." (See Appendix G regarding the transfer for value rule.)

   Second, a client who borrows on a life insurance contract should note that, in most cases, there will be no income tax deduction for interest on policy loans.

4. See Leimberg, et al., *The Tools and Techniques of Estate Planning*, 13th ed. (Cincinnati, OH: The National Underwriter Company, 2004) for information on these trusts.

5. See Chapter 28 regarding revocable trusts.

6. Skerik, 38th Annual N.Y.U. Institute, ¶35.05[6].

7. Planners are urged to check state law to determine whether it is possible to name "my spouse" as opposed to a specific individual as the holder of a special power.

8. Treasury Regulation §20.2042-(1)(c)(4) provides that

   "A decedent is considered to have an incident of ownership in an insurance policy on his life in trust if, under the terms of the policy, the decedent (either alone or in conjunction with another person or persons) has the power (as trustee or otherwise) to change the beneficial ownership in the policy or its proceeds, or the time or manner of enjoyment thereof, even though the decedent has no beneficial interest."

   Some authorities say the potential for this problem is reduced or eliminated by Revenue Ruling 84-179, 1984-2 CB 195, which holds that a decedent will not be deemed to possess incidents of ownership held in a fiduciary capacity if:

   (1) the insured's powers over the trust are not exercisable for his personal benefit;

   (2) the insured did not transfer the policy, nor did any consideration for purchasing or maintaining it come to the trust from the insured's personal assets; and

   (3) the trust powers held by the insured were not part of a prearranged plan.

   So, if the insured did not provide the consideration (premium payments) and can't use trust assets for his own benefits, it appears that the grantor insured could safely be the trustee.

   But it would be impossible for an insured who creates a life insurance trust to meet the last two tests, since it is usually the insured who is both the grantor and the party who dictates the terms of the trust. It is, therefore, likely that the IRS will claim that any insured grantor personally holds incidents of ownership held by him as trustee (regardless of a claim that the powers held by the client are limited due to his fiduciary duty to the beneficiaries of the trust and even though he can't personally benefit from the trust in any way).

   The solution to the cautious practitioner is obvious: Do not allow the insured to serve as trustee of a trust that holds life insurance on his life.

   Where the trust was created by someone other than the insured, if the insured is to also be the trustee, these precautions should reduce the potential for estate tax inclusion:

   (1) Do not give the insured any beneficial interest in the trust.

   (2) Preclude trust distributions to anyone (such as the insured's children) to the extent those payments are in satisfaction of a legal obligation of support under state law.

   (3) Provide a source of premium payments (e.g., fund the trust with income producing assets) other than the insured (in order to support an argument that the insured did not furnish consideration for maintaining the policies).

9. IRC Sec. 2041.

10. IRC Sec. 2513.

11. IRC Secs. 2503(b), 2502.

12. *Crummey v. Comm.*, 397 F2d 82 (9th Cir. 1968).

13. Rev. Rul. 73-405, 1973-2 CB 321.

14. IRC Sec. 2041.

15. IRC Sec. 2041.

16. *Est. of Holland v. Comm.*, TC Memo 1997-302; *Est. of Kohlsaat v. Comm.*, TC Memo 1997-212.

17. IRC Section 2514, according to the IRS, refers to the lapse of powers during a calendar year. So, the IRS position is that a beneficiary's demand powers must be aggregated to decide whether their lapse exceeded the permissible five-or-five limit.

18. IRC Section 2041.

19. Technically, the amount includable is the sum of the products obtained by multiplying the value of the trust share (using the federal estate tax value) by the following fraction:

$$\frac{\text{Amount of each lapse in excess of the greater of \$5,000 or 5\% of trust corpus}}{\text{Value of the trust share at the date of lapse}}$$

   There is a maximum inclusion amount: The includable amount can't exceed the federal estate tax value of the assets from which the power could have been satisfied.

20. 94 TC 74 (1991).

21. IRC Sec. 2513.

22. IRC Secs. 6019, 6075.

23. See discussion in Appendix A.

24. IRC Sec. 2206.

25. IRC Sec. 673. Note that if the interest is held by the grantor, it will probably result in the inclusion of trust assets in the grantor's estate. However, if the interest is held by the grantor's spouse, it will not result in estate tax inclusion even if the income is taxed to the spouse.

26. IRC Sec. 674. This will also cause estate tax inclusion of the policy proceeds if the power is held by the grantor, but not if it is held solely by the grantor's spouse.

27. IRC Sec. 675.

28. IRC Sec. 676. This would also cause estate tax inclusion.

29. IRC Sec. 677(a).

30. IRC Sec. 678(a).

31. IRC Sec. 2036

32. IRC Sec. 2035.

33. Technically, the value of a gift of an interest in group term coverage is the lower of the actual cost or the Table I cost. If the group coverage discriminates in favor of certain key employees, the actual cost of coverage will determine the gift. The value of the gift includes the actual cost or Table I cost (as appropriate) of the full amount of coverage (including the first $50,000 of coverage).

34. IRC Sec. 2036.

Chapter 24

KEY EMPLOYEE LIFE INSURANCE

WHAT IS IT?

Key employee life insurance is a life insurance policy owned by and payable to a business that insures the life or lives of employees (or outsiders) whose death(s) would cause a significant economic loss to the business, upon whose skills, talents, experience, or business or personal contacts the business is dependent, and who would be difficult to replace.[1]

WHEN IS THE USE OF SUCH A DEVICE INDICATED?

1. When the profits or the financial soundness of a client's business would be threatened or when a client's business will have a difficult period of adjustment following the death of a key employee such as a leading salesperson or an employee instrumental in the development of new products.

2. When the success of a business is dependent upon the unique skills and abilities of one or more key employees and the business' creditors insist that its indebtedness be collateralized through the purchase of key employee life insurance.

3. When a business desires to fund one or more obligations of the business at the death of a group of key employees (for example, the funding of large health and retirement benefits).

4. When business owners have been required by creditors to co-sign or guarantee that if the corporation defaults, they will personally be responsible for paying off the debt. Key employee insurance will protect those individuals and their estates.

5. Publicly held businesses quite often use key employee coverage to assure shareholders that the price of stock will not plummet nor will dividends fall at the death of a president or other senior executive.

6. Where the nature of the business involves the rendition of personal services (e.g., legal, medical, or other licensed professionals), the death of a key person can cause a drop in business income.

7. Where the psychological impact of the unexpected death of a key employee may be accompanied by the disproportionately large costs involved in meeting the time table for work-in-progress, pending negotiations, and incomplete projects. There are almost always significant costs of searching for, finding, and hiring a successor. Key employee coverage can reimburse the business for these costs.

8. Although it is rare that the death of a key person creates a void that cannot competently be filled given enough time, there are cases (especially in closely held businesses) in which key individuals "are the business." At the death (or long term disability) of such a driving force, the business will often fail entirely. Key employee coverage can protect the financial interests of investors.

9. Key employee coverage is particularly indicated in a closely-held business where profits are often dependent on the ability, initiative, judgment, or "rainmaking" ability of a single individual or small group of persons.

WHAT ARE THE REQUIREMENTS?

Key employee insurance should be owned by and payable to the corporation, which should also pay the premiums. As will be noted below under the discussion of taxation, adverse consequences are likely when the proceeds of an employer-owned policy are paid to a party other than the corporation or its creditors.

A corporate resolution should be entered into the corporate minutes stressing that the coverage has been purchased to indemnify the business for potential loss at the death of a key person and to serve any other corporate purpose. The resolution of the board of directors might stress the loss in words similar to the following:

> "The death or permanent disability of Jo-Ann Egly, Senior Vice President, would result in the loss of her unique fishing experience, special management abilities, dealer contacts, and understanding of the sports fishing industry and its economic direction."

HOW IS IT DONE – AN EXAMPLE

Steve and Bob form a computer software company called "L and L." At first, the firm has only one product, but after a number of years it has created several financial and estate planning programs and markets client-oriented brochures as well.

Steve is the creative and marketing genius but has little patience for the day-to-day details required in the actual operation of the business nor does Steve have the business background to handle the bookkeeping and accounting for the firm – and wouldn't want to even if he could. Bob on the other hand is brilliant at methodically organizing every detail of the production and distribution process and manages to maximize the profit-making potential of the firm's strong cash flow. Bob, however, does not have the marketing expertise, contacts, or technical skill of his co-shareholder.

Neither individual could, on his own, physically accomplish what both men do. Nor could either in any profitable degree match the skills of the other. At the death or long term disability of either, the remaining shareholder of L and L would suffer an incredible economic loss and would be faced with the costly burden of trying to replace the lost associate and paying for the mistakes and lost business incurred during that aggravating process.

L and L's board of directors, in recognition of these costs, signs a corporate resolution that provides authorization for the purchase of key employee life insurance coverage on both men's lives. The corporation will be the applicant, owner, premium payor, and beneficiary of the coverage. At either person's death, the insurance proceeds will be received by the corporation and can be used for any of the corporation's needs.

WHAT ARE THE TAX IMPLICATIONS?

1. Premiums paid by the corporation are not tax deductible.[2]

2. Generally, policy proceeds are free of federal income taxes.[3]

3. Where a key employee policy – or an interest in a key employee policy – has been transferred for any type of valuable consideration, proceeds may lose their income tax free status. (See Appendix G, "The Transfer for Value Rule," for more information.) Fortunately, even if there has been a transfer for value, there are exceptions which, if met, will enable the policy proceeds to maintain their income tax free status. These exemptions allow transfers to the following transferees: (1) the insured; (2) the insured's partner; (3) a partnership in which the insured is a partner; or (4) a corporation in which the insured is a shareholder or officer.[4]

It should be noted that transfers *to* co-shareholders of the insured are *not* among the protected transfers. Also, transfers *to* a corporation in which the insured is merely a director but is not an officer or shareholder are *not* among the protected transfers.

The transfer for value tax trap is so deadly (both in complexity and potential expense to all parties) that no transfers of life insurance policies should be made without careful review of the transfer for value rules by competent legal counsel.

4. In spite of the general rule that life insurance proceeds will generally be received income tax free, life insurance death benefits received by a "large" C corporation will generate "adjusted current earnings and profits" for purposes of computing the corporation's alternative minimum tax (AMT) liability. In a nutshell, this means that about 75% of the death proceeds in excess of the cash value received by a large corporation at the date of the insured's death will be treated as an adjustment for AMT purposes.

Therefore, roughly 75% of the total proceeds may be subject to a 20% surtax in a "worst case" scenario. This is essentially equivalent to a 15% tax (20% x 75%) on 100% of the proceeds.[5] So, in a worst case situation, about $150,000 will be lost out of a $1,000,000 death benefit.

To compensate for a worst possible case AMT loss, multiply the "target" or net amount needed by 118% to arrive at the necessary amount of insurance. For instance, if the corporation predicted a loss or cash need of $1,000,000 at the death of its president, it should purchase $1,180,000 of life insurance on the president's life.

No AMT is imposed on a "small corporation." A corporation qualifies as a "small corporation" for purposes of the small business exemption from the AMT if its average gross receipts for all three-tax-year periods (starting in tax years beginning after 1993) were $7.5 million or less. The $7.5 million threshold amount is reduced to $5 million for the corporation's first three-year period (or part of that period) beginning after December 31, 1993.[6]

5. A corporation's earnings and profits (E&P) will be increased to the extent that the death proceeds exceed (a) total premiums in the case of term insurance or (b) corporate owned cash values in the case of permanent coverage. This is important because the amount and character of income distributed from a corporation to its shareholders is determined in large part by reference to the firm's E&P.[7]

Also, C corporations are subject to the accumulated earnings tax – a 15% surtax on "unreasonable" accumulations of earnings and profits.[8] The accumulated earnings tax may be imposed on a corporation that has E&P in excess of the reasonable needs of the business. A corporation is allowed to accumulate up to a safe harbor amount of $250,000 ($150,000 for certain personal service corporations).

During the lifetime of the insured, the internal build-up of cash values should not trigger an accumulated earnings tax problem. Many courts have agreed that an accumulation of earnings is appropriate to pay for insurance (or to self insure) as a means of protecting the business against such contingencies as unsettled business conditions and the loss of a key employee. Generally, therefore, the cash values inside of permanent coverage should not create a problem under the accumulated earnings tax.[9]

A corporation typically acquires a key person life insurance policy to assure adequate working capital after a key employee's death. To the extent key employee death proceeds are used up in ordinary business operations, they should not cause an accumulated earnings tax problem.

6. Premiums paid by the corporation will not be taxable to the insured employee as long as that person is given no current rights in either the policy or its values.[10]

But if the proceeds are payable to the employee's estate or personal beneficiary, the result changes. In that case, premiums will *likely* be taxable to the employee where the policy is owned by the corporation[11] and the premiums will be taxable to the employee where the policy is owned by the employee.[12]

7. Generally, interest paid on loans secured by a key employee life insurance policy is not deductible unless one or more of the following exceptions are met:[13]

a. *"Four out of seven" exception* – At least four of the first seven annual premiums are paid without recourse to policy loans.

b. *"$100 a year" exception* – If the interest does not exceed $100 for any taxable year, the interest deduction will not be disallowed even if there is a systematic plan of borrowing.

c. *"Unforeseen event" exception* – If the debt was incurred because of an unforeseen substantial loss of income or substantial increase in obligations, the deduction will not be disallowed even though the policy loan was used to pay premiums.

d. *"Trade or business" exception* – If the debt is incurred in connection with the client's trade or business, the interest deduction will not be summarily disallowed. Generally, amounts to finance key employee coverage will not be considered to fall within this exception and in any event interest deductions for company-owned life insurance are severely restricted. See Appendix F, Taxation of Benefits.

Generally, with respect to contracts issued after June 8, 1997, no interest deduction is allowed for any interest paid or accrued with respect to a policy loan on a contract owned by a business. Almost all exceptions making an interest deduction possible on newly issued policies have been eliminated and the IRS is currently attacking interest deductions on many older contracts on the grounds that in reality the taxpayer did not meet at least one of the four tests above.[14]

Obviously, corporations in a relatively low tax bracket will have little interest in systematic borrowing in any event.

8. If the insured key employee holds no equity interest in the business, at his or her death, there should be no estate tax inclusion due to the payment of the key employee life insurance proceeds.[15]

9. The death proceeds of a corporate-owned life insurance policy on the life of a sole or "controlling" (one who owns more than 50% of the voting stock) shareholder will not be included separately as life insurance in the insured's gross estate to the extent that the proceeds are paid to – or for the benefit of – the corporation.[16]

Instead, the life insurance paid to the corporation (or to its creditors) is considered together with all other "non-operating assets" in the valuation process. That cash which includes what was policy proceeds is therefore part of the weighing that occurs in the determination of corporate net worth, prospective earning power, and dividend earning capacity.

10. To the extent the proceeds of a corporate owned life insurance policy on the life of a controlling shareholder are payable to a party other than the corporation or its creditors, those proceeds will be includable separately from the valuation of the business – as life insurance – in the insured shareholder's estate.

11. When a corporation owns a policy on the life of a non-controlling (50% or less) shareholder, the proceeds when paid to the corporation at the insured's death impact the value of the business. The life insurance paid to the corporation or its creditors is added together with all other "non-operating assets" in the valuation process. That cash is therefore part of the weighing that occurs in the determination of corporate net worth, prospective earning power, and dividend earning capacity.

12. Proceeds payable to or for the benefit of a partnership that owns a policy on the life of a partner are not included separately as life insurance in the gross estate of the key partner. The partnership rather than its partners is considered owner of the policy and its incidents of ownership. Of course, the proceeds increase the value of the insured partner's proportionate interest in the partnership for estate tax purposes.[17]

13. If proceeds of a partnership owned policy are payable to someone other than the partnership (or its creditors), they will be included separately as life insurance proceeds in the gross estate of an insured partner since the insured is deemed to hold incidents of ownership actually possessed by the partnership. The proceeds will be fully includable in the insured partner's estate (even if the insured is a minority partner).[18] Contrast this with the requirement of control (more than 50% of the voting power) required in the case of corporate-owned life insurance.

14. When an employee retires, quits, or is fired, a business owning insurance on his or her life may choose to sell it to the employee. If a key employee policy is sold to the insured at retirement or other termination of employment, even though it is a transfer and

is for valuable consideration, since it is to the insured, it falls within an exception to the transfer for value rule.[19] Planners should beware of transfers of key employee coverage by the business to others and check to be sure such assignments fall within one or more of the exceptions to the transfer for value rule.

15. Consideration should be given to the income tax implications when a corporation transfers a key employee policy to a former employee:

    a. If the business transfers the policy to the former employee for less than its value at that time, the employee will realize taxable income equal to the difference between the fair market value of the policy and the amount paid by the employee.[20] If the employee owns stock in the corporation, the IRS could classify the excess as a dividend rather than as compensation.

    b. If the employee pays nothing for the policy, the entire fair market value is taxable to the employee.[21]

    c. If the amount paid by the employee exceeds the corporation's net premium cost, the corporation will realize taxable income equal to that excess.

    d. If the amount paid by the employee is equal to or less than the corporation's net premium cost, no taxable gain will be realized by the transferring corporation.

16. A key employee sometimes sells a policy on his life to the corporation that will use it as key employee coverage. This transaction not only has the practical disadvantage of reducing personal coverage that may be needed but also has a number of serious adverse tax implications:

    a. If the insured is neither an officer nor shareholder of the company, the transfer for value rule is triggered. (See Appendix G, "The Transfer for Value Rule.")

    b. Taxable gain (ordinary income) will be realized by the seller to the extent that the amount paid by the corporation exceeds his net premium cost.[22]

    c. If the insured sells the policy to the corporation for less than his net premium cost, he will not be able to claim a deductible loss.

QUESTIONS AND ANSWERS

Question – What are the advantages of key employee life insurance?

Answer – There are a number of advantages of key employee life insurance. These include:

1. The value of the business owners' investment (and the ongoing credit of the business itself) is stabilized and maximized immediately by the existence of key employee life insurance coverage. During the insured's lifetime, policy cash values are carried as a corporate asset and can easily, quickly, and inexpensively be made available to the corporation for a business emergency or opportunity. At death, the infusion of large amounts of cash will serve as a "shock absorber" to cushion the impact of the key employee's loss.

2. From the time the first premium is paid, the business and its creditors have the assurance of "instant capital" at the death of a key employee. In this sense key employee coverage can serve both as a form of commercial loan protection as well as collateral for securing future commercial loans. Many banks and other lending institutions will refuse to make large loans to closely-held corporations unless life insurance in appropriate amounts can be obtained on pivotal personnel in the business.

3. A business receiving life insurance at the death of an employee is not restricted as to the manner in which that cash can be utilized. Key employee proceeds can be used for many purposes including finding a qualified replacement for the deceased key employee, paying for the training of the replacement, replacing lost profits, protecting the firm's credit rating, providing benefits under one or more employee benefit plans, and financing a buy-out of one or more deceased or disabled business owners.

Question – What are the disadvantages or costs of key employee coverage?

Answer – Key employee life insurance has disadvantages and costs which include:

1. The instant discounted capital provided by business-owned life insurance comes at a cost. Premiums must be paid with after-tax dollars. Also, the corporation must pay an opportunity cost: it cannot use money allocated to premiums for any other corporate purpose.

2. To the extent that the corporate AMT applies, the utility of key employee coverage is diminished.

Question – Is there a way around the non-deductibility of insurance premiums for key employee life coverage?

Answer – As a practical matter, the answer is no. This limitation extends to both term and permanent coverage. As a general rule, a client will not be allowed an income tax deduction for the payment of key employee life insurance premiums.

Question – How much insurance should be purchased by a business on its key employee?

Answer – A common method of calculating the economic effect of the loss of a key employee is the "discount approach." This technique applies a percentage discount to the fair market value of the business. The discount approach requires an appropriate discount factor. Some authorities believe that if the business will survive the loss of the key employee and, in time, will hire a competent replacement, an appropriate discount factor is 15 to 20%. But if the business will fail at the death of a specified key person, or will be placed in jeopardy from the loss of the key employee, an appropriate discount factor is from 20 to 45%. The officers of the company and the firm's accounting and legal advisors, however, should determine the exact discount factor.

Consider the following questions when determining the discount factor:

1. How long will it take the replacement to become as efficient and productive as the lost key employee was?

2. How much will it cost to locate, situate, and train a replacement, and will the new employee want a higher salary?

3. Is the replacement likely to make costly mistakes during the training period?

4. Will the loss of the employee result in a loss of clientele?

5. What percent of the firm's current net profits are attributable to the key employee?

While there are other methods of calculating the value of a key employee's contribution to a corporation, the discount approach illustrated below, courtesy of NumberCruncher Software, is a quick and effective method that sidesteps many of the difficulties posed by alternative methods.

KEY EMPLOYEE VALUATION

Fair Market Value of Business with Key Employee: $750,000

Discount Percent	Value without Key Employee	Value of Key Employee
17.000%	$622,500	$127,500
18.000%	$615,000	$135,000
19.000%	$607,500	$142,500
20.000%	$600,000	$150,000
21.000%	$592,500	$157,500
22.000%	$585,000	$165,000
23.000%	$577,500	$172,500

Computation Courtesy: *NumberCruncher Software*

Question – Should the insurance under a key employee policy be term or permanent?

Answer – As in every business planning problem, the "product must match the problem." If the need is for a short period of time, term insurance is indicated. Likewise, if the firm has a cash flow problem or is a recent start-up business, term coverage is generally indicated.

But in most cases the value of the truly "key" employee to a business increases over time. Therefore, the need is long-term. Often, key employee coverage will be converted to solve a long-term need such as funding a buy-sell agreement with an indeterminate time span or to finance the employer's obligation under a nonqualified deferred compensation plan. Thus, the preferred coverage is almost always some form of permanent insurance.

Question – How does a business account for key employee life insurance coverage?

Answer – Accounting for key employee life insurance depends on the type of policy. Term insurance premium payments represent a pure current expense. Such costs should be charged against income rather than retained earnings.

Insurance premiums paid on a permanent (cash value) type of policy are bifurcated. To the extent a premium payment generates an increase in the policy's cash value, a charge should be made to an asset account. To the extent the premium paid exceeds the increase in the policy's cash value, a charge should be made to expense.

The firm's balance sheet should show policy cash values as a "non-current" asset. When an insured dies, the gain upon the receipt of the insurance payment is typically reflected as a "special entry for nonrecurring amounts" on the Annual Statement of Operations. Alternatively, a corporation's gain on the receipt of death proceeds may be carried directly to the Retained Earnings Account.

It is the opinion of the authors that the method of accounting described above is antiquated and does not reflect the economic reality of the transactions over time considering the present products and riders available to businesses in the late 1990s and early twenty-first century.

An alternative method of accounting, called the "ratable charge" method, seems to provide a more realistic approach and has been used by a number of accounting firms even though it is not officially accepted. In essence, under the ratable charge method total premiums to be paid over a predetermined period (such as for 10 years or to age 55) are determined on the assumption that the insured is likely to live and will continue to remain an employee of the business that long. The guaranteed cash surrender value at the end of the selected period is then subtracted from the total premiums to be paid. The result is a "net cost" which is then amortized (ratably) as a level annual charge over the premium paying period.

This prime assumption upon which the ratable charge method relies becomes more likely if the policy in question contains what is often called a "policy exchange" rider, which is an option the client's firm has to continue the policy on another life if the insured employee should decide to leave the firm. In other words the company could substitute a new key employee for the one no longer employed. (In most cases the rider allows the exchange with no additional costs to the client's company.) The existence of an exchange rider would seem to offer an answer to the criticism that if the policy is discontinued prior to the end of the selected premium payment period, the ratable charge method would result in a large write-off of an unamortized deferred charge.

Question – Is there an income tax problem where a policy on the life of a controlling shareholder is payable to someone other than the corporation or its creditor?

Answer – Yes. There is a potential adverse tax consequence in this situation. If a policy death benefit that otherwise could (and should) have been paid to the corporation is in fact paid to the beneficiary of a shareholder, in the opinion of the authors, the IRS is almost certain to argue that the entire amount was constructively paid to that shareholder and is taxable as a dividend. If this argument should fail, the IRS is likely to claim the entire proceeds should be taxed to the recipient as compensation. Should that argument be deflected, the IRS could also argue that premiums for any open tax years should have been charged to the insured as dividends or at least as compensation.[23]

Question – What are the tax implications where a corporation attaches a disability income rider to a key person life insurance policy?

Answer – If the disability income policy is payable to the policyowner corporation, the premium payments for the disability portion as well as the life insurance portion will be nondeductible.[24] Income, when paid to the corporation upon the disability of the insured key employee, is income-tax free to the corporation.[25] Upon the payout to the disabled key employee, assuming the amount and terms of the payout are reasonable, the corporation should be able to deduct the payments as ordinary and necessary business expenses. Upon receipt by the key employee, the payments would be considered salary rather than proceeds from a disability income policy and therefore subject to ordinary income tax.

If the employee is named directly as payee of the disability income generated from the rider on a policy owned by the corporation, the taxation will probably be as follows:

1. Premiums paid by the corporation for the disability coverage should be deductible by the business as an ordinary and necessary business expense.

2. The key employee should not have to report as income premiums paid by the corporation on the disability coverage.

3. Income, when payable to the disabled key employee, would be treated as salary and subject to ordinary income tax when and as received.

Question – Does a corporation have an "insurable interest" in a key employee?

Answer – Insurable interest is essentially the expectation of a financial benefit from the continued life of the proposed insured. The question in basic terms is, "Does the business expect to benefit financially from its relationship with the proposed insured?" Generally, a corporation has an insurable interest in the life of a key employee if the continued success of the corporation depends upon the special skills and talents of the key employee, and the policy is purchased to protect the corporation against loss in the event of the key employee's death.

Generally, if a corporation has insurable interest in an individual when the policy is purchased, the issue is not again raised when the insured dies. However, the definition of insurable interest and its requirements is determined by state law. Practitioners must look to the law of the proposed insured's domicile to determine if the business does in fact have an insurable interest. If there is no insurable interest, the IRS might claim that the proceeds are not paid "by reason of the insured's death" but instead are paid "from a wagering contract" and therefore are taxable at ordinary income rates.[26]

Question – What is a "policy exchange rider" and how is it used in key employee insurance?

Answer – A "policy exchange rider" (often called a "substituted insured rider" or "exchange of insureds" option) provides that at the termination of the insured's employment, a new key employee can be substituted as the insured under the original policy (assuming the new person can provide evidence of insurability). Of course, appropriate adjustments in premium, cash value, or face value are made to the policy to reflect differences in age or insurability between the original insured and the new insured. Typically, there is no additional charge by the insurer at the time the new insured is substituted nor are commissions paid to the agent at that time. For these reasons, the corporate owner of the key employee coverage saves both underwriting and commission costs and receives an actuarially equivalent policy on the life of the new key employee.

Unfortunately, to be protected by Internal Revenue Code section 1035, an exchange must be on the life of the *same* insured. So the substitution of one insured for another under a policy exchange rider on a corporate-owned key employee life insurance contract will be taxed as if the corporation sold the first policy and used the proceeds to purchase the new contract. The corporation will have to report gain at ordinary income rates on the difference between the fair market value of the policy at the time of the exchange and the net premiums it had paid to that date.[27]

Question – If an "S" corporation purchases a policy on the life of a key employee, are the tax implications different from those of a "C" corporation?

Answer – In an S corporation, the income of the business flows through directly to its owners, the shareholders. Generally, when a policy's proceeds are paid to the corporation as death proceeds, they are received income-tax free, and each shareholder's pro rata share of the proceeds flows through income-tax free. The basis of each shareholder's stock is increased by his or her share of the tax-free proceeds.[28]

Question – Can a federally regulated bank purchase a life insurance policy on the life of a key employee?

Answer – A national bank may purchase key employee life insurance for the benefit of the bank if the bank has an insurable interest in the key employee's life.[29] According to the Office of the Comptroller of the Currency (OCC), key employee life insurance on the lives of executives and directors of banks is an appropriate investment when purchased as a funding mechanism for non-qualified deferred compensation plans. The OCC held that it was appropriate for banks to purchase the insurance to meet the bank's contractual obligations of payments upon early, normal, or late retirement as well as to families of covered employees at their deaths. It also held that life insurance could be properly held by a federal bank to serve as an actuarial cost recovery vehicle.[30]

CHAPTER ENDNOTES

1. Once, this was called "key man" insurance. Note that the term has no relationship to "key employee" as it is used for "top-heavy" pension and profit sharing rules.

2. IRC Sec. 264(a).
3. IRC Sec. 101(a); Treas. Reg. §1.101-1(a).
4. IRC Sec. 101(a)(2).
5. IRC Secs. 55-59. There is a flat 20% tax imposed on the company's alternative minimum taxable income (AMTI), after subtracting out a $40,000 exemption. The exemption starts to phase out beginning at an AMTI of $150,000, and is completely phased out at an AMTI of $310,000. Life insurance proceeds are added to a corporation's earnings and profits, becoming part of an adjustment added to a corporation's ordinary taxable income to determine its AMTI and, therefore, its potential alternative minimum tax liability.
6. IRC Sec. 55(e).
7. Rev. Rul. 54-230, 1954-1 CB 114.
8. IRC Secs. 531-537.
9. *Vuono-Lione, Inc. v. Comm.*, TC Memo 1965-96; *Harry A. Koch Co. v. Vinal*, 228 F. Supp. 782 (D. Neb. 1964); see also *Emeloid Co. v. Comm.*, 189 F.2d 230 (3rd Cir. 1951); *Bradford-Robinson Printing Co. v. Comm.*, 1 AFTR 2d 1278 (D. Colo. 1957).
10. *Casale v. Comm.*, 247 F.2d 440 (2d Cir. 1957); Rev. Rul. 59-184, 1959-1 CB 65.
11. Treas. Reg. §1.61-2(d)(2)(ii)(a); *Comm. v. Bonwit*, 87 F.2d 764 (2nd Cir. 1937).
12. Treas. Reg. §1.61-2(d)(2); *Canaday v. Guitteau*, 86 F.2d 303 (6th Cir. 1936); *Yuengling v. Comm.*, 69 F.2d 971 (3rd Cir. 1934); *Lee v. U.S.*, 219 F. Supp. 225 (W.D. S.C. 1963); *Jameson v. Comm.*, TC Memo 1942.
13. IRC Sec. 264(d).
14. See *IRS v. CM Holdings, Inc.*, 2002-2 USTC ¶50,596 (3d Cir. 2002); TAM 199901005; TAM 9812005.
15. IRC Sec. 2042.
16. Treas. Reg. §20.2042-1(c)(6).
17. IRC Sec. 2033.
18. IRC Sec. 2042(2); Rev. Rul. 83-147, 1983-2 CB 158.
19. See Appendix G, "The Transfer for Value Rule."
20. IRC Sec. 83; Treas. Reg. §1.83-3(e).
21. *Parsons v. Comm.*, 54 TC 54 (1970); *Thornley v. Comm.*, 41 TC 145 (1963).
22. *Gallun v. Comm.*, 327 F.2d 809 (7th Cir. 1964).
23. *Golden v. Comm.*, 113 F.2d 590 (3rd Cir. 1940). But see *Ducros v. Comm.*, 272 F.2d 49 (6th Cir. 1959); Rev. Rul. 61-134, 1961-2 CB 250.
24. IRC Sec. 265(a)(1).
25. IRC Sec. 104(a)(3).
26. *Atlantic Oil Co. v. Patterson*, 331 F.2d 516 (5th Cir. 1964); see also *U.S. v. Supplee-Biddle Hardware Co.*, 265 U.S. 189 (1924).
27. Rev. Rul. 90-109, 1990-2 CB 191.
28. IRC Secs. 1366(a)(1)(A), 1367(a)(1)(A).
29. Letter by John H. Noonan, Director, Commercial Activities, Administrator of National Banks, Comptroller of the Currency, October 28, 1986. See also Interpretive Ruling 7.7115, "Insuring Lives of Bank Officers."
30. OCC Interpretive Letter No. 848 and OCC Bulletin 96-51 (which supersedes a 1983 Letter to the contrary).

Chapter 25

LIFE INSURANCE IN QUALIFIED PLANS

WHAT IS IT?

Life insurance can often be purchased under favorable terms and conditions through a qualified pension or profit sharing plan.[1] The insurance is purchased and owned by the plan, using employer contributions to the plan as a source of funds.

WHEN IS THE USE OF THIS TECHNIQUE INDICATED?

1. When a substantial number of employees covered under a qualified plan have an otherwise unmet life insurance need, either for family protection or estate liquidity.

2. When there are gaps and limitations in other company plans providing death benefits, such as group term life insurance plans, nonqualified deferred compensation plans, and split dollar plans. Planners should consider using life insurance in a qualified plan to fill those gaps or supplement those plans.

3. When a qualified plan for a closely held business or professional corporation is overfunded or close to the full funding limitation for regular trusteed plans, the addition of an incidental life insurance benefit, or a change to fully insured (IRC Section 412(i)) funding, may permit future deductible contributions at a higher rate than before.

4. When life insurance would be attractive to plan participants as an additional option for investing their plan accounts. This technique is most often used in a profit sharing or 401(k) plan but can be used in other types of defined contribution plans as well.

5. When an employer wants an extremely secure funding vehicle for a plan, with guarantees as to future plan costs and benefits.

6. Life insurance in a plan can provide funds to pay estate taxes, if any, thereby enhancing the ability of plan proceeds to provide financial security for the participant's survivors.

ADVANTAGES[2]

1. The premium is deductible by the employer as part of its annual contribution on behalf of covered employees.

2. Life insurance products in a qualified plan can provide employees with retirement benefits at more favorable terms than would be available through individually purchased products.

- *Lower premiums and higher dividends* – In many cases, the economies of scale and efficiency of operation combined with a lower lapse rate make life insurance sold through a qualified plan highly cost effective for the insurer. This administrative savings can be passed through to the plan in the form of lower premiums and/or higher dividends than would otherwise be payable (even on individual products).

- *"Locking in" present mortality standards* – Upon retirement, the employee's balance in the plan can be converted into an annuity for life at rates guaranteed today. When life insurance with a built in conversion to an annuity feature is acquired long before retirement, the employee may achieve more favorable guaranteed rates than might be offered in the future. The reason is that yearly payouts from life annuities may decrease as insurance companies adjust their mortality tables to account for longer life spans. But through life insurance purchased now, there is a rate guarantee that the annuity purchase rate will not increase in spite of longer life expectancies. Locking in at current rates may increase ultimate retirement income.

- *No sales fees or other costs to purchase annuities* – Unlike the case of a noninsured plan where the trustee must eventually sell trust assets (and incur attendant costs) and then purchase annuities to provide lifetime benefits (and incur yet another round of costs), when there is insurance in the plan, no extra fee or commission is paid for the purchase of lifetime annuities for retirees if done through the life insurance contract.

3. The "pure insurance" portion of a qualified plan death benefit (i.e., the death proceeds less any policy cash values) is not subject to regular income tax. In other words the tax is not imposed on death benefits in excess of the cash surrender value immediately before the employee's death. This makes it, dollar for dollar, a more effective means of transferring wealth than any other type of plan asset.

4. A fully insured plan (i.e., an IRC Section 412(i) plan holding only life insurance policies or annuity contracts and meeting certain other requirements) is "tax privileged." Fully insured plans generally are not subject to the Internal Revenue Code's "minimum funding" standards[3] and:

   a) are exempt from costly actuarial certification requirement – reducing the administrative overhead and complexity of a defined benefit plan; and

   b) generate a higher initial level of deductible plan contributions than a regular trusteed plan.

5. Some life insurance companies provide low cost installation and administrative services for plans using their investment products. This also reduces the employer's cost for the retirement plan.

6. In comparison to group term life insurance costs, life insurance within a qualified plan may be less expensive to the employee. This is because the employee can report the lower of the Table 2001 costs (see Figure 25.1; formerly P.S. 58 costs were used) or the insurance company's rate (which in almost every case will be significantly lower than the reportable Table 2001 cost). That reportable amount can be lower than the reportable income under Table I for the same amount of group term insurance.

7. From the employer's perspective, life insurance within the qualified plan may be less expensive than comparable group term insurance because the employer in a qualified plan saves the conversion cost of group insurance. In a large group insurance plan of 1,000 employees, the group conversion charge may range from $60 to $100 per thousand. Overall, this could result in a significant charge against dividends.

8. Greater amounts of life insurance can be provided to owner-employees through creative pension formulas than through group term plans. This is because there is more plan design flexibility in pension law than with respect to group term life law.

9. Substandard risks can obtain insurance that might otherwise not be available on an individual basis. The additional diversification and spreading of risk available in a retirement plan often enables an insurer to accept a risk that would be turned down on an individual basis. This "guaranteed issue" leverage can be quite important where the owner-employee is the individual who is considered a higher than standard risk.

10. Even if the life insurance company is not willing to issue life insurance on a "guaranteed issue" basis (generally starting at five or more insured lives), any ratings that must be paid are part of the employer's contribution to the plan and, thus, income tax deductible to the employer. If the additional rating is significant, the fact that the employer can deduct it may be extremely important.

11. Substandard ratings costs are not taxed to the insured employee. Not only is the employer paying the premium (through the plan) but the employer is also paying for any rating. Yet, in reporting taxable income, the employee reports the lower of Table 2001 (formerly P.S. 58) costs or the insurer's standard term rates – no matter how high the actual rating paid by the plan.

12. Life insurance in the plan transfers the death benefit risk to the insurer. This satisfies the moral obligation of the employer toward the family of the insured and will often provide significantly more dollars than if only the fund deposited to the employee's account were distributed at death.

13. In defined contribution plans, employees may elect to purchase insurance on the lives of certain relatives and even unrelated persons in whom they have an insurable interest. Within the statutory limits, the employee can buy as much as he wants to buy of the type of coverage he wants.[4] This makes creative planning and "matching the product to the problem" more likely. For instance, a plan participant can purchase insurance on a business partner and use the proceeds to fund a buy-sell agreement.

14. Life insurance within a defined benefit plan may create a larger deduction, even in plans that are "maxed out." Furthermore, it is possible to maintain a large death benefit in a defined benefit plan even if a participant's salary drops. For instance, if the plan's benefit formula is based on the employee's 3 highest consecutive years, the funding is based on those years even if currently the employee is earn-

ing significantly less. So the death benefit remains the same. Compare this with group coverage where the benefit drops if salary drops.

15. A qualified plan may be used to "incubate" (some say "season") a policy. In other words, the acquisition costs – the high up front costs in the early years of the policy when outlays are not reduced by dividends – can be supported by the pension plan at the cost of reporting the economic benefit of the term insurance. Assuming the covered employee then purchases the policy from the plan for its full value after – say eight years – the employee is receiving a policy with a lower premium than if he waited eight years and bought it on his own. If he has invested the money that he otherwise would have paid in premiums over those eight years, there should be enough to purchase the policy from the pension plan. At that time, dividends will be considerable and may even be enough to "vanish" the premiums.

16. At termination of employment for any reason or upon retirement, an employee can generally obtain an individual life insurance contract at original issue age rates. This makes coverage highly portable. It is also highly inexpensive in comparison to the conversion of group term insurance at the employee's then attained age. A policy "rolled out" to the insured can often be kept in force with little or no outlay at retirement.

17. It is often possible in a defined benefit plan to pay out both a benefit of 100 times and the auxiliary fund to the beneficiary of an older owner-employee participant.

DISADVANTAGES[5]

1. Some life insurance policies may provide a rate of return on their cash values which, as compared with alternative plan investments, may be relatively low. However, rates of return should be compared on investments of similar risk.

2. Policy expenses and commissions on life insurance products may be greater than for comparable investments.

3. Income tax is levied upon the death proceeds in an amount equal to the cash value portion of the policy immediately before the insured's death. This taxable amount may be lowered by the sum of any Table 2001 costs reported by the employee (for-

merly P.S. 58 costs were used). But this should be compared with the receipt of the entire proceeds income tax free when the policy is purchased outside a qualified plan with after-tax dollars.

4. Some authorities believe that since life insurance outside a qualified plan can definitely be kept from the insured's estate while exclusion of life insurance within a qualified plan from the insured's estate is uncertain (i.e., not tested), it makes sense from an estate tax viewpoint to purchase life insurance outside a qualified plan (assuming the insured is healthy and insurable at standard rates).

HOW IS IT DONE – AN EXAMPLE

Your client is the sole shareholder and president of a cash-rich, highly profitable closely held corporation that employs ten other individuals. The business has set up a qualified pension and a qualified profit sharing plan. The client is highly rated for insurance purposes and his attorney has suggested he increase his estate liquidity by purchasing at least $1,000,000 of additional life insurance. Although your client has a salary of $400,000 a year from the business, his standard of living is exceptionally high and he has six children, all in Ivy League colleges or graduate schools which leaves him with little spendable income.

Instead of purchasing the high premium life insurance with personal, after-tax dollars (of which he has little), he has both the pension and profit sharing plan amended to allow the purchase of life insurance on the lives of plan participants. The trustees then purchase life insurance on his life equal to the maximum amount allowable under current pension law and the client's irrevocable trust set up for his wife and children purchases the balance of the $1,000,000 his attorney suggested.

WHAT ARE THE TAX IMPLICATIONS?

1. Employer contributions to a qualified plan, including amounts used to purchase life insurance, are generally deductible. The amount of life insurance purchased must fall within "incidental limits."

   The "incidental" test – A qualified retirement plan must be primarily just that – a plan providing retirement benefits. But it may also provide for the payment of death benefits – through insurance or otherwise – as long as those benefits are "incidental." Life insurance can be used to provide an incidental death benefit to participants in a qualified retirement plan, either a defined contribution or defined benefit plan. The Service considers any nonretirement benefit in a qualified plan to be incidental so long as the cost of that benefit is less than 25% of the total cost of the plan. Stated as a fraction, this would be as follows:

Cost of providing current life and health insurance

Cost of providing all current and
deferred benefits under the plan

The ratio must be less than 25%. Since this standard by itself is difficult to apply, the IRS has developed two practical tests for life insurance in a qualified plan.

If the amount of insurance meets either of the following tests, it is considered incidental:

a) *"100 to 1" test* – The participant's insured death benefit must be no more than 100 times the expected monthly normal retirement age benefit,[6] or

b) *"Less than…" test* – The aggregate premiums paid over the life of the plan for any insured death benefit must at all times be less than the following percentages of the overall cost to provide plan benefits for that participant:

ordinary life[7]	50%
term insurance	25%
universal life	25%
variable life[8]	50%

Traditionally, defined contribution plans such as profit sharing plans have used the "percentage limits" in determining how much insurance to provide. Defined benefit plans have typically used the "100 times" limit. However, any type of plan can use either limit.

A profit sharing plan may be subject to slightly different rules. It may provide for the distribution of funds accumulated in the plan after a fixed number of years (as few as two).[9] If the plan provides that life insurance can only be purchased with funds that have been on deposit for the specified period, there is no statutory limit as to how much can be used to purchase life insurance.[10]

2. Some qualified retirement plans allow participants to supplement employer contributions with their own after-tax contributions. These after-tax contributions can be used to purchase life insurance without limit. Also, tax-exempt plan earnings can be used to purchase life insurance without regard to the incidental limitations discussed above. Note, however, that if amounts attributable to voluntary deductible contributions (VDECs) under prior law, including net earnings allocable to them, are used to purchase life insurance, such amounts are treated as distributed to the employee in the year so applied.[11]

3. In the case of life insurance purchased by a profit sharing plan on the life of a key individual who generated significant profits to the employer, the incidental test above should not apply to the extent the policy was payable to the profit sharing plan and shared with all plan participants as an "economic shock absorber," (i.e., as a key employee policy for the plan).

4. The economic value of pure life insurance coverage on a participant's life is taxed annually to the participant at the lower of (a) the IRS Table 2001 cost (see Figure 25.1 for Table 2001, which replaced the former P.S. 58 rates), or (b) the life insurance company's actual rates for individual one-year term policies available to all standard risks.[12] Any amount actually contributed to the plan by the participant is subtracted from this taxable amount if the plan provides for employee after-tax contributions to be applied to the purchase of life insurance.[13]

If the policy in question is a "survivorship" (so called second-to-die) contract, as long as both insureds are still alive, the imputed income is less than under a single life contract since the rates are lower and a different table (see Figure 25.2) with substantially lower rates is used.[14]

5. The income taxation of an insured death benefit received by a plan participant's beneficiary is as follows:

a) The "pure insurance" (also called "net amount at risk") element of an insured plan death benefit (i.e., the death benefit less any cash value) is income tax free to a participant's beneficiary.[15]

b) The total of all Table 2001 costs (formerly P.S. 58 costs were used) paid by the participant can be recovered tax free from the plan death benefit (if it is paid from the same insurance contracts that gave rise to the costs).[16]

Figure 25.1

TABLE 2001					
One Year Term Premiums for $1,000 of Life Insurance Protection – One Life					
Age	Premium	Age	Premium	Age	Premium
0	$0.70	34	$0.98	67	$15.20
1	0.41	35	0.99	68	16.92
2	0.27	36	1.01	69	18.70
3	0.19	37	1.04	70	20.62
4	0.13	38	1.06	71	22.72
5	0.13	39	1.07	72	25.07
6	0.14	40	1.10	73	27.57
7	0.15	41	1.13	74	30.18
8	0.16	42	1.20	75	33.05
9	0.16	43	1.29	76	36.33
10	0.16	44	1.40	77	40.17
11	0.19	45	1.53	78	44.33
12	0.24	46	1.67	79	49.23
13	0.28	47	1.83	80	54.56
14	0.33	48	1.98	81	60.51
15	0.38	49	2.13	82	66.74
16	0.52	50	2.30	83	73.07
17	0.57	51	2.52	84	80.35
18	0.59	52	2.81	85	88.76
19	0.61	53	3.20	86	99.16
20	0.62	54	3.65	87	110.40
21	0.62	55	4.15	88	121.85
22	0.64	56	4.68	89	133.40
23	0.66	57	5.20	90	144.30
24	0.68	58	5.66	91	155.80
25	0.71	59	6.06	92	168.75
26	0.73	60	6.51	93	186.44
27	0.76	61	7.11	94	206.70
28	0.80	62	7.96	95	228.35
29	0.83	63	9.08	96	250.01
30	0.87	64	10.41	97	265.09
31	0.90	65	11.90	98	270.11
32	0.93	66	13.51	99	281.05
33	0.96				

c) The sum of all nondeductible contributions toward the plan made by the employee in a contributory plan is tax free to the participant's beneficiary.[17]

d) Any loans made by the plan and taxed to the employee are recovered tax free by the beneficiary.

e) Any employer contributions to the plan that for some reason were taxed to the employee are tax free to the beneficiary.

f) The remainder of the distribution is taxed as a qualified plan distribution. This taxable portion of the distribution may be subject to the limited availability of 10-year averaging if the plan participant was over 59½ at death.[18] (10-year averaging is available only to plan participants born before 1936.)

6. Under 2004 guidance, the value of a life insurance contract sold or otherwise distributed from a plan is the contract's *cash value, without reduction for surren-*

Figure 25.2

AGE	5	10	15	20	25	30	35	40	45	50
			One Year Term Premiums for $1,000 of							
			*Joint and Survivor Life Insurance Protection**							
5	.00	.00	.00	.00	.00	.00	.00	.01	.01	.01
10	.00	.00	.00	.00	.00	.00	.00	.00	.01	.01
15	.00	.00	.00	.00	.00	.00	.00	.01	.01	.01
20	.00	.00	.00	.00	.00	.00	.01	.01	.01	.02
25	.00	.00	.00	.00	.00	.00	.01	.01	.01	.02
30	.00	.00	.00	.00	.00	.01	.01	.01	.02	.02
35	.00	.00	.00	.01	.01	.01	.01	.01	.02	.03
40	.01	.00	.01	.01	.01	.01	.01	.02	.03	.04
45	.01	.01	.01	.01	.01	.02	.02	.03	.04	.06
50	.01	.01	.01	.02	.02	.02	.03	.04	.06	.09
55	.02	.01	.02	.02	.03	.03	.05	.06	.09	.13
60	.03	.02	.03	.03	.04	.05	.07	.09	.13	.20
65	.04	.03	.04	.05	.06	.08	.10	.14	.20	.30
70	.06	.04	.06	.08	.10	.12	.16	.22	.31	.45
75	.09	.06	.10	.12	.14	.18	.24	.33	.47	.69
80	.14	.09	.14	.18	.22	.28	.37	.50	.72	1.05
85	.21	.14	.22	.28	.33	.42	.55	.76	1.08	1.58
90	.31	.21	.32	.41	.49	.61	.81	1.12	1.59	2.33
95	.44	.30	.46	.59	.70	.88	1.17	1.61	2.29	3.36
100	.61	.42	.64	.81	.98	1.23	1.62	2.23	3.18	4.66

AGE	55	60	65	70	75	80	85	90	95	100
5	.02	.03	.04	.06	.09	.14	.21	.31	.44	.61
10	.01	.02	.03	.04	.06	.09	.14	.21	.30	.42
15	.02	.03	.04	.06	.10	.14	.22	.32	.46	.64
20	.02	.03	.05	.08	.12	.18	.28	.41	.59	.81
25	.03	.04	.06	.10	.14	.22	.33	.49	.70	.98
30	.03	.05	.08	.12	.18	.28	.42	.61	.88	1.23
35	.05	.07	.10	.16	.24	.37	.55	.81	1.17	1.62
40	.06	.09	.14	.22	.33	.50	.76	1.12	1.61	2.23
45	.09	.13	.20	.31	.47	.72	1.08	1.59	2.29	3.18
50	.13	.20	.30	.45	.69	1.05	1.58	2.33	3.36	4.66
55	.19	.29	.44	.68	1.03	1.56	2.35	3.47	5.00	6.94
60	.29	.44	.67	1.02	1.56	2.36	3.54	5.24	7.55	10.47
65	.44	.67	1.02	1.55	2.37	3.59	5.39	7.96	11.47	15.92
70	.68	1.02	1.55	2.37	3.61	5.47	8.22	12.14	17.49	24.28
75	1.03	1.56	2.37	3.61	5.50	8.33	12.52	18.50	26.65	37.00
80	1.56	2.36	3.59	5.47	8.33	12.64	18.98	28.05	40.42	56.10
85	2.35	3.54	5.39	8.22	12.52	18.98	28.51	42.13	60.70	84.26
90	3.47	5.24	7.96	12.14	18.50	28.05	42.13	62.26	89.70	124.52
95	5.00	7.55	11.47	17.49	26.65	40.42	60.70	89.70	129.26	179.42
100	6.94	10.47	15.92	24.28	37.00	56.10	84.26	124.52	179.42	249.05

* Rates are derived by a *Tax Facts* editor from U.S. Life Table 38. They are based on the underlying actuarial assumptions of the P.S. 58 rates. The method for deriving the rates is also based upon an unofficial informational letter of Norman Greenberg, Chief, Actuarial Branch, Department of the Treasury. The letter indicates that after the first death, the single life regular P.S. 58 rates are to be used. Due to space limitations, the table is presented in 5-year age increments. For planning purposes, it is suggested that each actual age be rounded to the nearest corresponding age in the table.

der charges, provided that amount is at least as large as the aggregate of: (a) premiums paid from the date of issue through the date of determination (generally the distribution date); plus (b) any amounts credited with respect to those premiums (e.g., dividends and interest, whether under the contract or otherwise); *or*, in the case of a variable contract, all adjustments made with respect to the premiums paid during that period (whether under the contract or otherwise) that reflect investment return and the current market value of segregated asset accounts; minus (c) reasonable mortality charges and reasonable other charges that are actually charged from the date of issue to the date of distribution, and that are actually expected to be paid.[19]

7. Qualified plan death benefits are, in general, included in a decedent's estate for federal estate tax purposes. However, some authorities (not including the authors) believe it may be possible to exclude the insured portion of the death benefit if the decedent had no "incidents of ownership" in the policy. This "subtrust" planning technique is discussed further in the "Questions and Answers," below.

QUESTIONS AND ANSWERS

Question – Can life insurance be used in a Keogh (HR-10) plan?

Answer – A Keogh plan is a qualified plan covering a proprietor or one or more partners of an unincorporated business. Life insurance can be used to provide a death benefit for regular employees covered under the plan, and the rules discussed in this chapter apply. Life insurance can also be provided under the plan for a proprietor or partners. However, slightly less favorable rules apply.[20] For example, amounts contributed to the plan for the purchase of life insurance for a self-employed person are not deductible,[21] nor can such amounts be recovered tax free from benefits received under the policy.[22]

Question – Can life insurance be used in an IRC Section 403(b) tax deferred annuity plan?

Answer – Life insurance can be provided as an incidental benefit under a tax deferred annuity plan.[23] It is provided on much the same basis as in a qualified profit sharing plan and subject to the same limits. Covered employees will have Table 2001 (formerly P.S. 58) costs to report as taxable income, as in a regular qualified plan.

Question – Why might it make sense to transfer life insurance from inside a plan to outside?

Answer – There are several reasons that a planner may consider removing life insurance from a qualified retirement plan. These include:

1. Fund assets can be invested more profitably in an alternative manner.

2. It is more likely that the assets can be safely excluded from the participant's estate.

Question – Assuming that the planning team feels that life insurance presently included in a qualified plan should be removed, how is this best accomplished?

Answer – A life insurance policy may be distributed from a plan to (a) the insured (who must also be a plan participant) or (b) a relative of the insured participant (who is also a beneficiary under the policy).[24]

The tactics to remove a policy from a qualified plan will depend on whether the policy is term or whole life.

If the policy is a *term* policy, the intended third party owner (e.g., the participant's irrevocable trust or child) should purchase a new term contract. Once it is in force, allow the term policy inside the retirement plan to lapse. (Of course, this assumes the participant is insurable at standard rates. If the participant is insurable only at a high rating or is uninsurable, use the procedure for whole life.)

If the policy is a *whole life* policy, sell the policy to the insured. However, note that under 2004 guidance, the value of the policy coming out of the plan is determined under special rules. See item 6 under "What are the Tax Implications." The insured can then make a gift (i.e., a transfer of the policy for "love and affection") to the third party who is meant to be the eventual owner and beneficiary. This two step process is vital to satisfy the "prohibited transaction" rules and to avoid the deadly impact (proceeds lose income tax free status) of the transfer for value rule.[25] Furthermore, the insured must survive more than three years from the date he or she makes a gift of the policy to its intended third party owner. (But this is of little additional risk since, had the participant done nothing, it would have been in the estate anyway.)

Question – Can a corporation or plan participant transfer personally-owned life insurance into a qualified plan?

Answer – Life insurance owned by a business or plan participant can (with care) be transferred by contribution or sale into a qualified retirement plan. This will generally make premiums "deductible" and relieve the corporation or participant from the burden of paying those premiums.

Before any such transfer, planners should consider:

- *The insurance needs of the transferor* – Perhaps the corporation that needs key employee coverage or the individual whose family needs coverage should not be assigning current coverage but should instead be encouraging the retirement plan to purchase additional coverage.

- *"Prohibited transaction" rules* – Ensure that the contribution of a life insurance policy to a plan by an employer or by the individual participant satisfies the prohibited transaction exemption.[26]

- *The taxation of life insurance proceeds from a qualified plan* – Payments made from the plan to the employee's beneficiary will not be totally income tax free (as they would have been had no transfer been made). Only the "pure life insurance" (i.e., the net amount at risk) will continue to be treated as life insurance. In other words, once an existing policy is transferred to the retirement plan, only the excess of the death benefit over the policy's cash value at the time of the participant's death will retain its income tax free status when paid out.[27]

Question – Can universal life insurance be used to provide an insured death benefit under a qualified plan?

Answer – Universal life and similar products may be used. However, even though universal life has an investment element like that in a whole life policy, the Service has taken the view that the incidental limits are applied as in the case of term insurance – that is, the aggregate premiums paid must be less than 25% of aggregate plan contributions for the participant. While this is clearly incorrect (since a portion of a universal life premium represents a savings or investment element), neither the Service nor the courts have yet offered relief from this 25% limitation.

Question – Can a participant in a qualified plan have the plan purchase life insurance on the life of a spouse or a business partner?

Answer – Yes. Some of the applications of this technique are: (1) the purchase of life insurance on a co-shareholder to help fund a buy-sell agreement; or (2) to provide for a beneficiary and avoid estate taxes on the death of the employee-participant. Second-to-die insurance is sometimes used for this latter purpose.

These "third-party" insurance techniques are primarily used in qualified profit sharing or stock bonus plans because of the need for an "earmarked" or "directed investment" account, as well as rulings prohibiting pension plans from providing third-party insurance.[28]

Question – Can a qualified plan trustee borrow against the cash value of life insurance policies held in the plan?

Answer – Yes, but borrowing by the plan creates "unrelated business taxable income" from any reinvestment of the loan proceeds. For example, if the loan proceeds are reinvested in certificates of deposit, the plan must pay tax on interest income from those certificates.[29]

Question – Why is life insurance in defined benefit plans particularly advantageous?

Answer – Life insurance is particularly advantageous in defined benefit plans because it *adds* to the limit on deductible contributions. This add-on feature allows greater tax deferred funding of the plan. A defined benefit plan can be funded to provide the maximum tax-deductible contribution for retirement benefits for each participant. The cost for life insurance can then be added to this amount and deducted.

By comparison, in a defined contribution plan, the costs of the life insurance must be part of the contributions to each participant's account. Using life insurance does not increase the IRC Section 415 annual additions limit for participants' accounts in defined contribution plans. That limit is the lesser of

(a) 100% of compensation or (b) $41,000 (in 2004, as indexed) whether or not life insurance is provided.[30]

Question – How can life insurance help to solve the problem of excessive taxation when a large distribution from a qualified plan is made upon the death of the participant to the participant's grandchild?

Answer – Rather than accept the imposition of three different taxes[31] (i.e., up to 55% estate tax, 55% generation-skipping transfer tax, and income tax at the beneficiary's rate), the participant should consider leveraging the qualified plan account to provide tax-free benefits for future generations. This can be accomplished by establishing an irrevocable trust to be the applicant-owner-beneficiary of insurance on the participant's life and taking early distributions[32] from the qualified plan to pay the annual premiums.

If the above plan were not undertaken and all three taxes applied, the participant's grandchild would likely receive less than 20¢ on the dollar. By withdrawing substantial sums and purchasing life insurance through an irrevocable trust, the grandchild would likely receive twice that amount (the net proceeds payable from the plan plus the tax free proceeds from the life insurance on the participant's life). If the participant were married, a survivorship life policy could be purchased by the trust that would pay off upon the death of the second to die. In such a case, much more insurance could be purchased with the same annual premium and the heirs could net as much as two or three times what they otherwise would have received.

Question – How can an employer cut turnover costs involved where life insurance is purchased on covered employees?

Answer – Turnover costs involved in buying cash value insurance policies can be minimized by having a longer waiting period for insurance than the plan's waiting period for entry. In the interim period, the death benefit for participants not covered by cash value policies can be provided by term insurance. In the past, many plans did not provide insurance for employees who were beyond a specified cutoff age. Under current age discrimination requirements, this probably is no longer allowed.

Question – Can insurance coverage be conditioned on the taking of a medical examination?

Answer – Yes. Insurance coverage can be conditioned on taking a medical exam if this does not result in discrimination in favor of highly compensated employees. For employees who do not "pass" the medical exam, insurance is typically limited to the amount, if any, that can be purchased for them using the amount of premium dollars that would be available if they were insurable. For example, if the plan's insurance formula provides insurance of 100 times the monthly benefit for standard risks (i.e., those employees who pass the medical exam), the insurance provided for a medically "rated" employee might be only 50 times the monthly benefit, since a 50 times benefit for that employee would cost as much to provide as a 100 times benefit for a standard risk.

Question – Does the Department of Labor (DOL) have a problem with whole life in pension plans?

Answer – The DOL has alleged that it is a breach of fiduciary duty to fund death benefits in qualified pension plans with permanent life insurance.[33] Their suggestion is that whole life insurance is too expensive to fund such death benefits and that "less expensive" term should be used. Planners should note, however, that in each of the cases where the DOL alleged a breach of fiduciary duties under the Employee Retirement Income Security Act (ERISA), the plans were very large, yet the policies purchased were individual contracts with relatively high loadings and commission structures.

In the authors' opinion, had the plans used low load group vehicles rather than individual contracts the DOL would not have objected nor would the courts have supported the DOL. The plan trustees, insurance agents, and insurer did not "match the product with the problem." The issue also gives fair warning to life underwriters not to serve as plan fiduciaries if a conflict of interest attack is to be avoided.

Question – Under the concept of "pension maximizing," how can life insurance be used for retirement planning as an alternative to the joint and survivor annuity?

Answer – If an individual participates in a qualified defined benefit plan or other pension plan maintained by his employer or business, the participant's spouse is generally entitled to a "survivor annuity" under the plan. Under most of these provisions, if the plan participant dies before the spouse, the plan pays the spouse an annuity (at least) equal to 50% or more of the "joint annuity" paid (or payable) during the participant's life.[34] This spousal benefit is a right guaranteed under federal law. However, the spouse generally has the option under the plan of "waiving" the right to the spousal benefit; the result of waiving this benefit is that the participant receives a larger monthly benefit during the participant's lifetime. Under a technique referred to as "pension maximizing," it may be better in a few cases to provide security for the spouse using life insurance on the participant's life. The spouse can then waive the survivor annuity, and the extra monthly income received during the participant's lifetime can help to recover, in part or fully, the cost of the life insurance. This concept is fully explained in Chapter 27.

Question – What is the "subtrust" concept and does it work?

Answer – Some authorities have suggested that it is still possible to avoid federal estate taxation on life insurance proceeds paid as part of a distribution from a qualified retirement plan through a "subtrust" concept.[35] One variation of this technique works like this:

- Step 1: The insured-participant makes an irrevocable beneficiary designation that divests him of the right to change the beneficiary of plan proceeds.

- Step 2: The qualified plan is amended to provide that the policy will not be distributed to the insured at retirement. This amendment is made to eliminate an IRS argument that the insured retained a reversionary interest in the policy.

- Step 3: The plan is amended to give the insured a right to purchase the policy for its full value at retirement.

- Step 4: To insulate an insured who is also a trustee of the plan from an incidents of ownership attack by the IRS, a special trust (subtrust) is created. Policies on the life of the insured-trustee are placed into the subtrust. The insured is given no control over the subtrust and cannot remove its independent trustee.

Will this subtrust concept work? Are there hidden tax problems associated with it? Because there are no cases on point nor at this date any rulings no one can be sure. One commentator has stated:

> …while the exclusion of life insurance from a participant's taxable estate is not impossible, sufficient consideration has not been given to the legal problems which this effort entails or to the legal procedures that must be followed if these problems are to be solved.[36]

If the insured has incidents of ownership and then divests himself of them as Step 1 of the subtrust technique suggests, a gift is made. This would seem to be the result if the irrevocable beneficiary designation is successful. There are several implications to such a gratuitous transfer:

- If the coverage itself has been given away, then the IRS could deem each future premium actually paid by the employer as though it were a gift made by the insured-participant to the new owner. This is consistent with the way group term life assignments are treated.

- Such gifts would not qualify for the gift tax annual exclusion since the beneficiary-owner does not have an immediate, unfettered, and ascertainable right to use, possess, or enjoy a policy that is presently inside a qualified plan.

- If neither the original assignment nor the annual premium payments can be considered present interest gifts, the transfers could not qualify for the "annual exclusion" exemption for generation skipping transfers.[37]

- If the plan participant dies within three years of the "gift" (the irrevocable beneficiary designation), the proceeds of the policy could be brought back into the estate under IRC Section 2035.

- In a small plan where the auxiliary fund is not sufficient by itself to fund the retirement benefit of the insured-participant without the cash values of the policy, it appears that the participant has a legal right to expect to get whatever it takes to pay the promised benefit – including any cash values necessary to "top off" the appropriate funding to adequate levels. That legal right may equate to a "reversionary interest" (i.e., a possibility that the policy or its proceeds may return to the decedent or his estate). This could pull the proceeds back into the insured's estate. Although there may be a solution to this dilemma, it is neither simple nor inexpensive and not certain to work.[38]

Step three of the subtrust plan indicates that the insured plan participant would be given a right to purchase the policy on his life. Although there is authority that such a right will not be considered an incident of ownership,[39] there is also evidence that the IRS may not agree. But if the insured does purchase the policy, the IRC Section 2035 three year clock begins ticking – not from the date of the original assignment or the participant's repurchase of the policy – but from the date of the second transfer of the policy. This, of course, endangers the estate tax savings goal of the entire technique.

If the trustee of the subtrust can be removed by the corporation and replaced by a new corporate appointee, will the corporation's power over the trustee be equated to an incident of ownership over the insurance in the subtrust? If so, will a controlling shareholder be deemed to control the policy in the subtrust by virtue of his control over the corporation?

What remains to be seen is: (i) whether the design and administration of these concepts can be made to work for clients who want *simple* solutions to their problems, (ii) whether clients are willing to pay for the design and implementation of these programs, (iii) whether an institutional framework can be developed to provide for the administration of these concepts, and (iv) if all the above is accomplished, whether a revenue-driven Congress will allow these concepts to remain available as a means of keeping life insurance out of a participant's taxable estate.[40]

Alternative to the subtrust concept – It is possible and sometimes desirable to remove life insurance from a qualified plan. The easiest way is for the trustee to allow the policy to lapse and for new insurance to be purchased outside the plan (preferably by adult beneficiaries or a trust for the intended recipient of the proceeds). A sale by the retirement plan of the policy to the insured is another possibility where the insured is in ill health, the policy in

question is beyond the incontestable period, or for whatever other reason the participant does not want the original policy to lapse (see discussion above).

Question – Can life insurance for key employees and business owners be made – at least indirectly – tax deductible by purchasing it through a welfare benefit (IRC Section 419) plan?

Answer – Not in the opinion of the authors. There are a number of individuals marketing a plan that provides death benefits and dismissal wage benefits to specified employees of participating employers, mostly very highly compensated owners of small business and professional practices with no more than ten or twelve employees. The plans promise "meaningful tax deferral to small businesses with few employees, tax deductible contributions for employee benefits, the accumulation of wealth to selected individuals through appreciation of assets purchased by the plan with their contributions," and fewer limitations on funding than a defined benefit pension plan, as well as promising to make it much easier for participants to reach plan assets and acquire benefits.

The tax benefits promised under these plans are based on the provisions of IRC Section 419, which sets forth certain limits on deductible contributions to welfare benefit plans (providing medical, disability, and life benefits for employees and independent contractors). These are generally plans established by large employers who are in essence self-insuring and creating a fund on behalf of their employees to which the employer makes contributions and deducts those payments. Money is paid out of the funds held inside the plan as claims are incurred by covered employees.

Generally, IRC Sections 419 and 419A limit the employer's deduction for contributions to a welfare benefits fund; however, an exception applies to "10 or more" employer plans.[41] To achieve their goals, the plans must qualify for this exception. The "10 or more" exception is not available to any plan that maintains experience-rating arrangements with respect to individual employers, no one of which made more than 10 percent of the trust's total contributions. The recurring issue is this: Is the plan an aggregation of individual plans and therefore not permitted to take advantage of the safe harbor exception to IRC Section 419A, or is the plan a single 10 or more employer plan that falls within the protection of the special safe harbor exception to IRC Section 419A?

Planners must remember that the principal purpose of a portion of IRC Section 419A is "to prevent employers from taking premature deductions, for expenses that have not yet been incurred." The exception for 10 or more employer plans was meant to apply only where there was genuine risk shifting into the pool, that is, an arrangement akin to the purchase of insurance (as opposed to self-funding of a risk). In each of the arrangements the authors have seen, there is an aggregation of individual, unique plans formed by separate employers who delegated to a common administrator their duties and responsibilities, but who expected that funds contributed to a trust fund would be disbursed according to each employer's contributions (and the earnings generated from those contributions) for the benefit of only that employer's employees. Each employer separately selected many of the relevant terms under which employees would receive benefits (e.g. vesting schedule, level of benefits, participation requirements) and no group of employees had any rights to the contributions or earnings on those contributions made by some other employer. There was no pooling of risks with other employers; only separate accounts and separate accounting. And "experience rating," the charging back of employee claims to the employer's account, was just what was done in most plans reviewed by the authors when the employee's benefits were adjusted to equal his or her employer's contributions. Benefits were limited to what was in an employer's account. So none of those plans could meet the spirit and letter of the law. Is it possible to design a plan that could meet both tests? Certainly. But the result may not be appealing to the smaller employer.[42]

Final regulations for 419A(f)(6) plans provide the following: (1) the basic requirements for a valid 10 or more employer plan; (2) the characteristics indicating when a plan is not a 10 or more employer plan; (3) which arrangements will be considered "experience-rating arrangements"; (4) special rules; and (5) definitions of key terms.[43]

Question – Can second-to-die insurance be used inside a qualified pension plan?

Answer – Many authorities seem to believe it should not. In a 1997 bulletin reporting on the American Society of Pension Actuaries Conference that year, the AALU reported that the IRS may question the acceptability of the acquisition by a qualified pension plan of a second to die contract – presumably on the lives of an employee participant and that person's spouse.

BNA (the Bureau of National Affairs, a private tax reporting service) has reported that "Employers considering second-to-die life insurance contracts inside defined benefit or money purchase plans would be well advised to reconsider."[44]

Question – Can springing value life insurance be safely used in qualified retirement plans?

Answer – In the authors' opinion, this is a dangerous practice and will almost certainly subject the client to an audit. The IRS has made it clear in 2004 guidance that new valuation rules will determine the tax treatment of such policies.[45] For details, see item 6 above, under "What are the Tax Implications."

CHAPTER ENDNOTES

1. For information on qualified plan rules, see S. Leimberg and J. McFadden, *The Tools and Techniques of Employee Benefit and Retirement Planning*, 8th Ed. (Cincinnati, OH: The National Underwriter Company, 2003). See also, H. Zaritsky and S. Leimberg, *Tax Planning with Life Insurance* (RIA Group, 1999).

2. For an excellent summary of over 40 such reasons, see Deppe, "Life Insurance in Qualified Retirement Plans," *The First Annual Henry A. Deppe Lecture* (Bryn Mawr, PA: The American College, 1990). See also, Zaritsky and Leimberg, note 1 above.

3. IRC Sec. 412(i), 412(h). The advantages of fully insured plans described in this chapter assume that the plan operates within the requirements of IRC Section 412(i) and satisfies the guidelines set forth in the following 2004 guidance: REG-126967-03, 2004-10 IRB 566; Rev. Proc. 2004-16, 2004-10 IRB 559; Rev. Rul. 2004-20, 2004-10 IRB 546, and Rev. Rul. 2004-21, 2004-10 IRB 544.

4. Where an individually allocated account exists, the participant may be able to decide whether or not to use employer dollars to pay premiums. For example, a young individual with family obligations can elect to have anything less than 50% of the employer profit sharing allocations paid as premiums on a low premium policy. An older participant with no family may direct that lesser amounts be used to purchase life insurance. Still others may choose to have none of the contributions directed toward life insurance.

5. In deciding whether to place needed life insurance inside or outside a qualified plan, the following steps should be taken: list the alternatives available, state the advantages and disadvantages of each, and assign a ranking of importance to each advantage and disadvantage. The final decision should be based on a quantitative assessment of economic value and psychological gains and costs.

6. Stated more completely, the "incidental" test is automatically satisfied if the death benefit will not be more than the amount of death benefit that would be payable if all plan benefits were funded through retirement income endowment policies that have a death benefit of $1,000, or the reserve, if greater, for each $10 per month of life annuity the policy guarantees at retirement age. See, e.g., Rev. Rul. 60-83, 1960-1 CB 157; Rev. Rul. 61-121, 1961-2 CB 65. So if a participant covered under a defined benefit pension earns $48,000 a year and the plan will pay $2,000 a month at normal retirement age, the pension can purchase up to $200,000

of life insurance. Technically, the 100 to 1 ratio test is not a Code imposed limitation, but a "safe harbor."

7. Certain types of whole life insurance with decreasing coverage generally will be treated as term insurance by the Service. In that case, the amount of employer contribution allocated to purchase insurance must be less than 25%. See, e.g., Rev. Rul. 76-353, 1976-2 CB 112.

8. See Let. Rul. 9014068.

9. A profit sharing plan may also provide for the distribution of plan assets at the attainment of a specified age or upon the prior occurrence of an illness, death, termination of employment, or even a layoff. Treas. Reg. §1.104-1(b)(ii).

10. See Rev. Rul. 61-164, 1961-2 CB 99; Rev. Rul. 66-143, 1966-1 CB 79.

11. IRC Sec. 72(o)(3)(B).

12. IRC Sec. 72(m)(3)(B); Treas. Reg. §1.72-16(b).

13. Rev. Rul. 68-390, 1968-2 CB 175.

14. After the first death, the single life Table 2001 should be used.

15. Treas. Reg. §1.72-16(c)(4). This portion will be taxed as ordinary income if the employee failed to report the Table 2001 costs.

16. Treas. Reg. §1.72-16(b)(4).

17. See Treas. Reg. §1.402(a)-1(a)(5).

18. If the decedent participated in the plan before 1987, there are also some favorable "grandfather" provisions that may apply. See Leimberg and McFadden, note 1 above, at p. 223-224.

19. See Rev. Proc. 2004-16, 2004-10 IRB 559.

20. For a discussion of these rules, see Leimberg and McFadden, note 1 above, at p. 73.

21. IRC Sec. 404(e).

22. Treas. Reg. §1.72-16(b)(4).

23. Treas. Reg. §1.403(b)-1(c)(3).

24. Ordinarily, a sale of any asset – including life insurance – by the retirement plan to a participant would be considered a "prohibited transaction." See IRC Sec. 4975(c)(1)(A); ERISA Sec. 406(a)(1)(A). However, PTE 92-6, 57 Fed. Reg. 5189, permits the sale of a life insurance contract by the plan to (a) the insured, (b) the insured's relative who is a beneficiary under the contract, (c) an employer whose employees are covered under the plan or (d) to another employee benefit plan if: (1) the contract would, but for the sale, be surrendered by the plan; (2) the amount received, in exchange for the policy, by the plan is at least equal to the amount necessary to put the plan in the same cash position it would have been had it retained the contract, surrendered it, and made any distribution owing to the participant; (3) the sale does not discriminate in form or operation in favor of plan participants who are officers, shareholders, or highly compensated employees; and (4) with respect to sales of the policy to anyone other than the insured, the participant is informed of the proposed sale, is given an option to purchase the policy before the plan can sell it to anyone else, and consents in writing to the sale.

25. For information on the transfer for value rule, see Appendix G.

26. PTE 92-5, 57 Fed. Reg. 5019.

27. IRC Sec. 72(m)(3)(C).

28. See Leimberg and McFadden, note 1 above, Chapters 15 and 18.

29. See, e.g., *Sisken Memorial Foundation, Inc. v. U.S.*, 790 F.2d 480 (6th Cir. 1986), *aff'g* 603 F.Supp. 91 (E.D. Tenn. 1984).

30. See IRC Sec. 415(c), Notice 2003-73, 2003-45 IRB 1017.

31. For decedents dying prior to 1997, there was also a 15 percent excess accumulations tax imposed on "excess" plan assets at the death of the participant. See IRC Sec. 4980A, repealed by TRA '97, Sec. 1073.

32. Income taxes and, possibly, the 10% early withdrawal penalty would apply. See IRC Sec. 72(t).

33. See, e.g., *Washington Report* (AALU 1992), Nos. 92-88, 92-80, 92-46, 92-22.

34. IRC Sec. 417(b).

35. See Eliasberg, "IRS Opens the Way Toward Favorable Estate and Income Tax Treatment of Plan Distributions," 10 *Estate Planning* 208, July 1983; "Here's How to Exclude Insurance in the Pension Plan from the Taxable Estate," *Life Association News*, August 1985, p. 179. See also Fair, "The Qualified Plan as an Estate Planning Tool," The Guardian Life Insurance Company of America.

36. See Pincus, "Subtrusts and Reversionary Interests: A Review of Current Options," *Journal of the Society of Financial Service Professionals*, September 1992, p. 64.

37. IRC Sec. 2642(c).

38. See Pincus, note 36 above, at p. 65.

39. See *Estate of John Smith v. Comm.*, 73 TC 307 (1979), *acq. in result*, 1981-1 CB 2.

40. See Pincus, note 36 above, at p. 68.

41. See IRC Section 419A(f)(6).

42. *Booth v. Comm.*, 108 TC 524 (1997); IRC Sections 419; 419A(f)(6); Notice 95-34, 1995-1 CB 309.

43. Treas. Reg. Sec. 1.419A(f)(6)-1; TD 9079, 69 Fed. Reg. 42254 (7-17-2003).

44. AALU Bulletin No. 97-99; BNA Pensions and Benefits Daily, November 6 1997.

45. See Rev. Proc. 2004-16, 2004-10 IRB 559, and REG-126967-03, 2004-10 IRB 566. Related guidance was provided Rev. Rul. 2004-20, 2004-10 IRB 546, and Rev. Rul. 2004-21, 2004-10 IRB 544.

Chapter 26

NONQUALIFIED DEFERRED COMPENSATION

WHAT IS IT?

Deferred compensation is a contractual arrangement between the employer and employee in which the employer generally makes an unsecured promise to pay benefits in a future tax year in exchange for services rendered currently. Nonqualified plans can also be set up for outside directors and other independent contractors. In general, the same tax rules that apply in employer-employee plans apply to plans that cover independent contractors.[1] One distinction with respect to plans covering only independent contractors is that ERISA does not apply.

A nonqualified deferred compensation plan is a deferred compensation plan that does *not* meet the tax and labor law requirements applicable to qualified plans.[2]

There are two major types of nonqualified deferred compensation plans: (1) "in addition" plans, also called "salary continuation" plans; and (2) "elective" plans, also called "salary reduction" plans.

"In addition" nonqualified deferred compensation plans are used to provide retirement benefits to a select group of executives (or other key employees), or to provide that select group with supplemental benefits *over and above* those provided by the employer's qualified plan. This is a nonelective form of deferred compensation; the employer provides it in addition to the key employee's salary and other compensation.

"Elective" nonqualified deferred compensation plans are those under which key employees voluntarily choose to defer a portion of their future salary (or bonus) as a means of tax deferred savings.

WHEN IS THE USE OF SUCH A DEVICE INDICATED?

A nonqualified deferred compensation plan should be considered by planners using the same critical overlay and analysis as is appropriate with any other life insurance planning tool. There are no clear cut "right or wrong" answers, and there are no "no cost" solutions.

The best course of action is to evaluate each of the viable alternative tools or techniques (such as Section 162 plans, split dollar life insurance, etc.) based upon the following six criteria:

1. What is the relative *tax* efficiency based upon current and probable future tax rates?

2. What is the probability of achieving the employer's objectives? In other words, what is the "cost efficiency"?

3. What security does the tool provide against employer insolvency?

4. Does the plan provide security in the event of management or ownership changes?

5. Can the employer keep or obtain the use of plan funds for an emergency or opportunity?

6. How easy is it to implement, explain, and maintain the plan?

A nonqualified deferred compensation plan is indicated in the following situations.

1. When an employer has had enough of the qualified plan "blues": increasing costs, decreasing employer discretion and control, and too many limitations on the benefits that may be provided to highly paid and owner-employees. In short, a nonqualified plan should be considered when an employer wants to decrease or eliminate the costs associated with a qualified plan.

2. When an employer would like to provide a retirement and/or death benefit to one or more key employees, but does not want the prohibitive cost or aggravation of a qualified plan or does not want to cover all the employees that must be covered under a qualified plan.

3. When an employer wants to provide *additional* benefits to an executive who is already receiv-

ing the maximum benefits or contributions under the employer's qualified plan. Supplemental benefits provided to key individuals under a nonqualified plan provide an excellent means of overcoming the IRC Section 415 limits placed upon a qualified plan.

4. When an employer wants certain key employees to have tax deferred compensation in different *amounts* or under different *terms* or different *conditions* from that provided to other employees.

5. When an employer seeks to establish an automatic and relatively painless investment program that uses *corporate* tax deductions to *leverage* the employee's future benefits. Because amounts paid by the corporation are generally deductible when paid, employer tax savings can considerably boost the amount payable to the key employee. For instance, suppose the employer is in a 40% combined federal and state bracket when benefits are paid. To pay benefits of $100,000 per year costs only $60,000, because a 40% deduction of the $100,000 distribution yields a $40,000 tax saving.

6. When an employer is seeking a tool to recruit, retain, retire, and reward key personnel without the limitations of a qualified plan.[3] Because nonqualified deferred compensation plans work in closely held corporations, smaller firms can use them as a replacement for (or to compete against) the equity-based compensation packages, such as company stock or stock options, that an employee of a publicly held company would expect to receive.

A nonqualified deferred compensation plan is generally not indicated when it is not likely that the business will survive the death, disability, or retirement of its key employees.

ADVANTAGES

1. There is much more *flexibility* in nonqualified deferred compensation plan design than in qualified plan design. For instance, an employer can pick and choose who will be covered, the levels of coverage (subject to the reasonable compensation limits on deductibility), and the terms and conditions of coverage. Also, an employer can provide that plan benefits will be forfeited *entirely* according to *any*

vesting schedule or upon any reasonable contingency. For instance, an employer can cut off all benefits if the employee terminates prior to a specified age or if the employee goes to work for a competitor. This means a nonqualified deferred compensation plan can be highly effective with respect to both costs and taxes.

Restrictions can be placed in the plan that will enable the employer to either (a) achieve its business goals or (b) recoup its funds, so that either the plan accomplishes what it was intended to accomplish or the employer gets its money back.

2. Nonqualified plans can escape (completely or in large part) a variety of government requirements imposed upon qualified plans, such as reporting and disclosure requirements, participation and vesting requirements, and fiduciary responsibility requirements.[4]

3. In general, covered employees are not taxed on benefits under nonqualified plans until they actually receive a distribution. Dollars growing over the deferral period currently grow tax free and, therefore, typically grow beyond the level that the employee would have realized, had the employee invested the after-tax dollars.

4. Employers using properly arranged nonqualified deferred compensation plans financed with life insurance are not currently taxed on the earnings, because tax on the inside buildup of cash surrender values is deferred until distribution.

5. The employer's deduction generally may be based upon benefits paid out of the plan, rather than upon contributions paid into the plan (this does not apply to a funded nonqualified deferred compensation plan). Consequently, the employer's deduction may be based upon an amount that is much larger than its original investment. So, if the employer's tax rates *do* increase between the date when the contributions are made to the plan and the payment of benefits, the value of the employer's deduction – and therefore its leverage – also increases.

6. The employee and employer may also take advantage of additional tax leverage. At the time when the payout period begins, the employer takes the cash it has and pays it out as tax deductible salary. Because of the employer's deduction, it can pay a larger amount to the employee. For example, if an employer is in a combined 40% state and federal

bracket and is obligated to pay out $10,000 a year, the after-deduction cost is only $6,000. But the employer could choose to incur a cost of $10,000 a year – and in fact pay out $16,667 [$16,667 - (.40 x $16,667) = $10,000].

The formula in the agreement between the employer and the covered employee could provide that the corporation would pay out a given percentage of earmarked cash funds on hand each year, multiplied by a fraction reflecting the employer's tax bracket that year.

DISADVANTAGES

1. The employer's income tax deduction is ordinarily deferred until the year in which income is taxable to the covered employee. This may be as many as 20 or more years from the time when the employer begins financing the obligation (for example, by paying premiums on a life insurance policy). However, if cash flow is a problem, the employer can reduce the contribution to the amount equal to the net, post-deduction contribution cost that the employer would have incurred, had an immediate deduction been available. For example, if the employer is in a 40% bracket (federal and state), and a deduction were allowed immediately, a contribution of $10,000 would result in a $4,000 deduction and an after-deduction cost of $6,000. So, in this example, a solution to cash flow problems might be to contribute only $6,000 each year.

2. From the employee's perspective, the right to assets in a nonqualified plan is ordinarily less than "bulletproof." The executive is relying mainly on the employer's unsecured promise to pay.

   To prevent current taxation of the employee, the plan is technically "unfunded" (i.e., no money or other assets are placed beyond the claims of the employer's other creditors). In essence, even if the employer has been regularly paying life insurance premiums to finance its obligation under the agreement, the employee relies not on the life insurance policy, but rather on the naked (albeit contractual) promise of the employer to pay the designated benefits.

   Other than that contractual promise, the employee has no assurance of being paid. When the time for payments comes, the employer may not be willing to make promised payments, or may not

have enough money to make them. Furthermore, if there is a corporate takeover, future management may not keep the prior management's promises, or at least not without a long, expensive, grueling lawsuit. The bottom line is that a nonqualified deferred compensation plan is generally not as secure as a qualified plan, from the retiring employee's perspective.

The current solution of choice to this lack of security is the "rabbi" trust (so called because the first such trust was established to provide post-retirement security for a rabbi). A rabbi trust is generally an irrevocable trust that holds the assets of the plan apart from the employer, but not apart from the employer's creditors. The employer gives up the use of plan investments and cannot reclaim those plan assets until all plan obligations have been met. Trust assets are dedicated solely to providing benefits to the employees covered under the plan, with one major exception: if the employer becomes insolvent or bankrupt, the assets become available to the general creditors of the employer, so that covered employees are compelled to "line up" with all other general creditors of the employer.

In short, the rabbi trust will protect employees against the employer's change of heart, and against change of management, but not against the employer's insolvency.

3. Life insurance payable to a "large" corporation may be subject to the alternative minimum tax (AMT) at the corporate level. This means that the employer must purchase enough insurance so that, even after any possible AMT, there will be enough cash to meet obligations under the plan. Although the AMT will be, at most, about 15% of the death benefit (and in most cases far less), it is suggested that the employer obtain about 18% more life insurance than the amount needed to meet cash flow demands under the plan. Any excess proceeds can be used as key employee coverage to cushion the financial shock of the loss of the key employee.

   Certain "small corporations" will qualify for an exemption from the AMT.[5] In order to initially qualify for the exemption, the corporation's average annual gross receipts for its first three-year period must not exceed $5 million. Thereafter, in order to continue to qualify for the exemption, the corporation's average annual gross receipts must not exceed $7.5 million in subsequent three-year periods. For a corporation that has not been in existence for three full years, its years of existence are substituted for the three-year period (with annualization of any short taxable year). A corporation will generally be exempt from the AMT in its first year of existence. Once a business fails to meet the gross receipts test, it cannot qualify as a small corporation in any later year. If a corporation fails to maintain its small corporation status, it loses the exemption from the AMT.

For example, assume that a calendar-year corporation started its business on January 1, 2003. The corporation will generally be exempt from the AMT in 2003. It will be exempt in 2004 if its gross receipts in 2003 do not exceed $5 million. It will continue to be exempt in 2005 if its average receipts for 2003 and 2004 do not exceed $7.5 million.

4. Required accounting disclosure reduces confidentiality.[6]

5. Not all employers can or should take advantage of these plans. An S corporation, a partnership, or a sole proprietorship generally cannot effectively utilize a nonqualified plan for its top employees, so that the use of such a plan is generally limited to a C corporation. Nonprofit corporations and governmental organizations can use these plans, but they are subject to special, highly restrictive rules under IRC Section 457. Second, there should be a high probability that the corporation will be fiscally sound long enough to be around when the promised payments are to be made. A nonqualified plan is of no use to either the employer or the covered employee if the business is no longer in existence when the distribution date arrives.

WHAT ARE THE REQUIREMENTS?

Cash value life insurance is an attractive vehicle for financing an employer's obligations under a nonqualified deferred compensation plan. There are essentially six steps necessary to implement a nonqualified deferred compensation plan financed by a company-owned life insurance policy.

1. The employer adopts a corporate resolution authorizing an agreement between the corporation and the employee (or independent contractor) to be covered, promising to make specified benefit payments upon the occurrence of certain triggering events, (e.g., retirement, death and, in some cases, disability) in return for the continuing services of the employee. The resolution usually will note the importance of the employee to the firm and the recruitment, retention, retirement, or reward benefits to be gained by implementing the plan.

2. A second and separate corporate resolution is adopted, authorizing the purchase of life insurance to indemnify the employer for the significant expenses it is likely to incur and the loss it is likely to realize at the death before retirement of the covered employee (or independent contractor).[7]

3. The appropriate amount of life insurance is purchased by and made payable to the employer. The employer is the owner, and no interest in the policy is given to the employee. The policy remains on the employer's books as a corporate asset, subject to the claims of the employer's creditors.

4. The employer's attorney drafts a nonqualified deferred compensation agreement, to be signed by an authorized officer of the employer and the covered employee. The plan should not mention how the employer will meet its obligations. In particular, when life insurance is used, the plan should contain no reference to or incorporation of the life insurance.[8]

5. A rabbi trust may also be established to hold the life insurance.[9]

6. A one-page ERISA notice should be completed and filed with the Department of Labor. Most nonqualified deferred compensation plans must satisfy the reporting and disclosure requirements established by the Employee Retirement Income Security Act (ERISA). However, these requirements are streamlined for plans financed exclusively through insurance purchased by the employer from its general assets and maintained primarily for the purpose of providing deferred compensation for a select group of management or highly compensated employees.[10]

HOW IT IS DONE – AN EXAMPLE

The Uncanny Corporation promises Jo-Ann Egly, a key executive, that, in return for her continued services until age 60, she will receive (in addition to her normal salary and other fringe and qualified pension or profit sharing benefits) $100,000 a year for 10 years, beginning at her retirement. Should she die prior to retirement, her children will be paid that amount, beginning at her death.

Like almost all nonqualified deferred compensation plans, the Uncanny Corporation's plan provides both lifetime retirement and "at death" payments. If the covered employee retires, the employer pays the promised annual payments from corporate surplus. The employer holds the life insurance policy until the employee's death, thus realizing income tax free proceeds that will help the employer's business recover its costs, and, in some cases, may even result in a net gain – even after figuring the time value of the employer's premium dollars. Insurance agents refer to this as "cost recovery" deferred compensation.

WHAT ARE THE TAX IMPLICATIONS?

1. In a properly drafted plan (one which avoids constructive receipt, the economic benefit doctrine, and IRC Section 83), the employee will not be taxed until benefits are actually received, at which time he reports the benefits as ordinary income. This same treatment also applies to survivors of the employee who receive benefits under the plan. No income averaging is available to either the employee or the employee's survivors.

2. Payments made to the employee (or his beneficiary) from a nonqualified plan – either directly by the employer or through a trust established to hold the financing vehicles for the plan – are deductible by the employer in the year that benefits are includable in the employee's (or beneficiary's) income, to the extent that they meet the "ordinary," "necessary," and "reasonable" tests applied to all compensation.[11]

   Contributions to a plan that is primarily for the benefit of shareholders are not deductible (and may be treated as dividends).[12] This emphasizes the importance of documenting the business purpose for the plan in a corporate resolution.

3. The internal buildup of value inside a life insurance contract is currently income tax deferred. By contrast, to the extent that the employer finances its obligation under the contract with mutual funds, stocks, bonds, or other assets producing taxable income, that taxable income is reportable – as earned – by the employer, at the employer's tax rate. This is another reason why life insurance is so often the principal (or an important auxiliary) financing vehicle.

When assets are held inside a rabbi trust designed to hold the financing mechanism, the tax consequences are essentially the same as when the assets are held directly by the employer. If properly drafted, the trust will be considered an employer grantor trust for income tax purposes. This means all trust income, deductions, and tax credits are treated as if earned by or allowable to the employer for tax purposes.

4. Amounts received from the plan by beneficiaries are taxable as received at ordinary rates, with one exception: to the extent that the inclusion of the benefit results in federal estate tax upon the covered employee's estate, an income tax deduction may be allowed to recipients under Code section 691 (for income in respect of a decedent).

5. Amounts deferred under a nonqualified plan are subject to Social Security tax when (1) the services are performed; or (2) when the employee no longer has a substantial risk of forfeiture, whichever is later.[13] It appears that outside directors who defer receipt of their fees for services performed must include their fees in net earnings for self-employment for Social Security tax purposes when the deferred fees are actually or constructively received.[14] Where an employee is fully vested in his benefit under a nonqualified deferred compensation plan, Social Security taxes apply immediately to deferred amounts – up to the applicable wage base ceilings. However, because most participants in nonqualified plans will earn more than the Social Security taxable wage base ($87,900 as indexed in 2004), a participant would pay little or no Social Security tax on such deferred benefits.

   Similarly, amounts deferred under a nonqualified deferred compensation plan are considered to be wages for federal unemployment tax (FUTA) purposes, as of the later of (1) the date when services are performed; or (2) the date when the employee no longer has a substantial risk of forfeiture.[15] However, because federal unemployment tax is imposed only on the first $7,000 of wages for the calendar year, an employee's nonforfeitable interest in a nonqualified plan should not create any FUTA tax liability.

6. The present value of any death benefit (or, if the payment is made in a lump sum, that lump sum amount) payable to a beneficiary is includable in a deceased employee's estate. The discount rate for computing the present value of the stream of income payments is the IRC Section 7520 interest rate

(basically 120% of Applicable Federal Midterm Rate or AFMR) and varies monthly.

Keep in mind that inclusion of this asset in the gross estate is moot if the annuity is payable solely to the surviving spouse, since it will qualify for the federal estate tax marital deduction. But planners should remember that if payments are contingent, or if they continue beyond the surviving spouse's death (as is usual in the case of payments for a fixed number of years), then, absent a timely and proper QTIP (Qualified Terminable Interest Property) election by the deceased employee's executor, there will be no marital deduction.

7. Subject to the annual exclusion deduction[16] and the $1,500,000 generation skipping transfer tax (GSTT) exemption (as indexed for inflation in 2004),[17] if nonqualified deferred compensation payments are made by a corporation to someone classified as being two or more generations below the employee (for example, the client's grandchild), GSTT will be imposed.

8. Gift tax implications depend upon whether the employee retains the right to change the designation of the beneficiary. Assuming that the employee retains the right to change the beneficiary designation (typically by notifying the employer in writing), and that the prior beneficiary's consent is not required to make such a change, there is no completed gift to the new beneficiary for gift tax purposes. So most nonqualified deferred compensation plans will not have any gift tax implications.

But, at the time when the employee makes an irrevocable assignment of the right to receive payments from the plan, the gift of the employee's property interest in the plan will be complete and gift tax will be imposed.[18] No annual gift tax exclusion would be allowed, because such a gift would be of a "future interest" as the beneficiary does not have the immediate, unfettered, and ascertainable right to use, possess, and enjoy the payments.

QUESTIONS AND ANSWERS

Question – Where does life insurance fit in a nonqualified deferred compensation plan?

Answer – Life insurance is the tool of preference to finance an employer's promises under a nonqualified plan. Typically, the employer purchases a life insur-

ance policy on the life of each covered employee. The employer owns each policy and names itself the beneficiary. The employee is given no rights in the policy and no right to name or change the beneficiary of the policy. In essence, the policy is held as a key employee contract (see Chapter 24), and will be subject to the same tax rules applicable to all such policies. In order to avoid both tax and ERISA problems, the agreement between the employer and the employee should not mention the life insurance.

Question – How have recent changes in pension law affected nonqualified deferred compensation?

Answer – The trend of tax law in the qualified retirement plan area is one of increasing costs, increasing limitation on the amount of benefits that may be provided to highly paid and owner-employees, and decreasing employer discretion and control.

Planners should point out that each of the following points pertaining to changes in the qualified retirement plan area makes nonqualified plans an appealing alternative:

First, regardless of how much the retiree was earning prior to retirement, the amount that can be paid to that person from a defined benefit pension plan is severely restricted. As of 2004, the maximum yearly benefit that can be distributed from a qualified retirement plan is only $165,000 (indexed for inflation), or, if lower, 100% of the participant's average three years' compensation.[19] Furthermore, a reduction must be made if the plan under which the payments will be made contains a pre-age 65 normal retirement age, or if the plan participant has fewer than 10 years of service.[20]

Second, as of 2004, the ceiling on the annual additions that can be added by an employer to the account of a plan participant in a qualified defined contribution (e.g., money purchase) plan – regardless of how much he or she is earning – is only $41,000 (indexed for inflation), or, if less, 25% of compensation.[21]

Third, all qualified retirement plans are limited with respect to the maximum compensation that can be used in computing either benefits or contributions. As of 2004, the maximum compensation that can be considered in computing a plan's permissible benefit distribution or annual additional contribution for an individual is the first $205,000 (indexed for inflation) of his annual compensation.[22]

The result of these rules is a severe restriction upon the benefits that may be provided to the highly paid and owners of the business – the people who work the hardest and add the most to the profits of the employer. Consequently, these same individuals will receive the least of all employees as a percentage of average pay before retirement. For example, an executive earning $500,000 a year who is covered under a 10% money purchase plan is credited with not 10% of $500,000, but only 10% of $205,000 (in 2004). He receives no credit for the other $295,000 of salary earned – even though he's taxed on all $500,000!

Fourth, participants in most qualified plans must become fully vested twice as quickly as was required under pension law just a few years ago. While this means fewer forfeitures from an employee viewpoint, benefit costs have increased significantly from an employer's perspective.

Fifth, tougher nondiscrimination rules place additional restraints on an employer's discretion with respect to who can be excluded from plan participation. This not only increases costs, but also reduces the employer's ability to direct cash flow to those who make the greatest contribution to it.

Sixth, Social Security integration rules (now referred to by the IRS as "permitted disparity") have been changed to further favor rank and file employees, which further adds to employer costs.

Question – What are the differences between "salary continuation" and "salary reduction" nonqualified deferred compensation plans?

Answer – These two types of plans involve significantly different design and drafting philosophies.

A *salary continuation* plan is a type of nonelective nonqualified deferred compensation plan that provides a specified deferred amount, payable in the future. A salary continuation plan is a fringe benefit provided by an employer with employer dollars in addition to other benefits and therefore requires *no* reduction in the covered employee's salary. For example, the contract might provide:

> "At retirement, disability, or death, the XYZ Corporation will pay you or your designated beneficiary $100,000 a year for 10 years."

The salary continuation plan is often used when an employer wants to provide something *in place of* or *in addition to* a qualified plan.

The salary continuation plan is usually a defined benefit type of plan. Plan benefits are often measured as a percentage of compensation. For instance, the employee will receive payments based upon average earnings over his final three years of service for the employer. Benefits may also be based upon years of service, so that the longer the employee has worked for the employer, the higher the benefit. Another possibility is that benefits may be based upon the achievement of specified goals.

A *salary reduction* plan is a true elective deferral of a specified amount of employee compensation.

Salary reduction plans typically utilize a defined contribution type of formula. An amount is added to the participant's account each year. That amount may be an actual accumulation of funds, or simply a bookkeeping account.

If the account is only a bookkeeping account, the employer will often guarantee a specified minimum rate of return on the money credited. The rate of return may be based upon some index beyond the employer's control – such as Moody's Bond Index. Alternatively, the rate of return may be tied to the value of the employer's stock.

Contributions are generally a specified percentage of the employee's compensation each year or can be designed to meet a "target" retirement benefit similar to a target benefit qualified retirement plan.

Question – What is meant by the terms "SERP" and "excess benefit" salary continuation plan?

Answer – A SERP (Supplemental Employee Retirement Plan) is a plan for a selected group of executives. A SERP generally provides extra retirement benefits for key personnel. An excess benefit plan is a special kind of supplemental plan. It is a creature of ERISA, and is a plan maintained by an employer solely for the purpose of providing benefits for certain employees in excess of the limitation on contributions and benefits imposed by IRC Section 415.[23] An excess benefit plan can restore parity between the percentage of pre-retirement pay provided to highly paid employees at retirement and the percentage of pre-retirement pay provided to rank and file employees at retirement.

Question – What is the "constructive receipt" doctrine?

Answer – Under the constructive receipt doctrine, an amount becomes currently taxable to a cash basis taxpayer, even before it is actually received, if it is *credited* to the employee's account, *set aside*, or *otherwise made available* to the employee.[24]

Once income is unconditionally subject to the taxpayer's demand, that income must be reported, even if the taxpayer has *not* chosen to reduce that income to his possession.

Amounts due from the employer will be includable in the income of an employee who is a cash basis taxpayer as soon as:

1. The money is available to him;

2. The employer is able and ready to pay;

3. The employee's right to payment is unrestricted; and

4. The failure to receive the money results from the exercise of the employee's own choice.[25]

Since the major advantage of a nonqualified deferred compensation plan to an employee is the deferral of tax (which deferral is analogous to an interest free loan from the government), it is essential that the plan avoid constructive receipt.

Question – How is it possible to avoid constructive receipt in establishing a nonqualified deferred compensation plan?

Answer – There is no constructive receipt if the employee's control over receipt is subject to a *substantial limitation or restriction*.[26] Perhaps the easiest way to avoid constructive receipt is to design the plan so that (1) the compensation is deferred before it is earned; (2) the employer's promise to pay benefits is completely unsecured; and (3) ultimate payment of the benefits is conditioned upon the passage of time or the occurrence of an event beyond the employee's control. Such actions will avoid constructive receipt even though the benefits are completely nonforfeitable.[27]

Question – Why must a salary reduction type plan provide that the employee's election to reduce salary be made *before* rendering the services for which the compensation is deferred?

Answer – If the covered employee's election to reduce his salary is made before rendering services for

which compensation is deferred, then, in order to avoid constructive receipt, all that is necessary is that there be a substantial limitation or restriction on the employee's ability to reach plan assets. But, according to the IRS, in order to defer compensation *after* services have been performed, the plan must provide *substantial risk of forfeiture* provisions, a much more severe standard than a mere substantial limitation or restriction.[28]

It is possible to build a great deal of flexibility into a salary reduction arrangement without triggering the constructive receipt doctrine, by permitting prospective adjustments to be made to the percentage of compensation to be deferred in future years on an annual basis.[29]

Question – What is meant by a "substantial risk of forfeiture"?

Answer – A substantial risk of forfeiture exists where rights in transferred property are conditioned directly or indirectly upon the performance (or nonperformance) of substantial services. For instance, if property must be returned to the employer should total earnings not increase in a given period of time, the property is subject to a substantial risk of forfeiture.[30]

When is a risk "substantial"? The answer will always depend upon the facts and circumstances of each case.[31] Planners must be sure that there is a clear line of demarcation between a mere contractual right to receive compensation in the future – which is safe from the application of the economic benefit theory – and a right that is secured and is not subject to a substantial risk of forfeiture.

Question – Can an employee make an election regarding the method of payment from the plan at the time of his retirement without triggering constructive receipt?

Answer – Many attorneys believe that an election regarding the mode of payment can safely be made without constructive receipt as long as it is made *before* any amount is actually *payable*.[32] However, the IRS refuses to rule favorably on a nonqualified plan that allows elections *after* the beginning of the period of *service* in which the compensation is earned – unless substantial forfeiture provisions are in effect.[33] Therefore, most plans require that participants must choose the time and manner in which benefits will be paid *before* the deferred amount is *earned*.

Question – How long does the constructive receipt problem last?

Answer – The problem of constructive receipt (keeping the time and manner of payment outside the employee's control) extends beyond the asset buildup period – plan provisions must also assure that the employee is not taxed on more than is actually received during the distribution period.

For example, assume that a plan provides for a distribution of benefits over 10 years in equal annual installments, starting at age 65. If the employee could elect, at any time during the distribution period, to accelerate the balance of payments, then the constructive receipt doctrine would require an immediate inclusion in income of the entire amount that the employee could elect to receive. Alternatively, assume that a plan provides for a 10 year distribution period, but allows the employee to elect, during the distribution period, to spread the ten annual payments over 15 years. Even if the employee chose the 15 year option, he would still be taxed as if plan assets were received over the original 10 year period.

Question – Does a controlling shareholder necessarily have constructive receipt of assets used to finance a nonqualified deferred compensation plan simply by virtue of his potential control of plan assets?

Answer – The IRS will not issue a private ruling with respect to the tax treatment of a controlling shareholder-employee's participation in a nonqualified deferred compensation plan.[34] The IRS seems to be concerned, in part, that a controlling shareholder, by virtue of his control, has the power to modify the terms of a deferral agreement at any time, and to access deferred amounts at will, and is therefore necessarily in constructive receipt of deferred amounts.[35]

It is the authors' opinion that if the plan is properly drafted, a controlling shareholder-employee should be able to participate and be taxed (or escape current taxation) in the same manner as a nonshareholder employee.[36]

Steps to thwart an attack on a plan in which a controlling shareholder is a participant include the following:

1. Separate the financing of the employer's obligation from the plan itself. For example, if a life insurance policy is to be used, do not match the policy benefit with the promises made. When the vehicle used to finance benefits is identical to and directly keyed into the benefits promised under the plan, the IRS may deny favorable tax treatment.[37] If the life insurance is maintained by the employer as key employee coverage and is kept totally separate from the agreement, there should be no constructive receipt or economic benefit issues.

2. If possible, include at least one highly compensated person who is not a shareholder-employee in the plan. The participation of a non-shareholder-employee greatly enhances the argument that the plan is for corporate, rather than shareholder, purposes, and will serve to justify a corporate income tax deduction when benefits are to be paid.

3. Create a full documentation of the corporate advantage to be gained and the business purpose to be served by the plan in corporate minutes and in the agreement itself. Use wording that indicates that other successful competitive companies are providing similar supplemental compensation in their benefit programs. Incorporate wording from trade journals evidencing that such plans are commonly used in the employer's industry or profession as a form of compensation for the recruitment, retention, retirement, and reward of key employees.

4. Consider using a rabbi trust. A rabbi trust can serve as a device that creates a substantial restriction or limitation upon the ability of even a controlling (however defined) shareholder to reach deferred amounts until the occurrence of specific events. Under state law, the independent trustee has the fiduciary responsibility to deny access to anyone until the covered person has satisfied the plan's triggering criterion (for example, disability, death, or attainment of a specified retirement age). Thus, the rabbi trust should negate any "raw power" that a controlling shareholder may have to reach benefits.

5. Establish an independent compensation review committee with the power to deny benefits to participants who do not meet

plan criteria. Have the committee actually meet and review the operation of the plan and police its provisions.

6. Do not provide a plan for shareholder-employees with terms and benefits more generous than would be provided to non-shareholder-employees. Provide that contributions or benefits on behalf of shareholder-employees cannot be proportionately greater than those provided to key employees who are not shareholders. In other words, base the plan benefit formula upon a reasonable and uniform percentage of salary.

Question – What is the economic benefit theory?

Answer – Under the economic benefit theory, an employee is currently taxable whenever he receives something of value that is the equivalent of cash.[38] In other words, if a compensation arrangement provides a current "economic benefit" to an employee, the employee must include the value of the benefit in income, even if there is no current right to receive cash or other property. The employee need only receive the *equivalent of cash* – something with a current, real, and measurable value – from his employer. As soon as such an event occurs, even if the employee *cannot* currently take possession of either the asset or the income it produces, he is taxable on the value of the benefit.

Question – How may IRC Section 83 cause the covered employee to be taxable on compensation even before it is actually received?

Answer – IRC Section 83 provides that the person who performed the services must include in income the amount by which the fair market value of property transferred in connection with the performance of such services exceeds the amount paid for such property. That amount is includable in the first taxable year in which the property becomes transferable or is no longer subject to a substantial risk of forfeiture.

The use of a rabbi trust will not cause the covered employee to be taxed under IRC Section 83.[39] The claims of participants and their beneficiaries to funds held in a rabbi trust are unsecured and the funds held in the rabbi trust can be reached by the employer's creditors. Because a rabbi trust does not cause the employer's promise to be other than

unfunded and unsecured, the IRS has repeatedly held that the adoption of a nonqualified deferred compensation plan and the creation of a related rabbi trust do not result in a transfer of property in connection with the performance of services.[40]

In the case of a life insurance policy, the plan should give no interest in the policy to the employee. The policy should remain on the employer's books as a corporate asset (i.e., subject to the claims of the employer's creditors) and the employer should be the sole applicant, owner, and premium payor. All of the favorable income and estate tax rulings in this area involve plans in which the employer owns the sole interest in the policy. Some authorities feel that the ability to defer taxation might, therefore, be threatened if the plan contemplates the use of split dollar contracts as an asset reserve.

Question – Is there a certain size or financial strength of the employer beyond which a "naked promise" is nevertheless viewed as "secured"?

Answer – Size of the employer makes no difference. A plan is not considered funded, even if a corporate employer as large as Microsoft makes a contractual promise to make payments in the future – as long as that promise is neither negotiable nor assignable. Such a promise is considered incapable of valuation and therefore not currently taxable because – regardless of the size or financial condition of the employer – the promise is subject to the hazards of economic and business conditions. There should be no taxation of the employee unless and until funds are placed beyond the reach of the employer or its creditors and the employee no longer runs a substantial risk of forfeiture.

The solution is to give an employee no greater rights than those of a general creditor. The earmarking of assets by the employer in order to meet its obligations under the plan will not cause the employee to be taxable. Even if cash or other property has been physically transferred to an irrevocable trust, the economic benefit theory will not apply, so long as the employee's rights to that asset remain subject to a substantial risk of forfeiture.

Question – What requirements does ERISA impose on nonqualified plans?

Answer – ERISA's requirements can be quite burdensome.[41] However, a properly designed nonqualified deferred compensation plan can escape all or most of the requirements applicable to qualified plans. For example, an unfunded excess benefit plan is freed from satisfying all of ERISA's reporting, disclosure, participation, vesting, funding, fiduciary responsibility, administrative enforcement and plan termination insurance requirements.[42]

Also, if a plan is unfunded and is limited to a select group of management or highly compensated employees, it will be exempt from ERISA's participation, vesting, funding, fiduciary responsibility, and plan termination insurance requirements.[43] However, such a plan will be subject to streamlined reporting and disclosure requirements, recordkeeping requirements and at least some of ERISA's administration and enforcement requirements (including the requirement that a claims procedure be established).[44] The streamlined reporting and disclosure rules require that a short statement be filed with the Secretary of Labor. The statement must include: (1) the name and address of the employer; (2) the employer's tax identification number; (3) a declaration that the employer maintains a plan (or plans) primarily for the purposes of providing deferred compensation to a select group of management or highly compensated employees; and (4) a statement of the number of such plans maintained and the number of employees participating in each such plan.[45] The streamlined reporting and disclosure rules also require that plan documents be provided to the Secretary of Labor upon request.[46]

Question – What factors should be considered by the attorney drafting the nonqualified plan?

Answer – The attorney drafting the nonqualified deferred compensation plan must first identify who is in control of the decision-making process – the employer or the employee.

The employer has three main objectives: (1) attracting new employees; (2) retaining highly productive key employees; and (3) providing incentives for superior performance.

If the attorney's mission is to maximize *employer* objectives, the plan should contain a vesting (forfeitability) schedule or other forfeiture of benefits provision desired by the employer. For example, many employer-controlled plans remain unvested for a number of years and then have only graduated vesting. ERISA's vesting requirements do not apply to a properly designed nonqualified deferred compensation plan. Planners, particularly

the attorneys who draft nonqualified plans, should keep in mind that, regardless of whether an employee's benefits are subject to forfeiture, the plan must never give the employee any right in the assets that the employer may have purchased to meet its obligations under the plan. Even if plan benefits are fully vested, there should be no adverse income tax implications to the covered employee, as long as: (1) the employer's promise to pay benefits is unsecured; and (2) the agreement is signed before the employee earns the income.

The individual drafting a nonqualified deferred compensation plan should consider the following:

1. Confining eligibility to certain key executives or technical or sales personnel;

2. Making plan eligibility either part of a predetermined company policy or adopting the plan for specific individuals as the need arises;

3. Including performance incentives (e.g., basing benefits or contributions on salary increases, profits, sales goals, the value of employer stock, or upon the satisfactory achievement of specified objectives);

4. Including clauses that trigger a forfeiture of benefits for termination of employment or for undesirable conduct;

5. Delaying vesting;

6. Establishing a two-tier interest rate on participant deferrals or employer contributions toward financing the benefit of a given employee (e.g., the plan could credit dollars at a lower rate of return if the employee retired or terminated employment prior to a given date, and at a higher rate if the employee stayed and met other employer conditions); and

7. Paying benefits only upon the same terms and conditions as in the employer's qualified plan.

Where an employee is the more powerful force in the bargaining process, his objectives are typically: (1) additional forms of compensation, the income tax on which is deferred as long as possible, so that money otherwise paid in taxes may continue to work for the employee for many years (this compounding of dollars otherwise paid in taxes is a major benefit of a nonqualified deferred compensation plan); (2) benefit certainty; and (3) immediate vesting of all benefits, without forfeiture provisions.

If the mission of the attorney who is drafting the nonqualified deferred compensation plan is meeting the *employee's* objectives, he should consider the following drafting points:

1. The inclusion of performance incentives (e.g., basing benefits or contributions on salary increases, profits, sales goals, the value of employer stock, or upon the satisfactory achievement of specified objectives);

2. The elimination of any clauses that trigger a forfeiture of benefits for termination of employment or for undesirable conduct; and

3. Immediate 100% vesting.

In addition, where the employee has a strong influence, planners should consider requiring the plan to pay benefits in the event of disability. Typically, such benefits should begin immediately upon disability. In addition, the definition of disability should be less stringent than the normal "total and permanent" disability required for Social Security payments. Possible disputes about disability status can be minimized by shifting the determination of disability to an insurance company or a physician chosen jointly by the employer and the employee.

Question – What vehicles are used to help an employer meet its obligations under a nonqualified plan?

Answer – Three methods are commonly used: (1) "pay-as-you-go;" (2) corporate-owned life insurance; and (3) alternative investments.

Pay-as-you go is, by definition, an obligation for the employer to use the working capital of the its business (or draw on its line of credit) every time a payment is due. This approach is simple and postpones the cash outflow as long as possible. The employer accrues a liability on its balance sheet under the category of deferred compensation. Some employers feel that this method makes sense as long as the employer itself can earn more after-tax return by reinvesting the money in its business than could be earned through an alternative investment.

This "opportunity cost of capital" decision-making tool is another way of saying that the employer expects to finance plan obligations through the future growth of its business. The problem with this thinking is that if expectations are not met, the necessary cash will not be there when needed. The obligation is then shifted to the future management of the business, and may fall due at the worst possible time (in terms of cash flow). It puts the financial security of the covered employees at the risk of the business. It must also be considered that future management may not be willing to make promised payments – even if able to.

Corporate-owned life insurance (COLI) is the preferred financing vehicle for most publicly-held and almost all closely-held businesses. Although there is no one type of contract that is "best" for nonqualified deferred compensation plans, most planners, after examining plan goals and other factors, tend to favor plans with high premium payment and investment flexibility and low mortality and expense costs. Permanent, rather than term, coverage is indicated where the plan contemplates use of some or all of policy values to finance retirement benefits.

COLI is attractive for many reasons, including: (1) tax-deferred build up inside the policy; (2) the fact that costs can almost always be recovered – including the after-tax cost of the use of corporate dollars; (3) a competitive internal rate of return, as compared with alternative investments; and (4) the ability to offer an immediate death benefit, with no risk to corporate cash flow.

Alternate investments are, of course, those investments other than life insurance that can be used to finance the employer's obligation. These should be long term conservative investments, such as mutual funds, that are highly liquid.

Question – Will the use of life insurance to finance an employer's obligation under a nonqualified deferred compensation plan cause the plan to be "funded"?

Answer – Generally, funding a nonqualified deferred compensation plan will result in current income taxation to the employee and will result in the imposition of onerous ERISA rules. Fortunately, a properly designed nonqualified deferred compensation plan will not be considered "funded" for tax or ERISA purposes merely because it is financed with life insurance.[47]

Question – If life insurance is selected as the means of financing the employer's obligation under a nonqualified deferred compensation plan, how much should be purchased?

Answer – The amount of life insurance purchased should be a function of (1) the plan benefits promised; (2) the alternative minimum tax (AMT), if any, expected to be applied to the proceeds; (3) the expected tax leveraging; and (4) the employer's goals with respect to the financial implications of the plan to its business.

The most generous plan, from the employee's viewpoint, is one in which all plan assets are leveraged with the employer's tax deduction to produce the maximum benefit. This is, of course, the least favorable to the employer and will result in the highest life insurance cost, since none of the proceeds are used to defray any of the employer's (1) premium outlay; (2) after-deduction cost of benefits, or (3) the time value of money during either the premium paying or benefit paying period.

It is, of course, appealing to the employer to be able to accomplish all of its recruitment, retention, retirement, and reward objectives without the limitations upon benefits for the highly compensated and owner-employees in a qualified plan. In addition, the employer can pay out all promised benefits to a covered employee and then recover some or all of the costs involved in the plan. These goals can all be accomplished through the purchase of corporate-owned life insurance.

Cost recovery nonqualified plans can be thought of as having at least three levels.[48]

1. Recovery of the net premiums paid, plus the after-deduction cost of the deferred salary paid to the employee or survivors, plus the cost of the use of money on the net premiums or the deferred benefits. This is the highest level of cost recovery and will therefore require the most life insurance to accomplish.

2. Recovery of the net premiums paid, plus the after-deduction cost of the deferred salary paid to the employee or survivors. This is the middle level of cost recovery and will require less life insurance.

3. Recovery of only the net insurance premium outlay or the after-deduction cost

of the deferred salary paid to the employee or survivors. This is the lowest level of cost recovery and will require the least amount of life insurance.

Question – What are the tax implications if a surety bond is used to provide additional security that the benefits under a nonqualified deferred compensation plan will be paid?

Answer – A surety bond is a contractual agreement by a bonding insurance company to pay the promised benefits in the event that the employer is unable or unwilling to make payments. If the employee purchases a surety bond and pays all premiums personally, and if the insurer requires some form of collateralization agreement with the employer, then, in the authors' opinion, the plan may be considered secured.[49] As a practical matter, few companies will issue such bonds; they are expensive, and so limited that they are of little interest to most covered employees.

Question – What are the tax implications if the employee purchases indemnification insurance to provide additional security that the benefits under a nonqualified deferred compensation plan will be paid?

Answer – The IRS has indicated that an employee can buy indemnification insurance to protect his deferred benefits without causing immediate taxation. The result is the same even if the employer reimburses the employee for the premium payments, as long as the employer has no other involvement in the arrangement. The employee's premium payments must be treated as nondeductible personal expenses, and any premium reimbursements must be included in the employee's income.[50] The consequences of such an arrangement under ERISA are not clear.

Question – Will guarantees made by a shareholder of the employer cause the plan to be considered "funded"?

Answer – A shareholder of the employer corporation can personally guarantee payment under a nonqualified deferred compensation plan *without* causing the employee to be taxed. A third party guarantee is merely a promise to pay, and, although it may broaden a participant's protection, it should not require the inclusion of the primary obligation amount in currently taxable income.[51] For example, where a parent corporation guaranteed payments under a subsidiary's contract with an executive, the IRS held that the guarantees would not cause the plan to be funded.[52] But if the employer's obligation is backed by a letter of credit from the employer or by a surety bond obtained by the employer, the promise may be considered to be secured, and thus cause current taxation.

Question – Can a third party, such as a parent corporation or a majority shareholder, guarantee payments to the employee under a nonqualified deferred compensation plan?

Answer – Under a third party guarantee, the employer obtains a guarantee from a third party to pay the employee if the employer defaults. This guarantor may be a shareholder, a related corporation, or a bank (through a letter of credit). There is precedent for a favorable IRS position on third party guarantees.[53] Unfortunately, too much *employer* involvement may cause the IRS to claim that the plan is formally funded for tax purposes. A better course of action is to have the employee, independent of the employer, obtain a third party guarantee.

Question – Why is the setting aside of assets described as "financing" rather than "funding"?

Answer – The use of the term "financed" is a reminder that the distinction between financing and funding is an important one. There is a way to finance the employer's obligations without the tax and ERISA problems associated with a "funded" plan: keep assets in the fund *accessible* to the employer and its creditors and provide no explicit security to the employee beyond that provided to other creditors of the employer. Note that, although for many purposes, the definitions of "unfunded" and "funded" are the same for both tax and ERISA purposes, in some important situations those definitions will differ.

The term "financing" implies that, regardless of the investment vehicle used, no money or other asset is placed beyond the reach of the employer or its creditors. Conversely, the term "funded" has adverse implications under both tax and ERISA law. A plan is funded if the employer has placed money or property credited to the employee's account in an irrevocable trust or otherwise placed restrictions upon the access to the fund by the employer and its creditors.

There are a number of problems presented by a funded plan.

First, once a plan is considered funded, the value of the employee's interest in the fund will become taxable to the employee as soon as his interest in the fund is substantially vested.[54] With funded salary reduction plans, this is almost always immediately. In other words, an employee could be taxed on benefits years before actually receiving any payments from the fund.

Second, funded plans may be subject to burdensome ERISA requirements, including the vesting and fiduciary requirements imposed on qualified plans.[55]

Thus, the question is, "How can an employee's security in his benefit be increased without triggering the adverse implications of a funded plan?" The easiest solution is an earmarked reserve account maintained by the employer. This means that the employer sets up an account invested in assets of various types. There is no trust – assets in the account are, at all times, fully accessible to both the employer and its creditors.

The employer could set up an actual reserve account with limited employee investment direction. Under such an arrangement, the employee is given the right to select the investments in the account. That right of direction must be limited to a choice of broad types of investment. If the employee is permitted to choose specific investments, the IRS could argue that the employee had constructive receipt of investment funds.[56] So the employee should be given the right to choose between equities, bonds, a family of mutual funds, etc.

The employer typically purchases, pays premiums on, and is the beneficiary of life insurance. Proceeds can be used to provide a death benefit if the employee dies in the early years of the plan. Employees should not be taxable on the current economic benefit of this type of security, because the insurance is strictly an employer asset.[57]

Question – Aside from financing the future obligation to an employee under a nonqualified deferred compensation plan by investing corporate dollars each year in life insurance, mutual funds, or some other asset, what can be done to increase employee security?

Answer – Security is an important goal for many reasons. Security of promised benefits is endangered by the possibility that the employer will be (1) unwilling to pay benefits as they come due (either because of a change of heart or a change of management); or (2) unable to pay benefits as they come due.

One partial answer to the desire for more security is the "rabbi trust." Rabbi trusts enhance employee security with minimal threat to the income tax advantages of the nonqualified deferred compensation plan. While there is some uncertainty in the area, the use of a rabbi trust (at least in the context of a nonqualified plan that is maintained for a select group of management or highly compensated employees or that is an excess benefit plan) should not cause the plan to be funded for ERISA purposes.[58]

A rabbi trust holds the assets of the plan apart from the corporation, but *not* apart from its creditors. The rabbi trust is generally an irrevocable trust that holds assets that will be used, wholly or partially, to satisfy the employer's obligation. The employer gives up the use of plan investments, so that those assets are dedicated solely to the employees covered under the plan, with one major exception: if the employer becomes bankrupt or insolvent, the assets become available to the general creditors of the employer. This means that covered employees must essentially "line up" with the employer's other general creditors.

Question – What factors would indicate that a rabbi trust should be coupled with a nonqualified deferred compensation plan?

Answer – Factors that would indicate the use of a rabbi trust include:

1. A fear that the management or ownership of the business is likely to change before all benefits will be paid;

2. A fear that hostile new management might renege on the employer's contractual obligations to its key employees; and

3. A perceived probability that if litigation were necessary, a win by key employees would come at a prohibitive cost.

Question – What, if any, are the downside risks or costs of setting up a rabbi trust?

Answer – The three costs of a rabbi trust (aside from the legal costs of creating the rabbi trust and the accounting costs of maintaining it) include:

1. The employer loses the use of plan assets (i.e., they are not available for a corporate emergency or opportunity);

2. The rate of return on plan assets in the trust may be less than what could have been earned had the money been invested in the employer's business; and

3. A rabbi trust does not provide any protection against the ultimate risk of employer insolvency.

A deferred annuity is probably an unsuitable investment for a rabbi trust, because increases in income inside the annuity would be currently taxable to the employer as grantor of the rabbi trust. Tax-advantaged investments, such as municipal bonds, preferred stocks, life insurance or a combination of these, are likely to be a better choice.

Question – What are some provisions that should be considered if an attorney will be drafting a rabbi trust for a nonqualified deferred compensation plan?

Answer – Generally, the rabbi trust documents that have previously received favorable rulings from the IRS are *irrevocable* and:

1. Require that plan assets be deferred until the participant's termination of employment;[59]

2. Preclude investment in employer stock;[60]

3. Make the assets available to all general creditors of the corporation should the employer become bankrupt or insolvent under state law (i.e., do not give the covered employee greater rights to trust assets than creditors have under state law);

4. Include a requirement that the employer (specifically, the CEO and the Board of Directors) must notify the trustee if the employer becomes "insolvent" or subject to bankruptcy proceedings;

5. Provide that if the employer notifies the trustee of its bankruptcy, the trustee must

suspend all payments to covered employees, hold all assets for the benefit of creditors, and provide that no further assets can be distributed to the covered employees until allowed by a bankruptcy court; and

6. Do *not* provide an "insolvency trigger," that is, a provision that triggers immediate payments to covered employees from the trust should the employer become insolvent or experience a drop in net worth below a specified level. The IRS views this type of provision as giving the employee greater rights to the assets than other corporate creditors, so that tax benefits are lost.

Drafters might also consider provisions that:

1. Provide that investment authority will automatically shift to the trustee of the rabbi trust in the event of an "unfriendly takeover," thus preventing the new management from making investments in illiquid employer-leased real estate or other employer-related ventures;

2. Include some type of acceleration provision that enables an employer, upon a change in tax law or an IRS audit with an unfavorable result that makes rabbi trust money taxable to participants, to immediately distribute trust assets. If neither the plan nor the trust has such a provision, the employee may incur a current tax, but have no cash with which to pay it.

3. Preclude the addition of new beneficiaries in the event of an unfriendly takeover and restrict the ability to make amendments. This avoids dilution of assets or the insertion of unfavorable provisions, and prevents new management from adding plan amendments that adversely affect already accrued plan benefits;

4. Make it clear that liability for promised benefits is joint and several between the trust and the employer. If plan liability is shifted completely to the trust, then aside from the obvious problems that arise if trust assets are insufficient, ERISA problems may also be triggered.

5. Do not condition the trustee's ability to pay benefits upon instructions from the employer.

6. Set up separate trusts if employees of both a parent and a subsidiary corporation are to be covered by salary continuation plans. This helps to keep creditors of an insolvent corporation from reaching assets that should go to employees of a financially sound related corporation.

7. Make the trust irrevocable, but specify a written procedure as to how the trustee and the employer can amend the trust with the consent of trust beneficiaries.

8. Provide that the trust will not terminate until all benefits promised under the nonqualified plan have been paid, and that any remaining trust assets will be returned to the employer at that time.

The IRS has released a model rabbi trust instrument intended to serve as a safe harbor for employers adopting rabbi trusts and to expedite the processing of requests for advance rulings on these arrangements. The IRS will no longer issue advance rulings on unfunded deferred compensation arrangements that use a trust other than the model trust, except in rare and unusual circumstances.[61]

Question – Can a nonqualified plan safely build in the right for an employee to make withdrawals in the event of hardship?

Answer – Yes. A number of IRS private letter rulings indicate that the withdrawal of funds from a rabbi trust pursuant to hardship withdrawal provisions is permissible, and will not, by itself, jeopardize the tax status of the plan. In fact, the IRS guidelines for giving advance rulings on unfunded deferred compensation plans expressly permit the use of hardship withdrawal provisions.[62] In IRS private letter rulings, "hardship" has been generally defined as an unforeseeable financial emergency caused by events beyond the participant's control. The amount that can be withdrawn is generally limited to the amount needed to satisfy the emergency. It is wise to provide that the hardship must not be reasonably relieved by reimbursement (by insurance or otherwise), liquidation of the participant's assets (to the extent such liquidation would not, in itself, cause a financial hardship), or cessation of deferrals under the plan.

Question – What are some of the "twists" on the rabbi trust technique?

Answer – Creative tax planners have improved the classic rabbi trust with a number of clever drafting concepts, as explained below.

The "standby rabbi trust" – A rabbi trust is established, but left virtually unfunded. A $10 deposit (to comply with state law) was all that was put into the trust. The employer established the trust so that if there was a change in corporate control, the employer would transfer assets equal to the present value of the benefits then payable to the trust.[63]

The "carry-on rabbi trust" – In addition to paying out deferred retirement benefits, a rabbi trust may hold funds for the purpose of continuing the same approximate level of life insurance, hospitalization, and major medical insurance that the employee enjoyed just prior to retirement.[64] This type of rabbi trust can be used to carry on an executive's post-retirement insurance needs.

The "double duty rabbi trust" – A single rabbi trust can be used to fund the assets of multiple deferred compensation plans.[65]

Question – Does it make sense in today's changing tax and economic environment to voluntarily defer compensation?

Answer – Many attorneys and accountants have asked just this question. In most cases, the answer is a very emphatic "YES!"

Here are some of the factors to consider:

1. Corporate tax rates may go up. When tax rates go down, the value of a corporate level tax deduction and the leverage it can produce when benefits are paid out is reduced. However, when rates go up, so does the employer's leverage. Higher tax brackets at distribution mean more benefits can be paid with the same post-deduction outlay, or that the same payments can be paid out at a lower net corporate cost.

2. A reduction in tax rates reduces the value of tax deferral to participating employees. However, when rates go up, so does the value of deferring next year's bonus.

3. The value of tax deferral is lower at a 36% bracket than at a 50% bracket. But as personal rates rise, so does the value of a deferral. From the employee's standpoint, deferral is advantageous even if rates rise to 40% (or even 45%), provided that the deferral period is long enough.

4. In a few situations, the employee may be better off taking the money, paying tax on it and investing on his own rather than risking being a general creditor of the employer for many years. But few employees would, year after year, invest the after-tax difference. If they did, *and* if they never touched the investment, *and* if it never suffered a capital loss, *and* if it always earned a specified after tax rate of interest, then they might be better off.

5. The mathematics of the deferral issue show that the benefit of deferral varies according to three factors: (a) the tax rate when the funds are distributed (if rates increase, the value of the "interest-free loan from the government" is offset by the amount of the increased tax that must be paid); (b) the length of the deferral; and (c) the interest rate that the deferred funds earn.[66] At what point will the deferral of current taxation offset the increase in tax rates? Under almost any scenario, a key employee is better off deferring compensation, assuming that tax rates will increase, if the deferral period exceeds 6 years and the interest rate is 6% or greater.[67]

6. When top corporate rates drop, the employer's cost of deferral can still be significant. In fact, the cost of deferral to the corporate employer can actually be greater than the value of deferral to the employee.

On the other hand, the employer can use the money it has on hand but is not paying out. It can put the earmarked investments to work at the corporation's earnings level, both during the accumulation period and during the distribution period. It could earn a rate of return sufficient not only to put the employee in a better position than he would have been had he taken current salary and invested it, but it can also retain a portion of the earnings to offset the cost of deferral.

With a salary continuation plan, the corporate client can set up the plan so that the employer maintains control and achieves its business purpose, or else it gets its money back. And, unlike the current payment of a salary, earmarked funds can be available for a corporate emergency or opportunity.

Question – What is a *secular trust* and what are its advantages and disadvantages?

Answer – A secular trust is an alternative to a rabbi trust.

It is generally an *irrevocable* trust designed to address the two major drawbacks of both the traditional naked promise by the employer to pay benefits and the rabbi trust: neither the employer's naked contractual promise nor the rabbi trust provides any protection against the employer's insolvency nor results in an up-front income tax deduction.

How does the secular trust give the employee protection against employer insolvency, and, at the same time, provide the employer with an immediate income tax deduction? The answer lies in the way that the secular trust is designed. First, the employer's creditors *cannot* reach assets placed in a secular trust. Second, as soon as funds are put into a secular trust, the employee is generally immediately taxed. As soon as the employee is taxed on funds placed in a secular trust, the employer can take an immediate income tax deduction.[68]

The purported advantages of the secular trust over the nonqualified deferred compensation plan (with or without a rabbi trust) include:

1. It is less expensive to create and maintain.

2. It can result in tax savings, since the contributions may generate an employer's deduction taken at a higher tax bracket than the bracket in which the contributions are taxed to the employee.

But there are potential problems involved with a secular trust, including:

1. Covered employees will generally be taxed each year on income that they have not received, so that they may not have the cash on hand to pay the taxes. This means that the employer may have to make additional cash payments, in order to enable the employee to pay the required tax.

2. A secular trust may create "double taxation," (i.e., both the trust and the highly compensated employees may be taxed each year on the trust's earnings).[69]

3. A secular trust is considered to be "funded" for ERISA purposes. As a result, a secular trust may have to satisfy a wide array of ERISA requirements, including reporting and disclosure, participation and vesting, funding, and fiduciary responsibility requirements.

Question – How are benefits paid under a nonqualified deferred compensation plan?

Answer – At retirement, benefits are generally paid either in a lump sum, or, more often, in a series of annual payments. For instance, payments for a fixed number of years (for example, 10 years) are common, as are life annuities and survivor annuities.

Planners must watch the constructive receipt doctrine, so that benefits are not taxed before they are actually received. Pay particular attention to "termination of employment" provisions.

Question – Can nonqualified deferred compensation plans be used by a partnership?

Answer – A partnership, for tax purposes, is essentially a conduit through which the income and deductions of the business flow directly to the owners. Income tax is imposed on each individual partner's distributive share of the partnership's income at the tax rate payable by each partner as an individual. The key point to note is that income tax is imposed whether or not that share is, in fact, distributed by the partnership to the partner.[70]

The general taxation of partnerships results in the absence of the tax deferral, which is a major reason for the deferral of compensation. To summarize:

1. No deduction is allowed to the partnership for any premiums paid on life insurance used to finance the nonqualified deferred compensation plan (the partnership is the beneficiary of the policy, and, therefore, deductions are not allowed under IRC Section 264(a)).

2. Amounts used to pay premiums remain part of the taxable income of the partner-

ship, since they cannot be deducted by the partnership. This means that amounts used to pay premiums will be currently taxable to the partners. Each partner will pay, at his personal tax rate, tax on those amounts divided between the partners according to his distributive share.[71]

3. Because the character of items of income is carried through from the partnership to its partners, when tax free life insurance proceeds are received by the partnership,[72] it remains income tax free to the partners.

4. A reduction in basis must be made by each partner for the amount of the (undistributed) premiums paid. Total premiums paid each year are allocated to each partner according to his distributive share.[73]

5. Each partner's adjusted basis is increased when the partnership tax conduit "distributes" those life insurance proceeds.[74]

Question – Can an S corporation use a nonqualified deferred compensation plan?

Answer – Like a partnership, an S corporation passes through directly and immediately all the income, losses, and deductions of the firm to its owners. This means that on a per-share, per-day basis, each shareholder of an S corporation is taxed on the income of the business. So, as is the case with partnerships, the ability of a shareholder in an S corporation to defer tax liability on income is lost (but only if the shareholder in question owns more than 5% of the corporation's stock).[75]

Question - Are there securities regulation issues with respect to nonqualified deferred compensation plans?

Answer - The answer is uncertain. At a meeting of the Securities and Exchange Commission (SEC), an SEC spokesperson stated that the SEC considered all nonqualified deferred compensation plans (with certain exceptions noted below) to be "registerable" and indicated that the SEC would be issuing a formal statement on its position. As of the date of this printing, that statement has not been issued. It is possible that the SEC may require the registration of nonqualified deferred compensation plans as "securities," but only if the plan involves employee contributions and the employees are motivated by "invest-

ment" rather than "tax deferral." If the employees making the contributions have "investment motives" (i.e., the plan involves investments in underlying securities whose return is credited to the employee), registration appears to be required. On the other hand, if employees are making contributions because of "tax deferral" motives (i.e., primarily to save income taxes), no registration with the SEC is necessary. In other words, an investment motivated nonqualified deferred compensation plan will be considered to be a security, while a nonqualified deferred compensation plan motivated by tax deferral need not be registered, because the plan will not be considered to be a security. In making its decision, the SEC will look at all the facts and circumstances. In the authors' opinion, most businesses which establish nonqualified deferred compensation plans for 20 or fewer key executives will probably qualify under one of the three safe harbor exemptions noted below, but plans covering a very large number of individuals or exceptionally large amounts of money may have to register. Certainly, no employer can ignore the issue and all should obtain competent legal advice on the registration issue.

The key registration exemptions that would apply to most small corporation plans are for "intrastate exemptions" (securities offered and sold only to persons resident within a single state), "small offerings", and "nonpublic offerings." Regulation D, Rules 505 and 506 are safe harbors which define the latter two exemptions, as follows:

(1) Offers and sales of securities with a total offering price of $5,000,000 or less, in which there are no more than 35 purchasers and which meet certain other rules will be protected from registration requirements.

(2) Offers and sales of securities which do not involve more than 35 purchasers are protected from registration requirements (regardless of the dollar amount of the offering) if every purchaser who is not considered an "accredited investor" is considered capable of evaluating the merits and risks of the prospective investment.[76]

Question – What is the impact of a nonqualified deferred compensation plan on the benefits payable under a qualified pension or profit sharing plan?

Answer – There is authority that might allow[77] and authority that might disallow[78] the inclusion of amounts deferred under a nonqualified deferred compensation plan in computing the amount that can be contributed to a qualified retirement plan on behalf of an employee.[79] In the authors' opinion, the IRS is most likely to argue that qualified retirement plan benefits discriminate in favor of the highly compensated where the qualified retirement plan takes into consideration amounts deferred under a nonqualified deferred compensation plan.[80]

Question – How does the elimination of the dollar limitation on wages subject to the Medicare hospital insurance (HI) tax affect nonqualified deferred compensation plans?

Answer – The Federal Insurance Contributions Act (FICA) tax is imposed upon both employees and employers. The base upon which that tax is levied has been a statutory maximum amount of employee wages. Actually, the tax is composed of OASDI (old-age, survivor and disability insurance) and HI (Medicare hospital insurance). The HI tax rate for wages paid to covered employees is 1.45% on both the employee portion and the employer portion (2.9% in total), and applies to all wages. The OASDI tax rate is 6.2% on both the employee portion and the employer portion (12.40% in total), and applies to the first $87,900 of wages.

Self-Employment Contributions Act (SECA) imposes a tax on an individual's self-employment income. The base is the same as for employees. The 15.3% self-employment tax rates are the same as the sum of the employee and employer rates above (2.9% for HI and 12.40% for OASDI).

The cap on wages and self-employment income subject to FICA and SECA taxes is indexed.

There is no dollar limit on wages and self-employment income subject to the HI portion of these taxes. High earners must now pay the HI tax on all wages and self-employment income. Employees and self-employed persons who have (or who establish) nonqualified deferred compensation plans or other types of supplemental retirement plans will be subject to the HI tax on ALL wages. The HI tax is imposed not when the money is received, but when it is earned. In other words, an employee covered under a nonqualified plan may be taxed at the HI rate on income he has not yet received.

Employers must now determine the present value of each year's deferred compensation accru-

als and be sure that employees satisfy the HI tax withholding rules.

Question – Can life insurance be used as a financing mechanism with respect to nonqualified deferred compensation plans for bank executives and directors?

Answer – Yes. The Office of the Comptroller of the Currency (OCC) has stated that life insurance purchased on the lives of executives and directors of banks is an appropriate investment when purchased as a funding mechanism for nonqualified deferred compensation plans. The OCC has held in an opinion letter that there were two legitimate justifications for banks to purchase insurance in this context. The first legitimate justification is to meet the bank's contractual obligation to make payments upon early, normal, or late retirement, as well as to families of covered employees at their deaths. The second legitimate justification is to serve as an actuarial cost recovery vehicle. In the opinion of the authors, the bank should own and name itself total beneficiary of the insurance. We feel it is essential for the parties to document (prior to the purchase of the life insurance) that the bank's obligation to make payments under the nonqualified deferred compensation plan would have existed with or without the presence of the insurance, and that the insurance was purchased to reduce or eliminate that previously existing liability.[81]

CHAPTER ENDNOTES

1. See e.g., IRC Sec. 404(d); Rev. Rul. 71-419, 1971-2 CB 220; Rev. Rul. 60-31, 1960-1 CB 174, Case 3. However, the IRS will not issue a private letter ruling with respect to the treatment of an independent contractor in an unfunded deferred compensation plans unless the independent contract is identified. Rev. Proc. 2004-3, Sec. 3.01(37), 2004-1 IRB 114.

2. For excellent coverage of the overall topic of nonqualified deferred compensation plans, see S. Leimberg and J. McFadden, *The Tools & Techniques of Employee Benefit and Retirement Planning*, 8th ed. (The National Underwriter Company, 1999); "A Fresh Look At Deferring Compensation: The Nonqualified Plan Alternative," *Pension Plan Guide No. 715* (Commerce Clearing House); Leimberg and McFadden, "Nonqualified Deferred Compensation: A Critical Look," *Journal of the American Society of CLU and ChFC*, May 1990, p. 32; Lewis and Skillman, "The Undeferring of Executive Compensation," *The Tax Executive*, Summer 1988, p. 313. See also L. Richey and L. Brody, *Comprehensive Deferred Compensation*, 3d ed. (The National Underwriter Company, 1997).

3. See "Meeting and Beating the 5R Problem," an employee benefit marketing brochure available from Leimberg & LeClair, Inc.

4. See, e.g., ERISA Secs. 4(b)(5), 104(a)(2)(A), 201(2), 301(a)(3), 401(a)(1); Labor Reg. §2520.104-23.

5   IRC Sec. 55(e).

6.   See FASB Statement No. 106 (December 1990). A complete discussion of accounting for deferred compensation is beyond the scope of this book. Plan sponsors should consult an accounting professional for advice regarding accounting for deferred compensation.

7.   See the example in Chapter 24, at "How It Is Done – An Example."

8.   See *Dependahl v. Falstaff Brewing Corp.*, 653 F.2d 1208 (8th Cir. 1981); *Goldsmith v. U.S.*, 586 F.2d 810, 78-2 USTC ¶9804 (Ct. Cl. 1978); *Frost v. Comm.*, 52 TC 89 (1969).

9.   Sample documents for nonqualified deferred compensation plans can be found in H. Zaritsky and S. Leimberg, *Tax Planning with Life Insurance*, 2d ed. (Warren, Gorham, Lamont, 1999), as well as in L. Richey and L. Brody, *Comprehensive Deferred Compensation*, 3d ed. (The National Underwriter Company, 1997).

10.   See ERISA Secs. 4, 101, 110; Labor Reg. §2520.104-23.

11.   See IRC Sec. 404(a).

12.   Treas. Reg. §1.404(a)-1(b).

13.   IRC Sec. 3121(v)(2). See TD 8814, 1999-9 IRB 4 and TD 8815, 1999-99 IRB 31.

14.   See IRC Sec. 1402(a).

15.   IRC Sec. 3306(r)(2).

16.   IRC Sec. 2642(e).

17.   IRC Sec. 2631.

18.   Rev. Rul. 70-514, 1970-2 CB 198.

19.   IRC Sec. 415(b).

20.   See IRC Sec. 415(b)(2)(c).

21.   IRC Sec. 415(c).

22.   IRC Sec. 401(a)(17).

23.   ERISA Sec. 3(36).

24.   See IRC Sec. 451(a); Treas. Reg. § 1.451-2(a). See generally Rev. Rul. 60-31, 1960-1 CB 174.

25.   See *Gullett v. Comm.*, 31 BTA 1067 (1935).

26.   Treas. Reg. §1.451-2(a).

27.   See Rev. Rul. 60-31, 1960-1 CB 174, as modified by Rev. Rul. 64-279, 1964-2 CB 121 and Rev. Rul. 70-435, 1970-2 CB 100. The IRS will not issue an advance ruling concerning the tax consequences of an unfunded arrangement if the arrangement fails to meet the guidelines set out in Rev. Proc. 99-3, Sec. 3.01(30), 1999-1 IRB 103, at 107; Rev. Proc. 71-19, 1971-1 CB 698, as amplified by Rev. Proc. 92-65, 1992-2 CB 428.

28.   See Rev. Proc. 71-19, 1971-1 CB 698. The Tax Court has been more lenient with elections to defer compensation after commencement of the earnings period. See, e.g., *Martin v. Comm.*, 96 TC 814 (1991); *Oates v. Comm.*, 18 TC 570 (1952), aff'd 207 F.2d 711 (7th Cir. 1953), acq.; *Veit v. Comm.*, 8 TCM 919 (1949); *Veit v. Comm.*, 8 TC 809 (1947), acq.

29.   See Let. Rul. 8607029.

30.   Treas. Regs. §§1.83-3(c)(1), 1.83-3(c)(2).

31.   Treas. Reg. §1.83-3(c)(1).

32.   There is some authority to support this belief. See, e.g., *Martin v. Comm.*, 96 TC 814 (1991); *Oates v. Comm.*, 18 TC 570 (1952), aff'd 207 F.2d 711 (7th Cir. 1953), acq.; *Veit v. Comm.*, 8 TCM 919 (1949); *Veit v. Comm.*, 8 TC 809 (1947), acq.

33.   Rev. Proc. 71-19, 1971-1 CB 698.

34.   See Rev. Proc. 99-3, Sec. 3.01(29), 1999-1 IRB 103, at 108.

35.   See TAM 8828004.

36.   See, e.g., *Commerce Union Bank v. U.S.*, 76-2 USTC ¶13,157 (M.D. Tenn. 1976); *First Trust Company of St. Paul v. U.S.*, 321 F.Supp. 1025 (D. Minn. 1970); and Rev. Rul. 77-139, 1977-1 CB 278 which support the proposition that a controlling shareholder's power to terminate a qualified pension plan does not cause the constructive receipt of the plan benefits for estate tax purposes. See also, *Moline Properties, Inc. v. Comm.*, 319 U.S. 436 (1943); *Casale v. Comm.*, 247 F.2d 440 (2nd Cir. 1957); and Rev. Rul. 59-184 which support the proposition that a corporation carrying on a valid business activity that is not a sham is a valid entity separate from its controlling shareholder.

37.   See *Goldsmith v. U.S.*, 78-1 USTC ¶9312 (Ct.Cl. Tr. Div. 1978), *adopted by full court w/out appeal*, 586 F.2d 810 (Ct. Cl. 1978). But see Let. Ruls. 8103089, 7940017. For a number of convincing arguments as to why *Goldsmith* should not be followed by the courts, see Richey and Brody, note 5 above, at p. 20.

38.   See, e.g., *Sproull v. Comm.*, 16 TC 244 (1951), aff'd. 194 F.2d 541 (6th Cir. 1952); *Goldsmith v. U.S.*, 78-1 USTC ¶9312 (Ct. Cl. Tr. Div. 1978), *adopted by full court w/out appeal*, 586 F.2d 810 (Ct. Cl. 1978).

39.   See, e.g., Let. Rul. 9214035.

40.   Under Treas. Reg. §1.83-3(e), an unfunded and unsecured promise to pay money or property is not property within the meaning of Sec. 83.

41.   Title I of ERISA imposes reporting and disclosure, participation and vesting, funding, fiduciary responsibility and other requirements on deferred compensation plans. Title IV of ERISA establishes plan termination insurance requirements.

42.   ERISA Secs. 4(b)(5), 4021(b)(8).

43.   ERISA Secs. 201(2), 301(a)(1), 401(a)(1), 4021(b)(6).

44.   See Labor Reg. §1.2520.104-23; ERISA Secs. 107, 503.

45.   Labor Reg. §1.2520.104-23(b)(1).

46.   Labor Reg. §1.2520.104-23(b)(2).

47.   See, e.g., Rev. Rul. 72-25, 1972-1 CB 127; Rev. Rul. 60-31, 1960-1 CB 174; DOL Advisory Opinion 81-11A. Compare *Dependahl v. Falstaff Brewing Corp.*, 491 F. Supp. 1188 (E.D. Mo. 1980), *aff'd in part*, 653 F.2d 1208 (8th Cir. 1981), *cert. denied*, 454 U.S. 968 (1981) and 454 U.S. 1084 (1981) (death benefit only plan financed with life insurance considered a funded plan) with *Belka v. Rowe Furniture Corp.*, 571 F. Supp. 1249 (D. Md. 1983) (nonqualified deferred compensation plan provided retirement and death benefit and financed with life insurance considered an unfunded plan) and *Belsky v. First National Life Insurance Company*, 818 F.2d 661 (8th Cir. 1987) (nonqualified deferred compensation plan providing retirement and disability benefits and financed with life insurance considered an unfunded plan).

48.   See Richey and Brody, note 5 above, at p. 11.

49.   But see Let. Rul. 8406012 (purchase by employer of surety bond does not by itself cause inclusion of deferred amounts before receipt). The IRS did not really understand that, in the typical situation, the employer must apply for the bond and consent to the employee's ownership. In reality it is the employer that stands behind the bond, and, for this reason, the authors believe the position of the IRS in the private letter ruling should not be relied upon.

50.   Unnumbered letter ruling, dated August 2, 1993, *reprinted in* 20 Pens. Ben, Rep. (BNA) 1802 (1993).

51.   See *Berry v. U.S.*, 593 F.Supp. 80, 85 (M.D.N.C., 1984), *aff'd* 760 F.2d 85 (4th Cir. 1985).

52. See Let. Rul. 8741078.

53. See, e.g., *Robinson v. Comm.*, 44 TC 20 (1965), (guarantees of boxer's deferred pre-fight payments by major owner of corporate fight promoter and by parent corporation of fight promoter did not cause the boxer to be other than an unsecured creditor) *acq.* 1970-2 CB xxi; Let. Rul. 8741078 (parent's guarantee of subsidiaries, deferred compensation obligations did not cause plan to be funded); Let. Rul. 7742098 (guarantees of corporation's deferred compensation obligations did not affect effectiveness of deferred compensation agreement). See also notes 42 and 43, above, and accompanying text.

54. See IRC Secs. 402(b), 83; Treas. Reg. §1.83-1(a)(1).

55. See, e.g., ERISA Secs. 201, 301(a), 401(a).

56. See Let. Ruls. 9815039, 9805030.

57. But see *Goldsmith v. U.S.*, 78-1 USTC ¶9312 (Ct. Cl. Tr. Div. 1978), *adopted by full court w/out appeal*, 586 F.2d 810 (Ct. Cl. 1978) (employee taxable on economic benefit of insurance protection).

58. See, e.g., DOL Advisory Opinions 92-13A, 91-16A, 90-14A, and 89-22A.

59. But see, e.g., Let. Rul. 9041053 (benefits payable after four, or fewer, years of employment).

60. For some time the IRS has refused to rule on rabbi trusts holding employer stock. This position seems to be changing, and the IRS apparently will now rule on the use of employer stock in a rabbi trust.

61. See Rev. Proc. 92-64, 1992-2 CB 422.

62. See Let. Ruls. 9242007, 9122034, 9121069. See also Rev. Proc. 92-65, Sec. 3.01(c), 1992-2 CB 428.

63. See Let. Rul. 8730041.

64. See Let. Rul. 8736045.

65. In Let. Rul. 8834041, the plans were sponsored by an employer and its subsidiary.

66. For an excellent in-depth discussion of the mathematics of deferral, see Doyle, "Employing Tax Leverage In a Time of Tax Uncertainty," in S. Leimberg, et al., *Financial Services Professional's Guide to The State of the Art* (The American College, 2nd ed., 1990).

67. See Tacchino, "Nonqualified Retirement Planning" in S. Leimberg, et al., *Financial Services Professional's Guide to The State of the Art* (The American College, 2nd ed., 1990).

68. See e.g., Let. Ruls. 9212024, 9212019, 9207010, 9206009.

69. See e.g., Let. Ruls. 9207010, 9206009.

70. Treas. Reg. §1.702-1(a).

71. IRC Sec. 702. A partner's capital interest in the partnership generally determines his or her distributive share.

72. IRC Sec. 101(a); Treas. Reg. §1.101-1(a).

73. IRC Sec. 705(a)(2)(B); Treas. Reg. §1.705-1(a)(3)(ii).

74. IRC Sec. 705(a)(1)(B); Treas. Reg. §1.705-1(a)(3)(ii). This Section provides that each partner's share of all undistributed amounts of income are included in basis adjustments.

75. IRC Sec. 1366.

76. AALU Bulletins No. 97-106, 97-97, 97-82, 97-51, 95-104, and 95-46; Securities Act of 1933; *SEC v. Howey*, 328 US 293 (1946).

77. Rev. Rul. 69-296, 1969-1 CB 127 (contributions made under IRC Sec. 403(b) annuity arrangement are compensation and can be considered in establishing contributions to a qualified money purchase pension plan).

78. Rev. Rul. 80-359, 1980-2 CB 137 (contributions to nonqualified plan may be used in computing benefits under qualified plan if such use does not result in discrimination against rank and file).

79. See Morrison and Hack, "Nonqualified Deferred Compensation Plans Can Reward Key Employees While Postponing Taxes," *Taxation for Lawyers*, March-April 1983, p. 291.

80. A private letter ruling is therefore suggested. See also, Treas. Regs. §§1.414(s)-1(c), 1.415-2(d)(3).

81. OCC Interpretive Letter No. 848 and OCC Bulletin 96-51 (which supersedes a 1983 Letter to the contrary). See also AALU Bulletin No. 99-5.

Chapter 27

PENSION MAXIMIZATION

WHAT IS IT?

A life insurance strategy called pension maximization or, sometimes, pension enhancement may provide a more attractive overall benefit package for married couples than the normal joint and survivor (J&S) annuity option from a qualified plan. The concept is simple. Rather than electing to receive the normal (normal default) J&S annuity from a pension plan, the retiring participant, with the consent of his or her spouse, selects the higher benefit payable under the single life (SL) annuity option. The couple purchases life insurance on the participant to assure the financial security of the spouse in the event the participant dies first and pension benefits cease. The difference between the pension benefit payable under the SL annuity and the lower joint benefit payable under the J&S annuity is available to pay premiums on the insurance.

A fundamental but often misperceived concept is that a J&S annuity is itself a type of insurance. Whenever a couple selects some form of J&S annuity, rather than the SL annuity, they are essentially buying insurance to assure survivor benefits for the spouse. The "premiums" they pay for this protection are equal to the difference between the benefit payable under the SL annuity and the joint benefit payable under the J&S annuity. For example, if the pension would pay $3,000 a month under the SL annuity option, but only $2,550 under the normal joint and 50% survivor annuity option, the couple is effectively paying a $450 monthly premium to insure that the spouse will be paid $1,275 per month (50% of the $2,550 joint benefit) in the event the plan participant dies first.

WHEN IS THE USE OF SUCH A DEVICE INDICATED?

1. When the participant and spouse wish or need to have more flexible survivor benefit options than those provided by a qualified plan's joint and survivor option.

2. When the participant's spouse is in poor health. In this case a qualified plan's joint and survivor option

may be an inefficient and expensive means to provide survivor benefits in the unlikely event the participant predeceases the spouse. The cost for the amount of insurance needed to provide income for the spouse who is in poor health for his or her remaining life in the event the participant predeceases the spouse may often be less than "cost" of the survivor benefit from the qualified plan.

3. When the participant's spouse has income and asset resources, such as his or her own retirement benefits, that can provide some of the spouse's required income needs if the participant predeceases the spouse. In this case, the cost of purchasing only so much life insurance on the participant as is necessary to supplement the spouse's other retirement income can be less expensive than the "cost" of the qualified plan's survivor benefit.

4. When the participant already has life insurance in place on his or her life that can provide the bulk of the surviving spouse's retirement income needs in the event the participant predeceases the spouse.

5. A pension maximization strategy is more likely to be feasible if the participant is a female. Pension benefits are computed based upon unisex mortality factors. Most life insurance policies are priced according to sex-based mortality factors. Since women still tend to live longer than men, the relative cost of survivor benefits acquired through insurance will generally be less than the cost of those same benefits acquired from a qualified plan.

ADVANTAGES

The principal advantage of a pension maximization strategy is planning flexibility as compared with the J&S annuity survivor benefit from a qualified plan.

The "insurance" feature of the J&S annuity has several unattractive elements. First, with this type of "insurance" the plan participant will generally have to continue paying the monthly "premium" (receive the lower J&S benefit payments rather than the higher SL benefit) even if the spouse dies first and the survivorship insurance is no longer necessary. Unless the plan has a "pop-up" feature where benefits payable to the participant jump or pop-up to the SL annuity amount in the event the spouse predeceases the participant, the participant will continue to receive the lower J&S benefit after the spouse's death. Typically, all else being equal, the joint benefit paid on J&S annuities with a pop-up feature is less than the joint benefit paid on normal J&S annuities. Either way, the couple must pay for the survivorship benefit by receiving lower joint benefits; it's just a matter of timing when the "premiums" are due.

A second unattractive element of the insurance feature of the J&S annuity is its lack of flexibility. Essentially the only option or choice a couple has with respect to the pension's survivor benefit is to select the survivor benefit ratio, that is, the percentage of the joint benefit that will be payable to the spouse in the event the participant dies first. The default ratio is 50%, but most plans will permit the couple to elect ratios of 66⅔%, 75%, or 100%. Of course, as the survivor benefit ratio goes up, the joint benefit typically goes down, effectively increasing the "premium" for the survivorship benefit.

Furthermore, a pensioner generally has no rights to (1) accelerate benefit payments if the need arises, (2) choose an alternative or substitute beneficiary if the spouse predeceases the participant, or (3) wait to select what type of benefit payout pattern will be paid to the surviving spouse if the participant dies first.

In contrast, the pension maximization plan is often attractive because a life insurance policy on the participant offers considerably more planning flexibility than the implicit "insurance" within the pension's J&S annuity.

If the spouse dies first, the participant has several alternatives as to what to do with the life insurance policy.

First, he may continue to pay premiums, keep the insurance in force, and name a new beneficiary, perhaps a child, grandchild, or even a favorite charity.

Second, he can suspend premium payments and effectively increase spendable retirement income. This is essentially a "home made" equivalent to the "pop-up" feature described above.

However, the participant still has several additional options with respect to the insurance coverage that are not available under the J&S annuity. If the policy has cash value, the participant may elect to keep the policy in force under either the reduced-face-amount fully-paid-up whole-life option or the full-face-amount term-life option. Alternatively, if life insurance is no longer needed or desired, he or she may surrender the policy and take cash value as a lump sum or under one of the many nonforfeiture (essentially annuity) options all life insurance policies must offer.

A life insurance policy also provides more flexibility than the J&S annuity with respect to the options available to the surviving spouse. Where the J&S annuity provides only one option – a life annuity for the spouse at some pre-specified proportion of the joint benefit – the life insurance provides many options as to how the proceeds may be distributed to the surviving spouse.

Although a couple may initially anticipate that a life annuity will be the best way to distribute the life insurance proceeds to the surviving spouse, circumstances may change. For example, if the spouse is not in good health, some form of higher-benefit, limited and guaranteed term annuity may be more suitable than a life annuity.

Alternatively, the couple may take a "wait and see" approach by setting up a trust to receive the life insurance proceeds. The trustee may be given discretion as to how to distribute the funds to best insure the surviving spouse's financial security. In such cases, payments could be accelerated to meet special needs, such as large medical expenses. Such flexibility is virtually never available under the pension's J&S annuity benefit.

Finally, a life insurance policy provides more flexibility to handle special or changing needs while both the participant and spouse are alive. For example, if the health of either partner begins to fail, they may borrow cash values from the policy to help pay medical expenses or simply to "accelerate" benefits that the couple may enjoy before deteriorating health eliminates that possibility. No such "acceleration" provision is generally available from the J&S pension option.

DISADVANTAGES

The life insurance option has its costs and risks. In general, the premium cost for an adequate amount of life insurance in a pension maximization plan that is implemented entirely when your client reaches retirement will be greater than the differential between the single and joint life annuity payouts from your client's pension. Whether the additional features and flexibility of the life insurance are worth the additional cost while the couple both live depends on what they want their plan to accomplish. Keep in mind that your client's financial needs will generally be greater when both the husband and wife are alive than when only one is alive. Also, a pension maximization plan that is implemented some years before retirement will generally cost less than one implemented later.

With the pension maximization plan, there is always a risk that premiums will not be paid and the insurance will not be in force when it is needed. Pension maximization should be employed only by those couples who are financially disciplined enough to see the plan through. Often, if the plan is implemented early enough, this risk can be reduced or eliminated altogether by paying enough up-front to entirely fund the life insurance policy at or soon after retirement.

WHAT ARE THE REQUIREMENTS?

The principal requirement involved in implementing a pension maximization strategy is compliance with the requirements of the Retirement Equity Act of 1984 (REA) for spousal benefits.

The law mandates that a spouse's interest in the participant's qualified retirement benefits must be protected and specifies that certain benefits must be paid to the spouse if the participant predeceases the spouse either before or after retirement. If these mandated benefits are not those desired by the participant and spouse, they may elect alternative forms of benefits or designate a beneficiary other than the spouse, but only by following strict compliance rules.[1]

Required (Default) Spousal Benefits – Unless expressly waived by both spouses in accordance with strict rules, qualified plans must generally automatically provide certain benefits for the participant's spouse. The first required benefit is a *qualified preretirement survivor annuity (QPSA)*. The QPSA is the automatic default benefit for the surviving spouse of a participant who dies before retirement, unless the participant and spouse have made a proper election otherwise. The second required benefit is a *qualified joint and survivor annuity (QJSA)*. The QJSA is the automatic default benefit for the participant and spouse at retirement, unless they have made a proper election otherwise.

Annuity starting date – The annuity starting date is a key date for purposes of determining whether benefits are payable as a QPSA, a QJSA, or another selected optional form of benefit payable under the plan. A participant who is alive on the annuity starting date must have benefits payable as a QJSA, unless the participant and

the spouse have made a qualifying election otherwise. The surviving spouse of a participant who dies before the annuity starting date must receive a QPSA, unless, once again, both the participant and the spouse made a qualifying election to waive the QPSA or to receive some other form of benefit in the event of the participant's death before the annuity starting date. The annuity starting date is also important for tax purposes, since "amounts received as an annuity" (periodic payments) and "amounts not received as an annuity" (nonperiodic payments) are subject to differing tax rules.

As a general rule, the annuity starting date is the first day of the first period for which an amount is paid as an annuity or in any other form as a retirement benefit to the participant under the plan.[2] In other words, it is the date at which payments are to commence to the participant under the QJSA or an alternative payout schedule, if properly elected with spousal consent. For most participants this date is the normal retirement age. However, for participants who retire early, it is the earliest date when benefit payments may begin for early retirement or the first date when benefits are payable after retirement, if later. For participants who continue to work beyond normal retirement age, the annuity starting date is generally the date when benefit payments are to begin under the plan once the participant retires.

REA requirements apply generally to all qualified pension plans – Plans that must meet the requirement include defined benefit, money purchase, target benefit, and cash balance plans. They also apply to benefits payable to a participant under a contract purchased by the plan and paid by a third party.[3]

Under a defined benefit plan, the survivor annuity requirements apply only to benefits in which the participant was vested immediately before death. They do not apply to benefits to which the participant's beneficiary becomes entitled by reason of the participant's death, or to proceeds of a life insurance contract, to the extent those proceeds exceed the present value of the participant's nonforfeitable benefits that existed immediately before death.[4]

The survivor annuity requirements also apply to nonforfeitable benefits payable under any defined contribution plan that is subject to the minimum funding standards of IRC Section 412 (money purchase pension plans but not profit sharing or stock bonus plans), including the proceeds of insurance contracts.[5] The rules also apply to profit sharing and stock bonus plans unless the plans meet the exception described below.

Exception for profit sharing and stock bonus plans and ESOPs – Profit sharing and stock bonus plans and ESOPs must conform unless *all* the following requirements are met:

- Each participant's vested benefit is payable on death to the surviving spouse, or, if there is no spouse, to a designated beneficiary (a spouse may consent to payments to a designated beneficiary);[6]

- The participant has *not* elected to receive benefits in the form of a life annuity; and[7]

- The qualified plan is not the recipient of a direct plan-to-plan transfer of benefits from a defined benefit, money purchase, target benefit, or cash balance pension plan. (If it is the recipient of a direct plan-to-plan transfer, then the general rules apply to the transferred benefit).[8]

In addition, the benefit must be available to the surviving spouse within a reasonable time after the participant's death. Access within a 90-day period following the participant's death is considered reasonable.[9] The benefit payable to the surviving spouse must also be adjusted for gains or losses occurring after the participant's death in accordance with plan rules governing the adjustment of account balances for other distributions.[10]

If these requirements are met, a participant does not need the spouse's consent to elect to take living benefits in some form other than a joint-and-survivor annuity. Permitted non-joint-and-survivor annuity distribution options would include:

- Term-certain annuities;

- Discretionary (nonannuity) installments; and

- Lump sum distributions.

Exception for certain benefits – Benefits are not required to be paid in the form of QPSA or QJSA if, at the time of death or distribution, the participant was vested only in employee contributions and the participant died, or distributions commenced, before October 22, 1986.[11] Also, if the present value of the participant's nonforfeitable benefit is $5,000 or less, a distribution may occur (usually a lump sum) without satisfying the spousal consent requirements for distributions other than the QPSA or QJSA.[12]

The REA requirements do not apply to IRAs.

Qualified preretirement survivor annuity (QPSA) – The QPSA is essentially a property right of the spouse created by law. The survivor benefit payable under the QPSA is an immediate annuity for the life of the participant's surviving spouse equal to the amount that would have been paid under the QJSA if the participant had either retired on the day before death or separated from service on the date of death and survived to the plan's earliest retirement age, then retired with an immediate joint and survivor annuity. If, before the participant's annuity starting date, the participant elects a form of joint-and-survivor annuity that satisfies the requirements for a QJSA and then dies before the participant's annuity starting date, the form of benefit elected is the QJSA, and the QPSA payable to the surviving spouse must be based on that form.[13]

Under a defined benefit plan, the plan must permit the surviving spouse to elect to receive payments under a QPSA no later than the month in which the participant would have reached the earliest retirement age. The plan may permit the surviving spouse to elect to begin receiving payments under the QPSA within a reasonable time after the participant's death (generally within 90 days), even if this date is before the plan's earliest retirement age.[14] If the surviving spouse elects to begin receiving payments before the earliest retirement date, the plan may actuarially adjust the value of the benefits to reflect the earlier distribution date.

The participant may elect an alternate form of benefit, if so offered by the plan, but only with spousal consent. Typically, considerable attention is paid to the form of benefit that will be paid at retirement and who should be named as beneficiary, but the form of benefit that will be paid and who should be named as the beneficiary in the event of the participant's death before retirement is often overlooked. It is important to coordinate elections regarding the QPSA with those anticipated regarding the QJSA. If, for example, the spouse has adequate pension benefits in the spouse's own right or other sources of retirement income, the participant may wish to name a child, parent, charity, or other person as the beneficiary of the retirement benefits. If this is desirable for retirement benefits, it is presumably also desirable for preretirement benefits. These objectives will be thwarted in the event of the participant's premature death unless the participant takes positive action to specify his intentions.

The participant may select a benefit other than the preretirement survivor annuity at any time after age

35 and can also change this election at any time before retirement. Generally, electing out of the preretirement survivor annuity entirely will increase the benefit payable at retirement, unless the plan specifically subsidizes the retirement benefit. The younger the participant is at the time the participant elects out, the greater, generally, will be the increase in the benefit payable at retirement.

Qualified joint and survivor annuity (QJSA) – The spouse's survivor benefit under the plan's default QJSA may be not less than 50% and not more than 100% of the joint benefit. For a married couple, the QJSA must be at least as valuable as any other optional form of benefit payable under the plan at the same time. Therefore, if a plan has two joint-and-survivor annuity options that would satisfy the requirements for a QJSA (e.g., a joint-and-50% survivor annuity and a joint-and-75% survivor annuity), but one has a greater actuarial value than the other (e.g., the joint and survivor annuity with 75% survivor benefit), the more valuable joint-and-survivor annuity is the QJSA.

If the plan offers two joint and survivor annuities that are actuarially equivalent, the plan must specify which is the QJSA. However, the participant may elect the other equivalent joint and survivor annuity without spousal consent. The participant may elect an alternate form of benefit, if so offered by the plan, but only with spousal consent.

An election to waive the normal form of joint and survivor benefit must be made during a 90-day period ending on the annuity starting date (the date on which benefit payments begin).[15] Notice of the election period must be provided to participants along with an explanation of the consequences of the election within a reasonable period of time before the annuity starting date, at least 90 days before the annuity starting date.

Spousal consent[16] – In general, any waiver of QJSA or QPSA benefits or election of an alternative benefit option will not be effective unless:

- The participant's spouse consents in writing to a change in either the QPSA or QJSA benefit;

- The election designates a beneficiary who may not be changed without spousal consent (unless the spouse expressly permits designation by the participant without further spousal consent);

- The election designates a form of benefit, which may not be changed without spousal consent;

- The consent acknowledges the effect of such election on benefit rights; and

- The consent is witnessed by a plan representative or a notary public.[17]

HOW IS IT DONE – AN EXAMPLE

The amount of insurance necessary to match the survivor benefits of the pension's J&S annuity can be estimated using the following present value of annuity due formula:[18]

$$InsAmt = SurBen \bullet (1-T) \bullet \left(\frac{1-(1+r^*)^{-N}}{r^*} \right) \bullet (1+r^*)$$

The terms of the formula are defined as follows:

InsAmt	=	Amount of insurance needed
SurBen	=	Initial annual survivor benefit from pension's J&S annuity (plus the dollar value of any other benefits, such as medical benefits, tied to continuation of pension payouts)
T	=	Assumed tax rate applicable to pension benefit (combined federal, state, and local tax rate)
N	=	Assumed number of years surviving spouse lives beyond participant's death
r*	=	Assumed aftertax inflation-adjusted rate of return on insurance proceeds
	=	$(r - I) \div (1 + I)$
r	=	Assumed aftertax investment rate of return on insurance proceeds
I	=	Inflation or cost-of-living adjustment (COLA, if any) for J&S survivor pension

The values for the assumptions should be conservative. This means the value for the assumed tax rate, *T*, should be at the high end of reasonable expectations. The assumed after-tax investment rate, *r*, should generally be at the low end of expectations. The COLA adjustment, *I*, (if any) should be at the high end of reasonable expectations (however, the COLA variable realistically should be less than *r*).

The appropriate assumption for N is a conservatively long estimate of the spouse's life expectancy.[19] This differs from the commonly-held wisdom that the appropriate assumption for N is a period considerably longer than the spouse's life expectancy in order to assure funds are not depleted in the event the spouse survives beyond his or her life expectancy. For example, one rule-of-thumb is to extend the period to 1 times the spouse's life expectancy at the date of the participant's retirement. However, this is overly conservative. The objective of the formula is to estimate the amount of insurance proceeds that would be necessary to reproduce the no-refund single-life survivor annuity that would otherwise be payable to the spouse under the pension plan's J&S annuity. The amount necessary to purchase (or receive as a life insurance settlement option) a no-refund single-life annuity can be estimated by using a conservatively long value for life expectancy together with conservative values for the other assumed variables. If an even longer period is used, the insurance need so calculated will be enough to provide not only a life annuity, but also a refund if the spouse dies before the end of the specified term. This overestimates the value of the spouse's survivor benefit from the pension plan.

The appropriate assumption for N depends initially not only on the spouse's age but also the spouse's health at the time the participant retires. If the spouse is in poor health with an expected life span that is shorter than normal for his or her age, the computation of the required insurance amount should use a value less than normal life expectancy.

For example, assume the spouse is age 60 when the participant retires. Assume also the survivor benefit under the pension's normal J&S annuity initially would be $24,000 (SurBen) per year, but the pension benefits are indexed for inflation, capped at a maximum of 4% per year. Assume a 5.5% after-tax return (r), a combined tax rate of 31% (T), a maximum COLA of 4% (L), and a life expectancy of 24.2 (N) years [the Table V value for age 60].

$$r^* = (r - I) \div (1 + I)$$

$$r^* = (.055 - .04) \div (1 + .04)$$

$$r^* = .01442$$

$$InsAmt = SurBen \bullet (1 - T) \bullet \left(\frac{1 - (1 + r^*)^{-N}}{r^*} \right) \bullet (1 + r^*)$$

$$InsAmt = \$24,000 \bullet (1 - .31) \bullet \left(\frac{1 - (1 + .01442)^{-24.2}}{.01442} \right)$$
$$\bullet (1 + .01442)$$

$$InsAmt = \$341,115$$

Based on the formula, the initial amount of required insurance would be $341,115. If the couple both survive for 10 years, the spouse's age would be 70, life expectancy declines to 16 years, and the required amount of insurance falls to $238,497. At the spouse's age 85, life expectancy is 6.9 years and the required insurance amount is $109,581. The amount of insurance required to finance the spouse's survivor benefit will generally decline each year that the participant and the spouse both survive. Figure 27.1 shows insurance requirements at various ages for three different assumed COLA rates.

WHAT ARE THE TAX IMPLICATIONS?

1. Survivor benefit distributions from a qualified plan and from a life insurance settlement option share some tax features, but differ in at least one important respect. In either case, income taxation on investment earnings is deferred until distributions are received. However, the distributions from a qualified plan will generally be subject to tax in their entirety, unless the participant acquired some nontaxable basis in the plan (for example, through nondeductible contributions, Table 2001 costs (formerly P.S. 58 costs) for insurance, or for loans that were treated as distributions and then repaid).

    Life insurance death proceeds are generally paid free of income tax. Consequently, if the death benefits are essentially used to purchase the equivalent of the qualified plan's survivor annuity under the settlement options, the survivor-annuitant will have a sizeable basis in the annuity. This basis will be recovered in a pro-rata fashion under the rules of IRC Section 72, leaving only a portion of each payment subject to income tax.

    Therefore, in determining the amount of insurance required so as to match the survivor benefit payable from a J&S annuity from the plan, planners have to consider the difference in the taxation of the benefits. Much less insurance is necessary to match the after-tax survivor payments from the qualified plan than to match the before-tax payments from the plan.

2. Similarly, planners must recognize that the amount that will be available to pay premiums on life insurance if the participant elects a SL annuity rather than a J&S annuity must be adjusted for taxes. The participant will only have the after-tax difference available to pay premiums.

Figure 27.1

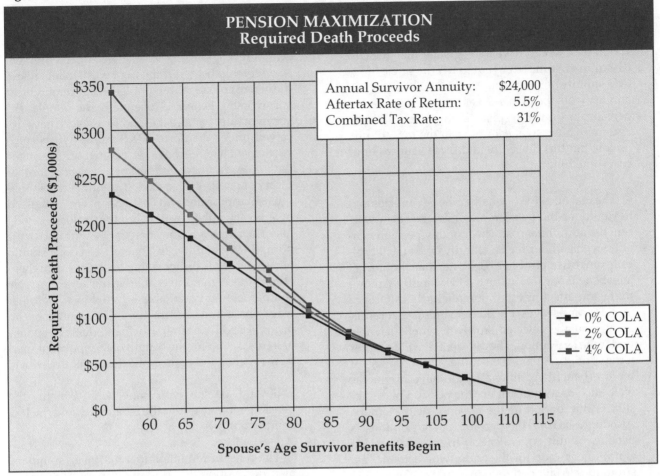

PENSION MAXIMIZATION
Required Death Proceeds

Annual Survivor Annuity:	$24,000
Aftertax Rate of Return:	5.5%
Combined Tax Rate:	31%

Y-axis: Required Death Proceeds ($1,000s)

X-axis: Spouse's Age Survivor Benefits Begin

Legend: 0% COLA, 2% COLA, 4% COLA

3. The value of the survivor benefit from a qualified plan J&S annuity will be included in the taxable estate of the participant. If the spouse is named as the beneficiary, it qualifies for the marital exclusion. However, if anyone other than the spouse is named as beneficiary, no exclusion applies.

If the participant retains any incidents of ownership in the life insurance policy, the death proceeds will be included in the estate. Similar to the survivor benefits from a qualified plan, if the spouse is named as beneficiary, the proceeds will qualify for the marital exclusion. If anyone else is named as beneficiary, the proceeds will be subject to estate tax.

However, if the participant creates an irrevocable life insurance trust, the death proceeds can escape inclusion in the estate. Often, even when the spouse is intended to be the primary beneficiary, an irrevocable life insurance trust can provide planning flexibility that is unavailable with the survivor benefit from a J&S annuity. For instance, the irrevocable life insurance trust can be arranged to handle contingencies, such as the possibility that the spouse

will predecease the participant, by naming contingent beneficiaries. Such planning options are generally unavailable with a J&S annuity survivor benefit from a qualified plan.

QUESTIONS AND ANSWERS

Question – How does one determine if a pension maximization strategy is feasible?

Answer – A pension maximization plan is not for everyone. The pension maximization plan is clearly advantageous if the extra pension benefit payable under the SL annuity option (as compared with the joint benefit payable under the standard J&S annuity option) is large enough to pay the premiums for a sufficient amount of life insurance. But this is not always, or even usually, the case.

The survivor benefits payable from a retirement plan are determined using actuarial methods and factors similar to those used to determine life insurance benefits. Assuming for argument's sake that all the assumptions used in the calculation of benefits for each alternative are identical, it is clear that the cost of the life insurance in the pension maximization plan would have to be greater than the cost (the difference in the payout under the single life or J&S annuity) of the insurance feature of the J&S annuity from the plan. As was described above, the pension maximization plan offers greater flexibility and more attractive features than the J&S annuity option, but this flexibility and these features must cost something.

The real question is whether the advantages and flexibility of the pension maximization plan warrant the additional cost. The monthly pension benefit payable under the SL annuity option will typically range from 10% to 25% greater than the normal joint benefit payable under the J&S annuity. Among the factors affecting this differential is the difference in the spouses' ages, the participant's age at retirement, and the selected survivor benefit payable under the J&S option. The differential will be larger if the survivor is paid 100% rather than only 50% of the joint benefit. Additional factors have an effect as well, such as whether or not the pension plan subsidizes one option at the expense of the others. Although each of the pension payout options is usually roughly equivalent on an actuarial basis, it is not uncommon for the underlying actuarial assumptions to favor one option over the others. Most often the normal joint and 50% survivor benefit annuity is the actuarially-favored option.

If the participant is insurable, a carefully designed pension maximizing plan can put the surviving spouse in a better position than just relying on the pension plan's survivor benefit and also provide the couple with a more attractive overall package of flexible options. Given the greater flexibility and the many advantages, a pension maximization plan may even be a desirable choice if the insurance premiums somewhat exceed the pension payout differential. But a bad design, or failure to follow through with the plan, can jeopardize the spouse's financial security in old age.

Question – What key points should planners keep in mind as they consider the pension maximization alternative for a client?

Answer – First, the spouse has rights to survivor benefits from the pension plan unless he or she expressly waives those rights in writing.

The normal form of pension benefit for married couples is a J&S annuity with a survivor benefit ranging from 50% to 100% of the joint benefit. In addition, a spouse is entitled to a preretirement survivorship benefit if the plan participant should die before normal retirement age. This preretirement survivorship benefit is essentially the same as the survivorship benefit the spouse would have received under the normal J&S annuity if the plan participant had retired or terminated service on the day of death. If a couple wishes to elect any other form of benefit, such as the SL annuity, the spouse must give informed and written consent (witnessed by a notary public or plan administrator) waiving his or her rights to the survivor benefit under the normal J&S annuity. In general, a spouse should never waive his or her rights to survivorship benefits without guarantees that he or she will receive comparable nonforfeitable benefits in some other way. These benefits are typically assured by an insurance policy on the participant's life. The spouse or a trust set up for the benefit of the spouse should be the owner and named beneficiary of the policy.

Second, be sure you know what benefits the pension will pay under the SL annuity and the J&S annuity options.

The pension administrator must give a summary plan description (SPD) to every plan participant. The SPD should describe all the options and participant rights under the plan. If necessary, the plan documents themselves can be reviewed to clarify the participant's and the spouse's rights. In addition, no later than within 90 days of retirement, the plan administrator must present retirees with a statement describing their options under the plan. Since it is advisable to begin planning sooner than 90 days before retirement, the participant may ask the plan administrator to estimate monthly benefits under various options before the 90-day period. The key factor is the relative difference between the single life and joint life payouts.

The differential between the SL and J&S annuities may be affected by whether the spouse is permitted to waive his rights to preretirement survivorship benefits and, if permitted, when he so elects. Typically, if the spouse waives rights to a preretirement survivor annuity, the value of the post-retirement J&S or SL annuity benefits are correspondingly increased. Therefore, it is often best to implement the pension maximization plan before retirement, especially if the plan permits the spouse to waive preretirement survivor benefits as well as post-retirement survivor benefits. The sooner the election to waive preretirement survivor benefits is made, the larger, generally, will be the upward adjustment of the post-retirement benefits. Once again, a spouse should generally not waive his rights to preretirement survivorship benefits until adequate insurance has been secured on the life of the plan participant.

Third, be sure to fully account for all of the benefits associated with the pension plan.

Some pension plans include specific cost-of-living adjustments (COLAs) or have a policy of making occasional ad hoc inflation adjustments to pension benefits. If the pension plan includes these adjustments, the couple's pension maximization plan will need a greater amount of insurance to provide benefits comparable to those offered by the inflation-adjusted pension.

In addition, employer-provided post-retirement medical benefits are sometimes tied to participation in the pension plan. In such plans, if the couple selects a J&S annuity, the company continues to pay certain medical benefits for both the participant and the spouse for as long as either one lives. However, if a couple selects the SL annuity from the pension plan, the spouse's medical benefits would typically cease upon the participant's death. Before proceeding with a pension maximization plan, check with the employer's benefits counselor to see how post-retirement medical benefits, if any, will be handled.

Fourth, a pension maximization plan is more likely to be a feasible alternative if some life insurance is already in force on the life of the participant before retirement. Often, the reasons for keeping life insurance in force change over time. For example, many people purchase life insurance to protect dependent children or to help finance their children's educations if the primary breadwinner dies. However, as the parents approach retirement age and the children leave the nest, these needs may diminish. Life insurance that was originally acquired for these kinds of purposes may then be used to help finance a pension maximization program. In such cases, the additional insurance required to fund the pension maximization program and its premium cost may be relatively low or zero.

Fifth, a pension maximization program is more likely to be feasible if insurance is acquired before retirement.

Keep in mind, the premium cost for insurance increases with the age of issue. The sooner an insurance program is implemented, the lower the average cost of coverage. Premiums must also be paid sooner, so there is an opportunity cost for setting up the program earlier rather than later. However, if a couple has legitimate life insurance needs before retirement, the purchase of life insurance with the anticipation of funding a pension maximization program at retirement becomes much more feasible.

One very important retirement reason for purchasing life insurance before retirement is to supplement the spouse's preretirement survivorship benefits from the pension plan.

Typically, pension benefits and, correspondingly, the spouse's survivorship benefits, will increase with the length of participation in the pension plan. If a participant dies before normal retirement age, contributions to the plan or benefit accruals for his or her account will be smaller than if the participant had survived to normal retirement age. Consequently, the spouse's survivorship benefits generally will be less than if the participant had survived to normal retirement age. However, the spouse's needs will actually be greater, since he will be younger and have a longer life expectancy than his life expectancy at the participant's normal retirement age. This deficiency can be corrected through the use of life insurance. If the participant survives to retirement age, at least a portion of the insurance needed for a pension maximization program will already be in place and have been partially or completely funded.

Sixth, a pension maximization strategy is more likely to be feasible if the participant is a female.

Despite some narrowing in the difference in longevity between men and women, women still exhibit longer life expectancies than men, on average. This enhances the feasibility of a pension maximization plan in two ways. First, private insurance uses sex-based mortality tables that are more favorable for females. Therefore, for a female the premium cost for life insurance purchased outside a pension plan will generally be less than that for a male, all else being equal. Second, since males of all relevant ages, on average, survive for a shorter period of years than females of the same age, less insurance is required to provide the same expected total survivor benefits until death for a male than for a female.

Seventh, a pension maximization strategy is more likely to be feasible if the participant's spouse is not in good health.

A J&S annuity is generally a poor "insurance" choice if the participant's spouse is less healthy than average for a person of his or her age. The greater the likelihood the spouse will not live as long as average for his or her age, the less insurance the pension maximization plan requires to assure a sufficient survivor benefit. For example, assume a participant-husband is in normal health, but the beneficiary-wife has advanced heart disease and is expected to survive, say, at most ten years. In this case the amount of insurance needed to provide survivor benefits for ten years in the event the husband predeceases the wife is considerably less than the amount needed for the normal duration of life for a healthy woman at normal retirement age.

Question – What information will be needed to analyze whether a pension maximization strategy should be implemented?

Answer – The types of information required are presented in the following checklist:

- A determination of what survivor elections are available from the pension plan, including joint and full survivor, joint and two-thirds, etc.;

- A comparison of the monthly dollar amount payable from the pension plan under the preferred joint and survivor option and under the single life option;

- Analysis of the current plan, including whether it provides cost-of-living increases and whether it requires a survivor election in order to maintain medical benefits if the participant predeceases the spouse;

- An assessment of the spouse's health;

- An assessment of the participant's health and insurability or rating classification;

- Standard information for insurance policies, including name, sex, date of birth, smoker/nonsmoker, physicals, etc.; and

- Generally, as Figure 27.1 demonstrates, the amount of insurance required declines as the couple ages, so some form of declining coverage, such as some combination of level premium whole life and decreasing term or universal life should be considered.

CHAPTER ENDNOTES

1. Retirement Equity Act of 1984 (REA). REA added Section 417 to the Code and made amendments to IRC Sec. 401(a). Technical and other corrections were made to REA by the Tax Reform Act of 1986. Additional guidance is provided in regulations issued under IRC Sections 401(a)(20), 411, and 417. See Treas. Regs. §§1.401(a)-20, 1.411(a)-11.
2. Treas. Reg. §1.401(a)-20, Q&A-10(b)(1).
3. Treas. Regs. §§1.401(a)-20, Q&A-1, 1.401(a)-20, Q&A-2.
4. Treas. Regs. §§1.401(a)-20, Q&A-3(a), 1.401(a)-20, Q&A-12(b).
5. Treas. Regs. §§1.401(a)-20, Q&A-3(a) and Q&A-12(b).
6. IRC Sec. 401(a)(11)(B)(iii)(1).
7. IRC Sec. 401(a)(11)(B)(iii)(2).
8. Treas. Reg. §1.401(a)-20, Q&A-3(a)(3).
9. Treas. Reg. §1.401(a)-20, Q&A-3(b)(1).
10. Treas. Reg. §1.401(a)-20, Q&A-3(b)(2).
11. Treas. Reg. §1.401(a)-20, Q&A-8(c).
12. Treas. Reg. §1.401(a)-20, Q&A-8(d).
13. Treas. Reg. §1.401(a)-20, Q&A-18.
14. Treas. Reg. §1.401(a)-20, Q&A-22.
15. Treas. Reg. §1.401(a)-20, Q&A-10(a).
16. IRC Sec. 417(a)(1).
17. Treas. Reg. §1.417(a)(2); Notice 97-10, 1997-1 CB 370.
18. To use a financial calculator to compute the InsAmt value, first set the calculator to payments at the beginning of each period (annuity due). Next, put the value of r^* into the interest rate register (usually designated r or I), the value of N into the years or periods register (usually designate n), the value of SurBen (1-T) into the payment register (usually designated Pmt), the value of 0 (zero) into the future value register (usually designated FV), and then *compute* the present value (usually designated PV), which is the estimated insurance need, *InsAmt*.
19. Table V - Ordinary Life Annuities - Expected Return Multiples, as provided in Treas. Reg. §1.72-9, is a useful source of conservative unisex life expectancy values. Table V is reproduced in Chapter 2.

Chapter 28

REVOCABLE LIFE INSURANCE TRUSTS

As one estate planning authority has stated:

> "As an estate planning tool, life insurance has no peer. It can create an estate where none otherwise exists or it can provide liquid funds to safeguard existing wealth. The benefits of life insurance as an estate planning tool can be increased through careful planning for the disposition of the life insurance itself. The personal life insurance trust is the premiere vehicle for achieving maximum flexibility in utilizing the death proceeds of life insurance to accomplish the decedent's personal and tax goals."[1]

This chapter should be read together with Chapter 23 on irrevocable life insurance trusts. Together, they will provide an excellent overview of how life insurance as a pivotal estate planning tool can be leveraged through another key tool, the trust.

WHAT IS A TRUST?

Picture in your mind a box.[2] Let's call that fictional box a "trust." Into that box you can put cash, stocks, bonds, mutual funds, the deed to your home, or even life insurance. You can put almost any asset into the box. When you do put property into the box, you are "funding" the trust (although some authorities restrict the definition of the term "funding" to the transfer of income producing assets into the trust). Funding (in the sense of adding income producing assets to a life insurance trust) is usually for the purpose of providing a source for premium payments where the trust will actually own and hold one or more policies.

State law determines the existence or nonexistence of a trust. In fact, a trust does not technically come into existence until the trust is at least nominally funded (often with little more than a small U.S. Savings Bond). Some states allow a trust to be considered funded merely by naming it the beneficiary of life insurance proceeds. Almost any type of asset can be placed into the trust. Assets typically found in trusts include cash, stocks, bonds, mutual funds, the deed to real estate, and life insurance. Additional assets can be placed into a trust even after it is initially

"funded." For example, a small government bond may form the initial funding of a trust but then later the same trust can be named as beneficiary of a life insurance policy, a pension plan, an IRA, or HR-10.

A trust is therefore a legal relationship that enables one party (called a trustee) to hold money or other property (the trust principal or "res" or "corpus") transferred to the trust by a second party (called the "grantor," "settlor," or "trustor") for the benefit of one or more third parties (the "beneficiaries") according to the terms and conditions of a legal document (called the "trust agreement"). In other words a trust is a means by which a property owner may separate the burdens of property ownership from the benefits of property ownership to whatever degree and upon whatever terms and for whatever period (within reasonable limits imposed by law) and for the benefit of whomever he pleases.[3]

Again, the key to understanding a trust is that for investment, management, and administration purposes the trustee holds full legal title to the property in the trust. But that trustee (or trustees, since there can be more than one) must use or distribute the property and the income it produces solely for and to the beneficiaries (or class of beneficiaries) selected by the grantor and named in the trust.

Should the trust fail (perhaps because the trust is declared invalid for technical reasons), the beneficiary holds the proceeds under what is called a "resulting trust." This is a fictitious trust created by law to prevent unjust enrichment. Usually, the proceeds held in such a resulting trust are eventually paid to or for the benefit of the would-be grantor's estate. However, if the trust is poorly drafted and there is not sufficient evidence to show that the presumptive grantor intended to create a trust, the beneficiary takes total and absolute title to the proceeds.[4]

LIVING TRUST DEFINED

A trust set up during the lifetime of the client is called an "intervivos" (living) trust. That trust can hold assets (including life insurance contracts) placed into the trust by its creator during his lifetime. It could also provide for the acceptance of additional assets at its creator's death. His will could "pour over" assets from the estate into the previously established trust. This is the "LITPOW" (Life Insurance Trust – Pour Over Will) combination that has been used as an effective estate planning tool for generations.

WHAT IS A REVOCABLE LIFE INSURANCE TRUST?

A revocable trust, as its name implies, is a trust established during a client's lifetime that can be revoked by the client. The client who sets up a revocable trust specifically reserves the right, at any time (until specifically making the trust irrevocable or until death at which time it becomes irrevocable), to alter or amend its terms or terminate the trust and recover its assets. In most states, a trust is irrevocable unless the trust document specifically provides otherwise. Also, a revocable trust is generally irrevocable while the grantor is incompetent.

If the revocable trust, through its trustee, is designated as the beneficiary (or as both the owner and beneficiary) of one or more insurance policies on the life of the trust's grantor, the trust is a revocable life insurance trust. The policy owner names the trust as beneficiary of the policy proceeds and the trustee is directed in the trust agreement to hold those proceeds for the beneficiaries of the trust to be distributed in the time and manner specified in the trust document.

When a revocable life insurance trust is created, the policy owner typically reserves all of the ownership rights in the policies and, unless the trust is funded with income producing assets, the policyowner will continue to be responsible to pay all premiums. If the trust is funded with income producing property, the trustee usually will be required to use the income from those assets to keep the insurance in force.

Actually, life insurance policies are seldom transferred to a revocable trust. Although the mere designation of a trust as the beneficiary of life insurance is sufficient in most states to create the trust, most cautious authorities suggest some other cash or other asset be placed into the trust as well to thwart an argument in a jurisdiction that may not clearly accept such a designation as adequate.

Note that a formal trust document should always be created since the mere designation of "trustee" as policy beneficiary will not, per se, establish a trust. Absent sufficient evidence to prove that a trust was intended, the policy proceeds will be paid outright (probably to the insured's estate if no other beneficiary was named). But if it can be shown that a trust was intended, even if the trust should fail for technical reasons, a "resulting trust" (a fictitious trust created by law to uphold the creator's wishes) occurs and the proceeds are held for the beneficiary.[5]

A revocable trust can be named as a contingent beneficiary of policy proceeds so that if the primary or even backup beneficiary died before the insured, there would be a receptacle for the money. For instance, a parent might name the other parent as primary beneficiary but provide in the insurance application that "If my spouse predeceases me, proceeds are to be paid to Thomas Trustworthy, trustee of the living trust I have established."

There is one good reason to transfer ownership of life insurance policies to a revocable trust and have the trustee name the trust as beneficiary: if the grantor becomes incapacitated, the trustee can, if necessary, borrow the cash value of the policies to keep them in force.

WHY SHOULD A CLIENT SET UP A TRUST?

There are many reasons why a client may want to make a gift in trust as opposed to outright. There are, of course, tax savings goals but, typically, these cannot be accomplished through revocable life insurance trusts.[6] Generally speaking, revocable life insurance trusts save neither income nor estate taxes. So it is the people oriented objectives of revocable trusts that provide the greatest incentive for their creation.

These can be categorized into the following broad terms of income and wealth:

1. management;

2. conservation; and

3. distribution.

More specifically, clients set up revocable trusts during their lifetime ("inter vivos" revocable trusts) to accomplish the following objectives:

1. *Postpone ownership during incapacity or inability of the beneficiary* – Quite often a client will feel that the beneficiary is unwilling or unable to invest, manage, or handle the responsibility of

an outright gift. Gifts to minors, for example, would fall into this category. But a trust should also be considered for persons who are legally adults but who lack the emotional or intellectual training, experience, physical capacity, or willingness to handle either large sums of money or assets which require constant and high level decision making ability. So a trust is often used to postpone full ownership until the donees are in a position to handle the income and the property itself properly.

2. *Maintain control over a beneficiary* – Some clients are reluctant to place all the ownership rights in the hands of a donee. They utilize trusts as the solution to the ambivalent position of wanting to institute a gift program but fear the possible results of an outright no strings attached transfer that lessens the donee's dependence on them.

3. *Avoid fragmentation of property* – A further impetus for the use of a trust is where the proposed gift property does not lend itself to fragmentation but the client wants to spread beneficial ownership among a number of people. For example, a large life insurance policy and the proceeds generated by it at the insured's death are often better held by a single trustee than jointly by several individuals.

4. *Retention of control over assets* – A revocable life insurance trust, which the client can alter, amend, revoke, or terminate at will, should be considered where conservation of assets and particular dispositive plans are important. In other words, if retention of lifetime control is essential to the client, such as where the client wants to limit the class of beneficiaries (e.g., no in-laws) or where the client wants to prevent the beneficiary from disposing of the property to persons outside the family, a trust provides a vehicle for a client to make a gift with minimal loss of lifetime control. At the same time, the client builds in flexibility to meet future contingencies and attain personal objectives.

5. *Unifying receptacle for other assets* – Because a trust can be named as recipient of almost any type of asset and because such property can be placed into trust at any time (and because parties other than the party who originally established the trust can make contributions of cash or property), a revocable trust makes an ideal vehicle for later contributions to "pour-over" into it. This unification of assets is particularly important if the client owns many different types of assets or owns property in more than one state. Bringing the assets together may save administrative costs and avoid multiple probates where property is owned in more than one state.

6. *Avoidance of publicity* – The terms of a trust are not public knowledge. Therefore, the amount placed into trust, the terms of the transfers, and the identity of the income and ultimate recipients does not become public knowledge. Privacy is particularly important where there are (or there is the potential for) intra family conflicts. Since there are no requirements that nonbeneficiary family members must be notified of the nature or extent of trust assets or the details of the dispositive plan of a revocable trust, the potential for family disputes is low. This is particularly important where the client wants to disinherit a particular family member or name a friend who is not a family member as a beneficiary.

7. *Opportunity for a trial run* – Setting up a trust during the client's lifetime affords an opportunity of seeing how well the trustee manages the property placed into the trust and how well the beneficiaries handle the income or other rights given to them. It also familiarizes the trustee with the client's assets, family, plans, and relationship of each to the others. If the client doesn't like what he sees, changes can be made.

8. *Selection of a favorable forum* – A revocable trust allows the client to select a state where the laws are most favorable to accomplishing his dispositive and administrative objectives. It is not necessary to use the laws of the client's domicile when creating a revocable living trust. To accomplish this objective, the trust should specify the state law that is to govern it. In some cases it may be necessary to have trust proceeds paid to a trustee in the selected state. Planners must, however, take care not to set up a multiple domicile issue when setting up a trust outside of the state of the grantor's domicile.

Cases where it may pay to shop for more favorable state law include (as well as where it may pay to use a trust rather than dispose of property by will) where the other (nondomiciliary) state has a more favorable (from the client's viewpoint) law regarding:

- *The rule against perpetuities* – This would allow the trust to continue longer than might be permitted otherwise.

- *Elective share (surviving spouse's rights to a statutory share of a deceased spouse's estate)* – For instance, in Florida, if property is placed into a revocable living trust, the surviving spouse has no right to it since the elective share is defined as a percentage of the probate estate.

- *Will contests* – If the client anticipates an attack on the will, a revocable trust should be considered. One reason is that the trustees of the trust can use trust assets to defend the trust against a challenger. On the other hand, in a will contest, until the validity of the will is determined, neither side has access to estate funds and each must personally bear the costs of litigation. Furthermore, the criterion for proper execution of a trust may be more lenient and therefore more easily defended than the requirements for a valid will.

- *Creditor's rights* – However, if the transfer is made to the trust in avoidance of existing or anticipated claims of creditors, it may be voidable.

- *Charitable bequests* – Some states contain charitable rules called "mortmain" statutes that nullify or otherwise limit gifts to charities if made within a specified period prior to death. The use of a revocable living trust may avoid this rule in some states.

- *Restrictions on qualification to serve as executor* – Careful selection of applicable state law may allow a party to serve who might not be qualified under the law in the client's state of domicile.

9. *Equalize risk and potential* – A living trust can be a great equalizer for both downside risk and upside potential. For instance, if a parent owned several parcels of land of equal value or used life insurance proceeds to purchase several parcels of land, he could make outright gifts of Parcel A to his daughter and Parcel B to his son. However, the children may be treated unequally since one property could drop in value while the other could rise. Alternatively, both proper-

ties could rise or fall at different rates. Placing both properties in trust could equalize the risks and potential rewards between the children. Investment results of life insurance proceeds invested in a pool by the trustee could be shared equally by the beneficiaries.

10. *Provide for ownership flexibility during beneficiaries' minority* – Major decisions and actions cannot be taken if property is placed directly in a minor's hands but can be taken if the same property is placed in trust for the minor. This generally makes it possible to sell, exchange, or mortgage a minor's property without the expensive, inflexible, and troublesome process of appointment of a guardian.

11. *Assure dispositive objectives* – An outright gift to a beneficiary will often return to the child's parents or go to the child's spouse or someone other than to whom the client would want it to go. This may defeat many of the client's non-tax objectives. A revocable trust would provide an assurance that the client's dispositive objectives could not be easily defeated.

12. *Provide for the helpless* – Physically, mentally, emotionally, and legally incompetent beneficiaries can be financially provided for though a revocable trust.

13. *Relieve the overburdened* – Even beneficiaries who are competent adults can be both protected against their own indiscretions and relieved of the burdens of investment, management, and record keeping.

14. *Back-up for the healthy* – A funded revocable trust can provide for the grantor in the event he is incapacitated and avoids the expensive, complex, aggravating, and embarrassing court process necessary to declare a person legally incompetent. A revocable trust, coupled with a durable power of attorney, can provide the basis for a contingency plan to deal with a client's inability to handle his own financial affairs.

15. *Multi-state administration can be avoided through the use of a revocable trust* – For instance, many clients will own property in more than one state. Ancillary administration (i.e., estate administration by a state other than the client's domicile state) is both expensive and aggravat-

ing. The client can unify the process and, in many cases, significantly cut down administration costs by placing title to out of state assets in a single revocable trust.

16. *Reduce the risk of a successful challenge* – Once an inter vivos (during lifetime) trust is created, its ability to perform the task for which it was designed is more certain than a will. This is at least one reason to establish an inter vivos rather than testamentary trust (one established under the grantor's will). Particularly, when one or more provisions of the client's will are controversial or likely to stir up a family dispute, a will is likely to be challenged or a surviving spouse may elect against (i.e., exercise a statutory right to take a share of the estate regardless of the terms of) the will. A trust is much less likely to be broken than a will based on the lack of capacity of the grantor or upon a claim of fraud or distress. Furthermore, the trustee can use trust assets to defend against a party who disagrees with the terms of the will.

ADVANTAGES OF A REVOCABLE LIFE INSURANCE TRUST

Among the advantages of a revocable life insurance trust, in addition to or as a consequence of making a revocable trust beneficiary of life insurance proceeds, are the following:

1. If a revocable trust is named as the beneficiary of all of a client's life insurance, a simple amendment to the trust can instantly achieve a redistribution of the proceeds of dozens of policies. This should save the client considerable time and aggravation compared to filling out a multiplicity of forms from numerous insurance companies.

2. Life insurance proceeds payable to a revocable trust are immediately available for the trustee's disposition. Conversely, insurance proceeds payable to a testamentary trust will not be available to the beneficiaries until the will has been admitted to probate and the trustee has accepted the trust. In some cases, there may be a delay of several years between admission of the will to probate and acceptance and final funding of the trust.

3. The transfer of a life insurance policy to the trust, the designation of the trustee as the ben-

eficiary, and even the distribution of the proceeds to the trustee can generally be structured as tax-free transactions.

4. Use of a trust makes the disposition of a policy easier where the beneficiary predeceases the insured. Compare this with an outright gift of the policy to a beneficiary who then dies before the insured. If a trust is used, it can continue to hold the policy after the predeceasing beneficiary's death and eventually transfer it to another party and in the way the insured client intended.

5. Probate is avoided with respect to a policy held by or payable to a revocable trust that continues after the beneficiary's death. Compare this with an outright gift of a policy to a beneficiary who then dies. If the intended individual beneficiary dies either prior to or after the insured, the policy or its proceeds are likely to be subjected to the costs, delays, and uncertainties of probate. Under the revocable trust document, interim distributions to the client's surviving spouse and/or children can be made without waiting for court approval.

    Use of a revocable life insurance trust assures continuation of the privacy of life insurance since there is no publicity and the amount of proceeds and other assets in the trust, as well as the terms of the trust, are not open to public scrutiny as are the reports and accounts filed with the probate court. Use of a revocable living trust as the receptacle for life insurance continues the exemption of proceeds from some states' death tax.

6. To some limited extent (varying widely from state to state)[7] life insurance proceeds payable to a revocable trust may be insulated from the claims of the grantor's creditors and the claims of the grantor's surviving spouse through an attack on the will or election against the will.

7. Using a trust continues the privacy afforded through life insurance. Confidentiality of who receives the proceeds and how much they receive is generally maintained for a longer period of time than if the proceeds were paid outright.

8. All the client's assets (such as life insurance, pension plan, IRA, and personal property) can be "poured over" into a revocable living trust.

The trust serves as a unifying receptacle for the collection of assets from a variety of sources and makes it easier to coordinate life insurance with other sources of financial security.

9. Compared to the use of settlement options, a trust provides significantly greater flexibility in terms of the trustee's ability to sprinkle income or spray capital when and as needed by the beneficiaries.

10. Compared to the use of settlement options, a trust makes it possible for the beneficiary to receive greater income and appreciation of capital. (Of course, both advantages entail greater risk.)

DISADVANTAGES OF A REVOCABLE TRUST

There is no tool or technique that is without cost and totally risk free. Trusts, even revocable trusts, are no exception. There are costs, paperwork, and other potential problems. These include:

- *Legal and accounting fees* – Legal fees to draft a trust may range from $500 to $5,000 or more depending on the degree of complexity in the trust, the expertise and reputation of the attorney, the prevailing legal fees in the area, and issues collateral to the creation of the trust that must be resolved. Compare these costs to buying an insurance policy and selecting a settlement option. In cases where the amount of insurance concerned is modest, a policy settlement option to provide for the management of insurance proceeds for the insured-grantor's family may prove to be a more cost efficient and objective effective mechanism than a revocable life insurance trust.

  Once a revocable trust is funded, filing of income tax returns may be required even though the trust may be treated as a grantor trust. IRS Form 1041, the Fiduciary Income Tax Return, is used to show the trust's income, deductions, and credits which must be reported by the grantor for taxable years beginning before the grantor's death. If the same person is both the grantor and the trustee (or co-trustee) or if one or both spouses are grantors and one or both spouses are trustees or co-trustees, Form 1041 is not required. If the trust has no income (as it typically would not as long as its only significant

asset was the potential receipt of life insurance proceeds), no income tax returns need be filed. At the insured's death, as long as the trust continues in existence, income earned from insurance proceeds payable to the trust must be reported on returns filed by the trust.

- *Trustee's commissions* – Although typically nominal when a trust is still unfunded, trustees' fees may run as high each year as 1.5 to 2% of trust assets and therefore must be considered. The younger the client is, the longer the trust will run and the higher the overall fees.

- *Hidden obstacles* – There are also hidden obstacles, such as the problem where a bank that holds a mortgage on property refuses to allow the mortgage to be carried over to the trust because a lender might have difficulty selling the mortgage on the secondary market. Will the client's property and casualty company insure cars and homes owned by a trust? (Consider the question of who has the right to drive trust owned cars?)

  Perhaps the biggest hidden obstacle is the time and trouble it takes to continually assign assets to the trust. Special forms must be completed at banks and brokerage houses and new deeds must be prepared (entailing conveyancing costs) and recorded (and in some cases transfer taxes must be paid) to transfer real estate to a revocable trust. Even if the client takes the time to transfer title to all his assets to the trust at its creation, after a number of years the client will often forget or not go to the trouble of titling new assets such as a car or personal effects in the name of the trust. Yet if such items are not transferred to the trust, the benefits of probate avoidance and property management and dispositive control for which the revocable trust is formed are unobtainable.

- *Estate taxes* – Since by definition, the trust is revocable, insurance proceeds paid to the trust will be includable in the insured-grantor's gross estate for federal estate, and generation-skipping transfer tax purposes. Of course, this may not be a disadvantage if the estate is less than the unified credit equivalent.

- *Panacea syndrome* – Many promoters of the revocable trust imply that somehow this tool is – by itself – a "magic pill" that can be purchased generically and once swallowed will solve all problems. "Buy my book, rip out the form, sign your name, and all your problems are solved." Not only is this incorrect; it is dangerous. Why? Because it deprives the estate owner of the advice of true estate planning professionals. It blocks questions about other problems the client may not know he has and eliminates the potential to use other tools and techniques, either as alternatives or complementary devices to the revocable trust.

ROLE OF THE TRUST DOCUMENT

Sometimes called a "Trust Indenture" or "Trust Agreement," this document sets forth the agreement between the parties (and serves as evidence for the "other parties in interest" in every trust agreement, the federal and state taxing authorities) and spells out:

1. how assets are to be managed;

2. who will receive income and capital from the trust;

3. how the trust income and capital is to be paid out; and

4. when (date or beneficiary's age) or under what circumstances (birth, death, marriage, etc.) the income and capital is to be paid to each beneficiary.

Where a trust is to be the beneficiary of life insurance or is to hold one or more policies, specific wording should be provided in the trust document to enable the trustee to accept the proceeds and hold the policies. Even more important, if the trustee is to purchase life insurance on the grantor's life or the lives of others, or is to pay premiums on one or more such policies, it is necessary that the terms of the trust specifically authorize such action. Many states do not permit the investment of trust assets in life insurance unless authorized by the terms of the trust or under provisions of the state's trust laws.[8]

WHAT IS THE JOB OF THE TRUSTEE?

The trustee is responsible for safeguarding and investing the assets in the trust and making payment as directed (or if given discretion, as appropriate under the guidance provided in the trust) to the named beneficiaries. This responsibility may run for as short as a few years or for generations.

Any natural person with the legal capacity to take and hold title to property and deal with it or any corporation which is authorized by its charter or articles of incorporation to act as trustee and which meets relevant state law requirements can be named as trustee. Unincorporated associations or partnerships cannot be trustees since they are not separate legal entities.

Although legally, there is no limit to the number of trustees, most clients select one, two (often a corporate trustee and an individual), or three (to avoid a voting tie). In some states, individuals and nonbank corporations serve as professional trustees. When more than one party is named, each is a co-trustee and all make decisions (and bear responsibility for mistakes) jointly. The authors recommend that at least two backup trustees be named in every trust in case the one named for some reason can't continue to act or refuses to serve.

A trustee's job can be a dangerous one depending on the funding of the trust. Life insurance is a relatively clean and safe asset to make payable to or have owned by the trust. But consider real estate, perhaps an apartment house, manufacturing business, or gas station placed into the trust to provide income and avoid probate. Consider the liability of the trustee for fines, cleanup costs, and damage to the environment if hazardous waste is found on the property, even if the hazard was created long before the trust and without the knowledge of the trustee.

WHO CAN BE THE BENEFICIARIES OF A TRUST?

Beneficiaries of a trust receive income from trust assets and/or principal at the ages and under the terms specified in the trust document. They can (and often do) include the person who established the trust. The first people to receive distributions are called "primary beneficiaries." The class of beneficiaries who receives what remains when a trust terminates are called "remainderpersons."

Although beneficiaries do not have to be identified by name, or even all be in existence at the date the trust is created, they must be an identifiable and definite class or group and must be in existence within the period measured by the appropriate state's rule against perpetuities. This makes it possible for a trust to be created for the "children of the grantor" even though all the members of that class of beneficiaries (the grantor's children) may not be in existence at the moment the trust is created since the grantor is presumed capable of having more children. As long as the class is limited and definite and all its members must be in existence within the period of the rule against perpetuities, the trust will be valid.

The rule against perpetuities is a state law restriction designed to limit the period during which a trust can withhold property or its income from outright ownership. The operation of the rule will vary from state to state but typically provides that a restriction will fail if it ties up property longer than a length of time equal to "lives in being" plus 21 years. In other words, the right to outright ownership of property must "vest" (can't be indefinitely restricted) within a given time frame.[9]

The Uniform Statutory Rule Against Perpetuities, which has now been adopted by a number of states, takes a slightly different approach. Rather than invalidating property interests at inception, this law adopts a flat period of 90 years from the creation of the interest (rather than a period measured by lives in being at the creation of the interest) and waits to see if the rule is violated before invalidating the interest.

SELECTION OF A TRUSTEE

When selecting a trustee, the major attributes to consider are the trustee's willingness to serve and at what cost; the trustee's experience with trust, financial, business, accounting, and tax matters; the trustee's temperament and relationship with the beneficiaries; and the tax effects of serving as trustee.

There are important tax considerations that go into the selection of a trustee. The grantor must consider whether a particular family member or related person can serve as trustee without creating unanticipated and adverse income, gift, or estate tax consequences.

During the grantor's lifetime, the trustee of an unfunded revocable life insurance trust has a relatively simple task. If the trust is merely the policy beneficiary, the trustee has virtually no responsibilities, not even to ascertain if premiums are paid or the policy is in danger of lapsing. If the trust is the policy owner and beneficiary, the trustee will have to use the trust funds and contributions by the grantor or others to pay the policy premiums. At the insured's death, the trustee must file the death claim, assuming the insured's executor hasn't already done so.

It is permissible, and often the case, that the person who establishes the trust names himself as the trustee while the only asset in the trust is the right to receive policy proceeds. But in such cases, there must be at least one other individual named as beneficiary of the trust. The reason is an ancient trust rule known as the "doctrine of merger." In a nutshell, this rule requires that the trustee and the beneficiary of the trust not be identical. Otherwise, the same party would hold both legal and equitable title, an event that nullifies the existence of the trust. If the sole trustee is the sole beneficiary, the trust is dissolved.

It is sometimes suggested that a trust should never have the following:[10]

1. one of two or more beneficiaries as sole trustee; or

2. one of two or more trustees as sole beneficiary; or

3. beneficiaries who are the same persons as the trustees.

Many expert planners suggest that someone other than the grantor be named as trustee because of the difficulty of accomplishing a smooth succession if the grantor becomes incapacitated. If the trustee is a corporate trustee, on the other hand, management of trust assets can continue without interruption even if the grantor becomes physically or mentally incapacitated. A potential compromise is for the grantor to be co-trustee. In any event, provision should be made for at least two or three successor trustees to take over administration of the trust in the event the current trustee, for whatever reason, cannot or will not continue to serve.

ESTATE TAX IMPLICATIONS

There are a number of estate tax related issues that must be considered with respect to revocable life insurance trusts. One concerns inclusion of trust assets. A second relates to the taxation of proceeds from policies owned by a third party but payable to the revocable trust. A third concerns the mechanism through which policy proceeds payable to a revocable trust can be used to provide estate liquidity.

1. *General estate tax inclusion issues* – Picture the box that represents a trust. Now imagine that the client retains a string on that box that enables him to pull back the assets in the box at any

time or use the income from the assets in the box for any purpose. Precisely because the client retains until death that right to alter, amend, revoke, and terminate the revocable trust, all the assets in such a trust will be included in the client's estate. The provision that encompasses such transfers is IRC Section 2038 which deals with lifetime gratuitous transfers in which the transferor retains the right to alter, amend, revoke, or terminate the gift. So revocable trusts, contrary to what is sometimes conveyed to the public, provide absolutely no shelter from the federal estate tax. Policy proceeds and any other assets in the trust at the client-grantor's death are estate tax includable.

2. *Third party owner issues* – Can the IRS include a life insurance policy in an insured-decedent's estate merely because it names a revocable trust established by the decedent as beneficiary? The IRS has (unsuccessfully) argued that by virtue of his power to "appoint" (i.e., direct the disposition of) trust property, the grantor of a revocable trust had to include in his estate a policy on his life purchased and owned by his spouse. In other words, through the ability to change the trust and its beneficiaries, the husband had the indirect ability to change the beneficiary of the life insurance. But the court held that unless the property over which one holds a power was in existence prior to the decedent's death, there is nothing to tax. In this case, the insured-decedent had a mere expectancy.[11]

But there are other traps for the unwary. For instance, the IRS will argue that even though the proceeds may not be estate tax includable under these facts, when the insured's death occurs, the surviving spouse (who was the policy owner) is deemed to have made a gift to the other beneficiaries. For instance, if the trust set up by the deceased insured provided income to the surviving spouse for life with the remainder passing at her death to her children, the IRS would claim that, at the moment the insured died, a gift equal to the present value of the children's remainder interest was made by the wife. Worse yet, since the surviving spouse is deemed to have made a gift (the remainder interest) but retained a lifetime income from the gift, the IRS would claim that the entire amount in the trust at the time of her death should be included in her estate.[12]

3. *Providing estate liquidity* – The trust document should provide that assets in the trust at the decedent-insured's death can (or even must) be used to (a) pay the expenses, administrative costs, and taxes of the estate, and (b) of the surviving spouse's estate if other funds are not available. But planners should note that if the surviving spouse is the trustee or has the power to appoint the trustee, the IRS could argue that the proceeds should be included in the surviving spouse's estate to the extent those proceeds could be used if the trustee is required (or even authorized) to pay the surviving spouse's debts, administrative expenses, or taxes.

Of course, the revocable life insurance trust, although not technically an estate tax planning vehicle, can save estate taxes and thereby enhance relative liquidity through use as a nonmarital trust and/or marital trust. In other words, there is no reason why a revocable life insurance trust established during a client's lifetime can't be used as part of an overall tax planning arrangement to lower estate taxes in the estates of a married couple. The trust can form either the marital or nonmarital share or even provide for both shares. This would allocate a portion of the estate into a CEBT (Credit Equivalent Bypass Trust), so that an amount equal to the credit equivalent (equal to $1,500,000 in 2004) would pass to it without tax, and the balance of the assets passing into the trust would pass to the surviving spouse in a manner qualifying for the marital deduction.

GIFT TAX IMPLICATIONS

There are only a few gift tax considerations with respect to revocable trusts. But they can be significant:

- *No gift until the client gives up power to revoke* – A direct gift of an asset from a client to a revocable trust will not cause any gift tax, because the client has never parted with dominion and control of the assets placed into the trust. This rule applies up until the moment when the client gives up the right to alter, amend, revoke, or terminate the trust. But if the trust becomes irrevocable for any reason during the client's lifetime, at that moment, since the client can no longer control the use, possession, or enjoyment of the property transferred into the trust, the client has made a gift.

Note that gift tax implications are based on the value of trust assets as of the date the grantor parts with dominion and control. For example, assume a client creates a revocable life insurance trust and retains the power to revoke the trust anytime until the youngest beneficiary reaches age 21. At that date, the client loses all dominion and control over the trust's assets and the gift becomes complete. Gift taxes will be based on the value of the assets in the trust at that time.

- *Third party payment of premiums is a gift* – If someone other than the grantor of the trust pays premiums while the trust is revocable, the IRS will treat such payments as gifts directly to the grantor even if the payor is a possible beneficiary of the trust or heir to the grantor.

- *Gift when policy owned by other than insured is paid to third party* – Whenever an insurance policy is owned by one party on the life of a second party and is payable to a third party, there is almost always a potentially serious and adverse tax consequence. For instance, suppose a revocable trust is set up by a client's wife for the benefit of her children. Suppose she contributed to that revocable trust a $1,000,000 policy on the life of her husband. The IRS will argue that, at the husband's death, the wife (who as owner, both before and after the transfer to the revocable trust) could have been the beneficiary of the proceeds. When instead, policy proceeds are paid to the trust (i.e., to her children), the wife is making a $1,000,000 (indirect but nevertheless taxable) gift to her children. Since she could have revoked the gift at any time, the gift from the mother to the children did not become complete at the moment of the husband's death. However, the gift does become complete when the trust becomes irrevocable (or the trust is included in her estate if the power to revoke is retained until death). Furthermore, the value of the gift includes proceeds, which are generally worth substantially more than the value of the policy or premiums when transferred to the trust.

INCOME TAX IMPLICATIONS

For most income tax purposes, there is no significant impact when assets are transferred to a revocable living trust. The client must report trust income, losses, deductions, and credits as though they were personally incurred. No fiduciary income tax return need be filed if the client who establishes the trust is also the trustee. (This suggests that the grantor of a revocable trust should be the trustee or co-trustee). This tax theory that the revocable trust is the income tax alter ego of the grantor is known collectively as the grantor trust rules. But if the grantor is not the sole or co-trustee, the trust must obtain a separate ID number and file information form 1041.

Usually, the holding period of the client is tacked on to the holding period of the trust for purposes of determining capital gain and loss when an asset transferred to a revocable trust is sold. But if, for any reason (such as the death or permanent incapacity of the grantor), the trust becomes irrevocable, a new holding period begins. That period starts on the day the trust becomes irrevocable. Planners should also note that if the trust becomes irrevocable during the grantor's lifetime, and then the grantor dies, the basis of the assets in the trust may not receive a step up.[13]

The ability to treat the grantor and the trust synonymously for most income tax purposes means that it is generally safe to transfer installment obligations,[14] a principal residence,[15] a partnership interest,[16] or a U.S. savings bond[17] to a revocable living trust.

There are, however, some important exceptions to the rule that generally transfers of assets to or from a revocable trust have no adverse income tax implications. There are several assets that, if transferred to a revocable trust, will not have the expected tax neutral effect and instead result in adverse consequences.[18] These assets include: (1) S corporation stock; (2) professional corporation stock; (3) Section 1244 stock; (4) Incentive Stock Options; and (5) IRAs, retirement plans, and annuities.

1. *S corporation stock problem* – The problem here is particularly dangerous since it occurs, not during the client's lifetime, but rather, after his death. If the revocable trust does not meet S corporation requirements under IRC Section 1361 (essentially requiring all income to be distributed currently to one beneficiary or that the trust be taxed at the highest income tax rate), the S election may be inadvertently terminated. S corporation stock can be owned by a revocable trust until the trust becomes (for whatever reason) irrevocable. So if the trust becomes irrevocable (for instance at the grantor's death), S corporation stock must generally be transferred out of the trust within two years.

2. *Professional corporation stock problem* – Most states allow only professionals to hold the stock of a professional corporation. This may not include a revocable trust.

3. *Section 1244 stock problem* – Ordinary, rather than capital loss, is allowed when stock in a small business corporation (defined in IRC Section 1244) is sold at less than its basis. But this favorable treatment does not apply if the seller is either an estate or trust. For favorable tax treatment, the seller must be an individual. So the loss on a sale by a revocable living trust of closely held stock would be a capital rather than an ordinary loss.

4. *Incentive stock option problem* – An incentive stock option (ISO) is a right to purchase stock issued to corporate employees and contain certain statutory tax advantages.[19] The ISO must be granted to a specific employee and must be expressly nontransferable as long as the employee lives. But if the options are held by a revocable trust, the tax advantages will be denied. The transfer to a revocable trust may be considered a taxable disposition.

5. *IRAs* – Although revocable trusts are often the beneficiary or contingent beneficiaries of IRAs and qualified retirement plans, some authorities caution that it may not be possible to roll benefits over tax free (as would be the case if the client's spouse were the recipient).

There may also be problems when trust assets are distributed to beneficiaries. One such potential problem concerns the loss disallowance rules. Losses may be disallowed when assets are distributed to beneficiaries after the grantor's death to fund a pecuniary (specific dollar amount) bequest.[20] Furthermore, the rental loss deduction allowed for losses incurred of up to $25,000 a year can be used to offset other income of an estate (provided the decedent actively participated in the property's management), but no such deduction is permitted to a trust.

CREDITOR IMPLICATIONS

It is a delusion to think that a client protects himself or his beneficiaries from creditors by placing assets in a revocable trust. The avoidance of probate does not equate to the avoidance of creditors. Creditors clearly have access to the assets in a revocable life insurance

trust until and unless the client dies or for some other reason the trust becomes irrevocable. All states currently allow creditors access to any assets the client can revoke or liberally amend. Furthermore, where creditors of an estate generally have a very short period of time to press their claims (4 to 6 months in many jurisdictions), creditors of a trust have no such abbreviated deadline and can file suits even years after the grantor's death as long as the time is within the statute of limitations (as long as 6 or 7 years in some states).

COORDINATING THE REVOCABLE TRUST WITH THE OVERALL ESTATE PLAN

No tool or technique, no matter how useful, should be employed in a vacuum. For this reason, the revocable life insurance trust must be meshed with the overall estate plan. Therefore, the planner must consider the following when suggesting the use of a revocable trust (no matter how it is to be funded).[21]

Importance of a will. A will is necessary in almost every estate plan for many reasons:

- Few clients will take the time or trouble to place all their assets into a revocable trust no matter what real or even perceived advantages there are.

- No matter how careful and diligent a client may have been about assigning assets to a revocable trust, there will almost always be some asset, such as a car, household items, or jewelry, that will unintentionally be missed and that will pass through intestacy absent a valid will. There may be some assets, such as the proceeds from a lawsuit arising out of the wrongful death of the client, that would be impossible for the client himself to assign to the trust. But if the will is coupled with a revocable trust, such assets can be poured over from the probate estate to the trust and unified with other estate assets. (Note that the trust should be in existence before the execution of the will since, in some states, a provision in a will referring to a trust created after the signing of the will is not recognized).

- There are certain objectives that can only be accomplished by will. For instance, a client can't appoint guardians of the person for his children in a trust, but a will can provide for both guardians and backups.

Importance of a Durable Power of Attorney. A power of attorney is a relatively simple and inexpensive legal document by which a client gives a spouse, child, other relative, or trusted friend (technically called the attorney-in-fact) the legal right to act on behalf of the client and in his place with respect to specified financial matters. The power of attorney can be drawn as broadly or as narrowly as desired.

The power of attorney should generally be "durable." This means the power given to the agent is not affected by the client's subsequent disability or incapacity. (Each state has slightly different magic words that make a power durable).

A well drafted power may negate the need to petition a court to have a guardian or conservator appointed to handle assets during the client's lifetime that have not already been placed into the revocable trust. In the case of a revocable life insurance trust where the trust has been formed but the only asset in the trust is the trust's right to receive life insurance proceeds, the coordination of the durable power with the trust is essential to protect the client. This planning is essential, not only if the client is suffering from a physical disability or illness that could lead to permanent or long term incapacity, but also by healthy clients who would like to assure continuity of management of assets if for any reason they can't handle their own affairs for a period of time. If the power is broad enough, the attorney-in-fact could transfer assets into the previously established revocable trust.[22]

CHAPTER ENDNOTES

1. Simmons, 210-2nd T.M., Personal Life Insurance Trusts.
2. From Leimberg, "Trust Me: A Nutshell Primer on Trusts," (Financial Data Center).
3. *Advanced Sales Reference Service*, Sec. 48, ¶10 (The National Underwriter Company).
4. *Advanced Sales Reference Service*, Sec. 48, ¶20 (The National Underwriter Company).
5. *Advanced Sales Reference Service*, Sec. 48, ¶20 (The National Underwriter Company).
6. Tax savings goals can often be accomplished with irrevocable life insurance trusts. See Chapter 23 on Irrevocable Trusts.
7. See the *Advanced Sales Reference Service* (The National Underwriter Company) for a summary of state laws in this area.
8. A list of statutes of the various states that permit fiduciaries to invest in life insurance can be found in the *Advanced Sales Reference Service*, Sec. 12, ¶10 (The National Underwriter Company).
9. For a discussion of the rule against perpetuities, see the *Advanced Sales Reference Service*, Sec. 51, ¶270.2 (The National Underwriter Company).
10. *Advanced Sales Reference Service*, Sec. 48, ¶20 (The National Underwriter Company).
11. *Est. of Margrave v. Comm.*, 45 AFTR 2d ¶148,393 (8th Cir. 1980); Rev. Rul. 81-166, 1981-1 CB 477.
12. IRC Sec. 2036(a).
13. See IRC Secs. 1014(b), 2511.
14. Were the trust considered a separate income tax entity, the transfer of a client's right to receive installment sales payments to the trust would be considered a taxable disposition of the obligation. That would trigger an immediate acceleration of the entire deferred gain.
15. Here, the client will not want to jeopardize the ability to exclude up to $250,000 ($500,000 in the case of certain married couples) of gain from the sale of a personal residence. Since the revocable trust and the grantor are considered for income tax purposes as the same entity, the holding period for the personal residence by the trust and the grantor can be added together making it more likely that the client can qualify for the exclusion for gain from a principal residence. But if the client is not considered the owner of the entire trust, the IRS may deny the exclusion for gain. Planners should also note that some states (such as Florida) will not honor a homestead exemption if the deed is registered in the name of a revocable trust.
16. One of the most important estate planning post death elections is the one that allows a step-up in basis of the underlying assets of a partnership upon the death of the partner. This IRC Section 754 election will not be lost though a transfer of a partnership interest to a revocable trust.
17. The holder of a Series E, EE, H, or HH bond need not worry that a transfer to a revocable trust will trigger an acceleration of income. All interest income will be reportable by the client when the trust cashes in the bonds or they mature.
18. See Gassman, Robinson, and Conetta, "Living Trust Checklist," *The Practical Lawyer*, Fall 1991, Pg. 89. Planners should also note that there are tax problems when the assets used to fund a living trust are generating passive activity losses.
19. For additional information on ISOs, see Leimberg and McFadden, *The Tools and Techniques of Employee Benefit and Retirement Planning*, (The National Underwriter Company, 8th ed. 2003).
20. IRC Sec. 267.
21. See Hira, "Revocable Trusts: Appealing But Beware," *Journal of Accountancy*, October 1991, Pg. 91.
22. For more on powers of attorney, see Leimberg et al., *The Tools and Techniques of Estate Planning*, (The National Underwriter Company, 13th ed. 2004).

Chapter 29

SECTION 162 PLANS

WHAT IS IT?

Often called an "Executive Bonus" plan, a Section 162 plan involves the purchase of a life insurance policy on the life of one or more employer-chosen employees. The employer pays premiums on the policy but charges the employee with a bonus in an amount equal to that payment.[1]

The employee (or the third party such as an irrevocable trust designated by the employee) purchases and owns the policy and names the beneficiary. The policyowner has all rights in the policy. The corporation never has any right to any part of the policy cash values, dividends, or death benefits and at no time does the corporation own any incident of ownership in the policy.

The arrangement is called a Section 162 plan because the corporation will take an income tax deduction under Internal Revenue Code section 162 for the amount of the bonus charged to the covered employee.[2] In some cases the corporation will pay premiums directly to the insurer while in other situations the corporation will actually pay the money to the employee or a trust for the payment to the insurer.

Usually, the bonus paid by the employer is the same as the premium on the selected policy but in some cases, to increase retirement and death benefits, employees will choose to add their own after-tax contributions to increase the premium amount.

WHEN IS THE USE OF SUCH A DEVICE INDICATED?

1. As an alternative for split dollar coverage.

2. When the business is in a relatively high income tax bracket and wants to provide fringe benefits to selected key employees.

3. When an employer would like to carve out large amounts of coverage under the group term life insurance plan and provide individual coverage to specified key employees.

4. When an employer seeks a replacement for, or a supplement to, a qualified pension or profit-sharing plan.

WHAT ARE THE REQUIREMENTS?

Assuming that the plan covers only one or two stockholder or top management executives, installation of a Section 162 plan is quite simple. There should be a corporate resolution by the company's board of directors adopted in writing before the agreement with the employee is signed. The resolution should specify the corporate objectives to be met and the general terms of the Section 162 plan.

A separate contract with the employee should state that the corporation is making a special benefit available to the employee in return for his or her past and continued services and will provide that benefit as a bonus over and above all other compensation. The agreement should retain for the employer the right to terminate the plan at any time and for any reason. The agreement should also list the amount of the death benefit, the type of policy to be purchased, and the terms upon which the employee will cease to be eligible for the benefit.

HOW IS IT DONE – AN EXAMPLE

Your client, Red Waggon, is an employee of Drywells Fargo, Inc. He enters into an agreement with his corporation that provides, in part:

> In consideration of Red Waggon's past service and continued performance of services, Drywells Fargo, Inc. will pay him an annual bonus equal to the amount of premium payable on the $300,000 whole life policy from the ABC Life Insurance Company. Drywells Fargo, Inc. will also pay an additional bonus in the amount of any income tax payable by Red Waggon on the first bonus (but not to exceed the tax payable assuming a 40% combined federal and state bracket).

Red's wife purchases a $300,000 policy on Red's life and names herself as beneficiary. Although the Fargo company's payment of premiums is considered income to Red and an indirect gift from him to his wife, because of the gift tax marital deduction there will be no gift tax liability. The policy will also be outside of Red's estate for federal estate tax purposes and not accessible by Red's creditors.

WHAT ARE THE TAX IMPLICATIONS?

The tax implications of a Section 162 plan include the following:

1. Payments made as a bonus to an employee, whether made directly by the employer to the insurer, or from the employer to the employee and then from the employee to the insurer, are currently deductible by the employer[3] even if the employer derives an indirect benefit such as the enhanced morale or increased efficiency of the employee.[4]

2. The entire bonus (premium) is reportable as income by the insured.[5]

3. If the employer pays premiums directly to the insurance company, the payments will probably be considered a "non-cash" fringe benefit for withholding purposes. Thus, the premiums should be added to regular cash wages paid during the year and the appropriate withholding adjustment made. In other words, employer payments of premiums are subject to both Social Security (FICA) tax and Federal Unemployment Tax (FUTA).

4. Since the employee has already paid tax on the full cost of the policy, he or she has a cost basis equal to the sum of all premiums paid by the employer. This basis, or "investment in the contract," can be used to offset income tax as amounts are withdrawn or when the policy is surrendered.

QUESTIONS AND ANSWERS

Question - What are the advantages of a Section 162 Plan?

Answer - There are a number of reasons a Section 162 Plan is a favored executive perquisite. These include:

1. The plan provides valuable life insurance for key employees at little or no out-of-pocket cost.

This results in less of an after-tax outlay for personal financial security.

2. The corporation has a great deal of freedom with respect to (a) who will be covered, (b) the amount of insurance offered to each selected individual, and (c) the terms and conditions of eligibility.[6]

3. The terms of a Section 162 plan are completely confidential. No one other than covered employees need to be informed about the plan nor does any covered employee need to be given information concerning the terms of benefits provided to other plan participants.

4. It is the authors' opinion that if the Section 162 plan covers only one or two employees who are shareholder or senior management employees, there should be no Department of Labor requirements for the employer to meet.[7] Even if a number of common law employees are covered and the plan is considered an employee welfare benefit plan under ERISA (Employee Retirement Income Security Act) and the employer has stated an intention to create a plan, requirements are minimal.[8]

5. A Section 162 plan can be terminated by an employer at any time for any reason without justification to the IRS or Department of Labor. No penalty is attached to a plan termination as is the case when a qualified plan is terminated.

6. Almost no employee benefit plan is as easy or as inexpensive as a Section 162 plan to implement and maintain. The authors suggest that in the agreement with the employer the employee request in writing (as a convenience) that the employer pay the bonus directly to the insurance company.

7. Section 162 plans are appreciated because they provide real benefits for employees, who know the benefits cannot be forfeited. For example, the employer corporation cannot take all or any part of what the employee owns away or even place policy values at risk of corporate financial problems, nor can the employer corporation's creditors reach the policy or its cash values because the employee (or a third party on the employee's behalf) owns the policy from inception and holds all rights to policy cash values and death proceeds.

8. Another factor that increases the employer appreciation of covered employees is the portability of the policy. The life insurance policy and all its benefits remain the employee's sole property. Termination of employment has no adverse impact on any of these values.

9. Present or future management can decide to discontinue premium payments but the employee will not lose anything he or she presently has if the business is sold or there is a corporate takeover.

10. Premium payments under a Section 162 plan will "self-complete" if the selected employee becomes sick or suffers an accident. If the covered employee is permanently and totally disabled, all premium payments will be taken over by the insurer and the policy's death benefits and cash values continue to grow as before.

11. Because the employee is the sole owner of the life insurance contract, its cash values (which accumulate income tax free) can be turned into supplemental retirement income at the employee's choice or be used for a child's college education or a variety of other cash needs.

Question - What are the disadvantages of Section 162 Plan?

Answer - There are several major problems or drawbacks to the Section 162 plan. These are:

1. Once each premium is paid, the employer no longer has any control over either the employee or the policy through the plan. The employee can literally "take the money and run."

2. The employer has no access to policy cash values for an emergency or business opportunity (let alone to use to supplement normal cash flow or ease a temporary shortage of cash).

3. None of the employer's outlay for the cost of a Section 162 plan will ever be recovered by the employer. Compare this with a split dollar plan, which allows recovery of the employer's costs.

Question - What is a "double bonus"?

Answer - Some employers pay not only an amount sufficient to pay premiums but also the tax on the bonus. This second bonus to pay the tax on the first payment is often called a "double bonus."

To compute the amount that the employer must pay the employee so that he or she will net an amount sufficient to pay both the premium and the tax on it, divide the premium by one minus the employee's combined income tax bracket. For instance, suppose the covered employee is in a combined federal and state income tax bracket of 30% and the premium is $10,000. The employer must bonus out $14,285.71 for the employee to net $10,000 after tax. [$10,000 divided by one minus .30 (.70) equals $14,285.71. Thus, $14,285.71 multiplied by .70 equals $10,000.]

Question - What type of life insurance policy is typically used to fund a Section 162 plan?

Answer - Any permanent or even term coverage can be used in a Section 162 Plan although almost always some form of permanent insurance is indicated to pay-up the policy by the time the insured reaches retirement age. Consider a policy on which cash dividends or the surrender of paid-up additional insurance can offset the employee's tax on the premiums paid by the employer or an arrangement that provides that after a period of time (twelve years, for example) future premiums will be paid through the surrender of paid-up additional insurance purchased with policy dividends.

CHAPTER ENDNOTES

1. See Christensen, "Several Methods Have Been Devised Which Allow Companies to Provide Life Insurance Benefits as an Executive Prerequisite [sic]," p. 83, *Trust and Estates* (February 1988).

2. IRC Sec. 162(a)(1).

3. No deduction will be allowed unless premiums paid on behalf of the key employee are considered, together with all other compensation paid on the employee's behalf, to be "reasonable." Treas. Reg. §1.162-9. Since this problem generally arises only where the employee in question is also a shareholder, if the total amount is more than what is considered "reasonable," the excess may be taxed as a dividend rather than as compensation. This would mean the corporation's deduction would be disallowed. For this reason, the business objective(s) to be met by a Section 162 plan should be detailed in a corporate resolution authorizing the arrangement.

4. Treas. Reg. §1.264-1(b). See also Treas. Reg. §1.162-9; Rev. Rul. 58-90, 1958-1 CB 88; *Brown Agency, Inc. v. Comm.*, 21 BTA 1111 (1931), Acq. 1931 CB 10; *Berizzi Brothers Co. v. Comm.*, 16 BTA 1307 (1929), Acq. 1931 CB 6; *Peerless Pacific Co. v. Comm.*, 10 BTA 103 (1928), Acq. 1931 CB 55.

5. IRC Sec. 61(a).

6. Neither the IRS nor the DOL impose rules in this area. The employer can select each desired plan provision with little concern as to anti-discrimination requirements.

7. Assuming the employer merely pays a cash bonus to selected employees who then use that extra money to pay life insurance premiums, no "plan" should come into existence merely because of this action. Likewise, if the employer pays the insurer directly as an administrative convenience for those covered employees who want to take advantage of that offer, there probably would still be no "plan." But at a certain point, as yet undefined by case law or ruling, employer involvement will become so great that the DOL could argue that a plan exists.

8. If a "plan" is found to exist by the Department of Labor, the "plan" would have to be in writing, a summary plan description would have to be provided to covered employees, plan documents would have to be furnished to participants upon request, and some party would have to be named as a "plan fiduciary" with specified fiduciary obligations. Written documents would have to spell out how the plan will meet its obligations and specify the terms of payment and the claims procedure.

Chapter 30

SPLIT DOLLAR LIFE INSURANCE

WHAT IS IT?

Split-dollar insurance is a popular benefit that has been provided to executives for almost 40 years and plays an integral role in financial and estate planning. Split-dollar insurance is not a kind of insurance like whole life or term. A split-dollar life insurance plan is a contractual arrangement under which the costs and benefits of life insurance are shared between the employer and the employee. The agreement will provide how the parties will share the premium payments and the benefits if the policy either matures in a death benefit or is surrendered for cash. The policy is a normal policy of permanent life insurance, but the two parties to the agreement execute a separate split-dollar contract. In this instance, we will be referring to the employer-employee agreement. For estate-planning purposes, the employee may choose to have the trustee of his or her irrevocable life insurance trust (ILIT) enter into the contract with the employer.

This chapter looks at the background of split-dollar insurance and the recent changes that have been made since 2001 that alter the application of this important tool.

WHEN IS THE USE OF SUCH A DEVICE INDICATED?

1. When an employer wants to provide a key employee or shareholder employee with a valuable benefit at a relatively low long-term cost. In fact, in certain situations the employer's only real cost (aside from the drafting of the documents) is the after-tax cost of the use of its money. In other words, the employer "pays" for a split dollar plan by giving up only the after-tax income the employer's portion would have earned had it been invested by the employer.

2. When an employer seeks an employee benefit that is highly flexible and avoids the aggravation involved in most other benefit plans, yet yields a high return in terms of employee appreciation. The employer can decide who will be covered and the terms and benefit levels each covered employee will receive. The plan can be designed so that the employer can modify or terminate it to meet changing circumstances.

3. When a corporation wants to facilitate a cross purchase of its stock. Two or more shareholders can purchase policies on each others' lives and split the premium outlay with the corporation. Each will pay the pure insurance cost for the insurance owned on the other shareholder's life based on the age of the insured shareholder (not the age of the policyowner-shareholder) (see "Tax Implications," below). At the death of the insured, the policyowner will receive the proceeds and use that cash to buy stock from the decedent shareholder's estate. Note that if the employee pays a part of the premiums in an endorsement arrangement, the employer will recognize income in the amount of the employee's contribution.

4. When a shareholder-employee needs estate liquidity and would like to tap corporate dollars to amass the available cash for his or her estate.

5. Whenever one party (such as a senior family member) is able and willing to help another party (such as a junior family member) subsidize the cost of providing financial security through life insurance.

6. When an income and estate tax free benefit is desired as an alternative to the taxable death benefit of a nonqualified deferred compensation plan.

7. When there is a significant income tax bracket differential between the employer and the employee. When the employer is in a lower tax bracket than the employee, the employer can pay the same premium with fewer taxable dollars than the employee. For example, suppose the premium is $10,000 a year. To an employer in a combined federal and state bracket of 30%, it costs only $14,286 to pay the premium. To an employee in a 40% combined bracket, it costs $16,667. (If the employer is in a significantly higher tax bracket than the employee, an IRC Section 162 executive bonus may be appropriate. See Chapter 29, "Section 162 Plans.")

8. When the client is in impaired health or for some other reason must pay a rating on a life insurance policy. The insured employee generally reports the economic benefit received just as a standard risk

insured would have to. Ironically, this is advantageous because the reportable income is based on standard rates no matter how much higher than normal the premium may be.

TYPES OF SPLIT-DOLLAR PLANS

Classic Split-Dollar

Classic split-dollar arrangements involve the splitting of a policy between a corporation and a participating executive. The corporation annually contributes the amount of premium equal to the increase in the cash-surrender value (CSV), while the participant pays the remainder of the premium. The corporation will receive the CSV at the earlier of the termination of the plan or the participant's death. The participant holds the right to designate the beneficiary of the policy. Although all of the initial tax authority on split-dollar involves the classic arrangement, it is rarely seen in practice. The typical modification of the classic split-dollar plan is for the employer to pay more of the annual premium — typically, an employer-pay-all arrangement.

Note, although the employee generally must pay a substantial part of the first premium, after the first year the employee's share of the premium decreases rapidly, and, in some cases, it even becomes zero after a relatively few years. The employee, thus, gets valuable insurance protection (decreasing each year, but still substantial for a long time) with a relatively small outlay for premiums in the early years and at little or no cost to the employee in later years.

If a split-dollar policy pays cash dividends, the employer and employee may agree to offset the declining coverage by reinvesting the dividends in term insurance on the employee's life.

Equity Split-Dollar

Equity split-dollar is a slight variation of the classic plan, but has created all of the controversy[1] (starting with a ruling in 1996) in the tax treatment of split-dollar life insurance. In the equity arrangement, the employee share of the premium is equal to the cost of the pure term insurance protection each year. (The calculation of this cost will also be discussed.) The employer's share is the remainder of the premium. At the time of the participating employee's death, or when the plan terminates, the employer is repaid the lesser of the policy's CSV or the

aggregate amount of the employer's premium. The employee, or his or her beneficiary, receives the excess of the total amount distributed from the policy over the employer's share of the benefits. The difference in the equity arrangement is that the employee will generally begin accruing an interest in the CSV. If the CSV exceeds the employer's aggregate share of the premiums, this excess belongs to the employee. Under the classic split-dollar plan, the entire CSV was returned to the employer at the earlier of employee's death or the termination of the plan. The tax controversy, discussed below, involves the income-tax treatment of the employee's component of the CSV.

Note, in the 1996 ruling, the employer paid for the employee's "share" of the premium in its entirety, a so-called single-premium policy. Under a collateral assignment of the policy to the corporate employer, the employer retained the right to recover from the proceeds of the policy the aggregate amount of net premiums paid. Such an arrangement is often called "equity split-dollar" because the employer's claim is more in the nature of a loan (without interest). In contrast, the employer's claim against the policy could be for the greater of cash-surrender value or net premiums paid; this permits the employer to enjoy the equity. Had the employer adopted this plain-vanilla approach, the issue in the ruling would not have arisen.

Reverse Split-Dollar

Reverse split-dollar is an employee benefit plan where the rules of the employer and employee are reversed for the purposes of sharing the premium costs and benefits from a permanent life insurance policy. The basic structure of reverse split-dollar requires the employer to pay the cost of the pure term insurance portion of the policy. The measure of the employer's premium share has typically been based on the P.S. 58 tables for the cost of insurance protection, but, as the discussion later indicates, after 2001 this is modified. The executive pays the balance of the premium. The employer's share at the employee's death under the reverse split-dollar plan is the pure insurance proceeds. The employee's beneficiary receives the CSV at the time of the employee's death. If the plan terminates prior to the employee's death, the CSV might be distributed to the employee. Or, the employee could keep the policy in force by paying all future premiums without contribution from the employer. The employer generally receives nothing if the plan terminates. The theory behind this method of sharing is that the employer has only contributed enough to the plan to provide the annual costs of pure term insurance.

Notice 2002-59[2] is believed to have ended the viability of reverse split dollar. In Notice 2002-59, the IRS stated that a party to a split dollar arrangement may use Table 2001 or the insurer's rates only for the purpose of valuing current life insurance protection when the protection is conferred as an economic benefit by one party on another party, determined without regard to consideration or premiums paid by the other party.

WHAT ARE THE REQUIREMENTS?

There are no nondiscrimination rules that must be met, nor is IRS approval required prior to or after a plan's installation. Split dollar can be established for as many employees as the employer desires. No notice must be given to any employee who is not covered. (Securities and Exchange Commission rules require publicly held corporations to disclose split dollar plans on the lives of members of the executive group, as noted below.)

Employers install a split dollar plan by:

1. Selecting the appropriate product to match the problem. In most cases this will be some type of permanent coverage to track with long-term needs, but in some cases it could be a term insurance product.

2. Selecting an ownership arrangement (a "collateral assignment," "endorsement," or "split-ownership" arrangement, as defined below) and drafting an agreement governing the terms and conditions between the parties. The agreement should answer the following questions:

   a) What will each party receive upon given events such as the insured's death?

   b) What are the respective rights and obligations of each party upon early and normal termination of employment by the employee?

   c) Who may terminate the plan and under what terms or conditions?

   d) Does the insured have the right to purchase the policy upon plan termination or upon termination of employment? If so, for what amount?

   e) How and under what circumstances may the plan be amended?

The agreement is strictly between the employer and the insured employee. The insurance company will respect its terms but is not privy to its terms or conditions. The Employee Retirement Income Security Act of 1974 (ERISA) may impose certain requirements with regard to the naming of a fiduciary, funding policy, claims procedure, and statement of the covered employee's rights under the plan.

3. Determining what (death benefit, premiums, cash values, and dividends) will be "split" and among what parties.

4. Drafting a corporate resolution authorizing the purchase of the life insurance and stating the business reasons and advantages to be gained by the action.

5. Completing beneficiary designations and filing the appropriate documents with the insurance company.

HOW IS IT DONE – AN EXAMPLE

Herb Hindes is the president, chief operating officer, and owner of 48% of the stock of Pin Wheels Inc., a manufacturer of children's toys. The remaining 52% of the corporation is owned equally by two unrelated individuals. Herb's attorney recently confirmed that his federal and state death taxes and other estate settlement costs would approximate $2,000,000. Because the business comprises almost all of Herb's net worth, a sale of the business to pay taxes would be inevitable absent some outside source of cash. Yet all the parties feared that such a sale would precipitate a break-up of the business, the loss of jobs, a forced sale turning into a fire sale of the stock at pennies on the dollar, and the end of Herb's dream of keeping the business he founded in his family.

An IRC Section 303 partial stock redemption and IRC Section 6166 estate tax deferral were investigated, but when the numbers were run – factoring in the corporate alternative minimum tax – all of the parties felt that an alternative solution should be considered. That alternative was to have Herb's daughters, Dianne and Laura, purchase insurance on Herb's life. At his death, the cash from the insurance could be used to purchase the stock from his estate. That would give the estate cash to pay taxes and other expenses and assure the children that no outsider could obtain the stock and that no other single shareholder could gain control of the business.

Dianne and Laura will be the original owners of the insurance, but cannot afford to pay the full premiums. To help them, Pin Wheels will split the premium dollars, with the company paying the premiums. None of that insurance will be in Herb's or his wife's estate. At Herb's death, Pin Wheels will recover every cent it advanced so its only cost will be the after-tax income its share of the premiums would have earned.

WHAT ARE THE TAX IMPLICATIONS?

The tax treatment of a split dollar arrangement depends on when the arrangement is first entered into. Generally, for split dollar arrangements entered into after September 17, 2003, the taxation of the arrangement is governed by regulations that were issued in 2003. Split dollar arrangements entered into before September 18, 2003, are generally governed by revenue rulings and other guidance issued by the IRS between 1964 and the issuance of the final regulations.

Treatment under Regulations

For split dollar arrangements entered into after September 17, 2003, the tax treatment will be under one of two mutually exclusive regimes; the arrangement will be treated either as the life insurance policy owner providing economic benefits to the non-owner, or as the non-owner making loans to the owner.[3] The person named on the policy as the owner is generally considered the owner of the policy. A non-owner is any person (other than the owner) having an interest in the policy (except for a life insurance company acting only as the issuer of the policy).[4] A split dollar arrangement will be treated as a loan if: (1) payment is made by the non-owner to the owner; (2) the payment is a loan under general principles of federal tax law or a reasonable person would expect the payment to be repaid to the non-owner; and (3) the repayment is made from, or secured by, either the policy's death benefit, cash value, or both.[5] Loan treatment will generally occur in a collateral assignment arrangement.

Economic Benefit Treatment

If the split dollar arrangement is not treated as a loan, the contract's owner is treated as providing economic benefits to the non-owner. Economic benefit treatment will generally occur in an endorsement arrangement. The non-owner (and the owner for gift and employment tax purposes) must take into account the full value of the

economic benefits provided to the non-owner by the owner, reduced by any consideration paid by the non-owner. Depending on the relationship between the owner and the non-owner, the economic benefits may consist of compensation income, a dividend, a gift, or some other transfer under the tax code. The value of the economic benefits is equal to: (1) the cost of life insurance protection provided to the non-owner; (2) the amount of cash value the non-owner has current access to (to the extent that amounts were not taken into account in previous years); and (3) the value of other benefits provided to the non-owner. The cost of life insurance protection will be determined by a life insurance premium factor put out by the IRS.[6] Presumably, Table 2001 will be used until the IRS issues another table.[7]

Under the economic benefit regime, the non-owner will not receive any investment in the contract with respect to a life insurance policy subject to a split dollar arrangement. Premiums paid by the owner will be included in the owner's investment in the contract. Also, any amount the non-owner pays toward a policy will be included in the income of the *owner* and increase the *owner's* investment in the contract.[8]

Death benefits paid to a beneficiary (other than the owner of the policy) by reason of the death of an insured will be excluded from income to the extent that the amount of the death benefit is allocable to current life insurance protection provided to the non-owner, the cost of which was paid by the non-owner or the benefit of which the non-owner took into account for income tax purposes.[9]

Upon the transfer of the policy to a non-owner, the non-owner is considered to receive generally the cash value of the policy and the value of all other rights in the policy, minus any amounts paid for the policy and any benefits that were previously included in the non-owner's income. However, amounts that were previously included in income due to the value of current life insurance protection that was provided to the non-owner may not be used to reduce the amount the non-owner is considered to receive upon roll-out. Thus, the taxation on the value of current life insurance protection will not provide the non-owner with any basis in the policy, while taxation for a previous increase in cash value will add basis for the non-owner.[10]

Loan Treatment

If the split dollar arrangement is treated as a loan, the owner is considered the borrower, and the non-owner is considered the lender.[11] If the split dollar loan is a below market loan, then interest will be imputed at the applicable federal rate (AFR), with the owner and the non-owner of the policy considered to transfer imputed amounts to each other.[12] In a split dollar arrangement between an employer and employee, the lender would be employer and the borrower the employee. Each payment under the split dollar arrangement will be treated as a separate loan. The employer is considered to transfer the imputed interest to the employee. This amount is considered taxable compensation, and generally will be deductible to the employer (however, no deduction will be allowed in a corporation-shareholder arrangement). The employee is then treated as paying the imputed interest back to the employer, which will be taxable income to the employer. This imputed interest payment by the employee will generally be considered personal interest and therefore not deductible.

The calculation of the amount of imputed interest differs depending on the type of below market loan involved. A below market loan is either a "demand loan" or a "term loan." A demand loan is a loan that is payable in full upon the demand of the lender. All other below market loans are term loans.[13] Generally, a split dollar term loan will cause more interest to be imputed in the early years of the arrangement, with the amount of imputed interest decreasing each year. In a split dollar demand loan, the imputed interest will be smaller in the early years of the arrangement, but will increase each year the arrangement is in place.

Effective Date of Regulations

These regulations apply to split dollar arrangements entered into after September 17, 2003, and arrangements entered into on or before September 17, 2003, that are materially modified after September 17, 2003.[14] The final regulations provide a "non-exclusive list" of changes that will not be considered material modifications. This list includes: (1) a change solely in premium payment method (for example, from monthly to quarterly); (2) a change solely of beneficiary, unless the beneficiary is a party to the arrangement; (3) a change solely in the interest rate payable on a policy loan; (4) a change solely necessary to preserve the status of the life insurance contract under IRC Section 7702; (5) a change solely to the ministerial provisions of the life insurance contract (such as a change in the address to send premiums); and (6) a change made solely under the terms of the split dollar agreement (other than the life insurance contract) if the change is dictated by the arrangement, is non-discretionary to the parties, and was made under a

binding commitment in effect on or before September 17, 2003.[15] An exchange of policies under IRC Section 1035 is not on the list of non-material modifications.

The final regulations also contain rules on when a split dollar arrangement is considered to be entered into. A split dollar arrangement is entered into on the *latest* of the following dates: (1) the date the life insurance contract is issued; (2) the effective date of the life insurance contract under the arrangement; (3) the date the first premium on the life insurance contract is paid; (4) the date the parties to the arrangement enter into an agreement with regard to the policy; or (5) the date on which the arrangement satisfies the definition of a split-dollar life insurance arrangement.[16]

Split Dollar Prior to Regulations

Split dollar arrangements that were entered into before September 18, 2003, are governed by various rulings and other guidance that have been issued by the IRS between 1964 and the issuance of final regulations on split dollar arrangements in 2003. This guidance includes Notice 2002-8,[17] which provides transition rules for arrangements not subject to the split dollar regulations. However, no inference is to be drawn from Notice 2002-8, or the proposed or final regulations regarding the appropriate tax treatment of split dollar arrangements entered into before September 18, 2003.

Notice 2002–8

For split dollar arrangements entered into before September 18, 2003:

1. The IRS will not treat an employer as having made a transfer of a portion of the cash value of a life policy to an employee for purposes of IRC Section 83 solely because the interest or other earnings credited to the cash value of the policy cause the cash value to exceed the portion payable to the employer.

2. Where the value of current life insurance protection is treated as an economic benefit provided by an employer to an employee, the IRS will not treat the arrangement as having been terminated (and thus will not assert that there has been a transfer of property to the employee by reason of termination of the arrangement) as long as the parties to the arrangement continue to treat and report the value of the life insurance

protection as an economic benefit provided to the employee. This treatment will be accepted without regard to the level of the remaining economic interest that the employer has in the life insurance contract.

3. The parties to the arrangement may treat premium or other payments by the employer as loans. The IRS will not challenge reasonable efforts to comply with the rules regarding original issue discount and below-market loans. All payments by the employer from the beginning of the arrangement (reduced by any repayments to the employer) before the first taxable year in which payments are treated as loans for tax purposes must be treated as loans entered into at the beginning of the first year in which payments are treated as loans.

For split dollar arrangements entered into before January 28, 2002, under which an employer has made premium or other payments under the arrangement and has received or is entitled to receive full repayment, the IRS will not assert that there has been a taxable transfer of property to an employee upon termination of the arrangement if: (1) the arrangement is terminated before January 1, 2004; or (2) for all periods beginning on or after January 1, 2004, all payments by the employer from beginning of the arrangement (reduced by any repayments to the employer) are treated as loans for tax purposes, and the parties to the arrangement report the tax treatment in a manner consistent with this loan treatment, including the rules for original issue discount and below-market loans. Any payments by the employer before the first taxable year in which payments are treated as loans for tax purposes must be treated as loans entered into at the beginning of the first year in which payments are treated as loans.

Notice 2001–10[18]

Notice 2001-10 was revoked by Notice 2002-8. However, for split dollar arrangements entered into before September 18, 2003, taxpayers may rely on the guidance contained in Notice 2001-10. Under Notice 2001-10, the IRS will generally accept the parties' characterization of the employer's payments under a split dollar plan, provided that: (1) the characterization is not clearly inconsistent with the substance of the arrangement; (2) the characterization has been consistently followed by the parties from the inception of the agreement; and (3) the parties fully account for all economic benefits conferred on the employee in a manner consistent with that characterization.

Under Notice 2001-10, there are three different ways that a split dollar plan may be characterized. First, the plan can be characterized as a loan, subject to the below market loan rules. Second, the plan could be characterized so as to be governed under the "traditional" split dollar rules of Revenue Ruling 64-328.[19] Finally, the plan could be characterized in such a way so that the employer's payments are treated as compensation.

Value of Economic Benefit

The employee is taxed on the value of the economic benefit he receives from his employer's participation in the split dollar arrangement.[20] One of the benefits the employee receives is current life insurance protection under the basic policy. The value of this benefit to the employee may be calculated by using government premium rates. For many years, "P.S. 58" rates were used to calculate the value of the protection.[21] However, the IRS revoked the use of P.S. 58 rates and provided new "Table 2001" rates. P.S. 58 rates may generally be used prior to 2002; Table 2001 rates may generally be used starting in 2001. Notice 2002-8 does provide for some "grandfathering" of P.S. 58 rates. For split dollar arrangements entered into before January 28, 2002, in which a contractual agreement between an employer and employee provides that P.S. 58 rates will be used to determine the value of current life insurance protection provided to the employee (or the employee and one or more additional persons), the employer and employee may continue to use P.S. 58 rates.

If the insurer publishes rates for individual, initial issue, one-year term policies (available to all standard risks), and these rates are lower than the P.S. 58 or Table 2001 rates (as applicable), these insurer rates may be substituted.[22] Only standard rates may be substituted, not preferred rates (e.g., those offered to non-smoking individuals).[23] The substituted rate must be a rate charged for initial issue insurance and must be available to all standard risks.[24]

For arrangements entered into before September 18, 2003, taxpayers may use the insurer's lower published premium rates that are available to all standard risks for initial issue one-year term insurance. However, for arrangements entered into after January 28, 2002, and before September 18, 2003, for periods after December 31, 2003, an insurer's rates may not be used unless: (1) the insurer generally makes the availability of the rates known to those who apply for term insurance coverage from the insurer; and (2) the insurer regularly sells term insurance at those rates to individuals who apply for

Figure 30.1

INTERIM TABLE 2001					
ONE-YEAR TERM PREMIUMS FOR $1,000 OF LIFE INSURANCE PROTECTION					
Attained Age	§79 Extended and Interpolated Annual Rates	Attained Age	§79 Extended and Interpolated Annual Rates	Attained Age	§79 Extended and Interpolated Annual Rates
0	$ 0.70	34	$ 0.98	67	$ 15.20
1	$ 0.41	35	$ 0.99	68	$ 16.92
2	$ 0.27	36	$ 1.01	69	$ 18.70
3	$ 0.19	37	$ 1.04	70	$ 20.62
4	$ 0.13	38	$ 1.06	71	$ 22.72
5	$ 0.13	39	$ 1.07	72	$ 25.07
6	$ 0.14	40	$ 1.10	73	$ 27.57
7	$ 0.15	41	$ 1.13	74	$ 30.18
8	$ 0.16	42	$ 1.20	75	$ 33.05
9	$ 0.16	43	$ 1.29	76	$ 36.33
10	$ 0.16	44	$ 1.40	77	$ 40.17
11	$ 0.19	45	$ 1.53	78	$ 44.33
12	$ 0.24	46	$ 1.67	79	$ 49.23
13	$ 0.28	47	$ 1.83	80	$ 54.56
14	$ 0.33	48	$ 1.98	81	$ 60.51
15	$ 0.38	49	$ 2.13	82	$ 66.74
16	$ 0.52	50	$ 2.30	83	$ 73.07
17	$ 0.57	51	$ 2.52	84	$ 80.35
18	$ 0.59	52	$ 2.81	85	$ 88.76
19	$ 0.61	53	$ 3.20	86	$ 99.16
20	$ 0.62	54	$ 3.65	87	$ 110.40
21	$ 0.62	55	$ 4.15	88	$ 121.85
22	$ 0.64	56	$ 4.68	89	$ 133.40
23	$ 0.66	57	$ 5.20	90	$ 144.30
24	$ 0.68	58	$ 5.66	91	$ 155.80
25	$ 0.71	59	$ 6.06	92	$ 168.75
26	$ 0.73	60	$ 6.51	93	$ 186.44
27	$ 0.76	61	$ 7.11	94	$ 206.70
28	$ 0.80	62	$ 7.96	95	$ 228.35
29	$ 0.83	63	$ 9.08	96	$ 250.01
30	$ 0.87	64	$ 10.41	97	$ 265.09
31	$ 0.90	65	$ 11.90	98	$ 270.11
32	$ 0.93	66	$ 13.51	99	$ 281.05
33	$ 0.96				

term insurance coverage through the insurer's normal distribution channels.[25]

There are no rulings on the amount of economic benefit to be included when the employee has not had a full year's benefit under a policy (e.g., the policy was purchased on September 1 for a calendar year employee). It would seem that the IRS would accept any reasonable attempt at allocating the cost in such a year. Also, there has been no formal guidance from the IRS as to which rates should be used to measure the economic benefit resulting from a split dollar arrangement using a policy which insures more than one life. The IRS has said that taxpayers should make appropriate adjustments to premium rates if life insurance protection covers more than one life.[26] Where the policy death benefit is payable at the second death, it is generally believed that following the first death, the Table 2001 or P.S. 58 rates for single lives should be used to measure the survivor's economic benefit.

Private Split–Dollar Plans

The use of private split-dollar life insurance has grown substantially as a result of favorable rulings.[27] It appears that private split-dollar remains viable, but the issues in the new Regulations related to the income-tax compensation measures (discussed above) should be applicable to the gift-tax treatment of private split-dollar. Thus, agreements entered into before January 28, 2002 would be unchanged. In fact, existing agreements using the P.S. 58 table rates could potentially be enhanced by switching to the Table 2001 rates. One advantage of private split-dollar is the smaller gift-tax cost associated with the transfer of the premium for the pure term insurance protection. The Table 2001 rates would create a lower gift-tax cost for entering into a split-dollar agreement with the insured's irrevocable life insurance trust. In fact, survivorship (second-to-die) coverage would result in an extremely low Table 2001 rate.

Estate and Gift Tax Issues

Many split-dollar arrangements were entered into with the goal of avoiding inclusion of the proceeds in the insured's gross estate. Under this type of agreement, the insured's irrevocable life insurance trust is the policyowner and a collateral-assignment agreement is formed with the insured's employer. Employer contributions to the plan are taxable to the employee under the economic-benefit theory. In addition, such contributions are treated as gifts by the employee to the trust to the extent of any economic benefit provided to the employee. Plans entered into prior to January 28, 2002 are grandfathered with respect to the measure of the economic benefit. However, plans entered into after that date would be subject to treatment under Table 2001 rates and the new restrictions with respect to the insurer's standard term rates. This should not be significant problem since lower economic-benefit rates result in a smaller income- and gift-tax cost. Again, pre-January 28, 2002 plans using P.S. 58 rates may consider the benefits of shifting to Table 2001 rates.

However, some critical issues are presented for the split-dollar agreements entered into by the employee's irrevocable trust. First, equity split-dollar agreements will provide the additional problem that the existence of the separate entity (that is, the trust) is the policyowner. All issues concerning the problems of dealing with these agreements must include the additional step of determining the gift-tax consequences for the employee. For example, switching to interest-free-loan tax treatment would raise the possibility that the imputed interest income would be a gift from the employee to the trust. If the rollout occurs, the employee may have to make a substantial gift to the irrevocable trust.

Collateral assignment is generally used to form a split-dollar agreement between the employee's irrevocable trust and the employer. This has been deemed essential to avoid inclusion in the insured employee's gross estate if the insured is a majority shareholder in the sponsoring corporation. It is unlikely that future split-dollar agreements will be designed in this fashion after final regulations require interest-free-loan tax treatment for collateral-assignment agreements.

PLANNING CONCEPTS

Endorsement Plans

Policies currently held under the endorsement plan allow employers to fund nonqualified deferred compensation while providing the employee's survivors with an income-tax-free benefit in lieu of the ordinary income compensation benefit. In many cases, such policies are intended to be held throughout the life of the covered employee. However, for those that will be terminated at retirement, the insurer's one-year term rates remain available to policies under a plan in place on or before January 28, 2002; plans entered into after that date will have access to those term rates after December 31, 2003 only if the rates are generally made known to applicants for term insurance and the insurer normally sells term insurance at such rates through its normal distribution channels (otherwise it must use Table 2001). Endorsement plans entered into after the effective date of the final regulations will be subject to the eventual valuation methodology adopted by the Service.

If the employee has constructed an estate plan utilizing third-party split-dollar (i.e., an irrevocable life insurance trust) with an endorsement policy, each year's economic benefit is taxable income to the employee and is also a gift to the trust, which gets larger and larger each year, and for even modest levels of coverage, it will ultimately exceed the annual exclusion.

A distribution of the policy to the employee will be taxable income to the employee to the extent its value exceeds the consideration paid by the employee, but annual income- and gift-tax charges will cease, and no further outlays may be required if the premiums have vanished at the time of the distribution. One major problem now is that the employee's ownership will cause estate-tax inclusion[28] (which was not the case under a properly drafted ILIT split-dollar prior to distribution) that can be rectified by transferring those rights to the trust with the hope that the employee survives the three-year period,[29] or by a sale of the policy to the trust if the exceptions to the transfer-for-value rule apply (e.g., the trust is a grantor trust, a partner of the employee, etc.), or by buying a three-year term policy in the amount of the potential estate-tax liability should the employee not survive.

The employee could make an additional gift to the ILIT in the amount of the value of the policy and have the trust purchase the employer's interest in the policy directly. This has the advantage of avoiding the three-year rule, but requires that an exception to the transfer-of-value rule be applicable to preserve the income-tax exclusion of the proceeds.

Collateral–Assignment Plans

Collateral-assignment plans typically provide for a rollout at retirement. They are typically designed with the anticipation that the policy will be projected to have sufficient cash value the employee can then borrow to finance the rollout or that the employer will give the employee the necessary cash as a bonus at retirement (and the policy will have sufficient cash value that can be borrowed to pay the taxes on the income). The annual cost of the former is substantially greater than the premium applicable to the latter.

Some collateral-assignment arrangements remain in place until death. The employee recognizes no taxable income at retirement even though the employer defers the enforcement of the employee's obligation until death. Here the use of insurer one-year term rates remains available for all plans entered into before January 28, 2002 as long as the annual economic benefit is reported. However, there is a substantial economic cost to the employer in this case that may preclude the arrangement surviving retirement. So a rollout is a typical eventuality (and most insurers design arrangements in anticipation of a rollout at 16 years of coverage). The employer funds the policy with a premium sufficient to enable the ILIT to repay the employer from the cash value and then support an adequate death benefit without further cash premiums.

Planners should be cautioned that the Internal Revenue Code can cause immediate taxation in the case of certain events occurring during the first 15 years.[30]

The employee does not report the policy equity at rollout under IRC Section 83 only if the plan is terminated before January 1, 2004, or the parties restructure the arrangement as an IRC Section 7872 below-market loan. The alternative to these safe harbors is taxation of the equity. Access to these safe harbors requires analysis of an in-force illustration that is based on current values and current policy assumptions by projecting how close the policy is to financing its own rollout from the cash value.

The loan and interest begin in 2004 when the arrangement is restructured as a loan. This will attribute interest income each year, which may or may not be higher than his reportable income based on the one-year term costs.

Simply having the employee returning the policy to the employer as a converted endorsement-method plan will not do, because it causes the employee to have income attributed under IRC Section 83. A death-benefit-only plan, in which the company is both owner and beneficiary of the policy, can avoid lifetime imputed income to the employee, but at the sacrifice of the tax-free nature of the benefits received by the employee's beneficiary.

If the plan stays put after 2003, the one-year term costs continue to be imputed, and the employee can utilize tax-free policy loans. However, if the agreement currently provides (as is usually the case) that the employer be repaid on the earlier of death or the sixteenth year of coverage, failure to do so can cause the employee to be subject to current taxation on income. However, the revision of the agreement triggering the repayment obligation only at the employee's death would appear to be a substantial modification to the terms and economics of the arrangement that could well vitiate the grandfathering protection of pre-January 28, 2002 arrangements; this would cause the policy's taxation to be based on Table 2001 rather than the insurer's one-year term rates after 2003.

With respect to existing collateral-assignment equity plans where the policies are owned by irrevocable life insurance trusts, a rollout financed by a combination of cash value and bonus has the following consequences: the bonus results in both income and a gift over to the irrevocable life insurance trust. If the plan is terminated from cash value, but premiums are still needed to maintain the death benefit, ascertain if the policy can be reconfigured for a lower outlay. If the clients are receptive to further estate planning, ask them to consider funding the trust now on a tax-efficient basis to enable it to rely more on cash value and trust capital to repay the company, and rely less on the less tax-efficient bonus course of action.

One strategy currently being suggested by commentators is a fairly short-term grantor retained annuity trust (GRAT) having an irrevocable life insurance trust as the remainder interest. Because the value of the remainder interest is based on the subtraction method, the taxable gift could be practically negligible, yet an appreciating asset in the GRAT would deliver significant value to the irrevocable life insurance trust at termination. Examples would include a minority interest in a pass-through entity that enables the valuation of the transfer to be pared down by a separate minority-interest discount in addition to the table discount for the deferred aspect of the remainder interest.

A simple bonus plan in which the executive owns the policy and the employer pays the premium nevertheless results in taxable income to the employee. This often results in a less-expensive policy than might otherwise be needed in a split-dollar context; the bonus plan involves a lot less tax and economic risk; the cash-value growth is tax-deferred, and withdrawals up to basis are free of income tax, as are loans.

QUESTIONS AND ANSWERS

Question – What are the advantages of a split-dollar arrangement?

Answer – There are a number of reasons that split-dollar life insurance arrangements are popular with both employers and key employees.

1. A split-dollar arrangement is an extremely cost effective tool that helps an employer to recruit, retain, and reward key employees.

    a) The major cost of the plan is the after-tax opportunity cost of the use of the employer's outlay.

    b) The employer will, in most cases, recover the entire amount advanced upon the employee's death (from the policy's death proceeds) or termination of the insured's employment (from the policy's cash value).

2. An employer can pick and choose who will be covered, the amounts of coverage, and the terms of the coverage, and vary these elements from employee to employee.

3. There are virtually no ERISA reporting and disclosure requirements for split-dollar plans because these plans are typically provided only to a select group of top-level employees.

4. In most types of split-dollar plans, the employer's outlay is fully secured at all times.

5. Split-dollar provides a way to guarantee the employee's insurability. For example, the employer could voluntarily sell the employee the insurance if the employee's health deteriorates in the future.

Question – What are the disadvantages, costs, and risks of a split-dollar arrangement?

Answer – There are, of course, costs associated with a split-dollar life insurance policy, including the following:

- Premium outlays are required by the parties to put and keep the insurance in force;

- Premiums are not tax deductible at any time by either party to a split-dollar arrangement;

- The covered employee must report, as income, the economic benefit received under a split-dollar life insurance arrangement. Reportable tax costs rise appreciably as the insured employee's age increases; and

- In most cases, a split-dollar plan must remain in effect for a relatively long period of time (10 to 15 years) before policy cash values and dividends maximize the economic efficiency of the plan.

Question – What are the income-tax results of various dividend options?

Answer – Generally, dividends paid under participating life insurance contracts are income-tax free because they are considered a return of the policy owner's capital due to favorable mortality, interest, and loading experience.

But in a split-dollar arrangement, dividends paid to the insured more closely resemble a transfer of capital from the employer to the employee and may be added to any other taxable economic benefit provided by the policy.

Generally, the results are as follows:

- If the employee receives the policy dividend in cash, the employee must report ordinary income in that amount and the employer will receive no deduction;

- If the dividend is paid in cash to the employer, the employee has no taxable income and the employer has no taxable income (until amounts received tax-free from the contract exceed the employer's premiums);

- If the dividend is used to reduce the employee's share of the premiums, the employee will have taxable income and the employer will receive no deduction;

- If the dividend is used to reduce the employer's share of the premiums, the employee will have no taxable income and the employer will have no taxable income;

- If the dividend is left on deposit at interest for the employee's account, both the dividend and the interest on it are taxable income to the employee. The employer receives no deduction;

- If the dividend is left on deposit at interest in the employer's account, the employee has no taxable income. The dividend is a nontaxable return of capital but any interest is taxable to the employer;

- If the employee owns and controls any paid-up additions (i.e., both the cash value and death benefits), the dividend is taxable to the employee and no deduction is allowable to the employer;

- Where the employer owns and controls the cash value of any paid-up additions but any death benefit in excess of the cash value is controlled by the employee, the employee is charged with the cost of insurance protection from the net amount at risk in the dividends. The employer receives no deduction;

- If the dividend is used to purchase one-year term insurance under the so-called "fifth dividend" option and the death benefit is payable to the employee, the full amount of the dividend is taxable as ordinary income to the employee. The employer receives no deduction; and

- If the dividend is used to purchase one-year term insurance under the so-called "fifth dividend" option and the death benefit is payable to the employer, the employee receives no taxable income and the employer receives no deduction.

Question – Which types of arrangements are specifically excluded from the application of the final split-dollar regulations?

Answer – The only arrangements excluded from the definition of split-dollar are group term life insurance plans under IRC Section 79 (other than those providing permanent protection to the employee), the purchase of life insurance between the policy owner and the life insurance company issuing the policy, and key person insurance where the corporation owns all of the rights in the policy. In addition, any plan under which there is no expectation of reimbursing the party advancing the premiums is not a split-dollar plan. In such situations, the premium payments will be treated as taxable income, a dividend, or a gift, depending on the relationship between the parties.

Question – What are the grandfathering provisions for equity split-dollar plans entered into prior to September 18, 2003?

Answer – The answer depends on when the parties entered into the equity split-dollar arrangement. If an employer and employee entered into an equity split-dollar plan before January 28, 2002, and the plan was terminated on or before December 31, 2003 by the employee repaying the employer's premium advances (i.e., a "rollout"), any then existing policy equity was not subject to tax. That provision was a big opportunity for employees in mature plans with a substantial equity buildup to roll out of the plan with no tax on the excess equity, but for more immature plans with little or no equity buildup this provision provided no real benefit. If the immature plan were terminated by December 31, 2003, the employee would be faced with the prospect of paying the full amount of future premiums with after-tax dollars (or finding some other source for future premium payments), and those same amounts would also be subject to gift taxation if the policy were owned by an ILIT.

As an alternative to terminating an equity split-dollar plan entered into prior to January 28, 2002 altogether (e.g., for one without substantial equity buildup), the parties to the plan could agree to switch to a loan regime January 1, 2004. Converting to a loan before January 1, 2004 avoided taxation to the employee of policy equity existing both at the time of the switch and at a later rollout. This loan safe harbor required that the beginning loan balance include all pre-2004 employer premium payments as of the beginning of the taxable year in which the switch occurs (although interest need not retroactively accrue on these prior employer payments), and that subsequent employer premium payments be treated as additional loans. This is the safe harbor that was most frequently used by immature old split-dollar plans and the technique has come to be called "switch-dollar."

Note, not all old plans needed to be rolled out or switched to a loan by December 31, 2003 to enjoy the benefits of taxation under the loan regime. Old plans that did not have equity by December 31, 2003 can delay the switch to a loan until just before the plan accrues equity in a future year without causing adverse tax consequences. The reason for delaying the switch to a loan and continuing in split-dollar is to preserve the use of favorable split-dollar term rates for as long as possible. This delayed switch is another facet of the switch-dollar technique.

Question – Are there any income tax consequences to the employer or the policy beneficiary in an endorsement plan when the death benefit is paid?

Answer – The amount, if any, received by the employer in excess of its aggregate premiums appears not to be taxable to the employer pursuant to the Code Sec. 101(a) death benefit exclusion. (This is a change from the proposed regulations.)

In contrast, the death benefit proceeds (despite IRC Section 101(a)) are excluded from the beneficiary's gross income only to a certain extent. The amount excluded is that portion of the current life insurance protection provided to the nonowner to the extent the cost for such protection was paid by the nonowner or the value of such protection was taxed to the nonowner as an economic benefit. Therefore, the entire employee death benefit would be taxed to the beneficiary if the employee never contributed or paid tax on the economic benefit.

Question – What if the employer loans with respect to premium payments under a split-dollar loan or collateral assignment regime include an adequate interest charge?

Answer – If adequate interest (based on the Applicable Federal Rate or AFR) is charged on a loan, then IRC Section 7872 generally does not apply. As a result, especially when interest rates are low, some planners suggest that the best course of action may be to arrange the transaction as a term loan that states adequate interest. Because adequate interest is stated, it can be paid annually, or even accrued until the end of the term, instead of being treated as transferred upon creation of the loan. However, if the employer directly or indirectly pays the interest to the employee (e.g., through bonus compensation), the stated interest is disregarded, and the loan is treated as a below-market loan under IRC Section 7872.

Question – What are the gift-tax consequences of split-dollar arrangements under the final regulations?

Answer – The regulations apply to private split dollar arrangements for gift tax purposes. In the usual private split-dollar arrangement, the donor makes premium payments on a life insurance policy owned by an irrevocable life insurance trust (ILIT). The arrangement is treated as a split-dollar loan from the donor to the ILIT if there is a reasonable expectation that the donor is to be repaid the premiums. If, as is frequently the case, the loan is repayable on the death of the donor, the term of the loan normally would be the donor's life expectancy. The value of each gift (assuming no stated interest) would be the total premium payment less the present value of the donor's right to receive repayment at life expectancy. If the premium payments are not split-dollar loans (i.e., there is not a reasonable expectation of repayment), then the payments are governed by general tax principles.

In employer-employee equity split-dollar where the policy is owned by the employee's ILIT, similar rules apply to the gift portion of the transaction. This arrangement is taxed the same as private equity split-dollar, treating the insured employee as the "donor."

In all non-equity donor/donee arrangements, gift tax consequences are determined under the economic benefit regime, regardless of who owns the policy.

Question – What life insurance rates are mandated for split-dollar arrangements involving survivorship life insurance?

Chapter 30 – Split Dollar Life Insurance

Answer – Table 2001 only provides individual, not survivorship, term rates, and Notice 2002-8 leaves it up to taxpayers to figure out survivorship rates based on the Table 2001 individual rates. It is anticipated that for new plans, the IRS will provide survivorship life insurance premium factors in addition to individual premium factors and will permit all of these new rates to be used to measure the term costs in plans entered into prior to September 17, 2003 as well as in new plans.

The author calculated the survivorship term rates based on Table 2001 factors and found that they are actually lower than one insurer's existing alternative survivorship term rates up to the age where a husband and wife are both 70. Thereafter, the rates cross over so that the insurer's alternative survivorship rates are lower than the survivorship rates based on Table 2001 factors. In addition, the survivorship rates based on Table 2001 factors will always be lower than the U.S. 38 rates commonly used in survivorship plans before the new regulations because the U.S. 38 rates are based on the higher P.S. 58 rate table. The favorable conclusion is that, in many if not most cases, survivorship split dollar plans will be able to use more favorable survivorship rates than the survivorship rates previously used in those plans.

Question – What new split-dollar plans are evolving as a result of the new regulations?

Answer – A number of planners have proposed a "hybrid" plan that has generally acquired the name "collateral endorsement switch-dollar." It is a hybrid plan since this technique starts as a nonequity endorsement plan, in the collateral assignment format, and then switches to a loan just before equity arises. By proceeding in this manner, the employee is taxed on the split-dollar term rates for as long as possible, assuming they are lower than interest costs.

This approach is sanctioned by the final regulations, which expressly cover modifying a nonequity split-dollar plan to change it to an equity plan. Under the regulations, if the employer, service recipient, or donor is not the owner of the policy immediately after the change to an equity plan, this modification is to be treated as a transfer of the policy to the employee, service provider, or donee. The policy transfer here would be in consideration for a note equal to the policy's then cash value (apparently, according to the regulations, determined without regard to surrender charges). This

note and future premium loans would comply with the new split-dollar loan rules.

Question – How are split-dollar plans affected by Sarbanes-Oxley Act of 2002, which prohibits a public company, either directly or indirectly, from providing any type of credit to any director or executive officer?

Answer – Since the Sarbanes-Oxley Act's interpretation and administration is within the jurisdiction of the Securities and Exchange Commission, the final split-dollar regulations do not address this issue. Most experts seem to think that collateral assignment split-dollar plans could fall under this Act, and some also believe the Act may cover endorsement arrangements as well. As of the date of this writing, the SEC has expressed no opinion on the matter.

Therefore, until the SEC provides further guidance, directors and executive officers of public companies should be very wary about continuing to participate in their companies' split-dollar plans. The plans may be beyond the reach of the Act if the plans can be considered as a binding commitment entered into prior to the Act's effective date and are grandfathered under the Act. Endorsement arrangements may not be subject to this prohibition, especially if they are non-equity arrangements that provide only a death benefit.

The Sarbanes-Oxley Act does not grandfather future executive loans (i.e., loans made after July 30, 2002) unless the plan is considered a binding commitment entered into before the Act's effective date and is grandfathered. The consequences of violating the Act can be severe — up to and including the imposition of fines and criminal penalties.

However, remember that Sarbanes-Oxley applies only to public companies and not to closely-held companies. Closely-held companies are probably the largest market for split-dollar plans.

CHAPTER ENDNOTES

1. TAM 9604001. This technical advice memorandum questions the tax treatment of equity split-dollar — the first time the IRS had done so. This received so much attention from the insurance industry, it became known as the "infamous TAM." In this private ruling, the IRS indicated that the buildup in the CSV accruing to the employee is taxable as ordinary income. To say the least, the IRS received a significant amount of commentary

from the insurance industry and even the American Bar Association. Notice 2001-10, 2001-1 CB 459, discussed below is the first official reaction of the IRS as a result of this commentary.

2. 2002-2 CB 481

3. Treas. Reg. §1.61-22(b)(3).

4. Treas. Reg. §1.61-22(c).

5. Treas. Reg. §1.7872-15(a)(2).

6. Treas. Reg. §1.61-22(d).

7. See Notice 2002-8, 2002-1 CB 398.

8. Treas. Reg. §1.61-22(f).

9. Treas. Reg. §1.61-22(f)(3).

10. Treas. Reg. §1.61-22(g).

11. Treas. Reg. §1.7872-15(a)(2).

12. See IRC Sec. 7872.

13. IRC Sec. 7872(f).

14. Treas. Regs. §§1.61-22(j), 1.7872-15(n).

15. Treas. Reg. §1.61-22(j)(2).

16. Treas. Reg. §1.61-22(j)(1)(ii).

17. 2002-1 CB 398.

18. 2001-1 CB 459.

19. 1964-2 CB 11

20. See Rev. Rul. 64-328, 1964-2 CB 11.

21. See Rev. Rul. 55-747, 1955-2 CB 228.

22. See Rev. Rul. 66-110, 1966-1 CB 12.

23. Let. Rul. 8547006.

24. Rev. Rul. 67-154, 1967-1 CB 11.

25. Notice 2002-8, 2002-2 CB 398.

26. Notice 2002-8, 2002-2 CB 398.

27. Rev. Rul. 81-198, 1981-2 CB 188; Rev. Rul. 78-420, 1978-2 CB 67

28. IRC Sec. 2042.

29. IRC Sec. 2035(d)(2).

30. IRC Sec. 7702(f)(7).

Appendix A

ESTATE TAXATION OF LIFE INSURANCE

AN OVERVIEW

Any one of seven reasons can cause life insurance to be includable in a decedent's gross estate. (Note that in some cases inclusion will result in the lifetime value being includable and in other situations the policy proceeds will be included). Planners should always consider the impact of state death taxation, which sometimes parallels federal estate tax law but often diverges significantly.

IRC Section 2033 Inclusion. The value of life insurance owned by the decedent on the life of another will be includable in the decedent's estate if the decedent dies first.

IRC Section 2035 Inclusion. Life insurance proceeds will be includable in the insured's estate if the insured held an "incident of ownership" (i.e., any significant ownership right) within three years of death, even if at the date of death the insured didn't own the policy or any policy rights.

IRC Sections 2036, 2037, 2038 Inclusion. Policy proceeds will be includable in the insured's estate if the insured transferred the policy to another party but retained a lifetime right to

1. enjoy the legal rights to the policy;

2. have the policy revert back to him or his estate under certain conditions; or

3. alter, amend, revoke, or terminate the policy.

IRC Section 2042 Inclusion. If (a) the policy proceeds were paid to (or for the benefit of) the insured's estate or (b) the insured owned at the date of his death an incident of ownership in the policy, the proceeds will be includable in the insured's gross estate.

IRC Section 2039 Inclusion. When a life insurance policy is used as part of the financing of an employee benefit, proceeds may be includable as an annuity.

IRC Section 2041 Inclusion. If the insured elected a settlement option for a beneficiary and also gave that person a general power of appointment over the policy proceeds, the proceeds will be includable in the beneficiary's gross estate.

IRC Section 2044 Inclusion. Life insurance proceeds may be includable in the estate of a beneficiary who was the insured's spouse and who had received the proceeds as a "qualifying income interest" for life under QTIP rules.

This Appendix will first briefly focus on the definition of life insurance for federal estate tax purposes and then examine in detail the most common reasons for estate tax inclusion of life insurance, IRC Sections 2033, 2035, and 2042.

LIFE INSURANCE DEFINED

Life insurance is a very broadly defined term for estate tax purposes. In its simplest definition, it is a contract under which the insurer agrees to pay a specified death benefit to a specified beneficiary at the death of the insured. The term encompasses life insurance of every description, as long as there is both (a) risk shifting and (b) risk sharing in the event of the policyowner's loss through the insured's death.

So accidental death benefits under a health insurance policy, payments under a fraternal society's lodge system, accidental death payments, group insurance, paid up additions, or other payments under a policy rider at the insured's death would all be considered life insurance for purposes of federal estate tax inclusion.

The element of risk must be present at the time of the insured's death for the proceeds of the contract to be includable as life insurance in the insured's gross estate.

Furthermore, to be considered life insurance for estate tax purposes, the death benefit must (a) be payable unconditionally and (b) have no effect on other legal liabilities or rights in connection with the insured's death. The issue arises most often in accident situations with respect to payments under automobile or air travel policies. For example, suppose a contract between an insurance company and the owner of an airplane provided that a specified payment would be made to the estate of any individual killed in an accident while flying in the owner's plane. If the contract further required that the passenger's estate would have to sign a release of all claims for damages against the owner or his estate in order to collect, that condition would affect other rights of the deceased. The contract would therefore not be considered life insurance.

Where there is no element of risk, the payment is not (at least for estate tax purposes) considered life insurance. It may, however, be subject to inclusion in the gross estate under one or more tax law provisions (for example as an annuity).

INSURANCE OWNED ON THE LIFE OF ANOTHER (IRC Section 2033)

Typical Situations: There are many situations in which one party purchases life insurance on the life of one or more other individuals. For instance, a business partner may purchase insurance on the lives of each of her three partners. Assume she dies before the three insureds do. The policies she owned on their lives would be includable in her estate (to the extent of the value of the policy as of the date of the insured's death) as "property in which the decedent had an interest." Likewise, a son may purchase insurance on the life of a parent. If the son predeceases the parent, the value of the unmatured policy will be in the son's estate.

Estate Tax Value: The estate tax value of third party owned unmatured policies includable in the estate of someone other than the insured is generally the replacement cost of the policy. Replacement cost is ascertained using the same rules governing valuation of policies for gift tax purposes (the date of death is substituted for the date of the gift in valuing the policy). In most cases, this approximates the sum of (a) the cash surrender value of the policy (technically, the interpolated terminal reserve of the policy is the amount includable and in early policy years this can significantly exceed the cash surrender value) plus (b) the unearned premium (any premium the insured paid but that was not earned by the insurer as of the date of the policyowner's death).

Common Disaster: Although the IRS has tried to include the entire proceeds in the insured's estate when the insured and the policy owner were killed in a common disaster, after a number of Circuit Court reversals, the IRS gave up. It now holds, in cases in which the

presumption of the Uniform Simultaneous Death Act applies (i.e., that the insured survived the beneficiary), that the policy's interpolated terminal reserve is the appropriate measure of inclusion rather than the death benefit. If, however, the presumed order of deaths is reversed (i.e., the presumption is that the beneficiary survived the insured), simultaneous deaths of the insured and the policyowner will cause the death proceeds to be includable in the policyowner's estate.

Excludable Growth: No inclusion is required for the increase in the value of a policy from the date of the policyowner's death to the valuation date resulting from the estate paying premiums or earning interest on a policy insuring a third party. So, if at the date of death a client owned a $1,000,000 policy insuring the life of a business associate and the interpolated terminal reserve (reflecting income earned by the policy reserve invested with the insurer during the period from the date of death) increased $2,000 from the owner's death to the valuation date, that increment would be excluded from the policyowner's gross estate.

Alternate Valuation Date Trap: But planners should beware of this situation: A decedent owns a life insurance policy insuring the life of a third party (such as a spouse or business associate). Within six months of the deceased policyowner's death, the insured dies. If the policyowner-decedent's executor uses the alternate valuation date to value assets in the estate, the increase in value caused by the insured's death, and not merely the interpolated terminal reserve plus any unearned premium, will be includable.

This alternate valuation date trap is especially dangerous with respect to last to die (also called second to die) life insurance in which a policy pays proceeds only when the second insured dies. When the first insured dies, the policy must be included as an asset in the estate of the decedent,[1] at its replacement value (essentially interpolated terminal reserve plus unearned premium). But if the decedent's executor elects the alternate date and the second insured has died between the first spouse's death and the alternate valuation date six months later, the entire proceeds will be includable in the first spouse's estate. The executor of the later dying spouse must include the entire amount of the proceeds again in that spouse's estate because of the incidents of ownership rules described below.[2]

Beneficiary Who Predeceases Insured: Typically, a primary beneficiary's rights to policy proceeds expire with his death. So, if the named beneficiary dies before the insured and no rights pass to the beneficiary's heirs, nothing will be in the beneficiary's estate. This assumes the beneficiary had no other rights in the policy and all rights in the proceeds terminated (as they usually do) upon predeceasing the insured. Note that state law determines the existence and extent of such ownership rights or interest in proceeds.

INCIDENT OF OWNERSHIP WITHIN THREE YEARS OF DEATH (IRC Section 2035)

The General Rule: IRC Section 2035 is entitled "Adjustments for certain gifts made within three years of decedent's death." The statute states that transfers in certain situations will be brought back into the gross estate for estate tax purposes if the decedent held at death an interest which would have been included under one or more of the following IRC sections

- Section 2036 (transfers with retained life estate),

- Section 2037 (transfers taking effect at death),

- Section 2038 (revocable transfers), or

- Section 2042 (proceeds of life insurance).

Inclusion is also mandated if the property would have been included under one of those four IRC sections but the decedent gave up fatal rights within three years of death.[3]

Section 2042 inclusion will be discussed in detail below. For purposes of Section 2035, it is sufficient to understand that Section 2042 requires inclusion if either (a) policy proceeds are payable to or for the benefit of the insured's estate or (b) the insured, at the time of death, held one or more incidents of ownership (i.e., valuable property rights) in the contract.

Adequate Consideration Rule: However, Section 2035 specifically excludes from estate tax inclusion a sale of property made for an adequate and full consideration in money or money's worth.[4] So, if life insurance is sold for adequate and full consideration in money or money's worth, it should not be included in the insured's gross estate under Section 2035 in any event.

It would appear at first glance that all problems under Section 2035 could easily be avoided by selling the policy rather than giving it away. Planners should proceed with caution because of (a) the transfer for value rule discussed in Appendix G and (b) the prob-lems inherent in a situation in which the IRS finds the consideration inadequate. Suppose, for example, a client was a doctor who knew he was dying of cancer. So, rather than give the policy on his life away, he sells them to his wife in return for her check in an amount equal to the policy's cash value. The IRS would claim that in the light of the actual circumstances, the policies were near to maturity and therefore worth much more than the cash values. It would include the difference between actual worth under the circumstances and the amount paid by the doctor's wife in the client's estate on the grounds that he had not in fact received adequate and full consideration.

"Adequate" is often (but not always) measured (by the IRS) relative to what would have been included in the estate had no transfer been made rather than the value of what was transferred. However, no one in the real world would pay, even on the life of a terminally ill insured, the full face amount because such a payment would ignore the cost of the time value of money. Some discount should be taken for the fact that some time (that proceeds could have been earning money) will pass before the proceeds are actually paid. Nevertheless, the courts have generally supported the IRS's interpretation of how adequate consideration is measured.

Premiums Not Brought Back: Does the language of the IRC encompass a "bring back" of cash the donor intended the donee use to pay premiums on life insurance? In other words, does the mere payment of premiums within three years of death cause the death proceeds of a policy to be brought back into the estate? It is clear now that it does not.

Gifts of Policies Within Three Years of Death: A gift of a life insurance policy or a release or transfer of any of the incidents of ownership in a life insurance policy by the insured within three years of the insured's death will result in inclusion under IRC Section 2035 regardless of the insured's motive for the transfer.

Note that IRC Section 2035 applies only to transfers of policies (or transfers or releases of incidents of ownership) by the insured. There will be no inclusion under IRC Section 2035 if someone else transfers a policy on the life of the insured within three years of the insured's death or within three years of the owner's death. (Section 2042 pertains only to proceeds of insurance on the decedent's life. A policy owned by a third party on the decedent's life would be includable, if at all, under IRC Section 2033. But Section 2035 pulls back the proceeds only if it would have been includable in the insured's gross estate under IRC Sections 2036, 2037, 2038, or

2042.) For instance, if a daughter owned a policy on the life of her 85 year old father and the daughter made a gift of the policy to her niece, no inclusion under Section 2035 would be required even if the father died within 3 years of the daughter's transfer to the niece.

In the case of second to die policies, the three year period is measured back from the death of the surviving insured since inclusion under Section 2035 is conditioned on a Section 2042 inclusion (but for the policy transfer). Since the only inclusion possible at the first death was under Section 2033, IRC Section 2035 does not begin to apply until the second death. For example, if a client and her husband purchase a second to die policy and assign it to an irrevocable trust for their children, there will be no Section 2035 inclusion unless both spouses have died within three years of the gift to the trust.

Gifts of Policies Beyond the Three Year Period: What if an insured pays premiums within three years of his death but the policy itself was purchased more than three years prior to the insured's death by a third party and the insured never had an incident of ownership? What if the insured pays premiums within three years of death and the policy was purchased by the insured but he transferred it to a third party more than three years prior to death? The answer to both questions is the same: there should be no inclusion since no Section 2042 rights were transferred within three years of death and none of the other (2036, 2037, or 2038) IRC Sections apply.

Payment of Premiums by Third Party Owner: What if the donee of the policy pays some or all of the premiums on the policy? According to several cases and regulations, if the donee rather than the insured pays premiums after the policy is received, even if the transfer from the insured occurred within three years of death, only a portion of the policy proceeds would be includable in the insured's estate. The inclusion ratio is

$$\frac{\text{PREMIUMS PAID BY DONOR}}{\text{TOTAL PREMIUMS PAID}}$$

For example, assume a client purchases a $1,000,000 policy on his life. Premiums are $25,000 payable semiannually. One year after purchasing the policy and paying $50,000 in premiums, she transfers the policy to her 38 year old son who pays – out of his own personal funds – the next four semiannual premiums of $25,000 each. If the insured client died at that point, she would have paid $50,000 out of the total of $150,000 (i.e., ⅓ of all premiums). Therefore, ⅓ of the $1,000,000 death benefit ($333,333) would be includable in her estate.

The Beamed Transfer Theory: Why has Section 2035 caused such a multiplicity of court cases? The answer lies in the less than clear manner in which Section 2035 was previously written and in this common fact pattern: A third party such as a spouse, child, or irrevocable trust purchases a life insurance policy on the life of a client but pays premiums with funds provided by the insured. In this scenario, the insured typically (but not always) has initiated the insurance purchase. The insured dies within three years of the issuance of the policy.

In the past, the IRS has argued that if the insured significantly participated in the procurement of a policy on his own life, that action, together with the transfer of amounts to pay premiums on the policy, was equivalent to purchase and transfer of the policy by the insured to the third party. This has been called the beamed transfer theory. After a number of losses in court, the IRS has announced that it will no longer pursue this theory.

Avoidance of Issue: For those preferring to play it safe, the odds of avoiding the issue generally increase if:

1. the insured never owns the policy (it should be owned from inception by a third party).

2. an adult beneficiary or independent trustee takes all the actions to purchase the policy on the life of the insured and place the policy into effect.

3. the trustee, if a trust is used, is authorized but not required, to purchase insurance on the life of anyone on whose life the trust's beneficiaries have an insurable interest.

4. the trust specifically prohibits the insured from obtaining any rights in any policy the trust may ever hold on the insured's life.

5. the trust permits, but does not require, the trustee to pay premiums.

6. the insured gives the trustee enough money to pay premiums for more than one year.

7. the cash gift to the trust (or adult policyowner) is given outright with no strings attached.

8. the gift is made well in advance of the date on which premiums are due.

9. the facts indicate that the trustee or adult policyowner is not acting mechanically as the insured's agent but is in fact making an inde-

pendent decision to purchase the insurance without direction from the insured.

10. the document (in the case of a trust) contains as few references as possible to life insurance and is not titled "Irrevocable Life Insurance Trust."

11. the actual policyowner could, for at least the first three years, pay premiums from a source other than from gifts from the insured and if necessary borrow from another relative or bank.

Exchange of Contracts Within Three Years of Death: What is the impact of an exchange of policies within three years of death? For instance, say the client transfers a policy on his life to an irrevocable trust or adult child. More than three years later, the trustee exchanges that policy with the insurer for a new one on the insured's life. Assume the client is not in any way involved in the replacement except for a written acknowledgement that the trustee's statements were correct. If the insured dies within three years of the exchange (i.e., the acquisition of the "new" policy), will the proceeds of the new policy be includable in the client's gross estate?

The answer is, "no." The exchange of policies by an irrevocable trust should not be treated as a transfer within three years of death if the original transfer occurred more than three years before death and the decedent possesses no interest in the policy at the date of the exchange. The key to success in policy exchanges is (a) be sure the facts don't indicate that the trustee's actions can be imputed to directions from the insured, and (b) be sure the facts indicate that there was no transfer from the insured.

Group Term Life: An employee can successfully transfer all incidents of ownership in group term life coverage if (a) the master contract or state law gives the employee a conversion privilege, and (b) both state law and the master contract allow assignment of all the covered employee's rights including the right to convert the contract to permanent coverage at termination of employment. An assignment of the policy must transfer all of the insured's interest in the group coverage including any right to convert the protection to permanent coverage. (These general rules are covered in more detail under the Section 2042 discussion).

In the context of the "Transfers within Three Years of Death" statute, it is clear that the transfer by the insured of group term life insurance to another within three years of the insured's death will result in federal estate tax inclusion under Section 2035. It is also certain that a transfer (within the scope of Section 2035) takes place when at the inception of coverage someone other than the insured employee is named as owner of the group term coverage.

Can the transfer of group term life ever escape the three year limit? The problem is that, by definition, group term life is typically annually renewable. Each year's premium automatically renews the coverage. If the IRS took the position that each payment created new coverage, it would be impossible to escape the three year limit.

Fortunately, the IRS has stated that the mere payment of the renewal premium does not create a new agreement. It merely continues the old agreement and therefore, with respect to an employee who has absolutely assigned his coverage, renewal is not a new transfer of insurance coverage for purposes of Section 2035. This favorable position is contingent on two conditions: First, no additional evidence of insurability can be required of the insureds in the group. Second, there can be no variation or break in the coverage.

One issue that often comes up pertains to a change in insurers. Assume, for example, that a corporate client finds the rates of one carrier more favorable than those of the current insurer and decides to switch. Each employee receives a new piece of paper with the name of a new insurer. Assume a client had transferred his coverage to his daughter more than three years ago. Does that transaction constitute new coverage and therefore start the three year clock ticking all over again? The answer depends on how much real change (if any) occurred from the covered employee's perspective.

In all probability, the clock will not start to tick again and the IRS will consider the three year period begun when the assignment of the first policy was executed if "the new arrangement is identical in all relevant aspects to the previous arrangement." So if the client dies more than three years after the first assignment, according to this ruling, there will be no inclusion of the group term life even if he dies within three years of the second assignment.

Practitioners should view this seemingly favorable viewpoint with caution, however, because of its unusual condition: a new arrangement must be identical in all relevant respects to the previous arrangement. In one favorable ruling, the employee did not use the company's standard assignment form. Instead, his attorney drew a form assigning not only all his rights in the original group coverage but also any right he might have in any future group term coverage. Although this technique of assigning present and future rights would seem to be a solution to the change in carriers issue, it creates a potential practical trap; if the employee assigns all present and future coverage to his current wife, for example, how will he feel if he later becomes divorced and his then ex-wife reaps the benefits of every increase he enjoys in group coverage, with him paying ever increasing Table I costs as well as possible gift taxes on the annual gifts?

Obviously, if the insured under a group contract is notified by the employer and the new carrier that any prior assignments are void because of the change of carriers and will not be recognized by a new insurer, the Section 2035 clock will tick anew when the new coverage begins. No protection would be afforded by the standard assignment of coverage form in this type of situation. The insured would have to make a new absolute assignment of his coverage and outlive the three year period beginning at the date of the new assignment.

Clients with substantial amounts of group term coverage who wish to remove that insurance from their estates should therefore consider an absolute assignment to a trust or named beneficiary and make the transfer as quickly as possible. A new assignment should be made every time an employer changes group carriers.

Corporate Owned Life Insurance: Section 2042 treats a shareholder who owns more than 50% of a corporation's stock as if he owned life insurance actually owned by the corporation. This provision applies only to the extent insurance owned by the corporation is payable to or for the benefit of a party other than the corporation or its creditor. If the corporation holds the policy insuring the controlling shareholder at such shareholder's death, the proceeds would be includable in his estate under Section 2042.

If the corporation transfers the policy to a third party within three years of the insured's death, for purposes of Section 2035, the insured would be deemed to have made a fatal transfer and inclusion of the proceeds would be the result.

For example, suppose a client owned 80% of the stock of a closely held corporation. The business owned a $1,000,000 life insurance policy on the client's life but the proceeds were payable to the client's children. Upon learning that IRC Section 2042 would require inclusion of the proceeds in the client's gross estate, the client's corporation immediately transfers ownership of the policy to the client's children but the client dies within several months of the transfer. The IRS would argue that

the corporation's transfer of the incidents of ownership was really an indirect transfer by the insured and since the transfer occurred within three years of the insured's death, Section 2035 applies.

Can a client who is a controlling shareholder avoid the 2035 problem by transferring just enough stock so that he no longer meets the "more than 50%" test and then have the corporation transfer the life insurance? The IRS has answered these questions by stating that a transfer of a majority shareholder's stock within three years of death could itself trigger taxation under Section 2035. A gift of a controlling interest in the stock of the corporation is considered a release of the incidents of ownership in the corporate owned policy on the insured's life that in turn is deemed to constitute a transfer of the policy by the insured. The IRS would make this argument even if the insured owned no stock in the corporation at death, because its argument rests on the constructive transfer within three years of the insured's death rather than on the insured's control of a corporation that owns insurance on his life when he dies.

Consider the following scenario: A corporation owns a $1,000,000 policy on the life of a client who owns 80% of the voting stock of the corporation. She is deemed to own the policy on her life that is actually owned by the corporation (to the extent that it was payable to someone other than the corporation or its creditors). Assume further that the proceeds are payable to the client's son. Two years ago, the company transferred the policy to the son who became owner as well as beneficiary. The client has contracted terminal cancer and has only days to live. She makes an immediate gift of 20% of her voting stock to her daughter who runs the business. Two days later, the client dies. The IRS would argue that by giving up control of her corporation, the client made a transfer of incidents of ownership in the life insurance and thereby made a transfer within three years of death and the $1,000,000 of proceeds are included in her estate. On the other hand, a sale of the stock for a price based on all the assets and liabilities of the corporation, i.e., for fair market value, is much more likely to be successful.[5]

Community Property Issues in Section 2035 Situations: Community property laws, if applicable, add another layer of complexity to the already difficult Section 2035 issues. These laws may work for or against the taxpayer. Assume a client lives and works in a community property state. The client's employer applies for a policy on the life of the client but all the facts, including the policy itself, indicate that the client's husband is the policy owner. Even if the client does not control the employer corporation, the IRS would argue that there was a constructive transfer of the insurance by the decedent to her husband. If the client died within three years of that constructive transfer, the IRS would include half the proceeds in her estate because the policy payments by the corporation would be deemed to be compensation to the client and under community property law only one half of that money would be hers to transfer.

Assume a policy was issued in which the insured's wife was named owner and beneficiary and the first premium was paid from the couple's community property checking account. Say the insured dies two months after the policy was issued. The use of community funds to pay the premium would be considered tantamount to a transfer by the insured of his interest in community funds that, in turn, would constitute a transfer of the policy itself. The IRS would include a percentage of the proceeds equal to the insured's community property portion of the premium multiplied by the insurance proceeds.

Techniques for Success: To obtain the highest probability of success, be sure the insured never possesses an incident of ownership. This technique will work in most cases where a policy is about to be issued.

But suppose a client transferred a policy to a trust more than three years ago and therefore has already outlived the statutory three year period. Assume a new insurer is willing to assume the obligations of the old insurer and issue a new policy to the trust with more favorable terms. Even if the insured died within three years of the issuance of the new policy, no inclusion would be required if the facts indicate that the exchange occurred strictly between the independent trustee and the insurance company. Note that from the date of the original transfer the insured never held an incident of ownership. Clearly no incident was held at the date of the exchange and therefore none could have been released or transferred by the insured. If this technique is used, it is important that the trustee be independent and act as trustee rather than as the insured's agent. The insured should not be involved in the transaction in any way except to sign as insured.

A sale of an existing policy may avoid the three year rule but result in the unfortunate income tax consequences discussed in Appendix G with regard to the transfer for value rule. Even if the transfer for value problem is not an issue, the IRS could argue that the amount paid for the policy was not a full and fair payment (especially if the insured was ill at the time of the transfer). But if the insured is healthy, the problem may be cured by transferring the policy to a spouse for full and adequate consideration (from the spouse's funds) and at some later date from the spouse to a trust for the couple's children or other mutually acceptable beneficiary (selected independently by the noninsured spouse). The transfer from the spouse to the trust would not be within the reach of IRC Section 2035.

PROCEEDS PAYABLE TO OR FOR BENEFIT OF INSURED'S ESTATE (IRC Section 2042(1))

Insurance Payable Directly To Estate: Regardless of who purchased the policy, owned the incidents of ownership, or paid premiums, if the proceeds are payable directly to the insured's estate (executor or administrator), they are includable for federal estate tax purposes. The entire value of the proceeds must be included.

Insurance Payable Indirectly To Estate: Likewise, regardless of who purchased the policy, owned incidents of ownership, or paid premiums, if the proceeds are for whatever reason payable "for the benefit of the estate," they are includable for federal estate tax purposes.

Insurance proceeds would be considered payable for the benefit of the estate if used to pay:

- federal estate tax;
- state death taxes;
- income or gift or any other taxes; or
- debts or other charges against the estate.

Inclusion of insurance proceeds payable for the benefit of the estate but not payable directly to the estate (executor or administrator) is conditioned on the following two tests.

First, the beneficiary to whom the proceeds are payable must be legally obligated to use the insurance money for one or more of the purposes described in the list of examples above. If there is no legal obligation for the beneficiary to use the money to meet the type of estate obligation described above, there should be no inclusion. So, for example, the mere power or authority to use insurance proceeds to satisfy debts of the insured will not cause inclusion since such a right does not amount to a legal obligation.

This makes the wording in a classic irrevocable life insurance trust crucial; if the trustee is given discretion to use or not use proceeds to purchase assets from the decedent's estate, the proceeds should not be includable. A loan from the trust to the estate, or even the purchase of assets by the trust from the estate, will not cause inclusion. But if the trustee is directed to pay the insured's estate taxes, debts, or administrative costs to the extent directed by the estate's executor, the proceeds required to pay those expenses will be includable to the extent so used.

Second, there must also be actual use of the insurance money to pay taxes or other claims against the estate. To the extent the trustee has the legal right to use the proceeds to pay taxes or other expenses but life insurance policy proceeds are not in fact used to pay off such claims, they will not be includable.

Insurance Payable To Beneficiary Barred From Collecting: What if the named beneficiary is barred by state law from collecting the policy proceeds? For example, what if the beneficiary murdered the insured in a state which provides that where a beneficiary takes the life of the insured and is convicted of a felony in the offense, the killer forfeits his beneficial interest in the insurance and the forfeited interest passes by law to the insured's other heirs at law unless otherwise disposed of by the insured.

Where state law diverts the proceeds to heirs of the insured's estate, the proceeds are treated for federal tax law purposes as if they had passed into the insured's estate first and were then paid out to the insured's heirs (even if the named beneficiary is convicted of voluntary manslaughter of the insured rather than murder). Thus, if a husband first insured and then murdered his wife and later killed himself, the murdered wife would be deemed to have the equitable right to dictate disposition of the proceeds even though she never owned the policy. The proceeds would probably be distributed according to the terms of the wife's will (as though her murderer had died first) and, for tax purposes, the IRS would tax the money in her estate as if it were paid to her estate's administrators.

Insurance Payable To Executor or Testamentary Trustee Payable To Others Under Governing Instrument: The implications of state law must be examined; there are a number of cases which hold that insurance should be considered payable to the ultimate beneficiary rather than to the estate even though the instrument itself appears to make the proceeds payable to the estate or its executor. This is particularly true where state law allows insurance on a parent's life to pass free from the claims against the estate even if payable to the

insured's estate. In such cases, federal law honors state law and treats the insurance as if it had been paid directly to the ultimate beneficiary.

Even more common is the case where insurance is payable to the trustee under a trust established in a will. Insurance payable to a testamentary trustee for the benefit of a named beneficiary other than the insured's estate will be treated as if received by the named beneficiaries rather than by the estate and will therefore be estate tax free (unless the insured held an incident of ownership in the policy).

But does the term "executor" mean anyone who happens to be an executor of the estate or does it mean only the person receiving the proceeds specifically as the estate's representative? If the proceeds are received in the new owner's individual capacity as beneficiary and not as the representative of the estate, proceeds are not deemed payable to or for the benefit of the estate. The test is whether or not the recipient is bound to the legal duty of then distributing the money according to the terms of the insured's will or state intestacy laws. If the recipient is so bound, then inclusion is mandated.

INSURANCE RECEIVABLE BY BENEFICIARIES OTHER THAN INSURED'S ESTATE (IRC Section 2042(2))

General Rule: If, at the insured's death, any "incidents of ownership" in a policy on his life were held by the insured, (regardless of the monetary value of the incident retained, whether exercisable alone or only in conjunction with another, or how the interest was acquired), the proceeds are includable in the insured's gross estate.

The physical ability of the insured to exercise the ownership right is immaterial; the IRS and the courts generally look to the insured's legal right to exercise ownership. Mere possession of the incident and not its exercise is all that is necessary for inclusion, but the insured must in fact hold legal right to exercise the power in question.

Amount Includable: If Section 2042(2) applies, the entire amount receivable by beneficiaries (other than the estate) is includable in the insured's gross estate. It is important to note that any incident of ownership will trigger inclusion; an insured does not have to possess all of the incidents of ownership nor does the incident of ownership have to be of great value to be fatal.

Incidents of Ownership Defined: Think of an incident of ownership as the right of the insured (or his estate) to one or more economic benefit from the policy. Such a benefit may take the form of the right to:

- cancel the policy;

- assign the policy;

- surrender the policy;

- obtain a policy loan;

- change the beneficiary;

- pledge the policy for a loan;

- change contingent beneficiaries;

- change beneficiaries' share of proceeds[6];

- require consent before change of beneficiary; or

- require consent before assignment of the policy.

Whether or not other rights will or will not be considered an incident of ownership is not always clear cut. Some of the more frequently litigated issues (and the typical results) have been:

1. the mere possession of the right to alter the time and manner of payment of the proceeds to a beneficiary (with no right to change the beneficiary or alter in any way the total amount of proceeds payable to that party)[7] (includable)

2. the right to require consent to the designation of a beneficiary who does not have an insurable interest in the life of the insured (includable)

3. the right to receive dividends on a mutual policy[8] (not includable)

4. the right to change the beneficiary of a policy held in trust[9] (includable)

5. the right to change the terms of a trust that holds a policy[10] (includable)

6. the right to exercise ownership rights only in conjunction with another (includable)

7. the naming by a third party owner as beneficiary "the person named by my husband (the insured) as the beneficiary of his will" (not includable)

8. the inability of the insured to exercise a retained power (includable)

9. the absence of intention on the part of the insured to retain an incident of ownership[11] (includable)

10. instructions to the insurance agent/and or insurer to divest the insured of any incident[12] (not includable)

11. the right to designate or make a change of beneficiary on a policy on the insured's life owned by the insured's employer even though the insured's employer retains the right to amend or cancel the policies without the insured's consent (includable)

12. the right to terminate a spouse's interest in a policy by divorcing her[13] (not includable)

13. the right to obtain cash values of a policy irrevocably assigned for the benefit of the insured's children to a trust (includable)

14. the right to cancel insurance payable to a trust providing income for life to the insured (including income from the proceeds of surrendered policies) (includable)

15. the right to cancel a no-fault auto insurance policy that provided survivors' loss benefits (not includable)

16. the right to purchase the policy from its owner[14] (generally includable)

17. the right to convert from term to whole life or from whole life to limited pay (includable)

18. the right to substitute policies of equal value for those held by a trust (not includable)

19. the right of one partner under a cross purchase buy-sell to veto another partner's right to borrow, surrender, or change beneficiaries (not includable)

20. the insured's right to alter, amend, or revoke a trust that is named as the beneficiary of a policy on the insured's life (not includable)

21. the right to select settlement options[15] (includable).

22. Loans made by the insured to an irrevocable life insurance trust to fund the premiums on a trust-owned life insurance contract were not considered incidents of ownership.[16]

23. The continuing power to determine the compensation of a trustee of an irrevocable life insurance trust was not considered the retention of an interest in the trust by the grantor and, therefore, did not cause federal estate tax inclusion of the trust's assets.[17]

24. the insured-grantor's right to remove a trustee for cause will not cause inclusion.[18]

Attribution of Ownership: In some cases, the IRS will attribute an entity's actual ownership of a life insurance policy to an owner of the entity. For instance, if a partnership owns a policy on the life of one of its partners, to the extent that policy is payable to a party other than the partnership or its creditors (for example to a partner's grandson), the insured partner will be deemed to hold an incident of ownership in the policy.

Because the partnership's actual incident of ownership is deemed constructively owned by the insured partner, it will be includable in his estate. There is no minimum partnership interest required for this result to occur. On the other hand, as long as the policy proceeds are payable to or for the benefit of the partnership, its incidents of ownership will not be attributed to its partners.

A partnership's ability to surrender or cancel its group term coverage will not be attributed to its partners. So, if a partner transfers (more than three years prior to his death) all of the incidents of ownership he holds in group term coverage, he will not be considered to constructively hold incidents of ownership through the partnership's ability to cancel the group term coverage.

When a corporation holds incidents of ownership in a life insurance policy, its ownership rights may be attributed to the insured. Here, the rule for corporations is slightly more formalized than is the case for a partnership: if (at death) the insured owns more than 50% of the total combined voting power of all classes of the corporation's shares entitled to vote, he is deemed to own incidents actually owned by the corporation to the extent proceeds are payable to anyone other than the corporation or its creditors.

For example, assume a client owns 80% of a corporation that owns an insurance policy on his life. If the policy is payable to the corporation (or its creditor), the client will be deemed to hold no incident of ownership in the policy. But if the proceeds of the corporate owned policy are payable to the client's daughter, then the policy actually owned by the corporation will be deemed to be owned by the client and includable in his estate. (The payment of the proceeds may also be considered a constructive dividend or compensation to the shareholder, followed by a gift from the shareholder to his daughter.)

If, however the proceeds were payable to a bank to which the client's corporation owed money and the proceeds were accepted in payment of that debt, to that extent the corporation's incidents of ownership would not be attributed to the client. Naturally, the payoff of the debt would have the affect of increasing the value of the corporation's stock.

There are at least two reasons why the difference (inclusion of proceeds in insured's estate as insurance versus inclusion of stock with higher value) is important: First, treating insurance proceeds as a corporate asset may result in a smaller increase than a dollar for dollar inclusion of insurance proceeds and only the decedent's proportionate share would be includable. For instance, if the decedent only owns 80% of the corporation, at worst 80% and not 100% of the proceeds would be includable. In many cases, since the net asset value of a corporation is not the predominant factor in valuing a going concern, there might not be a dollar for dollar increase in corporate value when insurance proceeds are payable to the corporation. Second, inclusion of life insurance in the insured's estate as life insurance makes qualification for a Section 303 stock redemption, a Section 6166 installment payment of estate tax, or a Section 2057 deduction for qualified family-owned business interests more difficult.

If corporate owned policy proceeds are used to redeem stock from a shareholder's estate, will the proceeds be considered payable to or for the benefit of the estate (and therefore includable separately as life insurance) or will the IRS treat the proceeds as payable to the corporation? The answer is that, in a classic stock redemption or Section 303 stock purchase, there will be no attribution of ownership even though indirectly the proceeds enhance the estate's liquidity and make stock held by the estate marketable. But if the decedent was a controlling shareholder of the corporation owning the policy and the proceeds are payable to a second corporate beneficiary to redeem its stock (or for general corporate purposes), the IRS would probably claim that the proceeds are not payable to or for the benefit of the (first) corporation and therefore should be included.

A corporation's ability to cancel group term life insurance coverage is not considered an incident of ownership held by its shareholder. Therefore, there should be no attribution, even in the case of a controlling stockholder.

Community Property Issues: When life insurance is purchased by community property domiciliaries, federal law usually recognizes it as being owned one half by the wife and one half by the husband. The result is that, where the insured spouse dies first, only half the proceeds are includable in his gross estate, regardless of who the beneficiary is. For example, if a client and his wife live in a community property state and purchase a $1,000,000 life insurance policy on the client's life, only $500,000 will be in the client's estate because the client never owned incidents of ownership over more than one half of the policy. This one half rule applies even if all the proceeds are payable to the insured's estate.

State community property law determines the extent to which the insured had incidents of ownership in a policy. For example, incidents of ownership do not apply merely because state law gives one spouse the right to manage a community owned policy and thus has the legal power to surrender the contract.

Likewise, regardless of whose name is listed on the policy application as owner, absent strong proof to the contrary, each spouse holds one half of all incidents of ownership. So generally, life insurance acquired by spouses in a community property state is presumed to be community property even if the title is held in only one spouse's name. However, the parties can establish, through clear and convincing evidence, that they intended to hold the property in some form other than all as community.

It is also possible that life insurance will be deemed to have been purchased partially with community property funds and partially with separate property funds. A common example is where the policy itself was purchased prior to marriage or before the couple moved to a community property state. Then, if premiums are paid from community funds, the proceeds have been generated by a mixture of separate and community premiums.

In Texas, Louisiana, New Mexico, and Arizona, the concept of "inception of title" is used to classify the proceeds; insurance proceeds on a policy purchased prior to the couple's marriage or move to a community property state remains as it was at inception, separate property, even though community funds were used to pay some premiums. Under state law, the proceeds would therefore be the insured's separate property, but the surviving spouse would have a right to be reimbursed for half of the community funds used to pay premiums. That, of course, would be the measure of federal estate tax inclusion; the entire proceeds would be includable less the one half of the community funds that were used to pay premiums.

California and Washington use a concept called the "premium tracing" rule; each spouse is deemed to own his share of the policy proportionate to his share of the premium contribution. Therefore, only the portion that belonged to the insured would be includable.

An unintended and unexpected gift tax trap may await the unwary; if the client names neither his estate nor his spouse as beneficiary of the proceeds, the IRS could argue that the uninsured spouse made a gift to the beneficiary when the proceeds are paid. The gift becomes complete upon the insured's death and the amount of the gift is one half the amount of the insurance proceeds.

Where the noninsured spouse dies first and the insurance is community property, half the value of the unmatured policy is includable in that spouse's gross estate. Then, if the insured spouse receives the policy under the noninsured spouse's will, the entire proceeds will be includable in his estate.

More Than 5% Test: In some situations, a client has made a conditional transfer, i.e., a gift of a policy coupled with a "but if…back to me" string. If certain events did (or did not) occur, the policy would revert (i.e., come back) to the donor insured (or his estate).

Such a reversionary interest in a policy held by the insured or the insured's estate will be considered an incident of ownership under Section 2042 if the actuarial value of that interest exceeds 5% of the value of the policy (measured immediately prior to the insured's death). This reversionary interest must be just that, a right retained by the insured (either in the policy provisions or by some other instrument or operation of law) when the insured transferred the policy. The mere possibility that a policy could return to the insured as a bequest by will at the donee's death or through the intestacy of the donee (or through the right of the insured to elect against a spouse's will) is not considered a reversionary interest and will therefore not cause inclusion.

Even if a reversionary interest exists, it must be actuarially (according to current monthly government discount rates) be worth more than 5% of the value of the policy as measured immediately before the insured's death. So, if someone else had an interest that lowered the value of the insured's interest, the value of the other person's interest could prevent estate tax inclusion in the insured's estate.

For example, suppose a client gave a policy on his life to his son and retained the right to regain the policy if the son died before the insured. Suppose, in the same transfer, the donor insured gave the son the unfettered right to surrender the policy for cash at any time. The son's power to completely eliminate the insured's right to regain the policy would reduce the value of the father's interest to zero.

As a practical matter, if the donee of a policy is the owner and has all rights normally associated with ownership except the right to name a successor owner (the reversionary right held by the insured), the value of the insured's reversionary right would be well below the more than 5% threshold. If the donee had the right to revoke the insured's successive ownership designation in addition to the ability to surrender the contract, the value of the insured's reversionary interest should approach zero.

Reversionary Interest and Death of Third Party Owner: What is the result where a third party owner of a policy on the insured's life dies before the insured does and the policy passes back to the insured? Here, state law must be examined very carefully. The results may be surprising. For example, suppose a client's wife purchased a $1,000,000 policy on the client's life. Assume the wife is killed in an automobile accident in which the client dies one hour later. As the beneficiary of his wife's will, the client becomes (if only for an hour) the owner of the insurance proceeds that are actually paid to the specified contingent beneficiaries.

Did the client have incidents of ownership? The answer will depend on state law. If title and legal right and possession of personal property pass to the estate's executor and that party is someone other than the client, the client would not have legal power to exercise incidents of ownership in the insurance. Therefore, nothing would be includable in his estate under Section 2042. But if he was the personal representative (executor) of the estate, as well as heir, he would have incidents of ownership since he would have immediate legal rights over the insurance. The same result would occur if the insured were named as contingent owner of the policy. Were he merely personal representative but not an heir of the wife's estate, there would be no inclusion because there would be no personally exercisable incidents of ownership.

Insured Also Trustee: Often, insureds have served as a trustee of a trust which held insurance on their lives. Unfortunately, such an arrangement has often led to expensive litigation and often federal estate tax inclusion of policy proceeds on these grounds: the trust owned the policy, the trustee controlled the trust, the insured was trustee, and therefore the insured is deemed to have held incidents of ownership in a policy on his life actually held by the trust. Of course, this argument conveniently overlooks the most basic premise of trust law: a fiduciary is barred from using such funds for personal benefit absent express provision in the governing instrument (assuming the fiduciary is not also a beneficiary).

Although it would appear a sound argument therefore, that incidents held purely and solely in a fiduciary capacity cannot be used except to benefit a trust's heirs (and therefore should not be included in the decedent's estate as insurance), the IRS doesn't see it that way. Fortunately, the courts don't always agree with the IRS. The result is a confusing and dangerous mix of cases and rulings that vary in result depending more on domicile than on facts.

Two types of situations may trigger the problem: The most common is where the client creates a trust and transfers life insurance to it and insists on being named trustee. But the problem can also occur where the policy on the insured is owned by a third party (such as the insured's spouse) and, at that third party's death, the policy passes to a trust over which the insured is trustee.

The following will summarize the Section 2042(2) issues with respect to life insurance trusts where the IRS will act aggressively against the deceased taxpayer's estate:

- If the decedent (acting alone or in conjunction with others) had the power as trustee to change the time or manner of enjoyment, even if the decedent had no beneficial interest in the trust, the IRS will treat him as having held an incident of ownership in a policy on his own life held in a trust if he was trustee.

- If the decedent transferred the policy to the trust or paid premiums, the IRS will treat him as having held an incident of ownership in a policy on his own life held in a trust if he was trustee.

- If the decedent could have exercised his powers as trustee for his own benefit, regardless of how those powers were acquired and regardless of whether or not the decedent transferred property to the trust, the IRS will treat him as having held an incident of ownership in a policy on his own life held in a trust if he was trustee.

The following will summarize the Section 2042(2) issues with respect to life insurance trusts where the IRS will not claim the deceased taxpayer held incidents of ownership:

- If (1) the decedent held powers only in a fiduciary capacity and could not exercise those powers for his personal benefit, (2) he did not transfer the policy or any of the premiums or other consideration for purchasing or maintaining the policy from personal assets, and (3) the return of powers to the decedent was not part of a prearranged plan.

The following will summarize the Section 2042(2) issues with respect to life insurance trusts where the courts in some jurisdictions are likely to agree with the IRS that the deceased taxpayer had held incidents of ownership:

- According to the Fifth Circuit,[19] a decedent has incidents of ownership in a policy on his life held in trust if the decedent is trustee, even if incidents of ownership are possessed only in a fiduciary capacity and the insured made no transfer of the policy to the trust.

The following will summarize the Section 2042(2) issues with respect to life insurance trusts where the courts in some jurisdictions are likely to agree with the IRS that the deceased taxpayer had held incidents of ownership:

- According to the Second,[20] Sixth,[21] and Eighth Circuits[22], a decedent does not have incidents of ownership in a policy on his life held in trust if the decedent transfers policies on his life to a trust, even though the decedent is named trustee, as long as he cannot exercise his fiduciary powers for his own benefit.

What is certain is that this confusion and danger can be avoided by naming someone other than the insured as the trustee of a trust that has or could have insurance on his life. As a next best alternative, planners should consider the following provisions:

1. Specifically forbid an insured serving as trustee from taking any action with respect to a policy on his life held by a trust over which the insured is trustee or co-trustee.[23]

2. Be sure the insured has no beneficial interest in the trust.

3. Specify that the insured, as trustee, cannot use trust income or assets to satisfy his legal obligation to support his children.

4. Place assets in the trust to generate sufficient income to pay premiums.

5. Follow the terms of the trust closely and avoid conflict fact patterns which indicate that the insured acting as trustee can use trust property for personal gain.

Insured as Fiduciary Other Than Trustee: When the insured becomes the executor or administrator of an estate or the custodian of a minor or otherwise legally incompetent person's assets, there is a strong possibility that an incident of ownership problem may arise if the estate or custodial account holds a policy on the insured's life. For example, assume a wife purchased a policy on her husband's life but the wife predeceased her husband. The policy would be considered personal property in her estate. Assume the wife's will left the entire estate to the husband, if living, otherwise to the couple's children.

When the insured becomes the administrator or executor of an estate and is also a beneficiary of the estate, as is the case in this example, it is highly likely that should the insured die, even before distribution of the policy, the IRS will claim he had incidents of ownership in a policy on his life held by the estate. It would argue that, as executor, the insured could exercise powers over the insurance for his own benefit. Inclusion is clear where the husband was the sole beneficiary of the estate. But what if the estate was split in thirds between the insured husband and the couple's two children? What if the wife's estate was payable entirely to the three children?

In the authors' opinion, these two later situations do not meet the three tests the IRS itself set out: (1) the insured must have transferred the policy or provided consideration for purchasing or maintaining it from the insured's personal assets; (2) the rights and powers the insured obtained were part of a prearranged plan involving the participation of the insured; and (3) the insured can personally benefit from the powers held as fiduciary. Even if the first and third tests were met (i.e., if the insured paid premiums from personal funds to keep the policy on his life in force and personally could benefit from the arrangement), it would be difficult for the IRS to argue that the wife and the husband colluded and she died first so that he could obtain control without inclusion of the policy in his estate.

Many states' version of the UGMA (Uniform Gifts to Minors Act) or UTMA (Uniform Transfers to Minors Act) allows a custodian for a child to purchase and/or maintain life insurance. It is clear that, if a client transfers life insurance on his life to a custodial account for his child and names himself as the custodian, assets in the account will be includable in his estate if he died before the minor child reaches the age where the custodial funds must be paid out under state law. If life insurance is one of the custodial account's assets, it will be included in the insured-custodian's estate. Likewise, if the client becomes successor custodian and then dies, the value of the property transferred will be includable in the client's estate.

There are situations in which an individual gives another person a power of attorney over assets in order to care for and protect the individual. Assume a client's mother owned a life insurance policy on the client's life. To protect herself against incompetency, the mother gave her son a general durable power of attorney with wide boilerplate provisions. Would the power given to the son amount to an incident of ownership in the policy on his life?

There appear to be no cases or rulings directly on point. If the insured could exercise powers over the life insurance as holder of the power, at the very least, the IRS could engage his estate in costly litigation. The authors conclude that the best course of action is to provide in the power of attorney that the holder of the power is barred from exercising any right whatsoever with respect to a policy of life insurance on his life.

Split Dollar Insurance: In the classic split dollar arrangement in which a corporation makes an outlay equal to the annual increase in policy cash values and a selected employee pays the balance of the premium, if any, the insured is given the power to name and change the beneficiary of the portion of the proceeds not going to the corporation (usually an amount at least equal to its cumulative outlay). That ability to name and change the beneficiary is an incident of ownership and will cause inclusion of the proceeds. The right to name the beneficiary of proceeds in excess of the cash value (or in the case of reverse split dollar, the right to name the beneficiary of the policy's cash value) would seem to be sufficient to warrant inclusion of the entire proceeds.

All the proceeds would be includable even if the insured possessed only one incident of ownership and even though a portion of the proceeds were payable to someone other than the insured's beneficiaries. For example, assume a client owned 40% of the stock of a company that provided $1,000,000 of life insurance on his life. The corporation paid an amount equal to each year's increase in cash values and the client paid the balance of the premium. At the client's death, the proceeds were to be paid to the corporation in an amount up to its total outlay and any balance would be paid to the client's daughter. Assuming the client doesn't assign the policy to his daughter more than three years prior to his death, the entire proceeds would be included in his estate.

However, a "claims against the estate" deduction might be allowed for proceeds paid to the corporation (or other party receiving a portion of the proceeds in return for having paid a portion of the premiums). This claim against the estate deduction should apply whenever:

1. the insured owned 50% or less of the corporation (i.e., was not a controlling shareholder);

2. there was a bona fide written agreement as to the reimbursement arrangement; and

3. the agreement was entered into initially for full and adequate consideration as part of a business transaction. This implies that the client's estate may not be allowed an estate tax deduction where the client merely names a family trust as beneficiary.

A much more difficult problem is faced when an individual controls (owns more than 50% of the combined voting stock in) a closely held corporation. In that case, to the extent proceeds of a corporate owned policy are payable to or for the benefit of a party other than the corporation, such proceeds are includable as insurance in the insured's estate (because the insured is deemed to possess incidents of ownership).

As the law stands today, it appears that the only way to remove a split dollar life insurance policy from the gross estate of a controlling shareholder is to insulate all incidents of ownership from the corporation (since once the corporation owns any incident, including the right to borrow against the cash surrender value, that incident is attributed to its controlling shareholder).

But how is it possible to set up a split dollar plan with the corporation advancing the bulk of the premium and yet not providing security for the corporation's outlays? One answer lies in the problem itself; there is only a problem if the shareholder is controlling (i.e., owns more than 50% of the vote). By definition, therefore, that person should be able to persuade the corporation to forego the customary protection or right to borrow against the policy's cash value or veto a loan against or surrender of the policy.

If the policy is owned by a third party, such as a trust for the client's children (or if adult children own the policy), from inception or the policy is assigned to an irrevocable trust (or to adult children) more than three years prior to the client's death, the insured would hold no incidents of ownership either personally or through the corporation (since the corporation would have no rights whatsoever except the right to receive that portion of the proceeds equal to its premium outlay).

If the insured owned more than 50% of the corporation which is splitting the premium and proceed dollars, it is appropriate (but not certain at this point) that since the amount payable to the corporation will already be included in the insured's gross estate due to the impact it will have increasing corporate value, those proceeds should not again be includable separately as insurance.

Although most split dollar arrangements are between corporations and employees, there are many agreements to split premiums, cash values, and death proceeds of life insurance that are made between individuals. Such an arrangement is often called "private split dollar." A father in law, for example, may protect his daughter and grandchildren by entering into a split dollar agreement with his son in law. The father would help the son in law obtain more insurance at a lower cost than might otherwise be possible.

If the insured is given or retains any incident of ownership in the policy, the proceeds will be includable in his estate. Suppose a parent, for instance, sets up a trust for his children and the trust purchases a life insurance policy on the father's life. To help the trustee pay premiums (and to lower gift tax costs), the father advances amounts equal to the annual increase in the policy's cash surrender value. The trustee must pay the balance of each year's premium. The father retains the right to recover an amount equal to his cumulative outlays or to borrow against the policy for up to that amount. That retained right will cause inclusion of the proceeds in his estate.[24]

INCLUSION OF LIFE INSURANCE IN RETIREMENT PLANS (IRC Section 2039)

Background: At one time, IRC Section 2039(c) provided an unlimited exclusion for the amount distributed at a participant's death from a qualified retirement plan to the extent attributable to employer contributions. That exclusion has been eliminated.

Subject to certain transition (grandfathering) rules, a decedent's executor must include in the gross estate the value of any payment "receivable by any beneficiary by reason of surviving the decedent under any form of contract or agreement…(other than as insurance under policies on the life of the decedent)," if certain other conditions are met. So Section 2039 will not cause the inclusion of the proceeds of a life insurance policy on a plan participant's life. Does this mean the proceeds are estate tax free? The answer is "yes," only if inclusion is not warranted under any other IRC section.

The Subtrust Concept: Some authorities have suggested that it is still possible to avoid federal estate taxation on life insurance proceeds paid as part of a distribution from a qualified retirement plan through a subtrust concept. One configuration of the technique works like this:

1. The insured employee makes an irrevocable beneficiary designation that divests him of the right to change the beneficiary of plan proceeds.

2. The qualified plan is amended to provide that the policy will not be distributed to the insured at retirement. This amendment is made to eliminate an IRS argument that the insured retained a reversionary interest in the policy.

3. The plan is amended to give the insured a right to purchase the policy for its full value at retirement.

4. To insulate an insured who is also a trustee of the plan from an incidents of ownership attack by the IRS, a special trust (subtrust) is created. Policies on the life of the insured-trustee are placed into the subtrust. The insured is given no control over the subtrust and cannot remove its independent trustee.

Will this subtrust concept work? Are there hidden tax problems associated with it? Because there are no cases on point, or, at this date, any public rulings, no one can be sure. Here are some issues to consider:

If the insured has incidents of ownership and then divests himself of them as step 1 of the subtrust technique suggests, a gift is made. This would seem to be the result if the irrevocable beneficiary designation is successful. There are several implications to such a gratuitous transfer:

First, if the coverage itself has been given away, then the IRS could deem each future premium actually paid by the employer as though it were a gift made by the insured employee to the new owner. This is consistent with the way group term life assignments are treated.

Second, such gifts would not qualify for the gift tax annual exclusion since the beneficiary-owner does not have an immediate, unfettered, and ascertainable right to use, possess, or enjoy a policy that is presently inside a qualified plan.

Third, if neither the original assignment nor the annual premium payments can be considered present interest gifts, the transfers could not qualify for the annual exclusion for generation-skipping purposes.[25]

Fourth, if the plan participant dies within three years of the gift (i.e., at the irrevocable beneficiary designation), the proceeds of the policy could be brought back into the estate under IRC Section 2035.

Step 3 of the subtrust plan indicates that the insured plan participant would be given a right to purchase the policy on his life. Although there is authority that such a right will not be considered an incident of ownership,[26] there is also evidence that the IRS may not agree.[27] But if the insured does purchase the policy, the Section 2035 three year clock begins ticking, not from the date of the original assignment or the participant's repurchase of the policy, but from the date of the second transfer of the policy. This, of course, endangers the estate tax savings goal of the entire technique.

If the trustee of the subtrust can be removed by the corporation and replaced by a new corporate appointee, will the corporation's power over the trustee be equated to an incident of ownership over the insurance in the subtrust? If so, will a controlling shareholder be deemed to control the policy in the subtrust by virtue of his control over the corporation?

Alternative to the Subtrust Concept: It is possible and sometimes desirable to remove life insurance from a qualified plan. Advantages of life insurance outside of a qualified plan include: (1) the ability to invest in more assets producing otherwise currently taxable income and have the income on such assets grow income tax free; and (2) the ability to exclude life insurance purchased outside the plan from federal estate taxes and be assured that, if arranged properly, exclusion is a very high probability if not a certainty.

The easiest way to remove life insurance from a qualified plan is for the trustee to allow the policy to lapse and for new insurance to be purchased outside the plan (preferably by adult beneficiaries or a trust for the intended recipient of the proceeds). A sale by the retirement plan of the policy to the insured is another possibility. This is a more appealing choice where the insured is in ill health, the policy in question is beyond the incontestable period, or, for whatever other reason, the client does not want the original policy to lapse.

A sale to the insured or to the policy's beneficiary is permissible under an exception to the prohibited transaction rules.[28] In most cases, the preferred course of action is to have the insured purchase the policy to nullify the danger under the transfer for value rule (see Appendix G). It is extremely important to document evidence that: (1) the contract would have been surrendered by the plan even if the sale had not taken place; and (2) the plan was placed financially in the same position it would have been in had it surrendered the contract and made a distribution of the amount the plan owed to the insured participant.

There are disadvantages to the "sale to the insured" technique: One is that the insured does not receive credit for the income tax paid on the costs of life insurance protection. In other words, the plan participant cannot count as part of his basis the taxes paid for the term insurance protection he received year after year. A second possible disadvantage is that the purchase by the insured does not solve the estate tax inclusion problem. That can only be accomplished if the insured then divests himself of all incidents of ownership and lives for more than three years after the transfer. A third potential problem lies with valuation issues; if the insured is terminally ill or in exceptionally poor health, the amount necessary to purchase the policy may be significantly more than its interpolated terminal reserve plus unearned premiums.

ESTATE TAX MARITAL DEDUCTION (IRC Section 2056)

General Rules: An unlimited deduction is allowed for property includable in the gross estate that passes in a qualifying manner to the surviving spouse of the decedent. The surviving spouse must be a U.S. citizen or the property must pass to a qualified domestic trust (QDOT) for the benefit of the surviving spouse. No deduction is allowed, however, for certain "nondeductible terminable interests," in general, interests which may terminate or fail to vest upon the lapse of time or upon the occurrence or nonoccurrence of a specified event or contingency. A spouse's interest in life insurance proceeds is terminable and would be nondeductible if (1) there is any possibility that her interest will terminate upon the occurrence or nonoccurrence of a contingency or event, (2) some other person or persons will receive the property as a result of the termination, and (3) that other person or persons will receive the property interest without paying consideration in money or money's worth. If all three tests are met, the interest will not qualify for the marital deduction.

Generally, proceeds will qualify for the federal estate tax marital deduction if they are paid in the form of a:

- Lump sum

- Life annuity ending at spouse's death

- Life annuity with principal remaining paid to spouse's estate

- Payment to spouse (interest only or installments) and principal remaining paid to specified beneficiary coupled with surviving spouse given general power of appointment over principal

- Payment to spouse of interest only, with remaining principal qualifying under QTIP rules

- Outright payment under insured's will

- Outright payment under state intestacy laws

- Payment of proceeds to trust which itself qualifies for marital deduction

Lump Sum To Spouse: Life insurance will qualify for the federal estate tax marital deduction if payable in a lump sum to the decedent-insured's surviving (U.S. citizen) spouse. Since the spouse will receive the entire interest in the proceeds rather than a nondeductible terminable interest, the marital deduction will be allowed even if the insured names secondary or other contingent beneficiaries in the event the noninsured spouse does not survive the insured. The marital deduction will also be allowed if the surviving spouse chooses to receive proceeds under a settlement option rather than take a lump sum, as long as the choice is hers.

Income To Spouse, Balance To Spouse's Estate: A marital deduction will be allowed if the insured or the surviving spouse selects a settlement option with the insurer giving the surviving spouse income from the proceeds for her life with the balance of the proceeds going to her estate. This follows the principle that a nondeductible terminable interest is one in which someone other than the surviving spouse might take her interest with no consideration upon the occurrence or nonoccurrence of a specified event. Since no one other than the spouse will take an interest (payment to the spouse's estate is equated to payment to the spouse), the interest is not a nondeductible interest. Therefore, a life annuity to the spouse with no refund or no period certain guarantee would qualify for the marital deduction. Likewise, a life annuity to the spouse coupled with a period certain guarantee (for example, a guarantee that at least 15 years' payments will be made) with the balance of any payments going to the spouse's estate will qualify.

Income To Spouse, Power of Appointment: As another exception to the nondeductible terminable interests rule, the interest can be payable to the spouse and then to some other beneficiary and still qualify, if the surviving spouse is given a general power of appointment over the proceeds and certain other requirements are met.

There are five conditions that must be met:

1. "All income to spouse" rule: There must be an agreement with the insurer that the proceeds (or a specified portion of the proceeds) will be paid in installments to the surviving spouse, or that the surviving spouse will receive all the income and no one else will receive installment or interest for as long as such spouse lives.

2. "Annually or more frequently" rule: The installments or interest payable solely to the surviving spouse must be payable annually or more frequently. Payments must begin no later than 13 months after the insured's death. As long as payment can begin within 13 months after the decedent's death, and the only person with any choice in that decision is the surviving spouse, the 13 month test is met even if, in fact, no payment is elected for more than 13 months. This condition is satisfied even if the insurance contract requires the surviving spouse to provide proof of death before the first payment is made.

3. "Power to Appoint" rule: The surviving spouse must have the general power to appoint all or a

specific portion of the amounts held by the insurer to either herself, her estate, her creditors, or the creditors of her estate. The power will be considered general if the surviving spouse can revoke the contingent beneficiaries the insured had named and substitute her estate. Likewise, if she can require the trustee to pay her principal for her own use, she will be deemed to have a general power.

4. "Alone and in All Events" rule: The power to make appointments of principal must be exercisable by the surviving spouse without the need to consult or obtain anyone else's consent. This requirement will not fail merely because the insurer places administrative restrictions on withdrawal rights. For example, the requirement that the beneficiary give formal written notice, or that some reasonable time interval must be allowed between partial exercises of the surviving spouse's powers, will not be considered to thwart the spouse's right to withdraw in all events. The power can be exercised either by will or by an instrument during the spouse's lifetime, but must be an unconditional right exercisable without limitations.

5. "No Power Except to Provide for Spouse" rule: The amounts payable under the arrangement with the insurer cannot be subject to a power of appointment in anyone's hands other than the surviving spouse, except for a power in the hands of another to appoint some or all of the insurance proceeds to the surviving spouse.

QTIP Rules: Another exception to the nondeductible terminable interests rule is qualified terminable interest property (QTIP). Under this exception, "income only" payments to the spouse with payments to a beneficiary following the termination of her interest can qualify for a marital deduction even if the surviving spouse is given no general power of appointment.

QTIP rules require that the proceeds "pass from the decedent," that the surviving spouse be given a "qualifying income interest for life," and that the original decedent's executor make an irrevocable election on the federal estate tax return to have the marital deduction apply. Any principal left at the time the surviving spouse dies will be includable in her estate.

Payment Under Insured's Will: In some instances, life insurance is payable to an insured's estate. Most often, this occurs where the insured has neglected to name a

specific beneficiary or contingent beneficiary or where the beneficiary named has predeceased the insured and the insured died before naming a new beneficiary.[29] But even such payments can qualify for the marital deduction if assets in the estate pass outright by will to the surviving (U.S. citizen) spouse.[30] Likewise, if the insured's life insurance is payable to his estate and he dies intestate, the proceeds will qualify for the federal estate tax marital deduction even though passing under state inheritance tax laws to the surviving spouse rather than by will or through specific direction in the policy itself.

Payment To Estate Trust or Marital Deduction Trust: Payment of life insurance proceeds directly to a trust which otherwise qualifies for a marital deduction will qualify the proceeds for the marital deduction. Therefore, payments to an "estate trust" (income may be paid out to the spouse or may be accumulated at the trustee's discretion, but principal remaining at the surviving spouse's death is payable to her estate) or "power of appointment" trust (the surviving spouse receives all income annually or more frequently and has the general power to appoint principal to herself or her estate) will qualify for a marital deduction.

Time Delay Clause: To qualify for the marital deduction, property must pass to a surviving spouse. If the beneficiary spouse does not survive the insured, the marital deduction is not allowed. In some situations, the beneficiary spouse may survive the insured spouse and yet the proceeds will not pass to the surviving spouse and so the marital deduction is lost. Planners must therefore make sure when using a time delay clause or common disaster provision that, if the marital deduction is important, that its requirements are met.

A time delay clause is a provision that can be inserted in an insurance company's beneficiary form that provides payment will be made to the surviving spouse of the insured, but only if such spouse is living at the end of a given period of time, typically 30 or 60 days[31] after the death of the insured. If the surviving spouse does not survive the time delay clause period, the proceeds are paid to contingent beneficiaries. Such a clause is designed to assure that the proceeds don't fall into the hands of a surviving spouse's relatives or to avoid a needless probate in the surviving spouse's estate (and perhaps needless state death taxes) if she doesn't survive the specified period of time.

The problem with a time delay clause is that probate costs and state inheritance taxes may be saved at the expense of much higher federal estate taxes; the marital deduction is denied if the surviving spouse dies before the end of the specified time period, since the proceeds will not pass to her. For instance, if a client provides in his life insurance beneficiary designation that his wife must survive him by 30 days in order to receive the proceeds of his $1,000,000 policy and she dies 18 days after he does, the money will not be paid to her or to her estate and will pass to the secondary beneficiary. The marital deduction will be lost.

Will a marital deduction be allowed even if the surviving spouse does survive the time delay period? The problem is that a time delay clause creates a condition which may terminate the surviving spouse's interest and result in property passing to someone other than the surviving spouse's estate and no consideration would be paid to her or her estate for the transfer. In other words, a time delay clause is a classic nondeductible terminable interest.

Fortunately, however, there is a specific statutory provision that enables the marital deduction to be obtained even if a time delay clause is used.[32] There are two requirements:

1. the delay period can not exceed 6 months, and

2. the spouse must actually survive whatever period is specified.

If both requirements are met, the marital deduction will be allowed. On the other hand, if under the clause there is any possibility that the surviving spouse may have to survive longer than 6 months to receive the proceeds, no matter how remote that possibility is, the marital deduction will be disallowed. The deduction will be disallowed even if the spouse does survive the specified period and the proceeds in fact pass to her.

A good example of such a fatal clause is one that paid the proceeds to the insured's wife "if she were living at the time the insurer received proof of the decedent's death." Proof of death was provided to the insurer within six months and payment of the proceeds was made to the widow. However, the IRS ruled that the marital deduction would not be allowed because proof of death might not have been made within the requisite six month period.

A time delay clause must be carefully considered because it can result in a "lose-lose" situation: if the spouse lives longer than the minimum time, the clause is inoperative. If the spouse outlives the insured but does not survive the specified period, the marital deduction is forfeited. Selection by the insured of a settlement option that qualifies for the marital deduction or payment of proceeds to a trust qualifying for the marital deduction may be a better choice.

Common Disaster Clause: A common disaster clause provides a presumption as to the order of death. If both the insured and the beneficiary die in the same accident, the insured will be deemed to have survived the beneficiary. In other words, a common disaster clause is triggered, not by an arbitrarily specified length of time the survivor must live, but rather by whether or not the beneficiary died in a common accident with the insured. No matter by how long the beneficiary survives the insured, if the beneficiary subsequently dies as the result of the accident which killed the insured, the proceeds will pass to the contingent beneficiary (or the insured's estate) and will therefore not qualify for the marital deduction.

A common disaster clause therefore would appear to cause a loss of the marital deduction; there is always a possibility that the surviving spouse's interest may terminate. The marital deduction will be lost if at the final audit of the estate tax return "there is still a possibility that the surviving spouse may be deprived of the property interest by operation of the common disaster provision as given effect by the local law."

But under a special exception to the normal rules disqualifying terminable interests, the deduction will be allowed if in fact the noninsured spouse does survive and receives the proceeds. Planners should not count on this occurrence if the federal estate tax marital deduction is important.

Uniform Simultaneous Death Act (USDA): Almost all the states have adopted the USDA. This law provides that if the insured and the beneficiary die at so nearly the same time that the order of their deaths cannot be ascertained, there is a legal presumption that the beneficiary died first. This, of course, would cause the loss of the marital deduction with respect to the proceeds. Note that the cause of death is irrelevant. In fact, the insured and the beneficiary can be at the opposite ends of the earth; if they die about the same time and the facts don't clearly indicate who died first, the presumption is that the beneficiary died first and therefore no marital deduction would be allowed.

In smaller estates, where federal estate taxes are not a major issue, this presumption would be favorable, since it would eliminate an unnecessary probate (and perhaps state taxation) of the proceeds in the beneficiary's estate. In a larger estate, the USDA could be a disaster.

Fortunately, a client can reverse the presumption of order of deaths merely by stating that desire in the insurance policy application or in a separate beneficiary agreement. This so called "reverse simultaneous death clause" nullifies the effects of a statutory presumption that the noninsured died first. Specifically, a reverse simultaneous death clause would state that if it cannot be determined who died first, the beneficiary will be deemed to have survived. Such a clause will be recognized by the IRS. Of course, if the facts show that the beneficiary did die first, a reverse simultaneous death clause will be worthless and the marital deduction will be lost.

ESTATE TAX CHARITABLE DEDUCTION (IRC Section 2055)

An unlimited charitable deduction is allowed for the net amount of life insurance proceeds included in the insured's estate if they are then paid to a qualified charity. If the proceeds are reduced by a policy loan, only the net amount includable in the estate and payable to the charity will qualify for the charitable deduction.

If the policyowner is not the insured but dies first, a charitable deduction will be allowed if the unmatured policy passes to a qualified charity. The inclusion and value of the deduction will be measured by the same rules governing a lifetime gift to a charity. In most cases, the deduction will be measured by the sum of the interpolated terminal reserve plus the unearned premium (as of the date of the policyowner's death).

APPORTIONMENT RULES: WHO PAYS THE ESTATE TAX ON INSURANCE PROCEEDS?

This is an extremely important issue that is often overlooked or that falls between the cracks of an otherwise good estate plan.

General Rule: As a general rule, to collect the federal estate tax, the IRS can follow life insurance proceeds as far as it can trace them. Any person who receives includable property is personally liable to the IRS for a deficiency in the estate tax. Each life insurance beneficiary is liable for that deficit, up to the full amount of the proceeds payable to him that were included in the insured's gross estate, regardless of a direction in the will exonerating the beneficiary from payment of the tax or a direction that the tax be paid from the probate estate. The IRS can follow any person who received life insurance proceeds and collect its tax from other property even if the proceeds themselves have been spent. If the proceeds have been spent, the government's lien extends to any property bought by or for the beneficiary with the proceeds.

Ordinarily, this tracking is not necessary because the executor, who is primarily liable, usually pays estate taxes out of probate funds. But what happens when significant nonprobate assets such as life insurance generate a tax but the proceeds are not payable to the executor to pay that tax?

Executor's Right To Recover: The Internal Revenue Code specifically authorizes an executor to recover from named beneficiaries of life insurance proceeds on the decedent's life a proportionate share of the taxes. The executor cannot claim reimbursement or contribution until after the executor pays the tax. Each beneficiary must (absent direction otherwise under the decedent's will or local law) reimburse the executor for his proportionate share of the federal estate tax. The IRS technically can't go against an insurance company for the tax regardless of how the proceeds are payable. But the executor may be able to reach the insurance proceeds held by the insurer to the extent the executor is entitled to contribution from the insurance beneficiary.

In the apportionment formula, total tax paid is multiplied by:

$$\frac{\text{proceeds included in estate \& received by beneficiary}}{\text{taxable estate}}$$

For instance, assume a client died and a $1,000,000 policy on his life was paid in equal shares to his two children. Assume further that the insurance was equal to about one half the client's taxable estate (total taxable estate was $2,000,000) and that the total estate tax was $600,000. The insurance in this simplified example would have generated ½ of the $600,000 tax, $300,000. Each child received ½ of the $1,000,000 proceeds, so each would be liable for about $150,000, ½ of the $300,000 tax.

Marital Share Exception: If life insurance proceeds were paid to the insured's surviving spouse in a manner qualifying for the estate tax marital deduction, the rule is different. There, the executor can require reimbursement by the beneficiaries only for the tax attributable to the excess of proceeds over the aggregate amount of marital deductions.[33] So, if the entire amount of proceeds payable to the surviving spouse qualified for the marital deduction, the spouse would have no duty to contribute toward the payment of the federal estate tax.

If only a portion of the proceeds paid to the surviving spouse qualified for the marital deduction, then the surviving spouse would be liable to reimburse the executor for the proportionate share of tax on the balance. For instance, if $200,000 of life insurance was payable to a spouse but only $120,000 qualified for the marital deduction, the executor would be entitled to reimbursement on the $80,000 taxable difference. If the total taxable estate were $250,000, then $80,000/$250,000 would be multiplied by the total tax payable to ascertain the spouse's required contribution.

Apportionment Provisions by Client: Clients can engineer a different result through a combination of state law and careful will planning. For instance, if the will directs how the tax burden is to be apportioned, those directions will generally be followed by both state and federal authorities (to the extent tax collection is not jeopardized). For example, if the client's will provides that "my son and daughter shall pay all death taxes," they would end up paying even the estate tax on life insurance payable to other beneficiaries. This can obviously lead to unintended results and emphasizes the importance of co-ordination between the attorney drafting the client's will and the client's life insurance agent.

Use of Disclaimers: A disclaimer is an unqualified refusal to accept property (such as assets left under a will or trust or life insurance proceeds). Can a disclaimer avoid a potential tax disaster? For example, assume a client's will provides that all estate taxes will be paid out of the residue (what's left after specific gifts) of the probate estate. The client's spouse was the beneficiary of the residue (which would qualify for an estate tax marital deduction.) The client's son was the beneficiary of a $10,000,000 policy on the client's life (which obviously would generate a very sizable federal estate tax). The client died. The son received $10,000,000 of insurance proceeds and the mother received a notice from the estate's executor that the tax on that money had to come out of her share of the estate (thus dramatically increasing the federal estate tax). To increase the size of the marital deduction and therefore decrease the amount of the estate tax, the client's son disclaims his right to have his mother pay the federal estate tax on the insurance he received.

Will the son be successful? The answer is "Yes," if the right steps are taken at the right time. A bequest is a direction to the executor to pay someone a part of the probate estate's assets. A common form of bequest is the forgiveness of a debt owed the testator. If, under state law, the decedent's allocation of estate taxes to the wife in the example above is from the son's perspective a valuable property interest tantamount to forgiving a debt, it may be disclaimed.

No Exception for Charity: Suppose a client named a charity as beneficiary of a large life insurance policy. Assuming the charity was qualified, the payment of the insurance, no matter how large, would not generate any federal estate tax. Yet, absent specific provision in a state law apportionment statute or in the decedent's will, the charity may have to bear (to the extent of the insurance it received) a portion or all of the federal estate tax on assets paid to other beneficiaries.

This doesn't seem to mesh with the rules exonerating a surviving spouse from a reimbursement obligation; to the extent life insurance payable to a surviving spouse qualifies for a marital deduction, it is exempted from the reimbursement obligation under federal law. Yet federal law provides no comparable protection for proceeds payable to charities.[34]

If the charity's share of life insurance proceeds is reduced by the reimbursement requirement, than the decedent's charitable deduction will be decreased. This in turn increases the decedent's estate tax burden, which increases the charity's burden, which… results in complex calculations.

Where Planning Should Be: Estate tax apportionment of life insurance should be arranged deliberately and carefully while the client is alive and his wishes can be known. The place to do this planning is in the client's will or revocable trust so that estate taxes and other expenses are shouldered by the parties the client wishes to carry them. It is important to be sure that in the attempt to lower the tax burden to its minimum legal level, the planning team does not lose sight as to what is necessary to uncover and effectuate the intended dispositive plan of the client.

ENDNOTES

1. IRC Sec. 2033.

2. IRC Sec. 2042(2).

3. IRC Sec. 2035(a).

4. IRC Sec. 2035(d).

5. FSA 1998-328.

6. If not includable under Section 2042, then under Section 2038(a)(1) as a transfer with a retained right to alter, amend, revoke, or terminate a gift. Section 2036(a) may also apply since the insured retains the power to select who will possess or enjoy the income from the property transferred.

7. The IRS holds that it is an incident of ownership and will include proceeds under that argument in all states except in Pennsylvania, Delaware, New Jersey, and the Virgin Islands.

8. Typically, this right has been held to be merely a reduction in premium cost, rather than an incident of ownership. However, the right to take dividend accumulations or surrender dividend additions for their cash value would be considered an incident of ownership.

9. An insured will have an incident of ownership if he can change the policy's beneficiary, even if he has no right to change the terms of the trust which itself holds the policy and even if the insured has no beneficial interest in the trust.

10. If the insured can change the terms of a trust (either alone or in conjunction with another), he will be deemed to have an incident of ownership in a policy held by the trust even though he holds no rights under the policy.

11. The existence of an incident of ownership is a fact ascertainable only under state law. Of course, where the insured intended never to possess an incident of ownership but an agent's mistake resulted in one, an exception (appropriately called the "agent's mistake" exception) may be made by the courts (after much legal expense and aggravation).

12. An insured will not be considered to have held incidents of ownership where the insured requested that the beneficiary be the owner and hold all incidents of ownership but by mistake the policy read otherwise. Likewise, if the insurance agent without authority and contrary to the instructions of a third party applicant fills in the application and names the insured as owner, no inclusion will be required.

    The issue is one of "policy facts versus intent facts" where the terms of the policy as to ownership conflict with the apparent intention of the insured. State law is determinate and usually it looks to the terms of the policy, although sometimes courts will apply principles of equity and contract law in concluding that the insured held none of the incidents of ownership.

    An insured would not be considered to hold incidents of ownership, even though he was named as owner, if his corporation carried the policies on its books as key man coverage and paid all the premiums and the other facts corroborate that the insured merely acted as the corporation's agent and that the designation of the insured as owner was an error.

13. A decedent will not be considered to have an incident of ownership in a policy merely by virtue of a trust provision that would terminate his wife's interest in the event of a divorce. The act of divorcing one's spouse is an act of independent significance and the termination of the spouse's interest would be an incidental consequence of that act.

14. This problem is especially important when dealing with key employee coverage and with insurance used to fund a buy-sell. It is the authors' opinion that a right to purchase existing life insurance in return for the then fair market value of the coverage should not be considered an incident of ownership. But the IRS continues to claim that the right to purchase an existing life insurance contract is an incident of ownership when that right is created in an employment or business ownership context even though, on almost identical facts, the Tax Court has reached the opposite result. For instance, the power to "veto" the cancellation of a policy by purchasing it at its fair market value was held not to be an incident of ownership.

    Practitioners can feel most safe when the insured's right to purchase is based on the occurrence of a prior event of "independent significance." For instance, if the insured's right to

purchase the insurance on his life was predicated on the corporation's prior purchase of his stock in the event of disability or other termination of employment, that act, being (a) contingent, (b) dependent on the occurrence of events which did not occur, and (c) beyond the control of the insured, should eliminate the incident of ownership problem.

15. The retention of the right to select settlement options is viewed by the IRS as a right to alter the timing of the payment of the proceeds, which is considered an incident of ownership.

16. Let. Rul. 9809032. Here, the trustees of the irrevocable trust borrowed amounts from the insured's revocable trust which they then used to pay premiums on the policies the irrevocable trust held on the insured-grantor's life. These loans were fully documented with notes, five of which were outstanding when the insured died. The IRS properly held that the identity of the premium payor is irrelevant in determining whether a decedent retained any incidents of ownership in the policy for estate tax purposes.

17. Let. Rul. 9809032. Conceivably, this power could provide the insured with the ability to encourage the trustees to resign by controlling the trustee's compensation. But according to the IRS, the grantor's right in this instance did not amount to a retention to affect the beneficial enjoyment of the trust property, since the grantor did not have the power to appoint a successor trustee.

18. Let. Rul. 9832039.

19. The Fifth Circuit includes Louisiana, Mississippi, and Texas. The Fifth Circuit may even be more difficult to live or die with than the IRS itself.

20. The Second Circuit includes New York, Vermont, and Connecticut.

21. The Sixth Circuit includes Michigan, Ohio, Kentucky, and Tenn.

22. Arkansas, Mo., Iowa, Minn., Neb., S.Dak., N. Dak.

23. The issue can occur in any fiduciary relationship. Planners must therefore be wary in fiduciary situations other than trusts.

24. Actually, the portion of the proceeds paid to the father's estate in repayment of the father's outlays would be included under IRC Section 2042(1). The balance of the proceeds, even though payable to the children's trust, would be included in the father's estate under IRC Section 2042(2). Note also, that the parent is making annual gifts of the economic benefit to the trust's beneficiaries.

25. IRC Sec. 2642(c).

26. See *Est. of Smith*, 73 TC 307 (1979).

27. See Rev. Rul. 79-46, 1979-1 CB 303.

28. See Prohibited Transaction Exemption 77-8 and PTE 92-5.

29. Some authorities have suggested that naming the estate as beneficiary of a modest amount of life insurance to satisfy creditors and pay death taxes and other estate settlement costs may be appropriate. In the authors' opinion, there are few situations that suggest that a client's estate be named as beneficiary of life insurance. There is almost always a more suitable designation than an insured's estate.

30. IRC Secs. 2056(a), 2056(d).

31. The insurer can't settle its obligation to the beneficiary until the end of whatever period of time has been specified. As a practical matter, this suggests that the time delay be kept to no more than 60 days, and in most cases 30 days.

32. IRC Sec. 2056(b)(3).

33. IRC Sec. 2206.

34. IRC Sec. 2206.

Appendix B

GIFT TAXATION OF LIFE INSURANCE

WHY A GIFT OF LIFE INSURANCE?

Planners must be constantly aware of the gift tax implications of transactions involving life insurance. Gifts of life insurance, as opposed to gifts of income producing property, are favored vehicles for many reasons. These include:

1. A gift of life insurance may increase the donor's spendable income since, after the gift, the donee often pays the premiums and the donor then can spend, invest, or give away the money that otherwise would have been paid in life insurance premiums. Conversely, a gift of income producing property will deprive the donor of the net after tax income from that property.

2. The donee is less inclined to surrender a policy for its cash value than to dispose of income producing property. This increases the probability that the policy, and therefore the proceeds, will be available to the beneficiaries. The likelihood of achieving the client's objectives (enhancement of the beneficiary's financial security or creation of a source of liquidity for the client's estate) will be met.

3. The gift tax cost of the transfer, when the gift is life insurance, is relatively low since essentially only the replacement value, rather than the face amount, is subject to gift tax. When income producing property is given, the entire fair market value is subject to gift tax. In other words, for the same gift tax cost a much larger amount can be excluded from a client's gross estate. For example, a ten year old whole life policy that will generate $1,000,000 of death benefit could be removed from a client's estate at the cost of a relatively low gift tax based on the policy's value at the date of the gift.

4. There is no gain for income tax purposes when a life insurance policy matures at death, even if that policy was obtained by gift. If any other type of property is given away, the recipient takes as his basis the donor's basis (with certain adjustments). In other words, the donor's basis is carried over from the donor to the recipient. Thus, no step up from the donor's basis is allowed to the donee on a gift except for perhaps a portion of any gift tax paid on the transfer. So, a gift of property other than life insurance results in a carryover basis and, upon a later sale by the donee, the entire gain inherent in the property must be recognized.

5. The client's personal financial security is diminished only by the transferred cash value and even this potential problem can be minimized by a carefully measured pre-transfer loan.[1]

6. A gift of life insurance may be a way to assure children of a first marriage of financial security and a share of their parent's wealth in the event of a second marriage.

7. Assume a client has a large estate and wants to provide children with an amount greater than the unified credit equivalent during the lifetime of his spouse. The client is going to leave all but the unified credit equivalent to his spouse, but doesn't want his children to have to wait until the surviving parent dies to receive their inheritance. A gift of life insurance from the client to the children more than three years before the client's death would help assure the achievement of the multiple goals.

THE FOUR QUESTIONS

As is the case with any other gift tax analysis, when life insurance is the subject of a transfer, the planner must ask four questions:

1. Was there a gift, a gratuitous transfer for less than adequate and full consideration?

2. Was the gift completed?

3. What is the value of the gift?

4. Is there an exclusion (such as the annual exclusion) or a deduction (such as the marital or

charitable deduction)[2] that can reduce or eliminate the taxable gift or a credit (such as the unified credit) that can reduce or eliminate the tax on the gift?

Typically, most gift tax problems with respect to life insurance arise where a client makes a gratuitous transfer of a policy. But several other situations can also trigger gift tax problems. The first is the case where a policy on one person's life is owned by a second person and payable to a third.[3] Another scenario that triggers gift tax is where one party pays premiums on behalf of another. Each of these and other gift tax generating types of transactions will be covered in detail below.

OUTRIGHT GIFTS OF POLICIES

An outright gift of a life insurance policy is a time tested technique for accomplishing a number of estate planning objectives including, but not limited to, saving federal and state death taxes and protecting proceeds from the claims of the original policyowner's creditors. The primary advantage of an outright gift of a life insurance policy is incredible leverage; the gift tax value of the lifetime transfer is considerably less than the death proceeds removed from the client's estate. If the future value of the gift tax (if any) actually payable currently is exceeded by the future value of the estate tax saved, the gift is advantageous.

For instance, assume a client is in a 50% federal estate tax bracket. Assume further that the client owns a $1,000,000 life insurance policy on his own life with a gift tax value of $200,000. If the client does nothing, $500,000 (1/2 of $1,000,000) will be lost in federal estate taxes. But if the client makes a gift of the policy and survives the gift by more than three years, none of the proceeds will be in the client's estate.[4]

Of course, if the lifetime value of the policy is large enough, there will be (assuming the transfer does not qualify for the gift tax annual exclusion or the client has used up the allowable unified credit) federal gift tax payable currently on the transfer. In the example above, the gift tax is 50% of the $200,000 value of the policy at the time it was transferred. Assuming a long term growth rate of 8% or less over a 20 year life expectancy, the tradeoff of paying a small tax today to save a much larger tax in the future makes sense. If any current gift tax is payable, the future value of this gift tax must be calculated and compared against the potential estate tax savings to measure the true advantage of a gift of the policy.

When is a gift of a life insurance policy a completed gift? In other words, at what point does the taxable gift occur? The IRS has held that the relinquishment of every right that would normally cause a life insurance policy to be included in the insured or in the policyowner's estate would mark the completion of a gift of the contract. So as long as the insured held any incident of ownership that would cause the policy proceeds to be included in his estate or as long as a client owned a policy on the life of another, no gift is yet made. A completed gift occurs at the moment every interest the insured and/or policyowner held is surrendered or otherwise assigned. So the insured must give up the right to the policy's cash value, to borrow on the contract, pledge it as collateral, name, change or veto a change of beneficiary, and every other right of any significant value. Until then, no completed gift occurs.

What is the effect of a reversionary interest on whether or not a completed gift of a policy has been made? Will the possibility of a reversion back to the donor of a life insurance policy render the gift incomplete? For example, the insured makes an absolute assignment of life insurance on his life to his wife. Assume the wife then names the insured's estate as beneficiary in the event the insured dies before the new policyowner (the wife) dies. There is a possibility that the proceeds would revert back to the insured. But that possibility is not enough to prevent the gift from being considered complete and therefore taxable. However, a possibility of reverter may allow a reduction in the value of the taxable gift assuming recognized actuarial standards can be applied to measure the value of the reversion.

When a gift of a life insurance policy is made or an individual is named as beneficiary, the new owner's (or beneficiary's) right to receive the policy's proceeds is conditioned on surviving the insured. This does not, however, affect the completeness of the gift. It merely affects the valuation.

Of course, if the trust to which a life insurance policy is transferred is revocable, so is the gift and therefore no completed gift has been made.

But what if the policy is given to an irrevocable trust? Is there a gift (and, if so, will it qualify for and be sheltered by the annual exclusion)? Both the transfer of a policy to such a trust and the payment of premiums subsequent to the transfer will be considered completed gifts subject to the gift tax. Absent special provisions, no annual exclusion would be allowable in either case because the typical irrevocable trust, by design, limits the time or manner in which the beneficiaries of the trust enjoy the property (including any life insurance policy transferred to the trust).

Assume, for example, a father transferred life insurance on his own life to a trust he created for his daughter's benefit. The trust provides that upon the father's death, policy proceeds are to be invested and the income paid to the daughter for the rest of her life. The daughter does not have the immediate, unfettered, and ascertainable right to use, possess, and enjoy that income or any other right inherent in the life insurance policy until after the death of her father. Since the donee daughter's interest does not take affect until some time in the future (i.e., at her father's death), the donor father will not be allowed an annual exclusion for either his gift of the policy or for future premiums he pays to keep it in force.

Do the results differ if the policy in question is group term insurance? Will a gift of a group term policy be considered a gift of a present interest? The answer depends again upon the terms and conditions of the irrevocable trust rather than upon the type of insurance involved. The gift of a life insurance policy will not be considered a future interest or fail to qualify for the annual exclusion merely because it is a term insurance policy.

A gift tax annual exclusion would be allowed, for example, if the rights to a $50,000 group term contract together with cash were contributed to the trust. The annual exclusion could be obtained through a trust provision which allows the beneficiary the noncumulative right to withdraw a specified amount each year and provides that any asset in the trust, including life insurance coverage, could be used to satisfy that demand right. Furthermore, since the coverage itself should qualify for the annual exclusion as a present interest, so should subsequent premium payments on the group coverage.

Assume that the terms of a trust provide that immediately upon the death of the insured covered under a group term contract, the trust's only beneficiary is to receive the entire policy proceeds as soon as they are received by the trust. As soon as the proceeds are transferred and the deemed gift occurs, the beneficiary has the immediate, unfettered, and ascertainable right to use, possess, and enjoy the money. So an annual exclusion should be allowed for the value of the coverage at the moment of transfer. Gifts deemed to be made by the employee insured each time the employer made an actual premium payment on the group term should be considered gifts of a present interest and qualify for the annual exclusion.

Would the result have been the same had the terms of the trust required the trustee to hold and invest policy proceeds and pay only the income to the trust's beneficiary? The answer is that such a gift (each actual payment by the employer and deemed payment by the insured employee) would be considered a gift of a future interest and would therefore not qualify for the annual exclusion.

Particular care must be used when a life insurance policy is contributed to an IRC Section 2503(c) trust, an irrevocable trust for a minor beneficiary. Gifts of a life insurance policy to an IRC Section 2503(c) trust for a minor will typically qualify for the annual exclusion if (a) policy values can be used for the minor's benefit and if (b) the policy will pass to the minor at age 21 (or, if the minor dies prior to that date, the policy will pass to the beneficiary named in his will or to the person(s) appointed by the minor during lifetime or by will). Premiums paid on the policy by the trust's grantor should also qualify for the annual exclusion.

Planners should also note the following points about life insurance and the gift tax:

- Gifts to minors can qualify for the annual exclusion even if the child has no legal right to exercise ownership privileges under the policy and even if no guardian has been appointed.

- Generally, gifts of life insurance to minors in states that have adopted the UGMA (Uniform Gifts to Minors Act) or UTMA (Uniform Transfers to Minors Act) will qualify for the gift tax annual exclusion. (There may be some question of qualification, however, if the state statute departs from one of these two Uniform Acts and allows custodianship to extend beyond the donee's 21st birthday.)

- Clients making gifts of large policies should consider splitting the contract into two or more smaller policies and transferring one policy in one year and the other(s) in other years so that all gifts fall within annual exclusion limits. (This technique may slightly increase the total premium cost and administrative burden.)

- An outright gift of a life insurance policy from one spouse to another will qualify for the gift tax marital deduction and eliminate any gift tax on intraspousal transfers.

THREE PARTY SITUATIONS

Planners should red flag every situation where one party owns a life insurance policy on the life of another and the proceeds are payable to a third party. Sometimes, in business cases, the situation results in income tax problems, while in other situations it causes serious and unexpected gift tax problems. Indirect, but nevertheless taxable, gifts can occur where one party (e.g., a wife) owns a policy on the life of a second party (e.g., a husband) and makes the proceeds payable to a third party (e.g., the couple's children). For example, Charlee Sterling purchases a $1,000,000 policy on the life of her husband Rob and names their son Max as beneficiary.

At the death of the husband, the wife is deemed to have made a gift to her son in the amount of the $1,000,000 policy proceeds. The reason for this harsh result is this: Every time a policy-owner-client names a beneficiary (other than the client or the client's estate) as beneficiary, the client is technically making a gift to that party. The reason no gift tax is imposed at that moment, in most cases, is because that gift remains incomplete until the policyowner no longer has the right to change that beneficiary designation. Retention of a power to revoke a gift renders the gift incomplete and therefore not taxable until the power is released or lapses.

Conversely, if the policyowner makes the policy beneficiary designation irrevocable, at that moment, a completed gift has been made. From that point on, every time a premium is paid, a further gift is made. Worse yet, since the gift is contingent upon the insured's death, it would be considered a future interest gift and therefore will not qualify for the annual exclusion.

When there is a three party situation, the gift becomes irrevocable when the insured dies. The gift that the policyowner makes when a third party is designated as beneficiary changes from uncompleted to completed at the insured's death. Thus, a taxable event occurs in that instant. The amount of the gift is the entire amount of proceeds paid to someone other than the policyowner. So, in the example above, the wife Charlee is deemed to be making a gift of $1,000,000 to her son Max at the moment of her husband's death.

The following common examples of the gift tax version of the three party situation will serve both as a warning and a review for planners:

1. A wife owns a policy on her husband's life. She names her children as beneficiaries. When the husband dies, she is deemed to have made a gift to the children in the amount of the entire policy proceeds.

2. A wife purchases a policy on her husband's life. She revocably names a trust she previously established as beneficiary of the proceeds. The trust provides that income from trust assets is to be paid to her husband for life, but upon his death principal is to be split in equal shares between the couple's children. A simultaneous death provision states that if the couple dies simultaneously, the wife would be presumed to have survived her husband. If the husband dies first or the couple does in fact die simultaneously, the wife will be deemed to have made a gift of the proceeds to her children. Had the trust been irrevocable, the annual premiums rather than the proceeds would have been the measure of the gifts.

3. A husband creates a revocable living trust. Under the terms of the trust, income was payable to his wife for life. At her death, any principal in the trust was to pass to the couple's children. The wife purchases a life insurance policy on her husband's life and names the revocable trust established by her husband as beneficiary. Upon the husband's death, the wife is deemed to have made a completed gift to her children equal to the entire proceeds less the present value of her right to a life income from the trust. If the wife had named the trust as irrevocable beneficiary, a completed gift would have been made at that time, but it would have been significantly less than the value of the proceeds.

The solution to all of the three party problems is relatively simple: Where one party will purchase a policy on the life of another from an insurer, name the purchaser as both policy owner and beneficiary.

PAYMENT OF PREMIUMS ON BEHALF OF ANOTHER

Payment by a client of one or more premiums would be considered a gift if the policy itself was owned by another person or party. The amount of the gift is the full premium paid. A reduction in the amount of the taxable gift would be allowed for the actuarial value of any interest in the policy's benefits retained by the donor.

For example, if a father paid premiums on a policy owned by his daughter, he is making gifts to her each time he pays a premium. Of course, where the parties are husband and wife, the gift may qualify for the unlimited marital deduction and no adverse gift tax implications will result.

Likewise, if a client makes cash transfers to an irrevocable trust to enable the trustee to pay premiums on one or more policies owned by the trust (or if the client makes payments directly to the insurance company), each premium payment would constitute a gift to the beneficiaries of the trust.

If a client funds an irrevocable trust by transferring income producing property to the trust to pay premiums, the fair market value of that property (in addition to the value of any policy transferred to the trust) would be subject to gift tax. But as soon as the income producing property is owned by the trust, income it produces is not deemed to be an additional gift – even if the client is considered the owner of trust income for income tax purposes.

Premiums paid by one of several beneficiaries of an irrevocable life insurance trust will be considered gifts to the other beneficiaries to the extent the payor's payments cover their share of the premiums. Intent to make a gift is irrelevant. The IRS would determine the value of the gifts by subtracting the actuarial value of the share retained by the premium paying beneficiary from the total premiums paid.

Usually, the donor of the gift will be the party making the actual premium payments. However, if an individual assigns group term coverage to a beneficiary or to a trust on behalf of one or more beneficiaries, group term premiums subsequently paid by the individual's employer will be deemed to be gifts from the employee to the beneficiary or to the beneficiaries of the trust. If the group insurance plan is nondiscriminatory (or if the client is not a key employee) the amount of each gift is found under Table I rates. If the employee chooses not to use the Table I rates, or the plan is found to be discriminatory (and the client is a key employee), the gift will be the actual cost of insurance on that employee. In any case, the gift would be based on the full face amount of the insurance and not merely the amount in excess of the first $50,000 of coverage.

There are many hidden gift situations. For instance, split dollar life insurance (an arrangement under which different parties share costs and benefits of a life insurance policy, see Chapter 30) often involves gift tax implications. For instance, assume a client has assigned his cash value interest in a policy in a split dollar arrangement to an irrevocable trust for his daughter. The client is making a gift of the policy, just as if he had made a gift of a previously purchased premium paying policy. So, the interpolated terminal reserve plus any unearned premium less amounts, if any, repayable to the employer would be the value of the gift.

Obviously, if, after the transfer of his interest in the policy to the trust, the client also pays premiums (including premiums paid by an employer), either directly to the insurer or as cash contributions to the trust, further gifts are made. The treatment of the split dollar arrangement depends on whether the client is the owner of the policy. Even if the trust is named as the policy owner, the client may be treated as the owner if the only economic benefit provided to the trust is the value of current life insurance protection.

If the client (or employer) is treated as owner of the policy, the employee client is deemed to have received premiums paid by the employer and then made a gratuitous transfer. What is the value of such annually recurring gifts? It appears that the value of those transfers would be measured by the same amount the employee reports each year as income.

If the trust is treated as the owner, the client (or employer) makes premium payments, and the client (or employer) is entitled to recover premiums, the client (or employer) is treated as making a loan to the trust. The client is treated as making a gift of interest on the loan to the trust. If there is no right to repayment, the entire value of the premium would be treated as a gift.

GIFT THROUGH SETTLEMENT OPTION

Assume a client died and the proceeds were payable to his surviving spouse in a manner that provided that she would receive only the income on the proceeds with the balance going to the couple's children at the client's death. Coupled to the widow's right to income for life was a general power of appointment that gave her the right to draw down unlimited amounts of principal at any time. To the extent she failed to exercise that right, she would be making gifts to her children, the remainder persons.

Since the children's right is neither immediate nor certain, it would be a future interest gift and, therefore, would not qualify for the gift tax annual exclusion. Under a de minimis rule, a gift would be made only to the extent that the amount subject to a right of withdrawal exceeded the greater of $5,000 or 5% of the principal held by the insurance company. The total value of the gift would be measured by the actuarial value of the children's interest.

HOW IS THE GIFT VALUED?

When a policy is transferred from one party to another, to the extent the transferor receives less than full and adequate consideration, the transfer is a gift. In other words, the difference between the value of the policy and the amount received in exchange for it is a gift.

Usually, this gift is taxed at its replacement value, the hypothetical amount it would cost to replace the contract with an identical contract issued by the same insurer on an insured of the same age and insurance rating. To simplify the procedure (since seldom, if ever, are identical contracts ever found in real life), several rules have been established.

Generally, most gift transactions break down into one of these three types:

1. gift of an established policy in premium paying status,

2. gift of a paid up or single premium policy, or

3. gift of a policy just purchased.

If the transaction involves a policy on which further premiums are payable, the value of the policy is the sum of (a) the "interpolated terminal reserve" plus (b) the value of any "unearned premiums" less the amount of any outstanding loan.[5] Interpolated terminal reserve is essentially the reserve held by the insurer to meet its claims under the policy, but adjusted from the contract's anniversary to the date of the gift. The unearned premium is the value of the unearned portion of the last premium payment made to the insurer prior to the gift.

IRS regulations give the example of a gift made four months after the last premium due date of an ordinary life policy. The policy itself is nine years and four months old at the date of the gift.

To compute the value of the gift (in this example):

State the terminal reserve at the end
of the (10th) year .... ($14,601)
State the terminal reserve at the end
of the (9th) year .... ($12,965)

The difference is annual increase
in terminal reserve .... ($ 1,636)

If the gift was made X/12s (4/12) of a year after
the premium due date, than Y/12 (1/3)
of annual reserve is .... ($ 545)
State the terminal reserve at premium
payment date .... ($12,965)
Sum of beg of yr terminal reserve
& increase in reserve .... ($13,510)

Unearned premium (8/12ths) of ($2,811)
annual premium .... ($ 1,874)

Gift value = (a) reserve at gift + (b) unearned
premium .... ($15,384)

If the transaction involves a previously purchased single premium or paid up policy, its gift tax value is the single premium the insurer would charge at the time of the gift for a comparable contract of equal face value on the life of a person the insured's age at the time of the gift.[6]

If the transaction involves a new policy purchased by one person or party on behalf of another or if a new policy is transferred as a gift immediately after its purchase, the gross premium paid to the date of the transfer is the gift.

Planners should advise clients to minimize the gift tax implications of a transfer by (1) making gifts as close to the premium paying date as possible so as to minimize any unearned premiums, and (2) borrow on the policy up to but not more than the client's basis.[7]

Life insurance companies will provide a statement of the gift tax value of any one of the three types of policies described above. Request IRS forms 712 or Form 93 S.

If the subject of the gift is group term life insurance, the IRS in a questionable but favorable ruling stated that there was no taxable gift because the policy had no ascertainable value.[8] Note, however, that in that ruling the coverage was assigned one day before a monthly premium was due. Stated differently, the IRS probably reasoned that the benefit of the prior month's premium payment had essentially expired. Thus, the value may, in fact, have been quite low but clearly had some value.

If the insured is an impaired risk or has become uninsurable by the date of the gift, the value of the policy for gift tax purposes may be increased. Likewise, if the insured is terminally ill or otherwise uninsurable at the time of the gift, it is likely the IRS would argue that the policy could be expected to mature shortly and, therefore, the replacement value should more closely approximate the face amount. Since these same valuation principles should apply for purposes of the income tax charitable deduction, the gift of a policy to a charity by a dying individual should result in a value that approaches the face amount of the policy.

COLLECTION OF GIFT TAX

A donee of any of the types of gifts described above is liable for the full gift tax to the extent it is not collected from the donor. The donee's liability is not limited to the cash value of the policy.

ENDNOTES

1. The authors suggest that the loan be somewhat less than the client's net cost. Otherwise, the client will be deemed to have received an amount equal to the loan in a constructive sale. The difference between the sales proceeds (i.e., the loan) and the client's basis would be immediately taxable at ordinary income tax rates.

2. To qualify a transfer of a life insurance policy for the gift tax marital deduction, the assignment to the insured's spouse must be: (a) outright or (b) consist of the transfer of a life interest coupled with a general power of appointment vested in the spouse, or (c) meet qualified terminable interest property (QTIP) rules.

   Typically, a gift of a life insurance policy to charity will qualify for the charitable deduction and therefore no gift tax will be payable regardless of the size of the policy or its value.

   However, the gift tax charitable deduction is allowed only if the client assigns his entire interest (or an undivided portion of the donor's entire interest). Thus, if a client gives a charity the right to the death benefit but keeps the policy cash values or gives the charity the right to policy cash values and retains the right to name the beneficiary of the death benefit, no gift tax (or income tax) deduction would be allowed.

   A further tax trap pertains to insurable interest. If the law in the state of the donor's domicile doesn't recognize that the charity has an insurable interest in the donor's life, the IRS may argue that the insured's estate may have rights in the policy or its proceeds. This in turn could thwart both the income tax deduction and the gift tax deduction since the donor's gift to charity would be considered a transfer of a partial interest rather than a gift of the donor's entire interest. A lack of insurable interest may also result in the disallowance of a charitable gift tax deduction for future premium payments made by the client to charity after the transfer of an existing policy or purchase by the charity of a new one.

   For a detailed discussion of the marital and the charitable deduction, see Leimberg et al., *The Tools and Techniques of Estate Planning*, 13th ed. (Cincinnati, OH: The National Underwriter Company, 2004).

3. Alternatively, adverse income tax treatment can be triggered. For instance, if a corporation owns a policy on the life of an employee but makes it payable to a party other than the corporation or a corporate creditor, payment of the death proceeds could be considered a dividend.

4. Both the policy and any gift tax paid on the policy will be included in the gross estate if death occurs within three years of the transfer. IRC Sec. 2035.

5. See IRS form 712, Part II.

6. What if the cash value of the policy given away is significantly larger than the replacement cost of a similar policy? If a 20 year old single premium life policy had a replacement cost well below the actual policy's cash value, would the replacement contract be comparable? Absent information as to what a truly comparable contract would cost, the policy's value should be found by reference to its interpolated terminal reserve.

7. A loan in excess of basis would result in an income tax gain upon transfer of the policy.

8. In the authors' opinion, this conclusion is at best risky to rely on since no matter how little value the right to death proceeds on a given employee might be it will always have some value. Secondly, it is actuarially always possible to assign a value to life insurance even if it is term coverage.

Appendix C

LIFE INSURANCE AND THE GENERATION–SKIPPING TRANSFER TAX

The GSTT in a Nutshell: A generation-skipping transfer tax (GSTT) is levied, in addition to any gift or estate taxes that apply to the transfer, on the value of life insurance (and/or any other property) transferred during lifetime or at death without adequate consideration to a transferee who is in (or who is assigned by statutory law to) a generation that is at least two generations below the transferor's generation (such a transferee is called a "skip person").[1] For example, the GSTT will be imposed when an exceptionally large life insurance policy (and/or other asset) is payable to (or for the benefit of) a client's grandchild.

The GSTT does not apply to transfers to "nonskip" persons, such as the client's child, brother, or sister or to anyone in a generation higher than the transferor's generation (e.g., a gift made by a grandchild to a grandparent). Likewise, a transfer to a trust for a nonskip person would not be subject to the GSTT. On the other hand, if all the beneficiaries of a trust are skip persons, a transfer to a trust for such people would be considered a transfer to a skip person. And, as discussed below, certain transfers from trusts to skip persons are subject to the GSTT.

The GSTT tax is broadly applied to life insurance transfers. It can be imposed regardless of whether proceeds are paid outright, in a lump sum, under settlement options, or in trust.[2] The GSTT may also be imposed upon a transfer of a large policy with substantial cash values to a trust during the insured's lifetime. The value upon which the tax will be based is the same as the value of the policy or the proceeds for gift or estate tax purposes.

In general, when life insurance (or other property) is transferred to a trust that has one or more skip persons as beneficiaries, the GSTT is imposed when distributions are made from the trust to those skip persons or when the interests of any nonskip persons terminate. For instance, if life insurance proceeds were left to a trust that provided income to the client's son for life and then paid the income and principal to the client's grandchildren, the tax would be imposed when the nonskip person (son) died.

As mentioned above, the GSTT may be levied in addition to any applicable federal estate or gift tax and is imposed as a flat tax at the highest federal estate tax level, 48% (in 2004).[3] Note that the GSTT rate applies regardless of the taxpayer's actual estate or gift tax bracket. In other words, even if the client is in only a 45% estate tax bracket, to the extent that the GSTT applies, a 48% GSTT rate is levied.

Fortunately, through careful planning it is possible to shelter all or a portion of even a very large transfer to a skip person through the use of one or both of two devices, the annual exclusion and the GSTT exemption:

GSTT Annual Exclusion: Certain direct gifts that qualify for the $11,000 (as indexed in 2004) gift tax annual exclusion (or the unlimited exclusion allowed for direct payment of tuition or medical expenses) may also qualify for an annual exclusion that can be applied against the GSTT.[4] This means an outright transfer of a policy or of premium dollars to a skip person will be subject to the GSTT only to the extent the value of the gift exceeds the $11,000 ($22,000 if gifts are split between spouses) annual exclusion limit. So the easiest and most certain way to take advantage of the GSTT annual exclusion is for the client to make gifts of cash each year of up to $11,000 to a skip person, who then leverages the gift by purchasing life insurance on the life of the client and/or the client's spouse.

For example, suppose a wealthy client, who has made large gifts and used up his gift tax unified credit and GSTT exemption in prior years, gives a granddaughter a $2,000,000 policy on his life in 2004. At the time of the gift, the policy has a gift tax replacement value of $200,000. The gift would qualify for the gift tax annual exclusion and also qualify for the GSTT annual exclusion. So there would be no gift tax imposed on the first $11,000 ($22,000 if the client were married and split the gift) of value. Likewise, there would be no GSTT imposed on the same amount.

Only direct skips (outright transfers to skip persons or transfers to trusts that have only skip persons as beneficiaries and meet certain other criterion) can qualify for this GSTT annual exclusion. So, if the transfer is to a trust, it can still qualify for the GSTT annual exclusion but only if (1) all trust beneficiaries are skip persons, (2) no distributions could ever be made to nonskip persons, and (3) each skip person's share is held in an account separate from the others or there are separate trusts for each.[5] Such entities are often called "vested" or "subtrust" trusts since the trust can benefit only one beneficiary and, at that person's death, assets in the trust must be included in the vested beneficiary's estate. Planners should note that the typical life insurance trust will not qualify.

Even if the transfer otherwise qualifies for the gift tax annual exclusion, if a trust benefits beneficiaries other than skip persons, it will not qualify for the GSTT annual exclusion. For example, assume the same facts as above, but the gift is made to a trust for the benefit of the client's son (a nonskip person) for life and then granddaughter. Even if the granddaughter is given a valid Crummey power and $11,000 of the gift to her qualifies for the gift tax annual exclusion from gift taxes, it will not qualify for the GSTT annual exclusion.

To leverage the annual exclusion, an irrevocable life insurance trust receiving the client's money could purchase life insurance on his life using the entire contribution as the policy premium. During the client's lifetime, neither federal gift tax nor GSTT would be imposed on the cash used as premiums. At the client's death, there would be neither federal estate tax nor GSTT imposed on the policy proceeds.

Either split dollar or the use of survivorship type contracts (or both techniques) can be used to pack the trust and squeeze in as much GSTT free life insurance as possible to maximize the leverage of the nontaxable gift technique. The trust can purchase insurance on the life of any person on whom the beneficiaries have an insurable interest, including parents as well as grandparents. Insuring a younger/healthier life than the beneficiary's grandparent would further the packing possibilities (at the cost of a potentially longer wait for the proceeds). But such sophisticated planning requires extremely careful drafting and the use of highly competent counsel in order to achieve all of its tax and personal objectives.

Another way to compound the advantage of the annual exclusion is to have the transferor's spouse make an identical gift or to have the transferor split the gift with his spouse.

There are downsides to qualifying for the GSTT annual exclusion:

1. If the beneficiary dies before the client-grantor, the cash values of the policies in the trust will be included in the beneficiary's estate. Of course, if the beneficiary survives the insured and then dies, the proceeds shielded from the GSTT may still generate significant federal estate tax in the beneficiary's estate. However, the estate tax at a lower generational level may not be a significant disadvantage where the older generation possesses substantially greater wealth than the lower generation.

2. Many Crummey power techniques, such as the hanging power, will not qualify for the GSTT annual exclusion, since there can be no indirect skip (i.e., the trust beneficiaries must include only skip persons). If nonskip persons, such as the client's children, are beneficiaries of the trust, this GSTT exclusion is denied. So, where there are several generations of beneficiaries and some are nonskip persons, the nontaxable gift exclusion is not available, and the client should use the GSTT exemption described below.

3. This exclusion requires undue dispositive rigidity. In other words, this exclusion, though appealing, will only work where the client is willing to set up a separate trust or allocate separate shares for each beneficiary and therefore precludes the flexibility inherent where a trustee is given discretion to spray principal or sprinkle income within a family unit. As a practical matter, few transfers will qualify for the GSTT annual exclusion and few clients will use the exclusion, even if they could qualify, because of these inflexible and impractical rules.[6] Most clients must therefore place all or most of their planning efforts on the next level of defensive measures.

4. The trust can't provide financial security for the intervening skipped generation, since the client's contributions to the trust must pass directly to the skip person.

GSTT Exemption: Over and above any allowable annual exclusion from the GSTT, each transferor is allowed to make a total of $1,500,000 (in 2004) of generation-skipping transfers and pay no tax.[7] This exemption can be used during lifetime or at death.[8] If a married client makes a generation-skipping transfer during lifetime, gift splitting (similar to the way gift tax split-gifts works) is allowable.[9] This enables a doubling of the $1,500,000 exemption to as much as $3,000,000 (in 2004) even though the transfer was made only by one spouse.

How the GSTT is Triggered: Three situations can trigger a GSTT: (1) a direct skip, (2) a taxable termination, and (3) a taxable distribution.

Direct Skip – A direct skip could occur when a client writes a check payable to a skip person, gives property outright during lifetime, leaves property by will directly to a skip person, or names a skip person as a direct beneficiary of a life insurance policy.[10] Therefore, if a client assigns an existing life insurance policy on his life to a grandchild, that gift would constitute a generation-skipping transfer. Assuming the entire transfer is taxable, the GSTT would be imposed on an amount equal to the policy's interpolated terminal reserve plus any unearned premium (less any gift tax payable on the transfer). Likewise, if a client died and the $1,000,000 proceeds of a policy on the father's life were paid to the grandson and the full $1,000,000 was taxable, a 48% (in 2004) tax would be imposed (after reducing the $1,000,000 by the $345,800 of estate tax also payable on the transfer, see below).

Taxable Termination – A taxable termination occurs when there are no more nonskip persons ahead of the skip person. In essence, the client's generation-skipping transfer to the skip person is deemed to occur at the moment nothing stands between the skip person and the transferred cash or other asset. Assume, for example, that a client creates a life insurance trust that provides, "Income from this trust is to be paid to my three children for life. At the death of the last survivor, principal is to be distributed to my six grandchildren." When the last nonskip person's (children's) interest terminates (in this example, by death), the property in the trust is subjected to the GSTT.

Taxable Distribution – A taxable distribution occurs when either income or principal is distributed from a trust to a skip person.[11] Such a distribution can occur while nonskip beneficiaries are still alive. For example, suppose a client created a life insurance trust that directed the trustee (during the lifetime of the client's three children) to pay income and principal to the client's three children and to the client's six grandchildren. The payments made by the trustee to grandchildren while the children were still alive would be considered a taxable distribution. Again, the taxable event occurs at the moment nothing stands between the skip person and the property transferred by the client.

Computing the Taxable Amount: The taxable amount is computed differently depending upon the type of taxable transfer involved.

Direct Skips – In a direct skip, the amount subject to the GSTT (i.e., the taxable amount) is generally equal to the value of the transfer reduced first by the gift or estate tax imposed on it.[12]

Example. A client dies in 2004 and a $2,000,000 policy is payable directly to his grandson. Assume the property would bear the estate tax and the GSTT. Assuming the client's estate was large and pushed the proceeds into the 48% federal estate tax bracket, the estate tax would be $960,000. The 48% GSTT would be imposed, not on $2,000,000, but on the $1,040,000 left after the federal estate tax ($2,000,000 proceeds less $960,000 federal estate tax imposed on the proceeds). The GST tax would be $337,297 $[(($1,040,000 \times .48) \prod (1 + .48))$ where transfer bears GSTT]. In total, the federal taxes levied would amount to $1,297,297 ($960,000 + $337,297)! The grandson receives a net transfer of $702,703 ($2,000,000 – $1,297,297).

Example. Assume, instead, that other property would bear the estate tax and the GSTT and that only $702,703 of the proceeds would be payable to the grandson. At a 48% federal estate tax bracket, the estate tax on $2,000,000 would be $960,000. The 48% GSTT would be imposed on $702,703 (there is no reduction for estate tax since the transfer to the grandson does not bear the estate tax). The GSTT would be $337,297 ($702,703 x .48). In total, the federal taxes levied would amount to $1,297,297 ($960,000 + $337,297)!

Thus, different methods are used to determine the GSTT depending on whether or not the GST bears the estate tax and the GSTT. However, as can be seen, the amount of the total tax ($1,297,297) on the direct skip is the same for the same net transfer ($702,703).

Of course, transfers to grandchildren made during the client's lifetime will also be subjected to the GSTT.

Example. Suppose a wealthy client who has made many large taxable gifts in prior years gives his granddaughter a policy on his life in 2004. Assume it is a policy with a face value of $2,000,000 and a replacement value of $200,000. The GSTT would be imposed on $200,000 at a 48% rate. The GST tax would be $96,000 (.48 x

$200,000). For gift tax purposes, the $200,000 gift is increased by the amount of the GST tax imposed on the transferor to $296,000 ($200,000 + $96,000). The gift tax on the gift (assuming the transfer is taxed at a 48% federal gift tax bracket) would be $142,080 ($296,000 x .48). Federal taxes would therefore total $238,080 ($96,000 + $142,080).

Taxable Terminations – In a taxable termination, the amount on which the tax is computed is the value of the property to which the termination pertains.

Example. Assume a client dies and $2,000,000 in policy proceeds are paid to a trust providing income to the client's son for life. At the son's death, the entire amount in the trust is to be paid to the client's grandson. Assuming the client's estate was large and pushed the proceeds into the 48% federal estate tax bracket in 2004, the estate tax would be $960,000 ($2,000,000 x .48). Assume this estate tax is paid by the trust and reduces the net proceeds in the trust to $1,040,000. In addition, when the son's interest terminates on his death (in 2004), that taxable termination generates a GSTT equal to 48% of the assets paid to the client's grandchild (ignoring for illustrative purposes the GSTT exemption). Assuming no growth or loss in the funds, the tax on the $1,040,000 termination would be $499,200 (.48 x $1,040,000). The total federal tax on the $2,000,000 proceeds would be $1,459,200 ($960,000 + $499,200).

Taxable Distributions – In a taxable distribution, the amount upon which the tax is computed is the value of the property the transferee receives.[13]

Example. A client dies in 2004 and $2,000,000 in policy proceeds are payable to a trust providing that the trustee can sprinkle income or spray principal to either the client's son or grandson or both. The federal estate tax on the $2,000,000 (assuming the client's estate was large and pushed the $2,000,000 into a 48 percent bracket) would be $960,000. Assume this estate tax is paid by the trust and reduces the net proceeds in the trust to $1,040,000. Also, assume the trustee immediately distributes the entire $1,040,000 to the client's grandson. In addition, a $499,200 GSTT would be payable (48% x

$1,040,000); a total federal tax of $1,459,200 ($960,000 + $499,200)!

Inclusion Ratio: Technically, the amount of a generation-skipping transfer that is subject to the GSTT is found through an inclusion ratio. The formula is:

$$1 - [\text{AMOUNT OF EXEMPTION} \div \text{TOTAL VALUE OF GIFT (or BEQUEST)}]$$

For example, if in 2004 the value of the gift was $1,500,000 and there were no exemptions or exclusions,[14] all of it would be subject to the GSTT. If the client had only $150,000 of his $1,500,000 per grantor exemption remaining, the inclusion ratio would be .900 [1 – ($150,000 ÷ $1,500,000)]. Ninety percent of the transfer would be subject to the GSTT. If the value of the gift was $1,500,000 and the amount of the exemption was also $1,500,000, the inclusion ratio would be 0. This would mean, not only that none of the transfer is taxable at the time it is made,[15] but also that the transfer (indeed, whatever it grows to by the date it is actually distributed to the skip person) will generally never be subjected to the GSTT. If a transfer to a trust, for example, has an inclusion ratio of zero, no future distributions or terminations from that trust will generally ever be subjected to the GSTT. However, if a trust beneficiary were to be treated as a transferor because property in the trust is included in his estate or the person is treated as making a taxable gift, a new inclusion ratio based upon the new transferor's GSTT exemption may be required.

This inclusion ratio concept has enormous leverage implications with respect to contributions of cash to irrevocable life insurance trusts. Assuming the annual exclusion is not sufficient or is for some reason not available to shield a transfer from the GSTT, clients should consider allocating a portion of the GSTT exemption to any transfer involving life insurance. The reason is that, once the exemption shields a gift of life insurance premiums or a gift of a life insurance policy, the proceeds generated by those protected premiums or policy will not be subjected to the GSTT when paid out. Applying the exclusion against the discounted future dollars represented by the premiums can save a client's estate literally millions of dollars.

Example. Assume an irrevocable trust for a client's grandchildren purchased a $20,000,000 policy on his life. If his premium outlay is $100,000 a year for 10 years and he allocates $100,000 of his GSTT exclusion against each year's premium payments, the inclusion ratio would be zero [1 - ($100,000 ÷ $100,000)]. None of the $20,000,000 proceeds would ever be subjected to the GSTT.[16] Had the client not allocated the exemption to protect the premiums from inclusion, the proceeds would have been subjected to the GSTT and the client's personal representative would be able to exclude only $1,500,000 (assuming death in 2004) of the $20,000,000, a difference in tax of $8,880,000 (.48 x $18,500,000)!

In the example, the client retained a zero inclusion ratio each year and guaranteed total exclusion of the policy proceeds by using a policy that became paid up before the transfers to the trust exhausted the GSTT exemption. The use of limited payment life insurance is essential in this regard. Had the premium payment period continued beyond the protection of the GSTT exemption, the inclusion ratio would have grown year by year with more and more of the proceeds becoming subject to the GSTT each year.

REVERSE QTIP ELECTION

It is currently possible to obtain a marital deduction for property that is not left outright to a spouse. In fact it is possible to specify that the principal of a client's estate must pass to his children or some selected party other than the surviving spouse and still obtain the marital deduction. The vehicle for such planning is called a QTIP trust, a trust that holds qualifying terminable interest property. Through a QTIP trust a client can provide income for life to a spouse but at that spouse's death the client can be sure it will pass to the person or persons he has selected.

There is a cost to this flexibility and tax deferral; whatever assets remain in the QTIP trust at the surviving spouse's death must be included in the surviving spouse's estate just as if the surviving spouse had transferred the property. The problem is (aside from the obvious estate tax and liquidity problem) that this same fiction applies for GSTT purposes. The surviving spouse is treated as if she was the transferor of property really transferred by her husband. This might cause a portion or all of her husband's GSTT exemption to be wasted.

For instance, a client, David Littell, died in 2004 leaving $3,000,000 of life insurance. Assume for simplicity that this was his entire estate. David had previously made gifts using $500,000 of his unified credit equivalent. $1,000,000 passed into a CEBT (credit equivalent bypass

trust for his five children and their five children). The balance of the proceeds ($2,000,000) was paid into a QTIP trust for his wife. So no federal estate tax was payable on any of his $3,000,000 estate. But absent a reverse QTIP election, David's wife is deemed to be the transferor of $2,000,000 and so none of David's GSTT exemption can be applied against the assets in the QTIP trust.

With a reverse QTIP election, the first spouse to die (David) will be treated as the transferor of both trusts and therefore his GSTT exemption can be allocated to both trusts. David's executor would allocate $1,000,000 of his $1,500,000 GSTT exemption to the CEBT and entirely eliminate the GSTT tax on this portion of his estate. The remaining $500,000 could then be applied against the $2,000,000 remaining portion. Of course, only $500,000/$2,000,000 of the future value of that trust would be protected against the GSTT. The surviving spouse could not use her $1,500,000 exemption against the GSTT since she was not the transferor (because of the reverse QTIP election).

Perhaps a better course of action to fully utilize both spouse's GSTT exemptions would be to split the QTIP trust into two trusts, one by formula equal to the amount of the GSTT exemption left after funding the CEBT ($500,000 in this example) and the other equal to the remaining estate ($1,500,000 in this example). The predeceased spouse's estate would make a reverse QTIP election and wipe out the GSTT in the first trust. The surviving spouse could then apply her $1,500,000 exemption to this second trust since she would be treated as its creator. In this way, all trusts have been fully sheltered from GSTT. This splitting of trusts for the purpose of making a reverse QTIP election must be made before the due date of the estate tax return of the first spouse to die.

GSTT AND IRREVOCABLE LIFE INSURANCE TRUSTS

Almost all individuals who establish irrevocable life insurance trusts are wealthy individuals. Many of these are superwealthy and are attempting to transfer many millions of dollars of assets downstream, not only to their children, but also to their grandchildren. A classic arrangement is for a client to place assets (including life insurance) into a trust and direct that income is to be paid to the client's spouse for life and then to the client's children for life and when they died, principal would be distributed to the client's grandchildren. The trust might give the client's children limited access to and control over some or all of the principal.

A trust such as this might last for several generations and, absent any GSTT, the IRS would receive no tax when the children died. This is the reason Congress imposed a generation-skipping transfer tax – so that even if a trust or a transfer skips an outright distribution (or vesting of rights) to the next generation down, a tax is nevertheless imposed on that skip at the time of the skip.

Transfers from irrevocable life insurance trusts are potentially subject to the GSTT. Where distributions from an irrevocable trust will be made to a client's grandchild or other skip person, a planner must consider potential GSTT problems. Unfortunately, transfers to the typical irrevocable life insurance trust will not qualify for the GSTT annual exclusion because such a trust usually gives a trustee sprinkle and spray powers to distribute income and principal among, not only grandchildren, but also children and the spouse of the client-transferor. Mere Crummey powers will not be enough to save the GSTT annual exclusion since, as mentioned above, the trust must have only one beneficiary and must terminate in favor of that beneficiary to qualify for the GSTT annual exclusion.

Three ways to utilize the GSTT exemption with an irrevocable life insurance trust include:

1. Use it immediately! Allocate the exemption (a) to the gift of the policy itself and any remaining exemption to (b) one or more of the premium payments;

2. Wait until the client dies. Save the GSTT exemption and use it then against the much larger death benefit; or

3. Wait until the client dies. Use the GSTT exemption to shelter transfers of other estate assets.

From a leveraging standpoint, the preferred choice is, obviously, the first of these three. In most cases, if there is any chance that the assets in the trust will be subjected to the GSTT, the client should consider immediately allocating a portion of his GSTT exemption to protect each transfer (and what it grows to) from the GSTT tax. The allocation is generally made by an election on the gift tax return for the year in which a transfer is made.[17]

It is the timely and creative use of the GSTT exemption, coupled with life insurance, that is the key to maximizing the exemption. This combination of exemption and life insurance provides the single most effective and pragmatic solution to the GSTT problem.

It is the technique that superwealthy clients with multimillions will use most to make an irrevocable trust into a dynasty trust and, thereby, keep great wealth within a family.

For instance, suppose a client and the client's spouse wanted to set up a trust that would last for the lives of their children, grandchildren, and great grandchildren, but wanted to avoid the confiscatory GSTT. They could set up an irrevocable trust. The trustee could purchase $15,000,000 of survivorship life insurance on their lives. Assume the clients pay 10 annual $200,000 premiums and, as each premium is paid, they allocate $200,000 of their combined GSTT exemptions to the payments. (Some gift tax may be due to the extent gifts are not covered by the gift tax annual exclusion or the unified credit.)

The results? Since the GSTT exemption protects not only the money contributed to the trust but also whatever that money generates, none of the $15,000,000 should be subject to GSTT taxes at either spouse's death. Nor should the GSTT be imposed when later generations terminate. Assuming the $15,000,000 in assets grow at the rate of 5 percent per year and are held intact for the nearly 100 years the trust is projected to last, over $1 billion dollars would ultimately be distributed to the client's great grandchildren!

By insulating a relatively small amount of premiums (say up to $100,000 a year for 10 years), an incredibly large amount of insurance proceeds can be protected forever.

For example, suppose a client establishes an irrevocable trust and the trustee applies for and becomes the owner and beneficiary of a $10,000,000 policy on the client's life. Each year, the client pays an annual premium that is shielded by a portion of the GSTT exemption. It is projected that $100,000 a year for 10 years is required before premiums vanish and the $10,000,000 policy is paid up. Assume the trust provides that the client's son is to receive income for life at the client's death and at the son's death, principal in the trust is to be distributed to the client's four children in equal shares if all are living. If a child dies, his share is to go in equal shares (per stirpes) to that child's child or children (the client's grandchildren).

If the client dies, predeceased by a child with three children, a transfer subject to the generation-skipping transfer tax has occurred. But since the inclusion ratio has always been zero, that is, since each transfer of premiums was covered by the GSTT exemption, none of the $10,000,000 will be subject to the GSTT. Alternatively, had the client not taken the trouble to allocate the GSTT exemption as each premium was paid, it could have been used at his death in 2004. But at that time, it could only have protected $1,500,000 of the total $10,000,000! The remaining $8,500,000 would have been subjected to a 48 percent tax! Careful planning and timely allocation of the GSTT exemption is worth about $4,000,000 in tax savings in this example.

Because of the incredible leverage that life insurance makes possible (by sheltering a relatively small amount of premiums, a disproportionately larger amount of proceeds can be protected), a client should almost always allocate the GSTT exemption against each premium, year by year. This forever protects the proceeds, regardless of how large they are. In a nutshell, by sheltering a million dollars of premiums, tens of millions of dollars of life insurance are freed from the GSTT tax because of the "once exempt, always exempt" character of the GSTT exclusion.

There are, of course, costs to using the exclusion to shelter premium payments:

1. The GSTT exemption is not available to avoid the tax on other transfers to skip persons.

2. Because the client will be required to file annual tax returns to make this allocation, the client will have to pay an advisor a relatively small fee for this mostly administrative task.[18]

3. There is an opportunity cost. If, for some reason, the transfers from the trust are not considered generation-skipping, the allocation of the GSTT exemption to the trust may result in its being wasted. If it's not likely that the trust will make such distributions, clients may want to save the GSTT exemption for a taxable transfer. This "save it for a rainy day" approach is not for the superwealthy who, almost inevitably, will have to face the GSTT problem in order to preserve great family wealth.

ENDNOTES

1. IRC Sec. 2613.

2. IRC Section 2663(3) gives the IRS authority to issue regulations that might provide that the beneficiary of an insurance policy be required to pay any GSTT.

3. IRC Sec. 2641.

4. IRC Sec. 2642(c).

5. IRC Section 2642(c) provides that transfers after March 31, 1988 qualify for the annual exclusion from the GSTT only if the following requirements are met:

(1) the transfer must be considered a direct skip,

(2) during the life of the skip person, no portion of the trust corpus or income may be distributed to or for the benefit of any other person, and

(3) the trust assets must be included in the estate of the skip person's estate if that person's death occurred prior to the trust's termination.

This necessitates the use of either separate shares for each skip person or the creation of a separate trust. This separate share rule applies to trusts established before April 1, 1988 if the client transfers assets (such as policies or cash for premium payments) after March 31, 1988. A possible solution is to have any life insurance policies in such a trust be made paid up. A new trust could then be created which meets the three requirements described above.

As a substitute for the use of the annual exclusion against the GSTT, in more modest estates where the client is not willing or able to meet the three requirements above, consider the use of the GSTT exemption.

6. A married client will usually want to provide his surviving spouse, in addition to the Crummey withdrawal power necessary to obtain the gift tax annual exclusion for a gift to the trust, a lifetime income interest after the grantor's death. This would violate both the second and third requirements above.

Most clients with more than one child or grandchild provide multiple Crummey withdrawal powers and beneficial interests to the grantor's several children (if for no other reason than to multiply the annual exclusions and reduce the gift tax cost of the transfer). This also violates at least two of the three rules above.

Few clients would want large amounts of cash and/or other investments to be paid to the estate of a grandchild with no direction as to the eventual beneficiary. So few clients will sacrifice this control to gain GSTT savings.

7. IRC Sec. 2631.

8. If the gift is made during lifetime, the client takes the GSTT exemption on his gift tax return. If the gift is made at death, the exemption is taken by the decedent's executor or administrator on the federal estate tax return. The exemption can be taken partially during lifetime and partially at death. But if no allocation is made, the exemption is deemed to have been allocated to lifetime direct skips in the order of their occurrence. IRC. Sec. 2632(a). Once made, the GSTT allocation is irrevocable. IRC Sec. 2631(b).

9. IRC Sec. 2652(a)(2).

10. IRC Sec. 2612(c).

11. IRC Sec. 2612(b).

12. IRC Sec. 2623.

13. IRC Sec. 2621.

14. As noted below, the annual exclusion can be used as an offset in the calculation of the inclusion ratio only with respect to direct skips.

15. IRC Sec. 2631.

16. The client should be given no interest that would cause the policy or other trust property to be included in his estate. Care should be taken with regard to the client's spouse; no interest should be given to the spouse that would cause the property to be included

in her estate had she been the grantor. The reason for this later precaution is that if the proceeds would have been included in her estate had she been the grantor, and the proceeds are received before her death, the GSTT exemption must be allocated against the proceeds rather than merely the policy premiums. The benefit of the GSTT exemption would be diluted and much more of the proceeds will become subject to the GSTT.

17. The election is not automatic. A client should generally take affirmative steps to secure the allocation's protection. It should be made on a timely filed gift tax return, which is typically due on April 15th of the year following the transfer.

18. Gift tax returns should generally be filed for most gifts to irrevocable life insurance trusts – even if the gifts are within the gift tax annual exclusion, they may be subject to the GSTT. Filing would allow the client to allocate a portion of his GSTT exemption to the annual gifts and thereby insure that the trust will be subject to neither current GSTT on the premiums nor GSTT on the policy proceeds.

MODIFIED ENDOWMENT CONTRACTS

INTRODUCTION

To counteract what was perceived as an abusive use of single-premium, limited-pay, and universal life policies as short-term tax-sheltered cash accumulation or savings vehicles, Congress passed legislation modifying Internal Revenue Code section 7702, which provides the tax law definition of a life insurance contract, and creating Internal Revenue Code (IRC) section 7702A, which defines a new class of insurance contracts called modified endowment contracts (MECs).[1]

The basic difference between MECs and other life insurance contracts is the federal income tax treatment of amounts received during the insured's life. Certain "distributions under the contract" that are not generally subject to tax when received from other life insurance contracts are subject to income tax and, in some cases, a 10% penalty when received from MECs.

In other respects, MECs are treated and taxed under the same rules that apply to other life insurance contracts that are not MECs. Basically, compared with policies that are not classified as MECs, MECs have detrimental tax consequences for some living benefits but the tax treatment of cash accumulations within the policy and death benefits is no different than for other policies.

What is a MEC? A MEC is a policy that meets the IRC Section 7702 definition of life insurance and is funded more rapidly than a paid-up policy based on seven statutorily-defined level annual premiums. (See Appendix F for more information on IRC Section 7702.)

The basic rules are:

1. Policies "entered into" before June 21, 1988, are grandfathered from the MEC rules unless they undergo a "material" change.

2. All policies entered into after June 20, 1988, and any policy, whenever issued, that undergoes a material change must be tested under the MEC classification rules.

3. Once a policy is classified as a MEC, it remains a MEC. A MEC will not change its MEC status if it is changed, adjusted, or reconfigured as a policy that would otherwise not be classified as a MEC.

4. A policy received in exchange for a MEC is also a MEC, even if the policy that is received would otherwise not be classified as a MEC.

MEC TAX TREATMENT

The tax treatment of certain amounts received from MECs prior to death – called distributions under the contract – is generally the same as the tax treatment afforded to annuity distributions. To the extent of gain in the policy, distributions are taxed on an income-first basis. In other words the first distributions out of the contract are not considered a tax free return of the policyowner's cost but rather the investment earnings on the contract. Those earnings are deemed to be withdrawn, and therefore become taxable, before the policyowner can recover his or her tax free basis. So, only after all income or gain in the policy has been received are additional amounts treated as nontaxable return of the policyowner's cost basis or investment in the contract.

In addition to the tax on distributions under the contract, a second tax is imposed in certain cases. This second tax is a 10% penalty tax. It is imposed on amounts received that are included in gross income.[2]

This 10% penalty tax does not apply to any distribution:

1. made on or after a taxpayer attains age 59½ years of age;

2. attributable to a taxpayer's becoming disabled; or

3. that is part of a series of substantially equal periodic payments made for the life (or life expectancy) of the taxpayer or for the joint lives (or life expectancies) of the taxpayer and beneficiary.[3]

Generally, gain in the contract is determined by subtracting adjusted premiums paid from policy cash values. Adjusted premiums are total premiums paid (excluding premiums paid for supplementary benefits such as waiver of premium and accidental death benefit features) less any dividends received in cash or credited against premiums and less the nontaxable portion of any previous withdrawals. Cash value is computed without regard to surrender charges and so, for this purpose, is really the policy's reserve or account value. Therefore, gain may exist and result in taxation of a distribution even though a policyowner cannot actually access it. Also, in some cases a full surrender could yield less tax than a partial withdrawal.

Amounts received that are treated as income-first distributions under the contract include:[4]

- policy loans (to pay premiums as well as for all other purposes);

- loans secured by the contract;

- interest accrued on a policy loan;

- withdrawals;

- cash dividends; and

- dividends retained by the insurer as principal or interest on a policy loan.

Amounts received that are not treated as income-first distributions under the contract include:[5]

- dividends retained by the insurer to pay premiums or other consideration for the contract;

- dividends used to purchase paid-up additions, term insurance, or other qualified additional benefits; and

- surrender of paid-up additions to pay premiums. However, it should be noted that the status of surrendering paid-up additions to pay premiums is uncertain. Most commentators feel they are not income-first distributions under the contract, but the issue has not yet been completely settled.

MEC tax treatment applies to amounts received during the contract year in which a policy effectively becomes a MEC as well as to amounts received in any subsequent contract year. It also applies to any distributions in the two years before the policy fails the seven-pay test.[6]

Example. Kathy purchased a life insurance contract on January 1, 2004. As of January 1, 2006, her basis in the policy is $100,000. The contract has a cash value of $140,000. The policy is a MEC. She borrows $50,000 from the policy's cash value on her 50th birthday. Kathy's taxable gain from the loan is $40,000 ($140,000 cash value - $100,000 basis in the policy). If Kathy is in the 25% income tax bracket, she must pay an income tax of $10,000 ($40,000 x 0.25). She must also pay a 10% penalty on the taxable amount. The penalty will be $4,000 ($40,000 x .10). Therefore Kathy's total tax bill on the loan from the policy is $14,000 ($10,000 + $4,000). Note that all amounts included in Kathy's gross income as a result of taking a loan from the policy will be added to her basis in the policy for purposes of determining future taxable amounts. Therefore Kathy's basis in the policy after taking the loan will be $140,000 ($100,000 original basis + $40,000 taxable portion of loan). The $10,000 nontaxable portion does not affect Kathy's basis in the contract because the transaction is a loan and not a withdrawal.

TECHNICAL DEFINITION OF A MODIFIED ENDOWMENT CONTRACT

A MEC is a life insurance contract that meets the requirements of IRC Section 7702 and:

1. was entered into on or after June 20, 1988, and fails to meet the seven-pay test; or

2. is received in exchange for a MEC.[7]

A policy that originally satisfies the seven-pay test in its first seven contract years may nonetheless become a MEC if it undergoes certain material changes, which are described below. Policies that undergo material changes are subjected to a new seven-pay test.

THE SEVEN-PAY TEST

The test for MEC status is called the "seven-pay" test. The seven-pay test must be applied in basically three situations:

1. To initially test policies entered into after June 20, 1988;

2. To retest policies entered into after June 20, 1988 if death benefits are reduced within the first seven contract years; and

3. To test or retest *any* policy, even those entered into before June 21, 1988, when there is a material change in future benefits.

INITIAL TEST FOR POLICIES ENTERED INTO AFTER JUNE 20, 1988

A contract fails to meet the seven-pay test if the accumulated amount paid under the contract at any time during the first seven contract years exceeds the sum of the "net level premiums" that would have been paid on or before such time if the contract provided for paid-up future benefits after the payment of seven level annual premiums.[8] Generally, "amount paid" is defined as the premiums paid under the contract reduced by any distributions but not including amounts includable in gross income. For purposes of this test, the death benefit for the first contract year is deemed to be provided until the maturity date without regard to any scheduled reduction after the first seven contract years. However, certain limited scheduled increases in death benefits may be taken into account.[9]

Example. If the annual net level premium for a $100,000 seven-pay policy is $4,500, then any $100,000 policy for the same insured on which aggregate premiums exceed $4,500 during the first year, $9,000 during the first 2 policy years, $13,500 during the first 3 policy years, $18,000 during the first 4 policy years, $22,500 during the first 5 policy years, $27,000 during the first 6 policy years, or $31,500 during the first 7 years of the policy will be considered a modified endowment contract.

The seven-pay test does not require that a policy provide for seven level annual premiums to be paid over seven years. Rather, the test limits the cumulative amount that may be paid for each of the first seven years. Premiums may not be paid in advance in an amount that violates the annual premium limit. However, it is possible to make up for premiums paid in prior years that were less than the maximum amount permitted.

If the aggregate premiums paid during the first seven years are less than aggregate premiums that would have been paid on a level annual-premium basis using the net level premium amount ($4,500 a year in the example) for a seven-pay policy (for the same insured), the policy will not be a modified endowment contract and will receive the same tax treatment previously applicable to all policies.

Definition of Net Level Premium

The definition of a net level premium under these new rules is based on the guideline level premium concept under IRC Section 7702. The net level premium is not the same as the actual premium payable under the contract. It is also not the same as what many life insurance agents refer to as a net premium. "Net level premium" is a technical term of art that refers to an artificially constructed net level premium that is computed using mandated interest, mortality, and expense assumptions.[10] Therefore, it is possible that even policies that require seven level annual premiums will not pass the seven-pay test in some cases because the artificial net level premium (as calculated under the regulations) will be less than the actual premium. In other words, if the net level premium is less than the actual premium payable, the payment of the actual premium due will cause the policy to fail the seven-pay test.

Actuarial studies show that the seven-pay test is generally quite generous in the amount of permitted premiums. For nonsmoker universal life policies under option A, the net level premium limits under the seven-pay test are higher than the guideline annual premium limits under IRC Section 7702 at all ages and for either sex. Under option B, the crossover age where the seven-pay test limits are more restrictive than the IRC Section 7702 limits is in the mid-50's for male nonsmokers and early 50's for male smokers. For females, it is in the mid-60's for nonsmokers and slightly earlier for smokers.[11] All term insurance policies and virtually all guaranteed premium whole life policies without paid-up additions premium riders will meet the seven-pay test.

Riders to policies are considered part of the base insurance policy for purposes of the seven-pay test. Since the cost of such riders will be included in the calculation of the seven-pay test, a term rider may help a policy avoid classification as a MEC. Examples of such riders would be guaranteed insurability, family term, accidental death or disability, disability waiver, or other allowed benefits.

Contracts with Death Benefits under $10,000

There is a variation on the application of the net level premium amount in the seven-pay test that applies to policies under $10,000 in face amount. For such policies, $75 a year can be added to the seven-pay-test premium.[12] The $75 additional allowance permits some small seven-pay policies to pass the seven-pay test that otherwise might not. The smaller the policy is, the more likely it is that the actual premium will be less than the net level premium plus $75. The full $75 can be used for any amount of coverage between $1,000 and $10,000, resulting in a maximum allowable additional expense loading of $7.50 per $1,000 of coverage on a $10,000 policy.

Congress anticipated the added attractiveness of this small policy expense allowance and its potential abuses. Therefore the statute requires that all policies issued by the same insurer for the same policyowner be treated as one policy for purposes of determining that the face amount does not exceed $10,000.[13] This prevents policyowners from purchasing a large number of small policies to take advantage of the allowable expense loading. Note that the statute does not require that policies from different insurers be aggregated for this purpose. This may present a planning opportunity for taxpayers purchasing several small policies from different insurance companies.

Refund of Excess Premiums

If the insurer returns premiums paid in excess of the net level annual premium limit plus the interest on the excess premiums within a 60-day grace period of the end of the contract year in which the excess occurs, the contract will not fail the seven-pay test. The returned amount will reduce the sum of premiums paid under the contract during such contract year for purposes of the seven-pay test. Interest paid will be includable in the gross income of the recipient.[14]

BENEFIT REDUCTIONS WITHIN THE FIRST SEVEN CONTRACT YEARS

If death benefits are reduced within the seven-year testing period, there is a look-back requirement. The seven-pay test must be reapplied as if the contract originally had been issued for the reduced benefit amount.[15]

Example. Assume the guideline annual premium is $10,000 based on the original death benefit. The policyowner pays $9,000 each year for the first 6 years. In year seven, the policyowner withdraws $36,000, with a corresponding decrease in the death benefit. The

recomputed guideline premium is $8,000. The policy now fails the seven-pay test and is a MEC since cumulative premiums paid in just the first year, $9,000, (and through year 6 as well) exceed the sum of the recomputed guideline annual premiums of $8,000. The $36,000 withdrawal will be subject to tax to the extent of gain in the policy. If the policyowner is under age 59½, a 10% penalty will also be imposed on the taxable portion of the distribution.

The seven-year rule for benefit reductions appears to apply only during the first seven contract years unless there is a material change. Therefore, absent a material change, a benefit reduction after the first seven years has no effect. A benefit reduction itself is not a material change. However, a material change may restart the seven-year look-back period for benefit reductions because a material change is treated like a new policy issuance. Apparently, benefit reductions within the first seven years after a material change will require a recomputation of the seven-pay test back to the date of the material change rather than the policy's original issue date, even if the periods overlap.

Distributions Affected

If a policy fails the seven-pay test as a result of the look-back rule, certain distributions are treated as potentially taxable distributions from a MEC. These distributions include all future distributions, distributions in the contract year the policy is treated as failing the seven-pay test, and prior distributions taken in anticipation of failure of the test. The statute authorizes the IRS to promulgate regulations defining what are distributions taken in anticipation of failure of the test, but it specifically states that any distribution that is made within two years before the failure will be treated as made in anticipation of such failure.[16]

Reductions of Benefits Attributable to Nonpayment of Premiums

Any benefit reductions attributable to the nonpayment of premiums due are not taken into account if the benefits are reinstated within 90 days after being reduced.[17] This rule applies to a nonforfeiture option of reduced paid-up insurance within the first seven contract years. In other words, if a policy that is put on reduced paid-up status fails the seven-pay test as a result of the look-back rule, the failure may be reversed if the policy is reinstated to its original death benefit within 90 days. Alternatively, failure of the test could probably be avoided by electing the extended term option rather than the reduced paid-up option. The policy could also be surrendered without adverse consequences since the complete surrender of a life insurance policy during the policy's first seven years is generally not considered to cause the policy to be treated as a MEC.

MATERIAL CHANGE RULES

Policies entered into prior to June 21, 1988, and policies entered into on or after that date with low enough premiums to avoid being classified as MECs are generally treated the same as life insurance policies have been treated in the past. This means there will generally be no income tax applicable to withdrawals until the policyowner's cost basis has been recovered (tax free). This is the cost-recovery rule or first-in-first-out (FIFO) treatment long associated with life insurance policy taxation.[18] Distributions or withdrawals that are subject to tax are not subject to the additional 10% penalty unless the policy is reclassified as a MEC.

However, a grandfathered policy or a policy that originally passed the seven-pay test when it was issued can become a MEC if there is a material change in the policy. A material change, in itself, does not cause a policy to become a MEC. A material change only subjects the policy to the seven-pay test. It is reclassified as a MEC only if it fails the test. For example, a single-premium life insurance policy acquired before June 21, 1988 is not a MEC. However, if there is a material change in the policy, it is subjected to the seven-pay test, which it would probably fail. It would then be a MEC.

Similarly, an elective increase in the death benefit (requiring evidence of insurability) of a universal life policy that was acquired before June 21, 1988 would also subject the policy to testing. However, depending on the timing and level of premium payments and the cash value in the policy, the policy after the change, in many cases, would pass the test. The policy would continue to be treated under the normal rules for life insurance contracts.

Changes That Are Not Material

What constitutes a material change under the law? What is not a material change is somewhat clearer than what is a material change, so the changes that are specifically excluded from consideration as material changes

are addressed first. The statute provides the following specific exceptions to the material change rules:[19]

1. cost-of-living increases in death benefits that are based on a broad-based index (such as the consumer price index) if the increase is funded ratably over the remaining life of the contract;

2. increases in death benefits due to the premiums paid for the policy to support the first seven contract years' level of benefits; and

3. death benefit increases inherent in the policy design due to the crediting of interest or other earnings.

Exception (1) would be met by the standard cost-of-living rider where there is a level step-up of future annual premium charges for cost-of-living increases in death benefits. Exception (2) appears to exempt any increase in death benefits necessary to keep the required relationship between the death benefit and the policy guideline cash value or guideline premiums as specified in IRC Section 7702 from being classified as a material change. Exception (3) appears to exempt the increasing death benefits of an option II universal life policy or a variable life policy from being classified as a material change.

Also, certain changes will not be treated as material which, by inference, adds the following exceptions to the material change rules:[20]

1. increases in death benefits, without limit, on policies which, as of June 21, 1988, required at least seven level annual premium payments and under which the policyowner continues to make at least seven level annual premium payments; and

2. increases in death benefits (or the purchase of an additional qualified benefit after June 21, 1988) if the policyowner had a unilateral right under the contract to obtain such increase or addition without evidence of insurability.

The first exception means that level premium whole life policies entered into before June 21, 1988, are permanently grandfathered from the material change rules as related to increases in death benefits (but other material changes, such as an exchange, would make them subject to seven-pay testing). Universal life or other flexible-premium policies are, presumably, not included since they do not require the payment of level premiums. The second exception appears to be a "grace amount" or "safe harbor" for death benefit increases that the policyowner had a contractual right to obtain without evidence of insurability such as might be provided by guaranteed insurability riders.

Material Change Defined

The statute says "the term 'material change' includes any increase in the death benefit under the contract or any increase in, or addition of, a qualified additional benefit under the contract."[21]

Material Increases in Death Benefits

Any increase in death benefits under a policy (excluding the exceptions mentioned above) will be treated as a material change if:

1. before June 21, 1988, the policyowner did not have a unilateral right under the contract to obtain such increase or addition without providing evidence of insurability;[22] or

2. the policyowner has a unilateral right under the contract to obtain increases or additions without evidence of insurability but such increases exceed the death benefit under the contract in effect on October 20, 1988, by more than $150,000;[23]

Basically, any increases in benefits that require evidence of insurability and even contractually-guaranteed increases that do not require evidence but that cumulatively exceed the amount in (2) will be treated as material changes. Shifting a universal life policy from death benefit option I to option II would be a material change since the election usually requires evidence of insurability.

On the other hand, increases without evidence of insurability may not be considered "material." Examples of such "could be safe" contractual rights include increases pursuant to guaranteed insurability riders, guarantee issue offers, scheduled option II face amount increases, and IRC Section 7702 cash value corridor increases. Death benefit increases for grandfathered policies due to premium payments, reserve earnings, cash value corridor, and/or regular option II increases should not cause loss of grandfathering, even if over $150,000, because they are covered by the "necessary premium" exception to the material change rules.

Other Material Changes

The following other types of changes are also considered material:

1. term life insurance conversions to permanent forms of coverage;[24] and

2. exchanges of one policy for another, whether or not tax free under IRC Section 1035.[25]

It is uncertain whether changes in contract mortality charges or interest rate guarantees are material changes.

Seven–Pay Test as Applied to Material Changes

A material change in a contract's benefits (or other terms) that was not reflected in any previous determination under the seven-pay test requires seven-pay testing. Apparently, a material change may take place anytime during the policy's existence. When a material change occurs, the contract is treated as if it were a new contract entered into on the date when the change takes effect. The seven-pay test, as described above, is applied as of the date of the material change, not the issue date of the policy. In addition, the seven-pay test is adjusted by a "rollover" rule that takes account of the contract's existing cash surrender value at the date of change.[26]

The procedure is as follows:

1. Determine the seven-pay premium (based on the insured's then attained age) for each of the next seven contract years after the material change.

2. Multiply (a) the cash surrender value as of the date of the material change (determined without regard to any increase in the cash surrender value that is attributable to the amount of premium that is not necessary) by (b) a specified fraction. The fraction is the ratio of:

    i) the seven-pay premium for the future benefits under the contract after the change to

    ii) the net single premium for such benefits computed using the same assumptions used in determining the seven-pay premium.

3. Subtract the product of the multiplication in step (2) from the amount determined in step (1).

The remainder is the adjusted seven-pay premium used to test actual premiums paid in each of the next seven contract years.

The adjusted seven-pay premium so determined could be negative if the cash value is large enough. This should not automatically make the contract a MEC. However, payment of additional premiums in the next seven years might make the policy a MEC.

ENDNOTES

1. The Technical and Miscellaneous Revenue Act of 1988 (TAMRA '88), P. L. 100-647. TAMRA '88 Section 5011 amended IRC Section 7702. TAMRA '88 Section 5012(c) created IRC Section 7702A which defines a modified endowment contract.

2. IRC Sec. 72(v).

3. IRC Sec. 72(v).

4. IRC Sec. 72(e); H.R. Conference Rep. No. 100-1104, (TAMRA '88) *reprinted in* 1988-3 CB 592. There is an exception under IRC Section 72(e)(10)(B) for loans made solely to cover burial expenses if the policy's maximum death benefit does not exceed $25,000.

5. H.R. Conference Rep. No. 100-1104, (TAMRA '88) *reprinted in* 1988-3 CB 592.

6. IRC Sec. 7702A(d).

7. IRC Sec. 7702A.

8. IRC Sec. 7702A(b).

9. IRC Section 7702A(c)(1)(B) with reference to IRC Section 7702(e)(2)(A) allows that "... an increase in the death benefit which is provided in the contract may be taken into account but only to the extent necessary to prevent a decrease in the excess of the death benefit over the cash surrender value of the contract,". This provision is essentially provided to accommodate option II of universal life policies where the death benefit is the cash value plus a level pure insurance amount.

10. IRC Sec. 7702A(c)(1)(B).

11. *Estate & Business Planning Technical Release*, Report No. 23, November 1988, State Mutual Companies, 440 Lincoln Street, Worcester, Massachusetts 01605.

12. IRC Sec. 7702A(c)(4).

13. IRC Sec. 7702A(c)(4).

14. IRC Sec. 7702A(e)(1). The rate of interest is an open issue. The consensus is that the interest rate should be that which was credited to premiums while in the policy. Administrative expenses and losses, such as commissions that are not recoverable, should be able to be factored into the ultimate interest amount paid. The net refund would then equal the excess premium plus the inside buildup thereon less the cost of the refund.

15. IRC Sec. 7702A(c)(2)(A).

16. IRC Sec. 7702A(d).

17. IRC Sec. 7702A(c)(2)(B).

18. It is important to remember that withdrawals from policies that are associated with a reduction in policy benefits during the first 15 policy years are currently subject to a limited income-first or LIF0-type federal income taxation. The MEC rules have been imposed *in addition to* the existing rules that were imposed by the Tax Reform Act of 1986. However, the 1986 rules do not apply to policy loans. The MEC rules *do* apply to loans as well as to withdrawals. Therefore a policy withdrawal can result in income tax liability even if the policy is not a MEC. However, the 10% penalty tax does not apply unless the policy is a MEC.

19. IRC Secs. 7702A(c)(3)(B)(i), 7702A(c)(3)(B)(ii).

20. TAMRA '88, P.L. 100-647, Sec. 5012(e).

21. IRC Sec. 7702A(c)(3)(B).

22. TAMRA '88, P.L. 100-647, Sec. 5012(e)(3).

23. TAMRA '88, P.L. 100-647, Sec. 5012(e)(2).

24. TAMRA '88, P.L. 100-647, Sec. 5012(e)(3).

25. H.R. Conf. Rep. No. 100-1104, (TAMRA '88) *reprinted in* 1988-3 CB 596; Let. Rul. 9044022.

26. IRC Secs. 7702A(c)(3)(A)(i), 7702A(c)(3)(A)(ii).

Appendix E

SECTION 1035 EXCHANGES

━━━ ███ ━━━

WHY AN EXCHANGE?

Insurance programs must be flexible enough to change as an insured's financial status, family responsibilities, and business needs changes. Furthermore, as new types of policies are developed, ethical agents will seek, when appropriate, to "match the product to the problem." If a new product solves the problem in a more cost effective manner than the old product, a client should be apprised of the opportunity and should be given the chance to exchange the old policy for the new. This is particularly important if the insurer that sold the existing contract is financially unstable. Federal income tax law facilitates certain exchanges by providing that in some instances they may be made without the immediate recognition of gain. Although such transactions are sometimes referred to as "Section 1035 tax-free exchanges" the gain at the time of the transaction is deferred rather than forgiven.

Factors indicating that an IRC Section 1035 exchange should be considered include:

1. A client feels that a higher rate of return can be realized with a new policy.

2. A client is concerned that the present insurer may become insolvent or that its investment experience will not warrant the dividends projected and that a more stable insurer can be obtained through a policy exchange or that diversification of insurance carriers will increase safety or return.

3. The client's current policy is subject to a substantial loan, the interest paid on the policy is nondeductible, costs are increasing, and the client needs to continue coverage.

4. The client would like to change from an individual to a group product.[1]

5. The death benefit under a new product will exceed the death benefit under the old product.[2]

6. The client would like to change an ordinary life policy into a single premium policy to eliminate the premium paying burden, obtain a higher rate of return on the underlying cash values, and obtain a higher death benefit.

7. A newly-developed type of policy (perhaps one with a more flexible premium structure or with a more adjustable death benefit) is more suitable to the client's needs, circumstances, or investment philosophy than the policy presently owned. For instance, a client may want to exchange an ordinary life contract for a universal, variable, or interest sensitive policy.[3]

8. Premium rates on the new policy are lower due to such factors as improved mortality tables, a non-smoking discount, a volume discount for several policies aggregated into one[4], or other factors.[5]

BASIC INCOME TAX IMPLICATIONS OF AN EXCHANGE

The Internal Revenue Code provides generally that all income, from whatever source derived, is reportable by the recipient.[6] So if an existing life insurance policy or annuity is surrendered, the gain, i.e., the excess of the "amount received" over the policyowner's basis, is taxable at ordinary rates.[7] Gain can therefore be thought of generally as the excess of amounts distributed under the policy over the amounts paid in. For example, assume a client surrenders a policy after paying $100,000 in premiums. If the client receives $130,000, the $30,000 excess over basis would be considered an ordinary income gain and would be immediately reportable. This same result (absent a proper exchange under IRC Section 1035) will occur even if the client immediately uses the proceeds to purchase a new insurance policy that is far more appropriate for his needs, purposes, and for the satisfaction of his goals than the old policy.

But mere appreciation in property does not result in taxation. There must be a disposition of the property, typically a sale or exchange, before that gain becomes taxable. Sometimes, when there is ostensibly a disposition but in reality the taxpayer has merely changed the form of investment without in fact "closing the books on the original purchase," the Internal Revenue Code will acknowledge that the gain, even though technically "realized," should not have to be "recognized" (i.e., reported as taxable).

Section 1035 of the Internal Revenue Code is such a provision. It allows the tax that would otherwise be imposed on a lump sum disposition of certain life insurance policies and annuities to be postponed. Specifically, the law provides that no gain (or loss) is recognized on the exchange of:

1. a life insurance contract for another life insurance contract[8] (one that the face amount or death benefit is not ordinarily payable in full during the insured's life[9]);

2. a life insurance contract for an endowment contract (one that depends in part on the life expectancy of the insured but which may be payable in full in a single payment during the insured's lifetime[10]);

3. an ordinary life insurance contract for an annuity (one payable during the life of the annuitant only in installments[11]);

4. an endowment contract for another endowment contract that provides for regular payments beginning at a date not later than the date payments would have begun under the contract exchanged[12];

5. an endowment contract for an annuity contract[13]; or

6. an annuity contract for an annuity contract.[14]

There is, of course, a cost for the privilege of postponing the reporting the gain. When any of the above tax-deferred exchanges occur, the new contract received takes the basis of the policy exchanged for it. The new policy's basis will be the cost basis of the old policy plus any premiums paid after the exchange minus any excludable dividends received after the exchange. In other words, as noted above, the tax on the gain is delayed rather than forgiven. For this reason, Section 1035 exchanges are referred to in this chapter as "tax-deferred" rather than "tax-free."

Although losses are not deductible, it is possible that IRC Section 1035 can be used to the client's advantage when a policy is in a loss position. Assume the following facts:

X has paid $10,000 a year for 10 years into a whole life contract and therefore has a $100,000 basis. Assume the policy cash value at that time is only $80,000. He exchanges the old policy for a new policy.

Because of the carryover of basis rules, X's entire $100,000 basis carries over into the new policy he receives in a Section 1035 exchange. So if he later begins to draw money out of the new contract, the first $100,000 he draws out is considered income tax free return of cost. Had X surrendered his contract and then purchased a new contract with the $80,000, his new basis would be only $80,000 rather than $100,000, a $20,000 difference in tax free recoveries.

Can this concept be carried further by combining a term conversion with a Section 1035 exchange? For instance, assume:

Y had paid $10,000 a year for term insurance for 10 years and at the end of that time the policy had no cash value. He decides to convert the term to whole life. Simultaneous with a conversion of the term to whole life insurance, the insured requested a Section 1035 exchange of the whole life to a "new" contract.

There would be no gain, of course, nor a deductible loss. But would the Section 1035 carryover of basis requirement mean the $100,000 of premiums he had paid for term insurance could be added to whatever additional amount he paid to convert the term to whole life? If so, he significantly boosts the amount that can later be withdrawn during lifetime as an income tax free recovery of basis. If this simultaneous conversion/exchange technique works, a client can recover in tax savings a great deal of the otherwise wasted outlay for term insurance. The answer is uncertain at this point.

PARTIALLY TAX-DEFERRED EXCHANGES

Tax law does not cause a Section 1035 exchange to "crash" merely because the client receives cash or some other property "to boot" which is not "of like-kind" in addition to the new policy or annuity. But if cash or any "in kind" payment of value such as a life insurance contract in return for an annuity is received as part of the exchange, gain must be currently recognized to the extent of such "boot" (i.e., cash or in kind property.[15]) "Cash" includes repayment of any outstanding loans at surrender. In other words, if a taxpayer sells or exchanges property subject to a debt, relief from that debt is treated in the same manner as if cash were received by the seller.

Where the transaction is largely tax-deferred but involves some boot such as cash, additional property, or the extinction of debt, gain is equal to the amount realized by the client less the client's basis.

Where boot (other than cash or the payoff of debt) is received, the client's basis must be split proportionately between the tax-deferred contract received in the exchange and the taxable in kind boot (i.e., the taxable asset).[16] For instance, if the client exchanges one annuity with a basis of $10,000 for another annuity worth $10,000 but "to boot" receives a small life insurance contract worth $2,000 from the new insurer, the value of the life insurance policy would be currently taxable. The client's $10,000 basis for both the annuity and the new policy would be apportioned according to their value ($10,000/ $12,000 of the $10,000 basis going to the new annuity and $2,000/$12,000 of the $10,000 basis going to the life insurance policy). To the extent the life insurance policy is taxable, that amount should be added to its basis.

TAXABLE EXCHANGES

The policy behind IRC Section 1035 is not to allow a tax-free exchange but rather to defer the tax on any gain. Therefore, IRC Section 1035 will not apply if the exchange (a) increases the possibility of eliminating the tax by extending the period of life insurance protection or (b) by providing life insurance protection where none previously existed.[17] For this reason, in the opinion of the authors, a Section 1035 exchange of term insurance for whole life will be viewed by the IRS as an attempt to do just that – extend the period of life insurance protection. Although nothing in the Code or regulations specifically denies the taxpayer the right to make such an exchange under IRC Section 1035, it is likely the IRS will make this claim anyway.

Any gain inherent in a contract must be reported by the client in any transaction that does not fully meet IRC Section 1035 rules. Therefore, if an endowment or annuity contract is exchanged for a life contract, any gain will be currently reportable. This is because if either an endowment or annuity contract matures, the proceeds would be taxable. If a contract owner could exchange either policy for one that provides income tax free death benefits by holding on to the policy until death, the owner could avoid tax on the gain forever.

For this same reason, an endowment contract may not be exchanged tax free for a life insurance contract. While an endowment contract will pay tax-exempt death benefits only if the insured dies before the endowment

maturity, a life insurance policy (unless it is surrendered) will assuredly pay tax-exempt death benefits. Any gain on this type of exchange is fully taxable since to allow a deferral would defeat the intent of the law.[18] Similarly, an exchange of an endowment policy is not protected under IRC Section 1035 for another endowment policy with a later maturity date since the extended date increases the chances of the insured's dying prior to maturity and the proceeds being paid income tax free.

How much is taxable if the exchange does not meet IRC Section 1035 requirements? The gain is the value of the new policy plus the cash (or in kind property), if any, received minus the net premium cost of the old policy (gross premiums less excludable dividends).

The value of the new policy depends on its premium paying status. If the policy is a single premium or a paid-up policy, it is valued at its "replacement cost," the single premium a person of the same sex and age as the insured would pay for a similar policy from the same company.[19] The value of a premium paying policy is the policy's interpolated terminal reserve plus any unearned premium.[20]

ISSUES UNDER IRC SECTIONS 7702 AND 7702A

Life insurance contracts considered "modified endowment contracts" (MECs) receive less favorable income tax treatment than those that are not so classified.

First, any lifetime distribution from a MEC is includable in the income of the recipient to the extent of the built-in gain in the contract at the time the distribution occurs. "Distribution" is defined broadly to include all loans and partial surrenders and even dividends. Only dividends retained by the insurer to pay premiums or purchase paid-up additions are excluded from the definition of distributions. Second, a 10% penalty tax is imposed on the amount of a distribution, unless the distribution is due to the death or disability of the policyowner or is made after the policyowner is 59 1/2 or is paid over the life expectancy of the taxpayer or the joint life expectancies of the taxpayer and the beneficiary. (See Appendix D for more on MECs.)

Therefore, MECs are more expensive contracts from a tax standpoint and should be avoided if possible.[21] So to the extent possible, planners should not taint a non-MEC contract through a policy exchange.

What is the tax implication if a MEC is exchanged for a new contract? If a contract is issued in exchange for a

MEC, the new contract is also considered a MEC. The exchange does not change the policy's characterization or remove the taint.[22]

What are the implications of exchanging a non-MEC policy for a new contract? Since policies issued prior to June 21, 1988, are not subject to the MEC seven-pay test, if such a protected policy is exchanged for a new policy the question is whether the new policy loses its "grandfathered" status? The answer seems to be yes. For purposes of the "seven-pay" test, the IRS appears to have taken the position that a life insurance contract received in a Section 1035 exchange in which the old policy was issued prior to June 21, 1988, should be treated as if it were a new contract issued on the date of the exchange. This means the new policy would be fully subject to the seven-pay test. Grandfathering would be lost.[23]

MECHANICS OF THE EXCHANGE

If a client were to sell property to one person and use the proceeds from the sale to purchase new property from a second party, the first transaction would be considered a "sale" rather than an exchange. The IRS will follow this same reasoning even if the client intended from the beginning to use the proceeds from the first transaction to purchase the second asset. How does this reasoning apply when the asset is a life insurance policy?

Take, for example, Gary who owns a life insurance policy on his life with a current cash value of $90,000. He has paid a total of $60,000 in premiums but has received back a total of $20,000 in dividends. If he were to surrender the policy, his realized gain would be $50,000 calculated as follows. He receives $90,000. His basis is $40,000 ($60,000 paid in less $20,000 recovered income tax free). So his realized gain is $50,000, the $90,000 received less the $40,000 basis. But if he had exchanged this policy for a new one under IRC Section 1035, no tax would be payable in the current year. His basis would be the same $40,000 as the basis he had in the original policy increased by any premiums he pays subsequent to the exchange.

For this reason, when a client owns a policy issued by one company, rather than cash it in and use the proceeds to purchase another company's product, the client should, if possible, assign his present contract to the new insurer in return for the new contract.

At times, planners are tempted to avoid this classic approach and use what seem to be less complicated and time consuming methods. In most of these, the policyholder first cashes in the old contract, obtains the policy

surrender value and then either pays it over to the new insurer or directs the insurer of the old policy to pay the proceeds directly to the new insurer. Under either approach, the old policy is never transferred to the new insurer. Will the IRS be kind to this type of transfer and call it an exchange or will it insist the transaction is first a sale followed by a purchase of a new contract? Some authorities say "no."[24]

There is an exception to this approach for tax deferred annuities (TDAs). A significant difference between TDAs and other types of policies is that the Internal Revenue Code itself requires a tax deferred annuity to be non-transferable. Thus, an employee is barred from assigning such a contract in exchange for one more financially advantageous or otherwise more appropriate for the employee's needs and is, in effect, "locked in." The IRS has provided that the holder of a TDA may make a direct transfer of the funds in the annuity between two insurers if the transferred funds continue to be subject to distribution requirements at least as strict as those that applied under the old contract.[25]

Although each company may have its own procedure, in general the mechanics are as follows:

1. An absolute assignment and exchange agreement form should be signed by the client transferring all rights to the old policy to the insurer that will issue the new policy. The legal name of the insurer should be used. The client's social security number or taxpayer ID number should accompany or be included in these forms.

2. An unsigned copy of the old company's surrender form (to be signed by an officer of the company that will surrender the old policy and issue the new policy) should accompany the assignment of the policyowner's interest.

3. The original policy is attached to the above forms.

4. A new policy is issued before the company issuing the new policy surrenders the old policy. This procedure ensures that the insured is covered by at least one policy during the transaction. If the old policy was surrendered before the new one was issued, and the insured died during the exchange process, there would be no coverage.

5. If the requested exchange is not a valid life to life, endowment, or annuity exchange or if the

issuance of the new policy is declined (or issued "rated" or issued at a premium or under terms other than as applied for), the insured should be notified immediately by the insurer.

6. If the new policy is issued, the old policy is then surrendered. The insured should then receive a letter from the insurer stating the Section 1035 cost basis of the new policy and the amount of any "boot" reportable as income.

    Form 1099R (Total Distributions From Profit-Sharing, Retirement Plans, Individual Retirement Arrangements, Insurance Contracts, etc.) is sent by the insurer to the IRS showing basis and distribution as well as the taxable amount for each policy surrendered by the insurer in a Section 1035 exchange. If a policy surrendered as part of a Section 1035 exchange had no loan at the time of surrender, no entry will be made in the "taxable income" box.

Planners should be aware of the pros and cons of the "inside" versus the "outside" procedure in the exchange of policies. The major advantage of the inside approach is safety and reliability of tax result. Although there appears to be nothing in the Internal Revenue Code or regulations as to how a Section 1035 exchange must be structured, the IRS appears to be comfortable with this procedure. The disadvantage is that the insurer that issued the old contract may take an undue amount of time to process the new company's request for surrender proceeds. Both normal time delay and a healthy resistance to a loss of business and an attempt to buy time to conserve the business may result in an inordinate amount of aggravation and uncertainty.

The outside procedure involves a surrender of the old contract by the client. The cash proceeds are used immediately to purchase a new contract from the new insurer. The advantage of the outside approach is that it is faster and simpler than the inside technique. But it is almost certain to result in a claim by the IRS that the policyholder had actual or constructive receipt of the proceeds and should therefore be taxed on the gain.

EXCHANGES INVOLVING LOANS

As mentioned above, if all the policyowner receives is the new policy, generally no gain will be realized if all the IRC Section 1035 requirements are met. But even if all the IRC Section 1035 requirements are met, if the policyowner receives the new policy and cash "to boot," the cash will be taxable to the extent of any gain.[26] So where any of the surrender proceeds from the old policy are paid in cash to the policyholder, that amount will be taxable to the extent of gain.

Extinction of indebtedness is boot. Surrender proceeds include payment of any outstanding loans on the old policy at surrender. That is, if a loan on the old contract is paid off pursuant to the exchange, the retirement or assumption of that liability is treated as boot.[27] Why? It would be very easy to avoid tax on a life insurance policy surrender if there were no such rule.

Example: Z had paid $80,000 in premiums for a life insurance policy on his life. The policy cash values total $100,000 so the policy has a built-in gain of $20,000. Were there no boot rule that applied on the extinction of debt, Z could first borrow $99,000 and then make a tax deferred Section 1035 exchange, and when the old policy was surrendered by the new insurer and the net equity of $1,000 paid to Z, only $1,000 (the cash boot received by Z) would be taxable.

Because extinction of indebtedness is boot, if there is a policy loan on the old policy, the exchange agreement should provide that the loan (including any accrued loan interest) is outstanding and that the new carrier will assume the liability on the loan and the new policy will serve as security for that loan. In other words to the extent the old debt is not carried over to the new policy, the policyowner will be subjected to current income tax. On the other hand to the extent the property received in the exchange is substantially a continuation of the old investment, no income is recognized. So when there is indebtedness against the old policy, if possible it should be exchanged for a new policy subject to the same amount of debt. The transaction will not result in a current tax.[28]

This favorable result will apply even if one policy is exchanged for another subject to the same indebtedness and the client was planning to make withdrawals or partial surrenders from the policy to reduce the debt.[29] An alternative is for the client to use other cash assets or borrow money from a bank or from other life insurance policies to pay off the debt. That way, there will be no loan outstanding and the problem is eliminated. The payment increases the cash values of the new policy so that after the exchange, the client can borrow the same amount out.

What about exchanges of minimum deposit plans? What pitfalls apply here? Since an income tax deduction for consumer loan interest is no longer available, non-business policyholders who have systematically "minimum deposited" (taken out maximum loans to pay premiums) and maintained a low after-tax outlay through deductible interest payments can no longer deduct interest outlays. To many, this disallowance of the interest deduction made the cost of continuing the policy (depending on the size of the outstanding loan) prohibitive. Of course, the client could continue to borrow more money from the policy but eventually substantial payments would be required to keep the policy in force. If the policy lapses, the lapse may be considered a taxable event.

Some companies have created "policy loan rollovers," cash value riders that facilitate a Section 1035 exchange as an alternative to a continuation of borrowing, a lapse of the old policy, or the surrender of the old policy followed by a purchase of a new policy. In essence the existing loan is "rolled" into the new policy. It appears that a loan transferred from the old policy to the new policy does not amount to a taxable distribution (boot). The client's basis in the old policy is carried over intact into the new policy and there is no taxable boot (because the loan is not canceled).[30]

How should exchanges of trade or business-owned insurance be handled? A trade or business can take an income tax deduction for interest incurred on a life insurance policy loan. With respect to policies purchased on or before June 21, 1986, there is no limitation as to the amount of the deduction. That liberal rule no longer applies to newly-issued policies. Now, with regard to policies purchased after June 20, 1986, interest deductions are either denied or severely limited.[31] (See the discussion in Appendix F under Policy Loan Interest.)

A grandfathering provision continues the unlimited deduction for interest payable on a life insurance policy loan incurred by a trade or business for policies issued before this date. The question is, will the grandfathering be lost if the policy is now exchanged? The answer is both yes and no. The new policy will probably be treated as just that, a new policy, if it is issued by a new insurer. However, if the new policy received in exchange is issued by the original insurer, the grandfathering protection may continue.

EXCHANGES INVOLVING QUALIFIED PENSION OR PROFIT SHARING PLANS

If a qualified pension or profit sharing plan owned a life insurance policy and exchanged it for one of the permissible types, it could qualify under IRC Section 1035 for a tax-deferred exchange. But as a tax exempt entity,[32] it does not need to qualify under the IRC Section 1035 safe harbor.

However, another and much more serious problem is possible with respect to a seemingly innocuous exchange. Specifically, if a qualified plan exchanges a whole life policy for a universal life product, it might violate the rule requiring that a qualified plan must exist primarily to provide retirement benefits to participants and that life insurance, while permissible, must be incidental.[33] The problem is that if certain percentages are exceeded (49.9% of total aggregate contributions to the plan for "ordinary life" and 25% for all other than ordinary life), the plan may be disqualified.

Some industry experts believe that universal life products should be considered "other than ordinary" life products. This is a dangerous situation since, as mentioned above, what appears to be a routine exchange could result in a disqualification of the entire plan.

FATAL FLAW CHECKLIST

The following is a checklist of the major tax traps incurred in Section 1035 exchanges:

1. *Failure to meet "same insured" requirement* – The tax deferred nature of a Section 1035 exchange presumes that both the old and the new contract are on the life of the same insured.[34] In the case of an exchange of annuity contracts the contracts exchanged must be payable to the same person or persons.[35]

   A taxable event will occur if the policies are on the lives of different insureds. For instance, a wife cannot exchange a policy on her life for a similar policy on the life of her husband. It is permissible, however, for the exchange to involve the policies of two different insurance companies. (There is no rule that requires the insurer of the new contract received in the exchange to be the same as the insurer of the old contract.)

   A "Change of Insureds Provision" (also called "Substitution of Insureds" Option or "Business Exchange Rider") allows a business to purchase a policy on one individual (typically a key employee or shareholder) but if that person leaves the firm, the firm has the option to substitute another key employee as the insured under the policy. The provision is advantageous because it does not require the policyowner business to incur new costs but the insurer does usually require medical evidence of the new person's insurability.

But the exercise of a change of insured option is a taxable event because it does not meet the "same insured" requirement.[36] Instead, when a new individual becomes insured under the old policy, a taxable event has occurred because the IRS treats the transaction as a surrender of the old contract. It's as if the policy on the terminating executive had been canceled.

The employer is liable for the difference between the policy's cash surrender value and the amount of premium the employer paid. Such riders will continue to be highly useful despite this unfavorable taxation since it takes the form of an option that can be used only when it is deemed appropriate by the client's advisers and the tax costs are minimal.

It is the opinion of the authors that the same insured logic would prevent a tax deferral when a single life is exchanged in return for a joint life contract or visa versa. The essence of a life insurance contract is the life that is insured under it. Therefore, when a contract goes from one life to two or two lives to one, the "same insured" test could not be met.

It is permissible, however, to exchange two contracts for one – as long as they are all on the same life. For example, suppose an individual wants to exchange a non-participating flexible premium life insurance policy with an adjustable death benefit, issued by company A, and a similar contract issued by company B solely for a non-participating flexible premium variable deferred annuity contract issued by company C. The IRS has held that IRC Section 1035 allows for situations other than only a one for one exchange. The Service pointed out in a private letter ruling that IRC Section 1031 (which deals with real estate exchanges) allows exchanges of more than one property for one property and also that, unless the specific words or context indicates to the contrary, words stated in the singular can be construed in the plural.[37]

2. *Poor timing* – Another fatal flaw is where there has been something other than an "exchange"

of insurance contracts. The discussion above regarding the "mechanics of the exchange" implies that a major key to success is the timing and manner in which the transaction occurs; "neatness counts" in avoiding litigation. It is preferable (if not essential) that the existing contract be assigned to the insurer that will issue the new contract "in exchange." This evidences that the transaction was "in kind" rather than "in cash." Unfortunately, it is not always easy to discern between an exchange and a "surrender and purchase."

If the IRS takes an extremely conservative (harsh) view, it would hold that IRC Section 1035(a) would not apply if a new life insurance policy has been issued prior to the surrender of the old policy.[38] But as a practical matter, it would be foolish to surrender an in force policy before obtaining new coverage. To blindly require the surrender of the old before the issuance of the new policy is a "form over substance" mentality that would seem to defeat the Congressional purpose of IRC Section 1035: to allow a taxpayer to defer the reporting of income if he has merely substituted one policy for another without truly reducing the built-in gain in the policy to his possession. Perhaps the key to success is to keep the interval between the issuance of the new policy and the surrender of the old policy as short as is mechanically feasible.

3. *Failure to give up the old policy in exchange for the new contract* – For there to be an "exchange," the old policy must be relinquished by the policyholder. Where the taxpayer borrows on the old policy and sends the loan check from the old policy to the new insurer as a premium payment for the new policy (either with the old insurer or a new insurer), since the old policy is still in force (even though subject to the loan) IRC Section 1035 should not be available.

Closely akin to this problem is the failure to physically obtain the new policy in exchange for the old. For instance, suppose the IRS can show that the new policy was put in force through the payment of new premiums rather than from cash received from the surrender of the old policy. The IRS could argue that the new contract of insurance was not received in exchange for the old policy but rather in exchange for the first premium which was paid from an outside source. This would seem to be a red flag against company assignment forms which indicate that the first premium is to be paid with funds other than those received from the "old" contract and with the amount received upon the surrender of the old contract being applied to future premiums.

A partial exchange of contracts will be allowed in the proper circumstances. For example, in one case, the Tax Court held that a woman's exchange of only a portion of one annuity contract for an annuity contract issued by another company was a nontaxable exchange. When the court looked at the regulations promulgated under IRC Section 1035, it noted that in order for an exchange to qualify for nonrecognition treatment, it is required only that the contracts be of the same type, e.g., an annuity for an annuity and that the obligee under the two contracts be the same person. The regulations do not state any other requirements. The court noted that for deferral to be allowed, the only requirements are that (a) the contracts be of the same type and (b) that the obligee(s) be the same person(s). Here, the contract owner was in the same economic position after the exchange as she was in prior to the transaction. The same funds are invested in annuity contracts and none of the money was reduced to the taxpayer's possession. So the exchange remained nontaxable even though partial.[39]

4. *Exchanges of unexchangeable* – "Government policies" are technically owned by the government. Since they cannot be assigned, they cannot be exchanged and therefore cannot be protected under IRC Section 1035.

ALTERNATIVES

There is an alternative to almost every tool or technique in life insurance planning, each with its attendant advantages and disadvantages. Planners contemplating an IRC Section 1035 tax-deferred exchange of life insurance policies should also consider the judicious use of cash dividend options or reduced paid-up insurance. Cash dividends can be used to purchase new insurance coverage. Placing an old policy on "reduced paid-up" or "extended term" makes it possible to free up significant premiums that can then be used to purchase new coverage without surrendering existing contracts or facing the uncertainty inherent in an unsettled area.

CHAPTER ENDNOTES

1. See Let. Rul. 9017062. There, the IRS sanctioned the exchange of two individual life insurance policies for two participating interests in a GULP (group universal life insurance policy). The ruling noted that at no time did the insured have the chance to elect to receive cash or any other type of property in exchange for his individual policies.

2. Generally, there seems to be no requirement that the contracts have the same face amount but care should be taken to assure that overall the new contract is not significantly more valuable than the old one so as to permit an argument that the difference should be taxable to the policyholder. See IRC Secs. 1035(d)(1), 1031(b).

3. See Manno and Nolan, "Internal Revenue Code Section 1035 and the Other Side of Exchange Programs," *Journal of the American Society of CLU & ChFC*, November 1985, p. 66.

4. There is no logical reason for the IRS to prohibit the exchange of multiple policies and there does not appear to be a prohibition. However, some commentators argue that the use of the term "exchange" implies a one-for-one transaction. But see Letter Ruling 9708016 discussed below.

5. See Mercer, "The Life Insurance Revolution: New Reasons for Using Section 1035 Exchanges," *Estates, Gifts, & Trusts Journal* 65 (March 14, 1991) and the follow-up entitled "Section 1035 Life Insurance Exchanges: Case Study" published in the May 9, 1991 issue of the *Estates, Gifts, & Trusts Journal* on page 112.

6. IRC Sec. 61.

7. IRC Sec. 72(e); Treas. Reg. §1.72-11(d). Taxable sales or exchanges of policies do not qualify for capital gain or loss treatment. See *W. Stanley Barrett v. Comm.*, 42 TC 993 (1964), aff'd 348 F.2d 916 (1st Cir. 1965).

8. The definition of life insurance is fairly broad and it appears to make no difference if the contracts exchanged are different varieties such as variable or universal or are whole life and limited pay. (See Rev. Rul. 68-235, 1968-1 CB 360.) Also, changes from individual to group do not seem to pose a problem. See Let. Rul. 9017062.

    At this point, it is not clear as to the direction the IRS would take on an exchange of term coverage into some form of permanent coverage such as ordinary or universal life. It is the authors' opinion that the IRS will claim that this is an attempt to artificially extend the tax free nature of the contract and will claim that such exchanges should not be afforded Section 1035 protection. However, the authors also feel this position is not justified by the Code itself.

9. IRC Sec. 1035(b)(3).

10. IRC Sec. 1035(b)(1).

11. IRC Sec. 1035(b)(2). Revenue Ruling, 68-235, 1968-1 CB 360, and Revenue Ruling, 72-358, 1972-2 CB 473, state that the exchange of a life insurance policy, endowment contract, or fixed annuity contract for a variable annuity contract with the same company or a different company qualifies as a tax-deferred exchange under IRC Section 1035(a).

12. IRC Sec. 1035(a)(2).

13. IRC Sec. 1035(a)(2).

14. IRC Sec. 1035(a)(3).

15. In TAM 8905004 the taxpayer purchased an annuity from an insurance company. Later, through a series of transactions, the taxpayer received both an annuity contract and a life insurance

contract in exchange. The IRS held that the transaction was governed by the "step transaction" doctrine. The IRS therefore re-characterized the transaction as an exchange of annuity contracts with the taxpayer receiving "boot" in the form of a life insurance contract. The taxpayer was therefore charged with income to the extent of the fair market value of the life insurance contract he received.

16. Treas. Reg. §1.1031(b)-1(c).

17. See Treas. Reg. §1.1035-1.

18. It is thought by some that the exchange is fully taxable even if the new policy is issued as of the old policy's original issue date and pursuant to a plan exchange option. See Lynch, "Exchanges of Insurance Policies Under Internal Revenue Code Section 1035: The Myths and the Realities," *Journal of the American Society of CLU & ChFC*, October, 1983, p. 32.

19. *Charles Cutler Parsons v. Comm.*, 16 TC 256 (1951); *W. Stanley Barrett v. Comm.*, 348 F.2d 916 (1st. Cir. 1965) *aff'd* 42 TC 993; Rev. Rul. 54-264 1954-2 CB 57; Reg. §25.2512-6(a), Example 3.

20. Rev. Rul. 59-195, 1959-1 CB 18; Treas. Reg. §25.2512-6(a), Example 4.

21. See Friedman, "Section 1035 Exchanges and Modified Endowment Contracts", *Journal of the American Society of CLU & ChFC*, July 1989, p. 62 for an excellent discussion of this topic.

22. IRC Sec. 7702A(a)(2).

23. Let. Rul. 9044022. See H.R. Conf. Rep. No. 100-1104, (TAMRA '88) *reprinted in* 1988-3 CB 596.

24. See Rev. Rul. 72-358, 1972-2 CB 473, Let. Ruls. 8344029, 8343010, 8501012, 8526038, 8741052, 9233054. Compare Let. Ruls. 8310033, 8515063. See Lynch, "Exchanges of Insurance Policies Under Internal Revenue Code Section 1035: The Myths and the Realities", *Journal of the American Society of CLU & ChFC*, October 1983, p. 32.

25. Rev. Rul. 90-24, 1990-1 CB 97.

26. IRC Secs. 1035(d)(1), 1031(b), 1031(c).

27. See Treas. Reg. §1.1031(b)-1(c).

28. Let. Ruls. 8604033, 8816015.

29. Let. Rul. 8816015.

30. Let. Rul. 8604033.

31. IRC Sec. 264(a)(4).

32. IRC Sec. 401.

33. Treas. Reg. §1.401-1(b)(1)(ii).

34. Treas. Reg. §1.1035-1.

35. Treas. Reg. §1.1035-1. In the authors' opinion, this suggests that in an exchange of an annuity for another annuity the obligee (or obligees) under the contracts must be the same. If an old annuity contract has no contingent annuitant, it cannot safely be exchanged for one in which there is a contingent annuitant. It is good practice to make sure that in each exchange situation that the parties (and their rights) are identical both before and after the transaction.

36. Rev. Rul. 90-109, 1990-2 CB 191. Note that this ruling does not appear to imply that IRC Section 7702 grandfathering is lost by exercise of the option.

37. IRC Sec. 1035(b); Rev. Rul. 85-159, 1985-1 CB 29; Let. Rul. 9708016; Let. Rul. 9644016.

38. For instance, See Let. Rul. 8810010.

39. *Conway v. Comm.*, 111 TC No. 20 (1998). The Service has also ruled on the proper way to allocate investment in the contract when one annuity is "split up" into two annuities. Rev. Rul. 2003-76, 2003-33 IRB 355. The Service has also said that it is considering issuing regulations to prevent abuse when one annuity is split into two annuities using Section 1035. Notice 2003-51, 2003-33 IRB 361.

TAXATION OF BENEFITS

"Bottom line" planning requires that a client focus only on the financial security he (or his beneficiaries) will have "below the line." This forces a concentration on the impact of taxes and other reasons for "slippage" in retaining and transferring income and wealth. If the planner and client cannot identify where losses will occur, they cannot take the proper steps to avoid, reduce, or compensate for those outflows. The consequential result of not understanding the forces that erode income and wealth and taking the proper action is obvious.

This appendix will cover two areas with respect to life insurance:

1. taxation of benefits during the insured's lifetime; and

2. taxation of benefits at the insured's death.

Because of their particular importance to planners, the subjects of estate, gift, and generation-skipping taxation, IRC Section 1035 exchanges, and transfers for value all are covered in separate appendices.

No deduction is allowed for premiums paid on any life insurance policy when the taxpayer is directly (or indirectly) a beneficiary under the policy. In fact, with the exception of an employer's deduction for premiums to pay group term life insurance, there is no situation where life insurance premiums, per se, are directly deductible. There are, of course, situations such as a donor's charitable gifts of money to pay premiums and an employer's bonus or compensation to an employee that takes the form of life insurance premiums. But in each of these cases, the deduction, to be allowed, must meet charitable or ordinary and necessary business expense tests and in neither case is the deduction allowed because the gift or payment is life insurance.[1]

TAXATION DURING THE INSURED'S LIFETIME

Life Insurance Defined

All currently issued contracts[2] must contain elements of both risk shifting and risk distribution in order to be considered "life insurance" and be taxed for federal purposes according to the rules that follow.[3] Currently issued contracts must also meet IRC Section 7702 requirements of either a "cash value accumulation" test or fall within a "cash value corridor" and meet certain guideline premium requirements.[4] These tests are incredibly complex and require actuarial determinations beyond the practical ability of most practitioners. It is wise, therefore, in the case of a large policy to obtain a written assurance from the home office of the insurer that the contract will in fact meet the current definition of life insurance in all respects and will continue to do so.

If a contract meets the definition of life insurance, the year by year increase in cash surrender value will not be subject to current income taxation. If the contract is not considered life insurance, each year the policyowner will be taxed on the annual increase in the policy's value.

Cash Value Increases

As noted above, as the cash value in a policy grows each year, the owner of the policy is not currently taxed on the increase.[5] No current income tax is payable no matter how large the internal build up may be.

Dividends

Dividends are considered the result of favorable insurer experience in mortality, income, and loading that make possible a return of a policyowner's outlay and are usually income tax free. Until total dividends received exceed the policyowner's cost, whether or not the policy is paid up, these distributions are income tax free regardless of whether received in the form of cash, used to purchase "paid-up additions," one year term insurance, or left to accumulate at interest. But any interest earned under this last alternative will be taxable in the year it is earned.[6]

Once dividends, together with any other nontaxable distributions, exceed the premiums paid by the policyowner, the excess is taxable each year at ordinary income rates.[7] In other words, once a policyowner has recovered his investment in the contract (generally total premiums less any tax-free distributions received), dividends as well as any other distributions are taxable as ordinary income.

Election to Make Policy Paid–Up

A policyowner can elect to make an existing contract "paid-up" by applying cash values to, in effect, purchase a single premium permanent plan of the same type as the existing plan but with a lowered death benefit. Since the cash values are never either actually or constructively received by the policyowner at that time, no gain must be recognized and the transaction results in no income taxation. However, if an outstanding loan is reduced during this transaction, the policyowner may incur some taxation.

National Service Life Insurance

No gain realized during the policyowner's lifetime from government life insurance is subject to income tax. The income enjoyed at the surrender or maturity of such a policy or any paid-up additional insurance is completely free of income tax.[8] Dividends paid from these policies are exempt,[9] as are those from other nongovernment issued contracts. Furthermore, interest on dividends is also income tax free.[10]

Policy Withdrawals

A withdrawal is the partial surrender of a policy. A policyowner will not have taxable income until withdrawals (including previous withdrawals and other tax free distributions from the policy such as dividends) made from the cash reserves of a "flexible premium" (i.e., universal or adjustable life) policy exceed the policyowner's cost (accumulated premiums). Until the policyowner has recovered his aggregate premium cost, he will generally be allowed to receive withdrawals tax free under what is known as the "cost-recovery first" rule.

But, this income tax liability is accelerated if a cash distribution occurs within 15 years of the policy's issue and that distribution is coupled with a reduction in the policy's contractual death benefits. A withdrawal within 15 years of policy issuance coupled with a drop in death benefits triggers income. Subject to a statutory ceiling, all the income growth in the cash surrender value is deemed to have been received by the policyowner.[11]

Once the 15-year period expires, no immediate taxation will occur upon a withdrawal.

This 15-year rule does not apply to policies issued prior to 1985. Nor does this 15-year rule apply to policy loans. This is because loans are not treated as distributions and do not reduce policy death benefits.

A notable exception to the cost-recovery rule applies to life insurance contracts classified as modified endowment contracts (MECs) which are covered in more detail in Appendix D. Generally, distributions from MECs are taxed under the interest-first rule which provides that the first distributions out of the contract are deemed to be taxable interest.

Surrender, Redemption or Maturity of a Policy

Gain, in the form of ordinary income,[12] is realized in many surrender, redemption, or maturity situations. These include:

1. *Lump sum cash-in* – The excess of the amount received by a policyholder in the complete surrender of a policy (or upon its redemption or maturity) over the policyowner's "investment in the contract" (i.e., cost) is taxable as ordinary income.[13] The policyowner determines the amount of lump sum payable and then subtracts from it the "cost" of the contract.

   A "lump sum" generally includes the cash value of paid-up additions, dividend accumulations, termination dividend, and unrepaid policy loans. Any interest previously paid on policy dividends that has already been taxed reduces taxable amount of the lump sum.

   Generally, "cost" is net premiums (gross premiums less the total of tax-free dividends received by the policyowner). Any dividends paid by the insurer that were accumulated at interest or used to purchase paid-up additional insurance must be included in the lump sum amount as part of the policyowner's cost.

2. *Interest only option* – If the lifetime proceeds are left intact with the insurer to earn interest, that interest is taxable each year as received or credited.[14] The gain on the proceeds is taxable immediately (assuming it can be withdrawn by the policyowner) even if the "interest only" election is made prior to surrender or maturity.

A policyowner's "investment in the contract" is defined as the total premiums (or other consideration) paid less the total amount of nontaxable distributions (i.e., dividends, unrepaid loans, and tax free withdrawals) received.[15]

Thus, investment in the contract includes:

1. Dividends used to purchase paid-up additions (actually, the cash values in paid-up additions are part of the "amount realized" by the policyowner and, thus, do not reduce his investment in the contract).

2. The economic benefit reportable income from the term insurance portion benefit received under a qualified retirement plan.[16]

These items would not be included in the investment in the contract:

1. premiums for disability income:

2. premiums for accidental death benefits;

3. premiums for waiver of premium;[17] and

4. interest paid on policy loans.[18]

Annuity Taxation

An annuity is a systematic liquidation of principal and interest over a fixed or contingent period of time.[19] Thus, the term "annuity" includes payments for a fixed period or payments of a fixed amount in addition to payments lasting for one or more lives. Payments of "interest only" will not qualify for annuity taxation because there is no liquidation of principal.[20]

"Amounts received as an annuity" are taxed under special rules that allow the annuitant to exclude from tax a fixed (return of cost) portion of each payment from gross income each year and require the payment of income tax at ordinary rates on the balance of each payment. Stated in another manner, a fixed portion of each payment received can be excluded from income as a return of capital while the balance of each payment is reportable as taxable income. See Chapter 8, "Annuities" for a complete discussion of these taxation rules.

Deductibility of Premium Payments

No deduction is allowed for the premiums paid on a personally owned life insurance policy, regardless of who is the premium payor or who is the policyowner. Such outlays are considered a nondeductible personal expense.[21] This rule applies even where the owner of the policy is someone other than the insured.

Business policyowners generally fare no better. No deduction is allowed for premiums paid on any life insurance policy if the taxpayer is directly or indirectly a beneficiary under the policy.[22] This "all or nothing"[23] prohibition blocks the deduction of premiums even if they would otherwise be deductible as ordinary and necessary business expenses.[24]

Policy Loan Interest

Depending on the disbursements of the loan to specific expenditures, the IRS will classify interest incurred on a loan as: (a) trade or business interest; (b) investment or passive activity interest; or (c) personal interest.[25]

1. *Trade or business situations* – Contracts purchased before June 21, 1986 are not subject to any limit on deductibility of interest.[26] Severe limitations on interest deductions apply in all other policy loan situations making it almost impossible to obtain an interest deduction.

   After 1996 legislation, the general rule of nondeductibility for policy loan interest on company owned policies does not apply to policy loan interest paid on policies insuring a "key person" up to $50,000 of indebtedness. A key person is an officer or 20% owner of the taxpayer. The number of persons who may be treated as a key person is limited to the greater of: (1) five persons; or (2) the lesser of 5% of the total officers and employees or 20 individuals. Generally, this rule of nondeductibility is applicable to interest paid or accrued after October 13, 1995, but there are several transitional provisions.[27]

   Additionally, the Internal Revenue Code imposes an interest rate cap for interest paid or accrued after December 31, 1995. Interest in excess of that which would have been paid had the "applicable rate of interest" been used cannot be deducted. The applicable rate of interest is that rate described in Moody's Corporate Bond Yield Average – Monthly Average Corporates as published by Moody's Investors Service. The Code also specifies a manner in which to determine the applicable rate of interest for pre-1996 contracts.[28]

After 1997, the rule concerning the deduction of policy loan interest states that no deduction shall be allowed for "... any interest paid or accrued on any indebtedness with respect to 1 or more life insurance policies owned by the taxpayer covering the life of any individual."[29]

Although the exception from the general disallowance rule for policies on key employees and the interest rate caps put in place by 1996 legislation remain unchanged, 1997 legislation added a new provision[30] which generally provides that no deduction will be allowed for the part of the taxpayer's interest expense that is "allocable to unborrowed policy cash values." This portion that is "allocable to unborrowed policy cash values" is an amount that bears the same ratio to the interest expense as the taxpayer's average unborrowed policy cash values of life insurance policies and annuity and endowment contracts issued after June 8, 1997 bears to the sum of: (1) in the case of assets that are life policies or annuity or endowment contracts, the average unborrowed policy cash values; and (2) in the case of assets of the taxpayer that do not fall into this category, the average adjusted bases of such assets.

"Unborrowed policy cash value" is defined as the excess of the cash surrender value of a policy or contract (determined without regard to surrender charges) over the amount of the loan with respect to the policy or contract.

Finally, there is an exception to the general rule of nondeductibility of interest expense allocable to unborrowed policy cash values. The exception applies to policies and contracts owned by entities if the policy covers only one individual who, at the time first covered by the policy, is: (1) a 20% owner of the entity; or (2) an individual who is an officer, director or employee of the trade or business. A policy or contract will not fail to come within this exception simply because it covers both the owner and the owner's spouse. Apparently, spouses of officers, directors, or employees who are not also 20% owners cannot be covered and still have the policy or contract qualify for this exception.

2. *Investment or passive activity situations* – In the authors' opinion where the policyowner can document that the proceeds of a policy loan were used to purchase an investment or expended on a passive activity, the interest should be considered investment interest or passive activity interest. For instance, if a policy loan was used to help the policyowner purchase land to be used for development, the loan interest should be deductible subject to investment interest limitations.[31]

3. *Personal situations* – In personal situations, the rule is simple and absolute. Interest on a policy loan is not deductible if it is neither trade or business nor investment interest.[32]

4. *Single premium contracts* – Even if a deduction is otherwise allowable, no deduction is allowed for interest paid or accrued on indebtedness incurred to purchase or continue in effect a single premium life insurance contract.[33] The term "single premium" is defined broadly. Essentially it is a policy on which substantially all the premiums are paid within four years of the date the policy was purchased or a policy on which an amount is deposited with the insurer for the payment of a substantial number of premiums.[34]

The interest deduction prohibition applies to existing as well as to newly-issued policies. If an existing policy which falls into the definition of "single premium" is pledged as collateral for a loan, it is likely that interest on that loan will not be deductible.[35]

5. *Financing the policy through policy loans* – Generally, even if a deduction is otherwise allowable, when premium payments are financed through policy loans, no deduction is allowed for interest payments.[36] There are four exceptions to this general rule:

Four-out-of-seven premiums paid without borrowing (the "four-out-of-seven" rule) – As its name implies, if no part of four of the first seven years' annual premium, measured after the date of issue (or after the last "substantial increase in premiums" if later) are paid through a loan, the interest deduction will be allowed (if otherwise deductible).[37] Stated in the reverse manner, if more than three premiums are borrowed during the first seven policy years (or during the first seven years after the last "substantial increase in premiums), even if the interest would otherwise be deductible, it may not be deducted. Once the four-out-of-seven test is failed, not only are prior interest deductions lost but all future deductions are barred as well.

Repayment of the loans during or after the seven-year period will not wash the taint. Once the four-out-of-seven rule is violated by the payment of more than three premiums by loans, interest can never qualify for a deduction.[38] Nor can the taint be removed by a gift or even a sale of the policy. The new owner carries over both payments by loan and payments by debt from the prior owner. So if the old owner borrowed two years' premiums, the new owner can borrow only one more without jeopardizing the interest deduction. Conversely, if the old owner had paid four premiums without borrowing, the new owner can borrow all of the next three years' premiums. The bottom line is that a new seven-year period does not begin merely because of a change of ownership.[39]

If the seven-year rule is met during the first seven years, there is no limit to the amount that can be borrowed in subsequent years (assuming no "substantial increase"[40]) in premiums. This means the policyowner could borrow the policy's entire cash value for any purpose whatsoever every year starting in the eighth policy year. Assuming the interest was otherwise deductible, it would not be barred by the tax prohibition regarding financing of premiums through loans.

Most experts feel that the IRS would not bar interest deductions on loans from universal life contracts merely because there is no specified premium that must be paid during each of the first seven years. Some say that the safest course of action is for the policyowner to pay four out of the first seven of the lowest premiums necessary to sustain the policy. Others say that no borrowing is permissible in a universal life policy.

The $100 exception – Even if there is found to be a systematic plan of borrowing to pay premiums, the interest deduction will not be disallowed if the interest does not exceed $100 for the policyowner's taxable year. This is an "all or nothing" exception. The entire deduction, not merely the excess, will be disallowed if the interest incurred in a year is more than $100.[41] So, for most business-owned policies, this exception is a minor one.

The unforeseen events exception – A deduction is not disallowed even if there is a loan and even if that loan is used to pay premiums if the reason for the systematic plan of borrowing was either that (a) there was an unforeseen substantial increase in the policyowner's financial liability or (b) the policyowner suffered an unforeseen substantial loss in income.

The interest deduction will be disallowed if the economic shock was foreseeable at the time the policy was purchased.[42] For instance, college education or retirement expenses are both foreseeable events. On the other hand, a layoff or firing is not.

Trade or business exception – An otherwise allowable interest deduction will not be disallowed if the loan was incurred in connection with the taxpayer's trade or business. But this requires that the policyowner prove that the amounts borrowed against the life insurance contract were actually used for business purposes. Business purposes, however, do not include outlays for key employee, buy-sell coverage, split dollar agreements, or retirement plans. Thus, the policyowner must be able to document (perhaps by a tracing of cash flows showing how the funds were used) not only an indebtedness but also a business purpose other than the purchase of cash value life insurance.[43]

The IRS will look at all the facts and circumstances of each case. If it finds that other business loans increase annually by the same amount as the premiums on a new policy, it will probably disallow the interest deduction. But probably the interest deduction on regular business loans (for instance indebtedness to purchase new equipment) will not be disallowed merely because the business used money in a year to buy life insurance instead of paying off or paying down the loan.

6. *Interest paid on conversion of a term policy* – Where a term policy is converted into a permanent contract, in some cases that conversion is made on an "original age" basis. This means the new contract is issued as though the policy were originally permanent coverage. The advantage is that premiums will be much lower than if the new policy were issued on an "attained age" basis. But to restore the insurer to where it would have been had the policy really been issued at the insured's original age, the policyowner must pay "back premiums" plus interest (the difference between the premiums

that have actually been paid on the term policy and the premiums that would have been paid on the permanent policy had it been issued instead of the term contract plus interest on that difference at a specified annual rate). This interest is not deductible.[44]

7. *Policy loan to purchase tax exempt securities* – No deduction is allowed for interest on a loan incurred or continued to purchase or carry tax exempt securities. If the loan is taken out to finance the purchase of any type of tax exempt asset, an interest deduction is barred. On the other hand, if the deduction is otherwise allowable, it will not be blocked merely because the policyowner also held tax exempt securities.[45]

Timing of Interest Deduction

In those rare cases where policy loan interest is allowable as a deduction, the timing of the deduction becomes important. Some of the basic rules concerning the timing of the interest deduction and the party who can take it:

1. Accrual basis policyowners take the deduction in the year interest "accrues" even if payment of the interest has not been made in that year.[46]

2. Cash basis policyowners take the deduction only in the year that the interest is paid.[47]

3. Only the policyowner may take a deduction and only if the policyholder has paid the interest. A father, for example, cannot pay and deduct interest on a policy owned by his son nor can a shareholder pay and deduct interest on a policy owned by his corporation.[48] But interest otherwise deductible will not be disallowed if the loan (including interest) reduces the benefit paid at an insured's death. The IRS will treat the situation as though interest were paid at the time of the insured's death.[49]

4. An assignee cannot deduct interest that accrued before the policy was transferred to him.[50]

Taxation of Policyowner or Insured in Business Situations

If the employer is directly or indirectly the beneficiary of the insurance contract, the insured-employee is not taxed on the corporation's payment of policy premiums.[51]

But the policyowner may be subject to income tax in a number of situations. These include:

1. Where an insured's employer pays premiums on a policy owned by employee (or employee's third party assignee) and proceeds are paid to employee's named beneficiary or estate.[52]

2. Where the proceeds of a policy owned by the corporation are payable to the personal beneficiary or estate of an employee.[53]

Where a corporate owned policy will be used to fund a stock redemption agreement in which the corporation will use the proceeds to buy back its own stock, premiums the corporation pays will not be taxed to any shareholder.

Where a policy to fund a buy-sell agreement is personally owned by a shareholder and the shareholder has named a personal beneficiary or designated his or her estate as recipient of policy proceeds, premium payments by the corporation may be considered a distribution of dividends.[54]

Likewise, where a policy on one person's life (e.g., another shareholder) is owned by a co-shareholder (for instance to fund a buy-sell agreement), premium payments made by the corporation will be considered dividends or compensation paid on a shareholder-employee's behalf.[55]

Taxation of Policyowner in Creditor Situation

If a creditor receives life insurance proceeds as payment of the debt, the IRS may claim that the proceeds should not be considered tax free life insurance proceeds.[56] For instance, in a collateral assignment (non-split dollar) case where a creditor must prove the existence and amount of debt in order to collect the proceeds, proceeds are received because of the indebtedness rather than because of the insured's death. Of course, the creditor could still receive the proceeds income tax free as a recovery of basis (the sum of any unpaid debt and premiums paid but not deducted) except to the extent the creditor already enjoyed a bad debt deduction.[57]

Taxation of Policyowner in Alimony Situations

Where the insured pays premiums on a life insurance policy pursuant to a divorce or separation agreement signed after 1984, payments are taxable as alimony to the non-insured spouse owner.[58]

Taxation of Advance Premium Deposits

A discount is allowed to a policyowner who pays premiums more than one year before they fall due. The IRS taxes the interest increment earned on those prepaid premiums.[59]

This makes the fund set aside by the policyowner and placed in the insurer's hands taxable before it is applied to pay premiums. Each year, as the interest on the remaining discounted fund is applied toward the payment of a new year's premium (or when it becomes available to be withdrawn by the policyowner without substantial restrictions or limitations), it is considered constructively received and therefore taxable. If the interest cannot be taken by the policyowner, it becomes taxable each year when it is applied toward the payment of the next due annual premium. If the policyowner cashes in a policy or it matures, the policyowner can lower taxable gain by any advance premiums paid and any interest increments that were already taxed. In other words, the policyowner can include in his basis the sum of discounted premiums plus interest upon which he paid tax.

Taxation of Accelerated Death Benefits

Amounts received under a life insurance contract on the life of a terminally ill insured or a chronically ill insured will be treated as an amount paid by reason of the death of the insured and are therefore not includable in the insured's gross income.

Amounts paid to a chronically ill individual are subject to the same limitations that apply to long-term care benefits. Generally, this is a $230 per day limitation (for 2004, as indexed for inflation). Accelerated death benefits paid to terminally ill individuals are not subject to this limit.

There are several special rules that apply to chronically ill insureds. Generally, the favorable tax treatment outlined above will not apply to any payment received for any period unless such payment is for costs incurred by the payee (who has not been compensated by insurance or otherwise) for qualified long-term care services provided to the insured for the period. Additionally, the terms of the contract under which such payments are made must comply with the requirements of IRC Section 7702B plus several other requirements.

"Terminally ill" is defined as an illness or physical condition that can reasonably be expected to result in death within 24 months following certification by a doctor. A chronically ill individual is a person who is not terminally ill and who has been certified by a physician as being unable to perform, without substantial assistance, at least two activities of daily living for at least 90 days or a person with a similar level of disability. Further, a person may be considered chronically ill if he requires substantial supervision to protect himself from threats to his health and safety due to severe cognitive impairment and this condition has been certified by a health care practitioner within the previous 12 months.

There is one exception to this general rule of non-includability for accelerated death benefits. The rules outlined above do not apply to any amount paid to any taxpayer other than the insured if the taxpayer has an insurable interest in the life of the insured because the insured is a director, officer or employee of the taxpayer or if the insured is financially interested in any trade or business of the taxpayer.

These provisions are effective for amounts received after December 31, 1996.[60]

Sale of a Life Insurance Policy

Gain on the sale of a life insurance contract is taxable as ordinary income.[61] Gain is determined as if the contract were surrendered by the policyowner. So the excess of the sales proceeds over the net premium cost (premiums paid less tax free dividends received) will be taxable. Generally, no loss deduction is allowed since most courts have characterized the portion of the policyowner's premium going toward pure insurance protection as a current expense rather than an investment. The balance of the premium is directed toward policy reserves so to the extent that policy reserves and cash value are the same, no loss has been incurred.[62]

If the policy is sold at less than its fair market value, the difference in this "bargain" sale may be taxable income to the buyer. For instance, if a business sells a key employee policy to the insured employee, the excess of the policy's fair market value over the price paid will be taxed to the buyer as additional compensation.

Suppose a corporation pays an annual premium today and then tomorrow sells a policy on an employee's life to her in return for an amount equal to its cash value. The difference between the value received and the amount paid is treated as a bonus to the employee. Since the policy's value will often exceed the cash surrender value, even a sale of a policy for its cash value on the last day of a policy year may result in taxable income to the employee.

These same rules apply where an employee or shareholder sells a policy to a corporation; ordinary income is realized by the seller to the extent that the value of the policy exceeds net premium cost.[63]

Corporate Distribution of Policy

In some situations, life insurance policies have been used by a corporation to "pay" for the purchase of stock or other assets. For instance, assume a corporation buys back its own stock or purchases land and in return pays for the purchase by distributing a life insurance policy on the life of the selling shareholder or landowner. Here, the transaction is considered an "exchange" of the policy for stock (or land).

The seller of the stock would realize gain equal to the excess of (1) the value of the policy over (2) the seller's basis in the stock (or land). That gain would be capital gain if the parties can prove that the policy was given in exchange for the property the corporation receives. Otherwise, the value of the policy might be treated as compensation if the "seller" was a common law employee or perhaps as a dividend if the "seller" was a shareholder.[64] Of course, if there was no consideration at all for the corporation's transfer of the policy, it would be taxable as compensation or as a dividend. For instance, where a buy-sell agreement required a corporation to distribute without cost a policy on the life of the surviving shareholder at the death of the first of two co-shareholders to die, the value of the policy was taxed as a dividend to the surviving shareholder.[65]

TAXATION AT AND AFTER THE INSURED'S DEATH

Implications of Meeting Definition

Essentially, what is defined as life insurance under income tax law will be treated as life insurance under federal tax law. If a contract meets the definition of life insurance, death benefits will be (generally[66]) exempt from income tax.[67]

Proceeds Payable at Insured's Death

Generally, the recipient of life insurance proceeds payable at the insured's death will receive those proceeds income tax free.[68] This favorable tax treatment applies even if the proceeds are paid to the insured's estate or to a corporation, partnership, trust, LLC, or other entity rather than to one or more individual(s). Proceeds are also income tax free regardless of whether paid in a lump sum or in installments, although any interest earned is taxable. Death benefits paid from term riders or paid-up additional insurance are likewise income tax free as are payments from an accidental death ("double indemnity") rider and group term life insurance. The exclusion is applicable regardless of who owned the policy or who paid premiums.

Proceeds Payable at a Date Later than Death

There are many times when life insurance policy proceeds are paid at a time later than the insured's death. Where that delay results in the payment of interest (as it almost always does), regardless of the reason for the delay, interest is taxed to the recipient at ordinary rates.[69] So no matter what the cause or who made the decision to postpone payment of the proceeds (the insured, the beneficiaries, or the insured's estate), interest is taxable at ordinary income tax rates.

Payments Taken in Installments

A beneficiary can choose to "settle" the debt owed by the insurer at the death of an insured in several forms other than a lump sum. The most common are the selection of payments for life (a "life income" option) and payments for a specified period of time (term certain). In either event, the amount of proceeds is systematically liquidated over the appropriate period of time. Part of each payment will be considered tax free and part will be taxable, in much the same way that annuity payments are taxed.[70]

The tax free portion is called the "amount held by the insurer." This is the total amount that may be recovered by the beneficiary income tax free. This consists of the face amount of the policy, supplementary insurance, and accumulated dividends if applied to increase guaranteed payments. When computing the ratio that follows, the value of a guarantee must be subtracted from the amount held by the insurer.

Taxable interest is determined through a subtractive method. First, calculate the principal (tax free) portion of each payment. Second, subtract that result from the payment. The difference is the taxable interest. The amount of each payment's income tax free principal portion is found by the following process:[71]

1. Compute the "amount held by the insurer";

2. Determine the number of years in the payment period;[72]

3. Divide the step one answer by the step two answer.

Life Income Option Elected

This tax free amount remains tax free regardless of how long the beneficiary lives. So even if the beneficiary outlives the life expectancy assumed in step two, these amounts remain income tax free. But anything in excess of the tax free principal calculated under this formula is taxable interest.[73]

Assume the beneficiary elected to take payments for life but agreed to take smaller amounts in return for the insurer's guarantee that if the beneficiary should die before receiving a specified amount of guaranteed payments, the balance would be paid to a secondary beneficiary. The secondary beneficiary would be allowed to receive the balance of the payment guaranteed by the insurer income tax free.[74]

For instance, assume a beneficiary is entitled to receive $80,000 but instead of a lump sum chooses to take $5,000 a year for life with the guarantee that regardless of when he dies, payments will continue until at least that amount has been paid out. Assume that the commuted value of the refund guarantee by the insurer is $15,000. This would lower the "amount held by the insurer" to $65,000 ($80,000 - $15,000). If the beneficiary has a 30-year life expectancy, the excludable amount would be about $2,167 ($65,000 ÷ 30). This would leave about $2,833 of each $5,000 payment ($5,000 - $2,167) taxable at ordinary income rates. If the beneficiary died before receiving the full $80,000, the balance of that guaranteed amount would be received tax free by the secondary beneficiary.

Fixed Period Option Elected

A beneficiary can choose to take the insurance proceeds in installments over a number of years. The total amount of proceeds – plus interest – is paid pro-rata over the fixed period. The same three step procedure used above to determine nontaxable and taxable amounts in the case of a life income option is used here. The number of installment payments to be made in the fixed period is "the number of years in the payment period."

Fixed Amount Option Elected

Here, the beneficiary selects an amount to be paid to him each month (or year). The length of time over which the lump sum will be paid depends on the size of the proceeds and the amount selected to be paid. Once again, the three step procedure used above applies. In this case the "amount held by the insurer" is divided by the number of payments the insurer will guarantee based on the fixed amount selected. The number of payments is that number which, using the insurer's guaranteed interest rate, is required to exhaust both principal and the guaranteed interest specified by the insurer. But if "excess interest" increases the number of payments, all additional payments made by the insurer after the guaranteed number of payments are fully taxable since the exclusion ratio no longer applies.

If the primary beneficiary dies before the end of the guaranteed payment period, the same amount of pro-rated principal can be excluded from gross income by the secondary beneficiary.[75]

Interest Only Option Elected

If the beneficiary chooses to leave the proceeds with the insurer and takes only interest, that interest is fully taxable but the proceeds are income tax free.[76] The result is the same even if the insured elected the interest only option. Generally, interest is taxable as soon as it is credited to the policy even if it is not in fact taken out by the beneficiary.[77]

Exception for Government Life Insurance

None of the interest element payable under a life income or installment settlement option is subject to income tax if the proceeds are payable under government life insurance.[78]

Exception to the General Rule for Transfer for Value

Where a policy or an interest in a policy is transferred in return for any type of valuable consideration in money or money's worth, the proceeds, except to the extent of the dollar value of that consideration and any premiums paid after the transfer by the new policyowner, lose their income tax free status. This extremely important rule is the subject of Appendix G.

Exception Where Proceeds Considered Compensation or Dividends

Often, the insured is an employee and/or a shareholder-employee of a corporation. Here, payment of the policy proceeds may be considered payment of compensation (deductible by the corporation and taxable as ordinary income in full to the recipient) or as the payment of a dividend (nondeductible by the corporation and taxable, at generally capital gain rates, to the extent of the corporation's earnings and profits to the recipient). The exact result will depend to a great extent upon facts, circumstances, and the existence or nonexistence of documentation of those facts and circumstances:

1. If the insured employee never reported income from the corporation's payment of premiums on a policy owned by the employee or a third party and it was discovered after his death by the IRS, the tax on the corporate-paid premiums plus interest and penalties would be payable by the employee's estate but the proceeds should remain income tax free. The income tax liability to the estate would be the same whether the payment was considered compensation or a dividend but if the payment was made on behalf of a shareholder-employee with respect to his stock, the premium payments would be considered nondeductible dividends.[79]

2. If the corporation owns and is beneficiary of the policy and pays all premiums, the proceeds will be received by the corporation income tax free (except to the extent of any corporate AMT). However, if it then pays out those proceeds for any reason to an employee (for instance in payment of the corporation's obligation under a nonqualified deferred compensation agreement), the payments would lose their life insurance status and be treated as taxable compensation.[80]

3. If the corporation owns the policy and pays all premiums but the proceeds are payable to an employee or employee-shareholder's beneficiary, payments would be considered compensation in the case of a common law employee or dividends in the case of a shareholder employee.[81]

In summary, where income is not reported during lifetime, at an insured's death where the corporation paid premiums on a policy payable to the insured employee's personal beneficiary or estate, the IRS will first argue that the proceeds are dividends (where the insured was a shareholder-employee) or compensation (where the insured held no stock). Failing that argument, the IRS will argue that the estate must pay income tax on the income that should have been reported during lifetime year after year. The IRS will likely assess interest and penalties on the unpaid tax as well.

The best solution is to name the corporation as owner and beneficiary of any insurance for which it pays premiums or to report corporate payments as bonuses year after year as the corporation pays premiums on a personally owned contract.

Exception Where Policy Owned by Qualified Retirement Plan

A portion of the proceeds equal to the cash surrender value of the policy immediately before the insured's death will be taxable as ordinary income when death benefits are paid from a qualified annuity plan or employee benefit trust at the death of the insured. The "net amount at risk" ("pure insurance") portion of the proceeds is income tax free.[82]

ENDNOTES

1. *Edward E. Thorpe and Co. v. Commissioner*, T.C. Memo. 1998-115 [1998 RIA TC Memo ¶98,115], Tax Ct. Dkt. No. 23900-95; IRC Sec. 264(a)(1).

2. No statutory definition must be met by a policy issued prior to January 1, 1985 assuming the policy is not a flexible premium contract. Internal Revenue Code section 7702(j) exempts certain plans or arrangements provided by churches to their employees or their beneficiaries from the requirement that the arrangement must meet the local law definition of life insurance.

3. See *Helvering v. LeGierse*, 312 U.S. 531 (1941). State law requirements must also be met. IRC Sec. 7702(a).

4. IRC Sec. 7702(a).

5. See *Theodore H. Cohen v. Comm.*, 39 TC 1055 (1963), acq. 1964-1 CB 4; *Abram Nesbitt II v. Comm.*, 43 TC 629 (1965).

6. As soon as there are no restrictions on a policyowner's right to receive the interest, under the doctrine of constructive receipt, it becomes taxable whether or not actually taken. Treas. Reg.

§1.451-2; *Theodore H. Cohen v. Comm.*, 39 TC 1055 (1963), acq. 1964-1 CB 4.

7. IRC Sec. 72(e)(5); Treas. Reg. §1.72-11(b)(1).

8. 38 U.S.C. §3101(a); Rev. Rul. 72-604, 1972-2 CB 35.

9. Rev. Rul. 71-306, 1971-2 CB 76.

10. Rev. Rul. 91-14, 1991-1 CB 18.

11. IRC Secs. 7702(f)(7)(A), 7702(f)(7)(B). This rule applies only to policies issued after 1984.

12. Capital gain is not available upon the surrender or maturity of a life insurance contract. See *Avery v. Comm.*, 111 F.2nd 19 (9th Cir. 1940); *Ralph Perkins v. Comm.*, 41 BTA 1225 (1940); *Blum v. Higgins*, 150 F.2nd 471 (2nd Cir. 1945).

13. IRC Sec. 72(e); Treas. Reg. §1.72-11(d).

14. IRC Sec. 72(j); Treas. Reg. §1.72-14(a).

15. IRC Sec. 72(c)(1); Treas. Reg. §1.72-6(a)(1).

16. Treas. Reg. §1.72-16(b).

17. Rev. Rul. 55-349, 1955-1 CB 232.

18. *Chapin v. McGowan*, 271 F.2nd 856 (2nd Cir. 1959).

19. Treas. Reg. §1.72-1(b).

20. Rev. Rul. 75-255, 1975-2 CB 22.

21. IRC Sec. 262; Treas. Reg. §1.262-1(b)(1).

22. IRC Sec. 264(a)(1).

23. Even if the premium payor may only receive a small part of the proceeds, if IRC Section 264(a)(1) applies, none of the premium is deductible. Rev. Rul. 66-203, 1966-2 CB 104.

24. Treas. Reg. §1.264-1(a)(1).

25. Temp. Treas. Reg. §1.163-8T.

26. See IRC Sec. 264(a)(4).

27. IRC Sec. 264; Health Insurance Portability and Accountability Act of 1996, Sec. 501.

28. IRC Sec. 264(e).

29. IRC Sec. 264(a)(4).

30. This provision is applicable to contracts issued after June 8, 1997. Taxpayer Relief Act of 1997, Sec. 1084; IRC Sec. 264(a); IRC Sec. 264(f).

31. Not all authorities agree. See Brody, Weinberg, Jansen, Asmar, and Kahn, *Federal Income Taxation of Life Insurance*, The American Bar Association, Real Property, Probate, and Trust Law Section, p. 50.

32. IRC Sec. 163(h)(1).

33. IRC Sec. 264(a)(2). This denial of deductibility applies for contracts purchased after March 1, 1954.

34. IRC Sec. 264(c). See *Frederick Dudderar v. Comm.*, 44 TC 632 (1965), acq. 1966-2 CB 4; *Campbell v. Cen-Tex Inc.*, 377 F.2d 688 (5th Cir. 1967).

35. See Rev. Rul. 79-41, 1979-1 CB 124.

36. IRC Sec. 264(a)(3). The Internal Revenue Service is attacking corporate-owned life insurance (COLI) interest deductions. Technical Advice Memorandum (TAM) 199901005 and Letter Ruling 9812005 are both situations where the IRS held that a corporation's deductions for interest claimed under COLI should be disallowed. The IRS stated in the 1999 TAM that the corporation did not really make policy loans to pay premiums but merely arranged for the appearance of cash transfers that flowed in both directions. The IRS looked behind the form the parties created to the substance: The facts indicated that a significant portion of amounts the corporation paid and classified as premiums were returned by the insurer concurrently with their payment. The result was a circular cash flow. So, the IRS treated the "interest" payments as amounts paid to support an interdependent and circular structure of charges and credits designed to increase the corporation's tax deductions while simultaneously increasing amounts credited to the COLI policies' tax deferred cash values rather than as interest payments for the use or forbearance of money. The Service has also been successful in litigation regarding COLI interest deductions. See *American Electric Power Co. v. U.S.*, 2003-1 USTC ¶50,416 (6th Cir. 2003); IRS v. CM Holdings, Inc., 2002-2 USTC ¶50,596 (3rd Cir. 2002).

37. IRC Sec. 264(d)(1); Treas. Reg. §1.264-4(d)(1).

38. Rev. Rul. 72-609, 1972-2 CB 199.

39. For more information on this "tack on" of previous history, see Rev. Rul. 71-309, 1971-2 CB 168.

40. Neither the Code nor the regulations provide guidance as to what will be considered a "substantial increase" in premiums. But in the opinion of the authors, only net premiums will be considered.

41. Treas. Reg. §1.264-4(d)(2).

42. Treas. Reg. §1.264-4(d)(3).

43. Treas. Reg. §1.264-4(d)(4). *American Body and Equipment Co. v. U.S.*, 511 F.2nd 647 (5th Cir. 1975).

44. See *Samuel J. Johnson*, TC Memo 1943; *J.I. Fleischer*, TC Memo 1943. The interest is not deductible mainly because it is not payable on indebtedness but rather as part of the cost of the permanent contract.

45. See *Levitt v. U.S.*, 517 F.2nd 1339 (8th Cir. 1975).

46. *M.G. Corlett v. Comm.*, TC Memo 1946-046.

47. IRC Sec. 163(a). See *Keith v. Comm.*, 139 F.2nd 596 (2nd Cir. 1944); *Nina Cornelia Prime, Exec. v. Comm.*, 39 BTA 487 (1939).

48. *J. Simpson Dean v. Comm.*, 35 TC 1083 (1961).

49. *Estate of Pat E. Hooks*, 22 TC 502 (1954), acq. 1955-1 CB 5.

50. *Agnes I. Fox*, 43 BTA 895 (1941).

51. *Casale v. Comm.*, 247 F.2nd 440 (2nd Cir. 1957); Rev. Rul. 59-184, 1959-1 CB 65.

52. *Yuengling v. Comm.* 69 F.2nd 971 (3rd Cir. 1934); Treas. Reg. §1.61-2(d)(2)(ii)(a). Only net premiums are includable in the employee's income when policy dividends are used to reduce premium payments. *Nelson H. Sturgis, Jr. v. Comm.*, TC Memo (1951).

53. Treas. Reg. §1.61-2(d)(2)(ii). *Comm. v. Bonwit*, 87 F.2nd 764 (2nd Cir. 1937). See *Ruth C. Rodebaugh v. Comm.*, TC Memo 1974-36, aff'd 75-2 USTC ¶9526 (6th Cir. 1975).

54. *Thomas E. Brock, Jr. v. Comm.*, TC Memo 1982-335. See also Rev. Rul. 79-50, 1979-1 CB 138 where a split dollar plan was held to result in dividend payments to a nonemployee stockholder.

55. Rev. Rul. 59-184, 1959-1 CB 65.

56. Treas. Reg. §1.101-1(b)(4).

57. *St. Louis Refrigerating & Cold Storage Company v. U.S.*, 162 F.2nd 394 (8th Cir. 1947); *T.O. McCamant v. Comm.*, 32 TC 824 (1959).

58. Temp. Treas. Reg. §1.71-1T, A-6.

59. Rev. Rul. 65-199, 1965-2 CB 20; Rev. Rul. 66-120, 1966-1 CB 214.

60. IRC Sec. 101(g).

61. See *Century Wood Preserving Co. v. Comm.*, 69 F.2nd 967 (3rd Cir. 1934); *London Shoe Co.*, 80 F.2nd 230 (2nd Cir. 1935).

62. *Gallun v. Comm.*, 327 F.2nd 809 (7th Cir. 1964).

63. *George W. Parsons v. Comm.*, 54 TC 54 (1970).

64. See *Peter J. Wilkin v. Comm.*, TC Memo 1969-130.

65. *Charles J. Thornley v. Comm.*, 41 TC 145 (1963).

66. If a contract issued after 1984 does not meet the definition of life insurance under IRC Section 7702, only the "pure insurance" (excess of death benefit over net surrender value) portion will be income tax free. IRC Sec. 7702(g)(2).

67. IRC Sec. 101.

68. IRC Sec. 101(a)(1).

69. IRC Sec. 101(c).

70. IRC Sec. 101(d)(1); Treas. Reg. §1.101-4(a)(1)(i).

71. Treas. Reg. §1.101-7 provides that life expectancy (the number of years in the payment period in the case of life income option) is found by using IRS Table V (one life) and VI (two lives).

72. An exclusion of up to $1,000 of interest is allowed to the surviving spouse of an insured who died prior to October 23, 1986. IRC Sec. 101(d)(1)(B) prior to repeal by TRA '86, Sec. 1001(a).

73. Treas. Reg. §1.101-4(d) provides that in the case of a joint and survivor option, the "amount held by the insurer" is divided by the life expectancy of the beneficiaries as a group in computing the annually excludable amount. This tax free amount can be excluded as long as any survivor lives.

74. Treas. Reg. §1.101-4(a).

75. See Treas. Reg. §1.101-4(g), Example 7.

76. Taxability applies to both guaranteed and excess interest. IRC Sec. 101(c).

77. Treas. Regs. §§1.61-7, 1.451-2. If the beneficiary has no contractual right to make a withdrawal of either principal or interest for a given period of time, interest is not taxable until that date. At that time, whatever interest has gone untaxed becomes immediately taxable. Treas. Reg. §1.101-4(g), Example 1. As soon as the beneficiary can take principal, the interest earned by that principal becomes taxable even if contractually the beneficiary cannot actually take it. Rev. Rul. 68-586, 1968-2 CB 195. See also *Rubye R. Strauss v. Comm.*, 21 TC 104 (1953).

78. 38 U.S.C. §3101(a).

79. See *Estate of J.E. Horne v. Comm.*, 65 TC 1020 (1975), acq. in result, 1980-1 CB 1.

80. *Essenfeld v. Comm.*, 311 F.2nd 208 (2nd Cir. 1962).

81. *Golden v. Comm.*, 113 F.2nd 590 (3rd Cir. 1940). See also Rev. Rul. 61-134, 1961-2 CB 250; *Ducros v. Comm.*, 272 F.2nd 49 (6th Cir. 1959).

82. IRC Sec. 72(m)(3)(C); Treas. Reg. §1.72-16(c)(4).

Appendix G

THE TRANSFER FOR VALUE RULE

INTRODUCTION

The utility of life insurance diminishes in direct proportion to any tax burden it must bear. Any planner dealing with life insurance must therefore obtain a strong working knowledge of the "transfer for value" rule – a tax trap that can cause all or a major portion of the death proceeds to become subject to ordinary income taxes.

For this reason, *The Tools and Techniques of Life Insurance Planning* devotes an entire appendix chapter to the transfer for value rule.[1]

This appendix chapter will:

1. define and explain the rule;

2. list its exceptions; and

3. analyze common factual situations in

   a) personal planning,

   b) buy-sell planning, and

   c) employee benefit planning.

Planners should suspect a potential problem in any transfer where a policy, or any interest in a policy, is transferred for any type of valuable consideration. To fail to identify this tax trap could be the most expensive mistake a practitioner can make.

THE RULE DEFINED

The transfer for value rule, contained in Internal Revenue Code section 101(a)(2), provides:

In the case of a transfer for a valuable consideration, by assignment or otherwise, of a life insurance contract or any interest therein, the amount excluded from gross income by [the beneficiary of death proceeds under a life insurance contract] shall not exceed an amount equal to the sum of the actual value of such consideration and the premiums and other amounts subsequently paid by the transferee.

So if transfers of a life insurance policy fall within the transfer for value rule, the result is a harsh penalty: with the exceptions listed below, transferees for value of life insurance policies are taxable at ordinary income rates on receipt of the policy proceeds less the sum of (a) amounts paid by them to acquire the policy, (b) later premiums, and (c) other amounts. The term "other amounts" includes any interest paid or accrued by the transferee on indebtedness with respect to a contract, but only if the interest is not allowable as a deduction under IRC Section 264(a)(4).[2]

The questions the planner must ask are:

1. Is there a transfer? and

2. Will the transferee pay any type of consideration for that transfer?

If the answer to both questions is yes, the results are likely to be harsh. For example, if a $1,000,000 term life insurance policy on an insured's life is transferred from the insured to his or her son for $10,000, there is a transfer of an insurance contract for valuable consideration. If the transferee, the son, then pays four $5,000 premiums before the insured's death, the amount excludable from the owner's gross income for amounts received under the policy will be limited to the value of the consideration paid for the policy ($10,000) plus the four $5,000 premiums paid after the transfer ($20,000), a total of $30,000. This means $970,000 ($1,000,000 less $30,000) would be subject to ordinary income tax! So instead of receiving $1,000,000 net, the son could owe a federal income tax of over $300,000 and net less than $700,000!

Planners should be aware of the following points:

1. It does not matter whether the policy is term insurance or permanent insurance.

2. The transfer for value rule applies to every type of life insurance contract and encompasses group as well as individually purchased coverage.

3. The method by which the policy is transferred is irrelevant for purposes of this rule.

4. The transfer for value rule can apply even if ownership of a policy has not been transferred. A mere shift in an interest in the contract may be sufficient to trigger the rule. So a transfer for value can occur from an absolute assignment of all the transferor's rights, a transfer of some lesser degree of policy rights, or a different type of transfer.

5. For the rule to apply there must be both a transfer of a policy or an interest in a policy and valuable consideration paid for that transfer to the transferor.

THE REQUIREMENT OF TRANSFER

The Internal Revenue Code does not define the term, "transfer for valuable consideration." But the regulations provide that a transfer for valuable consideration occurs whenever any absolute transfer for value of a right to receive all or any part of the proceeds of a life insurance policy takes place. This includes, as mentioned above, the creation for value of an enforceable right to receive all or part of the proceeds of a policy, but excludes any pledge or mere assignment of a policy as collateral security.[3]

So the pledge or assignment of a policy (or an interest in a policy) as collateral security is not a "transfer." A pledgee or assignee who receives the pledge or assignment of a policy as collateral for a loan will be able to recover proceeds income tax free (but as a repayment of capital, rather than as the proceeds of a life insurance policy).

The IRS defines the phrase "transfer for valuable consideration" broadly. The term encompasses any absolute transfer – for value – of a right to receive all or any part of a life insurance policy, including the creation for value of an enforceable contractual right to receive all or any part of the proceeds. If the insured in the above example had merely named his or her son as the policy beneficiary (for valuable consideration), that alone would constitute a transfer for purposes of the rule.

Planners should remember that any shifting of a beneficial interest in a policy is sufficient to trigger the transfer for value rule. No physical "transfer" of the policy or the policy's ownership is necessary, nor does every interest in the policy have to be transferred for the trap to be set.

THE REQUIREMENT OF CONSIDERATION

It is impossible to fall within the trap unless there is a transfer of a policy or an interest in a policy. It is also clear that even if there is a transfer, the transfer for value trap will not be triggered if there is no consideration given for that transfer.

So even if there is a nominal promise by the transferee to pay value and even if the policy assignment says, "for one dollar," the proceeds will be tax free – if in fact no consideration is ever paid – regardless of the formal recitation of consideration in the assignment form furnished by the insurer. Of course, the better and recommended practice is to show that a gift and only a gift is intended. To be safe, the assignment form should state that the transfer is solely "for love and affection."

If, in exchange for any kind of valuable consideration, a policy beneficiary of all or any portion of the proceeds is named or changed, there will be a transfer for value. This rule applies even if:

*   there is no assignment of the policy;

*   the policy has no cash surrender value at the time of the transfer; and

*   the policy is term insurance, so that it never has and never will have any cash value.

Even though the transfer is found to be for a valuable consideration and none of the exceptions to the transfer for value rule apply, if the consideration paid for the transfer plus any amounts paid subsequent to the transfer by the transferee equal or exceed the policy proceeds, the entire amount of the proceeds will be excludable from gross income. But it will be rare that the transferee will pay a sum equal to the proceeds for the policy.

It is not necessary that cash change hands for the trap to be set. Any consideration sufficient to support an enforceable contract right will be sufficient. For example, in the leading case in the buy-sell area, the mutuality of shareholders' agreements to purchase each others' stock in the event of death and relieve the business from the burden of paying premiums was held to be enough consideration to invoke the rule.[4]

Planners should therefore always inquire – whenever there is a transfer of either a policy or an interest in a policy – whether the transferring party will receive anything of any value in exchange for the transfer. A quid pro quo ("I'll do this for you if you do this for me") type transaction is consideration just as surely as if $1,000,000 changes hands. The quid pro quo does not have to be in writing, nor does it have to be explicitly stated by the parties. If it is logical to assume that the transfer of a policy or an interest in a policy would not have been made absent some consideration and that action or inaction was in fact taken, the IRS will presume that valuable consideration did pass to the transferor.

EXCEPTIONS TO THE RULE

It is essential that planners understand why the rule exists: Congress wanted to discourage speculation in human life through insurance via the sale of policies to those who do not have an insurable interest in the life of the insured (essentially, a stronger preference for the continued life of the insured than for receipt of the insurance proceeds).[5] The parties specified below as exempt from the transfer for value rule are those who are likely to have an insurable interest.

But it is equally important for practitioners to note that the mere fact that the beneficiary should or does have an insurable interest in the life of the insured is not sufficient. Even some parties who clearly have an insurable interest are not included in the exempt categories described below. For instance, the following individuals are not exempt from the rule:

- the policyholder's children;

- the policyholder's parents; and

- the policyholder's co-shareholders.

Furthermore, even if the beneficiary can show that there is no risk or intent of speculation on the death of the insured and the only violation is a technical one, proceeds will be taxable under the transfer for value rule.

Do not try to use logic as a working guideline to this rule. Read the Internal Revenue Code and the Treasury regulations. Again, suspect a problem whenever there is:

- a transfer of a policy or any interest in a policy; and

- any type of valuable consideration is (or could be) given in return for that transfer.

The safe course is to consider every transfer as suspect until scrupulously examined. As noted below, even what appears to be an outright "gift" of life insurance

may incorporate a fatal element of consideration in certain circumstances.

Five safe-harbor exceptions may shelter a transfer from the transfer for value rule penalty – even if there is a transfer for valuable consideration.

These five "safe harbors" consist of the following:

1. the "transferor's basis" ("in whole or in part") exception;

2. the "transfer to the insured" exception;

3. the "transfer to a partner of the insured" exception;

4. the "transfer to a partnership in which the insured is a partner" exception; and

5. the "transfer to a corporation in which the insured is a shareholder or officer" exception.

Exception 1: The Transferor's Basis

Internal Revenue Code section 101(a)(2)(A) provides that the transfer for value rule does not apply if the transferee's basis for determining gain or loss upon a subsequent sale of a policy or an interest in a policy is determined "in whole or in part" by reference to the transferor's basis. In a nutshell this means that if the basis in the contract is carried over from the transferor to the recipient the death proceeds will remain income tax free.

The rule above states that the beneficiary will receive tax free proceeds if basis is determined "in whole or in part" by reference to the transferor's basis. There are two common examples of the "in whole" portion of this exception. One is the case of outright gifts of policies that generally take the form of an absolute assignment of a policy for "love and affection." Here, no consideration of any kind changes hands. The transferor merely gives the policy to the transferee.

Example. Assume an insured sells his son a $100,000 policy on his life for $100 when the policy's gift tax value is $1,000. The son's basis for determining gain or loss upon a subsequent sale will be the father's basis (the net premiums he has paid) with an adjustment for any gift taxes the father may pay on the transfer. Here, the son's basis is determined in part by his father's basis. Even though there is a sale by the father of a policy worth $1,000 in return for $100 cash paid by the son, to the extent of the $900 balance ($1,000 value less $100 consideration paid) there is a gift from the father to the son. Tax law requires that the son carry over the father's basis (cost) for the portion of the transfer that was a gift. The proceeds are income tax free at the father's death because the tests of the "transferor's basis" exception are met.

The other common example of a clear carryover basis situation is when a policy is transferred from one business to another in a tax-free corporate reorganization.

So where the transferee's basis is determined by carrying over the donor's basis (with an adjustment for any gift taxes paid), the proceeds will be income tax free even if there is a transfer and even if it is made in return for valuable consideration.

Planners must be wary of the seeming simplicity of this exception. Many think that as long as the transfer is characterized by the taxpayer as a gift or part gift-part sale, the proceeds will be exempt from the transfer for value rule. This is a very dangerous and misleading presumption.

The problem is based on the technical way the basis laws work. In some cases, the transferee's basis is determined in whole or in part by reference to the transferor's basis (and therefore the transfer for value rule is avoided due to this first exception).

But in other cases, the transferee's basis is not determined by reference to the transferor's basis even though at least part of the transfer constitutes a gift and is considered so by the parties. Instead, basis is determined by the amount deemed paid by the transferee for the property.[6] This falls outside the protective safe harbor.

In the example above where an insured sells his son a $100,000 policy for $100 when the policy's gift tax value is $1,000, there is clearly a $900 gift and the son will determine his basis at least in part by carrying over his father's basis (plus any gift tax payable). (The son can then add to his basis the $100 he paid, plus any premiums he pays after the transfer.) The entire proceeds will be received income tax free because the son's lifetime basis in the policy is determined at least "in part" by referring back to the basis of the policy in his father's hands.

Now let's look at the result where the son's basis may be determined by what he "pays." Remember, the part gift-part sale protective rule only applies when it results in a carryover of all or a portion of the transferor's basis.

The problem is the transferee is considered to pay not only what he actually pays for the policy, but also any amount the transferee is deemed to pay by relieving the transferor of the obligation to pay a policy loan.

Here is where the trap lies: If the policy loan (and any cash or other property received in the exchange) is *greater* than the transferor's basis, the transferee takes as his basis the higher of (1) the amount the buyer actually pays for the policy *plus* the amount he is deemed to "pay" by reason of relieving the transferor of the obligation to repay the loan, or (2) the transferor's basis. Any gift tax payable is then added to the contract's basis.[7] So in this situation, the transfer is treated as if the transferee-buyer acquires the policy in a sale and not a gift!

Example. Assume a client has a $28,000 basis in a policy that he gives to his son. The basis is due to premiums he paid net of any dividends. At the time he gives the policy to his son, it is subject to a policy loan of $25,000. The client's basis is $3,000 greater than the loan. At the date of the gift, the replacement value of the policy is $30,000. In this situation there will be no transfer for value problem. The father is deemed to "sell" his son $25,000 worth of policy (the amount of the loan debt he is relieved of) for consideration in that amount. The father is deemed to make a gift of $5,000 (the difference between the policy's $30,000 value at the time of the transfer and its sale portion of $25,000). The son takes the policy at least partially with reference to his father's basis. So the proceeds will be received income tax free.

Example. Now assume the same facts as above except the father's basis is only $22,000 rather than $28,000. The $25,000 loan against the policy exceeds the $22,000 basis by $3,000. If the father sells the policy for its loan amount rather than gives it to his son, the father will realize a $3,000 gain. Under this circumstance, the son's basis is determined solely by the $25,000 amount he is deemed to have paid his father (i.e., the debt he is considered to have relieved his father of and assumed in the transaction). For purposes of computing the son's basis, the father's basis is irrelevant. Unfortunately, this means the son's receipt of the proceeds will be subject to the transfer for value rule because the son does not determine his basis "in whole or in part" by reference to the transferor's (his father's) basis. He determines it solely on the amount "paid" for the policy. There is a transfer of a policy, for valuable consideration received, with none of the exceptions met, and therefore the entire proceeds are subject to ordinary income tax.

Under the "transferor's basis" exception, it is generally safe to transfer life insurance to the insured's spouse or ex-spouse (if the transfer is incident to a divorce).[8] Why is such a transfer safe even if cash changes hands? IRC Section 1041 treats interspousal transfers as nontaxable events, so in the case where one spouse transfers a life insurance contract to another spouse, the consequences are:

1. No gain is recognized by either party for income tax purposes even if the policy is received in exchange for a surrender of marital rights.

2. The transferee spouse (or ex-spouse) takes as her basis the transferor's basis and therefore falls within the "transferor's basis" exception.

Under the "transferor's basis" exception, the transferee stands in the shoes of the transferor. This means that a transfer of a policy to a "transferor's basis" category of transferee carries over and retains the same tax treatment of the policy that it had in the hands of the transferor. In other words, if the proceeds were exempt before the transfer, they remain exempt after the transfer.

The opposite is also true. If the proceeds of a policy were subject to tax under the transfer for value rule before the present transfer, they continue to be tainted. A transfer to a "transferor's basis" transferee is not enough to eliminate the taint. Where the last owner's basis is determined in whole or part by reference to the prior owner's basis, the income tax exclusion is limited to the sum of:

• the amount which the transferor could have excluded had no transfer taken place; plus

• any premiums and other amounts paid by the final transferee.

Example. Assume that an insured purchases a $500,000 policy on his own life and gives it to his daughter, who later sells it to the insured's son. Here, the son must report the entire $500,000 (less the amount he pays for the policy and any premiums he later pays) as ordinary income when his father dies. Although the transfer from father to daughter is protected because of the daughter's carryover of the father's basis, that protection does not extend to the sale from her to the insured's son.

Example. Assume an insured gives the policy on his life to his daughter, who later gives it to her own daughter. Here, the granddaughter's basis is determined by a carryover of her mother's basis which, in turn, is carried over from (and therefore determined by reference to) the insured's basis. The proceeds will be income tax free.

Example. Assume a transfer of a policy from a corporation to X, a co-shareholder of Y, the insured. X pays the corporation an amount equal to the policy's value at the time of transfer. Assume further that X, the new policyowner, then transfers the policy on his co-shareholder's life to W, X's wife, for love and affection. Although a transfer of a policy on X's life to W, his wife, would be protected (because of the "in whole or in part" exception), the transfer of the policy on Y's life was tainted even before X transferred it. The subsequent transfer to W from X does not cleanse the taint.

There is a solution. Make the next-to-last transfer to one of the four "protected" parties (the insured, a partner of the insured, a partnership in which the insured is a partner, or a corporation in which the insured is a shareholder or officer). At that point, the transfer for value taint is washed away.[9] Proceeds will be income tax free if that party then makes an untainted gift.

Exception 2: Transfers to the Insured

IRC Section 101(a)(2)(B) provides that the transfer for value rule will not apply to transfers to the insured, to a partner of the insured, to a partnership in which the insured is a partner, or to a corporation in which the insured is a shareholder or officer. These "protected party" exceptions are obviously the safest of all the exceptions because they require the least verification and are easy to implement.

Of all of these protected party safe harbors, the most certain is the insured. The clearest, safest, most positive way to avoid the transfer for value rule is to be sure that the last transfer for valuable consideration is to the insured. No matter how little or how much money or other consideration is paid by the insured to obtain the policy, once the insured becomes the transferee, all prior transfer for value taint is eliminated and the proceeds regain (or retain) their income tax free status.

Exception 3: Transfers to a Partner of the Insured

If the transfer is to someone who is the insured's partner in a legitimate partnership, proceeds will be income tax free even if the transfer is for valuable consideration. Assume two individuals are partners in a real estate development partnership and each partner owns a policy on his own life. Each partner purchases the policy on the other's life.

There is a transfer for value because there is a transfer of a policy for valuable consideration. However, because the transfer is to a partner of the insured, the proceeds will be received income tax free.

It appears that the only requirement under this safe harbor is that the transferee partner must own a legitimate (no matter how small) share of a legitimate operating or investment partnership.[10] Even though the life insurance policy is in no way connected with the partnership or its operation, as long as the recipient partner is a partner of the insured (presumably at the date of receipt of the policy or the interest in the policy), the insurance proceeds should be income tax free.

Exception 4: Transfers to a Partnership in Which the Insured is a Partner

This exception, like the one above, has become quite popular in recent years because of its planning flexibility.[11] It requires only that the policy be transferred to a partnership in which the insured is a partner.

Example. Assume two individuals are partners in a real estate development partnership, and each partner owns a policy on his own life. Each partner sells the policy on his life to the partnership. Based on these facts there is a transfer for value, but it is exempt from the transfer for value rule because it is made to the insured's partnership.

Practitioners often ask if a client can establish a partnership "in name only" to avoid the sting of the transfer for value rule. The IRS has approved a transfer of a policy to a partnership established specifically to receive and hold policies insuring the lives of its partners.[12] However, a safer and suggested course is to transfer the policy to a partnership (or LLC electing taxation as a partnership) established for independent business or investment purposes.[13]

Exception 5: Transfers to a Corporation in Which the Insured is a Shareholder or Officer

Under this safe harbor, the transfer for value rule does not apply to a transfer to a corporation if the insured is either (1) an officer; or (2) a shareholder in the corporation (presumably on the date the policy is transferred).

Example. Assume an individually owned policy is transferred to the insured's corporate employer to be used as key employee coverage or to fund a stock redemption buy-sell agreement. The insured at the time of the transfer is the treasurer of the company and owns 30% of the company's stock. Thus, the transfer for value rule does not apply because the insured is both an officer (treasurer) and a shareholder.

Beware: This exemption does not protect transfers to persons who are merely:

- co-shareholders of the insured;

- key employees (no matter how important); or

- directors who are neither officers nor shareholders.

Summary of Safe Harbors

Transfers to the following persons are protected:

- anyone whose basis is determined by reference to transferor's basis;

- the insured;

- the spouse of insured;

- the ex-spouse of insured, if the transfer is pursuant to a divorce or separation agreement;

- a partner of the insured;

- a partnership in which insured is a partner; and

- a corporation in which insured is a shareholder or officer.

Transfers to any of the following are not protected and may set the transfer for value trap:

- a co-stockholder of insured;

- a purchaser who takes the policy subject to a loan in excess of the transferor's basis; or

- any other person or entity not listed above.

TYPICAL PERSONAL LIFE INSURANCE PLANNING PROBLEMS

Transfers of life insurance policies between family members other than spouses are a quicksand pit for clients and their planners.

Assume an insured purchases a policy on his life from his corporate employer. He then immediately names his wife as beneficiary. She collects the policy proceeds upon the insured's death. The proceeds should be exempt because the transfer is to a "proper party," the insured.

Not so easy to recognize are the much more deadly part gift-part sale situations discussed above which are usually triggered by policy loans. If a transferred policy is subject to a policy loan, the amount of that loan is treated as an "amount paid" for the policy. In most cases the insured's basis (net premiums paid) exceeds the amount of the loan. Therefore, the transferee's basis is determined by reference to the transferor's and there will be no problem.

But where the amount of the policy loan exceeds the transferor's basis, two adverse results are likely:

1. To the extent the loan exceeds the transferor's net cost, ordinary income is realized just as if the policy is sold to the transferee for a payment in the amount of the loan.

2. The transferee's basis is determined, neither in whole nor in part by reference to the transferor's basis but by the "sale" price – the amount of the loan. The result? The "transferor's basis" exception is not applicable.

There is a solution to the policy loan tax trap: Limit the amount of any proposed loan to some level that is clearly less than the transferor's basis. Then there will be no taxable sale and the transferee's basis will clearly be determined by reference to the transferor's basis.

TRANSFER FOR VALUE PROBLEMS IN BUY–SELL PLANNING

In planning for corporate or partnership buy-sell agreements funded with life insurance, as in any of the other "high risk" areas discussed below, it is essential to examine (and suspect) any transfer of a life insurance policy funding the buy-sell arrangement.[14]

Here is a checklist of potential transfer for value traps in the buy-sell planning area.

The "Uninsurable Shareholder" Trap

An uninsurable shareholder sells her individually owned insurance to a co-shareholder to help fund a cross purchase agreement. The transaction clearly falls within the transfer for value rule – as do the following two transfers.

The "Switch from Stock Redemption to Cross Purchase" Trap

A corporation sells a policy to a co-shareholder of the insured because the company wants to switch from a stock redemption plan to a cross purchase agreement and sells its corporate-owned policies on the lives of its shareholders to their co-shareholders.

The "Gift of Policies by Corporation Double Trouble" Trap

Two shareholders want to change an insured stock redemption agreement to a cross purchase plan. But instead of selling the policies, they intend merely to have the corporation give each shareholder the policy on the life of the insured.

Although the shareholders may call this transaction a gift to each other, the IRS is not likely to accept this transaction as a gift (and will probably challenge the distribution from the corporation as a dividend or as compensation).

The "Purchase by Insured Followed by Gift" Trap

Two shareholders want to change an insured stock redemption agreement to a cross purchase plan. They intend to avoid the transfer for value rule by a purchase of the policy from the corporation by the insured followed by a "gift" of the policy from the insured to the other shareholder.

They will probably not succeed. The IRS will doubtlessly argue that the double transfer is really one directly from the corporation. Failing that argument, the IRS will claim the reciprocity – I'll "give" you the policy on my life if you "give" me the policy on yours – constitutes consideration for the transfers.

The "Sale by Estate" Trap

Assume there are three shareholders, X, Y, and Z. The buy-sell agreement is set up on a cross purchase basis so that each owns policies on the other shareholders' lives. If X dies, the policy X owned on Y is sold by X's estate to Z. The policy X owned on Z is sold by X's estate to Y.

The proposed transactions will trigger the trap because Y and Z, as mere co-shareholders, are not protected parties. There are several possible indirect solutions to this problem:

1. Both policies can be sold to the corporation. A sale of a policy to a corporation in which the insured is an officer or shareholder is a safe transfer. The corporation can then establish a stock redemption or IRC Section 303 partial stock redemption plan that meshes with the existing cross purchase agreement. The result would be a hybrid plan, because the survivors, Y and Z in the example above, would still own policies on each other's lives. Of course, they can also transfer those policies to the corporation and use a stock redemption agreement.

2. The decedent's estate can surrender each policy for cash or can keep the policies in force, or place the policies on extended term or make the policies paid up for a lower face amount.

3. The survivors can purchase the policies on their own lives and continue them as personal insurance.

The Sale by a Trust Trap

A trust's sale of an interest in a life insurance policy to trust beneficiaries other than the insured can trigger the trap. For example, suppose a couple creates an irrevocable life insurance trust and places cash inside the trust for the trust to purchase and pay premiums for a second-to-die life insurance policy on their lives. At some later date, the couple decides to discontinue contributions. Since the trust does not have sufficient funds to keep the insurance in force, the couple's children decide to purchase the policy and pay premiums. There would be a transfer of a policy and it would be for valuable consideration.

In many of these situations, the solution is to make the buyers partners with the insured prior to the transaction. It is essential in these situations that the partnership be created and actively managed for reasons other than to merely to shield the transaction from the transfer for value rule. Be sure the entity is recognized as a partnership under state law. Also be sure that the partnership files federal income tax returns. It is also important to show that the parties intend to continue operating as a partnership at least through and including the year in which the purchase of the life insurance policy is consummated. Overall, create evidence that the firm is a legitimate operating entity.[15]

The "Policy Saving Trust" Trap

Assume a cross purchase buy-sell agreement is established and a trust is created to facilitate the transaction and assure an orderly transfer of the corporate stock. A corporate-owned life insurance policy on each shareholder's life is then transferred to the trustee who is to collect the proceeds and pay them to shareholder's estate.

The buy-sell agreement requires the insured's co-shareholders to pay premiums on the policy. At the insured's death, the trustee will collect the proceeds (on behalf of the surviving shareholders) and, in exchange for the stock held by the insured stockholder, pay the estate the appropriate amount of cash.

There is a transfer of a life insurance policy. But is there valuable consideration? If so, what is it and when is it "paid"? At least one court has held under these facts that the agreement of the co-shareholders to relieve the business of the burden of making premium payments and to buy the insured's stock at his death with the policy proceeds was sufficient consideration to give rise to a transfer for value – even though no cash was paid for the policies.[16]

In another example, assume six shareholders, all related, would like to establish a buy-sell agreement. But they are concerned about the bookkeeping and costs of the 30 policies needed to insure each shareholder individually.[17] Their attorney suggests that they form a trust, contribute cash to the trust to pay the premiums, have the trust buy one policy on each shareholder's life, and use the proceeds to buy the stock for the surviving shareholders. When a shareholder dies, his interest in the policies on the lives of the surviving shareholders "disappears" (according to the contract).

In the authors' opinion, trouble awaits those who fund a cross purchase buy-sell in a trust which provides that, at the death of one shareholder, the interest he had in the policies on the lives of the others "terminates" (vanishes into thin air) and "magically" the survivors end up with an interest (through the trust) in the remaining policies on the other survivors lives. This "one trust – one policy on each shareholder's life" cross purchase technique (unless the shareholders are also partners) is almost certain to attract litigation with the IRS.

Why? Upon the first death, there will be no physical transfer, and legal title to the policies on the lives of the survivors will not change. The trust will still be the legal owner of the policies. But the beneficial interest in the decedent's share of the policies on his co-shareholders' lives will shift to them. Each survivor will gain a beneficial interest he did not have before on the life or lives of his co-shareholders. Furthermore, on each subsequent death, there will be an additional transfer of equitable ownership to the surviving co-shareholders.

Where is the valuable consideration? No policyowner would allow the beneficial interest in a policy he or she owned on another shareholder's life to pass to the other shareholders unless each of the other shareholders did the same. That reciprocity would be consideration enough for the IRS.

The "Group Funded Cross Purchase Buy–Sell" Tax Trap

Abe and Sadie are unrelated shareholders. Each is insured for $100,000 under a corporate-owned group term life contract paid for by the corporation. They name each other as beneficiaries of their respective group term life coverage in order to fund the buy-sell with (from the corporation's perspective) tax deductible dollars. Each agrees to accept the proceeds of the other's group term life insurance as payment for his share of the business.

There is clearly a transfer of an interest in a policy and, although no cash is paid in return for the policies and even though the coverage is pure term insurance, there is the requisite valuable consideration. That consideration is reciprocity. Abe would not have named Sadie as his beneficiary without her agreement to do the same.

The "Endorsement Type Split Dollar" Tax Trap

Ted and Carol want to set up a cross purchase buy-sell agreement. Neither has the after-tax cash to pay premiums. Their corporation sets up a split dollar arrangement to assist them in funding the buy-sell. The corporation will purchase a policy on the life of each shareholder. At the death of either insured, the corporation will recover its outlay first. Any death benefit in excess of the corporation's interest (i.e., its cumulative outlay) will be payable to the insured's co-shareholder. The net proceeds of the policy on Ted's life will be paid to Carol and the net proceeds of the policy on Carol's life will be paid to Ted.

In the authors' opinion, when the corporation as policyowner names each insured's co-shareholder as beneficiary of part of the proceeds, there is a transfer of part of the corporation's interest in the policy, a portion of the death proceeds. In reality the corporation shifts the beneficial right to the death proceeds from itself to each insured's co-shareholder in consideration of the insured's continuing services as an employee. Thus, there is a transfer of an interest in a policy from the corporation to the co-shareholder of the insured employee (i.e., the corporation allows the insured to name the policy beneficiary) in return for the valuable consideration of the employee's services.

A further argument the IRS could make is that – to the extent each shareholder recognizes income (economic benefits) – it is as if the corporation purchases term insurance on his behalf. Normally, such a transaction would not be a problem because the term insurance purchased is usually on the insured's life and, if it is transferred to someone other than the insured, it is typically done without consideration. In a cross purchase endorsement split dollar, however, the employer owns each policy at inception. The policy insures the life of a co-shareholder of the person to whom the company endorses (shifts an interest in) a portion of the policy proceeds. This is clearly a transfer of an interest in a policy and the reciprocity, the fact that each shareholder tacitly allows the other to do so, provides the requisite consideration.

Avoiding the transfer is the answer to the problem. Instead of using the endorsement method in which the corporation is the original owner of the policy, the collateral assignment method eliminates any need to transfer an interest in the policy. Under the collateral assignment method, each shareholder purchases a policy on the life of his co-shareholder and owns it from the beginning. He then collaterally assigns it to the corporation (a "protected party") as security for the loan. Because there is no transfer of a policy or an interest in a policy (except to a protected party), the transfer for value rule will not apply.

The "Perhaps not so Safe Gift" Tax Trap

Assume a father gives a policy on his life to his son and the father pays the gift tax. After the gift of the policy, the father and son enter into a cross purchase agreement for the purchase of the father's stock in a corporation at the father's death. The father dies and the son, in fact, uses the policy proceeds to purchase the father's stock.

Does the son take the insurance income tax free? At first glance, the answer seems to be yes: the father intends the transfer of the policy to be a gift to his son (even though the father enters into a buy-sell agreement) and even files a gift tax return on the transaction and pays a gift tax.

But wise practitioners will ask some additional questions.[18] These include:

1. Do the transfer of the policy and the execution of the agreement occur contemporaneously?

2. How far apart do the two transactions occur? In other words, are the two events part of the same transaction? If so, the IRS can argue that the son pays a price (kept the policy in force) as part of his agreement to buy the father's stock.

3. Is there further evidence (such as continued gifts from the father) that establishes an intent to make the life insurance transfer a gift rather than part of a business transaction?

4. Is there an explicit agreement between the parties that the son will use the insurance proceeds to buy the father's stock at his death?

The IRS may try to prove that, although the transaction is cast as a gift, it is really part of a larger arrangement in which the transfer of the policy was bargained for by the son. Could it then be argued that even if the son's agreement constitutes some consideration for the transfer of the policy, so long as the son's basis is – at least in part – determined by reference to his father's basis, the proceeds retain their income tax free status? In the authors' opinion this technique is dangerous unless the facts are exactly right.

TRANSFER FOR VALUE PROBLEMS IN EMPLOYEE BENEFIT PLANNING

There are a number of situations in which clients can fall into the transfer for value trap in the employee benefit planning area. One is where there is a transfer of life insurance policies to the trustee of a qualified retirement plan. The transfer may take place as a part of the corporate employer's contribution to the plan on behalf of the participant or as a part of a participant's voluntary contribution to the plan.

In most cases the client will succeed if the transaction is properly structured and the following "no significant change of ownership" rationale is employed.

1. Assume an agreement between an employee, his employer, and a trust that provides for the employer to purchase an existing life insurance policy from the employee for its cash value. The employer proposes to transfer the policy to the trust as a part of the employer's required annual contribution to the trust. The trustee will pay the premiums on the policy. At the employee's death the trustee will pay the insurance proceeds to his designee. Assume the proceeds are in fact paid to the plan trustee, who turns them over to the insured's designee.

   There is no transfer for value problem here because there is no significant change in beneficial ownership. The proceeds retain their income tax free status because, in essence, there is no transfer and therefore the transfer for value rule cannot apply.

2. Assume a successor corporation's retirement plan buys life insurance contracts from a predecessor employer's Keogh plan. Here, the purchase of the insurance by the new trustee from the old trustee for the policy's cash value at the date of purchase should not be a transfer for value because no significant change in the beneficial interest of the contract occurs.

3. Assume an employee-participant personally owns a life insurance contract with a cash value. The employee-participant wants to transfer that policy (as a voluntary employee contribution) to a profit sharing trust of which she is a participant. Under the plan terms, the proceeds continue to be payable to the employee's beneficiary and the policy's cash surrender value is payable to the participant upon her retirement or other termination of employment.

   Because the proceeds are payable to the employee's designated beneficiary upon her death and the cash surrender value is payable to the participant upon her retirement or other termination of employment, there is no significant change in the policy's beneficial ownership. Therefore, the IRS should conclude that there is no transfer for value.

4. Assume a corporation establishes an irrevocable "rabbi trust" with a third party trustee. Assets in the rabbi trust remain subject to creditors of the corporation if it becomes insolvent or bankrupt. Participants receive only an unsecured right to the assets in the trust. The employer transfers certain life insurance contracts to the trust. The employer or the trust will pay the premiums and the trust will become the nominal owner and beneficiary of the contracts upon their transfer to the trust.

   Is there a transfer of a policy or an interest in a policy by the corporation? Here, the proceeds should be excludable from income tax of the trust and of the employer because there is never the requisite transfer. The trust should be viewed not as a trust but as an agency or alter ego of the employer. There is no change in equitable ownership of the policies, so the death benefits of the policies will retain their income tax free status.

Split dollar life insurance arrangements are tricky and, as noted above, are potential transfer for value problem areas.

1. Assume the insured's wife owns a policy on his life. She then collaterally assigns the policy to the insured's solely-owned corporation to fund a split dollar arrangement. Thereafter, the wife transfers her interest in the policy, subject to the corporation's rights under the split dollar arrangement, to the insured.

   The insured and the corporation propose to enter into a new split dollar agreement. The insured intends to assign his interest in the policy to his wife. She will then name herself as beneficiary of the proceeds in excess of the amount due the corporation under the split dollar plan.

   Is there a problem with this arrangement? The transfer of rights in the policy to the corporation qualify for the "proper party" exemption provided for transfers to a corporation in which the insured is either an officer or shareholder. So any amounts received under the policy upon the death of the insured should be entirely income tax exempt. The transfer of any rights in the policy to the insured should be similarly exempt. The final transfer, a gratuitous transfer of the insured's policy rights to his wife, should also be exempt because she takes as her basis in the contract an amount determined in whole or part by reference to the insured's basis.

2. Assume an insured owns all of the stock of a professional corporation. The firm owns a $1,000,000 life insurance policy on the shareholder's life. The insured purchases the policy from the corporation in exchange for its cash value. The insured then gives the policy to his wife. The wife sets up a split dollar arrangement with the insured's corporation and collaterally assigns the policy to the corporation.

   Here, the beneficiary should collect the proceeds free of income tax because the first transfer from the corporation to the insured is a transfer to the insured and the second transfer is one in which the transferee's basis is determined in whole or in part by reference to the transferor's.

3. Assume a corporation owns several policies on the life of its shareholder, M. The corporation sells the policies on M's life to an irrevocable trust established for his spouse and children. The trust is a partner of the insured and

his son in a business venture and has been so for almost 20 years.

Here, the IRS will probably hold that because the trust is the insured's business partner, the proceeds will be income tax free as long as the partnership itself has an independent business or investment reason for existence separate and apart from meeting the transfer for value exception.

SUMMARY

1. Suspect a transfer for value problem in every transfer of an existing policy – or any shift of an interest in a policy.

2. Whenever possible, make transfers only to "protected parties" (those excepted from the rule).

3. Do not transfer a policy with a loan in excess of the policyowner's basis. Reduce the loan below the transferor's basis or do not make the transfer.

4. Eliminate prior tainted transfers by making a further transfer to a protected party. If the insured is in good health (likely to live more than three years), consider a transfer to the insured followed by a gift.

ENDNOTES

1. For more information, see Brody and Leimberg, "The Not So Tender Trap – The Transfer for Value Rule," *Journal of the American Society of CLU & ChFC* (May 1984), p. 32, and Commito, "Transfer for Value Rulings Offer Planning Opportunities," *Journal of the American Society of CLU & ChFC* (Nov. 1991), p. 38.

2. This provision applies to contracts issued after June 8, 1997. TRA '97, Sec. 1084(d); IRC Sec. 101(a)(2).

3. Treas. Reg. §1.101-1(b)(4).

4. *Monroe v. Patterson*, 197 F. Supp. 146 (N.D. Ala. 1961).

5. "Insurable interest" is a term covered in more detail in Chapter 5 of this text.

6. See "Rearranging the Ownership of Life Insurance, The Part Gift, Part Sale Exception to the Transfer for Value Rule," *Keeping Current*, Vol. 12, Number 1 (December 1981), and "Careless Financial Planning By Violating the Transfer for Value Rule Can Transform Tax-Free Life Insurance Proceeds into Taxable Income," *Trusts and Estates* (January, 1989), p. 56.

7. Treas. Reg. §1.1015-4.

   "Perhaps it could be argued that even if the indebtedness is greater than the transferor's basis, the transferee's basis is still determined in part by the transferor's basis because the computation required by Treas. Reg. §1.1015-4 to determine the transferee's basis involves reference to the transferor's basis.

Nevertheless, until the matter is resolved, it may be advisable to either avoid the transfer of a policy where the indebtedness exceeds the transferor's basis or to reduce the indebtedness below the transferor's basis prior to the transfer." 111-4th T.M. *Estates, Gifts, and Trusts Portfolio*, p. A-40.

8. A transfer of property between spouses is considered a gift, with the transferee taking the basis of the transferor. IRC Sec. 1041(b). A transfer is "incident to a divorce" if the transfer occurs within one year after the date the marriage ends or is related to the cessation of the marriage. IRC Sec. 1041(c). A transfer is generally treated as related to the cessation of the marriage if it is pursuant to a divorce or separation instrument and the transfer occurs not more than 6 years after the date on which the marriage ends. Temp. Treas. Reg. §1.1041-1T(A-7). This protection does not extend to nonresident alien spouses. IRC Sec. 1041(d). IRC Section 1041 applies to transfers of property after July 18, 1984, or after December 31, 1983, if both spouses so elect.

9. Where the transfer is made to one of the "proper party" individuals or entities described in IRC Section 101(a)(2)(B), the entire amount of the proceeds will be excludable from the transferee's gross income. Treas. Reg. §1.101-1(b)(3).

10. The size of that share can be relatively small. The IRS has approved a transfer of a life insurance policy to a partner owning a 1% interest in a partnership in which the insured was a partner. Let. Rul. 9045004.

11. See for example, Let. Ruls. 9725009, 9725008, and 9725007.

12. Let. Rul. 9309021.

13. See *Swanson v. Comm.*, 518 F.2d 59 (8th Cir. 1975).

    See Let. Rul. 9843024 for an example of how a sale of a life insurance policy from an irrevocable trust to a limited partnership in which the insured is a partner fell within a safe harbor to the transfer for value rule. Here, a family limited partnership (FLP) was formed to acquire, hold, invest in, manage, trade, sell, or otherwise deal with real and personal, tangible and intangible property – expressly including life insurance. The partnership indicated that it wanted partnership rather than corporate income tax treatment. The previously established irrevocable life insurance trust created by the insured (who is also the general partner of the FLP) proposed to sell its interest in the insurance on the insured's life to the FLP. Each policy will be sold for an amount equal to the fair market value of the policies, i.e., their interpolated terminal reserve plus any unearned premium on the date of the sale. Here, the partnership held substantial assets in addition to the insurance.

    This ruling contained a number of warnings that should be considered by planners before relying on the "transfer to a partnership in which the insured is a partner" safe harbor exception. Specifically, the IRS refused to express an opinion on whether the insured partner reduces his interest in the FLP. Likewise, the IRS was noncommittal regarding the FLP's federal tax classification as a partnership if it disposes of all assets other than life insurance. As the authors have noted in the past, it appears that the "check-the-box" regulations may not be a total and absolute solution to transfer for value problems – at least not at this point. This means a partnership that owns only life insurance and has no purpose other than to hold that life insurance and thus escape the orbit of the transfer for value rule might be something other than a partnership for purposes of the exception to the rule. The solution is simple and one the authors have been advocating since the first edition of this book: Don't rely upon a partnership to fall within a transfer-for-value safe harbor unless the insured has some real and meaningful partnership interest and unless you can show the entity is doing something more than just holding assets, particularly if the only assets consist of life insurance contracts that require nothing more than the payment of premiums.

14. Let. Rul. 9727024. See "Cross-Purchase Life Policies Did Not Result in Transfers for Value," *Journal of Taxation* (October, 1997), pg. 250.

15. Let. Rul. 199903020.

16. *Monroe v. Patterson*, 197 F. Supp. 146 (N.D. Ala. 1961).

17. The number of policies needed in a cross purchase grows every time the business grows and the formula in the agreement calls for a revaluation. That number is N x (N-1) where N is the number of shareholders. With 6 shareholders, 30 policies are needed – every time the company is revalued.

18. "Questions and Answers on Estate Planning and Administration," *Trusts and Estates* (November, 1985), p. 47.

ACCOUNTING FOR LIFE INSURANCE

INTRODUCTION

Selecting the appropriate risk management and funding strategies in business planning ordinarily requires at least some input from other advisors to the client. Attorneys are integrally involved in drafting agreements and explaining the legal ramifications of transactions. Accountants provide insight into the effects that specific solutions will have for tax as well as financial reporting purposes. The client will best be served when all the client's advisors work as a team and are able to communicate.[1]

In order to minimize any communication problems due to technical terms or a misunderstanding regarding the impact of a specific solution on a specific financial statement, it is useful to review accounting fundamentals and language. Costly or incorrect policies, adverse tax consequences, or an adverse impact on the company's financial statement that is used to obtain corporate loans can each cause the client great distress and possibly cause the client to seek professional guidance elsewhere.

Financial reporting and income tax reporting are two separate and distinct methodologies. Companies will often keep two sets of books to meet the different requirements. Tax reporting is determined by the Internal Revenue Code, the regulations issued by the Internal Revenue Service, the outcome of judicial cases, and various informative rulings and releases. Financial reporting must meet the standards of Generally Accepted Accounting Principles (GAAP) which are a body of rules and interpretations no less voluminous or nebulous than the tax laws.

The rules and interpretations currently embody statements from the Accounting Principles Board (APB) and the body which replaced it, the Financial Accounting Standards Board (FASB). The American Institute of Certified Public Accountants develops issues through its Emerging Issues Task Force (EITF) and makes recommendations to the FASB. The FASB issues informative releases that may come in the form of Accounting Opinions, Accounting Interpretations, and Technical Bulletins. This appendix chapter will focus on accounting for financial statement purposes.

FINANCIAL REPORTING

A complete set of financial statements includes:

1. an "accountant's report" (also called a "cover letter") indicating the level of assurance provided by the accountants and any departures from Generally Accepted Accounting Principles (GAAP);

2. an income statement;

3. a balance sheet;

4. a statement of changes in stockholders' equity;

5. a statement of cash flows; and

6. notes to the financial statements.

Additional supplementary information may be provided, for which the accountants may (or may not) provide any assurance.

Accountant's report – The accountant's report is the best place to begin reading the financial statements. It will explain whether the accountants have compiled, reviewed, or audited the financial statements.

- A "compilation" is an engagement in which the accountant presents the client's information in the appropriate financial statement format without expressing any assurance as to whether the numbers provided by the client are correct.

- A "review" ordinarily includes analytical review, inquiries of management, and other procedures designed to give limited assurance as to whether the statements are prepared in accordance with GAAP.

- An "audit" includes an understanding of internal controls and assessment of risk that will lead to auditing procedures designed to provide the highest degree of assurance that the statements are prepared in conformity with

GAAP. Accountant's reports for audits are of four types: "unqualified," "qualified," "no opinion," and "disclaimer."

Other important information in the accountant's report includes any departures from GAAP and will explain the accountant's position, if any, regarding the effect of the departure on the financial statements. It will indicate any omission, such as the notes to the financial statements or perhaps the statement of cash flows. It may also indicate if there is a concern or uncertainty as to whether the company will continue operating. This concern or uncertainty is expressed as a "going concern" issue.

Income statement – The income statement shows the current period's income and expense activities since the prior period's financial statements. It may be on an interim, or part-year basis, or a full year basis. It is ordinarily broken down into operating activities and non-operating activities so that the user may segregate recurring and unusual (referred to as "extraordinary") activities from typical day-to-day operations. It provides the income and loss information for the activity.

The following is an example of an income statement:

INCOME STATEMENT
For the Year Ended December 31, xxxx

Gross Sales	$1,000,000
Less: Returns and Allowances	10,000
Net Sales	$ 990,000
Less: Cost of Goods Sold	490,000
Gross Profit	$ 500,000
Less: General Selling and Administrative	300,000
Net Profit from Operations	$ 200,000
Less: Nonoperating activities	0
Income before taxes and extraordinary item	$ 200,000
Less: Income taxes	30,000
Income before extraordinary item	$ 170,000
Less: Loss from extraordinary item	100,000
Net Income	$ 70,000

Balance sheet – The balance sheet is a snapshot of the company's financial condition at the end of business activity on a given day. It will ordinarily include the company's assets, liabilities, and the owner's or shareholders' equity. Basically, the balance sheet shows what the company owns. Assets are shown at "historical cost" (defined below). The balance sheet also shows what is owed on those assets. It shows in report form the fundamental accounting equation:

$$ASSETS = LIABILITIES + EQUITY$$

This means that what the business has – less what it owes – leaves the owners' equity (what they own). This principle can be easily understood in terms of a simple personal asset like a residence. Because of the "=" sign, one side of the equation *must* equal the other side for the equation to balance. This, of course, is the derivation of the name "balance sheet."

As mentioned above, most of the information included in the balance sheet is stated at historical cost, the price originally paid by the business for the asset. The theory of historical cost has a number of weaknesses, but continues on until a better solution can be found.

There are a number of exceptions to the historical cost rule. Among these are:

- obsolescent inventory;

- a loss on marketable securities such as stocks or an impairment of fixed assets; and

- fixed assets, such as real estate or equipment, that are shown at original cost less an allowance for depreciation (which is used to reflect the accounting expression of the recovery of the cost of an asset over its useful life).[2]

The key point to understand is that balance sheet figures are not necessarily intended to represent the current fair market or net realizable values of the assets (and often are quite different from those figures). The balance sheet is based on the "going concern" concept that assumes the business will remain in existence rather than be liquidated.

The following is an example of a balance sheet:

BALANCE SHEET
As of December 31, xxxx

ASSETS

Current Assets	
Cash and cash equivalents	$ 40,000
Accounts Receivable-trade	100,000
Inventories	50,000
Prepaid Insurance	10,000
Total current assets	$200,000
Property, Plant and Equipment, Net of Depreciation	300,000

Other Asset-Cash Surrender		
Value of Insurance		10,000
Total Assets		$510,000
Liabilities and Stockholders' Equity		
Current Liabilities:		
Accounts payable		$ 25,000
Total current liabilities		$ 25,000
Long-term Debt		75,000
Deferred Income Taxes		10,000
Total Liabilities		$110,000
Stockholders' Equity		
Common Stock		100,000
Retained Earnings		$300,000
Total stockholders' equity		$400,000
Total Liabilities and Stockholders' Equity		$510,000

Statement of changes – The statement of changes in stockholders' equity reflects all activity occurring to equity accounts during the financial statement period. This activity is usually related to the issuance or repurchase of the company's stock.

The following is an example of a statement of changes:

STATEMENT OF CHANGES IN STOCKHOLDERS' EQUITY
For the Year Ended December 31, xxxx

	Common Stock	Retained Earnings	Total Stockholders' Equity
Balance as of January 1, xxxx	$100,000	$250,000	$350,000
Net Income		70,000	70,000
Dividends		(20,000)	(20,000)
Balance as of December 31, xxxx	$100,000	$300,000	$400,000

Statement of cash flows – The statement of cash flows shows changes in the cash element (in terms of sources and uses of cash) and cash flows of the company that took place during the financial statement period. It is particularly relevant to the planner in determining whether sufficient cash flow is available to meet the needs of the business and fund other objectives such as life insurance premiums, nonqualified deferred compensation contributions, or contributions to employee benefit or retirement plans.

The following is an example of a statement of cash flows:

STATEMENT OF CASH FLOWS
For the Year Ended December 31, xxxx

Cash Flows Provided from (Used by) Operating Activities

Income from continuing operations	$170,000
Adjustments to reconcile income from continuing operations to net cash provided from continuing operations	10,000
Depreciation and amortization	10,000
Changes in assets and liabilities:	
Accounts receivable-trade	1,000
Inventories	(2,200)
Accounts payable	1,000
Other assets and liabilities	250
Net cash provided from Operating Activities	$180,050
Cash Flows Provided from (Used by) Investing Activities Capital additions	$(120,000)
Net Cash (Used by) Investing Activities	$(120,000)
Repayment of long-term debt	$(10,000)
Cash dividends paid	(20,000)
Net Cash (Used by) Financing Activities	$(30,000)
Increase (Decrease) in Cash and Cash Equivalents	$ 30,050
Cash and Cash Equivalents as of January 1, xxxx	9,950
Cash and Cash Equivalents as of December 31, xxxx	$ 40,000
Interest Paid (Continuing Operations)	$ 7,500
Income Taxes Paid (Continuing Operations)	$ 30,000

Notes to the financial statement – The notes to the financial statement will ordinarily contain vast amounts of useful information including, but not limited to:

- the accounting methods utilized;
- leases and terms;
- loans and loan repayment terms;
- detailed fixed asset information;
- related party transactions;
- income taxes; and

- information regarding "subsequent events" that occurred after the financial statement closing but before the financial statement release.

ACCOUNTING BASICS

Business accounting systems ordinarily use what is commonly referred to as "double-entry" accounting. Double entry accounting is based on a notion similar to that put forth by Sir Isaac Newton in his third law of motion: "For every action, there is an equal and opposite reaction." These actions are given the names "debit" and "credit" in accounting. And just as Newton's Laws of Motion carried no particular connotation of "good" or "bad," debits and credits are generally interpreted in a similarly neutral manner.

Once the professional is able to put aside the good and bad connotation of debits and credits, the mind is free to comprehend how the accounting system functions (even if nobody understands why it functions that way!).

Staying in general terms and referring to the balance sheet equation:

$$ASSETS = LIABILITIES + EQUITY$$

we must accept another general truth:

$$DEBITS = CREDITS$$

So, for every debit entry, there must be an equal and opposite credit entry. There must always be a balancing of the books.

One final general rule necessary to understand the environment is the bridge across the first two equations:

Certain accounts generally carry debit balances while other accounts (equal and opposite but not good or bad) generally carry credit balances.

Here are some general rules of thumb:

- Assets generally have debit balances. Therefore, liabilities and equity accounts must have credit balances.

- Expense and loss accounts ordinarily have debit balances. Revenue and gain accounts must therefore ordinarily have credit balances.

DEBIT BALANCE ACCOUNTS	CREDIT BALANCE ACCOUNTS
Assets	Liabilities
Expenses	Equity
Losses	Revenue
	Gains

Specific transactions, commonly referred to as "journal entries," may adjust a debit or credit type account. The key to understand what impact the transaction has on a specific account is to note what accounts ordinarily have debit and credit balances. Some specific examples may serve to clarify the rules:

Debit (Dr.) Cash	100	
Credit (Cr.) Sales		100

The above would be a journal entry to reflect a sale for cash. The debit to cash, a debit balance account in the balance sheet, would serve to *increase* the debit balance, or show *more* cash. The credit to sales in the income statement, a credit balance account, would serve to *increase* the credit balance, or show *more* sales.

(Dr.) Insurance Expense	50	
(Cr.) Cash		50

The above entry is an example of a debit and a credit that both affect debit balance accounts. The debit entry to "insurance expense" in the income statement serves to increase the debit balance or increase insurance expense. The credit entry to "cash" in the balance sheet, a debit balance account, serves to reduce the debit balance in the cash account. This is logical because the balance in the cash account is reduced when the expense is paid.

This background is necessary to understand accounting for life insurance. The basic rules are:

1. Cash surrender values will generally be assets of the company if the company owns the policy and is the beneficiary.

2. Cash values will carry debit balances on the balance sheet.

3. The current insurance expense will also carry a debit balance on the income statement.

4. Any income from the policy, including a death benefit, or any increase in the cash surrender value in excess of the premium paid in the current period will be a credit entry to an income (credit) account.

ACCOUNTING RULES SPECIFICALLY AFFECTING LIFE INSURANCE

The most common forms of life insurance that companies carry on their officers and stockholders are term and permanent insurance (including limited pay, ordinary whole life, universal, or variable life). Term insurance generally has no cash surrender value and thus represents only a pure insurance expense. Permanent insurance may have a cash surrender value and a loan value in addition to the insurance expense.

If the insured officers or their heirs are the beneficiaries of the policy, the premiums paid by the company represent compensation expense (or possibly a dividend) rather than insurance expense and represent income to the officer insured. In this case, the cash surrender value may not be an asset of the corporation. (If the company is both owner and beneficiary of the policy, then the policy may be an asset of the company.)

Here are some accounting guidelines for life insurance:

1. Unearned premiums (prepaid insurance) are classified as part of "working capital,"[3] but cash surrender values are not.[4]

2. "Loans accompanied by pledge of life insurance policies should be classified as current liabilities when, by their terms or by intent, they are to be repaid within twelve months."[5] (So short-term loans that are based on the policy as collateral should be shown as current liabilities.)

3. When a loan on a life insurance policy is obtained from the insurance company with the intent that it will not be paid but will be liquidated by deduction from the proceeds of the policy upon maturity or cancellation, the obligation should be excluded from current liabilities. (So loans that are not intended to be repaid in the short-term, such as loans that will be satisfied at the time of the maturity of the policy, should not be treated as short-term liabilities, which means that those loans do not reduce working capital).

4. If a company takes out policy loans from the insurance company on life insurance policies that it owns and if there is no intention to repay the loan during the ensuing operating cycle of the business, such loan may be excluded from current liabilities.[6]

5. The amount of the loan should be shown to reduce the cash surrender value, with disclosure of the amount so offset.[7]

6. Where a corporation maintains life insurance policies on its principal stockholders to fund the purchase of stock in the event of a stockholder's death, the footnote disclosure should first show the cash surrender value on the balance sheet[8] and then indicate disclosure of any commitments. For example:

    The company is the owner and beneficiary of key employee life insurance policies carried on the lives of X, Y, and Z bearing face value amounts of $500,000, $500,000 and $450,000 respectively. No loans are outstanding against the policies, but there is no restriction in the policies regarding loans. These life insurance contracts are accompanied by mandatory stock purchase agreements to the amount of the proceeds of the life insurance. In the event of the insured's death, the 'fair market value' of the stock will, by previous action, be established by the A Appraisal Company. The insured's estate will be obligated to sell, and the company will be obligated to purchase the insured's stock up to the appraisal value of the stock or the proceeds of insurance, whichever is the lesser. The purpose is to protect the company against an abrupt change in ownership or management.

So the original position taken by the accounting profession was that the cash surrender value, less any policy loans that were intended to be satisfied by set-off, should be shown as a noncurrent asset. Also, the portion of the insurance premium shown as an expense would be the difference between the premium payment and the increase in cash surrender value.

Examples of Accounting Journal Entries

If Corporation X pays an insurance premium of $4,800 on a $100,000 policy that covers its president and the policy's cash surrender value increases from $20,000 to $22,000, the proper journal entry would be:

Life Insurance Expense (Dr.)	2,800	
Cash Surrender Value of Insurance (Dr.)	2,000	
Cash (Cr.)		4,800

If the insured officer died half-way through the most recent period of coverage for which the $4,800 premium was made, the following entry would be made (assuming cash surrender value of $21,000 and refund of a pro rata share of the premium paid):

Cash	102,400
Cash Surrender Value of Insurance	21,000
Life Insurance Expense	2,400
Gain on Life Insurance Coverage	79,000

The gain on life insurance coverage is not generally reported as an extraordinary item because it is considered to be an ordinary business transaction.

Alternative Methods

This line of thinking came under attack a number of times and for a number of reasons. During the late 1960's and throughout the 1970's, new methods for expensing the insurance cost were offered to try to cure what was perceived as a significant flaw. This flaw is best highlighted by way of an example:[9]

TABLE 1
$100,000 LIFE PAID-UP AT AGE 65

Year	Annual Premium	Cash Value Increase	Total Premiums	Total Cash Value
1	$7,767	$1,344	$ 7,767	$ 1,344
2	7,767	6,119	15,534	7,463
3	7,767	6,308	23,301	13,771
4	7,767	6,514	31,068	20,285
5	7,767	6,741	38,835	27,026
6	7,767	6,991	46,602	34,017
7	7,767	7,272	54,369	41,289
8	7,767	7,589	62,136	48,878
9	7,767	7,951	69,903	56,829
10	7,767	8,365	77,670	65,194

Note: Maximum premium deposits	$77,670
Guaranteed cash value at age 65	65,194
Aggregate net cost	$12,476

Which would provide the following charges against income:

Year	Annual	Cumulative
1	$6,423	$ 6,423
2	1,648	8,071
3	1,459	9,530
4	1,253	10,783
5	1,026	11,809
6	776	12,585

Year	Annual	Cumulative
7	495	13,080
8	178	13,258
9	184 Cr.	13,074
10	598 Cr.	12,476

The example clearly shows that the charge to "income" is significantly higher in the early years, particularly year 1, and yet the benefit provided in each year is the same. One solution that has been proposed is called the "Ratable Charge Method." This method amortizes, or expenses the true cost of the insurance coverage in a straight line (i.e., ratably in equal increments) over the period of coverage. In the example this would mean that the $12,476 cost would have been expensed over the 10 years at the rate of $1,247.60 per year.

This solution was based on the premise that a company buys a policy to cover a fixed period of time and the net costs should be recognized evenly over that period of time. A variation of the ratable charge method adjusts the charge against income by taking into account the time value of the money involved.

One method follows the treatment of policies on the books of the life insurance company. The flaw with a small company using the same accounting as a life insurer is that the actuarial assumptions appropriate when a large group of policies is involved breaks down when the employer company holds just one or only a relatively few policies. Yet another accounting method charges an amount against earnings measured by the pure insurance portion of the payment (similar to the term insurance costs, such as P.S. 58 or Table 2001, used by the IRS).

It is important to understand that these alternative methods do *not* fall within the realm of generally accepted accounting principles (GAAP). This means that although they may provide a more desirable (and perhaps realistic) result in the early policy years than would be available under GAAP, the use of any of these alternatives would require a cover letter explaining the deviation and could prevent the accountant from providing an "unqualified" opinion (the equivalent of an "A").

On November 14, 1985 the Financial Accounting Standards Board issued FASB Technical Bulletin No. 85-4, Accounting for Purchases of Life Insurance.[10] This Bulletin stated the FASB's position (effective for insurance policies acquired after November 14, 1985). The Technical Bulletin clearly stated in response to the question of how an entity should account for an investment in insurance:

- "The amount that could be realized under the insurance contract as of the date of the statement of financial position should be reported as an asset."

- "The change in cash surrender or contract value during the period is an adjustment of premiums paid in determining the expense or income to be recognized under the contract for the period."

The Technical Bulletin was intended to apply to "all entities that purchase life insurance in which the entity is either the owner or the beneficiary of the contract, without regard to the funding objective of the purchase. Such purchases would typically include those intended to meet loan covenants or to fund deferred compensation agreements, buy-sell agreements, or post-employment death benefits."

The Technical Bulletin recognized that an insurance contract is significantly different from most investments and that payment may take a number of different forms. It concluded that the

"...pattern of premium payments is a decision that does not alter the underlying nature of the insurance contract. ... A portion of the premium [is for the] mortality risk and provides for recovery of the insurers contract acquisition, initiation, and maintenance costs. Another portion of the premium contributes to the accumulation of cash values. ... The relative amounts of premium payment credited to various contract attributes change over time as the age of the insured party increases and as earnings are credited to previously established contract values."

Respondents to this proposed technical bulletin argued that the primary objective of a life insurance contract is investment. Some argued that the company acquiring the policy is, in many cases, economically or contractually committed to maintain the contract in force. Both positions concluded that different values should be assigned than the settlement or cash surrender values because of the significant factors.

But both arguments were flatly rejected. The FASB found no compelling justification for departure from the contractually agreed upon settlement values between the buyer and seller (company and insurer) and stated that the arguments either had to do with future events, in which case it would be inappropriate to address them now, or that they just did not change the measurement of the agreed upon settlement values.

The FASB also rejected the argument that a business exchange rider made the accounting for life insurance incorrect. The FASB noted that:

"Such a provision does not affect the realization of future benefits under the insurance contract, nor does it change the traditional underwriting decisions involved in insuring a new life. Instead, the provision only reduces the cost of obtaining those benefits by allowing a new employee to be insured without the costs that are typically associated with obtaining a new policy."

FASB 96, Accounting for Income Taxes, indicates that the temporary difference for the excess of cash surrender value of life insurance over premiums paid is an example of the type of transaction that must be analyzed to determine the deferred income tax consequences. Conservatism requires that the deferred tax computation take into account any taxable income that would be recognized if a policy was surrendered.

SUMMARY

Generally Accepted Accounting Principles (GAAP) continue to recognize conservatively only the cash surrender value method of accounting for life insurance policies.[11] Any other method will be deemed to be a departure from GAAP if based on future possible events and assumptions applicable to unamortized deferred charges and should be discussed with the company's accountants.

Policy loans may, under certain circumstances, be set off against the cash surrender value rather than be reported as a liability on the balance sheet. The general reporting rules apply whether the policy is funding a buy-sell, a nonqualified deferred compensation plan,[12] or just protecting the interests of the business like a key employee policy.

Accounting for key employee life insurance depends on the type of policy:

- *Term insurance* – Premium payments represent a pure current expense. Such costs should be charged against income rather than retained earnings.

- *Permanent (cash value)* – Premium payments are bifurcated. To the extent a premium payment generates an increase in the policy's cash value, a charge should be made to an asset account. To the extent the premium paid exceeds the increase in the policy's cash value, a charge should be made to expense.

- *Cash values* – The firm's balance sheet should show policy cash values as a "non-current" asset.

- *Death proceeds* – When an insured dies, the gain upon the receipt of the insurance payment is typically reflected as a "special entry for nonrecurring amounts" on the Annual Statement of Operations. Alternatively, the gain on receipt by a corporation of death proceeds may be carried directly to the business's Retained Earnings Account since it is in effect adjusting prior years' activities.

WHERE CAN I FIND OUT MORE ABOUT IT?

1. *Accounting Standards – Original Pronouncements Issued Through June 1973* (Financial Accounting Standards Board), Chapters 2 and 3.

2. *AICPA Technical Practice Aids – As of June 1, 1989* (AICPA), p. 1391.

3. *Accounting Standards – Original Pronouncements July 1973-June 1, 1987* (Financial Accounting Standards Board), pp. 1441-1443.

4. Louis Richey and Lawrence Brody, *Comprehensive Deferred Compensation*, 3rd ed. (Cincinnati, OH: The National Underwriter Company, 1997).

5. Stephan R. Leimberg and John McFadden, *The Tools and Techniques of Employee Benefit and Retirement Planning*, 8th ed. (Cincinnati, OH: The National Underwriter Company, 2003).

ENDNOTES

1. This appendix chapter was written expressly for *The Tools and Techniques of Life Insurance Planning* by Barton Francis, CPA, CFP, of Ernst and Young, and edited by the authors. We express appreciation to Warren Martin, CPA, Rockville, Maryland, and Charles S. DiLullo, CPA, for their significant assistance.

2. This is not intended to be a clear and complete explanation of depreciation, but rather a familiarization with the concept that a piece of equipment, such as a business car, will benefit a number of accounting periods and the original cost or the reduction in value should not be charged against the income statement of one period. The depreciation allowance attempts to expense the vehicle over the periods that it is used to match the annual expense of its use against operating activities.

3. According to ARB (Accounting Research Bulletin) 43, the balance sheet is "...the connecting link between successive income statements." Working capital is defined as "...the excess of current assets over current liabilities, the relatively liquid portion of total enterprise capital which constitutes a margin or buffer for meeting obligations within the ordinary operating cycle of the business." It identifies current assets as specifically including "prepaid expenses such as insurance."

4. According to ARB 43, "This concept of the nature of current assets contemplates the exclusion from that classification of such resources as: (a) cash and claims to cash which are restricted as to withdrawal or use for other than current operations, are designated for expenditure in the acquisition or construction of noncurrent assets, or are segregated for the liquidation of long-term debts; ...(d) cash surrender values of life insurance policies..."

5. Footnote to ARB 43. The pledging of life insurance policies does not affect the classification of the asset any more than does the pledging of receivables, inventories, real estate, or other assets as collateral for a short-term loan.

6. Technical Practice Aids – Section 2240, Paragraph 7-1 of Accounting Principles Board Opinion No. 10 states: "It is a general principle of accounting that the offsetting of assets and liabilities in the balance sheet is improper except where a right of setoff exists." See also AICPA Technical Practice Aids Section 2240.

7. This is appropriate since the owner of a policy normally has the right to offset the loan against the proceeds received on maturity or cancellation of the policy.

8. A question was raised as to whether showing the cash surrender value as an asset was misleading if the company never intended to use the cash surrender value in operating. The response was: "If the enterprise retains all valuable contract rights incident to ownership of the life insurance policy, then it is mandatory from the standpoint of full accountability to reflect the asset status of the cash surrender value of the policy. Not to reflect the cash surrender value would be tantamount to creating a hidden reserve which would be contrary to generally accepted accounting principles."

9. See Gatewood, "Accounting for Business Life Insurance: The Ratable Charge Method," *CLU Journal*, July, 1967, p. 11; Tolan, "An Accrual Basis Alternative to Cash Basis Accounting for Corporate Life Insurance," *CLU Journal*, July, 1967, p. 60; Hodges, "Accounting for Corporate Owned Life Insurance," *CLU Journal*, January, 1978, p. 44, and Chapter 6 (Accounting for Deferred Compensation) in L. Richey and L. Brody, *Comprehensive Deferred Compensation*, 3rd ed. (Cincinnati, OH: The National Underwriter Company, 1997).

10. The Technical Bulletin included information regarding the thinking behind continuing to account for policies using the cash surrender value method and explained the thinking behind the rejection of other methods. The Technical Bulletin was released in response to the AICPA's Accounting Standards Executive Committee (AcSEC) concern that a number of different methods would be utilized in practice if GAAP was not clarified.

11. The authors' opinion is that the GAAP method of accounting described above is antiquated and does not reflect the economic reality of the transactions over time considering the present products and riders available to businesses in the early 21st century.

The alternative "ratable charge" method seems to provide a more realistic approach and has been used by a number of accounting firms even though it is not officially accepted. (See the unofficial statement of the Accountancy Principles Board in the *Journal of Accountancy*, November, 1970.)

In essence, under the ratable charge method total premiums to be paid over a predetermined period (such as for 10 years or to age 55) are determined on the assumption that the insured is likely to live and will continue to remain an employee of the business that long. The guaranteed cash surrender value at the end of the selected period is then subtracted from the total premiums to be paid. The result is a "net cost" which is then amortized (ratably) as a level annual charge over the premium paying period.

This prime assumption upon which the ratable charge method relies becomes more likely if the policy in question contains what is often called a "policy exchange" rider, an option the client's firm has to continue the policy on another life if the insured employee should decide to leave the firm. In other words the company could substitute a new key employee for the one no longer employed (in most cases the rider allows the exchange with no additional costs to the client's company). The existence of an exchange rider would seem to offer an answer to the criticism that if the policy is discontinued prior to the end of the selected premium payment period, the ratable charge method would result in a large write-off of an unamortized deferred charge.

12. FASB 106 should be reviewed where life insurance policies are funding vehicles for nonqualified deferred compensation plans. This release affects the accounting for these plans and may directly impact the timing of the recognition of the liability for postretirement benefits, while having no direct impact on the accounting for the underlying insurance product.

GLOSSARY[1]

absolute assignment: A transfer of a policy through which the policyowner shifts full and absolute control and all policy rights to the assignee. See also: assignment; collateral assignment.

absolute ownership: All legal rights and control of the incidents of ownership (e.g., selection of beneficiaries, settlement options, etc.) in a policy, without limitation, qualification, or restriction, are held by the policyowner.

accelerated option: Accumulated dividends and cash value are used to pay-up a life insurance policy sooner than scheduled.

accidental death benefit: An optional provision that provides an additional payment for loss of life due to an accident that was the direct cause of death. If the additional amount equals the face amount of the policy, this provision is frequently called a "double indemnity" provision. Some companies issue "ADB" in multiples of two or three times the face amount. See also: double indemnity.

account: The individual cash-value investment funds in a variable life insurance product. Also the cash-value accumulation account of universal or current-assumption policies.

accumulated dividends: Dividends left with the insurer to accumulate at interest. These dividends are generally income tax free but the interest is taxable as earned.

actuarial assumptions: An insurer, in establishing premium rates, scheduling policy cash values, and projecting future dividends must make certain estimates. The most important assumptions are based on probabilities of death using large numbers of insureds (so called mortality assumptions) and assumptions about interest and capital gains as well as sales commissions and other expenses.

actuarial cost: Projected cost as ascertained through assumptions and reduced to present values.

actuarial equivalent: Mathematically equivalent from an actuarial cost standpoint. For any type of life insurance policy or annuity issued by an insurer there are (theoretically at least) actuarial equivalent (i.e., mathematically equal) policies or annuities with different features or terms. For example, for any particular level-premium whole life policy with a given premium level

there is some (higher) level of premium that will make a 10-pay life policy its actuarial equivalent.

actuarial present value: The present worth of an amount or stream of payments receivable in the future, where each future amount is discounted at an assumed rate of interest and adjusted for the probability that it will in fact be received.

actuary: A professional highly educated in a number of fields such as mathematics, statistics, and accounting. An actuary must have superior knowledge as to the underlying principles of life insurance and their mirror image, annuities. Actuaries are responsible for creating new life insurance products and their pricing, value, and profit structures.

additional death benefit: See also: accidental death benefit; double indemnity.

additional premium: The amount of gross premium in excess of the recommended or "target premium" for the policy in universal and variable universal life policies.

additional provisions: Each life insurance contract contains "insuring" and "benefit" provisions as well as "uniform" provisions that define and limit coverage. Additional (general) provisions are often inserted into a contract to add to the protections, options, or flexibility of the policyowner.

adhesion: There is no true bargaining or "meeting of the minds" in a life insurance contract. Bluntly, a policyowner can "take it or leave it" but may not bargain for specific terms or conditions. In other words, the party who buys life insurance must adhere to an established, preexisting standard contract and its terms. The law provides special protection to one forced to accept a contract of adhesion and, other things being equal, will interpret the terms of such a document in favor of the policyowner rather than the insurer.

adjustable death benefit: Certain life insurance products allow the policyowner to increase or decrease the face amount (within limits and often only with evidence of insurability). For instance, universal and adjustable life policyowners can increase or decrease the amount of death benefit payable by adjusting the level of their premium payments.

adjustable life insurance: Many of the most attractive features of both term and whole life are contained in this highly flexible type of coverage. Premiums, death benefits, duration of coverage, and cash value levels can all be adjusted (both upward and downward within limits) by the policyowner to meet changing needs and circumstances.

adjustable premium: Term applicable to policies where the company has the contractual right to modify or change premium payments under certain specified conditions or to policies where the policyowner has the right to change scheduled premiums in universal or adjustable life.

adjusted gross estate: The adjusted gross estate is the gross estate less debts, funeral costs, and administrative expenses. This adjusted gross estate is the starting point for the balance of the federal estate tax computation and serves planners as a rough approximation of the before-death tax amount of assets that heirs might receive.

adjusted taxable gifts: Sum of taxable portion of post-1976 gifts other than those for any reason included in a deceased's gross estate.

administrator: The person or persons appointed by the probate (also called Surrogates' or Orphans') court to settle the estate of a person who died without a valid will. See also: executor.

admitted assets: In regulating insurers, a state insurance department will carefully examine and document as existing so called "admitted assets," i.e., all the assets of the insurer countable in ascertaining the insurer's financial soundness under state law. Such assets generally include all funds, securities, property, equipment, rights of action, or resources of any kind owned by the company or held in trust for others.

advanced life underwriter: This term refers to the agent marketing products and services where a sophisticated knowledge of law and high degree of creativity is required. Estate and financial planning, retirement planning, business insurance, and employee benefit planning are good examples of the fields in which an advanced life underwriter will work.

advance premium: Any premiums paid before their due date.

adverse selection: The tendency of people who are less than standard insurance risks to seek or continue insurance to a greater extent than other individuals. This so called "selection against the insurer" is a form of stacking the deck and is also found in the tendency of policyowners to take advantage of favorable options in insurance contracts.

age: The age in years of an applicant, insured, or beneficiary. Some companies use the age at the last birthday. Other companies use the age at the nearest birthday (last or next).

age at issue: The age of an insured at the time coverage goes into effect. Some insurers define issue age as the age at the insured's last birthday. In others, it is defined as the insured's age at the nearest birthday.

age limits: Minimum or maximum age limits for the insuring of new applicants or for the renewal of policies.

agency: The legal relationship empowering one party to act on behalf of another in dealing with third parties. (A life insurance agent does not generally have the authority to bind the insurance company.) The term agency is also defined as a sales office under the direction of either a general agent or a branch manager. A third definition of the term "agency" is an office operated by an independent agent who has an agent's contract with at least one insurer.

agent: A person who solicits insurance or aids in the placing of risks, delivery of policies, or collection of premiums on behalf of an insurer. Typically, a person placing products for a specific insurer is considered the insurer's agent rather than an agent of the policyowner.

agent of record: Typically, the agent who takes the initial policy application and who is entitled to any and all commissions on the issued insurance contract is considered the agent of record. If an insurer assigns an agent to service its "orphans" (policyowners who no longer have a servicing agent), the newly assigned agent will become the agent of record. Many times an agent will obtain a written authority from a current or prospective policyowner to be the sole party with the right to investigate and negotiate life insurance contracts. If any other agent does sell insurance to the client, the agent of record usually receives a percentage of the commission earned on the new policy. In this later case, the agent of record legally represents the interests of the client.

aggregate mortality table: A mortality table where the mortality rates at any age are based on all insurance in force at that age, without reference to the duration of insurance. See also: select mortality table and ultimate mortality table.

aleatory contract: Where a contract between two parties depends upon an uncertain event and where one party may pay a very small amount and receive a very large amount upon the occurrence or nonoccurrence of the specified event, it is called an aleatory contract. Life insurance is such a contract.

alternate valuation date: Typically, for federal estate tax purposes, assets are valued as of the date of a decedent's death. However, the estate's personal representative (executor or administrator) may elect to value all property in the estate as of its value six months from the date of death. If property is sold between the date of death and the date six months after death, that date becomes the alternate valuation date.

amount at risk: The pure insurance element of a life insurance policy. The net amount at risk is equal to the difference between the face value of a policy and its accrued cash value at a given time. The net amount at risk decreases as the cash value increases each year. If the cash value becomes the face value, the policy is said to mature or endow.

annual premium: The premium amount required on an annual basis under the contractual requirements of a policy to keep a traditional level premium whole life or term policy in force.

annuity: A systematic liquidation of principal and interest over a specified period. An annuity can be measured by a fixed duration (e.g., 20 years) or by the lifetime of one or more persons. A second definition for the term is the contract providing such an arrangement. An annuity can be commercial (e.g., such as the annuity an individual can purchase from an insurer) or private (e.g., a son can promise to pay his father an income for life that the father can never outlive but that ends at the father's death).

annuity, cash refund: See: cash refund annuity.

annuity certain: An annuity that pays a specified amount for a definite and specified period of time, such as 5 or 10 years, with remaining payments going to a designated beneficiary if the annuitant dies before the end of the specified period.

annuity certain, life: An annuity payable for a specified minimum number of periods or, if longer, for as long as the annuitant lives; a combination of an annuity certain and a life annuity.

annuity, deferred: See: deferred annuity.

annuity due: An annuity under which payments will be made at the beginning, rather than at the end, of each period (i.e., monthly, quarterly, yearly, et al.) For contrast, see: immediate annuity.

annuity, flexible premium: See: flexible premium annuity.

annuity, installment deferred: See: installment deferred annuity.

annuity, installment refund: See: installment refund annuity.

annuity, joint and survivor: See: joint and survivor annuity.

annuity, joint life: See: joint life annuity.

annuity, life: See: life annuity.

annuity, private: See: private annuity.

annuity, refund: See: refund annuity.

annuity, single-premium deferred: See: single-premium deferred annuity.

annuity, temporary: See: temporary annuity.

annuity, variable: See: variable annuity.

anti-rebate laws: State laws that prohibit an agent or company from giving part of the premium, or any other valuable consideration, back to the insured as an inducement to purchase life insurance.

applicant: The person(s) or party(ies) applying for and signing the written application for a contract of life insurance either on his or her own life or that of another.

application: A written form provided by an insurer typically completed by the insurer's agent and its medical examiner (in most cases) on the basis of information on the physical condition, occupation, and avocation of the proposed insured. The policy application is signed by the applicant (typically, but not always, the insured) and becomes a legal part of the insurance contract. The application is the major source of information for the insurer in deciding whether or not or on what terms and conditions a contract should be issued.

assign: To transfer a right or risk.

assignee: The person or party who receives a transferred right or risk when a life insurance policy is assigned.

assignment: The shift of rights and benefits of a life insurance contract from a policyowner to an assignee.

assumed interest rate: The rate of interest used by an insurance company to calculate its reserves.

attained age: Most insurers base premium rates on the age an insured has attained as of the application for insurance or its issue date, i.e., the age an insured has reached on a specific date. Generally, this is the age of the proposed insured based on his or her nearest (or, in some cases, last) birthday.

automatic premium loan provision: An option that will allow the insurer to automatically borrow money from a policy's cash value to pay any premium in default at the end of the grace period in order to keep a policy from lapsing.

aviation exclusion: A contract provision that excludes from coverage deaths due to airline accidents unless the insured was a passenger on a regularly scheduled commercial airline.

back-end load: A load is a charge against policy values for business expenses of the insurer in issuing the contract. These charges can be imposed at the inception of the contract (i.e., a "front-end" load) or at the termination of the contractual relationship (i.e., a "back-end" load). In the case of most variable, universal, and current-assumption life insurance products, the load is imposed when the policy is surrendered. Back-end loads typically decrease each year and disappear completely after the number of years specified in the contract.

banding: Banding refers to the recovery of ongoing administrative and handling costs. Insurers generally "band" premiums by policy size. This is a "cheaper by the dozen" concept in which larger policies are charged a more favorable rate than smaller policies. In other words a $1,000,000 policy will be charged significantly less per year than ten $100,000 policies for ongoing administrative and handling costs. Fewer policies are less expensive than more policies of the same aggregate amount. This is one reason why buy-sell policies may be purchased on a stock redemption rather than cross-purchase basis.

beneficiary: The recipient of life insurance proceeds at the death of the insured is the policy's beneficiary. A primary beneficiary is first in line to receive that money. A secondary beneficiary is entitled to payment only if no primary beneficiary is alive when the insured dies. Final beneficiaries are those entitled to proceeds if no primary

or secondary beneficiaries are alive at the death of the insured. These "backup" beneficiaries are often called "alternate" or "contingent" beneficiaries, since their claims are contingent on the deaths of everyone in the higher class of primary beneficiaries.

binding receipt: The receipt for payment of the first premium. This assures the applicant that if he or she dies before receiving the policy, the company will pay the death proceeds if the policy is in fact issued (or would have been issued) as applied for had death not intervened.

broker: A broker differs from an agent since the broker legally represents the customer rather than the insurer. Brokers may purchase policies on behalf of their clients though almost any insurer.

brokerage agency: A life insurance general agency servicing business of agents other than full-time (career) agents of the company represented by the agency.

broker-agent: A business entity licensed and registered with the Securities and Exchange Commission (SEC) with the legal right to offer securities products to the public. An agent selling variable life products and related securities (such as mutual funds) must be registered with a broker-dealer.

business insurance: Coverage concerned primarily with the protection of an insured's business against the economic loss incurred at the death or disability of a key executives and/or other key employees. Business insurance is also designed to stabilize and maximize the value of a business by assuring a practical plan for business owners to be bought out and receive fair value for their interests at the death of one or more of the owners.

buy-sell agreement: An agreement in which either the business or the surviving owners (or both) will purchase the shares owned by a deceased or retiring shareholder at a value or formula previously agreed upon by the parties and stipulated in the agreement.

capital conservation method: When an individual's needs for insurance are ascertained, there are two choices for determining how much income a given amount of capital will produce. One method assumes only income will be used so as to protect (conserve) capital. The capital conservation method, therefore, assumes only the earnings on principal (not the principal itself) will be used to satisfy those needs. The other approach is to annuitize capital (i.e., break down capital and pay out both income and capital to meet needs). This will generally result in a lower amount of capital needed (but at the expense of less future security and inheritance for others). See also: capital need analysis.

capitalization of policy loans: The process of increasing the policy loan in order to "pay" unpaid loan interest.

capital needs analysis: Capital needs analysis (CNA) is an appraisal of needs system popularized by super-salesman Tom Wolf. A client's financial needs are met though the economic value and income-producing capabilities of current and future assets.

capital stock insurance company: An insurance company owned by its stockholders (similar to the ownership of IBM by its shareholders). This form of corporate ownership should be contrasted with a mutual insurance company that is owned by its policyowners and operated solely for their benefit. See also: mutual company.

capital utilization method: A life insurance "needs computation" method based on the assumption that both the earnings and principal will be used up over the period during which the income will be needed. This method should be compared and contrasted with the capital conservation method of needs analysis.

cash accumulation policy: A contract that builds significant cash value or equity. Such policies include whole life policies, endowment policies, universal life, and the various variable life products.

cash refund annuity: A cash refund annuity pays a lump-sum cash benefit to a beneficiary if the annuitant dies before a recovery of premiums paid. The lump-sum cash benefit is equal to the difference between the total amount paid by the purchaser over the total annuity payments received before the annuitant's death.

cash surrender value: Cash surrender value is the amount available to the policyowner when a life insurance policy is surrendered. It is also the amount upon which a policy loan is based. In the first 8 to 10 years after a policy is issued, the cash value is typically the insurer's reserve to meet future liabilities reduced by a surrender charge that enables the insurer to recover expenses incurred in setting up the policy. If a policy is surrendered in later years, the cash surrender value usually equals or closely approximates the reserve value of the policy.

change of beneficiary provision: A provision that gives a policyowner the right to change the beneficiary at any time he or she chooses (unless an irrevocable beneficiary designation has been made).

classified risk: Most insureds are classified as "standard" risks. Those who are less likely to die (based on their health) than the standard risk may qualify for "preferred risk" classification, while those who are more likely to die than standard risks their age are called "substandard" risks and pay premiums accordingly. See also: substandard risk.

clause: A specific provision of a life insurance contract (or rider attached to it) dealing with a particular subject in that policy.

collateral assignee: The person or party to whom a collateral assignment is made.

collateral assignment: When a life insurance contract is transferred to an individual or other party as security for a debt, this usually temporary assignment does not transfer all policy rights. Under a collateral assignment, the creditor is entitled to be reimbursed only to the extent "his interest may appear," i.e., policy proceeds will be payable only for the amount owed by the policyowner at that time. Any death benefit in excess of the debt owed by the policyowner to the creditor is paid to the policy's beneficiary. For comparison, see: absolute assignment.

collateral assignment plan: A collateral assignment plan is a variation in a split dollar life insurance arrangement in which the insured initially applies for and owns the policy and names the beneficiary but collaterally assigns the policy to the payor of the bulk of the premiums as security for that party's outlays.

collateral loan: A loan guaranteed by the pledge of the life insurance contract as collateral.

commission: The percentage of the premium paid to an insurance agent or broker by the insurer as compensation.

commissioner: Also called superintendent in some states, a commissioner of insurance is the head of a state insurance department who supervises the insurance business in the state and administers insurance laws.

Commissioners Standard Ordinary Mortality Table (CSO): A standard mortality table approved by the National Association of Insurance Commissioners and used in life insurance rate calculations.

commissions, graded: This is the typical life insurance commission arrangement in which larger commissions are paid to the agent or broker during the first policy year than in renewal years.

commissions, level: This is a commission arrangement in which an agent is paid commissions of equal amounts over several years and is favored in ultra large cases in order to spread out the taxable commissions and thereby reduce taxes paid on the commissions.

commutation rights: The right of the beneficiary to receive – in one lump sum – the value of the remaining stream of future payments under a settlement option selected by the insured of a life insurance policy.

commute: To compute and pay – as of a given date – the lump-sum actuarial equivalent to a series of future payments that would be due under a life insurance contract.

commuted value: The present (i.e., discounted) actuarial value of a series of installments payable at fixed future dates. The commuted value is ascertained on the basis of an assumed rate of interest and mortality factors (if payments are contingent on the life or lives of one or more individuals).

compound interest: Interest earned on interest.

concealment: Intentional failure of the insured to disclose a material fact to the insurance company at the time application is made.

conditional assignment: An assignment made solely for the purpose of securing a debt. A conditional assignment is typically automatically terminated when the obligation is repaid. See also: assignment.

conditional premium receipt: This is the receipt given to a policy applicant if all or part of the premium is paid at the time of application. This receipt does not provide absolute interim insurance until the company acts on the application. It provides that the insurer will assume the risk of the death or a change in the health of the insured after the date of the application if it later approves the application or, more frequently, if the insured meets with the company's rules of insurability for the plan applied for as of the date of the application. See also: interim term insurance.

consideration: Consideration is an essential element of a binding contract. In a life insurance contract, the policyowner's consideration is the first premium payment and the application; the insurance company's consideration is the promise(s) contained in the contract. Future premiums are not consideration but rather a condition precedent to the insurer's obligation.

contestable clause: Sometimes called the incontestable clause. The provision in the insurance contract that states the time (called the contestable period) the insurer has to contest and the grounds under which the policy may be contested or voided by the insurer. By law, the maximum contestable period is two years, but many policies limit the period to one year.

contingent beneficiary: A contingent beneficiary is one who will receive death proceeds if the principal beneficiary predeceases the insured.

contract of insurance: A legally binding agreement in which an insurer agrees to pay a death benefit upon the death of the insured in return for the consideration of the policyowner's payment of an initial premium and the policy application. Once the insurer issues the contract, the policyowner pays premiums as a condition which precedes the insurer's duty to pay the death benefit upon the demise of the insured. This legally enforceable agreement comprises more than just the policy. The application and any attached supplements, riders, or endorsements form the entire contract.

contract rates: Life insurance settlement option rates (i.e., the guaranteed rates at which the policyowner's dollars can be converted into one or more forms of annuity payouts) are listed in the policy. In fact, the insurer may allow the purchase to be made at current rates if those are more favorable to the policyowner but because of increased longevity trends, guaranteed (contract) rates are often more favorable than current rates.

conversion: One type of life insurance contract can be exchanged for a different type assuming the contract is "convertible." For instance, term insurance can be converted to whole life or some other form of permanent insurance. Conversion occurs under a group policy when an insured individual applies for an individual policy without evidence of insurability within a stipulated period of time before the group insurance coverage terminates.

conversion, attained age: The premiums for the converted policy are based on the insured's age attained at time of conversion.

conversion, original age: Premiums for the converted policy are based on the insured's original age at issue. The policyowner must pay the difference in premiums, plus interest, for the time the policy has been in force.

convertible: A provision giving the policyowner the right to exchange the policy for another without evidence of insurability.

convertible term insurance: A term contract that may be converted to a permanent form of insurance without a medical examination, if conversion is made within a limited period as specified in the contract. The premium is usually based on the attained age of the insured at the time of conversion.

cost of insurance: In the case of a split dollar arrangement or life insurance in a qualified plan, the value of the pure insurance protection in any year is the difference between the face amount of the policy and its cash value multiplied by a life insurance premium factor provided by the IRS (currently Table 2001; formerly P.S. 58 rates) or, (in certain cases) if lower, the insurer's rates for individual one-year term policies available to all standard risks (initial issue insurance).

cost of living adjustment (COLA): A rider available with some policies that provides for automatic, periodic increases in benefits based on increases in the consumer price index (CPI) or other index of inflation.

credit life insurance: A policy issued on the life of a borrower with the creditor named as beneficiary to cover the repayment of a loan in the event the borrower dies before the loan has been repaid. Usually written using monthly decreasing term based on a relatively small, decreasing balance installment loan.

cross purchase: A buy-sell arrangement that provides that in the event of one owner's death, the surviving shareholders or partners are bound to purchase, and the estate of the deceased is bound to sell, the deceased's interest in the business. A cross-purchase agreement is often funded with life insurance policies owned by each owner on the life or lives of all other owners.

current-assumption policy: Current-assumption policies reflect the insurer's current interest, mortality, and expense experience directly in cash value credits and charges rather than indirectly through dividends. As a result, actual cash values accumulations are uncertain, although there is a minimum cash value guarantee. The most prevalent type of current-assumption policy is universal life, although it is also sold in fixed-premium modes. Although inaccurate, the term "interest-sensitive" is sometimes used synonymously with "current-assumption." Current-assumption is actually a broader concept implying direct sensitivity not only to current interest rates but also to mortality and expense experience. Although traditional participating whole life policies may reflect the company's current performance with respect to investment, mortality, and expenses through its declared dividends, these policies are not classified as current-assumption policies.

current interest rate: This is the interest rate credited to current-assumption and universal life products (versus the fixed rate of traditional life insurance policies).

current value: The fair market value of a security or other property at the present time.

date of maturity: The date upon which a life insurance policy endows if the insured is still living.

date of policy: The date appearing on the front page of an insurance policy indicating when the policy went into effect.

death benefit: The amount stated in the policy as payable upon the death of the insured.

death claim: When the insured dies, this is the form that must be signed by the policy beneficiary and, along with the death certificate, sent to the insurer to provide proof of the date the insured died and to establish the beneficiary's right to the policy's proceeds.

declared interest rate: In a universal life policy (or in the general account of a variable universal life or interest-sensitive whole life policy), cash values earn a minimum interest rate. However, they will actually be credited with a current rate of return that may be substantially higher. This rate is declared by the insurance company and may be periodically changed.

decreasing term insurance: If the face value of term insurance decreases over time in scheduled increments until the policy expires, the insurance is a form of decreasing term. Typically in such policies, the premium remains level.

default: If a policyowner fails to make a premium payment by a policy's final due date or by the end of its grace period, the policy is in default and will lapse.

deferred annuity: A series of payments that are not begun until the lapse of a specified period of time or until the annuitant reaches a specific age.

delivery of policy: Delivery is, in general and nonlegal terms, the presentation of the policy to the policyowner. Actual delivery is legally determined by the intent of the parties and, therefore, does not necessarily require that the policy physically change hands. For instance, a conditional binding receipt (or, at times, verbal acknowledgement) may constitute delivery.

dependency period: In computing life insurance needs, the years when children are dependent upon parents, usually until the youngest is 18 years old, is called the dependency period.

deposit term life insurance: Deposit term is a form of temporary coverage, normally sold for ten-year terms, with the first-year premium more than twice the amount of the annual premiums paid for the remaining years. This higher first-year premium is called a deposit. If the insured dies, double the deposit is added to the death benefit; if the insured lives, double the deposit is returned at the end of the term. The insured forfeits the deposit and receives no refund if the policy lapses. A form of tontine, most states now severely restrict or totally prohibit this type of policy.

disability premium waiver insurance: This is an important option or rider in a life insurance policy that provides that if an insured becomes totally disabled for six months or longer, no further premiums will be due and the policy will be continued in full force until death or recovery occurs. Upon recovery, the policyowner does not have to repay premium payments made by the insurer on behalf of the policyowner during the disability period.

dividend: When a policy participates in the favorable investment, mortality, and expense experience of the insurer (so called "par" policies), the policyowner receives "dividends" as a refund of an "overcharge" in premiums. For tax and other purposes, these dividends are considered a return of capital rather than a profit payment.

dividend additions: Participating policies provide that their dividends may be used as single premiums to purchase paid-up insurance at the insured's attained age as additions to the amount of insurance specified on the face of the contract. These additions are purchased at net rates (no commissions or other charges) to the policyowner. See also: paid-up additions.

dividend class: All policyowners are grouped into categories in which members who bought the same type of contract at the same age are classed. This classification method allows precise determination of how much premium should be returned to each class as a dividend.

dividend deposits: Cash dividends and interest arising from the policy left on deposit with the company under the terms of the dividend option.

dividend, extra: A dividend that is paid in addition to any regular, periodic dividends. See also: dividend.

dividend options: The different ways in which the insured, under a participating policy, may elect to receive dividends. The dividend options generally include receiving payments in cash, applying them to reduce premiums, purchasing additional paid-up insurance, having them held by the insurer to earn interest for the policyowner, or purchasing additional term insurance.

divisible surplus: The amount of the company's surplus earnings available for distribution among the policyowners in the form of dividends.

earned premium: The amount of premium that would compensate the insurance company for its loss experience, expenses, and profit year to date.

economic benefit: The economic benefit is, in a split-dollar or other employer-provided insurance plan, the amount that the insured employee or party must report currently as income.

emergency fund: When calculating the amount of life insurance needed, the amount figured into the client's needs that should be kept on hand by survivors as a fund for emergencies (similar to the reserve all clients should hold for an emergency such as an accidents or an unexpected but potentially profitable business opportunity). The increasing loan value of a life insurance policy also constitutes, and is often referred to as, an emergency fund for the insured during lifetime.

endorsement: A written modification to an insurance policy, usually written on the printed policy page. An endorsement may also be in the form of a rider. No endorsement is valid unless signed by an executive officer of the company and attached to and made a part of the policy. See also: rider.

endow: A life insurance policy is said to endow when its cash value equals the face amount. The policyowner then receives, in cash, the face amount.

endowment: A life insurance contract that provides for the payment of the face amount at the end of a fixed period, or at a specified age of the insured, or at the death of the insured before the end of the stated period.

evidence of insurability: A statement or proof of a person's physical condition, occupation, etc., affecting the acceptance of the applicant for insurance.

exceptions provision: An insurance policy provision that limits the insurance company's liability by excluding coverage for certain losses, such as death in an aviation accident other than on a regularly scheduled commercial airline.

excess initial expenses: An insurer's first-year expenses that exceed first-year expense loading. These are generally a result of higher first-year commission rates and the expense of selection and issue.

excess interest: The positive difference between the rate of interest an insurer guarantees to pay on proceeds left under settlement options and the higher interest actually paid. A second meaning of the term is the difference between the guaranteed rate of return on cash value and the higher, current rate in universal life and other interest-sensitive policies.

exclusion clause: A policy provision that excludes certain risks from coverage, such as aviation, war, or preexisting conditions. See also: exceptions provision.

exclusion ratio: A fraction used to determine the amount of annual annuity income exempt from federal income tax. The fraction is generally found by dividing the policyowner's investment in the annuity contract by the expected return.

expense charge: In variable, universal life, and other current-assumption policies, all costs are individually deducted and accounted for within the policies. These expense charges are fixed amounts or percentages deducted from gross premiums paid and cash value, as specified in the policy.

expense loading: The amount added to the premium during the rate-making process to cover the expenses of maintaining the business, commissions, administration, and overhead.

experience: The loss record of a type of insurance written. This record is used in adjusting premium rates and predicting future losses.

experience modification: The adjustment of premiums as a result of the application of experience rating; usually expressed as a percentage.

extended term option: A nonforfeiture option that provides that the net cash surrender value of a policy may be used as a net single premium at the attained age of the insured to purchase term insurance at the face amount of the original policy for as long a period as possible.

extra dividend: A dividend that is paid in addition to regular, periodic dividends.

extra premium: The amount charged in addition to the regular premium to cover an extra hazard, special or substandard risk.

extra protection benefit: An insurance policy provision that provides an extra amount of insurance payable if death occurs during the term of the provision.

face amount: The amount payable in the event of death, as stated on the front page of the policy. The face amount may be decreased by loans or increased by additional benefits payable under specified conditions, or as stated in a rider.

family income policy: A life insurance policy that combines whole life and decreasing term to provide income protection against the premature death of the family breadwinner. If the insured dies within a specified period, the family will receive a stated amount of income from date of death until the end of the period. The face amount of the policy is then paid to the family. For comparison, see: family maintenance policy.

family income rider: Similar to a family income policy except that the decreasing term coverage is written as a rider to a whole life policy rather than as combination of both coverages.

family maintenance policy: A life insurance policy combining level term and whole life to provide income protection against the premature death of the family breadwinner. If the insured dies within a specified period (say, 20 years) the family will receive a stated monthly amount from the date of death to 20 years in the future. The face amount of the policy is then paid to the family. For comparison, see: family income policy.

family policy: A policy that combines whole life and convertible term to provide insurance on each family member in units of coverage. Each unit generally consists of $5,000 of whole life on the wage earner, $1,250 of convertible term on the spouse and $1,000 of convertible term on each child.

family rider: An optional policy supplement attached to the insurance policy issued to the head of a family and insuring other members of the family, generally the spouse and children.

fifth dividend option: Because this option is usually listed after four other possibilities, it is often called the "fifth dividend" option. If selected, each year the insurer will use the prior year's dividend to purchase (at no commission or expense charge) one-year term insurance up to specified limits (usually no more than the policy's cash value) with the balance applied toward one or more of the other options. The fifth dividend option is useful to maintain level or increasing protection, to keep coverage high even if a policy loan has been taken out, or where the parties are involved in a split dollar arrangement.

final expenses: Costs incurred during a last illness, funeral and burial costs, debts, probate expenses, death taxes and any other taxes or obligations that must be paid in order to settle the estate of a decedent.

financed insurance: The payment of insurance premiums, in whole or in part, with funds obtained by systematic borrowing, usually from the cash value of the contract.

first-year premium: Insurance premiums that are due during the first policy year, regardless of whether they are paid annually, semiannually, quarterly, monthly, or weekly. Premiums due after the first year are known as renewal premiums.

fixed-amount settlement option: A life insurance policy beneficiary can request that proceeds be paid in regular installments of a fixed dollar amount. The number of payment periods is determined by the policy's face amount, the amount of each payment, and the interest earned. For contrast, see: fixed-period settlement option.

fixed annuity: An annuity that provides fixed payments during the annuity period. For contrast, see: variable annuity.

fixed-period settlement option: A life insurance settlement option in which the number of payments is set by the payee, with the amount of each payment determined by the amount of proceeds. For contrast, see: fixed-amount settlement option.

flexible premium annuity: An annuity that allows the owner of the contract to vary premium payments (within limits) from year to year.

flexible premium variable life: See: variable universal life.

fraternal insurance: Life or health insurance protection provided by fraternal benefit societies. Before purchasing fraternal insurance, an individual must become a member of the organization.

fraud: An act of deceit; misrepresentation of a material fact made knowingly, with the intention of having

another person rely on that fact and consequently suffer a financial hardship.

free-look provision: A provision in life insurance policies that gives the policyowner a stated amount of time (usually ten days) to review a new policy. It can be returned within this time for a 100% refund of premiums paid, but cancellation of coverage is effective from date of issue.

front-end load: A contract is front-end loaded when certain of the insurer's expenses are deducted from the gross premium before the remaining net premium goes into the cash value account.

full disclosure: The requirement that prospective purchasers of variable and universal life products be fully informed of the charges and costs and provided with all important information about their policies. Also includes the requirement that they are given a current prospectus and that no statements or guarantees are made by the agent regarding cash values or interest rates.

fully insured plan: Pension plans that are funded entirely through individual insurance contracts issued on the lives of participants. The insurance company products provide any pre-retirement death benefits and the entire retirement benefit for the employee.

general account: Traditionally, the term describing a company's overall investment portfolio. More recently, it also refers to the separate investment funds upon which the declared rate of return in a universal life policy is based. Also, with variable and variable universal life policies, one of the investment account options that earns a declared rate of return.

grace period: Most life insurance contracts provide that premiums may be paid at any time within a period of generally 30 or 31 days following the premium due date, during which time the policy remains in full force. If death occurs during the grace period, the insurer will pay the face amount less the amount of the earned but unpaid premium (and any outstanding loan). Generally, an insurer will not charge interest on overdue premiums if they are paid before the end of the grace period.

graded death benefits: A life insurance policy provision that provides for death benefits that, in the early years of the contract, are less than the face amount of the policy, but that increase with the passage of time.

graded premium life insurance: To make life insurance premiums more affordable (and therefore marketable), some insurers sell a form of modified life insurance that starts with relatively low premiums that increase slowly each year. After a period of years, the premium remains level. The death benefit remains level throughout the term of coverage.

gross premium: This is the premium paid by the policyowner. More technically, the gross premium is the net premium, plus the expense of operation less the interest factor. For contrast, see: net premium.

group life insurance: A form of life insurance covering a group of persons generally having some common interest or activity, such as employees of the same company or members of the same union or association. Most group insurance is issued using yearly renewable term, without requiring medical examinations.

group ordinary life insurance: Level premium ordinary life insurance issued on a group basis.

guaranteed cash value: The guaranteed amount available to the insured on surrender of a policy according to a table of guaranteed values scaled to the number of years in which the policy is in force. In a universal or variable policy, there is no guaranteed cash value.

guaranteed cost: This is another term for nonparticipating (non par) insurance. Guaranteed cost can also be defined as the maximum costs that can be deducted from cash value under the terms of the policy in universal or variable universal life contracts.

guaranteed insurability rider: A rider, now offered on most life insurance policies, that gives the policyowner the right to purchase additional insurance at specified future times without evidence of insurability. Rates are generally based on attained age at the time of purchase.

guaranteed interest rate: The minimum annual rate of interest used in calculating policy reserves from year to year, or annual increases in dividend accumulations, or the interest factor in proceeds held under a settlement option, or the amount payable under the interest income option, etc. This term also refers to the minimum rate credited to cash value in interest-sensitive policies.

guaranteed purchase option: See: guaranteed insurability rider.

human life value: One method of determining how much insurance a person should own is to measure his or her "human life" value, an estimate of the present value of a person's remaining economic worth. In gen-

eral terms, this projects future net after-tax salary and other earnings, reduces them by future expenses, and then discounts these future net values at interest to determine a lump-sum present value.

immediate annuity: An annuity contract that pays the annuity at the *end* of each period of payment. The interval may be monthly, quarterly, semiannually, or annually.

incidents of ownership: The right to exercise any of the privileges in the insurance policy (e.g., change the beneficiary, withdraw cash values, make loans on the policy, etc.). Any retention of an incident of ownership will cause federal estate tax inclusion of policy proceeds.

incontestable clause: See: contestable clause.

increasing term insurance: Term life insurance coverage that increases in face value each year (or certain period) from the date of policy issue to the date of expiration. For contrast, see: decreasing term insurance and level term insurance.

indeterminate premium: Refers to policies where the actual premium charged may be lower than the guaranteed premium stated in the policy. Policies with indeterminate premiums generally make reference to the *guaranteed* (or maximum) premium that can be charged, and the *current* (or lower) premium, based on the current and projected mortality and/or investment experience.

individual life insurance: Life insurance contract that covers only one insured, but that may sometimes cover several people, such as the members of a family, through the use of riders. The term "individual" is often used to distinguish this type of life insurance from group life insurance.

industrial life insurance: Often called debit or home service insurance, life insurance issued on individual lives from birth to age 70 in small amounts. Weekly or monthly premiums are collected at the individual's home by a home service agent. Usually, no medical examination is required.

initial death benefit: In flexible feature life insurance policies, the original face value of the policy; the specified amount.

initial premium: The first premium, generally payable with the application or upon delivery of the policy.

initial reserve: The reserve amount determined at the beginning of the policy year. It equals the preceding year's ending reserve, plus the annual net premium.

installment deferred annuity: An annuity in which the annuitant pays into the annuity fund over a period of time, after which (usually starting immediately) annuity payments begin coming back to the annuitant and continue for life.

installment premiums: Premiums paid over time rather than as a single premium.

installment refund annuity: A life annuity that will continue to make payments to a stipulated beneficiary after the death of the annuitant until the total payments equal the consideration paid to the insurer. For contrast see: cash refund annuity.

installment settlement: A series of periodic payments of proceeds instead of payment in a lump-sum. Any of the income settlement options in a policy. A policy clause allowing the beneficiary to choose to receive proceeds in installments.

insurability: The term insurability encompasses all conditions pertaining to an individual that affect his or her health, susceptibility to injury, as well as life expectancy and other factors considered by the insurer in its underwriting and rating process. If the risk is too high, the insurance company will refuse coverage.

insurable interest: A person who has a reasonable expectation of benefiting from the continuance of another person's life or of suffering a loss at his or her death is said to have an insurable interest in that life.

insurance reserves: The present value of future claims minus the present value of future premiums. Reserves are balance sheet accounts set up by insurers to reflect actual and potential liabilities under outstanding insurance contracts.

insured: The individual or group covered by the contract of insurance.

interest-adjusted cost method: A method of comparing costs of similar policies by using an index that takes into account the time value of money due at different times through interest adjustments to the annual premiums, dividends, and cash value increases at an assumed interest rate.

interest factor: One of three factors taken into consideration by an insurance company when calculating pre-mium rates. This is an estimate of the overall average interest that will be earned by the insurer on invested premium payments over a long period of time.

interest-only option: A settlement option under which all or part of the proceeds of a policy are left with the insurance company for a definite period at a guaranteed minimum rate of interest. Interest may be paid (usually subject to certain minimums) annually, semiannually, quarterly, or monthly – or, in some cases, may be added to the proceeds left with the insurer.

interest-sensitive whole life: A traditional whole life policy with fixed premiums and traditional nonforfeiture values where interest is credited directly to the cash value at current rates. Often used somewhat erroneously to refer to current-assumption policies. Generally loads, mortality costs, and interest credits are separately stated. The cash value of the policy is the greater of this fund less surrender charges, and the guaranteed cash values.

interim term insurance: Term life insurance issued to an applicant during the period between submission of the application and the time the insurance company either issues a permanent insurance policy or rejects the application. See also: conditional premium receipt.

interpolated terminal reserve: A reserve fund that an insurance company uses to cover its liability in a particular policy. It is used in determining the value of certain life insurance policies for gift tax purposes.

investment account: A separately managed cash value investment fund (usually similar to a mutual fund) into which variable and variable universal life insurance policyowners allocate the premiums and cash value. Policies generally have several of these accounts, each with its own investment objective and degree of risk.

investment portfolio: A list detailing the securities owned by a person, business, or mutual fund. Most insurance companies carry a broadly varied investment portfolio. Also refers to the equity-based accounts in variable and other interest-sensitive products.

investment year method of dividend calculation: Any dividend calculation method that recognizes differences in earned interest rates depending upon the year in which the investment is made. For contrast, see: portfolio method of dividend calculation.

issue: A term applying to the insurer's approving and forwarding new policies to the agent for delivery to applicants.

issue limit: The maximum amount of coverage a company is willing to extend on a given risk.

joint and survivor annuity: A life annuity payable over the lives of two or more annuitants that continues to make payments until the death of the last surviving annuitant.

joint and X-percent survivor annuity: An annuity that pays an income to two individuals. The specified percentage of the joint income continues to the survivor for life if the principal annuitant dies first. If the secondary annuitant dies first, the unreduced joint benefit continues to the principal annuitant for life. In its second-death form, X percent of the joint income is paid to the survivor regardless of which individual dies first. Common percentages are 100% (full), 75% (three-fourths), 66% (two-thirds), or 50% (one-half).

joint and survivorship option: A contract option that permits policy proceeds to be paid out as a joint and survivor annuity.

joint control: A life insurance policy provision that states that a person, persons, or organization other than the insured, usually the beneficiary, has a joint right with the insured to the exercise of the rights, powers, benefits, privileges, and options of the policy.

joint insurance: A life insurance contract covering two or more lives that pays death proceeds and terminates at the first death among the insured lives. Often used to fund cross purchase buy-sell agreements among more than two partners or shareholders.

joint life annuity: A life annuity payable to two or more annuitants that continues payments until one of the two annuitants dies.

jumbo risk: An insurance contract with exceptionally high limits, such as $250,000 or more.

juvenile insurance: Life insurance policies written on the lives of minors within specified age limits, generally with the parents or grandparents as the policyowners and premium payors.

key employee (sometimes called key executive or key man) insurance: Provides cash to absorb the financial loss caused by the death or disability of a vital individual in a business.

lapse: Termination of an insurance policy because of nonpayment of premiums or, in the case of variable and universal life policies, the depletion of cash value below that amount needed to keep the policy in force.

last survivor insurance: A life insurance contract on two or more persons that pays proceeds only upon the death of the last insured. Also called second-to-die insurance, last-to-die insurance, or survivorship life.

level premium: A life insurance premium that remains fixed through the life of a policy. It must be large enough so that in early years the insurer will develop a surplus large enough so that in later years – together with interest and future premiums – there will be enough to pay all death claims.

level term insurance: Term life coverage on which the face value remains the same from the date the policy is issued to the date the policy expires. For contrast, see: decreasing term insurance; increasing term insurance.

life annuity: An annuity contract that pays only until the annuitant dies. Payments cease at that time even if the amount paid by the insurer does not equal the total premiums paid by the annuity owner.

life expectancy: The average remaining term of life for a number of persons of a given age, according to probability statistics of a mortality table.

life income option: One of the settlement options under which the proceeds of a life insurance or annuity policy may be applied to buy an annuity payable to the beneficiary for life.

life income with period certain option: A life insurance proceeds settlement option that will pay at least a minimum specified number of periodic installments in a guaranteed amount whether the named beneficiary lives or dies.

life paid-up at age ( ): A form of limited payment life insurance that provides protection for the whole of life, with premium payments stopping at the indicated age. For example, if a 45-year old bought a life paid-up at age 65 policy, premiums would be payable for 20 years and coverage would continue for the insured's life.

limited-payment (limited-pay) policy: A life insurance policy that provides for payment of the premium for a period of years less than the period of protection provided under the contract.

loading charge: The additional charge for overhead costs added to the net premium. This charge is required by actuarial tables to cover mortality and interest factors.

loan: Money loaned at interest by the insurance company to a policyowner on the security of the cash value of his or her policy. See also: automatic premium loan provision; loan value.

loan value: A specified amount that can be borrowed from the insurance company by the policyowner, using the cash value of the policy as collateral.

lump sum: Payment of the entire proceeds of a life insurance policy at one time. This is the method of settlement provided by most policies, unless an alternate settlement is elected by the policyowner before the insured's death or thereafter by the beneficiary before receiving the payment.

mature: The time when a policy becomes payable. A whole life policy matures upon the death of the insured or when its cash value equals its face amount (usually at age 100).

Medical Information Bureau (MIB): This is an entity that collects and stores medical data on life and health insurance applicants. The information is exchanged among member insurance companies. Its purpose is to guard against fraud and concealment by helping insurers discover pertinent yet undisclosed health facts.

minimum deposit policy: A cash value life insurance policy having a first-year loan value that is available for borrowing immediately upon payment of the first-year premium. These types of contract are much less popular since Congress disallowed the deduction for personal interest.

minimum premium: A minimum premium is the smallest amount of premium the insurer requires to be paid in the first year of a universal life contract.

minor beneficiary: A beneficiary who is under the state's legal age of majority and, thus, not considered competent to make certain financial transactions on his or her own. A legal guardian must be appointed to accept death benefits on behalf of a minor beneficiary.

misrepresentation: A false statement as to a past or present material fact made in an application for insurance intended to induce an insurance company to issue a policy it would not otherwise issue, or to rate the policy more favorably than it otherwise would have, or to issue the policy with a larger face amount than it otherwise would have.

misstatement of age: Giving the wrong age for oneself in an application for insurance or for a beneficiary who is to receive benefits on a basis involving a life contingency. Also, a provision in most life policies setting forth the action to be taken if a misstatement of age is discovered after policy issue.

mode of payment: The frequency with which premiums are paid (e.g., annually, semiannually, etc.)

modified life: Whole life insurance with reduced premiums payable during the first few years (usually three to five) that are only slightly higher than the rate for term insurance. Thereafter, the annual premiums are higher than that for a comparable whole life policy.

moral risk: Moral condition as reviewed by a study of habits, environment, mode of living, and general reputation that an underwriter must take into consideration in determining whether an applicant for insurance is a standard insurable risk. This information is usually obtained from inspection reports.

mortality factor: One of the basic factors needed to calculate basic premium rates. It utilizes mortality tables in attempting to determine the average number of deaths at each specific age that will occur each year.

mortality risk: The risk of death. The risk carried by a life insurance company and sometimes called the pure insurance risk. The degree of risk is the difference between the policy reserve (usually equal to the cash value of a permanent life policy) and the face amount of the policy.

mortality table: A table of the mortality experience of groups of individuals categorized by age and sex that is used to estimate how long a male or female of a given age is expected to live. Some tables are required to be unisex, i.e., those used for actuarial calculations involving qualified pension plans. The mortality table is the primary starting point for calculating the risk factor, which in turn determines the gross premium rate.

multiple life policy: A life insurance policy taken out on the lives of three to five persons, with benefits payable upon the death of each person, except, generally, the last one to survive. Also called a last-to-die policy, its most popular use is to fund buy-sell agreements.

mutual company: A life insurance company that has no capital stock or stockholders. Rather, it is owned by its policyowners and managed by a board of directors chosen by the policyowners. Any earnings in addition to those necessary for the operation of the company and contingency reserves are returned to the policyowners in the form of policy dividends. For contrast, see: stock company.

National Association of Insurance Commissioners (NAIC): An association of state insurance commissioners attempting to solve insurance regulatory problems, create uniform legislation and regulations, and promote life insurance company solvency and responsibility.

net amount at risk: The difference between the face amount of an insurance contract and the policy's cash value.

net cost: A term ordinarily referring to the actual cost of insurance to a policyowner in a mutual company after the policy dividends are deducted from the premiums deposited. Since there are no dividends on nonparticipating policies, the net cost of these policies is equal to the total premiums paid. In determining the true net cost (sometimes called net ledger cost) of a life insurance policy over a period of years, allowance should also be made for the cash surrender value at the end of the given period. See also: net premium.

net level premium: The pure annualized level mortality cost of a life insurance policy from age of entry to maturity date. It is determined by dividing the net single premium for the policy by the present value of an annuity due for the premium-paying period.

net premium: This term has several meanings, depending on context: (1) premium paid minus agent's commission; (2) the original premium minus any returned premium; (3) the net charge for insurance cost only minus expenses or contingencies; or (4) a participating premium minus dividends paid or anticipated.

new money interest rate: See: investment year method of dividend calculation.

nonassignable contract or policy: A policy that the owner cannot legally assign to a third party.

nonconvertible term insurance: A term policy that may not be converted to a permanent policy.

nonforfeiture values: Those values or benefits in a life insurance policy that by law the policyowner does not forfeit, even if he or she chooses to discontinue payment of premiums. It usually includes cash value, loan value, paid-up insurance value, and extended term insurance value.

nonmedical insurance: Life insurance issued on a regular basis without requiring the applicant to submit to a medical examination. The insurer relies on the applicant's own answers to questions regarding his or her physical condition, and on personal references or inspection reports to decide whether to issue the policy.

nonparticipating life insurance: So called "non par" life insurance does not pay policy dividends. The policyowner is not in any way an owner and therefore is not entitled to share in any divisible surplus of the company. Any profits from the excess of the premium over the costs of insurance accrue to the nonpar company's stockholders, which is fair since they would be the ones to absorb any losses. For contrast, see: participating insurance.

nonrenewable contract: An agreement or policy written for a specific period and purpose and that does not contain an option to be renewed for successive terms. For contrast, see: renewable and convertible term.

nontransferable: A contract in which the benefits or any of its value cannot be sold, assigned, discounted, or pledged as collateral for a loan or as security for the performance of an obligation or for any other purpose, to any person other than the insurance company.

offer and acceptance: An offer is made by the life insurance policy applicant when he or she signs the application, submits to a physical examination, and pays the first premium. That offer is accepted by the insurer when the policy is issued and delivered. Sometimes the offer will be deemed to be made by the insurer and acceptance will be by the applicant in the form of a premium payment on the offered contract.

optional benefit: An additional benefit offered by the company, which may be included in a policy at the applicant's request, usually for an additional premium. Waiver of premium, accidental death benefit, and cost-of-living riders are examples of optional benefits.

optional paid-up insurance: One of the guaranteed nonforfeiture options in a policy where the cash value of the policy is used to buy a single premium paid-up insurance at the attained age.

ordinary life: Also referred to as straight life and whole life insurance. These three synonymous terms refer to the type of life insurance policy that continues during the whole of the insured's life, generally with level premiums payable each year until death or until age 100 when the policy endows if the insured is still living.

override: An override is the commission paid to a general agent or manager in addition to the commission paid the agent or broker who sells the policy.

ownership provision: A provision stating who the owner is when the owner is someone other than the insured.

paid-up additions: A dividend option that allows the policyowner to use policy dividends to purchase paid-up additional insurance on a net single premium basis at the insured's attained age.

paid-up policy: A policy on which the policyowner has completed payments, but that has not yet matured. This may be (1) reduced paid-up insurance provided under the nonforfeiture provision, (2) a limited payment policy under which all premiums have been paid, or (3) a policy on which accumulated dividends have been applied to pay the net single premium required to pay up the difference between the policy's reduced paid-up insurance and its face amount.

partial withdrawals (surrenders): The policyowner's right in universal and variable universal life insurance policies to receive a portion of the accumulated cash value without a policy loan and without terminating the policy. Some insurers also permit surrenders of paid-up additions from traditional participating policies without terminating the underlying policy. Partial withdrawals may incur a surrender charge and/or a processing fee.

participating insurance: An insurance policy, usually issued by mutual companies, that shares a portion of the surplus of the company with policyowners through dividends. The dividends represent the difference between the premiums charged and the actual costs (i.e., claims, expenses, earnings, etc.) experienced during the period for which the premiums were charged. For contrast, see: nonparticipating life insurance.

payor: The person who pays the premiums on a policy. Also, the applicant for a policy insuring the life of a juvenile.

permanent insurance: Any form of life insurance in which the insured has the guaranteed right to keep the policy in force as long as he or she pays the premium. Also refers to any life insurance policy that builds cash value. For contrast, see: term insurance.

persistency: Perhaps the most important objective test of a good insurance agent, persistency is a measure of the number of policies sold that "stay on the books." This "staying quality" is an indication that the policyowners were satisfied with their contracts, were not oversold, and have found the means and the desire to keep the policies in force over a long period of time. A low persistency (i.e., a high percentage of policies that have lapsed) is an indication that products were not matched with clients' problems or abilities to pay or that clients did not understand (or were allowed to forget) the importance of the coverage.

pledge: The placing of policy cash values as collateral for a loan.

policy: The basic written contract between the insurer and the policyowner. The policy together with the application and all endorsements and attached papers, constitutes the entire contract of insurance. See also: contract of insurance.

policy anniversary: The anniversary of the date of issue of a policy, as shown in the policy schedule.

policy change provision: A life insurance provision stating that the policyowner has the right to change his or her coverage from a term policy to a permanent, cash value policy, such as whole life, without providing evidence of insurability. To protect the company against adverse selection, evidence of insurability is usually required to change coverage from a permanent policy to a term plan.

policy date: The date on which coverage becomes effective, as shown in the policy.

policy fee: A small annual charge (sometimes a one-time charge) to the policyowner, in addition to the premium, to cover the costs of policy administration (premium collection and tax payments).

policyholder: The person or organization having rightful possession of a policy, irrespective of ownership rights or life insured. See also: policyowner.

policy loan: A loan to the policyowner by the insurer with the cash value of the policy assigned as the only security for the loan.

policyowner: The person who has ownership rights in an insurance policy and who may or may not be the insured. See also: policyholder.

policy period: The length of time during which the policy contract provides protection. Also called policy term.

policy proceeds: The amount payable in a single sum (if so elected) to the beneficiary or policyowner under a policy at death, surrender, or maturity. Policy proceeds generally may be applied under the policy's settlement options to provide income rather than a single lump sum.

portfolio method of dividend calculation: The method whereby dividends are calculated based on the average interest rate earned on total portfolio of investments. For contrast, see: investment year method of dividend calculation.

preferred risk: A person whose physical condition, occupation, mode of living, and other characteristics (including the size of policy to be purchased) indicate an above-average life expectancy and, therefore, who qualifies for a premium rate that is more favorable than that offered to standard risks. For contrast, see: standard risk.

preferred risk policies: Policies warranting a lower premium charge on the basis of rigid underwriting criteria that indicate better-than-average mortality risk. Certain classes of insureds may be favorably selected, such as business or professional people, for example, where the mortality experience is expected to be better than average. Typically, such policies are of larger than normal size.

preliminary term insurance: Term insurance attached to a newly issued permanent life insurance policy extending term coverage for a preliminary period of one to 11 months, until the permanent insurance becomes effective. The purpose of preliminary term insurance is to provide full life insurance protection immediately, but to delay the start of the larger permanent insurance premium and the policy anniversary to a later date.

premium: The periodic payment required to keep a specific insurance policy in force.

premium loan: Payment of the premium by taking a loan against the cash value of a policy. Frequently referred to as an automatic premium loan, a provision found in many life policies. See also: automatic premium loan provision.

premium mode: The frequency with which premium payments are made, as selected by the policyowner. Typical premium modes are annual, semiannual, quarterly, or monthly (or weekly in industrial insurance).

premium payment period: The number of years during which premiums are payable. For example, a 10-pay life policy has a 10-year premium payment period.

premium refund: A life insurance provision or rider that is a form of increasing term insurance. The beneficiary receives an amount equal to the premiums paid to date in addition to the face amount if death occurs during a stipulated period.

premium return: A return of premium may occur as a result of cancellation, rate adjustment, or calculation that an advance premium is in excess of actual premium.

primary beneficiary: The beneficiary specifically designated by the insured as the first in priority to receive policy proceeds.

private annuity: Annuity issued by an individual or organization other than an insurer or other company regularly engaged in annuity sales.

proceeds: The net amount of money payable by the insurance company at the death of an insured or at the maturity of a policy.

prohibited provisions: Life insurance policy provisions that are not allowed in the contract under state law, such as a provision eliminating the insured's right to sue the insurance company.

protection: A term synonymous with the term "coverage" that denotes the amount of insurance provided by the policy.

pure endowment: A theoretical contract that provides for payment only if a specific person survives to a certain date and not in event of that person's prior death. It contains no insurance elements and can be viewed mathematically as the actuarial opposite of a term contract, which provides for payment only in event the insured person dies within the term period specified.

ratable charge method: A method of accounting for policy cash values, policy loans and premiums. This method calls for amortization of the *cost of life insurance* on a straight-line basis over the policy life.

rated: A rated policy is one issued on a substandard risk with higher than standard premiums.

rating: The premium classification given to a person who applies for life insurance. The term is usually used when an applicant is designated as a substandard risk. A higher premium reflects the increased risk.

rebating: Generally, the return of part of the agent's commission to the policy purchaser but it also includes any form of inducement, favor, or advantage to the purchaser of a policy that is not available to all under the standard policy terms. Rebating is prohibited by law in most states. Both the agent and the person accepting the rebate can be punished by fine or imprisonment, and in most states the agent is subject to revocation of license.

reduced paid-up option: A nonforfeiture option that permits the insured to have the cash surrender value of his or her policy used to purchase a paid-up policy for, generally, a reduced amount of insurance.

re-entry term: Renewable term insurance that will charge lower new-issue term premiums if the insured periodically provides suitable evidence of insurability.

refund annuity: An annuity that will make payments after the death of the annuitant to a designated beneficiary, either as a lump-sum or in installments, until the total amount paid equals the total premiums paid for the annuity.

reinstatement provision: A policy provision defining a policyowner's right to reinstate a lapsed policy within a reasonable time after lapse, as well as the conditions necessary for reinstatement such as evidence of insurability and payment of back premiums and interest. The right is usually forfeited once a policy has been surrendered for its cash value.

renewable and convertible term: Term life insurance offering the policyowner both the option to renew the coverage at the end of the term period and the option (within the term period) to convert it to a permanent form of insurance.

renewal: Continuance of coverage under an insurance policy beyond its original term. Also, the payment of premiums after the first year of a policy or the agent's commissions on such second and subsequent years' premiums.

renewal commission: The commission paid or credited to an agent after the first policy year for premiums received by the company on business written by the agent.

renewal premium: Any premium due after the first policy year.

representations: Statements made by an applicant on the application that the applicant attests are substantially true to the best of his or her knowledge and belief, but which are not warranted as exact in every detail, as compared to warranties. See also: warranties and representations.

required provisions: Certain provisions must be included under state law in an insurance policy. Such provisions include the incontestability clause, misstatement-of-age clause, a provision for a grace period, as well as others mandated by state insurance laws.

reserve: The funds held by the company for all policies which, together with future premiums and interest earnings, are sufficient to meet all future claims.

reserve basis: The mortality and interest rate assumptions used in the computation of premiums and necessary reserves.

retirement income policy: A type of limited-pay life insurance contract designed to build cash values with the principal objective of funding a desired level of guaranteed monthly income for life, beginning at a certain age, usually 65. Unlike annuities, they also provide a death benefit.

retroactive conversion: Conversion of a term life insurance policy to a permanent policy with premiums determined as if the permanent policy were issued at the insured's original issue age rather than at the insured's attained age at the time of conversion. It usually requires payment of back premiums and interest from the original date of issue.

return of premium rider: A type of increasing term rider that will pay an amount equal to the sum of all premiums paid to date if the insured dies within a specified term, such as within the first 20 years after policy issue.

return premium policy: A life insurance policy that pays a death benefit equal to the face amount upon maturity plus all or a portion of the premiums paid.

risk factor: One of the three principal factors entering gross premium calculations. It is the estimated mortality costs of a group of policies, based on the mortality tables for life insurance. The factors insurers consider when estimating the chance of loss are age, sex, physical impairments, medical history, habits, occupation, and finances. See also: gross premium.

scheduled premium: The recommended or ideal premium in variable and universal life policies.

Section 79 plan: Merely a group-term life insurance plan but so called because of the favorable taxation under Internal Revenue Code section 79. The employee must report as gross income only the economic benefit (i.e., the Table I cost) of insurance over $50,000. When properly arranged, the cost of the premiums is also fully deductible by the employer.

select mortality table: A mortality table showing better-than-average mortality rates in the initial years after issue as a result of the insurer's ability to screen out bad risks through its underwriting process.

separate account: An investment account that is segregated from the general investment portfolio of the insurer. Required by law for assets backing variable products.

settlement: A term that is synonymous with the payment of a claim. It implies that both the policyowner and the insurance company are satisfied with the amount and the method of payment.

settlement dividend: A special or extra dividend payable at the time of termination of a policy by death, surrender, or maturity. Also called a terminal dividend.

settlement options: The various methods by which policy proceeds may be paid to the beneficiary. The options include: (1) a lump-sum cash payment; (2) leaving proceeds with the insurer at interest; (3) installment payments for a fixed period; (4) installment payments for life; and (5) installment payments of a fixed income as long as proceeds and interest will last.

single-premium deferred annuity: Annuity purchased with one premium, well in advance of the time the income period is to begin.

single-premium policy: A policy that is paid-up with one premium.

spendthrift provision: A policy provision to shelter policy proceeds, to the extent permitted by law, from the claims of creditors of any beneficiary or contingent beneficiary or to any legal process against any beneficiary or contingent beneficiary.

split-dollar insurance: An arrangement between two parties (often employer and employee) where there is a sharing or splitting of premiums, cash values, dividends, and / or death benefits.

standard policy: A policy issued with standard provisions and at standard rates; not rated or with special restrictions.

standard risk: A person who meets the insurer's underwriting criteria for standard policies. For contrast, see: rated; substandard risk.

stock company: A company that is owned and controlled by stockholders rather than policyowners. See also: mutual company.

straight life policy: See: ordinary life. For contrast, see: limited-payment policy.

straight term: A basic form of term life insurance, written for a specific number of years, having a level premium and automatically terminating at the end of the period.

substandard insurance: Life insurance issued at premium rates higher than standard, to applicants who are rated or substandard risks. For contrast, see: standard policy.

substandard risk: A person whose mortality risk is greater than average for his or her age. Substandard rating factors include various medical conditions such as diabetes, hypertension, and heart ailments; high risk occupations such as airline pilots, race car drivers, miners, and high-altitude construction workers; high risk avocations or hobbies such as scuba diving or sky diving; detrimental habits or addictions such as smoking, a history of drug use or alcohol abuse; and possible moral turpitude as evidenced by excessive gambling, criminal convictions, and bankruptcy. Substandard risks, if covered at all, are usually charged additional premium.

suicide provision: Life insurance policies include a provision that if the insured commits suicide within a specified period, usually one or two years after date of issue, the company is not liable to pay the face amount of coverage. Generally, liability is limited to a return of premiums paid.

supplemental term insurance: A supplemental agreement or rider available in some policies, providing for the payment of an additional specified sum in event the insured dies during the given term period. In general, any coverage purchased in addition to ongoing, base plans.

surplus account: The difference between a company's assets and liabilities. Net surplus includes contingency reserves and unassigned funds, while gross surplus also includes surplus assigned for distribution as dividends.

surrender: The policyowner's return of a policy to the insurance company in exchange for the policy's cash surrender value or other equivalent nonforfeiture values. See also: nonforfeiture values.

surrender charge: In a variable or universal life policy, a special charge that is levied on the available cash value to reimburse the insurer for the unrecovered costs of issuing the policy.

surrender dividend: See: terminal dividend.

surrendered policy: A life insurance policy that has been returned to the insurance company and terminated, generally under the nonforfeiture provisions of the policy after surrender values have become available.

target premium: The suggested or recommended annual premium for a universal life policy that will maintain the plan of insurance if the actual interest, mortality, and expense experience matches the underlying assumptions used to compute the premium.

temporary level extra premiums: A type of rating most frequently used with physical impairments where the risk is considered to be a temporary nature.

temporary life annuity: A life annuity that terminates at the earlier of the end of a stipulated period or the death of the annuitant.

term contract or policy: See: term insurance.

terminal dividend: Dividends that may be payable upon termination of a policy at death, maturity, or surrender for its cash value, usually after the policy has been in force for at least a specified number of years.

termination: Refers to a policy's becoming of no effect. No more premiums are payable on the policy after termination, and it no longer has any value. Termination can occur in a number of ways, including failure to pay premiums as required or surrendering the policy for its cash value.

term insurance: Life insurance protection that expires after a specified term without any residual value if the insured survives the stated period. The protection period may be as short as 30 days (as in temporary insurance agreements) or as long as 20 years or more. For contrast, see: whole life insurance.

term insurance rider: A form providing term life insurance that is attached to a permanent life insurance policy, with the purpose of increasing the total amount of protection during the term period.

term of policy: The period for which a policy is in force. This is to the end of the term period for term insurance, the maturity date for endowments, and to the insured's death (or, usually, age 100) for whole life policies.

term to age ( ): A form of long-term life insurance continuing to the designated age of the policyowner. If the insured survives the term, there is no residual value as would be the case with a cash-value policy that endows if the insured survives the term of coverage.

tontine: A type of insurance policy whereby a group of policyowners share various advantages on such terms that upon the death or default of any policyowner in the group, his or her advantages are distributed among the remaining policyowners on the expiration of an agreed period. See with respect to: deposit term.

traditional net cost comparison method: A method of determining policy cost over a stipulated period by adding a policy's premiums and subtracting dividends and the cash value at the end of the stipulated period.

traditional product: A life insurance product with fixed premiums, death benefit, and cash value growth. For contrast, see: universal life; variable life.

ultimate mortality table: A mortality table based on average life insurance experience after the period when the benefit of favorable "selection" attributable to the insurer's underwriting process has worn off.

unbundled fees: Refers to the legal requirement that variable, universal, and other current-assumption life insurance policy costs and deductions be clearly stated and explained.

underwriter: Technically, the person who writes his or her name under an insurance agreement, accepting all or part of the risk. Often refers to the home office employee who reviews the facts about the risk, accepts or declines the risk, and assigns the rate – the home office underwriter. Also, used in reference to the agent offering the insurance, since the agent does exercise underwriting discretion in selecting the risks (prospects) he or she contacts.

unearned premium: The portion of the premium applicable to the unexpired or unused part of the period for which the premium has been charged. Thus, in the case of an annual premium, at the end of the third month of the premium period, three-fourths of the premium is unearned.

uniform policy provision: A provision that is required by state statute to be in all insurance contracts of a given type; generally taken from or patterned after the model provisions provided by the National Association of Insurance Commissioners (NAIC).

Uniform Simultaneous Death Act: This law states that, when an insured and beneficiary die at the same time, or when they die together and it cannot be determined who died first, it is presumed that the insured survived the beneficiary. The insurance company then pays the proceeds to the next beneficiary in line, the secondary or contingent beneficiary, or to the insured's estate if the policyowner has not named a secondary beneficiary.

unilateral contract: A contract in which only one party pledges anything. A life insurance is a unilateral contract since only the insurance company can be sued for breach of contract.

universal life: A flexible-premium, current-assumption, adjustable-death-benefit policy. Similar to traditional policies, universal life pays a death benefit and accumulates cash value. Unlike traditional products, universal life completely separates the protection element from the accumulation element of the policy.

vanishing point: In some cash value policies, such as variable life, the projected time that all premium payments will end permanently, based on premium amount and assumed rate of return on cash value.

vanishing premium: A feature in some cash value policies whereby the premium, which is based on premium amount and assumed interest rates, will end after a specified period of time, usually as a result of applying dividends as additional premiums.

variable annuity: An annuity that invests the contract holder's funds in security-type investments and that does not guarantee the level of payments. Instead, payments may fluctuate up and down in relation to the earnings and market value of the assets in a separate account. Thus, the investment risk is assumed by the contract holder.

variable annuity accumulation unit: A unit similar to a share in a mutual fund that represents a share of a contract owner's ownership in the separate account backing the contract during the years prior to the annuity starting date. The value of the unit fluctuates in relation to changes in the market prices of the separate variable annuity portfolio securities owned by the insurance company and with investment income earned on these securities.

variable death benefit: A death benefit option in most variable life policies. The death benefit varies based on a formula relating the cash value to the death benefit. The death benefit is also variable in variable universal life policies under option B (or II) which pays a pure level death benefit plus the cash value at the time of the insured's death.

variable life insurance: Life insurance that provides a guaranteed minimum death benefit, but the actual ben-

efit paid may be more, depending on the fluctuating market value of investments in the separate account backing the contract at the time of the insured's death. The cash surrender value generally fluctuates with the market value of the investment portfolio.

variable universal life: The generic name for a flexible-premium universal life insurance policy, distinguished by a flexible premium and separate cash value investment accounts.

waiver of premium provision: See: disability premium waiver insurance.

waiver of premium with disability income rider: A life insurance rider that not only waives the premiums but also pays a specified monthly income if the insured becomes totally and permanently disabled.

war clause: A clause in an insurance contract limiting the insurance company's liability for specified loss caused by war.

warranties and representations: Almost every state provides that all statements made by a life insurance policy applicant, whether in the application blank or to the medical examiner, are considered, in the absence of fraud, to be representations and not warranties. The distinction is crucial since a warranty must be literally true. Even a small breach of warranty, even if by error, could be sufficient to render the policy void, whether the matter warranted is material or not and whether or not it had contributed to the loss. See also: representations.

whole life insurance: A form of life insurance offering protection for the whole of life, proceeds being payable at death. Premiums may be paid under a continuous premium arrangement or on a limited payment basis for virtually any desired period of years (e.g., 1, 10, 20, 30, or to ages 60 or 65). See also: ordinary life.

yearly renewable term insurance: A 1-year term insurance contract that may be renewed each year at, generally, successively higher premiums corresponding to the insured's attained age with no evidence of insurability. The right of renewal may extend to ten years or more or to an age such as 60 or 65. See: renewable term insurance.

ENDNOTE

1. The authors highly recommend Ingrisano and Ingrisano, *The Insurance Dictionary*, 3rd ed. (Longman Financial Services Publishing). Their text, which was extremely useful in the creation of this glossary, contains an extensive and highly practical list of almost every technical term commonly used in life insurance parlance and should be considered essential for the life insurance professional.

INDEX

Index

TOOLS & TECHNIQUES
Print • Online • CE Filed

The *Tools & Techniques Online Library* covers the following printed titles:

Charitable Planning

Employee Benefit & Retirement Planning

Estate Planning

Financial Planning

Life Insurance Planning

The *Tools & Techniques Online Library* provides you with immediate access to information across the financial services titles - increasing your ability to plan for your clients' needs. Other features of this annual service include advanced searching, cross-title analysis, results ranked as needed and more.

The *Tools & Techniques* titles are filed for CE credit in most states. Go to www.nationalunderwriter.com/educationservices to sign up for your CE exam today.

PAYMENT INFORMATION AND GUARANTEE

Add shipping & handling charges to all orders as indicated. If your order exceeds total amount listed in chart, or for overseas rates, call 1-800-543-0874. Any order of 10 or more items or $250.00 and over will be billed for shipping by actual weight, plus a handling fee. Any discounts do not apply to shipping and handling. Unconditional 30-day guarantee. Product(s) damaged in shipping will be replaced at no cost to you. Claims must be made within 30 days from the invoice date. Price, information, and availability subject to change.

SHIPPING & HANDLING

ORDER TOTAL			S&H
$0.00	TO	$59.00	$7.00
$60.00	TO	$149.00	$10.00
$150.00	TO	$250.00	$16.00

SALES TAX (Additional)
Residents of CA, DC, FL, GA, IL, KY, NJ, NY, OH, PA, and WA must add sales tax.

Please send me the following : *(please indicate quantity)*

The Tools & Techniques of Life Insurance Planning _____ Book (#2700003) $74.95
The Tools & Techniques of Estate Planning _____ Book (#2850013) $74.95
The Tools & Techniques of Practice Management _____ Book (#2690000) $74.95
The Tools & Techniques of Investment Planning _____ Book (#2730000) $74.95
The Tools & Techniques of Income Tax Planning _____ Book (#2740000) $74.95
The Tools & Techniques of Employee Benefit and Retirement Planning _____ Book (#2710008) $52.95
The Tools & Techniques of Financial Planning _____ Book (#2770007) $74.95
The Tools & Techniques of Charitable Planning _____ Book (#2500000) $52.95
The Tools & Techniques Online Library _____ 1 Year Subscription(TTLIB) $195.00

❏ Check enclosed*　　Charge My ❏AMEX ❏MC ❏VISA (check one) ❏Bill me

*Make check payable to The National Underwriter Company. Please include the appropriate shipping & handling and any applicable sales tax.

**For Visa/MC, the three-digit CVV# is usually printed on the back of the card. For American Express, the four-digit CVV# is usually on the front of the card.

Card #_____ CVV#**_____ Exp. Date _____
Signature_____
Name_____ Title_____
Company_____
Address_____
City_____ State_____ Zip+4_____
Business Phone (_____)_____
E-mail _____

BB

The National Underwriter Company
A Unit of Highline Media LLC

Please send me the following : *(please indicate quantity)*

The Tools & Techniques of Life Insurance Planning _____ Book (#2700003) $74.95
The Tools & Techniques of Estate Planning _____ Book (#2850013) $74.95
The Tools & Techniques of Practice Management _____ Book (#2690000) $74.95
The Tools & Techniques of Investment Planning _____ Book (#2730000) $74.95
The Tools & Techniques of Income Tax Planning _____ Book (#2740000) $74.95
The Tools & Techniques of Employee Benefit and Retirement Planning _____ Book (#2710008) $52.95
The Tools & Techniques of Financial Planning _____ Book (#2770007) $74.95
The Tools & Techniques of Charitable Planning _____ Book (#2500000) $52.95
The Tools & Techniques Online Library _____ 1 Year Subscription(TTLIB) $195.00

❏ Check enclosed*　　Charge My ❏AMEX ❏MC ❏VISA (check one) ❏Bill me

*Make check payable to The National Underwriter Company. Please include the appropriate shipping & handling and any applicable sales tax.

**For Visa/MC, the three-digit CVV# is usually printed on the back of the card. For American Express, the four-digit CVV# is usually on the front of the card.

Card #_____ CVV#**_____ Exp. Date _____
Signature_____
Name_____ Title_____
Company_____
Address_____
City_____ State_____ Zip+4_____
Business Phone (_____)_____
E-mail _____

BB

The National Underwriter Company
A Unit of Highline Media LLC

Order the *Tools & Techniques Series* and other titles by The National Underwriter Company.

Save 5% Instantly when you order online at **www.NationalUnderwriterStore.com.**

Include code BB at checkout.

The National Underwriter Company
A Unit of Highline Media LLC

ORDERS DEPARTMENT
THE NATIONAL UNDERWRITER COMPANY
PO BOX 14448
CINCINNATI OH 45250-9786

ORDERS DEPARTMENT
THE NATIONAL UNDERWRITER COMPANY
PO BOX 14448
CINCINNATI OH 45250-9786